NEW OXFORD STYLE MANUAL

NEW OXFORD STYLE MANUAL

The World's Most Trusted Reference Books

OXFORD
UNIVERSITY PRESS

OXFORD
UNIVERSITY PRESS

Great Clarendon Street, Oxford, OX2 6DP,
United Kingdom

Oxford University Press is a department of the University of Oxford. It furthers the University's objective of excellence in research, scholarship, and education by publishing worldwide. Oxford is a registered trade mark of Oxford University Press in the UK and in certain other countries

First edition published as *The Oxford Style Manual* in 2003
Second edition published as *New Oxford Style Manual* in 2012
First edition of *New Hart's Rules* published in 2005 and adapted from *The Oxford Guide to Style* (2002) by R.M. Ritter
Second edition of *New Hart's Rules* published in 2014
First edition of the *New Oxford Dictionary for Writers and Editors* published in 2005 and adapted from *The Oxford Dictionary for Writers and Editors*, second edition (2000), edited and compiled by R.M. Ritter
Second edition of the *New Oxford Dictionary for Writers and Editors* published in 2014

Impression: 7

Published in the United States of America by Oxford University Press
198 Madison Avenue, New York, NY 10016, United States of America

British Library Cataloguing in Publication Data
Data available

Library of Congress Cataloging in Publication Data
Data available

ISBN 978–0–19–876725–1

Printed and bound in Great Britain by
Clays Ltd, Elcograf S.p.A.

Contents

Preface

The *Oxford Style Manual* is the essential handbook for anyone who works with text, or who just seeks fast, authoritative guidance on matters of style, spelling, and presentation. This new second edition combines updated and revised versions of *New Hart's Rules* and the *New Oxford Dictionary for Writers and Editors*, both of which first appeared in 2005. In addition, with each revised impression, updates of spelling and factual information are applied to the *New Oxford Dictionary for Writers and Editors*, based on the online *Oxford Dictionary of English*.

Oxford Dictionaries are responsible for the largest language research programme in the world, which constantly monitors English of all types. The primary source for new and revised material is the Oxford English Corpus, a dynamic database of several billion words which provides a detailed picture of 21st-century English from around the world.

Consulting a book can still be the quickest and most convenient way of finding the information you want, as well as being an enjoyable method of browsing in its own right. But to explore the language further try Oxford Dictionaries online. This free site is updated regularly and allows you to search the *Oxford Dictionary of English* and its US counterpart, the *New Oxford American Dictionary*. It also offers information on usage, grammar, and writing, a Word of the Day, a language blog, audio pronunciations, synonyms, and example sentences.. Find Oxford Dictionaries at *www.oxforddictionaries.com*.

PART I

NEW HART'S RULES

Contents

Preface

New Hart's Rules is a guide to style designed for people writing or working with text in English. Its twenty-one chapters give a full account of such matters as capitalization, hyphenation, abbreviation, italicization, notes and references, work titles, quotations, bibliography, and publishing terms. Advice is given on dealing with scientific and foreign-language material, and on preparing lists, tables, and illustrations. The text is clearly written and laid out, with short paragraphs and many illustrative examples.

Hart's Rules for Compositors and Readers at the University Press, Oxford was first printed in 1893. Horace Henry Hart (1840–1916) was Printer to the University of Oxford and Controller of the University Press between 1883 and 1915. *Hart's Rules* was originally a slim twenty-four-page booklet intended only for staff of the printing house at the Clarendon Press, the learned imprint of Oxford University Press, but Hart decided to publish it for the public after finding copies of it for sale. In all, *Hart's Rules* was published in thirty-nine editions. Over time its size and influence grew, and it came to be regarded as the essential handbook for editors and typesetters. In 2002 a new edition was published under the name *The Oxford Guide to Style*. It revised and expanded *Hart's Rules*, and was published in a larger format. *New Hart's Rules* marked a return to the *Hart's Rules* name and small 'handbook' format that have been renowned for more than a hundred years.

New Hart's Rules has been written for contemporary writers and editors of all kinds. Whereas the original *Hart's* concentrated on style appropriate to academic publications, *New Hart's Rules* responds to the challenge of a wider constituency. Authors, including self-publishers, copy-editors, proofreaders, designers, typesetters, and anyone working on ebooks, websites, and other digital products, newspapers, magazines, reports, or theses will find here the advice they need on the language and presentation of their text.

New Hart's Rules continues to explain the 'house style' traditionally used at Oxford University Press, but it also gives a full account of widely used contemporary practices in all areas of writing and publishing, and makes clear the differences, where they exist, between British and American style; a new chapter focusing exclusively on this topic has been added in this edition.

Most of the illustrative examples in *New Hart's Rules* are taken from the Oxford English Corpus, a database containing hundreds of millions of words of real English, or from the Oxford Reading Programme. The book's spellings and recommendations are consistent with those given in the current range of Oxford dictionaries, and with those in the *New Oxford Dictionary for Writers and Editors*.

New Hart's Rules forms part of a trio of books designed specifically for writers and editors, along with the *New Oxford Dictionary for Writers and Editors* and the *New Oxford Spelling Dictionary*. These three books continue to form the complete reference set for everyone who is concerned to reach the highest standards in producing written works. They are intended to be used alongside a current Oxford dictionary such as the newly relaunched Oxford Dictionary website (www.oxforddictionaries.com), the *Concise Oxford English Dictionary* (twelfth edition, 2011) or the slightly larger *Oxford Dictionary of English* (third edition, 2010), which also includes encyclopedic material. For copy-editors the standard reference is Judith Butcher's *Copy-Editing: The Cambridge Handbook for Editors, Authors and Publishers* (fourth edition, 2006).

This edition of *New Hart's Rules: The Oxford Style Guide* is also available online, on the Oxford Dictionaries website. The site is updated regularly and gives you free access to our largest dictionary and thesaurus of current English as well as bilingual dictionaries for many languages. It also offers information on usage, grammar, and writing, our Word of the Day, a language blog, and more. In addition, the Gold subscription package features millions of example sentences and specialist language reference resources—including this book and the *New Oxford Dictionary for Writers and Editors*. Find Oxford Dictionaries online at www.oxforddictionaries.com.

Editorial team

Editor in chief of 2014 edition
Anne Waddingham

Editor in chief of 2005 edition
Rosemary Roberts

Project managers
Jamie Crowther
Rebecca Lane

Project manager of 2005 edition
Angus Stevenson

Contributors to both editions
Jane Bainbridge
Roger Bennett
Anthony Esposito
Ralph Evans
Nicola Freshwater
Carolyn Garwes
Orin Hargraves
Jacqueline Harvey
Leofranc Holford-Strevens
Simon Lancaster
Richard Lawrence
Ray Loughlin
Dorothy McCarthy
Susan Ratcliffe
Nick Rollin
Julian Roskams
Tom Stableford
Anne Waddingham
Maurice Waite

Design
Michael Johnson

Special thanks to
Nick Allen
Melinda Babcock
Sarah Barrett
Katrina Campbell
Nic Gibson
Barbara Horn
Veronica Hurst
Rebecca Kaye
Elizabeth Knowles
Judith Luna
Kathleen Lyle
Katherine Martin
David MacDonald
Maureen MacGlashan
Don McConnell
Peter Momtchiloff
Sandy Nicholson
Sarah Price
Kim Richardson
David Shirt
Melissa Spielman
Della Thompson
Bill Trumble
George Tulloch
Jane Ward
Kieran Waddingham
Sean Waddingham
Francis Whistler
John Woodruff

CHAPTER 1

The parts of a book

1.1 General principles

A book usually consists of three sections: **preliminary matter** (also called **prelims** or **front matter**), the **main text**, and **end matter**. All books have some kind of prelims, all have a text, and most works of non-fiction have end matter. The prelims and end matter usually contain a number of items or sections, subject to a given order and to conventions that control their presentation.

In discussing the parts of a printed book the following terms are used:

- **spread** or **double-page spread**—the pair of pages (left-hand and right-hand) exposed when the book is opened at random; the term **opening** is also used. The terms are sometimes distinguished, with a 'spread' being a pair of pages that are designed as an entity, for example in a highly illustrated book, and an 'opening' being any pair of facing pages.
- **recto**—the right-hand page of a spread: a recto always has an odd page number.
- **verso**—the left-hand page of a spread: a verso always has an even page number.

The recto is regarded as the 'more important' of the two pages of a spread. The main text always begins on a recto, and in a book divided into parts (Part I, Part II, etc.) a new part begins on a fresh recto, even though the preceding page may be blank. The design of a book may require that a new chapter begin on a fresh recto. The main items or sections in the prelims customarily begin on a fresh recto.

Readers of ebooks and other nonprint materials are often able to adjust the display of text to their preferences, and consequently the concepts of double-page spreads, rectos, and versos are not as meaningful in digital contexts. Publishers and authors need to consider carefully how material that depends on highly designed spreads in print will transfer to nonprint publication.

1.2 Preliminary matter

1.2.1 **Constituents**

Preliminary matter is any material that precedes the main text of the book. Preliminary pages are usually numbered with lower-case Roman numerals (rather than Arabic numerals) so that any late changes to the content or extent of the prelims will not affect the pagination of the main text. Page numbers (called **folios**) are not shown on every page of the prelims, though every page has its number (see also 1.5.1).

Prelims will always include some, and may include all, of the following items or sections, usually (but not always) in this order:

half-title page
half-title verso
frontispiece
title page
title page verso
dedication
foreword
preface
acknowledgements
contents
lists of illustrations, figures, and maps
list of tables
tables of cases and legislation (law books)
list of abbreviations
list of contributors
note to the reader
epigraph

Some but not all of these sections have headings in print, which are usually set to the same design as chapter headings. To facilitate navigation, digital or online versions may differ from print in having items in a different order (moving copyright information to the back, for example), or may include headings such as *Dedication* that don't traditionally appear in print.

Besides prelims and end matter, a hardback (or **case-bound**) book may have **endpapers** at both ends of the book, often of slightly stronger paper than the text; endpapers consist of a single sheet, half of it pasted to the inside of the case and half forming a **flyleaf** or blank page at the beginning or end of the book. Figures, maps, or other illustrations are sometimes printed on the endpapers; any that are essential should be repeated within the text, because endpapers may be obscured or removed altogether in library copies of the book or when it is published in paperback or as a digital edition.

1.2.2 **Half-title**

The half-title page is the first page (p. i) of the book (after a flyleaf, if any) and thus falls on a recto. It contains the main title, and only the main title, of the book (or the title of the volume if the work is in more than one volume).

Not all books now have a half-title, and it may sometimes be dispensed with as a space-saving measure (see 1.8).

1.2.3 **Half-title verso**

The verso of the half-title page (p. ii) is often blank, though it may carry announcements from the publisher such as a list of other books in the series to which the volume belongs, or a list of other works by the same author. Sometimes it will be given over to a frontispiece (see below). The half-title verso falls opposite the title page and may be incorporated into a special design for this important spread.

1.2.4 **Frontispiece**

A frontispiece is an illustration that, in print, faces the title page, an important position that is justified by the significance or representative content of the image. In a biography a frontispiece is usually a portrait of the subject, in a work of history it might be a map or a facsimile of a document, and so on.

If the book has integrated illustrations (see 16.1.1), the frontispiece is likely to be printed on text paper like all the other illustrations. If the book has plates, the frontispiece, like other pictures, will usually be printed on glossy art paper; in this case the frontispiece will appear on the verso of a single leaf **tipped in** (that is, inserted and pasted) between the half-title verso and the title page. Note that tipping-in is a costly process and is best avoided if possible.

Like any illustration, a frontispiece will generally be identified by a caption, which may be printed beneath the image or close by (at the foot of the title page verso, for example). The frontispiece is, exceptionally, listed on the contents page (see 1.2.11 below).

As a frontispiece may not always be reproduced in all subsequent editions of a book (a paperback edition, for example), the author should avoid referring to it in the text.

1.2.5 **Title page**

The title page (p. iii) presents at least the following details:

- the complete title and subtitle of the work
- a volume number, if any
- the name of the author or editor
- the publisher's name (called the **imprint**).

It may also include other, similar, information: for example a series title; the names of other people involved in the book's preparation, such as a translator or an illustrator; the place of publication or the cities in which the publisher has offices; the publisher's logo or **colophon** (device or emblem); and the date of publication.

The roles of people other than the author are defined by an introductory phrase, such as:

> Selected and edited by
> Translated by
> With illustrations by

1.2.6 **Title page verso**

The title page verso (p. iv, also, variously, called the **copyright**, **biblio**, or **imprint** page) contains the essential printing and publication history of the work. It presents at least the following details:

- publisher's imprint
- date of publication

- publishing history
- copyright line
- copyright notice(s)
- assertion of moral rights
- limitations on sales
- cataloguing in publication data
- ISBN
- statements concerning performing rights
- printer's name and location.

Publisher's imprint

The imprint consists of:

- the publisher's name (or the name of a subdivision of the company if this bears a separate name)
- the publisher's full registered postal address
- the place of publication.

It may also include the names of associated companies or offices, and the cities in which they are located.

Date of publication

The date of publication is given on the title page verso, whether or not it appears on the title page. For the first edition of a work the date of publication is usually the same as the copyright date (see below).

Publishing history

The publishing history of the book includes:

- reference to simultaneous co-publications of the work (with the name and location of the co-publishers)
- a description of the current version of the work (for example its edition number, if other than the first, or its status as a reprint)
- the sequence of editions, reprints, and publication in different bindings that has preceded the current version of the work, each of which is dated.

An **edition** is a version of a book at its first publication and at every following publication for which more than minor changes are made: a book goes into a new edition when it is revised, enlarged, abridged, published in a new format, or published in a different binding. A new edition requires a new ISBN (see below).

A **reprint** or **impression** is a republication of a book for which no corrections or only minor corrections are made. The publishing history usually distinguishes between these two states, describing them as 'reprinted' and 'reprinted with corrections'. The publishing history usually details the issuing of multiple reprints in a single year: *Reprinted 2004 (twice)*.

Copyright line

To qualify for protection under the Universal Copyright Convention, and for reasons of best practice, copyright ownership in a work must be stated in a particular form, giving the copyright holder's name and the year of first publication, preceded by the copyright symbol:

© Ann Jones 2014

A work may have multiple copyright holders, such as co-authors, an illustrator, a translator, or the contributor of an introduction; the rights of each of them must be separately stated.

Copyright may be held by the publisher rather than by the creator(s) of the work, who in this case will have assigned the rights permanently, rather than have licensed them to the publisher.

For guidelines on copyright see Chapter 20.

Copyright notice(s)

Many publishers include one or more copyright notices in their books, explicitly reserving certain rights in the work. Such notices relate to reproduction, electronic storage, transmission in other forms, and rebinding. An example may be seen on the title page verso of this book.

Assertion of moral rights

Under the UK's Copyright Act 1988 certain 'moral rights' in the work are enjoyed by its creator. Of these the right of paternity (the right to be identified as the author of the work) does not exist unless the author has explicitly asserted it. The assertion of this right, or of the author's moral rights in general, is recorded on the title page verso in a form such as:

The author's moral rights have been asserted

For an explanation of moral rights see Chapter 20.2.4.

Cataloguing in publication (CIP) data

Some national libraries, notably the British Library and the Library of Congress, compile catalogue records of new books before their publication. Publishers may include such records in full on the title page verso of the book, or may simply note that they are available. CIP data may not be altered in any way, even if it contains errors, without the written permission of the issuing library.

The CIP data is usually the means of stating the **ISBN** (International Standard Book Number), because this number is essential to the catalogue record. If CIP data is not reproduced in full the ISBN must be included elsewhere on the title page verso. The ISBN uniquely identifies the book in the particular edition to which it is attached. A new ISBN is needed for every new edition of the book, including reissue in a different binding and ebook editions. Each volume of a multi-volume work usually has its own ISBN, as may the set as a whole, though in some cases (notably where the volumes are not separately available for sale) a single number may be used for the whole set. The previous ten-digit ISBNs were replaced by thirteen-digit ISBNs in 2007; during the transition period, both were included.

A serial publication, such as a journal, magazine, or yearbook, has an **ISSN** (International Standard Serial Number), which is the same for all issues of the work.

The CIP data will often be accompanied by an indication of what impression a particular book represents. This may be a single number, or a series of numbers, the lowest number of which is that of the current impression. So the following line denotes a second impression:

10 9 8 7 6 5 4 3 2

Performing rights agencies

The public performance of dramatic and musical works is generally controlled on behalf of copyright holders by agents whom they empower to license performing rights. A clause stating that the right to perform the work is restricted, and giving the name and address of the agent to whom application must be made for permission to mount a performance, usually appears on the title page verso of printed plays and music.

Printer's name and location

The printer's name and location must be included on the title page verso.

Other information

The title page verso may present further information about the book as a publication. Typical elements include details of the design and production of the book, including the name and size of the typeface used and the name and location of the typesetting firm.

1.2.7 **Dedication**

The dedication is a highly personal expression on the part of the author. The publisher usually accepts its wording and content unchanged, and its design is usually subject to the author's approval when that of the rest of the book is not. Whenever possible the dedication falls on a recto (usually p. v), but if, for reasons of space, it must be relocated to a verso, one must be chosen that gives it sufficient prominence (for example the last verso preceding the first page of the text).

1.2.8 **Foreword**

The foreword is a recommendation of the work written by someone other than the author. He or she is usually named at the end of the piece, or in its title, and in the contents list. The distinction between the foreword and the preface (see below) should be noted and the correct title given to each of these sections of the front matter. The foreword usually begins on a fresh recto.

1.2.9 **Preface**

The preface is the section where the author sets out the purpose, scope, and content of the book. In the absence of a full acknowledgements section, the author may include in the preface brief thanks to colleagues, advisers, or others who have helped in the creation of the work.

In a multi-author work the preface may be written by the work's editor (*Editor's preface*). All works in a series may contain the same preface by the series editor (*Series editor's preface*), which precedes the preface by the author of each work. Successive editions of a work may have their own prefaces, each of which is appropriately titled (for example *Preface to the second edition*). If one or more earlier prefaces are reprinted in a new edition, they follow, in reverse numerical order, the preface belonging to that new edition; for example:

> Preface to the paperback edition
> Preface to the second edition
> Preface to the first edition

The preface usually begins on a fresh recto, as do each of multiple prefaces unless reasons of economy dictate otherwise.

1.2.10 **Acknowledgements**

Acknowledgements (or, in US spelling, *Acknowledgments*) are of two types: those recognizing the ideas, assistance, support, or inspiration of those who have helped the author to create the work; and those listing the copyright holders in material (such as quotations and extracts) reproduced in the book. The first type may, if those acknowledged are few, be included in the preface (see above). The second type relate to the legal requirement to acknowledge the sources of reproduced material and in many cases to gain permission from copyright holders or their licensees for its use, and as such the wording printed should be exactly as required by the copyright holder, even if this is inconsistent with style used elsewhere in the book. (For guidelines on copyright see Chapter 20.)

It is best to separate the two types of acknowledgement. The author's personal thanks follow the preface and are called simply 'Acknowledgements'. The names of those who hold copyright in verbal material (such as epigraphs or quotations) are listed in a separate section headed 'Copyright acknowledgements', which can appear either in the prelims or in the end matter. Acknowledgement lines for figures, tables, and similar illustrations reproduced in the text are best listed alongside the illustration's caption rather than on a separate page, unless otherwise specified by the copyright holder

1.2.11 **Contents**

The list of contents (headed *Contents*) always falls on a recto. It records the title and initial page number of every titled section that follows it in the prelims, part titles, chapter titles, and all sections in the end matter, including the index. It usually includes reference to the frontispiece if one is present (see 1.2.4). Lists in the prelims are referred to on the contents page as *List of Illustrations*, *List of Abbreviations*, etc., even though their own headings are best formulated simply as *Illustrations*, *Abbreviations*, etc.

Part titles, preceded by the word *Part* and a number, are listed in full, and a page number is given unless it is that of the following chapter in the part. The word *Chapter* may, but need not, appear before the number and title of each chapter, though if it is used in the list of contents it should also appear at the head of each chapter in the text. It is customary to use upper-case Roman numerals for part numbers (see 1.3.3) and Arabic numerals for chapter numbers (see 1.3.4).

In complex works, such as textbooks, headings within chapters may be included on the contents page or even as a subsidiary table of contents at the start of each chapter. In a multi-author volume authors' names as well as chapter titles are given in the contents list.

The wording, punctuation, capitalization, use of italics, and form of authors' names in the contents list must match the headings as they appear in the text itself. No full point is needed at the end of any heading, nor are leader dots wanted between titles and page references. The numerals on the contents page at the editing stage will be those of the script, or 'dummies' such as xxx or 000; on hard copy they should be circled to indicate that they are not to be printed; in electronic files they can be omitted as they will be inserted automatically by the publishing software, along with the table of contents (so it may not be necessary for an editor to compile one—check with the client). At page-proof stage the typesetter should have inserted the correct page references, but they must be checked by the proofreader.

The first volume of a multi-volume work published simultaneously or at short intervals should contain a contents list and list of illustrations (if relevant) for the entire set. Each subsequent volume needs lists only for that volume.

1.2.12 **Lists of illustrations, figures, and maps**

Illustrations numbered sequentially through the work are presented in a single list. Different types of illustrative material, numbered in separate sequences, are presented in separate lists, usually in the order illustrations, figures, maps.

Such a list consists of the captions, which may be shortened if they are discursive, and the sources or locations of the illustrative material where relevant. As with the contents, the correct page numbers for all illustrative material that is integrated with the text (though not those of plates in a separate section) may need to be inserted at page-proof stage, if not done automatically by the publishing software.

1.2.13 **List of tables**

A list of tables is useful only when the work contains many tables of particular interest. The list gives the table headings, shortened if necessary, and page numbers; sources appear in the text beneath each table.

Tables of cases and legislation

In most law books the judgments referred to in the text are listed, usually alphabetically by significant name, with the corresponding pagination or section number. The table may be subdivided according to jurisdiction, especially if there is a large number of cases. International cases may be listed by country.

Tables of legislation are ordered in a similar way but may be listed either alphabetically or chronologically.

1.2.14 **List of abbreviations**

The text of a book should be so presented as to 'explain' itself without recourse to external sources of information. Abbreviations that readers may be unable to interpret must be included in a list with the full form spelled out alongside each one. Well-known abbreviations that need no explanation (such as AD, BC, *UK*, and *US*) are not included in the list, nor are any that will be common knowledge to the expected readership of the work, although even here, for an international readership, it is safest to include all the abbreviations. In a multi-author book or work that will not be read serially, a list of abbreviations can obviate the need to spell them out the first time they are used in every chapter. If a term occurs only very rarely in the text it is better to spell it out at each occurrence than to use an abbreviation. The practice of spelling out a short form at the first instance of its use does not obviate the need for inclusion of a list of abbreviations. See also Chapter 10.

If the abbreviations are used in text or notes the list is best placed in the prelims of the book; if, however, abbreviations are used only in the bibliography, endnotes, or appendices, the list may be presented at the head of the relevant section. Arrange the list alphabetically by abbreviated form.

1.2.15 **List of contributors**

In a multi-author work it is customary to list the contributors and provide relevant information about each one, such as institutional affiliation or post held, a short biography, or details of other publications. The more detailed and discursive the entries are, the more appropriate it will be to place the list in the end matter of the work rather than the preliminary pages.

The list should be ordered alphabetically by contributor's surname (though names are presented in natural order, not inverted), and names should match the form in the contents list and the chapter headings. The presentation of each entry should as far as possible be standardized.

1.2.16 **Epigraph**

An epigraph is a relevant quotation placed at the beginning of a volume, part, or chapter, and is distinguished typographically from other displayed quotations. An epigraph relating to the entire volume is placed on a new page, preferably a recto, immediately before the text or in another prominent position within the prelims. Epigraphs for parts or chapters may be placed on the verso facing the part or chapter title or under the heading of the part or chapter to which they relate. The use of epigraphs and their positioning must be consistent throughout the work.

Epigraph sources are usually ranged right (see 2.5.1) under the quotation. The author's name and the title and date of the work are usually sufficient: further details are not normally included because readers are not expected to want to verify the quotation.

1.2.17 **Other sections**

Many publications need a short explanation of conventions, terminology, or forms of presentation used in the text, or guidance on how to use the book. Such information is best placed as near as possible to the beginning of the text and often carries the title *Note to the reader* or *How to use this book*.

1.3 Text

The text of a work, whether it is in a single volume or multiple volumes, should ideally unfold in a form in which each division is of equivalent scale and consistent construction. As part of marking up the text on-screen or on hard copy, the copy-editor will need to identify the hierarchy of headings that articulate the structure and all displayed elements of the text—those elements such as quotations, lists, notes, text boxes, tables, equations, and so on that need special presentation on the page. The designer specifies an appropriate typographic treatment for the body text and for each displayed element, and the typesetter applies the appropriate design and layout. For digital products, the elements are tagged electronically for later conversion. See 2.1 for further details.

1.3.1 **Volumes**

It is usual for each volume of a work published in multiple volumes to have its own pagination, index, bibliography, and so on. Even if the numbering of text pages is consecutive from one volume to the next, the preliminary pages of each volume begin with page i. Volumes may be numbered or titled or numbered and titled, as appropriate to the content of the work: each volume in a collection of correspondence or a biography, for instance, may be distinguished by a range of years, the volumes in a complete edition of an author's works by the names of different genres such as *Poems*, *Plays*, *Essays*.

Large scholarly works, especially those published over many years, are sometimes made available in **fascicles** (or **fascicules**) rather than volumes. While fascicles are technically separate works, each with its own ISBN, they are designed to be bound together and are, accordingly, through-paginated. The first fascicle contains preliminary material for the whole publication and the last the index or other end matter; any front matter or end matter included with the intermediate fascicles is discarded when the fascicles are combined into a book or books.

1.3.2 **The introduction**

The introduction is properly part of the text of the book (except in special contexts such as editions of literary texts, where the editor's introduction forms part of the prelims). The Arabic pagination begins with the first page of the introduction, which therefore must fall on a recto. The introduction may be treated (and numbered) as the first chapter of the work, or it may be headed simply *Introduction*, the numbered chapters following thereafter; when an introduction (or conclusion) addresses the work as a whole, it is usually left unnumbered.

1.3.3 **Parts**

It is useful to arrange a long or complex work in parts when the text falls into logical divisions of similar length. Parts should be numbered and may be titled; although Roman numerals are traditionally used for parts (*Part I*, *Part II*), Arabic numerals may be used or numbers spelled out (*Part One*, *Part Two*). The part number and title are best placed on a recto with a blank verso following; part title pages are included in the Arabic pagination of the book but the page numbers are not shown. Text describing the purpose of the part, or a part table of contents, may appear on the part opening page.

Parts are divided into chapters, which are numbered consecutively throughout the work.

1.3.4 **Chapters**

Most works in prose are divided into chapters, which usually have a number (customarily in Arabic numerals) and often—especially in nonfiction—a title. The use of the word *Chapter* before the number is optional (see 1.2.11). Chapter titles should be of similar length and style throughout a work and as succinct as possible—overlong titles cause design difficulties at chapter openings and may need to be cut down for running heads (see 1.5.3). Note numbers and similar cues should not appear in chapter titles but be moved to the text proper.

New chapters are usually allowed to begin on either a verso or a recto (unlike new parts—see above); exceptionally, when chapters are short or economical setting is required, they may run on—start on the same page as the end of the preceding chapter—after a specified number of lines' space. This is more common in fiction than in non-fiction. The first page of a new chapter lacks a running head, and the **folio** (page number) is either omitted or appears at the foot of the page (as a **drop folio**), even when on other pages it falls in the head margin (see 1.5.1).

The first line following the chapter heading is set **full out** (flush with the left-hand margin), with no paragraph indentation. In some designs large and small capitals are used for the first word or line of a chapter, as in 'HE was gone'. If the first word is a single capital letter (for example *I*, *A*), then the second word is printed in small capitals, with no further capital. If the chapter starts with a personal name, then the whole name is in capitals and small capitals, not just the first name or title: 'MR THORNTON had had some difficulty…'.

1.3.5 **Sections and subsections**

Chapters may be divided into sections and subsections by the use of **subheadings** (or **subheads**). There may be more than one level of subheading, though only complex works such as textbooks will generally need more than three. Too many levels of subheading are difficult to design and may be more confusing than helpful to the reader. Headings should not contain note numbers or similar cues.

Sections, subsections, or even individual paragraphs may be numbered if this will be useful to the reader—as it will when the text contains numerous cross-references. As in the present book, section headings are 'double-numbered', with the two numbers closed up either side of a full point; subsection headings are triple-numbered, the number reflecting the different levels of the headings: within Chapter 9 the first A-level heading is numbered 9.1, and the first B-level heading within section 9.1 is numbered 9.1.1, and so on.

The first line after a subheading is set flush with the left-hand margin, with no paragraph indentation. If the first sentence of a new section refers to the subject articulated in the heading it must begin by reiterating the subject rather than referring back to it with a pronoun. Not:

> **1.3 Text**
> This should ideally unfold in a form in which each division is of equivalent scale and construction.

but

> **1.3 Text**
> The text of a work should ideally unfold in a form in which each division is of equivalent scale and construction.

1.3.6 **Paragraphs**

Paragraphs are units of thought reflecting the development of the author's argument, and no absolute rules control their length. In the most general terms, one-sentence paragraphs are likely to be too short and paragraphs that exceed the length of a page of typeset material are likely to be too long to hold the reader's attention. However, it is inadvisable for an editor to alter the author's delivery by running together short paragraphs or splitting long ones without fully considering the effect on the integrity of the text, and the author should normally be consulted about such changes. Different considerations apply to websites, where readability is improved by short paragraphs and frequent headings (shorter and more frequent than would be normal in print). See also Web editing in 2.1.2 and Print versus Web style in 2.3.2.

The first line of text after a chapter, section, or subsection heading is set full out to the left-hand margin, with no paragraph indentation. The first line of every subsequent paragraph is normally indented; the style in which paragraphs are separated by a space and the first line of every paragraph is set full out is characteristic of documents and some reference works, and also of material on the Internet. In fictional dialogue it is conventional (though by no means obligatory) to begin a new paragraph with every change of speaker (see 9.2.4).

Complex works, such as textbooks and practitioner texts, sometimes have numbered paragraphs throughout, the numbers being set against headings or simply at the beginnings of paragraphs; this device facilitates all kinds of internal referencing. In this case the double- and triple-numbering system outlined in 1.3.5 above is applied. Numbered paragraphs may also be used when an author wishes to enumerate long points in an argument. Equations referred to in the text should be numbered and displayed; the numbering is enclosed in parentheses and set full right, aligned with the last line of the equation (see also 14.6.6).

1.3.7 **Conclusion, epilogue, afterword**

A conclusion sums up the work's findings and puts them in context. It may be numbered and titled as the final chapter of the work or (as with the introduction) headed simply *Conclusion*.

An epilogue or an author's note is nothing more than a short concluding comment on the text. An afterword is much the same, though it is typically written by someone other than the author. Neither of these sections bears a chapter number, though the headings are usually set to the same design as the chapter headings. One would not normally have more than one or two of these concluding sections in any book.

1.4 End matter

End matter (also called **back matter**) consists of any material that supplements the text. Sections in the end matter are, generally speaking, placed in order of their importance to the reader in using and interpreting the text, with the proviso that the index is always placed last. A series of sections might be ordered as follows:

appendix
glossary
endnotes
bibliography
notes on contributors
index

End matter is paginated in sequence with the text, and the sections carry headings that are usually set to the same design as the chapter headings, though the material itself is often set in smaller type than the text, in keeping with its subsidiary position. As noted in 1.2.1, ebooks may have some traditional front-matter items relocated to the back.

1.4.1 **Appendix**

An appendix (or **annex**, as it is sometimes called in the publication of documents) presents subsidiary matter that relates directly to the text but cannot comfortably be accommodated within it, such as a chronology or the texts of documents discussed. Multiple appendices appear under the collective heading *Appendices*, each with its own subheading and descriptive title. Appendices may be numbered with Arabic or Roman numerals or marked with letters.

1.4.2 **Glossary**

A glossary is an alphabetical list of important terms found in the text, with explanations or definitions. It is not a substitute for explaining terms at their first occurrence in the text. The glossary may simply repeat the textual explanation or it may expand upon it, but in any event the definitions in text and glossary must conform.

Each entry in a glossary begins a new line. Entries may be arranged in two columns (terms on the left and definitions on the right), or the definition may run on from the headword term; in the latter case turnover lines are often indented and entries spaced off from one another to make the headwords more prominent. Bold type is often used for headwords.

1.4.3 **Endnotes**

Endnotes are an alternative to footnotes, used in a single-author work where it is not essential (or customary in the discipline concerned) to position notes on the same page as the text to which they refer. In multi-author volumes, notes and other apparatus are usually placed at the end of each chapter or essay to preserve the integrity of the author's work: it would be inappropriate in these circumstances to position the reference material in a sequence at the end of the work. For the decision to place notes at the foot of the page, the end of the chapter, or the end of the work see 17.2.2; for setting out notes see 17.2.4; for running heads in endnotes see 1.5.3.

1.4.4 **Bibliography**

There are many ways of presenting citations of other works and materials of potential interest to the reader. The simplest is to list them alphabetically by authors' surnames (in which case names are inverted to expose the ordering principle) or, in specialist works that require it, chronologically. In some cases a bibliographic essay is more appropriate—as the name suggests, a discussion of sources with the citations embedded—or an annotated bibliography, in which comments on some or all of the sources are included.

A list that contains only works cited in the book is properly called *References* or *Works cited.* A list called *Bibliography* contains the works cited in the book and additional works of likely interest to the reader. A *Select bibliography* may be limited to works thought important by the author, or works cited multiple times in the text. A list of *Further reading* usually contains works not cited in the text. In general-interest non-fiction works a more seductive heading, such as *Now read on*. . ., may be used for a similar list. For choice and preparation of bibliographies see Chapter 18.

1.4.5 **Index**

The subject index, an alphabetical list of topics covered in the book, with references to the pages on which discussion occurs, is the last element in the end matter. A single index is preferred unless there is a strong case for subdivision into (say) an *Index of works* and a *General index*. Other indexes that may be needed include an alphabetical list of names (in a biography for example), first lines (of poetry), or an index locorum (an index of places) in a classical work. See Chapter 19.

1.5 Folios and running heads

1.5.1 **Introduction**

The term **folio** has two meanings in print production: it is used of the sheets of a script and also of the page number as a designed element on a typeset page. The latter meaning is the one relevant to this section. A **running head** (or **running headline, headline, header,** or **running title**) is a book title, chapter title, or other heading which appears at the top of every page or spread. Folios and running heads usually fall on the same horizontal line in the head (or top) margin of the page, though the designer may decide to position them in the foot (bottom) margin—in which case the text is called a **running foot** (or **running footline** or **footer**)—or even at the fore-edge (outer margin). They thus appear outside the text area of the page. Another option is to use running heads but to place folios at the foot of the page. Technically the entire line is the running head, but in editorial parlance the term is restricted to the textual material, excluding the folio.

1.5.2 **Folio**

The folio (set in lower-case Roman numerals in the prelims and in Arabic numerals for the text and end matter of the book) usually appears at the outer top edges of the spread, or centred at the foot.

All pages are counted in the pagination sequence, but the folio is not shown on some pages, including some in the prelims, turned pages (that is, those on which material is printed in landscape format), those taken up entirely by illustrations, figures, or tables, and blank pages. On a chapter opening page the folio usually appears in the foot margin (see 1.3.4).

1.5.3 **Running heads**

Running heads are not found in all books: for instance, they may not appear in modern fiction or in highly designed illustrated books.

Running heads, like folios, are omitted from some pages of the book. These include: any section of the prelims that has no section heading (half-title, title, and imprint pages, the dedication and epigraph); part titles; any page on which a chapter heading occurs (including sections in the front matter and end matter); blank pages. They are often omitted on turned pages and on full-page illustrations, figures, or tables.

The content of the running heads depends on the nature of the book. As a general rule, if the same running head is not used on verso and recto, the larger section generates the head on the verso and the smaller that on the recto: for example, the book or part title may be used on the verso, the chapter title on the recto; in a textbook the chapter title might be used on the verso and a numbered subheading on the recto (though running heads that change every few pages should if possible be avoided for the sake of economy). In a multi-author work authors' names normally appear on the verso and chapter titles on the recto. In encyclopedias it is common to reflect the first headword on the verso and the last on the recto in the running heads, whereas dictionaries tend to give the first and last headword on each page in that page's running head.

Sections in the prelims and end matter generally carry the same running head on the verso and recto. Ideally, however, running heads for endnotes should change on every page, indicating the text pages or chapters to which each page of notes refers: for example *Notes to pages 157–99*, or *Notes to Chapter 6*, rather than just *Notes*.

Running heads should match the material from which they are derived in every respect—wording, capitalization, and so on. This is usually generated automatically by desktop publishing software; however, if the book, chapter, or other titles used are very long they must be truncated for the running heads, which should not exceed about forty characters (including spaces) for most books, as a very rough rule of thumb—in this case, supply a list of shortened heads with the copy for the rest of the book.

1.6 Errata slips

An errata slip lists errors in a printed book and their corrections; if there is only one correction the correct term is *erratum slip*. A slip inserted loose in a book should be labelled with the author's name, book title, and ISBN; alternatively the slip may be tipped (pasted) in. In a later printing or edition, if the text itself has not been corrected, the errata may be set as part of the prelims or end matter. When fixed to, or printed in, the book the errata may be called **corrigenda** (singular *corrigendum*). Note that errata slips should be used only in the event of there being serious mistakes or errors of fact in the book.

A list of errata should be as concise as possible, making clear the location, the substance of the error, and the form of the correction. Italic type is used for editorial directions, and punctuation is included only where it is part of the error and/or the correction.

> p. 204, line 15: *for* live wire *read* earth wire
> p. 399, line 2: *for* guilty *read* 'not proven'

For ebook and other digital editions, it is much easier to correct the error than to prepare an errata slip.

1.7 Paper and book sizes

1.7.1 **Paper sizes**

The dimensions of a book depend on the dimensions of the sheet (the **quad sheet**) on which it is printed. For many centuries the dimensions of the common sizes of sheet have been proportioned so that they can be folded to produce viable page sizes without wastage (a small allowance is made for trimming the folded sheet). For example, quarto (4to or 4to) and octavo (8vo or 8vo) are obtained by folding standard sizes two and three times respectively.

Measured in millimetres the common metric paper sizes (untrimmed) are:

Size	**Quad sheet**	**4to**	**8vo**
metric crown	768 × 1,008	252 × 192	192 × 126
metric large crown	816 × 1,056	264 × 204	204 × 132
metric demy	888 × 1,128	282 × 222	222 × 141
metric royal	960 × 1,272	318 × 240	240 × 159

International paper sizes have been standardized still further by the ISO (International Standards Organization): A is the commonest, used for business correspondence, photocopying, etc.; B is used for posters, wall charts, and similar large items; C is used for envelopes and folders to fit A-series sizes. Measured in millimetres A and B (trimmed) sizes are:

A series		**B series**	
A0	841 × 1,189	B0	1,000 × 1,414
A1	594 × 841	B1	707 × 1,000
A2	420 × 594	B2	500 × 707
A3	297 × 420	B3	353 × 500
A4	210 × 297	B4	250 × 353
A5	148 × 210	B5	176 × 250
A6	105 × 148	B6	125 × 176
A7	74 × 105	B7	88 × 125
A8	52 × 74		
A9	37 × 52		
A10	26 × 37		

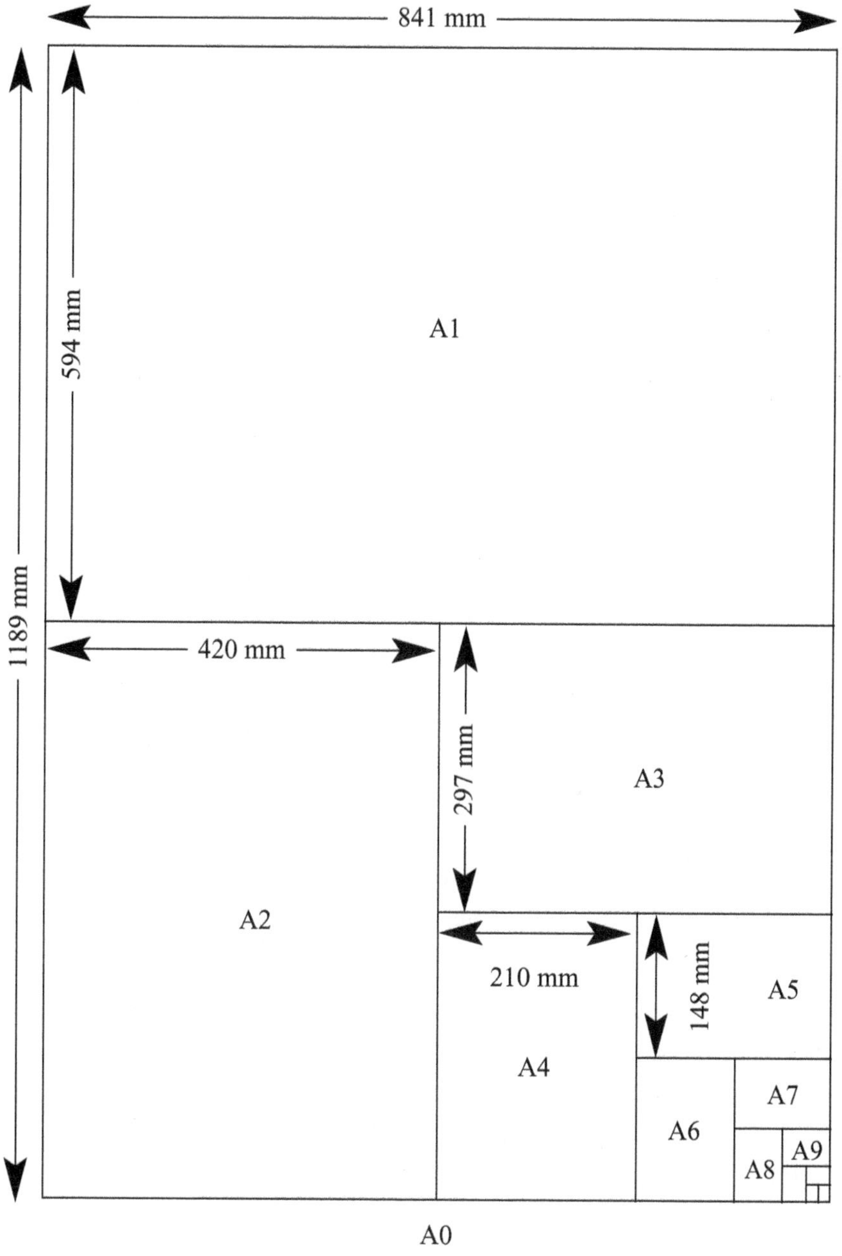

Figure 1.1 **International paper sizes A**

1.7.2 Book sizes

The following are the standard octavo trimmed and untrimmed page sizes, and the dimensions of the quad sheets from which they are derived, in millimetres:

Size		Millimetres
metric crown 8vo		
	trimmed	186 × 123
	untrimmed	192 × 126
	quad	768 × 1,008
metric large crown 8vo		
	trimmed	198 × 129
	untrimmed	204 × 132
	quad	816 × 1,056
metric demy 8vo		
	trimmed	216 × 138
	untrimmed	222 × 141
	quad	888 × 1,128
metric royal 8vo		
	trimmed	234 × 156
	untrimmed	240 × 159
	quad	960 × 1,272
A5		
	trimmed	210 × 148
	untrimmed	215 × 152.5
	quad	860 × 1,220

Dimensions are always given with height before width; for landscape formats reverse the pairs of numbers.

Mass-market paperbacks are often produced in what are known as **A format** and **B format** sizes. The first of these is 178 × 111 mm, B format is 196 × 129 mm.

1.8 Even workings

The pages of the publication are printed on the quad sheet in an order determined by the pattern of folding to be applied to it during the binding process; the arrangement or 'imposition' of the pages on both sides of the sheet is complex.

Each sheet forms a section or **signature** of the finished book; depending on the size of the sheet and the format of the book, the signature may consist of four, eight, sixteen, thirty-two, sixty-four, or even more pages. In the interests of economy it is desirable to ensure that the entire text of the book fits neatly into an exact multiple of the number of pages in each signature so that there are no blank pages at the end of the final section. At a late stage in the production of a print book it may be necessary to restrict the extent of the text in order to fit it exactly, or as nearly as possible, into signatures—that is, to achieve an 'even working'. This must be done without disrupting the pagination of the main text. The usual recourse is to reduce the number of pages in the prelims (which are not part of the main sequence of pages), often by sacrificing the luxury of blank versos and using them for sections that would ideally be placed on rectos; another option is to limit the extent of the end matter, normally by shortening the index or setting it in smaller type.

CHAPTER 2

Preparing copy

2.1 Definitions

2.1.1 **Introduction**

Historically, handwritten **copy** (the text) was called **manuscript** and the term lingers on even today, although text printed out should more properly be called **typescript** or **script**.

Production workflow

The technical stages of the traditional production process, which transforms the material from typescript to printed work, are, very generally speaking (and not always in this order):

- development editing
- copy-editing
- design
- typesetting
- proofreading
- correction (the last two stages may be repeated on successive sets of 'revised proofs')
- proof checking
- indexing
- final correction
- printing and binding.

Some of these steps may be omitted, depending on the readership or on budget and time constraints. See the following sections for a brief description of development editing and copy-editing (2.1.2), design (2.1.3), reading and checking of the proofs (2.1.5), and typesetting

(2.1.4). These specialist operations are frequently outsourced. Indexing is detailed in Chapter 19.

Modern production methods rarely proceed in such a linear fashion and are focused on creating content that can be repurposed for many different publishing outputs, not just print.

The content is stored in a neutral format, which means that it is typically coded with **XML tags**. XML allows the creation of customized **markup languages**. It allows content to be structured, stored, and transmitted in a form that is independent of software or hardware. Crucially, the XML tags describe content rather than presentation, e.g. a tag such as <strong> can be rendered as bold text in print or as red text on a website. The XML can subsequently be transformed to generate outputs as diverse as **HTML** for web publication, **EPUB** files for ebooks, interactive whiteboard material for classrooms, online learning environments, and archive files, as well as traditional print. XML files can also be packaged along with, or accessed by, custom software in the form of an app.

The preparation of files in a digital workflow usually starts with pre-editing (basic file cleanup and tagging), and the processes involved in editorial quality control (editing, checking, testing) are flexible and can take place in parallel as well as serially. This means that, in web publishing especially, traditional boundaries between editing as an initial stage and proofreading as a final stage have been eroded as these roles have merged and a web editor may be required to do several additional tasks (see 2.1.2). Nevertheless, editing and proofreading remain discrete tasks in many publishing houses, so are treated separately in 2.1.2 and 2.1.5.

2.1.2 **Copy-editing**

Whereas a development editor liaises closely with the author during the writing stage, the copy-editor is responsible for the technical preparation of the author's material for publication. These responsibilities, at their simplest, comprise:

- Correcting, or raising queries about, the author's spelling, word use, grammar, punctuation, and sentence structure
- standardizing the presentation of the material in respect of its 'editorial style' and conventions (see 2.3)

- ensuring all elements of the work—that is, headings, displayed quotations, lists, figure captions, references, note copy, etc.—are tagged correctly. These tags are often applied at the pre-editing stage by the XML supplier, but the copy-editor must verify their accuracy. If pre-editing has not been performed, the copy-editor must code or tag the material in the first instance. The tag can be in the form of a word-processor paragraph style or a tag inserted in the file, such as <H1> closed up to a main heading, or an encircled code written in the margin of hard copy. This is a key task for generating correct XML tagging (see 2.1.1); it also highlights features that require the designer's attention (2.1.3)
- indicating where items such as tables, figures, and illustrations should appear in the text to ensure that they are introduced in appropriate places when the pages are assembled
- cross-checking the material to ensure that elements purporting to be identical or related match each other (for example that the chapter titles on the contents page match the chapter openings, that the discussion in text relates accurately to the content of pictures and their captions), cross-references lead the reader to the right destination, note numbers refer correctly to the notes themselves, and so on
- monitoring the factual integrity of the material (for example keeping track of and regularizing the spelling of proper names, ensuring that columns of numerical data add up, checking that the author defines and uses special terms consistently)
- correcting the electronic file accurately or marking the typescript clearly to ensure that the material can be set in type or converted to digital format with minimum difficulty
- being alert to any material that has unsuitable cultural references, or seems potentially defamatory (see 20.5), blasphemous (20.10), or contravenes copyright (20.1–20.4) or that is not inclusive, i.e. is biased with regard to gender, race, sexual orientation, or disability, or that deals with sensitive areas in an offensive or outmoded way.

Dictionaries such as the *Oxford Dictionary of English* or the *Concise Oxford English Dictionary* discuss debatable points of usage, such as the split infinitive and the use of *hopefully* as a sentence adverb, and may usefully be consulted by editors who are uncertain whether an author's phrasing is acceptable English or appropriate to the given context.

It is now generally regarded as old-fashioned or gender biased to use *he* in reference to a person of unspecified sex, as in *every child needs to know that he is loved. He or she* is often preferred, and in formal contexts is probably the best solution, but can become tiresomely long-winded when used frequently. Alternatively use of *they* in this sense (*everyone needs to feel that they matter*) is generally accepted in speech and in writing, especially where it occurs after an indefinite pronoun such as everyone or someone, but should not be imposed by an editor if an author has used *he or she* consistently.

The level of responsibility the copy-editor carries for the structure of the material, factual accuracy, clarity of expression, and other authorial concerns is determined by the publisher, and should be clearly articulated in the brief. The editor should always be sensitive to the author's voice, and not undertake substantive editing or rewriting without discussing it with the author or publisher first.

On-screen (online) editing

Most copy-editing is done in word-processing software, although an editor may also be required to work in spreadsheet or presentation software, text editors, and in content management system editing interfaces (see 2.1.1). The copy-editor should be aware of the internal software tools that allow more efficient and accurate editing, such as templates and styles, global search and replace, macros, revision marking, and shortcut keys, as well as the pitfalls that can accompany these features. For example, it is unwise to replace text globally in documents containing quotations or bibliographic references, where original spelling must be retained. Add-ons can also usefully contribute to the editor's arsenal, such as consistency checkers, bibliographic software, clipboard managers, and third-party macros. Although copy-editing can be successfully completed without any of these tools or features, an editor practised in these techniques can work more effectively, and produce files that are optimized for the next production stage, whether print or digital.

See also 2.4 for a discussion of proofreading on-screen.

Web editing

Copy-editing and proofreading may be required at any stage in the creation and maintenance of websites, a cyclical process that may see the roles merged (see 2.1.1). Web editors should be aware of the differences between how a web page is used compared with print (more information can be found in the many works on usability) and bear in mind that the user may access the material from one of several portals (links), and not in the linear fashion found in printed matter. In essence this involves breaking up the information into smaller chunks that focus on the essentials, interspersed with concise headings and well-planned links.

In addition to the copy-editing tasks described earlier in 2.1.2, web editors may also be required to:

- repurpose existing text into a more suitable form for the website
- write links and summaries
- compose metadata to optimize the site for search engines
- source images and other media
- test and comment on interactive elements such as video
- check for accessibility issues, including writing alternative labels (**alt tags**) for images, for interpretation by screen readers
- create or update the site map.

Proof-editing

Proof-editing is the process whereby unedited material that is laid out in pages, with any figures, tables, notes, and running heads in situ, is corrected. The layout may have been done in word-processing or desktop-publishing software; sometimes only PDFs are supplied. The source is usually a corporate or self-publishing author, typically seeking proofreading services. It may not be apparent at first that more in-depth treatment is needed, so such material should be assessed carefully. If the word-processor files are available, amendments are usually done with revision tracking. It is essential that the author/client understands that the level of intervention needed is likely to be greater than a 'normal' proofread, so it is advisable to send them some sample marked pages to make this clear, as this may also affect negotiations over time and budget. Otherwise the usual requirements for a copy-edit or substantive edit apply, coupled with suggestions for improvements in layout if applicable. PDFs will need to be marked like a page proof (see 2.1.5), although if extensive changes are needed, it may be preferable to convert the files into word-processor documents to work with more efficiency on-screen; you may need to explain your reasons for this and seek approval before proceeding.

2.1.3 **Design**

The designer's role is to determine the appearance of the material on the printed page or screen. The designer creates a design template in which are included the typefaces, type sizes, spacing, and position on the page of all the elements of the material identified earlier. Much of this is done via the template styles, and if the documents have been prepared correctly, the word-processor paragraph and character styles can be imported into the typesetting template and mapped to the designer's styles, saving a great deal of time. This is one reason why it is desirable to format a document with word-processor styles. The designer may also produce specimen pages for approval by the publisher and author, and as guidance for the typesetter.

2.1.4 **Typesetting**

The typesetter produces a **proof**, by applying the design to the material in the electronic file (see 2.1.3), or by rekeying the material if the file is not available, or is incompatible, or unsuitable for some reason.

2.1.5 **Proofreading**

A proof is, as the name suggests, the means of 'proving' (or trying out) the typesetter's work. Most books today are 'set straight to page' and the first proof is a **page proof**.

Historically, text was set as a galley proof, in which the typographic design was applied but the material was not paginated and extraneous items such as footnotes, tables, figures, and illustrations were not integrated. The purpose was to allow the textual material to be checked and corrected—that is, to be finalized—before pages were made up because corrections after pagination might cause expensive disruption to the layout. This was especially true for books with complex layout but now it is easier to generate page proofs with low-resolution image scans (see 16.4.1) and adjust the text (**copy-fitting**) and other elements accordingly; another round of page proofs is then generated for further checking. Although modern systems make page make-up much more flexible, corrections should still not be made unless essential because they can cause delay, and run the risk of introducing new errors.

The proofreader's task is to read and correct the proof. If material has been rekeyed, it is best to read the proof 'against copy' but usually it is set from XML generated from word-processor files (see 2.1.3 and 2.1.4), so is read without reference to the typescript, known as reading 'cold' or 'blind' or 'by eye'. In general terms the proofreader's responsibilities comprise:

- checking for errors—either the typesetter's, in rekeyed material, or ones the copy-editor has missed, or the author's, in text that is being proof-edited (see 2.1.2)
- ensuring that the transformation of the material into typeset and paginated form has not resulted in poor presentation (such as bad word breaks where words are hyphenated at line endings, a short line at the top of a page, a table, figure, or illustration wrongly positioned, or a running head on a page that should have none)
- checking the integrity of the design—that is, ensuring that all like elements have been set in like manner (the proofreader is not asked to verify the technical implementation of the design, only to check by eye that it has been consistently applied)
- ensuring that page references (for example on the contents page or in cross-references) have been correctly inserted.

Most of the first two points are dealt with by the typesetting software, and copy-editors and proofreaders should be aware that page makeup is now frequently wholly automated so they should not work on the assumption that the typesetter will see any comments left in the copy-edited file. Prefer to send an accompanying email with the files if there is anything that needs to be brought to the typesetter's attention.

The changes marked on the first proof are executed by the typesetter and a revised proof is generated for checking by the proofreader. One or more further stages of correcting and checking may be needed before the material can be **passed for press** or signed off as ready to be printed and bound. See 2.1.1 for discussion of conversion of electronic files into digital products.

2.2 Making changes to copy

Most copy is amended on-screen (sometimes called **online editing**) in word-processing software or in a **content management system**. If changes need to be approved by, for example, the author or a production editor, revision tracking is used; queries can be inserted as comments or presented in a separate document or email. It is essential that all comments and revision histories are removed before the next stage of production.

When material must be edited on paper, a form of markup adapted from the proof-correction symbols (see 2.4) is used. Codes identifying the different elements are written in the left-hand margin. Cues locating the position of non-text items, such as illustrations and figures, are best placed in the right-hand margin. Instructions for the typesetter may be written in any convenient position where they will be seen before amending or keying the matter to which they relate. Codes, cues, and instructions should all be circled: by convention, circled material is observed by the typesetter but is not itself set in type. The typesetter is sent the electronic files and a printout marked with the copy-editor's changes: the setter does not rekey the material but needs only to intervene where a change is wanted.

The copy-editor should mark amendments very clearly in the body of the text, as the typesetter will only be glancing down the page looking for changes, not reading line by line. Red pen is favoured as it is obvious and scannable; however, some publishers prefer blue for text changes and red for codes, cues, and instructions. Ambiguous characters, especially if handwritten, should be clarified with a circled comment.

Similarly, if the script is to be entirely rekeyed, all corrections to the text itself are best positioned in the body of the material, above or (if there is space) on the line of type, so that the setter can readily see how they are to be integrated.

An example of marked up typescript is shown in Figure 2.1

2.3 Editorial style and house style

2.3.1 **Editorial style and decision-making**

Editorial style controls the way in which words, individual characters, and numbers are presented on the printed (or electronic) page. Stylistic consistency is an important characteristic of published material because it removes one possible cause of interference between the text and the reader. Inconsistent styling, whether of the words themselves or their presentation on the page, may distract or even mislead, and can affect the credibility of a publication, just as a work that is well finished in these respects can project an air of general reliability.

The essential features of editorial style relate to:

- spelling (including the use of hyphens)
- punctuation
- capitalization
- abbreviations
- treatment of numbers, dates, and time
- use of italic and bold type
- use of quotation marks.

All of these matters are dealt with elsewhere in this book. For spelling and hyphenation see Chapter 3; for punctuation see Chapter 4; for capitalization see Chapter 5; for abbreviations see Chapter 10; for numbers see Chapter 11; for the uses of italic type see Chapter 7; for quotation marks see 4.14 and 9.2.3.

Other conventions that are the subject of editorial decisions include:

- the components and typographic style of bibliographic citations
- the content of notes and in-text references and their relation to bibliographic citations
- the editorial treatment of displayed epigraphs and quotations and their sources
- the punctuation of lists
- the style of in-text references to non-text items such as illustrations, figures, and tables, and cross-references

- the order and contents of prelims and end matter
- the content of running heads.

For coverage of bibliography see Chapter 18; for notes and in-text references see Chapter 17; for quotations see Chapter 9; for lists and tables see Chapter 15; for illustrations and figures see Chapter 16; for prelims, end matter, and running heads see Chapter 1.

Stylistic precepts come into play only where there are alternative solutions of equal or comparable validity. For example, a style decision is needed between 'co-operate' and 'cooperate', each of which is a viable spelling of the word; a choice must be made between 'sine qua non' (roman) and '*sine qua non*' (italic), either of which can be defended. It follows, therefore, that no appeal need be made to stylistic conventions or record kept of them where text is incorrect—for example, a place name beginning with a lower-case letter is not in normal circumstances the subject of a style decision—or where orthodox practice makes a mode of presentation all but incorrect: for example, to style the title of a published book other than in italic in open text would be so unusual as to be tantamount to an error in most book publishing contexts.

It is important to recognize that style decisions are 'made' by leaving text unchanged as well as by changing it; the copy-editor must identify forms that are diagnostic of particular style points and record them explicitly for application throughout the script. The following example contains a number of implicit style decisions:

> In 1539 the monastery was 'dissolved', and the Abbot, in distress of mind—recognising that there was no alternative but to co-operate with the King's officers—blessed his monks (they numbered fifty-seven), prayed with them, and sent them out from the abbey gates to follow their vocation in the world.

If this passage were left unaltered the editor would have 'decided':

- to use single quotation marks
- to capitalize the titles of office holders (*Abbot*, *King*)
- not to capitalize informal references to institutions (*monastery*, *abbey*)
- to use closed em rules for parenthetical dashes
- to use *-ise* not *-ize* endings

- to spell out numbers (or, at least, those up to 100)
- to use the serial comma.

2.3.2 House style

A publisher's house style embodies its preference for how copy is set and laid out on the page. It thus encompasses some elements that control design as well as editorial presentation, including:

- the layout of headings, paragraphs, quotations, lists, and notes
- the make-up of typeset pages
- the application of hyphenation at line endings.

Some or all aspects of the publisher's house style are usually set out in a **style sheet** or **style guide**. Ideally this document will form part of the instructions sent to authors, so that they can follow the house style in creating the work. If this is not done, or if authors follow a different style, it may be necessary for the copy-editor to change the editorial style of the work in the course of editing it.

In some cases—where consistency across multiple publications is important to the integrity of the material—house style or an appropriate adaptation of it should always be imposed; examples include:

- issues of a journal
- individual volumes in a multi-volume publication (including reference works)
- closely integrated series.

How much importance is attached to house style in the case of separate works, however, depends on the policy and traditions of the publisher. In some cases it may be unnecessary or even unwarrantable to impose house style. Where an author has attended carefully and consistently to editorial style and the conventions pose no practical difficulties they may be best left alone: the copy-editor can probably spend editorial time more usefully than in overturning a serviceable and watertight system of editorial decisions, and an imperfect conversion of the author's to the publisher's style will damage rather than improve the work. On the other hand two factors should be noted: it is easier for an experienced copy-editor to impose a familiar house style than to learn an author's style and to check that it has, in fact, been consistently applied; further, those handling the work in the later stages of production may assume that house style has been used and may unwittingly compromise the consistency of the text by making corrections that match house style rather than the author's own style.

Even when house style is in use, it may need to be adapted to the special requirements of particular works. For example, in a historical context modern spellings of place names might be inappropriate; and in a specialist context general practice should not supplant scholarly usage of foreign words or technical terms.

Print versus Web style

The copy-editor should be aware that different stylistic considerations hold sway when working with web pages (see Web editing in 2.1.2), and house style may reflect this. For example, to improve readability on-screen, a house style might stipulate a maximum length for sentences; encourage shorter paragraphs, and more bulleted lists and headings; and minimize the use of punctuation, hyphens, and capitals to reduce visual distractions. Link style may be prescribed, e.g. substituting *click here* with a descriptive target, such as *book online*. These may run counter to the house style for print, so it is helpful to make these differences clear.

2.3.3 **Editorial style sheets**

No house style, however detailed, will cater for all the editorial or design decisions needed to set a publication in type. Just as the designer needs to specify typography for every book, so the copy-editor needs to record particular decisions on editorial style for every book, sometimes supplementing the house-style guidelines, sometimes preparing a completely new set of 'rules' that govern the text. When the editing task is complete this file, setting out the editorial decisions that have been made and applied to the text as a whole, has many uses. It is, of course, crucial to the copy-editor's own work as a record of decisions that have been made—no editor can hold the minutiae of editorial style in his or her head through an entire script. It may be sent to the author as a convenient means of accounting for minor changes made throughout the work. Some publishers send the editorial style sheet to the typesetter for reference. The proofreader ought to receive the style sheet with the proofs so that he or she can tell whether particular style points have been considered and decided by the copy-editor. And the style sheet should be preserved for use by the editor of a future edition of the book or of a related volume.

There are different ways of presenting editorial decisions in a style sheet—a simple alphabetical list, for example, in a word-processed document or a spreadsheet—but for purposes of easy retrieval and comprehension by those who work on the text after the copy-editor a generic approach is clearest. Under headings such as:

- spelling and hyphenation
- punctuation
- capitalization
- abbreviations
- numbers
- italics
- quotation marks

the copy-editor should record high-level decisions, subordinate decisions, and individual examples. So, for example, the section on spelling and hyphenation might begin with a statement that British English spelling is used and that a particular dictionary is taken as the authority; next, decisions on particular words or groups of words should be recorded (such as those with the suffix *-ize* or *-ise*); and finally a list of examples (ordered alphabetically) will be needed. The section on numbers would start with a general statement about the threshold chosen for changing from words to numerals, and go on to list exceptions (such as dates, round numbers, numbers used with units of measure).

2.4 Marking proofs

The requirement of any proof correction marks is that they be comprehensible to the person who must implement the changes they represent. In publishing houses, the use of standard proofreading symbols has been long established, and they represent an efficient means of communicating what needs to be done to a file (typically by the typesetter, in a traditional workflow). In wider contexts, however, such as websites, corporate literature, and self-publishing, the symbols are frequently unfamiliar to the individual amending the files, so instructions must be used instead. This section discusses both situations and applies equally to hard-copy proofs or PDFs, where markup is achieved with the software's commenting tools.

Markup with proofreading symbols

The symbols used to correct proofs in British publishing are those set out in BS 5261, Part 2: 2005. An earlier, 1976 standard, vestiges of which persist in many authors' and proofreaders' practice, used instructions such as 'itals' to change the type style to italic, and some different symbols such as # to indicate a word space. The US and Australian systems are similar to the 1976 UK standard.

The task of the proofreader in marking proofs is to attract the typesetter's attention to the presence of a correction, to locate the correction accurately in the body of the material, and to mark the correction clearly in the margin of the proof. A minimal mark is made in the body of the text and the substance of the correction in either margin. Traditionally, literal errors made by the typesetter are marked in red, and alterations and instructions made by the editor or proofreader in blue, although nowadays publishers may not impose this system because for text set from authors' files, typesetters' errors are confined to rekeyed matter, if any.

Figure 2.2 shows the folio illustrated in Figure 2.1 as a marked proof. Figure 2.3 shows the same page in finalized form.

Adding BSI symbols to PDFs with the commenting tools is slow compared with manual mark-up but it can be expedited using preformed 'stamps'. Alternatively hand-marked hard copy can be scanned and transmitted electronically to the typesetter. The choice will depend on the extent of amendments and the availability of a sheet-fed scanner.

Markup with instructions

Instead of using BSI symbols, proofs can be marked with instructions, e.g. *change 'nad' to 'and'*, or *insert comma after 'however'*. On PDFs this can be achieved with sticky notes or text boxes, different colour boxes

CHAPTER 2

ORIGINAL TYPESCRIPT COPY

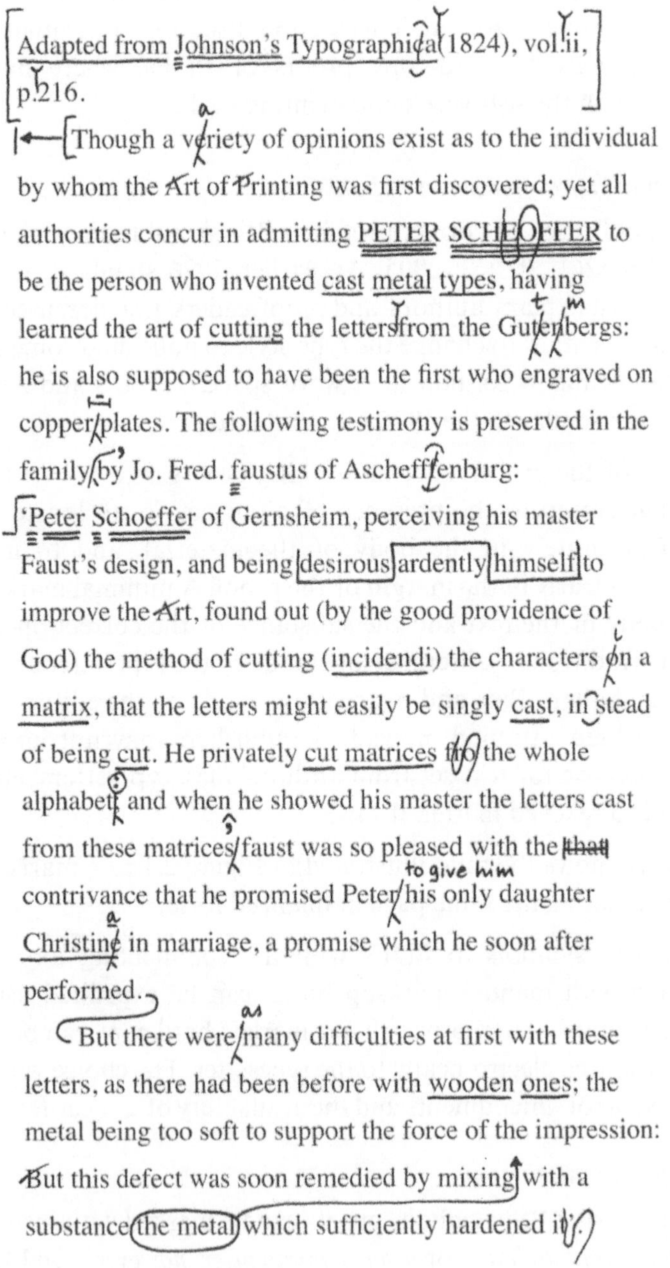

Adapted from Johnson's Typographica (1824), vol. ii, p. 216.

Though a veriety of opinions exist as to the individual by whom the Art of Printing was first discovered; yet all authorities concur in admitting PETER SCHEOFFER to be the person who invented cast metal types, having learned the art of cutting the letters from the Gutenbergs: he is also supposed to have been the first who engraved on copperplates. The following testimony is preserved in the family by Jo. Fred. faustus of Ascheffenburg:

'Peter Schoeffer of Gernsheim, perceiving his master Faust's design, and being desirous ardently himself to improve the Art, found out (by the good providence of God) the method of cutting (incidendi) the characters on a matrix, that the letters might easily be singly cast, in stead of being cut. He privately cut matrices fro the whole alphabet and when he showed his master the letters cast from these matrices faust was so pleased with the that contrivance that he promised Peter his only daughter Christine in marriage, a promise which he soon after performed.

But there were many difficulties at first with these letters, as there had been before with wooden ones; the metal being too soft to support the force of the impression: But this defect was soon remedied by mixing with a substance the metal which sufficiently hardened it.

Figure 2.1 **Marked-up typescript copy**

MARKS USED IN THE CORRECTION OF PROOFS

Adapted from Johnson's *Typographia* (1824), vol. ii, p. 216.

Though a variety of opinions exists as to the individual by whom the Art of printing was first discovered; yet all authorities concur in admitting PETER SCHOFFER to be the person who invested *cast metal types*, having learned the art of *cutting* the letters from the Gutterbergs: he is also supposed to have been the first who engraved on copper-plates. The foll owing testimony is preserved in the family by Jo.Fred. Faustus of Ascheffenborg:

'PETER SCHOEFFER of Gernsheim, perceiv-ing his master Faust's design, and being himself ardently desirous to improve the art, found out (by the good providence of god) the method of cutting (*incidendi*) the characters in a *matrix*, that the letters might easily by singly *cast*, instead of bieng *cut*. He privately cut *matrices* for the whole alphabet: and when he showed his master the letters cast from these matrices, faust was so pleased with the contrivance that he promised Peter to give him only his daughter *Christina* in marriage, a promise which he soon after performed. But there were as many difficulties as first with these *letters* as there hadbeen before with wooden *ones*; the metal being too soft to support the force of the impression: but this defect was soon remeded by mixing the metal with a substance which sufficiently hardened it.'

Figure 2.2 **Proofread proof**

CHAPTER 2

THE PROOFREAD PAGE CORRECTED

Adapted from JOHNSON's *Typographia* (1824), vol. ii, p. 216.

Though a variety of opinions exist as to the individual by whom the art of printing was first discovered; yet all authorities concur in admitting PETER SCHOEFFER to be the person who invented *cast metal types*, having learned the art of *cutting* the letters from the Guttembergs: he is also supposed to have been the first who engraved on copper-plates. The following testimony is preserved in the family, by Jo. Fred. Faustus of Ascheffenburg:

'PETER SCHOEFFER of Gernsheim, perceiving his master Faust's design, and being himself ardently desirous to improve the art, found out (by the good providence of God) the method of cutting (*incidendi*) the characters in a *matrix*, that the letters might easily be singly *cast*, instead of being *cut*. He privately *cut matrices* for the whole alphabet: and when he showed his master the letters cast from these matrices, Faust was so pleased with the contrivance that he promised Peter to give him his only daughter *Christina* in marriage, a promise which he soon after performed. But there were as many difficulties at first with these letters, as there had been before with *wooden ones*; the metal being too soft to support the force of the impression: but this defect was soon remedied by mixing the metal with a substance which sufficiently hardened it.'

Figure 2.3 **Final proof**

being used to distinguish queries from instructions. Frequently used instructions can be copied and pasted from a 'master' file. Heavily corrected text can be copied *en bloc* and pasted into a text box, then corrected by the proofreader so that the recipient can copy and paste it into the source file without further amendment, although formatting may need to be reinstated.

Note that some PDF editors allow direct editing of the text but for published works it is generally better for the amendments to be made in the source file, i.e. in the software that was used to create the file before conversion to PDF, particularly if the changes involve reflowing text.

For a discussion of proof-editing, see 2.1.2.

2.5 Technical issues for the copy-editor and proofreader

A note about Unicode

Unicode is an international encoding system by which each letter, digit, and symbol is assigned a unique numeric value that applies across different platforms and programs. Each character is assigned a code point and a character name (conventionally written in small caps), e.g. capital A is U+0041 LATIN CAPITAL LETTER A and a degree symbol is 00B0 DEGREE SIGN. The Unicode standard contains over 100,000 characters (with capacity for over a million), and is intended to cover most writing systems worldwide. Unicode-compliant fonts are now widely used; none contains all of the characters but the most common accents and symbols that were once a problem to transfer from one type of hardware or software to another can now be successfully reproduced.

There are several input methods for inserting non-keyboard characters into a document, including character mapping applets, or certain keyboard combinations that involve the Alt key and the hexadecimal code point, or the decimal equivalent. For example, in a Windows application, type the hexadecimal code point after a space, then press Alt and X together, and release the keys to insert the character. In HTML special sorts are inserted with an entity tag, such as for a nonbreaking space. Use your preferred input method but strive to use the correct Unicode character, especially for special sorts, as many look very similar, for example the Greek lower-case β and the German eszett ß. Code points and character names for various symbols and spaces are therefore used in Hart's to encourage good practice (see Table 14.4 for various mathematical symbols), although a successful outcome will depend on that character being available in the chosen font. There are various websites that list the characters, their code points, and their HTML entity tags.

2.5.1 Spacing

The height of type and of vertical spaces is measured in **points**. A **pica** is the standard unit of typographic measurement, equal to 12 points; the pica is used particularly to express the total amount of space a text will require, and the text measure (or width of a full line of type) is usually defined in picas.

Vertical spacing

Vertical or interlinear spacing within the body of the text is called **leading** (from the strips of lead formerly inserted between lines of type). The amount of leading affects readability—text that is 'set solid' (that is, without interlinear space) can be tiring to the eye, but too much leading also interferes with ease of reading, and of course takes up more space. The term 'leading' is sometimes also used to refer to the distance from the bottom of one line of type to the bottom of the next, but to avoid confusion it is better to refer to this as the **linefeed**.

The description of the type size is sometimes found on a title page verso. '11 on 12 point' or '11/12 point', for example, indicates that the lines of type are 12 points apart and the text is set in 11 point; in this case, therefore, there is leading of 1 point between the lines of type.

Justification

Copy can be arranged within the text area in one of four ways: **ranged left** (or **flush left**) so that the left-hand side is aligned but the right is uneven (**ragged right** or **unjustified**); **ranged right** so that the right-hand side is aligned and the left ragged; **justified** so that both left- and right-hand sides are aligned to the limits of the 'text measure'; or **centred** so that each line is balanced on the midpoint of the text measure.

Justified copy is produced by evenly varying the spaces between words on each line; spaces that are not permitted to vary in this way are called 'fixed' spaces (such as that between a note cue and the first word of the note). Ragged and centred text has invariable word spacing, as does poetry. Justified text characteristically employs line-end hyphenation to avoid excessive word spacing; ragged text characteristically does not employ it, or uses it to only a limited extent.

Horizontal spacing

An **em** is a unit for measuring the width of printed matter, originally reckoned as the width of a capital roman M, but in digital fonts equal to the current typesize, so an em in 10 point text is 10 points wide. An em space is indicated in hard-copy markup by the symbol □. The Unicode code point is U+2003. An **en** space (U+2002) is a unit of horizontal space equal to half an em. For em rules and en rules see 4.11.

A **thin space** (U+2009) is a fifth (sometimes a sixth) of an em space and is usually indicated in hard-copy markup by the symbol ꝭ. A **hair space** (U+200A) is a very thin space, thinner (sometimes by half) than a thin space. Both are used in contexts where the visual relationship of characters requires some spacing but not full word spacing (for example, where two punctuation marks follow each other). Both are fixed or invariable, and both generally behave as nonbreaking (that is, the matter preceding and following them cannot be separated at a line ending but is treated as a single character). A popular alternative to the thin space is the character **no-break space** (U+00A0).

A single word space is used after all sentence punctuation (not a double space, as was conventional in typewritten text). TeX (specialist software for composing technical material such as mathematics; see 14.6.6) inserts a sentence space that is slightly wider than a single space. It should be noted that most browsers will ignore multiple consecutive spaces. The typesetter should use a non-breaking word space between a pair of initials to prevent their being split across a line: for example, *T. S.* | *Eliot* (not *T.* | *S. Eliot*). Some styles use the same device to link abbreviations and numbers that belong together: *3 km*, *pp. 6–10*, etc. (see also 14.1.4, 14.1.5).

The first line of a paragraph after a heading, epigraph, or section break should be set full out to the left, and subsequent paragraphs indented.

For work that is to be typeset or converted to XML, it is preferable to apply a word-processor style with a built-in indent rather than keying spaces or tabs. Alternatively some styles prefer paragraphs separated by a space with the first line of each new paragraph set full out to the left. This is most commonly found on websites, in reports and some kinds of reference work (such as this one).

2.5.2 **General principles for typeset matter**

Besides checking the accuracy of the typesetter's work, the proofreader is charged with ensuring that the page is presented so as to be easy to read and pleasing to the eye. To this end some generally accepted rules have become established, though the extent to which they are adhered to depends on circumstances and design considerations.

Short lines

Traditionally, printers ensured that the last line of a paragraph did not consist of a single syllable, or numerals alone, or a word of fewer than five characters. This rule is no longer followed strictly, but others controlling the position on the page of short lines are still usually observed. The last line of a paragraph should not fall at the top of a new page or column: this is known as a **widow**. An **orphan**—the first line of a paragraph that falls at the bottom of a page or column—is undesirable, though it is now tolerated in most bookwork.

Line endings

No more than two successive lines should begin or end with the same word. Although practice is now less carefully controlled than formerly, many publishers set a limit to the number of lines in succession that may end with hyphens (typically, not more than three or four). The last line on a recto page should not end with a hyphen. Columns, lists, etc. should ideally not be split; if they are split the break should be in as unobtrusive a place as possible. For information on word division see 3.4.

Page depth

Pages should all be the same depth, so that matter aligns across the head and foot of the spread. The same provision applies to columns in multi-column setting. If absolutely necessary to avoid awkward page breaks, facing pages may be made a line short or long. Complete pages of material set in a type size different from that of the main text (appendices, notes, etc.) should be made up to the depth of the text page, to the nearest line.

Vertical spacing

Interlinear spacing between the lines of type should be uniform in normal texts. Where non-text items occur, extra space (or 'style space') is left between the illustration, figure, or table and the surrounding text. In the interests of preserving a constant page depth or avoiding awkward page breaks, style space may be slightly reduced or increased at need. Complex texts such as dictionaries may achieve equal page depth by varying the leading in adjacent columns of pages. See also 2.5.1.

Centred material

Centred displayed material should be set with invariable word spacing and each line should be separately centred. Wherever possible a short single word standing alone on the last line should be avoided.

CHAPTER 3

Spelling and hyphenation

3.1 Spelling

3.1.1 **General principles**

A good dictionary such as the *Concise Oxford English Dictionary* or the *Oxford Dictionary of English* should be consulted on matters of spelling and inflection; for US English texts a dictionary such as the *New Oxford American Dictionary* is indispensable. The dictionary will give guidance on recommended spellings and acceptable variants, and cover irregular or potentially problematic inflections. The main rules of spelling and inflection are outlined below.

English has an exceptional tolerance for different spellings of the same word. Some, such as *bannister* and *banister*, are largely interchangeable, although a dictionary will always indicate which is the preferred or dominant version. Other words tend to be spelled differently in different contexts: for instance, *judgement* is spelled thus in general British contexts, but is spelled *judgment* in legal contexts and US English. On the other hand, *accomodation* and *millenium* are commonly encountered in print but are not regarded as correct or acceptable spellings of *accommodation* and *millennium*.

Unless specifically instructed to follow the preferred spellings of a particular dictionary, an editor does not generally need to alter instances where a writer has consistently used acceptable variants, such as *co-operate* or *caviare*, rather than the preferred spellings, which in current Oxford dictionaries are *cooperate* and *caviar*. However, comparable or related words should be treated similarly: for instance, if *bureaus* rather than *bureaux* is used then prefer *chateaus* to *chateaux*, and standardize on *-ae-* spellings in words such as *mediaeval* if the author has consistently written *encyclopaedia*. For more on house style and editorial style see 2.3.1 and 2.3.2.

3.1.2 **British and US spelling**

Certain general tendencies can be noted in US spelling:

- *e* where British English has *ae* or *oe*: *estrogen, leukemia, hemoglobin*
- *-ense* for *-ence*: *defense, offense, pretense, license* (noun and verb)
- *-er* for *-re*: *caliber, center, maneuver, miter, scepter*
- *k* for *c*: *skeptic, mollusk*
- *-ll* for *-l*: *appall, fulfill, distill, enroll*
- *o* for *ou*: *mold, molt, smolder*
- *-og* for *-ogue*: *analog, catalog* (see 3.1.7)
- *-or* for *-our*: *color, honor, labor, neighbor, harbor, tumor*
- *z* for *s*: *analyze, paralyze, cozy* (but *advise, surprise*).

In British spelling *fetus* is used in technical texts but *foetus* in general readership; US usage is always *fetus*.

For *sulfur*/*sulphur* see 21.4.1.

Further details are given in sections 3.1.3 to 3.1.9 and in Chapter 21.

3.1.3 **Verbs ending in *-ise* or *-ize***

For most verbs that end with *-ize* or *-ise*, either termination is acceptable in British English. The ending *-ize* has been in use in English since the 16th century, and is not an Americanism, although it is the usual form in US English today. The alternative form *-ise* is far more common in British than it is in US English. Whichever form is chosen, ensure that it is applied consistently throughout the text.

Oxford University Press has traditionally used *-ize* spellings. These were adopted in the first editions of the *Oxford English Dictionary*, *Hart's Rules*, and the *Authors' and Printers' Dictionary* (the predecessor of the *Oxford Dictionary for Writers and Editors*). They were favoured on both phonetic and etymological grounds: *-ize* corresponds more closely to the Greek root of most *-ize* verbs, *-izo*.

For some words, however, *-ise* is obligatory: first, when it forms part of a larger word element such as *-cise* (= cutting), *-mise* (= sending), *-prise* (= taking), or *-vise* (= seeing); and second, when it corresponds to nouns with *-s-* in the stem, such as *advertise* and *televise*. Here is a list of the commoner words in which an *-ise* ending must be used in both British and US English:

advertise	advise	apprise	arise
chastise	circumcise	comprise	compromise
demise	despise	devise	disenfranchise
disguise	enfranchise	enterprise	excise
exercise	improvise	incise	merchandise
premise	revise	supervise	surmise
surprise	televise		

In British English, words ending *-yse* (*analyse*, *paralyse*) cannot also be spelled *-yze*. In US English, however, the *-yze* ending is usual (*analyze*, *paralyze*).

3.1.4 *-ie-* and *-ei-*

The well-known spelling rule '*i* before *e* except after *c*' is generally valid when the combination is pronounced *-ee-*:

believe	brief	ceiling	conceit	deceive	fiend
hygiene	niece	priest	receipt	receive	siege

There are exceptions, notably *seize*. *Caffeine*, *codeine*, and *protein* are all formed from elements ending in *-e* followed by *-in* or *-ine*, and *plebeian* is from the Latin *plebeius*.

The rule is not valid when the syllable is pronounced in other ways, as in *beige*, *freight*, *neighbour*, *sleigh*, *veil*, *vein*, and *weigh* (all pronounced with the vowel as in *lake*); in *eider*, *feisty*, *height*, *heist*, *kaleidoscope*, and *sleight* (all pronounced with the vowel as in *like*); and in words in which the *i* and *e* are pronounced as separate vowels, such as *holier* and *occupier*.

3.1.5 *-able* and *-ible*

The rules governing adjectives that end in *-able* or *-ible* relate to etymology: adjectives ending in *-able* generally owe their form to the Latin ending *-abilis* or the Old French *-able*, and words in *-ible* to the Latin *-ibilis*. When new adjectives are formed from English roots they take *-able*, as in *conceivable* and *movable*. New words are not generally formed with the *-ible* suffix.

With some exceptions, words ending in a silent *-e* lose the *e* when *-able* is added:

adorable excusable indispensable movable

However, in British English some words of one syllable keep the final *e* when its loss could lead to ambiguity:

blameable hireable likeable sizeable

In words ending *-ce* or *-ge* the *e* is retained to preserve the soft *c* or *g*:

bridgeable	changeable	knowledgeable
manageable	noticeable	serviceable

whereas if the word ends with a hard *c* or *g* the ending is always *-able*:

amicable navigable

In US usage, before a suffix beginning with a vowel the final *-e* is often omitted where in British usage it is retained, as in *blamable, likable,* and *sizable*. But it is always retained after a soft *c* and *g*, as in British usage.

3.1.6 Nouns ending in *-ment*

When *-ment* is added to a verb which ends in *-dge*, the final *e* is retained in British English:

abridgement
acknowledgement
judgement (but note that *judgment* is the usual form in legal contexts)

In US English the form without the *e* is more usual (*abridgment*, *acknowledgment*, *judgment*).

3.1.7 Nouns ending in *-logue*

Some—but not all—nouns that end in *-logue* in British English are often spelled *-log* in US English. *Analogue* and *catalogue* usually end in *-log* in America, and a few other words, such as *dialogue* and *homologue*, have the *-log* form as an accepted variant.

3.1.8 *-ce* and *-se* endings

Practice is the spelling of the noun in both British and US English, and it is also the spelling of the verb in the US. However, in British English the verb is spelled *practise*. *Licence* is the spelling of the noun and *license* of the verb in British English, whereas in US English both the noun and the verb are *license*.

US spellings of *defence* and *pretence* are *defense* and *pretense*.

3.1.9 *-ae-* in the middle of words

The *-ae-* spellings of *encyclopaedia* and *mediaeval* are being superseded by the forms *encyclopedia* and *medieval*, although they are still acceptable variants. The dated ligature *-æ-* should be avoided, although note that the title of the *Encyclopædia Britannica* is styled thus. *Archaean, haematology* and similar, largely technical words retain the *-ae-* in British English, but in US English are spelled *Archean, hematology*, etc. The *-e-* spelling is predominant in technical writing, whether British or US in origin.

3.2 Inflection

The chief rules whereby words change form to express a grammatical function are described below. In some cases there are acceptable variant forms in addition to those forms shown.

3.2.1 Verbs

Verbs of one syllable ending in a single consonant double the consonant when adding *-ing* or *-ed*:

beg, begging, begged
rub, rubbing, rubbed

When the final consonant is *w*, *x*, or *y* this is not doubled:

tow, towing, towed
vex, vexing, vexed

When the final consonant is preceded by more than one vowel (other than *u* in *qu*), or by a diphthong that represents a long vowel, the consonant is not normally doubled:

appeal, appealing, appealed
boil, boiling, boiled
clean, cleaning, cleaned
conceal, concealing, concealed
reveal, revealing, revealed

Verbs of more than one syllable ending in a single consonant double the consonant when the stress is placed on the final syllable:

allot, allotting, allotted
occur, occurring, occurred

Verbs that do not have stress on the final syllable do not double the consonant:

benefit, benefiting, benefited
budget, budgeting, budgeted
gallop, galloping, galloped
offer, offering, offered
profit, profiting, profited
target, targeting, targeted

Exceptions are:

input, inputting, inputted
output, outputting, outputted
kidnap, kidnapping, kidnapped
worship, worshipping, worshipped

Another exception is *focus, focusing, focused,* which can double the *s* as an acceptable alternative: *focussing, focused.*

Verbs ending in *-l* normally double the *l* in British English regardless of where the stress occurs in the word:

annul, annulling, annulled
enrol, enrolling, enrolled
grovel, grovelling, grovelled
travel, travelling, travelled

Exceptions in British English are:

parallel, paralleling, paralleled

In US English the final *l* generally doubles only when the stress is on the final syllable. So words such as *annul* and *enrol* inflect the same way in America as they do in Britain, but these verbs are different:

grovel, groveling, groveled
travel, traveling, traveled
tunnel, tunneling, tunneled

In some cases US English spells the basic form of the verb with *-ll* as well (*enroll*, *fulfill*).

Note that *install* has a double *l* in both British and US English, but *instalment* has a single *l* in British spelling and doubles it in US English.

Verbs generally drop a final silent *e* when the suffix begins with a vowel:

argue, arguing, argued
continue, continuing, continued

But a final *e* is usually retained to preserve the soft sound of the *g* in *ageing*, *twingeing*, *whingeing* (but not in US English). *Singeing* (from *singe*) and *swingeing* (from *swinge*) are thus distinguished from the corresponding forms *singing* (from *sing*) and *swinging* (from *swing*). *Raging* is an exception. An *e* is added to *dyeing* (from *dye*) to distinguish it from *dying* (from *die*).

A group of verbs—*burn*, *learn*, *spell*—have an orthodox past tense and past participle ending in *-ed*, but in British English also have an alternative form ending in *-t* (*burnt*, *learnt*, *spelt*). Note that the past of *earn* is always *earned*, never *earnt*, and that of *deal* is *dealt*, not *dealed*, in both British and US English.

3.2.2 **Plurals of nouns**

Nouns ending in *-y* form plurals with *-ies* (*policy, policies*), unless the ending is *-ey*, in which case the plural form is normally *-eys* (*valley, valleys*).

Proper names ending in *-y* retain it when pluralized, and do not need an apostrophe:

the Carys
the three Marys

Nouns ending in *-f* and *-fe* form plurals sometimes with *-fs* or *-fes*:

handkerchief, handkerchiefs
proof, proofs
roof, roofs
safe, safes

sometimes *-ves*:

calf, calves
half, halves
knife, knives
shelf, shelves

and occasionally both *-fs* and *-ves*:

dwarf, dwarfs *or* dwarves
hoof, hoofs *or* hooves

For nouns ending in *-o* there is no fixed system. As a guideline, the following typically form plurals with *-os*:

- words in which a vowel (usually *i* or *e*) precedes the final *-o* (*trios, videos*)
- words that are shortenings of other words (*demos, hippos*)
- words introduced comparatively recently from foreign languages (*boleros, placebos*)
- words of many syllables (*aficionados, manifestos*)
- proper names used allusively (*Neros, Romeos*).

Names of animals and plants normally form plurals with *-oes* (*buffaloes, tomatoes*). In other cases practice varies quite unpredictably: *kilos* and *pianos*, *dominoes* and *vetoes* are all correct. With some words a variant is well established; for example, both *mementoes* and *mementos* are used.

Compound nouns

Compound words formed by a noun and a following adjective, or by two nouns connected by a preposition, generally form their plurals by a change in the key word:

Singular	**Plural**
Attorney General	Attorneys General
brother-in-law	brothers-in-law
commander-in-chief	commanders-in-chief
court martial	courts martial *or* court martials
cul-de-sac	cul-de-sacs *or* culs-de-sac
father-in-law	fathers-in-law
fleur-de-lis	fleurs-de-lis
Governor General	Governors General
Lord Chancellor	Lord Chancellors
man-of-war	men-of-war
mother-in-law	mothers-in-law
passer-by	passers-by
Poet Laureate	Poets Laureate *or* Poet Laureates
point-to-point	point-to-points
sister-in-law	sisters-in-law
son-in-law	sons-in-law

Plurals of animal names

The plurals of some animal names are the same as the singular forms, for example *deer*, *grouse*, *salmon*, *sheep*. This rule applies particularly to larger species and especially to those that are hunted or kept by humans. In some contexts the *-s* is optional: the usual plural of lion is *lions*, but a big-game hunter might use *lion* as a plural. For this reason the style is sometimes known as the 'hunting plural': it is never applied to small animals such as mice or rats.

The normal plural of *fish* is *fish*:

a shoal of fish   he caught two huge fish

The older form *fishes* may still be used in reference to different kinds of fish:

freshwater fishes of the British Isles

Foreign plurals

Plurals of foreign (typically Latin, Greek, or French) words used in English are formed according to the rules either of the original language:

alumnus, alumni
genus, genera
nucleus, nuclei
stratum, strata

or of English:

arena, arenas
suffix, suffixes

Often more than one form is in use:

bureau, bureaus *or* bureaux
chateau, chateaus *or* chateaux
crematorium, crematoriums *or* crematoria
referendum, referendums *or* referenda

The plural of *formula* is now more commonly *formulas* than *formulae* in British and US English, even in mathematical or chemical contexts. In general the English form is preferred: for example, use *stadiums* rather than *stadia*, and *forums* rather than *fora*, unless dealing with the ancient world. Incidentally, *index* generally has the plural *indexes* in reference to books, with *indices* being reserved for statistical or mathematical contexts; conversely, *appendices* tends to be used for subsidiary tables and *appendixes* in relation to the body part. Always check such words in a dictionary if in any doubt.

Words ending in *-is* usually follow the original Latin form:

basis, bases
crisis, crises

3.2.3 **Adjectives**

Adjectives that form comparatives and superlatives through the addition of the suffixes *-er* and *-est* are:

- words of one syllable (e.g. *fast*, *hard*, *rich*)
- words of two syllables ending in *-y* and *-ly* (e.g. *angry*, *early*, *happy*) and corresponding *un-* forms when these exist (e.g. *unhappy*). Words ending in *-y* change the *y* to *i* (e.g. *angrier*, *earliest*)
- words of two syllables ending in *-le* (e.g. *able*, *humble*, *noble*), *-ow* (e.g. *mellow*, *narrow*, *shallow*), and some ending in *-er* (e.g. *clever*)
- some words of two syllables pronounced with the stress on the second syllable (e.g. *polite*, *profound*)
- other words of two syllables that do not belong to any classifiable group (e.g. *common*, *pleasant*, *quiet*).

Words of one syllable ending in a single consonant double the consonant when it is preceded by a single vowel

glad, gladder, gladdest
hot, hotter, hottest

but not when it is preceded by more than one vowel or by a long vowel indicated by a diphthong

clean, cleaner, cleanest
loud, louder, loudest

Words of two syllables ending in *-l* double the *l* in British English:

cruel, crueller, cruellest

Adjectives of three or more syllables use forms with *more* and *most* (*more beautiful*, *most interesting*, etc.).

3.2.4 **Adverbs**

Adverbs ending in *-ly* formed from adjectives (e.g. *richly*, *softly*, *wisely*) generally do not have *-er* and *-est* forms but appear as *more softly*, *most* *wisely*, etc. Adverbs that form comparatives and superlatives with *-er* and *-est* are:

- adverbs that are not formed with *-ly* but are identical in form to corresponding adjectives (e.g. *runs faster*, *hits hardest*, *hold it tighter*)
- some independent adverbs (e.g. *soon*, *likely*).

3.3 Hyphenation

3.3.1 **General principles**

Since hyphenation often depends on the word's or phrase's role and its position in a sentence, and because it is to an extent dependent on adopted style or personal taste, it cannot be covered fully in a dictionary. This section sets out the basic principles and current thinking on hyphens.

3.3.2 **Soft and hard hyphens**

There are two types of hyphen. The **hard hyphen** joins words or parts of words together to form compounds (e.g. *anti-nuclear*, *glow-worm*, *second-rate*). Use of the hard hyphen is described in the rest of this section. The **soft hyphen** indicates word division when a word is broken at the end of a line; for the soft hyphen and word division see 3.4.

3.3.3 **Compound words**

A compound term may be open (spaced as separate words), hyphenated, or closed (written as one word). However, there is an increasing tendency to avoid hyphenation for noun compounds: Oxford Dictionaries Online specifies *airstream* rather than *air-stream* and *air raid* rather than *air-raid*, for example.

It is, of course, vital to make sure that individual forms are used consistently within a single text or range of texts. If an author has consistently applied a scheme of hyphenation, an editor need not alter it, although a text littered with hyphens can look fussy and dated. Editors can find the dominant form of a particular compound in a suitable current dictionary such as the *New Oxford Dictionary for Writers and Editors*.

Some compounds are hyphenated where there is an awkward collision of vowels or consonants:

drip-proof take-off part-time

but even here some are now typically written as one word:

breaststroke earring hitchhiker

Formerly in British English, a rule was followed whereby a combination of present participle and noun was spaced if the noun was providing the action (*the walking wounded*) but hyphenated if the compound itself was acted upon (*a walking-stick*—that is, the *stick* itself was not *walking*). The so-called 'walking-stick rule' is no longer borne out in common use: *walking stick* and many other such combinations (*clearing house*, *colouring book*, *dining room*) are now written as two words.

Compound modifiers that follow a noun do not need hyphens:

the story is well known	the records are not up to date
an agreement of long standing	poetry from the nineteenth century

but a compound expression preceding the noun is generally hyphenated when it forms a unit modifying the noun:

a well-known story	up-to-date records
a long-standing agreement	nineteenth-century poetry

A distinction may be made between compounds containing an adjective, such as *first class* or *low level*, and compound nouns, such as *labour market*: when compounds of the first sort are used before a noun they should be hyphenated (*first-class seats, low-level radioactive waste*), but the second sort need not be (*labour market liberalization*).

Compound adjectives formed from an adjective and a verb participle should be hyphenated whether or not they precede the noun:

double-breasted suits Darren was quite good-looking

Where a compound noun is two words (e.g. *a machine gun*), any verb derived from it is normally hyphenated (*to machine-gun*). Similarly, compounds containing a noun or adjective that is derived from a verb (*glass-making, nation-builder*) are more often hyphenated than non-verbal noun or adjective compounds (*science fiction, wildfire*).

House styles vary greatly in their treatment of compound nouns and it is worth choosing a good dictionary such as the *Oxford Dictionary of*

English or Oxford Dictionaries Online for guidance, but if a specific preference is not stated, it is as well to decide on your own choices for, e.g., *decision maker/decision-making,* and apply them consistently. Most styles seem to agree on *policymaker* but not on which to use out of *policymaking, policy-making*, or *policy making* for example. Much depends on the familiarity of the readership with a particular usage, for example the compound noun *climate change* would be unacceptable if hyphenated and *jobseeker* would jar as two words, at least in the UK, where *Jobseeker's Allowance* is an accepted term. Agreement on the hyphenation of compound adjectives is more common:

decision-making process   cake-making equipment

but again there is a drift towards using one or two words

an international peacekeeping force   high quality teaching

unless ambiguous

cross-training of staff *rather than* cross training of staff

When a phrasal verb such as *to hold up* or *to back up* is made into a noun a hyphen is added or it is made into a one-word form (*a hold-up, some backup*). Note, however, that normal phrasal verbs should not be hyphenated:

continue to build up your pension   time to top up your mobile phone

not

continue to build-up your pension   time to top-up your mobile phone

Do not hyphenate adjectival compounds where the first element is an adverb ending in *-ly*:

a happily married couple   a newly discovered compound

Adverbs that do not end in *-ly* should be hyphenated when used in adjectival compounds before a noun, but not after a noun:

a tribute to the much-loved broadcaster
Dr Gray was very well known

Do not hyphenate italic foreign phrases unless they are hyphenated in the original language:

an *ex post facto* decision
an *ad hominem* argument
the collected *romans-fleuves*
a sense of *savoir-vivre*

Once foreign phrases have become part of the language and are no longer italicized, they are treated like any other English words, and hyphenated (or not) accordingly:

a laissez-faire policy
a bit of savoir faire

In general do not hyphenate capitalized compounds (although see 4.11.1):

British Museum staff
New Testament Greek
Latin American studies

Compound scientific terms are generally not hyphenated—they are either spaced or closed:

herpesvirus
radioisotope
liquid crystal display
sodium chloride solution

Capitalizing hyphenated compounds

When a title or heading is given initial capitals, a decision needs to be made as to how to treat hyphenated compounds. The traditional rule is to capitalize only the first element unless the second element is a proper noun or other word that would normally be capitalized:

First-class and Club Passengers
Anti-aircraft Artillery

In many modern styles, however, both elements are capitalized:

First-Class and Club Passengers
Anti-Aircraft Artillery

3.3.4 **Prefixes and combining forms**

Words with prefixes are often written as one word (*predetermine*, *anti-static*, *subculture*, *postmodern*), especially in US English, but use a hyphen to avoid confusion or mispronunciation, particularly where there is a collision of vowels or consonants:

anti-intellectual	de-ice	ex-directory	non-negotiable
pre-eminent	pro-life	re-entry	semi-invalid

but *predate* (existing before a certain date) despite potential confusion with the meaning *to catch prey*.

Note that *cooperate, coordinate*, and *microorganism* are generally written thus, despite the collision of *o*s, and *preoperative* is used to accord with *postoperative*.

A hyphen is used to avoid confusion where a prefix is repeated (*re-release*, *sub-subcategory*) or to avoid confusion with another word (*re-form/reform*, *re-cover/recover*).

Hyphenate prefixes and combining forms before a capitalized name, a numeral, or a date:

anti-Darwinism   pseudo-Cartesian   Sino-Soviet   pre-1990s

When it denotes a previous state, *ex-* is usually followed by a hyphen, as in *ex-husband*, *ex-convict*. There is no satisfactory way of dealing with the type *ex-Prime Minister*, in which the second element is itself a compound. A second hyphen, e.g. *ex-Prime-Minister*, is not recommended, and rewording is the best option. The use of *former* instead of *ex-* avoids such problems, and is more elegant. Note that in US style an en rule is used to connect a prefix and a compound (*the post–World War I period*).

The prefix *mid-* is now often considered to be an adjective in its own right in such combinations as *the mid nineteenth century*; before a noun, of course, all compounds with *mid* should be hyphenated:

a mid-grey tone   a mid-range saloon car

Email and *website* are commonly one word (but *web page*); *ebook* is gaining ground over *e-book* but less familiar terms such as *e-learning* are currently hyphenated.

3.3.5 **Suffixes**

Suffixes are always written hyphenated or closed, never spaced.

The suffixes *-less* and *-like* need a hyphen if there are already two *l*s in the preceding word:

bell-less   shell-like

Use a hyphen in newly coined or rare combinations with *-like*, and with names, but more established forms, particularly if short, are set solid:

tortoise-like	Paris-like	ladylike
catlike	deathless	husbandless

The suffixes *-proof*, *-scape*, and *-wide* usually need no hyphen:

childproof   moonscape   nationwide

When a complete word is used like a suffix after a noun, adjective, or adverb it is particularly important to use a hyphen, unless the word follows an adverb ending with -*ly*:

> military-style 'boot camps'
> some banks have become excessively risk-averse
> GPS-enabled tracking
> an environmentally friendly policy

There can be a real risk of ambiguity with such constructions: compare

> a cycling-friendly chief executive
> rent-free accommodation in one of the pokey little labourer's cottages

with

> a cycling friendly chief executive
> rent free accommodation in one of the pokey little labourer's cottages

3.3.6 **Numbers**

Use hyphens in spelled-out numbers from 21 to 99:

> twenty-three   thirty-fourth

For a full discussion of numbers see Chapter 11.

3.3.7 **Compass points**

Compass points are hyphenated:

> south-east   south-by-east   south-south-east

but the compound names of winds are closed:

> southeaster   northwesterly

In US usage individual compass points are compound words:

> southeast   south-southeast

Capitalized compounds are not usually hyphenated: note that, for example, *South East Asia* is the prevailing form in British English and *Southeast Asia* in US English.

3.3.8 **Other uses**

Use hyphens to indicate stammering, paused, or intermittent speech:

> 'P-p-perhaps not,' she whispered.
> 'Uh-oh,' he groaned.

Use hyphens to indicate an omitted common element in a series:

> three- and six-cylinder models   two-, three-, or fourfold
> upper-, middle-, and lower-class accents   countrymen and -women

When the common element may be unfamiliar to the reader, it is better to spell out each word:

ectomorphs, endomorphs, and mesomorphs

Hyphens are used in double-barrelled names:

Krafft-Ebing's *Psychopathia Sexualis* (*Krafft-Ebing* is one man's surname)

In compound nouns and adjectives derived from two names an en rule is usual (*Marxism–Leninism*), although for adjectives of this sort a hyphen is sometimes used (*Marxist-Leninist*). A hyphen, rather than an en rule, is always used where the first element of a compound cannot stand alone as an independent word, as in *Sino-Soviet relations*. See 4.11.1.

3.4 Word division

3.4.1 **General principles**

Words can be divided between lines of printing to avoid unacceptably wide spaces between words (in justified setting) or at the end of a line (in unjustified setting). The narrower the column, the more necessary this becomes. Some divisions are better than others, and some are unacceptable because they may mislead or confuse the reader. Rules governing division are based on a combination of a word's construction (i.e. the parts from which it is formed) and its pronunciation, since exclusive reliance on either can yield unfortunate results. The following offers general guidance only; for individual cases, consult the *New Oxford Spelling Dictionary*. See also 2.5.2 for a discussion of the general principles of page layout and proofreading. For word division in foreign languages, see Chapter 12, under the languages concerned.

A hyphen is added where a word is divided at the end of a line. This is known as a **soft hyphen** or **discretionary hyphen**:

con-
trary

If a word with a hard hyphen is divided after its permanent (keyed) hyphen, no further hyphen is added:

well-
developed

In most texts the hyphens in the examples above (*con-trary* and *well-developed*) will use the same symbol (-). Sometimes, as in dictionaries or other reference works in which it is important for the reader to know whether an end-of-line hyphen is a permanent one or not, a different symbol, such as ‐, is used when words are divided:

con‐
trary

A tilde (˜) is also occasionally used:

con˜
trary

In copy to be keyed, add a 'close up' mark (see Appendix Proofreading marks) to any permanent (hard) hyphen that falls at the end of a line, to indicate that it must be typed and set close to the next word. A stet mark (from Latin, 'let it stand') was formerly used, marked as three dots under the character.

3.4.2 **Principles of word division**

The main principle governing the guidelines that follow is that the word division should be as unobtrusive as possible, so that the reader continues reading without faltering or momentary confusion. All word divisions should correspond as closely as possible to a syllable division:

con-tact   jar-gon

However, syllable division will not be satisfactory if the result is that the first part is misleading on its own and the second part is not a complete recognizable suffix. For example, do not divide *abases*, as neither *aba-ses* nor *abas-es* are acceptable.

An acceptable division between two parts of one word may be unacceptable when applied to the same form with a suffix or prefix: *help-ful* is perfectly acceptable, but *unhelp-ful* is not as good as *un-helpful*.

The *New Oxford Spelling Dictionary* therefore uses two levels of word division—'preferred' divisions (marked |), which are acceptable under almost any circumstances, and 'permitted' divisions (marked ¦), which are not as good, given a choice. Thus *unhelpful* is shown as *un|help¦ful*.

The acceptability of a division depends to a considerable extent on the appearance of each part of the word, balanced against the appearance of the spacing in the text. For instance, even a division that is neither obtrusive nor misleading, such as *con-tact*, may be possible but quite unnecessary at the end of a long line of type, whereas a poorer division, such as *musc-ling*, may be necessary in order to avoid excessively wide word spaces in a narrow line. In justified setting, word spaces should not be so wide that they appear larger than the space between lines of type.

Whether the best word division follows the construction or the pronunciation depends partly on how familiar the word is and how clearly it is thought of in terms of its constituent parts. For instance, *atmosphere* is so familiar that its construction is subordinated to its pronunciation, and so it is divided *atmos-phere*, but the less familiar *hydrosphere* is divided between its two word-formation elements: *hydro-sphere*.

3.4.3 **Special rules**

Do not divide words of one syllable:

    though   prayer   helped

Do not leave only one letter at the end of a line:

    aground (*not* a-ground)

Avoid dividing in such a way that fewer than three letters are left at the start of a line:

    Briton (*not* Brit-on)
    rubbishy (*not* rubbish-y)

However, two letters are acceptable at the start of a line if they form a complete, recognizable suffix or other element:

    acrobat-ic   clean-er   vivid-ly   out-do

Nearly all words with fewer than six letters should therefore never be divided:

    again   coarse   hero   money

Divide words according to their construction where it is obvious, for example:

- between the elements of a compound word:

    table-spoon   railway-man

- between the root word and a prefix or suffix:

    un-prepared   wash-able

except where such a division would be severely at odds with the pronunciation:

dem-ocracy (*not* demo-cracy) chil-dren (*not* child-ren)
archaeo-logical *but* archae-ologist psycho-metric *but* psych-ometry
human-ism *but* criti-cism neo-classical *but* neolo-gism

When the construction of a word is no help, divide it after a vowel, preferably an unstressed one:

preju-dice mili-tate insti-gate

or between two consonants or two vowels that are pronounced separately:

splen-dour Egyp-tian appreci-ate

Divide after double consonants if they form the end of a recognizable element of a word:

chill-ing watt-age

but otherwise divide between them:

shil-ling soul-less admit-ting un-natural

Words ending in *-le*, and their inflections, are best not divided, but the last four letters can be carried over if necessary:

brin-dled rat-tled

With the present participles of these verbs, divide the word after the consonant preceding the *l*:

chuck-ling trick-ling

or between two identical preceding consonants:

puz-zling

Divide most gerunds and present participles at *-ing*:

carry-ing divid-ing tell-ing

Avoid divisions that might affect the sound, confuse the meaning, or merely look odd:

exact-ing (*not* ex-acting) co-alesce (*not* coal-esce)
le-gend (*not* leg-end) lun-ging (*not* lung-ing)
re-appear (*not* reap-pear) re-adjust (*not* read-just)

Words that cannot be divided at all without an odd effect should be left undivided:

breeches cliquey preaches sluicing

Hyphenated words are best divided only at an existing hard hyphen but can, if necessary, be divided a minimum of six letters after it:

counter-revolution~
ary

Even where no hyphen is involved, certain constraints must be observed on line breaks:

- Divide abbreviations and dates only after a hard hyphen or an en rule:

  UNESCO
  AFL-|CIO
  1914–|18

- Numbers should not be divided, even at a decimal point: *643.368491*. However, very large numbers containing commas may be divided (but not hyphenated) after a comma, though not after a single digit: *6,493,|000,000*. They cannot be divided at the same places if written with spaces instead of commas: *6 493 000 000*.
- Do not separate numbers from their abbreviated units:

  15 kg   300 BC

- If possible, do not separate a person's initials from their surname, and do not split two initials; a single initial should certainly not be separated from the surname.
- Do not separate a name from a following modifier:

  Louis XIV   Samuel Browne, Jr.

CHAPTER 4

Punctuation

4.1 Introduction

This chapter deals with particular situations where punctuation can be problematic or may be treated in different ways. It does not attempt to give a full account of the ways that punctuation is used in English. Some sections—such as those on the comma splice and on the use of apostrophes to form plurals—give guidance on correct usage, and explain styles that must be followed in order to write good English. Other sections, for example that on the serial comma, describe situations where a number of styles are possible but where a particular one should be adopted in order to produce a consistent text or adhere to a particular house style. See 21.2 for more details of US English usage.

4.2 Apostrophe

4.2.1 **Possession**

Use *'s* to indicate possession after singular nouns and indefinite pronouns (for example *everything*, *anyone*):

the boy's job   the box's contents   anyone's guess

and after plural nouns that do not end in *s*:

people's opinions   women's rights

With singular nouns that end in an *s* sound, the extra *s* can be omitted if it makes the phrase difficult to pronounce (*the catharsis' effects*), but it is often preferable to transpose the words and insert *of* (*the effects of the catharsis*).

Use an apostrophe alone after plural nouns ending in *s*:

our neighbours' children   other countries' air forces

An apostrophe is used in a similar way when the length of a period of time is specified:

a few days' holiday   three weeks' time

but notice that an apostrophe is not used in adjectival constructions such as *three months pregnant*.

Use an apostrophe alone after singular nouns ending in an *s* or *z* sound and combined with *sake*:

for goodness' sake

Note that *for old times' sake* is a plural and so has the apostrophe after the *s*.

Do not use an apostrophe in the possessive pronouns *hers*, *its*, *ours*, *yours*, *theirs*:

a friend of yours   theirs is the kingdom of heaven

Distinguish *its* (a possessive meaning 'belonging to it') from *it's* (a contraction for 'it is' or 'it has'):

give the cat its dinner   it's been raining

In compounds and *of* phrases, use *'s* after the last noun when it is singular:

my sister-in-law's car   the King of Spain's daughter

but use the apostrophe alone after the last noun when it is plural:

the King of the Netherlands' appeal   Tranmere Rovers' best season

A **double possessive**, making use of both *of* and an apostrophe, may be used with nouns and pronouns relating to people or with personal names:

a speech of Churchill's   that necklace of her mother's

In certain contexts the double possessive clarifies the meaning of the *of*: compare *a photo of Mary* with *a photo of Mary's*. The double possessive is not used with nouns referring to an organization or institution:

a friend of the Tate Gallery   a window of the hotel

Use *'s* after the last of a set of linked nouns where the nouns are acting together:

Liddell and Scott's *Greek–English Lexicon*
Beaumont and Fletcher's comedies

but repeat *'s* after each noun in the set where the nouns are acting separately:

Johnson's and Webster's lexicography
Shakespeare's and Jonson's comedies

An *'s* indicates residences and places of business:

at Jane's   going to the doctor's

In the names of large businesses, endings that were originally possessive are now often acceptably written with no apostrophe, as if they were plurals: *Harrods*, *Currys*. This is the case even when the name of the company or institution is a compound, for example *Barclays Bank*, *Citizens Advice Bureau*. Other institutions retain the apostrophe, however, for example *Levi's* and *Macy's*, and editors should not alter a consistently applied style without checking with the author.

An apostrophe and *s* are generally used with personal names ending in an *s*, *x*, or *z* sound:

Charles's   Thomas's   Marx's   *Bridget Jones's Diary*

but an apostrophe alone may be used in cases where an additional *s* would cause difficulty in pronunciation, typically after longer names that are not accented on the last or penultimate syllable:

Nicholas' or Nicholas's   Lord Williams's School

Jesus's is the usual non-liturgical use; *Jesus'* is an accepted archaism.

It is traditional to use an apostrophe alone after classical names ending in *s* or *es*:

Euripides'   Herodotus'   Mars'   Erasmus'

This style should be followed for longer names; with short names the alternative *Zeus's*, for instance, is permissible. When classical names are used in scientific or other contexts their possessives generally require the additional *s*:

Mars' spear

but

Mars's gravitational force

Use *'s* after French names ending in silent *s*, *x*, or *z*, when used possessively in English:

Dumas's   Descartes's

When a singular or plural name or term is italicized, set the possessive *'s* in roman:

the *Daily Telegraph*'s Brussels correspondent   the *Liberty*'s crew

Do not use an apostrophe in the names of wars known by their length:

Hundred Years War

It is impossible to predict with certainty whether a place or organizational name ending in *s* requires an apostrophe. For example:

Land's End	Lord's Cricket Ground
Offa's Dyke	St James's Palace
St Thomas' Hospital (not 's)	

but

All Souls College	Earls Court
Johns Hopkins University	St Andrews

Check doubtful instances in the *New Oxford Dictionary for Writers and Editors*, or on the institution's own website (other websites may be unreliable), or in a gazetteer or encyclopedic dictionary.

4.2.2 **Plurals**

Do not use the so-called 'greengrocer's apostrophe', for example *lettuce's* for 'lettuces' or *video's* for 'videos': this is incorrect. The apostrophe is not necessary in forming the plural of names, abbreviations, numbers, and words not usually used as nouns:

the Joneses	several Hail Marys	three Johns
CDs	the three Rs	the 1990s
whys and wherefores	dos and don'ts	the Rule of 9s

However, the apostrophe may be used when clarity calls for it, for example when letters or symbols are referred to as objects:

dot the i's and cross the t's   she can't tell her M's from her N's
find all the number 7's

Such items may also be italicized or set in quotes, with the *s* set in roman outside any closing quote:

subtract all the *x*s from the *y*s
subtract all the '*x*'s from the '*y*'s

4.2.3 **Contraction**

Use an apostrophe in place of missing letters in contractions, which are printed without spaces:

won't   we'll   will-o'-the-wisp   bo'sun

Except when copying older spellings, do not use an apostrophe before contractions accepted as words in their own right, such as *cello*, *phone*, *plane*, and *flu*.

When an apostrophe marks the elision of an initial or final letter or letters, such as *o'*, *'n'*, or *th'*, it is not set closed up to the next character, but rather followed or preceded by a full space:

rock 'n' roll
R 'n' B
it's in th' Bible
how tender 'tis to love the babe that milks me

In contractions of the type *rock 'n' roll* an ampersand may also be used: see 10.2.2.

There is no space when the apostrophe is used in place of a medial letter within a word:

learn'd ev'ry ma'am o'er

Formerly *'d* was added in place of *-ed* to nouns and verbs ending in a pronounced vowel sound:

concertina'd mustachio'd subpoena'd shanghai'd

but a conventional *ed* ending is now usual in such words:

subpoenaed shanghaied

The *'d* construction is still found, usually in poetry and older typography, especially to indicate that an *-ed* is unstressed—*belov'd, bless'd, curs'd, legg'd*—rather than separately pronounced—*belovèd, blessèd, cursèd, leggèd.*

An apostrophe is still used before the suffix when an abbreviation functions as a verb:

KO's OK'ing OD'd

4.3 Comma

4.3.1 **Restrictive and non-restrictive uses**

There are two kinds of relative clause, which are distinguished by their use of the comma. A defining or restrictive relative clause cannot be omitted without affecting the sentence's meaning. It is not enclosed with commas:

Identical twins who share tight emotional ties may live longer
The people who live there are really frightened

A clause that adds information of the form *and he/she is*, *and it was*, or *otherwise known as* (a non-restrictive or non-defining clause) needs to be enclosed with commas. If such a clause is removed the sentence retains its meaning:

> Identical twins, who are always of the same sex, arise in a different way
> The valley's people, who are Buddhist, speak Ladakhi

Note that in restrictive relative clauses either *which* or *that* may be used in British English, but in non-restrictive clauses only *which* may be used. Restrictive:

> They did their work with a quietness and dignity which he found impressive
> They did their work with a quietness and dignity that he found impressive

Non-restrictive:

> This book, which is set in the last century, is very popular with teenagers

In US English *which* is not used for restrictive clauses, unlike British usage of *which* or *that*.

Similar principles apply to phrases in parenthesis or apposition. A comma is not required where the item in apposition is restrictive or defining—in other words, when it defines which of more than one people or things is meant:

> The ancient poet Homer is credited with two great epics
> My friend Julie is absolutely gorgeous

Note, however, that when the name and noun are transposed commas are then required:

> Homer, the ancient poet, is credited with two great epics
> Julie, my friend, is absolutely gorgeous

Use a comma or commas to mark off a non-defining or non-restrictive word, phrase, or clause which comments on the main clause or supplies additional information about it. Use a pair of commas when the apposition falls in the middle of a sentence; they function like a pair of parentheses or dashes, though they imply a closer relationship with the surrounding text:

> I met my wife, Dorothy, at a dance
> Their only son, David, was killed on the Somme

Ensure that a parenthetical phrase is enclosed in a pair of commas; do not use one unmatched comma:

> Poppy, the baker's wife, makes wonderful spinach and feta pies

not

Poppy, the baker's wife makes wonderful spinach and feta pies

Do not use a comma when what follows has become part of a name:

Dave, the builder from down the road, said …

but

Bob the Builder

4.3.2 **Comma splice**

A comma alone should not be used to join two main clauses, or those linked by adverbs or adverbial phrases such as *nevertheless*, *therefore*, and *as a result*. This error is called a comma splice. Examples of this incorrect use are:

I like swimming very much, I go to the pool every week

or

He was still tired, nevertheless he went to work as usual

This error can be corrected by adding a coordinating conjunction (such as *and*, *but*, or *so*) or by replacing the comma with a semicolon or colon:

I like swimming very much, and go to the pool every week
He was still tired; nevertheless he went to work as usual

or by splitting it into two full sentences.

4.3.3 **After an introductory clause or adverb**

When a sentence is introduced by an adverb, adverbial phrase, or subordinate clause, this is often separated from the main clause with a comma:

Despite being married with five children, he revelled in his reputation as a rake
Surprisingly, Richard liked the idea

This is not essential, however, if the introductory clause or phrase is a short one specifying time or location:

In 2000 the hospital took part in a trial involving alternative therapy for babies
Before his retirement he had been a mathematician and inventor

Indeed, the comma is best avoided here so as to prevent the text from appearing cluttered.

Use a comma when a preposition is used as an adverb:

> In the valley below, the villages looked very small

If commas are omitted, be vigilant for ambiguities:

> In 2000 deaths involving MRSA in males increased by 66 per cent

Prefer *In 2000,* ... or recast the sentence.

A comma should never be used after the subject of a sentence except to introduce a parenthetical clause:

> The coastal city of Bordeaux is a city of stone
>
> The primary reason that utilities are expanding their non-regulated activities is the potential of higher returns

not

> The coastal city of Bordeaux, is a city of stone
>
> The primary reason that utilities are expanding their non-regulated activities, is the potential of higher returns

When an adverb such as *however*, *moreover*, *therefore*, or *already* begins a sentence it is usually followed by a comma:

> However, they may not need a bus much longer
>
> Moreover, agriculture led to excessive reliance on starchy monocultures such as maize

When used in the middle of a sentence, *however* and *moreover* are enclosed between commas:

> There was, however, one important difference

However is, of course, not followed by a comma when it modifies an adjective or other adverb:

> However fast Achilles runs he will never reach the tortoise

4.3.4 **Commas separating adjectives**

Nouns can be modified by multiple adjectives. Whether or not such adjectives before a noun need to be separated with a comma depends on what type of adjective they are. **Gradable** or **qualitative** adjectives, for example *happy*, *stupid*, and *large*, can be used in the comparative and superlative and be modified by a word such as *very*, whereas **classifying** adjectives such as *annual*, *mortal*, and *American* cannot.

No comma is needed to separate adjectives of different types. In the following examples *large* and *small* are qualitative adjectives and *black* and *edible* are classifying adjectives:

a large black gibbon native to Sumatra
a small edible fish

A comma is needed to separate two or more qualitative adjectives:

a long, thin piece of wood
a soft, wet mixture

No comma is needed to separate two or more classifying adjectives where the adjectives relate to different classifying systems:

French medieval lyric poets
annual economic growth
randomized controlled trial

Writers may depart from these general principles in order to give a particular effect, for example to give pace to a narrative or to follow a style, especially in technical contexts, that uses few commas.

4.3.5 **Serial comma**

The presence or lack of a comma before *and* or *or* in a list of three or more items is the subject of much debate. Such a comma is known as a serial comma. For a century it has been part of Oxford University Press style to retain or impose this last comma consistently, to the extent that the convention has also come to be called the **Oxford comma**. However, the style is also used by many other publishers, both in the UK and elsewhere. Examples of the serial comma are:

mad, bad, and dangerous to know
a thief, a liar, and a murderer
a government of, by, and for the people

The general rule is that one style or the other should be used consistently. However, the last comma can serve to resolve ambiguity, particularly when any of the items are compound terms joined by a conjunction, and it is sometimes helpful to the reader to use an isolated serial comma for clarification even when the convention has not been adopted in the rest of the text. In

cider, real ales, meat and vegetable pies, and sandwiches

the absence of a comma after *pies* would imply something unintended about the sandwiches. In the next example, it is obvious from the grouping afforded by the commas that the Bishop of Bath and Wells is one person, and the bishops of Bristol, Salisbury, and Winchester are three people:

the bishops of Bath and Wells, Bristol, Salisbury, and Winchester

If the order is reversed to become

the bishops of Winchester, Salisbury, Bristol, and Bath and Wells

then the absence of the comma after *Bristol* would generate ambiguity: is the link between Bristol and Bath rather than Bath and Wells?

In a list of three or more items, use a comma before a final extension phrase such as *etc.*, *and so forth*, *and the like*:

potatoes, swede, carrots, turnips, etc.
candles, incense, vestments, and the like

It is important to note that only elements that share a relationship with the introductory material should be linked in this way. In:

the text should be lively, readable, and have touches of humour

only the first two elements fit syntactically with *the text should be*; the sentence should rather be written:

the text should be lively and readable, and have touches of humour

4.3.6 **Figures**

In general text most styles use commas to separate large numbers into units of three, starting from the right:

£2,200
2,016,523,354

but it will depend on the nature of the material; for example technical texts use a thin or non-breaking space as a thousands separator; for more about numbers see Chapter 11 and 14.1.3.

4.3.7 **Use in letters**

In formal contexts commas are used after some salutations in letters and before the signature:

Dear Sir, …
Yours sincerely, …

US business letters use a colon after the greeting. On both sides of the Atlantic, however, punctuation is now sometimes omitted, particularly after email salutations (if any) and in informal writing. For more on addresses see 6.2.4.

4.3.8 **Other uses**

A comma is often used to introduce direct speech: see 9.2.2.

A comma is placed after *namely* and *for example* when part of a parenthetical phrase:

> We categorized them into three groups—namely, urban, rural, or mixed
>
> Take, for example, the shutting of a small girl in a locker by three older girls

but no comma is needed when introducing an item or list:

> The theoretical owners of the firm, namely the shareholders ...
>
> If they are off the road, for example on a grass verge, the district council then has to be notified

A comma is generally required after *that is*. Oxford style does not use a comma after *i.e.* and *e.g.* to avoid double punctuation, but US usage does (see 21.2.1).

4.4 Semicolon

The semicolon marks a separation that is stronger than a comma but less strong than a full point. It divides two or more main clauses that are closely related and complement or parallel each other, and that could stand as sentences in their own right. When one clause explains another a colon is more suitable (see 4.5).

> Truth ennobles man; learning adorns him
>
> The road runs through a beautiful wooded valley; the railway line follows it closely

In a sentence that is already subdivided by commas, a semicolon can be used instead of a comma to indicate a stronger division:

> He came out of the house, which lay back from the road, and saw her at the end of the path; but instead of continuing towards her, he hid till she had gone

In a list where any of the elements themselves contain commas, use a semicolon to clarify the relationship of the components:

> They pointed out, in support of their claim, that they had used the materials stipulated in the contract; that they had taken every reasonable precaution, including some not mentioned in the code; and that they had employed only qualified workers, all of whom were very experienced

This is common in lists with internal commas, where semicolons structure the internal hierarchy of its components:

> I should like to thank the Warden and Fellows of All Souls College, Oxford; the staff of the Bodleian Library, Oxford; and the staff of the Pierpont Morgan Library, New York

Since it can be confusing and unattractive to begin a sentence with a symbol, especially one that is not a capital letter, the semicolon can replace a full point:

> Let us assume that *a* is the crude death rate and *b* life expectancy at birth; *a* will signal a rise in …

4.5 Colon

The colon points forward: from a premise to a conclusion, from a cause to an effect, from an introduction to a main point, from a general statement to an example. It fulfils the same function as words such as *namely*, *that is*, *as*, *for example*, *for instance*, *because*, *as follows*, and *therefore*. Material following a colon need not contain a verb or be able to stand alone as a sentence:

> That is the secret of my extraordinary life: always do the unexpected
>
> It is available in two colours: pink and blue

Use the colon to introduce a list; formerly a colon followed by a dash :— was common practice, but now this style should be avoided unless you are reproducing antique or foreign-language typography:

> We are going to need the following: flashlight, glass cutter, skeleton key, …
>
> She outlined the lives of three composers: Mozart, Beethoven, and Schubert

The word following a colon is not capitalized in British English (unless it is a proper name, of course), but in US English it is often capitalized if it introduces a grammatically complete sentence:

> Mr Smith had committed two sins: First, his publication consisted principally of articles reprinted from the *London Review* …

A colon should not precede linking words or phrases in the introduction to a list, and should follow them only where they are introduced by a main clause:

> She outlined the lives of three composers, namely, Mozart, Beethoven, and Schubert
>
> She gave this example: Mozart was chronically short of money

Do not use a colon to introduce a statement or a list that completes the sentence formed by the introduction:

> Other Victorian authors worth studying include Thackeray, Trollope, and Dickens

A dash can also be used in a similar way to a colon, but they are not interchangeable: a dash tends to be more informal, and to imply an afterthought or aside (see 4.11.2).

A colon is used after the title of a work to introduce the subtitle. It may be followed by a capital or a lower-case letter (Oxford style uses a capital):

> *Finding Moonshine: A Mathematician's Journey through Symmetry*
> *Monster: The Autobiography of an L.A. Gang Member*

A colon may introduce direct speech: see 9.2.2.

4.6 Full point

The full point is also called **full stop** or, particularly in US use, **period**. Full points are used to mark the end of sentences, and in some classes of abbreviation. Do not use a full point in headings, addresses, or titles of works, even where these take the form of a full sentence:

> *All's Well that Ends Well*
> *Mourning Becomes Electra*

If the full point of an abbreviation closes the sentence, there is no second point:

> a generic term for all polished metal—brass, copper, steel, etc.
> I came back at 3 a.m.

For more on abbreviations see Chapter 10. See 9.2.3 for a discussion of the relative placing of full points and closing quotation marks.

4.7 Ellipses

An ellipsis (plural *ellipses*) is a series of points (…) signalling that words have been omitted from quoted matter, or that part of a text is missing or illegible. Omitted words are marked by three full points (*not* asterisks) printed on the line. They can be set as a single character (Unicode code point U+2026 HORIZONTAL ELLIPSIS), and many word processors will autocorrect three dots into a single glyph. Some publishers prefer either normal word spaces or fixed (narrower) spaces between the points (. . . or ...). A normal word space is set either side in running text:

I will not ... sulk about having no boyfriend

Political language ... is designed to make lies sound truthful

An ellipsis at the end of an incomplete sentence is not followed by a fourth full point. When an incomplete sentence is an embedded quotation within a larger complete sentence, the normal sentence full point is added after the final quotation mark:

I only said, 'If we could ...'.

A comma immediately before or after an ellipsis can generally be suppressed, unless it is helpful to the sense. If the sentence before an ellipsis ends with a full point it is Oxford practice to retain the point before the ellipsis, closed up to the preceding text. Every sequence of words before or after *four* points should be functionally complete. This indicates that at least one sentence has been omitted between the two sentences. If what follows an ellipsis begins with a complete sentence in the original, it should begin with a capital letter:

I never agreed to it. ... It would be ridiculous.

For more details on the use of ellipses in presenting quoted material see 9.3.3.

Sentences ending with a question mark or exclamation mark retain these marks before or after the ellipsis:

Could we ...?

Could we do it? ... It might just be possible ...!

An ellipsis can be used to show a trailing off on the part of a speaker, or to create a dramatic or ironic effect:

The door opened slowly ...

I don't ... er ... understand

It is also used, like *etc.*, to show the continuation of a sequence that the reader is expected to infer:

in 1997, 1999, 2001 ...

the gavotte, the minuet, the courante, the cotillion, the allemande, ...

Note that other languages use ellipses in different ways: Chinese and Japanese, for example, use six dots in two groups of three. For ellipses in mathematical notation see 14.6.2.

4.8 Question mark

4.8.1 **Typical uses**

Question marks are used to indicate a direct question. Do not use a question mark when a question is implied by indirect speech:

> He wants to know whether you are coming
> She asked why the coffee hadn't materialized

Requests framed as questions out of idiom or politeness do not normally take question marks:

> May I take this opportunity to wish you all a safe journey
> Will everyone please stand to toast the bride and groom

although a question mark can seem more polite than a full point:

> Would you kindly let us know whether to expect you?
> I wonder if I might ask you to open the window?

Matter following a question mark begins with a capital letter:

> You will be back before lunch, right? About noon? Good.

although short questions that are embedded in another sentence are not followed by a capital:

> Where now? they wonder

Embedded questions that are not in quotation marks are often not capitalized. The question mark follows the question at whatever point it falls in a sentence:

> The question is, what are the benefits for this country? What about the energy?

When the question is presented as direct speech (whether voiced or formulated in someone's mind), it should be capitalized and set in quotation marks:

> 'Why not?' she wondered
> She wondered, 'Why not?'

Note that a question mark at the end of a sentence functions like a full point, and that double punctuation should not be used. For a full account of the use of punctuation with quotation marks see 9.2.3.

4.8.2 Use to express uncertainty

Use a question mark immediately before or after a word, phrase, or figure to express doubt, placing it in parentheses where it would otherwise appear to punctuate or interrupt a sentence. Strictly, a parenthetical question mark should be set closed up to a single word to which it refers, but with a normal interword space separating the doubtful element from the opening parenthesis if more of the sentence is contentious:

> The White Horse of Uffington (? sixth century BC) was carved ...
> Homer was born on Chios(?)

However, this distinction is probably too subtle for all but specialized contexts, and explicit rewording may well be preferable. The device does not always make clear what aspect of the text referred to is contentious: in the latter example it is Homer's birthplace that is in question, but a reader might mistakenly think it is the English spelling (*Chios*) of what is *Khios* in Greek.

A question mark is sometimes used to indicate that a date is uncertain; in this context it may precede or follow the date. It is important to ensure that the questionable element is clearly identified, and this may necessitate the use of more than one question mark. In some styles the exact spacing of the question mark is supposed to clarify its meaning, but the significance of the space may well be lost on the reader, who will not grasp the difference between the following forms:

> ? 1275–1333 ?1275–1333

or

> 1275–1333 ? 1275–1333?

It would be clearer to present the first form with two question marks and the second with one only; and in general the question mark is better placed in the after position:

> 1275?–1333? 1275?–1333

Similarly, care must be taken not to elide numbers qualified by a question mark if the elision may introduce a false implication: in a context where number ranges are elided, *1883–1888?* makes clear that the first date is certain but the second in question; *1883–8?* suggests that the entire range is questionable.

More refined use of the question mark, with days and months as well as years, is possible but tricky. While *10? January 1731* quite clearly throws only the day into question, *10 January? 1731* could, in theory, mean that the day and year are known but the month is only probable. In such circumstances it is almost always preferable to replace or supplement the form with some explanation:

> He made his will in 1731 on the 10th of the month, probably January (the record is unclear)

or

> He made his will on 10 January? 1731 (the document is damaged and the month cannot be clearly read)

A distinction is usually understood between the use of a question mark and *c.* (*circa*) with dates: the former means that the date so qualified is probable, the latter that the event referred to happened at an unknown time, before, on, or after the date so qualified. (Note that the period implied by *c.* is not standard: *c.*1650 probably implies a broader range of possible dates than does *c.*1653.)

A question mark in parentheses is sometimes used to underline sarcasm or for other humorous effect:

> With friends (?) like that, you don't need enemies

4.9 Exclamation mark

The exclamation mark—also called an **exclamation point** in the US—follows emphatic statements, commands, and interjections expressing emotion. In mathematics, an exclamation mark is the factorial sign: $4! = 4 \times 3 \times 2 \times 1 = 24$; 4! is pronounced 'four factorial'. In computing it is a delimiter symbol, sometimes called a 'bang'. See Chapter 14.

Avoid overusing the exclamation mark for emphasis. Although often employed humorously or to convey character or manner in fiction, in serious texts it should be used only minimally.

As with a question mark, an exclamation mark at the end of a sentence functions like a full point, and double punctuation should not be used. For a full account of the use of punctuation with quotation marks see 9.2.3.

4.10 Hyphen

For the use of hyphens in compound words and in word division see Chapter 3.

4.11 Dashes

4.11.1 **En rule**

The en rule (US **en dash**) (–) (Unicode code point U+2013 EN DASH) is longer than a hyphen and half the length of an em rule. (See 4.11.2 for a definition of an em). Many British publishers use an en rule with space either side as a parenthetical dash, but Oxford and most US publishers use an em rule.

Use the en rule closed up in elements that form a range:

pp. 23–36   1939–45   Monday–Saturday   9.30–5.30

In specifying a range use either the formula *from ... to ...* or *xxxx–xxxx*, never a combination of the two (*the war from 1939 to 1945 or the 1939–45 war*, but not *the war from 1939–45*). For more on ranges see Chapter 11.

The en rule is used closed up to express connection or relation between words; it means roughly *to* or *and*:

Dover–Calais crossing	Ali–Foreman match
editor–author relationship	Permian–Carboniferous boundary

It is sometimes used like a solidus to express an alternative, as in *an on–off relationship* (see 4.13.1).

Use an en rule between names of joint authors or creators to show that it is not the hyphenated name of one person. Thus *the Lloyd–Jones theory* involves two people (en rule), *the Lloyd-Jones theory* one person (hyphen), and *the Lloyd-Jones–Scargill talks* two people (hyphen and en rule).

In compound nouns and adjectives derived from two names an en rule is usual:

Marxism–Leninism (Marxist theory as developed by Lenin)
Marxist–Leninist theory

although for adjectives of this sort a hyphen is sometimes used. Note the difference between *Greek–American negotiations* (between the Greeks and the Americans, en rule) and *his Greek-American wife* (American by birth but Greek by descent, hyphen). Elements, such as combining forms, that cannot stand alone take a hyphen, not an en rule: *Sino-Soviet*, *Franco-German* but *Chinese–Soviet*, *French–German*.

Spaced en rules may be used to indicate individual missing letters:

the Earl of H – – w – – d

'F – – – off!' he screamed

The asterisk is also used for this purpose (see 4.15).

4.11.2 **Em rule**

The em rule (US **em dash**) (—) (Unicode code point U+2014 EM DASH) is twice the length of an en rule. (An **em** is a unit for measuring the width of printed matter, originally reckoned as the width of a capital roman M, but in digital fonts equal to the current typesize, so an em in 10 point text is 10 points wide.) Oxford and most US publishers use a closed-up em rule as a parenthetical dash; other British publishers use the en rule with space either side.

No punctuation should precede a single dash or the opening one of a pair. A closing dash may be preceded by an exclamation or question mark, but not by a comma, semicolon, colon, or full point. Do not capitalize a word, other than a proper noun, after a dash, even if it begins a sentence.

A pair of dashes expresses a more pronounced break in sentence structure than commas, and draws more attention to the enclosed phrase than brackets:

The party lasted—we knew it would!—far longer than planned

There is *nothing*—absolutely nothing—half so much worth doing as simply messing about in boats

Avoid overuse of the dash in this context and the next; certainly, no more than one pair of dashes should be used in one sentence.

A single parenthetical dash may be used to introduce a phrase at the end of a sentence or replace an introductory colon. It has a less formal, more casual feel than a colon, and often implies an afterthought or aside:

I didn't have an educated background—dad was a farm labourer

Everyone understands what is serious—and what is not

They solicit investments from friends, associates—basically, anyone with a wallet

Do not use it after a colon except in reproducing antique or foreign-language typography.

Use an em rule spaced to indicate the omission of a word, and closed up to indicate the omission of part of a word:

> We were approaching — when the Earl of C— disappeared

Asterisks or two or more en rules are also employed for this purpose (see 4.11.1, 4.15).

An em rule closed up can be used in written dialogue to indicate an interruption, much like an ellipsis indicates trailing off:

> 'Does the moon actually—?'
> 'They couldn't hit an elephant at this dist—'

A spaced em rule is used in indexes to indicate a repeated word (see Chapter 19). Two spaced em rules (——) are used in some styles (including Oxford's) for a repeated author's name in successive bibliographic entries (see Chapter 18).

4.12 Brackets

The symbols (), [ ], {}, and < > are all brackets. Round brackets () are also called **parentheses**; [ ] are **square brackets** to the British, though often simply called **brackets** in US use; { } are **braces** or **curly brackets**; and < and > are **angle brackets**. For the use of brackets in mathematics see 14.6.5.

4.12.1 **Parentheses**

Parentheses or round brackets are used for digressions and explanations, as an alternative to paired commas or dashes. They are also used for glosses and translations, to give or expand abbreviations, and to enclose ancillary information, references, and variants:

> He hopes (as we all do) that the project will be successful
> Zimbabwe (formerly Rhodesia)
> They talked about power politics (Machtpolitik)
> *TLS* (*Times Literary Supplement*)
> £2 billion ($3.1 billion)
> Geoffrey Chaucer (1340–1400)

Parentheses are also used in enumerating items in a list (see Chapter 15).

4.12.2 **Square brackets**

Square brackets [ ] are used chiefly for comments, corrections, or translations made by a subsequent author or editor:

They [the Lilliputians] rose like one man
Daisy Ashford wrote The Young Visiters [*sic*]

For more on the use of brackets in quotations see Chapter 9.

4.12.3 **Braces**

Braces or curly brackets { } are used chiefly in mathematics, computing, prosody, music, and textual notation; their usage varies within each of these fields. A single brace may be used set vertically to link two or more lines of material together:

The High Court of Justice {
Queen's Bench
Chancery
the Family Division

4.12.4 **Angle brackets**

Angle brackets < >, the less-than or greater-than signs (Unicode code points U+003C and U+003E respectively), sometimes known as wide angle brackets, are used in pairs to enclose computer code or tags. They are used singly in computing, economics, mathematics, and scientific work to show the relative size of entities, the logical direction of an argument, etc. In etymology they are used singly to mean 'from, derived from' (<) and 'gives' or 'has given' (>):

< Urdu *murġī* hen > *murġ* bird, fowl

In mathematics and science narrow angle brackets ⟨ ⟩ are used (U+27E8 and U+27E9 MATHEMATICAL LEFT and RIGHT ANGLE BRACKET respectively); in these fields < >, respectively, signify 'less than' and 'greater than'. See 14.6.5.

Narrow angle brackets are also used to enclose conjecturally supplied words where a source is defective or illegible:

He came from *Oxon*: to be ⟨pedagogue⟩ to a neighbour of mine

Avoid angle brackets around URLs (see 18.8.3).

4.12.5 **Punctuation with brackets**

Rules governing punctuation are the same regardless of the type of bracket used. A complete sentence within brackets is capitalized and ends in a full point unless the writer has chosen to place it within another sentence:

The discussion continued after dinner. (This was inevitable.)
The discussion continued after dinner (this was inevitable).

No punctuation precedes the opening parenthesis except in the case of terminal punctuation before a full sentence within parentheses, or where parentheses mark divisions in the text:

> We must decide (*a*) where to go, (*b*) whom to invite, and (*c*) what to take with us

4.12.6 **Nested brackets**

In normal running text, avoid using brackets within brackets. This is sometimes inevitable, as when matter mentioned parenthetically already contains parentheses. In such cases Oxford prefers double parentheses to square brackets within parentheses (the usual US convention). Double parentheses are closed up, without spaces:

> the Chrysler Building (1928–30, architect William van Alen (*not* Allen))
>
> the album's original title ((*I*) *Got My Mojo Working* (*But It Just Won't Work on You*)) is seldom found in its entirety

References to, say, law reports and statutes vary between parentheses and square brackets; the prescribed conventions should be followed (see also Chapter 13).

4.13 Solidi and verticals

4.13.1 **Solidus**

The solidus (/, plural *solidi*) is known by many terms, such as the **slash** or **forward slash, stroke, oblique, virgule, diagonal,** and **shilling mark**. It is in general used to express a relationship between two or more things. The most common use of the solidus is as a shorthand to denote alternatives, as in *either/or*, *his/her*, *on/off*, *s/he* (she or he). The solidus is generally closed up, both when separating two complete words (*and/or*) and between parts of a word (*s/he*).

The symbol is sometimes misused to mean *and* rather than *or*, and so it is normally best in text to spell out the alternatives explicitly in cases which could be misread (*his or her*; *on or off*). An en rule can sometimes substitute for a solidus, as in *an on–off relationship*. In addition to indicating alternatives, the solidus is used in other ways:

- to form part of certain abbreviations, such as *a/c* (account), *c/o* (care of), *n/a* (not applicable), and *24/7* (twenty-four hours a day, seven days a week)
- to indicate line breaks when successive lines of poetry are run on as a single line, though Oxford traditionally prefers to use a vertical (|) instead (see 4.13.2, 9.4.1)
- to replace the en rule for a period of one year reckoned in a format other than the 1 January to 31 December calendar extent: *49/8 BC*, *the fiscal year 2000/1*
- to separate the days, months, and years in dates: *5/2/99* (see also 11.5)
- to separate elements in a URL: http://www.oup.com/oeddicref.

In scientific and technical work the solidus is used to indicate ratios, as in *miles/day*, *metres/second.* In computing it is called a **forward slash,** to differentiate it from a **backward slash**, **backslash**, or **reverse solidus** (\): each of these is used in different contexts as a separator (see 14.5.3,14.6.3).

4.13.2 **Vertical**

The vertical rule, line, or bar (|), also called the **upright rule** or simply the **vertical**, has specific uses as a technical symbol in the sciences (see 14.5.3, 14.6.5) and in specialist subjects such as prosody. More commonly, it may be used, with a space either side, to indicate the separation of lines where text is run on rather than displayed, for instance for poems, plays, correspondence, libretti, or inscriptions:

> The English winter—ending in July | To recommence in August

A solidus may also be used for this purpose. When written lines do not coincide with verse lines it may be necessary to indicate each differently: in such cases use a vertical for written lines and a solidus for verse.

When more than one speaker or singer is indicated in a run-together extract, the break between different characters' lines is indicated by two verticals (set closed up to each other).

In websites, spaced vertical lines are sometimes used to separate elements in a menu:

> News | History | Gallery | Music | Links | Contact

The vertical line is used in the syntax of some computing languages and scripts, and is sometimes referred to as a **pipe**.

4.14 Quotation marks

Quotation marks, also called **inverted commas**, are of two types: single (‘’) and double (“ ”). Upright quotation marks (' or ") are also sometimes used. People writing for the Internet should note that single quotation marks are regarded as easier to read on a screen than double ones. British practice is normally to enclose quoted matter between single quotation marks, and to use double quotation marks for a quotation within a quotation:

> ‘Have you any idea’, he said, ‘what “red mercury” is?’

The order is often reversed in newspapers, and uniformly in US practice:

> “Have you any idea,” he said, “what ‘red mercury’ is?”

If another quotation is nested within the second quotation, revert to the original mark, either single–double–single or double–single–double.

Displayed quotations of poetry and prose take no quotation marks. In reporting extended passages of speech, use an opening quotation mark at the beginning of each new paragraph, but a closing one only at the end of the last. For more on quotations see Chapter 9, which also covers direct speech and the relative placing of quotation marks with other punctuation.

Use quotation marks and roman (not italic) type for titles of short poems, short stories, and songs (see Chapter 8):

> ‘Raindrops Keep Falling on my Head’
> ‘The Murders in the Rue Morgue’

Use quotation marks for titles of chapters in books, articles in periodicals, and the like:

> Mr Brock read a paper entitled ‘Description in Poetry’

But omit quotation marks when the subject of the paper is paraphrased:

> Mr Brock read a paper on description in poetry

not

> Mr Brock read a paper on ‘Description in Poetry’

Quotation marks may be used to enclose an unfamiliar or newly coined word or phrase, or one to be used in a technical sense:

'hermeneutics' is the usual term for such interpretation
the birth or 'calving' of an iceberg
the weird and wonderful world of fan fiction, or 'fanfic'

They are often used as a way of distancing oneself from a view or claim, or of apologizing for a colloquial or vulgar expression:

Authorities claim to have organized 'voluntary' transfers of population
I must resort to a 'seat of the pants' approach
Kelvin and Danny are 'dead chuffed' with its success

Such quotation marks should be used only at the first occurrence of the word or phrase in a work. Note that quotation marks should not be used to emphasize material.

Quotation marks are not used around the names of houses or public buildings:

Chequers the Barley Mow

4.15 Asterisk

A superscript asterisk * is used in text as a pointer to an annotation or footnote, especially in books that have occasional footnotes rather than a formal system of notes (see also 14.1.6). It can also indicate a cross-reference in a reference work:

Thea *Porter and Caroline *Charles created dresses and two-piece outfits based on gypsy costume

Asterisks may be used to indicate individual missing letters, with each asterisk substituting for a missing letter and closed up to the next asterisk: *that b******!* En rules are also used for this purpose (see 4.11.1).

On websites and in emails asterisks are sometimes used to indicate emphasis, in place of quotation marks, or to show where italicization would normally be used, for example in the titles of books or other works that are mentioned:

The engagement, the debate, the willingness to engage—*that's* what's important
Maybe some people can handle these little romances as *harmless fun*, but I can't

Asterisks should not be used in place of dots for ellipsis.

For uses in computing see 14.5.3; for other uses see 10.3.

CHAPTER 5

Capitalization

5.1 General principles

Capital letters in English are used to punctuate sentences, to distinguish proper nouns from other words, for emphasis, and in headings and work titles. It is impossible to lay down absolute rules for all aspects of capitalization; as with hyphenation, the capitalization of a particular word will depend upon its role in the sentence, and also to some extent on a writer's personal taste or on the house style being followed. Also, certain disciplines, especially history, have their own particular styles of capitalization. However, some broad principles are outlined below. Editors should respect the views of authors, except in cases of internal discrepancies. Both authors and editors should strive for consistency: before writing or editing too much of a work, consider the principles that should govern capitalization, and while working through the material create a style sheet showing capitalization choices, and stick to it.

Excessive use of capitals in emails and on online forums is frowned upon (it is regarded as 'shouting'); on websites, words in capitals can be difficult to read, and it is better to use colour for emphasis.

For the use of capitals in work titles see 8.2.2 and 8.8. For capitalization in lists and tables see Chapter 15, in quotations and verse Chapter 9, in legal references 13.2.3, and in bibliographies 18.2.5. Small capitals are discussed at 7.5.2. For capitalization in languages other than English see Chapter 12 under the language concerned.

5.2 Sentence capitals

Capitalize the first letter of a word that begins a sentence, or the first of a set of words used as a sentence:

> This had the makings of a disaster. Never mind.
> Come on. Tell me!

Capitalize the first letter of a syntactically complete quoted sentence. If, as occasionally happens in fiction or journalism, quotation marks are not used, the first word is generally not capitalized:

> Sylvie replied, 'She's a good girl.'
> I thought, 'There goes my theory.'
> The question is, does anyone have an antidote?

Quoted single words or phrases that do not constitute a sentence are not capitalized:

> He'd say 'bye' and run down the wide school steps
> Certain young wines do not 'travel well'

For a full discussion of quotation marks and the punctuation that accompanies them see 9.2.

In British English, matter following a colon begins with a lower-case initial, unless it is a displayed quotation or extract, but in US style a capital letter may be used after a colon if it introduces a complete sentence.

5.3 Use to indicate specific references

5.3.1 **Use to create proper names**

Initial capitals mark out the status of words so that the reader interprets them correctly. Ordinary proper names are usually recognizable even when they are set (through error or because of the preference of the person named) with lower-case initials. However, where a proper name consists of common nouns and qualifiers, initial capitals are needed to distinguish the specific usage from a general descriptive usage. Consider the difference in meaning, conferred by the application of initial capitals, between the following usages:

> Tate Britain is the national gallery of British art
> the National Gallery contains incomparable examples of British art
> the city of London attracts millions of visitors every year
> the City (London's financial district)
> the sun sets in the west
> nationalist movements that posed a threat to the interests of the West

Some words are capitalized to distinguish their use in an abstract or specific sense. In the names of religious denominations the word *church* is capitalized, as in *the Baptist Church*, but *church* has a lower-case initial in general references to buildings, as in *a Baptist church*. (Note, however, that it would be usual to capitalize the full name of a specific building, as in *Pond Street Baptist Church*.)

Similarly, *State* is capitalized when it is used in an abstract or legal sense, as in *the separation of Church and State*, and in specific names of US states (*New York State*), but a reference to states in general will have a lower-case initial: *seven Brazilian states*. There is no need to capitalize the word *government*, whether it refers to a particular body of persons or to a general concept or body.

Historians commonly impose minimal capitalization on institutional references; this may sometimes appear unconventional and should not be permitted if it will obscure genuine differences in meaning (as, for example, between *the catholic church* and *the Catholic Church*), although readers will seldom misunderstand lower-case forms in context. The style is common in, and appropriate to, much historical work, but editors should not introduce it without consulting with the author and/or publisher.

It is as well, generally, to minimize the use of initial capitals where there is no detectable difference in meaning between capitalized and lower-case forms. *Left* and *right* are generally capitalized when they refer to political affiliations, but no reader would be likely to misinterpret the following in a book about British political life:

> He is generally considered to be on the left in these debates

simply because it was not capitalized as

> He is generally considered to be on the Left in these debates

Overuse of initial capitals is obtrusive, and can even confuse by suggesting false distinctions.

Capitals are sometimes used for humorous effect in fiction to convey a self-important or childish manner:

> Poor Jessica. She has Absolutely No Idea.
> Am irresistible Sex Goddess. Hurrah!

5.3.2 **Formal and informal references**

When one is referring back, after the first mention, to a capitalized compound relating to a proper name, the usual practice is to revert to lower case:

Cambridge University	their university
the Ritz Hotel	that hotel
Lake Tanganyika	the lake
National Union of Mineworkers	the union
the Royal Air Force	the air force

Capitals are sometimes used for a short-form mention of the title of a specified person, organization, or institution previously referred to in full:

the Ministry
the University statute
the College silver
the Centre's policy
the Navy's provisions

This style is found particularly in formal documents. Over the course of a book it is important to keep the practice within bounds and maintain strict consistency of treatment; it is easier to apply the rule that full formal titles are capitalized and subsequent informal references downcased.

Plural forms using one generic term to serve multiple names should be lower case:

Lake Erie and Lake Huron
lakes Erie and Huron
the Royal Geographical Society and Royal Historical Society
the Royal Geographical and Royal Historical societies
Oxford University and Cambridge University
Oxford and Cambridge universities

The rationale for this practice is that the plural form of the generic term is not part of the proper name but is merely a common description and thus ought not be capitalized.

5.4 Institutions, organizations, and movements

Capitalize the names of institutions, organizations, societies, movements, and groups:

the World Bank	the British Museum
the State Department	the House of Lords
Ford Motor Company	the United Nations

the Crown War On Want
the Beatles

Generic terms are capitalized in the names of cultural movements and schools derived from proper names:

the Oxford Movement the Ashcan School

Notice that the word *the* is not capitalized.

The tendency otherwise is to use lower case unless it is important to distinguish a specific from a general meaning. Compare, for example:

the Confederacy (the secessionist side in the American Civil War)
confederacy (*as in* 'a federation of states')
Romantic (nineteenth-century movement in the arts)
romantic (*as in* 'given to romance')

Certain disciplines and specialist contexts may require different treatment. Classicists, for example, will often capitalize *Classical* to define, say, sculpture in the fifth century BC as opposed to that of the Hellenistic era; editors should not institute this independently if an author has chosen not to do so.

5.5 Geographical locations and buildings

Capitalize names of geographical regions and areas, named astronomical and topographical features, buildings, and other constructions:

the Milky Way (*but* the earth, the sun, the moon, *except in astronomical contexts* (*see 14.7.1*) *and personification*)
New England the Big Apple the Eternal City
Mexico City (*but* the city of Birmingham)
London Road (*if so named, but* the London road *for one merely leading to London*)
the Strait of Gibraltar the Black Forest
the Thames Estuary (*but* the estuary of the Thames)
the Eiffel Tower Trafalgar Square
the Bridge of Sighs Times Square

River, *sea*, and *ocean* are generally capitalized when they follow the specific name:

the East River the Yellow River
the Aral Sea the Atlantic Ocean

However, where *river* is not part of the true name but is used only as an identifier it is downcased:

the Danube river

When *river* precedes the specific name it can be either upper or lower case, depending on the style adopted:

the River Tamar *or* the river Tamar

'The River Plate' is always capitalized, being a conventional mistranslation of *Río de la Plata* ('Silver River'). Names of well-known or previously mentioned rivers may be written without the specifying word (*the Amazon, the Mississippi*). A lower-case identifier may be added where some clarification is required—to differentiate between the Amazon river and forest, or the Mississippi river and state.

Capitalize compass directions only when they denote a recognized political or cultural entity:

North Carolina	Northern Ireland (*but* northern England)
the mysterious East	the West End

Usage in this area is very fluid, and terms may be capitalized or downcased depending on context and emphasis. For example, a book dealing in detail with particular aspects of London life might capitalize *North London, South London*, etc., while one mentioning the city merely in passing would be more likely to use *north London* and *south London*. Adjectives ending in *-ern* are sometimes used to distinguish purely geographical areas from regions seen in political or cultural terms: so

Kiswahili is the most important language of East Africa

but

Prickly acacia is found throughout eastern Africa

For treatment of foreign place names see 6.2.

5.6 Dates and periods

Capitalize the names of days, months, festivals, and holidays:

Tuesday	March	Easter
Good Friday	Ramadan	Passover
Thanksgiving	Christmas Eve	the Fifth of November
New Year's Day		

Names of the seasons are lower case, except where personified:

William went to Italy in the summer
O wild West Wind, thou breath of Autumn's being

Capitalize historical periods and geological time scales:

the Devonian period	Early Minoan
the Upper Palaeozoic era	
the Bronze Age	
the Middle Ages (*but* the medieval period)	the Renaissance
the Dark Ages	

Modern periods are more likely to be lower case; check such instances with the *New Oxford Dictionary for Writers and Editors*:

the space age
the age of steam
the jazz age
the belle époque

Use lower case for millennia, centuries, and decades (see also 11.6):

the first millennium the sixteenth century the sixties

5.7 Events

Initial capitals are generally used for the formal names of wars, treaties, councils, assemblies, exhibitions, conferences, and competitions. The following examples are indicative:

the Crucifixion	the Inquisition
the Reformation	the Grand Tour
the Great Famine	the Boston Tea Party
the Gunpowder Plot	the Great Fire of London
the First World War	the Siege of Stalingrad
the Battle of Agincourt	the French Revolution
the Treaty of Versailles	the Triple Alliance
the Lateran Council	the Congress of Cambrai
the Indian and Colonial Exhibition	the One Thousand Guineas

Note that *war* and equivalent terms are capitalized when forming part of the conventional name of a specific conflict, but are lower case when part of a looser, more descriptive designation:

the Peninsular campaign
the Korean conflict

After the first mention, any subsequent references to *the war* etc. are in lower case.

5.8 Legislation and official documents

The names of laws and official documents are generally capitalized:

the Declaration of Independence   the Corn Laws

Act is traditionally capitalized even in a non-specific reference; *bill* is lower case if it is not part of a name:

a bill banning unlicensed puppy farms
the Bill of Rights
the requirements of the Act
the Factory and Workshop Act 1911

For legal citations see Chapter 13.

5.9 Honours and awards

The full formal names of orders of chivalry, state awards, medals, degrees, prizes, and the like are usually capitalized, as are (in most styles) the ranks and grades of award:

the George Cross
Companion of the Order of the Bath
Dame Commander of the Order of the British Empire
Bachelor of Music
Licentiate of the Royal Academy of Dancing
Fellow of the Royal Society
Nobel Prize for Physics
the Royal Gold Medal for Architecture

but

an Olympic gold medal

Honours relating to a non-English-speaking country usually appear with an initial capital but with all other words in lower case; ranks may be translated or given in the original language, but in either case are best set lower case:

grand officer/*grand officier* of the Légion d'honneur

5.10 Titles of office, rank, and relationship

Words for titles and ranks are generally lower case unless they are used before a name, as a name, or in forms of address:

Winston Churchill, the prime minister	Prime Minister Winston Churchill
he was elected prime minister	Yes, Prime Minister
the US president	President Obama
the king of England	King Henry
the queen of Castile	Queen Elizabeth
an assembly of cardinals	Cardinal Richelieu
the rank of a duke	the Duke of Wellington
a feudal lord	Lord Byron
a professor of physics	Professor Higgins
Miss Dunn, the head teacher	Head Teacher Alison Dunn
a Roman general	Good evening, General!

Exceptions to this principle are some unique compound titles that have no non-specific meaning, which in many styles are capitalized in all contexts. Examples are:

Advocate General	Attorney General
Chancellor of the Exchequer	Chief Justice
Dalai Lama	Foreign Secretary
Governor General	Holy Roman Emperor
Home Secretary	Lord Chancellor
Prince of Wales	Princess Royal

Regardless of their syntactic role, references to specific holders of a rank or title are often capitalized:

a letter from the Prime Minister
the Archbishop of Canterbury

Use of this style can lead to difficulties in contexts where titles of office appear frequently: in such cases it is generally clearer and more consistent to stick to the rule that the title of office is capitalized only when used before the office-holder's name.

It is usual to capitalize *the Pope* and the reigning monarch (*the King/Queen*) but not all styles do. When it refers to Muhammad, *the Prophet* is capitalized (but note *an Old Testament prophet*). See also 5.11 for religious names.

Historians often impose minimal capitalization, particularly in contexts where the subjects of their writing bear titles: *the duke of Somerset*. This style can be distracting in works for a general readership.

Capitalize possessive pronouns only when they form part of the titles of a holy person, or of a sovereign or other dignitary:

Her/His Majesty   Their Excellencies   Our Lady   Your Holiness

Personal pronouns referring to the sovereign are capitalized only in proclamations: *We*, *Us*, *Our*, *Ours*, *Ourself*, etc.

Words indicating family relationships are lower case unless used as part of a name or in an address:

he did not look like his dad	Hello, Dad!
she has to help her mother	Maya tried to argue with Mother
ask your uncle	Uncle Brian

5.11 Religious names and terms

Use capitals for all references to the monotheistic deity:

Allah	the Almighty	God	the Holy Spirit
the Holy Trinity	Jehovah	the Lord	the Supreme Being

Use lower case for pronouns referring to God where the reference is clear, unless the author specifies otherwise. In any event, write *who*, *whom*, *whose* in lower case. Capitalize *God-awful* and *God-fearing* but downcase *godforsaken*.

Use lower case for the gods and goddesses of polytheistic religions:

the Aztec god of war   the goddess of the dawn

Capitalization of religious sacraments or rites in different religions (and contexts) is not uniform. Note, for example:

a mass   baptism   compline   bar mitzvah

but

the Mass   the Eucharist   Anointing of the Sick

5.12 Personification

Personified entities and concepts are capitalized:

O Freedom, what liberties are taken in thy name!
If the Sun and Moon should doubt, they'd immediately go out

Ships and other craft are traditionally female

he left the *Titanic* before she foundered on her maiden voyage

Formerly, it was also conventional to use *she* of nations and cities in prose contexts, but this is old-fashioned, and the impersonal pronoun is now used:

Britain decimalized its (*not* her) currency in 1971

The device is still found in poetic and literary writing:

And that sweet City with her dreaming spires
She needs not June for beauty's heightening

The names of characters in a play who are identified by their occupation are capitalized in stage directions and references to the text (in the text their names would generally be in small capitals):

[**First Murderer** appears at the door]

5.13 People and languages

Adjectives and nouns denoting place, language, or indigenous people are capitalized:

American	Austrian	French	Catalan
Cornish	Swahili	Aboriginal	

Related verbs tend to retain the capital (*Americanize*, *Frenchify*, *Hellenize*), but note that *anglicize* and *westernize* are usually lower case.

As a very general rule, adjectives based on nationality tend to be capitalized where they are closely linked with the nationality or proper noun, and lower case where the association is remote or merely allusive. For example:

Brussels sprouts	German measles	Irish setter
Turkish delight	Shetland pony	Michaelmas daisy
Afghan hound	Venetian red	Portuguese man-of-war

but

venetian blinds   morocco leather   italic script

However, there are many exceptions, such as *Arabic numbers*, *Chinese whispers*, *Dutch auction*, *French kissing*, and *Roman numerals*, and any doubtful instances need to be checked in a dictionary. *Caesarean* (section) can take either an initial capital or (more commonly in medical texts) lower case.

Note that in many European languages adjectives of nationality are lower case: the English word 'French' translates as *français* in French and *französisch* in German. See Chapter 12.

5.14 Words derived from proper nouns

Capitals are used for a word derived from a personal name or other proper noun in contexts where the link with the noun is still felt to be alive:

an Adonis	a Casanova	Dantesque	Dickensian
Homeric	Kafkaesque	Orwellian	Shakespearean

Lower case is used in contexts where the association is remote, merely allusive, or a matter of convention:

gargantuan	pasteurize	protean
quixotic	titanic	wellington boots

Some words of this type can have both capitals and lower case in different contexts:

Bohemian (of central Europe) *but* bohemian (unconventional)
Philistine (of biblical people) *but* philistine (tastes)
Platonic (of philosophy) *but* platonic (love)
Stoic (of ancient philosophy) *but* stoic (impassive)

Retain the capital letter after a prefix and hyphen:

pro-Nazi anti-British non-Catholic

Use lower case for scientific units (see also 14.1.4) and poetic metres derived from names:

ampere	joule	newton	volt
watt	alcaics	alexandrines	sapphics

In compound terms for concepts such as scientific laws the personal name only is capitalized:

Planck's law Hodgkin's lymphoma Occam's razor Halley's comet

In medical texts, eponymic derivations may be downcased: *Parkinson's disease, parkinsonism, parkinsonian.* See 14.3.6.

5.15 Trade names

In general proprietary terms should be capitalized:

Velcro	Google	Persil	Jacuzzi
Kleenex	Coca-Cola	Levi's	Skype

but write related verbs, for example *to skype* and *to google*, with a lower-case initial, although it is preferable to use generic verbs and nouns if possible (*use a VoIP service, do an online search*).

Some company and proprietary names use unusual configurations of upper- and lower-case letters; these should be followed:

iPad PlayStation PostScript QuarkXPress
GlaxoSmithKline PricewaterhouseCoopers

5.16 Ships, aircraft, and vehicles

Capitalize names of ships and vehicles, using italics for individual names but not for types, models, or marques:

the *Cutty Sark*
HMS *Hood*
The Spirit of St Louis
a Boeing 747 Jumbo Jet
the Supermarine Spitfire Mk Ia
a Mini Cooper S
the International Space Station
the *Curiosity* Mars rover

It is worth noting that people serve *in* not *on* ships and the definite article is omitted when using the ship prefix (HMS, RRS, SS, etc.):

He went aboard HMS *Victory not* He went aboard the HMS *Victory*

5.17 Names including a number or letter

It is usual to capitalize names that include a number or letter:

Route 66 Form 3b Flight 17 Gate 16 Room 101 Act I

CHAPTER 6

Names

6.1 References to people

6.1.1 **General principles**

Use the form of name individuals are most commonly known by, or known to prefer:

J. K. Rowling (*not* Joanne Rowling)
k. d. lang (*all lower-case*)
George Orwell (*not* Eric Arthur Blair)
Tom Hanks (*not* Thomas Hanks)

When mentioned in passing, a person's name usually need appear only in the form by which the bearer is best known. For example, a writer's married name or hereditary title is important only if the person wrote or was known by it (e.g. *Alfred, Lord Tennyson*). In text, authors need clarify titles and names altered by marriage or by any other means only to avoid confusion or to make a point:

Michael (later Sir Michael) Tippett
Laurence (later Lord) Olivier
George Orwell (born Eric Arthur Blair)
George Eliot (pseudonym of Mary Ann, later Marian, Evans)

Initials before a surname are separated by full points, with a space after each:

J. S. Bach E. H. Shepard Hunter S. Thompson

although some designs, particularly those of newspapers and scientific publications, omit the full points and spaces:

JRR Tolkien PJ Harvey George W Bush

Normally, names given entirely in initials have points but no spaces (*J.A.S.*, *E.H.S.*, *J.R.R.T.*). When people are commonly known by their free-standing initials, these forms have neither points nor spaces (*FDR*, *JFK*).

6.1.2 **Alternative names**

Distinguish between adopted names, pseudonyms, nicknames, and aliases.

- The owner of an **adopted name** uses it for all purposes, and may have adopted it legally. In this case, 'born', 'né(e)', 'formerly', or the like may be used:

  Marilyn Monroe, born Norma Jean Mortensen
  Joseph Conrad (formerly Teodor Józef Konrad Korzeniowski)

- **Né** (feminine form **née**), meaning 'born' in French, is used to indicate a previous forename or surname. In English it is most commonly applied to indicate a married woman's maiden name, after her adopted surname. It is not italicized:

  Susan Wilkinson (née Brown)
  Frances (Fanny) d'Arblay, née Burney
  Baroness Thatcher of Kesteven, née Margaret Roberts

  Do not use 'née' in conjunction with pseudonyms, aliases, or nicknames, but only where the new name is adopted. Some writers differentiate between using 'née' for a married woman's maiden name and 'born' for a person's previous name changed by a process other than marriage. This distinction is acceptable, and should not be changed when consistently applied.

- A **pseudonym** is a name adopted for a specific purpose, such as a pen name or stage name. It can be derived from the bearer's true name, or be wholly distinct from it:

  Boz (Charles Dickens)
  Q (Sir Arthur Quiller-Couch)
  Alain-Fournier (Henri-Alban Fournier)

- A **nickname** (more formally, **soubriquet**) can supplement or supplant the owner's original name

  the Sun King (Louis XIV of France)
  the Fat Controller (Sir Topham Hatt)
  Charlie 'Bird' Parker

  Through use it can eventually replace the owner's name, either occasionally (*Ol' Blue Eyes*, *Il Duce*), partially (*Fats Waller*, *Capability Brown*, *Grandma Moses*), or entirely (*Muddy Waters*, *Twiggy*, *Banksy*). While no rules govern whether a nickname is put in quotation marks, the tendency is for quotation marks to be used when the nickname is inserted within or precedes another name (Eldrick 'Tiger' Woods), and not when used alone.

Nicknames and other familiar terms of address are capitalized:

the Admirable Crichton	Capability Brown	the Famous Five
the Iron Duke	Al 'Scarface' Capone	Uncle Sam

6.1.3 **Identifiers**

Junior and *senior* are added to differentiate a son and father with the same name. Each has several abbreviations (*Jun.*, *Jnr*, *Jr*; *Sen.*, *Senr*, *Snr*, *Sr*). Use the abbreviation *Jr* (with a point in US use) for Americans, prefaced by a comma unless it is known that the bearer of the name did not use one. In British usage *Jun.* is more common, although rarely used, and the comma is not usual. In both cases the identifier precedes any abbreviations indicating degrees, honours, or scholarly affiliations.

Unlike *junior*, *senior* never forms part of the bearer's name and is therefore used only as an ad hoc designation for purposes of clarifying identities. Although abbreviated forms exist (see above), the spelled-out form, with a lower-case initial, is normally used.

In French '*fils*' is an ad hoc designation added after a surname to distinguish a son from a father, as 'Dumas *fils*'; '*père*' does the same to distinguish a father from a son, as 'Dumas *père*'. Both are italic in English.

6.1.4 **Titles**

Titles that follow a name are separated from it by a comma. Abbreviated titles of honour, such as *MBE* and *FRS*, are usually in capitals, with a comma preceding the first and separating each subsequent title; occasionally the first comma is dropped. As with other such abbreviations (see Chapter 10), abbreviated titles composed of all-capital letters have no full points in modern style (e.g. *DFC*, *FRA*); those with a combination of upper- and lower-case letters traditionally do (e.g. *B.Sc.*, *D.Phil.*, *Ph.D.*), but today are usually rendered without the points (*BSc*, *DPhil*, *PhD*), as are *Mr*, *Mrs*, *Dr* (see 21.4.4 for US usage).

Mr Joseph Andrews
Joseph Andrews, Esq.

Mrs Abigail Andrews
Dr John Andrews
Mary Andrews, DPhil
Admiral of the Fleet Viscount Jellicoe, GCB, OM, GCVO, SGM

Do not combine *Mr*, *Mrs*, *Miss*, *Ms*, *Dr*, etc. with any other title. Note that *Esq.* is now rarely used but, if present, should not be combined with *Mr* and comes before all other titles that follow a name. (Formerly *Mr* was used for manual workers or those without a university degree, and *Esq.* for professional men or those with a degree.) For titles of judges see 13.8.

There is no comma in some combinations of titles:

His Grace the Archbishop of Armagh   His Honour Judge Perkins

Orders, decorations, degrees, or fellowships are not usually included in title pages, although some academic books use them, excluding first degrees if the author has a postgraduate qualification. They are also not normally used in text except at first mention—and then only in the proportion required by the subject matter. For example, HRH The Prince of Wales, KG, KT, GCB, OM, AK, CD, QSO, PC is more simply styled *Prince Charles*, *the Prince of Wales*, or just *the Prince*.

6.1.5 **Peers and courtesy titles**

The peerage of the United Kingdom has five grades—for men: duke, marquess (*not* marquis), earl, viscount, and baron; for women (either in their own right or as the wife, widow, or former wife of a peer): duchess, marchioness, countess, viscountess, and baroness. Note that *count* is not a British title.

Dame is the equivalent of a knight of the Orders of Chivalry, and is always used with a forename with or without the surname, depending on context.

Downing Street announced MacArthur would now be known as Dame Ellen
Dame Vera Lynn, widely known as "The Forces' Sweetheart"

The title *Lady* is used in reference to female peers, the female relatives of peers, and the wives and widows of knights. It is used with or without a forename and surname, depending on her title.

Lord is a title given formally to a baron, and is used less formally to refer to a marquess, earl, or viscount, prefixed to a family or territorial name (*Lord Derby*). It is also used, prefixed to a forename, as a courtesy title for a younger son of a duke or marquess (*Lord John Russell*). Dukes are not referred to as *Lord* —, but as *the Duke of* —. Baronets (and knights) are entitled to the prefix *Sir*. *The Hon.* is a courtesy title used by a younger son of an earl, and all sons and daughters of a viscount or baron.

The courtesy title *Master* (or *Mistress*) is used by heirs of Scottish peerages.

Debrett's website or *Correct Form* (Debrett's, 2010) are useful sources of guidance on forms of address.

6.1.6 **Saints' names**

Saints' names can be problematic, as they exist as titles for individuals, as place names, and as surnames.

- In British usage, English 'saint' is abbreviated as *St* (*St.* for 'street' is conventionally distinguished by having a full point). US usage retains the full point (see 21.4.4). It is not hyphenated except in some personal names such as *St-John*. It is always capitalized in names.
- In French a capital *S* and hyphen are used if the name refers to the name of a place, institution, or saint's day, or is a family name or title: for example, *Saint-Étienne*, *Sainte-Beuve*, *Saint-Christophe-en-Brionnais*, *la Saint-Barthélemy*. A lower-case *s* with no hyphen is used if the reference is to the person of a saint, for example *saint Jean*, *sainte Jeanne d'Arc*. Abbreviations are *S.*, feminine *Ste*, for the persons of saints, in other contexts *St-*, feminine *Ste-*.
- In German use *Sankt*, abbreviated *St.*; for the saints themselves *hl.* (*heilig*).
- In Italian 'saint' before a consonant in the masculine form is *San* (for example *San Filippo*); before impure *S* (that is, an *s* followed by another consonant), the form is *Santo*: *Santo Stefano*. The feminine form before a consonant is *Santa*, as in *Santa Maria*. In both genders before a vowel the form is *Sant'* and the words are elided: *Sant'Agostino*, *Sant'Agnese*.
- In Portuguese 'saint' is masculine *São*, sometimes *Santo* before a vowel; feminine *Santa*.

- In Spanish 'saint' is masculine *San* (before *Do-*, *To-* it is *Santo*); the feminine is *Santa*.

Abbreviations of names derived from saints' names are generally alphabetized under the full form (that is, *St Andrews* would be found under *Saint* rather than under *St* or *A*).

6.1.7 **Welsh, Scottish, and Irish names**

Welsh names

Surnames were not used in Welsh culture until the Tudor period and became standard practice only from the seventeenth century. Before that both men and women took their names from their fathers. The male patronymic particles are *ap* (preceding a consonant) and *ab* (preceding a vowel), both meaning 'son of'. The female patronymic particle is *ferch*, meaning 'daughter of'. All are lower case. Sometimes the patronymic is doubled, naming the person's father and grandfather in the form 'son/daughter of X son of Y':

Gruffudd ap Madog
Llywelyn ab Owain
Hywel Fychan ap Gruffydd ap Hywel
Angharad ferch Morgan

Alphabetizing such names can be complex but general guidance is to organize them in the first instance on the personal (first) name. Alternatively use the particle (the system used in Welsh phone books, for example) but not on the capitalized 'surname', which is actually the antecedent's name.

Irish and Scottish names

The Irish prefix *O'* means 'grandson of'. In the English form use a closing quotation mark (apostrophe) with no space, as *O'Brien*, *O'Neill*. In Irish one alternative to this is the capital *O* and full space; another is the more authentic Gaelic *Ó*, followed by a full space: *Ó Cathasaigh*, *Ó Flannagáin*. Women's surnames begin with Ní or Nic. Follow the bearer's preference, if known.

Mac means 'son of'. Styling names with *Mac* can lead to problems, depending on whether they are rendered in Gaelic or English forms, or somewhere in between. Spelling rests on the custom of the person bearing the name, and variations in English spelling (*MacDonald*,

Macdonald, McDonald, M'Donald, etc.) must be followed, even though they do not reflect any variation in the Gaelic forms. In Irish, names with *Mac* are written as two words, for example *Michéal Mac Mathúna* (or *Mac Mathghamhna*) 'Michael MacMahon'. As a general rule, leave alone spelling variants found within a text unless you have good reason to believe that the same person's name is being spelled in different ways. However spelled, any name so prefixed is treated as *Mac* in alphabetical arrangement.

6.1.8 **Names containing prefixes**

With prefixes to proper names such as *de*, *du*, *van den*, or *von*, follow the bearer's preference, if known. Within an alphabetical listing supply cross-references where necessary.

de

In accordance with French practice *de* should not have an initial capital (*de Candolle*, *de Talleyrand-Périgord*), except when anglicized (*De Quincey*) or at the beginning of a sentence. Before a vowel *d'* is used (*d'Alembert*). When the surname is used by itself, without given name, initials, or title, *d'* should be retained (*d'Alembert*), but *de* only if the following element is monosyllabic (*de Thou*) or disyllabic ending in a syllable with mute *e* (*de Gaulle*); otherwise omit (*Toqueville* not *de Toqueville*). Names prefixed with a lower-case *de* or *d'* should be alphabetized under the surname:

Alembert, Jean le Rond d'
Chazelles, Jean-François, comte de
Mairan, Jean-Jacques de

Anglicized names of this form are alphabetized on the prefix.

In Netherlands Dutch, *de* (which is the definite article) is capitalized when the bare name is used alone, to distinguish it from its ordinary use. In English that is not necessary, though not wrong if followed consistently. The prefix does not form the basis for alphabetization, as *Groot, Geert de*. In Belgium the reverse is true, with *De Bruyne, Jan*.

Prefixes in Italian names are capitalized and are the basis for alphabetization:

De Sanctis, Gaetano
Del Corno, Francesco
Della Casa, Adriana
Di Benedetti, Vittorio

An exception is made for aristocratic names beginning *de'*, or *degli*: *Medici, Lorenzo de'*; these are capitalized under the main name rather than the prefix. This also applies to *De*, which is sometimes a dialectal form of *di* (*De Simone*), or sometimes a Latinism (*De Sanctis*).

In Spanish names *de* is lower case and omitted in bare surname references, and does not form the basis for alphabetization. For example *Luis Barahona de Soto* (alphabetized under *B*), *Diego de Hurtado de Mendoza* (under *H*), *Lope de Vega Carpio* (under *V*). The prefix *del*, as in *del Castillo*, is a contracted form of *de el*.

de la

In modern French the compound particle *de La* has only one capital (*de La Fontaine*). The *de* is dropped in the absence of a forename: *La Fontaine said*... When anglicized the prefix may deviate from this practice (*de la Mare*, *De La Warr*); follow established convention or the bearer's preference. Names prefixed with *de La* are alphabetized under *La*: *La Fontaine, Jean de*.

In Spanish *de la* is lower case: *Claudio de la Torre* but the short form is *La Torre* (alphabetized under *T*). Similarly *Bartolomé de las Casas* is shortened to *Las Casas*.

du

Du normally has an initial capital, and names are alphabetized under *D* accordingly: *Du Deffand, Marie, marquise*. Variations exist with lower-case *du*, with the name alphabetized according to the surname; this is also the case where the surname is actually formed from a title: *Maine, Louise de Bourbon, duchesse du*.

le, la

The definite article is capitalized when it occurs at the beginning of a French surname: *Le Pen*. (Note, however, that it is lower case in place names except at the beginning of a sentence.) In both cases the names are alphabetized on the article.

van, van de, van den, van der

In the Netherlands, *van*, *van de*, *van den*, and *van der*, prefixed to a surname, are not capitalized except when there is no given name, initial, or title before *Van*, to distinguish it from the ordinary preposition meaning 'of' or 'from'. In Belgium the reverse is usually true, with a capital *V* used in alphabetizing; Afrikaans employs both conventions. In Britain and the US well-known names of Dutch origin, such as *Vincent Van Gogh*, are usually alphabetized on the prefix: *Van Gogh, Vincent*.

von, von dem, von den, von der, vom

As a Germanic prefix to a proper name *von* usually has no initial capital, except at the beginning of a sentence. In some Swiss names the *Von* is capitalized (*Peter Von der Mühll*). Where the surname stands alone *von* is omitted (*Liebig*, not *von Liebig*), and the name is not alphabetized on the prefix (*Liebig, Gertrud von*). The related forms *von dem, von den, von der*, and *vom* are usually retained, however, and form the basis for alphabetization.

6.1.9 **Foreign names**

Arabic

Names beginning with the definite article *al* (or variants such as *el*, *ul*, or *an*) should always be hyphenated: *al-Islām*, *al-kitāb*. The *a* is capitalized at the start of a sentence but is otherwise lower case. In alphabetizing, the article is ignored and the person is listed under the capital letter of their last name. Thus *Aḥmad al-Jundī* would be listed as *al-Jundī, Aḥmad*, and alphabetized under *J*; the article is not inverted, and can even be deleted if the style is imposed consistently. Compound place names of the type *Shajar al-Durr* would be listed thus, however, not transposed as *al-Durr, Shajar*.

Familial prefix elements such as *abū* (father of), *umm* (mother of), and *ibn* or *bin* (son of) may appear as part of ordinary names. They are then in lower case and do not determine alphabetical position: *Muḥammad bin Aḥmad* would be listed as *Aḥmad, Muḥammad bin*. The prefix elements are not connected to the following name by hyphens. *Ibn* or *bin* is often abbreviated to *b.* in indexes and bibliographical references, and *bint* (daughter) may be abbreviated to *b.* or *bt*. On the other hand, such constructs may appear in established surnames, in which case the prefix should be capitalized and should determine alphabetical position: for example, the medieval author Muḥammad Ibn Saʿd would be listed as *Ibn Saʿd, Muḥammad*.

Transliterated modern Arabic names often employ established westernized spellings that may not follow normal rules of transliteration: *Hussein* rather than *Husayn*, *Nasser* rather than *Nāṣir*, *Naguib* rather than *Najīb*. In each case the most commonly occurring spelling of the bearer's name is acceptable, except in specialist contexts. Sometimes *Ibn* is used to indicate that the following name is not the father's (but e.g. the grandfather's) or is a nickname; this attempts to reproduce a distinction made in Arabic script, where lower-case *ibn* corresponds to *bn* without the initial *alif*.

Chinese

Chinese personal names normally consist of a single-syllable family name or surname, followed by a two-syllable personal name (*Ai Weiwei*). In formal contexts the family name should be used (*Ai* or *Mr Ai*). In romanization capitals are used for the first letter, both of the family and of the personal name. In the Wade–Giles transliteration system the two elements of the personal name are separated by a hyphen (for example *Mao Tse-tung*), whereas in the Pinyin system they are run together as a single word (*Mao Zedong*). When a form of name has a long-established history, for example *Sun Yat-sen* or *Chiang Kai-shek*, this should be preferred. Names are not inverted for alphabetization.

In pre-modern times two-syllable names were frequently found, for example *Wang Wei*. More recent figures may use a westernized form of surname, giving the initials for the personal name first and placing the family name last, for example *T. V. Soong*, *H. H. Kung*. In indexing and alphabetizing such names the order should be inverted in Western fashion.

French

The definite article (*le*, *la*) is capitalized when it occurs at the beginning of a French surname, and the name is alphabetized under *L*. Do not confuse this with the use of an article to refer to a person whose name itself does not incorporate it:

le Guerchin (Guercino)　　la Delaporte (Marguerite Delaporte)

Note that the article only accompanies the surname, not the forename. See also **de, de la, du** at 6.1.8.

When a first name is abbreviated in a French text, if the second letter of the name is an *h*, the *h* is retained:

Th. Gautier (Théophile Gautier) Ch. Mauron (Charles Mauron)

The honorifics *Monsieur* (Mr), *Madame* (Mrs), and *Mademoiselle* (Miss) can be used alone or in conjunction with a surname. They are abbreviated as *M*, *Mme*, and *Mlle* (no point). *Mademoiselle* as a form of address for adult women has now largely given way to *Madame* in everyday contexts.

German

Honorifics are *Herr* (Mr), *Frau* (Mrs), and *Fräulein* (Miss): these are abbreviated as *Hr.*, *Fr.*, and *Frl.* Unmarried women are now also usually called Frau; usage may differ regionally and according to the age of the speaker.

Whether individuals include the *Eszett* (ß) in their names is a matter of personal style in German or Austrian names, though it is rare in Swiss names. See also **von, von dem, von den, von der, vom** at 6.1.8.

Greek

Traditional practice is to write ancient Greek names in a Latinized form (for example *Hercules* rather than *Herakles*), although the Greek form is often used when discussing Greek literature, art, religion, etc. One would discuss the twelve labours of *Herakles* in Greek art and poetry, but in a general context one would refer to the labours of *Hercules*. A further rule is to give familiar names in their traditional English—that is, Latinized—form, but retain the Greek spelling for less familiar ones. It is difficult to give guidance as to which names are familiar and which are not, but in nonspecialist contexts, avoid Greek spelling when the Latinized name is a household name.

Some scholars differentiate separate bearers of the same name through Latinizing and Hellenizing alone, using *Thucydides* for the historian but *Thoukydides* for his uncle the politician; *Callimachus* for the poet but *Kallimachos* for the Athenian general. Probably no one would call the philosopher *Platon*; on the other hand, a lesser light by that name would normally be called *Platon* by modern scholars. No one would call the philosopher *Aristotle* anything else, though another man of the same name would be *Aristoteles*; similarly with *Homer* and *Hesiod* (*Homeros* and *Hesiodos*).

The following is a basic guide to Latinized forms of Greek names:

Greek	Latin
ai	ae
k	c
kh	ch
ei	i or ei
oi	oe
-os	-us
-ros	-er
ou	u
u	y

Some examples:

Greek	Latin
Achilleus, Akhilleus	Achilles
Aias	Aiax, (*English*) Ajax
Kallimachos, Kallimakhos	Callimachus
Lusandros, Lysandros	Lysander
Odysseus	Ulixes, (*English*) Ulysses
Oidipous	Oedipus
Thoukydides	Thucydides

For transliteration see 12.7.

Hebrew and Jewish

A Hebrew name may be rendered in English in a variety of ways: *Jacob*, for example, may also be *Ya'acov* or *Ya'akov*; similarly *Haim*, *Hayyim*, *Chaim*, and *Chayim* are all variants. Beyond ensuring that the same person is always referred to in the same way, one cannot standardize automatically throughout a text because any variant may represent the personal preference of the individual concerned or an established convention regarding how their name is spelled.

The *ben* that occurs in many Hebrew names means 'son of'; this is the traditional Jewish way of naming Jewish males. The female form is *bat* 'daughter of'. In pre-modern times a man would usually be known simply as the son of his father: *Avraham ben David* (Avraham the son of David). In scholarly works this is often abbreviated to *Avraham b. David*; for works aimed at a more general readership, the full form is probably clearer. The *Ben* that often figures in modern Israeli names represents a different usage: now part of the surname, it should be hyphenated to it and capitalized, as in *David Ben-Gurion*, and alphabetized under *B*. The unhyphenated *David Ben Gurion* is wrong, as it suggests that *Ben* is a middle name.

Italian

The forms of address are *Signor* (Mr), *Signora* (Mrs), and *Signorina* (Miss), abbreviated as *Sig.*, *Sig.ra*, and *Sig.na*. *Signor* adds an *-e* when it is not followed by a name. Adult women may be addressed as *Signora*, regardless of marital status, particularly in formal contexts. *Dottor* ('Doctor', though used also of any graduate) adds an *-e* in similar circumstances; the feminine form is *Dottoressa*. Those with higher degrees are *Professore* or *Professoressa*. Titles followed by a surname are lower case: *la signora Cappelletti, il dottor Ferro*. See also **de** at 6.1.8.

Japanese

Japanese names usually take the form of a single surname, followed by a personal name: *Itō Hirobumi, Omura Mizuki*. The surname forms the basis for alphabetization. The suffixes *-san* (gender-neutral), *-sama* (polite form), *-chan* (affectionate diminutive), and *-kun* (for addressing an inferior; also used by boys in addressing one another) are used only in speech, or transcriptions of speech.

In Western contexts it is conventional, especially in translations, to transpose the names—*Mizuki Omura*. (The writer known in the West as Kazuo Ishiguro would be Ishiguro Kazuo in Japan.) Well-known artists are often identified only by the personal name element, leaving out any reference to family, for example *Hokusai* rather than *Katsushika Hokusai*. Similarly, writers who are well known by their personal name may be so identified: *Bashō* rather than *Matsuo Bashō*.

Historically, it is common for two elements of a name to be separated by *no*, indicating the subordination of the second element to the first: *Ki no Tsurayuki*. Here, too, the name should appear in direct order.

Korean

In Korean names the surname precedes the personal name, unless a particular individual's name has become westernized. There are five predominant surnames in Korea—*Kim*, *Yi*, *Pak*, *Chŏng*, and *Ch'oe*—and more than a third of people will use one of the first three. Note that Anglicizations sometimes introduce variants, e.g. *Lee* or *Rhee* for *Yi*,

Park for *Pak*, *Cheung* for *Chŏng*. Personal names usually consist of two elements separated from one another by a hyphen: *Kim Jong-Un*.

Portuguese

As in Spanish practice, the surname is normally composed of two elements: the mother's maiden name and the father's surname, the latter forming the basis for alphabetization. Unlike Spanish, however, the mother's maiden name comes before the father's surname. Alphabetization is according to the last element in the surname: *Manuel Braga da Cruz* is ordered under *Cruz, Manuel Braga da.*

Standard forms of address are *Senhor* (Mr), *Senhora* (Mrs or Miss), *Minha Senhora* (a more polite form of Mrs), or *Dona* (Mrs or any older woman). *Menina* (Miss) is used only before a given name. Professional or conferred titles normally come after the *Senhor*, *Senhora*, etc.: *Senhor Professor*, *Senhora Doutora*. In Brazilian usage *Senhorita* is used for 'Miss', and it is considered more polite to use *Senhor* and *Senhora* in conjunction with the first name rather than surname.

Russian

The gender-neutral honorific *tovarishch* (Comrade) is now rarely used; it has been supplanted by the pre-Revolution forms *gospodin* (Mr) and *gospozha* (Mrs or Miss), which are used mostly in writing, and then only with the surname following. Russian names follow the patronymic pattern of given name, father's name with the suffix *-ovich* (son of) or *-ovna* (daughter of), and surname. While the surname is inherited, it is rarely used in speech. Correctly, transliterated abbreviated names with initials composed of two letters, one capital and one lower-case, should not be further reduced, as they are derived from a single Cyrillic letter, for example *Ya.* for Yakov, *Yu.* for Yuri, and *Zh.* for Zhores. For transliteration see 12.15.

Scandinavian

The ancient Scandinavian traditions of conferring patronymic names from one generation to the next—whereby, for example, *Magnus Pálsson* (Magnus, son of Pál) names his son *Pál Magnusson* and his daughter *Björk Magnúsdóttir*—are still found in Iceland, although they have not been used consistently elsewhere for the past one or two centuries; since

1923 only existing surnames have been allowed to be used in Iceland. Icelandic alphabetization is still by given name rather than surname, with *Finnur Jónsson* under *F* and *Vígdís Finnbogadóttir* under *V*. After using a person's full Icelandic patronymic name, it is customary to use their personal name in subsequent references, even in formal contexts. Other Scandinavian names follow the usual pattern; Danish and Norwegian surnames often end in *-sen* but Swedish in *-sson*, where the first *s* is the genitive ending (*Pettersson*, Peter's son).

Spanish

Standard forms of address are *Señor* (Mr), *Señora* (Mrs), *Señorita* (Miss), abbreviated as *Sr*, *Sra*, and *Srta*. *Señorita* as a form of address has now largely given way to *Señora* in everyday contexts.

Surnames are usually composed of two elements, the father's family surname followed by the mother's family surname (derived from her father's family name). So if, for example, *Señor Roberto Caballero Díaz* marries *Señorita Isabel Fuentes López*, their son might be *Jaime Caballero Fuentes*. The wife's surnames normally do not alter with marriage. In unofficial contexts the second half of a married woman's compound surname may be replaced by the husband's first surname and joined to her first surname by the conjunction *de*, although this is becoming rare: in the case above, *Isabel Fuentes López* could be *Isabel Fuentes de Caballero*, or *Señora de Caballero*.

Compound surnames may be joined with a *y*, or in Catalan surnames *i*:

José Ortega y Gasset   Josep Lluís Pons i Gallarza

The second element may be dropped in everyday use; Cervantes's full name was *Miguel de Cervantes Saavedra*, and prominent figures in Spanish public life may be referred to with only one surname:

Mariano Rajoy   Javier Bardem

In journalistic shorthand they would be referred to as *Rajoy* and *Bardem*.

Conversely, a person may become known by the second element of their surname, particularly if the expected one is very common: the poet Federico García Lorca is generally known as *Lorca*, the politician José Luis Rodríguez Zapatero is referred to as *Zapatero*, or *Rodríguez Zapatero* (but never just *Rodríguez*), and Pablo Ruiz

Picasso, son of José Ruiz Blasco and María Picasso, is known universally as *Picasso*.

Where two elements are used, alphabetization is normally according to the first element in the surname.

6.2 Place names

6.2.1 **General principles**

Choosing the appropriate spelling of a name for a town, city, country, or geographical feature can be a tricky and sensitive matter. Consulting an authoritative recent atlas, or a dictionary that includes encyclopedic information, such as the *Oxford Dictionary of English* or the *New Oxford Dictionary for Writers and Editors*, will help to establish the currently accepted form, but in many cases a choice must be made between alternative spellings.

Note that place names are always rendered in roman type, even if the form used is a foreign, unnaturalized one with unfamiliar spelling or accents:

rue St-Honoré   Biblioteca Nazionale Centrale di Roma

The modern tendency is to replace English versions of place names by the correct form in the local language, but it is far from being a universal rule: few writers in English would refer to *Roma* or *München* for Rome or Munich, for example. Be aware, also, that some local forms closely resemble their anglicized variant: be wary with *Lyon* and *Lyons*, *Marseille* and *Marseilles*, *Reims* and *Rheims*.

The following list provides examples of current Oxford preference for the names of some foreign cities when given in general—as opposed to specialist or historical—context:

Ankara (*not* Angora)	Beijing (*not* Peking)
Brussels (*not* Bruxelles *or* Brussel)	Florence (*not* Firenze)
Gdansk (*not* Danzig)	Geneva (*not* Geneve)
Livorno (*not* Leghorn)	Lyons (*not* Lyon)
Marseilles (*not* Marseille)	Reims (*not* Rheims)
Sichuan (*not* Szechuan *or* Szechwan)	Vienna (*not* Wien)

It is important to be aware of the sensitivities and contentious issues reflected in choices of name. Some particular points are expanded below:

- The island containing England, Wales, and Scotland is *Britain*; *Great Britain* is more usual when these countries are considered as a political unit; *Great* is a historical geographical term, to contrast it with Lesser Britain, an ancient name for Brittany. The *United Kingdom* is a political unit that includes these countries and Northern Ireland (but not the Isle of Man and the Channel Islands). The *British Isles* is a geographical term that refers to the United Kingdom, Ireland, and the surrounding islands, and does not connote ownership.
- *America* is a land mass consisting of the continents of North and South America. It should be used to mean 'the United States' only when the context is very clear. *North America* is a continent that contains Canada, the United States, Mexico, and the countries of *Central America* (which is classed as the southernmost part of North America).
- The official names of some Indian cities have changed since 1995, with *Mumbai* replacing *Bombay*, *Chennai* superseding *Madras*, *Kolkata* supplanting *Calcutta*, and *Bengaluru* succeeding *Bangalore*. A book about modern India should certainly use the new forms, although if the work is intended for a general readership the names may be glossed with their traditional forms.
- The country between Poland and Russia is *Belarus*, not *Belorussia* or *Byelorussia* and certainly not *White Russia*.
- In contemporary contexts place names in China should be spelled with the Pinyin rather than the Wade–Giles system (see 12.3.3): *Beijing* and *Guangzhou* rather than *Peking* and *Kwangchow*. The old name of the latter, *Canton*, may be felt to be more appropriate in historical contexts.
- The area of the Congo in Africa needs particular care. The country known as Zaire between 1971 and 1997 is the *Democratic Republic of Congo* (capital, Kinshasa), whereas its much smaller neighbour is *Congo* or *Republic of Congo* (capital, Brazzaville); the latter is sometimes distinguished as *Republic of Congo-Brazzaville*.

Names of features such as lakes, oceans, seas, mountains, and rivers can lay traps for the unwary: strictly speaking, a descriptive term should not be added to a name in which it is already present. For example the *meer* in *IJsselmeer* and *mere* in *Windermere* mean 'lake', and the first part of the name of the *Rio Grande* means 'river' in Spanish.

Romanization can cause difficulties with place names; some guidance is given in Chapter 12 under the individual language.

6.2.2 **Chronology**

Places where the official language has changed owing to historical events may need to be identified or benefit from a gloss: *Breslau* (*now Wrocław*). In specialist or historical works the subject, historical period, and prospective readership will govern which language or form is used for a particular place name, though the usage for any given region must be consistent; editors should not automatically change a name given in the text to its modern equivalent. When the place name itself—not merely its linguistic form—has changed, do not use the new name retrospectively: refer to the Battle of *Stalingrad*, even though since 1961 the city has been *Volgograd*. This applies no less when the old name is restored: the *Petrograd Soviet* and the *Siege of Leningrad* should not be placed in *St Petersburg*, though naturally '(now St Petersburg)' may be added if readers are thought to need it.

6.2.3 **Locating places**

It is sometimes necessary to distinguish places of the same name, to identify small places, or to clarify the name of a place when it has changed. In general it would be pedantic to refer to 'Paris, France' on the off-chance that one reader in a million might assume that 'Paris' standing alone referred to the place in Texas. Context will often make plain which of two places of the same name is meant: in a book about English churches it would be unnecessary to refer to 'Boston, Lincolnshire'. However, in the same book, a reference to 'Richmond' would require identification (unless, of course, the surrounding matter located it unambiguously in Surrey or Yorkshire).

A small place may be located by reference to a larger place, a county, a surrounding area, or a country:

Fiesole near Florence
Newton, Warwickshire
St-Julien-de-Jonzy in Burgundy
Kinshasa, the capital of the Democratic Republic of Congo

It is important to avoid anachronisms in these cases: a modern reference to Hampstead might identify it as 'in north London', but a reference to John Constable's taking a house there in the nineteenth century should identify Hampstead as 'near London' or 'north of London', or 'in Middlesex'. Similarly, care should be taken with historical subject matter not to 'correct' references because they do not conform with modern reality: for example, the town of Abingdon was in Berkshire until boundary changes in 1974 'moved' it to Oxfordshire.

6.2.4 **Addresses**

Use a comma to separate the elements in a run-on postal address, although the comma preceding the postcode may be omitted:

Great Clarendon Street, Oxford OX2 6DP, UK

Commas should be omitted altogether if the address is on separate lines, as on an envelope:

Great Clarendon Street
Oxford
OX2 6DP
UK

There is no comma after the street number:

23 Arnold Road

Postcodes are printed in capitals with no points or hyphens: *OX2 6DP*. Ensure that the letter *O* and the number *0* are distinguished. Postcodes are frequently set in small capitals rather than full capitals.

North American

US addresses have a zip code after the name of the town or city and the postal abbreviation of the state. The standard zip code consists of five numerals (with an optional further code of four more numerals, introduced by a hyphen) and is separated from the state abbreviation by a space:

198 Madison Avenue, New York, NY 10016 (*or* 10016-4314)

On an envelope this address would be laid out as:

198 Madison Avenue
New York, NY 10016 (*or* 10016-4314)

Note that the convention for Manhattan addresses is to spell out numbers for avenue names and use figures for street names:

25 W. 43 St.
the corner of Fifth and 59th

In Canadian addresses the postal code is placed on the last line. The postal abbreviation of the province is written on the same line as the town or city name:

202 Hanson Street
Toronto, ON
Canada
M4C 1A7

Apartment addresses are written as, for example:

310-99 Gerard St

or

99 Gerard St, Apt 310

or

99 Gerard St, #310

European

The words *rue*, *avenue*, *boulevard*, etc. are not capitalized in French street names:

56 rue de Rivoli   12 boulevard Louis Pasteur
place de la République

The definite article in place names is lower case except at the start of a sentence (*le Havre*). Street numbers precede the name in France but follow it in Belgium.

Composite French place names are hyphenated:

Saint-Étienne-du-Mont   Vitry-le-François
Saint-Denis-de-la-Réunion   rue du Faubourg-Montmartre

In German, Dutch, and Swedish addresses the equivalent of the word 'road' or 'street' is amalgamated with the name, so the issue of capitalization does not arise. Street numbers follow the name:

Friedrichstraße 10   Eriksgatan

Italian and Spanish street names take lower-case initials, and street numbers follow the name; Portuguese street names take upper-case initials:

piazza Luigi di Savoia 20   glorieta Puerta de Toledo 4
Travessa das Amoreiras

CHAPTER 7

Italic, roman, and other type treatments

7.1 General principles

7.1.1 Introduction

In most contexts roman type is the standard typeface used for text matter, but it can be varied, for reasons of emphasis, additional clarity, or common convention, through the use of other typographic styles or forms. Each of these—italic, roman text in quotation marks, bold, capitals and small capitals, and underlining—is used to indicate a departure of some sort from normal text or to alert the reader to interpret the words so distinguished in a particular way. Initial capitals are also used to delineate particular classes of word; see Chapter 5.

7.1.2 Punctuation and typography

All internal punctuation within a phrase or work title set in a different type style is set in that style, including colons between titles and subtitles, and exclamation or question marks that form part of the quoted matter. Punctuation not belonging to the phrase or title is set in roman. Ensure that formatting is precise. In

> Have you read *Westward Ho!*?

the exclamation mark is in italics because it is part of the title, but the question mark is in roman because it belongs to the surrounding context. Similarly, the plurals *s* and *es* and the possessive *'s* affixed to italicized or other typographically distinguished words are set in roman:

> several old *Economist*s and *New Yorker*s
> the *Majestic*'s crew

They are set in the variant typography where they form part of the word:

> It's not *John's* fault but *Mary's*
> We fitted several of the *blancs* in our luggage

Occasionally it may be necessary to indicate italics in text that is already italicized, especially in foreign text. In this instance the opposite font—roman type—is chosen:

> *Discuss the principle* caveat emptor *in common-law jurisdictions*
> He hissed, '*Do you have the slightest* idea *how much trouble you've caused?*'

Some publishers indicate italics in italicized text by putting it within quotation marks:

> *A study of Dickens's 'Hard Times'*

Not all styles do this, however, especially in blocks of italic text, such as a caption.

Within italic titles Oxford style does not convert to roman any material that would be italic in open text (for example ships' names or other work titles):

> *The Voyage of the Meteor* (not *The Voyage of the* Meteor)

but other styles do. Where italic type is shown on hard copy by underlining or italic type, editors should indicate the opposite font by encircling the word or words and inserting the 'change italic to roman type' mark (see Appendix Proofreading marks) in the margin.

Use of underlining in this context is not recommended: see 7.6 below. For a further discussion of titles within titles see 8.2.8.

7.2 Italic type

Italic type is used to indicate emphasis or stress; to style titles, headings, indexes, and cross-references; to indicate foreign words and phrases; and in specific technical contexts (see Chapter 14).

7.2.1 **Emphasis and highlighting**

Setting type in italics indicates emphasis by setting off a word or phrase from its context:

An essay's *length* is less important than its *content*
I don't care *how* you get here, just *get here*
Such style, such *grace*, is astounding

Employ italics sparingly for emphasis. It may be better to achieve the same effect by making the emphasis clear through the sentence structure, or by using intensifying adjectives and adverbs:

The actual purpose of her letter remained a mystery

rather than

The *purpose* of her letter remained a mystery

Italic may also be used to highlight a word, phrase, or character where it is itself the object of discussion:

the letter *z*   spell *labour* with a *u*   the past tense of *go* is *went*

Quotation marks may also be used in this way (see 7.3 below): decide which will be clearer and more intelligible to the reader, and apply that style consistently in comparable contexts.

Technical or recently coined terms and words being introduced, defined, or assigned a special meaning are often italicized at first mention:

The unit of cultivation was the *strip*... a bundle of strips made up what was known as a *furlong*
a pair of endocrine structures termed the *adrenal glands*

Bold type is also used for this purpose in some contexts (see 7.4 below).

When an author or editor adds italics to a quotation for emphasis, indicate that this has been done by adding 'my italics', 'author's italics', or 'italics added' in square brackets after the italicized word or words, or in parentheses at the end of the quotation or in the relevant footnote or endnote. (Using 'my emphasis' or 'emphasis added' is an acceptable alternative where italics are the only form of emphasis used.)

The committee had decided not to put it in the petition, 'but intimate it *to the prince*' (BL, Harley MS 6383, fo. 122a: my italics)

7.2.2 **Foreign words and phrases**

Italic type is used in English texts for words and phrases that are still regarded as foreign or need to be distinguished from identical English forms:

the *catenaccio* defensive system employed by the Italians
an *amuse-gueule* of a tiny sardine mounted on a crisp crouton

When a foreign word becomes naturalized into English (that is, no longer regarded as distinctively foreign) it is usually printed in roman like other English words:

> the phrase is repeated ad nauseam throughout the book
> Mortimer describes the scene with characteristic brio

Convention and context rather than logic determine when foreign words are sufficiently assimilated into English to be printed in roman type. In modern English the use of italics for foreign words is less prevalent than it used to be, and newly adopted foreign terms may pass into roman text very quickly. The best advice is to treat any one item consistently within a given text and follow the newest edition of a suitable dictionary, such as the *New Oxford Dictionary for Writers and Editors* or the *Shorter Oxford English Dictionary*. Take into account also the subject's conventions and the intended readers' expectations: if in doubt over the degree of assimilation of a particular word, the more cautious policy is to italicize, but in a work written for specialists whose terminology it may be a part of, it may be wiser not to.

On the other hand, consistency or context may require words normally romanized in general English to revert to italicization (or, as in German, capitalization), to avoid their looking out of place among related but less assimilated foreign words.

> A *coup d'état* depends upon the predisposition of the people to accept the *fait accompli* [fait accompli].

It is also sometimes important to go on italicizing a foreign word, however familiar, where there is an English word with the same spelling, as with *Land* for a province of Germany or *pension* for a Continental boarding house.

When a word is sufficiently assimilated to be printed in roman, it may still retain its accents, as with 'pâté', 'plié', and 'crèche'; or it may lose them, as with 'cafe', 'denouement', 'elite', and 'facade' (these forms are the ones shown in current Oxford dictionaries).

Foreign words assimilated into English tend to lose gender inflections, so that the English 'rentier'—now assimilated into the language in roman type—applies to both male and female, though the French feminine form of *rentier* is *rentière*. While in English the default gender is normally masculine, the dominant anglicized form of some words may be the feminine one: an example is 'blonde', which in British English is the usual form for both sexes, although 'blond' is still sometimes used for a man and is the dominant US form.

The explanation or translation of a foreign word or phrase may be presented in any of a number of ways, using roman type in quotation marks or parentheses, as appropriate:

> *bracchium* means 'arm'
>
> Old French *dangier* is derived from Latin *dominium* 'power', 'authority', which is the basic sense of Middle English *daunger*
>
> Napoleon said England was a nation of *boutiquiers* (shopkeepers)

Complicated contexts will require greater diversity: any sensible system is acceptable so long as it is consistently applied and is clear to the reader.

Foreign proper names are not italicized, even when cited in their original language:

> rue St-Honoré   Biblioteca Nazionale Centrale di Roma

7.2.3 **Titles of works**

Work titles are discussed fully in Chapter 8. Use italics for titles of books, periodicals, plays, films, TV and radio series, and music albums:

The Electric Kool-Aid Acid Test	*Past & Present*
Look Back in Anger	*West Side Story*
Fawlty Towers	*La dolce vita*

Italics are used for long poems (those of book length, or divided into books or cantos), but roman in quotation marks is used for shorter poems, songs, articles, and individual episodes in broadcast series. The titles of paintings, sculptures, and other works of art are also italicized, as are titles of operas, oratorios, collections of songs, etc.

7.2.4 **Other uses of italic**

Italic type is also found in the following contexts:

- stage directions in plays
- dictionaries, for part-of-speech markers, foreign words in etymologies, usage labels, and example sentences
- in some styles, for introducing cross-references as in *see* or *see under*, and other directions to the reader, such as *opposite* and *overleaf*

- enumeration such as (*a*), (*b*), (*c*) in lists, in some styles (see 15.1.5)
- names of ships, aircraft, and vehicles (see 5.16)
- names of parties in legal cases (see Chapter 13)
- biological nomenclature (see Chapter 14)
- science and mathematics (see Chapter 14).

7.3 Quotation marks

Quotation marks are discussed at 4.14 and 9.2.3. They are used with roman type in the titles of short poems, songs, chapters in books, articles, and individual episodes in broadcast series; the names of the Bible, the Torah, the Koran, and other religious texts and their subdivisions are written in roman without quotation marks. They are also used to distinguish colloquialisms in formal contexts and to give the implication 'so-called'.

7.4 Bold type

Bold or boldface is a thick typeface **like this**. **Bold type** is indicated on hard copy by a wavy underline. Where a distinction is to be made between two bold typefaces (e.g. bold and semibold), the convention is to use a double wavy line for bold and a single one for semibold.

Bold may be used instead of italic to highlight a newly introduced term, often one that is going to be defined or explained:

> **Percale** is a fine weave that produces a relatively fine and strong fabric for sheets.
>
> The **Pharisees** were sincere and pious Jews... The **Sadducees** were a group of aristocratic Jews... The **Essenes** had serious disagreements with both the Pharisees and the Sadducees.

This device is used particularly in textbooks, guidebooks, and other educational or instructional texts, less so in more literary contexts:

> The village of **Avrolles** (14 km), where the road changes from D943 to D905, has a church with a detached bell tower.

Bold is often used for headwords in dictionaries and encyclopedias; for certain components of citations in bibliographies and reference lists; in indexes to draw attention to types of reference or important references; to indicate cross-referencing generally; for vectors and matrix symbols in science and mathematics; and in titles and headings.

Avoid using bold for emphasis in the course of normal printed matter, as the effect is usually too startling in running text; avoid typographical distinction altogether, or prefer instead the less obtrusive italic.

7.5 Capitals

7.5.1 **Full capitals**

Full capitals are usually used for initialisms (*MA, ECG, RSS*; see Chapter 10), and for people known by their initials (*JFK, J. K. Rowling*; see Chapter 6); acronyms may be all capitals or initial capital (*UNESCO/ Unesco*; see also 10.2.4 and 21.4.5).

The use of initial capitals is discussed in Chapter 5.

Full capitals (and small capitals) may be used for displaying text on half-title and title pages, for logos and imprints, and for other types of special presentation and display. They are indicated on hard copy by a triple underline. In word processing prefer upper case to the attribute 'All Caps'.

Full capitals are usually too prominent to be used for emphasis in open text, but they are sometimes used, as are small capitals, to mimic inscriptions or to reproduce original orthography:

> The earliest Scandinavian coins, inscribed 'CNVT REX ÆNOR' ('Cnut, king of Danes'), seem to have been struck . . . no later than 1015

7.5.2 **Small capitals**

Small capitals are about two-thirds the size of large capitals, as in THIS STYLE OF TYPE, and are indicated on hard copy by a double underline. In typography, the term 'even s. caps.' instructs that the word(s) should be set entirely in small capitals, rather than a combination of capitals and small capitals.

Although small capitals are traditionally used in a number of set contexts, which are described below, they are not available in certain typefaces. It is possible to reduce capital letters to the size of small capitals, but this method is not suitable for ebooks and other electronic publications. For a text that requires a great many small capitals, a typeface that already includes them should be selected.

The main uses of small capitals are as follows:

- for specifying eras (AD, BC, BCE, AH; see Chapter 10). In an italic context they may be set in italics; otherwise, small capitals are generally set only in roman type
- for displayed subsidiary titles and headings, for signatures in printed correspondence, for academic qualifications following names displayed in a list, and sometimes for postcodes
- for reproduced all-capital inscriptions, headlines, notices, and so forth, if these are not reduced to capital and lower case. Formerly, full-capital abbreviations (such as *BBC*) were often set in even small capitals. While this practice has fallen out of widespread use, it remains a convenient alternative for those disciplines routinely requiring full-capital abbreviations in text, which otherwise can look jarring on the printed page
- in some styles, for the first word or words of chapters: these may be styled with spaced capital and small capital letters 'THUS' to introduce the text (see 1.3.4)
- in chemistry to denote molecular configurations D and L and oxidation states
- for cross-references and indexing:

  sing the praises of see PRAISE
- in some styles, for authors' names in bibliographies
- for characters' names in plays:

  CECILY When I see a spade I call it a spade.

  GWENDOLEN I am glad to say that I have never seen a *spade*.
- for Roman numerals in references, sigla (letters or symbols used to denote a particular manuscript or edition of a text), and play citations with more than one level
- for centuries in French and generally in Latin:

  le $\text{XI}^{\text{ème}}$ [*or* XIe] siècle

7.6 Underlining

In word processor files, do not use underlining when italic is intended. Underlining text on hard copy or proofs indicates that it is to be set in italics. When underlining matter in this way, ensure that the underlining includes all matter that is to be italicized, but nothing else. Mistakes are particularly common with internal and surrounding punctuation. Consider:

> 'The novel Bell, Book, and Candle', *not* 'The novel Bell, Book, and Candle'
>
> 'The colours were red, white, and blue', *not* 'The colours were red, white, and blue'

In typeset material it is undesirable to use underlining, as it cuts through the descenders of the characters and in some typefaces may obscure the identity of similar letters (*g* and *q*, for example). Italic type is preferable as a distinguishing mark, though in some cases underlining is required or is uniquely useful—for example in some scientific and mathematical notation, or in the precise reproduction of a manuscript, inscription, or correspondence, where it is needed to approximate underlining in the original.

As underscoring on hard copy or proofs indicates to the typesetter that italic is wanted, any instances where underlining is required must be marked in a different way: for example, with a highlighted underscore, which can be explained to the designer and typesetter in a note.

In non-print contexts such as websites avoid underlining as a substitute for (or in addition to) italics to indicate work titles or for emphasis, as users expect underlining to indicate a hyperlink. Browsers have their own styles for the display of hyperlinks so it is not necessary to add underlining to links in copy.

CHAPTER 8

Work titles in text

8.1 General principles

The text of one work often contains references to others. They may be discussed at length or mentioned fleetingly in passing, with extended bibliographic information or none at all. Work titles mentioned in the text should be styled according to consistent conventions, which will normally match those used in the notes or bibliography, if these are present. It should be noted that newspapers and magazines often follow their own style, which differs from other non-fiction works.

'Work titles' is a category of convenience, the boundaries of which may be indistinct. The works considered here are often in written form, but also include broadcast works, film, digital works (including games, apps, and podcasts), musical works, and works of art. The definition of a title is by no means unproblematic, especially outside the area of printed works, not least because the distinction between a formal title and a description is to some extent a matter of convention and arbitrary decision.

8.2 Titles of written works

8.2.1 **Introduction**

The typography and capitalization of the title of a written work depend on whether or not it was published and on the form in which it was published. Publication is not synonymous with printing: works were widely disseminated before the invention of printing and, in the modern era, many ebooks do not exist in hard copy form. Conversely, material that is printed is not necessarily published.

For capitalization of titles see 8.2.3; for use of 'the' see 8.2.7.

8.2.2 **Typography**

Free-standing publications

The title of a free-standing publication is set in italic type. This category comprises works whose identity does not depend on their being part of a larger whole. Such works may be substantial but they may also be short and ephemeral, if published in their own right. They thus include not only books of various kinds (for example novels, monographs, collections of essays, editions of texts, or separately published plays or poems) but also periodicals, pamphlets, titled broadsheets, and published sale and exhibition catalogues:

For Whom the Bell Tolls
Gone with the Wind
The Importance of Being Earnest: A Trivial Comedy for Serious People
Sylvie and Bruno
A Tale of Two Cities
The Merchant of Venice
the third canto of *Childe Harold's Pilgrimage*
The Economist
Farmer and Stockbreeder
a pamphlet, *The Douglas System of Economics*, which found a wide sale
Essay toward Settlement, a broadsheet petition published by 19 September 1659

The names of albums, CDs, and collections of songs are given in italic, whereas those of individual songs are in roman with quotation marks: see 8.6.

Digital resources (ebooks, apps, video games, podcasts etc.) should also be in italic: see 8.5.1.

Branded board and card games (Scrabble, Magic: The Gathering) are capitalized and usually roman with no quotation marks; generic names (chess, bridge) are roman lower case.

The names of sacred texts (see 8.3) are set in roman; the titles of ancient epic poems are usually set in italic (the *Iliad*, Ovid's *Metamorphoses*). The Mahābhārata is both a sacred text and an epic poem—roman can be used when reference is made in general terms and italic for a particular published text.

The titles of works published in manuscript before the advent of printing are italicized. They may be consistently styled like those published in print (it is pointless to ask whether, for example, a medieval work that survives in a unique copy was widely distributed, and irrelevant to inquire whether it has been printed in a modern edition):

the document we now call *Rectitudines singularum personarum*, which originated perhaps in the mid-tenth century

Items within publications

The title of an item within a publication is set in roman type within single quotation marks. This includes titles of short stories, chapters or essays within books, individual poems in collections, articles in periodicals, newspaper columns, individual texts within larger editions, sections within websites, and individual blog articles (see 8.5.1):

'The Monkey's Paw'
'The Old Vicarage, Grantchester'
'Sailing to Byzantium'
'Tam o' Shanter'
'Three Lectures on Memory', published in his first volume of essays, *Knowledge and Certainty*
she began writing a weekly column, 'Marginal Comments', for *The Spectator*
today's recommendation is 'Oxford Dictionaries Word of the Year' from OUPblog

There is room for flexibility here. For example, the titles of longer poems—such as Byron's *Don Juan* or Tennyson's *In Memoriam*—are usually italicized, as are individual Canterbury tales:

the first true editor of the *Canterbury Tales*
the aristocratic noble love of *The Knight's Tale* gives way to the more earthy passions of *The Miller's Tale* and *The Reeve's Tale*

Series titles

A series of books is not itself a work, and its title is not given the same styling as its component works. The overall title of a series is not normally needed when a book is mentioned, but if given should be set in roman type with the first and principal words capitalized:

the Rough Guides
Studies in Biblical Theology
The Social Structure of Medieval East Anglia, volume 9 of Oxford Studies in Social and Legal History

Descriptions of an edition should not be considered series titles and should not be capitalized, but a publisher's named edition of the works of a single author may be treated as a series title:

the variorum edition of her *Complete Poetry*

Dent published the Temple Edition of the Waverley Novels in forty-eight volumes

Titles of series of works of fiction may either be italicized like book titles or set in quotation marks, but loose descriptions of fictional series should not be treated as titles:

The Forsyte Saga — the 'His Dark Materials' trilogy, *or* the *His Dark Materials* trilogy

the Barsetshire novels

Style the titles of series of works of art like those of series of books (with the exception of series of published prints, which are given italic work titles):

a series of paintings entitled Guyana Myths

a series of prints, in issues of six, *Studies from Nature of British Character*

Unpublished works

The title of an unpublished work is set in roman type within single quotation marks. This category includes titles of such unpublished works as dissertations and conference papers, and longer unpublished monographs. (However, don't assume that all doctoral dissertations, for example, remain unpublished: in some universities, publication accompanies the awarding of the degree, or dissertations may be available online only.) The same styling is applied to internal reports, provisional titles used for works before their publication, and titles of works intended for publication but never published, or planned but never written:

his undergraduate dissertation, 'Leeds as a Regional Capital'

'Work in Progress' (published as *Finnegans Wake*)

Forster later planned to publish an 'Essay on Punctuation'

an unpublished short play, 'The Blue Lizard'

This treatment is accorded to unpublished works that are essentially literary compositions. Do not style descriptions of archival items as work titles. References to such material as unpublished personal documents, including diaries and letters, and legal, estate, and administrative records should be given in descriptive form with minimal capitalization:

Dyve's letter-book is valuable evidence

the diary of Robert Hooke for 3 April

the cartulary of the hospital of St John

the great register of Bury Abbey
the stewards' accounts in the bursars' book for 1504–5

Capitalized names are sometimes given to certain manuscripts. It is best to follow the author's usage (provided it is consistent on its own terms).

the marginal illustrations in the Luttrell Psalter
poems contained in the Book of Taliesin (a thirteenth-century manuscript then preserved at Peniarth)

8.2.3 **Capitalization**

The capitalization of work titles is a matter for editorial convention; there is no need to follow the style of title pages (many of which present titles in full capitals).

The initial word of a title is always capitalized. The traditional style is to give maximal capitalization to the titles of works published in English, capitalizing the first letter of the first word and of all other important words (for works in other languages see Chapter 12 and 8.8 below). Nouns, adjectives (other than possessives), and verbs are usually given capitals; pronouns and adverbs may or may not be capitalized; articles, conjunctions, and prepositions are usually left uncapitalized. Exactly which words should be capitalized in a particular title is a matter for individual judgement, which may take account of the sense, emphasis, structure, and length of the title. Thus a short title may look best with capitals on words that might be left lower case in a longer title:

An Actor and his Time
All About Eve
Six Men Out of the Ordinary
Through the Looking-Glass and What Alice Found There
What a Carve Up!
Will you Love me Always?

The first word of a subtitle is traditionally capitalized, whatever its part of speech (this is the Oxford style):

Small is Beautiful: Economics as if People Mattered
Film Theory: An Introduction

Alternatively, full capitalization may be applied to the main title while the subtitle has simply the capitalization of normal prose:

Rebirth, Reform and Resilience: universities in transition 1300–1700

In titles containing a hyphenated compound capitalize all parts (*Through the Looking-Glass*, *A Behind-the-Scenes Account of the War in Cuba*).

It is possible to give minimal capitalization to very long titles (usually from older sources) while applying full capitalization to most titles:

> *Comfort for an afflicted conscience, wherein is contained both consolation and instruction for the sicke, against the fearfull apprehension of their sinnes, of death and the devill, of the curse of the law, and of the anger and just judgement of God*

And it is usual to apply minimal capitalization to the titles of works, most especially poems or traditional songs, that are in fact their opening words:

> 'Wish me luck as you wave me goodbye'

If the traditional style is to capitalize the principal words within a work title, a more modern practice—in line with a general tendency to eliminate redundant capitalization—is to capitalize the first word of a title and then to apply the capitalization of normal prose. This style of minimal capitalization, which has long been standard in bibliography, has been adopted more quickly in academic and technical publishing than in general contexts. Even in academic contexts it is applied more frequently to items in roman (such as the titles of articles) than it is to italic titles, and maximal capitalization may be retained for the titles of periodicals after it has been abandoned for the titles of books:

> *Sheep, their breeds, management and diseases*
> *When champagne became French: wine and the making of a national identity*
> 'Inequality among world citizens' in the *American Economic Review*

8.2.4 **Spelling**

The original spelling of a title in any language should generally be preserved. US spellings should not be replaced by British ones, or vice versa. However, as with direct quotations from text (see 9.3.1), a limited degree of editorial standardization may be acceptable where the exact original orthography is of no particular relevance. Thus in the titles of early modern works:

- orthographic signs (including the ampersand) and abbreviations may be retained or expanded, and superscript letters reproduced or brought down, according to editorial preference
- the original's use of the letters *i* and *j*, and of *u* and *v*, may be consistently modernized, though it is generally safest to retain the printed forms

- a double *v* (*vv*) may be changed to the letter *w*
- the long *s* should always be regularized to *s* (*Perspective Practical*, 1672, not *Perſpective Practical*).

However, before implementing any of these changes, it is important to consult with the author, and to accede to their wishes if they prefer the original forms to be reproduced.

8.2.5 **Punctuation**

The original punctuation of work titles should generally be retained. However, some punctuation may be inserted to articulate a title in a way that is achieved on a title page by means of line breaks. In addition, title page forms may be made to run more smoothly by amending archaic semicolons and colons to commas; similarly, full points within a title may be changed to commas, semicolons, or colons:

> The Great Arch
> English State Formation as Cultural Revolution

on a title page may be rendered in text as

> *The Great Arch: English State Formation as Cultural Revolution*

and

> *The mathematicall divine; shewing the present miseries of Germany, England and Ireland: being the effects portended by the last comet*

may be rendered as

> *The mathematicall divine, shewing the present miseries of Germany, England and Ireland, being the effects portended by the last comet*

Similarly,

> *A treatise of the bulk and selvedge of the world. Wherein the greatness, littleness, and lastingness of bodies are freely handled*

may be rendered as

> *A treatise of the bulk and selvedge of the world, wherein the greatness, littleness, and lastingness of bodies are freely handled*

Again, particularly with archaic titles, it is important to explain your proposed practice to the author.

Two other changes should be made systematically:

- Use a colon to separate the main title from a subtitle (replace a dash or rule of any kind in this position with a colon).

- Place a comma before and after the word *or* (or its equivalent in any language) between parallel alternative titles. The second title should be given an initial capital, whether maximal or minimal capitalization is employed:

  The Construction of Nationhood: Ethnicity, Religion and Nationalism
  Parkinson's law, or, The pursuit of progress
  Senarius, sive, De legibus et licencia veterum poetarum

8.2.6 **Truncation**

A long title may be silently truncated, with no closing ellipsis, provided the given part is grammatically and logically complete (use a trailing ellipsis if the shortened title is grammatically or logically incomplete). Do not insert the abbreviation *etc.* or a variant to shorten a title (but retain it if it is printed in the original). Use an ellipsis to indicate the omission of material from the middle of a title.

Opening definite or indefinite articles may be omitted from a title to make the surrounding text read more easily. More severely shortened forms are acceptable if they are accurately extracted from the full title and allow the work to be identified; this is particularly helpful if a work is mentioned frequently and a full title given at its first occurrence.

8.2.7 **Use of *the***

It is a common convention in referring to periodicals to include an initial capitalized and italicized *The* in titles which consist only of the definite article and one other word, but to exclude the definite article from longer titles. Even when this convention is adopted, the definite article must be omitted from constructions where the article does not properly modify the title (see also 8.9):

> *The Economist*
> the *New Yorker*
> he wrote for *The Times* and the *Sunday Times*
> he was the *Times* correspondent in Beirut
> in the next day's *Times*

In the name of the Bible, other sacred texts, and ancient epic poems the definite article is lower case roman, and may be dropped if syntactically expedient:

> he spent tuppence on a secondhand *Iliad*, and was dazzled

8.2.8 **Titles within titles**

When the title of one work includes that of another this should be indicated with a minimum of intervention in the styling of the main title. The subsidiary title is sometimes placed within single quotation marks:

> *The History of 'The Times'*

Or, if the main title is italic, the subsidiary title may be set in reverse (roman) font:

> *Hardy's Tragic Genius and* Tess of the D'Urbervilles

Of course, whichever system is used, practice should be consistent throughout the work.

Underlining text to distinguish it is not recommended: see 7.6.

When one Latin title is incorporated in another the subsidiary title will be fully integrated grammatically into the main title, and there should be neither additional capitalization nor quotation marks:

> *In quartum librum meteorologicorum Aristotelis commentaria*

8.2.9 **Italics in titles**

Within italic titles containing a reference that would itself be italic in open text (for example ships' names), do not revert to roman in Oxford style (see 7.1.2):

> *The Voyage of the Meteor* (not *The Voyage of the* Meteor)

8.2.10 **Editorial insertions in titles**

See 4.12.2 for a discussion of square brackets. Use square-bracketed insertions in titles very sparingly. The editorial *sic* should be used only if it removes a real doubt; *sic* is always italic, while the brackets adopt the surrounding typography:

> his *Collection of* [*Latin*] *nouns and verbs … together with an English syntax*
>
> one of them, 'A borgens [bargain's] a borgen', setting a text written in a west-country dialect
>
> *The seven cartons* [*sic*] *of Raphael Urbino*

8.2.11 **Bibliographic information and locations**

A work mentioned in text may or may not be given a full citation in a note; in either case bibliographic detail additional to its title may be included in the text. Broadly speaking, the elements that are given in the text should be styled according to the conventions that govern citations in the notes or bibliography, but some minor variation may be appropriate (an author's full forename, for example, may be used rather than initials). Dates of publication are sometimes useful in text, and may be given in open text or in parentheses. Do not include place of publication routinely, but only if relevant to the discussion. Likewise STC (short-title catalogue) numbers may be given in specialist contexts or if helpful in the identification of a rare early work.

Bibliographic abbreviations and contractions used in the notes (e.g. *edn*, *vol.*, *bk*, *pt*, *ch.*) are generally acceptable in parenthetical citations in text but should be given in full in open text (*edition*, *volume*, *book*, *part*, *chapter*). Do not capitalize words representing divisions within works (*chapter*, *canto*, *section*, and so on). Abbreviations used for libraries or archival repositories in notes may be retained in parenthetical citations but should be extended to full forms in open text.

Locations within works can be described in a variety of ways in open text ('in the third chapter of the second book'; 'in chapter 3 of book 2'; 'in book 2, chapter 3'). Parenthetical references may employ the more abbreviated styles used in notes. In some contexts, for example where a text is discussed at length, short citations (for example 2.3.17 to represent book 2, chapter 3, line 17) may be acceptable even in open text. In such forms the numbers should be consistently either closed up to the preceding points or spaced off from them. The text should follow the conventions of the notes as to the use of Arabic or Roman numerals for the components of locations, for example acts, scenes, and lines of plays, or the divisions of classical or medieval texts. In the absence of parallel citations in the notes it is best to use Arabic numerals for all elements.

8.3 Sacred texts

8.3.1 **The Bible**

General considerations

It is the normal convention to set the title of the Bible and its constituent books in roman rather than italic type, with initial capitals.

Terms for parts or versions of the Bible are usually styled in the same way (the Old Testament, the Pentateuch, the Authorized Version). Specific modern editions of the Bible (for example the *New English Bible*) should be given italic titles. Terms such as *scripture* or *gospel* should not be capitalized when used generically, but may be either upper or lower case when applied to a particular book of the Bible. It is not necessary to capitalize the adjective *biblical*, or the word *bibles* used of multiple copies of the Bible:

the Acts of the Apostles
the Gospel of St Luke
a commentary on one of the gospels

Formerly, biblical references to chapters and verses used lower-case Roman numerals for chapter, followed by a full point, space, and verse number in Arabic (ii. 34). Modern practice is to use Arabic numerals for both, separated by a colon and no space (Luke 2:34). Fuller forms (the second epistle of Paul to the Corinthians) are generally more appropriate to open text, and more or less abbreviated citations (2 Cor. or 2 Corinthians) to notes and parenthetical references in text, but the degree of abbreviation acceptable in running text will vary with context.

Versions of the Bible

The Bible traditionally used in Anglican worship, called the Authorized Version (AV), is an English translation of the Bible made in 1611. The Vulgate, prepared mainly by St Jerome in the late fourth century, was the standard Latin version of both the Old Testament (OT) and New Testament (NT). Two modern English versions are the *English Standard Version* (*ESV*), an update of the 1971 *Revised Standard Version*, most recently revised in 2011, and the *New International Version* (*NIV*), first published in 1973–8, and revised in 1985 and 2011. The Roman Catholic Bible was translated from the Latin Vulgate and revised in 1592 (NT) and 1609 (OT); the *New Jerusalem Bible* is a modern English translation (1985). Many versions are available in digital format.

The Septuagint (LXX) is the standard Greek version of the Old Testament, originally made by the Jews of Alexandria but now used (in Greek or in translation) by the Orthodox Churches. Neither Septuagint nor Vulgate recognizes the distinction between 'Old Testament' and 'Apocrypha' made by Protestants.

Books of the Bible

Names of books of the Bible are conventionally abbreviated as follows:

Old Testament

Genesis	Gen.
Exodus	Exod.
Leviticus	Lev.
Numbers	Num.
Deuteronomy	Deut.
Joshua	Josh.
Judges	Judg.
Ruth	Ruth
1 Samuel	1 Sam.
2 Samuel	2 Sam.
1 Kings	1 Kgs
2 Kings	2 Kgs
1 Chronicles	1 Chr.
2 Chronicles	2 Chr.
Ezra	Ezra
Nehemiah	Neh.
Esther	Esther
Job	Job
Psalms	Ps. (*pl.* Pss.)
Proverbs	Prov.
Ecclesiastes	Eccles.
Song of Songs (*or* Song of Solomon)	S. of S.
Isaiah	Isa.
Jeremiah	Jer.
Lamentations	Lam.
Ezekiel	Ezek.
Daniel	Dan.
Hosea	Hos.
Joel	Joel
Amos	Amos
Obadiah	Obad.
Jonah	Jonah
Micah	Mic.
Nahum	Nahum
Habakkuk	Hab.
Zephaniah	Zeph.
Haggai	Hag.
Zechariah	Zech.
Malachi	Mal.

The first five books are collectively known as the Pentateuch (Five Volumes), or the books of Moses. Joshua to Esther are the Historical books; Job and Psalms are the Didactic books. The remainder of the Old Testament contains the Prophetical books. The major prophets are Isaiah, Jeremiah, and Ezekiel; the minor prophets are Hosea, Joel, Amos, Obadiah, Jonah, Micah, Nahum, Habakkuk, Zephaniah, Haggai, Zechariah, and Malachi.

New Testament

Matthew	Matt.
Mark	Mark
Luke	Luke
John	John
Acts of the Apostles	Acts
Romans	Rom.
1 Corinthians	1 Cor.
2 Corinthians	2 Cor.
Galatians	Gal.
Ephesians	Eph.
Philippians	Phil.
Colossians	Col.
1 Thessalonians	1 Thess.
2 Thessalonians	2 Thess.
1 Timothy	1 Tim.
2 Timothy	2 Tim.
Titus	Titus
Philemon	Philem.
Hebrews	Heb.
James	Jas.
1 Peter	1 Pet.
2 Peter	2 Pet.
1 John	1 John
2 John	2 John
3 John	3 John
Jude	Jude
Revelation	Rev.

Apocrypha

1 Esdras	1 Esdras
2 Esdras	2 Esdras
Tobit	Tobit
Judith	Judith
Rest of Esther	Rest of Esth.
Wisdom	Wisd.
Ecclesiasticus	Ecclus.
Baruch	Baruch
Song of the Three Children	S. of III Ch.

Susanna	Sus.
Bel and the Dragon	Bel & Dr.
Prayer of Manasses	Pr. of Man.
1 Maccabees	1 Macc.
2 Maccabees	2 Macc.

8.3.2 **Other sacred texts**

As with the Bible, the names of Jewish and Islamic scriptures, and of other non-Christian sacred texts, are cited in roman rather than italic.

In references to the texts of Judaism and Islam, as with the Bible, there are alternative conventions for naming, abbreviating, and numbering the various elements. The forms adopted will depend on the nature of the work and on authorial and editorial preference.

Jewish scriptures

The Hebrew Bible contains the same books as the Old Testament, but in a different arrangement. The Torah or Law has Genesis, Exodus, Leviticus, Numbers, Deuteronomy; Prophets has Joshua, Judges, Samuel, Kings, Isaiah, Jeremiah, Ezekiel, the Twelve; Writings or Hagiographa has Psalms, Proverbs, Job, Song of Songs, Ruth, Lamentations, Ecclesiastes, Esther, Daniel, Ezra, Nehemiah, Chronicles. Although nowadays divided as in Christian bibles, Samuel, Kings, and Chronicles were (and still may be) each traditionally counted as one book; similarly Ezra-Nehemiah.

The Talmud is the body of Jewish civil and ceremonial law and legend, comprising the Mishnah and the Gemara. The Talmud exists in two versions: the Babylonian Talmud and the Jerusalem Talmud. In most non-specialist works only the former is cited.

Islamic scriptures

The Islamic sacred book is the Koran, or Qu'ran/Quran. The Koran is divided into 114 unequal units called 'suras' or 'surahs'; each sura is divided into verses. Every sura is known by an Arabic name; this is sometimes reproduced in English, sometimes translated, for example 'the Cave' for the eighteenth. The more normal form of reference is by number, especially if the verse follows: '*Sura* 18, v. 45', or simply '18. 45'. References to suras have Arabic numbers with a full point and space before the verse number, though the older style of a Roman numeral or colon is also found.

The Sunna or Sunnah is a collection of the sayings and deeds of the Prophet; the tradition of these sayings and deeds is called Hadith.

8.4 References to Shakespeare

The standard Oxford edition of Shakespeare is *The Complete Works*, edited by Stanley Wells and Gary Taylor (Oxford University Press, 1986, compact edn 1988). No single accepted model exists for abbreviating the titles of Shakespeare's plays and poems, although in many cases the standard modern form by which the work is commonly known may be thought to be abbreviated already, since the complete original titles are often much longer. For example, *The First Part of the Contention of the Two Famous Houses of York and Lancaster* is best known as *The Second Part of King Henry VI*, and *The Comical History of the Merchant of Venice, or Otherwise Called the Jew of Venice* as *The Merchant of Venice*. The table below shows the more commonly found forms used by scholars. Column two gives the forms used in the *Shorter Oxford English Dictionary*; column three gives those specified for the Oxford editions series. Column four lists still shorter forms, which are useful where space is at a premium and in the references of specialist texts where familiarity with the conventions is assumed.

Title of work	**Standard abbreviations**		**Short abbrev.**
All's Well that Ends Well	*All's Well*	*All's Well*	*AWW*
Antony and Cleopatra	*Ant. & Cl.*	*Antony*	*Ant.*
As You Like It	*AYL*	*As You Like It*	*AYL*
The Comedy of Errors	*Com. Err.*	*Errors*	*Err.*
Coriolanus	*Coriol.*	*Coriolanus*	*Cor.*
Cymbeline	*Cymb.*	*Cymbeline*	*Cym.*
Hamlet	*Haml.*	*Hamlet*	*Ham.*
The First Part of King Henry IV	*1 Hen. IV*	*1 Henry IV*	*1H4*
The Second Part of King Henry IV	*2 Hen. IV*	*2 Henry IV*	*2H4*
The Life of King Henry V	*Hen. V*	*Henry V*	*H5*
The First Part of King Henry VI	*1 Hen. VI*	*1 Henry VI*	*1H6*

The Second Part of King Henry VI	*2 Hen. VI*	*2 Henry VI (Contention)*	*2H6*
The Third Part of King Henry VI	*3 Hen. VI*	*3 Henry VI (True Tragedy)*	*3H6*
The Famous History of the Life of King Henry VIII	*Hen. VIII*	*Henry VIII (All Is True)*	*H8*
The Life and Death of King John	*John K.*	*John*	*Jn.*
Julius Caesar	*Jul. Caes.*	*Caesar*	*JC*
King Lear	*Lear*	*Lear*	*Lr.*
A Lover's Complaint	*Compl.*	*Complaint*	*LC*
Love's Labour's Lost	*LLL*	*LLL*	*LLL*
Macbeth	*Macb.*	*Macbeth*	*Mac.*
Measure for Measure	*Meas, for M.*	*Measure*	*MM*
The Merchant of Venice	*Merch. V.*	*Merchant*	*MV*
The Merry Wives of Windsor	*Merry W.*	*Merry Wives*	*Wiv.*
A Midsummer Night's Dream	*Mids. N D.*	*Dream*	*MND*
Much Ado about Nothing	*Much Ado*	*Much Ado*	*Ado*
Othello	*Oth.*	*Othello*	*Oth.*
Pericles	*Per.*	*Pericles*	*Per.*
The Passionate Pilgrim	*Pilgr.*	*P. Pilgrim*	*PP*
The Phoenix and the Turtle	*Phoenix*	*Phoenix*	*Ph.T.*
The Rape of Lucrece	*Lucr.*	*Lucrece*	*Luc.*
The Tragedy of King Richard II	*Rich. II*	*Richard II*	*R2*
The Tragedy of King Richard III	*Rich. III*	*Richard III*	*R3*
Romeo and Juliet	*Rom. & Jul.*	*Romeo*	*Rom.*
Sonnets	*Sonn.*	*Sonnets*	*Son.*
The Taming of the Shrew	*Tam. Shr.*	*Shrew*	*Shr.*
The Tempest	*Temp.*	*Tempest*	*Tmp.*
Timon of Athens	*Timon*	*Timon*	*Tim.*
Titus Andronicus	*Tit. A.*	*Titus*	*Tit.*
Troilus and Cressida	*Tr. & Cr.*	*Troilus*	*Tro.*
Twelfth Night	*Twel. N*	*Twelfth Night*	*TN*
The Two Gentlemen of Verona	*Two Gent.*	*Two Gentlemen*	*TGV*
The Two Noble Kinsmen	*Two Noble K.*	*Kinsmen*	*TNK*
Venus and Adonis	*Ven. & Ad.*	*Venus*	*Ven.*
The Winter's Tale	*Wint. T.*	*Winter's Tale*	*WT*

'F1 and 'F2' are sometimes used to mean the First Folio and Second Folio respectively, and 'Q' to mean the Quarto edition.

8.5 Films, broadcast works, and digital media

Content may be experienced by the user in many ways other than through print. Electronic games, ebooks, audio books, websites, and apps are a few examples. The treatment of titles is generally similar to that of printed works.

8.5.1 **Films and broadcast works**

The titles of films and broadcast works (both individual programmes and series) are set in italic. The titles of episodes in series are set in roman in quotation marks. They are commonly given full capitalization, though minimal capitalization is acceptable if applied consistently. If necessary further information about the recording may be included in open text or within parentheses:

> *Look Back in Anger*
> *West Side Story*
> the film *A Bridge Too Far* (1977)
> his first radio play, *Fools Rush In*, was broadcast in 1949
> the Granada TV series *Nearest and Dearest*
> the American television series *The Defenders* ('The Hidden Fury', 1964)
> the video *Stones in the Park* (1969)

8.5.2 **Digital media**

The titles of apps and podcasts should be treated like free-standing publications, set in italics with important capitals. Titles of ebooks and audio books should follow the same style as a print edition.

> Discover great days out with the new *Trust Trails* app for iPhone and iPad
>
> From altruism to Wittgenstein, philosophers, theories and key themes, download the *In Our Time* philosophy podcast
>
> *The Adventures of Sherlock Holmes* is available in a variety of ebook formats from Project Gutenberg
>
> Thomas Hardy's *The Return of the Native*, in a new reading by Nicholas Rowe

Website titles are set roman, without quotation marks, although websites that also have a print version are treated in the same way as their hard-copy cousins; weblog (blog) titles may be roman or italic but should be treated consistently.

Please join me on Facebook, and follow me on Twitter.
Hans Rosling's Gapminder blog
The *British National Formulary* is available as a book, a website and a mobile app.

Titles of web pages (within a website) and individual blog posts or podcast items are roman with quotation marks:

the 'Morris Dance' page of Wikipedia
in the Language blog post 'Lincoln's rhetoric in the Gettysburg Address'

Titles of periodicals such as *Slate* and the *Huffington Post*, which are published online only, are treated like print titles, in italics with essential capitals; sites that feature their domain names as part of their title are usually treated similarly with important capitals even if the URL is rendered in lower case: *Politics.co.uk, NYTimes.com.*

Electronic games include video games, arcade games, and console games. Their titles are set in italic and given maximal capitalization:

Team Fortress 2
the *Pikmin* series
The Sims 3: University Life is the ninth expansion pack

Database names are set roman with essential capitals, e.g. the British Armorial Bindings database. Computer filenames, when referenced in running text, should be set roman and should include the file extension (filename.docx).

8.6 Musical works

8.6.1 **General principles**

The styling of musical work titles is peculiarly difficult because of the diversity of forms in which some titles may be cited, issues related to language, and longstanding special conventions. The most comprehensive source for the correct titles of musical works is *The New Grove Dictionary of Music and Musicians*, 2nd edition, edited by Stanley Sadie and John Tyrrell (London, 2001), available as part of Oxford Music Online.

8.6.2 **Popular music and traditional songs**

Song titles in English are set in roman type with quotation marks, capitalized according to the style adopted for titles in general:

'Three Blind Mice' 'Brown-Eyed Girl'

This is irrespective of whether the title forms a sentence with a finite verb:

'A Nightingale Sang in Berkeley Square'
'Papa's Got a Brand New Bag'

In contrast, traditional ballads and songs, which draw their titles directly from the first line, may follow the rules for poetry. Here, only the first and proper nouns are capitalized:

'Come away, death' 'What shall we do with the drunken sailor?'

The names of albums, CDs, and collections are given in italic, with no quotation marks:

A Love Supreme *Forever Changes*
Younger Than Yesterday *In the Land of Grey and Pink*

This results in the combination of, for example, 'Born to Run', from *Born to Run* (roman in quotation marks for song, italic for album).

8.6.3 **True titles**

A distinction is usually made between works with 'true' titles and those with generic names. The boundary between the two types of title is not always clear, but, as with all other difficult style decisions, sense and context provide guidance, and consistency of treatment within any one publication is more important than adherence to a particular code of rules.

True titles are set in italic type with maximal or minimal capital initials according to the prevailing style of the publication:

Britten's *The Burning Fiery Furnace* Elgar's *The Apostles*
Tippett's *A Child of our Time*

Foreign-language titles are usually retained (and styled according to the practice outlined in 8.8 below). By convention, however, English publications always refer to some well-known works by English titles, especially when the original title is in a lesser-known language:

Berlioz's *Symphonie fantastique* Schubert's *Die schöne Müllerin*
Liszt's *Années de pelerinage*

but

Berg's *Lyric Suite*
Bartók's *Music for Strings, Percussion and Celesta*
Stravinsky's *The Rite of Spring*

Operas and other dramatic works may be named in the original language or in English according to any sensible and consistent system—for example, in the original language if the reference is to a performance in that language, in English if the reference is to a performance in translation. A translated title may be given if the reader may not otherwise recognize the work:

> Mozart's *The Magic Flute*
> Janáček's *Z mrtvého domu* ('From the house of the dead')

Some works, however, are by convention always named in the original language:

> Puccini's *La Bohème* Weber's *Der Freischütz*

The titles of individual songs, arias, anthems, and movements are styled in roman in quotation marks, as are nicknames (that is, those not provided by the composer):

> 'Skye Boat Song'
> 'Dove sono' from *The Marriage of Figaro*
> the sacred madrigal 'When David heard that Absalom was dead'
> the 'Rigaudon' from *Le Tombeau de Couperin*
> the 'Jupiter' Symphony
> the 'Enigma Variations'

It is customary to use minimal capital initials for titles derived from the words of a song (see 8.6.2).

8.6.4 **Generic names**

Titles derived from the names of musical forms are set in roman type with initial capitals. Identifying numbers in a series of works of the same form, opus numbers, and catalogue numbers are all given in Arabic numerals; the abbreviations 'op.' and 'no.' may be capitalized or not, while the capital abbreviations that preface catalogue numbers are often set in small capitals without a full point and closed up to the numeral (though Oxford style is to use full capitals and a full point and to space off the numeral). The names of keys may use musical symbols # and ♭ or the words 'sharp' and 'flat'. Note the capitalization, punctuation, and spacing in the examples below:

> Bach's Mass in B minor *or* B Minor Mass
> Brahms's Symphony no. 4/Fourth Symphony
> Handel's Concerto Grosso in G major, op. 3, no. 3
> Mozart's Piano Trio, K496

Beethoven's String Quartet in C sharp minor, op. 131 *or* ... C# minor, op. 131

Tempo marks used as the titles of movements are also set in roman type with initial capitals, as are the sections of the mass and other services:

the Adagio from Mahler's Fifth Symphony
the Credo from the *Missa solemnis*
the Te Deum from Purcell's Morning Service in D

8.6.5 **Hybrid names**

Certain titles are conventionally styled in a mixture of roman and italic type. They include works that are named by genre and title such as certain overtures and masses:

the Overture *Portsmouth Point*   the Mass *L'Homme armé*

Note, however, that in other styles the generic word is treated as a descriptor:

the march *Pomp and Circumstance*, no. 1   the *Firebird* suite

Instrumentation that follows the title of a work may be given descriptively in roman with lower-case initials, or as part of the title. A number of twentieth-century works, however, include their instrumentation as an inseparable part of the title.

Three Pieces for cello and piano

but

Serenade for Strings   *Concerto for Orchestra*

8.7 Works of art

8.7.1 **General principles**

The formal titles of works of visual art, including paintings, sculptures, drawings, posters, and prints, are set in italic. Full capitalization is still usual, though with longer titles there may be difficulties in deciding which words should be capitalized:

Joseph Stella, *Brooklyn Bridge*
The Mirror of Venus
the etching *Adolescence* (1932) and the painting *Dorette* (1933)
the huge chalk and ink drawing *St Bride's and the City after the Fire, 29th December 1940*
the wartime poster *Your Talk may Kill your Comrades* (1942)

Consistently minimal capitalization is also possible for works of art:

Petrus Christus's *Portrait of a young man*

Works may be referred to either by a formal title or by a more descriptive form:

he painted a portrait entitled *James Butler, 2nd duke of Ormonde, when Lord Ossory*

he painted a portrait of James Butler (later second duke of Ormonde) when the subject was Lord Ossory

Titles bestowed by someone other than the artist or sculptor are usually given in roman with no quotation marks:

La Gioconda   the Venus de Milo

Works that discuss numerous works of art need consistent conventions and abbreviations for the parenthetical presentation of such information as the medium, dimensions, date of creation or date and place of first exhibition, and the current ownership or location of the works mentioned:

Andromeda (bronze, *c.*1851; Royal Collection, Osborne House, Isle of Wight)

The Spartan Isadas (exh. RA, 1827; priv. coll.)

8.7.2 **Series of works of art**

Place the titles of series of unique works of art in roman type with maximal capitalization and without quotation marks. Series of published prints may be given italic titles:

a series of paintings of children, Sensitive Plants, with such names as *Sweet William* and *Mary Gold*

his finest series of prints, *Gulliver's Travels* and *Pilgrim's Progress*

8.8 Non-English work titles

For general guidance on works in languages other than English see Chapter 12. The rules governing the capitalization of titles in some languages, such as French, are complex, and in less formal contexts it is acceptable to treat foreign-language titles in the same way as English ones.

Take care to distinguish the title, date of publication, and author of the original from the title, date, and translator of an English version. Ideally the title of the translation should not be used as if it were the title of the original work, but this rule may be relaxed in some contexts.

English titles may be used for works performed in English translation. The common English titles of classical works may be used in place of the Greek or Latin originals, and common English or Latin titles may be used for ancient or medieval works originally written in Greek, Arabic, or Persian:

> Virgil's *Eclogues*
> Avicenna's *Canon of Medicine*
> Aristotle's *De caelo et mundo*

The title in the original language may be accompanied by an English translation, especially if its sense is not implied by the surrounding text. Place such translations in quotation marks within parentheses (square brackets are sometimes used), in roman type with an initial capital on the first word. The true titles of published translations are set in italics, like those of other publications.

> *Auraicept na n-éces* ('The primer of the poets')
> the lament 'O, Ailein duinn shiùbhlainn leat' ('Oh, brown-haired Allan, I would go with you')
> a translation of Voltaire's *Dictionnaire philosophique* (as *A Dictionary of Philosophy*, 1824)

Except in specialist contexts the titles of works in non-Roman alphabets are not reproduced in their original characters but are transliterated according to standard systems (with minimal capitalization) or replaced by English translations. Words actually printed in transliteration in a title are rendered as printed, not brought into line with a more modern style of transliteration:

> Ibn Sīnā's *Kitāb shifā' al-nafs*
> Chekhov's *The Cherry Orchard*
> his translation of the Bhagavadgita was published in London (as *The Bhagvat-geeta*) in 1785

8.9 Integration of titles into text

Integrate the title of a work syntactically into the sentence in which it is mentioned.

Do not separate an author's name from a work title simply by a comma; where appropriate employ a possessive form. An initial definite or indefinite article may be omitted from a title if this helps the sentence to read more smoothly:

> the arguments in Darwin's *Origin of Species*

Always treat the title of a work as singular, regardless of its wording:

> his *Experiences of a Lifetime* ranges widely

Phrasing that places the title of a work as the object of the prepositions *on* or *about* (as in the third of the following examples) should be avoided. The style should be:

> a paper on the origins of the manor in England
> a paper, 'The origins of the manor in England'

not

> a paper on 'The origins of the manor in England'

When part or all of a book's title or subtitle, or any other matter from the title page, is quoted it should be styled as a quotation, not as a work title, that is in roman not italic type and with the original punctuation and capitalization (unless full capitals) preserved:

> *The Enimie of Idlenesse*, printed in 1568, was presented as a manual 'Teaching the maner and stile how to endite, compose, and write all sorts of Epistles and Letters'

CHAPTER 9

Quotations and direct speech

9.1 General principles

A direct quotation presents the exact words spoken on a particular occasion or written in a particular place. It can be of any length, but there are legal restrictions on how much of another's work one may repeat; for more on copyright see Chapter 20.

A direct quotation or passage of direct speech should be clearly indicated and, unlike a paraphrase, should exactly reproduce the words of the original. Although the wording of the quoted text should be faithfully reproduced, the extent to which the precise form of the original source is replicated will vary with context and editorial preference.

Quotations from early manuscripts may call for more or less complex and specialist conventions that are not discussed here.

9.2 Layout of quoted text

9.2.1 Displayed and run-on quotations

Quotations can be run on in text or broken off from it. A prose quotation of fewer than, say, fifty words is normally run on (or **embedded**) and enclosed in quotation marks, while longer quotations are broken off without quotation marks. But there is no firm rule, and the treatment of particular quotations or groups of quotations will depend on editorial preference, context, and the overall look of the displayed text. A passage that contains multiple quotations, for example, may be easier to read if all are displayed, even if some or all of them contain fewer than fifty words. Or it may be thought helpful to display a single, short quotation that is central to the following argument.

Quotations that are broken off from text (called **displayed** or **block** quotations, or **extracts**) begin on a new line, and can appear in various formats: they may be set in smaller type (usually one size down from text size), or in text-size type with less leading (vertical space between the lines); set to the full measure, or to a narrower measure; set with all lines indented from the left, or block centred (indented left and right); or set justified or unjustified. A commonly encountered style is shown below; the text is indented one em left and right:

> Most of those who came in now had joined the Army unwillingly, and there was no reason why they should find military service tolerable. The War had become undisguisedly mechanical and inhuman. What in earlier days had been drafts of volunteers were now droves of victims. I was just beginning to be aware of this.

Displayed quotations should not be set entirely in italic type even if they appeared thus in the original publication (although individual words may of course be italicized). If two or more quotations that are not continuous in the original are displayed to follow one another with none of the author's own text intervening, the discontinuity is shown by extra leading.

More than one line of quoted verse is normally displayed, line by line. Some other material, for example lists, whether or not numbered, and quoted dialogue, is suitable for line-by-line display. For verse quotations see 9.4 below; for extracts from plays see 9.5.

Because displayed quotations are not enclosed by quotation marks, any quoted material within them is enclosed (in British style) by single quotation marks, not double. A quotation within a run-on quotation is placed within double quotation marks:

> These visits in after life were frequently repeated, and whenever he found himself relapsing into a depressed state of health and spirits, 'Well', he would say, 'I must come into hospital', and would repair for another week to 'Campbell's ward', a room so named by the poet in the doctor's house.

> Chancellor was 'convinced that the entire Balfour Declaration policy had been "a colossal blunder", unjust to the Arabs and impossible of fulfillment in its own terms'.

If a section consisting of two or more paragraphs from the same source is quoted, quotation marks are used at the beginning of each paragraph and the end of the last one, but not at the end of the first and intermediate paragraphs.

9.2.2 **Introducing quotations and direct speech**

When quoted speech is introduced, interrupted, or followed by an interpolation such as *he said*, the interpolation is usually separated from the speech by commas:

> 'I wasn't born yesterday,' she said.
> 'No,' said Mr Stephens, 'certainly not.'
> A voice behind me says, 'Someone stolen your teddy bear, Sebastian?'

A colon may also be used before the quoted speech. A colon is typically used to introduce more formal speech or speeches of more than one sentence, to give emphasis to the quoted matter, or to clarify the sentence structure after a clause in parentheses:

> Rather than mince words she told them: 'You have forced this move upon me.'
> Philips said: 'I'm embarrassed. Who wouldn't be embarrassed?'
> Peter Smith, general secretary of the Association of Teachers and Lecturers, said: 'Countries which outperform the UK in education do not achieve success by working teachers to death.'

Very short speeches do not need any introductory punctuation:

> He called 'Good morning!'

and neither does a quotation that is fitted into the syntax of the surrounding sentence:

> He is alleged to have replied that 'our old college no longer exists'.

The words *yes* and *no* and question words such as *where* and *why* are enclosed in quotation marks where they represent direct speech, but not when they represent reported speech or tacit paraphrasing:

> She asked, 'Really? Where?'
> He said 'Yes!', but she retorted 'No!'
> The governors said no to our proposal.
> When I asked to marry her, she said yes.

9.2.3 **Quotation marks**

Modern British practice is normally to enclose quoted matter between single quotation marks, and to use double quotation marks for a quotation within a quotation:

> 'Have you any idea', he said, 'what "red mercury" is?'

The order is often reversed in newspapers, and uniformly in US practice:

> "Have you any idea," he said, "what 'red mercury' is?"

If another quotation is nested within the second quotation, revert to the original mark, either single-double-single or double-single-double.

Quotation marks with other punctuation

When quoted speech is broken off and then resumed after words such as *he said*, a comma is used within the quotation marks to represent any punctuation that would naturally have been found in the original passage. Three quoted extracts—with and without internal punctuation—might be:

> Go home to your father.
> Go home, and never come back.
> Yes, we will. It's a good idea.

When presented as direct speech these would be punctuated as follows:

> 'Go home', he said, 'to your father.'
> 'Go home,' he said, 'and never come back.'
> 'Yes,' he said, 'we will. It's a good idea.'

The last example above may equally be quoted in the following ways:

> He said, 'Yes, we will. It's a good idea.'
> 'Yes, we will,' he said. 'It's a good idea.'
> 'Yes, we will. It's a good idea,' he said.

In US practice, commas and full points are set inside the closing quotation mark regardless of whether they are part of the quoted material (note in the US example the double quotation marks):

> No one should 'follow a multitude to do evil', as the Scripture says.
> *US style*: No one should "follow a multitude to do evil," as the Scripture says.

This style is also followed in much modern British fiction and journalism. In the following extract from a British novel the comma after 'suggest' is enclosed within the quotation marks even though the original spoken sentence would have had no punctuation:

> 'May I suggest,' she said, 'that you have a bath before supper?'

Traditional British style would have given:

> 'May I suggest', she said, 'that you have a bath before supper?'

When a grammatically complete sentence is quoted, the full point is placed *within* the closing quotation mark. The original might read:

> It cannot be done. We must give up the task.

It might then be quoted as

He concluded, 'We must give up the task.'

'It cannot be done,' he concluded. 'We must give up the task.'

When the quoted sentence ends with a question mark or exclamation mark, this should be placed within the closing quotation mark, with no other mark outside the quotation mark—only one mark of terminal punctuation is needed:

He sniffed the air and exclaimed, 'I smell a horse!'

When the punctuation mark is not part of the quoted material, as in the case of single words and phrases, place it outside the closing quotation mark:

Why does he use the word 'poison'?

When a quoted sentence is a short one with no introductory punctuation, the full point is generally placed outside the closing quotation mark:

Cogito, ergo sum means 'I think, therefore I am'.

He believed in the proverb 'Dead men tell no tales'.

He asserted that 'Americans don't understand history', and that 'intervention would be a disaster'.

9.2.4 **Dialogue**

Dialogue is usually set within quotation marks, with each new speaker's words on a new line, indented at the beginning:

'What's going on?' he asked.

'I'm prematurely ageing,' I muttered.

In some styles of writing—particularly fiction—opening quotation marks are replaced with em rules and closing quotation marks are omitted:

— We'd better get goin', I suppose, said Bimbo.

— Fair enough, said Jimmy Sr.

In other styles, marks of quotation are dispensed with altogether, the change in syntax being presumed sufficient to indicate the shift between direct speech and interpolations:

Who's that? asked Russell, affecting not to have heard.

Why, Henry, chirped Lytton.

Dialogue in fiction is often not introduced with 'say' or any other speech verb:

I decide it's Spencer's fault, and sit up grumpily.

'Who let you in?'

Thought and imagined dialogue may be placed in quotation marks or not, so long as similar instances are treated consistently within a single work.

9.2.5 **Sources**

The source of a quotation, whether run on or displayed, is normally given in a note if the work uses that form of referencing, or it may be presented in an author-date reference. The source of a displayed prose quotation may be given in the text. It may, for example, follow the end of the quotation in parentheses after an em space, or be ranged right on the measure of the quotation, either on the line on which the quotation ends, if there is room, or on the following line:

> Troops who have fought a few battles and won, and followed up their victories, improve on what they were before to an extent that can hardly be counted by percentage. The difference in result is often decisive victory instead of inglorious defeat (*Personal Memoirs*, 355).

> He brought an almost scholarly detachment to public policy—a respect for the primacy of evidence over prejudice; and in retirement, this made him a valued and respected member of the scholarly community. Those of us privileged to know him will always remember him as an exemplar of standards and qualities in public life.
>
> *The Times*, 8 Nov. 1999

9.3 Styling of quoted text

9.3.1 **Spelling, capitalization, and punctuation**

In quotations from printed sources the spelling, capitalization, and punctuation should normally follow the original. However:

- Such obvious errors as a missing full point or unclosed parentheses or quotation marks may be silently corrected.
- Forms of punctuation that differ from house style may be silently regularized. Thus foreign forms of question mark or quotation mark (for example « » or „“) should be replaced, and the use of double and single quotation marks and of em rules, en rules, and hyphens standardized.
- It is acceptable to change a capital on the first word of a quotation to lower case, to integrate it into the surrounding sentence.

- Orthographic signs (including the ampersand) and abbreviations may be retained or expanded, and superscript letters reproduced or brought down, according to editorial preference.
- The original's use of the letters *i* and *j*, and of *u* and *v*, may be consistently modernized, though it is generally safest to retain the printed forms.
- A double *v* (*vv*) may be changed to the letter *w*.
- The long *s* (roman ſ, italic *ſ*) is a variant form rather than a distinct letter and is always regularized to *s*.
- Text that is printed in full caps may be rationalized to upper and lower case (or caps and small caps).

Preserve if possible the Old and Middle English letters ash (æ), eth (ð), thorn (Þ), yogh (ȝ), and wyn (ƿ) in quotations from printed sources (see 12.13.1). Ligatured œ and æ in quoted text may be retained or printed as two separate letters according to editorial policy.

9.3.2 **Interpolation and correction**

Place in square brackets any words interpolated into a verbatim quotation that are not part of the original. Use such interpolations sparingly. Editorial interpolations may be helpful in preserving the grammatical structure of a quotation while suppressing irrelevant phrasing, or in explaining the significance of something mentioned that is not evident from the quotation itself. The Latin words *recte* (meaning 'properly' or 'correctly') and *rectius* ('more properly') are rare but acceptable in such places:

> he must have left [Oxford] and his studies
>
> as though they [the nobility and gentry] didn't waste enough of your soil already on their coverts and game-preserves
>
> the Duke and Duchess of Gloucester [*recte* Cumberland] are often going to a famous painters in Pall Mall; and 'tis reported that he [Gainsborough] is now doing both their pictures

The Latin word *sic* (meaning 'thus') is used to confirm an incorrect or otherwise unexpected form in a quotation; it is printed in italics within square brackets. Do not use *sic* simply to flag erratic spelling, but only to remove real doubt as to the accuracy of the quoted text. Do not use [!] as a form of editorial comment:

> Bulmer established his Shakspeare [*sic*] Press in London at Cleveland Row

In some contexts editorial policy may allow the silent correction of trivial errors in the original, judging it more important to transmit the content of the quoted matter than to reproduce its exact form.

9.3.3 **Omissions**

Mark the omission of text within a quotation by an ellipsis (...). Do not place an ellipsis at the start or end of a quotation, even if this is not the beginning or end of a sentence; the reader must accept that the source may continue before and after the text quoted. See 4.7 for a full discussion of ellipses.

Punctuation immediately before or after an ellipsis can generally be suppressed unless it is helpful to the sense, as might be the case with a question or exclamation mark; style in similar contexts should be consistent within a work. It may, however, be retained in some contexts—for purposes of textual analysis, for example, or where the author has some other particular reason for preserving it. If the preceding sentence ends with a full point it is Oxford practice to retain the point before the ellipsis, closed up to the preceding text:

> Writing was a way of understanding ... world events.
>
> Where is Godfrey? ... They say he is murdered by the papists.
>
> Presently a misty moon came up, and a nightingale began to sing.... It was strange to stand there and listen, for the song seemed to come all the more sweetly and clearly in the quiet intervals between the bursts of firing.

Do not delete an ellipsis that is part of the original text if the words on either side of it are retained in the quotation. In a quotation that contains such an original ellipsis any editorial ellipsis should be distinguished by being placed within square brackets:

> The fact is, Lady Bracknell [...] my parents seem to have lost me ... I don't actually know who I am [...] I was ... well, I was found.

An ellipsis can mark an omission of any length. In a displayed quotation broken into paragraphs mark the omission of intervening paragraphs by inserting an ellipsis at the end of the paragraph before the omission. For omissions in verse extracts see 9.4.3 below.

9.3.4 **Typography**

A quotation is not a facsimile, and in most contexts it is not necessary to reproduce the exact typography of the original. Such features as change of font, bold type, underscoring, ornaments, and the exact layout of the text may generally be ignored. Italicization may be reproduced if helpful, or suppressed if excessive.

9.4 Poetry

9.4.1 **Run-on verse quotations**

More than one line of quoted verse is normally displayed line by line, but verse quotations may also be run on in the text. In run-on quotations it is Oxford style to indicate the division between each line by a vertical bar (|) with a space either side, although a solidus (/) is also widely used:

> 'Gone, the merry morris din, | Gone the song of Gamelyn', wrote Keats in 'Robin Hood'

When set, the vertical or solidus must not start a new line. See also 4.13.

9.4.2 **Displayed verse**

In general, poetry (including blank verse) should be centred on the longest line on each page; if this is disproportionately long the text should be centred optically. Within the verse the lines will generally range on the left, but where a poem's indentation clearly varies the copy should be followed: this is particularly true for some modern poetry, where correct spacing in reproduction forms part of the copyright. In such instances it is useful to provide the typesetter with a PDF or photocopy of the original to work from. It is helpful to indent turnovers 1 em beyond the poem's maximum indentation:

> Pond-chestnuts poke through floating chickweed on the green
> brocade pool:
> A thousand summer orioles sing as they play among the roses.
> I watch the fine rain, alone all day,
> While side by side the ducks and drakes bathe in their crimson
> coats.

Do not automatically impose capitals at the beginnings of lines. Modern verse, for example, sometimes has none, and the conventions commonly applied to Greek and Latin verse allow an initial capital to only a few lines (see 12.8.5, 12.12.3).

9.4.3 **Omissions**

Omissions in verse quotations run into text are indicated like those in prose. Within displayed poetry the omission of one or more whole lines may be marked by a line of points, separated by 2-em spaces; the first and last points should fall approximately 2 ems inside the measure of the longest line:

> Laboreres þat haue no lande, to lyue on but her handes,
> Deyned nouȝt to dyne a-day, nyȝt-olde wortes.
>
> . . . .
>
> Ac whiles hunger was her maister, þere wolde none of hem chyde,
> Ne stryve aȝeines his statut, so sterneliche he loked.

Use an ellipsis when the end of a line of displayed verse is omitted; indicate the omission of the start of the first line of displayed verse by ranging (usually right with the next line):

>   a great beau,
> that here makes a show,
> and thinks all about him are fools

9.4.4 **Sources**

If there is sufficient room a short source—such as a book, canto, or line number, or a short title—can be placed in parentheses on the same line as the last line of verse. Oxford practice is to begin the reference 1 em to the right of the end of the quotation's longest line:

> The world was all before them, where to choose
> Their place of rest, and providence their guide:
> They hand in hand with wandering steps and slow
> Through Eden took their solitary way   (xii. 648–9)

If the source is longer place it on the next line down, ranged to the right with the end of the quotation's longest line:

> They hand in hand with wandering steps and slow
> Through Eden took their solitary way
>   *Paradise Lost*, xii. 648–9

9.5 Plays

Publishers have their own conventions for the presentation of plays, quotations from which may be treated as run-on quotations, or as prose or poetry extracts, with no strict regard to the original layout, spacing, or styling of characters' names. Any sensible pattern is acceptable if consistently applied. If a speaker's name is included in the quotation it is best printed as a displayed extract.

To follow Oxford's preferred format in extracts from plays, set speakers' names in small capitals, ranged full left. In verse plays run the speaker's name into the first line of dialogue; the verse follows the speaker's name after an em space and is not centred; indent subsequent lines by the same speaker 1 em from the left. Indent turnovers 2 ems in verse plays, 1 em in prose plays:

> Her reply prompts Oedipus to bemoan his sons' passivity:
>
> OEDIPUS But those young men your brothers, where are they?
>
> ISMENE Just where they are—in the thick of trouble.
>
> OEDIPUS O what miserable and perfect copies have they grown to be of Egyptian ways!
>
> For there the men sit at home and weave while their wives go out to win the daily bread.

> This is apparent in the following exchange between them:
>
> WIPER We've had ballistics research on this. No conceivable injury could from this angle cause even the most temporary failure of the faculties.
>
> BUTTERTHWAITE You can't catch me. I've read me Sexton Blake. I was turned the other way.
>
> WIPER Are you in the habit, Alderman, of entering your garden backwards?

Particularly in verse plays a single line is sometimes made up of the speeches of more than one character and is set as more than one line of type. The parts are progressively indented, with an interword space clear to the right of the previous part's end, repeating as necessary. Ideally this layout should be preserved in the quoted extract, as in the following extreme example:

KING JOHN	Death.
HUBERT	My lord.
KING JOHN	A grave.
HUBERT	He shall not live.
KING JOHN	Enough.

Do not include stage directions in extracts from plays unless they are relevant to the matter under discussion (in which case their styling in the original may be preserved or adapted). Similarly, line numbers should not normally be included.

9.6 Epigraphs

In publishing, an epigraph is a short quotation or saying at the beginning of a book or chapter. Publishers will have their own preferences for the layout of epigraphs. In Oxford's academic books they are set in small type, verse epigraphs being treated much like displayed verse quotations and optically centred. A source may be placed on the line after the epigraph, ranged right on the epigraph's measure:

> To understand history the reader must always remember how small is the proportion of what is recorded to what actually took place.
>
> Churchill, *Marlborough*

An epigraph's source does not usually include full bibliographic details, or even a location within the work cited (though such information can be given in a note if it seems helpful). The date or circumstances of the epigraph, or the author's dates, may be given if they are thought to be germane:

> You will find it a very good practice always to verify your references, sir!
>
> Martin Joseph Routh (1755–1854)

9.7 Non-English quotations

Quotations from languages other than English are commonly given in English translation, but they are sometimes reproduced in their original language, for example when their sense is thought to be evident, in specialist contexts where a knowledge of the language in question is assumed, or where a short quotation is better known in the original language than it is in English:

> *L'État c'est moi* ('*I* am the State')
> *Après nous le déluge* ('After us the deluge')
> *Arbeit macht frei* ('Work liberates')

Quotations in other languages follow the same rules as those in English. The wording, spelling, punctuation, capitalization, and layout of non-English quotations should be treated like those in English, and omissions, interpolations, and sources presented in the same way:

> Asked about the role of the new Spanish government in his release, Raúl Rivero replied:
>
> Tengo un sentimiento de gratitud con el Gobierno de [José María] Aznar por lo que hizo cuando caí preso. Pero, efectivamente, me parece que la

nueva politica española ha sido más efectiva. La confrontación nunca en política resuelve nada. Creo que el cambio sí ha favorecido . . . que en Cuba hubiera más receptividad en las autoridades cubanas.

El País, 1 Dec. 2004, 33e

Le Monde reported that 'Raúl Rivero a exprimé sa "gratitude éternelle" envers le gouvernement espagnol'.

In the second example the original wording, including the French rendering of a Spanish name, has been reproduced exactly, but French quotation marks and italicization of quotations (« *gratitude éternelle* ») have been adapted to British conventions.

Sometimes it seems desirable both to retain the original—perhaps because its exact sense or flavour cannot be captured by a translation—and to provide an English version for readers unfamiliar with the language in question. It is always worth asking in such cases whether the original is genuinely helpful to the reader. The English equivalent may take the form of an explanation or paraphrase, but if it too is presented as a direct quotation, whether loose or literal, it should be enclosed in quotation marks and will normally be placed within parentheses after the original. Alternatively the translation may be given first, followed by the original in quotation marks within parentheses. If sources of quotations are given in parentheses, a source may follow a translation within a single set of parentheses, separated from it by a comma, semicolon, or colon, according to house style:

It provided accommodation for 'candidates às magistraturas superiores das Faculdades', those eligible for senior posts in the university.

The cyclist Jean Bégué was 'de ces Jean qu'on n'ose pas appeler Jeannot' ('one of those men named John one dare not call Johnny').

He poses the question 'Wie ist das Verhältnis des Ausschnitts zur Gesamtheit?' ('What is the relationship of the sample to the whole group?': Bulst, 'Gegenstand und Methode', 9).

Inter needed to develop 'a winning attitude and an attractive style of play' ('un'identità vincente e un bel gioco').

Where a displayed translation is followed by a displayed original—or vice versa—place the second of the two quotations in parentheses. Where the second of the two displayed quotations is the original, some authors prefer to have it set in italics. A displayed verse original may be followed either by a verse translation set in lines or by a displayed prose translation:

Rufus naturaliter et veste dealbatus
Omnibus impatiens et nimis elatus
(Ruddy in looks and white in his vesture,
Impatient with all and too proud in gesture)   (Wright, i. 261)

Gochel gwnsel a gwensaeth
a gwin Sais, gwenwyn sy waeth
(Beware the counsel, fawning smile and wine of the Englishman—it is worse than poison)

In most contexts quotations from other languages should be given in translation unless there is a particular reason for retaining the original. On occasion it is helpful to include within a translation, in italics within parentheses, the untranslated form of problematic or specially significant words or phrases:

> Huntington, 'obsessed with the idea of purity, does not recognize the cardinal virtue of... Spanish: the virtue of coexistence and intermixing (*mestizaje*)'.

Isolated non-English words or phrases generally look best italicized rather than placed in quotation marks (see 7.2.2), especially if they are discussed as set terms rather than quotations from a particular source. For inflected languages this has the advantage of allowing the nominative form of a word to be given even when another case is used in the passage cited. The non-English term may be used untranslated or with an English equivalent (perhaps on its first occurrence only if it is used frequently):

> This right of common access (*Allemansrätten*) is in an old tradition
>
> As early as 1979 the status of *denominação de origem controlada* was accorded to Bairrada
>
> In this document he is styled *magister scolarum*
>
> Montella was *capocannoniere* (top scorer), with eleven goals

In some works appropriate conventions will be needed for quotations transliterated from non-roman alphabets and for the rendering of German Fraktur type. The German *Eszett* (ß) can normally be regularized as double *s* (ss). For advice on transliteration see Chapter 12.

CHAPTER 10

Abbreviations and symbols

10.1 General principles

Abbreviations fall into three categories. Strictly speaking, only the first of these is technically an abbreviation, though the term loosely covers them all, and guidelines for their use overlap. There is a further category, that of symbols, which are more abstract representations.

- **Abbreviations** in the strict sense are formed by omitting the end of a word or words (*Lieut.*, *cent.*, *assoc.*).
- **Contractions** are formed by omitting the middle of a word or words (*Dr*, *Ltd*, *Mrs*, *Revd*, *St*). Informal contractions (*I've*, *he's*, *mustn't*) are widely used but are not always appropriate (see 10.2.3).
- **Acronyms** are formed from the initial letters of words. Acronyms are sometimes defined specifically as words formed from the initial letters of other words and pronounced as words themselves (*AWOL*, *PIN*, *BOGOF*), as opposed to **initialisms**, which are formed from the initial letters of words but not pronounced as words (*BBC*, *QED*). Some acronyms are now treated as orthodox nouns: examples include *laser* (from *l*ight *a*mplification by *s*timulated *e*mission of *r*adiation) and *scuba* (*s*elf-*c*ontained *u*nderwater *b*reathing *a*pparatus). Another class can be presented in all caps or can retain just the initial capital: *AIDS*/*Aids* is an example. Oxford dictionaries, in particular the *New Oxford Dictionary for Writers and Editors*, give the meanings of a great many abbreviations. (See also 10.2.4.)
- **Symbols** or **signs** may be letters assigned to concepts (π, Ω), or special typographical sorts (%, +, #). They are typically used in conjunction with words, numbers, or other symbols (πr^2, £100, © Oxford University Press), although they may be used on their own as, for example, note markers.

In work for a general audience do not use abbreviations or symbols in open text (that is, in the main text but not including material in parentheses) unless they are very familiar indeed (*US*, *BBC*, *UN*), or would be unfamiliar if spelt out (*DNA*, *SIM card*), or space is scarce, or terms are repeated so often that abbreviations are easier to absorb. Abbreviations are more appropriate in parentheses and in ancillary matter such as appendices, bibliographies, captions, figures, notes, references, and tables, and rules differ for these.

It is helpful to spell out abbreviations at first mention, adding the abbreviation in parentheses after it:

> the Economic and Social Research Council (ESRC)

It is generally better to avoid an abbreviation in a chapter title or heading but, if unavoidable, spell it out at the first mention in the text proper. Some house styles for specialist works make exception for abbreviations that are so familiar to a technical readership they do not need to be defined, such as *RAM* (random-access memory) in an academic computer book. It is helpful to authors and editors if the house style lists these exceptions. (See 14.3.1.)

It is not necessary to define an abbreviation at first mention in each chapter unless the book is likely to be read out of sequence, as in a multi-author work or a textbook. If this is the case, or simply if many abbreviations are used, including a list of abbreviations or a glossary is a good way to avoid repeatedly expanding abbreviations (see 1.2.14). Titles of qualifications and honours placed after personal names are an exception to the general rule that initialisms should be spelled out; many forms not familiar to most people are customarily cited:

> Alasdair Andrews, Bt, CBE, MVO, MFH

For more on titles see 6.1.4.

It is possible to refer to a recently mentioned full name by a more readable shortened form, rather than—or in addition to—a set of initials: *the Institute* rather than *IHGS* for the Institute of Heraldic and Genealogical Studies. (See also 5.3.2.)

As a general rule, avoid mixing abbreviations and full words of similar terms, although specialist or even common usage may militate against this, as in *Newark, JFK, and LaGuardia airports*.

For lists of abbreviations see 1.2.14; for legal abbreviations see 13.2.2; for abbreviations in or with names see 6.1.1. For Latin bibliographic abbreviations such as 'ibid.' see 17.2.5.

10.2 Punctuation and typography

10.2.1 **Full points?**

Traditionally, abbreviations end in full points while contractions do not, so that we have *Jun.* and *Jr* for Junior, and *Rev.* and *Revd* for Reverend. This rule is handy and in general is borne out, although there are some exceptions: for example *St.* (= Street) is often written with a point to avoid confusion with *St* for Saint, and *no.* (= *numero*, Latin for number). Note that everyday titles such as *Mr*, *Mrs*, and *Dr*, being contractions, are written without a point, as is *Ltd*; editors need not attempt to establish how a particular company styles *Ltd* in its name. US style uses more points than British style does, even with contractions, thus giving *Jr.* instead of *Jr* (no point). (See 6.1.3.)

A problem can arise with plural forms of abbreviations such as *vol.* (volume) or *ch.* (chapter): these would strictly be *vols* and *chs*, which are contractions and should not end with a point. However, this can lead to the inconsistent-looking juxtaposition of *vol.* and *vols* or *ch.* and *chs*, and so in some styles full points are retained for all such short forms. Similarly, *Bros*, the plural form of *Bro.* 'brother', is often written with a point.

Technical and scientific writing uses less punctuation than non-technical English. Metric abbreviations such as *m* (metre), *km* (kilometre), and *g* (gram) do not usually have a full point, and never do in scientific or technical writing. Purely scientific abbreviations (*bps* = bits per second; *mRNA = messenger ribonucleic acid*) are presented without full points.

There are other exceptions to the principle that abbreviations have full points. For example, abbreviations for eras, such as AD and BC (traditionally written in small capitals), have no points. Arabic and Roman ordinal numbers take no points (*1st*, *2nd*, *3rd*); similarly, monetary amounts (*£6m*, *50p*) and book sizes (*4to*, *8vo*, *12mo*) do not have points. Note also that there are no points in colloquial abbreviations that have become established words in their own right, such as *demo* (demonstration) or *trad* (traditional).

If an abbreviation ends with a full point but does not end the sentence, other punctuation follows naturally: *Gill & Co., Oxford.* If the full point of the abbreviation ends the sentence, however, there is no second full point: *Oxford's Gill & Co.*

10.2.2 **Ampersands**

Avoid ampersands except in established combinations (e.g. *R & B*, *T & C*) and in names of firms that use them (*M&S, Mills & Boon*). There should be spaces around the ampersand except in company names such as *M&S* that are so styled; in journalism ordinary combinations such as *R&B* are frequently written with no spaces.

10.2.3 **Apostrophes**

Place the apostrophe in the position corresponding to the missing letter or letters (*fo'c's'le, ha'p'orth, sou'wester, t'other*), but note that *shan't* has only one apostrophe. Informal contractions such as *I'm*, *can't*, *it's*, *mustn't*, and *he'll* are perfectly acceptable in less formal writing, especially fiction and reported speech, and are sometimes found even in academic works. However, editors should not impose them except to maintain consistency within a varying text.

There are no apostrophes in colloquial abbreviations that have become standard words in the language, such as *cello*, *flu*, *phone*, or *plane*. Retain the original apostrophe only when archaism is intentional, or when it is necessary to reproduce older copy precisely. Old-fashioned or literary abbreviated forms such as *'tis*, *'twas*, and *'twixt* do need an opening apostrophe, however: make sure that it is set the right way round, and not as an opening quotation mark.

10.2.4 **All-capital abbreviations**

Abbreviations of a single capital letter normally take full points (*G. Lane*, *Oxford U.*) except when used as symbols (see 10.3 below); abbreviated single-letter compass directions have no points, however: *N*, *S*, *E*, *W*.

Acronyms or initialisms of more than one capital letter take no full points in British and technical usage, and are closed up:

TUC MA EU NE SW QC DFC

In some US styles certain initialisms may have full points (*US*/*U.S.*). In some house styles any all-capital proper-name acronym that may be pronounced as a word is written with a single initial capital, giving *Basic*, *Unesco*, *Unicef*, etc.; some styles dictate that an acronym is written thus if it exceeds a certain number of letters (often four). Editors should avoid this rule, useful though it is, where the result runs against the common practice of a discipline or where similar terms would be treated dissimilarly based on length alone.

Where a text is rife with full-capital abbreviations, they can be set all in small capitals to avoid the jarring look of having too many capitals on the printed page. Some abbreviations (e.g. BC, AD) are always set in small capitals (see 7.5.2).

For treatment of personal initials see 6.1.1; for postcodes and zip codes see 6.2.4.

10.2.5 **Lower-case abbreviations**

Lower-case abbreviations are usually written with no points (*mph*, *plc*), especially in scientific contexts.

In running text lower-case abbreviations cannot begin a sentence in their abbreviated form. In notes, however, a group of exceptions may be allowed: *c.*, *e.g.*, *i.e.*, *l.*, *ll.*, *p.*, *pp.* are lower case even at the beginning of a note.

Write *a.m.* and *p.m.* in lower case, with two points; use them only with figures, and never with *o'clock*. see 11.3 for more on times of day.

Short forms of weights and measures are generally not written with a point, with the exception of forms such as *gal.* (gallon) and *in.* (inch) that are not in technical use:

oz lb g dwt
pt qt ft m (miles *or* metres)

Note that *min.*, and *sec.* have a point in general contexts but are not used in scientific work.

When an abbreviated unit is used with a number there is usually a space between them (see 14.1.4):

a unit of weight equal to 2,240 lb avoirdupois (1016.05 kg)

10.2.6 **Upper- and lower-case abbreviations**

Contracted titles and components of names do not require a full point:

Dr	Mr	Mrs	Ms
Mme	Mlle	Ft (= Fort)	Mt (= Mount)

St. meaning 'street' is traditionally written with a point to distinguish it from *St* meaning 'saint'.

Shortened forms of academic degree are usually written without punctuation (*PhD*, *MLitt*). For plurals, see 10.5.

British counties with abbreviated forms take a full point (*Berks.*, *Yorks.*), with the traditional exceptions *Hants*, *Northants*, and *Oxon*, whose abbreviations were derived originally from older spellings or Latin forms.

Names of days and months should generally be shown in full, but where necessary, as in notes and to save space, they are abbreviated thus:

Sun.	Mon.	Tue.	Wed.	Thur.	Fri.	Sat.
Jan.	Feb.	Mar.	Apr.	May	June	July
Aug.	Sept.	Oct.	Nov.	Dec.		

10.2.7 **Work titles**

Italic text (e.g. titles of books, plays, and journals) usually produces italic abbreviations:

DNB (*Dictionary of National Biography*)
Arist. *Metaph.* (Aristotle's *Metaphysics*)

Follow the forms familiar in a given discipline; even then permutations can exist, often depending on the space available or on whether the abbreviation is destined for running text or a note.

For legal references see Chapter 13.

10.3 Symbols

Symbols or signs are a shorthand notation signifying a word or concept. They may be special typographical sorts, or letters of the alphabet. Symbols are a frequent feature of scientific and technical writing, but many are also used in everyday contexts, for example to denote copyright (©), currencies (£, $, €), degrees (°), feet and inches (′, ″), and percentages (%).

Do not start a sentence with a symbol: spell out the word or recast the sentence to avoid it:

Sixteen dollars was the price	The price was $16
Section 11 states ...	As §11 states, ...

Symbols formed from words are normally set close up before or after the things they modify (*GeV*, Σ^+), or set with space either side if standing alone for words or concepts (*a W chromosome*). Symbols consisting of or including letters of the alphabet never take points. Abstract, purely typographical symbols follow similar rules, being either closed up (° # ¿ » %) or spaced. In coordinates, the symbols of measurement (degrees, seconds, etc.) are set close up to the figure, not the compass point (see 14.1.8):

52° N 15° 7′ 5″ W

Authors should use Unicode-compliant fonts (such as Times New Roman) when creating special sorts in their typescripts (see also 2.5). If there are many special sorts present, authors should create a PDF showing the special sorts correctly and provide it to the publisher.

As an alternative to superior numbers the symbols *, †, ‡, §, ¶, || may be used as reference marks or note cues, in that order. This system is based on print-page conventions and does not translate well into ebooks or online publishing.

The signs + (plus), – (minus), = (equal to), > ('larger than', in etymology signifying 'gives' or 'has given'), < ('smaller than', in etymology signifying 'derived from') are often used in biological and philological works, and not only in those that are scientific or arithmetical in nature. In such instances +, –, =, >, < should not be printed close up, but rather separated by the normal space of the line or a thin space (be consistent). (See also 4.12.4 and 14.6.3.)

The use of symbols can differ between disciplines. For example, in philological works an asterisk (*) prefixed to a word signifies a reconstructed form; in grammatical works it signifies an incorrect or non-standard form. A dagger (†) may signify an obsolete word, or 'deceased' when placed before a person's name.

The distinction between abbreviation and symbol may sometimes be blurred in technical contexts: some forms which are derived directly from a word or words are classed as symbols. Examples are chemical elements such as *Ag* (silver) from *argentum* and *U* from *uranium*, and forms such as *E* from *energy* and *m* from *mass* which are used in equations rather than running text. For the use of symbols in science, mathematics, and computing see Chapter 14.

10.4 The indefinite article with abbreviations

The choice between *a* and *an* before an abbreviation depends on pronunciation, not spelling. Use *a* before abbreviations beginning with a consonant sound, including an aspirated *h* and a vowel pronounced with the sound of *w* or *y*:

a BA degree	a KLM flight	a BBC announcer
a YMCA bed	a U-boat captain	a UNICEF card

Use *an* before abbreviations beginning with a vowel sound, including unaspirated *h*:

an MCC ruling	an FA cup match	an HDTV
an IOU	an MP	an RAC badge
an SOS signal	an NHS hospital	

This distinction assumes the reader will pronounce the sounds of the letters, rather than the words they stand for (*a Football Association cup match, a high-definition television*). *MS* for manuscript is normally pronounced as the full word, *manuscript*, and so takes *a*; MS for multiple sclerosis is often pronounced *em-ess*, and so takes *an*. 'R.' for rabbi is pronounced as *rabbi* ('a R. Shimon wrote').

The difference between sounding and spelling letters is equally important when choosing the article for abbreviations that are acronyms and for those that are not: *a NASA launch* but *an MC's toast*.

10.5 Possessives and plurals

Abbreviations form the possessive in the ordinary way, with an apostrophe and *s*:

a CEO's salary   MPs' assistants

Most abbreviations form the plural by adding *s*; an apostrophe is not needed:

DVDs   MCs   SOSs   VIPs

In plural forms of a single letter an apostrophe can sometimes be clearer:

A's and S's
the U's
minding your p's and q's

When an abbreviation contains more than one full point, put the *s* after the final one (*Ph.D.s, the d.t.s*).

For abbreviations with one full point, such as *ed.*, *no.*, and *Adm.*, see 10.2.1.

A few abbreviations have irregular plurals (e.g. *Messrs* for *Mr*). In some cases this stems from the Latin convention of doubling the letter to create plurals:

ff. (folios *or* following pages)	pp. (pages)
ll. (lines)	MSS (manuscripts)
opp. cit.	

10.6 e.g., i.e., etc., et al.

Do not confuse 'e.g.' (from Latin *exempli gratia*), meaning 'for example', with 'i.e.' (Latin *id est*), meaning 'that is'. Compare

hand tools, e.g. hammer and screwdriver

with

hand tools, i.e. those able to be held in the user's hands

Although many people employ 'e.g.' and 'i.e.' quite naturally in speech as well as writing, prefer 'for example', 'such as' (or, more informally, 'like'), and 'that is' in running text. Conversely, adopt 'e.g.' and 'i.e.' within parentheses or notes, since abbreviations are preferred there.

A sentence in text cannot begin with 'e.g.' or 'i.e.'; however, a note can, in which case they remain lower case.

Take care to distinguish 'i.e.' from the rarer 'viz.' (Latin *videlicet*, 'namely'). Formerly some writers used 'i.e.' to supply a definition or paraphrase, and 'viz.' to introduce a list of items. However, it is Oxford's preference either to replace 'viz.' with 'namely' or to prefer 'i.e.' in every case.

Write 'e.g.' and 'i.e.' in lower-case roman, with two points and no spaces. In Oxford's style they are not followed by commas, to avoid double punctuation; commas are often used in US practice. A comma, colon, or dash should precede 'e.g.' and 'i.e.' A comma is generally used when there is no verb in the following phrase:

> different fruits, e.g. apples, oranges, bananas, and cherries
> part of a printed document, e.g. a book cover

Use a colon or dash before a clause or a long list:

> digital cameras have the advantage of being solid-state devices— i.e. they don't have moving parts

In full 'etc.' is *et cetera*, a Latin phrase meaning 'and other things'. 'Et al.' is short for Latin *et alii*, 'and others'. In general contexts both are lower-case roman, with a full point, though 'et al.' is sometimes italicized in bibliographic use. Do not use '&c.' for 'etc.' except when duplicating historical typography. 'Etc.' is preceded by a comma if it follows more than one listed item: *robins, sparrows, etc.*; it is best to avoid using 'etc.' after only one item (*robins etc.*), as at least two examples are necessary to establish the relationship between the elements and show how the list might go on. The full point can be followed by a comma or whatever other punctuation would be required after an equivalent phrase such as *and the like*— but not by a second full point, to avoid double punctuation.

Use 'etc.' in technical or scholarly contexts such as notes and works of reference. Elsewhere, prefer *such as*, *like*, *or for example* before a list, or *and so on*, *and the like* after it; none of these can be used in combination with 'etc.' It is considered rude to use 'etc.' when listing individual people; use 'and others' instead; use 'etc.' when listing *types* of people, however. In a technical context, such as a bibliography, use 'et al.':

> Daisy, Katie, Alexander, and others
> duke, marquess, earl, etc.
> Smith, Jones, Brown, et al.

Do not write 'and etc.': 'etc.' includes the meaning of 'and'. Do not end a list with 'etc.' if it begins with 'e.g.', 'including', 'for example', or 'such as', since these indicate that the list is to be incomplete. Choose one or the other, not both.

10.7 Abbreviations with dates

In reference works and other contexts where space is limited the abbreviations 'b.' (born) and 'd.' (died) may be used. Both are usually roman, followed by a point, and printed close up to the following figures:

> Amis, Martin (Louis) (b.1949), English novelist ...

An en rule may also be used when a terminal date is in the future:

> *The Times* (1785–) Jenny Benson (1960–)

A fixed interword space after the date may give a better appearance in conjunction with the closing parenthesis that generally follows it:

> *The Times* (1785–) Jenny Benson (1960–)

For people the abbreviation b. is often preferred, as the bare en rule may be seen to connote undue anticipation.

The Latin *circa*, set roman or italic, meaning 'about', is used in English mainly with dates and quantities. Set the abbreviation, *c.* or *ca*, in roman or italic close up to any figures following (*c.*1020, *c.*£10,400), but spaced from words and letters (*c.* AD 44). In discursive prose it is usually preferable to use *about* or *some* when describing quantities, although *approximately* is better in scientific text:

> about eleven pints some 14 acres approximately 50 kg

With a span of dates the abbreviation must be repeated before each date if both are approximate, as a single abbreviation is not understood to modify both dates:

> Philo Judaeus (*c.*15 BC–*c.* AD 50)

Distinguish between *c.* and ?: the former is used where a particular year cannot be fixed upon, but only a period or range of several years; the latter where there are reasonable grounds for believing that a particular year is correct. It follows therefore that *c.* will more often be used with round numbers, such as the start and midpoint of a decade, than with numbers that fall between. See 4.8.2.

A form such as '*c.*1773' might be used legitimately to mean 'between 1772 and 1774' or 'between 1770 and 1775'. As such, it is best in discursive prose to indicate the earliest and latest dates by some other means. Historians employ a multiplication symbol for this purpose: *1996* × *1997* means 'in 1996 or 1997, but we cannot tell which'; similarly,

1996 × *2004* means 'no earlier than 1996 and no later than 2004'. Figures are not generally contracted in this context:

the architect Robert Smith (b.1772 × 1774, d.1855)

The Latin *floruit*, meaning 'flourished', is used in English where only an approximate date of activity for a person can be provided. Set the italicized abbreviation *fl.* or *flor.* before the year, years, or—where no concrete date(s) can be fixed—century, separated by a space:

William of Coventry (*fl.* 1360) Edward Fisher (*fl.* 1627–56)
Ralph Acton (*flor.* 14th c.)

CHAPTER 11

Numbers and dates

11.1 Numbers: general principles

11.1.1 **Introduction**

This chapter mainly covers general texts and the humanities; more detailed information about dealing with numbers in scientific contexts can be found in Chapter 14, particularly 14.1, and 14.6.1 discusses typography in mathematical notation.

11.1.2 **Figures or words?**

The main stylistic choice to be made when dealing with numbers is whether to express them in figures or in words. It is normal to determine a threshold below which numbers are expressed in words and above which figures are used; depending on the context, the threshold may vary. In non-technical contexts, Oxford style is to use words for numbers below 100; in technical contexts numbers up to and including ten are spelled out. In specialist contexts the threshold may, with good reason, be different: in some books about music, for example, numbers up to and including twelve are spelled out (there being twelve notes in the diatonic scale). The threshold provides only a general rule: there are many exceptions to it, as described below. On websites different rules may apply: figures tend to be used more than words.

Large round numbers may be expressed in a mixture of numerals and words (*6 million*; *1.5 million*) or entirely in words (*six million*; *one and a half million*). In some contexts it makes better sense to use a rounded number than an exact one, such as *a population of 60,000* rather than *of 60,011*. This is particularly true if the idea of approximation or estimation is expressed in the sentence by such words as *some*, *estimated*, or *about*. Rounded approximations may be better expressed in words if the use of figures will confer a false sense of exactitude:

about a thousand *not* about 1000
some four hundred *not* some 400

Particularly where quantities are converted from imperial to metric (or vice versa), beware of qualifying a precise number with *about*, *approximately*, etc.: *about three kilometres* should not be converted to *about 1½ miles*.

In expressing approximate figures some styles traditionally preferred *more than* to *over*. Modern usage tends to treat them as synonyms:

She was born in Oxford and has lived in Ireland for over twenty-five years
She was born in Oxford and has lived in Ireland for more than twenty-five years

although there are certain contexts in which one or the other is syntactically correct:

We spent a lot of time together, well over two months, and so we really got to know each other
There's more than one way of tackling this problem

or sounds more natural, e.g. in reference to age:

Applicants must be over 25 and have had a clean driving licence for more than five years

Use words in informal phrases that do not refer to exact numbers:

talking nineteen to the dozen
I have said so a hundred times
she's a great woman—one in a million
a thousand and one odds and ends

When a sentence contains one or more figures of 100 or above, a more consistent look may be achieved by using Arabic numerals throughout that sentence: for example, *90 to 100* (not *ninety to 100*) and *30, 76, and 105* (not *thirty, seventy-six, and 105*). This convention holds only for the sentence where this combination of numbers occurs: it does not influence usage elsewhere in the text unless a similar situation exists.

In some contexts a different approach is necessary. For example, it is sometimes clearer when two sets of figures are mixed to use words for one and figures for the other, as in *thirty 10-page pamphlets* or *nine 6-room flats*. This is especially useful when the two sets run throughout a sustained expanse of text (as in comparing quantities):

the manuscript comprises thirty-five folios with 22 lines of writing, twenty with 21 lines, and twenty-two with 20 lines

Anything more complicated, or involving more than two sets of quantities, will probably be clearer if presented in a table.

Spell out ordinal numbers—*first, second, third, fourth*—except when quoting from another source. In the interests of saving space they may also be expressed in numerals in notes and references (see also 11.6.2 below). Use words for ordinal numbers in names, and for numerical street names (apart from avenue names in Manhattan—see 6.2.4):

the Third Reich	the Fourth Estate	a fifth column
Sixth Avenue	a Seventh-Day Adventist	

It is customary to use words for numbers that fall at the beginnings of sentences:

> Eighty-four different kinds of birds breed in the Pine Barrens
> 'How much?' 'Fifty cents'

In such contexts, to avoid spelling out cumbersome numbers, recast the sentence, writing for example *The year 1849* … instead of *Eighteen forty-nine* …

Use figures for ages expressed in cardinal numbers, and words for ages expressed as ordinal numbers or decades:

a girl of 15	a 33-year-old man
between her teens and twenties	in his thirty-third year
in the twenty-first century	

In less formal or more discursive contexts (especially in fiction), ages may instead be spelled out, as may physical attributes:

> a two-year-old   a nine-inch nail

Words can supplement or supersede figures in legal or official documents, where absolute clarity is required:

> the sum of nine hundred and forty-three pounds sterling (£943)
> a distance of no less than two hundred (200) yards from the plaintiff

Figures are used for:

- parts of books, including chapters, pages, and plates (*p. 14*, *Chapter 7*)
- numbers of periodicals (*Language* 61)
- scores of games and sporting events (*a 3–1 defeat*, *37 not out*)
- distances of races (*the 400 metres*)
- house or building numbers (*47 Marston Street*)
- road or highway numbers in a national system (*A40*, *M25*, *Route 66*).

11.1.3 **Punctuation**

When written in words, compound numbers are hyphenated (see 11.1.6 for fractions):

ninety-nine   one hundred and forty-three
in her hundred-and-first year

In non-technical contexts commas are generally used in numbers of four figures or more:

1,863   12,456   1,461,523

In technical and foreign-language work use a thin space (see 14.1.3):

14 785 652   1 000 000   3.141 592

In tabular matter, numbers of only four figures have no thin space, except where necessary to help alignment with numbers of five or more figures.

There are no commas in years (with the exception of long dates such as 10,000 BC), page numbers, column or line numbers in poetry, mathematical workings, house or hotel-room numbers, or in library call or shelf numbers:

1979   1342 Madison Avenue
Bodl. MS Rawl. D1054   BL, Add. MS 33746

11.1.4 **Number ranges**

Numbers at either end of a range are linked with an en rule. A span of numbers is often elided to the fewest figures possible:

30–1   42–3   132–6   1841–5

but retain as many digits as necessary where they change across the range:

65–71   352–62   1491–560   89,999–90,000

In any event, do not elide digits in (or ending with) the group 10 to 19 because of the way they are read or spoken:

10–12   15–19   114–18   310–11

However, some editorial styles vary greatly in their treatment: for example some require no elision, some elide to the final two digits, and some don't elide multiples of 10 or 100 (*30–32; 100–101*).

Even in elided styles all digits may be preserved in more formal contexts, such as titles and headings, and in expressing people's vital dates:

Charles Dickens (1812–1870)
The National Service of British Seamen, 1914–1918
Turbulent years, 1763–1770

Dates that cross the boundary of a century should not be elided: write *1798–1810, 1992–2001*. Spans in BC always appear in full, because an elided second date could be misread as a complete year: *185–22 BC* is a century longer than *185–122 BC*, and dates for, say, Horace (65–8 BC) might appear to the unwary to express a period of three rather than fifty-seven years.

When referring to events known to have occurred between two dates, historians often employ a multiplication symbol: *1225 × 1232* (or in some styles *1225 × 32*) means 'no earlier than 1225 and no later than 1232'. The multiplication sign is also useful where one element in a range is itself a range: *1225 × 32–1278*.

In specifying a range use either the formula *from xxxx to xxxx* or *xxxx–xxxx*; take care to avoid the mistake of combining the two. It is *the war from 1939 to 1945* or *the 1939–45 war*, never *the war from 1939–45*. The same applies to the construction 'between … and …': *the period between 1998 and 2001* or *the period 1998–2001*, but not *the period between 1998–2001*. For ranges that include a negative value, it is best to use words to avoid confusion between a negative number and a dash, or to prevent an en rule clashing with a minus sign: *95% confidence interval = −743.23 to −557.28* not *95% CI = −743.23 – −557.28*.

When describing a range in figures, repeat the quantity as necessary to avoid ambiguity:

1000–2000 litres   1 billion to 2 billion light years away

The elision *1–2000 litres* means that the amount starts at only 1 litre, and *1 to 2 billion light years away* means that the distance begins only 1 light year away.

For ranges that include a unit, the unit symbol does not need to be repeated (*45.6–50.2 kg*) unless the symbol is normally closed up (*14°–18°* [of angle])

A solidus replaces the en rule for a period of one year reckoned in a format other than the normal calendar extent: *49/8 BC, the tax year 1934/5*. A span of years in this style is joined by an en rule as normal: *1992/3–2001/2*.

Use a comma to separate successive references to individual page numbers: *6, 7, 8*; use an en rule to connect the numbers if the subject is continuous from one page to another: *6–8*.

11.1.5 **Singular or plural?**

Whether they are written as words or figures, numbers are pluralized without an apostrophe (see also 4.2.2):

the 1960s	the temperature was in the 20s
they arrived in twos and threes	she died in her nineties

Plural phrases take plural verbs where the elements enumerated are considered severally:

Ten miles of path are being repaved
Around 5,000 people are expected to attend

Plural numbers considered as single units take singular verbs:

Ten miles of path is a lot to repave
More than 5,000 people is a large attendance

When used as the subject of a quantity, words like *number*, *percentage*, and *proportion* are singular with a definite article and plural with an indefinite:

The percentage of people owning a mobile phone is higher in Europe
A proportion of pupils are inevitably deemed to have done badly

None in the sense *no one person* takes the singular:

Later, 26 children and one teacher went to hospital, but none was seriously injured

but in the sense of *not any* takes the plural verb:

He had hoped to receive parking permits for residents but none were forthcoming

The numerals *hundred, thousand, million, billion, trillion*, etc. are singular unless they refer to indefinite quantities:

two dozen	about three hundred
some four thousand	more than five million

but

dozens of friends	hundreds of times
thousands of petals	millions of stars

Note that a **billion** is a thousand million (1,000,000,000 or 10^9), and a **trillion** is a million million (10^{12}). In Britain a billion was formerly a million million (10^{12}) and a trillion a million million million (10^{18}); in France, Germany, and elsewhere these values are still used.

11.1.6 **Fractions and decimals**

Fractions in mathematical contexts are discussed in 14.6.6. In other material, spell out simple fractions in running text. When fractions are spelled out they are traditionally hyphenated:

two-thirds of the country   one and three-quarters
one and a half

although they are increasingly written as open compounds (*three quarters*).

Hyphenate compounded numerals in compound fractions such as *nine thirty-seconds of an inch*; the numerator and denominator are hyphenated unless either already contains a hyphen. Do not use a hyphen between a whole number and a fraction: *one and seven-eighths* rather than *one-and-seven-eighths*. Combinations such as *half a mile* and *half a dozen* should not be hyphenated, but write *a half-mile* and *a half-dozen*.

In statistical matter use specially designed fractions where available (½, ¾, etc.), which have a diagonal bar—the Unicode block 'Number Forms' has a range of single-character fractions. The form of fraction with a horizontal bar (e.g. $\frac{19}{100}$) is satisfactory—even in running text—if presented in TeX, which subtly adjusts interline spacing and character size and spacing, but if not set in TeX, seldom looks elegant. In non-technical running text, set complex fractions in text-size numerals with a solidus between (*19/100*).

Decimal fractions may also be used: *12.66* rather than *12⅔*, *99.9* rather than *99 and 9/10*. Decimal fractions are always printed in figures. They cannot be plural, or take a plural verb. For values below one the decimal is preceded by a zero: *0.76* rather than *.76*. Exceptions are quantities (such as probabilities) that never exceed one, although authorities differ on this; if house style does not specify, it is best to follow the author's notation.

Decimals are punctuated with the full point on the line. In the UK decimal currency was formerly treated differently, with the decimal point set in medial position (*£24·72*), but this style has long been out of favour.

Note that European languages, and International Standards Organization (ISO) publications in English, use a comma to denote a decimal sign, so that *2.3* becomes *2,3*.

For the use of decimals in tables see Chapter 15.

11.2 Numbers with units of measure

11.2.1 **General principles**

Generally speaking, figures should be used with units of measurement, percentages, and expressions of quantity, proportion, etc.:

a 70–30 split
6 parts gin to 1 part dry vermouth
the structure is 83 feet long and weighs 63 tons
10 per cent of all cars sold

Note that *per cent* rather than % is used in running text in non-technical work, and that US English has *percent*, closed up.

Use figures, followed by a space, with abbreviated forms of units, including units of time, and with symbols:

winds gusted to 100 mph   250 BC   11 a.m.   13 mm

although % is commonly closed up, contrary to SI guidelines.

11.2.2 **Singular and plural units with numbers**

Note that units of measurement retain their singular form when part of hyphenated compounds before other nouns:

a five-pound note	a two-mile walk
a six-foot wall	a 100-metre race

Elsewhere, units are pluralized as necessary, but not if the quantity or number is less than one:

two kilos *or* 2 kilos	three miles *or* 3 miles
0.568 litre	half a pint

For a fuller discussion of scientific units see Chapter 14. Do not add 's' to unit symbols (*cm, ml*) in scientific work; see 14.1.3 and 14.1.4.

11.2.3 **Currencies**

Amounts of money may be spelled out in words with the unit of currency, but are more often printed in numerals with the symbols or abbreviations:

twenty-five pounds	thirteen dollars	seventy euros
£25	$13	€70

Round numbers lend themselves to words better than do precise amounts, though even these may need to be spelled out where absolute clarity is vital, as in legal documents. For amounts of millions and above, and for thousands in financial contexts, it is permissible to combine symbols, numerals, words, and abbreviations, according to the conventions of the context in which they appear: *£5 million, US$15 billion.*

Where symbols or abbreviations are used, such as *£* (pounds), *$* (dollars), € (euros), ₹ (rupees), they precede the figures. As several countries use the dollar, if there is any ambiguity use the accepted prefix (*A$*, US$). There is no space after symbols, but some styles use a space after abbreviations; this is acceptable if imposed consistently within a work:

> £2,542 £3 m $4,542 €11.47 m

Use *00* after the decimal point only if a sum appears in context with other fractional amounts:

> They bought at £8.00 and sold at £11.50

Amounts in pence, cents, or other smaller units are set with the numeral close up to the abbreviation, which has no full point: *56p* or *56¢* rather than *£0.56 or $0.56*. Mixed amounts do not include the pence/cent abbreviation: *£15.30* rather than *£15.30p.*

Amounts in pre-decimal British currency (before February 1971) are expressed in pounds, shillings, and pence—*£.s.d.* In Oxford style these are italic with a normal space separating the elements:

> Income tax stood at 8*s.* 3*d.* in the £
> The tenth edition cost £1 10*s.* 6*d.* in 1956

Other styles render them closed up, in roman with full points:

> The statue was sold at auction for £76.10s.9d. in Manchester

The international standard three-letter currency code (ISO 4217:2008) is used in trade, commerce, and banking, and the commonest currencies are well known enough to be used without explanation even in lay texts; the amount is prefixed by the code and a normal space: *GBP 500; EUR 40,000; USD 1 million.* Less familiar currencies will need explanation at first mention: *Macanese pataca (MOP) 1600.*

11.3 Times of day

The formulation of times of day is a matter of editorial style, and different forms are more or less appropriate to particular contexts. It is customary to use words, and no hyphens, with reference to whole hours and to fractions of an hour:

> four (o'clock) half past four a quarter to four

Use *o'clock* only with the exact hour, and with time expressed in words: *four o'clock*, not *half past four o'clock* or *4 o'clock*. Do not use *o'clock* with *a.m.* or *p.m.*, but rather write, for example, *eight o'clock in the morning*. Use figures with *a.m. or p.m.*: *4 p.m.* Correctly, *12 a.m.* is midnight and *12 p.m.* is noon; but since this is not always understood, it may be necessary to use the explicit *12 midnight* and *12 noon*. The twenty-four-hour clock avoids the use of *a.m.* and *p.m.*: *12.00* is noon, *24.00* is midnight. In British English either a colon or a full point as a separator is acceptable if applied consistently.

In the twelve-hour clock, use figures when minutes are to be included: *4.30 p.m.* For a round hour it is not necessary to include a decimal point and two zeros: prefer *4 p.m.* to *4.00 p.m.* In North America, Scandinavia, and elsewhere the full point is replaced by a colon: *4:30 p.m.* This is often seen in British usage too. Some styles omit the punctuation in *a.m.* and *p.m.*

11.4 Roman numerals

The base numerals are I (1), V (5), X (10), L (50), C (100), D (500), and M (1,000). The principle behind their formation is that identical numbers are added (II = 2), smaller numbers after a larger one are added (VII = 7), and smaller numbers before a larger one are subtracted (IX = 9). The I, X, and C can be added up to four times:

I, II, III, IV, V, VI, VII, VIII, IX, X (10)
XI, XII, XIII, XIV, XV, XVI, XVII, XVIII, XIX, XX (20)
MCCCCVIII (1408)

If possible, avoid eliding Roman numerals. To save space in certain circumstances two consecutive numerals may be indicated by *f.* for 'following': *pp. lxxxvii–lxxxviii* becomes *pp. lxxxvii f.*

Roman numerals can be difficult to interpret and may cause design problems because of the variable number of characters needed to express them. For example, they may be best avoided in tabulated lists, such as contents pages, because the alignment of the numerals and the following matter can produce excessive white space on the page:

I . . .
II . . .
III . . .
IV . . .

V ...
VI ...
VII ...
VIII ...
IX ...
X ...

Oxford's use of Roman numerals is described below:

- Capital Roman numerals are used for the chapters and appendices of a book, for acts of plays or sections of long poems, and for volume numbers of multi-volume works:

  Act I of *The Tempest* Book V
  Chapters III–VIII Volume XVI Soot–Styx

- The division label (part, book, chapter, appendix, etc.) is styled in the same height as the numeral, capital with capital, lower case with lower case, and small capital with small capital. Thus *Chapter XI*, *chapter xi*, CHAPTER XI.

- Lower-case Roman numerals are used to number the preliminary pages in a book, and for scenes of plays:

  pp. iii–x *Hamlet*, Act I, sc. ii

- When Roman numerals are used in references, they are lower case if there is only one level, small capital and lower case in that order if there are two (*II. i*), full capital, small capital, and lower case in that order if there are three (*III. II. i*).

- Capital Roman numerals are used after the names of monarchs and popes: *Henry VIII* (no full point). The number should not be written as an ordinal (*Henry the VIIIth*), although the style *Henry the Eighth* is an acceptable alternative to figures in running text.

- Capital Roman numerals are similarly used in American personal names, where the male of a family bears the same name: *Adlai E. Stevenson III*, *Daniel P. Daly V*. A male bearing his father's name is styled *Jr*, whereas a male bearing his grandfather's name—but not his father's—is styled *II*.

- Roman numerals in manuscript sometimes have a final or single *i* replaced by a *j*, for example *ij*, *viij*. This style need be retained only when reproducing copy in facsimile.

- In editions of Latin texts, Roman numerals should generally be set in small capitals. Classical scholars tend to make little use of Roman numerals, both in classical reference (*Ovid*, Amores *3.1.15* not *III.i.15*) and in volume numbers of books.

11.5 Date forms

Figures are used for days and years in dates. Use cardinal numbers not ordinal numbers for dates:

12 August 1960 2 November 2003

Do not use the endings *-st*, *-rd*, or *-th* in conjunction with a figure, as in *12th August 1960*, unless copying another source: dates in letters or other documents quoted verbatim must be as in the original. Where less than the full date is given, write *10 January* (in notes *10 Jan.*), but *the 10th*. If only the month is given it should be spelled out, even in notes. An incomplete reference may be given in ordinal form:

They set off on 12 August 1960 and arrived on the 18th

In British English style dates should be shown in the order day, month, year, without internal punctuation: *2 November 2003*. In US style the order is month, day, year: *November 2, 2003*.

A named day preceding a date is separated by a comma: *Tuesday, 2 November 1993*; note that when this style is adopted a terminal second comma is required if the date is worked into a sentence:

On Tuesday, 2 November 1993, the day dawned frosty

There is no comma between month and year: *in June 1831*. Four-figure dates have no comma—2001—although longer dates do: *10,000 BC*.

Abbreviated all-figure forms are not appropriate in running text, although they may be used in notes and references. The British all-figure form is *2/11/03* or *2.11.03* (or the year may be given in full). In US style the all-figure form for a date, which is always separated by slashes rather than full points, can create confusion in transatlantic communication, since *11/2/03* is 2 November to an American reader and 11 February to a British one. Note that the terrorist attacks of 11 September 2001 are known by the shorthand *September 11* or *9/11* not only in the US but also in Britain and around the world.

The dating system promoted by the ISO is year, month, day, with the elements separated by hyphens: *2003-11-02*. This style is preferred in Japan and increasingly popular in technical, computing, and financial contexts. Another alternative, common on the Continent and elsewhere, is to use (normally lower-case) Roman numerals for the months (*2. xi. 03*). This system serves to clarify which number is the day and which the month in all contexts—a useful expedient when translating truncated dates into British or US English.

For precise dates in astronomical work, use days (*d*), hours (*h*), minutes (*m*), and seconds (*s*) (*2001 January 1d 2h 34m 4.8s*) or fractions of days (*2001 January 1.107*). See also 14.7.2.

For abbreviations of days and months see 10.2.6.

11.6 Decades, centuries, and eras

11.6.1 **Decades**

References to decades may be made in either words or figures:

the sixties   in his seventies   the 1960s   in his 70s

Write either *the sixties* or *the 1960s*, not *the '60s*. Similarly, when referring to two decades use *the 1970s and 1980s*, even though *the 1970s and '80s* transcribes how such dates may be read out loud.

When the name of a decade is used to define a social or cultural period it should be written as a word (some styles use an initial capital). The difference between labelling a decade *the twenties* and calling it *the 1920s* is that the word form connotes all the social, cultural, and political conditions unique to or significant in that decade, while the numerical form is simply the label for the time span. So, *the frivolous, fun-loving flappers of the twenties*, but *the oyster blight of the 1920s*.

11.6.2 **Centuries**

Depending on the editorial style of the work, refer to centuries in words or figures; Oxford style is to use words:

the nineteenth century   the first century BC

Centuries may be abbreviated in notes, references, and tabular matter; the abbreviation may be either *c.* or *cent.*: *14th c., 21st cent.* Both spelled-out and abbreviated forms require a hyphen when used adjectivally:

> an eighth-century (*or* 8th-c.) poem
> the early seventeenth-century (*or* 17th-c.) dramatists

In dating medieval manuscripts, the abbreviation *s.* (for *saeculum*, pl. *ss.*) is often used instead: *s. viii*.

Centuries BC run backwards, so that the fifth century BC spanned 500–401 BC. The year 280 BC was in the third century BC.

Conventions for numbering centuries in other languages vary, though for the most part capital Roman numerals are used, with two common exceptions: French uses small capitals in roman, full capitals in italic. In either case the figures are followed by a superior *e* or *ème* to indicate the suffix: *le XVIIe siècle, le XVIIème siècle*. German uses Arabic numerals followed by a full point: *das 18. Jahrhundert*. Occasionally capital Roman numerals are used; these too must be followed by a full point.

11.6.3 **Eras**

The two abbreviations most commonly used for eras are BC and AD. Both are written in small capitals. The abbreviation BC (before Christ) is placed after the numerals, as in *72 BC*, not *BC 72*; *AD* (*anno domini*, 'in the year of our Lord') should be placed before the numerals, as in *AD 375* (not *375 AD*). However, when the date is spelled out it is normal to write *the third century AD* rather than *AD the third century*.

Some writers prefer to use AD for any date before the first millennium. While this is not strictly necessary, it can be handy as a clarifying label: *This was true from 37* may not instantly be recognized as referring to a year. Any contentious date, or any year span ranging on either side of the birth of Christ, should be clarified by BC or AD: *this was true from 43 BC to AD 18*. Conversely, a date span wholly in BC or AD technically needs no clarification, since *407–346* is manifestly different from *346–409*, though it is customary to identify all BC dates explicitly.

The following eras should be indicated by the appropriate abbreviation before the year:

- *a.Abr.* (the year of Abraham), reckoned from 2016 BC and used in chronicles by Eusebius and Jerome; not written AA.
- AH (*anno Hegirae*, 'in the year of the Hegira'), the Muslim era, reckoned from 16 July 622 (the date of Muhammad's departure from Mecca).
- AM (*anno mundi*, 'in the year of the world') will normally represent the Jewish era, reckoned from 7 October 3761 BC.
- AS (*anno Seleuci*), the Seleucid era, variously reckoned from autumn 312 BC and spring 311 BC, formerly current in much of the Near East.
- AUC (*anno Urbis conditae*, 'in the year of the foundation of the City'), the supposed Roman era from 753 BC. This was actually used only rarely by the Romans (who had several different dates for the foundation of Rome, and designated the year by the names of the consuls).

The following eras should be indicated by the appropriate abbreviation after the year:

- BCE (Before Common Era) and CE (Common Era) are used instead of BC and AD, mainly by writers who wish to avoid specifying dates in Christian terms.
- BP (Before Present) is used by geologists and palaeontologists for dates not accurate within a few thousand years; AD 1950 is fixed as the conventional 'present'. It is customary to use BP when discussing periods before 10,000 years ago. Some authors favour BP as a matter of course, since it does not presuppose any Christian reckoning on the reader's part. This is acceptable, provided BP is not intermingled with BC and other references of this kind within the same text.

For all era abbreviations other than *a.Abr.*, use unspaced small capitals, even in italic.

11.7 Regnal years

Regnal years are marked by the successive anniversaries of a sovereign's accession to the throne. Consequently they do not coincide with calendar years, which up to 1751 in England and America—though not in

Scotland—began legally on 25 March. All Acts of Parliament before 1963 were numbered serially within each parliamentary session, which itself was described by the regnal year or years of the sovereign during which it was held. Regnal years were also used to date other official edicts, such as those of universities.

Regnal years are expressed as an abbreviated form of the monarch's name followed by a numeral. The abbreviations of monarchs' names in regnal-year references are as follows:

Car. *or* Chas. (Charles)
Hen. (Henry)
Steph. (Stephen)
Edw. (Edward)
Jac. (James)
Will. (William)
Eliz. (Elizabeth)
P. & M. (Philip and Mary)
Wm. & Mar. (William and Mary)
Geo. (George)
Ric. (Richard)
Vic. *or* Vict. (Victoria)

The names of John, Anne, Jane, and Mary are not abbreviated. See 13.5.1 for details of citing statutes including regnal years.

11.8 Calendars

11.8.1 **Introduction**

The following section offers brief guidance for those working with some less familiar calendars; fuller explanation may be found in Bonnie Blackburn and Leofranc Holford-Strevens, *The Oxford Companion to the Year* (Oxford University Press, 1999).

Dates in non-Western calendars should be given in the order day, month, year, with no internal punctuation: *25 Tishri AM 5757*, *13 Jumada I AH 1417*. Do not abbreviate months even in notes.

11.8.2 **Old and New Style**

The terms **Old Style** and **New Style** are applied to dates from two different historical periods. In 1582 Pope Gregory XIII decreed that, in order to correct the calendar then used—the **Julian calendar**—the days 5–14 October of that year should be omitted and no future centennial year (e.g. 1700, 1800, 1900) should be a leap year unless it was divisible by 400 (for example 1600, 2000). This reformed **Gregorian calendar** was quickly adopted in Roman Catholic countries, more slowly elsewhere: in Britain not till 1752 (when the days 3–13 September were omitted), in Russia not till 1918 (when the days 16–28 February were omitted). Dates in the Julian calendar are known as Old Style, while those in the Gregorian are New Style.

Until the middle of the eighteenth century not all states reckoned the new year from the same day: whereas France adopted 1 January from 1563, and Scotland from 1600, England counted from 25 March in official usage as late as 1751. Thus the execution of Charles I was officially dated 30 January 1648 in England, but 30 January 1649 in Scotland. Furthermore, although both Shakespeare and Cervantes died on 23 April 1616 according to their respective calendars, 23 April in Spain (and other Roman Catholic countries) was only 13 April in England, and 23 April in England was 3 May in Spain.

Confusion is caused on account of the adoption, in England, Ireland, and the American colonies, of two reforms in quick succession: the adoption of the Gregorian calendar and the change in the way the beginning of the year was dated. The year 1751 began on 1 January in Scotland and on 25 March in England, but ended throughout Great Britain and its colonies on 31 December, so that 1752 began on 1 January. So, whereas 1 January 1752 corresponded to 12 January in most Continental countries, from 14 September onwards there was no discrepancy. Many writers treat the two reforms as one, using *Old Style* and *New Style* indiscriminately for the start of the new year and the form of calendar. In the interests of clarity *Old Style* should be reserved for the Julian calendar and *New Style* for the Gregorian; the 1 January reckoning should be called 'modern style', that from 25 March 'Annunciation' or 'Lady Day' style.

It is customary to give dates in Old or New Style according to the system in force at the time in the country chiefly discussed. Any dates in the other style should be given in parentheses with an equals sign preceding the date and the abbreviation of the style following it:

23 August 1637 NS (= *13 August OS*) in a history of England, or *13 August 1637 OS* (= *23 August NS*) in one of France. In either case, *13/23 August 1637* may be used for short. On the other hand, it is normal to treat the year as beginning on 1 January: modern histories of England date the execution of Charles I to 30 January 1649. When it is necessary to keep both styles in mind, it is normal to write *30 January 1648/9*; otherwise the date should be given as *30 January 1648* (= *modern 1649*).

11.8.3 **Greek calendars**

In the classical period years were designated by the name of a magistrate or other office-holder, which meant nothing outside the city concerned. In the third century BC a common framework for historians was found in the Olympiad, or cycle of the Olympic Games, held in the summer every four years from 776 BC onwards. Thus 776/5 was designated the first year of the first Olympiad; 775/4 the second year; and 772/1 the first year of the second Olympiad. When modern scholars need to cite these datings, they are written *Ol. 1, 1*, *Ol. 1, 2*, and *Ol. 2, 1* respectively.

11.8.4 **French Republican calendar**

The Republican calendar was introduced on 5 October 1793, and was discontinued with effect from 1 January 1806. On its introduction it was antedated to begin from the foundation of the Republic (22 September 1792). The months of the new calendar were named according to their seasonal significance. Though difficult to translate, approximations are included in parentheses:

Autumn	**Winter**	**Spring**	**Summer**
vendémiaire (vintage)	nivôse (snow)	germinal (seed time)	messidor (harvest)
brumaire (mist)	pluviôse (rain)	floréal (flowers)	thermidor (heat)
frimaire (frost)	ventôse (tempest)	prairial (meadows)	fructidor (fruit)

The months are not now capitalized in French, though they were at the time and may still be so in English. Years of the Republican calendar are printed in capital Roman numerals: *9 thermidor An II*; *13 vendémiaire An IV*; in English *Year II*, *Year IV*.

11.8.5 **Jewish calendar**

The Jewish year consists in principle of twelve months of alternately 30 and 29 days; in seven years out of nineteen an extra month of 30 days is inserted, and in some years either the second month is extended to 30 days or the third month shortened to 29 days. The era is reckoned from a notional time of Creation at 11.11 and 20 seconds p.m. on Sunday, 6 October 3761 BC.

11.8.6 **Muslim calendar**

The Muslim year consists of twelve lunar months, so that thirty-three Muslim years roughly correspond to thirty-two Christian ones. Years are counted from the first day of the year in which the Prophet made his departure, or Hegira, from Mecca to Medina, namely Friday, 16 July AD 622.

CHAPTER 12

Languages

12.1 General principles

This chapter provides guidelines on the editing and presentation of material in foreign languages and Old and Middle English. Languages are listed alphabetically, either separately or, for clarity and convenience, with related languages: for instance, there is one section for Slavonic languages rather than separate sections for Belarusian, Bosnian, Bulgarian, etc.

The sections stress common pitfalls and conundrums in spelling, punctuation, accents, syntax, and typography, and are intended to offer guidance to users across a broad spectrum of familiarity with the languages. A full account of each language is not the aim; rather, it seeks to aid authors and editors who are dealing with foreign-language material within English-language contexts. Overall, those languages most often met with in English-language publishing are covered in greatest depth, though not all languages of equal frequency are—or can usefully be—addressed equally: with editorial concerns foremost, distinctions between related languages have been highlighted. Help is given on setting non-Roman alphabets in English-language texts, as well as on transliteration and romanization.

Typescripts containing extensive non-roman characters should be created with a Unicode-compliant font (see 2.5) to facilitate typesetting. Authors should consult their publisher about any font requirements specific to non-roman alphabets.

For information on foreign personal names and place names see Chapter 6.

12.2 Arabic

12.2.1 **Alphabet**

Arabic is written from right to left in a cursive script consisting of twenty-eight letters, all representing consonants; their form varies according to position within the word, and several are distinguished only by dots. Some letters cannot be joined to the next even within a word; the space between them should be smaller than that between words, and unbreakable. A horizontal extender on the baseline is often added to a letter that would otherwise seem too close to the next. In verse it is conventional to give all lines the same visual length, so that the rhyming letter is aligned on the left throughout.

The same script, with additional letters, is or has been employed for other languages spoken by Muslims, such as Persian, Pashto, Urdu, Turkish, and Malay; these last two are now written in the Roman alphabet.

There is no standard system of transliterating Arabic.

12.2.2 **Accents and punctuation**

Vowel marks and other guides to pronunciation are used in editions of the Koran, in schoolbooks, and usually in editions of classical poetry; otherwise they are omitted except where a writer thinks they are needed to resolve ambiguity. Strict philological usage requires the underline in *ḏ*, *ṯ*; the under-dot in *ḥ*, *ṣ*, *ḍ*, *ṭ*, *ẓ*; the over-dot in *ġ*; the inferior semicircle in (*ḫ*); the háček in *ǧ* (often written *j*) and *š*, and the macron in *ā*, *ī*, *ū* (do not use the acute or circumflex instead). Less learned systems will dispense with some or all of these diacritics. There are also two independent characters, ʿayn (ʿ) and hamza (ء) (corresponding to Hebrew ʿayin and aleph) which should be used if available; if not, substitute Greek asper (ʽ) and lenis (ʼ) respectively. These should be distinguished from the apostrophe, mainly found before *l*-, e.g. in *ʿAbdu ʾl-Malik*; insert a hair space (see 2.5.1) between them and quotation marks.

The definite article *al* or *ʾl*- (or regional variants such as *el*- and *ul*-) is joined to the noun with a hyphen: *al-Islām*, *al-kitāb*. Do not capitalize the *a* except at the beginning of a sentence; it should not be capitalized at the start of a quoted title.

Table 12.1 **Arabic alphabet**

Alone	Final	Medial	Initial			Alone	Final	Medial	Initial		
ا	ـا			'alif	'	ض	ـض	ـضـ	ضـ	ḍād	ḍ
ب	ـب	ـبـ	بـ	bā'	b	ط	ـط	ـطـ	طـ	ṭā'	ṭ
ت	ـت	ـتـ	تـ	tā'	t	ظ	ـظ	ـظـ	ظـ	ẓā'	ẓ
ث	ـث	ـثـ	ثـ	thā'	th	ع	ـع	ـعـ	عـ	ʿayn	ʿ
ج	ـج	ـجـ	جـ	jīm	j	غ	ـغ	ـغـ	غـ	ghayn	gh
ح	ـح	ـحـ	حـ	ḥā'	ḥ	ف	ـف	ـفـ	فـ	fā'	f
خ	ـخ	ـخـ	خـ	khā'	kh	ق	ـق	ـقـ	قـ	qāf	q
د	ـد			dāl	d	ك	ـك	ـكـ	كـ	kāf	k
ذ	ـذ			dhāl	dh	ل	ـل	ـلـ	لـ	lām	l
ر	ـر			rā'	r	م	ـم	ـمـ	مـ	mīm	m
ز	ـز			zāy	z	ن	ـن	ـنـ	نـ	nūn	n
س	ـس	ـسـ	سـ	sīn	s	ه	ـه	ـهـ	هـ	hā'	h
ش	ـش	ـشـ	شـ	shīn	sh	و	ـو			wāw	w
ص	ـص	ـصـ	صـ	ṣād	ṣ	ي	ـي	ـيـ	يـ	yā'	y

Columns 5 and 6 list the names and romanized characters respectively.

12.2.3 **Word division**

In Arabic script words should not be divided even at internal spaces; if the spacing of the line would otherwise be too loose, use extenders within words. In transliteration, avoid dividing except at the hyphen following the article; if absolutely necessary, take over no more than one consonant. In loose transcription, note that *dh kh sh th* may represent either the single consonants strictly transliterated ḏ, ḫ, š, and ṯ respectively, or combinations of *d k s t* plus *h*. When in doubt, do not divide.

12.3 Chinese

12.3.1 **Introduction**

The forms of Chinese spoken in areas occupied by those of Chinese origin differ so widely from one another that many may be deemed to constitute languages in their own right. The principal dialects are Northern Chinese (Mandarin), Cantonese, Hakka, the Wu dialect of Suzhou, and the dialect of Min (Fukien). All of these, however, share a common written language consisting of thousands of separate ideographs or 'characters'. The language traditionally used for the compilation of official documents is totally unlike the spoken language, as is the language in which the classic texts of Chinese literature are expressed. For these, also, the same script is used.

12.3.2 **Scripts**

The structure of individual ideographs can sometimes be very complicated in script, involving the use of as many as twenty-eight separate strokes of the brush or pen. A code of simplified characters is in use on the mainland, but more traditional forms are found in Hong Kong, Taiwan, Singapore, and areas beyond Chinese jurisdiction.

The language is monosyllabic, one ideograph representing a syllable. Each ideograph is pronounced in a particular inflection of voice, or 'tone'. The National Language (the standard spoken form of modern Chinese) uses four separate tones, Cantonese, nine. The National Language is derived from the pronunciation of northern China (notably that of the Beijing area), which has traditionally been adopted for the transaction of official business—hence the term 'Mandarin', which is sometimes used to categorize it. Alternative names for it are *putonghua* ('speech in common use') or *Kuo-yü* (otherwise *Guoyu*, 'National Language').

The many thousand Chinese characters are traditionally written from top to bottom in vertical columns running right to left across the page, but nowadays, especially in mainland China, are printed in left-to-right lines like the Western alphabet. This has always been the practice when Chinese phrases are set within a Roman text.

12.3.3 **Transliteration**

Although the pronunciation of characters varies markedly from dialect to dialect (the surname pronounced *Wu* in Mandarin is *Ng* in Cantonese), romanization is normally based on Beijing ('Mandarin') usage. There are two main systems: **Wade–Giles,** formerly the norm in English-language publications, and **Pinyin,** the official transliteration in the People's Republic. The name, in Wade–Giles, would be spelled *P'in-in*.

Wade–Giles gives forms such as T'ien-tsin and *Mao Tse-tung*, whereas Pinyin gives Tianjin and *Mao Zedong*.

Wade–Giles separates the syllables of compounds with hyphens; Pinyin runs them together, with an apostrophe where the break would not be obvious (*Xi'an* = Wade–Giles *Hsi-an*, since *Xian* would be read as Wade–Giles *Hsien*). Wade–Giles distinguishes aspirated from unaspirated consonants with a Greek asper (ʽ), which is sometimes replaced by an opening quote or an apostrophe, and is often omitted in popular writing; Pinyin uses different letters. Wade–Giles uses *ü* more often than Pinyin, which requires it only in the syllables *lü* and *nü*; only Wade–Giles uses *ê* (e.g. *jên* = Pinyin *ren*) and *ŭ* (*ssŭ* = Pinyin *si*). Neither consistently indicates the syllabic tone, despite its importance; when they do so, Wade–Giles writes a superior figure after the syllable (i^1 i^2 i^3 i^4), Pinyin an accent on the vowel (*yī yí yǐ yì*; note the need to combine these with the umlaut).

12.4 Dutch and Afrikaans

12.4.1 **Introduction**

Dutch is the language of the Netherlands. The Dutch spoken in northern Belgium, formerly called Flemish, is now officially called Dutch (*Nederlands* in Dutch). Afrikaans is one of the official languages of South Africa, and was derived from the Dutch brought to the Cape by settlers in the seventeenth century.

12.4.2 **Dutch**

Alphabet

The alphabet is the same as English, but *q* and *x* are used only in foreign loanwords. In dictionaries *ij* precedes *ik*; in directories and encyclopedias it is sometimes treated as equivalent to *y*. The apostrophe occurs in such plurals as *pagina's* ('pages'), but not before *s* in the genitive.

Accents

The acute is used to distinguish *één* ('one') from een ('a'), and *vóór* ('before') from *voor* ('for'). The only other accent required—except in foreign loanwords—is the diaeresis:

knieën 'knees' *provinciën* 'provinces' *zeeën* 'seas'

Punctuation and capitalization

Punctuation is less strict than in, for example, German. Capitals are used for the pronouns *U* 'you' and *Uw* 'your', for terms indicating nationality (*Engelsman* 'Englishman', *Engels* 'English'), and for adjectives derived from proper nouns, but not for days or months; in institutional names capitalize all words except prepositions and articles.

The abbreviated forms of *des* and *het* (*'s* and *'t* respectively) take a space on either side except in the case of towns and cities, where a hyphen follows: *'s-Gravenhage*. When a word beginning with an apostrophe starts a sentence, it is the following word that takes the capital: *'t Is*.

Word division

Do not divide the suffixes *-aard*, *-aardig*, *-achtig*, and any beginning with a consonant. This applies to the diminutive suffix *-je*, but note that a preceding *t* may itself be part of the suffix: *kaart-je* ('ticket'), but *paar-tje* ('couple').

Take over single consonants; the combinations *ch*, *sj*, *tj* (which represent single sounds) and *sch*; and consonant + *l* or *r* in loanwords. Take over the second of two consonants (including the *g* of *ng* and the *t* of *st*); when more than three come together take over those combinations that may begin a word. Do not divide double vowels or *ei*, *eu*, *ie*, *oe*, *ui*, *aai*, *eei*, *ieu*, *oei*, *ooi*.

12.4.3 **Afrikaans**

Alphabet, accents, and spelling

There is no *ij* in Afrikaans, *y* being used as in older Dutch; *s* is used at the start of words where Dutch has *z*, and *w* between vowels often where Dutch has *v*.

The circumflex is quite frequent; the grave is used on paired conjunctions (*òf* … *òf*, 'either … or') and a few other words. The acute is found in the demonstrative *dié* to distinguish it from the article *die*, and in certain proper nouns and French loan-words. There is no diaeresis with *ae* (*dae* 'days').

Capitalization

As in Dutch, when a word beginning with an apostrophe starts a sentence in Afrikaans, the following word is capitalized. This rule is important, since the indefinite article is written *'n*:

> *'n Man het gekom*, 'A man has come'

The pronoun *ek* 'I' is not capitalized.

12.5 French

12.5.1 **Accents**

The acute (´), the most common accent in French, is used only over *e*; when two *e*'s come together the first always has an acute accent, as in *née*. The grave (`) is used mainly over *e*, but also on final *a*, as in *voilà*, and on *u* in *où* ('where'), but not *ou* ('or'). The circumflex (ˆ) may be used over *a, e, i, o,* and *u*. The cedilla *c* (*ç*) is used only before *a*, *o*, and *u*. The diaeresis (¨) is found on *i*, *e*, and *y*.

Although they are recommended by the Académie française, accents on capital letters are often omitted in everyday French, except when they are needed to avoid confusion:

POLICIER TUÉ 'Policeman killed'
POLICIER TUE 'Policeman kills'

12.5.2 **Orthographic reform**

Les Rectifications de l'orthographie, drafted by the Conseil Supérieure de la Langue Française, was published in 1990. It is a controversial document and ignored by many. From an editor's point of view the main changes are those affecting circumflex accents and hyphens. Since the document recommends the removal of the circumflex on *i* and *u*, except in verb endings and a few words where it distinguishes meaning, the lack of this accent may indicate the author's support for the reform, and it would be wise to ascertain whether or not this is the case; if this is not possible, assume that the reforms are not being followed.

12.5.3 **Abbreviations**

As in English, place a full point after an abbreviation (*chap.*, *ex.*) but not after a contraction (*St*, *Mlle*). Retain the hyphen when a hyphenated form is abbreviated:

J.-J. Rousseau (Jean-Jacques Rousseau)
P.-S. (post-scriptum)

Some common examples of abbreviations in French:

abrév.	abréviation
apr.	après
av.	avant
c.-à-d.	c'est-à-dire
chap.	chapitre
Cie, Cie	compagnie
conf.	confer (Lat.)
d°	dito
Dr	docteur
éd.	édition
etc.	et cætera
ex.	exemple
f°	folio
Ier, Ier	premier
IIe, 2e, $\text{II}^{\text{ème}}$, $2^{\text{ème}}$	deuxième
ill.	illustration
in-4°	in-quarto
in-8°	in-octavo
inéd.	inédit
in-f°	in-folio
in pl.	in plano (Lat.)
l.c.	loc. cit. (Lat.)
liv.	livre
M.	monsieur
Me, M^{e}	maître
Mlle, Mlle	mademoiselle
MM.	messieurs
Mme, Mme	madame
ms.	manuscrit
mss.	manuscrits
n°	numéro
p.	page
p., pp.	pages
P.-S.	post-scriptum
qqch	quelque chose
qqn	quelqu'un
s., ss., suiv.	suivant
s.d.	sans date
s.l.	sans lieu
t.	tome
TVA	taxe à la valeur ajoutée
v.	voyez, voir
Vve	veuve

12.5.4 **Capitalization**

Capitalize only the first element (or first element after the article) in compound proper names. If the first element has a following adjective linked by a hyphen, capitalize the adjective also:

l'Académie française	*la Comédie-Française*
le Palais-Royal	*la Légion d'honneur*
le Conservatoire de musique	*Bibliothèque nationale*

Note that a following adjective is lower case, while an adjective preceding the noun is capitalized:

Le Nouveau Testament *les Saintes écritures*
l'Écriture sainte

Use lower-case letters for: days of the week; names of months; the cardinal points (*le nord*, *le sud*, etc.); languages; adjectives derived from proper nouns (*la langue française*); ranks, titles, regimes, religions, adherents of movements, and their derivative adjectives (*calvinisme, chrétien(ne), le christianisme, humaniste, les sans-culottes, le socialisme, les socialistes*).

Use capitals for nationalities when used as nouns: *le Français* ('the Frenchman'), *la Française* ('the Frenchwoman'), as opposed to *le français* ('French') (the language). Note that when referring to an adherent of Judaism *un juif* should be lower-case like *un chrétien* and *un musulman*, but capitalized as a member of a people: *un Juif* like *un Turc* and *un Arabe*. In practice, the capital seems to be used more widely.

In names for geographical features common nouns such as *mer* ('sea') are lower case, but there are traditional exceptions:

le Bassin parisien	*le Massif central*	*le Massif armoricain*
la Montagne Noire	*le Quartier latin*	

12.5.5 **Punctuation**

Hyphen

Use hyphens to connect cardinal and ordinal numbers in words under 100:

vingt-quatre *trois cent quatre-vingt-dix*

but when *et* joins two numbers no hyphen is used:

vingt et un *cinquante et un* *vingt et unième*

Quotation marks

Texts set wholly in French should use quotation marks called **guillemets** (« »); these need not be used for French text in English-language books. A space is inserted inside the guillemets, separating the marks from the matter they contain; prefer a thin or no-break space (see 2.5.1) to avoid awkward line breaks but a normal word space is acceptable.

A guillemet is repeated at the head of every subsequent paragraph belonging to the quotation. In conversational matter guillemets are sometimes put at the beginning and end of the remarks, and the individual utterances are denoted by a spaced dash:

> *« — Nous allons lui écrire, dis-je, et lui demander pardon.*
> *— C'est une idée de génie. »*

Many modern authors dispense with guillemets altogether, and denote the speakers by a dash only, although this is officially frowned upon.

English-style inverted commas are often used to mark a quotation within a quotation.

Where guillemets are used, only one » appears at the end of two quotations concluding simultaneously.

12.5.6 **Work titles**

Capitalize the initial letter of the first word of a title and of a following noun, if the first word is a definite article:

> *Les Femmes savantes* *Au revoir les enfants*

Where the title occurs within a sentence, a lower-case *l* for the definite article (*le*, *la*, *les*) beginning a title may be used; the article is construed with the surrounding sentence:

> *La mise en scène de la Bohème* 'The production of *La Bohème*'

If a noun following an initial definite article is itself preceded by an adjective, capitalize this also:

> *Le Petit Prince* *Les Mille et Une Nuits* (two adjectives)

but downcase any following adjective:

> *Les Mains sales*

If the title begins with any word other than *le*, *la*, *les*, or if the title forms a complete sentence, downcase the words following, unless they are proper nouns:

Une vie
A la recherche du temps perdu
La guerre de Troie n'aura pas lieu
Les dieux ont soif

A parallel title is treated as a title in its own right for the purposes of capitalization:

Emile, ou, De l'éducation

As these rules are complex, some English styles merely capitalize the first word and any proper nouns.

12.5.7 **Word division**

Divide words according to spoken syllables, and in only a few cases according to etymology. A single consonant always goes with the following vowel (*amou-reux*, *cama-rade*); *ch*, *dh*, *gn*, *ph*, *th*, and groups consisting of consonant + *r* or + *l* count as single consonants for this purpose.

Other groups of consonants are divided irrespective of etymology (*circons-tance, tran-saction*, *obs-curité*) but divide a prefix from a following *h* (*dés-habille*). Always divide *ll*, even if sounded *y*: *travaillons, mouil-lé*. Do not divide between vowels except in a compound: *anti-aérien, extra-ordinaire* (but *Moa-bite*). In particular, vowels forming a single syllable (*mon**sieu**r*) are indivisible. Do not divide after a single letter (*émettre*) or before or after an intervocalic *x* or *y* (*soi**x**ante*, *mo**y**en*, *Ale**x**andre*), but divide after *x* or *y* if followed by a consonant: *dex-térité, pay-san*. Do not divide abbreviated words (*Mlle*), within initials (la *CRS*), or after an abbreviated forename (*J.-Ph.* Rameau) or personal title (le *Dr* Suchet).

Do not divide after an apostrophe within compound words (*presqu'île*, *aujour-d'hui*). Divide interrogative verb forms before *-t-*: *Viendra-|t-il?*

12.5.8 **Numerals**

Use words for times of day if they are expressed in hours and fractions of hour:

six heures 'six o'clock'   *trois heures et quart* 'a quarter past three'

but use figures for time expressed in minutes: *6 h 15*, *10 h 8 min 30 s*.

Set Roman numerals indicating centuries in small capitals:

le xième siècle   xie siècle

but they should be in full capitals when in italic.

Use upper-case Roman numerals for numbers belonging to proper nouns (*Louis XIV*), but Arabic numerals for the numbers of the arrondissements of Paris: *le 16ᵉ arrondissement.*

In figures use thin spaces to divide thousands (*20 250*), but do not space dates, or numbers in general contexts (*l'an 1466, page 1250*).

Times of day written as figures should be spaced as *10 h 15 min 10 s* (10 hrs 15 min. 10 sec.); formerly this was also printed *10ʰ 15ᵐ 10ˢ*.

12.6 Gaelic

12.6.1 **Alphabet and accents**

Both Irish and Scots Gaelic are written in an eighteen-letter alphabet with no *j, k, q, v, w, x, y, z* (except in some modern loanwords); in Irish the lower-case i is sometimes left undotted. Until the middle of the twentieth century Irish (but not Scots Gaelic) was often written and printed in **insular** script, a medieval form of Latin handwriting, in which a dot was marked over aspirated consonants. In Roman script aspirated consonants are indicated by the addition of *h* after the letter, in both Irish and Scots Gaelic (Irish *an chos* 'the foot', Scots Gaelic *a' chas*). Irish marks vowel length with an acute accent (*á, é, í, ó, ú*), Scots Gaelic with the grave (*à, è, ì, ò, ù*). Apostrophes are frequent in Scots Gaelic, less so in Irish.

12.6.2 **Mutations**

In Irish Gaelic, as in Scots Gaelic and Welsh, initial consonants are replaced by others in certain grammatical contexts, in a process called **mutation.** In Irish the mutation known as **eclipsis** is indicated by writing the sound actually pronounced before the consonant modified: *mb, gc, nd, bhf, ng, bp, dt*. If the noun is a proper name, it retains its capital, the prefixed letter(s) being lower case:

> *i mBaile Átha Cliath* 'in Dublin' (*Baile Átha Cliath = Dublin*)
> *na bhFrancach* 'of the French'

The same combination of initial lower-case letter followed by a capital occurs when *h* or *n* is prefixed to a name beginning with a vowel—*go hÉirinn* 'to Ireland', *Tír na nÓg* 'the Land of the Young'—or *t* is prefixed to a vowel or *S*: *an tAigéan Atlantach* 'the Atlantic Ocean', *an tSionnain* 'Shannon'. Before lower-case vowels, *h* is prefixed directly (*na hoíche* 'of the night'), as is *t* before *s* (*an tsráid* 'the street'), but *n* and *t* take a hyphen before a vowel (*in-áit* 'in a place', *an t-uisce* 'the water'). Except in dialects, eclipsis is not found with consonants in Scots Gaelic.

Prefixed *h*-, *n*-, and *t*- always take a hyphen:

an t-sràid 'the street'	*Ar n-Athair* 'Our Father'
na h-oidhche 'of the night'	*na h-Eileanan an Iar* 'the Western Isles'

12.7 German

12.7.1 **Accents and special sorts**

German uses the diacritics *Ä*, *Ö*, *Ü*, *ä*, *ö*, *ü*, and the special sort *Eszett* (ß) (see 12.7.2): *Eszett* differs from a Greek beta (β), which should not be substituted for it.

12.7.2 **Orthographic reform**

A new orthography agreed by the German-speaking countries came into force on 1 August 1998. The seven-year transitional period, during which both systems were official, ended on 31 July 2005, and the older orthographic forms are now considered incorrect, although they are still widely used. The reform's main tendency is to eliminate irregularities that caused difficulty for the native speaker. At the same time, more variations are permitted than under the old rules, though these options are restricted: it is not acceptable to mix and match old and new spellings at will.

Under the new orthography, certain words were adjusted to resemble related words, so that, for instance, the verbs *numerieren* and *plazieren* become *nummerieren* and *platzieren* to coincide with the related nouns *Nummer* ('number') and *Platz* ('place').

In verbal compounds, nouns and adjectives regarded as retaining their normal functions are written separately:

radfahren → *Rad fahren* 'to ride a bicycle'

but

irreführen ('to mislead') and *wahrsagen* ('to predict')

Long-established loanwords have been Germanized (*Tip* → *Tipp*, 'tip'), and ee substituted for *é* in such words as *Varietee* for *Varieté* ('music hall').

The optional use of *f* for *ph* is extended: *Delfin* ('dolphin'), *Orthografie* ('orthography'), but not to words deemed more learned: *Philosophie* ('philosophy'), *Physik* ('physics').

The *Eszett* was traditionally used in place of a double *s* at the end of a syllable, before a consonant (whatever the vowel), and after long vowels and diphthongs. The new rules allow the ß only after a long vowel (including *ie*) or diphthong:

> *Fuß, Füße* 'foot, feet'

after a short vowel *ss* is to be used:

> *Kuss, Küsse* 'kiss, kisses'

but:

> *ihr esst, ihr aßt* 'you [pl.] eat, ate'
> *wir essen, wir aßen* 'we eat, ate'

The *Eszett* is considered an archaism in Swiss German, *ss* being preferred in all circumstances. No corresponding capital and small capital letters exist for *ß*, and *SS* and *ss* are used instead; in alphabetical order *ß* counts as *ss* and not *sz*.

In the absence of specific instructions to the contrary, or of evidence from the nature of the text itself, the new rules should be applied in all matter not by native speakers of German. Quotations from matter published in the old spelling should follow the old style (except in respect of word division), but new editions will normally modernize.

The new orthography's effects in other areas are mentioned under the headings below.

12.7.3 **Abbreviations**

Use a full point:

- after an abbreviation that would be read out in full; a space after any points within it is optional (but usual in formal writing):

> *d. h.* (*das heißt*, 'that is')
> *Dr.* (*Doktor*, 'Dr')
> *Prof.* (*Professor*, 'Prof.')

usw. (*und so weiter*, 'and so on')
z. B. (*zum Beispiel*, 'for example')

- after numerals used for days of the month and ordinal numbers:

Montag, den 12. August 'Monday, 12 August'
der 2. Weltkrieg (*der Zweite Weltkrieg*, 'the Second World War')

Do not use points in abbreviations that are pronounced as such:

DM (*die Deutsche Mark*, 'the German mark')
KG (*Kommanditgesellschaft*, 'limited partnership')

Some common examples of abbreviations in German:

a. a. O.	am angeführten Ort
Abb.	Abbildung
Abt.	Abteilung
Anm.	Anmerkung
Aufl.	Auflage
Ausg.	Ausgabe
Bd., Bde.	Band, Bände
bes.	besonders
bzw.	beziehungsweise
d. h.	das heißt
d. i.	das ist
ebd.	ebenda, ebendaselbst
Erg. Bd.	Ergänzungsband
etw.	etwas
Hft.	Heft
hrsg.	herausgegeben
Hs., Hss.	Handschrift, Handschriften
Lfg.	Lieferung
m. E.	meines Erachtens
m. W.	meines Wissens
Nr.	Nummer
o.	oben
o. Ä.	oder Ähnliche(s)
o. O.	ohne Ort
R.	Reihe
s.	siehe
S.	Seite
s. a.	siehe auch
s. o.	siehe oben
sog.	sogenannt
s. u.	siehe unten
u. a.	unter anderem
u. ä.	und ähnliches

usf., u. s. f.	und so fort
usw., u. s. w.	und so weiter
verb.	verbessert
Verf., Vf.	Verfasser
vgl.	vergleiche
z. B.	zum Beispiel
z. T.	zum Teil

12.7.4 **Capitalization**

All nouns in German are written with initial capital letters, as are other words (adjectives, numerals, and infinitives) that are used as nouns:

Gutes und Böses 'good and evil'
Die Drei ist eine heilige Zahl 'Three is a sacred number'

The basic rule of capitalizing nouns remains untouched by the orthographic reform, but whereas all nouns used as adverbs were previously lower case, some changes have been implemented: for example, *heute abend* ('tonight') is now *heute Abend, morgen abend* ('tomorrow evening') becomes *morgen Abend*, and *gestern morgen* ('yesterday morning') becomes *gestern Morgen.*

Adjectives used as nouns are capitalized with fewer exceptions than before: *alles übrige* becomes *alles Übrige* ('everything else').

In the new rules the familiar forms of the second person pronouns *du, dich, dir, dein, ihr, euch, euer* are not (as they formerly were) capitalized in letters and the like. The old rule remains that pronouns given a special sense in polite address are capitalized to distinguish them from their normal value: these are (in medieval and Swiss contexts) *Ihr* addressed to a single person; (in early modern contexts) *Er* and *Sie* (feminine singular); and (nowadays) *Sie* (plural). In all of the above the capital is used also in the oblique cases and in the possessive, but not in the reflexive *sich.*

Capitalize adjectives that form part of a geographical name (or are formed from a place name), the names of historic events or eras, monuments, institutions, titles, special days and feast days. Otherwise do not capitalize adjectives denoting nationality:

das deutsche Volk 'the German nation'

or the names of languages in expressions where their use is considered adverbial:

italienisch sprechen 'to speak Italian'

Traditionally, adjectives derived from personal names were capitalized in certain contexts, but according to the new rules all adjectives derived from personal names are to be lower case, except when the name is marked off with an apostrophe:

das ohmsche Gesetz or *das Ohm'sche Gesetz* 'Ohm's Law'

In work titles the first word and all nouns are capitalized, with all other words having a lower-case initial.

12.7.5 **Punctuation**

There are very specific rules about the placing of commas in German. Do not interfere in the punctuation of quoted matter without reference to the author or the source.

Sentences containing an imperative normally end in an exclamation mark. The traditional practice of ending the salutation in a letter with an exclamation mark—*Sehr geehrter Herr Schmidt!* ('Dear Herr Schmidt')—has largely given way to the use of a comma, after which the letter proper does not begin with a capital unless one is otherwise required.

German rarely employs the en rule in compounds in the way that it is used in English, preferring a hyphen between words:

die Berlin-Bagdad-Eisenbahn 'the Berlin–Baghdad railway'

The en rule is used for page and date ranges (*S.348–349, 1749–1832*): do not elide such ranges. It is also used, with a word space on each side, as a dash.

Quotation marks

German quotation marks (*Anführungszeichen*) take the form of two commas at the beginning of the quotation, and two opening quotation marks (turned commas) at the end („“), or reversed guillemets are used (»…«). Mark quotations within quotations by a single comma at the beginning and a single opening quotation mark at the end (‚ ‘). No space separates the quotation marks from the quotation.

Expect a colon to introduce direct speech. Commas following a quotation fall after the closing quotation mark, but full points go inside if they belong to the quotation.

Apostrophe

The apostrophe is used to mark the elision of *e* to render colloquial usage:

Wie geht's? 'How are things?'/'How are you?'

When the apostrophe occurs at the beginning of a sentence, the following letter does not become a capital:

's brennt! 'Fire!' (not *'S brennt*)

The apostrophe is also used to mark the suppression of the possessive *s* (for reasons of euphony) after names ending in *s*, *ß*, *x*, *z*:

Aristoteles' Werke   *Horaz' Oden*

Hyphen

Traditionally, a noun after a hyphen begins with an initial capital:

das Schiller-Museum 'the Schiller Museum'

but the new orthography allows words to be run together:

das Schillermuseum

The hyphen was used to avoid the double repetition of a vowel (*Kaffee-Ersatz*, 'coffee substitute') but not to avoid the similar repetition of a consonant (*stickstofffrei*, 'nitrogen-free'). The new rules no longer require a hyphen—groups of three identical consonants are written out even before a vowel and when *sss* results from the abolition of β after a short vowel:

Brennnessel   *Schifffahrt*
Schlußsatz → *Schlusssatz*

It is permissible to make such compounds clearer by using a hyphen:

Brenn-Nessel   *Schiff-Fahrt*   *Schluss-Satz*

12.7.6 **Word division**

For the purpose of division, distinguish between simple and compound words.

Simple words

Do not divide words of one syllable. Divide other simple words by syllables, either between consonants or after a vowel followed by a single consonant. This applies even to *x* and mute *h*: *Bo-xer, verge-hen.*

Do not separate *ch, ph, sch, ß,* and *th* (representing single sounds). Correct examples are *spre-chen, wa-schen, So-phie, ka-tholisch, wech-seln,*

Wechs-ler. Traditionally *st* was included in this group, but under the new rules it is no longer, and should be divided: *Las-ten, Meis-ter, Fens-ter*.

At the ends of lines, take over *ß*: *hei-ßen, genie-ßen*.

Take over as an entity *ss* if used instead of *ß*, but divide *ss* when it is not standing for *ß*: *las-sen*.

Traditionally, if a word was broken at the combination *ck* it was represented as though spelled with *kk*: *Zucker* but *Zuk-ker, Glocken* but *Glok-ken*. According to the new orthography, the combination *ck* is taken over whole, as it was traditionally after a consonant in proper nouns or their derivatives: *Zu-cker, Glo-cken, Fran-cke, bismar-ckisch*.

Treat words with suffixes as simple words and divide in accordance with the rules above: *Bäcke-rei, le-bend, Liefe-rung*.

Compound words

Divide a compound word by its etymological constituents (*Bildungs-roman, Kriminal-polizei, strom-auf*) or within one of its elements: *Bundes-tag* or *Bun-destag*. Divide prefixes from the root word: *be-klagen, emp-fehlen, er-obern, aus-trinken*.

12.7.7 **Numerals**

Separate numbers of more than four figures with thin spaces by thousands: *6 580 340*.

A full point after a numeral shows that it represents an ordinal number:

> *14. Auflage* (14th edition)
> *Mittwoch, den 19. Juli 1995* (Wednesday, 19 July 1995)

The full point also marks the separation of hours from minutes: *14.30 Uhr* or *14*^{30} *Uhr*.

Germans use Roman numerals rarely: even when citing Roman page numbers, they often convert them into Arabic and add an asterisk: *S. 78** (p. lxxviii). Distinguish this from *1**, denoting the first page of an article that is in fact (say) the third or fifth page of a pamphlet.

12.7.8 **Historical and specialist setting**

The traditional black-letter German types such as Fraktur and Schwabacher were replaced by the Roman Antiqua in 1941. They are now

Table 12.2 **German Fraktur alphabet**

𝔄	𝔄̈	𝔅	ℭ	𝔇	𝔈	𝔉	𝔊	ℌ	ℑ	𝔎	𝔏	𝔐	𝔑	𝔒	𝔒̈	𝔓	𝔔	ℜ	𝔖	𝔗	𝔘	𝔘̈	𝔙	𝔚	𝔛	𝔜	ℨ
A	Ä	B	C	D	E	F	G	H	I *or* J	K	L	M	N	O	Ö	P	Q	R	S	T	U	Ü	V	W	X	Y	Z

𝔞	𝔞̈	𝔟	𝔠	𝔡	𝔢	𝔣	𝔤	𝔥	𝔦	𝔧	𝔨	𝔩	𝔪	𝔫	𝔬	𝔬̈	𝔭	𝔮	𝔯	ſ	𝔰	𝔱	𝔲	𝔲̈	𝔳	𝔴	𝔵	𝔶	𝔷
a	ä	b	c	d	e	f	g	h	i	j	k	l	m	n	o	ö	p	q	r	s	s	t	u	ü	v	w	x	y	z

𝔠𝔥	𝔠𝔨	𝔣𝔣	𝔣𝔦	𝔣𝔩	𝔩𝔩	ſ𝔦	ſſ	ſ𝔱	ß	𝔱𝔷
ch	ck	ff	fi	fl	ll	si	ss	st	ß	tz

found only to a limited extent in German-speaking countries, mostly in decorative or historical contexts, or in approximating earlier typography. Any matter to be set in them should be deemed a quotation. Word division should follow the pre-1998 rules, not the new; in particular the *st* ligature should be taken over. The long *s* (ſ) in Fraktur type is used at the beginnings of words, and within them except at the ends of syllables. The short final *s* (𝔰) is generally put at the ends of syllables and words, except before *p* (*Knospe*).

12.8 Greek

12.8.1 **Introduction**

Ancient and modern Greek show a remarkable similarity, and much of what follows covers both. Modern Greek may be divided into two forms, **katharevousa** (literally 'purified'), a heavily archaized form used in technical and Church contexts, written in polytonic script, and **demotic,** the form which is spoken and used in everyday contexts. Demotic, which uses monotonic orthography, has been the official form since 1976, and is employed in official documents.

12.8.2 **Alphabet**

Ancient and modern Greek are written in an alphabet that consists of twenty-four letters: seventeen consonants and seven vowels (α, ε, η, ι, ο, υ, ω). Modern Greek is written from left to right, as was ancient Greek from the classical period onwards.

In ancient Greek the 'final' sigma (i.e. the form used at the end of words) must be distinguished from ϛ stigma [*sic*], which was used for the numeral 6 and in late manuscripts and early printed books for στ.

Table 12.3 **Greek alphabet**

Upper-case	Lower-case	Name	Translit-eration	Upper-case	Lower-case	Name	Translit-eration
Α	α	alpha	a	Ν	ν	nu	n
Β	β	beta	b	Ξ	ξ	xi	x
Γ	γ	gamma	g	Ο	ο	omicron	o
Δ	δ	delta	d	Π	π	pi	p
Ε	ε	epsilon	e	Ρ	ρ	rho	r
Ζ	ζ	zeta	z	Σ	σ (ς final)	sigma	s
Η	η	eta	ē	Τ	τ	tau	t
Θ	θ	theta	th	Υ	υ	upsilon	u or y
Ι	ι	iota	i	Φ	φ	phi	ph
Κ	κ	kappa	k	Χ	χ	chi	kh
Λ	λ	lambda	l	Ψ	ψ	psi	ps
Μ	μ	mu	m	Ω	ω	omega	ō

Stigma is also used in scholarly work (especially on Latin authors) to denote 'late manuscripts'. In papyri and inscriptions sigma is normally printed Ϲ ϲ ('lunate sigma'), with no separate final form; this is also sometimes used in other ancient contexts, but never in modern Greek.

Texts of early inscriptions may require Latin *h* (to be italic with a sloping fount), and the letters Ϝ (wau or digamma) and Ϙ (koppa).

In ancient Greek an iota forming a 'long diphthong' with a preceding *α*, *η*, or *ω* is traditionally inserted underneath the vowel: *ᾳ ῃ ῳ* ('iota subscript'). Some modern scholars prefer to write *αι, ηι, ωι* ('adscript iota'), in which case accents and breathings should be set on the first vowel; in the case of *αι* this means that the accent may fall on either letter depending on the pronunciation. When a word is set in capitals, iota is always adscript (i.e. written on the line rather than beneath it); when the word has an initial capital but is otherwise lower case, an initial long diphthong will have the main vowel as capital, the iota adscript lower case; hence *ᾧ* will become *ΩΙ* in capitals (for the absence of accent and breathing see below), but Ὧι at the start of a paragraph. In modern Greek the iota is omitted even in phrases taken bodily from the ancient language.

12.8.3 **Transliteration**

Whether or not to transliterate ancient or modern Greek must of course depend on the context. In general contexts any use of Greek script will be very off-putting to the majority of people, but readers who know Greek will find it far harder to understand more than a few words in transliteration than in the Greek alphabet. If the work is intended only for specialists, all Greek should be in the Greek alphabet; in works aimed more at ordinary readers, individual words or short phrases should be transliterated:

> *history* comes from the Greek word *historiē*

although longer extracts should remain in Greek script, with a translation. Table 12.3 shows how Greek letters are usually transliterated.

12.8.4 **Accents**

The accents in ancient and modern Greek are acute ´, used on any of the last three syllables of a word; grave ` used only on final syllables; circumflex ^, used on either of the last two syllables of a word. The diaeresis ¨ is also used, to show that two vowels occurring together do not form a diphthong.

All words of three or more syllables, and most others, carry an accent. Most unaccented words cause the majority of preceding words to take an acute on their final syllable; they are known as **enclitics**, the others (all monosyllables) as **proclitics**. An acute accent on a final syllable or a monosyllable will be found before an enclitic, before punctuation, and in the two words *τίς* and *τί* when they mean 'who?' and 'what?'; otherwise it is replaced by a grave, although in modern Greek it is sometimes retained.

Greek uses marks known as **breathings** to indicate the presence or absence of an aspirate at the beginning of a word: they are ‘ (**asper** or **rough breathing**) and ’ (**lenis** or **smooth breathing**). Breathings are used on all words beginning with a vowel or diphthong and also with *ρ*; in this case, and that of *υ* and *υι*, the breathing will nearly always be the asper.

Table 12.4 **Greek accents**

’	lenis (smooth breathing)	῎	lenis acute	῏	circumflex lenis
‘	asper (rough breathing)	῍	lenis grave	῟	circumflex asper
΄	acute	῞	asper acute	¨	diaeresis
`	grave	῝	asper grave	΅	diaeresis acute
		͂	round circumflex	῭	diaeresis grave

Each of the accents may be combined with either breathing or with the diaeresis; but breathing and diaeresis never stand on the same letter. The accent always stands over the diaeresis; the breathing stands to the left of the acute or grave, but underneath the circumflex. Except in the case of long diphthongs (see above), accents are placed over the second vowel of a diphthong (which is always ι or υ).

Accents and breathings are regularly used when words are set in capital and lower-case style; they precede capitals and are set over lower-case letters. They are omitted when words are set wholly in capitals.

In modern Greek many printers now dispense with breathings and use only a single accent, either a small downward-pointing filled-in triangle or simply the acute; as before, the accent is omitted in capitals, but otherwise precedes capitals and stands over lower-case letters. Monosyllables, even if stressed, do not have an accent, save that ή 'or' is distinguished from η 'the' (nominative singular feminine), in traditional spelling ἤ and ἡ respectively. The diaeresis remains in use; however, it is used to show that ᾳϊ and οϊ *are* diphthongs, as opposed to the digraphs αι (pronounced ϵ) and οι (pronounced ι).

In both ancient and modern Greek a final vowel or diphthong may be replaced at the end of a word by an apostrophe when the next word begins with a vowel or diphthong; occasionally it is the latter that is replaced. Traditionally setters have represented the apostrophe by a lenis; but if the font has a dedicated apostrophe that should be used. Do not set an elided word close up with the word following. It may be set at the end of a line even if it contains only one consonant and the apostrophe or lenis.

12.8.5 **Capitalization and punctuation**

In printing ancient Greek, the first word of a sentence or a line of verse is capitalized only at the beginning of a paragraph. In modern Greek, capitals are used for new sentences, though not always for new lines of verse.

For titles of works in ancient Greek, it is best to capitalize only the first word and proper nouns, or else proper nouns only. In modern Greek the first and main words tend to be capitalized; first word and proper nouns only is the rule in bibliographies.

In ancient Greek, it is conventional to capitalize adjectives and adverbs derived from proper nouns, but not verbs:

Ἕλλην 'a Greek'
Ἑλληνιστί 'in Greek'

but

ἑλληνίζω 'I speak Greek/behave like a Greek'

In modern Greek, lower case is the rule:

ελληνικὸς 'Greek (adj.)'
ελληνικὰ 'in Greek'

The comma, the full point, and the exclamation mark (in modern Greek) are the same as in English; but the question mark (;) is the English semicolon (italic where necessary to match a sloping Greek font), and the colon is a raised full point (·). Use double quotation marks, or in modern Greek guillemets.

12.8.6 **Word division**

In ancient Greek the overriding precept should be that of breaking after prefixes and before suffixes and between the elements of compound words. This requires knowledge of the language, however, since many prefixes cannot be distinguished at sight: *ἔν-αυε* 'lit' contains a prefix, *ἔναιε* 'dwelt' does not.

A vowel may be divided from another (*λύ-ων*) unless they form a diphthong (*αι, αυ, ει, ευ, ηυ, οι, ου, υι*). Take over any combination of 'mute' (*β, γ, δ, θ, κ, π*, τ, *φ, χ*) followed by 'liquid' (*λ, μ, ν, ρ*), also *β δ, γ δ, κτ, πτ, φθ, χθ*, or any of these followed by *ρ*; *μν*; and *σ* followed by a consonant other than *σ* or by one of the above groups: *ἑλι-κτός, γι-γνώ-σκω, μι-μνή-σκω, κα-πνός, βα-πτί-ζω*.

Any doubled consonants maybe divided; *λ, μ, ν*, and *ρ* maybe divided from a following consonant, except in *μν*. Divide *γ* from a following *κ* or *χ*; take over *ξ* and *ψ* between vowels (*δεί-ξειν, ἀνε-ψιός*).

Modern Greek word division follows ancient principles, but the consonant groups taken over are those that can begin a modern word. Therefore *θμ* is divided, but *γκ, μπ, ντ, τζ, τσ* are not.

12.8.7 **Numerals**

Two systems of numerals were in use in ancient Greek. In the older system (the 'acrophonic' system, used only for cardinal numbers), certain numbers were indicated by their initial letters. This was eventually

Table 12.5 **Alphabetic Greek numbers.**

αʹ	1	νʹ	50	ϡʹ	900
βʹ	2	ξʹ	60	͵α	1,000
γʹ	3	οʹ	70	͵β	2,000
δʹ	4	πʹ	80	͵γ	3,000
εʹ	5	ϙʹ	90	͵δ	4,000
ϛʹ	6	ρʹ	100	͵ε	5,000
ζʹ	7	σʹ	200	͵ϛ	6,000
ηʹ	8	τʹ	300	͵ζ	7,000
θʹ	9	υʹ	400	͵η	8,000
ιʹ	10	φʹ	500	͵θ	9,000
κʹ	20	χʹ	600	͵ι	10,000
λʹ	30	ψʹ	700		
μʹ	40	ωʹ	800		

replaced by the alphabetic system, shown in Table 12.5, which could be used of either cardinals or ordinals. The Greek numeral sign (ʹ) is used to denotes numbers; the Greek lower numeral sign (͵) signifies thousands. The symbols ϛ and ϡ, are known as 'stigma' and 'sampi' respectively.

Modern Greek uses Arabic numerals: if a sloping font is being used they should be set in italic, but with upright fonts they should be set in roman, in both cases ranging. Alphabetic numerals are still employed, however, in much the same way as Roman numerals are in Western languages; *vi* is commonly written *στʹ*.

12.9 Hebrew

12.9.1 **Alphabet**

The Hebrew alphabet consists exclusively of consonantal letters. Vowels may be indicated by dots or small strokes ('points') above, below, or inside them, but Hebrew is generally written and printed without vowels. Hebrew written without vowels is described in English as 'unpointed' or 'unvocalized'.

Each letter has a numerical value. Letters are therefore often used in Hebrew books—especially in liturgical texts and older works—to indicate the numbers of volumes, parts, chapters, and pages. Letters are also used to indicate the day of the week, the date in the month, and the year according to the Jewish calendar.

The consonantal letters are principally found in two different forms: a cursive script, and the block ('square') letters used in printing.

Table 12.6 **Hebrew alphabet**

Consonants

Block*	Cursive*	Name	Simplified transcription	Numerical value	Scholarly transcription
א	א	alef	—†	1	ʾ
בּ	בּ	beit	b	2	b
ב	ב	veit	v		ḇ
ג	ג	gimmel	g	3	g/ḡ
ד	ד	dalet	d	4	d/ḏ
ה	ה	hé	h	5	h
ו	ו	vav	v	6	w
ז	ז	zayin	z	7	z
ח	ח	chet	ch, ḥ	8	ḥ
ט	ט	tet	t	9	ṭ
י	י	yod	y, i‡	10	y
כּ	כּ	kaf	k	20	k
כך	כך	khaf, khaf sofit	kh		ḵ
ל	ל	lamed	l	30	l
מם	מם	mem, mem sofit	m	40	m
נן	נן	nun, nun sofit	n	50	n
ס	ס	samekh	s	60	s
ע	ע	ʿayin	—†	70	ʿ
פּ	פּ	pé	p	80	p
פף	פף	fé, fé sofit	f		p
צץ	צץ	tsadi, tsadi sofit	ts	90	ṣ
ק	ק	kof	k	100	q
ר	ר	resh	r	200	r
שׁ	שׁ	shin	sh	300	š
שׂ	שׂ	sin	s		ś
ת	ת	tav	t	400	t/ṯ

Vowels

Form	Name
ָ	kamats
ַ	patah
ֶ	segol
ֵ	tseré
ִ	hirik
ְ	sheva
ֻ	kubutz
ֲ	hataf patah
ֱ	hataf segol
וֹ	holam
וּ	shuruk

* Where two forms are given, the second is that used in final position.
† The letters *alef* and *ʿayin* are not transliterated in the simplified system. Where they occur in intervocalic position an apostrophe is used to indicate that the vowels are to be pronounced separately.
‡ Transliterated 'y' as a consonant, 'i' as a vowel.

12.9.2 **Transliteration**

Different systems of transliterated Hebrew may require the following diacritics: ś (and sometimes the acute is also used on vowels to indicate stress); *ā*, *ē*, *ī*, *ō*, *ū*; *ê*, *î*, *ô*, *û*; *ă*, *ĕ*, *ŏ* (in some systems represented by superiors, $^{a\,e\,o}$); ḥ, ṣ, ṭ, ẓ (in older system also ḳ for *q*); *š*; ḇ, ḏ, g̱, ḵ, p̱, ṯ (less strictly *bh*, *dh*, *gh*, *kh*, *ph*, *th*). Special characters are *schwa* ə, *aleph* ʾ, *ʿayin* ʿ; in loose transliteration from modern Hebrew the latter two may be replaced by an apostrophe or omitted altogether.

12.9.3 **Word division**

In Hebrew script, words are short enough not to need dividing; transliterated words should be so divided that the new line begins with a single consonant. In loose transliteration, *ts* and combinations with *h* may or may not represent single consonants; when in doubt avoid dividing.

12.10 Italian

12.10.1 **Accents**

The use of accents in the Italian language is not entirely consistent; editors should as a general rule follow the author's typescript. There are two accents, acute and grave. The acute accent is used on a 'closed' *e* and very rarely on a closed *o: perché*, 'because', *né*... *né*... 'neither... nor...'. The grave accent is used on the 'open' *e* and *o*: *è*, 'is', *cioè*, 'that is', *però*, but', 'however'. The grave is also used to indicate stress on a final syllable. An alternative convention does exist for *i* and *u*, whereby they are marked with an acute accent: *così* and *cosí* ('so'), *più* and *piú* ('more'). However, in normal, standard Italian it is considered good practice to use the grave accent on all vowels except the closed *e* and, very rarely, *o*.

The appearance in a single text of Italian extracts with several different systems of accentuation may indicate not ignorance or carelessness in the author, but rather scrupulous fidelity to sources. Any discretional accents should be left alone unless the copy-editor is expert in the language and the author is not. There are other respects in which Italian spelling is even now less regulated than, say, French, and zeal for consistency must be tempered by either knowledge or discretion.

Leave capital letters unaccented as a general rule, unless an accent is needed to avoid confusion. The grave accent on an upper-case *E* is marked as an apostrophe:

> *E' oggi il suo compleanno* 'It is his birthday today'

12.10.2 **Abbreviation**

Italian abbreviations are usually set with an initial capital only rather than in full capitals, with no full point following: *An* (*Alleanza Nazionale*), *Rai* (*Radiotelevisione Italiana*). When the expansion does not begin with a capital, neither does the abbreviation: *tv* (*televisione*).

12.10.3 **Capitalization**

Italian uses capital letters much less frequently than English. Capitalize names of people, places, and institutions, and some dates and festivals.

Use lower-case for *io* (*I*), unless it begins a sentence. *Lei*, *Loro*, and *Voi* (polite forms of 'you') and related pronouns and adjectives, *La, Le, Suo, Vi, Vostro*, are often capitalized, especially in commercial correspondence:

> *La ringraziamo per la Sua lettera* 'Thank you for your letter'

Note that polite *La* and *Le* may be capitalized even when suffixed to a verb: *ringraziarLa* 'thank you'.

When citing titles of works capitalize only the first word and proper nouns:

> *Il gattopardo* *La vita è bella*

Roman numerals indicating centuries are generally put in full capitals in both italic and roman:

> *l'XI secolo* 'the eleventh century'

Names of days and months (*lunedì, gennaio*) and languages, peoples, and adjectives of nationality are lower case:

> *Parlo inglese e francese* 'I speak English and French'
> *Gli italiani* 'the Italians'
> *un paese africano* 'an African country'

although the capitalization of the names of peoples (*gli Italiani*) is becoming more common.

12.10.4 **Punctuation**

Italian makes a distinction between points of omission (which are spaced) and points of suspension (which are unspaced). The latter equate with the French *points de suspension*, three points being used where preceded by other punctuation, four in the absence of other punctuation.

Put the ordinary interword space after an apostrophe following a vowel: *a' miei, ne' righi, po' duro, de' Medici*. Insert no space after an apostrophe following a consonant: *l'onda, s'allontana, senz'altro*. When an apostrophe replaces a vowel at the beginning of a word a space always precedes it: *e 'l, su 'l, te 'l, che 'l*. Note, however, that in older printing these rules may be reversed: *a'miei, l' onda, e'l*.

Single and double quotation marks, and guillemets, are all used in varying combinations. A final full point is placed after the closing quotation marks even if a question mark or exclamation mark closes the matter quoted:

«Buon giorno, molto reverendo zio!». 'Good day, most reverend Uncle!'

12.10.5 **Word division**

Do not divide the following compound consonants:

bl	*br*	*ch*	*cl*	*cr*	*dr*	*fl*	*fr*	*gh*	*gl*
gn	*gr*	*pl*	*pr*	*sb*	*sc*	*sd*	*sf*	*sg*	*sl*
sm	*sn*	*sp*	*sq*	*sr*	*st*	*sv*	*tl*	*tr*	*vr*
sbr	*sch*	*scr*	*sdr*	*sfr*	*sgh*	*sgr*	*spl*	*spr*	*str*

Divide between vowels only if neither is *i* or *u*. When a vowel is followed by a doubled consonant, including *cq*, the first of these goes with the vowel, and the second is joined to the next syllable: *lab-bro*, *mag-gio, ac-qua*. Apply the same rule if an apostrophe occurs in the middle of the word: *Sen-z'altro, quaran-t'anni*. In general an apostrophe may end a line if necessary, but in this case it may not, although it may be taken over along with the letter preceding it.

In the middle of a word, if the first consonant of a group is a liquid (*l*, *m*, *n*, or *r*) it remains with the preceding vowel, and the other consonant, or combination of consonants, goes with the succeeding vowel: *al-tero, ar-tigiano, tem-pra.*

12.11 Japanese

Japanese is expressed and printed in ideographs of Chinese origin (*kanji*), interspersed with an alphabet-based script (*kana*), of which there are two versions: the *hiragana* (the cursive form) is used for inflectional endings and words with grammatical significance, and the *katakana* (the 'squared' form) is used for foreign loanwords and in Western names. Both vertical columns running right to left and horizontal left-to-right layout are used.

The most frequently used system of romanization uses the macron ¯ to indicate long vowels; syllable-final *n* is followed by an apostrophe before *e* or *y*. The inclusion of macrons is optional in non-specialist works, and maybe omitted in well-established forms of place names, such as *Hokkaido*, *Honshu*, *Kobe*, *Kyoto*, *Kyushu*, *Osaka*, *Tokyo*.

12.12 Latin

12.12.1 **Alphabet**

The standard Latin alphabet consists of twenty-one letters, *A B C D E F G H I K L M N O P Q R S T V X*, plus two imports from Greek, *Y* and *Z*. *A*, *E*, *O*, *Y* are vowels. *I*, *V* may be either vowels or consonants.

Early modern printers invented a distinction between vocalic *i*, *u* and consonantal *j*, *v*; many scholars, especially when writing for general readers, still retain it with *u*/*v*, distinguishing *solvit* with two syllables from *coluit* with three (also *volvit* 'rolls/rolled' from *voluit* 'willed'), but others prefer to use *V* for the capital and *u* for the lower case irrespective of value. (However, the numeral must be *v* regardless of case.) By contrast, the use of *j* is virtually obsolete except in legal and other stock phrases used in an English context, such as *de jure*.

In classical Latin the ligatures *æ*, *œ* are found only as space-saving devices in inscriptions. They are found in post-classical manuscripts and in printed books down to the nineteenth century and occasionally beyond. They should not now be used unless a source containing them is to be reproduced exactly.

12.12.2 **Accents**

In modern usage Latin is normally written without accents. In classical Latin the *apex*, resembling an acute, was sometimes used on long vowels other than *I*, and until recently *ë* was used to show that *ae* and *oe* did not form a diphthong: *aëris* 'of air' (as opposed to *aeris* 'of bronze/money'), *poëta* 'poet'. Older practice used the circumflex on long vowels to resolve ambiguity: *mensâ* ablative of *mensa* 'table'; one may also find the grave accent on the final syllables of adverbs. In grammars and dictionaries vowels may be marked with the macron or the breve: *mēnsă* nominative, *mēnsā* ablative.

12.12.3 **Capitalization**

Classical Latin made no distinction between capital and lower case. In modern usage proper names and their derivatives are capitalized (*Roma* 'Rome', *Romanus*, 'Roman', *Graece* 'in Greek') except in verbs (*graecissare* 'speak Greek/live it up'); the first letter in a sentence may or may not be capitalized, that in a line of verse no longer so.

In titles of works, one may find (proper names apart) only the first word capitalized (*De rerum natura, De imperio Cn. Pompei*—Oxford's preference), first and main words (*De Rerum Natura, De Imperio Cn. Pompei*), or main words only (*de Rerum Natura, de Imperio Cn. Pompei*), even proper nouns only (*de rerum natura, de imperio Cn. Pompei*). For the treatment of Latin titles within titles see 8.2.8.

12.12.4 **Word division**

A vowel may be divided from another (*be-atus*) unless they form a diphthong, as do most instances of *ae*, *oe*, *ei*, *au*, and *eu*. When *v* is not used, the correct divisions with consonantal *u* are *ama-uit*, *dele-uit*. Likewise, a consonantal *i* is taken over (*in-iustus*).

Take over *x* between vowels (*pro-ximus*). Any doubled consonants may be divided; except in *mn*, the letters *l*, *m*, *n*, and *r* may be divided from a following consonant. Traditionally, any group capable of beginning a word in either Latin or Greek was not divided: for example *bl*, *br*, *ch*, *cl*, *cr*, *ct*, *dl*, *dr*, *gn*, *gu*, *mn*, *ph*, *pl*, *pr*, *ps*, *pt*, *qu*, *th*, *tl*, and *tr* (many of these are found in such English words as *ctenoid*, *gnomon*, *mnemonic*, *pneumonia*, *psychology*, and *ptomaine*).

However, as in Greek, these rules should be subject to the overriding precept that prefixes and suffixes are separated and compounds divided into their parts. This requires knowledge of the language, as some common prefixes may have different forms in different contexts.

12.12.5 **Numerals**

Latin, of course, uses Roman numerals, which are described at 11.5. They should generally be set in small capitals. The letter *C* was sometimes used in reversed form in numerals: IↃ 500 (normally written as D), CIↃ 1,000 (otherwise written M) or ī, which unlike M was already used in antiquity.

12.13 Old and Middle English

12.13.1 **Alphabet**

Old English is the name given to the earliest stage of English, in use until around 1150. Middle English is the name given to the English of the period between Old and modern English, roughly 1150 to 1500.

Several special characters are (or have been) employed in the printing of both Old and Middle English texts:

- the **ash** (*Æ*, *æ*), a character borrowed from the runic alphabet, pronounced approximately as in 'h*a*t'. This character should be printed as a single sort, not two separate letters.
- the **eth** or **edh** (*Ð*, *ð*), sometimes called a 'crossed *d*'. This character is used indiscriminately for the voiced *th* as in '*th*at' and the voiceless *th* of '*th*in'.
- the **thorn** (*Þ*, *þ*), a character borrowed from the runic alphabet, pronounced the same as eth. Authors and editors should ensure that the printer cannot mistake a thorn for a *p* or a wyn (see below).
- the **wyn** or **wynn,** formerly called the **wen** (*Ƿ*, *ƿ*), a character borrowed from the runic alphabet to represent the sound of *w*. It is now usual to substitute *w* for the wyn of the manuscript, as it is easily confused with a thorn, though it may be distinguished by the absence of an ascender. Note that a printer may also mistake a wyn for a *p*.
- the **yogh** (*Ȝ*, *ȝ*), a Middle English letter used mainly where modern English has *gh* and *y*. In Old English script the letter *g* was written ᵹ, so-called 'insular *g*', and pronounced, according to context, either hard (in the earlier period like Dutch *g* (the voiced equivalent of the German *ach* sound); in later Old English (like *g* in *go*) or soft (like *y* in *year*). In later manuscripts the 'Carolingian' *g* is found; after the Norman Conquest the influence of French, in which the letter was pronounced either as in *go* or as in *gentle*, caused this to be used in Middle English for those sounds, but a developed form of the insular shape (*Ȝ*, *ȝ*) for specifically English values, including the voiceless spirant in *niȝt* 'night' (still heard in Scots *nicht*); a combination of its two most characteristic sounds gave this character the name 'yogh'. Except in special circumstances, Old English ᵹ is now represented by *g*; in Middle English the distinction between *g* and yogh must be maintained; *ȝ* is to be used for yogh in all Middle English work. In some Middle English texts the same shape is also used for *z*. Note that a printer may mistake a yogh for a *g* in one form or a 3 or *z* in the other.

In printing Old and Middle English no attempt should be made to regularize the use of eth and thorn even in the same word; scribes used both letters at random. Whereas eth had died out by the end of the thirteenth century, thorn continued in use into the fifteenth century, and even later as the *y* for *th* of early Scots printing and in *ye* or *y*^{e} used for *the* and *yt*, *y*^{t}, *y*^{at}, for *that*; hence *Ye Olde* was originally read *The Old.*

12.13.2 **Punctuation**

Except in specialized texts, normal modern English punctuation conventions should be applied to Old and Middle English. In manuscripts, editors should not attempt to regularize or correct individual punctuation marks, especially as these marks do not necessarily perform functions equivalent to those of their modern counterparts: in the Old English of the late tenth and eleventh centuries a semicolon was the strongest stop and a full point the weakest.

12.14 Portuguese

12.14.1 **Introduction**

Brazilian Portuguese differs considerably in spelling, pronunciation, and syntax from that of Portugal, far more so than US English differs from British English. Attempts to achieve agreement on spelling have not been very successful, and important differences in practice have been indicated below. In contrast to the case in English, differences of spelling and pronunciation generally go hand in hand.

12.14.2 **Alphabet and spelling**

The letters *k*, *w*, and *y* are used only in loanwords. Apart from *rr* and *ss*, double consonants are confined to European Portuguese: *acção* 'action, share', *accionista* 'shareholder', *comummente* 'commonly', in Brazilian Portuguese *ação, acionista, comumente*. Several other consonant groups have been simplified in Brazilian Portuguese: *acto, amnistía, excepção, óptico, súbdito* (= subject of a king), *subtil* are *ato, anistia, exceção, ótico, súdito, sutil*.

In Brazilian Portuguese the numbers 16, 17, and 19 are spelled *dezesseis, dezessete, dezenove* in contrast to European Portuguese *deza-*; 14 may be *quatorze* beside *catorze*.

There are also many differences of vocabulary and idiom, such as frequent omission of the definite article after *todo* 'every' and before possessives.

12.14.3 **Accents**

European Portuguese uses four written accents on vowels: acute, grave, circumflex, and tilde (*til* in Portuguese); Brazilian Portuguese also uses the diaeresis. The acute may be used on any vowel; the grave only on *a*; the circumflex on *a*, *e*, and *o*; the tilde on *a* and *o*. The diaeresis is used on *u* between *q*/*g* and *e*/*i* to show that the vowel is pronounced separately.

Normal stress is unaccented; abnormal stress is accented. The rules of accentuation are complex, and cannot be fully described in a work of this type. Normal stress falls on the penultimate syllable in words ending in *-a*, *-am*, *-as*, *-e*, *-em*, *-ens*, *-es*, *-o*, *-os*; in all other cases (including words in *-ã*) the stress falls on the final syllable.

Note the use of the circumflex in words like *circunstância*, *paciência*, and *cômputo*, where *m* or *n* with a consonant follows the accented vowel. In Brazilian Portuguese the circumflex is also used when *m* or *n* is followed by a vowel: *Nêmesis*, *helênico*, *cômodo*, *sônico*. European Portuguese generally has an acute accent, so *Némesis*, *helénico*, *cómodo*, *sónico*. Thus we have *António* in European Portuguese but *Antônio* in Brazilian Portuguese; editors should ensure that any such names are correctly spelled according to their bearers' nationality.

12.14.4 **Punctuation**

The inverted question marks and exclamation marks which are characteristic of Spanish are not normally used in Portuguese.

12.14.5 **Word division**

Take over *ch*, *lh*, *nh*, and *b*, *c*, *d*, *f*, *g*, *p*, *t*, *v* followed by *l* or *r*; divide *rr*, *ss*, also *sc*, *sç*. Otherwise divide at obvious prefixes such as *auto-*, *extra-*, *supra-*, etc. When a word is divided at a pre-existing hyphen, repeat the hyphen at the beginning of the next line: *dar-lho* is divided *dar- -lho*.

12.15 Russian

12.15.1 **Alphabet and transliteration**

Russian is one of the six Slavonic languages written in Cyrillic script (see **Slavonic languages** at 12.17 for a list of the others). Table 12.7 includes 'upright' (*pryamoĭ*) and 'cursivĭ' (*kursiv*) forms and also a transliteration in accordance with the 'British System' as given in British Standard 2979 (1958). For a brief discussion of the problems of transliteration see 12.17.1.

12.15.2 **Abbreviations**

One of the distinctive aspects of non-literary texts of the Soviet period was the extensive use of abbreviations, used to a far lesser extent in the post-Soviet language.

In lower-case abbreviations with full points, any spaces in the original should be kept, for example и т. д., и пр., but с.-д. Abbreviations by contraction, such as д-р, have no points. Abbreviations with a solidus are typically used in abbreviations of unhyphenated compound words.

Table 12.7 **Russian alphabet**

Upright	Cursive	Translit-eration	Upright	Cursive	Translit-eration	Upright	Cursive	Translit-eration
А а	*А а*	a	Л л	*Л л*	l	Ч ч	*Ч ч*	ch
Б б	*Б б*	b	М м	*М м*	m	Ш ш	*Ш ш*	sh
В в	*В в*	v	Н н	*Н н*	n	Щ щ	*Щ щ*	shch
Г г	*Г г*	g	О о	*О о*	o	Ъ ъ	*Ъ ъ*	”
Д д	*Д д*	d	П п	*П п*	p	Ы ы	*Ы ы*	ȳ
Е е	*Е е*	e	Р р	*Р р*	r	Ь ь	*Ь ь*	’
Ё ё	*Ё ё*	ë	С с	*С с*	s	Э э	*Э э*	é
Ж ж	*Ж ж*	zh	Т т	*Т т*	t	Ю ю	*Ю ю*	yu
З з	*З з*	z	У у	*У у*	u	Я я	*Я я*	ya
И и	*И и*	i	Ф ф	*Ф ф*	f			
Й й	*Й й*	ĭ	Х х	*Х х*	kh			
К к	*К к*	k	Ц ц	*Ц ц*	ts			

Abbreviations consisting of capital initial letters, such as *ООО* ('Ltd'), are set close without internal or final points. Commonly used lowercase abbreviations that are pronounced syllabically and declined, for example вуз, are not set with points.

Abbreviations for metric and other units are usually set in cursive and are not followed by a full point; abbreviated qualifying adjectives do have the full point, however (5 *кв. км* etc.).

12.15.3 **Capitalization**

Capital initial letters are in general rarer in Russian than in English. Capitalize personal names, but use lower-case initial letters for nouns and adjectives formed from them:

троцкист 'Trotskyite'   марксизм 'Marxism'

and for nationalities, names of nationals, and inhabitants of towns:

татарин 'Tartar'   англичанин Englishman'

Ranks, titles, etc. are also lower case:

святой Николай 'Saint Nicholas'
князь Оболенский 'Prince Obolensky'

Each word in names of countries takes a capital:

Соединённые Штаты Америки 'United States of America'

Adjectives formed from geographical names are lower case except when they form part of a proper noun or the name of an institution:

европейские государства 'European states'

but

Архангельские воздушные линии 'Archangel Airlines'

Geographical terms forming part of the name of an area or place are lower case:

остров Рудольфа 'Rudolph Island'   Северный полюс 'the North Pole'

Capitalize only the first word and proper nouns in titles of organizations and institutions, and of literary and musical works, newspapers, and journals.

Days of the week and names of the months are lower case, but note Первое мая and 1-е Мая for the May Day holiday.

The pronoun of the first-person singular, я = I, is lower case (except, of course, when used at the beginning of a sentence).

12.15.4 **Punctuation**

Hyphen

The hyphen is used in nouns consisting of two elements:

интернет-сайт 'website'
вице-спикер Думы 'The Deputy Speaker of the Duma'

It is also used in compound place names, Russian or foreign, consisting of separable words.

Dash

En rules are not used in Russian typography; em rules set close up take their place. Spaced em rules are much used in Russian texts; they may indicate that a word needs to be understood, or represent the rarely used present tense of быть 'to be'.

линия Москва — Киев 'the Moscow–Kiev line'
Иван играет на рояле, а Людмила — на скрипке 'Ivan plays the piano, Lyudmila the violin':
Волга — самая большая река в Европе 'the Volga is the longest European river'

Dashes are also used to introduce direct speech.

Quotation marks

Guillemets, set close, are used to indicate direct speech and special word usage and with titles of literary works, journals, etc.

12.15.5 **Word division**

Russian syllables end in a vowel, and word division is basically syllabic. However, there are many exceptions to this generalization, most of which are connected with Russian word formation. Consonant groups may be taken over entire or divided where convenient (provided at least one consonant is taken over), subject to the following rules.

- Do not separate a consonant from the prefix, root, or suffix of which it forms a part: род | ной, под|бежать, мещан |ство are correct divisions. Divide between double consonants (клас|сами), except where this conflicts with the preceding rule (класс |ный).
- Do not leave at the end of a line—or carry over—a single letter, or two or more consonants without a vowel: к|руглый, ст|рела,

жидко|сть are incorrect. The letters ъ, ь, and й should never be separated from the letter preceding them (подъ|езд).

12.15.6 **Numerals**

Arabic numerals are used. Numbers from 10,000 upwards are divided off into thousands by thin spaces, and not by commas (*26 453*); below 10,000 they are set closed up (*9999*). The decimal comma is used in place of the decimal point (*0,36578*). Ordinal numbers are followed by a contracted adjectival termination except when they are used in dates (5-й год but 7 ноября 1917 г.).

12.16 Scandinavian languages

12.16.1 **Danish, Norwegian, and Swedish**

Forms of Norwegian

Norway, which until the middle of the nineteenth century used Danish as its literary language, now has two written languages: **bokmål** (also called **riksmål),** a modified form of Danish, and **nynorsk** (also called **landsmål),** a reconstruction of what Norwegian might have been but for the imposition of Danish. Each of these has several variants, and the only safe rule for the non-expert is to assume that all inconsistencies are correct.

Alphabets and accents

Modern **Danish** and **Norwegian** have identical alphabets, the twenty-six letters of the English alphabet being followed by *æ*, *ø*, *å*; in their place **Swedish** has *å*, *ä*, *ö*. The letter *å*, found in Swedish since the sixteenth century, was adopted in Norway in 1907, and in Denmark in 1948; previously these languages used *aa* (cap. *Aa*).

Acute accents are found in loanwords and numerous Swedish surnames, and occasionally for clarity, for example Danish *én* 'one', neuter *ét* (also *een*, *eet*) as against indefinite article *en*, *et*. The grave accent is sometimes used in Norwegian to distinguish emphatic forms.

Capitalization

Until 1948 Danish nouns were capitalized as in German, a practice also found in nineteenth-century Norwegian. All the languages now tend to favour lower-case forms, for example for days, months, festivals, and historical events. This also applies to book titles; but periodical and series titles are legally deposited names, complete with any capitals they may have.

Institutional names are often given capitals for only the first word and the last; but in Danish and Norwegian some names begin with the independent definite article, which then must always be included and capitalized, *Den*, *Det*, *De* (= *Dei* in Nynorsk).

Capitalize the polite form of the second person in Danish and Norwegian: *De*, *Dem*, *Deres* (Nynorsk: *De*, *Dykk*, *Dykkar*). In Danish capitalize also the familiar second person plural, *I*, to distinguish it from *i* ('in').

Word division

Compounds are divided into their constituent parts, including prefixes and suffixes. In Danish take over *sk*, *sp*, *st*, and combinations of three or more consonants that may begin a word (including *skj*, *spj*). In Norwegian or Swedish take over only the last letter; *ng* representing a single sound is kept back, and in Swedish *x*; other groups that represent a single sound are taken over (Norwegian *gj*, *kj*, *sj*, *skj*, Swedish *sk* before *e*, *i*, *y*, *ä*, *ö*). In Swedish compounds three identical consonants are reduced to two, but the third is restored when the word is broken: *rättrogen* ('orthodox'), divided *rätt|trogen*.

12.16.2 **Icelandic and Faeroese**

Alphabets and accents

In both languages the letter *d* is followed by *ð*. Icelandic alphabetization has *þ*, *æ*, *ö* after *z*; Faeroese has *æ*, *ø*. The vowels *a*, *e*, *i*, *o*, *u*, *y* may all take an acute accent. Icelandic uses *x*, Faeroese *ks*; the Icelandic *þ* corresponds to the Faeroese *t*.

Capitalization

Icelandic capitalization is minimal, for proper nouns only. In institutional names only the initial article (masculine *Hinn*, feminine *Hin*, neuter *Hið*) should be capitalized. Faeroese follows Danish practice, though polite pronouns are not capitalized.

12.17 Slavonic languages

12.17.1 **Scripts and transliteration**

Of the Slavonic languages Russian, Belarusian, Ukrainian, Bulgarian, and Macedonian are written in the Cyrillic alphabet, Polish, Czech, Slovak, Sorbían, Croatian, Bosnian, and Slovene in the Latin. At the time of writing Serbian is written in either.

See 12.15.1 and Table 12.7 for details of the Cyrillic alphabet. The extra sorts called for by the languages other than Russian that use Cyrillic are Belarusian *i* (= *i*) and ў (= *w*); Macedonian ѓ (= *ǵ*), ѕ (= *dz*), *j* (= *j*), Љ (= *lj*), Њ, (= *nj*), Ќ (= *ḱ*), and џ (= *dž*); Serbian Ђ, ђ (= đ), j (=*j*), Љ (= *lj*), Њ, (= *nj*), Ћ, ћ (= *ć*), and џ (= *dž*); and Ukrainian ґ (= *g*), є (= *ye*), *i* (= *i*), and *ї* (= *yi*). In some Macedonian and Serbian fonts cursive *г*, *п*, and *т* are in the form of superior-barred cursive *ī*, *ū*, and *ш̄* respectively.

Transliteration systems are largely similar for those languages written in Cyrillic, but at the time of writing there is still no internationally agreed, unitary system. Of the three currently most favoured systems, the ALA-Library of Congress, International Scholarly, and British, the ALA-LC system seems to be gaining ground because of its increasing use in national and academic libraries, spurred on by developments in information technology and standardized, machine-readable cataloguing systems.

Wherever possible, adhere to a single transliteration system throughout a single work. In texts using transliterated Russian, as well as Belarusian, Bulgarian, and Ukrainian, authors and editors should avoid mixing, for example, the usual British *ya*, *yo*, *yu*, the Library of Congress *ia*, *io*, *iu*, and the philological *ja*, *jo*, *ju*. (Note that the transliteration of Serbian and Macedonian operates according to different rules.)

12.17.2 **Belarusian**

In standard transliteration of Belarusian (also called Belorussian), the diacritics ĭ, ŭ, è (or ė, é), and ʹ (soft sign) are used. In specialist texts, the philological system requires č, ë, š, ž. The Library of Congress system requires ligatured *i͡a*, *i͡o*, *i͡u*, *z͡h* In practice the ligature is often omitted, as many non-specialist typesetters have difficulty reproducing it; this is the case for all languages that employ this system.

12.17.3 **Bosnian, Croatian, and Serbian**

Linguistic nomenclature in the former Yugoslavia is still very contentious. Serbo-Croat was the main official language of Yugoslavia: although the term Serbo-Croat is still used by some linguists in Serbia and Bosnia–Herzegovina, the ISO has assigned codes to Bosnian, Croatian, and Serbian. Oversimplifying, Bosniaks (Bosnian Muslims) in Bosnia–Herzegovina use Bosnian, Croats in Croatia and Bosnia–Herzegovina use Croat, while Serbs in Serbia and Montenegro and in Bosnia–Herzegovina use Serbian.

The Roman alphabet used for Bosnian and Croatian is the standard *latinica* that is to be used for transliterating Serbian even for lay readers: thus четници will be *četnici* not *chetnitsi.*

The Cyrillic alphabet is ordered а б в г д ђ е ж з и ј к л љ м н њ о п р с т ћ у ф х ц ч џ ш; both in transliterated Serbian and in Croatian, the *latinica* order is a b c č ć d dž đ e f g h i j k l lj m n nj o p r s š t u v z ž.

Diacritics for transliterated Serbian are *ć*, *č*, *š*, *ž*; special characters are *Đ đ*.

12.17.4 **Bulgarian**

The ALA-LC system of transliteration uses the diacritics *ĭ*, *ŭ*, and the letter combinations *zh*, *kh*, *eh*, *sh*, *sht*. It also requires the ligatures *i͡a*, *i͡u*, *t͡s* The philological system requires *č*, *š*, *ž*.

12.17.5 **Czech and Slovak**

Czech and Slovak are written using the Roman alphabet, which in Czech is a á b c č d ď e é ě f g h ch i í j k l m n ň o ó p r ř s š t ť u ú ů v y ý z ž; in alphabetizing, ignore accents on vowels and on *d*, *n*, and *t*. The Slovak alphabet is a á ä b c č d ď e é f g h ch i í j k l ĺ ľ m n ň o ó ô p r ŕ s š t ť u ú v y ý z ž; in alphabetizing, ignore acute, circumflex, and accents on *d*, *l*, *n*, *r*, and *t*.

The diacritics used in Czech are *á*, *é*, *í*, *ó*, *ú*, *ý*, *ů*, *č*, *ď*, *ě*, *ň*, *ř*, *š*, *ť*, *ž*. The palatalization of *d*, *t* is always indicated by a háček in upper case (*Ď*, *Ť*) and in lower case either by a háček (*ď*, *ť*) or—preferably—a high comma right (*d’*, *t’*). Slovak uses the diacritics *ä*, *á*, *é*, *í*, *ĺ*, *ó*, *ŕ*, *ú*, *ý*, *ô*, *č*, *d’*, *l’*, *ň*, *š*, *t’*, *ž*. The palatalization of *d* and *t* is the same as for Czech; that for the Slovak *l* can be either a háček or high comma right in upper case (*Ľ*, *L’*) and a high comma right in lower case (*ľ*).

12.17.6 **Macedonian**

Macedonian is written in the Cyrillic alphabet, with a transliteration system similar to that used for Serbian. The diacritics used are *ǵ*, *ḱ*, *č*, *š*, *ž*, and the apostrophe; the letter combinations *lj*, *nj*, *dž* should not be broken in word division.

12.17.7 **Old Church Slavonic**

Also called Old Bulgarian, Old Church Slavonic was written in the Cyrillic alphabet as well as the older Glagolitic alphabet. The regional variants that developed from it are known collectively as Church Slavonic.

The diacritics and ligatures used in the Library of Congress's transliteration of Church Slavonic are *ǵ*, *ḟ*, *v̇*, *ẏ*, *ż*, *ě*, *i͡a*, *i͡e*, *i͡u*, *k͡s*, *p͡s*, *t͡s*, *i͡ę*, *i͡ǫ* (with ogonek or right-facing hook on *e*, *o*), *o͡t*, *ē*, *ī*, *ō*, *ū*, *ȳ*, *ǐ*, *ę*, *ǫ* (ogonek). In Russian Church Slavonic, *ja*/*ya*/*ia* may correspond to *ę* and *i͡ę*, *u* to *ǫ*, and *ju*/*yu*/*iu* to *i͡ǫ*. The philological system uses *č*, *š*, *ž*. Special characters are *′* (soft sign), *″* (hard sign).

12.17.8 **Polish**

Polish is written in the Roman alphabet, as in English without *q*, *v*, and *x*. It employs the diacritics *ć*, *ń*, *ó*, *ś*, *ź*, *ż*, and *Ą*, *ą*, *Ę*, *ę* (ogonek, hook right); in addition there is one special character, the crossed (or Polish) *l* (*Ł ł*).

Alphabetical order is: a ą b c ć d e ę f g h i j k l ł m n ń o ó p r s ś t u w y z ź ż. The digraphs *ch*, *cz*, *dz*, *dź*, *dż*, *rz*, and *sz* are not considered single letters of the alphabet for ordering purposes; however, these letter combinations should not be separated in dividing words.

12.17.9 **Slovene**

Slovene (also called Slovenian) is written in the Roman alphabet and uses the háček on *č*, *š*, *ž*; the digraph *dž* is not considered a single letter.

12.17.10 **Ukrainian**

The philological system requires *č*, *š*, *ž*, *ǐ*, *ï*, *′* (soft sign), and the letter combinations *je*, *šč*, *ju*, *ja*. The Library of Congress system requires ligatured *i͡a*, *i͡e*, *i͡u*, *z͡h* as with Belarusian, the ligature is often omitted. The Ukrainian и is transliterated as *y*, not *i* (which represents Ukrainian *i*).

12.18 Spanish

12.18.1 **Introduction**

The Spanish used in Spain and the Spanish spoken in Latin America are mutually intelligible in much the same way that American and British English are. However, there are important differences in vocabulary and usage both between Spain and Latin America and among the Latin American countries—it is a mistake to think that Latin American Spanish is a uniform variant of the language.

12.18.2 **Alphabet and spelling**

In older works *ch* and *ll* were treated as separate letters for alphabetical purposes, but this is now very dated. The letter *Ñ*, *ñ* is treated as a separate letter. The letters *k* and *w* are used only in loanwords from other languages and their derivatives.

The only doubled consonants in Spanish are *cc* before *e* or *i*, *rr*, *ll*, and *nn* in compounds. They can be remembered as the consonants appearing in CaRoLiNe. Where an English speaker might expect a double consonant, Spanish normally simply has one, as in *posible* 'possible'.

12.18.3 **Accents**

Normal stress in Spanish falls on either the penultimate or the last syllable, according to complex rules. Normal stress is not indicated by an accent; an acute accent is used when the rules for normal stress are broken. The only other diacritical marks used are the tilde on the *ñ*, and the diaeresis on *ü*, following *g* before *e* or *i*, where *u* forms a diphthong with *e* or *i*. Accents are normally used on capitals.

The accent is used to show interrogative and exclamatory use in the following words:

cuál 'what', 'which'	*cómo* 'how'	*cuándo* 'when'
cuánto 'how many/much'	*dónde* 'when'	*qué* 'what'
quién 'who'		

The accented forms are used in indirect questions. In 1959 the Real Academia decreed that, except in ambiguous cases, the accent is not needed on demonstrative pronouns *este* ('this one'), *ese* ('that one'), *aquel* ('that one, further away') with their feminine equivalents, *esta*, *esa*, *aquella*, and plurals *estos/estas*, *esos/esas*, *aquellos*, *laquellas*. This ruling is not universally accepted, however, and both conventions will be found. The neuter forms *esto*, *eso*, *aquello* are never accented.

12.18.4 **Capitalization**

Capitals are used in much the same way as in English in proper names. Practice differs in titles of books, poems, plays, and articles, where normally the first word and proper nouns are capitalized:

Cien años de soledad
La deshumanización del arte
Doña Rosita la soltera, o El lenguaje de las flores
El ingenioso hidalgo don Quijote de la Mancha.

Capitalize names of high political or religious authorities—when not followed by their first name—and references to God:

el Rey *la Reina* *los Reyes* *el Papa* *creer en Dios*

but

el rey Carlos III *el papa Juan XXIII*

Roman numerals indicating centuries are generally given in full capitals: *el sigh XI*.

Lower case is usually used for names of posts and titles:

catedrático	*doctora*	*duquesa*	*general*
juez	*ministro*	*presidente*	

This may include non-Spanish titles such as *sir* or *lord*: *el embajador británico sir Derek Plumbly*.

Also written in lower case are:

- nouns and adjectives denoting nationalities, religions, and peoples and ethnic groups: *francés/francesa*, *católico/-a*, *dominicano/-a*, *asiático/-a*, *amerindio/-a*
- names of artistic and literary movements: *romanticismo*, *gótico*, *surrealismo*
- names of streets and roads: *calle de Hortaleza*, *avenida de Navarra*, *puente de Santiago*; but *la Gran Via*
- names of administrative divisions and geographical features, and cardinal points when they are not part of a name: *provincia de Toledo*, *estado de Nueva York*, *condado de Lancashire*, *cordillera de los Andes*, *lago Titicaca*, *el sur de Francia*.

Traditionally names of the days of the week, months, and seasons take a lower-case initial letter, but the use of capitals for these words is now very common and cannot be assumed to be a mistake.

12.18.5 **Punctuation**

The most obvious differences from other European languages are the inverted exclamation mark and question mark inserted at the place where the exclamation or question begins:

> *¡Mire!* 'Look!' *¿Dónde vas?* 'Where are you going?'

This need not be the start of the sentence:

> *Si ganases el Gordo, ¿qué harías?* 'If you won the jackpot what would you do?'

Quotation marks take the form of guillemets (called *comillas*), set closed up (e.g. *«¡Hola!»*). However, it is more common—especially in fiction—to dispense with *comillas* altogether and indicate speakers by a dash.

Colons are used before quotations (*Dijo el alcalde: «Que comience la fiesta.»*), in letters (*Querido Pablo:*), and before an enumeration (*Trajeron de todo: cuchillos, cucharas, sartenes, etc.*). Points of suspension are set closed up with space following but not preceding them.

12.18.6 **Word division**

The general rule is that a consonant between two vowels and the second of two consonants must be taken over to the next line. The combinations *ch*, *ll*, and *rr* are indivisible and must be taken over: *mu-chacho, arti-llería, pe-rro*.

The consonants *b*, *c*, *f*, *g*, *p* followed by *l* or *r* must be taken over as a pair: *ha-blar* 'to speak', *ju-glar* 'minstrel'; so must *dr* and *tr*, as in *ma-drugada* 'dawn', *pa-tria* 'fatherland'.

The letter *s* must be divided from any following consonant: *Is-lam, hués-ped* 'guest, host', *Is-rael, cris-tiano*; similarly *Es-teban* 'Stephen', *es-trella* 'star', even in a compound (*ins-tar* 'to urge', *ins-piración*).

Divide compounds into their component parts, except where they contain *s* + consonant or *rr* (*des-hacer* 'to undo', *sub-lunar*, but *circuns-tancia, co-rregir* 'to correct', *inte-rrumpir* 'to interrupt'). Never divide diphthongs and triphthongs; if possible, avoid dividing between vowels at all.

12.19 Welsh

12.19.1 **Alphabet and accents**

The Welsh alphabet consists of twenty-eight letters, alphabetized as a b c ch d dd e f ff g ng h i j l ll m n o p ph r rh s t th u w y. The letters *k* and *v* are very frequent in medieval texts but are now obsolete.

Rh counts as a separate letter at the start of a word or syllable only, i.e. after a consonant but not a vowel: *route* comes before *rhad* 'cheap', *cynrychioli* 'to represent' before *cynrhon* 'maggots', but *arholi* 'to examine' before *arian* 'money'; *w* is usually, y always, a vowel.

All vowels (including *w* and *y*) may take a circumflex. Acute, grave, and diaeresis are also found: most frequent are *á* in final syllables (*casáu* 'to hate') and *ï* before a vowel (*copïo* 'to copy'). The letter with the diaeresis always precedes or follows another vowel.

A word consisting of an apostrophe followed by a single letter must be set close up to the preceding word:

> *cerddai'r bachgen a'i fam i'ch pentref*, 'the boy and his mother used to walk to your village'

12.19.2 **Word division**

Do not divide the digraphs *ch*, *dd*, *ff*, *ll*, *ph*, *rh*, *th*. Note that *ng* is indivisible when a single letter, but not when it represents *n* + *g*: this happens most frequently in the verb *dangos* 'to show' and its derivatives, compounds ending in *-garwch* or *-garwr* (e.g. *ariangarwr* 'money-lover'), place names beginning with *Llan-* (*Llangefni*, *Llangollen*), and in *Bangor*. Thus *cyng-aneddol* but *dan-gosol*.

Do not divide *ae*, *ai*, *au*, *aw*, *ayw*, *ei*, *eu*, *ew*, *ey*, *iw*, *oe*, *oi*, *ou*, *ow*, *oyw*, *wy*, *yw*, and other combinations beginning with *i* and with *w* when this letter is a consonant. The presence of a circumflex or an acute does not affect word division, but it is legitimate to divide after a vowel bearing the diaeresis, as also after a diphthong or triphthong before another vowel. Thus *barddoï-aidd* 'bardic', *gloyw-ach* 'brighter', *ieu-anc* 'young'.

Generally, take back a single consonant other than *h*, except after a prefix (especially *di-*, *go-*, *tra-*): *g-l* but *s-gl* (and so similar groups). A suffix beginning with *i* plus a vowel must be broken off: *casgl-iad* 'collection'.

It is always safe to divide *l-rh*, *ng-h*, *m-h*, *n-h* (but *n-nh*), *n-n*, *n-rh*, *r-r*, and after a vowel *r-h*. Initial *gwl-*, *gwn-*, *gwr-*, and their mutated forms must not be divided, since the *w* is consonantal: *gwlad* 'country', (*hen*) *wlad* '(old) country', *gwneud* 'to do', (*ei*) *wneud* 'to do (it)'. *Gwraig* 'woman', (*y*) *wraig* '(the) woman', cannot be divided.

12.19.3 **Mutations and other changes**

As in Irish Gaelic, initial consonants are replaced in certain grammatical contexts by others in a process called **mutation:** *cath* ('cat') but *fy nghath* ('my cat'), *ei gath* ('his cat', *ei chath* ('her cat'). *Caerdydd* (Cardiff), *Dinbych* (Denbigh), *Gwent* give *i Gaerdydd* ('to Cardiff'), *yng Nghaerdydd* ('in Cardiff'), *i Ddinbych* ('to Denbigh'), *yn Ninbych* ('*in Denbigh*'); *i Went* ('to Gwent'), *yng Ngwent* ('in Gwent'). 'Oxford' is *Rhydychen*, but 'from Oxford' is *o Rydychen*. The full range of mutations is *b* to *f* or *m*; *c* to *ch*, *g*, or *ngh*; *d* to *dd* or *n*; *g* to zero or *ng*; *ll* to *l; m* to *f*; *p* to *b*, *mh*, or *ph*; *rh* to *r*; *t* to *d*, *nh*, or *th*.

Initial vowels may acquire a preliminary *h* (*offer* 'tools', *ein hoffer* 'our tools') and changes of stress within a word may cause *h* to appear or disappear and double *n* or *r* to be simplified:

brenin 'king'	*brenhinoedd* 'kings'
brenhines 'queen'	*breninesau* 'queens'
corrach 'dwarf'	*corachod* 'dwarfs'
cynneddf 'faculty'	*cyneddfau* 'faculties'
cynnin 'shred'	*cynhinion* 'shreds'
dihareb 'proverb'	*diarhebion* 'proverbs'

12.20 Yiddish

Yiddish originated in German as spoken by Jews; since the later eighteenth century it has been based on dialects spoken to the east of Germany proper. It is written in an adaptation of the Hebrew alphabet, with extra characters for use in writing the basic German-derived vocabulary, and loanwords taken from surrounding (mostly Slavonic) languages; several other letters are used only in words taken from Hebrew and Aramaic, which are spelled as in their languages of origin.

CHAPTER 13

Law and legal references

13.1 Introduction

Often the standards adopted in the legal discipline are at variance with those of other subjects. Additionally, practices common in one aspect of the law may be unfamiliar in another. However, there is no reason why the following general guidelines cannot be applied across a broad range of legal studies. Given the variety of legal citations in use, this section cannot purport to be wholly definitive, nor to resolve every stylistic point that may occur. Options are given for those aspects of citation on which there is no widespread consensus.

13.2 Typography

13.2.1 **Italics**

Law uses more foreign—particularly Latin—words than many other subjects. For that reason law publishers may deviate from the usage of general reference works when determining which words and phrases to italicize. Only a handful of foreign-language law terms have become so common in English that they are set as roman in general use. Some publishers use this as a basis for determining styles: the well-known 'inter alia' and 'prima facie' are in roman, for example, but *de jure* and *stare decisis* are in italic. Others prefer to set all Latin words and phrases in italic, rather than appear inconsistent to readers immersed in the subject, for whom all the terms are familiar. Regardless of which policy is followed, words to be printed in roman rather than italic include the accepted abbreviations of *ratio decidendi* and *obiter dictum/dicta*: 'ratio', 'obiter', 'dictum', and 'dicta'.

Traditionally, the names of the parties in case names are cited in italics, separated by an italic or roman 'v.' (for 'versus'): *Smith* v. *Jones*. The 'v.' may have a full point: any style is acceptable if consistently applied.

13.2.2 **Abbreviations**

There are four possibilities regarding the use of full points in abbreviations:

- there should be no points at all, or no points only in legal abbreviations
- all points should be put in ('Q.B.D.')
- points should be in abbreviations of fewer than three letters ('A.C.')
- points should not appear between or after capitals, but should appear after abbreviations that consist of a mixture of upper- and lower-case letters ('Ont. LJ', 'Ch. D' but 'QBD', 'AC').

References, especially familiar ones, and common legal terms (paragraph, section), may be abbreviated in the text as well as in notes, but all other matter should be set out in full. Where a term is repeated frequently and is unwieldy when spelled out, such as 'International Covenant on Civil and Political Rights', then refer to it at first mention in full, with '(ICCPR)' following it, and thereafter simply as 'ICCPR'. Be careful that the abbreviations chosen do not confuse institutions with conventions (for example, use 'ECHR' for 'European Convention on Human Rights' and 'ECtHR' for 'European Court of Human Rights'). Both the Court of Justice of the European Union and the European Court of Human Rights are frequently referred to as 'the European Court': the European Court of Human Rights should always be referred to in full, unless the text in question is specifically about human rights and there is no possibility of confusion.

In cases, use 'Re' rather than 'In re', 'In the matter of', etc. Abbreviate *ex parte* to *ex p*, with the letter *e* capitalized when it appears at the beginning of a case name but in lower case elsewhere:

> *R* v. *Acton Magistrates, ex p. McMullen*

When citing a law report, generally do not include expressions such as 'and another' or 'and others' that may appear in the title, but use 'and anor', or 'and ors' in cases such as '*Re P and ors* (*minors*)' to avoid the appearance of error. To avoid unnecessary repetition, shorten citations in the text following an initial use of the full name: 'in *Glebe Motors plc v Dixon-Greene*' could subsequently be shortened to 'in the *Glebe*

Motors case'. In criminal cases it is acceptable to abbreviate 'in *R v Caldwell*' to 'in *Caldwell*'. Where a principle is known by the case from which it emerged, the name may no longer be italicized: for example, 'the Wednesbury principle'.

Law notes tend to be fairly lengthy, so anything that can be abbreviated should be. Thus 'HL', 'CA', etc. are perfectly permissible, as are 's', 'Art', 'Reg', 'Dir', %, all figures, 'High Ct', 'Sup Ct', 'PC', 'Fam Div', etc., even in narrative notes.

13.2.3 **Capitalization**

Capitalize 'Act', even in a non-specific reference; 'bill' is lower case except in the name of a specific bill. Unless it is beginning a sentence, 'section' always has a lower-case initial. 'Article' should be capitalized when it refers to supranational legislation (conventions, treaties, etc.) and lower case when it refers to national legislation.

'Court' with a capital should be used only when referring to international courts such as the Court of Justice of the European Union (CJEU) and the International Court of Justice, or for relating information specific to a single court. For instance, in a book about the Court of Appeal, Criminal Division, that court may be referred to as 'the Court' throughout. It is a common shorthand convention in US law to refer to the Supreme Court as 'the Court' and to a lesser court as 'the court'.

A capital may also be used in transcripts where a court is talking about itself, but not necessarily where it refers to itself in a different composition. Thus members of a Court of Appeal would refer to 'a judgment of the Court' when citing a previous judgment by themselves, but to 'that court' when referring to a Court of Appeal composed of others. Where, however, the reference is to a court in general, the *c* should always be lower case. For spelling of 'judgment' in legal contexts, see 13.8.

The word 'judge' should always begin with a lower-case letter, unless it is referring to a specific person's title or the author has contrasted the Single Judge with the Full Court (as in criminal appeals and judicial review proceedings), where they both have specific parts to play and almost constitute separate courts in themselves.

13.3 References

The names of books and non-law journals and reports should be in italic, following the standard format (see Chapter 8). Abbreviated references to reports and reviews should be in roman—in text, references, and lists of abbreviations. Full names of law journals and reports are in roman in Oxford style (e.g. Solicitors Journal), the reference following the date. Some publishers style the full name in italics but even here the abbreviated form is always roman: *All England Reports* but All ER.

References to journals, reports, or reviews should be cited with the date and volume number first, followed by the abbreviation of the report or review name, and then—without a comma in between—the page number. Where a specific page within an article is referred to, the initial page number should be followed by a comma plus the specific page number, or no comma and 'at' followed by the specific page number (choose one style or the other and use it consistently).

P Birks, 'The English Recognition of Unjust Enrichment' [1991] LMCLQ 473, 490–2

SC Manon, 'Rights of Water Abstraction in the Common Law' (1965) 83 LQR 47 at 49–51

Some legal writers cite others' works without a place of publication, or without first names or initials, for example 'Smith & Hogan *Criminal Law* (13th edn, 2011)'. This is an established convention in at least parts of the discipline, the expectation being that the work will be read by those who are already immersed in the relevant texts. However, editors should not impose it, and if the expected readership is more general or more elementary (as in an undergraduate or introductory text), full references must be given.

Certain textbooks have been accorded such eminence that in references the name of the original author appears in italics as part of the title, for example *Chitty on Contracts* and *Dicey and Morris on Conflict of Laws*. In full references it is not necessary to give the name of the current editor, although the edition number and the date of that edition must be stated.

Abbreviate only titles of well-known books, journals, or reports (for example Smith & Hogan, the NLJ); all others should appear in full. Variations exist in the way that many periodicals are abbreviated or punctuated. Providing authors are consistent, such variations are acceptable; in works for non-specialists, readers may benefit from expanded versions of very terse abbreviations.

Setting all abbreviated titles in roman does leave some pitfalls, of which one must be wary: 'CMLR', for instance, refers to Common Market Law Reports (which publishes only reports and never articles), while 'CMLRev' refers to Common Market Law Review. Unfortunately, where authors cite the latter as the former the only indication of the error is that the reference is to an article.

If a book, journal, report, or series is referred to very frequently in a particular work, certain common abbreviations (such as 'Crim', 'Eur', 'Intl', 'J', 'L', 'Q', 'R', 'Rev', 'U', 'Ybk') may be used; give them in full at their first occurrence but abbreviated thereafter, and include in the List of Abbreviations.

13.4 Citing cases

13.4.1 General principles

Where a specific page within a report is referred to, the initial page number should be followed by a comma plus the specific page number, or no comma and 'at' followed by the specific page number: the decision is a matter of personal choice but should be applied consistently throughout a particular work:

> *Ridge v Baldwin* [1964] AC 40, 78–9

or

> ... [1964] AC 40 at 78–9

In reports a date is in square brackets if it is essential for finding the report, and in parentheses where there are cumulative volume numbers, the date merely illustrating when a case was included in the reports:

> *R v Lambert* [2001] 2 WLR 211 (QBD)
> *Badische v Soda-Fabrics* (1897) 14 RPC 919 (HL)

No brackets are used in cases from the Scottish Series of Session Cases from 1907 onwards, and Justiciary Cases from 1917 onwards, but instead the case name is followed by a comma:

> *Hughes v Stewart*, 1907 SC 791
> *Corcoran v HM Advocate*, 1932 JC 42

It is usual to refer to Justiciary Cases (criminal cases before the High Court of Justiciary) simply by the name of the panel (or accused).

In US, South African, and some Canadian cases the date falls at the end of the reference:

Michael v Johnson, 426 US 346 (1976)

Quote extracts from cases exactly. Do not amend to improve the sense, and clearly indicate if you correct obvious errors. Omitted text should be indicated by ellipses.

Neutral citations

Since 2001 most UK cases have been given a neutral citation, which is the official number attributed to the judgment by the court. Give the neutral citation first, followed by a citation of the best report (see 13.4.3):

R v G [2003] UKHL 50, [2004] 1 AC 1034

To cite a specific paragraph of a judgment, enclose the paragraph number in square brackets:

R v G [2003] UKHL 50 at [13]

13.4.2 **Unreported**

Cite a newspaper report if there is no other published report. The reference should not be abbreviated or italicized:

Powick v Malvern Wells Water Co., The Times, 28 September 1993

When a case has not (yet) been reported and there is no neutral citation, cite just the name of the court and the date of the judgment. The word 'unreported' should not be used:

R v Marianishi, ex p London Borough of Camden (CA, 13 April 1965)

Unreported EU cases are handled differently (see 13.4.4 below).

13.4.3 **Courts of decision**

Unless the case has a neutral citation, was heard in the High Court or was reported in a series that covers the decisions of only one court, the court of decision should be indicated by initials at the end of the reference:

Blay v Pollard [1930] 1 AC 628, HL
Bowman v Fussy [1978] RPC 545, HL
Re Bourne [1978] 2 Ch 43

References to unreported cases, however, should be made in parentheses to the court of decision first (even if it is an inferior court), followed by the date. Reference is not normally made to the deciding judge (for example '*per* Ferris J'), except when wishing to specify him or her when quoting from a Court of Appeal or House of Lords decision.

Where a case has been included in a report long after it was heard, both the report and hearing dates may be included in the citation so the reader knows there has been no error:

> *Smith v Jones* [2001] (1948) 2 All ER 431

A single 'best' reference should be given for each case cited. For UK cases, the reference should be to the official Law Reports; if the case has not been reported there, the Weekly Law Reports (WLR) are preferred, and failing that the All England Reports (All ER). In certain specialist areas it will be necessary to refer to the relevant specialist series, for example Family Law Reports and Industrial Cases Reports.

13.4.4 **European Union**

Where it is available, cite a reference to the official reports of the EU, the European Court Reports (ECR), in preference to other reports. If an ECR reference is not available, the second-best reference will usually be to the Common Market Law Reports (CMLR). However, where a case is reported by the (UK) official Law Reports, the WLR, or the All ER, that may be cited in preference to CMLR, particularly if readers may not have ready access to CMLR. If the case is not yet reported it should be cited with a reference to the relevant notice in the *Official Journal*.

The case number should always be given before the name of a case in the Court of Justice of the European Union (which consists of the Court of Justice, the General Court (formerly the Court of First Instance), and the Civil Service Tribunal):

> Case C-118/07 *Commission of the European Communities v Finland* [2009] ECR I-10889

Treat Commission Decisions—but not Council Decisions—as cases.

Judgments of the courts are uniformly translated into English from French, sometimes inexactly. If the meanings of such judgments are not clear, refer to the original French for clarification.

13.4.5 **European Human Rights**

For decisions of the European Court of Human Rights cite official reports or the European Human Rights Reports (EHRR), providing one in preference to the other throughout. Until 1 November 1998 the official reports were known as Series A and numbered consecutively. The official reports were then renamed as Reports of Judgments and Decisions and they are cited as ECHR. The EHRR series is consecutively numbered, but from 2001 case numbers replaced page numbers:

> *Young, James and Webster v UK* (App no 7601/76) (1982) 4 EHRR 38
> *Plattform 'Artze für das Leben' v Austria* (App no 10126/82) (1988) Series A no 139
> *Osman v UK* (App no 23452/94) ECHR 1998-VIII 3124

Decisions and reports of the European Commission of Human Rights (now defunct) should cite the relevant application number, a reference to the Decisions and Reports of the Commission series (or earlier to the Yearbook of the ECHR), and—if available—a reference to the EHRR:

> *Zamir v UK* (App no 9174/80), (1985) 40 DR 42

13.4.6 **Other cases**

The citation of laws in other jurisdictions is too big a subject to cover in any great detail here. Authors and editors unsure of the relevant conventions should consult *The Bluebook: A Uniform System of Citation* (19th edn, 2010). This is a useful guide to citing legal sources from a wide range of jurisdictions.

13.5 Legislation

13.5.1 **UK legislation**

A statute's title should always be in roman, even where a foreign statute is in italics in the original. Older statutes, without a short title, will require the appropriate regnal year (see 11.7) and chapter number. Use Arabic numerals for chapter numbers in Public (General) and Private Acts:

> 3 & 4 Geo V, c 12, ss 18, 19

Use lower-case Roman numerals in Public (Local) Acts:

> 3 & 4 Geo V, c xii, ss 18, 19

Scots Acts before the Union of 1707 are cited by year and chapter: 1532, c 40. All Acts passed after 1962 are cited by the calendar year and chapter number of the Act; commas before the date were abolished retroactively in 1963. There is no need for the word 'of'—except perhaps when discussing a number of Acts with the same title (for example, to distinguish the Criminal Appeals Act of 1907 from that of 1904). Provided the meaning is clear, it is permissible even in text to refer to 'the 1904 Act'.

Some UK statutes are almost invariably abbreviated, for example PACE (Police and Criminal Evidence Act) and MCAs (Matrimonial Causes Acts). Where such abbreviations will be familiar to readers they may be used, even in text, although it is best to spell a statute out at first mention with the abbreviation in parentheses before relying thereafter simply on the abbreviation. Use an abbreviation where one particular statute is referred to many times throughout the text.

Except at the start of a sentence or when the reference is non-specific, use the following abbreviations: 's', 'ss', 'Pt', 'Sch'. For example, paragraph (k) of subsection (4) of section 14 of the Lunacy Act 1934 would be expressed as 'Lunacy Act 1934, s 14(4)(k)'. There is no space between the bracketed items. In general, prefer 'section 14(4)' to 'subsection (4)' or 'paragraph (k)'; if the latter are used, however, they can be abbreviated to 'subs (3)' or 'para (k)' in notes.

Statutory instruments should be referred to by their name, date, and serial number:

> Local Authority Precepts Order 1897, SR & O 1897/208
> Community Charge Support Grant (Abolition) Order 1987, SI 1987/466

No reference should be made to any subsidiary numbering system in the case of Scots instruments, those of a local nature, or those making commencement provisions.

Quote extracts from statutes exactly. Do not amend to improve the sense, and clearly indicate if you correct obvious errors. Omitted text should be indicated by ellipses.

13.5.2 **European Union legislation**

For primary legislation, include both the formal and informal names in the first reference to a particular treaty:

EC Treaty (Treaty of Rome, as amended), Art 3b
Treaty on European Union (Maastricht Treaty), Art G5c

Cite articles of the treaties without reference to the titles, chapters, or subsections. As part of a reference, abbreviate 'Article' to 'Art', in roman. Cite protocols to the treaties by their names, preceded by the names of the treaties to which they are appended:

Act of Accession 1985 (Spain and Portugal), Protocol 34
EC Treaty, Protocol on the Statute of the Court of Justice

References to secondary legislation (decisions, directives, opinions, recommendations, and regulations) should be to the texts in the *Official Journal* of the European Union. The title of the legislation precedes the reference to the source:

Council Directive (EC) 97/1 on banking practice [1997] OJ L234/3
Council Regulation (EEC) 1017/68 applying rules of competition to transport [1968] OJ Spec Ed 302

While it is always important to state the subject matter of EU secondary legislation, the long official title may be abbreviated provided that the meaning is clear. For example, the full title

Commission Notice on agreements of minor importance which do not fall under Article 85(1) of the Treaty establishing the EEC [1986] OJ C231/2, as amended [1994] OJ C368/20

may be abbreviated to

Commission Notice on agreements of minor importance [1986] OJ C231/2, as amended [1994] OJ C368/20

13.6 International treaties, conventions, etc.

Apart from EU treaties, where the short name usually suffices (see above), set out the full name of the treaty or convention with the following information in parentheses:

- the date of signature or adoption and, if available, the date it entered into force
- the Treaty Series number (or if not yet published, the International Legal Materials (ILM) citation) or, if earlier, other relevant number
- the familiar name
- any relevant protocols.

For example, a reference to the Refugee Convention should be expressed as follows:

> Convention Relating to the Status of Refugees (adopted 28 July 1951, entered into force 22 April 1954) 189 UNTS 137 (Refugee Convention)

A short title will suffice for subsequent references in the same chapter.

References to the Uniform Commercial Code (UCC) and US Restatements should be set in roman, for example 'UCC ss 2–203'.

13.7 Other materials

13.7.1 **Reports of Parliamentary select committees**

Refer to such papers by name and number:

> Defence Select Committee, 'Iraq: An Initial Assessment of Post-Conflict Operations' HC (2004–05) 65-I

13.7.2 **Law Commission**

Cite Law Commission reports by name and Commission number, with the year of publication and any Command Paper number:

> Law Commission, *Intoxication and Criminal Liability* (Law Com No 314, Cm 7526, 2009) para 1.15

13.7.3 **Hansard**

Hansard (not italic) is the daily and weekly verbatim record of debates in the British Parliament (its formal name being *The Official Report of Parliamentary Debates*). There have been five series of Hansard: first, 1803–20 (41 vols); second, 1820–30 (25 vols); third, 1830–91 (356 vols); fourth, 1892–1908 (199 vols); fifth, 1909– . It was only from 1909 that Hansard became a strictly verbatim report; prior to that time the reports' precision and fullness varied considerably, particularly before the third series.

Since 1909 reports from the House of Lords and the House of Commons have been bound separately, rather than within the same volume. References up to and including 1908 are 'Parl. Deb.' Hansard is numbered by column rather than page. Full references are made up of HC or HL, volume number, column number, and date (in parentheses):

> Hansard, HC vol 357, cols 234–45 (13 April 1965)

For pre-1909 citations, use the following form:

Parl. Deb. (series 4) vol. 24, col. 234 (24 March 1895)

13.7.4 **Command Papers**

In references, the abbreviations given before the numbers of Command Papers vary according to the time period into which the paper falls. Consequently they should *not* be made uniform or changed unless they are clearly incorrect. The series, abbreviations, years, and number extents are as follows, with an example for each:

1st	(*none*)	(1833–69)	1–4,222	(C (1st series) 28)
2nd	C	(1870–99)	1–9,550	(C (2nd series) 23)
3rd	Cd	(1900–18)	1–9,239	(Cd 45)
4th	Cmd	(1919–56)	1–9,889	(Cmd 12)
5th	Cmnd	(1957–86)	1–9,927	(Cmnd 356)
6th	Cm	(1986–)	1–	(Cm 69)

The references themselves are set in parentheses:

Secretary of State for Health, 'Government Response to the House of Commons Health Committee Report on the Provision of Allergy Services' (Cm 6433, 2005)

13.8 Judges' designations and judgments

In text it is correct either to spell out the judge's title (Mr Justice Kennedy) or to abbreviate it (Kennedy J). It is best to follow the author's preference, providing it is consistently applied in similar contexts. It is a matter of house style whether or not the abbreviation takes a full point. The following table shows various titles and their abbreviated forms, where they exist:

Mr Justice	J
Lord Justice	LJ
Lords Justice	LJJ
Lord Chief Justice Parker	Parker LCJ, Lord Parker CJ
The Master of the Rolls, Sir F. R. Evershed	Evershed MR
His Honour Judge (County Court)	HH Judge
Attorney General	Att. Gen.
Solicitor General	Sol. Gen.
Lord . . ., Lord Chancellor . . .	LC
Baron (*historical, but still quoted*)	B
Chief Baron Blackwood	Blackwood CB
The President (Family Division)	Sir Stephen Brown, P
Advocate General (of the CJEU)	Slynn AG
Judge (of the CJEU)	*no abbreviation*

Law Lords are the Justices of the Supreme Court; their names are not abbreviated. Do not confuse them with Lords Justice. 'Their Lordships' can be a reference to either rank. There is in legal terms no such rank as 'member of the Privy Council': the Judicial Committee of Privy Council is staffed by members of the Supreme Court.

'Judgment' spelled with only one *e* is correct in the legal sense of a judge's or court's formal ruling, as distinct from a moral or practical deduction. A judge's judgment is always spelled thus, as judges cannot (in their official capacity) express a personal judgement separate from their role. In US style 'judgment' is the spelling used in all contexts.

CHAPTER 14

Science, mathematics, and computing

14.1 General principles

14.1.1 **Official guidelines**

Authors and editors involved in publishing scientific material must be aware of the intended readership and its level of expertise when considering what specialist terminology and stylistic conventions to adopt. Authors of texts involving the 'harder' sciences, such as astronomy, biology, chemistry, computing, mathematics, and technology, commonly employ practices different from those in the humanities and social sciences, particularly in those texts aimed at a specialist readership. Authors should follow the standards common in their discipline, as well as any set out for specific contexts, such as series or journal articles. In general, authors and editors should follow the recommendations of the Royal Society and the Système International d'Unités (SI), particularly those for styling symbols and units, which can vary between disciplines. Internal consistency is vital where more than one standard is acceptable, or where recommendations conflict.

If an author has good reason for using a convention different from the norm, they should mention this to the editor early on. As common usage changes more frequently in the sciences than in other disciplines, it is particularly important to clarify variations before editing begins. Many scientific journals have developed their own house style: this will vary according to the subject's conventions and the readership's requirements. Authors should be aware that, for reasons of efficiency and speed, this style may be imposed—often automatically by computer software—without the author being consulted.

Authors should avoid introducing a novel notation or non-standard symbols. If non-standard terms are essential to the notation system, authors should consider including a list of symbols in the preliminary matter and supplying the editor with printed examples or a PDF, so that there is no danger of misunderstanding what is intended.

As a requirement of submission, journal authors in particular may need to write in a template downloaded from a publisher's website. This framework ensures that the document is structured in such a way that encoding for output as print or digital product can be achieved without manual intervention.

14.1.2 **Clarity**

Clarity in the presentation and explanation of difficult scientific concepts is to be valued. The principle of maximum clarity underpins most scientific style guidance and should be used to discriminate between alternative solutions to presentational problems.

Authors and editors should take care that hard copy, if used, is clear and unambiguous, and any handwritten notation is kept to a minimum. Whether hard copy or on-screen, ensure the correct character is used for special sorts (accented characters, Greek letters, mathematical symbols). For example, distinguish between:

- numbers 0 and 1 and the letters O and 1
- single (′) and double (″) primes and single (’) and double (”) closing quotation marks
- multiplication signs (×) and roman x.
- narrow angle brackets and inequality signs < and > (see 14.6.7 and Table 14.4).

Do not underline the inequality signs < and > to create less-than/greater-than or equal to symbols ≤ and ≥, and degree symbols should not be typed as lower-case superscript 'o's. See Table 14.4 for the corresponding Unicode code points.

Likewise, in electronic documents do not underline text to be set in italic. On hard copy, ensure that any hand-drawn rules above or below letters or whole expressions are not mistaken for underlining for italic.

There are particular issues of clarity involved in typesetting mathematics which affect the choice of typeface (see 14.6.1).

Scientific illustrations should adhere to the principle of maximum clarity: all unnecessary graphic effects should be eschewed. As far as possible, illustrations and their captions should be self-contained and require no reference to text material to make interpretation of them possible. See Chapter 16.

14.1.3 **Numerals**

Numbers in general are dealt with in Chapter 11. In science and mathematics figures are set close up, without a comma, in numbers up to 9999. In larger numbers thin spaces (see 14.1.5) are introduced after each group of three digits to the right or left of a decimal point (*1 234 567.891 011 12*); to permit alignment, spaces can also be introduced into four-figure numbers in columnar and tabular work. Decimal points are set on the baseline, not medially. Numbers less than one must be preceded by a zero (0.75), except where specific style guidance allows quantities that never exceed unity (such as probabilities) to be typeset without.

The SI guidelines state that it is preferable to use only numbers between 0.1 and 1000. It is better, therefore, to write *22 km* rather than *22 000 metres*, or *3* mm^3 rather than *0.003 cubic centimetres*. Powers of units can be represented exponentially, for example m^2 for square metre and cm^3 for cubic centimetre.

14.1.4 **Units**

There are internationally agreed abbreviations for many units (unit symbols), including all those in the SI. When used in full, a unit takes lower case (*kilogram, nanometre*), even eponymous ones (*newton, tesla*); when assigned a value, the unit symbol is used, standardly followed by a space (*10 kg, 1.435 m*), preferably a non-breaking or thin space (see 14.1.5). Unit symbols must not be pluralized (not *cms*). Table 14.1 shows SI units, prefixes, and their symbols.

Table 14.1 **SI units**

1. Base units

Physical quantity	**Name**	**Abbreviation or symbol**
length	metre	m
mass	kilogram	kg
time	second	s
electric current	ampere	A
temperature	kelvin	K
amount of substance	mole	mol
luminous intensity	candela	cd

2. Supplementary (dimensionless) units

Physical quantity	Name	Abbreviation or symbol
plane angle	radian	rad
solid angle	steradian	sr

3. Derived units with special names

Physical quantity	Name	Abbreviation or symbol
frequency	hertz	Hz
energy	joule	J
force	newton	N
power	watt	W
pressure	pascal	Pa
electric charge	coulomb	C
electromotive force	volt	V
electric resistance	ohm	Ω
electric conductance	siemens	S
electric capacitance	farad	F
magnetic flux	weber	Wb
inductance	henry	H
magnetic flux density	tesla	T
luminous flux	lumen	lm
illuminance	lux	lx
absorbed dose	gray	Gy
activity	becquerel	Bq
dose equivalent	sievert	Sv

4. SI prefixes

Submultiple	Prefix	Symbol	Multiple	Prefix	Symbol
10^{-1}	deci	d	10^{1}	deca	da
10^{-2}	centi	c	10^{2}	hecto	h
10^{-3}	milli	m	10^{3}	kilo	k
10^{-6}	micro	µ	10^{6}	mega	M
10^{-9}	nano	n	10^{9}	giga	G
10^{-12}	pico	p	10^{12}	tera	T
10^{-15}	femto	f	10^{15}	peta	P
10^{-18}	atto	a	10^{18}	exa	E
10^{-21}	zepto	z	10^{21}	zetta	Z
10^{-24}	yocto	y	10^{24}	yotta	Y

Some units not defined by SI are still compatible with SI units, such as *hours, minutes, days, litres*. The unit symbol for hour is *h* not *hr* and either *L* or *l* is acceptable for *litre*; if L is preferred it should also be used with prefixes such as mL for millilitres.

The unit symbol does not need to be repeated when en rules (dashes) are used to indicate a range (*45.6–50.2 kg*) unless the unit symbol is closed up (*14°–18°* [of angle]; see also 14.1.8).

Units are derived from other units by multiplication or division (m^2, *m/s*). A product of two or more different units may be separated with a fixed thin or hair space (narrower than a thin space; see 2.5.1), for example *N m*, or with a medial dot (*N·m*, set closed up; U+22C5 DOT OPERATOR) but not *Nm*. Use a solidus or negative index (*m/s* or ms^{-1}) for division but no more than one solidus in the same expression, to avoid ambiguity (instead of *J/K/mol* use $JK^{-1}\ mol^{-1}$ or spell out the final expression, *J/K per mole*).

14.1.5 **Punctuation and spaces**

Oxford style is to omit full points at the end of a displayed formula or equation, and internal punctuation is limited to that in or following any interpolated text. Other styles treat formulas and equations as an integral part of the sentence and punctuate accordingly. Text set on the same line as a displayed equation that qualifies some aspect of the equation should be spaced off from the equation by at least one em.

The presence or absence of spaces can alter the meaning of scientific text so care must be taken that they are used appropriately: *+5* is a positive integer; *+ 5* indicates an addition. Spaces come in various widths, either breaking or non-breaking; Unicode fonts have a variety of spaces between 2000 to 200A (hexadecimal) but the two that are used most frequently in technical texts, other than the word space, are the non-breaking space (U+00A0) and the thin space (U+2009) (see also 2.5.1).

14.1.6 **Notes**

It is good practice in scientific writing for all important information to be worked into the text, leaving only matter of secondary interest in notes, such as references, interpretations, and corrections. Since authors in many technical subjects choose to use an author–date (Harvard) style of references (see Chapter 17), notes occur infrequently. If a note is needed, however, make every effort to avoid adding the cue to a formula or equation, where it may be mistaken for part of the notation. For this reason superscript numerical note cues are not used except in contexts where equations are sparse. Where non-numerical note cues are required, the cue should be one of the marks of reference († ‡ § ¶ ||) in that order, repeated as necessary (††, ‡‡, etc.) throughout the chapter. The asterisk (*) reference mark used in other disciplines is not found in scientific or mathematical contexts, where that symbol may be assigned special uses. For more on notes and references see Chapter 17.

14.1.7 **Eponymic designations**

Names identified with specific individuals may be treated in several ways. Traditionally a disease, equation, formula, hypothesis, law, principle, rule, syndrome, theorem, or theory named after a person is preceded by the person's name followed by an apostrophe and *s*:

Alzheimer's disease	Bragg's law	Caro's acid
Gödel's proof	Newton's rings	

Any variation follows the normal rules governing possessives (see 4.2.1):

Charles's law	Descartes's rule of signs
Archimedes' principle	Chagas's disease

An apparatus, coefficient angle, constant, cycle, effect, function, number, phenomenon, process, reagent, synthesis, or field of study named after a person is usually preceded by the name alone or its adjectival form:

Leclanché cell	Salk vaccine
Cartesian coordinates	Newtonian telescope

Eponymic anatomical or botanical parts may incorporate the name either as a possessive (*Cowper's glands*, *Bartholin's gland*, *Wernicke's area*) or adjectivally (*Casparian strip*, *Eustachian tube*, *fallopian tube*). Something named after two or more people is known by the bare surnames, joined by an en rule:

Cheyne–Stokes respiration	Epstein–Barr virus
Stefan–Boltzmann law	Haber–Bosch process
Creutzfeldt–Jakob disease	

although the en rule is often erroneously replaced by a hyphen, especially in digital text—internet usage is an unreliable indicator in this regard.

Particularly in medical use, British technical practice increasingly is to use bare surnames, so as to avoid the possessive's proprietary effect:

Angelman syndrome	Kawasaki disease
	Rous sarcoma

This is the typical form for toponymic designations:

Borna disease	Coxsackie virus	East Coast fever
Ebola fever	Lyme disease	

For guidance on capitalization of words derived from proper nouns, see 5.14.

14.1.8 **Degrees**

Degrees are of three types: degrees of inclination or angle, abbr. *d.* or *deg.*; degrees of temperature, symbol ° (U+00B0 DEGREE SIGN); and degrees of latitude and longitude, abbr. *lat.* and *long.* (no points in scientific work). For degrees of temperature see 14.1.9.

- A degree of inclination or angle is reckoned as 1/360th of a circle. The degree symbol (°) is set close up to the numeral. Decimal subdivisions of degree are preferred to minute (*1/60 degree*) or second (*1/3600 degree*), as in *60.75°*.
- In geography, degrees of latitude and longitude are the angular distances on a meridian north or south of the equator (**latitude**), or east and west of the prime or Greenwich meridian (**longitude**). They maybe expressed in degrees (°), minutes (′), and seconds (″). The degree symbol is set closed up to the figure, for example *40° 42′ 30″ N74° 1′ 15″ W*. In discursive and non-technical contexts there are generally spaces between each item. In display work and technical contexts the figures may be closed up, and the seconds given as decimal fractions, for example *40° 42.5′ N 74° 1.25′ W*. The *N*, *S*, *E*, and *W* (no points) make the addition of *lat.* or *long.* superfluous in most instances, though especially in precise coordinates the reverse holds, with, for example, *Lat. 40.980818, Long. −74.093665*.
- In non-technical writing it is usually best to spell out the word *degree*. Where degrees of inclination and temperature occur in the same writing it may be advantageous to use the degree symbol for one and the word for the other.

14.1.9 Temperature and calories

The various common scales of temperature are **Celsius** (or **centigrade**), **kelvin**, and **Fahrenheit**; in scientific work only the Celsius and kelvin scales are used. Generally, use Arabic numerals for degrees of temperature, but words for degrees of inclination and in ordinary contexts for temperature. SI guidelines stipulate a space between the value and the degree symbol used with the scale abbreviation (*10 °C*) but it is commonly closed up (*10°C*). The degree symbol itself is printed close up to its scale abbreviation (*°C* not *° C*); alternatively use Unicode code point U+2103 for the glyph degree Celsius (℃). For a range of temperatures repeat the unit if closed up but not if a space is normally used (*15°C–17°C* or *15–17 °C*). Do not use the degree symbol with the kelvin scale.

- Degree **Celsius** (abbreviation °C) is identical in magnitude to the kelvin. To convert Celsius into kelvin add 273.15. It is the equivalent of degree centigrade, which it officially replaced in 1948. It is used as the common measure of temperature in most of the world outside the US.
- The **kelvin** (abbreviation K) is used in expressing kelvin temperatures or temperature differences: 0 K = absolute zero, or −273.15 °C. It officially replaced degree Kelvin (abbreviation °K) in 1968 as the SI unit of thermodynamic temperature (formerly called 'absolute temperature'). It is used in certain scientific writing.
- Degree **Fahrenheit** (abbreviation °F) is the commonly used temperature unit in the US. The Fahrenheit scale was originally calibrated at the ice (32 °F) and steam points (212 °F).
- The term **calorie** stood for any of several units of heat and internal energy, originally relating to the gram of water and the degree Celsius. The calorie used in food science is actually a **kilocalorie**. Sometimes called a **large calorie**, it is often written with a capital *C* to distinguish it from the **small calorie**. Because of these uncertainties and potential confusions the SI unit of energy, the **joule**, is preferred in all scientific contexts.

14.2 Biological nomenclature

14.2.1 **Capitalization of English names**

In general contexts the English names of animal or plant species should not be capitalized, unless one of the words is a proper name:

red deer	greater spotted woodpecker	lemon balm
mock orange	Pallas's cat	Camberwell beauty

In specialized contexts such as field guides and handbooks capitalization is more usual, especially in ornithology. A third style is to capitalize only the first word of the compound. In most contexts, however, the use of lower case is still preferable. This could give rise to ambiguities—a little gull could be a particular species or just 'a small gull'—but these are avoidable by careful wording.

14.2.2 **Structure of taxonomic groups**

In descending order, the hierarchy of taxonomic groups is:

kingdom
phylum (in botany, division)
class
order
family
genus
species

All organisms are placed in categories of these ranks: the domesticated cat, for example, is described in full as Carnivora (order), Felidae (family), *Felis* (genus), *Felis catus* (species). In addition, intermediate ranks may be added using the prefixes *super, sub*, and *infra*, and sub-families may be further divided into tribes. All taxonomic names are Latin in form, though often Greek in origin, except for the individual names of cultivated varieties of plant.

Rules for naming taxonomic groups are published in the following guides: for animals, the International Code of Zoological Nomenclature (ICZN); for wild plants and fungi, the International Code of Botanical Nomenclature (ICBN); for cultivated plants, the International Code of Nomenclature for Cultivated Plants (ICNCP); for bacteria, the International Codes of Nomenclature of Bacteria (ICNB); for viruses, the International Committee on Taxonomy of Viruses (ICTV).

14.2.3 **Groups above generic level**

Names of groups from kingdom to family are plural and printed in roman with initial capitals (Bacillariophyceae, Carnivora, Curculionidae). The level of the taxon is usually indicated by the ending: the names of botanical or bacteriological families and orders, for example, end in *-aceae* and *-ales*, while zoological families and sub-families end in *-idae* and *-inae* respectively. (Ligatures such as æ and œ are not now used in printing biological nomenclature.)

14.2.4 **The binomial system**

Living organisms are classified by genus and species according to the system originally devised by Linnaeus. This two-part name—called the **binomial** or **binomen**—is printed in italic, and usually consists of the capitalized name of a genus followed by the lower-case specific name. Thus the forget-me-not is *Myosotis alpestris*, with *Myosotis* as its generic name and *alpestris* as its specific epithet; similarly the bottlenose dolphin is *Tursiops* (generic name) *truncatus* (specific name). Specific names are not capitalized even when derived from a person's name: *Clossiana freija nabokovi* (Nabokov's fritillary), *Gazella thomsoni* (Thomson's gazelle).

A genus name is printed in italic with an initial capital when used alone to refer to the genus. If, however, it also has become a common term in English for the organism concerned it is printed in roman and lower case (rhododendron, dahlia, tradescantia, stegosaurus); thus '*Rhododendron* is a widespread genus' but 'the rhododendron is a common plant'. Specific epithets are never used in isolation except in the rare cases where they have become popular names (japonica), when they are printed in roman.

Latin binomials or generic names alone may be followed by the surname of the person who first classified the organism. These surnames and their standardized abbreviations are called 'authorities' and are printed in roman with an initial capital: '*Primula vulgaris* Huds.' shows that this name for the primrose was first used by William Hudson; '*Homo sapiens* L.' shows that Linnaeus was the first to use this specific name for human beings. If a species is transferred to a different genus, the authority will be printed in parentheses. For example, the greenfinch, *Carduelis chloris* (L.), was described by Linnaeus but placed by him in the genus *Loxia*.

14.2.5 **Abbreviation**

After the first full mention of a species, later references may be shortened by abbreviating the generic name to its initial capital, followed by a full point: *P. vulgaris, E. caballus*. If two organisms with the same single-letter abbreviation occur in the same sentence or paragraph, a multiple-letter abbreviation is sometimes used (*Staphylococcus* and *Streptococcus* may become *Staph*. and *Strep*. for example) but is best avoided as there are very few 'official' multiple-letter abbreviations so inconsistencies between publications can occur. The species names are usually sufficient to avoid confusion, or use the full version.

14.2.6 **Subspecies and hybrids**

Names of animal subspecies have a third term added in italic to the binomial, for example *Motacilla alba alba* (white wagtail), *M. alba yarrelli* (pied wagtail). Plant categories below the species level may also have a third term added to their names, but only after an abbreviated form of a word indicating their rank, which is printed in roman:

subspecies (Latin *subspecies*, abbreviation subsp.)
variety (Latin *varietas*, abbreviation var.)
subvariety (Latin *subvarietas*, abbreviation subvar.)
form (Latin *forma*, abbreviation f.)
subform (Latin *subforma*, abbreviation subf.)

So '*Salix repens* var. *fusca*' indicates a variety of the creeping willow, and '*Myrtus communis* subsp. *tarentina*' a subspecies of the common myrtle.

Other abbreviations are occasionally printed in roman after Latin names, such as 'agg.' for an aggregate species, 'sp.' (plural 'spp.') after a genus name for an unidentified species, 'gen. nov.' or 'sp. nov.' indicating a newly described genus or species, and 'auctt.' indicating a name used by many authors but without authority.

The names attached to cultivated varieties of plants follow the binomial, printed in roman within single quotation marks (*Rosa wichuraiana* 'Dorothy Perkins'). The cultivar name may be preceded by the abbreviation 'cv.', in which case the quotation marks are not used (*Rosa wichuraiana* cv. Dorothy Perkins). The names of cultivated varieties may also appear after variety or subspecies names, or after a genus name alone: for example, the ornamental maple *Acer palmatum* var. *heptalobum* 'Rubrum', and the rose *Rosa* 'Queen Elizabeth'. Names of hybrid plants are indicated by a roman multiplication sign (×): *Cytisus* × *kewensis* is a hybrid species, × *Odontonia* is a hybrid genus. Horticultural graft hybrids are indicated by a plus sign (+*Laburnocytisus adami*).

14.2.7 **Bacteria and viruses**

Bacteria

Genera used adjectivally are lower case roman (salmonella poisoning, streptococcal infection); plural noun forms can add -s or take the Latin form (rickettsias, salmonellae, staphylococci). Bacterial strains are usually designated by capitals and numbers in roman (*Escherichia coli* K12) but consult the relevant authority as nomenclature changes.

Viruses

The International Committee on Taxonomy of Viruses (ICTV) has developed a system of classifying and naming viruses. The ranks employed for animal, fungal, and bacterial viruses are order, *family*, *subfamily*, *genus*, and *species*. Wherever possible, Latinized names are used for the taxa; hence names of genera end in the suffix *-virus*, subfamilies end in *-virinae*, families end in *-viridae*, and orders end in *-virales*. Latinized specific epithets are not used, so binomial nomenclature does not obtain. The ICTV recommends italicizing and capitalizing the first word of all Latinized names when used in a taxonomic sense, but not in vernacular usage.

taxonomic: a newly acquired virulence of several bee viruses belonging to the family *Dicistroviridae* has been observed worldwide

vernacular: measuring the impact of herpes zoster and post-herpetic neuralgia on quality of life

However, not all publishers (including OUP) follow this guidance, italicizing only genera and species, so check which style is used. Those genera or higher groups that do not yet have approved Latinized names are referred to by their English vernacular names. Capitalization is used only for proper nouns:

We have focused our interest on acute bee paralysis virus, which shares some antigenic and sequence similarities with Kashmir bee virus and Israeli acute paralysis virus.

The ranks of genus and species are not used in the taxonomy of plant viruses, which are classified in groups—not families—with the approved group name ending in *-virus*. Existing names employ various combinations of Roman or Greek letters, Arabic or Roman numerals, and superscript and subscript characters. Many names are prefixed with a capital P or lower-case phi (PM2, ϕ6, ϕX, Pf1). It is important therefore to follow carefully the conventions employed in the original name.

14.2.8 **Enzymes**

Enzyme nomenclature has several forms, depending on context. Most enzyme trivial names are based on the name of the type of reaction they catalyse and the name of the substrate or product they are associated with. Most end in *-ase*, though some do not.

A systematic nomenclature has been devised by the International Union of Biochemistry and Molecular Biology. Each enzyme has a systematic name incorporating its type designation (i.e. group name), the name of its substrate(s), and a unique four-digit numerical designation called the EC (Enzyme Commission) number. For example, the systematic name of glutamate dehydrogenase is L-glutamate:NAD^+ oxidoreductase (deaminating), EC 1.4.1.2.

Because systematic names are so unwieldy, they tend to supplement or clarify trivial names rather than replace them. In most contexts trivial names alone suffice, though the EC number and full systematic name should follow at first occurrence in formal usage.

Although restriction endonucleases also have EC classifications, they have additional nomenclature that is based on the genus, species, and strain from which they are derived (such as *Bam*HI from *Bacillus amyloliquefaciens* strain HI).

14.2.9 **Genes and chromosomes**

Conventions for naming genes and gene products (the proteins they code for) vary widely among species or type of organism, and also change rapidly. Authors and editors are advised to check the website of the relevant nomenclature committee or other authority for current guidelines—many organisms now have dedicated online databases containing a searchable catalogue of genes with annotated gene sequence data, plus descriptions of gene functions. The *New Oxford Dictionary for Scientific Writers and Editors* has a helpful summary of the basic rules of gene nomenclature for selected groups of organisms or species.

The following is some general guidance but there are many exceptions so editors with limited knowledge of the subject should not be tempted to standardize capitalization, hyphenation, and italicization for example, without checking the relevant authority. As an example, acute myeloid leukaemia genes in humans and mice are *AML1* and *Aml1*, respectively, and their protein products are AML1 and Aml1.

- Gene names and their more commonly used symbols are usually italicized; most symbols are given three letters (such as *CDH1* for cadherin 1), although older symbols may differ (*w* for the *white* gene in white-eyed fruit flies *Drosophila* for example).
- For dominant traits, the name and symbol generally begin with a capital letter, whereas for recessive traits the initial letter is lower case (in baker's yeast *Saccharomyces cerevisiae,* for example, *CUPI, arg2*).
- Plus and minus signs are used in some organisms to indicate normal (wild type) or mutant forms, such as the cyc^{+} *Cyclops* wild-type gene in zebrafish; others use all capitals (*AGAMOUS-LIKE*, symbol *AGL*) for wild types and lower case for mutants (*accelerated cell death, acd*) in wall cress *Arabidopsis thaliana.*
- Protein products usually follow the corresponding gene symbol but are set roman (for example, the protein product of the *trpA* gene required for tryptophan synthesis in *E. coli* is TrpA).
- Human gene names are roman but the symbols are italic capitals and Arabic letters (G-protein coupled receptor, *GPR1*). The Gene Nomenclature Committee Human Genome Organization (HUGO) is responsible for assigning gene symbols; their website genenames. org is a database of approved nomenclature and associated resources. For the major histocompatibility complex see 14.3.5.

Each community also has its own convention for designation of genetic markers and transgenic strains.

Chromosomes are designated by a roman letter or number (in humans 1 to 22, X, Y); different regions and bands on the short (p) or long (q) chromosome arms are specified with Arabic numbers and letters, in roman, for example 14q32.2. Duplicated, deleted, or translocated regions are designated dup, del, or t respectively; for example t(9;22)(q34;q11.2) refers to a reciprocal translocation between bands 34 and 11.2 of the long arms of chromosomes 9 and 22. Gain or loss of a chromosome is indicated by a plus or minus sign, so +21 indicates an extra chromosome 21. The length of DNA sequences is cited in base pairs (bp), kilobases (kb), or megabases (Mb); the centiMorgan (cM) is a measure of genetic distance and relates to recombination frequency.

14.3 Medical terminology

14.3.1 **Abbreviations**

Abbreviations should be defined when first used. Avoid using clinical-style shorthand in formal writing (US for ultrasound; Hb for haemoglobin unless referring to specific types; see 14.3.3).

Abbreviations of Latin terms are now discouraged, particularly in pharmacology, where clarity of meaning is paramount. In addition, British and US usage differs in some cases (see Table 14.2).

The same abbreviations may be used for different terms: CSF may be *cerebrospinal fluid* or *colony-stimulating factor*. Which of these abbreviations should be employed in a text depends on the type of work and its expected readership.

Some abbreviations will be so familiar to the readership that they do not need to be defined (*DNA, HIV*) but be aware that some well-known English abbreviations may be known by a different abbreviation in other languages (*AIDS, SIDA* in French). It is useful to have a house style list of those that do not need to be defined for a particular specialty but, if in doubt, it is best to define it at some point.

Table 14.2 **Dosage abbreviations**

British	US	
a.c		ante cibum (before food)
b.d	b.i.d.	bis die (twice daily)
o.d	q.d	omni die (every day)
o.m		omni mane (every morning)
o.n	q.h.s	omni nocte (every night)
p.c		post cibum (after food)
p.r.n.		pro re nata (when required)
q.d.s.	q.i.d.	quater die sumendum (to be taken four times daily)
q.q.h.		quarta quaque hora (every four hours)
stat		statim (immediately)
t.d.s.	t.i.d.	ter die sumendum (to be taken three times daily)
t.i.d.		ter in die (three times daily)

14.3.2 **Blood groups**

Blood-group antigens are designated by capital letters, sometimes combined with a lower-case letter or letters, such as A, B, AB, O, Rh. Note that while A, for example, is defined as a blood group, *not* blood type, blood is described as being type A, *not* group A.

14.3.3 **Haemoglobin**

The types of normal human haemoglobin are designated Hb A, Hb A_2, and Hb F. Their component globin chains are designated by a Greek letter (α, β, γ, or δ); subscript numerals indicate the number of chains. Abnormal haemoglobins are designated either by letters (C–Q, S) or by the name of the place where they were first identified (e.g. Hb Bart's, Hb Chad).

14.3.4 **Vitamins**

The group of organic compounds that form vitamins may be known by their chemical names or by a single capital letter; those forming part of a group are identified further by subscript Arabic figures (e.g. vitamin B_1). (Dietary minerals are known only by their chemical names.)

14.3.5 **Immunology**

Symbols for human histocompatibility leukocyte antigens are HLA followed by a letter to designate the class (e.g. HLA-A). Classification is complex and ongoing; consult the website of the World Health Organization Nomenclature Committee for Factors of the HLA System, which changed the way HLA alleles are designated and named in 2010. Symbols for human immunoglobulins are Ig also followed by a class letter (e.g. IgA); do not use Ig as an abbreviation for immunoglobulin. T cell is not hyphenated unless used adjectivally (T-cell receptor). The gene symbols for immunoglobulins and T-cell receptors are assigned by the ImMunoGeneTics (IMGT) Nomenclature Committee; lists of human and murine gene names can be found on their website. Symbols for many other molecules such as interferons consist of capital letters to designate the molecule, prefixed by the source, and followed by other designations (rhIFN-α1, recombinant human interferon-α1).

14.3.6 **Diseases**

Disease names may be descriptive or eponymic (e.g. *Parkinson's disease*). Derived words do not take a capital letter (e.g. *parkinsonism*). See also 14.1.7 on eponymic designations. Note that descriptive names are now preferred (*reactive arthritis* over *Reiter's disease*). Avoid using nouns derived from disease names to describe patients (*diabetics, epileptics*); use *people with diabetes* or *epileptic patients* for example.

14.3.7 **Drug nomenclature**

In professional or technical contexts, prefer a drug's generic name (in lower case) to its proprietary name (with an initial capital), which may differ over time and between countries. Even generic names can vary, however, and there are several conventions worldwide, chiefly British Approved Names (BANs), Recommended International Non-Proprietary Name (rINNs), US Adopted Names (USANs), and Japanese Approved Names (JANs). European legislation requires the use of rINNs for medicinal product labelling and in 2003 all British Approved Names (BANs) were harmonized with rINNs with the exception of adrenaline (in rINN epinephrine) and noradrenaline (norepinephrine). Publishers should therefore impose rINNs/new BANs as a matter of policy. In a historical context, and for lidocaine (lignocaine) where changeover has been slower, it may be useful to add the original BAN as a gloss. The *British National Formulary* retains original BANs as synonyms and the Medicines and Healthcare Products Regulatory Agency (MHRA) website has a complete list of the BANs changed. A dictionary that includes all the international systems is published annually by the US Pharmacopeial Convention.

14.4 Chemistry

14.4.1 **Introduction**

The International Union of Pure and Applied Chemistry (IUPAC) generates comprehensive advice on chemical nomenclature, terminology, standardized methods for measurement, and atomic weights. By their recommendations, symbols for the elements are set in roman with an initial capital, no point at the end; spelled-out names of chemical compounds are in lower-case roman; and symbols for the elements in formulas are printed in roman without spaces:

H_2SO_4 $Cu(CrO_2)_2$

Table 14.3 lists the IUPAC-accepted names and abbreviations of chemical elements.

14.4.2 **Roman and italic**

In certain kinds of name, symbols are printed in italic (*O*-methylhydroxylamine, *fac*-triamine-trinitrosylcobalt(III)). Italic is also used for certain prefixes, of which the commonest are *o*-, *m*-, *p*-, *cis*-, and *trans*- (*o*-tolidine, *p*-diethylbenzene, *cis*-but-2-ene). Retain the italic, but not

the *cis* isomer   position *a* is *ortho* to the methyl group

the hyphen, when the prefix is used as a separate word:

The prefixes *d*-, *l*-, and *dl*- are no longer used for labelling stereoisomers, which are expressed either by small capitals or by symbols: D-(+), L-(−), and DL-(±) respectively; for example 'DL-lactic acid', '(+)-tartaric acid'. In each case the hyphens must be retained, although not when expressing their absolute configuration.

14.4.3 **Formulas and structural drawings**

A chemical formula shows the elements present in a compound and their relative proportions (H_2O, C_2H_6O); a chemical equation represents the changes that occur in a chemical reaction, in words or symbols:

glucose + oxygen→carbon dioxide + water

$C_6H_{12}O_6(aq) + O_2(g) \rightarrow CO_2(g) + H_2O(g)$

Table 14.3 **Chemical elements**

Element	Symbol	Atomic no.	Element	Symbol	Atomic no.	Element	Symbol	Atomic no.
actinium	Ac	89	germanium	Ge	32	potassium	K	19
aluminium	Al	13	gold	Au	79	praseodymium	Pr	59
americium	Am	95	hafnium	Hf	72	promethium	Pm	61
antimony	Sb	51	hassium	Hs	108	protactinium	Pa	91
argon	Ar	18	helium	He	2	radium	Ra	88
arsenic	As	33	holmium	Ho	67	radon	Rn	86
astatine	At	85	hydrogen	H	1	rhenium	Re	75
barium	Ba	56	indium	In	49	rhodium	Rh	45
berkelium	Bk	97	iodine	I	53	roentgenium	Rg	111
beryllium	Be	4	iridium	Ir	77	rubidium	Rb	37
bismuth	Bi	83	iron	Fe	26	ruthenium	Ru	44
bohrium	Bh	107	krypton	Kr	36	rutherfordium	Rf	104
boron	B	5	lanthanum	La	57	samarium	Sm	62
bromine	Br	35	lawrencium	Lr	103	scandium	Sc	21
cadmium	Cd	48	lead	Pb	82	seaborgium	Sg	106
caesium	Cs	55	lithium	Li	3	selenium	Se	34
calcium	Ca	20	livermorium	Lv	116	silicon	Si	14
californium	Cf	98	lutetium	Lu	71	silver	Ag	47
carbon	C	6	magnesium	Mg	12	sodium	Na	11
cerium	Ce	58	manganese	Mn	25	strontium	Sr	38
chlorine	Cl	17	meitnerium	Mt	109	sulphur	S	16
chromium	Cr	24	mendelevium	Md	101	tantalum	Ta	73
cobalt	Co	27	mercury	Hg	80	technetium	Tc	43
copernicium	Cn	112	molybdenum	Mo	42	tellurium	Te	52
copper	Cu	29	neodymium	Nd	60	terbium	Tb	65
curium	Cm	96	neon	Ne	10	thallium	Tl	81
darmstadtium	Ds	110	neptunium	Np	93	thorium	Th	90
dubnium	Db	105	nickel	Ni	28	thulium	Tm	69
dysprosium	Dy	66	niobium	Nb	41	tin	Sn	50
einsteinium	Es	99	nitrogen	N	7	titanium	Ti	22
erbium	Er	68	nobelium	No	102	tungsten	W	74
europium	Eu	63	osmium	Os	76	uranium	U	92
fermium	Fm	100	oxygen	O	8	vanadium	V	23
flerovium	Fl	114	palladium	Pd	46	xenon	Xe	54
fluorine	F	9	phosphorus	P	15	ytterbium	Yb	70
francium	Fr	87	platinum	Pt	78	yttrium	Y	39
gadolinium	Gd	64	plutonium	Pu	94	zinc	Zn	30
gallium	Ga	31	polonium	Po	84	zirconium	Zr	40

Formulas and reaction schemes may be numbered separately from figures, often with a sequence of bold numbers or letters in square brackets or parentheses, ranged right.

When expressing formulas, the order of brackets normally follows that in mathematics: {[( )]}. Parentheses are used to define the extent of a chemical group, as in $(C_2H_5)_3N$; square brackets are used to denote, for example, chemical concentration in complex formulas: $[H_2SO_4]$. This sequence will vary in certain circumstances, for example in the use of square brackets in denoting coordination compounds:

$K_3[Fe(CN)_6]$ $[Ni(CO)_4]$

In organic chemical nomenclature, it is usual to write a formula as a series of groups (known as a structural formula):

$CH_3COC_2H_5$ RCH_2COOCH_3

Medial dots can be used to divide off the groups, if clarification of a formula is needed (usually in textbooks). Unicode code point U+00B7 MIDDLE DOT is acceptable.

$(CH_3CO{\cdot}C_2H_5;$ $R{\cdot}CH_2{\cdot}COOCH_3)$

In most other contexts they can be dispensed with, although dots are required in formulas of addition compounds ($Na_2CO_3{\cdot}10H_2O$). Indicate a single bond with a closed-up en rule or a minus sign (C–H), a double bond by an equals sign ($CH_3CH{=}CH_2$), and a triple bond by an equivalence sign (U+2261 IDENTICAL TO) ($CH_3C{\equiv}CH$).

In chemical equations, different types of arrows are used to represent reactions or electron movement; arrows may be single or double barbed—each has significance. For example, a long double-barbed arrow is used to indicate the direction of a reaction

$$CO_2 + 2H_2O \rightarrow CH_4 + 2O_2$$

and two single-barbed arrows pointing in opposite directions indicate a reversible reaction, which may be in balanced equilibrium (same length arrows)

$$N_2 + 3H_2 \rightleftharpoons 2NH_3$$

or favour either the reactants or products (different length arrows).

Equations and displayed or skeletal formulas can be created in dedicated chemistry drawing packages; anything other than simple, single-line formulas that can be word processed will be treated as artwork (for details see Chapter 16). There are also TeX macro packages that can be used for creating chemistry graphics or typesetting chemistry according to a publisher's style (see 14.6.1).

14.4.4 **Superscripts and subscripts**

Superscripts and subscripts need not occur only singly, and need not follow what they modify. In specifying a particular nuclide, the atomic (proton) number is printed as a left subscript (${}_{12}Mg$). Similarly, the mass (nucleon) number of an element is shown with its symbol and printed as a left superscript (${}^{235}U$, ${}^{14}C$)—not to the right, as formerly. If it is given with the name of the element no hyphen is necessary (uranium 235, carbon 14).

In inorganic chemical nomenclature the relationship between the superscripts and subscripts surrounding a chemical symbol is important: superscript expresses the electrical charge and subscript the number of atoms for each molecule. These should be staggered so as to indicate the ions present ($Na^+{}_2CO_3{}^{2-}$ (sodium carbonate) but $Hg_2{}^{2+}Cl_2{}^-$ (dimercury(I) chloride)). A medial dot is used to indicate coordinated species ($CuSO_4{\cdot}5H_2O$). Ionic charge is shown by a right superscript ($SO_4{}^{2-}$). Indicate complex ions by square brackets: $K^+{}_3[FeCl_6]^{3-}$.

Indicate oxidation states by a small-capital Roman numeral, set in parentheses close up to the spelled-out name, for example 'manganese(IV)'; or by a superscript Roman numeral set in capitals to the right of the abbreviated name, for example 'Mn^{IV}'.

Atomic orbitals, designated s, p, d, f, g, are roman, and can have subscript letters with superscript numbers attached ($d_z{}^2$, $d_x{}^2$–$d_y{}^2$).

14.5 Computing

14.5.1 **Terminology**

The influence of the US on the computing field has resulted in US spelling being adopted for much of the standard vocabulary, such as *analog*, *disk*, and *program* rather than *analogue*, *disc*, *programme* (but note *compact disc*, *digital versatile disc*). Phrases such as *object-oriented* should not be changed to British usage (*orientated*). Other spellings not forming part of computing terminology should be normalized to British spelling for texts intended wholly or mostly for the UK market.

In the main, the names of programming languages, including acronyms, are styled in upper and lower case (Unix (trademark UNIX), Java, Python, Lisp); capitals are used for abbreviations (PHP, SQL). The plus signs in C++ are styled on the line, not superscripted, and C# (pronounced C sharp) uses a hash on the line, not a sharp sign. While it is acceptable to style different language names differently, ensure that the same style is adopted for the same language throughout a work. Styling of programming language names and many of the other computing abbreviations and terms can be found in the *New Oxford Dictionary for Scientific Writers and Editors* or the *New Oxford Dictionary for Writers and Editors*.

Data storage is measured in *bytes* (symbol B), which is usually defined as 8 *bits* (b); multiples may appear to use the same prefixes as the SI, including K (not k) for kilo-, M for mega-, G for giga-, T for tera-, but they are in fact binary so a kilobyte (1 KB) is 1024 bytes, a megabyte (1 MB) is 1024 × 1024 bytes, and so on. Note that this usage is confined to data storage—other measurements such as data transmission rates take the standard SI prefixes. Linux and open-source communities often use the International Electrotechnical Commission standard, which uses the prefixes

kibi- (Ki) =	mebi- (Mi) =	gibi- (Gi) =	tebi- (Ti) =	pebi- (Pi) =
210	220	230	240	250

14.5.2 **Representation**

The text of a computer program or textual data file such as an XML file may be presented in a work in several ways: in whole or in part, displayed or run into text. Not being a prose extract in the traditional sense, any such material is treated rather like an equation, with no minimum size and no small type needed for display.

Where the features of the program or mark-up language require character-literal syntax and precise line breaks, display, indentation, spacing, or special sorts, these must be reproduced exactly. It is wise to insert any lengthy code directly from the source rather than retype it, which can introduce error. It is useful to set any selected material in a distinctive typeface—a sans-serif font, or a monospace typeface such as

Courier—one advantage of the latter being that fixed-width fonts preserve alignment of code elements, such as end-of-line comments, as they would appear on-screen in a text editor.

```
<body bgcolor = "#000033" text = "#000033"
  link = "#FF0000" vlink = "#66CC33" alink = "#FFFF00"
  onLoad = "MM_displayStatusMsg('welcome'); return
         document:MM_returnValue">
```

If the font chosen to indicate programming or mark-up language text is sufficiently different from the font used for normal text, it is unnecessary to delimit it further by quotation marks, even when run into text. If, however, quotation marks are needed, note that computing practice matches standard British usage in the relative placement of punctuation and quotation marks. The punctuation falls outside the closing quotation mark, so that in citing parts of

```
x=0;
for (i-0;i++;i < n)
x+=V[i];
```

in text, the punctuation does not interfere with the syntax: 'x = 0;', and 'x += V[i]'. This style, which would be imposed naturally in British publishing, should also be imposed in US computing texts, though not extended to normal quotations. US computing books can also reserve British-style single quotation marks for programming and mark-up language text, using double quotes for normal quotations.

In-text or displayed formulas and equations are best described and set so far as possible according to the rules governing mathematics. Any visual representations of structures or hierarchical classifications (use-case and activity diagrams, screen shots, tree grammars, Venn diagrams) will be treated as artwork (see Chapter 16).

14.5.3 **Computing symbols**

Mathematical material in computing contexts is usually treated in the same way as in other texts, although the sense of, for example, some logic symbols may differ from standard practice. In programming, the different types of bracket have various specific uses and order, depending on the language. In computing, the **slash** (/) is used as a separator, as with URLs for example. When a **backslash** (\) separator is used, the slash can be called a **forward slash** to differentiate it further.

Code tags in SGML-based languages are enclosed by angle brackets < >: note that the narrow angle brackets ⟨ ⟩ generally employed in technical contexts should not be used here (see 14.6.5 for mathematical brackets).

Other symbols have various context-specific functions: the asterisk, for example, is a Kleene star in BNF, a multiplication operator in C, and a wildcard character in various command-line shells. In some computing languages multi-symbol operators are used—for example, a combined colon and equals sign := is used as the assignment symbol ('gets' or 'becomes'); in others ::= means 'is defined as' and :- means 'if'. These symbols constitute a single unit and are set close up, with space either side:

$$\{\mathrm{A}[x] := y,\ \mathrm{B}[u, v] := w\}.$$

⟨decimal fraction⟩ ::= ⟨unsigned integer⟩

but not all languages require space around operators. It is important to be aware of the specific rules regarding spaces, indentation, commenting, spelling and capitalization, and the meanings of symbols used alone or in combinations in programming and mark-up languages—if working in an unfamiliar language, find out the rules online or raise a query with the originator.

14.6 Mathematics

14.6.1 **Introduction**

The *de facto* standard for mathematical typesetting is T$_{\mathrm{E}}$X (usually reproduced as TeX), a mark-up language available for many computing platforms, which consists of a coded, plain-text file that can be output to a device-independent file for printing or to PDF to produce high-quality results in terms of the complex layout, formatting, and special characters often demanded in mathematical work. LaTeX is the most popular TeX-based system. Some mathematical societies and publishers have their own plain TeX or LaTeX style files to help authors prepare their submissions according to the required specifications. Mathematical mark-up languages such as MathML and TeXML can be used to embed formulas in webpages, ebooks, and apps.

As a result, former constraints in setting 'difficult' material such as embellishments, fractions, fences, and overbars have been overcome, and digital product has removed the necessity to minimize displayed matter to reduce page extents and production costs.

When mathematical notation is required in text that is not created in a TeX-based system, authors should prepare their files using a word-processor equation editor or a stand-alone WYSIWYG (graphical) application for creating mathematical notation based on MathML.

In a mathematical equation each letter represents a quantity or operation, but the style (bold, italic, script, sans serif) and the relative positioning and sizes of the symbols (subscript, superscript) also convey important information.

Some typefaces are not suited to setting mathematics and should be avoided: sans-serif faces often suffer from indistinguishable characters (l, I, 1 are common examples). Subscripts and sub-subscripts must be legible and the distinction between roman, italic, bold, and sans serif clear even in one isolated character. Plain serifed faces such as Times, Computer Modern, and Lucida Math are generally to be favoured for mathematical work. The choice of typeface should be carried through to headings and labelling of figures where maths may occur. The typography of equations should not be altered to conform with design specifications for headings and labels.

14.6.2 **Notation**

The established style is to use roman type for operators and certain numerical constants, and to label points in a diagram. Italic is used for letters expressing a variable, and bold is used for vectors and matrices. Each description should be represented by a single symbol: avoid using abbreviated words. Here are some specific points:

- It is common to set the headword of definitions, theorems, propositions, corollaries, or lemmas in capitals and small capitals, with the remaining text of the heading in italic. The full text of the proof itself is set in roman.
- Avoid starting a sentence with a letter denoting an expression, so that there is no ambiguity about whether a capital or lower-case letter is intended.

- Most standard abbreviations, for example 'log(arithm)', 'max(imum)', 'exp(onential function)', 'tan(gent)', 'cos(ine)', lim(it)', and 'cov(ariance)', are set in roman, with no full points.
- Distinguish between a roman 'd' used in a differential equation ($\mathrm{d}x/\mathrm{d}y$), the symbol ∂ for a partial differential, and the Greek lower-case delta (δ). Authors should preclude further potential for confusion by avoiding an italic *d* for a variable. US authors may use italic for differential *d*
- The exponential 'e' remains in roman (but may be italic in US texts); sometimes it may be preferable to use the abbreviation 'exp' to avoid confusion. The letters i and j are roman when symbolizing imaginary numbers, and italic when symbolizing variables.
- In displayed equations, the integral, summation, and product symbols ($\int$ Σ Π) may have limits set directly above them (upper limit) or below them (lower limit). In running text, the convention is to place these after the symbol wherever possible (as in the first example)

$$\int_a^b x^2\,dx \qquad \sum_{m=0}^{\infty} \qquad \prod_{r\geq 1}$$

- Missing terms can be represented by three dots which are horizontal ($\cdots$), vertical ($\vdots$), or diagonal ($\ddots$), as appropriate. Include a comma after the three ellipsis dots when the final term follows, for example $x_1, x_2, \ldots, x_{\mathrm{n}}$.

14.6.3 **Symbols**

Operational signs are of two types: those representing a verb (e.g. $= \approx \neq \geq$) and those representing a conjunction (e.g. $+ - \supset \times$). All operational signs take a space on either side, consistently either a thin space or a word space. (If setting in TeX, such spaces are built in, so there is no need to add any.) They are not closed up unless they are being used to modify a value, for example, a difference of ±2; magnification ×200.

Set a multiplication point as a medial point (·) (U+22C5 DOT OPERATOR) but it should be used only to avoid ambiguity and is not needed between letters, unless a vector product is intended (e.g. **a**·**b**), in which case U+2219 BULLET OPERATOR should be used; there are no spaces either side of a medial point.

In print product where space-saving is desirable, any symbol that involves setting a separate line of type should be avoided when an alternative form is available. So, for angle *ABC*, prefer $\angle ABC$ to

$\widehat{ABC}$,

and for vector r, prefer **r** (in bold) to $\vec{r}$ to prevent uneven line spacing, unless using TeX, which can handle this.

The space around a colon used as a ratio sign (mixed in the proportion 1:2) is narrower than that used around an operational sign, so when using either word or thin spaces around operators, use a thin or hair space respectively on either side of the colon; some styles set the colon closed up. A colon in a set or function such as $\{x: x > 0\}$ is closed up to the preceding letter with a non-breaking space after.

A solidus is set closed up to the characters either side (12/28, *a*/*b*) and there is no space before a factorial (12!). In TeX-based systems there is no constraint in using the vinculum or overbar—the horizontal rule above the square-root sign ($\sqrt{2}$), although it is still best avoided in tightly leaded text, in which case √2 is sufficient or the extent covered by the rule may be shown by parentheses:

$$\surd\left(\frac{x^2}{a^2}+\frac{y^2}{b^2}\right)$$

is sufficient for

$$\sqrt{\left(\frac{x^2}{a^2}+\frac{y^2}{b^2}\right)}$$

14.6.4 Superscripts and subscripts

Reserve superscript letters for variable quantities (set in italic); reserve subscript letters for descriptive notation (set in roman). Asterisks and primes are not strictly superscripts and so should always follow immediately after the term to which they are attached, in the normal way.

When first a subscript and then a superscript are attached to the same symbol or number, mark the subscript to align with the superscript in a 'stack'.

If it is necessary to have multiple levels of superscripts or subscripts, the relationships must be made clear for the typesetter if rekeying is necessary.

Wherever possible, it is customary—and a kindness to the reader's eyesight—to represent each superscript or subscript description by a symbol rather than an abbreviated word. Those subscript descriptions that are standardly made up of one or more initial letters of the word they represent are set in roman type.

14.6.5 Brackets

The preferred order for brackets is {[( )]}. When a single pair of brackets has a specific meaning, such as $[n]$ to denote the integral part of n, they can, of course, be used out of sequence. The vertical bars used to signify a modulus— $|x|$ —should not be used as brackets.

Two further sorts of mathematical brackets may be used: double square brackets ⟦ ⟧ and 'narrow' angle brackets ⟨ ⟩. Angle brackets are used singly in Dirac bra and ket notation and in pairs they may be used to indicate the value of a quantity over a period of time, but they can also be used generally. Note that in mathematical work, the inequality signs < and > are not used as brackets. Double square brackets can be placed outside, and narrow angle brackets inside, the bracket sequence, and are handy for avoiding the re-arrangement of brackets throughout a formula or, especially, a series of formulas. Thus for comparison's sake the formula

$$\left\{1 + [2(a^2 + b^2)(x^2 + y^2) - (ab + xy)^2]\right\}^2 =$$
$$\left\llbracket 1 + \left\{[(a + b)^2 + (a - b)^2](x^2 + y^2) - (ab + xy)^2\right\}\right\rrbracket^2$$

is perhaps better put

$$= \left\{1 + [(\langle a + b\rangle^2 + \langle a - b\rangle^2)(x^2 + y^2) - (ab + xy)^2]\right\}^2$$

14.6.6 Fractions, formulas, and equations

Definitions

The terms *equation*, *formula*, and *expression* are sometimes confused by non-mathematicians; the following explanations may help to clarify usage.

An *equation* is a statement in which two mathematical expressions are linked by an equals sign:

$$y = 12a + b \text{ or } 10 \div 5 = 2$$

A mathematical *expression* does not have an equals sign—

$$v^2 + f \text{ or } 3 - 7i$$

—or can be a single term such as exponential e.

A *formula* is a mathematical rule expressed in words or symbols:

(in words) the circumference of a circle is equal to twice the radius multiplied by pi

(in symbols) $c = 2\pi r$

Layout

As discussed in 14.6.1, digital product has fewer constraints on space than the printed page, so displaying equations where it helps clarity of meaning is desirable; even inline expressions can be satisfactorily presented in TeX, which subtly adjusts interline spacing and character size and spacing. If not set in TeX, simplification remains desirable for equations embedded in text material that would otherwise require extra leading to be introduced. For example,

$$\frac{a}{b} \text{ can be written as } a/b, \text{ and } \frac{x-1}{3} \text{ as } |(x-1)/3|$$

and simple fractions such as ${}^{\pi}\!/_{2}$, ${}^{x}\!/_{3}$, ${}^{a+b}\!/_{4}$ can be written as $\frac{1}{2}\pi$, $\frac{1}{3}x$, $\frac{1}{4}(a+b)$.

But just because the equations can have complex formatting, it does not necessarily mean that they should: work can be reduced and appearance improved by writing such a formula as

$$\lim_{n\to\infty}\left[1-\sin^2\frac{\alpha}{n}\right]^{\frac{-1}{\sin^2\frac{\alpha}{n}}} \quad \text{in the form} \quad \lim_{n\to\infty}[1-\sin^2(a/n)]^{-1/\sin 2(a/n)}$$

In printed product, displayed formulas three or four lines deep can thus be reduced to a space-saving, neater, and more manageable two-line form in almost all instances.

Displayed formulas are usually centred on the page. If there are many long ones, or a wide discrepancy in their length, it may be better to range them all left with a 1- or 2-em indent.

If it is necessary to break a formula—whether displayed or run-in—at the end of a line, it should be done at an operational sign, with the sign carried over to the next line. If an equation takes up two or more lines it should be displayed, with turnover lines aligned on the operational sign (preferably =):

$$\begin{aligned}\mu_0 &= 4\pi \times 10^{-7}\,\mathrm{H\,m^{-1}} \\ &= 12.566\,370\,614\,4 \times 10^{-7}\,\mathrm{H\,m^{-1}} \qquad (2.1)\end{aligned}$$

Any equation referred to at another point in the text should be numbered; any numbered equation should be displayed. It is usually better to include the chapter number in front of the sequence number, such as 2.1 for the first equation in Chapter 2. If, however, the total number of equations is very small, it is possible to use a single sequence of numbers throughout the text. As illustrated above, these numbers are enclosed in parentheses and set full right, aligned on the same line as the final line of the equation.

14.6.7 **Mathematical symbols**

Table 14.4 **Some mathematical symbols and corresponding Unicode code points**

	Unicode U+	**Unicode character name**	**Alternative common name (where different)**
=	003D	EQUALS SIGN	
≠	2260	NOT EQUAL TO	
≡	2261	IDENTICAL TO	identically equal to
≢	2262	NOT IDENTICAL TO	not identically equal to
≈	2248	ALMOST EQUAL TO	approximately equal to
≉	2249	NOT ALMOST EQUAL TO	not approximately equal to
≃	2243	ASYMPTOTICALLY EQUAL TO	
≄	2244	NOT ASYMPTOTICALLY EQUAL TO	
∼	223C	TILDE OPERATOR	equivalent to, of the order of
≁	2241	NOT TILDE	not equivalent to, not of the order of
∝	221D	PROPORTIONAL TO	
→	2192	RIGHTWARDS ARROW	approaches
⇒	21D2	RIGHTWARDS DOUBLE ARROW	implies
⇔	21D4	LEFT RIGHT DOUBLE ARROW	two-way implication
>	003E	GREATER-THAN SIGN	
≯	226F	NOT GREATER-THAN	
<	003C	LESS-THAN SIGN	
≮	226E	NOT LESS-THAN	
≫	226B	MUCH GREATER-THAN	
≪	226A	MUCH LESS-THAN	
≥	2265	GREATER-THAN OR EQUAL TO	
≤	2264	LESS-THAN OR EQUAL TO	
π	03C0	GREEK SMALL LETTER PI	pi
∞	221E	INFINITY	
( )	0028 and 0029	LEFT PARENTHESIS (and RIGHT)	
[ ]	005B and 005D	LEFT SQUARE BRACKET (and RIGHT)	
{ }	007B and 007D	LEFT CURLY BRACKET (and RIGHT)	braces

(*continued*)

Table 14.4 **(Continued)**

	Unicode U+	**Unicode character name**	**Alternative common name (where different)**
⟨ ⟩	27E8 and 27E9	MATHEMATICAL LEFT ANGLE BRACKET (and RIGHT)	narrow angle brackets
⟦ ⟧	27E6 and 27E7	MATHEMATICAL LEFT WHITE SQUARE BRACKET (and RIGHT)	double brackets
˄	02C4	MODIFIER LETTER UP ARROWHEAD	vector product
∅	2205	EMPTY SET	
+	002B	PLUS SIGN	
−	2212	MINUS SIGN	
⋅	22C5	DOT OPERATOR	medial or multiplication dot
ab, $a{\cdot}b$, $a \times b$			*a* multiplied by *b*
a/b, $a \div b$, ab^{-1}			*a* divided by b
a^n			*a* raised to the power of *n*
$\lvert a \rvert$			the modulus (or magnitude) of *a*
$\sqrt{a}$, $a^{1/2}$			square root of *a*
p!			factorial *p*
′	2032	PRIME	minute
″	2033	DOUBLE PRIME	second
°	00B0	DEGREE SIGN	
∠	2220	ANGLE	
∶	2236	RATIO	
∷	2237	PROPORTION	
∴	2234	THEREFORE	hence
∵	2235	BECAUSE	
$\exp x$, e^x			exponential of *x*
$\log_a x$			logarithm to base a of *x*
$\ln x$, $\log_e x$			natural logarithm of *x*
$\lg x$, $\log_{10} x$			common logarithm of *x*
$\sin x$			sine of *x*
$\cos x$			cosine of *x*
$\tan x$			tangent of *x*
$\sin^{-1} x$, $\arcsin x$			inverse sine of *x*
$\cos^{-1} x$, $\arccos x$			inverse cosine of *x*
$\tan^{-1} x$, $\arctan x$			inverse tangent of *x*
∫	222B	INTEGRAL	
Σ	2211	N-ARY SUMMATION	summation
Δ	2206	INCREMENT	delta
Π	220F	N-ARY PRODUCT	product
$\Delta x x$			finite increase of *x*
δx			variation of *x*
dx			total variation of *x*
$f(x)$			function of *x*

Equivalent character and numerical entity codes can be sourced online.

14.7 Astronomy

14.7.1 **Conventions**

Most current astronomy texts follow those recommendations for style set out by the International Astronomical Union (IAU), though other styles may be found, especially in older works. Ensure consistency within a given work, preferring modern to older styles except when reproducing earlier texts.

Capitalize *Earth*, *Moon*, and *Sun* in astronomical contexts but not in general text; the definite article is omitted before *Earth* in technical texts:

> On Earth, valleys occur both on dry land and beneath the sea; there are also valleys on the Moon, Mars, and Venus.
>
> The members organise turtle walks everyday and during full moon and new moon days, intensify the patrols.
>
> Common sense seems to be disappearing off the face of the earth.

Use lower case for *suns* and *moons*. Capitalize *Galaxy* and *Solar System* when it refers to the Milky Way and our planetary system, but *galactic* and *solar* is lower case in all other contexts. While *minor planet* is preferable to *asteroid* in technical usage, *asteroid belt* is an accepted astronomical term.

14.7.2 **Units**

One-letter abbreviations for time units (*second, minute, hour, day, year*) are acceptable (*s, m, h, d, y*) if the context makes them clear. Time units can be written on the line with spaces (*5h 35m 45s*) or superscripted and closed up ($5^{h}35^{m}45^{s}$); aim for consistency. Dates are commonly written in the form *1954 March 31*. A year stated in the form *2000.0* represents an epoch; the '.0' is significant and should not be deleted. Angles are often written with the angle symbol immediately before the decimal point (*0″.001*). Conventional notation is also acceptable but be consistent.

Note *light year* is a unit of distance, not time, is abbreviated with points, *l.y.*, and is used in non-specialist texts. The distance unit *parsec*, symbol *pc*, is preferred in academic texts. SI prefixes (see 14.1.4) can be used with parsec (e.g. *5 Mpc*), unlike the light year. Within the Solar System, distances are measured in astronomical units, symbol AU.

14.7.3 **Stellar nomenclature**

Galaxies, nebulae, and bright star clusters can be designated by names (*Crab Nebula*, *Beehive Cluster*, *Sombrero Galaxy*) or by numbers in a catalogue such as that of Messier (*M1*, *M104*) or the New General Catalogue (*NGC 1952*, *NGC 4594*). Note the prefix M is closed up, whereas a space is inserted after NGC.

The eighty-eight constellations have been assigned official names by the IAU. Many bright stars within these constellations have traditional names (*Sirius*, *Canopus*, *Castor*, and *Pollux*), though astronomers tend to favour the Bayer letter system, in which Greek letters are allotted in alphabetical order by brightness as seen from Earth. The letter can be written in full or using the Greek character, and is used in combination with a three-letter roman abbreviation (no point) assigned by the IAU, so in the constellation Centaurus, for example, the brightest star is written as *Alpha Centauri, Centauri*, or *Cen*. The genitive form of the constellation name is used (*Orionis* not *Orion*), both capitalized when in full form (*Beta Crucis*). An alternative designation is the Flamsteed system, which uses a number and the constellation abbreviation (*61 Cyg, 58 Ori*).

CHAPTER 15

Lists and tables

15.1 Lists

15.1.1 **General principles**

Lists arrange related elements of text in a linear, structured form. Lists may be displayed or run into text; their characteristics are explicit when they are displayed (see 15.1.4), but should be no less rigorously applied when they are embedded in the text (see 15.1.3). Lists may be broken across pages, whereas most tables should not be broken unless their size makes a break unavoidable.

15.1.2 **Arrangement of items**

Regardless of presentation, the text should make it clear what the elements of a list have in common. An open-ended list should specify at least three items, which are sufficiently similar to show how the list might continue: *French, Spanish, Portuguese, etc.* A list comprising examples introduced by *includes*, *for example*, or *such as* should not end tautologically in *etc.*

Lists should be grammatically consistent and balanced—for example, *the zookeeper fed the elephant, a lion, and llamas* unsettles the reader because it is inconsistent in its use (or lack) of articles. Depending on context and emphasis, the first item alone may have an article (*what colours are the legs, eyes, and bill?*), all the items may have no article (*deciduous trees include oak, ash, sycamore, and maple*), or the article for each item may be repeated to emphasize its separateness:

> The government does not yet appear to have given much consideration to balancing the needs of the research community, the taxpayer, and the commercial sectors, for which it is responsible.

A list that is very complex, or just very long, may need to be broken off and displayed (see 15.1.4).

15.1.3 **Lists in running text**

A list occurring as part of a sentence or sentences (a **run-on** or **in-text** list) follows the same rules governing any other sentence. If a colon is used to warn the reader that a list comes next, the introduction should be a main clause:

> The product range expanded to include the following: soluble junior aspirin, gripe mixture, specially formulated children's shampoo and formulations for adults to relieve the symptoms of feverish cold, influenza, irritating coughs and stomach upsets.

Rearranged as *The product range expanded to include soluble junior aspirin, gripe mixture* etc.), a colon should not be used as *The product range expanded to include* is an incomplete sentence.

A straightforward list within a single sentence needs no numbers or letters to aid the reader:

> Rabbits are divided into four kinds, known as warreners, parkers, hedgehogs, and sweethearts

House style will dictate whether the serial, or Oxford, comma (see 4.3.5) is used before the final list item; in the examples below, the first has it, the second does not:

> Markets are held every Tuesday, Thursday, and Saturday
>
> A bridge provides passage over obstacles such as rivers, valleys, roads and railways

It is usually acceptable to arrange into lists information where each element has only a few simple components, so long as these are treated unambiguously; notice in the following example that each element has the same structure:

> Animals with specific medical problems that may be helped by special diets, for example renal disease (restricted protein and phosphorus), inflammatory bowel disease (select protein, limited antigen), or diabetes mellitus (high fibre), should be fed the most appropriate diet for their condition.

For a discussion of the use of commas and semicolons in run-on lists see 4.4 and 4.5.

Information in many run-on lists may equally be displayed (see below).

15.1.4 **Displayed lists**

There are three kinds of displayed list: lists marked by numbers or letters, lists with bulleted points, and simple lists with no markers. The purpose of a display is to draw the reader's attention and to make the material easy to find, consult, and digest; displaying also has the effect of breaking up the text. It is important to establish an underlying logic that determines whether lists are run on or displayed.

The introduction is usually a partial sentence finishing with a colon:

> An advertisement from this period promotes Fennings' Ointment for:
> - abrasions, abscesses, aching feet
> - blotches, bruises, burns, boils
> - chapped hands, chilblains, cuts

Opinions differ as to whether it is permissible to split an infinitive around a colon; Oxford style allows it, as here:

> The committee's overarching recommendations were to:
> - improve daily conditions
> - tackle the inequitable distribution of money, power, and resources
> - measure and understand the causes

the alternative being to repeat 'to' for each item (*to improve, to tackle, to measure*).

End punctuation may vary: full points if list items are sentences; commas or semicolons at the discretion of author or editor (usually none); full point or no full point at the end of the last item. It is worth bearing in mind that if there is no full point at the end of a list, screen-reading software will continue to read the next paragraph as though it were part of the final list point. Omit 'and' and 'or' at the end of the penultimate point in a displayed list.

The preceding sentence can end with a full point or a colon (but no dash). Items that are complete sentences generally start with capitals and end in full points:

> - Fino is a pale and delicate dry sherry of medium alcohol that is best drunk well chilled as an aperitif.
> - Manzanilla is a very dry fino, considered to be the best, and is only produced in Sanlúcar de Barrameda on the coast.
> - Amontillado is nuttier and fuller-bodied than the fino, between 17 and 18 degrees of alcohol.
> - Oloroso is darker and more fragrant, containing between 18 and 20 degrees of alcohol.

- Cream sherries are sweeter and range from the lighter-tasting pale creams to the darker and velvety varieties that make a great after-dinner drink.
- Palo Cortado is a cross between an oloroso and an amontillado, and is very rare as it occurs spontaneously in only a small percentage of fino barrels when the yeast does not form properly.

Sentence fragments are usually lower case, with no end punctuation; the final item may or may not consistently take a full point. In this example, it does:

Legislation will be effective only if it is:

- closely monitored
- comprehensive
- strictly enforced.

Where possible, choose a system and stick to it; if necessary, reword the stem or list items to conform to your choice. However, in a publication with many diverse lists it may be better to allow both types (complete and fragmentary sentences) rather than to impose an artificial uniformity—but avoid mixing both types in one list.

15.1.5 **Numbers, letters, and bullets**

When elements of a list are cited in text, or when it is desirable to show the order or hierarchy of the points being made, numbering the items clarifies the sense. Letters or numbers in italic or roman may be used in run-on or displayed lists. In run-on lists lower-case letters or Roman numerals are often used; they should be in parentheses:

> Problem-solving helps to: (*a*) define the problem; (*b*) divide it into manageable parts; (*c*) provide alternative solutions; (*d*) select the best solution; and (*e*) carry it out and examine the result.

In displayed lists numbers are often used; they may be in roman or bold, with or without a following point, depending on the design decisions made:

1. Activities and action happen extremely quickly when in a product-recall situation. It is suggested that a number of blank copies of the product-recall coordinator's log be held, allowing data to be recorded directly on to this document.
2. The log is a key document and it is extremely important that it is maintained at all stages during the product-recall process.

3. Information in the log must be accurate, clear, and concise.
4. In the product-recall coordinator's absence the log's continued maintenance must be given priority by the Incident Management Team.

There are no hard-and-fast rules about the sequence of number styles in lists of more than one level. In Oxford style Arabic numbers at the first level are followed by italic lower-case letters in parentheses, followed by lower-case Roman numerals in parentheses—1 (*a*) (i) (ii) (iii) (*b*) (i) (ii) (iii) 2 (*a*) (i) (ii) (iii) (*b*) (i) (ii) (iii), etc. But a hierarchy that ran 1 (i) (*a*) (*b*) (*c*) (ii) (*a*) (*b*) (*c*), etc., would be no less acceptable. More complex lists might require, in addition, upper-case letters and Roman numerals above the Arabic numerals in the hierarchy. Numbered sections and subsections are discussed in 1.3.5 and 1.3.6.

If there is no reason for items to be hierarchical, a typographical symbol such as a bullet is used:

The moons closest to Jupiter are:

- Metis
- Adrastea
- Amalthea
- Thebe
- Io
- Europa

Bullets may be ranged left or indented, with an en space separating them from the item. Each typeface has a standard bullet size, so there is normally no need to specify this.

15.1.6 **Simple lists**

Material may also be displayed in simple lists with neither numbers nor bullets:

9.00	arrive at meeting point
9.15	coach leaves
10.30	motorway stop (20 minutes)
11.30	arrival at destination
1.00	lunch in the picnic area
3.45	return to coach
4.00	coach departs for home
5.15	motorway stop (20 minutes)
6.30	arrive home.

15.2 Tables

15.2.1 **General principles**

A table is a set of data systematically displayed in rows and columns. Tables are best used for information that is too complex to be presented clearly in a list or in running text, and particularly for information intended for comparison, either within a single table or between similar tables.

Tables should be numbered by chapter or section in the order in which each is mentioned (*Table 1.1*, *Table 1.2*, etc.) If there are only a few tables they may be numbered in a single sequence throughout the text. Frequent or large tables may be better placed at the end of the chapter or as an appendix to text; tables in an appendix are numbered separately. Unlike lists, tables should not be broken across pages unless their size makes a break unavoidable.

Consider whether tabular presentation is the clearest means of setting out the material. It might be more digestibly presented in a few sentences, or as a figure or graph. Two or more tables might be better merged, or a large one split up. For example, large tables viewed on a small screen can be problematic as they can be unreadable if zoomed out to show the whole structure or hard to interpret if column and row headings are not visible at larger font settings; careful consideration should be given as to whether to split the table into smaller components, for example, or to display the data in a different way.

The information must be relevant to the textual argument and correspond to what the text describes. It should not merely repeat the text. The order of elements in the table should be transparent; if no other order can be imposed on the table as a whole, alphabetical or numerical order may be best.

Omit vertical rules in tables—presentation is clearer and less cluttered without them. Horizontal rules should be kept to a minimum, although head and tail rules are included in most cases.

Most word-processing programs have a tool to create and edit tables; most page layout software can import the result but success depends partly on how well the table has been prepared. In the table body remove unnecessary spaces and tabs, and avoid adding a new line with a hard return—introduce an extra row instead. (A swift way of cleaning up a badly prepared table is to copy it into a blank spreadsheet then back into the document.) Alternatively, present data as columns separated by single tabs, rather than in table cells; include a tab for every column including empty cells. Do not use multiple tabs or spaces between columns. For either method preferably apply word-processor styles to the different table elements: title, column headings, body other than final row, final row, and notes.

Tables can also be prepared efficiently as spreadsheets but authors and editors should be aware that cell formulas will not import into other types of software, only the result of the formula; this is not a problem provided the table is not pasted back into the spreadsheet, e.g. for amendment. Most spreadsheet file formats can be imported into page layout software; however, spreadsheets should not be embedded in word-processed documents but presented separately.

Be prepared for the fact that badly prepared tables may be rekeyed if quicker than tidying up after an unsuccessful import. It is helpful if hard copy or a PDF that shows intended layout accompanies the files, in case vertical alignment is lost. Drawn elements within a table, such as chemical structures, may need to be treated as artwork. When in doubt, flag problematic tables or seek advice from the publisher.

Page layout software treats tables as separate elements, which are positioned once the text has flowed into the page template; consequently it may be more convenient if tables are presented separately rather than in situ in the document—it is worth checking whether your designer or publisher has a preference. If no guidance is given, gather the tables together in one place, or group them by chapter for example, or present them in sequence at the end of the document if only a few. The approximate position of tables should be clearly flagged—by a placement indication in the margin of hard copy or on a separate line in an electronic text, for example:

<<TABLE 1 NEAR HERE>>

All tables should also be cited by number in the text. Citations can be of the style *Table 2.1 summarizes the planning processes*, or in the passive form *The planning processes are summarized* (*Table 2.1*)... Avoid positional references such as 'the table above' or 'the following table', as the final paginated layout is likely to be different from that in the script.

Running heads can be set normally over full-page **portrait** (upright) or **landscape** (turned or broadside) tables, or they can be omitted; consistency is important.

If the author-number reference system is used in the text (see 17.4), any references cited in the table should be numbered in sequence according to where the table appears on the page; if the final position is unknown, number according to where the table is first cited or where it is likely to appear—some adjustment may be needed on page proofs.

15.2.2 **Table headings**

Tables must have headings, which are usually positioned above the table, consisting of the table number and a title that describes what the table contains. The title may use minimal or maximal capitalization according to the style of the work as a whole; no full point is needed after the table number or at the end of the heading.

When units are the same throughout the table they may be defined in the heading, for example:

Table 15.1 Price of apples, by region, 1954–1976 ($/ton)

The heading may also be used to expose the logic behind the order in which the material is presented in the table, for example:

Table 8.1 Tree and shrub species used in hedging (ordered by frequency of use)

15.2.3 **Column and row headings**

The length of column and row headings should be reduced to a minimum, so any repeated information should be removed to the table heading. Similar tables should be treated similarly. Capitalize only the first word and proper names in each heading; do not include end punctuation. Do not number headings unless the numbers are referred to in the text. Spans in headings must not overlap: *1920–9, 1930–9, 1940–9* rather than *1920–30, 1930–40, 1940–50*.

Units, where needed, are usually in parentheses, and should not be repeated in the body.

Column headings with common elements can be combined over a 'straddle' or 'spanner' rule (see Table 15.1).

Table 15.1 **Per cent of deaths from cancer attributable to smoking, 1975 and 1995**

Country	**Male**		**Female**	
	1975	**1995**	**1975**	**1995**
Australia	39	32	4	14
Finland	46	37	1	4
France	33	38	0	2
Hungary	36	53	5	15
UK	52	40	12	20
US	42	43	10	25

Source: *Oxford Textbook of Medicine*, 4th edn, vol. 1 (Oxford University Press, 2003).

Totals may be set off by a space or a rule (see Table 15.2). The word 'Total' may be formatted differently from the body.

Table 15.2 **New Zealand casualties 1939–1945**

Branch	**Deaths**	**Wounded**	**Prisoners**	**Interned**	**Total**
Army	6,839	15,324	7,863	—	30,026
Navy	573	170	54	3	800
Air Force	4,149	255	552	23	4,979
Merchant navy	110	—	—	—	—
TOTAL	11,671	15,749	8,469	26	35,805

Source: R. Kay (ed.), *Chronology: New Zealand in the war, 1939–1945* (Wellington, 1968).

Row headings (also called stub or side headings) may or may not have a heading like other columns. If they do have a heading, ensure that it is appropriate and relevant to all of the stubs. Where row headings turn over to another line, data should be aligned consistently with either the last or the first line of the side heading.

15.2.4 **Body of table**

The body of a table is simply the tabular data introduced and ordered by the columns and stub. Where data drawn from a variety of sources has to be recast to allow comparison, ensure that this does not introduce inaccuracy or anachronism, or distort the material's integrity, especially if the source is in copyright.

The unit(s) used in the table should suit the information: for example, national agricultural production figures may be easier to compare if rounded to 1,000 tons. Rounding also saves space, but editors should not make wholesale changes without querying them with the author. Tables intended for comparison should ideally present their data consistently in similar units. Ensure that abbreviations are consistently applied from one table to another, and that all units and percentages are defined. Exclude end punctuation. Mathematical operators (+, –, >, etc.) may be close up to surrounding digits to save space if necessary. Ensure that the correct symbols are used for minus signs, hyphens, and en and em rules; on hard copy mark their first occurrence in each table. Add zeros in front of decimal points if omitted; the exception may be probability values, for example $p < .05$, as house styles vary.

Familiar abbreviations are acceptable, such as %, &, country abbreviations, and those well known in the reader's discipline. Ambiguous abbreviations such as *n/a* ('not applicable' or 'not available') and unfamiliar abbreviations must be explained in the notes (see 15.2.5): the reader should be able to understand the table independently of the text, particularly in digital product as the table may open in a separate window or screen. Repeat information rather than use ditto marks. Em rules or en rules are often used in empty fields, but can indicate either 'no data' or 'not available', so it may be better to specify which is the case.

Turn-lines in simple items in columns are indented 1 em, with no extra vertical space between items (see for example column 2 in Table 15.3). Turn-lines in discursive or run-on items (for example data in a chronology) can be set full left in a column as panels or blocks of text, not indented, with a space between each item (see for example column 4 in Table 15.3).

Related figures in a single column should have the same number of decimal places. Unrelated figures may have a different number of decimal places, but only if reflecting different levels of accuracy. Editors should check with the author before rounding them to a common level. Percentage totals may vary slightly above or below 100 per cent as a result of rounding.

Table 15.3 **Beaufort wind scale**

Force	Description of wind	Mean wind speed (*knots*)	Specification for use at sea
0	calm	less than 1	Sea like a mirror
1	light air	1–3	Ripples with appearance of scales are formed, but without foam crests
2	light breeze	4–6	Small wavelets, still short but more pronounced; crests have a glass appearance and do not break
3	gentle breeze	7–10	Large wavelets; crests begin to break; foam of glassy appearance, perhaps scattered white horses
4	moderate breeze	11–16	Small waves becoming longer; fairly frequent white horses
5	fresh breeze	17–21	Moderate waves, taking a more pronounced long form; many white horses are formed
6	strong breeze	22–7	Large waves begin to form; the white foam crests are more extensive everywhere (probably some spray)
7	moderate gale *or* near gale	28–33	Sea heaps up and white foam from breaking waves begins to be blown in streaks along the direction of the wind
8	fresh gale *or* gale	34–40	Moderately high waves of greater length; edges of crests begin to break into spindrift; foam is blown in well-marked streaks
9	strong gale	41–7	High waves; dense streaks of foam; crests of waves begin to topple, tumble, and roll over
10	whole gale *or* storm	48–55	Very high waves with long overhanging crests; the resulting foam is blown in dense white streaks; the sea takes a white appearance; the tumbling of the sea becomes heavy and shock-like; visibility affected
11	storm *or* violent storm	56–63	Exceptionally high waves at sea; the sea is completely covered with white patches of foam; visibility affected
12+	hurricane	64 and above	The air is filled with foam and spray; sea completely white with driving spray; visibility very seriously affected

Sources: Smithsonian Institution, *Smithsonian Meteorological Tables* (1966); Hydrographer of the Navy (UK).

When statistical matter within each column is unrelated, align it on the left with the column heading (see Table 15.4). Optionally, the longest line can be designed so that it is centred under the heading, if the result suits the material better.

When statistical matter within the columns is related, align it so that the longest item aligns with the column heading and other items align with the decimal point or with the final digit on the right (see Table 15.5).

Table 15.4 **Comparison of four forests with infection present**

	Forest			
	Black	**New**	**Sherwood**	**Speymouth**
Age	20	43	35	69
Area sampled, acres	6.9	11.2	7.5	27.6
No. of trees	10,350	4,702	2,650	945
No. of infected trees	163	98	50	23
Infected trees, %	1.63	0.9	20.3	10.7
Chi-square for observed values	7.83	11.09	4.98	too small

Table 15.5 **Working days lost through strikes per 1,000 workers, six countries, 1960–1999 (annual averages)**

	1960–4	**1971–5**	**1980–4**	**1990–5**	**1995–9**
France	352	232	90	36	98
Germany	34	57	50	17	1
Italy	1,220	1,367	950	148	33
Japan	302	188	10	3	2
United Kingdom	242	1,186	480	29	23
United States	722	484	160	33	13

Source: S. Ackroyd et al. (eds), *Oxford Handbook of Work and Organization* (Oxford University Press, 2005), derived from: J. Davies, 'International Comparisons of Labour Disputes in 1999', *Labour Market Trends*, 109/4; D. Bird, 'International Comparisons of Industrial Disputes in 1989 and 1990', *Employment Gazette*, 99/12; *Employment Gazette*, 90/2; *Department of Employment Gazette*, 79/2.

15.2.5 Notes to tables

Notes fall directly beneath the table to which they refer; they are not incorporated with the text's footnote system. Set notes to table width, normally one size down from table size. General notes, notes on specific parts of the table, and probability values should appear in this order; source notes may go first or last provided they are treated consistently. Ensure that notes to a table cannot be mistaken for text recommencing after the table. General and source notes are uncued and often preceded by *Note*: and *Source*: respectively. The reference structure of source notes matches that used elsewhere in the work. Each note should generally begin on a new line and end with a full point (see Table 15.6), although notes of a kind can run on, separated by semicolons, to save space:

CI = confidence interval; OR = odds ratio; SD = standard deviation

Mark specific notes with a system of indices different from that used in the text (for example * † §), as in Table 15.6, or superscript letters or numbers (italic or roman). Cues in a table read across; for example, a cue in the last column of the first row precedes a cue in the first column of the second row.

Probability values may be indicated by a system of asterisks, in which case the convention should be explained in a note: '*p < .05; **p < .01; ***p < .001'. Editors should not impose other symbols in this case.

Table 15.6 **Issues of the de luxe edition of *Ulysses*, copies 1–1,000**

		Price		
Copies	**Paper**	**France(FF)**	**UK(£/s./d.)**	**USA($)**
1–100*	Holland handmade	350	7/7/-	30
101–250	Verge d'Arches	250	5/5/-	22
251–1,000†	linen	150	3/3/-	12

* Autographed by Joyce.
† This issue, the cheapest of the three, was still 5–7 times costlier than the average book.

15.2.6 **Presentation on the page**

Tables may be placed on the page in portrait or landscape format. Authors are not responsible for determining the format in which tables will be set. A wide table may fit a page's measure if the arrangement of column and stub heads is reversed, but editors should consult the author first. Do not rearrange similar or related tables into differing structures.

Large portrait and landscape tables may be presented over two or more pages of text. Hard-copy editors should indicate preferred places where a large table may be split; on-screen editors can do the same on a PDF or in a note to the designer. Headings do not need to be repeated where continued tables can be read across or down a facing page. If the table continues on a verso page, however, indicate which headings need to be repeated. On-screen editors should not repeat headings in files that will be imported into page-layout software as that will be done automatically.

In page proofs insert a 'continued' line, such as 'Table 2 *cont.*', only if the table turns over to a verso page, not if it extends over facing pages. When several continued tables are given in succession, a short form of each table's title can be helpful.

CHAPTER 16

Illustrations and artwork

16.1 General principles

16.1.1 **Introduction**

Illustrations are non-textual graphic elements, commonly referred to as **artwork**, used to enhance publications of all kinds, and are an essential part of many works, from children's stories to technical manuals, in both conventional print and online/digital media. They may be, for example, photographic images, graphs, charts, maps, or drawings/cartoons, essential to the delivery of the ideas in the publication or purely cosmetic/decorative. They may be embedded in the main text or appear separately; they may be an integral part of the design. Multimedia publication also allows the integrated use of audio and video elements, although this aspect is beyond the scope of the present chapter.

Historically, original artwork was typically supplied to publishers as black and white drawings, tone photographs, or colour transparencies (hard copy; see 16.4). It is now standard publishing practice for illustrations to be handled as **digital artwork** (see 16.3), created by the author using digital photography or suitable graphics software packages, or produced by scanning existing hard copies.

There are different criteria for preparing/publishing illustrations in print and digital media—an illustration created for online use (e.g. an infographic; see 16.2.4) will generally not be suitable for high-quality printing. It is important that authors prepare and supply artwork in the correct format for the final output.

Illustrations not created by the author(s) for a specific publication (including illustrations previously published elsewhere or images taken from the web) may be subject to copyright, and permission to reproduce them must be obtained from the copyright holder (see 16.5).

The effective use of illustrations can significantly improve the clarity of the messages conveyed. Consult with your editor/publisher and prepare them at the same time as writing the text. Consider their layout in relation to the overall material, whether printed or digital. Do not let them be an afterthought!

16.1.2 **Numbering and citations**

Figures (illustrations together with their **captions**) may be numbered by chapter or section in the order in which they appear (e.g. the second figure in *Chapter 1* is *Figure 1.2* and the third figure in *Section III* is *Figure III.3*); if there are only a few, they can be numbered in a single sequence throughout the text. Figures in an appendix are numbered separately (e.g. the fourth figure in *Appendix A1* is *Figure A1.4*). Numbered **plates** also use a separate sequence (see 16.1.3).

Depending on the nature of the publication, figures may be subdivided into other graphic elements, such as schemes, flowcharts, structures, maps, etc. These can be included in the same sequence with other illustrations or numbered separately for the sake of clarity.

References to figures may be variously styled—consistency is most important, whichever style is adopted. They can be cited actively:

> Fig. 1.3 shows a flowchart of mass input/output.

or passively:

> A flowchart using boxes for the process units and arrows for the mass inputs/outputs provides an overview of the process (Fig. 1.3).

All the illustrations in the text should be cited (this will enable hyperlinks to be included in digital media).

Avoid positional references (*the figure above* or *the following illustration*) in the original text, as the configuration may change during make-up and on different viewing platforms (see 16.2.3).

16.1.3 **Page make-up**

The typesetter/designer is usually responsible for overseeing the placement of illustrations, ideally following as close as possible to their first citation in the text. The exceptions are plate sections (groups of high-quality images that benefit from the use of glossy art paper) in printed works—these will be inserted in the most convenient place for subsequent collation.

Page make-up/web design software is used by the typesetter/designer to assemble pages digitally to generate output suitable for printing or on-screen viewing. Various elements such as text and digital artwork are combined in a single file; the elements can be 'cut & pasted' on-screen.

Indicate the approximate position of figures with a **cue** (or **tag**) in square brackets in the original text, for example:

[FIGURE 1.3]

The aesthetics of page design often dictate the layout of illustrations for print output. Pictures generally appear at the bottom or top of a printed page, or may bleed over the cut edge. Illustrations to be set landscape should always be placed with the head of the illustration turned to the left. In double-column formats, multiple illustrations should follow the flow of the text on the page: down the left column and then down the right. Running heads and page numbers are generally omitted from full-page illustrations in books.

Space should be allowed for the caption, and between the illustration and the text or adjacent illustrations. Ensure that nothing important is lost in the gutter between two pages when illustrations span a two-page spread.

Different criteria may be applied to digital publications, such as web pages and ebooks, to take advantage of the opportunities offered by such media. For example, figures in academic journals may only appear as thumbnails in online versions—these are hyperlinked to full-size versions that open in a new page of a web browser. Be aware that illustrations may be resized and reformatted automatically to provide optimum viewing on different digital platforms (e.g. a large computer monitor or a smaller mobile device).

16.1.4 **Scaling (sizing)**

The final dimensions of the illustrations will depend on the type of publication (printed or digital) and the layout specifications (e.g. one or two columns) developed by the editor and designer.

Hard-copy original artwork may need to be enlarged/reduced to match the final dimensions (see 16.4.1). Digital artwork should be supplied at the final dimensions and resolution (see 16.3).

Similar illustrations need to be in proportion, especially when being compared. Cropping of hard copy may mean that an **original** does not have to be reduced as much. Be aware of possible cropping restrictions on copyright images (see 16.5 and Chapter 20).

16.1.5 **Labelling (lettering) and shading**

Traditionally, authors provided hard-copy roughs that were copy-edited and sent to an illustrator for redrawing, at which stage any essential changes could be made. However, most illustrations are now handled as author-prepared digital artwork (see 16.3) and the publisher may not want to have them redrawn, in which case the changes that can be made will be restricted (e.g. it may not be practical to match editorial style in the text with that of labels/lettering). It is therefore helpful for editors to know whether changes are possible.

Ensure final-size characters are large enough to remain sharply defined in the published version. **Labels** should be no smaller than 8 points (Helvetica, Arial, or a similar sans-serif font is commonly used). Line widths should be no less than ½ point.

If **lettering** would obscure an item, use leader lines pointing out the relevant features (Figure 16.1).

Spelling, hyphenation, symbols, and abbreviations for units should match those in the captions (see 16.1.7) and text.

Tints/shading may be used to differentiate areas of an illustration (Figure 16.2), but colour or similar effects should not be the only method used to convey meaning. Ensure that vital information is not lost if the image is displayed without colour. Avoid using solid black for large areas, as this may cause problems in conventional printed works.

16.1.6 **Key**

The key explains the symbols or conventions used in the illustration. It is usually part of the artwork, although if it is simple it may be included as part of the caption (see 16.1.7). Check that the key corresponds with

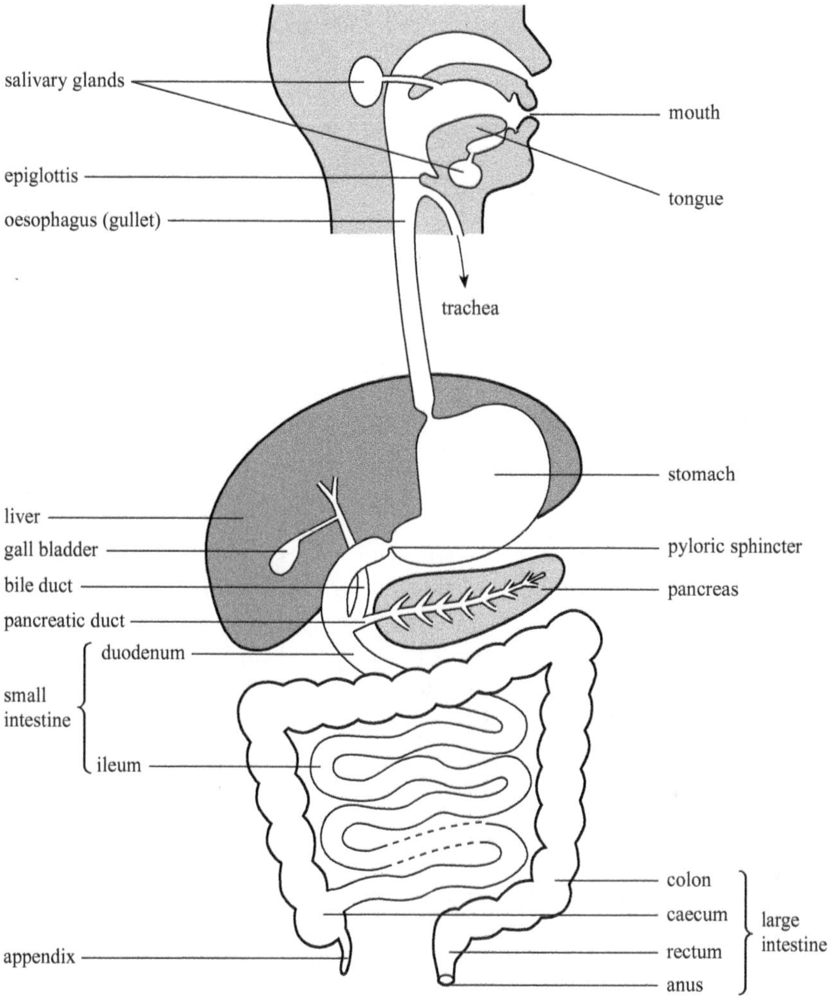

Figure 16.1 **The human alimentary canal.**

the caption and text; it may be necessary to relabel artwork taken from other sources accordingly.

16.1.7 **Captions**

Most illustrations (apart from purely decorative illustrations) require a caption (a complete sentence) or legend (an incomplete sentence, such as in Figure 16.3, although the terms are often used interchangeably), which should indicate the essential content of the illustration. These generally appear beneath (sometimes beside) the illustration, depending

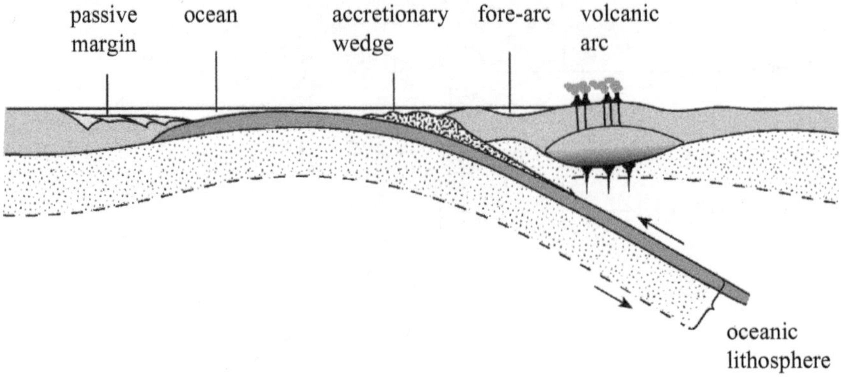

Figure 16.2 **Accretionary wedge.**

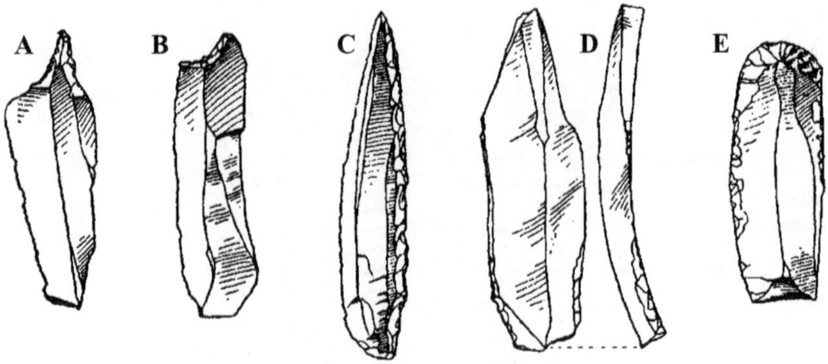

Figure 16.3 **Upper Palaeolithic blade tools in flint. (A) Solutrean piercer, Dordogne. (B) Magdalenian concave end-scraper, Dordogne. (C) Gravettian knife point, Dordogne. (D) Magdalenian burin, Dordogne. (E) End-scraper, Vale of Clwyd.**

on the page design. Captions or legends should begin with the number of the figure or illustration. Source lines or other wording required by the copyright holder should also appear as part of the caption.

Figures (i.e. the illustration and caption) should be able to stand alone from the text. Captions should explain the illustration in full. They should be concise and extraneous information should be removed. Remove or reduce labelling on the illustration by including explanations in the caption, as in Figure 16.3. Use of descriptive terms such as *above, below, top, bottom, left, right*, and *clockwise* can also help identify elements in an illustration or components of a group of illustrations.

Ensure the format of the caption text is consistent.

Supply captions as a list at the end of a chapter or in a separate file. Do not integrate them with the text or incorporate them in the artwork (see 16.1.6). Captions for unnumbered illustrations should be clearly identifiable.

Check that spellings, hyphenation, and symbols correspond to those used in the artwork and text.

16.2 Specific types of illustrations

16.2.1 **Maps**

Maps are difficult to execute and often require special attention. Information must be relevant, and presented in a clear and uncluttered fashion. The level of detail should relate to the reasons why the reader will consult the map. When a map is to be (re)drawn by the publisher (coordinated to match the design of a publication), supply a rough sketch or copy:

- *Geographical and political features* must be easily distinguishable by line weights, tints/shading, and typographic conventions: for example, countries in capitals (FRANCE), towns in capitals and lower case (Paris), major physical features such as mountain ranges and oceans in italic capitals (*PYRENEES, ATLANTIC OCEAN*), and individual mountains and smaller bodies of water (rivers and lakes) in italic capital and lowercase (*Seine, Aneto*). Spellings must agree with the text. Supply text for any key or note to appear on the map.
- Incorporate a *scale bar*.
- *North* is assumed to be at the top (usually the top of the page unless set landscape). If this is not the case, include an arrow to indicate north.
- Indicate any *cropping*, either to allow for enlargement of an area or to minimize peripheral features.
- If appropriate, give the *projection*.

16.2.2 **Graphs**

Graphs show the relationship between variable quantities. The horizontal (x) and vertical (y) axes should be labelled with a quantity (include any units in parentheses—ensure these match the caption and text). The labels should be parallel to the axis, reading from bottom to top for the y axis (Figure 16.4).

The intervals in the axis divisions should be consistent (unless it is a logarithmic scale). The numbers differentiating divisions should be horizontal for both axes. The numbers do not have to start at zero. A zero symbol should precede any decimal point for values less than one (e.g. *0.86* not *.86*)

Extra rules other than the x and y axes, such as gridlines, should be deleted unless there is a need to read off a specific value on a curve, but this is unusual. Arrowheads can be drawn at the ends of axes to indicate a trend but are superfluous if the axis has a scale.

Bar charts are used to represent categories of discrete data. They have vertical or horizontal columns where the column length is proportional to the quantity in that category; only the y axis has a scale. All the columns should be the same width and usually have a gap between.

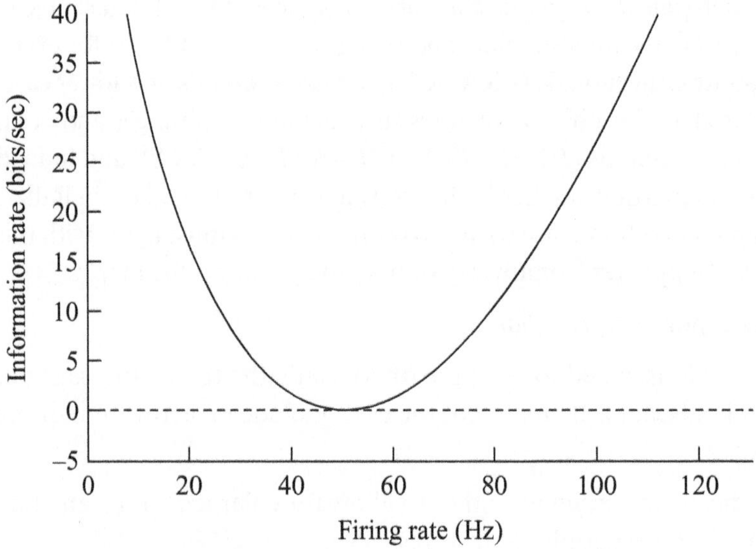

Figure 16.4 **Simple graph.**

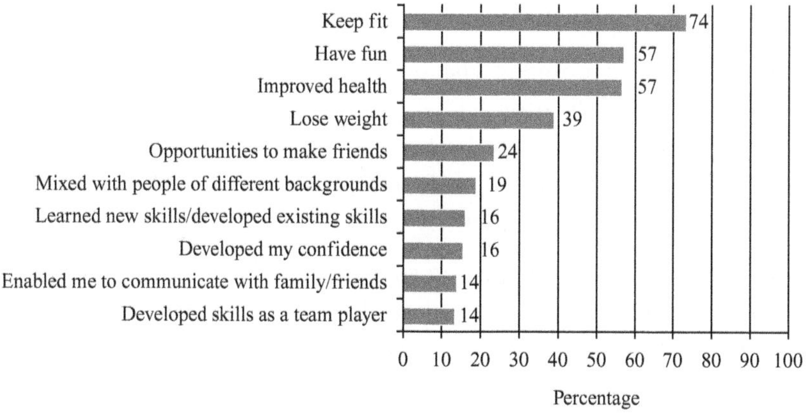

Figure 16.5 **Example of a bar chart. From *Experience of sport and physical activity in Northern Ireland 2011/12* (Department of Culture, Arts and Leisure, 2013).**

A *histogram* represents continuous data so the column widths may vary as their area is proportional to the frequency; the columns therefore have no gaps between. Both x and y axes have a scale.

The format should be consistent throughout a series of graphs, and be consistent with the text and caption.

Graphs created using generic word-processing, spreadsheet, or presentation software are not suitable for professional printing. Graphs produced using custom software for specific applications may be suitable provided the output settings match those required for digital artwork files (see 16.3).

16.2.3 Medical images

Radiographs (X-rays), scans, and other diagnostic images, as well as pictures of pathology specimens or micrographs, should be supplied as high-resolution digital files. Micrographs should contain internal scale markers.

Remove any patient identification details from such images (and accompanying text and captions). Use of a photograph of a patient will require a Patient Consent Form even if any identifying features have been removed/obscured.

16.2.4 **Infographics**

Infographics are a popular visual shorthand for conveying complex concepts (data visualization). They provide clear visual representations of data, integrating words and graphics to reveal patterns or trends (e.g. weather maps), or to provide information (e.g. maps of public transportation) that would be unwieldy in text form.

Static infographics may be produced using standard graphics packages. Online interactive infographics that allow the viewer to interact with data can be created using a range of software available on the Internet.

16.3 Digital artwork and graphics files

16.3.1 **Overview**

The preferred method of handling illustrations for publication in all types of media is via digital artwork. This route has many benefits to the author and the publisher, and has clear advantages over using hard copy. By originating and manipulating artwork, the author has complete control over the final illustration and the production times/costs are minimized for the publisher.

It is very important that digital artwork is prepared in the correct format. Many publishers have their own specific guidelines for authors and general guides/resources are available on the web.

Digital artwork can be created using graphics/image-editing software (see 16.3.2), by a digital camera (see 16.3.5), or by scanning original hard copy to produce digital files (see 16.3.6).

16.3.2 **Files and file types**

Graphics files can be bitmap (also known as raster) or vector based.

- *Bitmap graphics* consist of many small elements called pixels. **Bitmap images** are *continuous tone* images (see 16.4) produced when using a digital camera or scanning an existing illustration, or can be created and edited in raster graphics software.
- *Vector graphics* consist of separate mathematically described shapes called objects. **Vector images** are usually used for *line artwork* (see 16.4) and can be created using vector graphics software.

A final illustration may use a combination of vector and bitmap elements.

Graphics files are supported by many file formats. Standard image formats include:

JPEG A common bitmap file format produced by most digital cameras; best used for continuous tone illustrations. JPEG is a lossy format, meaning that it discards colour information to produce a compressed file. This is not normally an issue for online publication, but may be noticeable in print.

TIFF The preferred bitmap format for continuous tone illustrations. TIFF files are significantly larger than JPEG files and can be either uncompressed or compressed using lossless compression. Unlike JPEG, TIFF files can support multiple layered images, where elements of the image exist in separate layers that can be manipulated without affecting the others.

EPS A standard format for vector (line artwork) graphics. Bitmaps can also be embedded in EPS files, making this a recommended format for combined vector/bitmapped illustrations. EPS files are high-quality, very large memory files because of their lossless format.

These exchange formats can be viewed using most software packages.

Application-specific formats such as PSD (bitmap) and AI (vector) are designed to be understood only by the software in which they were created (Adobe Photoshop and Illustrator, respectively); however, they can be easily converted to exchange formats.

PDF files are used for creating and digitally transferring documents, including text and graphics, in the final intended layout. These may be suitable for print, depending on the quality of any embedded images and the output options selected.

Word-processor, spreadsheet, and presentation files are not suitable for high-quality print output. GIF files, which can also support *animated graphics*, and PNG files are useful for simple web images, but not for print. BMP files offer no advantage over other formats and should be avoided. RAW files are produced by high-end digital cameras, and require processing and conversion to a standard format such as JPEG or TIFF.

16.3.3 **Size and resolution**

Supply digital artwork at the same size as the final published illustration. Dimensions may be given in units of length for print output (e.g. 10 × 15 cm) or pixels for on-screen viewing (e.g. 800 × 600 pixels).

Resolution is the number of dots or pixels in a given area: dots per inch (dpi) or pixels per inch (ppi) (for most practical purposes the units are interchangeable). It is very important that digital artwork be supplied at the correct resolution to ensure high-quality output—low-resolution artwork is not suitable for print, and may result in requests for resubmission and delays in publication.

Minimum resolutions (at final image size) for print:

- line artwork: 600 dpi (simple) to 1200 dpi (detailed)
- tone artwork: 300 dpi
- combined line/tone: 600–900 dpi.

Be aware that the requirements for printed and on-screen images are very different. The resolution of a computer monitor is 72–96 dpi, meaning that although an image may look acceptable on a monitor and be suitable for online use, it may be of insufficient resolution for print purposes.

Resolution is not a set value—it is variable and is inversely proportional to visual size. If the visual size is doubled, the resolution halves, reducing the quality (Figure 16.5). The size and resolution of digital artwork can be determined and revised in most graphics software.

Images copied from the web are usually too low resolution for print. It may be possible to obtain high-resolution versions (and appropriate copyright clearance; see 16.5) from the website administrator.

16.3.4 **Handling colour**

Ensuring accurate reproduction of colour illustrations is an important consideration and is critical for certain types of fine art/photography publications.

Computer monitors/desk-top printers and conventional printers use different models (colour spaces) to handle colour. Computer monitors use RGB (Red, Green and Blue) mode to display colours, whereas conventional printing uses CMYK (Cyan, Magenta, Yellow, and Key

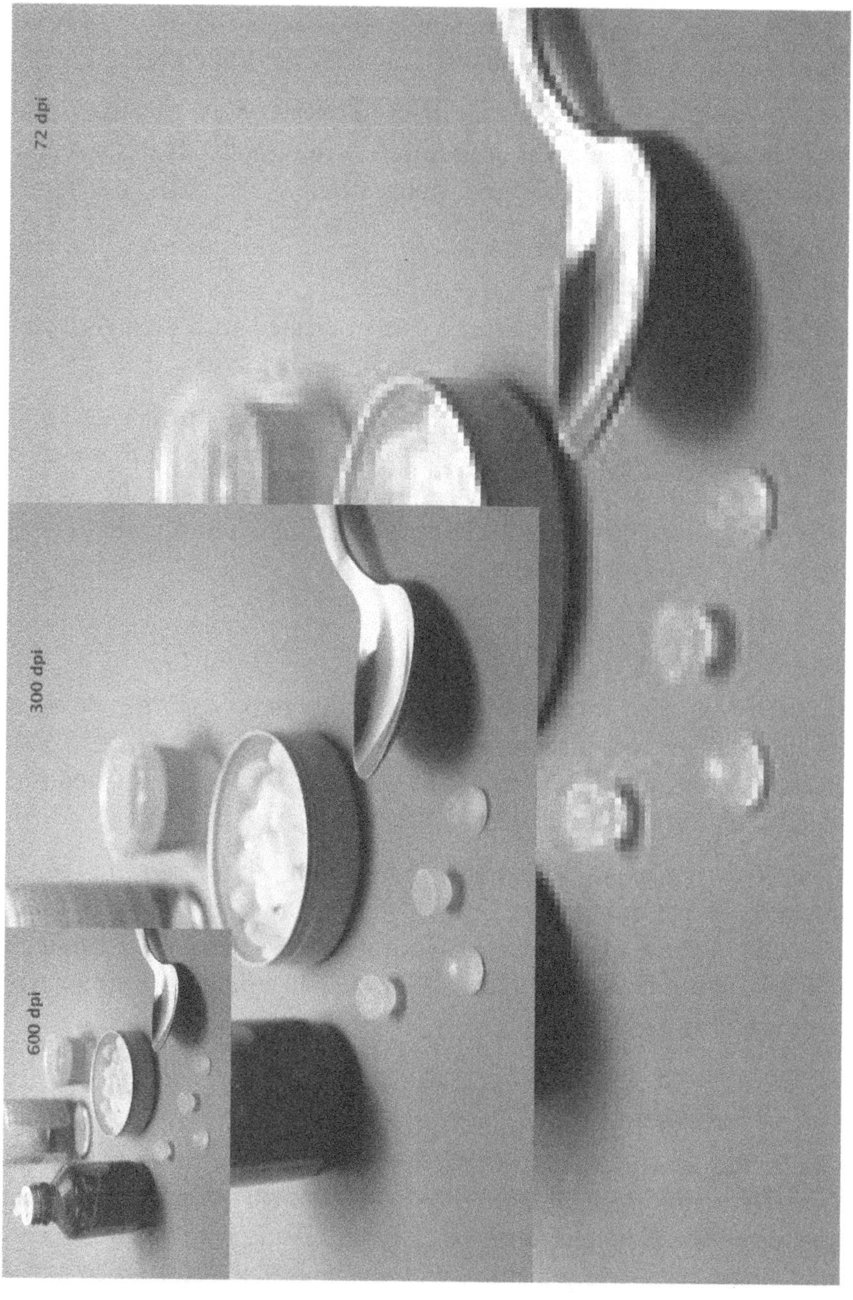

Figure 16.6 **The same photograph at different resolutions.**

(Black) mode. As a result, an image viewed on a computer monitor may not match the final colour rendition of the printed version.

Ideally, monitors should be calibrated to assess colour accuracy, and files should be created in the appropriate colour mode: RGB for online publication and CMYK for print publication.

16.3.5 **Digital cameras**

Image files of hard copy originals can be created with a good digital camera (at least 10 megapixels and a high-quality lens).

When taking digital photographs, ensure that the lighting is bright and even (without shadows), ISO is set to the lowest value, the image is sharply in focus, extraneous elements are cropped out and the camera is set to produce the largest file size possible. RAW files should be converted to a standard file format (see 16.3.2).

16.3.6 **Scanning**

Hard copy may be scanned to produce digital files. Scans should be at the final size and orientation, and at the correct resolution (see 16.3.3). The originals should be free from dust and other debris, and the scanned colours should match the original.

It is better to scan originals rather than scan a printed copy, to reduce interference patterns (moiré) caused by previous screening. A high-resolution scan of a poor original will not improve the quality, although it is possible to touch-up and relabel scanned originals using image-editing software.

16.3.7 **Submitting files**

Check that artwork files conform to any specified requirements. Individual illustrations (and parts) should be supplied as separate files. Do not embed the illustrations in text or other files. Ensure all layered files are flattened (the layers that make up the image are compressed into a single plane).

Name the files in a logical style following the conventions used in the text (e.g. in a simple format *Figure_1.1.tif* or with a project identifier

Smith_Fig_3.tif). If figures are not numbered, use a brief unambiguous descriptive name to match the corresponding citations and captions (e.g. *Ozone_distribution_2014.tif*).

Compile a separate artwork log listing all of figures (and parts) and corresponding file names, together with any notes (e.g. unusual file formats).

Final artwork files may be submitted on portable media (CD/DVD, flash drives, etc.) or over the Internet via file-sharing sites/FTP. Group large numbers of individual files in a logical directory/folder structure (e.g. by section/chapter). Keep a backup copy of all files.

16.4 Line and tone artwork: hard copy

Traditionally, publishers recognize two main types of illustration: line artwork and tone artwork, both of which may be black and white or colour. Final illustrations may be combinations of line and tone artwork.

- *Line illustrations* can be graphs, charts, plans, maps, pen-and-ink drawings, woodcuts/etchings or musical scores—typically, any illustration that has no continuous tone and cannot be typeset.
- *Continuous tone illustrations* are usually photographs, but may also be drawn and painted artwork. To simulate the subtle transitions of tone in print, the picture is broken up into a series of dots (half-tone). This was formerly done by screening; however, developments in digital reproduction technology enabling the production of print-ready material mean that this process has been largely superseded.

The distinction between line and tone illustrations has important consequences when creating digital artwork files (see 16.3).

16.4.1 **Submitting original hard copies**

Hard copy may be submitted only if it is not possible for an author to create digital artwork from existing material (through scanning or digital photography; see 16.3.5 and 16.3.6) or if originals need to be redrawn (check with your editor/publisher).

- Line artwork should be clear and crisply defined, mounted on card.
- Glossy photographic prints with good contrast produce the best results.
- Present slides as 35 mm (mounted) or larger-format colour transparencies.
- Previously screened illustrations and photocopies reproduce poorly.

Reductions/enlargements should be indicated as a percentage (e.g. '67 per cent' indicates a reduction of the artwork *to* 67 per cent of its original size—not reduced *by* 67 per cent).

Any relabelling and cropping should be marked on a photocopy—the original may be scanned to capture the image without redrawing from scratch. Supply an accompanying text file for each label. Avoid making any marks on the original.

Present a composite illustration with more than one part as individual pieces of artwork, clearly identified and accompanied by a photocopy showing the desired layout.

Identify all artwork with the title of the work and identification number, and include name/address details to enable the publisher to return the (often valuable) artwork. Originals should be securely packaged.

16.5 Permissions and acknowledgements

Most illustrations are protected by copyright law and permission (clearance) must be obtained in good time from the copyright holder to reproduce any illustrations not originated by the author specifically for a particular publication. These include illustrations from other publications, including your own material if it has been previously published elsewhere, pictures taken by professional photographers, and material taken from the Internet. Where there is any doubt (e.g. when a modified version of an illustration is to be used) it is prudent to ask for permission. Keep a record of all correspondence relating to obtaining permissions. For more information, see Chapter 20.

The moral rights (see 20.2.4) of any photographer/artist should be asserted because even if copyright has been assigned to a third party, the originator retains the moral rights to their work. When using your own photographs for commercial purposes you may need to use Release Forms to obtain permission from any individuals (or their guardian) in them or anyone who owns property in them. Patient Consent Forms should be obtained for any photographs of patients used in medical publications (see 16.2.3).

Illustrations may also be sourced through picture libraries. These are agencies that represent the creators or the assigned copyright holders of images and sell licences for the images they hold. Some picture libraries also provide images that are in the public domain.

The wording of the copyright information may be stipulated by the copyright holder. This should be included at the end of the caption itself, unless the copyright holder instructs otherwise.

CHAPTER 17

Notes and references

17.1 General principles

Publications of many kinds employ pointers within the main body of the text to refer the reader to explanatory or additional material either on the same page or elsewhere in the work. Academic publications in particular need an apparatus to provide references to support, and sometimes to clarify and amplify, what is said in the text. It is of course the responsibility of the author to ensure that the text is properly supported by appropriate sources, that the sources are correctly quoted or interpreted, and that the citations are accurate, complete, and follow an appropriate style. It is, however, the duty of the editor to ensure that the references in a work are presented in a clear and consistent manner. The reader may well see sloppy references as symptoms of generally careless scholarship.

The systems commonly adopted vary greatly between disciplines, and there may be considerable variation even within a single discipline, according to the preferences of particular publishers, editors, and authors. Furthermore, as in other aspects of editing, practice changes over time, and new styles may be taken up very unevenly. The most traditional system employs numbers, letters, or symbols as cues to direct the reader to notes which are printed either at the foot of the page to which they relate (**footnotes**) or in a group at the end of the text (**endnotes**). Alternatively, in what is known as the **author–date** or **Harvard** system, the cues may take the form of an author's name and date of publication (or in the **author–number** or **Vancouver** system simply a reference number) within parentheses that enable the reader to identify the work in a list of full references at the end of the text. Various permutations are possible. In some ways life is made easier for both author and editor if a commonly recognized system is adopted, but agreed adaptation to the needs of a particular work can prove beneficial. What matters most is that the necessary information should be conveyed to the reader (of both print and electronic materials) clearly and economically.

The primary function of scholarly annotation is to identify for the reader the sources of what is said in text. This may be the location of a verbatim quotation or—just as important in an academic work—the basis for a statement by the author. Simple references of this kind can be accommodated by systems that use brief parenthetical references in the text to take the reader to a consolidated bibliography (see 17.3 and 17.4). Such references are particularly well suited to scientific publications, but they are also used in the social sciences and increasingly in the humanities. In the humanities it is normally notes that are the essential feature of the supporting apparatus. Notes are a convenient vehicle not only for complex bibliographical citations but also, for example, for acknowledgements, further discussion, supporting original text, and bibliographical surveys (see 17.2.1). Notes may be used in conjunction with a bibliography or more selective suggestions for further reading, or with a list of abbreviations of frequently cited sources (see 17.2.6).

17.2 Footnotes and endnotes

17.2.1 **The use of notes in the humanities**

An apparatus based on notes is normal in the humanities, where more is often needed than a simple link to a consolidated list of published sources. For example, manuscript sources are more easily cited in notes than in the systems of parenthetical reference used in scientific publications (see also 18.6). Different sources, or versions of a source, may be compared and evaluated in a note. If a quotation is given in translation in the text the original may perhaps be given in a note, or conversely (this may be scrupulous scholarly practice where doubt is possible about the correctness of a translation, but it should not be adopted routinely without good reason). It is sometimes helpful to include in a note a brief survey of the literature on a particular topic, or a summary of a debate, though authors should be discouraged from needlessly transforming notes into bibliographies. Author's acknowledgements also fit neatly into notes. Also, notes can perform special functions in scholarly editions of original texts, where they may, for instance, supply variant readings from different manuscripts.

The flexibility that makes notes such a useful tool can be abused. Authors sometimes include in notes further discussion of a question raised in the text, or of some related issue. While this cannot be outlawed altogether, it should be avoided wherever possible. For the most part, if a point is important and relevant enough to be discussed at all it should be dealt with in the text. Notes should be kept as short as possible, and inessential material excluded. The best place for extensive but essential ancillary matter that cannot be accommodated in the text may be an appendix. The main function of notes (other than those in editions of texts) remains the clear and concise presentation of necessary references.

17.2.2 **Footnotes or endnotes?**

In printed material, notes may be either **footnotes**, placed at the foot of the page to which they relate, or **endnotes**, placed in a single sequence at the end of the text. In multi-author volumes and journals that employ endnotes they should be printed at the end of an individual chapter or article; otherwise they are normally placed at the end of the book, in a separately numbered sequence for each chapter.

Some categories of note, such as those that explain the meaning of words in the text or provide variant readings, have an especially strong claim to be placed at the foot of the page. Footnotes are in general much more convenient for the reader, who can keep track of them without the annoying disruption of flipping back and forth between text and notes in the course of reading. The setting of notes at the foot of the page can make page layout more complex than placing them together at the end of the text, depending on the length and number of footnotes.

In material presented in formats that do not rely on a fixed page, such as ebooks and some websites, the distinction between footnotes and endnotes becomes less meaningful. Notes in electronic formats will generally be connected to the text via a hyperlink. Authors should discuss with their publishers every format in which their text is likely to be published and plan for a notes system that will work across them all.

17.2.3 **Numbering and placement**

The reader is referred to a footnote or endnote by a cue in the text. This normally takes the form of a superior Arabic number. The cue is placed after any punctuation (normally after the closing point of a sentence). If, however, it relates only to text within parentheses it is placed before the closing parenthesis. The cue is repeated at the start of the note. Notes cued in the middle of a sentence are a distraction to the reader, and cues are best located at the end of sentences:

> He was a genuine Shropshire lad, as John H. Johnston reminds us.[51]
>
> Bergonzi quite correctly notes, 'Owen's attitude to the "boys" or "lads" destined for sacrifice has some affinity with Housman's.'[55]
>
> (Hopkins wrote defensively to Bridges: 'When you read it let me know if there is anything like it in Walt Whitman; as perhaps there may be, and I should be sorry for that.'[29])

Characters other than Arabic numerals may be used for note cues when there are relatively few notes in a sequence, but this should only be done when necessary. In mathematical or scientific contexts, for example, superior lower-case letters may be used to avoid confusion with superscript numbers in technical notation. Lower-case Roman numerals may also serve as note cues (though this quickly becomes unwieldy), as can reference marks (the traditional order is *, †, ‡, §, ¶, ||, repeated in duplicate as **, ††, and so on as necessary—but this too is a cumbersome method if there are more than a handful of notes). Occasionally different types of cue are employed on the same page for parallel sequences of notes serving different purposes: this should be avoided if possible but is sometimes required in complex editions.

Notes should be numbered continuously through each chapter or article. This allows the numbers in the author's copy to remain unchanged at typesetting; internal cross-references to notes thus do not require correction on page proof, and passages of text may even be located by reference to numbered notes (*Ch. 6 at n. 17*). Continuous numbering of notes through an entire book is to be avoided, as it can generate too many three-digit cues and will cause problems if a note is deleted or added at proof stage. Whether numbered page by page or chapter by chapter note cues must appear in strict numerical sequence; the same number must not be used twice within a sequence, even if the content of the note is the same.

An initial note consisting entirely of acknowledgements may be placed before the numbered notes and cued with an asterisk; the asterisk is placed at the end of the first sentence of text. Avoid asterisks, note numbers, or other cues within or at the end of titles, subtitles, and chapter subheadings. An initial uncued note may be used to provide the original location of a reprinted chapter or article.

A note giving the source for a displayed quotation is best placed at the end of the quotation itself rather than at the end of the preceding text. Where there are multiple quotations from or references to a particular source the locations should be given in a single note after the last quotation or reference, provided no other citation intervenes. The page numbers should be in the same order as the quotations or statements to which they relate, not rearranged into numerical sequence. If there are repeated citations of a single source (but no other) over several paragraphs it may be best to provide a separate note for each paragraph. The notes in three such successive paragraphs might, for example, be:

> 6. Smith, *Windham's Green Book*, 25, 17, 31.
> 7. Smith, *Windham's Green Book*, 87, 95, 103–5.
> 8. Smith, *Windham's Green Book*, 150, 75, 279.

Furthermore, where it can be done without ambiguity, it is good practice to group references to different sources in a single note after several sentences or at the end of a paragraph. The nature of the source will generally indicate to which statement in the text it relates, and any doubt may be removed by a parenthetical word or phrase after the references or by an introductory phrase before several related references. The editorial effort required is justified by the reduction in the number of notes and the improved readability of the text.

> Not even the best endowed colleges had incomes approaching those of such great Benedictine houses as... Westminster or Glastonbury... New College's estates probably yielded revenues of a similar magnitude to the Augustinian abbey of Oseney.... The estate income of All Souls... was probably slightly lower for example than that of Bolton Priory in Yorkshire, which supported merely fifteen canons... The college by contrast remained close to its statutory complement of a warden and forty fellows.[30]
>
> 30. D. Knowles and R. N. Hadcock, *Medieval Religious Houses: England and Wales* (1953), 80 (Westminster), 66 (Glastonbury), 149 (Oseney), 128 (Bolton); I. Kershaw, *Bolton Priory* (1973), 186; Cobban, 'Colleges and halls', 609.

17.2.4 **Layout of notes**

The layout and typography of notes is subject to considerable variation. Footnotes in particular are usually set in smaller type than text.

A note should begin with a capital initial and end with a full point. It may or may not contain grammatically complete sentences. Abbreviated forms (for example for the months of the year) and symbols that would not be acceptable in open text may be appropriate within citations in notes. Various forms of punctuation and wording may be used to group citations and to indicate how they relate to material in the text or to related questions; what is most efficient in any context is a matter for editorial judgement. The common abbreviation 'cf.' (Latin *confer*) means 'compare', and thus is not quite the same as 'see'.

The number preceding the note may be superscript or on the line:

> [40] Mokyr, *Why Ireland Starved*, 26.
> 40. Mokyr, *Why Ireland Starved*, 26.

Whether or not a point is needed after a number on the line is a design issue.

17.2.5 **Forms of citation**

Full guidance on the form of bibliographic citations is to be found in Chapter 18. For the most part the same considerations govern entries in a bibliography and citations in notes, with the important exception that in notes an author's initials or forename precede rather than follow the surname. Consistent systems for the formulation of notes are essential, but abstract rules should not be followed too slavishly: much can depend on editorial judgement in presenting particular references as clearly and economically as possible.

Author and short title

In addition to general bibliographic rules there are conventions, relating especially to multiple citations of the same work, that are intended to promote brevity and clarity within notes. Unless it is included in a list of abbreviations or a bibliography (see 17.2.6), full bibliographic details of a published work or the location of an unpublished source should be given when it is first cited in an article or book, and repeated at its first citation in any subsequent chapter in the same book. Subsequent citations should take a very abbreviated form, typically the author's surname and a shortened title of the work. The short title should be accurately extracted from the full title (not a paraphrase) and should be as brief as is compatible with the unambiguous identification of the work. Rather longer forms may be advisable if works of similar title are cited. Short titles alone may be used for works cited with no namedauthor. It is a matter of judgement whether an editor's name should be repeated with the title of an edited text. Short forms may also be devised for the multiple citation of unpublished sources whose full forms are unduly lengthy.

Once a short form has been established, the author's initials or the full title should not be reintroduced in later citations in the same chapter.

> 5. R. J. Faith, *The English Peasantry and the Growth of Lordship* (1997).
>
> 73. Faith, *English Peasantry*, 49–50.

Location within a work

Locations within a work should generally be given in the shortest unambiguous form. Publishers will have their own conventions for the various fields in which they produce books or journals. Lower-case Roman numerals were traditionally used for volume numbers, but Arabic numerals are now common; either system should be applied consistently. Roman page numbers must be retained and not converted to Arabic. Volume and page numbers may be linked by a point, consistently either closed up or spaced off. Abbreviations for pages or volumes (*p.*, *pp.*, *vol.*, *vols.*) are not strictly necessary in most cases, but they should be included before Arabic or Roman numerals if there is a risk of confusion as to what element is being cited. If a work has numbered columns rather than pages there is no need to use the abbreviation *col.* in citations, as there will be no ambiguity when the reader consults the source. Likewise compound locations consisting of several numbers (whether Arabic, lower-case Roman, or small capitals, depending on house style or general convention) may reasonably be used with no explanation of the elements they represent (book, chapter, paragraph, question, etc.) if there will be no ambiguity in the source itself.

> *Letters and Journals of Robert Baillie*, 2.110
>
> Brett-Smith, 1.xxviii–xxix
>
> *English Historical Documents*, i, 2nd edn, ed. D. Whitelock (London, 1979), no. 191
>
> *Liber de caesaribus*, v.39.20

Authors sometimes feel obliged to give the overall pagination of articles or chapters they cite in addition to the particular passage to which they are referring. This is no more logical or helpful than citing the total pagination of a book, and is an unnecessary complication of a citation.

For the treatment of abbreviations and contractions of terms such as 'page', 'chapter', and 'volume' see Chapter 10. The use of 'f.' after a page number to indicate 'and the following page' should be replaced with an explicit two-page span (*15–16*, not *15 f.*). A page number followed by 'ff.' to indicate 'and the following pages' should also be converted to a precise span if possible, but this form is acceptable when it is difficult for the author (or editor) to identify a final relevant page. The spacing, if any, before the abbreviation (*23ff.* or *23 ff.*) is a matter of house style; Oxford traditionally uses a thin space between a number and a following 'f.' or 'ff.', and between a number and a following 'n.' or 'nn.' in the absence of a subsequent note number (when a note number is included, normal space of the line is used: *23 n. 5*). When specific notes are cited, 'note' may be abbreviated to 'n.' and 'notes' to 'nn.' It is best to avoid punctuation between page number and note number. In the third of the following examples the notes cited contain information additional to that given in the text:

Marx, *Manifesto*, 37 n. 4.

Kleinhans, 'Marxism and Film', 106ff.

K. McRoberts, *Misconceiving Canada* (Toronto: OUP, 1997), 12 and nn. 37–8.

Recto and verso are sometimes abbreviated r and v, set roman, and may be used to indicate right- and left-hand pages respectively— *31r, 70r, 78v, 89r*.

A reference to another place within the work itself may be included in a note if it will be genuinely helpful to the reader, but such internal cross-references should be added judiciously. Where possible, cross-refer by chapter and chapter subheading in addition to using the page number: this will be more effective than the page number alone in an ebook or other unpaged format.

Abbreviations

Many abbreviations are used in note references, to aid or direct the reader as succinctly as possible. For the most part, a lower-case abbreviation that begins a note is capitalized, whether or not the note is a complete sentence. A handful of common abbreviations are, however, exceptions to this rule: *c.*, e.g., i.e., l., ll., p., pp. generally remain lower case:

20. *c.*1344, according to Froissart.
21. e.g. service outside the jurisdiction.
22. i.e. Copyright, Designs & Patents Act 1988, §4.
23. p. 7.
24. ll. 34–44 (Miller edn).

Certain Latin words or their abbreviations have been traditionally used to make citations in notes more concise. These abbreviations serve admirably in print but are far less useful in electronic formats, where the notes may appear (for example) in a pop-up rather than in a consecutive list. The reader hovering on a note link and receiving the abbreviation 'Ibid.' in a standalone pop-up gains no useful information. For this reason Oxford prefers the author and short-title system wherever possible. Exceptions are allowed for some specialist material (such as legal publications) where these abbreviations are rigidly followed throughout a discipline.

- The word *ibidem*, meaning 'in the same place', is normally abbreviated to 'ibid.', occasionally to 'ib.' Bibliographically, 'ibid.' means 'in the same work', or 'in the same place within that work', as in the immediately preceding citation (either in the same or the preceding note). 'Ibid.' is best avoided in favour of an author and short-title system.

- The abbreviations 'op. cit.' (*opere citato*, 'in the cited work') and 'art. cit.' (*articulo citato*, 'in the cited article') were once commonly used in place of a work title, normally after an author's name. In fact they are of little use. The author's surname and a short title create a more helpful citation. Avoid these forms.

- The abbreviation 'loc. cit.' (*loco citato*, 'in the cited place') is often misunderstood and misused. It can represent only a specific location within a work and is therefore of extremely restricted usefulness. It may occasionally save the repetition of a long and complex location involving multiple elements that cannot easily be compressed, but most often the repeated location (for example volume and page) will be no longer than 'loc. cit.' itself.

- *Idem* (commonly but not always abbreviated to 'id.') means 'the same person', and was formerly used in place of an author's name when works by the same author are cited one after the other. This is perhaps an excessive saving of space. Furthermore there are grammatical complications, as the form of the Latin pronoun varies with gender and number. While a male author is *idem* (id.) a female must be *eadem* (ead.); multiple female authors are *eaedem* (eaed.) and multiple authors of whom at least one is male are *eidem* (eid.). An author's gender is not always known, and editors cannot always be relied upon to apply the correct forms. Apart from the language problem, XML tagging of the author element will not work properly if the author's name is not repeated, so links to citation indexes are not formed correctly. Avoid this form and repeat an author's name in a new citation.

- The word *passim* may be placed after a span of pages, or a less specific location, to indicate that relevant passages are scattered throughout the overall location. This usage is of limited use to the reader and should be applied sparingly.

17.2.6 **Bibliographical abbreviations**

A list of bibliographical abbreviations is often printed in a book's preliminary matter, or at the start of a bibliography. An abbreviated citation assigned in this way will be used every time the work is cited in a note, even at its first citation in a chapter. Whether or not it is worth including such a list in a volume will depend not only on how often particular works are cited in the volume as a whole but also on how many works are cited frequently in more than one chapter. If a work is cited very many times in one chapter it will routinely be reduced to author and title after its first citation; a more irregular abbreviation of a complex source may be explicitly introduced at its first mention in a chapter:

> Bede, *Historia ecclesiastica gentis Anglorum* (hereafter *HE*)
> St John's College, Cambridge, archives (hereafter SJC)

If a source abbreviated in this way is cited in no other chapter in the volume an entry in an overall list of abbreviations may be superfluous.

17.3 Author–date system

An apparatus for references known as the **author–date** (or **Harvard**) system is normal in the scientific, technical, and medical fields, and is also used extensively in the social sciences. It is not based on notes but relies on brief parenthetical references in the text to take the reader to the appropriate point in a consolidated list of full citations, generally known as the reference section. A reference section includes only those works that are cited in the text; a more general list of works of related interest should be called *Bibliography* or *Further Reading*. This is an economical method of citing straightforward published sources.

It is possible to combine this arrangement with a separate sequence of numbered notes for explanatory or discursive matter:

text

a stoutly republican coalition that retained none the less a great deal of the administrative style of the old regime (see Stookey 1974). It was replaced by a government with a different style,[2] a style... not forgotten or revoked.

endnote 2

The usual explanation of the timing of the coup is that it forestalled a Ba'athist plot. That this was no simple question... we shall see when we quote the speeches given at a tribal meeting soon afterwards.

reference section

Stookey, R. W., 1974. 'Social Structure and Politics in the Yemen Arab Republic', *Middle East Journal*, 28/3: 248–60; 28/4: 409–19

In extreme cases where multiple references (and multiple authors) render a sentence unreadable, and the problem cannot be resolved by rewriting, a group of references may be relegated to a footnote. Bracketed author–date references to a bibliographic list are sometimes included within footnotes.

17.3.1 **Reference section**

In the author–date system the full references are listed alphabetically in a section at the end of the text (either chapter by chapter or in a consolidated list at the end of the book). As in bibliographies, authors' initials generally follow their surnames. To facilitate linking with the short references given in the text the date of publication immediately follows the authors' names. The styling of these references can vary considerably; scientific and medical publishers, for example, may use very different conventions from those adopted in the humanities. For example, end references may be fully or minimally punctuated and formatted:

Grinspoon, L., Bakalar, J. B. (1993), *Marijuana: The Forbidden* Medicine. London: Yale University Press.

Kalavala M, Mills CM, Long CC, et al. (2007). The fingertip unit: A practical guide to topical therapy in children. J Dermatol Treat 18:319–320.

There is a general preference for minimal punctuation in scientific work, to save space and keying time, while humanities publications usually prefer fuller punctuation. For further guidance see Chapter 18.

17.3.2 **References in text**

A typical reference in the text consists of an author's name and date of publication enclosed within parentheses (or occasionally square brackets), with or without a comma separating name and date, according to the style adopted. The reference is placed immediately after the statement to which it relates. If this happens to be at the end of a sentence the closing parenthesis precedes the closing point (but a reference at the end of a displayed quotation follows the closing punctuation). If the author's name is given in open text it need not be repeated in the parentheses, where the date alone suffices. Several references may be included within the same parentheses, separated by a comma or semicolon, depending on the style adopted:

text

While there was an extraordinary sense of optimism among people establishing their own farms in the early years of independence (Unwin 1994), this is rapidly withering away.

reference section

Unwin, T. (1994), 'Structural Change in Estonian Agriculture: From Command Economy to Privatisation', *Geography*, 79, 3: 246–61.

text

For years, most textbooks referred to the five stages of economic integration as defined by Balassa (1961).

reference section

Balassa, Bela (1961), *The Theory of Economic Integration*. London: Allen and Unwin.

text

They are also used to detect segmental hypermobility (Magarey 1988, Maitland 2001).

reference section

Magarey ME (1988). Examination of the Cervical and Thoracic Spine. In: R Grant (ed.) *Physical Therapy of the Cervical and Thoracic Spine*, pp. 81–109. Churchill Livingstone: New York.

Maitland G (2001) *Maitland's Vertebral Manipulation*, 6th edn. Butterworth–Heinemann: Oxford.

Multiple authorship is very common in scientific publication. Each work should have a consistent convention as to how many authors' names are given in full and what number, if any, should be reduced to 'et al.' (sometimes italicized) after the name of the first author (see Chapter 18). Some publishers use 'et al.' to shorten references in text even when the names are given in full in the corresponding entry in the reference section. Either an ampersand or 'and' should be used consistently to link dual authors or the last two of multiple authors, even though in the reference section they may be separated by a comma:

text

One of the biggest successes of the 1960s was transformed into an albatross hanging from the neck of an embattled Community (Rosenblatt et al., 1988).

reference section

Rosenblatt, Julius et al. (1988). *The Common Agricultural Policy of the European Community*, International Monetary Fund, occasional paper 62, November.

text

Prototypical birds, for instance, seem to be birds of average size and average predacity (Rips et al., 1973).

reference section

Rips LJ, Shoben EJ, Smith EE (1973). Semantic Distance and the Verification of Semantic Relations. *Journal of Verbal Learning and Verbal Behaviour* 12: 1–20.

text

It has been estimated that the human eye can discriminate no fewer than 7.5 million just noticeable colour differences (Brown and Lenneberg 1954).

reference section

Brown, R., and Lenneberg, E. H. (1954). 'A Study in Language and Cognition'. *Journal of Abnormal and Social Psychology* 49: 454–62.

If the reference section contains works by authors of the same surname their initials may be retained in the in-text reference to distinguish between them. If there is more than one work by an author in a single year they are distinguished by lower-case letters (either roman or italic depending on house style) appended to the year in the parenthetical reference and in the list. The dates of several works by a single author are separated by commas. Occasionally a parenthetical reference may be introduced by terms like 'see', 'see also', or 'cf.':

text

a diverse body of work has emerged which focuses on the 'governance' of socio-economic systems (see Jessop 1995a, 1997)

reference section

Jessop, B. (1995a) 'The Regulation Approach, Governance and Post-Fordism', *Economy and Society*, 24, 3: 307–33.

Jessop, B. (1995b) 'Regional Economic Blocs', *American Behavioral Scientist*, 38, 5: 674–715.

Jessop, B. (1997) 'The Governance of Complexity and Complexity of Governance', in A. Amin and J. Hausner (eds) *Beyond Markets and Hierarchy*, Aldershot: Edward Elgar.

How to style references to works that do not fit into the normal pattern of author and title is a matter for editorial judgement. A reference to an anonymous work, for instance, may place either 'anon.' or a short title before the date of publication; reference to a work produced by a corporate body may similarly use either the work title or the name of the body, abbreviated if the name is very long:

text

at the hands of the state, paramilitary and guerilla forces (CNRR/GMH, 2008a)

reference section

CNNR/GMH (Comisión Nacional de Reparación y Reconciliación y Grupo de Memoría Historica) (2008a) *Trujilla: Una Tragedia que no Cesa [Trujilla: A Tragedy Without End]*, Bogotá, Colombia: CNRR.

A reference to an unsigned item in a periodical may use its title and date. The crucial point is that all in-text references should be styled consistently with the reference section and should enable the reader easily to identify the source there.

A personal communication or an interview with the author may be so described in a parenthetical reference, but need not be included in the reference section:

text

By this time, industry had come to play a leading role (World Bank 1993).

reference section

World Bank (1993) *Vietnam: Transition to the Market*. Washington, DC: The World Bank.

text

in Uppsala 'the main aim is to create sustainable development, although there is no true consensus as to what this means' (Peterson, pers. comm.).

appendix: Informants

Agneta Peterson, environmental planning officer, Uppsala municipality.

The same is also true of academic papers submitted but not yet accepted for publication; see also 18.3.1

Broadly speaking, articles in scientific disciplines are shorter than those in the humanities, and often it is not necessary to specify a location within in-text references; locations are more commonly cited in references in the social sciences. When a location is given it is usually separated from the date by a colon.

17.4 Numbered references

Some scientific publications use the **author–number** (or **Vancouver**) system, which numbers the citations in a single sequence and dispenses with authors' names in the references in text; these consist simply of superscript numbers or numbers in parentheses or square brackets, multiple references being separated by commas, set close, with number ranges used as appropriate (*as found in similar studies.*[3, 5, 6, 14–18]). This arrangement has a superficial resemblance to endnotes, but the reference numbers do not necessarily occur in numerical sequence in the text, where any one may be repeated several times:

text

Issues of risk, choice, and chance are central to the controversy over the MMR vaccine that erupted in the UK in 1998 and has continued into the new millennium.[1]

reference section

1. Fitzpatrick M. *MMR and Autism: What Parents Need to Know*. London: Routledge, 2004.

text

The inter-individual variability in VO_2 measured at a given speed and rate can be as high as 15% [18].

reference section

18. Nieman, D. C. *Exercise Testing and Prescription*, 5th edn. New York: McGraw-Hill, 2003; 90.

The late addition or removal of a reference from a numbered list may require more or less extensive correction of the numbers in the reference section and the in-text citations.

17.5 Citation linking

17.5.1 **Reference management software**

The many software programs that can help with reference formatting can adapt citations to whichever system is required by the publisher with comparative ease. References can be downloaded from citation databases such as Copac in a form that can be imported into the reference management software, which then embeds the reference in the word-processor document. Editors should be aware that automatically formed references should always be checked for consistency, completeness, and accuracy, as some manual intervention may be necessary, particularly for sources that do not follow the usual pattern.

17.5.2 **References as an active resource**

Hyperlinks in digital texts can and have transformed the workhorse reference list into a dynamic resource providing access to multimedia material that enriches the user's experience to a far greater extent than a printed book. Authors and editors should be aware, however, that this will be successful only if the referencing is done accurately to enable linking to material that should be current and accessible.

CHAPTER 18

Bibliography

18.1 General principles

18.1.1 **Introduction**

Bibliography, specifically **enumerative bibliography**, is the discipline of citing reference matter in a consistent and accurate manner, so as to provide enough key material for readers to be able to identify the work and locate it in a library or a citation index (bibliographic database). Bibliographies occur in all types of publication, and are found in most non-fiction works (though depending on the type of publishing they may not be headed *Bibliography*—see 1.4.4).

The structure of bibliographic citations is determined by the referencing system in use in the publication concerned. In general publishing and academic publishing in the humanities, bibliographic citations are ordered (very broadly speaking):

author, title, place of publication, date of publication

This form supports the use of footnotes or endnotes for referencing (see 17.2). In these types of publishing the bibliographic list is likely to include works that are not referred to in the text.

Academic publishing in the sciences and social sciences uses **author–date** references in the text to source quotations and references to other authorities (see 17.3); this form requires bibliographic citations ordered:

author, date, title, place of publication

In these types of publishing the bibliographic list often includes only those works that are referred to in the text; the correct heading for such a list is not *Bibliography* but *References.*

A variation on the author–date system is the **author–number** system (see 17.4).

18.1.2 **Placement within a publication**

Citations are conventionally found in two different parts of an academic work:

- **Note citations** appear in footnotes and endnotes (see 17.2).
- **Bibliography citations** form a list of works that is usually placed at the end of a publication before an index, or at the end of a chapter in multi-contributor titles.

In the interests of simplicity it is best to keep stylistic differences between note citations and bibliography citations to a minimum. The following distinctions are useful, however:

- Note citations will frequently require a specific volume and/or page number. Apart from page ranges to identify the start and end of chapters in books or articles in journals, bibliography citations will usually cite a work in its entirety.
- In bibliography citations, if an author or editor is cited before the title the surname should appear first, aiding the reader in navigating through a list. In note citations this is an irritant that reduces readability, and should be avoided:

  note citation
  Joe Bailey, *Pessimism* (London, 1988), 35.
  bibliography citation
  Bailey, Joe, *Pessimism* (London, 1988).

Except when it is necessary to clarify a difference between the two types of citations, examples in this chapter follow bibliography style.

18.1.3 **Arrangement and ordering of a bibliography**

A bibliography is normally ordered alphabetically by the surname of the main author or editor of the cited work. It is sometimes advantageous to subdivide longer lists, for example by subject or type of work. A typical division is that of primary and secondary sources; also, a separate list of manuscripts and documents may be made. A bibliography of primary sources is sometimes more historically interesting if ordered chronologically, or more practical if arranged by repository. For ordering in the author–date system see 18.5.

Alphabetization follows the same principles as in indexing (see Chapter 19); ignore all accents (index *Müller* as *Muller*, not *Mueller*) and treat *Mc* as *Mac* and *St* as *Saint*. See 6.1.8 for the indexing of names with prefixes.

Single author

Entries by the same author may be ordered alphabetically by title, ignoring definite and indefinite articles, or chronologically by year, the earliest first, and alphabetically within a single year. Alphabetical order is advisable when many works by one author are cited, but chronological order may be preferred if it is important to show the sequence of works. In second and subsequent works by the same author do not replace the name with an em rule or rules: although this has been traditional print practice, it is not suitable for many types of electronic publication, so it is preferable to spell out the name in full for each entry.

> Rogers, C. D., *The Family Tree Detective* (Manchester, 1983).
> Rogers, C. D., *Tracing Missing Persons* (Manchester, 1986).

Works edited by an author are listed in a separate sequence following all works written by him or her, singly or with co-authors; works edited in collaboration are arranged according to the same rules as for multiple authors. Alternatively, it is possible to list all publications associated with a single person in a single sequence, ignoring the distinction between author and editor.

More than one author

It is usual to alphabetize works by more than one author under the first author's name.

When there is more than one citation of the same author, group references within these two categories (see 18.5 for a more detailed discussion of bibliographic order):

- works written by a single author
- works written by the same author with any co-authors, in alphabetical order by surname of the co-author:

> Hornsby-Smith, Michael P., *Roman Catholics in England: Studies in Social Structure since the Second World War* (Cambridge, 1987).
> Hornsby-Smith, Michael P., *Roman Catholic Beliefs in England* (Cambridge, 1991).

Hornsby-Smith, Michael P., and Dale, A., 'Assimilation of Irish Immigrants', *British Journal of Sociology*, xxxix/4 (1988), 519–44.

Hornsby-Smith, Michael P., and Lee, R. M., *Roman Catholic Opinion* (Guildford, 1979).

Hornsby-Smith, Michael P., Lee, R. M., and Turcan, K. A., 'A Typology of English Catholics', *Sociological Review*, xxx/3 (1982), 433–59.

18.1.4 **Bibliographic elements**

As a general rule, it is important for citations in a bibliography to be consistent in the level of detail provided. Inconsistency is a form of error and will not only reduce the overall integrity of an academic publication but may also prevent successful linking with citation indexes. Moreover, readers should be able to infer reliably that an absence of information from one citation but not another reflects the bibliographic detail available from the texts being cited.

For published matter, the key elements required for a 'complete' citation are:

- person or persons responsible for the work
- title of the work or serial
- the edition being used, if not the first edition
- place and date of publication.

Some citations require further details: these are covered in the various sections in this chapter. A decision to include other information (for example number of volumes, series title, publisher, or access dates) should be applied consistently to all citations where relevant.

All bibliographic information must be taken from the cited work itself, and not from a secondary source such as a library catalogue or other bibliography. Additional information not supplied by the work should generally appear within square brackets.

The means by which a reader distinguishes one element from the other is by its order within the citation, its typography, and its surrounding punctuation. It is therefore important to ensure that each part of the citation is presented correctly, and in the appropriate place.

For non-published material (so-called 'grey' literature), such as manuscripts, company reports, and some electronic sources, there are fewer established conventions, but efforts should be made to follow the style consistently using the general pattern applied to published matter (see also 18.6).

This is particularly important for automated XML tagging (see 2.1.1) because the process relies on the recognition of patterns in formatting and order of the elements. This can break down if the 'rules' for a particular citation system are not followed.

18.2 Books

18.2.1 **Introduction**

A complete book citation must include author or editor details, title, edition information (if an edition other than the first edition is cited), and date and place of publication:

> Demaus, Robert, *William Tyndale: A Contribution to the Early History of the English Bible*, new edn, rev. Richard Lovett (London, 1886).
> Watt, R. W., *Three Steps to Victory* (London, 1957).
> Bagnold, Enid, *A Diary Without Dates* (2nd edn, London, 1978).

See 18.8 for ebook citations.

18.2.2 **Author's name**

Some publishers, especially in the humanities, prefer to cite the author's name as it appears on the title page (the same applies to all personal names, whether of authors or others); this is because some authors insist on being known by their initials while others object to their forenames being cut down. Applying this practice requires the author to exercise the discipline of noting the form as it appears in the book, and not relying on secondary sources, such as library catalogues and other bibliographies. A more pragmatic approach (often adopted in scientific publication) is to systematically reduce forenames to initials, especially for multi-author works where different contributors may have adopted different practices.

The author's name should appear at the start of the citation. In bibliography citations the surname is given first, followed by a comma and the given names or initials:

> Bailey, Joe   Eliot, T. S.

In scientific works, initials and minimal punctuation are more usual in the reference list:

> Feynman R   Nurse PM

See 17.3 for more details of punctuation of authors' names.

Names that are best left unabbreviated and in natural order in bibliography citations include:

- medieval compound names that conjoin a personal name with a toponym, occupation, patronymic, or epithet:

  Hereward the Wake   Aelred of Rievaulx

- pseudonyms that lose their sense if altered:

  Dotted Crotchet   Afferbeck Lauder

- names given as initials only, even if the full name is known:

  BBC
  EA Games
  IBM

In a list, such examples would all be ordered by their first element.

If works of one author are cited under different names, use the correct form for each work, and in humanities texts, supply a former name after a later one in parentheses, adding a cross-reference if necessary:

Joukovsky, F., *Orphée et ses disciples dans la poésie française et néolatine du XVIe siècle* (Geneva, 1970).

Joukovsky, F. (= Joukovsky-Micha, F.), 'La Guerre des dieux et des géants chezles poètes français du XVIe siècle (1500–1585)', *Bibliothèque d'Humanisme et Renaissance*, xxix (1967), 55–92.

Unless the author's preference is known to be otherwise, when citing naturalized names that include particles keep the particle with the surname only if it is capitalized. For foreign names follow the correct usage for the language or person in question:

De Long, George Washington   Goethe, Johann Wolfgang von
Musset, Alfred de

Titular prefixes (*Sir*, *Revd*, *Dr*, *Captain*, etc.) are not needed unless their removal would mislead:

Wood, Mrs Henry, *East Lynne*, 3 vols (London, 1861).

Two or more authors

With two or three authors (or editors), cite in the order that appears on the title page. Either the first cited name only, or all names before the title, may be inverted so that the surname appears first. Whichever style is chosen must be applied consistently:

King, Roy D., and Morgan, Rodney, *A Taste of Prison* (London, 1976).

King, Roy D., and Rodney Morgan, *A Taste of Prison* (London, 1976).

When there are four or more authors, works in the humanities usually cite the first name followed by 'and others' or 'et al.' (from Latin *et alii* 'and others'; note that, depending on style, 'et al.' can appear in roman or italic type—consistency is important):

Stewart, Rosemary, and others, eds, *Managing in Britain* (London, 1994).

In some scientific journals, where it is not unusual for several names to be identified with an article or paper, the policy can be to cite up to six authors before reducing the list to a single name and 'et al.', either in roman or italic and sometimes dropping the full point.

Pseudonyms

Cite works published under a pseudonym that is an author's literary name under that pseudonym:

Eliot, George, *Middlemarch* (New York, 1977).

Twain, Mark, *A Connecticut Yankee at King Arthur's Court* (Harmondsworth, 1971).

In some contexts it may be useful to add a writer's pseudonym for clarification when a writer publishes under his or her real name:

Dodgson, C. L. [Lewis Carroll], *Symbolic Logic* (Oxford, 1896).

Conversely, an author known by his or her real name may need to be identified when he or she occasionally publishes under a pseudonym:

Afferbeck Lauder [Alistair Morrison], *Let Stalk Strine* (Sydney, 1965).

If the bibliography contains works under the author's true name as well as a pseudonym, the alternative names may be included in both cases to expose the identification:

Coulange, P. [J. Turmel], *The Life of the Devil*, tr. S. H. Guest (London, 1929).

Turmel, J. [P. Coulange], 'Histoire de l'angélologie du temps apostolique à la fin du Ve siècle', *Revue d'Histoire et de Littérature Religieuse*, iii (1898), 299–308, 407–34, 533–52.

Anonymous

For texts where the author is not known, in bibliography citations *Anon.* or *Anonymous* may be used, with like works alphabetized accordingly:

Anon., *Stories after Nature* (London, 1822).

Do not use *Anon.* for note citations; simply start the citation with the title:

Stories after Nature (London, 1822).

If the author's name is not supplied by the book but is known from other sources, the name may be cited in square brackets:

[Balfour, James], *Philosophical Essays* (Edinburgh, 1768).

[Gibbon, John], *Day-Fatality, or, Some Observations on Days Lucky and Unlucky* (London, 1678; rev. edn 1686).

18.2.3 **Editors, translators, and revisers**

Special XML tagging elements are created for editors, translators, and compilers so it is important that they are identified as such.

In books comprising the edited works of a number of authors, or a collection of documents, essays, congress reports, etc., the editor's name appears first followed by *ed.* (standing for 'editor'; plural *eds* or *eds.*) before the book title:

Dibdin, Michael, ed., *The Picador Book of Crime Writing* (London, 1993).

Ashworth, A., 'Belief, Intent, and Criminal Liability', in J. Eekelaar and J. Bell, eds., *Oxford Essays in Jurisprudence*, 3rd ser. (1987), 6–25.

Bucknell, Katherine, and Nicholas Jenkins, eds, *W. H. Auden, 'The Map of All My Youth': Early Works, Friends, and Influences* (Oxford, 1990).

Some styles, including Oxford, insert 'ed.' and 'eds' within parentheses:

SAMPSON, RODNEY (ed.), *Early Romance Texts: An Anthology* (Cambridge, 1980).

Editors of literary texts (or of another author's papers) are cited after the title; in this case *ed.* (standing for 'edited by') remains unchanged even if there is more than one editor:

Hume, David, *A Treatise of Human Nature*, ed. David Fate Norton and Mary J. Norton (Oxford, 2000).

For note citations, when an author is responsible for the content of the work but not the title (for example letters collected together posthumously), and the author's name appears as part of that title, there is no need to repeat the author's name at the start of the citation:

The Letters of Percy Bysshe Shelley, ed. F. L. Jones (Oxford, 1964).

rather than

Shelley, Percy Bysshe, *The Letters of Percy Bysshe Shelley*, ed. F. L. Jones (Oxford, 1964).

As with editors, translators and revisers are named after the title and are introduced respectively by *tr.* or *trans.* ('translated by'), *rev.* ('revised by'):

> Albert Schweitzer, *The Quest of the Historical Jesus*, tr. William Montgomery (n.p., 1910).

Translators or revisers whose contribution is sufficiently substantial for them to count as joint authors are named after the original author.

18.2.4 **Organization as author**

In the absence of an author or editor, an organization acting in the role of author can be treated as such. Do not use *ed.* or *tr.* in these instances:

> Amnesty International, *Prisoners Without a Voice: Asylum Seekers in the United Kingdom* (London, 1995).

18.2.5 **Titles and subtitles**

In general the treatment of titles in bibliography matches that of work titles mentioned in text (see Chapter 8). Always take the title from the title page of the work being cited, not the dust jacket or the cover of a paperback edition, and never alter spelling in order to conform to house style. Punctuation in long titles may be lightly edited for the sake of clarity.

Consider truncating long and superfluous subtitles, but not if that would significantly narrow the implied scope of a work. Subtitles are often identified as such on the title page by a line break or a change in font or font size; in a bibliography a subtitle is always divided from the title by a colon.

Capitalization

In most bibliographic styles traditional capitalization rules are applied to titles (see 8.2.3). In practice the choice between upper and lower case is usually instinctive, but will at least downcase the following:

a	at	from	on	to
an	be	in	that	under
and	by	is	the	which
as	for	of	then	

Unless the exact form is of bibliographic or semantic relevance your primary guide should be to style a title sensibly and consistently throughout a work.

The Importance of Being Earnest: A Trivial Comedy for Serious People
Twenty Years After
Moby-Dick, or, The Whale

Capitalization of foreign titles follows the rules of the language (see Chapter 12); however, the treatment of the first word of a title, subtitle, or parallel title conforms to the style used for English-language titles.

Titles within titles

Titles within titles may be identified by quotation marks. Always capitalize the first word of the nested title; this capitalized word is regarded in some styles as sufficient to identify the subsidiary work:

Grigg, John, *The History of 'The Times'*, vi (1993).
O'Conor, Roderick, *A Sentimental Journey through 'Finnegans Wake', with a Map of the Liffey* (Dublin, 1977).
Grigg, John, *The History of* The Times, vi (1993).

The convention of using roman instead of italic to identify nested titles is established but not recommended; see 7.6. For a further discussion of titles within titles see 8.2.8.

Foreign-language titles

Works should be cited in the form in which they were consulted by the author of the publication that cites them. If the work was consulted in the original foreign-language form, that should be cited as the primary reference; a published English translation may be added to the citation if that is deemed likely to be helpful to the reader:

J. Tschichold: *Typographische Gestaltung* (Basle, 1955); Eng. trans. as *Asymmetric Typography* (London, 1967).

Conversely, if a work was consulted in translation, that form should be cited; the original publication may also be included in the citation if that would be helpful (as it will be if the two forms of the title differ significantly):

R. Metz, *A Hundred Years of British Philosophy*, ed. J. H. Muirhead, trans. J. W. Harvey (1938) [Ger. orig., *Die philosophischen Strömungen der Gegenwart in Grossbritannien* (1935)]

When it is helpful to include a translation of a foreign-language title for information, the translation follows immediately after the title in roman, within square brackets; quotation marks are not necessary:

Nissan Motor Corporation, *Nissan Jidosha 30nen shi* [A 30-year history of Nissan Motors] (1965).

Care should be taken with consistency in capitalization in translations of this kind—some styles use essential capitals, others do not.

18.2.6 **Chapters and essays in books**

The chapter or essay title, which is generally enclosed in quotation marks and conforms to the surrounding capitalization style, is followed by a comma, the word *in*, and the details of the book. When citing a chapter from a single-author work there is no need to repeat the author's details:

> Ashton, John, 'Dualism', in *Understanding the Fourth Gospel* (Oxford, 1991), 205–37.

The placement of the editor's name remains unaffected:

> Shearman, John, 'The Vatican Stanze: Functions and Decoration', in George Holmes, ed., *Art and Politics in Renaissance Italy: British Academy Lectures* (Oxford, 1993), 185–240.

Quotation marks within chapter titles and essay titles become double quotation marks:

> Malcolm, Noel, 'The Austrian Invasion and the "Great Migration" of the Serbs, 1689–1690', in *Kosovo: A Short History* (London, 1990), 139–62.

See 9.2 for more on quotation marks.

If an introduction or foreword has a specific title it can be styled as a chapter in a book; otherwise use *introduction* or *foreword* as a descriptor, without quotation marks:

> Gill, Roma, introduction in *The Complete Works of Christopher Marlow*, 1 (Oxford, 1987; repr. 2001).

18.2.7 **Volumes**

A multi-volume book is a single work with a set structure. Informing readers of the number of volumes being cited is a useful convention that, if followed, must be applied consistently. The number of volumes is provided before the publication information, using an Arabic numeral. In references to a specific volume in a set, however, the number is usually styled in lower-case Roman numerals, although this style may vary: capital or small capital Roman numerals, or Arabic figures, may also be used.

There are two ways of citing a particular location in a multi-volume work: the entire work may be cited and the volume and page location given after the date(s) of publication; or the single relevant volume may be cited with its own date of publication, followed by the relevant page reference. Note in the examples below the use of Arabic and Roman numerals for different purposes:

Vander Straeten, Edmond, *La Musique aux Pays-Bas avant le XIXe siècle*, 8 vols (Brussels, 1867–88), ii, 367–8.

Vander Straeten, Edmond, *La Musique aux Pays-Bas avant le XIXe sièclè*, ii (Brussels, 1872), 367–8.

When the volumes of a multi-volume work have different titles, the form is:

Glorieux, P., *Aux origines de la Sorbonne*, i: *Robert de Sorbon* (Paris, 1966).

Ward, A. W. and A. E. Waller, eds, *The Cambridge History of English Literature*, xii: *The Nineteenth Century* (Cambridge, 1932), 43–56.

If only the volume title appears on the title page the overall title should still be included, either as directed above or within square brackets after the volume title:

David Hackett Fischer, *Albion's Seed: Four British Folkways in America* [vol. i of *America: A Cultural History*] (New York, 1989).

18.2.8 **Series title**

A series is a (possibly open-ended) collection of individual works. In book citations, a series title is optional but useful information. It always appears in roman type, fully capitalized, and before or within the parentheses that hold publication information. Most, but not all, series are numbered; the volume numbers in the series should follow the series title:

Stones, E. L. G., ed. and tr., *Anglo-Scottish Relations, 1174–1328: Some Selected Documents*, Oxford Medieval Texts (Oxford, 1970).

Dodgdon, J. McN., *The Place-Names of Gloucestershire*, 4 vols, English Place-Name Society, 38–41 (1964–5).

18.2.9 **Place of publication**

Publication details, including the place of publication, are usually inserted within parentheses. The place of publication should normally be given in its modern form, using the English form where one exists:

The Hague (*not* Den Haag)   Munich (*not* München)
Turin (*not* Torino)

Where no place of publication is given *n.p.* ('no place') may be used instead:

Marchetto of Padua, *Pomerium*, ed. Giuseppe Vecchi (n.p., 1961).

It is sufficient to cite only the first city named by the publisher on the title page. While other cities from which that imprint can originate may also be listed there, it is the custom for publishers to put in first place the branch responsible for originating the book. It is not necessary to include the name of the country, but US state abbreviations can be included, particularly if locations are globally less well known (*Boca Raton, FL*). Be consistent about the abbreviation system used (*FL* or *Fla.* etc.). For punctuation in association with publishers' names, see 18.2.10.

18.2.10 **Publisher**

The publisher's name is not generally regarded as essential information, but it may be included if desired; in the interests of consistency give names of all publishers or none at all. The preferred order is place of publication, publisher, and date, presented in parentheses thus:

(Oxford: Oxford University Press, 2005)

Publishers' names may be reduced to the shortest intelligible unit without shortening words (for example, *Teubner* instead of *Druck und Verlag von B. G. Teubner*), and terms such as *Ltd*, *& Co.*, and *plc* can be omitted. University presses whose names derive from their location can be abbreviated (*Oxford: OUP*; *Cambridge: CUP*; etc.), providing this is done consistently. See 18.2.9 for guidance on place of publication.

18.2.11 **Date**

The use of parentheses around a date in a bibliographic citation implies publication. See 18.4 and 18.6 for dates of unpublished works. Always cite the date of the edition that has been consulted. This date is usually found on the title page or the copyright page; for older books it may appear only in the colophon, a publishing device added to the last page of the book. Dates given in Roman numerals should be rendered into Arabic numerals.

When no date of publication is listed, use the latest copyright date. When multiple dates are given ignore the dates of later printings and impressions, but when using a new or revised edition use that date. If no date can be found at all, use *n.d.* ('no date') instead. Alternatively, if the date is known from other sources, it can be supplied in square brackets:

C. F. Schreiber, *A Note on Faust Translations* (n.d. [*c.*1930])

Works published over a period of time require a date range:

Asloan, John, *The Asloan Manuscript*, ed. William A. Craigie, 2 vols (Edinburgh, 1923–5).

When the book or edition is still in progress, an open-ended date is indicated by an en rule:

W. Schneemelcher, *Bibliographia Patristica* (Berlin, 1959–).

Cite a book that is to be published in the future as 'forthcoming' or 'in press'. Do not guess, or supply a projected publication date as these often prove inaccurate.

18.2.12 **Editions**

When citing an edition later than the first it is necessary to include some extra publication information, which is usually found either on the title page or in the colophon. This may be an edition number, such as *2nd edn*, or something more descriptive (*rev. edn, rev. and enl. edn*).

Placement

It is not necessary to identify first editions as such but subsequent editions should be numbered in ordinal form: *2nd, 23rd.* As a general rule, edition details should appear within parentheses, in front of any other publication information:

Baker, J. H., *An Introduction to English Legal History* (3rd edn, 1990).
Denniston, J. D., *The Greek Particles* (2nd edn, Oxford, 1954).

When the edition being cited is singularly identified with a named editor, translator, or reviser the editor's name appears at the head of the citation; the edition number directly follows the title and is not placed inside the parentheses that contain the publication details. This establishes that earlier editions are not associated with that editor:

Knowles, Elizabeth, ed., *The Oxford Dictionary of Quotations*, 5th edn (Oxford, 1999).

Citing more than one edition

Sometimes it is useful to include details of more than one edition. When this information is limited to publication details (edition, date and place of publication, and publisher) the information can remain within a single set of parentheses. When more information is needed (e.g. when a later edition has a different title and editor) it is clearer to close off the parentheses, insert a semi-colon, and continue:

Denniston, J. D., *The Greek Particles* (1934; 2nd edn, Oxford, 1954).

Denniston, J. D., *The Greek Particles* (Oxford, 1934; citations from 2nd edn, 1954).

Berkenhout, John, *Outlines of the Natural History of Great Britain*, 3 vols (London, 1769–72); rev. edn, as *A Synopsis of the Natural History of Great Britain*, 2 vols (London, 1789).

18.2.13 **Reprints, reprint editions, and facsimiles**

Reprint and facsimile editions are generally unchanged reproductions of the original book, perhaps with an added preface or index. It is always good practice to include the publication details of the original, especially the publication date if a significant period of time has elapsed between the edition and its reprint.

If the reprint has the same place of publication and publisher details as the original, these need not (though they may) be repeated. Best practice is to arrange the citation so that a reading from left to right follows the chronology of the work:

Gibbon, Edward, *Decline and Fall of the Roman Empire*, with introduction by Christopher Dawson, 6 vols (London, 1910; repr. 1974).

Allen, E., *A Knack to Know a Knave* (London, 1594; facs. edn, Oxford: Malone Society Reprints, 1963).

Joachim of Fiore, *Psalterium decem cordarum* (Venice, 1527; facs. edn, Frankfurt am Main, 1965).

Smith, Eliza, *The Compleat Housewife, or, Accomplished Gentlewoman's Companion* (16th edn, London, 1758; facs. edn, London, 1994).

Reprints that include revisions can be described as such:

Southern, R. W., *Saint Anselm: A Portrait in a Landscape* (rev. repr., Cambridge, 1991).

Title change

A changed title should be included: the parentheses that hold details of the original publication are closed off and the reprint is described after a semicolon in the same fashion as for a later edition with an altered title (see above):

Hare, Cyril, *When the Wind Blows* (London, 1949); repr. as *The Wind Blows Death* (London, 1987).

Lower, Richard, *Diatribæ Thomæ Willisii Doct. Med. & Profess. Oxon. De febribus Vindicatio adversus Edmundum De Meara Ormoniensem Hibernum M.D.* (London, 1665); facs. edn with introduction, ed. and tr. Kenneth Dewhurst, as *Richard Lower's 'Vindicatio': A Defence of the Experimental Method* (Oxford, 1983).

18.2.14 **Translations**

In a citation of a work in translation, the original author's name comes first and the translator's name after the title, prefixed by 'tr.' or 'trans.':

Bischoff, Bernhard, *Latin Palaeography: Antiquity and the Middle Ages*, tr. Dáibhí Ó Cróinín and David Ganz (Cambridge, 1990).

Martorell, Joanat, *Tirant lo Blanc*, tr. with foreword by David H. Rosenthal (London, 1984).

Details of the original edition may also be cited:

José Sarrau, *Tapas y aperitivos* (Madrid, 1975); tr. Francesca Piemonte Slesinger as *Tapas and Appetizers* (New York, 1987).

18.3 Articles in periodicals

18.3.1 **Introduction**

A complete periodical citation requires author or editor details that relate to the article being cited, the article title, the journal title, volume information, date, and page range:

Schutte, Anne Jacobson, 'Irene di Spilimbergo: The Image of a Creative Woman in Late Renaissance Italy', *Renaissance Quarterly*, 44 (1991), 42–61.

Authors' and editors' names in periodical citations are treated the same as those for books.

If a paper has been submitted for publication but has not yet been accepted, it should not be listed in the bibliography, as it may be rejected. Refer to the paper in the running text as *unpublished, in submission*, or *submitted for publication*. Personal communications should be referred to as such in the running text, and omitted from the bibliography. If a paper has been accepted for publication it can be cited in the end list as *in press*; do not guess the publication date. It is worth checking an online citation index to find out if works cited as *in press* have been published in the interim (particularly if not one of the author's own sources); if so, complete the publication details.

18.3.2 **Article titles**

Titles of articles—whether English or foreign—may be given in roman within single quotation marks; in some academic works quotation marks are omitted altogether. Quotation marks within quoted matter become double quotation marks:

Halil Inalcik, 'Comments on "Sultanism": Max Weber's Typification of the Ottoman Polity', *Princeton Papers in Near Eastern Studies*, 1 (1992), 49–72.

Pollard, A. F. 'The Authenticity of the "Lords' Journals" in the Sixteenth Century', *Transactions of the Royal Historical Society*, 3rd ser., 8 (1914), 17–39.

Titles of journals, magazines, and newspapers appear in italic with maximal capitalization, regardless of language. If the title starts with a definite article this can be omitted, except when the title consists of the word *The* and only one other word:

Downing, Taylor and Andrew Johnston, 'The Spitfire Legend', *History Today*, 50/9 (2000), 19–25.

Drucker, Peter, 'Really Reinventing Government', *Atlantic Monthly*, 275/2 (1995), 49–61.

Greeley, A. W., 'Will They Reach the Pole?', *McClure's Magazine*, 3/1 (1894), 39–44.

Henry James, 'Miss Braddon', *The Nation* (9 Nov. 1865).

See also 8.2.7.

18.3.3 **Periodical volume numbers**

Volume numbers are usually styled as Arabic numerals, but whatever you choose must be applied consistently: do not follow what is used by the journal itself.

Volumes usually span one academic or calendar year, but may occasionally cover a longer period of time. When a volume is published in issues or parts, some journals will separately paginate each issue, so that each new issue starts at page 1. Other publications paginate continuously through each volume, so that the first page number of a new issue continues from where the preceding issue left off. It is important to include issue numbers when citing separately paginated journals, because volume number and page number alone will not adequately guide a researcher to the appropriate location within the journal run.

Although issue numbers are superfluous with continuously paginated journals, best practice is to include issue numbers nevertheless: the information is not in error, the citation remains consistent with neighbouring journal citations, and in formulating the citation there is no need for you to determine which pagination system the journal follows at any given time (some journals switch from one system to another over the history of their publication).

Part or issue numbers follow the volume number after a solidus:

> Neale, Steve, 'Masculinity as Spectacle', *Screen*, 24/6 (1983), 2–12.
>
> Garvin, David A., 'Japanese Quality Management', *Columbia Journal of World Business*, 19/3 (1984), 3–12.

Magazines and newspapers are often identified (and catalogued) by their date, rather than a volume number:

> Lee, Alan, 'England Haunted by Familiar Failings', *The Times* (23 June 1995).
>
> Putterman, Seth J., 'Sonoluminescence: Sound into Light', *Scientific American* (Feb. 1995), 32–7.

Some publishing houses prefer to distinguish magazine and newspaper publications from academic journals by not inserting the date between parentheses:

> Blackburn, Roderic H., 'Historic Towns: Restorations in the Dutch Settlement of Kinderhook', *Antiques*, Dec. 1972, 1068–72.

Always follow the form used on the periodical itself: if the issue is designated *Fall*, do not change this to *Autumn*, nor attempt to adjust the season for the benefit of readers in another hemisphere, as the season forms part of the work's description and is not an ad hoc designation.

Series

Where there are several series of a journal the series information should appear before the volume number:

> Moody, T. W., 'Michael Davitt and the British Labour Movement, 1882–1906', *Transactions of the Royal Historical Society*, 5th ser., 3 (1953), 53–76.

New series can be abbreviated either to 'new ser.' or NS in small capitals. Avoid OS, which can mean either 'original' or 'old' series:

> Barnes, J., 'Homonymy in Aristotle and Speusippus', *Classical Quarterly*, new ser., 21 (1971), 65–80.

Barnes, J., 'Homonymy in Aristotle and Speusippus', *Classical Quarterly*, NS 21 (1971), 65–80.

18.3.4 **Page numbers**

As with chapters and essays in books, it is customary to end the citation with a page range showing the extent of a periodical article. This is particularly important when a through-paginated journal is cited without issue numbers, as it aids the reader in finding the article in a volume that has no single contents page. The page extent is also useful as an indicator of the scale and importance of the article. Whether or not to elide page ranges is a matter of house style; see 11.1.4 for guidance.

18.3.5 **Reviews**

Reviews are listed under the name of the reviewer; the place of publication and date of the book reviewed are helpful but not mandatory:

Ames-Lewis, F., review of Ronald Lightbown, *Mantegna* (Oxford, 1986), in *Renaissance Studies*, 1 (1987), 273–9.

If the review has a different title, cite that, followed by the name of the author and title of the book reviewed:

Porter, Roy, 'Lion of the Laboratory', review of Gerald L. Geison, *The Private Science of Louis Pasteur* (Princeton, 1995), in *TLS* (16 June 1995), 3–4.

18.4 Theses and dissertations

Citations of theses and dissertations should include the degree for which they were submitted, and the full name of the institution as indicated on the title page. Titles should be printed in roman within single quotation marks. The terms *dissertation* and *thesis*, as well as *DPhil* and *PhD*, are not interchangeable; use whichever appears on the title page of the work itself. The date should be that of submission; it should preferably not be placed within parentheses:

Hill, Daniel, 'Divinity and Maximal Greatness', PhD thesis, King's College, London, 2001.

Universities and institutions must always be cited using their full, official form, so as to avoid potential confusion between similar-sounding names (for example *Washington University* and *University of Washington*).

18.5 Citations to support author–date referencing

As explained in 18.1.1 and in Chapter 17, where the author–date referencing method is in use, bibliographic citations are reconfigured so that the publication date appears at the head after the author's name (this is the formula that the reader, trying to trace a work referenced in the text, will seek):

> Lakoff, R. (1975). *Language and Women's Place*. New York: Harper and Row.

A reference list in this system is ordered:

- alphabetically by author (for complications where multiple authors are named see 18.1.3)
- multiple works by a single author (or by the same combination of authors) are ordered chronologically by year of publication
- multiple works by the same author(s) published in the same year are ordered alphabetically by title, ignoring definite and indefinite articles.

Author–date references in the text must be able to identify each work uniquely by means of the author's surname and date of publication alone. Where more than one work by a particular author or authors is published in a single year, it follows that some further identifier is needed to distinguish them. In this case the dates of publication are supplemented by lower-case letters, which are used in the in-text references:

> Lyons, J. (1981a), *Language and Linguistics: An Introduction* (Cambridge: Cambridge University Press).
>
> Lyons, J. (1981b), *Language, Meaning and Context* (London: Fontana Paperbacks).

The letters are allocated according to the order in the reference list.

18.6 Manuscript and other documentary sources

18.6.1 **Introduction**

For non-published documentary sources that have been digitized, see 18.6.6 and 18.8.

Conventions for citing physical manuscripts and archival material are less well established than those for published works, partly because it is often necessary to formulate citations in a way that addresses the qualities and subject matter of the particular material at hand. When establishing how best to order and describe manuscript sources ensure that each citation:

- is consistent with others of the same kind
- conforms with the basic bibliographical principles that control the ordering of elements for citing published matter (authors are cited before titles, and titles before dates)
- includes the repository where the manuscript is stored, and, if possible, a shelf mark, piece number, or other unique identifier that allows the manuscript to be located within that repository.

The different elements that constitute a manuscript citation will normally fall into one of two categories:

- details that *describe* the item (author, title and/or descriptor, and date)
- details that *locate* the item (name and location of repository, collection name and/or shelf mark, page or folio number(s)).

Treat author details as for book details (see 18.2.2).

18.6.2 **Titles and descriptors**

When a manuscript has a distinct title it should be cited in roman, in single quotes. General descriptors appear in roman only, and usually take a lower-case initial:

> Chaundler, Thomas, 'Collocutiones', Balliol College, Oxford, MS 288.
> exchequer accounts, Dec. 1798, Cheshire Record Office, E311.

Depending on the readership and function of the bibliography, descriptors are not always necessary; sometimes a shelf mark is enough for an informed reader to comprehend the general nature of what is being cited. For example, in a specialist historical text it may be sufficient to provide piece numbers for documents in the National Archives without naming the collection to which they belong:

> PRO, FO 363   PRO, SP 16/173, fo. 48

18.6.3 **Dates**

Dates follow description details and are not enclosed in parentheses:

Smith, Francis, travel diaries, 1912–17, British Library, Add. MS 23116.

Bearsden Ladies' Club minutes, 12 June 1949, Bearsden and Milngavie District Libraries, box 19/d.

18.6.4 **Repository information**

The level of information required to identify the place accurately will depend upon the stylistic conventions of the work in which the citation occurs, the anticipated readership of the publication, and the size and general accessibility of the repository being cited. Repositories of national collections and archives may not require a country or city as part of the address. Some repositories include enough information within their name to render further address details otiose. If one particular repository is to be cited many times, consider creating an abbreviation that can be used in its place, with a key at the top of the bibliography, or group like citations together as a subdivision within the list.

In English-language publications names of repositories are always roman with upper-case initials, regardless of the conventions applied in the language of the country of origin:

Bibliothèque Municipale, Valenciennes, MS 393
Biblioteca Nazionale Centrale, Florence, cod. II.II.289

18.6.5 **Location details**

Any peculiarities of foliation or cataloguing must be faithfully rendered: a unique source is permitted a unique reference, if that is how the archive stores and retrieves it. For archives in non-English-speaking countries, retain in the original language everything—however unfamiliar—except the name of the city. Multiple shelf-mark numbers or other numerical identifiers should not be elided:

Bodleian Library, Oxford, MS Rawlinson D. 520, fol. 7
Paris, Bibliothèque Nationale de France, MS fonds français 146
Koninklijke Bibliotheek, The Hague, handschriften 34C18, 72D32/4

18.6.6 **Grey literature**

Grey literature is defined as 'manifold document types produced on all levels of government, academics, business and industry in print and electronic formats that are protected by intellectual property rights, of sufficient quality to be collected and preserved by library holdings or institutional repositories, but not controlled by commercial publishers i.e., where publishing is not the primary activity of the producing body'.

Such non-published material includes reports by companies, ministries, or research teams, theses (see 18.4), newsletters, technical notes, product catalogues, presentations, personal communications, working papers, academic courseware, and much more. Although there are fewer established conventions, efforts should be made to follow the style consistently using the general pattern applied to published matter, so that valid XML tagging can ensure that citation indexes will successfully acquire, analyse, and disseminate the information correctly.

18.7 Audio and audiovisual materials

18.7.1 **Introduction**

For broadcasts and recordings the ordering of elements within a citation may differ according to the content of the recording or the purpose for which it is cited: sound recordings, for example, might be best listed under the name of the conductor, the name of the composer, or even the name of the ensemble. As with all citations, sufficient information should be given to enable the reader to understand what type of work it is, and how to find it.

18.7.2 **Audio recordings**

Essential elements to include are title (see 8.5 for typographical treatment of titles), recording company and catalogue number, and, if available, date of issue or copyright. Other useful information includes details of performers and composers, specific track information, recording date (especially if significantly different from date of issue), authorship and title of any sleeve notes that accompany the recording, and the exact type of recording (e.g. wax cylinder, 78 rpm, compact disc, audio file format), and a Uniform Resource Indicator (URI) if accessed online. The following examples show an appropriate style for presenting such information:

Carter, Elliott, *The Four String Quartets*, Juilliard String Quartet (Sony S2K 47229, 1991).

Davis, Miles, and others, 'So What', in *Kind of Blue*, rec. 1959 (Columbia CK 64935, 1997) [CD].

Vitry, Philippe de, *Philippe de Vitry and the Ars Nova*, Orlando Consort (Amon Ra CD-SAR 49, 1991) [incl. sleeve notes by Daniel Leech-Wilkinson, 'Philippe de Vitry and the 14th-Century Motet'].

Audio recordings that combine different works without a clear single title may require more than one title:

Dutilleux, Henri, *L'Arbre des songes*, and Peter Maxwell Davies, *Concerto for Violin and Orchestra*, André Previn, cond., Isaac Stern, violin, and Royal Philharmonic Orchestra (CBS MK 42449, 1987).

In recording numbers a hyphen rather than an en rule is the norm. Where a range of such numbers is given they should never be elided:

Lightnin' Hopkins, *The Complete Aladdin Recordings* (EMI Blues Series CDP-7-96843-2, n.d.) [2-vol. CD set].

18.7.3 **Films, videos, and broadcasts**

See also 18.3. When citing audiovisual, video, and broadcast media, the three key elements that need to be included are:

- title of the piece (italic or single quotation marks), or a description of what the item is (roman):

  The Empire Strikes Back 'How to Play Women's Lacrosse'
  interview with Albert Einstein

- broadcasting or production details, including a date
- short description of the medium, unless this is already made clear by the context or a heading within the bibliography.

If the citation is of a digital version of a pre-digital film or broadcast, include details of the original work, the source type (video etc.), date of post, and URI.

'Tony Hancock Face to Face interview 01' with John Freeman [video], YouTube (televised by the BBC 7 February 1960, uploaded 17 March 2009), http://www.youtube.com/watch?v=lnkovGeASzE

Podcasts can be treated similarly:

Fay Weldon, interview with Kirsty Young, *Desert Island Discs Archive* [podcast], BBC Radio 4 (9 May 2010), http://www.bbc.co.uk/podcasts/series/dida05/all.

18.8 Websites and other digital media

18.8.1 **General principles**

The basic template for citing digital references might include some, or all, of the following classes of information (not always necessarily in this order):

- author's or editor's name (if no author, list under the title or website name)
- title of the article or other subsection used (roman in quotes) or description of the content if there is no title (roman, in square brackets)
- general title or title of the complete work (italic)
- volume or page numbers (when citing online journals that have no volumes the date may be cited here)
- general information, including type of medium (in square brackets)
- date on which the material was created or on which it was published or posted (day month year, in parentheses); use *n.d.* if the date is unknown, or *c.XXXX* if approximate date is known
- institution or organization responsible for maintaining or publishing the information (roman, with maximal capitalization)
- address of online source or digital object identifier (doi)
- pagination or online equivalent
- date accessed.

Examples of specific digital citations are presented in 18.8.5.

Electronic books, journals, magazines, newspapers, and reviews should be treated as much as possible like their print counterparts, with the same style adopted for capitalization, italics, and quotation marks. It is sometimes less straightforward to fit the pertinent information into the categories normally associated with print publications, such as author, title, place and date of publication, and publisher. Aspects such as pagination and publication date may differ between hard-copy and digital versions, so the reference must make clear which is meant.

Where print versions exist they can—but need not—be cited; similarly, citing digital versions of printed media is not mandatory. To provide the reader with both does, however, offer all possible options for following up a reference. When making citations for references with more than one online source, choose the one that is most likely to be stable and durable.

18.8.2 **Media**

Where the context or content of a citation does not make obvious the format or platform in which the data are held, give additional clarification (typically in square brackets):

[DVD]   [blog]   [abstract]

There is no need to add *online* or *available from* to the citation, since this will be apparent from the inclusion of an address.

18.8.3 **Resource locators**

URLs are unreliable as a medium- to long-term source locator for various reasons and some house styles preclude them from references. However, even if a web page no longer exists, the URL still constitutes a historical source if it is provided with a date of access (presumably, it existed at a point in the past, when the author accessed it), and there may not be an alternative source for the information.

If citing the whole of a document that consists of a series of linked pages, give the highest-level URL; this is most often the contents or home page. Give enough information to allow the reader to navigate to the exact reference. Many sites provide a search facility and regularly archive material; the search function will provide the surest method of reaching the destination if the document is relocated.

The protocol *http* is commonly omitted for websites that include *www* in the domain name as the browser will automatically insert it, and it is becoming more common to omit *www* as well; however, other protocols exist, such as *ftp* and the encrypted variant *https*, so if there is any risk of confusion, include the protocols for all.

It is also good practice to include the trailing forward slash (which points to a resource on the website) after the domain name (http://www.royal.gov.uk/).

It is not advisable to enclose a URL in angle brackets because it can interfere with XML tagging. Do not add underline formatting to URLs in word processor files. Normal punctuation can be used after a URL:

> The British Armorial Bindings database, begun by John Morris and continued by Philip Oldfield, is now available on the Web at http://armorial.library.utoronto.ca/.

If citing a long URL is unavoidable, never hyphenate the address at a line break, or at hyphens. Divide URLs only after a solidus or a %; where this is impossible, break the URL before a punctuation mark, carrying it over to the following line. Where space allows, setting a URL on a separate line can prevent those of moderate length from being broken.

18.8.4 **Access information**

Up to four dates can be significant in providing a complete citation for an electronic source:

- the date the information was originally **created**, released, or printed; this is of special interest when citing online reprints of previously published material
- the date the information was originally **posted** or made available online: mainly of relevance when citing large online reference works
- the date the information was last **updated** or revised: rarely required
- the date the information was last **accessed** by the author: always record this and include it in the citation; editors should not change the author's access date as the web page may have changed.

It is rarely necessary to include more than two of the above dates, and usually the access date, and maybe the last updated date, will suffice.

18.8.5 **Types of digital citation**

Depending on their importance, some Internet material (e.g. a passing reference to a tweet, a Facebook update, or an image) may simply be referred to in passing in the text or in notes, rather than included as a reference in the bibliography. Full details should be provided in a footnote or endnote. The principles remain the same as for a reference, except that the first name of the author/originator is not reversed as it is in a bibliographical reference.

Print publication available online

UNESCO, *The United Nations World Water Development Report 4*, vol. 1: *Managing Water under Uncertainty and Risk* (Paris: UNESCO, 2012), http://unesdoc.unesco.org/images/0021/002156/215644e.pdf, accessed 9 Nov. 2013.

Online journal article

Druin, A., 'The Role of Children in the Design of New Technology', *Behaviour & Information Technology*, 21/1 (2002), 1–25. doi: 10.1080/01449290110108659

Liu, Ya-Ming, Yea-Huei Kao Yang, and Chee-Ruey Hsieh, 'Regulation and Competition in the Taiwanese Pharmaceutical Market under National Health Insurance', *Journal of Health Economics*, 31 (2012), 471–83. doi: 10.1016/j.jhealeco.2012.03.003

Article in a database

Li, Shu, Chungkun Shih, Chen Wang, Hong Pang, and Dong Ren, 'Forever Love: The Hitherto Earliest Record of Copulating Insects from the Middle Jurassic of China', *PLoS ONE*, 8/11 (2013), e78188. doi: 10.1371/journal.pone.0078188

News report

BBC News, 'Colchester General Hospital: Police Probe Cancer Treatment' (5 Nov. 2013), http://www.bbc.co.uk/news/uk-england-essex-24819973, accessed 5 Nov. 2013.

BBC News, 'Inside India's Mars Mission HQ' [video] (5 Nov. 2013), http://www.bbc.co.uk/news/world-24826253, accessed 5 Nov. 2013.

Hooper, Richard, 'Lebanon's Forgotten Space Programme', BBC News Magazine (14 Nov. 2013), http://www.bbc.co.uk/news/magazine-24735423, accessed 14 Nov. 2013.

Interview

McEwen, Stephen, 'Tan Twan Eng Interview: "I Have No Alternative but to Write in English"', *The Spectator* (20 May 2013), http://blogs.spectator.co.uk/books/2013/05/tan-twan-eng-interview-i-have-no-alternative-but-to-write-in-english/, accessed 9 Nov. 2013.

Online book

Beckford, William, *Vathek*, 4th edn (London, 1823) [online facsimile], http://beckford.c18.net/wbvathek1823.html, accessed 5 Nov. 2013.

Online article

Allaby, Michael, 'Feathers and Lava Lamps', Oxford Reference (2013), http://www.oxfordreference.com/page/featherslavalamps, accessed 9 Nov. 2013.

Online reference

'Gunpowder Plot', *Encyclopaedia Britannica*, http://www.britannica.com/EBchecked/topic/249505/Gunpowder-Plot, accessed 5 Nov. 2013.

Wikipedia article

'Oxford University Press', Wikipedia (last modified 5 Nov. 2013), http://en.wikipedia.org/wiki/Oxford_University_Press, accessed 5 Nov. 2013.

Blog

Tan, Siu-Lan, 'Why does this Baby Cry when her Mother Sings?' [including video], OUPblog (5 Nov. 2013), http://blog.oup.com/2013/11/why-does-this-baby-cry-when-her-mother-sings-viral-video/, accessed 9 Nov. 2013.

Television programme

Berger, John, Episode 1, *Ways of Seeing*, BBC (1972), https://www.youtube.com/watch?v=0pDE4VX_9Kk, accessed 9 Nov. 2013.

Online video

Nicholson, Christie, 'A Quirk of Speech May Become a New Vocal Style' [video], *Scientific American*, 17 Dec. 2011, http://www.scientificamerican.com/podcast/episode.cfm?id=a-quirk-of-speech-may-become-a-new-11-12-17, accessed 4 Nov. 2013.

Webcast

Yousafzai, Malala, 'Making a Wish for Action on Global Education: Malala Yousafzai addresses Youth Assembly at UN on her 16th Birthday, 12 July 2013' [webcast], UN Web TV, 12 Jul 2013, http://webtv.un.org/search/malala-yousafzai-un-youth-assembly/2542094251001?term=malala, accessed 15 Feb. 2015.

YouTube video

Arthur Rubinstein, 'Rachmaninoff Piano Concerto No. 2, Op. 18, I Moderato. Allegro (Fritz Reiner)' [video], YouTube (recorded 9 Jan. 1956, uploaded 8 Nov. 2011), http://www.youtube.com/watch?v=0Vv0Sy9FJrc&list=PLDB11C4F39E09047F, accessed 9 Nov. 2013.

Online image

M. Clarke, 'Exports of Coal to the IFS' [poster], Manchester Art Gallery, http://www.manchestergalleries.org/the-collections/search-the-collection/display.php?EMUSESSID=70bd7f1a388d79a82f52ea9aae713ef2&irn=4128, accessed 5 Nov. 2013.

'Christ the God Shepherd', stained glass window, Church of St Erfyl, Llanerfyl, Powys, Imaging the Bible in Wales Database, http://imagingthebible.llgc.org.uk//object/1884, accessed 10 Nov. 2013.

Podcast

Grayson Perry, 'I Found Myself in the Art World' [podcast], Reith Lecture (5 Nov. 2013), BBC Radio 4, http://downloads.bbc.co.uk/podcasts/radio4/reith/reith_20131105-0940b.mp3, accessed 5 Nov. 2013.

The speaker's name may be replaced with that of a writer or producer, depending on the podcast.

Facebook post/update

Barack Obama, 'Tomorrow is Veterans Day' [Facebook post] (10 Nov. 2013), https://www.facebook.com/photo.php?fbid=10151936988101749&set=a.53081056748.66806.6815841748&type=1&theatre, accessed 13 Nov. 2013.

John Harvey, '"These are a Few of My Favourite Things", No. 28' [Facebook post] (13 Nov. 2013), https://www.facebook.com/photo.php?fbid=229786530530896&set=a.108896335953250.15125.100004986510149&type=1&theatre, accessed 13 Nov. 2013.

If there is no obvious 'heading' that can be used in place of a title for the post, it can simply be described as a '[Facebook post]'.

Twitter post/tweet

Shakespeare's Globe, 'On this day in 1611 first production of The Tempest was performed by King's Men at Whitehall Palace before James I' [Twitter post], 5.48 a.m., 1 Nov. 2013, https://twitter.com/The_Globe/status/396257422928400385, accessed 5 Nov. 2013.

The date and time of messages are always those of the reader's time zone, as it may not be possible to determine the exact date and time a tweet was posted. The tweet itself may be omitted and replaced with the description 'Twitter feed', 'Twitter post', or 'tweet'. If the tweeter is a named or known individual, the tweet can also be listed under his/her real name followed by the username in parentheses, or vice versa.

Ebook

Rankin, Ian, *Saints of the Shadow Bible* [Kindle edn] (London: Orion, 2013).

or

Rankin, Ian, *Saints of the Shadow Bible* (Kindle edn, London: Orion, 2013).

Austen, Jane, *Persuasion*, ed. Gillian Beer (London: Penguin, 2003; Kindle edn, 2006).

The pagination of an ebook is not always fixed; hence reference is best made to a chapter or section rather than a page number. Some ebook editions provide print page numbers to facilitate referencing. Avoid device-specific indicators such as Kindle location numbers. As with any resource that is relatively new, citation styles vary and will probably change fairly quickly, as the technology continues to evolve. The last example above includes the publication details of the print as well as the ebook version. Some styles (not Oxford) suggest including the device on which it is read, the database from which it has been downloaded, and the date of the download.

Mobile app

Simogo, *Device 6* (version 1.1) [mobile application for iPhone and iPad], downloaded 9 Nov. 2013.

Eliot, T. S., *The Waste Land* (version 1.1.1) [mobile application for iPad] (London: Touch Press, 2013), downloaded 9 Nov. 2013.

Some styles also include the web address of the download site.

CD-ROM/DVD

United Nations, *World Population Prospects: The 2010 Revision* [CD-ROM] (New York: United Nations Department of Economic and Social Affairs, Population Division, 2011).

CHAPTER 19

Indexing

19.1 Introduction

A good index enables the user to navigate sensibly through the work's main topics and facts. How long it needs to be to accomplish this depends on the size and complexity of the work and the requirements and expectations of the readership. In general, a short index for a general book can account for as little as 1 per cent of the text it catalogues, while an exhaustive index for a specialist book can take up as much as 15 per cent. The editor should be consulted before preparing the index to a printed book, as length constraints may apply, such as those needed to make an even working (see 1.8). In digital products, there are no such constraints, and a professional indexer will achieve a better result if allowed to determine the index length.

The index is a vital component of the work, directly affecting the text's usefulness for the reader. This chapter provides some general guidance on producing and checking an index for those not trained in indexing. However, if you are an author who needs an index, especially for a large or important work, it is strongly recommended that you consider using a professional indexer. Not only are they skilled at choosing, compiling, and ordering an index's content using specialized software but they also bring a fresh pair of eyes to the text, which is invaluable in assessing the content from the reader's viewpoint. Indexing software also reduces the problems associated with changes in pagination and ensures typographical consistency. Indexes are best submitted electronically, as rekeying errors are hard to spot.

19.1.1 **Indexing in the digital age**

Although at first glance free-text searching in digital products might seem to make indexes redundant, the chief disadvantages are that users must know precisely what they are looking for, and how to spell it; that multiple hits may be generated with no indication of which are of greatest relevance; and that underlying concepts which do not have obvious key terms are not retrieved. A well-formed index is therefore just as important in digital as in print publications.

Indexes are often created from first or second proofs, i.e. late in the production process, using page numbers as locators. With the exception of ebooks where fixed layout is desirable (such as highly illustrated titles), the possibilities offered by reflowing the same text into a great variety of digital formats means that the page is irrelevant as a concept other than for the print edition. This brings a major advantage to the indexing process as it can now start at a much earlier stage, as soon as a stabilized text becomes available. Two methods of indexing unpaged content are described here: embedded indexing and indexing to location markers.

Embedded indexing

Embedded indexing (EI) involves inserting actual index terms as hidden text marked with a functional identifier at appropriate locations in the electronic version of the indexed document. After pagination, EI software builds the index automatically by associating the final page locations with each embedded index entry and performing the sorting, suppression of duplication, and formatting necessary to produce a usable index. Most of the common word-processing packages, including LaTex, include an EI system. The default is usually to produce an index with page locations, but an embedded index can be presented with hyperlinks for use in digital product. Because of its availability in word-processing software, embedded indexing is preferred by some publishers and by many authors producing their own indexes. It may be more time consuming for a professional indexer than production of a conventional index using specialized software. Authors making their own embedded indexes should also be aware that, unlike specialized indexing software, the default alphabetization routines of the word-processing packages may not fully implement the principles outlined below under 19.3 (though some systems include mechanisms that can 'force' the correct order). Authors planning to submit an embedded index should consult their publisher early on in the production process.

Tagging with code markers

An alternative approach is to mark the point in the text to which an index term is to be linked using a location marker rather than a page number. The location marker (known also as an ID, unique number, or tag) must be unique to each point to be marked. Apart from the use of location codes rather than page numbers, the construction of the index follows exactly the same course as a traditional index. It differs from embedded indexing in that only the location codes, not index terms, are inserted in the electronic text and the indexer compiles a separate, stand-alone index file.

19.2 What to index

19.2.1 **General principles**

The indexer's job is to identify and analyse concepts treated in the text so as to produce a series of headings based on its terminology; to indicate relationships between concepts; to group together information that is scattered in the text; and to synthesize main headings and subheadings into entries. All items of significance (names, places, concepts) should be entered, with correct page numbers and spelling. The needs of the user of the index should always be kept in mind, particularly in terms of what and where things will be sought: for example, in all but the most technical books an entry for *humankind* or *mankind* will be more helpful than one for *homo sapiens*. Looking at indexes of related works in the field can provide useful guidance.

Usually a single index will suffice: multiple indexes can be unhelpful and should not be provided without being agreed with the editor beforehand.

Indexes comprise a list of single headings or multiword headings followed by one or more locators (a page or page range, section, numbered paragraph, or some other division) to indicate where the topic is discussed in the text, or by a cross-reference to another heading. Entries complicated enough to require further division may have **subentries** within the **main entry**. In all but the most complex indexes, subentries within subentries (sub-subentries) should be avoided.

In some works it is desirable to highlight those references that include the principal discussion of a heading, and this is usually indicated by the use of bold type:

miners **245–7**, 257, 346

Editors of multi-author works must ensure as far as possible that contributors' terminology and sources have been standardized to a single form throughout a work: the index may otherwise require frequent cross-references to guide the reader between variants.

19.2.2 **Main entries**

Main entries are those most likely to be first sought by the reader, and should be in a form that anticipates where the reader will look for them. They should be concise and consist of nouns modified if necessary by adjectives, verbs, or other nouns; unless house style dictates otherwise, they should start with a capital letter only if the word is capitalized in the text. Normally choose the plural form unless the noun is uncountable, e.g. *lightning*. If use of the singular is unavoidable, both can be accommodated through parentheses: *cake*(*s*). If singular and plural forms have different meanings, both forms may be used in the index.

Ignore passing or minor references that give no information about the topic. Do not include entries from the preface, contents, introduction, and other preliminary matter unless they contain information not found elsewhere that is relevant to the subject of the work. There is no need to index bibliographies or reference lists. There is usually no need to augment a heading with supplementary information from the text, though in some cases a gloss or other clarification in parentheses may prove necessary, such as in *vom* (proper name prefix).

Use cross-references or subentries where a single reference spans ten or more pages, or where lengthy strings of locators threaten to clutter the layout. An array of unqualified or undifferentiated locators several lines deep is tiresome and unhelpful to users, who will have to spend too much time trying to locate the information they seek. Any string should ideally be reduced to six or fewer numbers. For example,

habitat loss 83–5, 100–7, 114–16, 117–18, 121–2, 125–9

can be broken down into:

habitat loss:
  from development 83–5, 100–7
  from erosion 125–9
  from logging 114–16
  in Asia 117–18
  in England 121–2

It is advisable to avoid main headings that echo the title or subtitle of the book. If such entries are essential, they must be succinct. In biographies or collections of letters, keep subentries relating to the subject to a reasonable minimum, confining them to factors of relevance.

19.2.3 **Subentries**

Subentries are used chiefly to analyse a complex subject heading made up of two or more discrete categories:

life:
  beginnings of 2, 98
  DNA's role in 5–7, 10, 12–13
  and inorganic matter 7, 10, 28–9, 48
  as process, not substance 10, 11
  understanding 240–1

Run together a simple heading with no general page references and only one category:

life, beginnings of 2, 98

Sub-subentries can most effectively be bypassed by denesting the subentry containing the sub-subentry into a separate main heading of its own, cross-referring to it as necessary. For example, in the following

moorlands:
  enclosure 198, 200, 201
  industries 201, 205
    charcoal-burning 197
    coalmining 201
    tin-mining 197
  roads 201

the subheading *industries* under *moorlands* can be changed to a cross-reference '*see also* industries', leading to a main entry with subentries of its own.

It may not always be possible, or practical, to use subentries and sub-subentries to avoid long strings of locators in an exhaustive index—such as one containing numerous references to authors of cited publications, a separate index of authors, or an index of musical works.

An index is not intended to be an outline of the entire text: there should not be a subheading for every locator, and a list of subheadings all with the same locator should be condensed.

19.2.4 **Notes**

Notes should be indexed only if they give information not found elsewhere in the text. When there is a reference to a topic and a footnote to that topic on the same page, it is usually sufficient to index the text reference only. See 19.6.

19.2.5 **Cross-references**

Cross-references are used to deal with such things as synonyms, near-synonyms, pseudonyms, abbreviations, variant or historical spellings, and closely related topics; they fall into two classes. The first, introduced by *see*, directs attention from one possible entry to a synonymous or analogous one, under which the references will be found:

Canton, *see* Guangzhou
farming, *see* agriculture
Dodgson, C. L., *see* Carroll, Lewis
Severus, Sextus Julius, *see* Julius Severus

The second, introduced by *see also*, extends the search by directing attention to one or more closely related entries or subentries. Two or more cross-references are given in alphabetical order, separated by semicolons:

birds 21, 88–9; *see also* chickens
clothing 27, 44–6, 105–6; *see also* costume; millinery
housing 134–9, 152; *see also* shelter, varieties of
tread depth 109; *see also* routine maintenance; tyre condition, indicators

Except in the case of reference from a non-preferred to a preferred term, or cross-references between acronyms and their full forms (see later in this section), do not use a 'see' cross-reference to a heading that takes up the same space as that occupied by the cross-reference itself. In

authors, *see* writers
writers 25, 36–8

the reader would find it easier if the locators were repeated after both headings (a 'double entry'). Equally, do not cross-refer simply to the same references listed under a different heading, nor bewilder the reader by circular or redundant cross-referring:

authors 25, 36–8, 50; *see also* writers
writers 25, 36–8, 50; *see also* authors

There must be no 'blind' cross-references: in other words, ensure that every cross-reference is to an existing entry. Cross-references to general areas rather than specific headings are often in italic:

authors, *see under the individual authors*

In addition to inversion of proper names (see 19.3.2), wherever a heading (or subheading) consists of more than one word a decision must be made as to whether another heading in inverse form is also needed. As long as the first word is one that users will look for, the direct form of entry is better:

right of expression
secondary education
trial by jury

If the second and later words in the heading are also words that may be looked for, then additional inverse headings (and cross-references) can be made:

education, secondary
expression, right of
jury trials

Inverse headings need not be made automatically for every multiword heading, as applied consistently they can have a significant effect on the index length. The selection will depend on the context: for example, the heading *education, secondary* above is not needed if *education* is the subject of the whole text.

Terms such as names of organizations are often referred to in the text in an abbreviated form. The indexer must decide whether to make a heading under the shortened form or at the spelled-out version of the term. It is generally agreed that widely known terms such as UNICEF and NATO can be indexed in their shortened forms without cross references from the spelled-out forms. However, the indexer will need to decide how much cross-referencing is appropriate for the likely users of the index. It may be helpful to include the full form in parentheses after the shortened version:

OUP (Oxford University Press)
Oxford University Press, *see* OUP

A double entry may also be used:

OUP (Oxford University Press)
Oxford University Press (OUP)

although if space is an issue a cross-reference may be more economical. For reasons of neatness and apparent consistency, it will often be advisable to adopt a single practice (all entries cross-referred from shortened form to full title or vice versa; or all double entered) for all organization names in a given index.

19.3 Alphabetical order

19.3.1 **Systems of alphabetization**

The two systems of alphabetizing headings are **word by word** and **letter by letter**, with minor variations in each. The International and British Standard (BS ISO 999: 1996) advocates word-by-word indexing, which is the system usually employed in general indexes in Britain. Letter-by-letter indexing is preferred in British encyclopedias, atlases, gazetteers, and some dictionaries, and is more common in the US.

The word-by-word system alphabetizes compound terms (those that consist of more than one word or element) up to the first word space and then begins again, so separated words precede closed compounds (e.g. *high water* comes before *highball*). Hyphens are treated as spaces, and the two parts of a hyphenated compound are treated as separate words, except where the first element is not a word in its own right (e.g. *de-emphasis*, *iso-osmotic*, *proto-language*).

In the letter-by-letter system alphabetization proceeds across spaces, with separated (and also hyphenated) words being treated as one word.

In both systems the alphabetization ignores apostrophes, accents and diacritics. Parenthetical descriptions are also ignored: *high* (light headed) is treated as a simple heading (i.e. as *high* alone would be).

Alphabetization continues until a comma indicates inverted order: for instance, *High, J.* is treated as *High* for alphabetization, although if there were several instances of *High*, the form *High, J.* would come after *High* alone and also after *High, B. Bath, order of the* would come before *Bath bun* and *Bath chair*.

Where headings are identical, indexing software will order terms in strict alphabetical order. This is preferred to some systems that order entries according to what they are, such as people first, then subjects, concepts, objects, places, and titles of works.

Thus in the example below *High, J.* comes first, as the name of a person.

These are time consuming because they require manual intervention on the indexer's part and it can be argued that many index users will not be aware of these conventions.

The example below demonstrates alphabetization in the word-by-word and letter-by-letter systems:

Word by word	**Letter by letter**
High, J.	High, J.
high (light-headed)	high (light-headed)
high chair	highball
high-fliers	highbrow
high heels	high chair
High-Smith, P.	Highclere Castle
high water	high-fliers
High Water (play)	high heels
highball	highlights
highbrow	Highsmith, A.
Highclere Castle	High-Smith, P.
highlights	high water
Highsmith, A.	*High Water* (play)
highways	highways

In both systems, letter groups are treated as one word if—such as *NATO* and *NASA*— they are pronounced as such. Otherwise, the word-by-word system lists all sets of letters before any full word, ignoring any full points:

Word by word	**Letter by letter**
I/O	I/O
IOU	iodine
IPA	IOU
i.p.i.	Iowa
IPM	IPA
i.p.s	IP address
IP address	Ipanema
Ipanema	i.p.i.
iodine	IPM
Iowa	i.p.s.

Definite and indefinite articles at the beginning of entries are transposed in both systems:

Midsummer Night's Dream, A
Vicar of Wakefield, The

In works written in English, foreign words are conventionally alphabetized by ignoring accents and diacritics, so for example *ö* and *ø* are treated as *o*. Some information on alphabetization in languages other than English is given in Chapter 12.

19.3.2 **Names**

Personal names are generally given in inverted form to bring the significant element (the surname) forward: so *Meynell, Alice* rather than *Alice Meynell.*

Where people bear the same surname, initials are conventionally listed before full names; a name with a title that is otherwise identical with one without should follow it:

Meynell, A.
Meynell, Dr A.
Meynell, Alice
Meynell, F.
Meynell, Sir F.
Meynell, W.
Meynell, W. G.

List names prefixed with *Mc*, *Mac*, or *M*ᶜ as if they were spelled *Mac*:

McCullers
MacFarlane

McFingal
McNamee

Personal names given only by surname in the text require a fuller form in the index, even if mentioned only in passing: *Shepard's illustrations* is therefore expanded to the heading *Shepard, E. H.* Bare surnames should be avoided wherever possible: particularly for specialist subjects an author should anticipate inserting missing names in an index generated by an indexer, or checking for accuracy those the indexer supplies.

Personal names in a single numbered (usually chronological) sequence should be recorded in that sequence in spite of any surnames or other additions. Beware the omission of a number, especially of *I*; if others in the sequence appear duly numbered, restore the number when listing. Hence *Frederick Barbarossa* should become *Frederick I Barbarossa* and precede *Frederick II*. Where appropriate—especially for the period before *c.*1300—index people by their given names, with their titles, offices, etc. provided with suitable cross-references. Note again that descriptions in parentheses are disregarded for the purposes of alphabetization:

Henry
Henry (of France), archbishop of Reims
Henry, chaplain
Henry I, count of Champagne
Henry (the Lion), duke of Saxony
Henry, earl of Warwick
Henry II, emperor and king of Germany
Henry IV, emperor and king of Germany
Henry I, king of England
Henry II, king of England
Henry, king of England, the young king
Henry, scribe of Bury St Edmunds
Henry, son of John
Henry de Beaumont, bishop of Bayeux
Henry of Blois, bishop of Winchester
Henry Blund
Henry of Essex
Henry the Little
Henry de Mowbray
Henry Fitz Robert

Treat *St* as if it were spelled *Saint*, for both personal and place names. In alphabetical arrangement, saints considered in their own right as historical figures are indexed under their names, the abbreviation *St* being postponed:

Augustine, St, bishop of Hippo
Margaret, St, queen of Scotland
Rumwald, St, of Kings Sutton

When a place or a church is named after a saint, or the saint's name complete with prefix is used as a surname, alphabetize it under the word *Saint* as if spelled out, not under *St*. Thus for example *St Andrews, Fife*, *St Peter's, Rome*, and *St John, Olivier* are all treated as if they were written *Saint*—:

Saint, J. B.
St Andrews, Fife
St Benet's Hall
St James Infirmary
St John-Smythe, Q,
Saint-Julien
St Just-in-Roseland

When the saint's name is in a foreign language, alphabetize its abbreviation under the full form in that language: thus *Ste-Foy* is alphabetized as *Sainte-Foy*.

Foreign names are treated in the form familiar to the reader, so there is a comma in *Bartók, Béla* even though in Hungarian the surname comes first. Some information on alphabetizing non-English names is given at 6.1.8 and 6.1.9.

Alphabetize natural geographical features according to whether the descriptive component forms part of the name:

Graian Alps
Grampians, the
Granby, Lake
Granby River
Gran Canaria
Grand, North Fork
Grand, South Fork
Grand Bérard, Mont
Grand Canyon
Grand Rapids
Grand Ruine, La
Grand Teton

Always retain the component if it is part of the official name:

Cape Canaveral
Cape Cod
Cape of Good Hope
Cape Horn

Where confusion may result—in atlases, for example—cross references or multiple entries are common.

19.3.3 **Scientific terms**

If the first character or characters in a chemical compound is a prefix or numeral, such as O-, *s*-, *cis*-, it is ignored for alphabetizing but taken into account in ordering a group of similar entries. For example, '2,3-dihydroxybenzene', '2,4-dihydroxybenzene', and '*cis*-1,2-dimethyl cyclohexane' would all be found under *D*, and the abbreviation '(*Z,Z*)-7,11-HDDA', expanded as '*cis*-7,*cis*-11-hexadecadien-1-yl acetate', would be alphabetized under *H*. In chemical notation disregard subscript numerals except when the formulas are otherwise the same:

vitamin B_1
vitamin B_2
vitamin B_6
vitamin B_{12}

Greek letters prefixing chemical terms, star names, etc. are customarily spelled out (and any hyphen dropped): for example, α Centauri, α chain, and α-iron are alphabetized as *Alpha Centauri*, *alpha* (α) *chain*, and *alpha iron*. However, Greek letters beginning the name of a chemical compound are ignored in alphabetization: for example, 'α-oxo carbenes' is spelled thus but alphabetized under *O* for *oxo*.

19.3.4 **Symbols and numerals**

There are two systems for alphabetizing symbols and numerals: the International and British Standard advises listing them before the alphabetical sequence, but they are also commonly arranged as if spelled out, alphabetizing '=' as *equals*, '£' as *pounds*, '→' as *implies*, '&' as *ampersand*, '1st' as *first*, and '7' as *seven*. An ampersand *within* an entry is best treated either as if spelled out as *and* or ignored.

Before the alphabetical sequence	**As if spelled out**
1st Cavalry	1st Cavalry
2/4 time	*42nd Street*
3i plc	3i plc
42nd Street	2/4 time

Where the names of symbols may be problematic, it may be helpful to give an umbrella heading for symbols (for example *rules of inference*, *linguistic symbols*, *coding notation*) in addition to alphabetical listings. Whichever system is followed, maintain consistency throughout.

19.3.5 **Subentries**

Arrangement of subentries should normally be alphabetical by key words (but see 19.4), ignoring leading prepositions, conjunctions, and articles in alphabetical ordering. Ensure that subentries are worded so that they are unambiguous and 'read' from or to the heading in a consistent pattern. Arrange subentries beneath related or similar headings in parallel. Cross-references from a main heading with subentries may either follow the locators for the main entry:

monasticism 20–3, 69, 131, 158, 202; *see also* ascetism; religious orders
  cathedrals 112
  churches 206
  and mission 89, 90, 94, 134
  reform 112–14
  in Spain 287

or be given as the final subentry:

monasticism 20–3, 69, 131, 158, 202
  cathedrals 112
  churches 206
  and mission 89, 90, 94,134
  reform 112–14
  in Spain 287
  see also ascetism; religious orders

19.4 Non-alphabetical order

Some matter will call for ordering on some basis other than alphabetical, such as numerical, chronological, or hierarchical. Where this matter forms part only of an occasional group of subentries within an otherwise alphabetical index it may be ordered as necessary without comment; however, where a significant amount needs to be included in the form of headings it should be placed in a separate index where similar elements can be found and compared easily. Never arrange entries or subentries themselves by order of locator, as this is of least help to the reader.

Chronological ordering may be useful in arranging entries or subentries, for example according to the life and times of the subject in a biography:

dynasties, early:
  Legendary Period (prehistoric) 1–33, 66, 178
  Xia (*c.*2100–1600 BC) 35–60, 120
  Shang (*c.*1600–*c.*1027 BC) 61–84
  Zhou (*c.*1027–256 BC) 12, 85–100, 178
  Quin (221–207 BC) 109–35
  Han (206 BC–AD 220) 132,136–7, 141
Hart, Horace:
  birth 188
  apprenticeship 192, 195
  in London 195–9
  in Oxford 200, 201–60
  retirement 261
  illness and death 208, 277–9

Subjects may sometimes be ordered according to some recognized hierarchical system of classification (e.g. *BA, MA, MPhil, DPhil* or *duke, marquess, earl, viscount, baron*). Indexes of scriptural references are arranged in their traditional order rather than alphabetically.

19.5 Presentation of indexes

19.5.1 **Style**

Index matter is set in small type, one or two sizes down from text size, usually set justified left (ragged right) in two or more columns. Typically, the running heads are *Index* on both recto and verso, though two or more indexes can be differentiated according to their title, such as *Author index*, *General index*, *Index of first lines*.

Begin each entry with a lower-case letter unless it is for a word that is capitalized in the text. Carefully check hyphenation, italics, spelling, and punctuation for consistency with the text. Instructions for cross-referring (*see*, *see also*) should be italicized. However, 'see' and 'see also' commonly appear in roman when they are followed by italicized text:

> Plutarch's *Lives*, see *Parallel Lives*; *see also* biographies; Dryden
> Poema Morale, see *Selections from Early Middle English*
> *Poetics, see* Aristotle

In Oxford style there is an en space between the entry and the first locator; interposing a comma is less usual nowadays. If a heading ends with a numeral (*B-17, Channel 13, M25, uranium 235*), a colon or comma can be added to separate it from the locator but a space is acceptable if that is the chosen style for other entries. Oxford style separates an entry from a following cross-reference with a comma but others omit the punctuation in accordance with other entries.

Separate multiple cross-references from each other with commas or semicolons:

> earnings *see* income; taxation; wages

There is no punctuation at the end of entries. Oxford style inserts a colon after a main heading when there are no locators but instead a list of subentries

> earnings:
> income 12, 14–22, 45
> taxation 9, 11, 44–9
> wages 12–21, 48–50

but other styles only use the colon in this way in run-on entries but not in set-out style (see 15.5.2).

19.5.2 **Layout**

The first or only index in a work typically begins on a new recto, though subsequent indexes can begin on a new page.

The samples below show the two basic styles of typographic design for indexes, the subentries being either **set out** (or **indented**) or **run on** (or **run in**). The set-out style uses a new (indented) line for each sub entry; it is therefore clearer than the run-on style, though it takes up more room. In the set-out style, avoid further subdivision of subentries if possible, as this can result in complicated and space wasting structures. In the run-on style, subentries do as the name suggests: they run on and are separated from the main entry—and each other—by a semicolon. They are indented appropriately to distinguish them from the heading. Sub-subentries should be avoided entirely in run-on style. Take particular care that the arrangement is logical and consistent, since the style's density makes it more difficult to read.

Set out

shields 4, 78, 137, 140
  heraldic designs 82
  kite-shaped 199
  round 195
  Viking 43, 44, 53
ships/shipping 22, 68, 85, 230–52
  design and navigation 6
  pirate 23
  spending on 59
  see also galleys; longships; piracy
shipyards 234

Run on

shields 4, 78, 137, 140; heraldic designs 82; kite-shaped 199; round 195; Viking 43, 44, 53

ships/shipping 22, 68, 85, 230–52; design and navigation 6; pirate 23; spending on 59; see also galleys; longships; piracy

shipyards 234

Which style a publisher chooses depends on the length and number of subentries in the final index copy, and the conventions of related works. In any case, index copy must be submitted for setting with all entries and subentries in the set-out form for markup: it is easier for the typesetter to run these on afterwards, if necessary, than it is to set out an index from copy that was presented in the run-on format.

Turn-lines or turnovers (where text runs to more than one line of typescript) should be indented consistently throughout, and in set out style should be indented more deeply than the deepest subheading indentation. To save space, sub-subentries—where unavoidable—may be run on even in otherwise set-out indexes.

When an entry breaks across a page—most especially from the bottom of a recto to the top of a verso—the heading or subheading is repeated and a continuation note added during typesetting:

shields (*cont.*)
Viking 43, 44, 53

19.6 Number references

In references to pagination and dates, use the smallest number of figures consistent with clarity: see 11.1.4.

Be as specific as possible in your references. For this reason, do not use section or clause numbers instead of page numbers unless they are frequent and the entire index is to be organized that way. Avoid using 'f.' and 'ff.'; give instead the first and last pages of the material: *123–5*, for example, denotes one continuous discussion spanning three pages, whereas *123, 124, 125* denotes three separate short references. Avoid using *passim* ('throughout'). Cite the page extent of a chapter and not, for example, *Ch. 11*.

References to footnotes and endnotes may simply give the page number. If more detail is desired, give references to footnotes and endnotes in the form '*word* 90 n. 17' for one note and '*word* 90 nn. 17, 19' for two or more; each has a full point and a space after the abbreviation. There is no need to give the note number where there is only one note on the page cited; in such cases it is Oxford style to insert a thin space between page number and 'n.'

To provide the most effective help to the reader, a general index serving more than one volume must include the volume number as part of each locator, regardless of whether the pagination runs through volumes in a single sequence or begins anew with each volume. Volume numbers may be styled in Roman numerals, often in small capitals, separated by a full point: '*word* III. 90'. Indexes to a group of periodicals may have both the series and volume number as part of the locator.

Though simple page references are often sufficient, it may be appropriate to mark figures denoting references to illustrations in italic or bold, or with some typographic symbol (such as an asterisk or dagger), and provide an introductory note at the start of the index in the form *Italic/bold numbers denote reference to illustrations*. Some authors use a similar treatment to flag passages that are particularly significant or include definitions; again, explain this practice at the start of the index (but bear in mind that readers often ignore these explanatory notes).

CHAPTER 20

Copyright and other publishing responsibilities

20.1 Introduction

This chapter is not intended to provide legal advice, but as a general guide to copyright and other related areas, with emphasis on the position in the UK. It should alert readers to matters on which help may need to be sought from their publisher or legal adviser.

20.2 UK copyright

20.2.1 **General principles**

Copyright is a property right that attaches to an 'original' literary, dramatic, musical, or artistic work: examples of these are books, letters, drawings, book layouts, and computer programs. It arises when a work is created in permanent form such as in writing, or by visual, audio, or electronic means. Copyright initially belongs to the creator of the work unless the work is made in the course of employment, when it will generally belong to the employer. In the UK the test of 'originality' has been characterized as low: for example, a train timetable can attract copyright protection. In many other countries, such as France and Germany, a higher degree of originality has generally been required for copyright protection, as a copyright work is expected to demonstrate some aspect of the author's 'personality'. However, following developments in European case law, a certain convergence has come about, with 'originality' in all EU Member States requiring the work to be the 'author's own intellectual creation'. Broadly, copyright protects the expression of ideas, not ideas themselves, although the two do converge: for instance, incidents in a story have been protected.

In the UK the Copyright, Designs and Patents Act 1988 ('Copyright Act 1988') established the copyright period for most of types of work to be the life of the author plus fifty years from the end of the year in which the author died. From 1 July 1995 this was increased to the life of the author plus seventy years. Reference books, multi-author works, and other works with no named author are also covered by the Copyright Act 1988, and it can be very difficult to establish whether they are still in copyright.

A separate copyright, belonging to the publisher and lasting for twenty-five years from the end of the year of first publication, also exists. This right attaches to the typographical arrangement of a literary, musical, or dramatic work, irrespective of whether the underlying content of the work is still in copyright. This provides the publisher with protection from unauthorized reproduction of the printed page.

As from 1995, a new right akin to copyright was introduced. This right, called 'publication right', arises where a previously unpublished work is first published after the expiry of copyright. It lasts for twenty-five years from the end of the year of first publication.

Copyright confers on its owner the exclusive right to authorize certain acts in relation to their work, including copying, publishing, and adapting. Copyright owners can give third parties the right to use their works by licensing or assigning the work. Licensing means allowing a third party to use the work in a specified way, for example in a certain territory, for a certain length of time, in a specified language, or on a specific medium, or a combination of these. Generally, assigning a work means that the work is permanently given away. Copyright owners will usually only deal with their works in this way in return for financial compensation. This may be a one-off fee or royalties (which are payments linked to sales of the work). Authors' agreements with their publishers often provide that copyright transferred to the publishers revert to the author in certain circumstances, such as if the publisher allows the work to go out of print.

Copyright is infringed if the whole or a substantial part of the work is reproduced without the copyright owner's permission. (There are exceptions to this, described in 20.2.3.). Although the amount used will be relevant, the test is qualitative rather than quantitative. If the essential element of a work is copied, even if this constitutes only a small part of the work quantitatively, copyright will be infringed.

If authors or editors adapt or add to a copyright work, and in so doing exercise sufficient skill and care, demonstrating the efforts of their own intellectual creation, then a new copyright can arise in the revised work. Nevertheless, if the revised work incorporates a substantial part of the original work without the consent of the copyright owner, copyright in the original work will be infringed.

A joint copyright work is one in which the contributions of two or more authors are commingled. A collective work is one in which the contribution of each author, and initially the copyright for it, is separate from that of the other author(s). One party to a joint copyright cannot alone give consent binding on their co-authors to use a joint work.

Copyright is subject to national frontiers. Different copyright periods apply, and acts of infringement that take place outside the UK are not generally actionable in the UK. As a general rule, proceedings have to be brought in the jurisdiction in which the infringement took place.

20.2.2 **Illustrations**

Illustrations an author wishes to include, but that are not their own work, are governed by laws similar to those for writing. For example, in the main, the copyright in a painting belongs to the artist, and continues with their heirs or anyone to whom they have transferred their copyright until seventy years after their death. Although the owners of the painting may sell it, they may not generally reproduce it without the copyright owner's permission. The same law applies to commissioned works, including photographs, with copyright belonging to the creator and not the commissioner, unless otherwise agreed. Copyright in images is quite complex, especially in multimedia works and websites, and a specialist picture researcher may be needed to determine what may and may not be done with them. For example, although works of art are on show in a public place and are themselves often out of copyright, permission to reproduce must sometimes be sought from the gallery that owns or displays them. Also, the photographer of a painting can hold their own copyright in the photograph they have taken.

20.2.3 **Fair dealing**

The Copyright Act 1988 contains a list of various activities which permit substantial parts of a copyright work to be reproduced without the copyright owner's permission, in certain circumstances. Of most relevance to authors and publishers are the various 'fair dealing' exceptions which operate as a defence to an act that would otherwise be an infringement of copyright. In general, when reproducing a substantial part of a work using one of these defences sufficient acknowledgement to the copyright owner needs to be given. The forms of fair dealing are as follows: use for purposes of non-commercial research or private study, for the purposes of criticism or review (provided the work has already been made available to the public), or for the purposes of reporting current events. Photographs are excluded from the fair dealing provisions relating to the reporting of current events.

The amount of a work that can be copied within the fair dealing limits varies according to the particular circumstances of the works in question, although there is no fixed portion or percentage that may be copied from a work. Issues to take into account include whether the work could be considered by potential purchasers to constitute a substitute for the other work, and the number and extent of the proposed quotations or extracts in the context of the work in which they are to be incorporated. Trade practice may also be relevant. Various guidelines have been issued, for example by the Society of Authors, but these are not legally binding and are by way of general guidance only. As a general rule, copyists must reproduce the minimum necessary to achieve their purposes.

Separate provisions exist for dealing by librarians and for copying for the purposes of educational instruction or examination.

In summary, therefore, there are two steps to determining whether the use of a work infringes the copyright in it. It must be established whether a substantial part of the work has been used. If so, one must consider whether such use constitutes fair dealing.

20.2.4 **Moral rights**

Under the Copyright Act 1988, authors have four basic 'moral rights'; many other countries extend similar 'moral rights' to their authors. The rights apply to works entitled to copyright protection, and ownership of copyright is a separate issue: authors can sell their copyright without affecting their moral rights, which cannot be assigned but can be waived. (The Act itself gives specific information about when and to whom the rights do and do not apply, and how the right of paternity is asserted in the case of non-literary works.) The rights are:

- **the right of paternity**: the right to be identified as the work's author. This needs to be asserted, as it does not exist automatically; many publishers affirm the author's moral right to be identified as the author of the work as a matter of course, usually on the title verso. The right lasts for the same period as the copyright period.
- **the right of integrity**: the right to protest against treatment that 'amounts to distortion or mutilation of the work or is otherwise prejudicial to the honour or reputation of the author'. (Thus something done that is prejudicial to the author's honour or reputation will not generally be actionable unless there is *also* some modification to the work itself, although the context in which a work is placed can constitute a 'treatment'.) The right does not need to be asserted, as it exists automatically; it lasts for the same period as the copyright period. It is common practice for publishers to ask authors to waive by contract their right to protest against such treatment, where modification of the work is required for editorial or sub-licensing purposes.

The rights of paternity and integrity do not extend to works reporting current events, or to works where an author contributes to a periodical or other collective work of reference. In such cases the work may be trimmed, altered, and edited without the author's consent, subject to the general laws of copyright and any contractual obligations which may be owed to the authors.

- **the right of false attribution**: the right not to have a literary, dramatic, musical, or artistic work falsely attributed to one as author. This right lasts for twenty years after the person's death.
- **the right of privacy of photographs and films commissioned for private and domestic purposes**: the right not to have such photographs or films shown in public or issued to the public.

20.2.5 **Database rights**

In the EU a separate right that protects databases, akin to copyright, has existed since 1998. This right, which arises automatically, can exist alongside copyright in a database. Database right arises where a collection of data or other material is created which: (*a*) is arranged in such a way that the items are individually accessible; and (*b*) is the result of a substantial investment in either the obtaining, verification or presentation of the data. Database right is infringed by the extraction and/or re-utilization of the whole or a substantial part of the contents of the database.

Database right lasts for fifteen years from making, but if publication takes place during this time, the term is fifteen years from publication.

20.3 Copyright conventions

Most countries give copyright protection to foreign works under international copyright treaties, such as the Berne and Universal Copyright Conventions (see 20.3.1 and 20.3.2). Anomalies exist in the treatment afforded in different countries, however, for example because the qualification requirements and rules on ownership and duration differ.

20.3.1 **Berne Convention for the Protection of Literary and Artistic Works**

Most industrialized countries are signatories to the Berne Convention, including the UK, the US, and Russia. The Berne Convention does not require registration of copyright and there is no obligation to include a copyright statement or to use the © symbol (although doing so is good practice in any event).

20.3.2 **Universal Copyright Convention**

To claim copyright protection in signatories to the Universal Copyright Convention, the following formality must be complied with: the symbol ©, the name of the copyright owner, and date of first publication must appear in a prominent place in every copy of the work published with the authority of the copyright owner. There is no requirement to register the copyright. Very few countries are parties to the Universal Copyright Convention and not to the Berne Convention, and so in most of the world, to obtain copyright protection this © wording is not required, although, as said above, its use is good practice in any event.

Having said that there is no requirement to register copyright, in some countries, such as the US and China, it can be advisable to do so to avoid potential enforcement problems.

20.4 Permissions

20.4.1 **What needs permission**

As explained above, unless the fair dealing provisions apply the copyright owner's permission needs to be obtained when a substantial part of a copyright work is to be copied. Such permission may sometimes only be given on payment of a fee or some other form of consideration. Most publishers expect authors to secure permissions to reproduce any copyrighted work in their text.

There can be no hard-and-fast rules to allow authors to gauge when they have taken a 'substantial part' of a work. As stated in 20.2.1, substantiality is a qualitative measure and calculating the arithmetic proportion copied does not assist. An extract may be deemed to be a substantial part of a work, and therefore infringing, even where only a small part of the work has been taken. Careful consideration must always be given to the amount copied from a qualitative viewpoint. For example, one author was found to have infringed the copyright of another when he copied one page from a long book, and a thirty-two-line poem was deemed to have been infringed by the unauthorized use of four lines. If in doubt authors should seek guidance from their editor/publisher.

20.4.2 **Requesting permission**

In requesting permission, authors should describe the work in which the material is to be included, specifying the author, the title, the publisher, and the type of work, so the copyright owner understands where, and in what circumstances, their material will appear. Authors should give the copyright owner specific information about the work in which the material originally appeared, to aid identification.

Authors should make clear if they are translating, redrawing, or modifying copyright material. Care should be taken to request all the rights needed. Note that the rights for different territories may be separately owned. Also, care needs to be taken when issuing a new edition of a work to check whether the original permissions cover the new edition as well.

Crown copyright publications include bills and Acts of Parliament, command papers, reports of select committees, Hansard, non-parliamentary publications by government departments, naval charts published by the Ministry of Defence, and Ordnance Survey publications. The rules relating to Crown copyright are different from the general rules on copyright. Guidance can be obtained from the National Archives.

20.4.3 **Acknowledgements**

This section sets out general industry practice relating to acknowledgements. It applies where the copyright owner does not impose specific provisions relating to the acknowledgement. For details on setting out acknowledgements see 1.2.11.

The acknowledgement should identify: (*a*) the author of the work (remembering that under the fair dealing provisions, it is the author who has to be acknowledged, not the copyright owner—who could be different); and (*b*) the work by its title or other description.

The acknowledgement should be placed where practicable or logical, given the quantity and variety of material to be acknowledged. When an entire chapter or section is being reproduced, practice is for it to appear as an uncued note at the foot of its first page. When a smaller extract or series of extracts is being reproduced, details are generally listed in an acknowledgements section, either in the preliminary matter or—especially with anthologies or collections—at the end of the work.

For illustrations, acknowledgements should be set as part of the caption; for figures and tables they are often set in a separate note below the caption under the heading *Source*.

General practice is to credit the source, providing the elements in an acknowledgements format along these lines:

> [author], from [title of copyrighted text] [edition, if other than the first], [year of publication], © [copyright proprietor—this can be the author or another party]. Reprinted [*or* Reproduced] by permission of [usually a publisher or agent].

The publisher's name alone is generally given, without the address, city, or country. When it is in a foreign language it should not generally be translated, although romanization from a non-Roman alphabet is usually acceptable. When copyright illustrations are acknowledged, use *reproduced* instead of *reprinted*.

Wording, capitalization, and punctuation can generally be standardized, although not where the copyright holder specifies a particular form of words for the acknowledgement, or its position. An acknowledgement list may be prefaced by *We are grateful for permission to reproduce the following material in this volume*, to save space and avoid repetition.

As a general rule, permission should be obtained for *all* copyright material in an anthology, regardless of length. The result is usually a separate acknowledgements section, placed either in the preliminary pages or at the end of the book, before the index. Normally an acknowledgement must be in the exact form specified by the copyright holder and not standardized; reprint and copyright years must be given in full where indicated.

In some situations copyright owners cannot be located, despite real efforts having been made to trace and contact them. When this happens the author needs to decide whether to omit the extract or to include it and risk being the subject of a copyright infringement action. If the author chooses to include the extract, a 'disclaimer' at the end of the acknowledgements section should be included, for example:

> There are instances where we have been unable to trace or contact the copyright holder. If notified the publisher will be pleased to rectify any errors or omissions at the earliest opportunity.

It is important to understand that such a disclaimer is not a defence to copyright infringement; if an author chooses to include such material, however, the disclaimer together with the evidence of efforts made to trace and contact the copyright owners may mitigate the adverse consequences if a copyright owner should subsequently object.

20.5 Defamation

A defamatory statement is one that injures the reputation of another person by exposing that person to hatred, contempt, or ridicule, or is disparaging or injurious to that person in their business, or lowers a person in the estimation of right-thinking members of society generally. **Libel** is making a defamatory statement in permanent form (e.g. in writing); **slander** is making a defamatory statement in temporary form (e.g. in speech).

In essence an allegation is defamatory if it is untrue and a person's reputation is damaged by it. The claimant need not be named but must be identifiable. The defamatory statement need not be direct; it may be implied or by way of innuendo. A company has a reputation but can only sue if it can demonstrate that an allegation has resulted in financial loss. However, directors of a company—if named or identifiable—might be able to sue for untrue allegations made against the company, even if no financial loss has been suffered.

The dead cannot be libelled, but care must be taken to ensure that in statements about the dead the living are not defamed by association.

The author's intention is irrelevant in determining whether a statement is defamatory. A defamed person is entitled to plead any meaning for the words used that a 'reasonable' person might infer.

The clearest defence against a defamation action is that the statements can be proved to be true by direct first-hand evidence. It is no defence to a libel action that the defamatory statements have been published previously, although this might affect the level of damages payable.

Criticism or other expressions of opinion can be defended as fair comment provided the subject matter of the comment is one of public interest, the facts underlying the expression of opinion are true, the comment is one which an honest person could hold, and the statement is 'comment' rather than 'fact'.

20.6 Negligent misstatement

If an author makes a statement negligently (without due care) in circumstances where it is likely and reasonable that the reader will place reliance on it, in some, limited, circumstances, the reader could sue the author/publisher. It is not possible to exclude liability for death or personal injury caused by such negligence. It is for this reason that care needs to be taken when, for example, giving information about DIY or other potentially dangerous activities. A publisher will generally require the author to provide warranties in the author contract that any instructions contained in the book are accurate.

20.7 Passing off

'Passing off' occurs where a misrepresentation is made which causes or will likely cause damaging confusion. Passing off in publishing can arise in various different ways. Most disputes involve similar titles—especially series titles where customers may buy individual books on the strength of the series name—or similar jacket design, where books from different publishers have a similar appearance, logo, or brand. More specific examples include giving the impression that a biography has been authorized by its subject, or that a sequel was authorized or written by the author of the original book.

20.8 Trade marks

It is sometimes necessary to refer to a registered trade mark in a work. When referring to a trade mark care should be taken not to give the impression that it is being used with the approval of its owner, particularly when using in a trade mark in a title or on a cover. A registered trade mark is indicated by the symbol ®; ™ indicates rights that are claimed but not registered.

20.9 The Internet

It is a common misconception that copyright does not apply to material which appears on the Internet. This is untrue: copyright and other laws apply to works put on the Internet as much as printed publications. Hence, copying material from a website can constitute copyright infringement as much as copying material from a book, and the considerations set out earlier in this chapter apply. An added complication of posting to and using material from a website is the issue of jurisdiction: if a work is written in France, posted on to the Internet from a cybercafe in Germany with an ISP based in Ireland, and read by someone in Australia, ascertaining which country's laws apply can be problematic. A detailed analysis of this issue is beyond the scope of this book.

20.10 Blasphemy, obscenity, racial hatred, and official secrets

Publishing a work which contains contemptuous, scandalous, or insulting material relating to the Christian religion is a criminal offence, punishable by a fine or imprisonment. Note that only the Christian religion is covered by this law and that merely attacking Christianity is not blasphemy: the attack would be blasphemous only if it were contemptuous or insulting.

It is also an offence to publish an obscene work. A work is deemed to be obscene if its overall effect is to deprave or corrupt its readers. Lewd or repulsive material is not necessarily obscene: to be obscene the material must constitute a menace to public morals.

By publishing works which could stir up racial hatred publishers could commit another offence. Racial hatred means hatred against groups of people who are defined by their colour, race, nationality, or ethnic or national origins. A work could stir up racial hatred if it contained threatening, abusive, or insulting material, and if there was either an intention to stir up racial hatred or it was likely that the work would do so.

It is also an offence to publish certain types of material if publication could damage national security or interests: cases on this point have related to memoirs by former workers for the Foreign Office or members of the intelligence agencies.

CHAPTER 21

US and British English

21.1 Overview

While English continues to develop as the world's most important language and most common lingua franca, long-standing preferences and differences remain among its several varieties (see 21.7), and in particular between the two most widespread varieties considered here: British English and US English.

21.2 Punctuation

Note that there are some differences in the terminology of marks of punctuation between dialects. The British terms are used in the discussion below, but it is important to be aware of the following differences: the *full point* is called a *period* in US English; the *exclamation mark* may be called an *exclamation point*; the *em rule* and *en rule* are called an *em dash* and *en dash*; *curly brackets* (braces) are sometimes called *wavy brackets*; the *solidus* is called a *slash*. The term *inverted commas* is not used in US English for *quotation marks*, and *round brackets* is not used of *parentheses*.

21.2.1 **Comma**

See 4.3 for guidance that is pertinent to both dialects. US style is to insert a comma after the phrases *for example* and *that is*, whenever they occur and are not followed by stronger punctuation, such as a colon. US style also prefers commas after the common abbreviations of these phrases, *e.g.* and *i.e.*, even though this results in double punctuation. See 10.6.

US style places commas inside closing quotation marks. See 9.2.3.

21.2.2 **Colon**

As noted at 11.3, US style is to separate the hours and minutes in numerical representations of time with a colon, e.g. 5:23 am. British style often uses a full point: 5.23 am. In US style the first word of a sentence after a colon is often capitalized, but is lower case in British.

21.2.3 **Full point**

US style places full points inside closing quotation marks. See 9.2.3.

There is some variation within and between the dialects in the use of full points with abbreviations. This subject is covered in 21.4.4.

21.2.4 **Dashes**

See 4.11 for the main discussion of UK usage. En rules (dashes) in US usage are used to join open elements into compounds (for example, the post–Civil War armistice), and a hyphen rather than an en rule is used to create a compound derived from two names (Marxist-Leninist theory).

21.2.5 **Quotation marks**

See 4.14 for the main discussion. Changing the style and placement of quotation marks and their accompanying punctuation for correct localization of text can be a tedious exercise because of the stylistic variations between British and US English.

21.3 Quantities, units, and numerical information

21.3.1 **US units of measure**

For readers of non-technical documents (including journalism) in US English, the following units are the norm:

Linear measurement: imperial system (inches, feet, yards, miles)
Area measurement: imperial system (square inches, square feet, acres, square miles)
Cubic measurement: cubic inches and feet
Liquid and dry volume: pints, quarts, gallons, bushels
Units of mass: ounces, pounds, tons
Temperature: Fahrenheit scale

In US style, recipes use the imperial units of volume noted above and also the *cup*: equal to half a US pint, or eight ounces. There are numerous resources online for conversion to these from metric units by typing, for example

convert 450 ml to cups

in a search engine. This service works for any sort of conversion in commonly used units and is readily available in the absence of extensive tables that list the conversions.

21.3.2 **British units of measure**

For British readers use the metric system for linear, area, and volumetric measurements and the Celsius scale for temperature. Note that the phrase *below zero* in British text normally means below freezing. In US English, it normally means below zero in the Fahrenheit scale, or about –18° C.

In some non-technical contexts British readers may still prefer imperial units: distances in *miles*, for example, rather than in *kilometres*. The *stone* (plural *stone*, and equal to 14 pounds), with any fractional part reported in *pounds*, is often expected for reporting a person's weight, rather than *kilograms*.

The British and US imperial units of volume larger than the ounce are not precise equivalents; the British pint contains 20 ounces, the US pint only 16. There are few contexts in which these differences are pertinent because the larger imperial units (quart and gallon) are not commonly used in the UK today. Most readers of English in any dialect are familiar with the British use of *pint* in relation to beverages and no further explication is necessary. However, any measurements involving cookery in which pints are used should be carefully converted to an appropriate equivalent.

21.3.3 **Other numerical data**

See the note at the end of 11.1.5 concerning some variation in the use of *trillion* and *billion* between British and US English. This difference is now mainly historical.

The word *nought* is not used in US English to stand for *zero*. For technical contexts, *zero* is used; for scores in sports, *nothing* is used.

Telephone numbers

In all of the US and Canada, numbers for landline telephones or mobile phones contain 10 digits. The first three are called the area code. The two most popular styles for showing telephone numbers are:

(nnn) nnn-nnnn
nnn-nnn-nnnn

Occasionally a 1 appears at the beginning of a full number; this is required on most landline telephones when they are calling a number outside the local area code:

1-nnn-nnn-nnnn

UK telephone numbers vary in length and typically consist of two parts. The first part, most usually designating a geographical area or a particular grouping of mobile telephone numbers, may be set off in brackets:

(0nnnn) nnnnnn

Other styles may eliminate the brackets, or show a division in the non-geographical part of the number:

0nnnn nnnnnn
0nnn nnn nnnn

It is common in Britain and elsewhere, and increasingly so in the US, to prefix a country code with a + sign at the beginning of a foreign telephone number. In this case the leading zero is dropped:

+31 20 347 1111.

A US alternative is to show the country code in parenthesis at the beginning of a number:

(31) 20 347 1111.

Dates

These are discussed at some length in Chapter 11. It is important to ensure that dates in British format—*day/month/year*—are not misunderstood when Americanizing to *month/day/year*, and vice versa. Documents that may have readers in both or in multiple dialects should spell out the name of the month or use its standard abbreviation (see 10.2.6) to prevent confusion.

Buildings

The level of a building whose floor is at the same level as the ground may be called the *ground floor* in British or US English; it is also called the *first floor* in US English. The floor above this is the *second floor* in US English, the *first floor* in British English; and so forth.

21.4 Orthographic variation (spelling and hyphenation)

Orthographic variation constitutes the difference between the major dialects of English that is most obvious to readers. There are hundreds of orthographic variants (that is, differently spelled versions of the same word) between British and US English, and between any other two dialects of English. Fortunately, most of them fall into easily identifiable patterns. There are, however, many individual cases. These cases mostly involve variants in which one dialect uses a single spelling for different meanings while the other dialect uses different spellings to distinguish different meanings of a word.

21.4.1 **Spelling patterns**

The main spelling differences between British and US English are detailed in 3.1 and 3.2. Table 21.1 lists some words that do not conform to a single pattern of spelling differences and that may easily slip past editorial notice (though many will be detected with spellchecking software).

Table 21.1

US	**British**
adz	adze
ax	axe
behoove	behove
caliper	calliper
carburetor	carburettor
checkered	chequered
checkers (game)	chequers
chili	chilli
gelatin	gelatine
glycerin	glycerine
granddad	grandad
jewelry	jewellery
karat	carat
licorice	liquorice
maneuver	manoeuvre
mustache	moustache

(*continued*)

Table 21.1 **(Continued)**

US	**British**
novitiate	noviciate
pajamas	pyjamas
peddler	pedlar
phony	phoney
pita bread	pitta bread
plow	plough
pudgy	podgy
raccoon	racoon
tartar sauce	tartare sauce

Note that the spellings *aesthetic*, *archaeology*, *caesura*, *caulk*, *glamour*, *ochre*, *onomatopoeia*, *paean*, and *theatre* are acceptable in both dialects; these are exceptions to the rules laid out in 3.1.2.

Whisky is the British spelling for all varieties except Irish *whiskey*; US spelling has *whiskey* as standard and *whisky* as a common variant, and does not maintain this geographical distinction.

The US spelling for *sulfur* (*sulfide*, *sulfate*) is also the one recommended by the International Union of Pure and Applied Chemistry (IUPAC) and is used in most British English scientific texts but not all. Check with the publisher; in non-technical material, use *sulphur* in British English.

21.4.2 **Spelling ambiguities**

A few words deserve close scrutiny because different spellings are assigned to different meanings in one dialect while the other dialect uses a single spelling for all meanings. Some examples appear in Table 21.2.

Table 21.2

Meaning for which one dialect uses a particular spelling	**British spelling**	**US spelling**
an order for a bank to pay a sum	cheque	check
current of air; amount swallowed; depth of water; denoting beverages served from a barrel	draught	draft

Meaning for which one dialect uses a particular spelling	British spelling	US spelling
division between walking area and driving area	kerb	curb
unit of length in the metric system	metre	meter
all meanings except those connected with computing	programme	program
level of a building	storey	story
metal tool with movable jaws	vice	vise

It must be kept in mind that a number of spelling variants are in fact acceptable in both British and US English; most of these are discussed in Chapter 3. When this is the case, it should be ascertained whether house style dictates one spelling or another. If this is not the case, internal consistency is the rule, following the preferred spellings in a suitable dictionary.

21.4.3 **Compound words**

See 3.3 for general discussion. US English is much readier to use and to accept new compounds spelled solid (that is, with no space and no hyphen) than British English. A number of compound words are spelled open or with a hyphen in British English but solid in the US. These include

- the intermediate directions of the compass (*northeast, southwest*, etc.)
- compounds beginning with *anti-, non-,* and *semi-* (*antinuclear, noninvasive, semitrailer*)
- nonce compounds ending in *-like* (*adobelike*)
- *percent* (always solid in the US but *per cent* in British English)

An exception is *no one*, always two words in the US but sometimes spelled *no-one* in British English. In general, US English is ready to eliminate a hyphen in a word formed by addition of a prefix or suffix except when the hyphen serves to prevent the doubling of a vowel or the tripling of a consonant.

21.4.4 **Forms of abbreviations and initialisms**

Many frequently used abbreviations and contractions differ in punctuation between the two dialects. An important point to check, discussed in 10.2.1, is full points (or elimination of them) at the end of contractions such as *Mr, Ms, Dr, St,* and the like. Full points are expected in US English, absent in British English.

There is widespread conformity in the presentation of acronyms and abbreviations in US and British English, though see the note about punctuation of these at 10.2.4. British English often uses *Aids* in a non-technical context, and US English has *AIDS* for acquired immune deficiency syndrome.

21.5 Lexical variation (word choices)

21.5.1 **'-isms'**

Words and expressions that originated, or that are used exclusively, in one variety of English are often referred to as '-isms' of one kind or another: Canadianisms, Americanisms, Australianisms, and the like. Examples of the hundreds of such word pairs in British and US English, in which the dialects have a different word to designate the same thing, include *aubergine/eggplant*, *braces/suspenders*, *flat/apartment*, *lift/elevator*, *nappy/diaper*, *torch/flashlight*.

21.5.2 **Words used in similar contexts**

A few words have similar, contrasting, or quite different meanings in British and US English but are used in very similar contexts that may make it easy to overlook the fact that the writer intended something different from what the reader in another dialect would interpret. Common examples are set out in Table 21.3.

Table 21.3

Word	Usual British meaning	Usual US meaning
Asian *noun*	someone from India or the countries that border it	someone from China, Japan, Korea, or a neighbouring country
bailiff *noun*	executor of court orders such as eviction and repossession	court officer who maintains order and performs other duties in a courtroom
biscuit *noun*	a flat, somewhat dry, sweet cake (= US *cookie*)	a savoury quick bread, similar to a roll (like British *scone*)
carnival *noun*	seasonal celebration that typically precedes Lent	travelling, temporary amusement park (= British *funfair*)
chancellor *noun*	honorary patron of a university	senior administrative official of a university
chips *noun*	strips of potato fried in fat (= US *fries*)	dry, crisp snack food made from potato, cornmeal, or other vegetables (= British *crisps* when made from potatoes)
cider *noun*	fermented apple juice (= US *hard cider*)	unfiltered apple juice
corn *noun*	any cereal crop	*Zea maize*, as a human food, food crop, or industrial crop
crèche *noun*	day nursery; child care centre	representation of the Nativity
CV *noun*	summary of education, qualifications, employment (= US *résumé*)	similar to UK meaning, but typically used only in academia, medicine, and law
entrée *noun*	dish before the main course	the main course
football *noun*	association football (= US *soccer*)	American football

(*continued*)

Table 21.3 **(Continued)**

Word	Usual British meaning	Usual US meaning
government *noun*	the government currently in power; roughly equivalent to US *administration*	the institution and its components at the state or national level that persists through changes of leadership
homely *adjective*	simply furnished and comfortable (= US *homey*)	plain and unattractive (of a person)
judicial review *noun*	a procedure by which a court can review an administrative action by a public body and secure a declaration, order, or award.	review by a higher court or by the Supreme Court of the constitutional validity of a legislative act
lemonade *noun*	clear fizzy drink with lemon flavour	still drink made from lemon juice, water, sugar
lime (tree) *noun*	a tree of the genus *Tilia* (= US *linden*)	a tree that produces limes, *Citrus aurantifolia*
mad *adjective*	insane	angry
mean *adjective*	selfish	cruel
momentarily *adverb*	for a moment	in a moment
moot *adjective*	subject to debate	having no significance
osteopath *noun*	health practitioner who does spine and joint adjustments (like US *chiropractor*)	medical doctor with additional qualification in spine manipulation
ouster *noun*	eviction from a property	removal from public office
pants *noun*	underpants	trousers
paraffin *noun*	liquid combustible fuel (= US *kerosene*)	inert waxlike substance obtained from petroleum
pavement *noun*	walkway beside a road (= US *sidewalk*)	roadway made of asphalt or concrete

Word	Usual British meaning	Usual US meaning
pound sign *noun*	the symbol £	the symbol #
quite *adverb*	to some extent	very, really (see also 21.6)
smart *adjective*	fashionable	intelligent
solicitor *noun*	a lawyer who handles routine legal matters (= US *lawyer* or *attorney*)	a government lawyer, or in some contexts, a salesperson (e.g. on a sign that says 'No solicitors')
subway *noun*	walkway under a road	underground train or rail system
sycamore *noun*	*Acer pseudoplatanus*, the sycamore maple	Any tree of the genus *Platanus* (= British *plane tree*)
table *verb*	bring forward for discussion	remove from consideration
through *predicate adjective*	having successfully passed to the next stage of a competition	finished
trunk *noun*	luggage or storage container with hinged lid	storage compartment in the rear of a vehicle (= British *boot*)

21.5.3 **Preferred inflections**

A number of verbs show different behaviour between British and US English. Those that are merely spelling variants are discussed above in 21.4.1. Some other verbs have forms that are used exclusively or preferentially in only one dialect. A few verbs (some mentioned in 3.2.1) have a participle form ending in *-t* that is not used in US English when the verb appears as part of a finite verb phrase. These forms—*burnt*, *leant*, *learnt*, *smelt*, *spelt*, *spilt*, and *spoilt*—are not used in US English and should be replaced by their *-ed* equivalents when Americanizing text. *Burnt* is occasionally used in US English as an adjective.

Special attention should be given to the participles *got* and *gotten*, since British English does not use the latter as a past participle of *get*. When Briticizing text, all instances of *gotten* can simply be changed to *got*. When Americanizing, it is necessary to distinguish the various senses of *get*. US English uses *got* in verb phrases where the verb means 'possess' (*I've got a beach house in Florida*) and 'have as an obligation' (*I've got to go to Chicago next week*). *Gotten* is the preferred form when the verb means 'obtain' (*Have you gotten your results yet?*) and 'become' (*She hasn't gotten any prettier over the years*). *Gotten* is also more usual in US English in a number of idioms and phrasal verbs containing *get*, such as *get used to something*, *get over something*, *get through something*, *get rid of something*, *get nowhere/anywhere*.

21.5.4 **Variants with common etymology**

Several word pairs in British and US English derive wholly or partly from a common ancestor but have settled on distinct preferred forms in the two dialects. These are laid out in Table 21.4.

Table 21.4

US English	**British English**
airplane	aeroplane
aluminum	aluminium
candidacy	candidature
centennial	centenary
costumer	costumier
deviltry	devilry
doodad	doodah
edgewise	edgeways
elasticized	elasticated
expiration	expiry
furor	furore
hauler	haulier
hodge-podge	hotch-potch
hydroplane	aquaplane
math	maths
normalcy	normality
orient (verb)	orientate
polyethylene	polythene

US English	British English
raise (in pay)	rise
sailboat	sailing boat
sequester	sequestrate
snicker	snigger
specialty	specialism
tidbit	titbit

21.5.5 **Variability in function words**

Although it rarely gives rise to a misunderstanding, there are several minor differences between British and US English in the choice of function words such as prepositions, conjunctions, and articles. The main points to be aware of are:

- *around/round* US English does not use *round* as a preposition or an adverb; *around* is used in all cases.
- *around/about* Many phrasal verbs in the two dialects differ only by British English preferring *about*, and US English preferring *around*, for the particle. Examples include *mess around/about*, *hang around/ about*, *lie around/about*.
- *inside*, when used as a preposition, may be followed by *of* in US English, but not usually in British English.
- *amidst/amongst/whilst* These are generally not used in US English, which prefers *amid/among/while.*
- Both dialects use *different from* when contrasting two things. *Different than* is mainly used in US English; *different to* is used exclusively in British English.
- A number of idioms and set phrases use a different preposition in the two dialects: British *at the weekend*, US *on the weekend*; British *at school*, US *in school*; a vehicle *on tow* (British), or *in tow* (US).
- variable use of the definite article (British *in/to hospital*, US *in/to the hospital*; British *at table*, US *at the table*).
- *towards* occurs in both dialects but *toward*, preferred in US English, is rare in British.

21.5.6 **Offensive language**

Language that may be offensive to some readers, or regarded as insensitive to its intended audience, is largely the same among varieties of English and careful writers avoid it. Words in Table 21.5 are differently perceived and used by Britons and Americans and so should be scrutinized carefully when editing text from the opposite dialect.

Humorous puns in informal writing that play on the ambiguity of slang and informal terms with variable meanings in different dialects—such as *dick*, *fag*, *faggot*, *knock-up*, *randy*, *rear-ender*, *rubber*, *shag*, *willie*—should probably be left alone in localizing text unless it is suspected that an offensive misunderstanding may result.

Table 21.5

Word	**Use in British English**	**Use in US English**
fit *noun*	a sudden attack of convulsions	(regarded as offensive when used with reference to epilepsy; use *seizure* instead)
fanny *noun*	vulgar term for female genitalia	informal or humorous term for the buttocks
spunk *noun*	vulgar term for semen	pluck; spirit; mettle

21.6 Grammatical and syntactic variation

The subtlest area of variation between US and British English involves text that contains no spellings or words that would be unfamiliar or unclear to readers who are fluent in a different English variation, but that nonetheless contains a usage common in one dialect but not the other. Putting these right depends mainly on the 'ear' of the editor to recognize usages that don't quite sound right. Examples of these include:

- differences in the number and countability of nouns (British *accommodation*, US *accommodations*). Other classes of words showing variability in this respect include some common ailments (US uses an article *a toothache/cramp*), certain foods when cooked

(British *scrambled egg, mashed potato*; US uses plural forms), and a few other words that do not belong to a class: *main/mains* (as a conduit for water, electricity, etc.), *overhead/overheads, scale/scales* (weighing device), *math/maths* (mathematics).

- variability in predication of group nouns (a plural verb is used in British where individuality or corporateness are being emphasized, e.g. *Barclays are still recruiting in Poole*; US English would use *Barclays is ...*)
- variability in the preferential use of modal verbs (especially *must, would,* and *should*). The modal contractions *daren't* and *shan't* are uncommon in US English and are commonly regarded as Briticisms.
- different status with regard to the transitivity of some verbs (the most frequent verbs requiring attention here are *agree, appeal, approximate, bath/bathe, catchup, give, impact, loan/lend, notify, protest, provide*).
- variable usage and preferences for submodifiers (especially *rather* and *quite*). Many perfunctory uses of *quite* as a submodifier in British English are considered superfluous in US English and may be simply deleted. British English also shows greater frequency of *very* before adjectives when there is no clear reason for it to American ears, and it can often be deleted. Americans tend to use *fairly* and *somewhat* in many cases where British writers use *rather*.
- minor differences in the wording of some idioms (British *home from home*, US *home away from home*; British *write to me*, US *write me*). There are dozens of these and their rectification depends on the ear of the editor.
- variation in use of the subjunctive mood. US English more readily uses the subjunctive after nouns, verbs, and adjectives of requiring and demanding (*She insisted Jane sit here*). These uses are acceptable but not always idiomatic in British English, which uses modal verbs or the declarative form to say the same thing (*She insisted Jane should sit here*).
- variation in the uses of tenses. Informal US English often uses the simple past with adverbs such as *already, ever, just,* and *yet*; British English is more likely to use the present perfect. In conversational

US English it is acceptable to say *We already ate* or *She just got here.* British English and more formal US English uses perfect tenses in these constructions (*I've already eaten* or *She has just got here*).

- variable preferences for introducing subordinate clauses. See 4.3.1.

21.7 Other varieties of English

Although there is considerable variation in specific vocabulary among varieties of English other than US and British, nearly all varieties of English tend to follow one or the other closely with regard to orthography, grammar, and syntax. Countries that are former British colonies and members of the Commonwealth tend to follow British English, as is also the case for English used within the European Union. Former US colonies (notably the Philippines), Latin America, and other countries with strong cultural or trade relations with the US tend to follow US English. Two main varieties—Canadian and Australian—deserve mention because they both follow British English in some respects and US English in others. When localizing to either of these dialects, it is essential to have specific guidance in the form of a dictionary and a style document to ensure consistency.

PART II

NEW OXFORD DICTIONARY FOR WRITERS AND EDITORS

Contents

Preface

The *New Oxford Dictionary for Writers and Editors* is not an ordinary dictionary. It is designed for people who work with words—authors, copy-editors, proofreaders, students writing essays and dissertations, journalists, people writing reports or other documents, and website editors. It provides comprehensive coverage of those words that need to be referred to frequently on account of their spelling, capitalization, hyphenation, or punctuation, whether they are ordinary English words or foreign words, proper names, cultural references, abbreviations, proprietary terms, or rare words. Its compact size means that it can be accommodated on a crowded desk and can be referred to far more quickly than a standard dictionary.

The *Oxford Dictionary for Writers and Editors* (*ODWE*) is a title with a great deal of history. As the *Authors' and Printers' Dictionary* it was first published in 1905, under the editorship of F. Howard Collins, and eleven editions were produced before the book was revised and retitled the *Oxford Dictionary for Writers and Editors* in 1981. The last edition of *ODWE*, the second, was published in 2000, in a new larger format.

New ODWE marks a return to the traditional small 'handbook' form. It is a freshly compiled text that makes use of the latest evidence provided by the Oxford English Corpus, a database of two and a half billion words of current English, and by the Oxford Reading Programme. The dictionary's spellings and forms are consistent with those given in the current range of Oxford dictionaries and accurately reflect the way the English language is used today. The book also contains a great many entries that will not be found in traditional dictionaries—for example, proprietary terms, work titles, fictional characters, and abbreviated forms—and it draws on the heritage, accumulated over a century, of *ODWE*.

It remains an invaluable academic resource while providing broad coverage of today's world for a new generation of writers, editors, and students.

New ODWE is one of a trio of books designed specifically for writers and editors, along with *New Hart's Rules* (the Oxford style guide) and the *New Oxford Spelling Dictionary*. These three books combine to form the complete reference set for everyone who is concerned to reach the highest standards in producing written works.

This edition of *New ODWE* is also available online, on the Oxford Dictionaries website, www.oxforddictionaries.com. The site is updated regularly and gives you free access to our largest dictionary and thesaurus of current English as well as bilingual dictionaries for many languages. It also offers information on usage, grammar, and writing, our Word of the Day, a language blog, and more. In addition, the Gold subscription package features millions of example sentences and specialist language reference resources—including this book and *New Hart's Rules*.

Many people have helped put together this new book, and those most directly involved are listed below. We would also like to thank Val Rice, Jan Baiton, and other members of the Society for Editors and Proofreaders for their interest in and support of the project. Finally, the editors are indebted to the work of the second edition of the *Oxford Dictionary for Writers and Editors*, edited and compiled by Robert Ritter.

Editorial team

Editors
Angus Stevenson
Lesley Brown

Chief editorial consultant
Rosemary Roberts

Design
Michael Johnson

Thanks to
Catherine Soanes
Trish Stableford

Guide to the dictionary

Introduction

The *New Oxford Dictionary for Writers and Editors* is a book specifically designed for writers and editors: for all those people writing or working with texts in English. Unlike a standard dictionary, it focuses on words and names that cause difficulty or controversy and does not aim to cover all the common words in the language.

Defining style

Definitions, where given, are brief, since their principal purpose is simply to identify the item in question. Common words that are included on account of their form or abbreviation are not defined. The initial article in definitions is omitted where this does not lead to ambiguity.

Parts of speech

The part of speech (or word class) is not shown if an entry has only one. Abbreviated parts of speech are shown where there are two or more:

> **compliment** n. expression of praise or admiration. v. congratulate or praise

Parts of speech are also shown if only one of two or more is being dealt with explicitly:

> **blanket** v. (**blanketing, blanketed**)

In the interests of space, definitions for two parts of speech are occasionally combined by means of brackets:

> **feint** n. & v. (make) deceptive or pretended attack. adj. (of paper) printed with faint lines

Inflections

Regular, straightforward inflections and plural forms are not shown. Irregular or problematic verbal inflections are given in the order *present participle, past tense.*

Inflections and plurals that fall into the following categories are shown:

- plurals for nouns ending in *-o* (e.g. *manifestos, tomatoes*)
- inflections for verbs that double or might be expected to double consonants (e.g. *benefit, focus*)
- verb inflections that are different in British and US English (e.g. *label, travel*)
- plurals of nouns that have or that might be expected to have a Latinate plural (typically those ending in *-us* or *-um*, e.g. *cactus, stadium*).

Variants and errors

The main form of each word given is the standard British spelling or form. *New ODWE* distinguishes between allowed spelling variants and those which are not acceptable either because they are archaic or because they are non-standard and regarded as errors. Allowed variants are introduced by *also*, for example:

griffin (also **gryphon**) mythical creature

Errors and other non-standard variants are introduced with *not*, as in:

baklava Middle Eastern dessert (not **baclava**)

Edinburgh capital of Scotland (not **-borough**)

Variants and US forms are cross-referred to the main spelling of the item in the following way:

gryphon var. of **griffin**

armor US var. of **armour**

Unacceptable forms are cross-referred as follows:

baclava use **baklava**

Where verbs can be spelled with either an *-ize* or *-ise* ending, the *-ize* spelling is given as the main form, with the *-ise* spelling shown with the formula '*Brit.* also *-ise*'. Either spelling may be used, depending on the style or preference being followed. The form *-ize* has been in use in English since the 16th century and, although it is widely used in American English, it is not an Americanism. The form *-ise* is used particularly in British English.

Compound words

Compound terms may be spaced as separate words, hyphenated, or written as one word. There is no hard-and-fast rule saying whether, for example, *airbase*, *air base*, or *air-base* is correct: all forms are found in use and none is incorrect. However, it is important to make sure that individual forms are used consistently within a single text or range of texts, and for this reason information on compound words forms an important focus for *New ODWE*.

In general there is a tendency in modern English to avoid hyphenation for noun compounds: there is, for example, a preference for *airbase* rather than *air-base* and for *air raid* rather than *air-raid*. There is an additional preference in American English for the form to be one word and in British English for the form to be two words: for example, *end point* tends to be the commoner form in British English, while *endpoint* is commoner in American English. *New ODWE* indicates the usual or preferred form in British English for common compounds. Where consecutive entries for compound forms are included with the same gloss the entries are combined:

jelly baby, jelly bean (two words)

Capitalization

Nouns such as *king*, *queen*, *president*, and *prime minister* are generally written with a lower-case initial but may be capitalized in certain contexts. For example, the word *king* has a lower-case initial in ordinary use, as in *Canute became king of all England*, but when used as a title in a proper name it is capitalized, as in *King Henry VIII*. The note 'cap. in titles' indicates this for relevant entries. Chapter 5 of *New Hart's Rules* gives a full discussion of the issues involved in capitalization.

Abbreviations

Established acronyms and initialisms such as *BBC*, *CND*, and *NATO* are shown in capitals, without points. This is the usual style in British English, although points are permissible; in American English it is more usual to write such abbreviations with points (for example *L.A.*). Acronyms (abbreviations formed from the initial letters of other words and pronounced as words, such as *NATO*) are sometimes written with just an initial capital (*Nato*): this is an acceptable house style, but such alternatives are not indicated at individual entries.

Labelling

The label '*Brit.*' implies that the use is found in standard British English but not in standard American English, though it may be found in other English-speaking parts of the world. The labels '*US*' and '*N. Amer.*', on the other hand, imply that the use is typically US (or US and Canadian) and is not standard in British English, though it may be found elsewhere.

Italicized words

Words and phrases that have come into English directly from other languages are traditionally written in italics to show that they are not fully established as English words. As the word or phrase becomes more widely used it may eventually become regarded as part of the standard vocabulary of English, and the italics may no longer be used. In *New ODWE* words that are judged not to be fully assimilated are shown in bold italic:

cafard melancholia (Fr., ital.)

echt authentic and typical (Ger., ital.)

For words that have an accented character in the original language but whose main English form is now unaccented, the original form is shown at the end of the entry:

elan energy, style, and enthusiasm (not ital.) [Fr. *élan*]

The titles of novels, plays, long poems, and other complete works are shown in italic, according to standard convention. Short poems are given in roman type; when referred to in text these are generally enclosed in single quotation marks. Work titles are covered in full in Chapter 8 of *New Hart's Rules*.

Abbreviations used in the dictionary

adj.	adjective	Ir.	Irish
adv.	adverb	It.	Italian
arch.	archaic	ital.	italic
Anat.	anatomy	L.	Latin
Arab.	Arabic	Ling.	linguistics
Archaeol.	archaeology	mod.	modern
Archit.	architecture	Math.	mathematics
Astron.	astronomy	Med.	medicine
Austral.	Australian	Mil.	military
Biochem.	biochemistry	Mus.	music
Biol.	biology	Mythol.	mythology
Bot.	botany	n.	noun
Brit.	British	N. Amer.	North American
Canad.	Canadian		
cap.	capital	Naut.	nautical
caps	capitals	N. Engl.	northern English
cent.	century		
cents	centuries	Norw.	Norwegian
Chem.	chemistry	NZ	New Zealand
Chr. Theol.	Christian theology	obj.	object
		OE	Old English
Class.	classical	offens.	offensive
Comput.	computing	Philos.	philosophy
derog.	derogatory	Phonet.	phonetics
dial.	dialect	Photog.	photography
disp.	disputed	Phys.	physics
Du.	Dutch	Physiol.	physiology
Electron.	electronics	pl.	plural
esp.	especially	Port.	Portuguese
Fr.	French	prep.	preposition
Genet.	genetics	pron.	pronoun
Geol.	geology	Psychol.	psychology
Geom.	geometry	RC Ch.	Roman Catholic Church
Ger.	German		
Gk	Greek		
Gram.	grammar	ref.	reference
hist.	historical	Rhet.	rhetoric
Ind.	Indian	Rom.	Roman

Russ.	Russian	techn.	technical
S. Afr.	South African	usu.	usually
Sc.	Scottish	v.	verb
Scand.	Scandinavian	W. Ind.	West Indian
Sp.	Spanish	WWI	World War I
spec.	specifically	WWII	World War II
subj.	subject	Zool.	zoology

Note on trademarks and proprietary terms

A

A 1 pl. **As** or **A's** 1st letter of the alphabet **2** ampere(s) **3** answer **4** series of paper sizes each twice the area of the next, as *A0, A1, A2, A3, A4*, etc., A1 being 841 × 594 mm **5** a human blood type

Å¹ ångstrom(s)

Å² 1 (also **å**) Swedish letter, used also in Danish and Norwegian **2** village in northern Norway

a 1 arrives **2** atto- (10^{-18}) **3** before [L. *ante*]

a Phys. acceleration

@ 'at', used to indicate cost or rate per unit, and in Internet addresses

A3 size of paper, 420 × 297 mm

A4 size of paper, 297 × 210 mm

A$ Australian dollar(s)

AA 1 Alcoholics Anonymous **2** anti-aircraft **3** Automobile Association

AAA 1 Amateur Athletic Association **2** American (or Australian) Automobile Association

AAAS American Association for the Advancement of Science

Aachen city in western Germany; Fr. name **Aix-la-Chapelle**

Aalborg city and port in Denmark; Danish name **Ålborg**

A & E accident and emergency

A & M Hymns Ancient and Modern

A & R artists and repertoire (or recording)

aardvark ant-eating African mammal

aardwolf pl. **aardwolves** African mammal of the hyena family

Aarhus city in Denmark; Danish name **Århus**

Aaron (in the Old Testament) brother of Moses

A'asia Australasia (one cap.)

aasvogel S. Afr. vulture

AAU US Amateur Athletic Union

AB¹ a human blood type

AB² 1 able seaman **2** Alberta **3** US Bachelor of Arts [L. *Artium Baccalaureus*]

Ab (also **Av**) (in the Jewish calendar) eleventh month of the civil and fifth of the religious year

ABA 1 Amateur Boxing Association **2** American Bar Association **3** American Booksellers' Association

abacus pl. **abacuses**

Abadan oil-refining centre in Iran; cf. **Ibadan**

Abaddon hell or the Devil

abalone edible mollusc of warm seas

à bas down with! (Fr., ital.)

abattoir slaughterhouse

abaya full-length sleeveless garment worn by Arabs

Abba¹ 1 (in the New Testament) God as father **2** (in the Syrian Orthodox and Coptic Churches) title for bishops and patriarchs

Abba² Swedish pop group

Abbasids dynasty of caliphs who ruled in Baghdad 750–1258

abbatial relating to an abbey, abbot, or abbess

Abbe, Ernst (1840–1905), German physicist

abbé French abbot or other cleric (accent, not ital.)

Abbevillian Archaeol. dated term for earliest Palaeolithic culture in Europe, the Lower Acheulian

abbey pl. **abbeys** (cap. in names)

abbrev. pl. **abbrevs** or **abbrevs.** abbreviated; abbreviation

ABC¹ 1 the alphabet **2** alphabetical or simple guide

ABC² 1 American Broadcasting Company **2** Australian Broadcasting Corporation

ABC Islands the islands of Aruba, Bonaire, and Curaçao

abdabs informal nervous anxiety or irritation (not **habdabs**)

abdominal relating to the abdomen (not **abdomenal**)
abductor 1 person who abducts another **2** Anat. muscle; cf. **adductor**
abecedarian arranged alphabetically
à Becket, St Thomas, see **Becket, St Thomas à**
Abel (in the Old Testament) the second son of Adam and Eve, murdered by his brother Cain
Abelard, Peter (1079–1142), French scholar, lover of Héloïse
Aberdeen Angus (two caps)
Aberdeenshire council area and former county of NE Scotland
Aberdonian person from Aberdeen
Aberfan village in South Wales, site in 1966 of collapse of a slag heap
Abergavenny town in Monmouthshire, Wales
Abernethy town in Perthshire, Scotland
Aberystwyth town in Ceredigion, Wales
abet (**abetting, abetted**) □ **abetment, abettor**
ab extra from outside (L., ital.)
ABH Brit. actual bodily harm
abhor (**abhorring, abhorred**) □ **abhorrence, abhorrent**
abide (past **abided** or arch. **abode**)
Abidjan chief port of Côte d'Ivoire (Ivory Coast)
abigail arch. lady's maid (lower case)
Abilene name of cities in Texas and Kansas
ab initio from the beginning (L., ital.)
Abitur (in Germany) set of examinations taken in the final year of secondary school (cap., ital.)
abjure renounce (a belief or claim); cf. **adjure** □ **abjuration**
Abkhazia autonomous territory in NW Georgia □ **Abkhaz, Abkhazian**
ablation 1 melting, evaporation, or erosion **2** surgical removal of body tissue; cf. **ablution**
ablative 1 Gram. denoting a case indicating an agent, instrument, or source (abbrev. **abl.**) **2** involving ablation
ablaut Ling. alternation in the vowels of related word forms (e.g. in *sing, sang, sung*) (not ital.)
able-bodied (hyphen)
ablution 1 act of washing **2** (**ablutions**) Brit. room in army base for washing etc.; cf. **ablation**
ABM anti-ballistic-missile
abnegate renounce or reject □ **abnegation, abnegator**
Åbo Swed. name for **Turku**
abode arch. past of **abide**
abomasum pl. **abomasa** Zool. fourth stomach of a ruminant
A-bomb atom bomb (hyphen)
Abominable Snowman pl. **Abominable Snowmen** yeti (caps)
aboriginal, aborigine cap. with ref. to indigenous peoples of Australia
ABO system system of four basic types (A, AB, B, and O) into which human blood may be classified
aboulia var. of **abulia**
about-turn (N. Amer. **about-face**) (hyphen)
above board (two words)
ab ovo from the very beginning (ital.) [L., 'from the egg']
Abp Archbishop (no point)
abracadabra word said by conjurors when performing a magic trick
Abraham Hebrew patriarch
abridgement (US **abridgment**)
abrogate repeal or cancel (a law or agreement); cf. **arrogate**
abruption sudden breaking away from a mass
Abruzzi region of east central Italy
ABS 1 acrylonitrile-butadiene-styrene, a hard composite plastic **2** anti-lock braking system
abscess swollen area containing pus (not **abcess**)
abscissa pl. **abscissae** or **abscissas** Math. x-coordinate on a graph; cf. **ordinate**
abscission Bot. process by which parts of a plant break off naturally □ **abscise**
abseil (not **-sail**)
absent-minded (hyphen)
absinthe (also **absinth**) **1** the shrub wormwood **2** aniseed-flavoured liqueur
absit omen may this (evil) omen be absent (L., ital.)
absolute zero lowest temperature that is theoretically possible (zero kelvins, −273.15°C)

absorb soak up; cf. **adsorb**
□ **absorbent, absorption, absorptive**
abstemious indulging only moderately in food, drink, etc.
ABTA Association of British Travel Agents
abu means 'father of' in Arabic; lower case in the middle of personal names
Abu Dhabi largest member state of the United Arab Emirates
Abu Ghraib prison near Baghdad, Iraq
Abuja city in Nigeria, the capital since 1991
abulia (also **aboulia**) absence of will-power
Abu Simbel site of two huge ancient temples in Egypt
abut (**abutting, abutted**) □ **abutment, abutter**
ABV alcohol by volume
abysm literary abyss
abysmal 1 extremely bad **2** literary very deep; cf. **abyssal**
abyss very deep chasm
abyssal 1 of the depths of the ocean **2** Geol. plutonic; cf. **abysmal**
Abyssinia former name for **Ethiopia**
AC 1 Aircraftman **2** (also **a.c.**) alternating current **3** appellation contrôlée **4** athletic club **5** before Christ [L. *ante Christum*] **6** Companion of the Order of Australia
Ac the chemical element actinium (no point)
a/c 1 account **2** (also **A/C**) air conditioning
academe, academia academic world (lower case)
academician member of an academy
Académie française French literary academy (one cap., not ital.)
Academy award trademark an Oscar (one cap.)
Acadia former French colony in Nova Scotia
acanthus pl. **acanthuses** plant or shrub with spiny leaves
a cappella (also **alla cappella**) Mus. sung without instrumental accompaniment
Acapulco (also **Acapulco de Juárez**) port in Mexico
ACAS Advisory, Conciliation, and Arbitration Service
acc. Gram. accusative
Accademia della Crusca Italian literary academy (not ital.)
Accadian use **Akkadian**
accede 1 assent or agree to **2** assume an office or position
accelerando pl. **accelerandos** or **accelerandi** Mus. with a gradual increase of speed
accelerator (not **-er**)
accentor songbird of a family including the dunnock
acceptor Chem. & Phys. (not **-er**)
accessible (not **-able**)
accessorize (Brit. also **accessorise**)
accessory (Law also **accessary**)
acciaccatura pl. **acciaccaturas** or **acciaccature** Mus. grace note
accidence dated grammar concerned with the inflections of words
accident-prone (hyphen)
accidie spiritual or mental sloth (not ital.)
acclimatize (Brit. also **acclimatise**)
accommodate (two *c*s, two *m*s)
□ **accommodation**
accordion (not **-ian**)
accouchement arch. action of giving birth (not ital.)
accoucheur arch. male midwife (not ital.)
account (abbrev. **a/c**)
accoutred (US **accoutered**)
accoutrement (US **accouterment**)
Accra capital of Ghana
accredit (**accrediting, accredited**)
□ **accreditation**
accrue (**accruing, accrued**) be received in regular amounts □ **accrual**
accumulate (two *c*s, one *m*)
□ **accumulator**
accursed (arch. also **accurst**)
accusative Gram. case expressing the object of an action or the goal of motion (abbrev. **acc., accus.**)
AC/DC 1 alternating current/direct current **2** informal bisexual
acedia listlessness; accidie
acesulfame artificial sweetener
Achaean 1 an ancient Greek from Achaea

in the Peloponnese **2** (esp. in Homer) a Greek
Achaemenids (also **Achaemenians**) dynasty ruling in Persia 553–330 BC
acharnement arch. bloodthirsty fury (Fr., ital.)
Achates companion of Aeneas in the *Aeneid* (see **fidus Achates**)
ache v. (**aching, ached**)
Acheron Gk Mythol. one of the rivers of Hades
Acheulian (also **Acheulean**) Archaeol. main Lower Palaeolithic culture in Europe
à cheval on horseback (Fr., ital.)
Achilles Gk Mythol. hero of the Trojan War
Achilles heel, Achilles tendon (no apostrophe)
achy (not **achey**) □ **achiness**
acid substance that turns litmus red, neutralizes alkalis, etc.
acid drop, acid rain, acid test (two words)
ack-ack anti-aircraft gunfire (hyphen)
ackee (also **akee**) West African tree or its fruit
acknowledgement (US **acknowledgment**)
ACLU American Civil Liberties Union
acme highest point of excellence
Acmeist member of a 20th-cent. movement in Russian poetry (cap.)
acne skin condition marked by numerous red pimples
Acol system of bidding in bridge (one cap.)
acolyte **1** assistant or follower **2** person assisting a priest
acoustics **1** acoustic properties of a room or building (treated as pl.) **2** branch of physics concerned with sound (treated as sing.)
acquiesce, acquire, acquaint (not **aqu-**)
acquit (**acquitting, acquitted**) □ **acquittal**
Acre seaport of Israel; also called **Akko**
acre unit of land area equal to 4,840 square yards (0.405 hectare) □ **acreage**
Acrilan trademark acrylic textile fibre
acronym word formed from the initial letters of other words (e.g. *NATO*); cf. **initialism**
acrophobia fear of heights
acropolis fortified part of an ancient Greek city; (**the Acropolis**) the ancient citadel at Athens
acrostic poem or puzzle in which certain letters in each line form a word or words
ACT **1** advance corporation tax **2** Australian Capital Territory
Act written ordinance passed by Parliament (cap.)
Actaeon Gk Mythol. hunter killed by his own hounds
ACTH Biochem. adrenocorticotrophic hormone
acting lower case in e.g. *the acting Chief Constable*
actinia pl. **actiniae** or **actinias** sea anemone
actinium chemical element of atomic number 89 (symbol **Ac**)
action-packed (hyphen)
action painting style of painting in which paint is thrown on to the canvas (two words, lower case)
actor increasingly used to refer to a person of either sex, although **actress** is still acceptable; cf. **one-acter**
Actors' Studio acting workshop in New York (apostrophe)
Acts of the Apostles book of the New Testament (abbrev. **Acts**)
actualité (Fr., ital.) **1** news, current affairs **2** truth (this sense not found in Fr.)
actualize (Brit. also **actualise**)
actus reus Law conduct which is a constituent element of a crime (L., ital.); cf. ***mens rea***
acupressure, acupuncture (one word)
acushla affectionate Irish form of address (ital.)
acute accent the mark ´ placed over a letter
ACW aircraftwoman
AD Anno Domini (normally written in small capitals, and traditionally placed before the numerals (*AD 375*) unless the date is spelled out (*the third century AD*); cf. **BC, BCE, CE**

ad advertisement (no point)
Ada computer programming language
adagio pl. **adagios** Mus. piece in slow time
Adam[1] (in the biblical and Koranic traditions) the first man
Adam[2], Robert (1728–92) and James (1730–94), Scottish architects
Adams **1** Ansel (Easton) (1902–84), American photographer **2** John (1735–1826), 2nd president of the US 1797–1801 **3** John Quincy (1767–1848), 6th president of the US 1825–9
Adam's Peak mountain in Sri Lanka
adaptor (also **adapter**) **1** device for connecting pieces of equipment or electrical plugs **2** person that adapts something
Adar (in the Jewish calendar) the sixth month of the civil and twelfth of the religious year, known in leap years as **Second Adar**; preceded in leap years by the intercalary month **First Adar**
ADC **1** aide-de-camp **2** analogue to digital converter
ad captandum vulgus to appeal to the masses (L., ital.)
ADD attention deficit disorder
Addams, Jane (1860–1935), American social reformer
Addenbrooke's hospital in Cambridge, England (apostrophe)
addendum pl. **addenda** additional item at the end of a book (not ital.)
Addis Ababa (also **Adis Abeba**) capital of Ethiopia
Addison, Joseph (1672–1719), English writer and politician
Addisonian **1** relating to Joseph Addison **2** Med. relating to Addison's disease
Addison's disease (apostrophe)
Addled Parliament Parliament of James I of England, dissolved without having passed any legislation
add-on n. (hyphen, two words as verb)
addorsed Heraldry back to back
adduce cite as evidence; cf. **educe** □ **adducible**
adductor Anat. muscle; cf. **abductor**
Adelaide capital of South Australia
Adélie Land (also **Adélie Coast**) section of Antarctica (two caps)
Adélie penguin (one cap)
Aden port in Yemen
Adenauer, Konrad (1876–1967), first Chancellor of the Federal Republic of Germany 1949–63
adenoma pl. **adenomas** or **adenomata** benign tumour in epithelial tissue
ad eundem to the same degree at another university (L., ital.)
à deux involving two people (Fr., ital.)
ADF automatic direction-finder
ad fin. at or near the end of a piece of writing (point, ital.) [L. *ad finem* 'at the end']
ADHD attention deficit hyperactivity disorder
adhibit (**adhibiting**, **adhibited**) apply or affix
ad hoc arranged or done for a particular purpose (not ital., two words even before a noun)
ad hominem (not ital.) **1** associated with a particular person **2** (of an argument) personal
ad idem on the same point, in agreement (L., ital.)
adieu pl. **adieus** or **adieux** goodbye (not ital.)
Adi Granth principal sacred scripture of Sikhism (not ital.)
ad infinitum endlessly, forever (not ital.)
ad interim for the meantime (L., ital.)
adios Spanish for 'goodbye' (not ital.)
Adirondack Mountains range of mountains in New York State
Adis Abeba var. of **Addis Ababa**
adj. **1** adjective **2** (**Adj.** or **Adjt**) adjutant
adjunct **1** extra part **2** Gram. word or phrase other than the verb or predicate
adjure urge to do something; cf. **abjure**
adjutant assistant to a senior military officer (abbrev. **Adj.** or **Adjt**)
adjutant general pl. **adjutants general** high-ranking administrative officer (abbrev. **AG**)
adjuvant Med. (of therapy) applied to suppress secondary tumour formation
Adler, Alfred (1870–1937), Austrian psychologist and psychiatrist □ **Adlerian**
ad-lib v. (**ad-libbing**, **ad-libbed**)

speak without preparation (hyphen, two words as adj., adv., or noun)
ad libitum as much as desired (L., ital.)
ad litem Law acting on behalf of a person who cannot represent themselves (L., ital.)
Adm. Admiral or Admiralty
admin administration (no point)
administratrix pl. **administratrixes** or **administratrices** Law female administrator of an estate
Admirable Crichton, the 1 see **Crichton 2** (***The Admirable Crichton***) play by J. M. Barrie (1914)
admiral (cap. in titles; abbrev. **Adm.**)
Admiral's Cup yacht-racing competition held every two years
Admiralty former government department responsible for the Royal Navy (abbrev. **Adm.**)
ad misericordiam appealing to mercy or pity (L., ital.)
admissible (not **-able**)
admit (**admitting, admitted**) □ **admittance**
ad nauseam to a tiresomely excessive degree (not ital.)
ado fuss or difficulty (one word)
adobe clay used to make sun-dried bricks
Adonai a Hebrew name for God (not ital.)
Adonais elegy on death of Keats by Shelley (1821)
Adonis 1 Gk Mythol. youth loved by Aphrodite and Persephone **2** extremely handsome young man
Adorno, Theodor Wiesengrund (1903–69), German philosopher
ADP 1 Biochem. adenosine diphosphate **2** automatic data processing
ad personam on an individual basis (L., ital.)
ADR 1 alternative dispute resolution **2** American depository receipt
ad referendum subject to a higher authority (L., ital.)
ad rem to the point (L., ital.)
adrenaline (also **adrenalin**) synthetic drug is **Adrenalin** (US trademark)
Adrian IV (*c.*1100–59), the only Englishman to be pope (1154–9); born *Nicholas Breakspear*
Adrianople ancient name for **Edirne**
Adriatic Sea sea between the Balkans and the Italian peninsula
adroit clever or skilful
à droit to the right (Fr., ital.)
ADSL asymmetric digital subscriber line
adsorb hold (molecules of a gas or liquid) as a film on the surface of a solid; cf. **absorb** □ **adsorbent, adsorption, adsorptive**
ADT Atlantic Daylight Time
aduki var. of **adzuki**
Adullamite member of a dissident political group
adumbrate 1 give a faint or general idea of **2** be a warning of □ **adumbration**
adv. adverb
ad valorem in proportion to the value (L., ital.)
Advent 1 the Coming or Second Coming of Christ **2** season of the Church year leading up to Christmas
advent arrival of a notable person or thing (lower case)
adventitious 1 happening according to chance **2** coming from outside
adverse unfavourable; cf. **averse**
advertise (not **-ize**)
advice guidance with regard to future action
advise give advice to (not **-ize**) □ **advisable**
adviser (also **advisor**)
advocaat liqueur made with eggs, sugar, and brandy (not ital.)
advocate Sc. a barrister
Advocate Depute pl. **Advocates Depute** (in Scotland) officer assisting the Lord Advocate (caps)
Advocate General pl. **Advocates General** officer assisting the judges in the European Court of Justice (caps; abbrev. **AG**)
advowson right to recommend a member of the Anglican clergy for a vacant benefice
advt advertisement (no point)
Adygea autonomous republic in SW Russia
Adyghe (also **Adygei**) pl. same, member of a people of SW Russia

adytum pl. **adyta** innermost sanctuary of an ancient Greek temple
adze (US **adz**) tool with an arched blade
adzuki (also **aduki**) pl. **adzukis** dark-red edible bean
AE auto-exposure
Æ (also **æ**) Old English letter representing a vowel intermediate between *a* and *e*; ash
AEA Atomic Energy Authority
Aegean Sea sea between Greece and Turkey
aegis 1 protection or support **2** Class. Mythol. goatskin shield
aegrotat certificate stating that a student is too ill to take an exam (not ital.) [L., 'he is sick']
Aelfric (*c.*955–*c.*1020), Anglo-Saxon writer; known as **Grammaticus**
Aeneid Latin epic poem by Virgil about the Trojan prince Aeneas
aeolian (US **eolian**) Geol. relating to the action of the wind (lower case)
Aeolian Islands (US **Eolian Islands**) ancient name for **Lipari Islands**
Aeolian mode (US **Eolian mode**) Mus. (one cap.)
Aeolus Gk Mythol. god of the winds
aeon (US or tech. **eon**)
aepyornis extinct giant flightless bird (not **epyornis**)
AER annual equivalence rate
aerial n. device for transmitting or receiving signals. adj. in the air; cf. **ariel**
aerie US var. of **eyrie**
aerobics exercises intended to make the cardiovascular system more efficient
aerodrome Brit. small airfield
aerodynamic, aerofoil, aerogramme (one word)
aeronaut dated traveller in a flying craft
aeronautics study or practice of building or flying aircraft (treated as sing.)
aeroplane (Brit.; US form is **airplane**; **aircraft** is often preferred)
aerospace aviation and space flight (one word)
Aeschines (*c.*390–*c.*314 BC), Athenian orator and statesman
Aeschylus (*c.*525–*c.*456 BC), Greek dramatist
Aesculapius Rom. Mythol. god of medicine □ **Aesculapian**
Æsir the Norse gods and goddesses collectively
Aesop (6th cent. BC), Greek storyteller known for fables
aesthete (US **esthete**) □ **aesthetic**
Aesthetic Movement artistic movement of the 1880s (caps)
aestival (US **estival**) relating to summer
aestivate (US **estivate**) Zool. spend a dry period in a dormant state
aet. (also **aetat.**) of or at the age of (not ital.) [L. *aetatis* 'of age']
a.e.t. (in soccer) after extra time
aether arch. clear sky, the ether
aethereal use **ethereal**
aetiology (US **etiology**) **1** Med. cause of a condition **2** investigation of something's cause
Aetna, Mount use **Etna**
AF 1 audio frequency **2** autofocus
Afar pl. same or **Afars** member of a people of Djibouti and NE Ethiopia; also called **Danakil**
Afars and Issas, French Territory of the former name (1946–77) for **Djibouti**
AFC 1 Air Force Cross **2** Association Football Club
affaire (also ***affaire de cœur***) love affair (Fr., ital.)
affairé busy (Fr., ital., accent)
affect have an effect on; cf. **effect**
Affenpinscher small breed of dog (cap., not ital.)
afferent Physiol. conducting nerve impulses or blood inwards; cf. **efferent**
affetuoso Mus. with feeling
affianced engaged to marry (not ital.)
affidavit Law sworn written statement
affiliate (two *f*s, one *l*) □ **affiliation**
afflatus divine inspiration (not ital.)
afflux arch. flow of water or air
affranchise (not **-ize**)
affronté (also **affronty**) Heraldry facing the observer (accent, not ital.)
Afghan 1 person from Afghanistan **2** breed of hunting dog **3** sheepskin coat

Afghani pl. **Afghanis** person from Afghanistan
afghani pl. **afghanis** monetary unit of Afghanistan (lower case)
aficionado pl. **aficionados** enthusiast for particular subject (not ital.)
afield (one word)
AFL Australian Football League
AFL-CIO American Federation of Labor and Congress of Industrial Organizations (hyphen)
AFM Air Force Medal
à fond thoroughly, fully (Fr., ital.); cf. ***au fond***
aforementioned, aforesaid, aforethought (one word)
a fortiori with a yet stronger reason than a conclusion previously accepted (two words, not ital.)
afreet (also **afrit**) jinn or demon in Arabian mythology (not ital.)
African American the currently accepted term in the US for a black American (no hyphen even when attrib.)
Afrikaans language of southern Africa derived from Dutch
Afrika Korps German army force sent to North Africa in 1941
Afrikander (also **Africander**) South African breed of sheep or cattle
Afrikaner Afrikaans-speaking white person in South Africa
afrit var. of **afreet**
Afro pl. **Afros** frizzy hairstyle
Afro-American now superseded by **African American**
Afro-Caribbean (hyphen)
afterbirth, afterburner, aftercare (one word)
after-effect (hyphen)
afterglow (one word)
after-image (hyphen)
afterlife, aftermath, aftershave, aftershock, aftertaste, afterthought, afterword (one word)
AG 1 Adjutant General **2** Attorney General **3** Advocate General
Ag the chemical element silver (no point) [L. *argentum*]
Aga trademark type of stove (cap.)
aga Ottoman military commander or official (lower case)
Aga Khan spiritual leader of the Nizari sect of Ismaili Muslims
Agamemnon Gk Mythol. commander-in-chief of the Greeks against Troy
agape (not ital.) **1** Christian love **2** communal meal in token of Christian fellowship
Agassi, André (b.1970), American tennis player
Agassiz, Jean Louis Rodolphe (1807–73), Swiss-born American zoologist and geologist
à gauche to the left (Fr., ital.)
age group (two words)
ageing (US **aging**)
ageism discrimination on the grounds of a person's age (not **agism**)
agenda pl. **agendas** list of items to be discussed
Agent General pl. **Agents General** foreign representative of an Australian state or Canadian province
Agent Orange defoliant chemical used by the US in the Vietnam War (caps)
agent provocateur pl. **agents provocateurs** (not ital.)
age-old (hyphen)
Aggadah var. of **Haggadah**
aggiornamento bringing up to date (It., ital.)
aggrandize (Brit. also **aggrandise**)
aggressor (not **-er**)
Agincourt battle in France (1415) during the Hundred Years War
aging US var. of **ageing**
agio pl. **agios** charge made for the exchange of money into a more valuable currency
agism use **ageism**
agitato Mus. agitated in manner
agitprop political propaganda in art or literature (one word, lower case)
agley Sc. askew, awry
AGM annual general meeting
agma speech sound of 'ng' as in *thing*, or IPA symbol used to represent it, ŋ
agnail use **hangnail**
Agni Vedic god of fire
agnostic person who believes that nothing can be known of the existence

of God □ **agnosticism**

Agnus Dei **1** figure of a lamb bearing a cross or flag **2** invocation beginning with the words 'Lamb of God' (caps, not ital.)

a gogo in abundance (two words, not ital.) [Fr. *à gogo*]

agonize (Brit. also **agonise**)

agora[1] pl. **agorae** or **agoras** public open space in ancient Greece

agora[2] pl. **agorot** or **agoroth** monetary unit of Israel

agoraphobia fear of open or public places

agouti pl. same or **agoutis** large rodent of Central and South America

AGR advanced gas-cooled reactor

Agra city in northern India, site of the Taj Mahal

agriculturist (not **agriculturalist**)

agrimony plant of the rose family with yellow flowers

agrochemical (also **agrichemical**) chemical used in agriculture

agronomy science of soil management and crop production

agrostology branch of botany concerned with grasses

Aguascalientes city and state in Mexico

ague arch. illness involving fever and shivering

Agulhas, Cape most southerly point of South Africa

AH in the year of the Hegira, used in the Muslim calendar for reckoning years (small caps)

ahimsa (in the Hindu, Buddhist, and Jainist tradition) respect for all living things and avoidance of violence towards others (not ital.)

Ahmadabad (also **Ahmedabad**) city in western India

Ahriman Zoroastrian evil spirit, opponent of Ahura Mazda

Ahura Mazda Zoroastrian creator god

Ahvenanmaa Finnish name for **Åland Islands**

AI **1** Amnesty International **2** artificial insemination **3** artificial intelligence

AID artificial insemination by donor

Aida opera by Verdi (1871) (no accent)

aide assistant to a leader (not ital.)

aide-de-camp pl. **aides-de-camp** military officer assisting a senior officer (hyphens, not ital.)

aide-memoire pl. **aides-memoires** or **aides-memoire** book or note used to aid the memory (not ital.) [Fr. *aide-mémoire*]

Aids (also **AIDS**) viral disease [*acquired immune deficiency syndrome*]

aigrette headdress, esp. one consisting of an egret's feather (not ital.)

aiguille pinnacle of rock (not ital.)

aiguillette braided shoulder ornament on a military uniform (not ital.)

AIH artificial insemination by husband

aikido Japanese form of self-defence and martial art (not ital.)

ailanthus pl. **ailanthuses** tall tree of Asia and Australasia

aileron control surface on an aircraft's wing

ailurophobia fear of cats

Ainu pl. same or **Ainus** member of an aboriginal people of northern Japan

aioli garlic mayonnaise (not ital.)

airbag, airbase (one word)

airbed (one word)

airborne (one word)

air brake (two words)

airbrick, airbrush (one word)

Airbus trademark type of airliner (cap., one word)

air chief marshal RAF rank above air marshal

air commodore RAF rank above group captain

air conditioning (two words) □ **air-conditioned**

aircraft pl. same (one word)

aircraft carrier (two words)

aircraftman (or **aircraftwoman**) lowest RAF rank

airdrome US var. of **aerodrome**

Airedale **1** large rough-coated breed of terrier **2** area of Yorkshire

airfare, airfield, airflow (one word)

air force (two words)

Air Force One official aircraft of the US president

airframe, airfreight (one word)

air freshener (two words)

airgun (one word)
air gunner (two words)
airlift, **airline**, **airliner**, **airlock**, **airmail**, **airman** (one word)
air marshal RAF rank above air vice-marshal (two words)
air mile (two words) **1** nautical mile as a measure of distance flown by an aircraft **2** (**Air Miles**) trademark points accumulated from purchases
airplane N. Amer. aeroplane
airplay, **airport** (one word)
air raid (two words)
air-sea rescue (hyphen)
airship, **airside**, **airspace**, **airspeed**, **airstrip**, **airtight** (one word)
air-to-air, **air-to-ground**, **air-to-surface** (hyphens)
air traffic control (three words) □ **air traffic controller**
air vice-marshal RAF rank above air commodore (one hyphen)
airwaves, **airway**, **airwoman**, **airworthy** (one word)
airy-fairy informal idealistic and vague (hyphen)
ait (also **eyot**) small island in a river
aitchbone buttock or rump bone of cattle
Aix-en-Provence city in southern France (hyphens)
Aix-la-Chapelle Fr. name for **Aachen** (hyphens)
Ajaccio port in Corsica
Ajax Gk Mythol. name of two Greek heroes, one the son of Telamon, the other the son of Oileus
Ajman member state of the United Arab Emirates
Ajmer city in NW India
AK Alaska (postal abbrev.)
AK-47 type of assault rifle
aka also known as (no points)
akee var. of **ackee**
Akela adult leader of a group of Cub Scouts
Akhmatova, Anna (1889–1966), Russian poet; pseudonym of *Anna Andreevna Gorenko*
Akihito (b.1933), son of Emperor Hirohito, emperor of Japan since 1989
akimbo (one word)
Akita Japanese breed of dog (cap.)
Akkadian inhabitant of Akkad in ancient Babylonia (not **Acc-**)
Akko another name for **Acre**
Akmola former name for **Astana**
akvavit var. of **aquavit**
AL 1 Alabama (postal abbrev.) **2** American League (in baseball)
Al the chemical element aluminium (no point)
al- (also **el-** and other variants) Arabic definite article, used in proper names (lower case, hyphen)
ALA 1 American Library Association **2** all letters answered
à la in the specified style or manner (accent, not ital.)
Alabama (official abbrev. **Ala.**, postal **AL**)
à la carte available as separate items, rather than part of a set meal (accent, not ital.); cf. **table d'hôte**
Aladdin's cave (one cap.)
Alain-Fournier (1886–1914), French novelist; pseudonym of *Henri-Alban Fournier*
Alamein see **El Alamein**
à la mode (accent, not ital.) **1** up to date **2** (of beef) braised in wine
Åland Islands group of islands forming a region of Finland; Finnish name **Ahvenanmaa**
à la page up to date (Fr., ital.)
Alaric king of the Visigoths 395–410
alarm clock (two words)
alarums and excursions confused activity and uproar
Alaska (official abbrev. **Alas.**, postal **AK**)
alb long white clerical vestment
alba variety of rose
albacore kind of tuna
Albania republic in SE Europe □ **Albanian**
Albany state capital of New York
albedo pl. **albedos** proportion of light or radiation that is reflected
Albee, Edward Franklin (b.1928), American dramatist
albeit (one word)
Albert, Prince (1819–61), consort to

Queen Victoria

Alberta province in western Canada

Albigenses heretic French sect in the 12th–13th cents □ **Albigensian**

albino pl. **albinos** person or animal lacking pigment in the skin and hair □ **albinism**

Albinoni, Tomaso (1671–1751), Italian composer

Albinus another name for **Alcuin**

Albion Britain or England

Ålborg Danish name for **Aalborg**

albumen white of an egg

albumin protein found in blood serum and egg white

Albuquerque city in New Mexico

Alcaeus (*c.*620–*c.*580 BC), Greek lyric poet

alcahest var. of **alkahest**

alcaic of a verse metre in four-line stanzas (lower case)

alcalde magistrate or mayor in Spain, Portugal, or Latin America

Alcatraz island in San Francisco Bay, site of a prison 1934–63

alcazar Spanish palace or fortress of Moorish origin (not ital.) [Sp. *alcázar*]

Alcheringa (among Australian Aboriginals) 'Dreamtime' or golden age (cap.)

Alcibiades (*c.*450–404 BC), Athenian general and statesman

alcopop Brit. informal soft drink containing alcohol (one word)

Alcott, Louisa May (1832–88), American novelist

Alcuin (*c.*735–804), English scholar and theologian; also known as **Albinus**

Aldeburgh town in Suffolk, England

al dente cooked so as to remain firm (not ital.)

Aldermaston site in southern England of the Atomic Weapons Research Establishment

Alderney third largest of the Channel Islands

Aldis lamp lamp for signalling in Morse code

Aldiss, Brian (Wilson) (b.1925), English novelist

Aldrin, Buzz (b.1930), American astronaut; full name *Edwin Eugene Aldrin*

Aldus Manutius (1450–1515), Italian printer; Latinized name of *Teobaldo Manucci*; also known as **Aldo Manuzio**

aleatory (also **aleatoric**) depending on the throw of a die or on chance

Alecto (also **Allecto**) Gk Mythol. one of the Furies

alehouse (one word)

alembic apparatus formerly used for distilling

aleph first letter of the Hebrew alphabet, ʾ, typographically largely equivalent to the Arabic hamza or Greek lenis [Heb. *ʾālep̱*]

Aleppo city in northern Syria

Aleutian Islands chain of US islands in the Bering Sea

A level Brit. advanced level examination (two words)

alewife pl. **alewives** fish of the herring family (one word)

Alexander (356–323 BC), king of Macedon 336–323; known as **Alexander the Great**

Alexander Nevsky (*c.*1220–63), prince of Novgorod 1236–63; canonized as **St Alexander Nevsky**

alexanders plant of the parsley family (lower case, treated as sing.)

Alexander technique system designed to improve posture (one cap.)

Alexandria chief port of Egypt

alexandrine line of verse having six iambic feet (lower case)

alfalfa plant with clover-like leaves

Alfa Romeo Italian car company (two words, caps)

al-Fatah var. of **Fatah**

al fresco in the open air (two words, not ital.)

al-Fujayrah var. of **Fujairah**

Alfvén, Hannes Olof Gösta (1908–95), Swedish physicist

alga pl. **algae** simple plant, esp. seaweed

Algarve southernmost province of Portugal

algebra mathematics in which letters are used to represent numbers and quantities □ **algebraic**

Algeciras port in southern Spain

Algeria country in North Africa; capital, Algiers □ **Algerian**
ALGOL early computer programming language (caps)
Algol star in the constellation Perseus
algology study of algae
Algonquian (also **Algonkian**) large family of North American Indian languages
Algonquin (also **Algonkin**) member of an American Indian people
algorithm process or set of rules used in calculations (not **-rhythm**)
alguacil pl. **alguaciles** mounted official at a bullfight (not ital.)
alhaji pl. **alhajis** African Muslim who has been to Mecca as a pilgrim; cf. **haji** (not ital.)
Alhambra Moorish palace near Granada in Spain
Ali (600–61), cousin of the Prophet Muhammad, regarded by Shiites as the first imam
Ali, Muhammad, see **Muhammad Ali**
alias also known as (not ital.)
Ali Baba hero of a story from the *Arabian Nights*
alibi pl. **alibis** piece of evidence that one was elsewhere; disp. excuse or pretext
Alice's Adventures in Wonderland book by Lewis Carroll (1865)
alienist dated psychiatrist
Aligarh city in northern India
Alighieri, Dante, see **Dante**
alimentary relating to nourishment
alimony N. Amer. maintenance paid to a spouse after separation
A-line (of a garment) slightly flared (hyphen)
A-list list of the most celebrated individuals in show business (hyphen)
Alitalia Italian national airline
aliyah pl. **aliyoth** Judaism (not ital.) **1** immigration to Israel **2** honour of being called upon to read from the Torah
al-Jizah Arab. name for **Giza**
alkahest (also **alcahest**) hist. universal solvent sought by alchemists
alkali pl. **alkalis** compound that turns litmus blue and neutralizes or effervesces with acids
alla breve Mus. time signature indicating two or four minim beats in a bar
alla cappella var. of **a cappella**
Allah name of God among Muslims and Arab Christians [Arab. *'allāh*]
Allahabad city in north central India
allargando pl. **allargandi** or **allargandos** Mus. getting slower and broader
All Blacks New Zealand rugby union team (caps)
all-clear signal that danger is over (hyphen)
Allecto var. of **Alecto**
allée alley, avenue (Fr., ital.)
Allegheny Mountains mountain range in the eastern US
allegretto pl. **allegrettos** Mus. at a fairly brisk speed
Allegri, Gregorio (1582–1652), Italian priest and composer
allegro pl. **allegros** Mus. at a brisk speed
allele Genet. alternative form of a gene
alleluia var. of **hallelujah**
allemande (not ital.) **1** German court dance **2** figure in country dancing
all-embracing (hyphen)
Allen, Woody (b.1935), American actor; born *Allen Stewart Konigsberg*
Allenby, Edmund Henry Hynman, 1st Viscount (1861–1936), British soldier
Allen key (US **Allen wrench**) (one cap.)
Allerød Geol. second stage of the late glacial period in northern Europe
alleviate make less severe □ **alleviator**
alley pl. **alleys**
alleyway (one word)
All Fools' Day April Fool's Day (caps)
All Hallows All Saints' Day, 1 November (caps)
all-important, **all-in**, **all-inclusive**, **all-in-one** (hyphens)
allium pl. **alliums** plant of a genus that includes the onion, garlic, etc.
allochthonous Geol. originating at a distance from its present position; cf. **autochthonous**
allocution speech giving advice or warning; cf. **elocution**
allodium pl. **allodia** hist. estate held in absolute ownership
allosaurus carnivorous dinosaur (lower case)

allot (**allotting, allotted**) ◻ **allotment**

all-party, all-pervasive, all-powerful, all-purpose (hyphen)

all right (not **alright**)

all-round adj. having many abilities or uses (hyphen) ◻ **all-rounder**

all round prep. around all the parts of (two words)

All Saints' Day Christian festival held on 1 November (caps)

All Souls Oxford college (no apostrophe)

All Souls' Day Catholic festival held on 2 November (caps)

allspice (one word)

all-star (hyphen)

All's Well that Ends Well Shakespeare play (abbrev. ***All's Well***)

all together all in one place; all at once; cf. **altogether**

allusive using suggestion rather than explicit mention; cf. **elusive, illusive**

alluvion Law formation of new land by deposition of sediment; cf. **avulsion**

alluvium deposit left by flood water in a river valley or delta ◻ **alluvial**

ally (**allies, allying, allied**) with ref. to WWI and WWII use **the Allies**

Alma-Ata var. of **Almaty**

almacantar var. of **almucantar**

al-Madinah Arab. name for **Medina**

Almagest Arabic version of Ptolemy's astronomical treatise

alma mater one's former university, school, etc. (lower case, not ital.)

almanac (in titles also **almanack**)

Almanach de Gotha annual publication giving information about European royalty, nobility, and diplomats

Alma-Tadema, Sir Lawrence (1836–1912), Dutch-born British painter

Almaty (also **Alma-Ata**) former capital of Kazakhstan

Almería town and province in Andalusia, Spain (accent)

almighty as title for God use **the Almighty**

Almohads Berber dynasty that conquered the Almoravids in the 12th cent.

Almoravids Berber federation powerful in the 11th cent.

almshouse (one word)

almucantar (also **almacantar**) Astron. **1** circle on the celestial sphere **2** type of telescope

aloe vera (two words)

aloha Hawaiian word of greeting or parting (not ital., lower case)

alongshore along or by the shore (one word)

alopecia Med. baldness or absence of hair

ALP Australian Labor Party

alp high mountain; (**the Alps**) mountain range in Switzerland etc.

alpenhorn (also **alphorn**) very long wooden wind instrument (lower case)

alpha first letter of the Greek alphabet (**Α, α**), transliterated as 'a'

alphabetize (Brit. also **alphabetise**)

alphanumeric consisting of or using both letters and numerals (one word)

alpha particle (two words)

alpha test (two words, hyphen as verb)

alphorn var. of **alpenhorn**

alpine relating to high mountains; (**Alpine**) relating to the Alps

alpinist mountaineer (lower case)

al-Qaeda (also **al-Qaida**) Islamic fundamentalist group [Arab. *al-qāʿida*]

al-Qahira (also **el-Qahira**) Arab. name for **Cairo**

already (one word)

alright use **all right**

ALS autograph letter signed

Alsace region of NE France

Alsace-Lorraine area of France formerly ruled by Prussia (hyphen)

Alsatian (not **-ion**) **1** Brit. German shepherd dog **2** person from Alsace

also-ran pl. **also-rans** (hyphen)

alt. (point) **1** alternative **2** altitude

Alta Alberta (no point)

Altamira site in Spain of a cave with Palaeolithic rock paintings (one word)

altazimuth **1** Astron. type of telescope mounting **2** surveying instrument

alter ego secondary or alternative personality (not ital.)

alternate adj. **1** every other **2** N. Amer. alternative

alternating current (abbrev. **AC** or **a.c.**)
Althing legislative assembly of Iceland (not ital.)
althorn musical instrument of the saxhorn family
Althorp village and country house in Northamptonshire, England
Althusser, Louis (1918–90), French philosopher
altissimo Mus. very high in pitch
Alt key Comput. (no point)
alto pl. **altos** highest male or lowest female adult singing voice
altocumulus pl. **altocumuli** cloud (lower case)
altogether in total (one word); cf. **all together**
alto-relievo pl. **alto-relievos** Art high relief (hyphen, not ital.) [It. *alto-rilievo*]
aludel pot formerly used in chemical processes
aluminium (US **aluminum**) chemical element of atomic number 13 (symbol **Al**)
alumnus (fem. **alumna**) pl. **alumni** or **alumnae** former student of a particular school or college
al-Uqsur var. of **el-Uqsur**
alveolus pl. **alveoli** **1** Anat. tiny air sac in the lungs **2** socket for the root of a tooth □ **alveolar**
Alzheimer's (in full **Alzheimer's disease**) (apostrophe, one cap.)
AM **1** amplitude modulation **2** (**A.M.**) Hymns Ancient and Modern **3** US Master of Arts [L. *artium magister*] **4** Member of the Order of Australia
Am the chemical element americium (no point)
AM in the Jewish era, reckoned from 7 October 3761 BC (small caps) [L. *anno mundi* 'in the year of the world']
a.m. before noon [L. *ante meridiem*]
amadavat var. of **avadavat**
amah nursemaid or maid in the Far East or India (not ital.)
amanuensis pl. **amanuenses** person who takes dictation for writer
amaranth **1** tropical plant **2** purple colour □ **amaranthine**
amaretti Italian almond-flavoured biscuits (not ital.)
amaretto pl. **amarettos** Italian almond liqueur (not ital.)
Amarna, Tell el- see **Tell el-Amarna**
Amaryllis name for a country girl in Latin poetry
amaryllis plant with trumpet-shaped flowers (lower case)
Amaterasu principal deity of the Japanese Shinto religion
Amati family of Italian violin-makers
Amazon **1** river of South America **2** Gk Mythol. female warrior □ **Amazonian**
ambassador (cap. in titles) □ **ambassadress, ambassadorial**
ambergris wax-like secretion of the sperm whale
ambiance combination of the accessory elements of a painting to support the main effect of a piece (Fr., ital.)
ambidextrous (not **ambidexterous**)
ambience character and atmosphere of a place; cf. **ambiance** □ **ambient**
ambit scope, extent, or bounds
ambo pl. **ambos** or **ambones** pulpit with steps in an early Christian church
Ambon (also **Amboina**) Indonesian island
amboyna type of decorative wood
ambrosia Class. Mythol. food of the gods (lower case)
ambry var. of **aumbry**
AMDG to the greater glory of God [L. *ad maiorem Dei gloriam*]
ameba, amebiasis US vars of **amoeba, amoebiasis**
âme damnée pl. ***âmes damnées*** devoted adherent (ital.) [Fr., 'damned soul']
amen (lower case)
amend make minor improvements to; cf. **emend**
amende honorable pl. ***amendes honorables*** open apology and reparation (Fr., ital.)
amenorrhoea (US **amenorrhea**) abnormal absence of menstruation
amercement English Law, hist. a fine
America acceptable in general contexts as a name for the United States
American Indian in US official

contexts replaced by **Native American**; still acceptable in general use
Americanize (Brit. also **Americanise**)
American plan N. Amer. full board in a hotel etc.
American Revolution N. Amer. term for **War of American Independence**
America's Cup yachting race
americium chemical element of atomic number 95 (symbol **Am**)
Amerindian (also **Amerind**) American Indian
à merveille admirably, wonderfully (Fr., ital.)
Ameslan American Sign Language
Amex 1 trademark American Express **2** American Stock Exchange
Amharic official language of Ethiopia
amiable friendly and pleasant in manner
amicable characterized by friendliness and agreement
amice white cloth worn by a priest celebrating the Eucharist
amicus (in full **amicus curiae**) pl. **amici, amici curiae** impartial adviser to a court of law (not ital.)
amidships (one word)
amigo pl. **amigos** friend (not ital.)
Amin, Idi (1925–2003), Ugandan head of state 1971–9; full name *Idi Amin Dada*
amino acid (two words)
amir var. of **emir**
Amis 1 Sir Kingsley (1922–95), English novelist **2** Martin (Louis) (b.1949), English novelist, son of Kingsley Amis
Amish strict US Mennonite sect
amitriptyline Med. antidepressant drug
Amman capital of Jordan
ammeter instrument for measuring electric current in amperes
Ammon Gk and Rom. name of **Amun**
amoeba (US **ameba**) pl. **amoebas** or **amoebae** (not ital.)
amoebiasis (US **amebiasis**) Med. infection with amoebas
amok (also **amuck**) (in **run amok**) behave uncontrollably
Amon var. of **Amun**
amontillado pl. **amontillados** medium dry sherry (not ital.)
amoral lacking a moral sense; cf. **immoral**
amoretto pl. **amoretti** representation of Cupid (not ital.)
amoroso (not ital.) **1** Mus. in a tender manner **2** dark sweet sherry
amortize (Brit. also **amortise**) write off (an asset or debt) over a period
Amos 1 Hebrew minor prophet **2** book of the Old Testament (no abbrev.)
amour love affair or lover (not ital.)
amour courtois courtly love (Fr., ital.)
amour fou uncontrollable or obsessive passion (Fr., ital.)
amour propre self-respect (Fr., ital.)
amp (no point) **1** ampere **2** amplifier
Ampère, André-Marie (1775–1836), French physicist
ampere SI unit of electric current (no accent; abbrev. **A**)
ampersand the sign &, standing for *and* or Latin *et*; use in reproducing correct form of company names, e.g. *M&S*
amphetamine stimulant drug
amphibian Zool. cold-blooded vertebrate of the class Amphibia
amphibole mineral
amphibolite kind of rock
amphibology (also **amphiboly**) grammatically ambiguous phrase or sentence
amphisbaena mythical serpent with a head at each end
amphisbaenian Zool. worm lizard
amphitheatre (US **amphitheater**)
amphora pl. **amphorae** or **amphoras** ancient Greek or Roman jar
ampoule (US also **ampul** or **ampule**) capsule containing liquid for injecting
ampulla pl. **ampullae** ancient Roman flask
Amritsar city in NW India, centre of the Sikh faith
Amtrak trademark US passenger railway service
amuck var. of **amok**
Amun (also **Amon**) supreme god of the ancient Egyptians; Gk and Rom. name **Ammon**

Amundsen, Roald (1872–1928), Norwegian explorer, first to reach the South Pole (1911)

Amur a river of NE Asia

amuse-gueule pl. ***amuse-gueules*** or same, small savoury appetizer (Fr., ital.)

amygdala pl. **amygdalae** Anat. part of the brain

amygdalin Chem. bitter substance in almonds and fruit stones

AN Anglo-Norman

an use **a** not **an** before words such as *hotel* and *historical* where the initial *h* is sounded

ana arch. **1** anecdotes or literary gossip (treated as pl.) **2** collection of sayings (treated as sing.)

anabasis pl. **anabases 1** military advance into the interior of a country **2** (***Anabasis***) work by Xenophon

anacoluthon pl. **anacolutha** Gram. construction lacking the expected sequence, e.g. *while in the garden, the door banged shut*

Anacreon (*c.*582–*c.*485 BC), Greek lyric poet □ **Anacreontic**

anaemia (US **anemia**)

anaerobe Biol. organism able to grow without free oxygen

anaesthesia (US **anesthesia**)

anaesthetize (US **anesthetize**, Brit. also **anaesthetise**)

Anaglypta trademark embossed wallpaper, to be painted over (cap.)

Anaheim city in California

analects (also **analecta**) collection of short literary or philosophical extracts

analogous comparable (not **analagous**)

analogue (US **analog**) adj. using information represented by a continuously variable physical quantity. n. person or thing comparable to another

analyse (US **analyze**)

analysis pl. **analyses**

Anancy cunning spider in African and West Indian folk tales

anapaest (US **anapest**) metrical foot of two short or unstressed syllables followed by one long or stressed syllable

anaphora 1 Gram. use of a word referring back to a word used earlier; cf. **cataphora 2** Rhet. repetition of a word or phrase

anastomosis pl. **anastomoses** cross-connection between parts of a network

anathema pl. **anathemas** a curse

anatomize (Brit. also **anatomise**) **1** dissect **2** examine and analyse

ANC African National Congress

anchorite (fem. **anchoress**) hermit

ancien régime pl. ***anciens régimes*** old political or social system; (***the Ancien Régime***) system in France before the Revolution (Fr., ital.)

Ancient Mariner, The Rime of the poem by Coleridge (1798)

Ancient of Days, the biblical title for God (caps)

Ancyra ancient name for **Ankara**

Andalusia southernmost region of Spain; Sp. name **Andalucía**

Andaman and Nicobar Islands islands in the Bay of Bengal, a Union Territory in India

andante Mus. in a moderately slow tempo

andantino Mus. lighter than andante, and usually quicker

Andersen, Hans Christian (1805–75), Danish writer of fairy tales

Anderson, Elizabeth Garrett (1836–1917), English physician

Anderson shelter (one cap)

Andes mountain system in South America □ **Andean**

Andhra Pradesh state in SE India

Andorra autonomous principality in the Pyrenees

androecium pl. **androecia** Bot. stamens of a flower

androgen male sex hormone

androgynous of indeterminate sex □ **androgyny**

Andromeda 1 Gk Mythol. princess saved from a sea monster by Perseus **2** constellation

andromeda bog rosemary (lower case)

anechoic free from echo

anele arch. anoint

anemia US var. of **anaemia**

anemone 1 plant of the buttercup family **2** sea anemone

anent arch. or Sc. concerning, about

anesthesia etc. US var. of **anaesthesia** etc.

aneurysm (also **aneurism**) Med. swelling of the wall of an artery

Angeleno pl. **Angelenos** person from Los Angeles

Angelic Doctor nickname of St Thomas Aquinas

Angelico, Fra (*c.*1400–55), Italian painter and Dominican friar; born *Guido di Pietro*

Angelman syndrome Med. (not **Angelman's syndrome**)

angelus Roman Catholic devotion announced by bell (lower case)

Angevin **1** person from Anjou **2** Plantagenet king of England, esp. Henry II, Richard I, and John

angioma pl. **angiomas** or **angiomata** Med. growth composed of blood vessels or lymph vessels

Angkor Wat temple in NW Cambodia

angle brackets the marks < > or ⟨ ⟩

angle grinder, angle iron (two words)

anglepoise adjustable desk lamp (cap. as trademark)

anglerfish pl. same (one word)

Anglesey island and county of NW Wales; Welsh name **Ynys Môn**

Anglican Communion Christian Churches connected with the Church of England (caps)

anglice in English (not ital., lower case)

anglicize (Brit. also **anglicise**) (lower case)

Anglo-Catholic, Anglo-Indian, Anglo-Irish, Anglo-Latin, Anglo-Norman (hyphen)

Anglophile person fond of England (cap.)

anglophone English-speaking (lower case)

Anglo-Saxon prefer **Old English** for the language

Angola republic in southern Africa □ **Angolan**

Angora former name for **Ankara**

angora yarn from a long-haired goat (lower case)

Angostura former name for **Ciudad Bolívar**

Angostura bitters trademark kind of tonic (one cap.)

Angry Young Men group of British playwrights and novelists of the early 1950s (caps)

angst general anxiety or dread (not ital., lower case)

Ångström, Anders Jonas (1814–1874), Swedish physicist

angstrom (abbrev. **Å**) unit of length equal to one hundred millionth of a centimetre, 10^{-10} metre, now largely replaced by the **nanometre** (no accents)

Anguilla one of the Leeward Islands

anguilliform eel-like

Angus council area of NE Scotland

aniline liquid used in dyes, drugs, etc.

anima Psychol. **1** feminine part of a man's personality; cf. **animus** **2** inner part of the psyche; cf. **persona**

animalcule arch. microscopic animal

animato Mus. in an animated manner

anime Japanese film and television animation (not ital., no accent)

animé resin from West Indian tree (accent)

animus **1** ill feeling **2** Psychol. masculine part of a woman's personality; cf. **anima**

anion Chem. negatively charged ion; cf. **cation**

Anjou former province of western France

Ankara capital of Turkey since 1923; former names **Ancyra, Angora**

ankh ancient Egyptian symbol

ankylosing spondylitis Med. form of spinal arthritis

ankylosis Med. stiffening of joints due to fusion of the bones

anna former monetary unit of India and Pakistan (lower case)

an-Najaf var. of **Najaf**

Annam former empire and French protectorate in SE Asia □ **Annamese**

Annapurna ridge of the Himalayas

Ann Arbor city in Michigan

annatto pl. **annattos** orange-red dye

Anne (1665–1714), queen of England and Scotland (known as Great Britain from 1707) and Ireland 1702–14

Anne Boleyn see **Boleyn**

Anne of Cleves (1515–57), fourth wife of Henry VIII (divorced)
annex v. **1** add as an extra part **2** appropriate (territory). n. (Brit. also **annexe**) an addition to a building or to a document
Anno Domini of the Christian era; see AD (not ital.) [L., 'in the year of the Lord']
annul (**annulling, annulled**) ◻ **annulment**
annular ring-shaped
annulet 1 Archit. band encircling a column **2** Heraldry charge in the form of a ring
annulus pl. **annuli** ring-shaped object
Annunciation, the announcement of the Incarnation by the angel Gabriel to Mary, celebrated on 25 March
annus horribilis year of disaster (L., ital.)
annus mirabilis remarkable year (L., ital.)
anode positively charged electrode; cf. **cathode**
anodized (Brit. also **anodised**) coated with a protective oxide layer
anomia Med. inability to recall the names of everyday objects
anomie (also **anomy**) lack of social or ethical standards
anon soon, shortly (no point)
anon. anonymous (point)
anorexia (also **anorexia nervosa**) obsessive desire to lose weight by refusing food
anorexic (also **anorectic**) suffering from anorexia
A. N. Other Brit. sports player who is not named
Anouilh, Jean (1910–87), French dramatist
Anschluss annexation of Austria by Germany in 1938 (Ger., ital., cap.)
Anselm, St (*c.*1033–1109), Italian-born theologian, Archbishop of Canterbury 1093–1109
ANSI American National Standards Institute
answerphone Brit. telephone answering machine (lower case)
antagonize (Brit. also **antagonise**)
Antakya Turkish name for **Antioch**
Antananarivo capital of Madagascar
Antarctica continent round the South Pole ◻ **Antarctic**
ante stake in a card game (not ital.)
anteater (one word)
antebellum occurring or existing before a war, esp. the US Civil War (one word, not ital.)
antechamber, antedate, antediluvian (one word)
antemeridian occurring in the morning (one word, not ital.)
ante meridiem before noon; see **a.m.** (L., ital.)
ante mortem before death (two words, not ital.)
antenatal (one word)
antenna pl. **antennae 1** Zool. sensory appendage **2** pl. also **antennas** an aerial
antepartum Med. occurring not long before childbirth (one word, not ital.)
antepenultimate last but two (one word)
ante-post Brit. (of a bet) placed before the runners are known (hyphen)
anteroom (one word)
anthelmintic Med. used to destroy parasitic worms
anthill (one word)
anthologize (Brit. also **anthologise**)
anthropomorphism attribution of human characteristics to a god, animal, etc.
anthropomorphous (of a god, animal, etc.) human in form or nature
anthropophagus pl. **anthropophagi** cannibal
anthroposophy system established by Rudolf Steiner
anti-abortion, anti-aircraft, anti-apartheid (hyphen)
antibacterial, antibiotic, antibody (one word)
antic arch. grotesque or bizarre
Antichrist opponent of Christ (cap., one word)
anti-Christian (one cap., hyphen)
anticlimax (one word)
anticline Geol. fold of rock with downwards-sloping strata; cf. **syncline**
anticlockwise (one word)
anticyclone, antidepressant (one word)

antidisestablishmentarianism opposition to the disestablishment of the Church of England
antifreeze (one word)
Antigone Gk Mythol. daughter of Oedipus and Jocasta
Antigua and Barbuda country consisting of three islands (Antigua, Barbuda, and Redonda) in the Leeward Islands ◻ **Antiguan**
anti-hero (or **anti-heroine**) (hyphen)
antihistamine (one word)
Anti-Lebanon Mountains range of mountains along the Lebanon–Syria border
Antilles group of islands forming the greater part of the West Indies
antilog antilogarithm (one word, no point)
antimacassar (one word)
antimatter (one word)
antimony chemical element of atomic number 51 (symbol **Sb**)
antinomy paradox
anti-nuclear (hyphen)
Antioch 1 city in southern Turkey; Turkish name **Antakya 2** city in ancient Phrygia
antioxidant, antiparticle (one word)
antipasto pl. **antipasti** Italian hors d'oeuvre (one word, not ital.)
anti-personnel (hyphen)
antiperspirant (one word)
Antipodes, the Australia and New Zealand ◻ **Antipodean**
antipodes (also **antipode**) the direct opposite (lower case)
antipope rival to pope (one word)
antique v. (**antiquing, antiqued**) make (something) look old
anti-racism (hyphen)
antiretroviral drug which inhibits retroviruses such as HIV (one word)
anti-Semitism (hyphen, one cap.)
antisocial troublesome to others (one word); cf. **unsocial, unsociable**
antistrophe second section of an ancient Greek choral ode (one word); cf. **strophe**
antithesis pl. **antitheses 1** the direct opposite **2** rhetorical device involving an opposition of ideas ◻ **antithetical**
antitoxin (one word)
antitype person or thing representing the opposite of another (one word)
Antony, Mark (*c.*83–30 BC), Roman general; Latin name *Marcus Antonius*
Antony and Cleopatra Shakespeare play (abbrev. ***Ant. & Cl.***)
antonym word opposite in meaning to another; cf. **synonym** ◻ **antonymous**
Antrim county and town in Northern Ireland
Antwerp port in Belgium; Fr. name **Anvers**, Flemish name **Antwerpen**
Anubis dog-headed Egyptian god
anus Anat. pl. **anuses**
Anvers Fr. name for **Antwerp**
any- pronouns and adverbs beginning with *any-*, *every-*, and *some-* are usu. single words ('anyone you ask', 'everything I own', 'somebody to talk to'), but where each word retains its own meaning the words are printed separately ('any one item', 'every thing in its place')
anybody, anyhow (one word)
any more (two words, one word in US)
anyone, anyplace, anything, anyway, anywhere (one word)
Anzac soldier in the Australian and New Zealand Army Corps (1914–18)
Anzus alliance between Australia, New Zealand, and the US
AO Officer of the Order of Australia
AOB any other business
AOC appellation d'origine contrôlée
A-OK (caps, hyphen)
AONB Area of Outstanding Natural Beauty
aorist simple past tense of a verb, esp. in Greek
aorta main artery of the body
Aotearoa Maori name for **New Zealand** [lit. 'land of the long white cloud']
aoudad Barbary sheep
à outrance to the death or the very end (Fr., ital.)
AP Associated Press
Apache pl. same or **Apaches** member of an American Indian people

apache pl. **apaches** street ruffian in Paris (lower case)
apanage var. of **appanage**
apartheid (lower case)
apatosaurus herbivorous dinosaur; also called **brontosaurus** (lower case)
APB US all-points bulletin
APC armoured personnel carrier
ape v. (**aping, aped**) □ **apelike**
APEC Asia Pacific Economic Cooperation
Apelles (4th cent. BC), Greek painter
apeman (one word)
Apennines mountain range in Italy (one *p*, two *ns*)
aperçu pl. **aperçus** illuminating comment (accent, not ital.)
aperitif (not ital.)
Apex system of reduced airline and rail fares (one cap.) [*A*dvance *P*urchase *Ex*cursion]
apex pl. **apexes** or **apices**
apfelstrudel apple strudel (lower case, not ital.)
aphelion pl. **aphelia** Astron. point in an orbit that is furthest from the sun; cf. **perihelion**
apheresis pl. **aphereses** Gram. omission of the initial sound of a word, as when *he is* is pronounced *he's*
aphesis pl. **apheses** Gram. loss of a vowel at the beginning of a word (e.g. of *e* from *esquire* to form *squire*)
aphis pl. **aphides** aphid
Aphrodite Gk Mythol. goddess of beauty and love; Rom. equivalent **Venus**
aphtha pl. **aphthae** small mouth ulcer
API Comput. application programming interface
apian relating to bees
apiary place for keeping bees
apical relating to an apex
apices pl. of **apex**
Apis Egyptian bull god
aplenty (one word)
apnoea (US **apnea**) Med. temporary cessation of breathing
Apocalypse, the (esp. in the Vulgate) the book of Revelation (abbrev. **Apoc.**)
Apocrypha writings appended to the Old Testament in the Septuagint and Vulgate (treated as sing. or pl.; abbrev. **Apoc.** or **Apocr.**)
apocryphal 1 of doubtful authenticity **2** belonging to the Apocrypha
apodictic (also **apodeictic**) clearly established
apodosis pl. **apodoses** Gram. main clause of a conditional sentence; cf. **protasis**
apogee 1 culmination or climax **2** Astron. point in the moon's orbit at which it is furthest from the earth; cf. **perigee**
Apollinaire, Guillaume (1880–1918), French poet; pseudonym of *Wilhelm Apollinaris de Kostrowitzki*
Apollinaris (*c.*310–*c.*390), heretical bishop of Laodicea □ **Apollinarian**
Apollo 1 Gk Mythol. god of music **2** US space programme; ***Apollo 11*** was the first to land astronauts on the moon (1969)
Apollonian relating to the rational aspects of human nature; cf. **Dionysiac**
Apollonius (3rd cent. BC), Greek poet; known as **Apollonius of Rhodes**
Apollyon the Devil (Rev. 9:11)
apologia written defence of one's opinions or conduct (not ital.)
apologize (Brit. also **apologise**)
apophthegm (US **apothegm**) saying or maxim
aporia Rhet. the expression of doubt
aposiopesis pl. **aposiopeses** Rhet. device of suddenly breaking off
apostasy (not **-cy**)
apostatize (Brit. also **apostatise**)
a posteriori proceeding from experiences to the deduction of probable causes (two words, not ital.)
Apostle disciple of Jesus
apostle pioneering supporter of an idea (lower case)
Apostles' Creed statement of Christian belief (caps)
Apostolic Fathers Christian leaders succeeding the Apostles (caps)
apostrophize (Brit. also **apostrophise**) **1** address with an exclamation **2** punctuate with an apostrophe
apothecaries' measure (apostrophe)
apothegm US var. of **apophthegm**
apotheosis pl. **apotheoses** elevation to divine status
apotropaic averting bad luck

appal (US **appall**) (**appalling, appalled**)
Appalachian Mountains mountain system of North America
appanage (also **apanage**) hist. provision for the maintenance of the younger children of kings and princes
apparatchik pl. **apparatchiks** or **apparatchiki** member of a communist party administration (not ital.)
apparatus pl. **apparatuses**
apparatus criticus pl. **apparatus critici** notes accompanying a text (not ital.)
apparel v. (**apparelling, apparelled**; US one **-l-**)
apparitor officer of a Church court
appeasement (not **appeasment**)
appellant Law person appealing against a court ruling
appellation contrôlée (also ***appellation d'origine contrôlée***) guarantee as to the origins of a French wine (ital.)
appendectomy (Brit. also **appendicectomy**) operation to remove the appendix
appendix pl. **appendices** in ref. to books or **appendixes** in ref. to the body part
appetizing (Brit. also **appetising**)
Appian Way road southward from ancient Rome (two caps)
apple green, apple pie, apple sauce (two words)
appliqué v. (**appliquéing, appliquéd**) (accent, not ital.)
appoggiatura pl. **appoggiaturas** or **appoggiature** Mus. grace note
appraise assess the value or quality of
apprise inform (not **-ize**)
apprize (Brit. also **apprise**) arch. put a price on
appro approval (no point)
approx. approximate (point)
APR annual(ized) percentage rate
après coup after the event (ital.) [Fr., 'after stroke']
après-ski social activities after skiing (accent, not ital.)
April (abbrev. **Apr.**)
April Fool (two caps)
April Fool's Day (caps, apostrophe)
a priori based on deduction rather than observation (two words, not ital.)
apropos (one word, not ital.)
apse domed recess at a church's eastern end
apsis pl. **apsides** Astron. point in an orbit that is nearest to or furthest from the central body
apt. N. Amer. apartment (point)
Apuleius (born *c.*123 AD), Roman writer
Apulia region of SE Italy; It. name **Puglia**
aqua fortis arch. nitric acid (not ital.)
aqua regia mixture of concentrated nitric and hydrochloric acids (not ital.)
aquarium pl. **aquaria** or **aquariums**
Aquarius eleventh sign of the zodiac □ **Aquarian**
aquavit (also **akvavit**) alcoholic spirit made from potatoes
aqua vitae alcoholic spirit, esp. brandy (two words, not ital.)
aqueduct (not **aqua-**)
Aquinas, St Thomas (1225–74), Italian theologian and Dominican friar
Aquitaine region of SW France
AR 1 Arkansas (postal abbrev.) **2** Autonomous Republic
Ar the chemical element argon
ARA Associate of the Royal Academy
arabesque (lower case)
Arabian camel one-humped camel; cf. **Bactrian camel**
Arabian Nights (in full ***The Arabian Nights' Entertainment***) collection of Arabic stories
arabica type of coffee (lower case)
Arabic numeral the numerals 0, 1, 2, 3, etc. (one cap.)
arachnid Zool. arthropod of the class Arachnida, e.g. a spider (lower case)
Arafat, Yasser (1929–2004), Palestinian president 1996–2004
Aragon region of NE Spain; Sp. name **Aragón**
Araldite trademark kind of glue
Aral Sea inland sea on the border between Kazakhstan and Uzbekistan
Aramaean (also **Aramean**) member of an ancient people of Aram (Syria) and Mesopotamia in the 11th–8th cents BC
Aramaic ancient Semitic language

Aran Islands group of three islands off the west coast of Ireland, assoc. with a style of knitwear; cf. **Arran**
Arapaho pl. same or **Arapahos** member of a North American Indian people
Ararat, Mount pair of volcanic peaks in eastern Turkey, traditional resting place of Noah's ark
arbalest hist. crossbow
arbiter person who settles a dispute
arbiter elegantiarum (also ***arbiter elegantiae***) judge of taste and etiquette (L., ital.)
arbitrage simultaneous buying and selling of assets in different markets or forms ◻ **arbitrageur** (also **arbitrager**)
arbitrator person or body officially appointed to settle a dispute
arbitress arch. female arbiter
arbor[1] **1** axle **2** device holding a tool in a lathe
arbor[2] US var. of **arbour**
arboreal relating to or living in trees
arboretum pl. **arboretums** or **arboreta** botanical garden devoted to trees
arboriculture cultivation of trees and shrubs
Arborio variety of Italian rice used in risotto (cap.)
arbor vitae kind of conifer (not ital.)
arbour (US **arbor**) garden bower
arbutus pl. **arbutuses** evergreen tree or shrub
ARC 1 Agricultural Research Council **2** Aids-related complex
Arc, Joan of, see **Joan of Arc, St**
arc v. (**arcing, arced**)
Arcadia 1 mountainous district in southern Greece **2** (also **Arcady**) pastoral paradise ◻ **Arcadian**
arcana 1 secrets or mysteries **2** either of the two groups of cards in a tarot pack (the **major arcana** and the **minor arcana**)
arc cosine Math. inverse of a cosine (abbrev. **arcos**)
Arc de Triomphe arch in Paris
archaea Biol. microorganisms similar to bacteria (lower case) ◻ **archaean**
Archaean (US **Archean**) earlier part of the Precambrian
archaeology (US **archeology**)
archaeopteryx oldest known fossil bird
Archangel port of NW Russia; Russ. name **Arkhangelsk**
archangel (cap. in titles)
archbishop cap. in titles (*the Archbishop of Canterbury*, but *the archbishop said ...*); abbrev. **Abp**
archdeacon (cap. in titles)
archdiocese district for which an archbishop is responsible
archduchess, archduke (cap. in titles)
Archean US var. of **Archaean**
arch-enemy (hyphen)
archeology US var. of **archaeology**
archetype (not **architype**)
archidiaconal relating to an archdeacon
archiepiscopal relating to an archbishop
Archilochus (8th or 7th cent. BC), Greek poet
archimandrite superior of a monastery or group of monasteries in the Orthodox Church
Archimedes (*c.*287–212 BC), Greek mathematician ◻ **Archimedean**
archipelago pl. **archipelagos** or **archipelagoes**
Archipiélago de Colón Sp. name for **Galapagos Islands**
archon chief magistrate in ancient Athens
arc light (two words)
arc sine Math. inverse of a sine (abbrev. **arcsin**)
arc tangent Math. inverse of a tangent (abbrev. **arctan**)
Arctic, the regions around the North Pole
arctic very cold (lower case)
Arctic Circle (two caps)
Arctogaea (US **Arctogea**) Zool. zoogeographical region
Ardennes region of SE Belgium, NE France, and Luxembourg
ardour (US **ardor**)
are hist. unit of measurement equal to 100 square metres
area code N. Amer. dialling code
areca nut astringent seed chewed with betel leaves in Asia

areg pl. of **erg**
areola pl. **areolae** Anat. small area around the nipple; cf. **areole, aureole**
areole Biol. small area bearing spines or hairs on a cactus; cf. **areola, aureole**
areology study of the planet Mars
Areopagus hill in ancient Athens, site of council and court
Arequipa city in Peru
Ares Gk Mythol. god of war; Rom. equivalent **Mars**
arête sharp mountain ridge (accent, not ital.)
argent Heraldry silver
Argentina republic in South America ◻ **Argentine, Argentinian**
argentine arch. of silver
argon chemical element of atomic number 18, a noble gas (symbol **Ar**)
Argonauts Gk Mythol. heroes who accompanied Jason on the quest for the Golden Fleece
argosy hist. large merchant ship
argot slang of a group (not ital.)
arguable (not **-eable**)
argumentum ad hominem argument appealing personally to an opponent (L., ital.)
argumentum e silentio conclusion based on lack of contrary evidence (L., ital.)
Argus Gk Mythol. watchman with a hundred eyes (cap.)
argus 1 Asian pheasant **2** butterfly (lower case)
argy-bargy (hyphen)
argyle diamond pattern on knitted garments (lower case)
Argyll and Bute council area in the west of Scotland
Argyllshire former county in the west of Scotland
Århus Danish name for **Aarhus**
aria long solo song in an opera or oratorio
Arian[1] (also **Arien**) person born under the sign of Aries
Arian[2] adherent of Arianism
Arianism heresy denying the divinity of Christ
Ariel fairy in Shakespeare's *The Tempest*
ariel kind of gazelle; cf. **aerial**
Aries first sign of the zodiac
arioso pl. **ariosos** Mus. style of vocal performance less formal than an aria
Ariosto, Ludovico (1474–1533), Italian poet
Aristophanes (*c*.450–*c*.385 BC), Greek comic dramatist
Aristotle (384–322 BC), Greek philosopher and scientist ◻ **Aristotelian**
Arizona (official abbrev. **Ariz.**, postal **AZ**)
Arkansas (official abbrev. **Ark.**, postal **AR**)
Arkhangelsk Russ. name for **Archangel**
Ark of the Covenant (also **Ark of the Testimony**) chest which contained the law tablets of the ancient Israelites
Arlington county in northern Virginia, the site of the Pentagon
Armada (also **Spanish Armada**) fleet sent against England in 1588 by Philip II of Spain (cap.)
armadillo pl. **armadillos**
Armageddon (in the New Testament) the last battle between good and evil
Armagh county and town in Northern Ireland
Armagnac type of French brandy
Armalite trademark automatic rifle (cap.)
armband, armchair (one word)
Armenia country in the Caucasus ◻ **Armenian**
armful pl. **armfuls**
armhole (one word)
armiger person entitled to heraldic arms ◻ **armigerous**
armillary sphere revolving model of the celestial sphere
Arminian follower of the Dutch Protestant theologian Jacobus Arminius (1560–1609)
Armistice Day (caps)
armoire ornate cupboard or wardrobe (not ital.)
armor US var. of **armour**
armorial relating to heraldic devices
Armorica ancient region of NW France
armory[1] heraldry
armory[2] US var. of **armoury**

armour (US **armor**) ◻ **armour-plated**
armoury (US **armory**)
armpit, **armrest** (one word)
arm's length (two words, hyphen when attrib.)
arms race (two words
Armstrong 1 (Daniel) Louis (1900–71), American jazz musician; known as **Satchmo 2** Neil (Alden) (1930–2012), American astronaut, the first man to set foot on the moon (20 July 1969)
arm-wrestling (hyphen)
Army List official list of commissioned officers (caps)
Arnhem town in the Netherlands
Arnhem Land Aboriginal reservation in Northern Territory, Australia
ARP hist. air-raid precautions
arpeggio pl. **arpeggios** Mus. notes of a chord played in rapid succession
arpeggione 19th-cent. stringed instrument (not ital.)
arquebus (also **harquebus**) early gun
arr. (point) **1** arranged by **2** arrives
arraign call to answer a criminal charge ◻ **arraignment**
Arran island in the west of Scotland; cf. **Aran Islands**
arrant utter, complete; cf. **errant**
Arras town in NE France
arrester device on an aircraft carrier that slows down aircraft after landing
arrêt decree (Fr., ital.)
Arrhenius, Svante August (1859–1927), Swedish chemist
arrhythmia Med. irregular heart rhythm (two *r*s) ◻ **arrhythmic**
arrière-garde rearguard (Fr., ital.)
arrière-pensée pl. ***arrière-pensées*** concealed intention (Fr., ital.)
arrivederci Italian for 'goodbye' (not ital., not **arrividerci**)
arriviste ambitious and self-seeking person (not ital.) ◻ **arrivisme**
arrogate take or claim for oneself without justification; cf. **abrogate**
arrondissement division of a French government department (not ital.)
arrowhead, **arrowroot** (two words)
arroyo pl. **arroyos** US dry gully
arsenic chemical element of atomic number 33 (symbol **As**)
arsis pl. **arses** Prosody stressed syllable or part of a metrical foot; cf. **thesis**
art. article
Artaxerxes name of three kings of ancient Persia
art deco art style of the 1920s (two words, lower case)
artefact (US **artifact**)
artel pl. **artels** or **arteli** hist. Russian association of craftsmen (not ital.)
Artemis Gk Mythol. goddess of hunting; Rom. equivalent **Diana**
arteriosclerosis hardening of the arteries
Artex trademark textured plaster for walls and ceilings
art form, art history (two words)
arthropod Zool. invertebrate of the phylum Arthropoda, e.g. an insect
Arthurian relating to the legendary King Arthur of Britain
article (abbrev. **art.**)
artifact US var. of **artefact**
artilleryman pl. **artillerymen** (one word)
artisan (not **-izan**)
artiste singer, dancer, or entertainer
art nouveau art style of the early 20th cent. (two words, lower case)
Arts and Crafts Movement (caps)
artwork (one word)
arty (N. Amer. **artsy**)
Aruba island in the Caribbean Sea, a territory of the Netherlands
arugula N. Amer. rocket (salad vegetable)
Arundel town in West Sussex, England
Aryan 1 member of an ancient Indo-European people **2** (in Nazi ideology) white person not of Jewish descent **3** dated Proto-Indo-European language
AS Anglo-Saxon
As the chemical element arsenic (no point)
as pl. **asses** ancient Roman copper coin
ASA 1 Advertising Standards Authority **2** Amateur Swimming Association **3** American Standards Association
asafoetida (US **asafetida**) fetid resinous gum
Asante var. of **Ashanti**
asap as soon as possible (no points)

ASB Alternative Service Book
ASBO pl. **ASBOs** antisocial behaviour order
ascendancy (not **ascendency**) □ **ascendant**
ascender part of a letter that extends above the level of the top of an *x*
Ascension Day Thursday forty days after Easter (caps)
Ascension Island small island in the South Atlantic
ascetic austere, self-disciplined
Ascham, Roger (*c.*1515–68), English humanist scholar
ASCII Comput. American Standard Code for Information Interchange
Asclepius Gk Mythol. god of healing; cf. **Aesculapius**
ASDIC early form of sonar used to detect submarines (all caps)
ASEAN Association of South East Asian Nations
Asgard home of the Norse gods
ash Old English runic letter, ᚫ, represented by the symbol æ or Æ
Ashanti (also **Asante**) pl. same, member of a people of Ghana
ash blonde (also **ash blond**) (two words, hyphen when attrib.)
Ashby de la Zouch town in Leicestershire, England (no hyphens)
ashen-faced (hyphen)
Asher Hebrew patriarch
Ashgabat (also **Ashkhabad**) capital of Turkmenistan
Ashkenazi pl. **Ashkenazim** Jew of central or eastern European descent; cf. **Sephardi**
Ashkenazy, Vladimir (Davidovich) (b.1937), Russian-born pianist
ashlar masonry of square-cut stones
Ashmolean Museum museum of art and antiquities in Oxford
ashram Indian religious retreat
ashrama Hinduism any of the four stages of an ideal life
Ash Shariqah Arab. name for **Sharjah**
ashtray (one word)
Ashur var. of **Assur**
Ash Wednesday first day of Lent (caps)
ASI airspeed indicator
Asian in Britain refers to people from the Indian subcontinent; in N. Amer. refers to people from the Far East
Asiatic use only in scientific and technical contexts; offensive when used of people
A-side more important side of a pop single (hyphen)
asinine extremely stupid (not **ass-**)
Asir Mountains range of mountains in SW Saudi Arabia
askance with suspicion or disapproval (not **askant**)
askari pl. same or **askaris** East African soldier or police officer
asking price (two words)
ASL American Sign Language
ASLEF Associated Society of Locomotive Engineers and Firemen
AS level (in the UK except Scotland) advanced subsidiary level (examination) (two words)
Aslib Association of Special Libraries and Information Bureaux (one cap)
ASM 1 air-to-surface missile **2** assistant stage manager
Asmara (also **Asmera**) capital of Eritrea
ASP Comput. application service provider
aspartame artificial sweetener
asper sign (ʽ) of rough breathing in Greek
Asperger's syndrome (also **Asperger syndrome**) mild autistic disorder
asperges sprinkling of holy water at the beginning of the Mass
aspergillosis Med. condition of lungs being infected by fungi; farmer's lung
aspergillum pl. **aspergilla** or **aspergillums** implement for sprinkling holy water
asphalt (not **ashphalt**)
asphyxia deprivation of oxygen
aspirin pl. same or **aspirins** pain-relieving medicine (lower case)
assai Mus. very
Assam state in NE India
assassin cap. with ref. to Nizari Muslim fanatics at the time of the Crusades
assegai (also **assagai**) spear used in southern Africa
assemblé Ballet kind of leap (Fr., ital.)

assembly line (two words)
asses pl. of **as**
asset stripper (two words)
asseveration solemn or emphatic declaration
assigner person who assigns something in general senses
assignee 1 person to whom a right or liability is transferred **2** person appointed to act for another
assignor Law person for or by whom an assignee is appointed
Assisi town in central Italy
assize hist. court sitting at intervals in each county of England and Wales
Assoc. Associate; Associated; Association (point)
Associated Press New York news agency (abbrev. **AP**)
Association football Brit. formal term for **soccer** (one cap.)
ASSR hist. Autonomous Soviet Socialist Republic
Asst Assistant (no point)
Assumption reception of the Virgin Mary into heaven, celebrated on 15 August (cap.)
Assur (also **Asur** or **Ashur**) ancient city state of Mesopotamia
assurance Brit. insurance under whose terms a payment is guaranteed
assure 1 tell positively **2** make certain to happen **3** cover by assurance; cf. **ensure, insure**
Assyria ancient country in what is now Iraq
AST Atlantic Standard Time
Astana capital of Kazakhstan
Astarte Phoenician goddess of fertility and love
astatine chemical element of atomic number 85 (symbol **At**)
asterisk symbol (*) used as a pointer to an annotation or footnote; cf. **Asterix**
asterism group of three asterisks (⁂) drawing attention to following text
Asterix cartoon character; cf. **asterisk** [Fr. *Astérix*]
Asti 1 Italian white wine **2** province of NW Italy
astigmatism eye condition resulting in distorted images
Astrakhan city in southern Russia
astrakhan dark curly fleece of young karakul lambs (lower case)
AstroTurf trademark artificial grass surface (one word, two caps)
Asturias autonomous region of NW Spain
Asunción capital of Paraguay
Asur var. of **Assur**
ASV American Standard Version
Aswan city in southern Egypt, site of two dams across the Nile
asylum seeker (two words)
asymmetry lack of symmetry (one *s*, two *ms*)
asymptote line that continually approaches a curve but does not meet it
asynchronous not existing or occurring at the same time
asyndeton pl. **asyndeta** Gram. omission of a conjunction between parts of a sentence
As You Like It Shakespeare play (abbrev. ***AYL***)
At the chemical element astatine (no point)
Atahualpa last Inca ruler (*c.*1502–33)
Atalanta Gk Mythol. huntress
ataraxy (also **ataraxia**) serene calmness □ **ataractic, ataraxic**
Atatürk, Kemal (1881–1938), Turkish president 1923–38
ATB all-terrain bike
ATC 1 air traffic control or controller **2** Air Training Corps
atelier workshop or studio (not ital.)
a tempo Mus. in the previous tempo
ATF (US Federal Bureau of) Alcohol, Tobacco, and Firearms
Athabaskan (also **Athapaskan**) family of North American Indian languages
Athanasian Creed early summary of Christian doctrine; also called **Quicunque vult**
Athanasius, St (*c.*296–373), Greek theologian
atheist person who disbelieves in the existence of a god or gods
atheling prince or lord in Anglo-Saxon England [OE *ætheling*]
Athelstan king of England 925–39
Athenaeum, the London club
Athene (also **Athena**) Gk Mythol. goddess

of wisdom and craft; Rom. equivalent **Minerva**

Athens capital of Greece; Gk name **Athínai** ◻ **Athenian**

athlete's foot (apostrophe)

Atlanta state capital of Georgia (US)

Atlantic Ocean ocean lying between Europe, Africa, and America

Atlantis legendary lost island ◻ **Atlantean**

Atlas Gk Mythol. one of the Titans

atlas 1 pl. **atlases** book of maps **2** pl. **atlantes** carved column on a Greek building

ATM automated teller machine

atmosphere Phys. unit of pressure (abbrev. **atm**)

ATOL Air Travel Organizer's Licence

atoll coral reef or island chain

atomize (Brit. also **atomise**)

A to Z (two caps, no hyphens)

ATP 1 Biochem. adenosine triphosphate **2** automatic train protection

atrium pl. **atria** or **atriums 1** open central court, orig. in an ancient Roman house **2** Anat. each of the two upper cavities of the heart

atropine poisonous substance in deadly nightshade, used as a drug

Atropos Gk Mythol. one of the three Fates

ATS Auxiliary Territorial Service (for women in Britain, 1938–48)

at sign the symbol @

attaché person on an ambassador's staff (accent, not ital.)

attaché case (accent, two words, not ital.)

Attalids Hellenistic dynasty of the 3rd and 2nd cents BC

attar essential oil from rose petals

attendee use **attender**

Attic relating to Attica in eastern Greece

Attila (406–53), king of the Huns

attitudinize (Brit. also **attitudinise**)

Attlee, Clement Richard, 1st Earl Attlee (1883–1967), British prime minister 1945–51

attn attention (i.e. for the attention of) (no point)

atto- denoting a factor of 10^{-18} (abbrev. **a**)

attorn Law make or acknowledge a transfer

attorney pl. **attorneys** person appointed to act for another; US a lawyer

Attorney General pl. **Attorneys General** (two words, caps; abbrev. **AG**)

attributive Gram. (of an adjective) preceding a noun (abbrev. **attrib.**)

ATV 1 all-terrain vehicle **2** hist. Associated Television

Atwood, Margaret (Eleanor) (b.1939), Canadian novelist

AU 1 angstrom unit(s) **2** (also **a.u.**) astronomical unit(s)

Au the chemical element gold (no point) [L. *aurum*]

aubade poem or piece of music appropriate to the dawn (not ital.)

auberge French inn (not ital.)

aubergine Brit. purple egg-shaped fruit; N. Amer. name **eggplant**

aubretia (also **aubrietia**) plant named after French botanist Claude Aubriet (**aubretia** and **aubrietia** are now commoner than the strictly correct form **aubrieta**)

Aubusson 1 fine tapestry or carpet **2** town in central France

AUC used to indicate a date reckoned from 753 BC, the year of the foundation of Rome (small caps) [L. *ab urbe condita* 'from the foundation of the city']

au contraire to the contrary (Fr., ital.)

au courant well informed (Fr., ital.)

Auden, W(ystan) H(ugh) (1907–73), English poet

Audh var. of **Oudh**

Audi pl. **Audis** German make of car

audio cassette, audio tape, audio typist (two words)

audiovisual (one word)

audit v. (**auditing, audited**)

Audit Commission UK body that monitors public spending

auditorium pl. **auditoriums** or **auditoria**

Audubon, John James (1785–1851), American naturalist and artist

au fait thoroughly conversant (not ital.)

Aufklärung the Enlightenment (Ger., cap., ital.)

au fond in essence (Fr., ital.); cf. ***à fond***

auf Wiedersehen German for 'goodbye' (one cap., not ital.)
Aug. August
Augeas Gk Mythol. king whose filthy stables were cleaned by Hercules □ **Augean**
auger tool for boring holes; cf. **augur**
aught arch. anything at all
au gratin sprinkled with breadcrumbs or cheese and browned (not ital.)
augur v. portend a good or bad outcome. n. ancient Roman official who interpreted natural signs; cf. **auger**
August month (abbrev. **Aug.**)
august respected and impressive (lower case)
Augustan **1** relating to the Roman emperor Augustus **2** relating to 17th- and 18th-cent. English literature
Augustine Augustinian friar
Augustine, St **1** (died *c.*604), Italian churchman; known as **St Augustine of Canterbury** **2** (354–430), Doctor of the Church; known as **St Augustine of Hippo**
Augustinian relating to St Augustine of Hippo
Augustus (63 BC–AD 14), the first Roman emperor; born *Gaius Octavius*; also called (until 27 BC) **Octavian**
auk seabird
Auld Alliance alliance between Scotland and France in the 13th–16th cents
auld lang syne times long past (for song title use caps and quotation marks)
Auld Reekie 'Old Smoky', nickname for Edinburgh
aumbry (also **ambry**) recess or cupboard in a church
au mieux on intimate terms (Fr., ital.)
au naturel in a natural way (not ital.)
Aung San (1914–47), Burmese nationalist leader
Aung San Suu Kyi (b.1945), Burmese political leader, daughter of Aung San
auntie (also **aunty**) informal **1** aunt **2** (**Auntie**) Brit. the BBC
Aunt Sally (caps) **1** British pub game **2** easy target for criticism
au pair girl who helps with housework and childcare (not ital.)
au pied de la lettre literally (Fr., ital.)
aura pl. **auras** distinctive atmosphere or quality
aural relating to the ear or to hearing; cf. **oral**
Aurangzeb (1618–1707), Mogul emperor of Hindustan 1658–1707
aurar pl. of **eyrir**
aureole (also **aureola**) **1** (in paintings) halo on a holy person **2** circle of light around the sun or moon; cf. **areola, areole**
au revoir French for 'goodbye' (not ital.)
Aurignacian early stages of the Upper Palaeolithic culture in Europe and the Near East
aurochs pl. same, extinct wild ox
Aurora Gk Mythol. goddess of the dawn
aurora pl. **auroras** or **aurorae** appearance of lights in the sky near the poles, the **aurora borealis** or **Northern Lights** and **aurora australis** or **Southern Lights** (lower case)
Auschwitz town in Poland, site of a Nazi concentration camp; Pol. name **Oświęcim**
auscultation Med. listening to sounds from the heart etc. with a stethoscope
Auslese German white wine (not ital.)
auspicious conducive to success
Aussie informal Australian (not **Ozzie**)
Austen, Jane (1775–1817), English novelist
Austin **1** Alfred (1835–1913), Poet Laureate 1896–1913 **2** Herbert, 1st Baron Austin of Longbridge (1866–1941), English motor manufacturer **3** J(ohn) L(angshaw) (1911–60), English philosopher
Austin Friars Augustinian Friars
austral of the southern hemisphere; (**Austral**) of Australia or Australasia
Australasia region consisting of Australia, New Zealand, and islands of the SW Pacific (abbrev. **A'asia**)
Australian Capital Territory federal territory in New South Wales, Australia (abbrev. **ACT**)
Australian Labor Party (not **Labour**; abbrev. **ALP**)
Australian Rules (football) (two caps)
Austria country in central Europe; Ger. name **Österreich**

Austria–Hungary (en rule)
Austro-Hungarian (hyphen)
Austronesian family of languages spoken in the South Pacific
AUT Association of University Teachers
autarchy 1 autocracy **2** var. of **autarky**
autarky (also **autarchy**) economic self-sufficiency
auteur film director (not ital.)
author in most contexts prefer **author** to **authoress** for female writers □ **authorial**
author–date system form of referencing; also called **Harvard system** (en rule)
authorize (Brit. also **authorise**)
Authorized Version (abbrev. **AV**) Brit. English translation of the Bible made in 1611; King James Bible (not ital., caps)
autism condition characterized by difficulty in communicating □ **autistic**
autobahn German motorway (lower case, not ital.)
autochthonous indigenous; cf. **allochthonous**
autocracy absolute government
autocue television prompting device (cap. as trademark)
auto-da-fé pl. **autos-da-fé** burning of a heretic by the Spanish Inquisition (not ital.)
autogiro (also **autogyro**) pl. **autogiros** aircraft with freely rotating horizontal blades
autograph 1 celebrity's signature **2** manuscript in the author's handwriting
autoimmune Med. (one word)
automaton pl. **automata** or **automatons**
autonomy self-government □ **autonomous**
autonym author's own name
autopilot (one word)
autopista Spanish motorway (lower case, not ital.)
autopsy post-mortem examination
autoroute French motorway (lower case, not ital.)
autostrada pl. **autostradas** or **autostrade** Italian motorway (lower case, not ital.)
autumn chiefly Brit. season (lower case)
Auvergne region of south central France
AV 1 audio-visual (teaching aids) **2** Authorized Version
Av var. of **Ab**
avadavat (also **amadavat**) South Asian waxbill (bird)
Avalon place where King Arthur was taken after death
avant-garde (of the arts) experimental (hyphen, not ital.)
avatar 1 Hinduism manifestation of a deity or released soul **2** incarnation or embodiment
avaunt arch. go away!
Ave. Avenue
ave atque vale hail and farewell (L., ital.)
Ave Maria prayer to the Virgin Mary (caps, not ital.)
aver (**averring**, **averred**) assert to be the case
Averroës (*c.*1126–98), Spanish-born Islamic philosopher, judge, and physician; Arab. name *ibn-Rushd*
averse strongly disliking or opposed; cf. **adverse**
Avesta sacred texts of Zoroastrianism
avian relating to birds
aviator (fem. **aviatrix**, pl. **aviatrices**) dated pilot
Avicenna (980–1037), Persian-born Islamic philosopher and physician; Arab. name *ibn-Sina*
aviculture rearing of birds
Avignon city in SE France
Ávila, St Teresa of see **Teresa**
avizandum Sc. Law time taken for further consideration of a judgment
avocado pl. **avocados** fruit
avocation hobby or minor occupation
avocet wading bird
Avogadro, Amedeo (1776–1856), Italian chemist and physicist
Avogadro's constant, Avogadro's law (apostrophe, one cap.)
avoirdupois system of weights based on a pound of 16 ounces or 7,000 grains; cf. **troy**
Avon 1 name of various English rivers

2 former county of SW England
avulsion Law separation of land from one property and attachment to another; cf. **alluvion**
AWACS airborne warning and control system
Awadh var. of **Oudh**
award-winning (hyphen)
Awdry, Reverend W(ilbert Vere) (1911–97), English writer of the *Thomas the Tank Engine* books
aweigh Naut. (of an anchor) raised clear of the seabed (not **away**)
awe-inspiring (hyphen)
awestruck (also **awestricken**) (one word)
awhile for a short time (but **for a while**)
AWOL absent without (official) leave (caps)
AWS automatic warning system
axe (US **ax**)
axel jump in skating
axis pl. **axes 1** line about which a body rotates **2** (**the Axis**) WWII alliance between Germany and Italy
axolotl salamander which retains its larval form throughout life
ayah nanny employed by Europeans in India
ayatollah Shiite religious leader in Iran (cap. in titles)
Ayckbourn, Sir Alan (b.1939), English dramatist
aye¹ (also **ay**) pl. **ayes 1** yes **2** (**aye aye**) Naut. response accepting an order
aye² arch. or Sc. always
aye-aye Madagascan primate (hyphen)
Ayers Rock (no apostrophe); official name **Uluru**
'ayin (also ***ayin***) accent in Hebrew (ʿ), typographically largely equivalent to the Arabic *'ayn* or Greek asper (ital.)
AYL Shakespeare's play *As You Like It*
Aymara pl. same or **Aymaras** member of an American Indian people of Bolivia and Peru
'ayn (also ***ayn***) accent in Arabic (ʿ), typographically largely equivalent to the Hebrew *'ayin* or Greek asper (ital.)
Ayrshire former county of SW Scotland
Ayurveda traditional Hindu system of medicine □ **Ayurvedic**
A–Z (en rule)
azalea flowering shrub
Azerbaijan country in the Caucasus □ **Azerbaijani** pl. **Azerbaijanis**
Azeri pl. **Azeris 1** member of the majority population of Azerbaijan **2** language of Azerbaijan
Azikiwe, (Benjamin) Nnamdi (1904–96), first president of Nigeria 1963–6
Azilian early Mesolithic culture in Europe
Azores group of islands in the Atlantic Ocean
Azov, Sea of inland sea of southern Russia and Ukraine
Azrael (in Jewish and Islamic belief) angel who severs the soul from the body at death
AZT trademark in the UK azidothymidine (an anti-AIDS drug now called zidovudine)
Aztec member of the people dominant in Mexico before the Spanish conquest
azulejo pl. **azulejos** Spanish and Portuguese glazed tile (not ital.)

B

B 1 pl. **Bs** or **B's** 2nd letter of the alphabet **2** hist. baron **3** bel **4** Chess bishop **5** the chemical element boron **6** series of paper sizes each twice the area of the next, as *B0, B1, B2, B3, B4*, etc., B4 being 250 × 353 mm **7** a human blood type **8** black (grade of pencil lead)

b 1 Phys. barn(s) **2** Cricket bowled by; bye(s)

b. born (point, no space after)

BA 1 Bachelor of Arts **2** British Airways **3** British Association (for the Advancement of Science) **4** Buenos Aires

Ba the chemical element barium (no point)

BAA British Airports Authority

Baader–Meinhof Group Red Army Faction, a German terrorist group of the 1970s (en rule, hyphen in Ger.)

Baal (also **Bel**) Phoenician fertility god

Baalbek town in eastern Lebanon

baas S. Afr. offens. supervisor or employer

Baath Party (also **Ba'ath Party**) Iraqi and Syrian socialist party

baba ganoush aubergine dip

Babbitt novel (1922) by Sinclair Lewis, about the conformist businessman George Babbitt □ **Babbittry**

babbitt metal alloy of tin, antimony, copper, and usu. lead (lower case)

babel confused noise (lower case)

Babel, Tower of (in the Old Testament) tower built in an attempt to reach heaven

babirusa Malaysian wild pig

babu pl. **babus** Indian title of respect

baby boom, baby boomer (two words, lower case)

Babygro pl. **Babygros** trademark all-in-one garment for babies (cap.)

Babylonia ancient region of Mesopotamia, whose capital was Babylon

Babylonian Captivity captivity of the Israelites in Babylon (caps)

babysit (**babysitting, babysat**) □ **babysitter**

bacalao dried or salted cod

baccalaureate 1 examination taken to qualify for higher education **2** university bachelor's degree

baccarat gambling card game

Bacchae female devotees of Bacchus

bacchanal wild celebration (lower case)

Bacchanalia (treated as sing. or pl.) **1** festival of the god Bacchus **2** (**bacchanalia**) wild revelry □ **bacchanalian**

bacchant (fem. **bacchante**) priest, priestess, or follower of Bacchus

Bacchus Gk Mythol. the god Dionysus □ **Bacchic**

Bach, Johann Sebastian (1685–1750), German composer; of his twenty children **Wilhelm Friedemann Bach** (1710–84) was an organist and composer, **Carl Philipp Emanuel Bach** (1714–88) wrote church music and keyboard sonatas, and **Johann Christian Bach** (1735–82) was music master to the British royal family

bach Welsh term of endearment (ital., lower case)

Bacharach, Burt (b.1928), American songwriter

bacillus pl. **bacilli** rod-shaped bacterium

backache, backbeat (one word)

backbencher MP who does not hold office, who sits behind the front benches in the House of Commons (one word)

backbiting, backbone (one word)

back-breaking (hyphen)

back burner, back catalogue (two words)

backcloth, backdate (one word)

back door (two words)

backdrop, backfire, backhand (one word)

back matter the end matter of a book (two words)
back number (two words)
backpack, backpacker (one word)
back-pedal (hyphen)
backsheesh use **baksheesh**
backslapping (one word)
backslash oblique stroke (\) in printing or writing (one word); cf. **slash**
backslide (past and past part. **backslid**) (one word)
back-stabbing (hyphen)
backstage (one word)
back stairs (two words, one word as adj.)
backstroke, backtrack (one word)
backup n. (one word, two words as verb)
backwash, backwater, backwoods, backwoodsman, backyard (one word)
baclava use **baklava**
Bacon 1 Sir Francis, Baron Verulam and Viscount St Albans (1561–1626), English statesman and philosopher **2** Francis (1909–92), Irish painter **3** Roger (*c.*1214–94), English philosopher, scientist, and Franciscan friar □ **Baconian**
bactericide substance that kills bacteria
bacterium pl. **bacteria** microorganism
Bactrian camel two-humped camel; cf. **Arabian camel**
bade past of **bid**
Baden spa town in Austria
Baden-Baden spa town in Germany
Baden-Powell, Robert (Stephenson Smyth), 1st Baron Baden-Powell of Gilwell (1857–1941), English soldier and founder of the Scout movement
Baden-Württemberg state of western Germany
badger-baiting (hyphen)
badinage witty conversation (not ital.)
Badminton country seat of the Duke of Beaufort in SW England
badminton game with rackets and a shuttlecock (lower case)
bad-tempered (hyphen)
BAe British Aerospace (now **BAE Systems**)
Baedeker, Karl (1801–59), German publisher of guidebooks
Baffin Bay, Baffin Island in the Canadian Arctic (two caps)
BAFTA British Academy of Film and Television Arts
bagarre scuffle or brawl (Fr., ital.)
bagatelle (not ital.) **1** game in which balls are hit into holes on a board **2** something trifling or negligible
Bagehot, Walter (1826–77), English economist and journalist
bagel ring-shaped bread roll (not **beigel**)
Baghdad capital of Iraq
bagnio pl. **bagnios 1** arch. brothel **2** hist. prison in the Far East
bagpipe (one word)
baguette long French loaf (not ital.)
Baha'i pl. **Baha'is 1** a monotheistic religion **2** adherent of the Baha'i faith □ **Baha'ism**
Bahamas country consisting of an archipelago in the West Indies, independent since 1973 □ **Bahamian**
Bahasa Indonesia, Bahasa Malaysia official languages of Indonesia and Malaysia
Bahrain sheikhdom in the Persian Gulf
baht pl. same, monetary unit of Thailand
Bahutu pl. of **Hutu**
Baikal, Lake large lake in southern Siberia (not **Baykal**)
bail[1] temporary release of a person awaiting trial
bail[2] Cricket crosspiece over the stumps
bail[3] (Brit. also **bale**) **1** scoop water out of a boat **2** (**bail out**) make an emergency parachute descent from an aircraft
Baile Átha Cliath Ir. name for **Dublin**
bailee Law person to whom goods are delivered for a purpose
bailer person who bails water out; cf. **bailor**
bailey pl. **baileys** outer wall of a castle
bailie pl. **bailies** municipal officer in Scotland
bailiff sheriff's officer or landlord's agent (one *l*, two *f*s)
bailiwick district or jurisdiction of a bailie or bailiff
bailor Law person who entrusts goods to a bailee; cf. **bailer**

Baily's beads Astron. (not **Bailey's**)
bain-marie pl. **bains-marie** or **bain-maries** pan of hot water for slow cooking (hyphen, not ital.)
Bairam either of two annual Muslim festivals, **Greater Bairam** and **Lesser Bairam** (see **Eid**)
Baird, John Logie (1888–1946), Scottish pioneer of television
bait food used to entice fish etc.
baited see **bated**
Baja California peninsula in NW Mexico
baked Alaska dessert (one cap.)
Bakelite trademark early form of plastic (cap.)
Bakewell tart (one cap.)
baklava Middle Eastern dessert (not **baclava**)
baksheesh tip or bribe in the Middle and Far East (not **back-**)
Baku capital of Azerbaijan
Balaclava scene of a battle in the Crimean War (1854); now **Balaklava**
balaclava woollen hat with holes for the eyes and mouth (lower case)
balalaika Russian musical instrument
balancing act (two words)
Balboa, Vasco Núñez de (1475–1519), Spanish explorer, the first European to see the Pacific Ocean
balboa monetary unit of Panama (lower case)
baldachin (also **baldaquin**) ceremonial canopy over an altar, throne, etc.
Balder Scand. Mythol. god who was invulnerable to all things except mistletoe
Bâle Fr. name for **Basle**
bale[1] bound bundle of paper, hay, etc.
bale[2] arch. evil or torment
bale[3] Brit. var. of **bail**[3]
Balearic Islands group of Spanish islands in the Mediterranean
Bali island of Indonesia
balk (also **baulk**)
Balkanize (Brit. also **Balkanise**) divide into smaller mutually hostile states
Balkis name of the queen of Sheba in Arabic literature
ballade poem consisting of one or more triplets of stanzas with a refrain
Ballantyne, R(obert) M(ichael) (1825–94), Scottish writer for boys
ball bearing (two words)
ballet dancer (two words)
Ballets Russes ballet company formed by Sergei Diaghilev
ball game (two words)
Balliol College Oxford
Ballistic Missile Defense Organization see **Strategic Defense Initiative**
ballistics science of projectiles and firearms (treated as sing.)
ballon d'essai pl. ***ballons d'essai*** experiment to see how a new policy will be received (Fr., ital.)
ballot v. (**balloting, balloted**)
ballpark, ballpoint, ballroom (one word)
ballyhoo extravagant publicity or fuss
bal masqué pl. ***bals masqués*** masked ball (Fr., ital.)
balm in Gilead comfort in distress (Jer. 8:22)
balm of Gilead fragrant medicinal resin
bal musette pl. ***bals musettes*** dance hall with an accordion band (Fr., ital.)
balmy (of weather) pleasantly warm; cf. **barmy**
baloney nonsense; for the type of sausage use **bologna**
Balt speaker of a Baltic language
Balthasar one of the three Magi
Balthazar ancient king of Babylon
balthazar large wine bottle equivalent to sixteen regular bottles (lower case)
Balti person from Baltistan in the Himalayas
balti pl. **baltis** type of Pakistani cuisine (lower case)
Baluchi pl. same or **Baluchis** person from Baluchistan in western Asia
baluster upright forming part of a series supporting a railing
balustrade railing supported by balusters
Balzac, Honoré de (1799–1850), French novelist □ **Balzacian**
Bamako capital of Mali
bambino pl. **bambini** or **bambinos** baby or young child (not ital.)
ban pl. **bani** monetary unit of Romania

banana republic, banana skin, banana split (two words)
bancassurance (also **bankassurance**) selling of insurance by banks
Band-Aid trademark kind of sticking plaster (caps, hyphen)
bandana (also **bandanna**) coloured headscarf
Bandaranaike, Sirimavo Ratwatte Dias (1916–2000), prime minister of Sri Lanka 1960–5, 1970–7, and 1994–2000
B & B bed and breakfast (caps)
bandeau pl. **bandeaux** narrow band worn round the head or chest (not ital.)
banderole (also **banderol**) narrow flag with a cleft end
bandolero pl. **bandoleros** Spanish bandit (not ital.)
bandolier (also **bandoleer**) shoulder belt for cartridges
bandora kind of bass lute (not **bandore**)
bandsaw, bandsman, bandstand (one word)
Bandung city in Indonesia
bandwagon, bandwidth (one word)
Banff town in Alberta, Canada
Banffshire former county of NE Scotland
bang (cannabis) use **bhang**
Bangalore city in south central India
Bangkok capital of Thailand
Bangladesh country of the Indian subcontinent, formerly East Pakistan
Bangui capital of the Central African Republic
bani pl. of **ban**
banian use **banyan**
banister (also **bannister**) upright supporting a handrail on a staircase; (**banisters**) handrail and its uprights
banjo pl. **banjos** or **banjoes**
Banjul capital of Gambia
bankassurance var. of **bancassurance**
Ban Ki-moon (b.1944), South Korean Secretary General of the United Nations since 2007
banknote, bankroll (one word)
banneret hist. **1** knight who commanded his own troops in battle **2** knighthood given on the battlefield
Bannister, Sir Roger (Gilbert) (b.1929), the first man to run a mile in under 4 minutes (1954)
bannister var. of **banister**
banns notice of intended marriage
banquet v. (**banqueting, banqueted**)
banquette 1 upholstered bench **2** step behind a rampart
banshee wailing female spirit
bantamweight boxing weight between flyweight and featherweight (one word)
Bantu pl. same or **Bantus** offensive with ref. to a person; still used with ref. to a group of Niger–Congo languages
banyan Indian fig tree (not **banian**)
banzai Japanese battle cry (lower case, not ital.)
baobab African or Australian tree
BAOR British Army of the Rhine
Baptist member of a Protestant denomination advocating baptism by total immersion (cap.)
baptistery (also **baptistry**) part of a church used for baptism
baptize (Brit. also **baptise**)
Bar, the (cap.) profession of barrister
bar unit of pressure
Barbados one of the Caribbean islands, independent since 1966 □ **Barbadian**
Barbarossa 1 (*c.*1483–1546), Barbary pirate; born *Khair ad-Din* **2** see **Frederick I**
Barbary former name for the Muslim countries of North and NW Africa
barbecue (**barbecues, barbecuing, barbecued**) (also **-que**)
barbed wire (US **barbwire**)
barberry spiny shrub with red berries
barbet tropical bird
barbette housing on a gun turret
Barbican arts complex in London
barbican outer defence of a city or castle (lower case)
Barbie (also **Barbie doll**) trademark doll representing an attractive young woman
Barbirolli, Sir John (Giovanni Battista) (1899–1970), English conductor
barbitone (US **barbital**) sedative drug of the barbiturate type
Barbizon School 19th-cent. school of French landscape painters
Barbour trademark waxed outdoor jacket
Barbuda one of the Leeward Islands

(see **Antigua and Barbuda**) ◻ **Barbudan**

barbwire US var. of **barbed wire**

barcarole (also **barcarolle**) song of Venetian gondoliers

Barchester (in the novels of Anthony Trollope) cathedral city in the county of Barsetshire

Barclays bank (no apostrophe)

Bar-Cochba Jewish rebel leader; known as **Simeon** in Jewish sources

barcode (one word)

bard poet; (**the Bard** or **the Bard of Avon**) Shakespeare; (**Bard**) winner of a prize for Welsh verse at an Eisteddfod

Bardot, Brigitte (b.1934), French actress

bareback, barefaced, barefoot, bareheaded (one word)

Bareilly city in northern India

bare-knuckle (hyphen)

Barenboim, Daniel (b.1942), Israeli pianist and conductor

Barents Sea part of the Arctic Ocean to the north of Norway (no apostrophe)

bargainer person who bargains

bargainor Law person who sells

baritone male singing voice between tenor and bass; cf. **baryton**

barium chemical element of atomic number 56 (symbol **Ba**)

bark arch. ship or boat

barkentine US var. of **barquentine**

Barkly Tableland plateau region in Northern Territory, Australia

barleycorn former unit of measurement (one word); cf. **John Barleycorn**

barmaid, barman (one word)

Barmecide illusory or imaginary (cap.)

bar mitzvah initiation ceremony of a Jewish boy; cf. **bat mitzvah**

barmy mad, crazy; cf. **balmy**

barn Phys. unit of area (abbrev. **b**)

Barnabas, St Apostle who accompanied St Paul (not **-us**)

Barnard, Christiaan Neethling (1922–2001), South African heart surgeon

Barnardo's UK children's charity

barn dance, barn door, barn owl (two words)

Barnstaple town in Devon (not **-stable**)

Barnum, P(hineas) T(aylor) (1810–91), American showman

barograph barometer that records its readings

baron member of the lowest order of the British nobility, usu. addressed as 'Lord' (cap. in titles; abbrev. **Bn**)

baroness wife or widow of a baron, or woman holding the rank of baron, usu. addressed as 'Lady' (cap. in titles)

baronet member of the lowest hereditary titled British order, entitled to the prefix 'Sir' (cap. in titles; abbrev. **Bt**)

Barons Court area of London (no apostrophe)

baroque ornate style of architecture, music, and art of the 17th and 18th cents (lower case)

barouche hist. four-wheeled horse-drawn carriage

barque three-masted sailing ship; literary a boat

barquentine (US **barkentine**) sailing ship similar to a barque

barracouta slender food fish

barracuda large predatory fish

barratry 1 arch. fraud or gross negligence on the part of a ship's master or crew **2** Law malicious litigation ◻ **barrator**

Barrault, Jean-Louis (1910–94), French actor and director

barre horizontal bar used by ballet dancers (not ital., no accent)

barré method of playing a guitar chord with one finger across all the strings (not ital., in popular music no accent)

barrel n. measure of capacity for oil and beer (abbrev. **bl**). v. **barrelling, barrelled**; US one **-l-**

Barrie, Sir J(ames) M(atthew) (1860–1937), Scottish author of *Peter Pan*

barrio pl. **barrios** district of a town in a Spanish-speaking country

barrique small barrel

barroom (one word)

Barrow-in-Furness town in Cumbria (hyphens)

Barry, Comtesse du, see **Du Barry**

Barsetshire fictional county in the novels of Anthony Trollope

Bart (Baronet) prefer **Bt**
bartender (one word)
Barth 1 John (Simmons) (b.1930), American novelist **2** Karl (1886–1968), Swiss Protestant theologian
Barthes, Roland (1915–80), French writer and critic
Bartholomew, St Apostle
Bartók, Béla (1881–1945), Hungarian composer
Bartolommeo, Fra (*c.*1472–1517), Italian painter; born *Baccio della Porta*
Baruch book of the Apocrypha (do not abbreviate)
baryte (also **barite**) colourless or white mineral
baryton old stringed instrument; cf. **baritone**
bas bleu pl. ***bas bleus*** bluestocking (Fr., ital.)
bascinet var. of **basinet**
baseboard N. Amer. skirting board (one word)
Basel Ger. name for **Basle**
BASIC simple high-level computer programming language (caps)
basidium pl. **basidia** spore-bearing structure in certain fungi
Basie, Count (1904–84), American jazz bandleader; born *William Basie*
basilisk mythical reptile; cockatrice
Basil, St (*c.*330–79), Doctor of the Church, bishop of Caesarea; known as **St Basil the Great** □ **Basilian**
basinet (also **bascinet**) close-fitting steel helmet
basis pl. **bases**
Baskerville (1706–75), English printer, designer of a typeface
Basket Maker member of an ancient culture of the south-western US (caps)
Basle city in NW Switzerland; Fr. name **Bâle**, Ger. name **Basel**
Basque member of a people living in the Pyrenees of France and Spain (the **Basque Country**)
basque close-fitting bodice (lower case)
Basra port of Iraq
bas-relief Art low relief (hyphen, not ital.)
basset breed of hunting dog with a long body (lower case)
basso pl. **bassos** or **bassi** bass voice or vocal part (not ital.)
basso continuo see **continuo**
basso profundo pl. **bassos profundos** or **bassi profundi** bass singer with a low range (not ital.)
basso-relievo pl. **basso-relievos** Art low relief (not ital.) [It. *basso-rilievo*]
bastardize (Brit. also **bastardise**)
Bastille prison in Paris
bastinado (**bastinadoes, bastinadoing, bastinadoed**) punishment or torture by caning the soles of the feet (not ital.)
Basutoland former name for **Lesotho**
Batak pl. same or **Bataks** member of a people of Sumatra
Batavia former name for **Jakarta**
bateau-mouche pl. ***bateaux-mouches*** pleasure boat used on the Seine in Paris (Fr., ital., hyphen)
bated phr. is **bated breath**, not **baited breath**
Batesian mimicry Zool. (one cap.)
Bath spa town in SW England □ **Bathonian**
Bath bun (one cap)
bath chair (two words, lower case)
bathhouse (one word)
Bath Oliver trademark biscuit (caps)
bathos (in literature) unintentional change in mood from the serious to the trivial; cf. **pathos** □ **bathetic**
bathrobe, **bathroom**, **bathtub** (one word)
Bathurst former name for **Banjul**
bathwater (one word)
bathyscaphe type of manned submersible vessel
Batman US cartoon character
batman military officer's personal servant (lower case)
bat mitzvah initiation ceremony for a Jewish girl; cf. **bar mitzvah**
batrachian frog or toad
Batswana pl. of **Tswana**
battalion (abbrev. **Bn**)
battels (at Oxford University) account for food and accommodation expenses
battement Ballet movement of a leg outward from the body and in again (Fr., ital.)

batterie de cuisine equipment required for preparing meals (Fr., ital.)

battle cap. in names of battles, e.g. *Battle of Britain*

battleaxe (US **battleax**) (one word)

battlecruiser, battledress, battlefield, battleground, battleship (one word)

baud pl. same or **bauds** Comput. unit of transmission speed for signals (lower case)

Baudelaire, Charles (Pierre) (1821–67), French poet and critic □ **Baudelairean**

Bauhaus early 20th-cent. German school of applied arts

baulk var. of **balk**

Bavaria state of southern Germany; Ger. name **Bayern**

bayadère Hindu dancing girl (not ital.)

Bayard, Pierre du Terrail, Chevalier de (1473–1524), French soldier known as the knight 'sans peur et sans reproche'

Bayes' theorem Statistics (note apostrophe) □ **Bayesian**

Bayeux Tapestry embroidered cloth illustrating the Norman Conquest (two caps)

Baykal, Lake use **Baikal**

bay leaf (two words)

bayonet v. (**bayoneting, bayoneted**)

Bayreuth town in Bavaria where Wagner is buried

bazaar (one *z*, two *a*s)

BB double-black (pencil lead)

BBC British Broadcasting Corporation (write channel names *BBC1*, *BBC2*, etc. with the figure closed up)

bbl. barrels (esp. of oil)

BC 1 British Columbia **2** Berne Convention

BC before Christ (written in small capitals and placed after the numerals (*72 BC*)); cf. **AD, BCE, CE**

bcc blind carbon copy

BCD Comput. binary coded decimal

BCE before the Common Era; cf. **AD, BC, CE** (small caps, follows the numerals)

BCG Bacillus Calmette-Guérin, an anti-tuberculosis vaccine

BD Bachelor of Divinity

Bde Brigade

bdellium fragrant resin

Bdr Bombardier

BDS Bachelor of Dental Surgery

BE 1 Bachelor of Education **2** Bachelor of Engineering **3** bill of exchange

Be the chemical element beryllium (no point)

BEA 1 British Epilepsy Association **2** hist. British European Airways

beachcomber, beachhead (one word)

Beach-la-mar var. of **Bislama**

Beagle ship on which Darwin travelled around the southern hemisphere

Beaker folk late Neolithic and early Bronze Age people (one cap.)

beanbag, beanfeast, beanpole, beanstalk (one word)

bear-baiting (hyphen)

bear garden, bear hug (two words)

Béarnaise sauce rich white sauce (cap., accent, not ital.)

bearskin (one word)

beat generation (two words, lower case)

beatific blissfully happy

beatify RC Ch. announce that (a dead person) is in a state of bliss, the first step towards making them a saint

beatitude 1 supreme blessedness; (**the Beatitudes**) blessings listed by Jesus in the Sermon on the Mount **2** (**His/Your Beatitude**) title of patriarchs in the Orthodox Church

Beatles, the pop and rock group from Liverpool (lower-case 'the')

beatnik member of the beat generation (lower case)

beau pl. **beaux** or **beaus** (not ital.) **1** boyfriend or male admirer **2** dandy

Beaubourg Centre another name for **Pompidou Centre**

Beau Brummell see **Brummell**

Beaufort scale scale of wind speed ranging from 0 (calm) to 12 (hurricane) (one cap.)

beau geste pl. ***beaux gestes*** noble and generous act (Fr., ital.)

beau idéal highest possible standard of excellence (Fr., ital.)

Beaujolais Nouveau newly produced Beaujolais wine (two caps)

Beaulieu village in Hampshire, England

Beaumarchais, Pierre Augustin Caron de (1732–99), French dramatist
beau monde fashionable society (not ital.)
Beau Nash see **Nash**
Beaune red burgundy wine
beau sabreur pl. ***beaux sabreurs*** dashing adventurer (Fr., ital.)
Beauvoir, Simone de, see **de Beauvoir**
beaux pl. of **beau**
beaux arts fine arts; (**Beaux Arts**) relating to the decorative style of the École des Beaux-Arts in Paris (not ital.)
beaux esprits pl. of ***bel esprit***
beaux yeux good looks (Fr., ital.)
bebop type of jazz originating in the 1940s (one word)
béchamel rich white sauce (accent, not ital.)
bêche-de-mer pl. same or **bêches-de-mer** sea cucumber eaten in China and Japan (accent, hyphens, not ital.)
Bechstein, Friedrich Wilhelm Carl (1826–1900), German piano-builder
Bechuanaland former name for **Botswana**
Becket, St Thomas à (*c.*1118–70), English Archbishop of Canterbury 1162–70 (accent, one *t*)
Beckett, Samuel (Barclay) (1906–89), Irish dramatist and novelist (two *t*s) □ **Beckettian**
Becquerel, Antoine-Henri (1852–1908), French physicist
becquerel Phys. the SI unit of radioactivity (abbrev. **Bq**)
BEd (also **B.Ed.**) Bachelor of Education
bedbug, bedchamber, bedclothes (one word)
bedel university official with ceremonial duties (spelled **bedell** at Cambridge)
Bede, St (*c.*673–735), English monk, theologian, and historian; known as **the Venerable Bede**
bedevil (**bedevilling, bedevilled**; US one **-l-**)
Bedfordshire county of south central England (abbrev. **Beds.**)
bedlam scene of uproar (lower case)
Bedouin (also **Beduin**) pl. same, nomadic desert Arab (in specialized usage prefer the sing. form **Bedu** and pl. **Beduin**)
bedpan, bedpost, bedrock, bedroom (one word)
bedside, bedsit, bedspread, bedtime (one word)
Beeb informal the BBC
beef pl. **beeves** or US **beefs** Farming cow, bull, or ox fattened for its meat
beefburger, beefcake, beefeater, beefsteak (one word)
beehive (one word)
Beerbohm, Max (1872–1956), English caricaturist and critic; full name *Sir Henry Maximilian Beerbohm*
Beerenauslese German white wine (cap.)
beer glass, beer mat, beer money (two words)
beestings milk produced by a cow after giving birth (treated as sing.)
bee-stung (hyphen)
beeswax (one word)
Beethoven, Ludwig van (1770–1827), German composer □ **Beethovenian**
Beeton, Mrs Isabella Mary (1836–65), English writer on cookery
beeves see **beef**
BEF British Expeditionary Force
befall (past **befell**; past part. **befallen**)
befit (**befitting, befitted**)
beget (**begetting**; past **begot**; past part. **begotten**)
Beggar's Opera, The ballad opera by John Gay (1728)
begum Ind. Muslim woman of high rank; (**Begum**) title of a married Muslim woman
behaviour (US **behavior**)
behemoth enormous creature, in the Book of Job (40:15) prob. a hippopotamus or a crocodile
Behn, Aphra (1640–89), English novelist and dramatist
behold (past and past part. **beheld**)
behoof arch. benefit or advantage
behove (US **behoove**) be a duty or responsibility
beigel use **bagel**
beignet fritter (not ital.)
Beijing capital of China; formerly transliterated as **Peking**

Beirut capital of Lebanon
bejewelled (US **bejeweled**)
Bekaa Valley in central Lebanon
Bel var. of **Baal**
bel unit of sound intensity or electrical power level (abbrev. **B**)
belabour (US **belabor**)
Bel and the Dragon book of the Apocrypha (abbrev. **Bel & Dr.**)
Belarus country in eastern Europe; formerly called **Belorussia, White Russia** □ **Belarusian**
Belau var. of **Palau**
bel canto style of operatic singing (not ital.)
beldam (also **beldame**) arch. old woman
Belém city in northern Brazil
bel esprit pl. ***beaux esprits*** witty person (Fr., ital.)
Belgic relating to the ancient Belgae of Gaul
Belgium country in western Europe; Fr. name **Belgique**, Flemish name **België**
Belgrade capital of Serbia and former capital of Yugoslavia; Serbian name **Beograd**
Belial a name for the Devil
belie (**belying, belied**)
believable (not **-eable**)
Belisha beacon flashing light on a zebra crossing (one cap.)
Belitung Indonesian island; former name **Billiton**
Belize country in Central America; former name **British Honduras** □ **Belizean**
Bell, Currer, Ellis, and Acton, the pseudonyms used by Charlotte, Emily, and Anne Brontë
belladonna deadly nightshade (one word)
belle beautiful girl (not ital.)
Belleek 1 town in Fermanagh, Northern Ireland **2** kind of porcelain produced in Belleek
belle époque settled period before WWI (lower case, not ital.)
belle laide pl. ***belles laides*** fascinatingly ugly woman (Fr., ital.)
Bellerophon Gk Mythol. hero who killed the monster Chimera
belles-lettres literary works noted for their aesthetic effect (hyphen, not ital.; treated as sing. or pl.) □ **belletrist**
Bellini[1] family of 15th-cent. Italian painters
Bellini[2] pl. **Bellinis** cocktail of peach juice and champagne
Belloc, (Joseph) Hilaire (1870–1953), French-born British writer of *Cautionary Tales*
bellwether leading sheep of a flock (one word)
belly dancer (two words)
bellyful pl. **bellyfuls**
Belorussia (also **Byelorussia**) former name for **Belarus**
Belshazzar (6th cent. BC), viceroy of Babylon, whose death was foretold by writing on the palace wall (Dan. 5)
Beltane ancient Celtic festival celebrated on May Day
belvedere building positioned to command a good view
BEM British Empire Medal
Benares former name for **Varanasi**
benchmark (one word)
Benedicite canticle used in matins (cap.)
Benedick character in Shakespeare's *Much Ado about Nothing*
Benedict XVI (b.1927), German cleric, pope 2005–13; born *Joseph Alois Ratzinger*
Benedict, St (*c.*480–*c.*550), Italian hermit
Benedictine 1 member of a religious order following the rule of St Benedict **2** trademark liqueur based on brandy
Benedictus 1 invocation forming a set part of the Mass **2** canticle beginning *Benedictus Dominus Deus* (Luke 1:68–79)
beneficent (not **beneficient**)
benefit v. (**benefiting, benefited** or **benefitting, benefitted**)
Benelux collective name for Belgium, the Netherlands, and Luxembourg
BEng (also **B.Eng.**) Bachelor of Engineering
Bengali pl. **Bengalis 1** person from Bengal **2** language of Bangladesh and West Bengal
Benghazi port in NE Libya
Ben-Gurion, David (1886–1973), Israeli prime minister 1948–53 and 1955–63

Ben-Hur novel and two films (hyphen)
Benin country of West Africa
□ **Beninese**
Benn, Tony (1925–2014), British Labour politician; full name *Anthony Neil Wedgwood Benn*
Bennet surname of Elizabeth in Jane Austen's *Pride and Prejudice*
Bennett 1 Alan (b.1934), English dramatist **2** (Enoch) Arnold (1867–1931), English novelist **3** Sir Richard Rodney (1936–2012), English composer
Ben Nevis mountain in western Scotland, the highest in the British Isles
Bentham, Jeremy (1748–1832), English philosopher
ben trovato invented but plausible (It., ital.)
Benzedrine trademark drug used as a stimulant; amphetamine (cap.)
benzene liquid hydrocarbon present in petroleum
benzine mixture of liquid hydrocarbons obtained from petroleum
benzoin resin obtained from certain Asian trees
benzol crude benzene
Beograd Serbian name for **Belgrade**
Beowulf Old English epic poem
bequeath leave (property) by a will (not **-the**)
Berber member of the indigenous people of North Africa
berceau pl. ***berceaux*** arbour, bower (Fr., ital.)
berceuse pl. ***berceuses*** lullaby (Fr., ital.)
berg S. Afr. mountain or hill
bergamot 1 oily substance extracted from a variety of orange **2** kind of pear
Bergen 1 seaport in SW Norway **2** Flemish name for **Mons**
Bergerac[1] wine-producing region in SW France
Bergerac[2] see **Cyrano de Bergerac**
Bergman 1 (Ernst) Ingmar (1918–2007), Swedish film and theatre director **2** Ingrid (1915–82), Swedish actress
beriberi tropical disease (one word)
Bering, Vitus (Jonassen) (1681–1741), Danish navigator and explorer
Bering Sea, Bering Strait (two caps)
Berkeleian relating to George Berkeley
Berkeley[1] city in western California
Berkeley[2] **1** Busby (1895–1976), American choreographer and film director **2** George (1685–1753), Irish philosopher and bishop **3** Sir Lennox (Randall Francis) (1903–89), English composer
berkelium chemical element of atomic number 97 (symbol **Bk**)
Berkshire former county of southern England (abbrev. **Berks.**)
Bermuda (also **the Bermudas**) country consisting of small islands off the US, a British overseas territory □ **Bermudian** (also **Bermudan**)
Bernard of Clairvaux, St (1090–1153), French theologian and abbot
Berne (also **Bern**) capital of Switzerland
Berne Convention international copyright agreement (abbrev. **BC**)
Bernhardt, Sarah (1844–1923), French actress; born *Henriette Rosine Bernard*
Bernoulli Swiss family of mathematicians and scientists
Bernstein, Leonard (1918–90), American composer
bersagliere pl. ***bersaglieri*** Italian rifleman (ital.)
berserker ancient Norse warrior
Berwickshire former county of SE Scotland
Berwick-upon-Tweed town in NE England (hyphens)
beryllium chemical element of atomic number 4 (symbol **Be**)
Berzelius, Jöns Jakob (1779–1848), Swedish chemist
Besançon town in NE France
beseech (past and past part. **besought** or **beseeched**)
beset (**besetting**; past and past part. **beset**)
bespeak (past **bespoke**; past part. **bespoken**)
Bessarabia region of eastern Europe, now in Moldova and Ukraine
Bessemer process steel-making process (one cap.)
bestrew (past part. **bestrewed** or **bestrewn**)
bestride (past **bestrode**; past part. **bestridden**)

bestseller, bestselling (one word)
bet v. (**betting**; past and past part. **bet** or **betted**)
beta second letter of the Greek alphabet (**B, β**), transliterated as 'b'
beta blocker, beta decay (two words)
betake (past **betook**; past part. **betaken**)
Betamax trademark in the US obsolete format for video recorders
beta particle, beta ray (two words)
beta test (two words, hyphen as verb)
betatron Phys. apparatus for accelerating electrons
betel Asian plant whose leaves are chewed with areca nuts
Betelgeuse star in the constellation Orion (not **-geux**)
bête noire pl. **bêtes noires** one's pet aversion (accent, not ital.)
Beth Din (also **Beit Din**) Jewish religious court
bethel nonconformist chapel (lower case)
bethink (past and past part. **bethought**)
Bethlehem town near Jerusalem, the reputed birthplace of Jesus
bêtise foolish or ill-timed remark or action (Fr., ital.)
Betjeman, Sir John (1906–84), English poet, Poet Laureate 1972–84
betony plant of the mint family
better (also **bettor**) person who bets
Betws-y-coed town in Conwy, North Wales (hyphens, one cap.)
beurre blanc sauce made with butter, onions, etc. (not ital.)
Beuys, Joseph (1921–86), German artist
BeV another term for **GeV**
Bevan, Nye (1897–1960), British Labour politician; full name *Aneurin Bevan*
bevel v. (**bevelling, bevelled**; US one **-l-**)
beverage drink
Beveridge, William Henry, 1st Baron (1879–1963), British economist and social reformer
Beverley town in the East Riding of Yorkshire
Beverly Hills city in California
Bevin, Ernest (1881–1951), British Labour statesman
Bewick, Thomas (1753–1828), English wood engraver
Bexleyheath town in Greater London (one word)
bey governor of a district or province in the Ottoman Empire
Bey of Tunis hist. ruler of Tunisia
bezant 1 hist. coin orig. minted at Byzantium **2** Heraldry solid gold roundel
bezel ring holding the cover of a watch face etc.
bezique card game
b.f. 1 boldface (type) **2** (in bookkeeping) brought forward
BFI British Film Institute
BFPO British Forces (or Field) Post Office
BG Brigadier General
BGH bovine growth hormone
Bh the chemical element bohrium (no point)
Bhagavadgita poem in the Mahabharata
Bhagwan Ind. God
bhaji pl. **bhajis, bhajia** Indian fried cake of vegetables
B'ham Birmingham (England)
bhang (in India) cannabis leaves (not **bang**)
bhangra popular music combining Punjabi and Western elements
bharal Himalayan wild sheep (not **burhel**)
Bharat Hindi name for **India**
BHC 1 benzene hexachloride **2** British High Commission
Bhopal city in central India
bhp brake horsepower (no points)
bhuna (also **bhoona**) medium-hot dry curry
Bhutan small independent kingdom in the Himalayas □ **Bhutani**
Bhutto 1 Benazir (1953–2007), Pakistani prime minister 1988–90 and 1993–96, daughter of Zulfikar Ali Bhutto **2** Zulfikar Ali (1928–79), Pakistani president 1971–3 and prime minister 1973–7
Bi the chemical element bismuth (no point)
Biafra part of eastern Nigeria, proclaimed as a state in 1967

Białystok city in NE Poland
biannual occurring twice a year; cf. **biennial**, see also **bimonthly**
bias v. (**biasing, biased**)
Bible, the (not ital.; abbrev. **Bib.**)
bible authoritative book on particular subject (lower case)
Bible Belt (caps)
biblical (lower case) □ **biblically**
bibliophile collector or lover of books
bibliopole arch. dealer in books
bibliotheca library; book catalogue (not ital.)
Bibliothèque nationale de France French national library in Paris
bicameral (of a legislative body) having two chambers
bicentenary two-hundredth anniversary
bicentennial relating to a two-hundredth anniversary (two *ns*)
bichon frise pl. **bichon frises** or **bichons frise** breed of small dog with a curly white coat (not ital.)
bid[1] (past and past part. **bid**) offer (a price) for something
bid[2] (past **bid** or **bade**; past part. **bid**) **1** utter (a greeting etc.) to **2** arch. command to do something
Biedermeier 19th-cent. German style of furniture and decoration
biennale exhibition or festival held every other year
biennial occurring every other year; cf. **biannual**, see also **bimonthly**
biennium pl. **biennia** or **bienniums** period of two years
bien pensant right-thinking; orthodox (Fr., ital.)
Bierce, Ambrose (Gwinnett) (1842–*c.*1914), American writer
bifocal (one word)
Big Bang, Big Ben, Big Brother (caps)
big dipper 1 Brit. roller coaster **2** (**the Big Dipper**) N. Amer. the Plough (constellation)
big-headed (hyphen)
bigoted (one *t*)
bijou (not ital.) adj. small and elegant. n. pl. **bijoux** arch. jewel or trinket
bijouterie jewellery or trinkets (Fr., ital.)
bikini pl. **bikinis**
Bilbao seaport in northern Spain
bilberry (not **bill-**)
bilbo pl. **bilbos** or **bilboes** hist. sword with fine blade
bilboes iron bar with sliding shackles
Bildungsroman novel about a person's formative years (Ger., cap., ital.)
bilharzia tropical disease
bilingual (one word)
bill draft of a proposed law (lower case exc. in names of bills)
Billericay town in Essex
billet v. (**billeting, billeted**)
billet-doux pl. **billets-doux** love letter (hyphen, not ital.)
billion pl. **billions** or with numeral or quantifying word **billion** a thousand million (1,000,000,000); Brit. dated a million million (1,000,000,000,000) (abbrev. **bn**; for billions of pounds write e.g. £100bn)
Billiton former name of **Belitung**
bill of exchange (abbrev. **BE**)
bill of lading (abbrev. **BL**)
Bill of Rights (caps)
billy goat (two words)
Billy the Kid see **Bonney**
biltong dried meat
BIM British Institute of Management
bimbo pl. **bimbos**
bimetallic (one word)
bimonthly avoid **bimonthly** (and similar expressions such as **biweekly**) as ambiguous; prefer alternative expressions such as *every two months* and *twice a month*
bin means 'son of' in Arabic; lower case as a patronymic, but upper case in family names
bindi pl. **bindis** mark worn on the forehead by Indian women
binge v. (**bingeing** or US **binging, binged**)
binge drinking (two words)
bin Laden, Osama (1957–2011), Saudi-born Islamic militant
binnacle housing for a ship's compass
binocular for both eyes
binoculars optical instrument

binomial (one word)
bio pl. **bios** biography
biodegradable (one word)
bipartisan, biplane, bipolar (one word)
birdbrain, birdcage, birdlime (one word)
birdie Golf score of one stroke under par at a hole
bird-like (hyphen)
bird of paradise pl. **birds of paradise** (lower case)
birdseed (one word)
Birdseye, Clarence (1886–1956), American businessman and inventor; food company is **Birds Eye**
bird's-eye view (one hyphen)
birdsong, birdwatching (one word)
biretta square cap worn by Roman Catholic clergymen
biriani (also **biryani**) Indian dish
Birman long-haired breed of cat; cf. **Burmese**
Birnam village in Perthshire, Scotland; **Birnam Wood** features in *Macbeth*
biro pl. **biros** ballpoint pen (cap. as trademark)
birth certificate, birth control (two words)
birthmark, birthplace (one word)
birth rate (two words)
birthright, birthweight (one word)
Birtwistle, Sir Harrison (Paul) (b.1934), English composer
biryani var. of **biriani**
BIS Bank for International Settlements
bis Mus. to be repeated
biscotti small Italian biscuits (not ital.)
bisexual (one word)
Bishkek capital of Kyrgyzstan
bishop cap. in titles (*the Bishop of Oxford*, but *the bishop said ...*); abbrev. **Bp**, in chess **B**
Bishopbriggs town in southern Scotland
Bishop's Stortford town in Essex
Bislama (also **Beach-la-mar**) pidgin language used in Vanuatu
Bismarck[1] state capital of North Dakota
Bismarck[2], Otto Eduard Leopold von, Prince of Bismarck (1815–98), Chancellor of the German Empire 1871–90 □ **Bismarckian**
bismillah invocation used by Muslims, 'in the name of God'
bismuth chemical element of atomic number 83 (symbol **Bi**)
bison pl. same, humpbacked wild ox, *Bison bison* (N. Amer., also called **buffalo**) and *B. bonasus* (Poland, also called **wisent**)
bisque **1** rich seafood soup **2** extra turn allowed in croquet **3** biscuit pottery
Bissau capital of Guinea-Bissau
bistoury surgical knife
bistro pl. **bistros** small restaurant
bit[1] N. Amer. informal unit of 12½ cents
bit[2] Comput. unit of information expressed as either a 0 or 1 in binary notation; cf. **byte**
Bithynia ancient region of NW Asia Minor
bitmap Comput. (one word)
bitts posts on the deck of a ship for fastening mooring lines or cables
bituminize (Brit. also **bituminise**) treat with bitumen
bivouac v. (**bivouacking, bivouacked**)
biweekly, biyearly avoid as ambiguous: see **bimonthly**
bizarre (one *z*, two *r*s)
bizarrerie strange and unusual thing (not ital.)
Bizet, Georges (1838–75), French composer
Bk the chemical element berkelium (no point)
bk pl. **bks** book
BL **1** Bachelor of Law **2** bill of lading **3** hist. British Leyland **4** British Library
bl barrel
black use **black** (lower case) as an adj. for people with dark-coloured skin; do not use as a noun; avoid **coloured, Negro**, and **Negress**; see also **African American**
Black and Tans Irish armed force recruited by the government to fight Sinn Fein in 1920–1 (caps)
blackball, blackberry, blackbird, blackboard, blackcap (one word)
blackcock male black grouse (one word); cf. **greyhen**

Black Country, Black Death (caps)
black-figure type of ancient Greek pottery (hyphen)
blackfly (one word)
Blackfoot pl. same or **Blackfeet** member of a confederacy of North American Indian peoples
Black Forest wooded region of SW Germany; Ger. name **Schwarzwald**
Black Forest gateau (two caps)
Black Friar friar of the Dominican order (two words)
Blackfriars area of London (one word)
black game black grouse collectively
blackguard dated dishonourable man
Black Jew a Falasha
blacklead graphite (one word)
blackleg (one word)
black letter early bold style of type
blacklist, blackmail (one word)
Black Maria police vehicle for transporting prisoners (caps)
Blackmore, R(ichard) D(oddridge) (1825–1900), English novelist and poet
blackout n. (one word, two words as verb)
Black Prince (1330–76), Edward, the eldest son of Edward III of England
Black Rod (in full **Gentleman Usher of the Black Rod**) chief usher of the Lord Chamberlain's department of the royal household
blackshirt member of a Fascist organization (one word, lower case)
blacksmith (one word)
Black Watch the Royal Highland Regiment
blad promotional booklet of pages from a forthcoming book
blaeberry Sc. and N. Engl. bilberry
Blaenau Ffestiniog town in Gwynedd, Wales, home of the **Ffestiniog Railway** (not **Festiniog**)
blague joke or piece of nonsense (Fr., ital.)
blagueur person who talks nonsense (Fr., ital.)
Blair Atholl town in Perthshire, Scotland
Blairgowrie town in Perthshire, Scotland
Blake, William (1757–1827), English artist and poet □ **Blakean**
blameable (not **blamable**)
blancmange gelatinous dessert
blanket v. (**blanketing, blanketed**)
blanquette white meat in a white sauce (not ital.)
Blantyre city in Malawi
blasé indifferent to something because of overfamiliarity (accent, not ital.)
blast furnace (two words)
blast-off n. (hyphen, two words as verb)
blastula pl. **blastulae** or US **blastulas** embryo at an early stage of development (not ital.)
blatant (not **-ent**)
blather (also Sc. **blether**) talk at length without making much sense
Blaue Reiter group of German expressionist painters (Ger., ital.)
bleed Printing be printed so as to run off the page after trimming
Blenheim 1 village in Bavaria, site of a battle in which the English defeated the French and the Bavarians (1704) **2** Duke of Marlborough's seat at Woodstock near Oxford
Blenheim Orange orange-red variety of English apple (caps)
blent literary past and past part. of **blend**
Blériot, Louis (1872–1936), French pilot, the first person to fly the English Channel (1909)
blesbok South African antelope (not **blesbuck**)
blessed (not **blest** or **blessèd** exc. in poetry)
Blessed Virgin Mary title of Mary, the mother of Jesus (abbrev. **BVM**)
blether Scottish var. of **blather**
Blighty Britain or England
blindfold (one word)
blind man's buff (US **blind man's bluff**) (three words)
blini (also **blinis**) (sing. **blin**) Russian pancakes
BLitt (also **B.Litt.**) Bachelor of Letters [L. *Baccalaureus Litterarum*]
blitz sudden intensive attack; (**the Blitz**) German air raids on Britain 1940–1
blitzkrieg intensive military campaign

(lower case, not ital.)

Blixen, Karen (Christentze), Baroness Blixen-Finecke (1885–1962), Danish writer; also known as **Isak Dinesen**

bloc allied group of countries or parties

block Printing piece of wood or metal engraved for printing on paper or fabric

blockbuster, blockbusting (one word)

block capitals plain capital letters

blockhead (one word)

blocking impressing text or a design on a book cover

Bloemfontein judicial capital of South Africa

blonde in Britain **blonde** is commoner, in the US **blond**; spellings do not always correspond to the French fem. and masc. forms

Blondin, Charles (1824–97), French acrobat; born *Jean-François Gravelet*

bloodbath (one word)

blood brother, blood cell, blood count (two words)

blood-curdling (hyphen)

blood donor, blood feud, blood group (two words)

bloodhound, bloodletting, bloodline, bloodlust (one word)

blood poisoning, blood pressure, blood relation, blood sport (two words)

bloodstain, bloodstock, bloodstream, bloodsucker (one word)

blood test, blood transfusion, blood vessel (two words)

Bloody Mary[1] Mary I of England

Bloody Mary[2] pl. **Bloody Marys** drink of vodka and tomato juice (caps)

Bloody Sunday (caps)

Bloomsbury Group (caps)

blow (past **blew**; past part. **blown** or in sense 'damned, cursed' **blowed**)

blow-dry (hyphen)

blowfly, blowhole, blowlamp (one word)

blowout n. (one word, two words as verb)

blowpipe (one word)

blowsy (also **blowzy**) (of a woman) coarse and untidy-looking

blowtorch (one word)

blow-up n. (hyphen, two words as verb)

BLT bacon, lettuce, and tomato (sandwich)

Blücher, Gebhard Leberecht von (1742–1819), Prussian general

blue person who has represented Cambridge University or Oxford University in a match between the two universities (lower case)

Bluebeard fairy-tale character who killed several wives in turn (cap.)

bluebell, blueberry, bluebird (one word)

blue-black (hyphen)

Blue Book report issued by Parliament or the Privy Council (caps)

blue-chip (of a company) constituting a reliable investment (hyphen)

blue-collar N. Amer. relating to manual workers (hyphen)

bluegrass kind of country music (one word)

blue-green, blue-grey (hyphen)

blueing, blueish vars of **bluing, bluish**

bluejacket Royal Navy sailor (one word)

Blue Peter blue and white flag raised by a ship about to leave port (caps)

blueprint (one word)

blue riband (N. Amer. **blue ribbon**) badge awarded to the winner of a contest or worn by members of the Order of the Garter (lower case)

blues melancholic music (treated as sing. or pl.)

bluestocking (one word)

Bluetooth trademark standard for the wireless interconnection of mobile phones, computers, etc. (cap.)

bluey almost or partly blue

bluing (also **blueing**) blue powder formerly used in laundry

bluish (also **blueish**) having a blue tinge

Blu-Tack trademark blue sticky material for attaching paper to walls

B-lymphocyte Physiol. lymphocyte responsible for producing antibodies

Blyth town in Northumberland

BM **1** Bachelor of Medicine **2** British Museum

BMA British Medical Association

BMI body mass index

B-movie (hyphen)
BMR basal metabolic rate
BMus (also **B.Mus.**) Bachelor of Music
BMW German car company (*Bayerische Motoren Werke AG*)
BMX robust bicycle suitable for cross-country racing [f. *bicycle motocross*]
Bn 1 Baron **2** Battalion
bn billion
B'nai B'rith Jewish organization (two apostrophes)
BNC Brasenose College, Oxford
BNP British National Party
BO body odour
BOAC hist. British Overseas Airways Corporation
Boadicea var. of **Boudicca**
boarding house, boarding pass, boarding school (two words)
Board of Trade former British government department
boardroom, boardwalk (one word)
boatbuilder, boathouse, boatload, boatman (one word)
Boat Race annual boat race between Oxford and Cambridge universities (caps)
boatswain (also **bo'sun** or **bosun**)
bobby socks N. Amer. ankle socks
bobby-soxer N. Amer. dated teenage girl
bobolink North American songbird
bobsleigh (N. Amer. **bobsled**) mechanically steered and braked sledge
bocage modelling of plants and flowers in clay (not ital.)
Boccaccio, Giovanni (1313–75), Italian writer
Boccherini, Luigi (1743–1805), Italian composer
Boche dated Germans collectively
BOD biochemical oxygen demand
bodega Spanish cellar or shop selling wine and food (not ital.)
Bodensee Ger. name for **Lake Constance**
Bodhgaya (also **Buddh Gaya**) village in NE India where the Buddha attained enlightenment
bodhisattva (in Mahayana Buddhism) person who is able to reach nirvana
bodhrán Irish drum (accent, not ital.)
bodhi tree var. of **bo tree**
Bodleian Library library of Oxford University; informally known as **Bodley**
Bodoni, Giambattista (1740–1813), Italian printer
body Printing depth of a character or a piece of type
body blow (two words)
bodybuilder, bodyguard, bodywork (one word)
Boeing US aircraft manufacturers
Boeotia region of central Greece
Boer hist. Dutch or Huguenot settler in southern Africa
Boethius, Anicius Manlius Severinus (*c.*480–524), Roman philosopher
boeuf French for 'beef' (ital.)
boeuf bourguignon beef stewed in red wine (not ital.)
Bofors gun light anti-aircraft gun
Bogarde, Sir Dirk (1921–99), British actor
Bogart, Humphrey (DeForest) (1899–1957), American actor
bogey (not **bogy**) pl. **bogeys 1** Golf one stroke over par at a hole **2** evil or mischievous spirit
bogeyman (one word)
bogie wheeled undercarriage
Bogomil member of a heretical medieval sect
Bogotá capital of Colombia; official name **Santa Fé de Bogotá**
bog-standard (hyphen)
bohème bohemian person (Fr., ital.)
Bohemia western part of the Czech Republic
Bohemian person from Bohemia
bohemian unconventional artistic person (lower case)
Bohr, Niels Hendrik David (1885–1962) and his son, Aage Niels (1922–2009), Danish physicists
bohrium chemical element of atomic number 107 (symbol **Bh**)
boilermaker (one word)
boiler room, boiler suit (two words)
boiling point (two words; abbrev. **bp** or **BP**)
boîte small restaurant or nightclub

(Fr., ital.)
bok choy US var. of **pak choi**
Bokhara 1 Turkoman rug or carpet **2** var. of **Bukhara**
Bokmål form of the Norwegian language that is closer to Danish; also called **Riksmål**; cf. **Nynorsk**
bold (also **boldface**) typeface with thick strokes, like **this**
bolero pl. **boleros** Spanish dance in triple time
boletus (also **bolete**) pl. **boletuses** kind of toadstool
Boleyn, Anne (1507–36), second wife of Henry VIII (executed)
Bolingbroke surname of Henry IV of England
Bolívar, Simón (1783–1830), Venezuelan patriot (accent)
bolivar monetary unit of Venezuela (lower case, no accent)
Bolivia country in South America □ **Bolivian**
boliviano pl. **bolivianos** monetary unit of Bolivia (lower case)
Böll, Heinrich (Theodor) (1917–85), German writer
Bologna city in northern Italy
bologna N. Amer. smoked sausage (lower case)
Bolognese relating to Bologna; cf. **spaghetti bolognese**
Bolshevik member of the majority faction of the Russian Social Democratic Party, which seized power in the Revolution; cf. **Menshevik**
bolshie (also **bolshy**) deliberately uncooperative
Bolshoi Moscow ballet company
bolthole (one word)
Boltzmann's constant Chem. (symbol **k**)
bolus pl. **boluses 1** ball of food being swallowed **2** large pill
bombardier rank of non-commissioned officer in certain artillery regiments, equivalent to corporal (abbrev. **Bdr**)
Bombay city on the west coast of India; official name (from 1995) **Mumbai**
bombazine twilled dress fabric (not **bombasine**)
bombe frozen dessert (not ital.)
bombé (of furniture) rounded (accent, not ital.)
bombproof, bombshell, bombsight (one word)
bomb site (two words)
bona fide genuine, real (not ital.)
bona fides honesty and sincerity of intention (not ital.)
Bonaparte (Italian **Buonaparte**) Corsican family including the three French rulers named Napoleon
bon appétit enjoy your meal! (accent, not ital.)
bona vacantia Law unclaimed goods to which the Crown may have right (L., ital.)
bonbon a sweet (one word)
bonbonnière box or jar for confectionery (accent, not ital.)
bondholder (one word)
bondieuserie church ornament or devotional object (Fr., ital.)
bond paper high-quality writing paper (two words)
bone dry, bone idle (two words, hyphen when attrib.)
Bo'Ness town in West Lothian, Scotland [f. *Borrowstounness*]
bongo pl. **bongos** small drum
Bonhoeffer, Dietrich (1906–45), German Lutheran theologian
bonhomie good-natured friendliness (not ital.)
bonjour French for 'good day' (one word, not ital.)
bon mot pl. **bon mots** or **bons mots** witty remark (not ital.)
Bonn city in Germany, capital of the Federal Republic of Germany 1949–90
bonne nursemaid or housemaid (not ital.)
bonne bouche pl. ***bonnes bouches*** appetizing item of food (Fr., ital.)
bonne femme cooked in a simple way (Fr., ital.)
bonneted (one *t*)
Bonney, William H. (1859–81), American outlaw; born *Henry McCarty*; known as **Billy the Kid**
Bonnie Prince Charlie see **Stuart**[2]
bonsai pl. same, art of growing dwarf varieties of trees or shrubs

bonsoir French for 'good evening', 'goodnight' (one word, not ital.)
bontebok South African antelope (not **bontebuck**)
bon ton good style (Fr., ital.)
bon vivant pl. ***bon vivants*** or ***bons vivants*** person with a luxurious lifestyle (Fr., ital.)
bon viveur pl. **bon viveurs** or **bons viveurs** a *bon vivant* (not in Fr. use; not ital.)
bon voyage have a good journey! (not ital.)
bony (not **boney**)
booby trap n. (two words, hyphen as verb)
boogie v. (**boogieing, boogied**)
boogie-woogie (hyphen)
book (abbrev. **bk**)
bookbinder, bookcase, bookend (one word)
Booker Prize annual prize awarded for a novel published by a British, Irish, or Commonwealth citizen (caps); now called the **Man Booker Prize**
bookkeeper, bookmaker, bookmark (one word)
Book of Changes English name for **I Ching**
Book of Common Prayer official service book of the Church of England
bookplate, bookrest, bookseller (one word)
bookshelf pl. **bookshelves** (one word)
bookstall, bookwork, bookworm (one word)
Boole, George (1815–64), English mathematician
Boolean denoting a system of binary notation used to represent logical propositions
Boone, Daniel (*c.*1734–1820), American pioneer
Boötes northern constellation (the Herdsman) (accent)
bootlace, bootleg, bootmaker, bootstrap (one word)
Bophuthatswana former black homeland in South Africa
borborygmus pl. **borborygmi** Med. rumbling in the intestines
Bordeaux port of SW France
bordello pl. **bordellos** brothel
bordereau pl. **bordereaux** memorandum of contents, docket (not ital.)
borderland, borderline (one word)
Borders see **Scottish Borders**
bordure Heraldry broad border in a coat of arms
Boreas Gk Mythol. god of the north wind
Borges, Jorge Luis (1899–1986), Argentinian writer ◻ **Borgesian**
Borgia 1 Cesare (*c.*1476–1507), Italian statesman, cardinal, and general **2** Lucrezia (1480–1519), Italian noblewoman, sister of Cesare Borgia
Boris Godunov see **Godunov**
born (abbrev. **b.**) existing as a result of birth; cf. **borne**
born again (two words, hyphen when attrib.)
borne carried or endured; cf. **born**
Borneo large island of the Malay Archipelago ◻ **Bornean**
Borodin, Aleksandr (Porfirevich) (1833–87), Russian composer
Borodino village west of Moscow, the scene of a battle (1812) at which Napoleon's forces defeated the Russians
boron chemical element of atomic number 5 (symbol **B**)
borscht Russian or Polish beetroot soup [Russ. *borshch*]
borstal hist. custodial institution for young offenders (lower case)
borzoi pl. **borzois** Russian wolfhound
Bosch, Hieronymus (*c.*1450–1516), Dutch painter
Bosnia–Herzegovina (also **Bosnia and Herzegovina**) country in the Balkans, formerly a constituent republic of Yugoslavia (en rule)
Bosporus (also **Bosphorus**) strait separating Europe from the Anatolian peninsula of western Asia
bossa nova Brazilian dance (two words)
bosun (also **bo'sun**) var. of **boatswain**
Boswell, James (1740–95), Scottish biographer of Samuel Johnson ◻ **Boswellian**
botanize (Brit. also **botanise**)
Botany merino wool (cap.)
botfly fly whose larvae parasitize mammals (one word)

bothy Sc. hut or cottage (not **bothie**)

Botox trademark drug used to remove facial wrinkles (cap.)

bo tree (also **bodh tree**) fig tree sacred to Buddhists

Botswana country in southern Africa; former name **Bechuanaland** □ **Botswanan**

Botticelli, Sandro (1445–1510), Italian painter; born *Alessandro di Mariano Filipepi*

bottle bank, bottle green (two words)

bottleneck (one word)

bouchée small filled pastry (Fr., ital.)

bouclé yarn with a looped or curled ply (accent, not ital.)

Boudicca (d. AD 62), ruler of the Iceni in eastern England; also called **Boadicea**

boudin French black pudding (Fr., ital.)

boudoir (not ital.)

bouffant (not ital.)

bougainvillea (also **bougainvillaea**) tropical climbing plant

bouillabaisse Provençal fish soup (not ital.)

bouilli stewed or boiled meat (Fr., ital.)

bouillon thin soup or stock (not ital.)

boule legislative body of ancient or modern Greece

boules French form of bowls (not ital.)

boulevardier wealthy socialite (not ital.)

bouleversé overturned or upset (Fr., ital.)

Boulez, Pierre (b.1925), French composer and conductor

boulle (also **buhl**) material used for inlaying furniture (not ital.)

Boulogne ferry port in northern France

bouquet garni bunch of herbs for flavouring a stew or soup (not ital.)

Bourbon[1] branch of the royal family of France

Bourbon[2] biscuit with a chocolate cream filling (cap.)

bourbon kind of American whisky (lower case)

bourgeois pl. same (member of the) middle class (not ital.)

bourgeoise middle-class woman (not ital.)

bourgeoisie the middle class (not ital., treated as sing. or pl.)

Bourgogne Fr. name for **Burgundy**

bourn 1 dial. small stream **2** (also **bourne**) boundary or domain

Bournemouth town on the south coast of England

Bournville area of Birmingham

bourrée lively French dance (accent, not ital.)

Bourse Paris stock exchange

boustrophedon written alternately from right to left and from left to right

boutonnière spray of flowers worn in a buttonhole (accent, not ital.)

Boutros-Ghali, Boutros (b.1922), Egyptian Secretary General of the United Nations 1992–7

bouzouki pl. **bouzoukis** Greek form of mandolin

bowdlerize (Brit. also **bowdlerise**) remove improper material from (a text)

bowie knife long knife with double-edged blade (two words, lower case)

bowling alley, bowling green (two words)

bowser trademark tanker for fuelling aircraft or supplying water (not **bowzer**)

Bow Street Runners early London police (caps)

bow tie, bow window (two words)

boxcar (one word)

boxful pl. **boxfuls**

Boxing Day first day (strictly, first weekday) after Christmas Day (caps)

boxing glove (two words)

box number, box office, box room (two words)

boyar hist. Russian aristocrat

boycott withdraw from relations with (lower case)

boyfriend (one word)

Boy Scout official term is now **scout**

BP 1 blood pressure **2** boiling point **3** British Petroleum **4** British Pharmacopoeia

Bp Bishop (no point)

bp 1 Biochem. base pair(s) **2** basis point(s) **3** boiling point

BP before the present (small caps, placed after the numerals)
BPC British Pharmaceutical Codex
BPhil (also **B.Phil.**) Bachelor of Philosophy
bpi Comput. bits per inch
bpm beats per minute
bps Comput. bits per second
Bq becquerel
BR hist. British Rail (previously British Railways)
Br the chemical element bromine (no point)
Br. (point) **1** British **2** (in religious orders) Brother
braai pl. **braais** S. Afr. barbecue
brace Printing either of the marks { and }; curly bracket
bracket v. (**bracketing, bracketed**)
Braggadocchio braggart in Spenser's *The Faerie Queene*
braggadocio boastful behaviour
Brahe, Tycho (1546–1601), Danish astronomer
Brahma creator god in Hinduism
brahma short for **brahmaputra**
Brahman (also **Brahmin**) pl. **Brahmans** member of the highest Hindu caste, that of the priesthood
Brahmanism early form of Hinduism
Brahmaputra river of southern Asia
brahmaputra Asian breed of chicken
Brahmi one of the two oldest alphabets in the Indian subcontinent; cf. **Karoshthi**
Brahmin 1 var. of **Brahman 2** US socially superior person
Brahmoism Hindu reform movement
brail Naut. furl (a sail)
Braille written language for the blind (cap.)
brainchild pl. **brainchildren** (one word)
Braine, John (Gerard) (1922–86), English novelist
brainpower, brainstem, brainstorm (one word)
brains trust (no apostrophe)
brainwash, brainwave (one word)
braise stew (food) slowly; cf. **braze**
brake 1 device for slowing a vehicle **2** horse-drawn carriage **3** instrument for crushing flax **4** thicket; cf. **break**
brake horsepower pl. same (abbrev. **b.h.p.**)
Bramah, Joseph (1748–1814), English inventor
Bramley pl. **Bramleys** cooking apple
branch line (two words)
Brandenburg state of NE Germany
brand name (two words)
brand new (two words, hyphen when attrib.)
Brands Hatch motor-racing circuit in Kent (no apostrophe)
Brandt, Willy (1913–92), Chancellor of West Germany 1969–74
Brand X (caps)
brant N. Amer. brent goose
Brasilia capital, since 1960, of Brazil
brasserie inexpensive French restaurant
brassie Golf a number two wood
brassiere bra (no accent) [Fr. *brassière*]
Bratislava capital of Slovakia; Ger. name **Pressburg**; Hungarian name **Pozsony**
brat pack (two words)
brattice lining in a coal mine
Braunschweig Ger. name for **Brunswick**
bravo 1 pl. **bravos** expression of approval for a performer **2** pl. **bravos** or **bravoes** dated thug or assassin
braze join by soldering; cf. **braise**
brazier 1 pan holding lighted coals **2** worker in brass
Brazil country in South America □ **Brazilian**
Brazil nut (two words, one cap.)
Brazzaville capital of the Congo
BRCS British Red Cross Society
breadboard, breadcrumb, breadfruit, breadline (one word)
break (past **broke**; past part. **broken**) separate into pieces; cf. **brake**
breakdown n. (one word, two words as verb)
breakneck (one word)
Breakspear, Nicholas, see **Adrian IV**
breakthrough n. (one word, two words as verb)
break-up n. (hyphen, two words as verb)
breakwater (one word)

breastbone, breastfeed, breastplate, breaststroke (one word)
breathalyse (US **breathalyze**) test with a breathalyser
breathalyser (trademark **Breathalyzer**) device for measuring the amount of alcohol in a driver's breath
breathing sign in Greek (ʻ or ʼ) indicating the presence of an aspirate (**rough breathing**) or the absence of an aspirate (**smooth breathing**)
breccia Geol. rock consisting of angular fragments
Brecht, (Eugen) Bertolt (Friedrich) (1898–1956), German dramatist and poet □ **Brechtian**
Breconshire (also **Brecknockshire**) former county of south central Wales
breech birth (two words)
Breeches Bible Geneva Bible of 1560, with *breeches* used in Gen. 3:7 for the garments made by Adam and Eve
breeches buoy device for transferring a passenger from a ship (two words)
breech-loader (hyphen)
breeding ground (two words)
brent goose (N. Amer. **brant**)
bresaola Italian cured raw beef
Brescia city in northern Italy
Breslau Ger. name for **Wrocław**
Bretagne Fr. name for **Brittany**
Breton person from Brittany
Breughel use **Bruegel**
breve 1 Mus. a note equivalent to two semibreves **2** mark (˘) indicating a short or unstressed vowel
brevet former type of military commission
breviary book containing the Roman Catholic service for each day
Brezhnev, Leonid (Ilich) (1906–82), USSR president 1977–82
briar (also **brier**) **1** prickly shrub **2** tobacco pipe
bribable (not **bribeable**)
bric-a-brac (hyphens)
brickbat, brickfield, bricklayer (one word)
brick red (two words, hyphen when attrib.)
bridegroom, bridesmaid (one word)
bridgehead (one word)
Bridges, Robert (Seymour) (1844–1930), English poet, Poet Laureate 1913–30
Bridgetown capital of Barbados
Bridgnorth town in Shropshire, England (not **Bridgenorth**)
Bridgwater town in Somerset, England (not **Bridgewater**)
bridle path (two words)
bridleway (one word)
Brie creamy French cheese (cap.)
brier var. of **briar**
brigadier rank of army officer above colonel (cap. in titles; abbrev. **Brig.**)
brigadier general pl. **brigadier generals** US officer rank (cap. in titles; abbrev. **BG**)
Brillat-Savarin, Anthelme (1755–1826), French gastronome
brilliantine oil used on men's hair
brimful (one *l*, one word)
bring-and-buy sale (hyphens)
brio vigour or vivacity (not ital.)
brioche sweet French roll (not ital.)
briquette block of compressed coal dust or peat (not **briquet**)
brisé Ballet jump in which one leg is swept up to the side (Fr., ital.)
brisling Norwegian sprat
Britain island containing England, Wales, and Scotland; **Great Britain** is more usual for the political unit. The **United Kingdom** is a political unit that includes these countries and Northern Ireland (but not the Isle of Man and the Channel Islands). The **British Isles** is a geographical term that refers to the United Kingdom, Ireland, and the surrounding islands
Britannia personification of Britain (one *t*, two *n*s)
Briticism idiom confined to British English (not **Britishism**)
British Expeditionary Force British military force sent to France in 1914 and 1939 (abbrev. **BEF**)
British Honduras former name for **Belize**
British Indian Ocean Territory British overseas territory in the Indian Ocean, including Diego Garcia

British Isles see **Britain**
British Somaliland former British protectorate in East Africa, now part of Somalia
Briton British person
Britpop (one word)
Brittany region of NW France; Fr. name **Bretagne**
Britten, (Edward) Benjamin, Lord Britten of Aldeburgh (1913–76), English composer
Brittonic var. of **Brythonic**
Brno city in the Czech Republic
bro pl. **bros** informal brother; greeting
Bro. pl. **Bros.** Brother (in writing before name of monk)
broadband (one word)
Broad Church **1** Anglican tradition favouring a liberal interpretation of doctrine **2** (**broad church**) group encompassing a wide range of views
broadleaved (one word)
broad-minded (hyphen)
Broadmoor special hospital in southern England for potentially dangerous mentally ill patients
broadsheet, broadside, broadsword (one word)
Broadway street in New York famous for its theatres
Brobdingnag land in *Gulliver's Travels* where everything is of huge size □ **Brobdingnagian**
broccoli vegetable (two *c*s, one *l*)
brochette meat or fish chunks cooked on a skewer (not ital.)
broderie anglaise open embroidery on white cotton or linen (not ital.)
broil N. Amer. grill
broker-dealer person combining the former functions of a broker and jobber on the Stock Exchange (hyphen)
Bromberg Ger. name for **Bydgoszcz**
bromine chemical element of atomic number 35 (symbol **Br**)
bronchial relating to the bronchi or bronchioles
bronchioles Anat. minute branches into which a bronchus divides
bronchus pl. **bronchi** air passage of the lungs diverging from the windpipe
bronco pl. **broncos** US wild horse
Brontë **1** Charlotte (1816–55), author of *Jane Eyre* (1847) **2** Emily (1818–48), author of *Wuthering Heights* (1847) **3** Anne (1820–49), author of *The Tenant of Wildfell Hall* (1847)
brontosaurus another term for **apatosaurus**
Bronx borough of New York City
Bronze Age (caps)
Bronzino, Agnolo (1503–72), Italian painter; born *Agnolo di Cosimo*
Brooke, Rupert (Chawner) (1887–1915), English poet
Brooklyn borough of New York City
broomstick (one word)
Bros Brothers (in names of companies)
brother pl. in church contexts **brethren** (cap. in title of monk; abbrev. **Br., Bro.**)
brother-german pl. **brothers-german** arch. brother sharing both parents (hyphen)
brother-in-law pl. **brothers-in-law** (hyphens)
brougham horse-drawn carriage with an open driver's seat (lower case)
brouhaha commotion, fuss (one word)
Brown **1** Ford Madox (1821–93), English painter **2** John (1800–59), American abolitionist **3** Lancelot (1716–83), English landscape gardener; known as **Capability Brown** **4** Robert (1773–1858), Scottish botanist
Browne **1** Hablot Knight, see **Phiz** **2** Sir Thomas (1605–82), English writer and physician
brownfield site previously developed urban site; cf. **greenfield site**
Brownian motion random movement of microscopic particles in a fluid, observed by Robert Brown
Brownie (Brit. also **Brownie Guide**) member of the junior branch of the Guide Association (cap.)
brownie (lower case) **1** rich chocolate cake **2** benevolent elf
Brownshirt member of a Nazi militia suppressed in 1934 (cap.)
browse (not **browze**) **1** survey in a leisurely way **2** feed on leaves, twigs, etc. □ **browsable**
Bruckner, Anton (1824–96), Austrian composer
Bruegel (also **Brueghel**; not **Breughel**)

1 Pieter (*c.*1525–69); known as **Pieter Bruegel the Elder 2** Pieter (1564–1638), son of Pieter Bruegel the Elder; known as **Hell Bruegel 3** Jan (1568–1623), son of Pieter Bruegel the Elder; known as **Velvet Bruegel**

Bruges city in NW Belgium; Flemish name **Brugge**

Brummagem 1 relating to Birmingham **2** dated cheap or showy

Brummell, George (1778–1840), English dandy; known as **Beau Brummell**

Brunei oil-rich sultanate in Borneo □ **Bruneian**

Brunel 1 Isambard Kingdom (1806–59), English engineer **2** Sir Marc Isambard (1769–1849), French-born English engineer, his father

Brunelleschi, Filippo (1377–1446), Italian architect; born *Filippo di Ser Brunellesco*

brunette (US also **brunet**) woman with dark brown hair

Brunhild in the *Nibelungenlied*, the wife of Gunther; in Norse myth spelled **Brynhild**

Brunswick city and former duchy of Germany; Ger. name **Braunschweig**

bruschetta toasted Italian bread with olive oil (not ital.)

Brussels capital of Belgium; Fr. name **Bruxelles**; Flemish name **Brussel**

Brussels sprout vegetable (one cap., no apostrophe)

brut (of sparkling wine) very dry (not ital.)

brutalize (Brit. also **brutalise**)

Brylcreem trademark cream for men's hair (cap.)

bryology study of mosses

Brythonic (also **Brittonic**) group of Celtic languages consisting of Welsh, Cornish, and Breton (cf. **Goidelic**); also called **P-Celtic**

BS 1 Bachelor of Surgery or US Science **2** Blessed Sacrament **3** British Standard(s)

BSc (also **B.Sc.**) Bachelor of Science

BSE bovine spongiform encephalopathy

BSI British Standards Institution

B-side less important side of a pop single (hyphen)

BSL British Sign Language

BST British Summer Time

BT British Telecom

Bt Baronet

B2B business-to-business

Btu (also **BTU**) British thermal unit(s)

BTW by the way

bu. bushel (point)

Bual Madeira wine

buccaneer pirate

Buccleuch, Duke of (not **-eugh**)

Bucephalus favourite horse of Alexander the Great

Bucharest capital of Romania; Romanian name **Bucureşti**

Buchenwald Nazi concentration camp in eastern Germany

Buckingham Palace London residence of the British sovereign

Buckinghamshire county of south central England (abbrev. **Bucks.**)

buckram cloth stiffened with paste

Bucureşti Romanian name for **Bucharest**

Budapest capital of Hungary; formed in 1873 by the union of Buda and Pest

Buddha title of the founder of Buddhism, **Siddartha Gautama** (*c.*563–*c.*483 BC)

Buddh Gaya var. of **Bodhgaya**

buddleia shrub with clusters of lilac or white flowers

budgerigar Australian parakeet

budget (**budgeting, budgeted**) cap. with ref. to regular estimate of national revenue and expenditure

Buenos Aires capital of Argentina

buffalo pl. same or **buffaloes**

Buffalo Bill (1846–1917), American showman; born *William Frederick Cody*

buffer state, buffer zone (two words)

buffet v. (**buffeting, buffeted**)

buffo pl. **buffos** comic actor in Italian opera (not ital.)

Buffon, Georges-Louis Leclerc, Comte de (1707–88), French naturalist

Bugatti Italian car manufacturer

buhl var. of **boulle**

build-up n. (hyphen, two words as verb)

built-in, built-up (hyphen)

Bujumbura capital of Burundi
Bukhara (also **Bukhoro, Bokhara**) city in Uzbekistan
Bukharin, Nikolai (Ivanovich) (1888–1938), Russian revolutionary
bulbul African and Asian songbird
Bulgar member of an ancient Slavic people
bulgar (also **bulgur**) cereal food made from whole wheat
bulletin board (two words)
bullet point (two words)
bulletproof (one word)
bullfight, bullfighting, bullfinch, bullfrog, bullring (one word)
bullseye (also **bull's eye**) centre of a target
bulrush (also **bullrush**) reed mace or similar waterside plant
bulwark defensive wall
Bulwer-Lytton see **Lytton**
bumblebee (one word; not **humble-bee** (arch.))
bumf (also **bumph**) informal printed information
bumkin Naut. short boom
bumpkin country person
buncombe use **bunkum**
Bundesbank central bank of Germany
Bundesrat upper house of Parliament in Germany or Austria
Bundestag lower house of Parliament in Germany
bungee jumping (two words)
Bunker Hill first pitched battle (1775) of the War of American Independence
bunkum informal nonsense (not **buncombe**)
Bunsen burner gas burner (one cap.)
Buñuel, Luis (1900–83), Spanish film director
Buonaparte It. spelling of **Bonaparte**
Buonarroti see **Michelangelo**
buoy, buoyant (not **bou-**)
BUPA trademark British United Provident Association
bur see **burr**
Burbage, Richard (*c.*1567–1619), English actor
Burberry trademark garment made by the UK company Burberrys Ltd
bureau pl. **bureaux** or **bureaus**
bureau de change pl. **bureaux de change** (not ital.)
burette (US also **buret**) glass tube for delivering known volumes of a liquid
burgh hist. Scottish borough or chartered town
burgher arch. citizen of a town or city
burgomaster mayor of a Dutch, Flemish, German, Austrian, or Swiss town (one word)
burgrave hist. governor of a German town or castle
Burgundy region of east central France; Fr. name **Bourgogne**
burgundy red wine from Burgundy (lower case)
burhel use **bharal**
burial ground (two words)
burka (also **burkha, burqa**) enveloping garment worn by some Muslim women
Burke's Peerage guide to peers and baronets first published in 1826
Burkina Faso country in western Africa; former name **Upper Volta** □ **Burkinan**
burl lump in wool or cloth
Burma country in SE Asia; official name **Union of Myanmar**
Burmese pl. same **1** (also **Burman**) member of the largest ethnic group of Burma **2** person from Burma **3** language of Burma **4** short-coated breed of cat; cf. **Birman**
burn (past and past part. **burned** or Brit. **burnt**)
Burne-Jones, Sir Edward (Coley) (1833–98), English artist (hyphen)
burnet (one *t*) **1** plant of the rose family **2** day-flying moth
Burnett, Frances (Eliza) Hodgson (1849–1924), British-born American novelist (two *t*s)
Burney, Fanny (1752–1840), English novelist
burnous (US **burnoose**) hooded cloak worn by Arabs
burnt sienna reddish-brown pigment
bur oak North American oak formerly used in shipbuilding (not **burr**)
burqa var. of **burka**
burr 1 strong pronunciation of the

letter *r* **2** (also **bur**) prickly seed case or flower head **3** (also **bur**) rough edge left by a tool

burrito pl. **burritos** tortilla rolled round a savoury filling

burro pl. **burros** donkey

Burroughs 1 Edgar Rice (1875–1950), American writer, creator of Tarzan **2** William (Seward) (1914–97), American novelist

bursa pl. **bursae** or **bursas** Anat. fluid-filled sac or cavity

Burton 1 Richard (1925–84), Welsh actor; born *Richard Jenkins* **2** Sir Richard (Francis) (1821–90), English explorer and translator **3** Robert (1577–1640), English churchman and scholar

Burton upon Trent town in central England (three words)

Burundi central African country □ **Burundian**

bus n. pl. **buses**; US also **busses.** v. **busses, bussing, bussed** or **buses, busing, bused**

busby tall fur hat worn by hussars and artillerymen (lower case)

Bush 1 George (Herbert Walker) (b.1924), 41st president of the US 1989–93 **2** George W(alker) (b.1946), 43rd president of the US 2001–2009

bushbaby, bushbuck (one word)

bushel (abbrev. **bu.**)

bushido code of honour of the samurai

Bushman member of an aboriginal people of southern Africa

bushman person who lives in the Australian bush (lower case)

businesslike, businessman, businesswoman (one word)

business person (two words)

busman (one word)

buss arch. or N. Amer. kiss

bus shelter, bus station, bus stop (two words)

busybody (one word)

busy Lizzie plant (two words, one cap.)

busyness state of being busy

Buthelezi, Dr Mangosuthu (Gatsha) (b.1928), South African politician

Butler 1 Samuel (1612–80), English poet, author of *Hudibras* **2** Samuel (1835–1902), English novelist, author of *Erewhon*

buttercream, butterfingers, buttermilk, butterscotch (one word)

buttonhole (one word)

buyout n. (one word, two words as verb)

buzzword (one word)

BVI British Virgin Islands

BVM Blessed Virgin Mary

b/w black and white

BWI hist. British West Indies

BWR boiling-water reactor

by and by, by and large (no hyphens)

by-blow, by-catch (hyphen)

Bydgoszcz river port in Poland; Ger. name **Bromberg**

bye pl. **byes** Cricket (abbrev. **b**)

bye-bye (hyphen)

by-election (also **bye-election**) (hyphen)

Byelorussia var. of **Belorussia**

by-form (hyphen)

bygone (one word)

by-law (also **bye-law**) (hyphen)

byline (one word, not **byeline**) **1** line naming the writer of an article **2** part of the soccer goal line to either side of the goal

byname nickname (one word)

bypass (one word)

by-product (hyphen)

byroad, bystander (one word)

byte Comput. group of bits (usu. eight) as a unit; cf. **bit²**

by the by, by the way (no hyphens)

byway, byword (one word)

Byzantine 1 relating to Byzantium, the Byzantine Empire, or the Eastern Orthodox Church **2** excessively complicated or devious

Byzantine Empire empire formed from the eastern part of the Roman Empire (caps)

Byzantium ancient Greek city, from the 4th cent. called Constantinople and now Istanbul

C

C 1 pl. **Cs** or **C's** 3rd letter of the alphabet **2** Phys. capacitance **3** (**C.**) Cape **4** the chemical element carbon **5** Celsius or centigrade **6** Church **7** (**C.**) Command Paper (second series, 1870–99) **8** a computer programming language **9** Conservative **10** Phys. coulomb(s) **11** (also **c**) Roman numeral for 100 [L. *centum* 'hundred']

c 1 Cricket caught by **2** (also **¢**) cent(s) **3** centi- **4** the speed of light in a vacuum

c. century or centuries

c. circa (ital., point, set closed up to following figure)

© copyright

C$ Canadian dollar(s)

C2C consumer-to-consumer

CA 1 California (postal abbrev.) **2** Sc. & Canad. chartered accountant

Ca the chemical element calcium (no point)

ca (circa) use ***c.***

CAA Civil Aviation Authority

Caaba use **Kaaba**

caatinga thorny shrubs and stunted trees in dry areas of Brazil

CAB 1 Citizens' Advice Bureau **2** US Civil Aeronautics Board

cabal secret faction

Cabala, Cabbala vars of **Kabbalah**

caballero pl. **caballeros** Spanish gentleman (not ital.)

Cabernet Sauvignon red wine (caps)

cabin boy, cabin crew (two words)

cabinet sense 'committee of senior ministers' is usu. cap.

cabinetmaker (one word)

cable Naut. 200 yards (182.9 m) or (in the US) 240 yards (219.4 m)

cable car, cable stitch, cable television (two words)

cabochon gem polished but not faceted (not ital.); (***en cabochon***) treated in this way (ital.)

caboodle (in **the whole kit and caboodle**) not **kaboodle**

cabriole Ballet kind of jump (Fr., ital.)

cabriole leg curved leg on furniture

cabriolet 1 car with a roof that folds down **2** small carriage with a hood

ca'canny policy of deliberately limiting output at work (apostrophe)

cacao seeds from which cocoa and chocolate are made

cachalot dated sperm whale

cache v. (**cacheing** or **caching, cached**) □ **cacheable**

cache-sexe G-string or loincloth (Fr., ital.)

cachinnate laugh loudly

cachou pl. **cachous** lozenge sucked to mask bad breath

cachucha Spanish solo dance (not ital.)

cacique chief or boss in South America or the West Indies (not ital.)

cacodemon (also **cacodaemon**) malevolent spirit or person

cacoethes an urge to do something inadvisable

cacography bad handwriting or spelling

cacology bad choice of words or poor pronunciation

cacophony discordant mixture of sounds

cactus pl. **cacti** or **cactuses**

CAD computer-aided design

caddie (also **caddy**) person who carries a golfer's clubs

caddis fly insect with aquatic larvae

caddy 1 storage container **2** var. of **caddie**

cadence 1 modulation of the voice **2** close of a musical phrase

cadency Heraldry status of a younger branch of a family

cadenza Mus. virtuoso solo passage

cadi (also **kadi**) pl. **cadis** Muslim judge

Cadiz port in SW Spain; Sp. name **Cádiz**

cadmium chemical element of atomic

number 48 (symbol **Cd**)
Cadmus Gk Mythol. traditional founder of Thebes ◻ **Cadmean**
cadre group of activists or workers
caduceus pl. **caducei** wand of Hermes or Mercury
caducity frailty or infirmity
caducous Bot. easily detached and shed
CAE computer-aided engineering
caecum (US **cecum**) pl. **caeca** Anat. pouch connected to the intestines
Caedmon (7th cent.), Anglo-Saxon monk and poet
Caerdydd Welsh name for **Cardiff**
Caerfyrddin Welsh name for **Carmarthen**
Caernarfon (also **Caernarvon**) town in NW Wales
Caernarfonshire (also **Caernarvonshire**) former county of NW Wales (abbrev. **Caerns.**)
Caerphilly 1 town in South Wales **2** mild white cheese
caerulean use **cerulean**
Caesar title of Roman emperors
Caesarea ancient port of Palestine
Caesarean (also **Caesarian**) **1** (US **Cesarean** or **Cesarian**) effected by Caesarean section **2** relating to Julius Caesar or the Caesars
caesium (US **cesium**) chemical element of atomic number 55 (symbol **Cs**)
caesura metrical break in a line of verse
CAF N. Amer. cost and freight
cafard melancholia (Fr., ital.)
cafe (no accent) [Fr. *café*]
café au lait (Fr., ital.) **1** coffee with milk **2** light brown colour
café noir black coffee (Fr., ital.)
cafeteria self-service restaurant
cafetière coffee pot (accent, not ital.)
caffè Italian coffee or cafe (ital.)
caffeine (not **-ie-**)
caffè latte, caffè macchiato see **latte, macchiato**
CAFOD Catholic Fund for Overseas Development
caftan var. of **kaftan**
cagey (not **cagy**) ◻ **cagily, caginess**
cagoule (also **kagoul**) hooded waterproof jacket
cahier exercise book or notebook (Fr., ital.)
CAI computer-assisted (or -aided) instruction
Caiaphas Jewish high priest before whom Christ was tried
caiman (also **cayman**) tropical American reptile similar to an alligator
Cain (in the Old Testament) son of Adam and Eve and murderer of his brother Abel
Cainozoic use **Cenozoic**
caique 1 rowing boat on the Bosporus **2** Mediterranean sailing ship
Cairngorm Mountains mountain range in northern Scotland
Cairo capital of Egypt; Arab. name **al-Qahira** ◻ **Cairene**
caitiff arch. contemptible person
Caius Gonville and Caius College, Cambridge
Cajun person from Louisiana descended from French Canadians
CAL computer-assisted (or -aided) learning
Cal large calorie(s) (no point)
cal small calorie(s) (no point)
calabrese variety of broccoli
calamanco pl. **calamancoes** hist. woollen cloth
calamari (also **calamares**) squid as food
Calamity Jane (*c.*1852–1903), American frontierswoman; born *Martha Jane Cannary*
calamus pl. **calami** waterside plant
calando Mus. gradually decreasing in speed and volume
calcareous chalky
calceolaria plant with slipper-shaped flowers
calcium chemical element of atomic number 20 (symbol **Ca**)
calculator (not **-er**)
calculus 1 pl. **calculuses** branch of mathematics **2** pl. **calculi** Med. concretion of minerals in an organ
Calcutta port in eastern India; official name **Kolkata**
Calderón de la Barca, Pedro (1600–81), Spanish dramatist and poet
caldron US var. of **cauldron**

Caledonian Scottish
calendar chart of days and months
calender machine for glazing or smoothing cloth or paper
calends (also **kalends**) first day of the month in the ancient Roman calendar
calf love (two words)
calfskin (one word)
Caliban character in Shakespeare's *The Tempest*
calibre (US **caliber**)
calico pl. **calicoes** unbleached cotton cloth
Calicut former name for **Kozhikode**
California (official abbrev. **Calif.**, postal **CA**) □ **Californian**
californium chemical element of atomic number 98 (symbol **Cf**)
Caligula (AD 12–41), Roman emperor 37–41; born *Gaius Julius Caesar Germanicus*
caliper (also **calliper**)
caliph hist. chief Muslim civil and religious ruler (cap. in titles; not **khalif** exc. in specialist contexts)
calisthenics US var. of **callisthenics**
calix use **calyx**
calk US var. of **caulk**
call centre, call girl (two words)
calligraphy (not **caligraphy**)
Callimachus (*c.*305–*c.*240 BC), Greek poet and scholar
Calliope the Muse of epic poetry
calliope keyboard instrument (lower case)
calliper var. of **caliper**
callisthenics (US **calisthenics**) gymnastic exercises
callous 1 insensitive and cruel **2** var. of **callus**
calloused (also **callused**) having an area of hardened skin
callus (also **callous**) hardened area of the skin
Calor gas trademark liquefied butane in portable containers (one cap.)
calorie unit of energy needed to heat 1 gram of water by 1°C (**small calorie**, abbrev. **cal**) or 1 kilogram by 1°C (**large calorie**, abbrev. **Cal**); not now in scientific use
calque Ling. a loan translation
caltrop 1 spiked metal ball **2** creeping plant (not **caltrap**)
calumet American Indian peace pipe
calumniate defame □ **calumniator**
Calvados apple brandy (cap.)
Calvary hill on which Christ was crucified
Calvin, John (1509–64), French Protestant theologian
calx pl. **calces** oxide formed by heating an ore or mineral
Calypso nymph in the *Odyssey*
calypso pl. **calypsos** West Indian song on a topical theme (lower case)
calyx pl. **calyces** or **calyxes** Bot. sepals of a flower (not **calix**)
CAM computer-aided manufacturing
camaraderie mutual trust and friendship (not ital.)
Camargue region of SE France
Camb. Cambridge
cambium pl. **cambia** Bot. cellular plant tissue
Cambodia country in SE Asia; called the **Khmer Republic** 1970–5 and **Kampuchea** 1976–89
Cambrian 1 Welsh **2** Geol. first period in the Palaeozoic era
cambric white linen or cotton fabric
Cambridge (abbrev. **Camb.**)
Cambridgeshire county of eastern England (abbrev. **Cambs.**)
Cambridge University (two caps)
Cambyses king of Persia 529–522 BC
camcorder (one word)
camel the **Arabian camel** has one hump, the **Bactrian camel** two
camellia flowering shrub (two *ls*)
camelopard arch. giraffe (not **-leo-**)
Camelopardalis northern constellation
Camelot place where King Arthur held his court
Camembert creamy French cheese (cap.)
cameo pl. **cameos**
cameraman (one word)
camera-ready (hyphen)
camerawork (one word)
Cameroon country in West Africa; Fr.

name **Cameroun** ◻ **Cameroonian**
camiknickers (one word)
Camões (also **Camoëns**), Luis (Vaz) de (*c.*1524–80), Portuguese poet
camomile (also **chamomile**) plant of the daisy family
Camorra criminal society originating in Naples
campanile bell tower
Campari trademark pink aperitif
camp bed (two words)
Campbell-Bannerman, Sir Henry (1836–1908), British prime minister 1905–8
Camp David country retreat of the US president
Campeche port and state in SE Mexico
campfire (one word)
Campion, St Edmund (1540–81), English Jesuit priest
campsite (one word)
campus pl. **campuses** grounds and buildings of a university
Campus Martius open space in ancient Rome
CAMRA Campaign for Real Ale
camshaft (one word)
Camulodunum Roman name for **Colchester**
Can. Canada; Canadian
Canaan biblical name for Palestine west of the River Jordan, the Promised Land of the Israelites
canaille the common people, the masses (Fr., ital.)
Canaletto (1697–1768), Italian painter; born *Giovanni Antonio Canale*
canapé piece of bread or pastry with a savoury topping (accent, not ital.)
canard unfounded rumour (not ital.)
Canarese var. of **Kanarese**
canasta card game
Canaveral, Cape cape in Florida, from where the Apollo space missions were launched; known as **Cape Kennedy** 1963–73
Canberra capital of Australia
cancan dance (one word)
cancel n. Printing page or section inserted in a book to replace the original. v. **cancelling, cancelled**; US **-l-**
Cancer fourth sign of the zodiac ◻ **Cancerian**
Cancún resort in SE Mexico (accent)
candela SI unit of luminous intensity (abbrev. **cd**)
candelabrum pl. **candelabra** large branched candlestick or lamp-holder
Candide satire by Voltaire (1759)
candle (also **international candle**) unit of luminous intensity, superseded by the candela
candlelight (one word)
Candlemas Christian festival held on 2 February (one *s*)
candlepower illuminating power expressed in candelas or candles (one word; abbrev. **c.p.**)
candlestick, candlewick (one word)
candour (US **candor**)
C & W country and western (music)
candyfloss (one word)
canister round or cylindrical container (not **-nn-**)
cannabis (lower case exc. for the botanical genus)
cannellini bean, cannelloni (two *n*s, two *l*s)
Cannes resort in southern France
cannibalize (Brit. also **cannibalise**)
cannonball (one word)
cannon fodder (two words)
cannot prefer to **can not** exc. in constructions of the form *can not only ... but also ...*
canoe v. (**canoeing, canoed**)
canon (not **cannon**) **1** general rule or principle **2** member of the clergy
cañon US gorge, canyon (accent, not ital.)
canonize (Brit. also **canonise**)
can opener (two words)
Canova, Antonio (1757–1822), Italian sculptor
canst arch. (no apostrophe)
Cant. Canticles
Cantab of Cambridge University (no point) [L. *Cantabrigia* 'Cambridge']
cantabile Mus. in a smooth singing style
Cantabrigian of Cambridge University
cantaloupe variety of melon

cantata descriptive piece of music with vocal solos
Cantate Psalm 98 (97 in the Vulgate) as a canticle (cap.)
Canterbury city in Kent, SE England
canterbury cabinet for holding music or books (lower case)
Canterbury bell cultivated bellflower (one cap.)
cantharus pl. **canthari** ancient Greek and Roman drinking cup
canticle hymn; (**Canticles** or **Canticle of Canticles**, abbrev. **Cant.**) the Song of Songs (esp. in the Vulgate)
cantilever projecting beam fixed at only one end
canto pl. **cantos** section of a long poem
Canton former name for **Guangzhou**
canton subdivision of a country; Swiss state (lower case)
Cantonese pl. same **1** person from Canton (Guangzhou) **2** form of Chinese spoken in SE China and Hong Kong
cantonment military garrison or camp
cantoris section of a church choir on the north side; cf. **decani**
cantus firmus pl. **cantus firmi** Mus. basic melody in a polyphonic composition (not ital.)
Canute (also **Cnut** or **Knut**) Danish king of England 1017–35, Denmark 1018–35, and Norway 1028–35 (historians prefer the form **Cnut**)
canvas pl. **canvases** or **canvasses** coarse unbleached cloth
canvass solicit votes
caoutchouc unvulcanized rubber
CAP Common Agricultural Policy
cap. (point) **1** capacity **2** capital (city) **3** pl. **caps** or **caps.** capital letter
Capability Brown see **Brown**
Cape Agulhas, Cape Canaveral, etc. see **Agulhas, Cape**; **Canaveral, Cape**, etc.
Cape Breton NE part of Nova Scotia
Čapek, Karel (1890–1938), Czech writer
Cape Province former province of South Africa; known as **Cape Colony** 1814–1910
capercaillie (Sc. also **capercailzie**) large grouse of northern Europe
Capetian of the dynasty ruling France between 987 and 1328
Cape Town legislative capital of South Africa (two words) ◻ **Capetonian**
Cape Verde Islands country consisting of a group of islands off Senegal ◻ **Cape Verdean**
capias Law writ ordering a person's arrest
capital gains tax (abbrev. **CGT**)
capitalize (Brit. also **capitalise**)
capital letter (abbrev. **cap.**)
Capitol **1** seat of the US Congress in Washington DC **2** temple of Jupiter on the Capitoline Hill in ancient Rome
capitulary royal ordinance, esp. under the Merovingian dynasty
capitulum pl. **capitula** Anat. & Bot. compact head of a structure
cap'n captain (apostrophe)
capo pl. **capos** **1** (also **capo tasto**) clamp for raising the pitch of a stringed musical instrument **2** N. Amer. head of a crime syndicate
Capo di Monte type of porcelain
capoeira Brazilian martial art and dance form
Cappadocia ancient region of central Asia Minor
cappuccino pl. **cappuccinos** frothy coffee (two *p*s, two *c*s)
capriccio pl. **capriccios** lively piece of music
capriccioso Mus. in a free and impulsive style
Capricorn tenth sign of the zodiac ◻ **Capricornian**
caps (also **caps.**) capital letters
Capsian Palaeolithic culture of North Africa and southern Europe
capsicum pl. **capsicums** sweet pepper, chilli pepper, etc.
capsize (not **-ise**)
captain (cap. in titles; abbrev. **Capt.**)
Captivity, the the Babylonian Captivity of the Israelites (cap.)
Capuchin Franciscan friar (cap.)
capuchin South American monkey (lower case)
Capulets Juliet's family in Shakespeare's *Romeo and Juliet*; cf. **Montagues**
Car. Charles (regnal year) [L. *Carolus*]
carabineer (also **carabinier**) hist.

cavalry soldier armed with a carbine
carabiner var. of **karabiner**
carabiniere pl. ***carabinieri*** member of the Italian paramilitary police (ital.)
Caracas capital of Venezuela
Caractacus var. of **Caratacus**
caracul var. of **karakul**
carafe glass flask for wine
caramba! expr. surprise (Sp., ital.)
caramelize (Brit. also **caramelise**)
carat (abbrev. **ct**) **1** unit of weight for precious stones and pearls **2** (US **karat**) measure of the purity of gold
Caratacus (also **Caractacus**) (1st cent. AD), British chieftain
Caravaggio, Michelangelo Merisi da (*c.*1571–1610), Italian painter □ **Caravaggesque**
caravanserai (US **caravansary**) pl. **caravanserais** desert inn for travellers
caravel (also **carvel**) Spanish or Portuguese ship of the 15th–17th cents
caraway plant with edible seeds (one *r*)
car bomb n. (two words, hyphen as verb)
carbon chemical element of atomic number 6 (symbol **C**)
carbon-12, **carbon-14** (hyphen)
carbon copy (two words; abbrev. **cc** or **c.c.**)
carbon dating (two words)
Carboniferous fifth period of the Palaeozoic era
carbonize (Brit. also **carbonise**)
carburettor (US **carburetor**; not **-er**)
carcass (Brit. also **carcase**)
Carcassonne walled city in SW France
carcinoma pl. **carcinomas** or **carcinomata** a cancer
Card. Cardinal (point)
cardamom spice (not **cardamum**)
cardholder (one word)
Cardiff the capital of Wales; Welsh name **Caerdydd**
Cardiganshire former county of SW Wales; now **Ceredigion**
cardinal Roman Catholic Church dignitary (cap. in titles; abbrev. **Card.**)
card sharp, card table, card vote (two words)
careen **1** turn (a ship) for cleaning or repair **2** N. Amer. move fast, career
carefree (one word)
caret mark (^, ‸) placed below a line of text to indicate a proposed insertion
caretaker, careworn (one word)
carex pl. **carices** kind of sedge
cargo pl. **cargoes** or **cargos**
Carib member of an indigenous South American people
Caribbean (one *r*, two *b*s)
Cariboo Mountains mountain range in British Columbia, Canada
caribou pl. same, N. Amer. reindeer
CARICOM Caribbean Community and Common Market
carillon set of bells
carina pl. **carinae** or **carinas** Zool. keel-shaped structure
Carinthia state of southern Austria; Ger. name **Kärnten**
carioca **1** person from Rio de Janeiro **2** Brazilian dance
cariole var. of **carriole**
caritas Christian love of humankind, charity (not ital.)
carl (also **carle**) arch. peasant or villein
carline **1** kind of thistle **2** piece of timber supporting the deck of a ship
Carlisle city in Cumbria, NW England
Carlist supporter of Spanish pretender Don Carlos (1788–1855)
carload (one word)
Carlovingian var. of **Carolingian**
Carlyle, Thomas (1795–1881), Scottish writer □ **Carlylean**
carmaker (one word)
Carmarthen town in SW Wales; Welsh name **Caerfyrddin**
Carmarthenshire county of South Wales
Carmelite friar or nun of an order founded at Mount Carmel in Israel
Carnac Neolithic site in Brittany; cf. **Karnak**
Carnatic Engl. form of **Karnataka** in SW India
Carnaval des animaux suite by Saint-Saëns (1886)
Carné, Marcel (1906–96), French film director (accent)

carnelian (also **cornelian**) semi-precious stone
carnet (not ital.) **1** a permit **2** book of tickets for public transport
carnival festival (not **carne-**)
carol v. (**carolling, carolled**; US one **-l-**)
Caroline (also **Carolean**) of the reigns of Charles I and II of England
Carolingian (also **Carlovingian**) of the Frankish dynasty founded by Charlemagne's father
Carolinian person from South or North Carolina
carol-singing, carol-singer (hyphen)
carom N. Amer. shot in billiards or pool
carouse drink and enjoy oneself □ **carousal**
carousel N. Amer. merry-go-round
carpaccio pl. **carpaccios** thin slices of raw beef (not ital.)
car park (two words)
Carpathian Mountains mountain system of eastern Europe
carpe diem seize the day! (L., ital.)
carpet v. (**carpeting, carpeted**)
carpetbagger (one word)
carpet-bomb (hyphen)
car phone (two words)
carpus pl. **carpi** Anat. the wrist
Carracci family of 16th-cent. Italian painters
carrageen (also **carragheen**) edible red seaweed
carrageenan thickening agent extracted from carrageen
Carrara town in Italy, famous for the marble quarried there
carraway use **caraway**
carriageway (one word)
carriole (also **cariole**) horse-drawn carriage for one person
Carroll, Lewis (1832–98), English writer; pseudonym of *Charles Lutwidge Dodgson*
carryall, carrycot (one word)
carry-on n. (hyphen, two words as verb)
carsick (one word)
carte Fencing var. of **quart**
carte blanche complete freedom to use one's discretion (not ital.)
carte de visite pl. ***cartes de visite*** small photograph of someone (Fr., ital.)
Cartesian relating to René Descartes
Carthage ancient city on the coast of North Africa □ **Carthaginian**
carthorse (one word)
Carthusian monk or nun of an order founded by St Bruno
Cartier-Bresson, Henri (1908–2004), French photographer
cartouche decorative representation of a scroll
cartwheel, cartwright (one word)
carvel-built Naut. having external planks which do not overlap; cf. **clinker-built**
Carver US wooden chair with arms and a rush seat (cap.)
carver Brit. principal chair in a set of dining chairs (lower case)
Cary, (Arthur) Joyce (Lunel) (1888–1957), English novelist
caryatid pl. **caryatides** or **caryatids** pillar in the form of a female figure
Casablanca 1 largest city of Morocco **2** (***Casablanca***) Bogart film (1942)
Casals, Pablo (1876–1973), Spanish cellist; Catalan name *Pau Casals*
Casanova 1 Giovanni Jacopo (1725–98), Italian adventurer; full name *Giovanni Jacopo Casanova de Seingalt* **2** a notorious seducer (cap.)
casbah var. of **kasbah**
case Printing **1** partitioned container for loose metal type **2** capital or minuscule form of a letter
casebook (one word)
casebound (of a book) hardback (one word)
case history (two words)
casein protein in milk
case law (two words)
case-sensitive (hyphen)
case study (two words)
casework (one word)
cashback (one word)
cash card, cash crop, cash desk, cash flow (two words)
cashpoint trademark (one word)
cash register (two words)
casino pl. **casinos**
Caslon, William (1692–1766), English

type founder

Casnewydd Welsh name for **Newport**

Caspar one of the three Magi

Cassandra Gk Mythol. Trojan princess whose prophecies, though true, were disbelieved

cassata Neapolitan ice cream (not ital.)

cassation Mus. informal 18th-cent. composition

Cassation, Court of court of appeal in France

cassava tuberous root used as food in tropical countries; manioc

Cassell publishers

Cassiopeia 1 Gk Mythol. mother of Andromeda **2** constellation

cassis (not ital.) **1** (also **crème de cassis**) blackcurrant liqueur **2** wine from Cassis near Marseilles

Cassivellaunus ancient British chieftain of the 1st cent. AD

cast actors in a play or film

castaway n. (one word, two words as v.)

caste hereditary class of Hindu society

Castel Gandolfo summer residence of the Pope near Rome

castellated having battlements

Castell-Nedd Welsh name for **Neath**

caster 1 person or machine that casts **2** var. of **castor**

caster sugar (also **castor sugar**) finely granulated white sugar

Castile region of central Spain; Sp. name **Castilla** □ **Castilian**

cast iron (two words, hyphen when attrib.)

Castlereagh, Robert Stewart, Viscount (1769–1822), British Tory statesman

cast-off n. Printing final page produced before the whole book is proofed, to ascertain the book's length (hyphen, two words as verb)

Castor 1 Gk Mythol. twin brother of Pollux **2** second-brightest star in the constellation Gemini

castor¹ (also **caster**) **1** small swivelling wheel on furniture **2** container with holes for sprinkling the contents

castor² 1 arch. beaver **2** oily substance secreted by beavers

castrato pl. **castrati** hist. male singer castrated in boyhood

casual relaxed and unconcerned; cf. **causal**

casuist person who uses clever but false reasoning □ **casuistry**

casus belli pl. same, cause of a war (L., ital.)

casus foederis pl. same, event covered by the terms of an alliance (L., ital.)

CAT 1 clear air turbulence **2** computer-assisted testing **3** Med. computerized axial tomography

catabolism Biol. breakdown of complex molecules (not **katabolism**)

catachresis pl. **catachreses** incorrect use of a word

cataclasm violent break or disruption

cataclysm violent upheaval or disaster

catafalque decorated framework to support a coffin

Catalan relating to Catalonia

catalogue (US **catalog**) v. (**cataloguing, catalogued**; US **cataloging, cataloged**)

catalogue raisonné pl. **catalogues raisonnés** descriptive catalogue of works of art (accent, not ital.)

Catalonia autonomous region of NE Spain; Catalan name **Catalunya**; Sp. name **Cataluña**

catalyse (US **catalyze**)

catamaran yacht with twin hulls

cataphora Gram. use of a word referring forward to a later word; cf. **anaphora**

catarrh excess mucus (two *r*s, one *h*)

catarrhine Zool. denoting primates that lack a prehensile tail; cf. **platyrrhine**

Catawba pl. same **1** US variety of grape **2** member of a North American Indian people

catcall (one word)

catch-22 inescapable dilemma (lower case exc. as title of 1961 novel by Joseph Heller)

catch-all, catch-as-catch-can (hyphens)

catchline, catchphrase (one word)

catchup (one word) **1** old-fashioned term for **ketchup 2** var. of **catch-up**

catch-up an act of catching someone up (hyphen)

catchword (one word) **1** slogan or encapsulation **2** word placed in a prominent position

catechism religious instruction by question and answer
catechize (Brit. also **catechise**)
catechumen Christian preparing for baptism or confirmation
categorize (Brit. also **categorise**)
catena pl. **catenae** or **catenas** chain or series, esp. of early Christian texts
caters system of change-ringing using nine bells
Cath. 1 Cathedral **2** Catholic
Cathars medieval Christian sect
catharsis pl. **catharses** release of pent-up emotions
Cathay name for China in medieval Europe
cathedral (cap. in names; abbrev. **Cath.**)
Catherine de' Medici (1519–89), queen of France, wife of Henry II
Catherine II (1729–96), empress of Russia 1762–96; known as **Catherine the Great**
Catherine of Aragon (1485–1536), first wife of Henry VIII (divorced)
Catherine, Duchess of Cambridge (b.1982), wife of Prince William, born *Catherine Elizabeth Middleton*
Catherine, St (died *c.*307), early Christian martyr
Catherine wheel firework (one cap.)
cathode negatively charged electrode (not **kathode**)
cathode ray tube (abbrev. **CRT**)
Catholic of the Roman Catholic faith (abbrev. **Cath.**)
catholic wide or all-embracing (lower case)
Catholic Emancipation (caps)
Catholicism (cap.)
Catiline (*c.*108–62 BC), Roman conspirator; Latin name *Lucius Sergius Catilina*
cation Chem. positively charged ion; cf. **anion**
catlike (one word)
cat-o'-nine-tails whip (hyphens, apostrophe)
cat's cradle, cat's eye (two words, apostrophe)
Catskill Mountains range of mountains in New York State
cat's paw (two words, apostrophe)
catsuit (one word)
catsup US var. of **ketchup**
cat's whisker (two words, apostrophe)
cattleya tropical American orchid
Catullus, Gaius Valerius (*c.*84–*c.*54 BC), Roman poet
catwalk (one word)
Caucasian dated as an anthropological term; used esp. in the US to mean 'white or of European origin'
Cauchy, Augustin Louis, Baron (1789–1857), French mathematician
caucus pl. **caucuses 1** political meeting to select candidates or decide policy **2** group within a larger organization
caudillo pl. **caudillos** Spanish leader (cap. as title of General Franco)
cauldron (US **caldron**)
caulk (US also **calk**) seal, make waterproof
causal relating to a cause; cf. **casual**
'cause because (apostrophe)
cause célèbre pl. **causes célèbres** controversial issue (accents, not ital.)
causerie informal article or talk on a literary subject (not ital.)
cauterize (Brit. also **cauterise**)
cava Spanish sparkling wine (not ital.)
Cavafy, Constantine (1863–1933), Greek poet; born *Konstantinos Petrou Kavafis*
Cavalier hist. supporter of King Charles I
cavalier casual, offhand (lower case)
cavatina pl. **cavatine** or **cavatinas** Mus. simple operatic aria or lyrical instrumental piece
caveat warning or proviso (not ital.)
caveat emptor let the buyer beware (L., ital.)
caveman (one word)
caviar (also **caviare**)
cavil (**cavilling, cavilled**; US one **-l-**) make petty objections
Cavour, Camillo Benso, Conte di (1810–61), Italian statesman
Cawnpore former name of **Kanpur**
Caxton, William (*c.*1422–91), the first English printer
Cayenne capital of French Guiana
cayenne hot pepper (lower case)
cayman var. of **caiman**
Cayman Islands group of three islands

in the Caribbean

CB **1** Law Chief Baron **2** Citizens' Band **3** Companion of the Order of the Bath

CBC Canadian Broadcasting Corporation

CBE Commander of the Order of the British Empire

CBI Confederation of British Industry

CBS Columbia Broadcasting System

CC **1** City Council **2** Companion of the Order of Canada **3** County Council; County Councillor **4** Cricket Club **5** Roman numeral for 200

cc (also **c.c.**) **1** carbon copy **2** cubic centimetre(s)

CCC Corpus Christi College

CCF Combined Cadet Force

CCJ county court judgment

CCTV closed-circuit television

CD **1** civil defence **2** pl. **CDs** compact disc **3** corps diplomatique

Cd (no point) **1** the chemical element cadmium **2** Command Paper (third series, 1900–18)

cd candela

CDC **1** US Centers for Disease Control **2** Commonwealth Development Corporation

CD-R trademark in the US compact disc recordable

Cdr Commander

Cdre Commodore

CD-ROM compact disc read-only memory

CD-RW compact disc rewritable

CDT Central Daylight Time

CE **1** Church of England **2** civil engineer

Ce the chemical element cerium (no point)

CE Common Era (used instead of AD in non-Christian contexts; small caps, follows the numerals)

ceasefire (one word)

Ceauşescu, Nicolae (1918–89), president of Romania 1974–89

cecum US var. of **caecum**

cedilla mark ¸ under a letter, esp. to show that a *c* is pronounced like an *s*

Ceefax trademark BBC teletext service

ceilidh Scottish or Irish gathering with folk music and dancing

Celebes former name for **Sulawesi**

celestial hierarchy (in Christian angelology) seraphim, cherubim, thrones, dominations, principalities, powers, virtues, archangels, and angels

celiac US var. of **coeliac**

cellar (not **celler**)

Cellini, Benvenuto (1500–71), Italian goldsmith and sculptor

cello pl. **cellos** violoncello (no apostrophe) □ **cellist**

cellophane trademark transparent wrapping material

cell phone mobile phone (two words)

Celsius temperature scale; prefer to **centigrade** (abbrev. **C**, written after number)

Celt, Celtic (not **K-**)

celt Archaeol. prehistoric cutting tool (lower case)

Celtic Church (caps)

cembalo pl. **cembalos** harpsichord

cemetery (not **-try, -tary**)

CEng (also **C.Eng.**) chartered engineer

cenobite (also **coenobite**) member of a monastic community

Cenozoic Geol. most recent era (not **Cainozoic**)

censer container in which incense is burnt

censor suppress unacceptable parts of

censorious severely critical

censure criticize severely, reprove

census pl. **censuses** official count of a population

cent monetary unit equal to one hundredth of a dollar or other decimal currency (abbrev. **c** or **ct**; symbol **¢**)

cent. pl. **cents** or **cents.** century (point)

centaury plant of the gentian family

centavo pl. **centavos** monetary unit of Mexico, Brazil, etc.

centenarian person a hundred or more years old

centenary Brit. hundredth anniversary

centennial adj. relating to a hundredth anniversary. n. chiefly US hundredth anniversary

center US var. of **centre** etc.

centesimal relating to division into hundredths

centesimo pl. **centesimos** former

monetary unit of Italy
centésimo pl. **centésimos** monetary unit of Uruguay and Panama (accent)
centigrade (lower case; abbrev. **C**); prefer **Celsius**
centigram metric unit equal to one hundredth of a gram (abbrev. **cg**; not **-gramme**)
centilitre (US **centiliter**) metric unit equal to one hundredth of a litre (abbrev. **cl**)
centime one hundredth of a franc
centimetre (US **centimeter**) metric unit equal to one hundredth of a metre (0.394 in.) (abbrev. **cm**)
cento pl. **centos** compilation of quotations from different authors
Central African Republic country of central Africa
Central America Guatemala, Belize, Honduras, El Salvador, Nicaragua, Costa Rica, and Panama
central Europe (one cap.)
centralize (Brit. also **centralise**)
Central Powers 1 Germany, Austria-Hungary, Turkey, and Bulgaria in WWI **2** Germany, Austria-Hungary, and Italy 1882–1914
centre (US **center**)
centreboard, centrefield, centrefold (one word)
centre forward, centre half (two words)
centrepiece (one word)
centre spread, centre stage (two words)
cents (also **cents.**) centuries
centurion commander of an ancient Roman century
century (abbrev. **c.** or **cent.**)
CEO chief executive officer
ceorl var. of **churl**
cep edible mushroom
cephalic of the head
Cephalonia Greek island in the Ionian Sea; Gk name **Kefallinía**
Cerberus Gk Mythol. monstrous watchdog at the entrance to Hades
cerebellum pl. **cerebella** part of the brain at the back of the skull
cerebrospinal, cerebrovascular (one word)
cerecloth hist. waxed cloth for wrapping corpses
Ceredigion county of western mid Wales
Cerenkov, Pavel, see **Cherenkov**
Cerenkov radiation (also **Cherenkov radiation**) Phys.
Ceres Gk Mythol. goddess of agriculture; Rom. equivalent **Demeter**
cerium chemical element of atomic number 58 (symbol **Ce**)
CERN Conseil Européen pour la Recherche Nucléaire, former title of the European Organization for Nuclear Research
cert. (point) **1** certificate **2** certified
CertEd (also **Cert. Ed.**) Certificate in Education
certiorari Law writ by which a higher court reviews a case
cerulean of a deep blue colour (not **caerulean**)
Cervantes, Miguel de (1547–1616), Spanish author of *Don Quixote*; full name *Miguel de Cervantes Saavedra*
cervix pl. **cervices** Anat. **1** lower end of the womb **2** neck
Cesarean (also **Cesarian**) US var. of **Caesarean**
Cesarewitch annual horse race at Newmarket, England
cesium US var. of **caesium**
cesser Law termination or cessation
cesspit, cesspool (one word)
c'est la vie that's life! (Fr., ital.)
cestui que trust Law beneficiary of a trust
CET Central European Time
ceteris paribus other things being equal (L., ital.)
Cévennes mountain range in south central France
Ceylon former name for **Sri Lanka**
Cézanne, Paul (1839–1906), French painter
CF 1 Chaplain to the Forces **2** cystic fibrosis
Cf the chemical element californium (no point)
cf. compare with (point) [L. *confer*]
c.f. carried forward (points)

CFA Communauté Financière Africaine (African Financial Community)
CFC pl. **CFCs** chlorofluorocarbon
CFE College of Further Education
cg centigram(s)
CGI Comput. **1** Common Gateway Interface **2** computer-generated imagery
CGS Chief of the General Staff
cgs centimetre-gram-second
CGT capital gains tax
CH Companion of Honour
ch. (point) **1** pl. **chs** or **chs.** chapter **2** (of a horse) chestnut **3** church
Chablis dry white burgundy wine (cap.)
cha-cha (also **cha-cha-cha**) ballroom dance (hyphen)
chaconne composition or dance in slow triple time
chacun à son goût each to their own taste (Fr., ital.)
Chad country in northern central Africa □ **Chadian**
chador (also **chaddar** or **chuddar**) headscarf worn by Muslim women
chaffinch (one word)
Chagall, Marc (1887–1985), Russian-born French artist
chaîné pl. ***chaînés*** Ballet sequence of fast turns (Fr., ital.)
chain gang, **chain mail**, **chain reaction** (two words)
chainsaw (one word)
chain-smoke, **chain-smoker** (hyphen)
chairman, **chairperson**, **chairwoman** (one word)
chaise longue pl. **chaises longues** sofa with a backrest at one end (not ital.)
chal (fem. **chai**) Gypsy
chalaza pl. **chalazae** Zool. strip joining the yolk to the shell in a bird's egg
Chalcedon former city on the Bosporus, now part of Istanbul
chalcedony quartz occurring in a microcrystalline form
Chaldea ancient country in what is now southern Iraq □ **Chaldean**
Chaldee 1 language of the ancient Chaldeans **2** dated Aramaic
Chaliapin, Fyodor (Ivanovich) (1873–1938), Russian operatic bass
challenged uses as an alternative to **disabled** or **handicapped** (e.g. *physically challenged*) have gained little currency; found only in humorous contexts (e.g. *vertically challenged*)
chalumeau pl. **chalumeaux** 18th-cent. reed instrument
chamaeleon use **chameleon**
Chamberlain 1 (Arthur) Neville (1869–1940), British prime minister 1937–40 (Con.), son of Joseph Chamberlain **2** Joseph (1836–1914), British statesman
chambermaid (one word)
chamber music, **chamber pot** (two words)
Chambers's Encyclopaedia (two *s*s)
Chambertin red burgundy wine (cap.)
chambray gingham cloth
chambré (of red wine) at room temperature (Fr., ital.)
chameleon lizard with the ability to change colour (not **chamaeleon**)
chamois pl. same **1** goat-antelope found in mountainous areas **2** soft pliable leather (var. of **shammy**)
chamomile var. of **camomile**
Chamonix ski resort in the Alps of eastern France
champagne white sparkling wine from Champagne in NE France (lower case)
champaign flat open country
champerty Law illegal agreement
champignon mushroom or toadstool (Fr., ital.)
Champlain, Samuel de (1567–1635), French explorer and colonial statesman
champlevé enamelwork (Fr., ital.)
Champs-Élysées avenue in Paris
chancellery position or department of a chancellor (not **-ory**)
chancellor (cap. in titles)
Chancellor of the Exchequer (caps)
chance-medley Law accidental killing of a person in a fight (hyphen)
Chancery Lord Chancellor's court, a division of the High Court of Justice
chancre ulcer, esp. in venereal disease
Chandigarh city and Union Territory in NW India
Chanel, Coco (1883–1971), French

couturière; born *Gabrielle Bonheur Chanel*
changeable (not **-gable**)
changeover n. (one word, two words as verb)
change-ringing ringing of bells in a constantly varying order (hyphen)
Chang Jiang var. of **Yangtze**
channel v. (**channelling, channelled**; US one **-l-**)
Channel Islands group of islands in the English Channel (abbrev. **CI**)
chanson French song (ital.)
chanson de geste pl. ***chansons de geste*** French medieval epic poem (ital.)
chansonnier writer or performer of French songs (ital.)
chant (not **chaunt** (arch.))
chanteuse female singer of popular songs (not ital.)
chantey (also **chanty**) US or arch. var. of **shanty**
Chantilly town near Paris in France
chantry endowed chapel
Chanukah var. of **Hanukkah**
chap. pl. **chaps** or **chaps.** chapter
chaparajos (also **chaparejos**) fuller form of **chaps**
chapatti pl. **chapattis** (also **chapati**) cake of Indian unleavened bread (not **chupatty**)
chapbook (one word)
chapeau-bras pl. ***chapeaux-bras*** hist. three-cornered hat carried under the arm (Fr., ital.)
chapel royal pl. **chapels royal**
chaperone (also **chaperon**)
Chappaquiddick Island island off Massachusetts, scene of a car accident involving Senator Edward Kennedy
chaps[1] trousers worn by cowboys; chaparajos
chaps[2] (also **chaps.**) chapters
chapter (abbrev. **ch.** or **chap.**)
char[1] (**charring, charred**) partially burn
char[2] var. of **charr**
charabanc early form of bus (not **char-à-banc**)
characterize (Brit. also **characterise**)
charcuterie cold cooked meats, or a shop selling them (not ital.)
Chardonnay white wine (cap.)
chargé d'affaires pl. **chargés d'affaires** ambassador's deputy (accent, not ital.)
Charge of the Light Brigade, The poem by Alfred Tennyson (1854)
chargrill (one word)
charisma 1 compelling charm **2** pl. **charismata** divinely conferred power
charivari (US also **shivaree**) pl. **charivaris** mock serenade
Charlemagne (742–814), king of the Franks 768–814 and Holy Roman emperor (as Charles I) 800–14
Charles's Wain Astron. the Plough
Charleston[1] **1** capital of West Virginia **2** port in South Carolina
Charleston[2] dance of the 1920s (cap.)
charlotte, charlotte russe puddings (lower case)
Charolais pl. same, breed of white beef cattle (not **Charollais**)
Charon Gk Mythol. old man who ferried the dead to Hades
charpoy Ind. light bedstead
charr (also **char**) trout-like fish
Chartist advocate of UK parliamentary reform 1837–48 (cap.)
Chartres city in northern France
chartreuse pale green or yellow liqueur (lower case)
charwoman (one word)
Charybdis Gk Mythol. whirlpool opposite the cave of the sea monster Scylla
Chas. Charles (point as formal abbrev. and regnal year; no point when used as informal name)
Chasid, Chasidism (also **Chassid, Chassidism**) vars of **Hasid, Hasidism**
chasse liqueur drunk after coffee (not ital.) [Fr. *chasse-café*]
chassé (**chassés, chasséing, chasséd**) (perform) a gliding step in dancing (accent, not ital.)
chassis pl. same, base frame of a vehicle
chastise (not **-ize**)
chateau pl. **chateaux** castle (not ital., no accent) [Fr. *château*]
Chateaubriand, François-René, Vicomte de (1768–1848), French writer
chateaubriand thick fillet of beef steak (lower case, not ital.)
chatelain (fem. **chatelaine**) person in charge of a house [Fr. *châtelain(e)*]

chat room, **chat show** (two words)
Chattanooga city in Tennessee, scene of a battle in the American Civil War
Chatto & Windus publishers
Chaucer, Geoffrey (*c.*1342–1400), English poet □ **Chaucerian**
chauffeur (fem. **chauffeuse**) driver
chaunt use **chant**
chauvinism, **chauvinist** (lower case)
ChB (also **Ch.B.**) Bachelor of Surgery [L. *Chirurgiae Baccalaureus*]
Ch.Ch. Christ Church, Oxford
CHD coronary heart disease
cheapskate (one word)
Chechnya (also **Chechenia**) autonomous republic in SW Russia; also called **Chechen Republic**
check US var. of **cheque**
checkers N. Amer. the game draughts
check-in n. (hyphen, two words as verb)
checking account (Canad. **chequing account**) N. Amer. bank current account
checklist, **checkmate** (one word)
checkout n. (one word, two words as verb)
checkpoint (one word)
check-up n. (hyphen, two words as verb)
Cheddar kind of cheese (cap.)
cheekbone (one word)
cheerleader (one word)
cheeseboard, **cheeseburger**, **cheesecake**, **cheesecloth** (one word)
cheesy (not **-ey**)
chef a cook
chef d'école pl. ***chefs d'école*** initiator of a school of art etc. (Fr., ital.)
chef-d'œuvre pl. ***chefs-d'œuvre*** masterpiece (Fr., ital.)
cheiromancy var. of **chiromancy**
Cheka Soviet secret police 1917–22
Chekhov, Anton (Pavlovich) (1860–1904), Russian dramatist and short-story writer □ **Chekhovian**
Chellean former term for **Abbevillian**
Chelyabinsk city in southern Russia
chem. chemistry (point)
chemin de fer card game (not ital.)
chemise (not ital.) **1** woman's nightdress or undergarment **2** dress hanging from the shoulders
Chemnitz city in eastern Germany; former name **Karl-Marx-Stadt**
Chennai official name for **Madras**
cheongsam dress worn by Chinese and Indonesian women
Cheops (*fl.* early 26th cent. BC), Egyptian pharaoh
cheque (US **check**) order to a bank to pay a stated sum
chequer, **chequered** (US **checker**, **checkered**)
Chequers country seat in Buckinghamshire of the British prime minister
Cherbourg port in northern France
chère amie pl. ***chères amies*** female lover, girlfriend (Fr., ital.)
Cherenkov (also **Cerenkov**), Pavel (Alekseevich) (1904–90), Soviet physicist, discoverer of **Cerenkov radiation**
chéri (fem. ***chérie***) darling (Fr., ital.)
Chernobyl town in Ukraine, scene of an accident at a nuclear power station
chernozem fertile black soil
Cherokee pl. same or **Cherokees** member of an American Indian people
Chersonese ancient name for the Gallipoli peninsula
cherub pl. **cherubs** or **cherubim** angelic being
Cherubini, (Maria) Luigi (1760–1842), Italian composer
Cherwell river running into the Thames at Oxford
Chesapeake Bay inlet of the North Atlantic on the US coast
Cheshire county of NW England (abbrev. **Ches.**)
Chesil Beach shingle beach off the Dorset coast
chessboard, **chessman** (one word)
chess piece, **chess player**, **chess set** (two words)
Chester city in NW England
Chesterfield town in Derbyshire
chesterfield sofa with a padded back and arms (lower case)
Chester-le-Street town in County Durham (hyphens)
Chesvan var. of **Hesvan**
Chetnik WWII Serbian guerrilla (cap.)
chetrum pl. same or **chetrums** monetary unit of Bhutan

cheval glass tall mirror on a frame

chevalier French knight (not ital.)

chevet Archit. apse giving access to chapels behind the high altar

chevron V-shaped line or stripe

chevrotain deer-like mammal

Chevy pl. **Chevys** Chevrolet car

Chevy Chase, The Ballad of 15th-cent. English ballad

Cheyenne pl. same or **Cheyennes** member of an American Indian people

Cheyne–Stokes breathing Med. abnormal pattern of breathing (en rule)

chez at the home of (not ital.)

Chhattisgarh state in central India

chi¹ twenty-second letter of the Greek alphabet (**Χ**, **χ**), transliterated as 'kh' or 'ch'

chi² (also **qi** or **ki**) life force in Chinese philosophy

Chiang Kai-shek (also **Jiang Jie Shi**) (1887–1975), president of China 1928–31 and 1943–9 and of Taiwan 1950–75

Chianti pl. **Chiantis** red Italian wine

chiaroscuro pl. **chiaroscuros** treatment of light and shade

chiasma pl. **chiasmata** Anat. structure at the crossing of the optic nerves

chiasmus Rhet. inversion of the order of words

chibouk (also **chibouque**) Turkish tobacco pipe

chic (**chicer**, **chicest**) stylish (not ital.)

Chicago city in Illinois, US
□ **Chicagoan**

Chicano pl. **Chicanos**; fem. **Chicana**, pl. **Chicanas** North American of Mexican descent

Chichele, Henry (*c.*1362–1443), Archbishop of Canterbury 1414–43

Chichén Itzá site in Mexico, the centre of the later Mayan empire

Chichimec pl. same or **Chichimecs** member of a group of peoples formerly dominant in central Mexico

Chickasaw pl. same or **Chickasaws** member of an American Indian people

chickenpox (one word)

chickpea (one word)

chicory 1 plant with edible leaves and root **2** N. Amer. endive

chide (past **chided** or arch. **chid**; past part. **chided** or arch. **chidden**)

chiffchaff common warbler (one word)

chiffonier (not ital.) **1** Brit. low cupboard **2** N. Amer. tall chest of drawers

chignon coil of hair (not ital.)

Chihuahua state of northern Mexico

chihuahua very small breed of dog (lower case)

chilblain swelling on a hand or foot (not **chill-**)

childbearing, **childbed**, **childbirth**, **childcare** (one word)

Childe arch. youth of noble birth

Childermas arch. feast of the Holy Innocents, 28 December (not **-mass**)

childlike, **childminder**, **childproof** (one word)

Chile country in South America
□ **Chilean**

chiliad group of a thousand things

chilli (US also **chile** or **chili**) pl. **chillies**, US **chiles** or **chilies** hot-tasting pepper

Chiltern Hundreds Crown manor, whose administration is a nominal office for which an MP applies as a way of resigning from the House of Commons

chimera (also **chimaera**) **1** Gk Mythol. monster with a lion's head, a goat's body, and a serpent's tail **2** something hoped for but illusory

chimney pl. **chimneys**

Ch'in, **Ch'ing** vars of **Qin**, **Qing**

chin-chin drinking toast (hyphen)

Chindit member of the Allied forces in Burma in 1943–5

chinoiserie decoration with Chinese motifs (lower case, not ital.)

chinos casual trousers made from a cotton twill fabric

chip and PIN method of payment

chipboard (one word)

chipmunk ground squirrel (not **-monk**)

Chirac, Jacques (René) (b.1932), French prime minister 1974–6 and 1986–8 and president 1995–2007

chi-rho the symbol ☧, a monogram of chi (X) and rho (P), the first two letters of Greek *Khristos* 'Christ'

chiromancy (also **cheiromancy**) palmistry

Chiron Gk Mythol. wise centaur
chiropodist person who treats the feet (not **cheiro-**)
chiropractic complementary medicine based on treating misalignments of the joints (not **cheiro-**) □ **chiropractor**
chirrup (**chirruping, chirruped**)
chisel v. (**chiselling, chiselled**; US one **-l-**)
Chişinău capital of Moldova; Russ. name **Kishinyov**
Chittagong seaport in SE Bangladesh
chivvy (**chivvying, chivvied**) harass (not **chivy**)
chlamydia pl. same or **chlamydiae** parasitic bacterium
chlorine chemical element of atomic number 17 (symbol **Cl**)
chloroform liquid formerly used as a general anaesthetic
chlorophyll green pigment which allows plants to absorb light
chloroplast structure in green plant cells in which photosynthesis takes place
ChM (also **Ch.M.**) Master of Surgery [L. *Chirurgiae Magister*]
chock-a-block, chock-full (hyphens)
chocolatier maker or seller of chocolate (not ital.)
Choctaw pl. same or **Choctaws** member of an American Indian people
choirboy, choirmaster (one word)
choler arch. **1** bodily humour identified with bile **2** anger or irascibility
cholera bacterial disease of the small intestine
choleraic arch. infected with cholera
cholera morbus acute gastroenteritis
choleric bad-tempered or irritable
cholesterol fatty compound present in most body tissues
choliamb Prosody modification of the iambic trimeter, with a final spondee or trochee
Chomsky, (Avram) Noam (b.1928), American theoretical linguist □ **Chomskyan**
choosy (not **-ey**)
chop-chop hurry up! (hyphen)
Chopin, Frédéric (François) (1810–49), Polish-born French composer; Polish name *Fryderyk Franciszek Szopen*
chopstick (one word)
chop suey Chinese dish (two words)
choral sung by a choir or chorus
chorale stately hymn tune, or a composition based on one
chord Anat. var. of **cord**
choreography sequence of steps and movements in dance; cf. **chorography**
chorizo pl. **chorizos** spicy Spanish pork sausage
chorography description and mapping of regions; cf. **choreography**
chorus (**choruses, chorusing, chorused**)
chota peg Ind. small drink of whisky
choucroute sauerkraut (Fr., ital.)
Chou En-lai var. of **Zhou Enlai**
choux light pastry used for eclairs and profiteroles (not ital.)
chow mein Chinese dish (two words)
Chr. Chronicles
Chr. Coll. Cam. Christ's College, Cambridge
Chrétien de Troyes (12th cent.), French poet
Christ title given to Jesus, also treated as a name □ **Christlike**
Christchurch 1 city in New Zealand **2** town in Dorset
Christ Church Oxford college (not **Christ Church College**; abbrev. **Ch.Ch.**)
Christian, Christianity (cap.)
Christian era era beginning with the traditional date of Christ's birth
Christiania former name for **Oslo**
Christianize (Brit. also **Christianise**)
Christian name prefer **given name, forename**, or **first name**
Christie Skiing, dated type of sudden turn
Christie's auctioneers (apostrophe)
Christmas pl. **Christmases**
Christmas Day, Christmas Eve (caps)
Christ's College, Cambridge (abbrev. **Chr. Coll. Cam.**)
chromatography Chem. technique for the separation of a mixture
chrome yellow bright yellow pigment
chromium chemical element of atomic

number 24 (symbol **Cr**)
chromolithograph coloured picture printed by lithography
chromosome Biol. structure in a cell nucleus carrying genetic information
Chronicles either of two books of the Old Testament (abbrev. **1 Chr., 2 Chr.**)
chrysalis pl. **chrysalises** dormant insect pupa
chrysanthemum pl. **chrysanthemums** plant with bright ornamental flowers
chryselephantine (of ancient Greek sculpture) overlaid with gold and ivory
Chrysler US car company
chrysoprase green gemstone
Chrysostom, St John (*c.*347–407), Doctor of the Church, bishop of Constantinople
chs (also **chs.**) chapters
chthonic (also **chthonian**) of the underworld
chuddar var. of **chador**
chukka (US **chukker**) period of play in a game of polo
Chunnel, the informal the Channel Tunnel
chupatty use **chapatti**
church cap. in the names of institutions, e.g. the *Church of England*; abbrev. **C** or **ch.**
churchgoer, churchgoing (one word)
Churchill, Sir Winston (Leonard Spencer) (1874–1965), British prime minister 1940–5 and 1951–5 ◻ **Churchillian**
Church Slavonic language of the Orthodox Church in Russia, Serbia, etc.
churchwarden, churchyard (one word)
churinga sacred object among Australian Aboriginals
churl (also **ceorl**) hist. serf or low-ranking freeman
Churrigueresque of a lavishly ornamented Spanish baroque style
chutzpah self-confidence or audacity (not ital.)
chypre heavy sandalwood perfume
CI Channel Islands
Ci curie (no point)
CIA Central Intelligence Agency
ciabatta Italian bread made with olive oil (not ital.)
ciao Italian for 'hello' or 'goodbye' (not ital.)
Cibber, Colley (1671–1757), English comic actor and dramatist, Poet Laureate 1730–57
cicada bug that makes a droning noise
cicatrix (also **cicatrice**) pl. **cicatrices** scar
cicatrize (Brit. also **cicatrise**) heal by scar formation
Cicero, Marcus Tullius (106–43 BC), Roman orator ◻ **Ciceronian**
cicerone pl. **ciceroni** guide
cicisbeo pl. **cicisbei** or **cicisbeos** married woman's male companion or lover
CID Criminal Investigation Department
Cid, El see **El Cid**
cider (not **cyder** (arch.))
ci-devant former (Fr., ital.)
CIE hist. Companion (of the Order) of the Indian Empire
c.i.f. cost, insurance, freight
CIGS hist. Chief of the Imperial General Staff
cilantro N. Amer. coriander
cilium pl. **cilia** Biol. microscopic hair-like structure
cill var. of **sill**
cimbalom Hungarian dulcimer
C.-in-C. commander-in-chief
Cincinnati city in Ohio
cineaste (also **cineast**) fan of the cinema
cine camera (two words)
CinemaScope trademark cinematographic process (one word, two caps)
cinéma-vérité style of film-making characterized by realism (Fr., ital.)
cineraria plant of the daisy family
cinerarium pl. **cinerariums** place where funeral urn is kept
Cingalese use **Sinhalese**
cingulum pl. **cingula** **1** girdle or belt **2** Anat. bundle of nerve fibres
cinquecento the 16th cent. as a period of Italian art and literature (lower case, not ital.)
Cinque Ports medieval ports in Kent and East Sussex, orig. Hastings, Sandwich, Dover, Romney, and Hythe; later

also Rye and Winchelsea
cinques Bell-ringing system of change-ringing
Cintra var. of **Sintra**
Cinzano trademark an Italian vermouth
CIO Congress of Industrial Organizations
cion use **scion**
cipher (also **cypher**) **1** a code **2** dated a zero
cipolin Italian marble with white and green streaks [It. *cipollino*]
circa (with dates) approximately (abbrev. ***c.***, set closed up to figures)
Circe enchantress in Homer's *Odyssey*
circiter approximately, circa (L., ital.)
circuit board, circuit breaker (two words)
circularize (Brit. also **circularise**) distribute circulars to
circumcise (not **-ize**)
circumflex the mark ^ placed over a letter
Cirencester town in Gloucestershire
cire perdue method of casting bronze (Fr., 'lost wax', ital.)
cirque Geol. steep-sided hollow
cirrhosis chronic liver disease
cirrus pl. **cirri** **1** cloud forming wispy streaks **2** Zool. & Bot. tendril
CIS Commonwealth of Independent States
cis- on this side of
cis- Chem. denoting a type of isomer
cisalpine on the southern (Roman) side of the Alps (lower case exc. in **Cisalpine Gaul**)
cisatlantic on the same side of the Atlantic as the speaker
cislunar between the earth and the moon
cispontine on the north side of the River Thames; cf. **transpontine**
cist (also **kist**) Archaeol. coffin or burial chamber
Cistercian monk or nun of an order that is a branch of the Benedictines
cit. citation; cited
Citizens' Band range of radio frequencies (abbrev. **CB**)
Citlaltépetl highest peak in Mexico
citrine **1** lemon colour **2** variety of quartz
Citroën French car company
citrus pl. **citruses** lemon, lime, orange, etc. (tree or fruit)
city use **the City** for London's financial area; abbrev. in name of sports clubs **C**
City Company corporation descended from a trade guild of London (caps)
Ciudad Bolívar city in SE Venezuela; former name **Angostura**
civilize (Brit. also **civilise**)
Civil List annual allowance to meet the expenses incurred by the Queen in her role as head of state (caps)
civil servant (lower case)
civil service caps as the proper name of a particular country's administration
CJ Chief Justice
CJD Creutzfeldt–Jakob disease
Cl the chemical element chlorine (no point)
cl centilitre (no point)
Clackmannanshire council area and former county of central Scotland
clairvoyant (not ital.)
clamorous (not **clamour-**)
clamour (US **clamor**)
clampdown n. (one word, two words as verb)
clangour (US **clangor**) □ **clangorous**
claptrap nonsense, rubbish (one word)
claque group of people hired to applaud or heckle (not ital.) □ **claqueur**
clarabella organ stop
Clare College, Clare Hall Cambridge colleges
Clarenceux Heraldry second King of Arms
Clarendon Press former imprint used by Oxford University Press for academic books
Clare of Assisi, St (1194–1253), Italian abbess, founder of the 'Poor Clares'
claret red wine, esp. from Bordeaux (lower case)
clarinettist player of a clarinet
Clark, William (1770–1838), American explorer
Clarke, Sir Arthur C(harles) (1917–2008), English writer of science fiction

class. classic, classical; classification
classes botanical and zoological classes should be in roman with capital initials
classic 1 of acknowledged excellence **2** simple and elegant **3** very typical of its kind
classical 1 relating to the cultures of ancient Greece and Rome **2** representing the highest standard within a form **3** written in the tradition of formal European music, *c.*1750–1830 (after Baroque and before Romantic)
Classics study of ancient Greek and Latin literature, philosophy, and history (cap.)
classmate, classroom (one word)
Claude Lorrain (also **Lorraine**) (1600–82), French painter; born *Claude Gellée*
Claudius (10 BC–AD 54), Roman emperor 41–54; full name *Tiberius Claudius Drusus Nero Germanicus* □ **Claudian**
Clausewitz, Karl von (1780–1831), Prussian general □ **Clausewitzian**
Clay, Cassius, see **Muhammad Ali**
clayey of or resembling clay
clean-cut, clean-living, clean-shaven (hyphen)
clearcole hist. primer for distemper (one word)
clear-cut, clear-headed (hyphen)
clearing bank, clearing house (two words)
clear-out n. (hyphen, two words as verb)
clear-sighted (hyphen)
clearstory US var. of **clerestory**
clearway (one word)
cleave (past **clove, cleft**, or **cleaved**; past part. **cloven, cleft**, or **cleaved**)
cleft lip not **harelip**
cleistogamy Bot. self-fertilization within a permanently closed flower
Clemenceau, Georges (Eugène Benjamin) (1841–1929), French prime minister 1906–9 and 1917–20
Clemens, Samuel Langhorne, see **Twain**
Cleopatra (also **Cleopatra VII**) (69–30 BC), queen of Egypt 47–30
clepsydra pl. **clepsydras** or **clepsydrae** ancient water clock
clerestory (US **clearstory**) upper part of a church, containing a series of windows
clerihew short comic verse on a famous person
clerisy learned or literary people as a group
Clermont-Ferrand city in central France
Cleveland[1] 1 former county of NE England **2** city in NE Ohio
Cleveland[2], (Stephen) Grover (1837–1908), 22nd and 24th president of the US 1885–9 and 1893–7
clevis U-shaped or forked metal connector
clew 1 Naut. lower corner of a sail **2** arch. ball of thread **3** arch. var. of **clue**
cliché (accent) **1** unoriginal phrase etc. **2** Printing stereotype or electrotype □ **clichéd**
clientele clients collectively
Clifden nonpareil large moth
cliffhanger, cliffhanging (one word)
climacteric 1 critical period or event **2** Med. the menopause
climactic forming an exciting climax
climatic relating to climate
climbdown n. (one word, two words as verb)
cling film (two words)
clinker-built Naut. having external planks which overlap; cf. **carvel-built** (not **clincher-built**)
Clio the Muse of history
cliometrics technique for interpreting economic history (treated as sing.)
clipboard (one word)
clique small close-knit group □ **cliquey, cliquish**
CLit (also **C.Lit.**) Companion of Literature
clitoris part of the female genitals □ **clitoral**
Cllr Councillor
cloaca pl. **cloacae 1** Zool. cavity for the release of both excretory and genital products **2** arch. sewer
cloakroom (one word)
cloche 1 cover for plants **2** woman's close-fitting hat
clock face, clock radio, clock tower (two words)

clockwise, **clockwork** (one word)
cloisonné enamel work with colours separated by strips of wire (Fr., ital.)
closed-circuit television (hyphen; abbrev. **CCTV**)
close-knit (hyphen)
close season (N. Amer. **closed season**) **1** period when fishing or the killing of game is forbidden **2** Brit. part of the year when a sport is not played
closet v. (**closeting, closeted**)
closing time (two words)
clotbur plant with burred fruits
clothe (past and past part. **clothed** or arch. or literary **clad**)
Clotho Gk Mythol. one of the three Fates
cloture procedure for ending a debate; closure (not ital.) [Fr. *clôture*]
clou point of greatest interest (Fr., ital.)
cloud cuckoo land (three words, lower case; in ref. to the *Birds* of Aristophanes one word, cap.)
clough N. Engl. ravine
clove hitch a knot (two words)
club foot deformed foot (two words); also called **talipes** □ **club-footed**
clubhouse, **clubmate** (one word)
clue piece of evidence (not **clew** (arch.))
Cluniac monk of a Benedictine order founded at Cluny in France
Clwyd former county of NE Wales
Clyde, Firth of estuary of the River Clyde in SW Scotland
Clytemnestra Gk Mythol. wife of Agamemnon; in Gk contexts **Klytaimnestra**
CM 1 common metre **2** Member of the Order of Canada
Cm the chemical element curium (no point)
Cm. Command Paper (sixth series, 1986–) (point)
cm centimetre(s) (no point)
Cmd Command Paper (fourth series, 1918–56)
Cmdr Commander
Cmdre Commodore
CMEA Council for Mutual Economic Assistance
CMG Companion (of the Order) of St Michael and St George
Cmnd Command Paper (fifth series, 1956–86)
Cn the chemical element copernicium (no point)
CNAA Council for National Academic Awards
CND Campaign for Nuclear Disarmament
CNN Cable News Network
Cnossos use **Knossos**
cnr corner
CNS central nervous system
CN Tower tower in Toronto, Canada [*C*anadian *N*ational (Railways)]
Cnut var. of **Canute** (form preferred by historians)
CO 1 Colorado (in official postal use) **2** Commanding Officer **3** conscientious objector
Co the chemical element cobalt (no point)
Co. 1 company **2** county: *Co. Cork*
c/o care of
coachload, **coachman** (one word)
coagulum pl. **coagula** a clot
coal black (two words, hyphen when attrib.)
coalface, **coalfield**, **coalman** (one word)
coal tit small bird (not **cole tit**)
coastguard, **coastline** (one word)
coatimundi (also **coati**) pl. **coatimundis** raccoon-like animal
coat of arms (three words)
coat-tails (hyphen)
co-author (hyphen)
coaxial (of a cable) having two wires (one word)
cobalt chemical element of atomic number 27 (symbol **Co**)
Cobbett, William (1763–1835), English writer
cobblestone (one word)
Cobden, Richard (1804–65), English political reformer
coble flat-bottomed fishing boat
cobnut (one word)
COBOL (also **Cobol**) computer programming language
coca tropical American shrub whose leaves are the source of cocaine
Coca-Cola trademark soft drink (hyphen)
coccyx pl. **coccyges** or **coccyxes** Anat. bone at the base of the spinal column

Cochin-China former name for southern Vietnam
cochineal scarlet dye for colouring food
cochlea pl. **cochleae** Anat. cavity of the inner ear
cock-a-hoop overjoyed (hyphens)
Cockaigne imaginary country of ease and luxury
cock-a-leekie Scottish chicken soup (hyphens)
cockatiel small crested Australian parrot
cockatoo crested Australian parrot
cockatrice mythical reptile; basilisk
Cockcroft, Sir John Douglas (1897–1967), English physicist
cockcrow (one word)
Cockerell, Sir Christopher Sydney (1910–99), English inventor of the hovercraft
cockeyed, cockfight, cockpit, cockroach (one word)
cockney pl. **cockneys** (lower case)
cockscomb 1 crest or comb of a domestic cock **2** tropical plant; cf. **coxcomb**
cockswain use **coxswain**
cocoa powder made from cacao seeds
coconut (not **cocoanut** (arch.))
Cocos Islands group of islands in the Indian Ocean, an external territory of Australia
COD cash on delivery; N. Amer. collect on delivery
COD *Concise Oxford Dictionary* (now called the *Concise Oxford English Dictionary*)
codeine analgesic drug (not **-ie-**)
code name (two words)
codex pl. **codices** or **codexes** ancient manuscript in book form
codfish (one word)
cod liver oil (three words)
Cody, William Frederick, see **Buffalo Bill**
coed N. Amer. dated female student (one word)
co-editor, co-educational (hyphen)
coefficient (one word)
coelacanth marine fish known only from fossils until 1938
coelenterate Zool. aquatic invertebrate such as a jellyfish or sea anemone
coeliac (US **celiac**) Anat. relating to the abdomen
coenobite var. of **cenobite**
coenzyme substance necessary for the functioning of an enzyme (one word)
coeternal existing with something else eternally (one word)
Coetzee, J(ohn) M(axwell) (b.1940), South African novelist
Cœur de Lion name given to Richard I
coeval of the same age (one word)
coexist, coextensive (one word)
C of E Church of England (no points)
coffee bar, coffee cup, coffee shop, coffee table (two words)
cofferdam watertight enclosure in construction work (one word)
co-founder (hyphen)
cogito, ergo sum I think, therefore I am (said by Descartes)
cognac brandy (not ital.)
cognize (Brit. also **cognise**) become aware of
cognomen third name or family name of an ancient Roman citizen, as Marcus Tullius *Cicero*
cognoscenti well-informed people (not ital.)
cogwheel (one word)
cohabit (one word)
COI Central Office of Information
coiffeur (fem. **coiffeuse**) hairdresser (not ital.)
coign 1 angle of a wall **2** (**coign of vantage**) position for observation
Cointreau trademark orange-flavoured liqueur (cap.)
coitus, coitus interruptus (not ital.)
Coke trademark Coca-Cola
coke cocaine (lower case)
Col. 1 Colonel **2** Epistle to the Colossians
col. pl. **cols** or **cols.** column
cola (lower case) **1** carbonated soft drink **2** (also **kola**) African tree or its nut
colander strainer (not **collander**)
colcannon Irish dish of cabbage and potatoes
Colchester town in Essex; Roman name **Camulodunum**

Colchis ancient region south of the Caucasus
cold-blooded, cold-hearted (hyphen)
Colditz castle in Germany used as a camp for Allied prisoners in WWII
cold war (lower case)
coleopteran beetle
Coleraine town in Northern Ireland
Coleridge, Samuel Taylor (1772–1834), English poet
coleslaw (one word)
cole tit use **coal tit**
Colette (1873–1954), French novelist; born *Sidonie Gabrielle Claudine*
colic abdominal pain caused by wind in the intestines □ **colicky**
coliseum large theatre or stadium; (**Coliseum**) theatre in London; see also **Colosseum**
Coll. 1 Collected or Collection **2** College
collage form of art in which materials are stuck to a backing
collapsar Astron. star that has collapsed under its own gravity
collapsible (not **-able**)
collarbone (one word)
collect. collectively
collectable (also **collectible**, esp. in ref. to things of interest to collectors)
collectanea passages collected from various sources (not ital.)
collector's item (apostrophe)
college (cap. in names; abbrev. **Coll.**)
College of Arms corporation which records and grants armorial bearings
collegium pl. **collegia 1** society of amateur musicians, esp. at a German or US university **2** hist. administrative board in Russia
col legno Mus. played with the back of the bow
Colles fracture Med. kind of wrist fracture (no apostrophe)
collogue (**colloguing, collogued**) arch. talk confidentially
collop slice of meat
colloquial (of language) informal (abbrev. **colloq.**)
colloquium pl. **colloquiums** or **colloquia** conference or seminar
colloquy conversation
collotype printing process
Colo. Colorado (official abbrev.)
Cologne city in western Germany; German name **Köln**
cologne eau de cologne; toilet water (lower case)
Colombia country in South America; cf. **Columbia** □ **Colombian**
Colombo capital of Sri Lanka (not **Columbo**)
Colón chief port of Panama
colón pl. **colones** monetary unit of Costa Rica and El Salvador
colonel rank of army officer above lieutenant colonel (cap. in titles; abbrev. **Col.**) □ **colonelcy**
Colonel Blimp pompous reactionary person (caps)
colonel-in-chief pl. **colonels-in-chief** honorary head of a regiment in the British army (hyphens)
colonize (Brit. also **colonise**)
colonnade row of columns (two *ns*)
colophon publisher's emblem or imprint
colophony rosin
color US var. of **colour**
Colorado state in the central US (official abbrev. **Colo.**, postal **CO**) □ **Coloradan**
coloration (also **colouration**) arrangement of colour, colouring
coloratura elaborate ornamentation of a vocal melody (not ital.)
Colosseum amphitheatre in Rome, the *Amphitheatrum Flavium*; cf. **coliseum**
Colossians, Epistle to the book of the New Testament (abbrev. **Col.**)
colossus pl. **colossi** person or thing of enormous size
Colossus of Rhodes ancient bronze statue of the sun god Helios
colour (US **color**)
colourant (US **colorant**)
colouration var. of **coloration**
coloured (US **colored**) avoid using **coloured** of black people exc. in ref. to South Africa, where it denotes people of mixed-race parentage and is not generally considered offensive
colourist, colourless (US **colorist, colorless**)
colourway (US **colorway**) (one word)

colporteur seller or distributor of books or religious material
cols (also **cols.**) columns
colter US var. of **coulter**
colubrine of or resembling a snake
columbarium pl. **columbaria** room or building for storing funeral urns
Columbia 1 river in NW North America **2** state capital of South Carolina; cf. **Colombia**
Columbia, District of see **District of Columbia**
Columbus, Christopher (1451–1506), Italian-born Spanish explorer; Spanish name *Cristóbal Colón*
column (abbrev. **col.**)
coma[1] **1** state of prolonged unconsciousness **2** pl. **comae** Astron. cloud of gas and dust around the nucleus of a comet
Comanche pl. same or **Comanches** member of an American Indian people
combat v. (**combating, combated** or **combatting, combatted**)
combustible (not **-able**)
comeback n. (one word, two words as verb)
Comecon former association of east European countries
Comédie-Française, La French national theatre (caps, hyphen)
comedienne female comedian (but **comedian** is often preferred for both sexes)
Comedy of Errors Shakespeare play (abbrev. ***Comm. Err.***)
comedy of manners (lower case)
comeuppance (one word)
comfit arch. a sweet; cf. **confit**
COMINT communications intelligence
Comintern the Third International, a communist organization (1919–43)
comitia ancient Roman assembly
commander (abbrev. **Cdr**)
commander-in-chief pl. **commanders-in-chief** (hyphens; abbrev. **C.-in-C.**)
Commander of the Faithful one of the titles of a caliph (caps)
commando pl. **commandos**
Command Paper document laid before Parliament by order of the Crown (abbrev. **C.** (1870–99), **Cd** (1900–18), **Cmd** (1918–56), **Cmnd** (1956–86), **Cm.** (1986–))
comme ci, comme ça indifferent(ly), so-so (Fr., ital.)
commedia dell'arte Italian comic theatre of the 16th–18th cents (It., ital.)
comme il faut correct in behaviour or etiquette (Fr., ital.)
commemorate (three *ms*)
Commemoration annual celebration at Oxford University in memory of founders and benefactors
commencement (in North America and at Cambridge University) ceremony in which degrees are conferred
commentator (not **-or**)
commercialize (Brit. also **commercialise**)
commère female compère (Fr., ital.)
commingle (two *ms*)
commis chef junior chef (not ital.)
commissary deputy or delegate
commissionaire uniformed door attendant
commit (**committing, committed**)
commitment (one *t*)
commodore naval rank above captain (cap. in titles; abbrev. **Cdre, Cmdre**)
Common Entrance examination taken by candidates for public school (caps)
Common Era another term for **Christian era** (caps; abbrev. CE)
common law (two words, hyphen when attrib.)
Common Market the EEC
common metre metrical pattern for hymns (abbrev. **CM**)
commonplace (one word)
Common Pleas (in full **Court of Common Pleas**) court for hearing civil cases (abbrev. **CP**)
common room (two words)
Commons, the the House of Commons
common sense (two words, hyphen when attrib.) □ **commonsensical**
Common Serjeant circuit judge of the Central Criminal Court
commonwealth independent state or community; (**the Commonwealth** or **Commonwealth of Nations**) association of the UK and former countries of the British Empire

communard a member of a commune; (**Communard**) supporter of the Paris Commune of 1871
communion cap. in ref. to Holy Communion
communiqué official announcement (accent, not ital.)
communism, communist cap. in ref. to Marxist–Leninist system in the Soviet Union etc.
commutator device for reversing the direction of flow of electric current
commuter person who commutes to work
Comoros country consisting of a group of islands in the Indian Ocean □ **Comoran**
compact disc (abbrev. **CD**)
Companion member of the lowest grade of certain orders of knighthood
companion-in-arms (hyphens)
companionway set of steps leading down from a ship's deck (one word)
company (abbrev. **Co.** or Mil. **Coy**)
comparative (not **-itive**)
compare (abbrev. **cf.**)
compass point no points in abbrevs of compass points, e.g. *SE*
compatible (not **-able**)
compendious comprehensive but concise
compendium pl. **compendiums** or **compendia**
compère person who introduces variety acts (accent, not ital.)
complacent smug and self-satisfied
complaisant willing to accept the behaviour of others
Compleat Angler, The book by Izaak Walton (1653)
complement n. thing that contributes beneficial extra features. v. contribute extra features to □ **complementary**
complexion (not **complection**)
compliment n. expression of praise or admiration. v. congratulate or praise
complimentary **1** expressing praise or admiration **2** free of charge
compline Roman Catholic service of evening prayers (lower case)
compositor person who arranges type for printing or keys text into a composing machine
compos mentis in one's right mind (not ital.)
compote fruit cooked in syrup (not ital., no accent)
comprehensible (not **-able**)
comprise (not **-ize**; avoid construction **comprise of**)
compromise (not **-ize**)
compte rendu pl. ***comptes rendus*** formal report or review (Fr., ital.)
Compton-Burnett, Dame Ivy (1884–1969), English novelist
comptroller controller (used in the title of some financial officers)
computerize (Brit. also **computerise**)
computer-literate (hyphen)
Comte, Auguste (1798–1857), French philosopher □ **Comtean** (also **Comtian**)
comte (or ***comtesse***) French nobleman or noblewoman (cap. in titles; not ital. as part of name)
Con. **1** (of an MP) Conservative **2** constable
con¹ (**conning, conned**) **1** deceive **2** (US **conn**) Naut. steer (a ship)
con² disadvantage of, argument against (no point)
con³ a convict (no point)
Conakry capital of Guinea
con amore Mus. with tenderness
Conan Doyle see **Doyle**
con brio Mus. with vigour
concave curving inwards; cf. **convex**
concentre (US **concenter**) concentrate in a small space
Concepción city in Chile
concertgoer (one word)
concert hall (two words)
concertina v. (**concertinaing, concertinaed** or **concertina'd**)
concertino pl. **concertinos** simple or short concerto
concerto pl. **concertos** or **concerti** composition for a solo instrument accompanied by an orchestra
concerto grosso pl. **concerti grossi** composition for a group of solo instruments accompanied by an orchestra
concessionaire holder of a concession

or grant [Fr. *concessionnaire*]
conch pl. **conches** or **conchs** shell
conchie conscientious objector (not **conchy**)
concierge caretaker of a building (not ital.)
concinnity elegance of literary style
concision conciseness
Concord 1 capital of New Hampshire **2** town in NE Massachusetts; cf. **Concorde**
concord agreement, harmony [Fr. *concorde*]
concordance list of the words in a text or used by an author
concordat agreement or treaty
Concorde supersonic airliner; cf. **Concord**
concours d'élégance pl. same, exhibition of vintage motor vehicles (Fr., ital.)
concourse open area inside or in front of a building
concur (**concurring, concurred**)
condominium pl. **condominiums** **1** joint control of a state's affairs by other states **2** N. Amer. building or complex containing a number of individual flats or houses
condottiere pl. ***condottieri*** hist. leader of a troop of mercenaries (It., ital.)
conductor (not **-er**)
conductus pl. **conducti** medieval musical setting of a Latin text
coney (also **cony**) pl. **coneys** rabbit
Coney Island coastal resort in New York City
confectionary adj. relating to confectionery
confectionery n. sweets and chocolates
confederacy league or alliance; (**the Confederacy**) the Confederate States
confederate joined by an agreement or treaty; (**Confederate**) denoting the southern states which separated from the US in 1860–1
confer (**conferring, conferred**) ◻ **conferree, conferment, conferral**
confessor (not **-er**)
confetti small pieces of paper thrown at a wedding
confidant (fem. **confidante**) person in whom one confides (not ital.)
confit meat, esp. duck, cooked slowly in its own fat; cf. **comfit** (not ital.)
confrère colleague (not ital.)
Confucius (551–479 BC), Chinese philosopher; Latinized name of *Kongfuze* (*K'ung Fu-tzu*) ◻ **Confucian**
conga v. (**congaing, congaed** or **conga'd**)
congé dismissal or rejection (Fr., ital.)
congeries pl. same, disorderly collection (not ital.)
Congo country in central Africa; capital, Brazzaville; full name **Republic of Congo**; sometimes known as **Congo-Brazzaville** ◻ **Congolese**
Congo, Democratic Republic of large country in central Africa; capital, Kinshasa; former name (1971–97) **Zaire** ◻ **Congolese**
Congregationalist member of a Christian denomination (cap.)
Congress US legislative body, composed of the Senate and the House of Representatives (cap.)
conjoined twins prefer to **Siamese twins**
conjugate Gram. give the different forms of (a verb); cf. **decline**
conjunctiva pl. **conjunctivae** Anat. mucous membrane in front of the eye and inside the eyelids
conjuror (also **conjurer**) magician
con man (two words)
con moto Mus. with movement
Connacht (also **Connaught**) province of the Republic of Ireland
Connecticut state in the north-eastern US (official abbrev. **Conn.**, postal **CT**)
connection Brit. var. **connexion** is dated exc. in ref. to association of Methodist Churches
connector (not **-er**)
Connemara coastal region of Galway in the Republic of Ireland
connivance willingness to allow something wrong
connoisseur expert judge in matters of taste
connotation idea which a word invokes in addition to its primary meaning
connote imply or suggest (something) in

addition to the literal or primary meaning; cf. **denote**

Conquest, the invasion of England by William of Normandy in 1066

conquistador pl. **conquistadores** or **conquistadors** 16th-cent. Spanish conqueror of Mexico or Peru (not ital.)

Conrad, Joseph (1857–1924), Polish-born British novelist; born *Józef Teodor Konrad Korzeniowski*

Cons. (of an MP) Conservative

conscientious wishing to do what is right

consensus (not **concensus**)

conservative cap. in a political context; abbrev. **C**, **Con.**, or **Cons.**

Conservative Judaism, **Conservative Party** (caps)

conservatoire (N. Amer. **conservatory**) college of classical music (not ital.)

Consols British government securities with fixed annual interest

consommé clear soup (accent, not ital.)

con sordino Mus. using a mute

consortium pl. **consortia** or **consortiums** association of companies etc.

conspectus pl. **conspecti** overview of a subject (not ital.)

constable police officer (cap. in titles; abbrev. **Con.**, **Const.**)

Constance, Lake lake in SE Germany; Ger. name **Bodensee**

Constanţa (also **Constanza**) port in Romania

Constantine (*c.*274–337), Roman emperor; known as **Constantine the Great**

Constantinople name for Istanbul 330–1453

constitution cap. in ref. to the US principles of federal government

consuetude chiefly Sc. a custom, esp. one with legal force

consul 1 diplomat based in a foreign city **2** ancient Roman chief magistrate (lower case)

Consul General pl. **Consuls General** consul of the highest status (two words, caps)

cont. 1 contents **2** continued

contact lens (two words)

contadino pl. ***contadini***; fem. ***contadina***, pl. ***contadine*** Italian peasant (ital.)

***conte* 1** short story or medieval narrative tale [Fr.] **2** Italian count (cap. in titles; not ital. as part of name) [It.]

contemn arch. treat or regard with contempt

contemporaneous in the same period of time □ **contemporaneity**

contemporary (not **-pory**)

contemptible (not **-able**)

conterminous having the same boundaries; coterminous

contessa Italian countess (cap. in titles; not ital. as part of name)

continent, **continental** cap. in ref. to mainland Europe as distinct from Britain

continual constantly or frequently occurring; cf. **continuous**

continuo (also **basso continuo**) pl. **continuos** accompanying part in baroque music

continuous without interruption, unbroken; cf. **continual**

continuum pl. **continua** continuous sequence with gradual variation

contr. contracted; contraction

Contra opponent of the Nicaraguan Sandinista government 1979–90

contra prep. against

contrabass (also **contrabasso**) Mus. **1** a double bass **2** part of an octave below the normal bass range

contraction word shortened by elision or combination

contractor (not **-er**)

contralto pl. **contraltos** lowest female singing voice

contra mundum defying or opposing everyone else (L., ital.)

contrariwise in the opposite way (not **contrary-**)

contratenor Mus. singing part

contredanse French country dance (ital.)

contretemps minor dispute (not ital.)

contributor (not **-er**)

con trick (two words)

control (**controlling**, **controlled**)

control freak (two words)

contumacious arch. or Law wilfully disobedient to authority
contumelious arch. insolent
conundrum pl. **conundrums** puzzling problem
convener (also **convenor**) person who calls a meeting
conversazione pl. ***conversaziones*** or ***conversazioni*** gathering for learned conversation (It., ital.)
converter (also **convertor**)
convertible (not **-able**)
convex curving outwards; cf. **concave**
conveyor belt (not **-er**)
Convocation assembly of Church of England clergy or of certain universities (cap.)
convolvulus pl. **convolvuluses** twining plant
Conwy (also **Conway**) town and county in North Wales
cony var. of **coney**
cooee (**cooees, cooeeing, cooeed**) (make) a call
Cook 1 Captain James (1728–79), English explorer **2** Thomas (1808–92), English travel agent
cookbook (one word)
cookie N. Amer. sweet biscuit (not **cooky**)
coolibah (also **coolabah**) Australian gum tree
coolie 1 dated unskilled labourer in Asia **2** offens. person from the Indian subcontinent
Co-op name for the UK retail chain the **Co-operative Group**
coop cage for poultry
co-op a cooperative organization (hyphen)
Cooper, James Fenimore (1789–1851), American novelist
cooperate, cooperation, cooperative (one word, though hyphen also used)
co-opt (hyphen)
coordinate, coordination (one word, though hyphen also used)
co-own (hyphen)
Copacabana Beach resort in Brazil near Rio de Janeiro
coparcener Law joint heir □ **coparcenary**
copeck var. of **kopek**
Copenhagen capital of Denmark; Danish name **København**
copernicium chemical element of atomic number 112 (symbol **Cn**)
Copernicus, Nicolaus (1473–1543), Polish astronomer; Latinized name of *Mikołaj Kopernik* □ **Copernican**
copier (not **copyer**)
co-pilot (hyphen)
Copland, Aaron (1900–90), American composer (not **Copeland**)
copolymer Chem. (one word)
cop-out n. (hyphen, two words as verb)
copper chemical element of atomic number 29 (symbol **Cu**)
Copper Age (caps)
copperas crystals of hydrated ferrous sulphate
copperplate old style of round handwriting (one word)
Coppola, Francis Ford (b.1939), American film director
Copt 1 native Egyptian in the Hellenistic and Roman periods **2** member of the Coptic Church
Coptic language of the Copts
Coptic Church native Christian Church in Egypt
copula Logic & Gram. connecting word
copybook, copycat (one word)
copy-edit, copy-editor (hyphen)
copyholder 1 hist. type of feudal tenant **2** clasp or stand for holding sheets of text (one word)
copyright (one word; symbol ©)
copy typist (two words)
copywriter (one word)
coq au vin casserole of chicken in red wine (not ital.)
coquette a flirt □ **coquettish, coquetry**
Cor. Epistle to the Corinthians
coram populo in public (L., ital.)
cor anglais pl. **cors anglais** woodwind instrument (not ital.)
corbel projection jutting out from a wall to support a structure
Corcyra ancient name for **Corfu**
cord (Anat. also **chord**)
cordillera system of mountain ranges
Cordoba (also **Cordova**) **1** city in

southern Spain; Sp. name **Córdoba** **2** city in Argentina

cordoba monetary unit of Nicaragua

cordon-bleu pl. **cordon-bleus** African waxbill (bird) (hyphen)

cordon bleu (of cookery) of high class (two words, not ital.)

cordon sanitaire pl. **cordons sanitaires** line preventing anyone from leaving an infected area (not ital.)

Cordova var. of **Cordoba**

corduroy ribbed cotton fabric

CORE US Congress of Racial Equality

co-respondent person cited in a divorce case (hyphen)

corf pl. **corves** wagon or basket formerly used for coal

Corfu Greek island; ancient name **Corcyra**; modern Gk name **Kérkira**

corgi pl. **corgis** small breed of dog

Corinth city in Greece; mod. Gk name **Kórinthos** □ **Corinthian**

Corinthians, Epistle to the either of two books of the New Testament (abbrev. **1 Cor.**, **2 Cor.**)

Coriolanus Shakespeare play (abbrev. ***Coriol.***)

corn cereal crop, esp. (in England) wheat, (in Scotland) oats, (in the US) maize

corncob, corncrake (one word)

Corneille, Pierre (1606–84), French dramatist

cornelian var. of **carnelian**

cornerstone (one word)

cornetto pl. **cornetti** old woodwind instrument

cornfield, cornflour, cornflower (one word)

cornice moulding just below a ceiling

corniche road cut into a cliff; (**the Corniche**) the coast road from Nice to Genoa

Corn Laws 19th-cent. laws to protect British farmers (caps)

cornu pl. **cornua** Anat. horn-shaped projection (not ital.)

cornucopia horn of plenty (lower case)

Cornwall western county of England; Cornish name **Kernow**

corolla Bot. petals of a flower

corollary conclusion or consequence

corona pl. **coronae** Astron., Phys., Anat., Bot.

Corot, (Jean-Baptiste) Camille (1796–1875), French landscape painter

Corp. N. Amer. Corporation

corpora pl. of **corpus**

corporal[1] rank of non-commissioned army officer (cap. in titles; abbrev. **Cpl**)

corporal[2] relating to the body

corporeal physical as opposed to spiritual

corposant arch. an appearance of St Elmo's fire

corps pl. same, group or military subdivision

corps de ballet members of a ballet company who dance together (not ital.)

corps d'elite select group of people [Fr. *corps d'élite*]

corpus pl. **corpuses** or **corpora** **1** collection of texts **2** Anat. main body of a structure

Corpus Christi feast commemorating the institution of the Eucharist

Corpus Christi College Oxford, Cambridge (abbrev. **CCC**)

corpuscle red or white blood cell

corpus delicti Law circumstances constituting a crime

corpus luteum pl. **corpora lutea** Anat. ovarian body

Correggio, Antonio Allegri da (*c.*1494–1534), Italian painter; born *Antonio Allegri*

corregidor pl. ***corregidores*** Spanish magistrate (ital.)

correlation mutual relationship of interdependence (not **corelation**)

correspondence (not **-ance**)

corrida bullfight (not ital.)

corridor (not **-door**, **-der**)

corrigendum pl. **corrigenda** thing to be corrected

corroboree Australian Aboriginal dance ceremony

corrupter (not **-or**)

corselet piece of body armour (not **corslet**)

corselette woman's undergarment

corsetière woman who makes or fits corsets (accent, not ital.)

Corsica island off Italy, a region of France; Fr. name **Corse**
corso pl. **corsos** (not ital.) **1** street in Italy etc. **2** social promenade
cortège funeral procession (accent, not ital.)
Cortes legislative assembly of Spain
Cortés (also **Cortez**), Hernando (1485–1547), Spanish conquistador
cortex pl. **cortices** Anat. outer layer of an organ or structure
Corunna port in NW Spain; Sp. name **La Coruña**
corvée feudal labour (accent, not ital.)
corvette small naval escort vessel
corvine like a crow
corybant pl. **corybantes** ancient Phrygian priest
coryphaeus pl. **coryphaei** leader of a chorus
coryphée leader of a corps de ballet (accent, not ital.)
Cos var. of **Kos**
cos[1] variety of lettuce (lower case)
cos[2] cosine (no point)
cos[3] informal because (no apostrophe)
Cosa Nostra US criminal organization
cosecant Math. (abbrev. **cosec**)
cosh Math. hyperbolic cosine (no point)
Così fan tutte opera by Mozart (1790)
co-signatory (hyphen)
Cosimo de' Medici (1389–1464), Italian statesman and banker; known as **Cosimo the Elder**
cosine Math. (one word; abbrev. **cos**)
cosmogeny origin or evolution of the universe
cosmogony study of or theory about the origin of the universe
cosmos the universe (lower case)
COSPAR Committee on Space Research
cosseted pampered (one *t*)
co-star (hyphen)
Costa Rica republic in Central America □ **Costa Rican**
cost–benefit analysis (en rule)
cost-effective (hyphen)
costumier (US **costumer**) maker or supplier of costumes (not ital.)
cosy (US **cozy**)
cotangent Math. (one word; abbrev. **cot**)
cote shelter for mammals or birds
Côte d'Azur eastern Mediterranean coast of France
Côte d'Ivoire country in West Africa; former English name **Ivory Coast**
coterie small exclusive group of people (not ital.)
coterminous having the same boundaries; conterminous (one word)
Côtes-du-Rhône Rhône wine appellation (hyphens)
cotillion 18th-cent. French dance [Fr. *cotillon*]
cotoneaster shrub with red berries
cottar (also **cottier**) hist. tenant of a cottage
cotter pin fastening pin
cotton candy N. Amer. candyfloss
cottontail American rabbit (one word)
cotton wool (two words) **1** Brit. fluffy wadding **2** US raw cotton
cotyledon Bot. embryonic leaf
couch kind of coarse grass
coudé telescope in which the rays are bent to a focus (accent, not ital.)
cougar N. Amer. puma
couldst arch. could (no apostrophe)
coulee N. Amer. deep ravine [Fr. *coulée*]
coulis pl. same, thin fruit or vegetable purée (not ital.)
coulisse flat piece of stage scenery; (**the coulisses**) the wings
couloir narrow gully
Coulomb, Charles-Augustin de (1736–1806), French physicist, known for **Coulomb's law**
coulomb SI unit of electric charge (lower case; abbrev. **C**)
coulter (US **colter**) cutting blade in front of a ploughshare
council deliberative or administrative assembly
council estate, council house (two words)
councillor (US **councilor**) member of a council; cf. **counsellor** (abbrev. **Cr**)
counsel n. advice. v. (**counselling, counselled**; US one **-l-**) **1** advise **2** help to resolve personal problems
counsellor (US **counselor**) person trained to help with personal problems; cf. **councillor**

count foreign noble (cap. in titles; abbrev. **Ct**)
countdown n. (one word, two words as verb)
counteract (one word)
counter-attack (hyphen)
counterbalance, countercharge, counterclaim (one word)
counterclockwise N. Amer. anticlockwise (one word)
counterculture (one word)
counter-espionage, counter-intelligence, counter-intuitive (hyphen)
counterirritant, countermeasure, countermelody (one word)
Counter-Reformation reform of the Church of Rome in the 16th and 17th cents (caps, hyphen)
counter-revolution (hyphen)
countertenor Mus. highest male adult singing voice (one word)
countervail offset by countering with equal force
countess wife or widow of a count or earl, or woman holding the rank of count or earl (cap. in titles)
Count Palatine pl. **Counts Palatine** feudal lord with royal authority
countrified (not **countryfied**)
country dance, country house (two words)
countryman, countryside, countrywide, countrywoman (one word)
county (abbrev. **Co.**)
county council, county councillor, county court (two words; abbrev. **CC**)
County Durham see **Durham**
coup violent seizure of power (not ital. exc. in Fr. phrs)
coup de foudre pl. ***coups de foudre*** sudden unforeseen event
coup de grâce pl. ***coups de grâce*** blow or shot given to kill a wounded person or animal
coup de main pl. ***coups de main*** sudden surprise attack
coup de maître pl. ***coups de maître*** masterstroke
coup d'état pl. ***coups d'état*** a coup
coup de théâtre pl. ***coups de théâtre*** dramatically sudden act
coup d'œil pl. ***coups d'œil*** quick glance
coupe shallow glass dish
coupé sporty car with a sloping rear (accent, not ital.)
Couperin, François (1668–1733), French composer
courante rapid gliding dance
Courbet, Gustave (1819–77), French painter
courgette Brit. immature vegetable marrow; N. Amer. name **zucchini**
Courrèges, André (b.1923), French fashion designer
court cap. in names of specific courts, e.g. *Court of Appeal, Court of Claims*
Courtauld, Samuel (1876–1947), English industrialist
court bouillon stock used in fish dishes (not ital.)
courthouse (one word)
court martial n. pl. **courts martial** or **court martials.** v. **court-martialling, court-martialled**; US one **-l-**
Courtrai Fr. name for **Kortrijk**
courtroom, courtyard (one word)
couscous North African dish of steamed or soaked semolina; cf. **cuscus**
cousin-german pl. **cousins-german** one's first cousin (hyphen)
Coutts & Co. bankers
couturier (fem. **couturière**) maker and seller of couture clothes (not ital.)
covalent Chem. (one word)
Covenanter supporter of Presbyterianism in 17th-cent. Scotland
covenantor Law party entering into a covenant (not **-er**)
cover girl (two words)
covering letter (N. Amer. **cover letter**)
cover-up n. (hyphen, two words as verb)
covet (**coveting, coveted**)
covin arch. fraud, deception
Coward, Sir Noël (Pierce) (1899–1973), English dramatist
co-worker (hyphen)
Cowper, William (1731–1800), English poet
cowrie marine mollusc (not **cowry**)
co-write, co-writer (hyphen)
Cox (in full **Cox's orange pippin**) variety of eating apple
coxcomb arch. dandy; cf. **cockscomb**

coxswain steersman of a boat (not **cockswain**)
Coy (military) company (no point)
coyote North American wild dog
coypu pl. **coypus** large South American rodent
cozen trick or deceive
cozy US var. of **cosy**
CP 1 cerebral palsy **2** Law hist. (Rolls of the Court of) Common Pleas **3** Communist Party
cp. compare; prefer **cf.**
c.p. candlepower
CPA US certified public accountant
Cpl Corporal
CPO Chief Petty Officer
CPR 1 Canadian Pacific Railway **2** cardiopulmonary resuscitation
CPRE Campaign to Protect Rural England
CPS Crown Prosecution Service
cps (also **c.p.s.**) characters per second; cycles per second
CPU Comput. central processing unit
CR Community of the Resurrection
Cr (no point) **1** the chemical element chromium **2** Councillor **3** credit
crab apple (two words)
Crabbe, George (1754–1832), English poet
Cracow city in southern Poland; Pol. name **Kraków**
Crane 1 (Harold) Hart (1899–1932), American poet **2** Stephen (1871–1900), American novelist
crane fly long-legged fly (two words)
cranesbill plant (one word)
cranium pl. **craniums** or **crania** Anat. the skull
crank 1 eccentric person **2** N. Amer. bad-tempered person
crape black silk used for mourning clothes; cf. **crêpe**
craquelure network of fine cracks in the paint or varnish of a painting
crash-dive, crash-land (hyphen)
crasis pl. **crases** Phonet. a contraction of two adjacent vowels
crawfish pl. same **1** spiny lobster **2** N. Amer. freshwater crayfish
crayfish pl. same **1** freshwater crustacean **2** spiny lobster
CRC 1 Printing camera-ready copy **2** Comput. cyclic redundancy check or code
creation cap. in ref. to God's creation of the universe
crèche (accent) **1** Brit. nursery for babies and young children **2** N. Amer. representation of the nativity scene
Crécy battle (1346) between the English and the French in Picardy
credible able to be believed, convincing
credit (**crediting, credited**) (abbrev. **Cr**)
creditable deserving acknowledgement but not outstanding
credit card (two words)
creditor person or company that is owed money
creditworthy (one word)
credo pl. **credos** statement of beliefs (cap. in ref. to the Apostles' Creed or Nicene Creed)
crematorium pl. **crematoria** or **crematoriums**
crème anglaise, crème brûlée, crème caramel, crème de la crème, crème de menthe, crème fraiche (accents, not ital.)
Cremona city in northern Italy
crenellated (US also **crenelated**) having battlements
crenulate (also **crenulated, crenate**) Bot. & Zool. having a scalloped edge
Creole 1 person of mixed European and black descent **2** descendant of European settlers in the Caribbean, Central or South America, or the southern US **3** mother tongue combining a European and a local language
crêpe (accent, not ital.) **1** thin fabric with a wrinkled surface **2** wrinkled rubber **3** thin pancake; cf. **crape**
crêpe de Chine fine crêpe fabric
crêperie restaurant serving crêpes
crêpe Suzette pl. **crêpes Suzette** thin pancake flamed with alcohol
Cres. crescent (point)
crescendo adv. & adj. Mus. with a gradual increase in loudness (abbrev. **cresc.**, **cres.**). n. pl. **crescendos** or **crescendi** **1** gradual increase in loudness

2 loudest point
Cretaceous Geol. last period of the Mesozoic era
Crete Greek island; mod. Gk name **Kríti** □ **Cretan**
cretin informal stupid person
cretonne heavy cotton fabric
Creutzfeldt–Jakob disease degenerative disease affecting nerve cells in the brain (en rule)
crevasse deep fissure in ice
crevette shrimp or prawn
crew cut (two words, hyphen when attrib.)
Crichton, James (1560–*c*.1585), Scottish adventurer; known as **the Admirable Crichton**
cri de cœur pl. ***cris de cœur*** passionate appeal (Fr., ital.)
crime passionnel pl. ***crimes passionnels*** crime caused by sexual jealousy (Fr., ital.)
criminal conversation Law, hist. adultery (abbrev. **crim. con.**)
Crimplene trademark synthetic fabric
cringe (**cringing, cringed**)
crinkum-crankum arch. elaborate decoration
cripple, crippled avoid in ref. to disabled people; see **disabled**
crise de nerfs pl. ***crises de nerfs*** attack of anxiety (Fr., ital.)
crisis pl. **crises**
crispbread (one word)
criss-cross (hyphen)
criterion pl. **criteria** standard by which something may be judged
criticaster minor critic
criticize (Brit. also **criticise**)
critique analysis and assessment
Crna Gora Serbian name for **Montenegro**
Croat (also **Croatian**) **1** person from Croatia **2** Slavic language of the Croats, written in the Roman alphabet
Croatia country in SE Europe, formerly a republic of Yugoslavia
crochet (**crocheting, crocheted**)
Crockett, Davy (1786–1836), American frontiersman
Crockford (in full ***Crockford's Clerical Directory***) reference book of Anglican clergy
Crockford's London club
crocus pl. **crocuses** or **croci**
croeso welcome! (Welsh, ital.)
Croesus last king of Lydia *c*.560–546 BC, renowned for his wealth
Crohn's disease disease of the intestines
croissant flaky French roll (not ital.)
Cro-Magnon earliest form of modern human in Europe
Crome, John (1768–1821), English painter
Crome Yellow novel by Aldous Huxley (1921)
Crompton, Richmal (1890–1969), English writer
Cromwell 1 Oliver (1599–1658), Lord Protector of the Commonwealth 1653–8 **2** Thomas (*c*.1485–1540), chief minister to Henry VIII 1531–40 □ **Cromwellian**
Cronus (also **Kronos**) Gk Mythol. supreme god until dethroned by Zeus; Rom. equivalent **Saturn**
cronyism appointment of friends to positions of authority (not **croney-**)
Crookes, Sir William (1832–1919), English physicist and chemist
croque-monsieur French cheese and ham sandwich (hyphen, not ital.)
croquet v. (**croqueting, croqueted**)
croquette fried ball of meat, fish, etc.
crore pl. same, **crores** Ind. ten million; cf. **lakh**
crosier var. of **crozier**
crossbar (one word)
cross-bencher independent member of the House of Lords (hyphen)
crossbill, crossbones, crossbow (one word)
cross-breed, cross-check, cross-contamination, cross-country, cross-dress (hyphen)
crosse stick used in lacrosse
cross-examine, cross-eyed, cross-fertilize (hyphen)
crossfire (one word)
cross-question, cross-refer (hyphen)
cross reference (two words, hyphen as verb; abbrev. **xref.**)

crossroads pl. same (one word)
cross section, cross stitch (two words)
crosswind (one word)
crosswise (also **crossways**) (one word)
crossword (one word)
crotchet Brit. musical note
croupier person in charge of a gaming table
crouton piece of fried or toasted bread served with soup
crown 1 (**the Crown**) monarchy or reigning monarch (cap.) **2** former British coin with a value of five shillings (25p) **3** (in full **metric crown**) paper size, 384 × 504 mm; (in full **crown octavo**) book size, 186 × 123 mm; (in full **crown quarto**) book size, 246 × 189 mm
Crown court, Crown jewels, Crown prince (one cap.)
crow's foot, crow's nest (two words)
crozier (also **crosier**) bishop's hooked staff
CRT cathode ray tube
cru pl. ***crus*** French vineyard or wine-producing area (ital.)
Crucifixion, the (cap.)
crudités raw vegetables as an hors d'oeuvre (accent, not ital.)
cruel (**crueller, cruellest**; US **crueler, cruelest**)
Crufts annual dog show (no apostrophe)
Cruikshank, George (1792–1878), English illustrator
cruiserweight (in boxing) light heavy-weight (one word)
crumhorn var. of **krummhorn**
crusade, crusader cap. in ref. to medieval military expeditions to the Holy Land
cruse arch. pot or jar
Crusoe see **Robinson Crusoe**
crux pl. **cruxes** or **cruces** decisive point
cryogenics study of very low temperatures (treated as sing.)
cryonics freezing of a dead body in the hope of a future cure (treated as sing.)
cryptogam Bot., dated plant with no true flowers or seeds
cryptogram text written in code
cryptonym code name
cryptosporidium pl. **cryptosporidia** parasitic protozoan
crystallize (Brit. also **crystallise**)
CS 1 chartered surveyor **2** Civil Service **3** Court of Session
Cs the chemical element caesium (no point)
c/s cycles per second
CSA Child Support Agency
csardas (also **czardas**) pl. same, Hungarian dance
CSC Civil Service Commission
CSE hist. Certificate of Secondary Education
CS gas (two caps)
CSM Company Sergeant Major
CST Central Standard Time
CSU Civil Service Union
CT 1 computerized (or computed) tomography **2** Connecticut (postal abbrev.)
Ct Count
ct 1 carat **2** cent
Ctesiphon ancient city near Baghdad
CTT capital transfer tax
CU Christian Union
Cu the chemical element copper (no point) [late L. *cuprum*]
cu. cubic
Cub (also **Cub Scout**) junior member of the Scout Association (cap.)
Cuba libre pl. **Cuba libres** drink of lime juice and rum
cubbyhole (one word)
cube root (two words)
cubic (abbrev. **cu.**)
cubism early 20th-cent. style of painting (lower case)
Cúchulainn legendary Irish hero
cudgel v. (**cudgelling, cudgelled**; US one -l-)
cue v. (**cueing** or **cuing, cued**)
cufflink (one word)
Cufic var. of **Kufic**
cui bono? who stands to gain? (L., ital.)
cuirass piece of body armour
cuirassier cavalry soldier wearing a cuirass
cuisine cookery (not ital.)
Culdee monk of the Celtic Church
cul-de-sac pl. **culs-de-sac** or **cul-de-sacs**

street closed at one end (hyphens, not ital.)
culex pl. **culices** kind of mosquito
Culpeper, Nicholas (1616–54), English herbalist
cultivar Bot. variety produced by selective breeding (abbrev. **cv.**)
Cultural Revolution political upheaval in China 1966–8 (caps)
cum combined with (not ital.)
Cumberland former county of NW England
Cumbria county of NW England
cum dividend with a dividend about to be paid
cum grano salis with a pinch of salt (L., ital.)
cumin (also **cummin**) plant with aromatic seeds
cum laude with distinction (L., ital.)
cummerbund sash worn around the waist
cummings, e. e. (1894–1962), American poet and novelist (lower case); full name *Edward Estlin Cummings*
cumquat var. of **kumquat**
cumulonimbus pl. **cumulonimbi** cloud forming a towering mass
cumulus pl. **cumuli** cloud forming rounded masses
cuneiform denoting wedge-shaped characters used in Mesopotamian writing
Cunobelinus var. of **Cymbeline**
CUP Cambridge University Press
cup-bearer (hyphen)
Cup Final (caps)
cupful pl. **cupfuls**
Cupid Rom. Mythol. god of love; Gk equivalent **Eros**
cupric Chem. of copper with a valency of two
cupro-nickel alloy of copper and nickel
cuprous Chem. of copper with a valency of one
cup tie (two words) □ **cup-tied**
curable (not **-eable**)
Curaçao island in the Netherlands Antilles
curaçao pl. **curaçaos** liqueur flavoured with bitter oranges (not **curaçoa**)
curare poison obtained from some South American plants
curb 1 control or limit **2** US var. of **kerb**
curé French parish priest (accent, not ital.)
cure-all n. universal remedy (hyphen)
curettage Med. scraping of the lining of the uterus with a **curette** (surgical instrument)
curfuffle use **kerfuffle**
Curia papal court at the Vatican
Curie, Marie (1867–1934) and Pierre (1859–1906), pioneers of the study of radioactivity
curie unit of radioactivity, now replaced by the **becquerel** (abbrev. **Ci**)
curio pl. **curios** unusual and intriguing object
curiosa curiosities, esp. erotica or pornography (not ital.)
curium chemical element of atomic number 96 (symbol **Cm**)
curlicue decorative curl or twist
curly bracket bracket of the style { }; brace
currach (also **curragh**) coracle (small boat)
curragh Ir. stretch of marshy ground; (**The Curragh**) area of County Kildare with a racecourse and military camp
curriculum pl. **curricula** or **curriculums**
curriculum vitae pl. **curricula vitae** (abbrev. **CV**)
cursor movable indicator on a computer screen
curtain-raiser (hyphen)
Curtiss, Glenn (Hammond) (1878–1930), American air pioneer
curtsy (also **curtsey**) (**curtsies** or **curtseys**, **curtsying** or **curtseying**, **curtsied** or **curtseyed**)
curvet (**curvetting**, **curvetted** or **curveting**, **curveted**) (of a horse) leap
cuscus tree-dwelling marsupial; cf. **couscous**
cusec unit of flow equal to one cubic foot per second
Cushitic group of East African languages
customize (Brit. also **customise**)
cut and dried (hyphens only when attrib.)

cutback n. (one word, two words as verb)
cut-off, **cut-out** n. (hyphen, two words as verb)
cut-price (N. Amer. **cut-rate**) (hyphen)
cut-throat (hyphen)
Cutty Sark tea clipper preserved in London
cuvée type or batch of wine (accent, not ital.)
CV curriculum vitae
cv. cultivated variety; cultivar
CVO Commander of the Royal Victorian Order
Cwlth Commonwealth (no point)
Cwmbran town in SE Wales
CWO Chief Warrant Officer
c.w.o. cash with order
cwt hundredweight (no point) [L. *centum* 'a hundred']
cyan greenish-blue colour
Cybele Phrygian mother goddess
cybernetics study of communications and control systems in animals and machines (treated as sing.)
Cyclades group of islands in the Aegean Sea
cyclo-cross cross-country bicycle racing (hyphen)
cyclopedia (also **cyclopaedia**) arch. exc. in book titles encyclopedia
Cyclops pl. **Cyclops** or **Cyclopes** Gk Mythol. one-eyed giant
cyclops pl. same, minute freshwater crustacean (lower case)
cyder use **cider**
cymbal musical instrument □ **cymbalist**
Cymbeline 1 (also **Cunobelinus**) (died *c.*42 AD), British chieftain **2** (***Cymbeline***) play by Shakespeare (abbrev. ***Cymb.***)
Cymraeg the Welsh language
Cymric Welsh
Cymru Welsh name for **Wales**
Cynewulf (late 8th–9th cents), Anglo-Saxon poet
Cynic member of a school of ancient Greek philosophers
cynic cynical person (lower case)
cynosure centre of attention
cypher var. of **cipher**
cypress coniferous tree
Cyprian, St (d.258), Carthaginian bishop and martyr
Cypriot person from Cyprus
Cyprus island in the eastern Mediterranean, independent since 1960; part proclaimed itself the Turkish Republic of Northern Cyprus in 1983
Cyrano de Bergerac play by Edmond Rostand (1897)
Cyrenaic of an ancient Greek school of philosophy founded at Cyrene in North Africa
Cyrillic alphabet used esp. for Russian and Bulgarian
cyst Med. fluid-filled sac
Cytherean 1 Astron. relating to the planet Venus **2** relating to the goddess Cytherea (Aphrodite)
czar etc. var. of **tsar** etc.
czardas var. of **csardas**
Czech person from the Czech Republic or Czechoslovakia
Czechoslovakia former country in central Europe, divided between the Czech Republic and Slovakia since 1993 □ **Czechoslovak**, **Czechoslovakian**
Czerny, Karl (1791–1857), Austrian composer

D

D 1 pl. **Ds** or **D's** 4th letter of the alphabet **2** US Democrat or Democratic **3** depth **4** the hydrogen isotope deuterium **5** Chem. dextrorotatory **6** dimension(s) or dimensional: *3-D* **7** doctor **8** (also **d**) Roman numeral for 500

d 1 daughter **2** day(s) **3** deci- **4** departs **5** diameter **6** penny or pence (of pre-decimal currency) [L. *denarius*]

d. died (point, no space after)

d' lower case as prefix to a non-anglicized proper name, exc. at the beginning of a sentence

DA 1 deposit account **2** US district attorney

Da. Danish

da deca-

DAB digital audio broadcasting

dab hand (two words)

DAC digital to analogue converter

da capo Mus. repeat or repeated from the beginning

Dacca var. of **Dhaka**

dacha Russian country house (not ital.)

Dachau Nazi concentration camp in Bavaria

dachshund short-legged breed of dog

dacoit armed robber in India or Burma

dactyl metrical foot consisting of one long followed by two short syllables

Dada early 20th-cent. movement in art etc. □ **Dadaism**

daddy-long-legs (hyphens) **1** Brit. crane fly **2** N. Amer. harvestman

dado pl. **dados**

Daedalus Gk Mythol. craftsman who built the labyrinth, father of Icarus

daemon (also **daimon**) **1** Gk Mythol. a divinity or supernatural being **2** arch. demon **3** (also **demon**) Comput. background process

da Gama, Vasco (*c.*1469–1524), Portuguese explorer

dagger Printing obelus, †; used before a person's name to show that they are dead

Dagon deity of the ancient Philistines

Daguerre, Louis-Jacques-Mandé (1789–1851), French inventor of the first practical photographic process

daguerreotype early form of photograph (lower case)

dahabeeyah Nile sailing boat

dahlia plant of the daisy family

Dahomey former name for **Benin**

Dáil (in full **Dáil Éireann**) lower house of Parliament in the Republic of Ireland

Daily Express, Daily Mail, Daily Telegraph UK newspapers ('the' lower case and roman)

Daimler German car company

daimon var. of **daemon**

daimyo (also **daimio**) pl. **daimyos** feudal Japanese lord

daiquiri pl. **daiquiris** cocktail (lower case; not **daquiri**)

dais low platform (not **daïs**)

daisy chain (two words)

daisy-cutter (hyphen)

Dakar capital of Senegal

Dakota former territory of the US, now the states of North Dakota and South Dakota

dal decalitre (no point)

Dalai Lama spiritual head of Tibetan Buddhism

dalek hostile alien in the TV serial *Doctor Who* (lower case)

Dalí, Salvador (1904–89), Spanish surrealist painter □ **Daliesque**

Dalit another term for **Harijan**

Dallapiccola, Luigi (1904–75), Italian composer

Dalmatia region in SW Croatia

Dalmatian large spotted breed of dog (not **-ion**)

dal segno Mus. repeat or repeated from

the sign ℅ (abbrev. **DS**)
dalton unit expressing the molecular weight of proteins (lower case)
dam decametre (no point)
damage limitation (two words)
Damaraland region of central Namibia
Damascene 1 relating to Damascus **2** relating to the conversion of St Paul on the road to Damascus
damascene (also **damascened**) (of metal) inlaid or having a wavy pattern (lower case)
Damascus capital of Syria
damask figured lustrous fabric
Dame title given to a woman with the rank of Knight Commander or holder of the Grand Cross in the Orders of Chivalry
damnosa hereditas inheritance bringing more burden than profit (L., ital.)
damnum pl. **damna** Law a loss (not ital.)
Damocles legendary courtier who was seated with a sword hung by a single hair over his head □ **Damoclean**
Damon ancient Syracusan whose friendship with Pythias (also called Phintias) was legendary
Dampier, William (1652–1715), English explorer
Dan Hebrew patriarch
Dan. Daniel
Danae (also **Danaë**) Gk Mythol. mother of Perseus
Danaids (also **Danaïds**) Gk Mythol. daughters of Danaus, king of Argos, who murdered their husbands
Danakil another name for **Afar**
Da Nang port in Vietnam
dance band, dance floor, dance hall (two words)
D and C (also **D & C**) dilatation and curettage
Dandie Dinmont breed of terrier
dandruff scurf (not **-riff**)
Danegeld, Danelaw (one word)
Daniel 1 Hebrew prophet **2** book of the Old Testament (abbrev. **Dan.**)
Daniell cell voltaic cell (two *l*s)
Danish (abbrev. **Da.**)
Danmark Danish name for **Denmark**
d'Annunzio, Gabriele (1863–1938), Italian writer
danse macabre dance of death (Fr., ital.)
danseur (fem. **danseuse**) dancer (not ital.)
Dante (1265–1321), Italian poet; full name *Dante Alighieri* □ **Dantean, Dantesque**
Danube river of Europe; Ger. name **Donau** □ **Danubian**
Danzig Ger. name for **Gdańsk**
Daodejing var. of **Tao-te-Ching**
Daoism var. of **Taoism**
DAR Daughters of the American Revolution
Darby and Joan old married couple
d'Arc, Jeanne, see **Jeanne d'Arc**
Dardanelles strait between Europe and Asiatic Turkey; in ancient times called the **Hellespont**
daredevil (one word)
Dar es Salaam former capital of Tanzania (capital is now Dodoma)
Darfur region in the west of Sudan
Darien hist. the Isthmus of Panama
Darius I (also **Darius the Great**) king of Persia 521–486 BC
Darjeeling 1 (also **Darjiling**) hill station in NE India **2** kind of tea
Dark Ages period between the fall of the Roman Empire and the high Middle Ages, *c.*500–1100 AD (caps)
darkroom (one word)
darmstadtium chemical element of atomic number 110 (symbol **Ds**)
darshan Hinduism occasion of seeing a holy person or the image of a deity (ital.)
Darwen town in Lancashire
Darwin[1] capital of Northern Territory, Australia
Darwin[2] **1** Charles (Robert) (1809–82), English natural historian **2** Erasmus (1731–1802), English physician and scientist □ **Darwinian**
dashboard (one word)
DAT digital audiotape
dat. Gram. dative
data in specialized scientific fields treated as a plural; in non-scientific use treated as a mass noun with a singular verb (see also **datum**)
databank, database (one word)
datable (also **dateable**)

data processing, data set (two words)
Date Line (also **International Date Line**) (caps)
dateline statement of when and where a dispatch or newspaper article was written (one word)
date rape, date stamp n. (two words, hyphen as verb)
dative Gram. case indicating an indirect object or recipient (abbrev. **dat.**)
datum pl. **data 1** piece of information **2** assumption or premise; see also **data**
daube stew of braised meat (not ital.)
Daudet, Alphonse (1840–97), French novelist and dramatist
daughter-in-law pl. **daughters-in-law** (hyphens)
Daumier, Honoré (1808–78), French artist
dauphin eldest son of the king of France
Dauphiné former province of SE France
dauphinois (also **dauphinoise**) (of potatoes) sliced and baked in milk
Davies 1 Sir Peter Maxwell (b.1934), English composer **2** W(illiam) H(enry) (1871–1940), Welsh poet
da Vinci, Leonardo, see **Leonardo da Vinci**
Davis 1 Bette (1908–89), American actress **2** Miles (Dewey) (1926–91), American jazz trumpeter
Davis Cup annual tennis championship
Davy, Sir Humphry (1778–1829), English chemist, inventor of the **Davy lamp**
Davy Jones's locker the bottom of the sea (two caps)
Dayak (also **Dyak**) pl. same or **Dayaks** member of a group of peoples of Borneo
day boy (two words)
daybreak, daydream (one word)
Day-glo (also **dayglo**) trademark fluorescent paint
Day Lewis, C(ecil) (1904–72), English poet, Poet Laureate 1968–72 (no hyphen)
daylight (one word)
daylight saving time N. Amer. summer time (lower case; abbrev. **DST**)
day-long (hyphen)
Day of Atonement Yom Kippur
day off pl. **days off** (two words)
Day of Judgement Judgement Day (not **Judgment**)
day out pl. **days out** (two words)
daytime (one word)
Dayton city in western Ohio
Daytona Beach city in Florida
Db the chemical element dubnium (no point)
dB decibel(s)
DBE Dame Commander of the Order of the British Empire
DBS direct broadcasting by satellite; direct-broadcast satellite
DC 1 Mus. da capo **2** (also **d.c.**) direct current **3** District of Columbia **4** District Commissioner
DCA Department of Constitutional Affairs
DCB Dame Commander of the Order of the Bath
DCL Doctor of Civil Law
DCM Distinguished Conduct Medal
DCMG Dame Commander of the Order of St Michael and St George
DCMS Department for Culture, Media, and Sport
DCVO Dame Commander of the Royal Victorian Order
DD Doctor of Divinity
D-Day 6 June 1944 (hyphen)
DDR hist. German Democratic Republic (East Germany)
DDT dichlorodiphenyltrichloroethane, an insecticide
DE Delaware (postal abbrev.)
de lower case as prefix to non-anglicized French, Spanish, and Dutch names (alphabetize by surname, e.g. *Maupassant, Guy de*); capitalized in Flemish and most Italian names, apart from aristocratic names such as *Medici, Lorenzo de'*
de- generally forms solid compounds
DEA US Drug Enforcement Administration
deadbeat, deadhead (one word)
dead heat, dead leg (two words)
deadline, deadlock, deadpan (one word)

dead reckoning, dead ringer (two words)
dead weight (two words; usually one word in economics and shipping senses)
deaf mute avoid; prefer **profoundly deaf**
Dean of Faculty president of the Faculty of Advocates in Scotland
deasil Sc. clockwise; cf. **widdershins**
deathbed (one word)
death blow, death knell, death mask, death penalty, death row, death toll (two words)
deathtrap (one word)
death warrant (two words)
deathwatch beetle (one word)
death wish (two words)
deb informal debutante (no point)
debacle failure or disaster [Fr. *débâcle*]
debatable (not **debateable**)
debauchee debauched person
de Beauvoir, Simone (1908–86), French writer
debenture long-term security yielding a fixed rate of interest
debit card (two words)
debonair stylish and charming [Fr. *débonnaire*]
Debrett's Peerage guide to the British nobility
debris scattered remains [Fr. *débris*]
debut first appearance [Fr. *début*]
debutant person making a debut [Fr. *débutant*]
debutante girl making her first appearance in society [Fr. *débutante*]
Dec. December
dec. 1 deceased **2** Cricket declared
deca- (also **dec-** before a vowel) ten (abbrev. **da**)
decaffeinated (not **-ie-**)
decahedron pl. **decahedra** or **decahedrons** solid figure with twelve plane faces
decalitre (US **decaliter, dekaliter**) 10 litres (abbrev. **dal** or US **dkl**)
Decalogue, the the Ten Commandments
Decameron, The work by Boccaccio, written 1348–58
decametre (US **decameter, dekameter**) 10 metres (abbrev. **dam**, US **dkm**)
decani section of a church choir on the south side; cf. **cantoris**
Deccan plateau in southern India
deceased (abbrev. **dec.**)
December (abbrev. **Dec.**)
decennium pl. **decennia** or **decenniums** decade ◻ **decennial**
decentralize (Brit. also **decentralise**)
deceptively can mean both one thing and its opposite, e.g. in *a deceptively simple plan* and *a deceptively spacious room*; avoid if possible
deci- one-tenth (abbrev. **d**)
decibel unit expressing the intensity of a sound or the power of an electrical signal (abbrev. **dB**)
decigram (also **decigramme**) one-tenth of a gram (abbrev. **dg**)
decilitre (US **deciliter**) one-tenth of a litre (abbrev. **dl**)
decimalize (Brit. also **decimalise**)
decimate kill or destroy a large proportion of; only traditionalists insist on its original meaning 'kill one in every ten of' ◻ **decimator**
decimetre (US **decimeter**) one-tenth of a metre (abbrev. **dm**)
deckchair (one word)
deckle edge rough uncut edge of a sheet of paper ◻ **deckle-edged**
Declaration of Independence document declaring the US to be independent of the British Crown, signed on 4 July 1776 (caps)
declared Cricket (abbrev. **dec.**)
déclassé (fem. **déclassée**) having fallen in social status (accents, not ital.)
declension Gram. variation of the form of a noun, pronoun, or adjective
de Clerambault's syndrome erotomania
decline Gram. give the different forms of (a noun or adjective); cf. **conjugate**
deco art deco
decollate behead
décolletage woman's cleavage or low neckline (accent, not ital.) ◻ **décolleté** (also **décolletée**)
decolonize (Brit. also **decolonise**)
deconstructionism philosophical and literary theory (lower case)
decor furnishing and decoration

[Fr. *décor*]
Decorated stage of 14th-cent. English Gothic architecture (cap.)
Decoration Day US Memorial Day
découpage decoration with paper cut-outs (accent, not ital.)
decree nisi pl. **decrees nisi** stage in divorce proceedings (not ital.)
decrescendo pl. **decrescendos** Mus. diminuendo
decretum pl. ***decreta*** papal decree or judgement (L., ital.)
decriminalize (Brit. also **decriminalise**)
Dedalus, Stephen, character in James Joyce's *A Portrait of the Artist as a Young Man*
deducible able to be inferred (not **-able**)
deductible able to be subtracted (not **-able**)
de-emphasize (Brit. also **de-emphasise**) (hyphen)
deemster a judge in the Isle of Man
deep freeze (US trademark **deepfreeze**) n. (hyphen as verb)
deep-fry, deep-rooted, deep-seated (hyphen)
de-escalate (hyphen)
de facto in actual fact (not ital., no hyphen when attrib.)
defecate (not **defaecate**)
defector (not **-er**)
defence (US **defense**)
defendant (not **-ent**)
Defender of the Faith title conferred on Henry VIII by Pope Leo X; in Latin **Fidei Defensor**
defer (**deferring, deferred**) □ **deferment, deferral**
defibrillator Med. apparatus for regulating rhythm of heartbeats
deficient do not use in ref. to people with mental disabilities
definable (not **-eable**)
definiendum pl. ***definienda*** word etc. being defined (L., ital.)
definiens pl. ***definientia*** word etc. used to define something (L., ital.)
definite article Gram. (in English) the word 'the'
deflection (not **deflexion** (dated))
Defoe, Daniel (1660–1731), English novelist and journalist
DEFRA Department for Environment, Food, and Rural Affairs
defuse 1 remove the fuse from **2** reduce the danger or tension in; cf. **diffuse**
deg. degree(s)
dégagé unconcerned or unconstrained (accents, not ital.)
Degas, (Hilaire Germain) Edgar (1834–1917), French painter (no accent)
de Gaulle, Charles (André Joseph Marie) (1890–1970), French head of government 1944–6, president 1959–69
degauss Phys. remove unwanted magnetism from (one word)
degree symbol °, set closed up to the scale (10 °C) or, where none, figure (35°); abbrev. **deg.**
de haut en bas condescendingly (Fr., ital.)
de Havilland, Sir Geoffrey (1882–1965), English aircraft designer
Deianira Gk Mythol. wife of Hercules
de-ice (hyphen)
deictic Ling. having a meaning dependent on its context
Dei gratia by the grace of God (L., ital.; abbrev. **DG**)
deism belief in a supreme being, spec. of a creator who does not intervene in the universe; cf. **theism**
Deity, the cap. in ref. to the creator and supreme being
deixis Ling. function of deictic words
déjà vu feeling of having already experienced a situation (accents, not ital.)
de jure rightfully, by right (L., ital.)
dekaliter, dekameter US vars of **decalitre, decametre**
Dekker, Thomas (*c.*1570–1632), English dramatist
de Klerk, F(rederik) W(illem) (b.1936), South African president 1989–94
de Kooning, Willem (1904–97), Dutch-born American painter
Del. Delaware
del Math. operator used in vector analysis (symbol ∇)
del. delete
del. *delineavit* (ital.)
de La one cap. as prefix to non-anglicized French names, unless

starting a sentence (alphabetize under *La*); lower case in Spanish names

Delacroix, (Ferdinand Victor) Eugène (1798–1863), French painter

de la Mare, Walter (John) (1873–1956), English poet

Delaware state of the US on the Atlantic coast (official abbrev. **Del.**, postal **DE**) □ **Delawarean**

delete symbol ₰; abbrev. **del.** or **dele**

Delft town in the Netherlands

delft glazed earthenware (lower case)

Delhi state in central India, containing the cities of Old and New Delhi

Delibes, (Clément Philibert) Léo (1836–91), French composer

delicatessen shop selling cooked meats, prepared foods, etc.

Delilah (in the Old Testament) woman who betrayed Samson

delineavit drew this (L., ital.; abbrev. ***del.***)

delirium tremens condition in chronic alcoholics (not ital.; abbrev. **DTs**)

Delius, Frederick (1862–1934), English composer

Della Cruscan member of an 18th-cent. school of English poets

della Quercia, Jacopo (*c.*1374–1438), Italian sculptor

della Robbia, Luca (1400–82), Italian sculptor

Delos Greek island formerly sacred to Apollo; mod. Gk name **Dhílos** □ **Delian**

Delphi site of an ancient Greek oracle; mod. Gk name **Dhelfoí** □ **Delphic**

delphinium pl. **delphiniums** plant

delta fourth letter of the Greek alphabet (**Δ, δ**), transliterated as 'd'

delta rays, delta wing (two words)

deltiology hobby of collecting postcards

de luxe luxurious (two words, not ital.)

Dem. US Democrat

demagogue political leader (not **demagog**) □ **demagoguery**

démarche political step or initiative (accent, not ital.)

dematerialize (Brit. also **dematerialise**)

de Maupassant, Guy, see **Maupassant**

demeanour (US **demeanor**) bearing or behaviour

de' Medici¹ see **Medici**

de' Medici², Catherine, see **Catherine de' Medici**

de Médicis, Marie, see **Marie de Médicis**

démenti official denial of a published statement (Fr., ital.)

demesne 1 hist. land attached to a manor **2** arch. domain

Demeter Gk Mythol. corn goddess; Rom. equivalent **Ceres**

demigod, demigoddess, demijohn (one word)

demilitarize (Brit. also **demilitarise**)

de Mille, Cecil B. (1881–1959), American film producer and director

demi-mondaine woman belonging to the demi-monde (Fr., ital.)

demi-monde group on the fringes of respectable society (not ital.)

demi-pension half-board hotel accommodation (Fr., ital.)

demise death (not **-ize**)

demi-sec (of wine) medium dry (not ital.)

demisemiquaver Mus., Brit. note having the value of half a semiquaver; N. Amer. **thirty-second note**

demitasse small coffee cup [Fr. *demi-tasse*]

demiurge (one word) **1** (in Platonic philosophy) creator of the world **2** (in Gnosticism) heavenly being subordinate to the supreme being

demo pl. **demos**

demobilize (Brit. also **demobilise**)

Democrat cap. in ref. to the US Democratic Party (abbrev. **Dem.**)

democratize (Brit. also **democratise**)

Democritus (*c.*460–*c.*370 BC), Greek philosopher

démodé out of fashion (Fr., ital.)

demoiselle young woman (not ital.)

de Moivre, Abraham, see **Moivre**

demon evil spirit or devil; see also **daemon**

demonetize (Brit. also **demonetise**) deprive of status as money

demonize (Brit. also **demonise**)

demonstrable (not **demonstratable**)
demonstrator (not **-er**)
de Montfort, Simon, see **Montfort**
demoralize (Brit. also **demoralise**)
De Morgan, Augustus (1806–71), English mathematician
demos pl. **demoi** the common people (lower case, not ital.)
Demosthenes (384–322 BC), Athenian orator and statesman
demotic kind of language used by ordinary people; spec. the normal spoken form of modern Greek (cf. **katharevousa**) or a simplified form of ancient Egyptian script (cf. **hieratic**) (lower case)
demur (**demurring, demurred**) show reluctance
demutualize (Brit. also **demutualise**)
demy 1 (also **metric demy**) a paper size, 564 × 444 mm **2** (also **demy octavo**) a book size, 216 × 138 mm **3** (also **demy quarto**) a book size, 276 × 219 mm
demythologize (Brit. also **demythologise**)
Den. Denmark
denar monetary unit of Macedonia; cf. **dinar**
denarius pl. **denarii** ancient Roman coin
denationalize (Brit. also **denationalise**)
Denbighshire county of North Wales
dene (also **dean**) wooded valley
dengue tropical viral disease
Deng Xiaoping (also **Teng Hsiao-p'ing**) (1904–97), Chinese communist statesman, vice-premier 1973–6 and 1977–80
Den Haag Du. name for **The Hague**
denier 1 unit expressing the fineness of yarn **2** former French coin
denim cotton twill fabric
De Niro, Robert (b.1943), American actor
Denmark Scandinavian country (abbrev. **Den.**); Danish name **Danmark**
de nos jours contemporary (Fr., ital.)
denote be a sign of or name for; cf. **connote**
denouement final part of a play, film, etc. [Fr. *dénouement*]
de nouveau afresh, anew (Fr., ital.)
de novo afresh, anew (L., ital.)
dentelle ornamental tooling used in bookbinding (not ital.)
dentine (US **dentin**) hard tissue forming the bulk of a tooth
deoch an doris Sc. & Ir. drink taken before parting (not ital.) [Gaelic *deoch an doruis*]
deodar Himalayan cedar
deodorize (Brit. also **deodorise**)
Deo gratias thanks be to God (L., ital.; abbrev. **DG**)
Deo volente God willing (L., ital.; abbrev. **DV**)
dep. 1 departs **2** deputy
département French administrative district (ital.)
department (abbrev. **dept**)
departmentalize (Brit. also **departmentalise**)
dépaysé (fem. ***dépaysée***) out of one's usual surroundings (Fr., ital.)
dependant (US **dependent**) n. person who relies on another for support
dependent adj. relying on someone or something (not **-ant**)
depersonalize (Brit. also **depersonalise**)
depositary person to whom something is lodged in trust
depositor (not **-er**)
depository place where things are stored
depot place where things are stored [Fr. *dépôt*]
deprecate express disapproval of
depreciate 1 diminish in value over time **2** disparage or belittle
Depression, the cap. in ref. to the slump of 1929 and subsequent years
de profundis from the depths, the opening words of Psalm 130 (L., ital.)
dept department (no point)
depute n. Sc. official representative
député member of the French parliament (ital.)
deputize (Brit. also **deputise**)
De Quincey, Thomas (1785–1859), English writer
deracinated uprooted from one's usual environment [Fr. *déraciné*]

derailleur kind of bicycle gear (not ital.)
Derby, the annual horse race, run on Epsom Downs in England
derby (lower case) **1** sports match between two local teams **2** N. Amer. bowler hat
Derbyshire county of north central England (abbrev. **Derby.**)
de règle required by custom (Fr., ital.)
de rigueur obligatory (not ital.)
derisible laughable, contemptible
derisive expressing contempt or ridicule
derisory ridiculously small or inadequate
dermis (also **derm, derma**) Anat. layer of tissue below the epidermis
dernier cri the latest fashion (Fr., ital.)
derrick 1 kind of crane **2** framework over an oil well
Derrida, Jacques (1930–2004), French philosopher □ **Derridean**
derrière person's buttocks (accent, not ital.)
derring-do heroic actions (hyphen)
derringer small pistol, named after Henry Deringer (lower case)
Derry another name for **Londonderry**, preferred locally
derv diesel oil (lower case)
de Sade, Marquis, see **Sade**
desaparecido pl. ***desaparecidos*** person presumed killed by soldiers or police (Sp., ital.)
Descartes, René (1596–1650), French philosopher and mathematician
descendant n. person descended from a particular ancestor
descendent adj. descending
descender part of a letter that extends below the line (as in *g* and *p*)
descendible Law able to be inherited by a descendant (not **-able**)
desensitize (Brit. also **desensitise**)
desert n. desolate waterless area; cf. **dessert**
deserts what a person deserves
déshabillé (also Engl. form **dishabille**) state of being only partly clothed (accents, not ital.)
desiccate to dry (one *s*, two *cs*)
desideratum pl. **desiderata** something needed or wanted (not ital.)
desirable (not **-eable**)
desktop (one word)
Des Moines capital of Iowa
desorb Chem. cause the release of (an adsorbed substance) □ **desorption**
despatch var. of **dispatch**
desperado pl. **desperadoes** or **desperados**
desperate (not **-arate**)
de Spinoza, Baruch, see **Spinoza**
despise (not **-ize**)
des Prez (also **des Prés** or **Deprez**), Josquin (*c.*1440–1521), Flemish musician
des res desirable residence (no points)
dessert sweet course; cf. **desert**
dessertspoonful pl. **dessertspoonfuls** (one word)
destabilize (Brit. also **destabilise**)
de Staël, Madame (1766–1817), French writer; born *Anne Louise Germaine Necker*
De Stijl Dutch abstract art movement
desuetude state of disuse
detector (not **-er**)
detent a catch in a machine
detente easing of hostility between countries (no accent, not ital.) [Fr. *détente*]
deterrent (not **-ant**)
detestable (not **-ible**)
detonator, detractor (not **-er**)
de trop superfluous (not ital.)
de Troyes, Chrétien, see **Chrétien de Troyes**
deus ex machina unexpected power or event saving a situation (L., ital.)
Deut. Deuteronomy
deuteragonist person secondary to the protagonist in a drama
deuterium heavy isotope of hydrogen (symbol **D**)
Deutero-Isaiah the supposed later author of Isaiah 40–55
Deuteronomy fifth book of the Old Testament (abbrev. **Deut.**)
Deutschland Ger. name for **Germany**
Deutschmark (also **Deutsche Mark**) former monetary unit of Germany (abbrev. **DM**)
de Valera, Eamon (1882–1975), Irish

Taoiseach (prime minister) 1937–48, 1951–4, and 1957–9 and president of the Republic of Ireland 1959–73

Devanagari alphabet used for Sanskrit, Hindi, and other Indian languages

develop (not **-ope**) □ **development**

Devi supreme Hindu goddess

devi Ind. goddess (lower case)

Devil, the cap. in ref. to Satan

devilled (US **deviled**) (of food) cooked with hot seasoning

devilling (US **deviling**) working as a junior assistant

devilry (not **deviltry** (arch.))

devil's advocate (lower case, apostrophe)

Devil's Island former penal settlement off the coast of French Guiana

devise (not **-ize**) □ **deviser**

devisor Law person who bequeaths something to someone

devoir arch. person's duty

Devon county of SW England; old name **Devonshire** is retained in titles etc.

Devonian 1 relating to Devon **2** Geol. fourth period of the Palaeozoic era

devoré velvet fabric with a pattern in the pile (accent, not ital.)

de Vries, Hugo (1848–1935), Dutch botanist

DEW distant early warning

dewar kind of vacuum flask

Dewey 1 John (1859–1952), American philosopher **2** Melvil (1851–1931), American librarian, inventor of the **Dewey decimal system**

Dexedrine trademark form of amphetamine

dexter Heraldry on the bearer's right-hand side, i.e. the left as it is depicted; cf. **sinister**

dexterous (also **dextrous**) skilful

DF 1 Defender of the Faith **2** direction finder

DFC Distinguished Flying Cross

DfES Department for Education and Skills

DFID Department for International Development

DFM Distinguished Flying Medal

DfT Department for Transport

DG 1 by the grace of God [L. *Dei gratia*] **2** director general **3** thanks be to God [L. *Deo gratias*]

dg decigram(s) (no point)

Dhaka (also **Dacca**) capital of Bangladesh

dhal (also **dal**) (in Indian cookery) split pulses

dharma (in Indian religion) eternal law of the cosmos

Dhelfoí mod. Gk name for **Delphi**

Dhílos mod. Gk name for **Delos**

dhobi pl. **dhobis** Ind. person whose occupation is washing clothes

dhoti pl. **dhotis** Indian man's loincloth

dhow Arabian sailing ship (not **dow**)

DHSS hist. Department of Health and Social Security

dhurra use **durra**

dhurrie (also **durrie**) Indian rug

DI 1 Defence Intelligence **2** Detective Inspector **3** direct injection

dia. diameter

diablerie (not ital.) **1** recklessness, wildness **2** arch. sorcery

diachronic concerned with the way something develops over time; cf. **synchronic**

diaconate office of deacon

diacritic a sign such as an accent used to indicate a difference in pronunciation

diaeresis (US **dieresis**) pl. **diaereses** mark ¨ placed over a vowel to indicate that it is sounded separately, as in *naïve, Brontë*

Diaghilev, Sergei (Pavlovich) (1872–1929), Russian ballet impresario

diagnosis pl. **diagnoses**

diagram (not **diagramme**)

dial v. (**dialling, dialled**; US one **-l-**)

dialect (abbrev. **dial.**) □ **dialectal**

dialectic (also **dialectics**, usu. treated as sing.) investigation of ideas through argument □ **dialectical**

dialler (US **dialer**)

dialling code, dialling tone Brit. (N. Amer. **area code, dial tone**)

dialog box (Brit. also **dialogue box**) boxed area on computer screen

dialogue (US also **dialog**) conversation between people in a book, film, etc.

dial-up adj. used via a telephone line (hyphen, two words as verb)
dialyse (US **dialyze**) purify or treat by means of dialysis
dialysis pl. **dialyses** Chem. & Med. separation of particles in a liquid by filtration
diamanté (accent, not ital.)
diameter (abbrev. **dia.**) ◻ **diametral**
Diana Rom. Mythol. goddess of hunting; Gk equivalent **Artemis**
Diana, Princess of Wales (1961–97), former wife of Prince Charles; title before marriage *Lady Diana Frances Spencer*
diarchy (also **dyarchy**) government by two authorities
diarrhoea (US **diarrhea**) (two *r*s)
diaspora dispersion of a people from their homeland; (**the Diaspora**) dispersion of the Jews beyond Israel
diathesis pl. **diatheses** Med. tendency to suffer from a particular condition
dice small cube used in games of chance (traditionally the plural of **die**, but now used as both the sing. and the pl.)
dicey potentially dangerous (not **dicy**)
dichotomize (Brit. also **dichotomise**)
dichotomy division or contrast between two opposed or different things
Dickens, Charles (John Huffam) (1812–70), English novelist ◻ **Dickensian**
dickens used in exclamations (lower case)
dicky (also **dickey**) pl. **dickies, dickeys** **1** false shirt front **2** folding seat
dicky bird, dicky bow (two words)
Dictaphone trademark small speech recorder
dictum pl. **dicta** or **dictums** formal pronouncement
dicy use **dicey**
Diderot, Denis (1713–84), French philosopher and writer
didgeridoo (also **didjeridu**) Australian Aboriginal wind instrument
didicoi Gypsy or other nomadic person (not **diddicoy**)
didrachm ancient Greek coin worth two drachmas
didst arch. (no apostrophe)
die n. **1** device for moulding metal or for stamping a design **2** sing. of **dice**
die-cast (hyphen)
died (abbrev. **d.**) see also **dagger**
diehard (one word)
dieresis US var. of **diaeresis**
diesel-electric, diesel-hydraulic (hyphen)
Dies Irae Latin hymn sung in a Mass for the dead (caps, ital.)
diestrus US var. of **dioestrus**
dietician (also **dietitian**)
Dieu et mon droit God and my right (the motto of the British monarch) (Fr., ital.)
difference (not **-ance**)
differentia pl. **differentiae** distinguishing characteristic (not ital.)
differently abled proposed as an alternative to **disabled, handicapped**, etc. but has gained little currency
diffuse spread over a wide area; cf. **defuse**
digamma sixth letter of the early Greek alphabet (Ϝ, ϝ) (not used in classical times)
Digest, the compendium of Roman law compiled in the reign of Justinian
digestif alcoholic drink taken after a meal (Fr., ital.)
digital using information represented as digits using discrete values of a physical quantity such as voltage; cf. **analogue**
digitize (Brit. also **digitise**)
diglossia Ling. situation in which two languages are used within a community
dike US var. of **dyke**
diktat an order or decree (not ital.)
dilapidated (not **del-**)
dilatation Med. the action of widening or opening
dilate widen or open ◻ **dilatable, dilation**
dilator (not **-er**)
dilemma situation involving a choice between undesirable alternatives; disp. problem
dilettante pl. **dilettanti** or **dilettantes** person with a superficial interest in a subject; arch. amateur lover of the arts (not ital.)
diluvial (also **diluvian**) relating to a flood, esp. the biblical Flood
diluvium pl. **diluvia** material deposited

by glacial action
dim. diminuendo
DiMaggio, Joe (1914–99), American baseball player
dime N. Amer. ten-cent coin
diminuendo pl. **diminuendos** or **diminuendi** Mus. getting softer (abbrev. **dim.**)
dim sum Chinese dish of small savoury dumplings (not **dim sim**)
DIN technical standards used to designate electrical connections and film speeds [Ger. *Deutsche Industrie-Norm* 'German Industrial Standard']
dinar monetary unit of Bosnia, Serbia, Montenegro, and several countries of the Middle East and North Africa; cf. **denar**
Dinesen, Isak, see **Blixen**
Ding an sich Philos. thing as it is in itself (Ger., ital.)
dinghy small boat
dingo pl. **dingoes** or **dingos** Australian wild dog
dingy gloomy and drab
dining car, **dining hall**, **dining room**, **dining table** (two words)
dinosaur Mesozoic fossil reptile (species names lower case, as *allosaurus*)
diocese district under the care of a bishop □ **diocesan**
dioecious Biol. having the male and female reproductive organs in separate individuals; cf. **monoecious**
dioestrus (US **diestrus**) Zool. sexual inactivity between periods of oestrus
Diogenes (*c*.400–*c*.325 BC), Greek Cynic philosopher
Diogenes Laertius (3rd cent. BC), Greek biographer
Dionysiac relating to the emotional aspects of human nature; cf. **Apollonian**
Dionysian 1 relating to Dionysus **2** relating to Dionysius
Dionysius two rulers of Syracuse, **Dionysius the Elder** (ruled 405–367 BC) and his son **Dionysius the Younger** (ruled 367–357 BC)
Dionysus Gk Mythol. god of wine, nature, and ecstatic rites; also called **Bacchus**
dioptre (US **diopter**) unit of refractive power
Dioscuri Gk & Rom. Mythol. the twins Castor and Pollux
DIP 1 Comput. document image processing **2** Electron. dual in-line package
Dip. diploma
DipAD (also **Dip.AD**) Diploma in Art and Design
DipEd (also **Dip.Ed.**) Diploma in Education
DipHE (also **Dip.HE**) Diploma of Higher Education
diphtheria (not **dipth-**)
diphthong combination of two vowels in a single syllable (not **dipth-**)
diplodocus dinosaur (lower case)
diplomate chiefly US holder of a diploma, esp. a doctor certified as a specialist
dipsomania alcoholism
diptych painting on two hinged panels
Dirac, Paul Adrian Maurice (1902–84), English physicist
direct current (abbrev. **DC** or **d.c.**)
direction finder (two words)
Directoire of a neoclassical decorative style (cap., not ital.)
director general pl. **directors general** (two words)
Directory, the revolutionary government in France 1795–9 (cap.)
directress (also **directrice**) female director; but prefer **director**
directrix pl. **directrices** Geom. fixed line describing a curve or surface
dirigible adj. able to be guided or steered. n. airship
dirigisme state control of economic and social matters (Fr., ital.)
dirigiste relating to *dirigisme* (Fr., ital.)
dirndl dress with a full skirt
dirt cheap, **dirt poor**, **dirt track** (two words, hyphen when attrib.)
dis- expressing negation, removal, or separation; cf. **dys-**
disabled as an adjective, the standard term: prefer to **crippled**, **defective**, or **handicapped**; has not been replaced by coinages such as **differently abled** or **physically challenged.** Do not use as a noun (*the disabled*)
disaffirm Law reverse (a decision) or

repudiate (a settlement)
disappear, **disappoint** (one *s*, two *ps*)
disassemble take to pieces; cf. **dissemble**
disassociate var. of **dissociate**
disastrous (not **des-**, **-terous**)
disbound (of part of a book) removed from a bound volume
disc (US & Comput. **disk**)
discernible (not **-able**)
discerption arch. action of pulling something apart □ **discerptible**
disciple lower case for Apostles □ **discipular**
disc jockey (two words; abbrev. **DJ**)
disco pl. **discos**
discobolus pl. **discoboli** discus thrower in ancient Greece; the *Discobolus* is a lost statue by Myron
discoloration (not **discolouration**)
discolour (US **discolor**)
discomfit (**discomfiting, discomfited**) make uneasy or embarrassed
discomfort slight pain or awkwardness
disconnection (not **disconnexion**)
discotheque dance club [Fr. *discothèque*]
discreet careful and prudent
discrepancy difference or lack of compatibility (not **-ency**)
discrete separate and distinct
discus pl. **discuses**
disect use **dissect**
disembowel (**disembowelling, disembowelled**; US one **-l-**) □ **disembowelment**
disenfranchise (also **disfranchise**; not **-ize**)
disenthral (US **disenthrall**) (**disenthralling, disenthralled**) □ **disenthralment**
diseuse (masc. ***diseur***) female artiste who performs monologues (Fr., ital.)
dishabille Engl. form of **déshabillé**
dishevelled (US **disheveled**) □ **dishevelment**
dishonour, dishonourable (US **dishonor, dishonorable**)
disinterested impartial; cf. **uninterested**
disjecta membra scattered fragments, esp. of written work (L., ital.)
disk spelling in the US and in computing contexts of **disc**
disk drive (two words)
diskette floppy disk
Disneyland name of amusement parks in California and (**Disneyland Resort Paris**) France
Disney World amusement park in Orlando, Florida
disorganized (Brit. also **disorganised**)
disorient (Brit. also **disorientate**) cause to lose one's sense of direction
dispatch (also **despatch**)
dispensable (not **-ible**)
Dispersion, the the Diaspora (cap.)
display type bold or eye-catching type used for headings or advertisements
Disraeli, Benjamin, 1st Earl of Beaconsfield (1804–81), British prime minister 1868 and 1874–80
dissect (not **disect**) □ **dissector**
disseize (also **disseise**) Law wrongly dispossess
dissemble hide one's true motives or feelings; cf. **disassemble**
dissension disagreement leading to discord (not **dissention**)
Dissenter hist. a Nonconformist (cap.)
dissociate (also **disassociate**) disconnect or separate
dissyllable var. of **disyllable**
dissymmetry (not **disy-**) **1** lack of symmetry **2** symmetrical relation of mirror images
distension condition of being distended (not **-tion**)
distil (US **distill**) (**distilling, distilled**)
distingué (fem. ***distinguée***) distinguished (Fr., ital.)
distrait (fem. ***distraite***) distracted (Fr., ital.)
distributor (not **-er**)
district attorney US state prosecutor (caps in titles; abbrev. **DA**)
District of Columbia US federal district coextensive with the city of Washington (abbrev. **DC**)
disulphide (US **disulfide**)
disyllable (also **dissyllable**) word or metrical foot of two syllables
disymetry use **dissymetry**

ditchwater (one word)
ditheism belief in two gods
dithyramb wild ancient Greek hymn to the god Dionysus
ditto mark „ indicating a list item etc. is to be repeated
div Math. divergence (no point)
div. division (point)
Divali var. of **Diwali**
dive-bomb, dive-bomber (hyphen)
divers arch. several, sundry
diverse widely varied
diverticulum pl. **diverticula** Anat. blind tube leading from a cavity or passage
divertimento pl. **divertimenti** or **divertimentos** Mus. light composition, esp. suite for chamber orchestra
divertissement minor entertainment or diversion (not ital.)
Dives rich man [Luke 16]
dividing line (two words)
diving bell, diving board, diving suit (two words)
division (abbrev. **div.**; symbol ÷)
divisor Math. number by which another number is to be divided
divorcee (Brit. both male and female; US masc. **divorcé**, fem. **divorcée**, not ital.; no accents in Brit.)
Diwali (also **Divali**) Hindu festival
Dixie name for the Southern states of the US
DIY do-it-yourself □ **DIY'er**
DJ n. pl. **DJs 1** disc jockey **2** dinner jacket. v. (**DJ's, DJ'ing, DJ'd**) perform as a disc jockey
Djakarta var. of **Jakarta**
djebel var. of **jebel**
djellaba (also **djellabah** or **jellaba**) Arab hooded cloak
djibbah (also **djibba**) var. of **jibba**
Djibouti country on the NE coast of Africa (not **Jibuti**) □ **Djiboutian**
djinn var. of **jinn**
dkl, dkm US dekaliter(s); dekameter(s) (no point)
DL Deputy Lieutenant
dl decilitre(s) (no point)
D-layer layer of the ionosphere (hyphen, one cap.)
DLitt (also **D.Litt.**) Doctor of Letters [L. *Doctor Litterarum*]
DM (also **D-mark**) Deutschmark
dm decimetre(s) (no point)
DMs Dr Martens (shoes or boots)
dmu diesel multiple unit (railway vehicle)
DMus (also **D.Mus.**) Doctor of Music
DMZ US demilitarized zone
DNA deoxyribonucleic acid
DNB Dictionary of National Biography, completed in 1900; the new *Oxford Dictionary of National Biography* was published in 2004
Dnieper river of eastern Europe; Russ. name **Dnepr**, Ukrainian name **Dnipro**
Dniester river of eastern Europe; Russ. name **Dnestr**, Ukrainian name **Dnister**
D-notice government notice to news editors requiring them not to publish certain information (hyphen, one cap.)
DNS Comput. domain name server (or system)
do var. of **doh**
do. ditto
DOA dead on arrival
doable able to be done (one word)
Dobermann pinscher (US **Doberman**) large German breed of dog
doc informal **1** doctor **2** document **3** documentary
docent US **1** university teacher **2** museum guide
doch an dorris var. of **deoch an doris**
docket v. (**docketing, docketed**)
docklands (lower case, but **Docklands** in East London)
dockside, dockyard (one word)
doctor usu. lower case in ref. to a medical practitioner, but cap. for a holder of the highest university degree; abbrev. **D**, but **Dr** before a name
Doctor of Civil Law (abbrev. **DCL**)
Doctor of Divinity (abbrev. **DD**)
Doctor of Laws (abbrev. **LLD**)
Doctor of Letters (abbrev. **DLitt, LittD**)
Doctor of Medicine (abbrev. **MD**)
Doctor of Music (abbrev. **MusD, DMus**)
Doctor of Philosophy (abbrev. **PhD, DPhil**)

Doctor of Science (abbrev. **DSc**)
Doctor Who UK science-fiction TV series (no question mark, not ***Dr Who***)
doctrinaire seeking to impose a doctrine in all circumstances
docudrama television drama based on real events (one word)
DOD US Department of Defense
dodecahedron pl. **dodecahedra** or **dodecahedrons** solid figure with twelve plane faces
dodecaphonic Mus. of the twelve-note scale
dodgem (US trademark **Dodg'em**)
Dodgson, Charles Lutwidge, see **Carroll**
dodo pl. **dodos** extinct flightless bird
Dodoma capital of Tanzania
DoE hist. Department of the Environment
doest, doeth arch. (no apostrophe)
dogana custom house in Italy (ital.)
dog cart, **dog collar**, **dog days** (two words)
doge hist. chief magistrate of Venice or Genoa
dog-eared (hyphen)
dogfight, **dogfish** (one word)
doggerel badly written verse
Doggett's Coat and Badge trophy in an annual rowing contest among Thames watermen
doggy-paddle (hyphen)
doghouse (one word)
dogie N. Amer. motherless calf
dog Latin debased form of Latin
dogma pl. **dogmas** doctrine held to be authoritative
dogmatize (Brit. also **dogmatise**)
do-gooder (hyphen)
dogsbody (one word)
Dog Star the star Sirius
dog-tooth (hyphen) **1** architectural ornament **2** (also **dogstooth**) small check pattern
DoH Department of Health
doh (also **do**) Mus. note in tonic sol-fa
doily ornamental mat or napkin
do-it-yourself (hyphens; abbrev. **DIY**)
dol. dollar(s)
Dolby trademark noise-reduction system used in tape recording
dolce Mus. sweetly and softly
dolce far niente pleasant idleness (It., ital.)
Dolcelatte trademark Italian cheese
dolce vita life of pleasure and luxury (It., ital.); (***La dolce vita***) film by Fellini (1960)
doldrums, the (lower case) **1** state of stagnation or depression **2** region of the Atlantic Ocean
doleful (not **-full**)
Dolgellau town in Gwynedd, Wales
Dolittle, Dr hero of children's books by Hugh Lofting (1886–1947); cf. **Doolittle**
D'Oliveira, Basil (Lewis) (1931–2011), British cricketer
dollar monetary unit of the US, Canada, Australia, etc. (symbol **$**; different dollars differentiated as US$, A$ (Austral.), C$ (Canad.), etc.)
Dollfuss, Engelbert (1892–1934), Chancellor of Austria 1932–4
doll's house (N. Amer. **dollhouse**) (note apostrophe)
Dolly Varden **1** character in Dickens's *Barnaby Rudge* **2** woman's large hat **3** charr (fish) of the North Pacific
dolma pl. **dolmas** or **dolmades** stuffed vine or cabbage leaf
dolman long Turkish robe
dolmen megalithic tomb
dolorous sorrowful
dolour (US **dolor**) sorrow
dolphinarium pl. **dolphinariums**
Dom **1** title prefixed to the names of some Roman Catholic dignitaries and Benedictine and Carthusian monks **2** Portuguese title prefixed to a male forename; cf. **don**
domain **1** area controlled by a ruler or government **2** Comput. distinct subset of the Internet
domaine vineyard (Fr., ital.)
Domesday Book (not **Doomsday**)
domicile place of residence (not **domicil**)
dominatrix pl. **dominatrices** or **dominatrixes** dominating woman
Dominica one of the Windward Islands
Dominican Republic country in the Caribbean, the eastern part of the island of Hispaniola

dominie Sc. schoolmaster
domino pl. **dominoes**
don 1 university teacher, esp. at Oxford or Cambridge **2** (**Don**) Spanish title prefixed to a male forename; cf. **Dom**
Dona (also **Doña**) title prefixed to the forename of a Portuguese (or Spanish) lady; cf. **Donna**
Donatello (1386–1466), Italian sculptor; born *Donato di Betto Bardi*
Donau Ger. name for the **Danube**
Donegal county in the north-west of the Republic of Ireland (but **Donegall Street**, Belfast)
doner kebab (not **donor**)
Donets river of eastern Europe
Donetsk city in Ukraine
dong monetary unit of Vietnam
Donizetti, Gaetano (1797–1848), Italian composer
donjon 1 great tower or innermost keep of a castle **2** arch. dungeon
Don Juan legendary Spanish nobleman famous for seducing women
donkey pl. **donkeys**
Donna title prefixed to the forename of an Italian lady; cf. **Dona, Doña**
donna Italian lady (ital.)
Donne, John (1572–1631), English poet
donnée (Fr., ital.) **1** subject or theme of a narrative **2** basic fact or assumption
donor giver (not **-er**)
Don Quixote romance (1605–15) by Cervantes
donut US var. of **doughnut**
Doolittle, Hilda (1886–1961), American poet; pseudonym **H.D.**; cf. **Dolittle, Dr**
doomsayer, doomsday (one word)
Doomsday Book use **Domesday Book**
doorbell, doorknob, doorman, doormat, doornail, doorstep, doorway (one word)
Doornik Flemish name for **Tournai**
dopey (not **dopy**) **1** stupefied **2** silly
doppelgänger a double of a living person (accent, lower case, not ital.)
Dopper S. Afr. member of the Gereformeerde Kerk (Calvinistic denomination)
Doppler effect (also **Doppler shift**) Phys. apparent change in frequency of sound etc. waves as the source is approaching or receding (one cap.)
dopy use **dopey**
Dordogne river and department of western France
Doré, Gustave (1832–83), French illustrator
Dorian member of an ancient Hellenic people
Doric 1 Greek dialect of the Dorians **2** broad dialect, esp. the dialect of NE Scotland **3** plain order of classical architecture
Dormition Orthodox Church festival celebrating the passing of the Virgin Mary from earthly life (cap.)
Dormobile trademark motor caravan
dormouse pl. **dormice** (not **door-**)
dormy Golf ahead by as many holes as there are holes left to play
Dorneywood country house in southern England used by a Secretary of State or government minister
doronicum pl. **doronicums** leopard's bane (plant)
dorp S. Afr. rural town or village
Dorset county of SW England (not **-shire**)
dory 1 marine fish **2** flat-bottomed rowing boat
DOS Comput. disk operating system
DoS Comput. denial of service
dos-à-dos (Fr., ital.) **1** back to back **2** (of two books) bound together with a shared central board
dos and don'ts rules of behaviour (one apostrophe)
dose quantity of a medicine or drug taken at one time; cf. **doze**
do-si-do pl. **do-si-dos** figure in country dancing (hyphens)
dosimeter device for measuring an absorbed dose of ionizing radiation (not **dosemeter**)
Dos Passos, John (Roderigo) (1896–1970), American novelist
dossier collection of documents
Dostoevsky (also **Dostoyevsky**), Fyodor (Mikhailovich) (1821–81), Russian novelist
DoT 1 (in Canada and formerly in the UK) Department of Transport **2** US

Department of Transportation
dot arch. woman's dowry (Fr., ital.)
dot-com (also **dot.com**) company conducting its business on the Internet
dots (...) see **ellipsis**
Douai town in northern France
douane custom house in a Mediterranean country (Fr., ital.)
Douay Bible English translation of the Bible formerly used in the Roman Catholic Church
double agent (two words)
double-barrelled (hyphen)
double bass, double bill, double bluff (two words)
double-book, double-breasted, double-check, double-click, double-cross (hyphen)
double dagger (also **double obelus**) symbol (‡) used to introduce an annotation
double-dealing, double-decker, double-edged (hyphen)
double entendre pl. **double entendres** word or phrase open to two interpretations, one of which is indecent (not ital.) [obs. Fr., now *double entente*]
double-glazed (hyphen)
double glazing (two words)
double obelus var. of **double dagger**
doublespeak, doublethink (one word)
doubloon old Spanish gold coin
doublure ornamental inner lining of a book cover
doubting Thomas sceptical person (one cap.) [after John 20:24–9]
douceur a bribe (Fr., ital.)
douceur de vivre (also ***douceur de vie***) pleasant way of living (Fr., ital.)
douche shower of water directed at the body (not ital.)
doughboy 1 dumpling **2** US infantryman, esp. in WWI
doughnut (US also **donut**)
Douglas fir, Douglas pine, Douglas spruce (one cap.)
Douglas-Home, Sir Alec, Baron Home of the Hirsel of Coldstream (1903–95), British prime minister 1963–4
Doulton (also **Royal Doulton**) trademark decorative pottery or porcelain
Dounreay atomic research station in northern Scotland
douse 1 drench with liquid **2** extinguish; cf. **dowse**
dove N. Amer. past of **dive**
dovecote (also **dovecot**) (one word)
dow use **dhow**
dowager widow with a title or property derived from her late husband
dowelling (US **doweling**) cylindrical rods for cutting into dowels
dower 1 widow's share for life of her husband's estate **2** arch. dowry
Dow Jones index (also **Dow Jones average**) list of share prices on the New York Stock Exchange (two caps)
Down county of Northern Ireland
down and out destitute (three words; hyphenated as noun)
downbeat, downcast, downfall, downhill, download, downmarket (one word)
down payment (two words)
downpipe, downplay, downpour, downright, downriver, downshift, downside, downsize (one word)
Down's syndrome (also **Down syndrome**) congenital disorder (one cap.; not **mongolism**)
downstairs, downstream, downstroke (one word)
down to earth (three words, hyphens when attrib.)
downtown, downtrodden, downturn (one word)
down under (two words; usu. caps as noun meaning 'Australia and New Zealand')
downwind (one word)
dowse search for water by observing the motion of a pointer; cf. **douse**
doxology liturgical formula of praise to God
doyen (fem. **doyenne**) most prominent person in a particular field (not ital.)
Doyle, Sir Arthur Conan (1859–1930), Scottish creator of Sherlock Holmes
D'Oyly Carte, Richard (1844–1901), English impresario
doze sleep lightly; cf. **dose**
dozen pl. same exc. in informal contexts (abbrev. **doz.**)
DP 1 data processing **2** displaced person

DPhil (also **D.Phil.**) Doctor of Philosophy
DPP Director of Public Prosecutions
DPT Med. diphtheria, pertussis (whooping cough), and tetanus
Dr 1 debit [f. *debtor*] **2** (as a title) Doctor **3** (**Dr.**) (in street names) Drive
dr. 1 drachm(s) **2** drachma(s) **3** dram(s)
drachm former unit of weight equivalent to 60 grains (an eighth of an ounce) (abbrev. **dr.**)
drachma pl. **drachmas** or **drachmae** former monetary unit of Greece (abbrev. **dr.**)
Draco (7th cent. BC), Athenian legislator
draconian excessively harsh (lower case)
draft n. **1** preliminary version of a text **2** written order to pay a sum **3** (**the draft**) US conscription for military service **4** US var. of **draught.** v. **1** prepare a draft of (a text) **2** US conscript for military service
draftsman 1 person who drafts legal documents **2** US var. of **draughtsman**
drafty US var. of **draughty**
dragée sweet or silver cake decoration (accent, not ital.)
dragoman pl. **dragomans** or **dragomen** Arabic, Turkish, or Persian interpreter
dragonfly (one word)
dragonnade hist. persecution involving quartering troops on a population
dragoon member of any of several British cavalry regiments
drag queen, drag race (two words)
drainpipe (one word)
dram[1] 1 Sc. small drink of spirits **2** (abbrev. **dr.**) drachm
dram[2] monetary unit of Armenia
drama-documentary (hyphen)
dramatis personae the characters in a play (not ital.)
dramatize (Brit. also **dramatise**)
dramaturge (also **dramaturg**) **1** dramatist **2** literary editor at a theatre
Drambuie trademark whisky liqueur
Drang nach Osten former German policy of eastward expansion (ital.)
draught (US **draft**) n. **1** current of cool air **2** act of drinking or inhaling **3** depth of water needed to float a ship.
draughtboard, draughtproof (one word)
draughts Brit. game played on a chequered board; N. Amer. name **checkers**
draughtsman (US **draftsman**)
draughty (US **drafty**)
Dravidian (speaker of) a family of languages of India and Sri Lanka
drawback, drawbridge (one word)
drawing board, drawing pin, drawing room (two words)
dreadnought type of early 20th-cent. battleship; (***HMS Dreadnought***) ship completed in 1906
dream v. (past and past part. **dreamed** or **dreamt**)
dreamland (one word)
Dreamtime (also **Dreaming**) (among Australian Aboriginals) the golden age or Alcheringa (cap.)
dreich Sc. dreary, bleak
Dreiser, Theodore (Herman Albert) (1871–1945), American novelist
dressing-down n. (hyphen)
dressing gown, dressing room, dressing table (two words)
dressmaker (one word)
dress rehearsal, dress sense (two words)
drey squirrel's nest
drier[1] comparative of **dry**
drier[2] var. of **dryer**
drift ice, drift net (two words)
driftwood (one word)
drily (N. Amer. **dryly**) in an ironically humorous way
drink-driving Brit. driving a vehicle with an excess of alcohol in the blood; N. Amer. **drunk-driving** □ **drink-driver**
drip-dry, drip-feed (hyphen)
drivable (not **driveable**)
drive-by, drive-in adj. (hyphen, two words as verb)
drivel v. (**drivelling, drivelled**; US **-l-**)
driving licence (N. Amer. **driver's license**)
Dr Martens trademark boot or shoe with an air-cushioned sole (abbrev. **DMs**)

droit a right or due (Fr., ital.)
droit de seigneur supposed right of a feudal lord to have sex with a vassal's bride (Fr., ital.)
dromedary Arabian camel (with one hump)
drop capital (also **drop initial**) large opening capital letter occupying more than the depth of a line
drop kick n. (two words, hyphen as verb)
dropout n. (one word, two words as verb)
drosera sundew (plant) (not ital.)
droshky Russian four-wheeled open carriage (not **drosky**)
drosophila fruit fly used in genetic research (not ital.)
drouth arch. drought
druggist N. Amer. pharmacist
drugstore N. Amer. pharmacy also selling toiletries etc.
Druid ancient Celtic priest (cap.)
drumbeat, **drumhead** (one word)
drum kit, **drum major**, **drum majorette**, **drum roll** (two words)
drumstick (one word)
drunk driving N. Amer. drink-driving (two words)
drunkenness (three *ns*)
Druze pl. same or **Druzes** member of a sect linked with Islam, living in Lebanon and Syria (not **Druse**)
dry (**drier**, **driest**) □ **dryness**
dryad wood nymph (lower case)
dry-clean, **dry-cleaner** (hyphen)
dryer (also **drier**) person or thing that dries
dryly N. Amer. var. of **drily**
dryness (not **dri-**)
dry point work produced by engraving on a copper plate with a needle
DS 1 Mus. dal segno **2** detective sergeant **3** Mil. directing staff
Ds the chemical element darmstadtium (no point)
DSC Distinguished Service Cross
DSc (also **D.Sc.**) Doctor of Science
DSM Distinguished Service Medal
DSO Distinguished Service Order
DSP Comput. digital signal processor (or processing)
d.s.p. died without issue [L. *decessit sine prole*]
DSS hist. Department of Social Security
DST N. Amer. daylight saving time
DTI Department of Trade and Industry
DTP desktop publishing
DTp Department of Transport
DTs delirium tremens
Du usu. capitalized as prefix to a non-anglicized proper name, unless part of a title
Du. Dutch
dual-purpose, **dual-use** (hyphen)
Dubai state of the United Arab Emirates
Du Barry, Marie Jeanne Bécu, Comtesse (1743–93), French mistress of Louis XV
dubbin grease used for waterproofing leather (not **dubbing**)
Dubček, Alexander (1921–92), First Secretary of the Czechoslovak Communist Party 1968–9
Dublin capital of the Republic of Ireland
Dublin Bay prawns scampi (two caps)
dubnium chemical element of atomic number 105 (symbol **Db**)
Du Bois, W(illiam) E(dward) B(urghardt) (1868–1963), American writer and political activist
Dubonnet trademark sweet red vermouth
Dubrovnik port in Croatia; former It. name **Ragusa**
duc French duke (cap. in titles; not ital. as part of name)
Duce, Il title assumed by Benito Mussolini in 1922
Duchamp, Marcel (1887–1968), French-born artist
duchess duke's wife or widow, or woman holding a rank equivalent to duke (cap. in titles)
duchesse 1 soft heavy kind of satin **2** chaise longue **3** dressing table with a pivoting mirror
duchesse French countess (cap. in titles; not ital. as part of name)
duchesse lace, **duchesse potatoes** (two words)
duchy territory of a duke or duchess; (**the Duchy**) royal dukedom of Cornwall or Lancaster
duckbill animal with jaws resembling a duck's bill (one word)

duck-billed platypus (hyphen)
duckboard, ducktail, duckwalk, duckweed (one word)
ductus pl. **ducti** Anat. duct (not ital.)
duel v. (**duelling, duelled**; US one **-l-**)
dueller, duellist (US **dueler, duelist**)
duello rules or practice of duelling
duende (not ital.) **1** passion **2** an evil spirit
duenna chaperone in a Spanish family (not ital.) [Sp. *dueña*]
duet v. (**duetting, duetted**)
due to traditionally condemned as incorrect in the sense 'because of'; **on account of** is a better alternative
Dufay, Guillaume (*c.*1400–74), French composer; cf. **Dufy**
duffel (also **duffle**) coarse woollen cloth
duffel bag, duffel coat (two words)
Dufy, Raoul (1877–1953), French painter; cf. **Dufay**
dugout n. (one word)
duiker African antelope (not **duyker**)
du jour enjoying great but probably short-lived popularity (Fr., ital.)
duke male holding the highest hereditary title in the British and certain other peerages (cap. in titles)
DUKW amphibious transport vehicle
dulia RC Ch. reverence accorded to saints and angels; cf. **latria**
dullness (not **dulness**)
Duma Russian legislative body
Dumas 1 Alexandre (1802–70), author of *The Three Musketeers* and *The Count of Monte Cristo*; known as **Dumas *père*** **2** Alexandre (1824–95), author of *La Dame aux camélias*; known as **Dumas *fils***
du Maurier 1 Dame Daphne (1907–89), English novelist **2** George (Louis Palmella Busson) (1834–96), French-born novelist and artist
dumb avoid in the sense 'congenitally unable to speak': prefer alternatives such as **speech-impaired**
Dumbarton town in SW Scotland
Dumbartonshire var. of **Dunbartonshire**
dumb-bell (hyphen)
dumbfound (one word; not **dumfound**)
dum-dum informal stupid person (hyphen)
dumdum bullet (no hyphen)
Dumfries town in SW Scotland, in Dumfries and Galloway council area
Dumfriesshire former county of SW Scotland
dummy mock-up of a book or page
Dunbartonshire (also **Dumbartonshire**) former county of west central Scotland, now divided into **East Dunbartonshire** and **West Dunbartonshire** council areas.
Dunelm of Durham University (no point) [L. *Dunelmensis* 'of Durham']
dungeon 1 underground prison cell **2** arch. donjon
Dungeons and Dragons trademark fantasy role-playing game (two caps)
Dunkirk port in northern France; Fr. name **Dunkerque**
Dun Laoghaire port in the Republic of Ireland
Duns Scotus, John (*c.*1265–1308), Scottish theologian
duo pl. **duos**
duodecimal having twelve as a base
duodecimo pl. **duodecimos** page size resulting from folding a sheet into twelve leaves; twelvemo (abbrev. **12mo**)
duodenum pl. **duodenums** or **duodena** Anat. first part of the small intestine
duologue play or part of a play with only two speaking actors
duomo pl. **duomos** Italian cathedral
duotone half-tone illustration
dupondius pl. **dupondii** bronze or brass ancient Roman coin
Du Pont family of US industrialists
duppy W. Ind. malevolent spirit or ghost
du Pré, Jacqueline (1945–87), English cellist
dura use **durra**
durable (not **-eable**)
durchkomponiert Mus. (of a song) having different music for each verse (Ger., ital.)
Dürer, Albrecht (1471–1528), German engraver and painter
Durex pl. same, trademark condom
D'Urfey, Thomas (1653–1723), English playwright

Durham city and (also **County Durham**) county of NE England
Durkheim, Émile (1858–1917), French sociologist
durra variety of sorghum (not **dura, dhurra**)
durrie var. of **dhurrie**
Dushanbe capital of Tajikistan
Düsseldorf city in NW Germany
dustbin (one word)
dust bowl (two words)
dustcart (one word)
dust jacket (two words)
dustman, dustpan (one word)
dust storm, dust trap (two words)
Dutch (abbrev. **Du.**)
Dutch East Indies former name for **Indonesia**
Dutch Guiana former name for **Suriname**
duty-bound, duty-free (hyphen)
duumvir pl. **duumvirs**, L. **duumviri** (in ancient Rome) each of two officials holding a joint office
dux 1 chiefly Sc. top pupil in a school or class **2** Mus. subject of a fugue
duyker use **duiker**
DV *Deo volente* (God willing)
DVD digital versatile disc (formerly digital videodisc)
DVLA Driver and Vehicle Licensing Agency
Dvořák, Antonín (1841–1904), Czech composer
DVT deep-vein thrombosis
dwarf pl. **dwarfs** or (esp. in Tolkien and other fantasy writing) **dwarves**; considered offensive in the sense 'abnormally small person', but alternatives such as **person of restricted growth** have gained little currency
DWP Department for Work and Pensions
dwt 1 deadweight tonnage **2** pennyweight
Dy the chemical element dysprosium (no point)
dyad something consisting of two parts
Dyak var. of **Dayak**
dyarchy var. of **diarchy**
dybbuk pl. **dybbuks** or **dybbukim** malevolent spirit in Jewish folklore
dyeing colouring cloth etc.; cf. **dying** □ **dyeable**
dyer person who dyes cloth etc.
dyestuff (one word)
Dyfed former county of SW Wales
dying ceasing to live; cf. **dyeing**
dyke (US **dike**) **1** embankment holding back the sea **2** a lesbian
Dylan, Bob (b.1941), American singer; born *Robert Allen Zimmerman*
dynamo pl. **dynamos**
dyne Phys. unit of force (abbrev. **dyn**)
dys- bad or difficult (esp. in medical terms); cf. **dis-**
dysentery infection of the intestines
dyslexia Med. difficulty in recognizing written words or letters □ **dyslectic, dyslexic**
dyspepsia indigestion
dysphasia Med. difficulty in generating speech, due to brain disease or damage
dysphoria state of unease or general dissatisfaction
dysplasia Med. enlargement of an organ or tissue
dyspnoea (US **dyspnea**) Med. laboured breathing □ **dyspnoeic**
dyspraxia developmental disorder of the brain in childhood
dysprosium chemical element of atomic number 66 (symbol **Dy**)
dysrhythmia Med. abnormality in the rhythm of the brain or heart
dystopia imaginary place in which everything is bad
dystrophy Med. wasting disorder
Dzerzhinsky, Feliks (Edmundovich) (1877–1926), Russian Bolshevik leader
dzo pl. same or **dzos** hybrid of a cow and a yak (not **dzho** or **zho**)
Dzongkha official language of Bhutan; Bhutani

E

E 1 pl. **Es** or **E's** 5th letter of the alphabet **2** East or Eastern **3** complying with EU regulations; cf. **E-number 4** exa- (10^{18}) **5** energy: $E = mc^2$ **6** (**E.**) Earl

e (also **e**⁻) Chem. an electron.

è used in English in poetic and archaic contexts to indicate that an elided syllable is to be pronounced separately, as in 'Hence, loathèd Melancholy!'

e Math. base of Napierian or natural logarithms, approx. equal to 2.71828

€ euro or euros

each (abbrev. **ea.**)

earache, earbashing, eardrum, earful (one word)

Earhart, Amelia (1898–1937), American aviator

earhole (one word)

earl (cap. in titles; abbrev. **E.**)

Earl Grey type of tea (caps)

Earl Marshal pl. **Earl Marshals** officer presiding over the College of Arms

earlobe (one word)

Earl Palatine pl. **Earls Palatine** hist. earl with royal authority within his domain

Earls Court area of London (no apostrophe)

Early English earliest stage of English Gothic church architecture (caps)

earmark, earmuffs (one word)

earn past and past part. is **earned**, not **earnt**

Earp, Wyatt (1848–1929), American gambler and marshal

earphone, earpiece, earplug, earring, earshot (one word)

ear-splitting (hyphen)

earth cap. only in astronomical contexts and in a list of planets

earth-shattering (hyphen)

earthwork, earthworm (one word)

east (abbrev. **E**; cap. in ref. to the broad geographical region to the east of Europe, or to the former communist states of eastern Europe)

East Africa (caps)

East Anglia region of eastern England (caps)

eastbound (one word)

Eastbourne coastal town in East Sussex

East End area of London (caps)

East Ender (two words); British television programme is ***EastEnders***

Easter celebrated between 21 March and 25 April, on first Sunday after the first full moon following the northern spring equinox

eastern (abbrev. **E**; cap. in ref. to the broad geographical region to the east of Europe)

Eastern bloc (not **Eastern block**)

Eastern Church the Orthodox Church

Eastern Empire eastern part of the Roman Empire after its division in AD 395 (caps)

eastern hemisphere (lower case)

Easter Rising uprising in Ireland against British rule, Easter 1916

East Germany the German Democratic Republic, under Soviet control 1945–90

East India Company hist. trading company in SE Asia

East Indies 1 islands of SE Asia, esp. the Malay Archipelago **2** (also **East India**) arch. SE Asia as a whole

East London port in South Africa

East Lothian council area and former county of east central Scotland

East Riding of Yorkshire unitary authority in NE England

East River arm of the Hudson River in New York City (caps)

East Side part of Manhattan in New York City (caps)

East Sussex county of SE England (caps)

East Timor eastern part of the island of Timor, independent from Indonesia since 2002; official name **Timor Leste**

East–West (en rule)
easy-going (hyphen)
eau de cologne pl. **eaux de cologne** toilet water (not ital.)
eau de Nil pale greenish colour (not ital.)
eau de toilette pl. **eaux de toilette** toilet water (not ital.)
eau de vie pl. **eaux de vie** brandy (not ital.)
EB *Encyclopædia Britannica*
eBay Internet site for trading goods
Ebbw Vale town in South Wales; Welsh name **Glynebwy**
Ebla city of ancient Syria
Eblis var. of **Iblis**
E-boat German torpedo boat in WWII
Ebola (also **Ebola fever** or **Ebola virus**) infectious disease
e-book electronic version of printed book (hyphen)
Eboracum Roman name for York (abbrev. **Ebor.**)
Ebro river of NE Spain
EBU European Broadcasting Union
ebullient (not **-ant**)
EC 1 East Central (London postal district) **2** European Commission **3** European Community
écarté (Fr., ital.) **1** card game for two players **2** ballet position
ECB England and Wales Cricket Board
Ecce Homo painting of Christ wearing the crown of thorns [L., 'behold the man', said by Pontius Pilate]
eccentric 1 unconventional and slightly strange **2** (also **excentric**) tech. not placed centrally or symmetrically about a centre
Eccles cake cake of pastry filled with currants (one cap., no apostrophe)
Ecclesiastes book of the Old Testament attributed to Solomon (abbrev. **Eccles.**)
Ecclesiasticus book of the Apocrypha (abbrev. **Ecclus**)
ECG electrocardiogram or electrocardiograph
echelon level or rank (not ital.) [Fr. *échelon*]
echidna egg-laying mammal of Australia and New Guinea
echinacea plant used in herbal medicine
echo (**echoes, echoing, echoed**)
echt authentic and typical (Ger., ital.)
eclair choux pastry cake filled with cream (not ital.) [Fr. *éclair*]
éclaircissement an explanation (Fr., ital.)
éclat brilliant display or effect (accent, not ital.)
eclectic borrowing from a wide range of sources □ **eclectically**
ecliptic great circle representing the sun's apparent path during the year
eclogue pastoral poem, esp. (the *Eclogues*) a collection of ten by Virgil
E. coli *Escherichia coli*, bacterium which can cause food poisoning
e-commerce commercial transactions conducted on the Internet (hyphen)
Economist, The UK periodical (cap. and italic *The*)
economize (Brit. also **economise**)
ecossaise energetic country dance (not ital.) [Fr. *écossaise*]
ecosystem, **ecoterrorism** (one word)
eco-warrior (hyphen)
ecru fawn colour (not ital.) [Fr. *écru*]
ECSC European Coal and Steel Community
ecstasy (not **ex-**, **-cy**; cap. as drug)
ECT electroconvulsive therapy
ectomorph person with lean and delicate build
ecu (also **ECU**) former term for **euro¹**
Ecuador equatorial republic in South America □ **Ecuadorian** (or **Ecuadorean**)
ecumenical involving unity among Christian Churches
eczema condition in which the skin becomes rough and inflamed
ed. pl. **eds** or **eds.** edited by; edition; editor
edacious fond of eating
Edam 1 town in the Netherlands **2** round Dutch cheese
Edda either of two 13th-cent. Icelandic books, the *Elder* or *Poetic Edda* and the *Younger* or *Prose Edda*
Eddy, Mary Baker (1821–1910), US founder of Christian Science movement

Eddystone Rocks reef off coast of Cornwall, site of lighthouse
edelweiss alpine plant
edema US var. of **oedema**
Eden, Garden of (caps)
Edgbaston area of Birmingham (not **Edgebaston**)
Edgehill English Civil War battle in the Midlands (1642) (not **Edghill**)
edge tool (two words)
edgeways (US **edgewise**) (one word)
Edgeworth, Maria (1767–1849), Irish novelist (not **Edgworth**)
Edgware, Edgware Road in London (not **Edgeware**)
edh var. of **eth**
Edinburgh capital of Scotland (not **-borough**)
Edirne town in Turkey, capital of the Ottoman Empire 1361–1453; ancient name **Adrianople**
Edison, Thomas (Alva) (1847–1931), American inventor
edition (abbrev. **ed.** or **edn**)
editio princeps pl. ***editiones principes*** first printed edition of a book (L., ital.)
editor (not **-er**; abbrev. **ed.**)
editorialize (Brit. also **editorialise**)
editress (or **editrix**, pl. **editrices**) dated female editor
Edmonton 1 capital of Alberta, Canada **2** area of Greater London
Edmund Campion, St see **Campion**
edn pl. **edns** edition (no point)
Edo former name for **Tokyo**
Edom ancient region south of the Dead Sea □ **Edomite**
EDP 1 electronic data processing **2** editorial design and production
eds (also **eds.**) pl. of **ed.**
EDT Eastern Daylight Time
educe bring out (something latent or potential); cf. **adduce** □ **eduction**
Edw. Edward (regnal year)
Edward the Confessor, St (*c.*1003–66), king of England 1042–66
EEC European Economic Community
EEG electroencephalogram, electroencephalograph, or electroencephalography
Eelam proposed homeland of the Tamil people of Sri Lanka
e'en 1 literary even **2** Sc. even (evening)
e'er literary ever
eerie (not **eery**)
Eeyore gloomy donkey in *Winnie-the-Pooh* by A. A. Milne □ **Eeyorish**
effect n. a result. v. cause to happen; cf. **affect**
effector Biol. (not **-er**)
effectuate cause to happen
effendi pl. **effendis** educated or high-ranking man in eastern Mediterranean or Arab countries
efferent Physiol. conducting nerve impulses or blood outwards; cf. **afferent**
effluvium pl. **effluvia** unpleasant or harmful odour or discharge
effluxion 1 arch. action of flowing out **2** Law expiration of agreement
EFL English as a foreign language
EFTA European Free Trade Association
e.g. for example (not ital., comma before but not after) [L. *exempli gratia*]
egg cup (two words)
egghead (one word)
eggplant N. Amer. aubergine (one word)
eggshell (one word)
ego pl. **egos 1** person's sense of self-esteem **2** part of the mind responsible for sense of self
egoism 1 Philos. theory that treats self-interest as the foundation of morality **2** egotism
egotism excessive conceit
egregious outstandingly bad
egret small white heron; cf. **aigrette**
Eichmann, (Karl) Adolf (1906–62), German Nazi, executed in Israel
Eid (also **Id**) either of two Muslim festivals, **Eid ul-Fitr** at the end of the fast of Ramadan and **Eid ul-Adha** after the annual pilgrimage to Mecca (not ital.)
eider northern sea duck
eiderdown (one word)
eidetic (of mental images) unusually vivid
eidolon 1 idealized person or thing **2** phantom
Eifel region of western Germany

Eiffel Tower Parisian landmark erected 1889 (caps)
eigenvalue, eigenvector Math., Phys. (one word)
Eiger, the peak in the Swiss Alps
Eigg island of the Inner Hebrides in Scotland
eight (Roman numeral **viii** or **VIII**) □ **eightfold, eighth**
eighteen (Roman numeral **xviii** or **XVIII**) □ **eighteenth**
eighteenmo pl. **eighteenmos** another term for **octodecimo**
eighth note N. Amer. Mus. a quaver
eighties (also **1980s**) decade (lower case, no apostrophe)
eighty hyphen in compound numbers, e.g. *eighty-one*; Roman numeral **lxxx** or **LXXX** □ **eightieth**
Einstein, Albert (1879–1955), German-born American theoretical physicist
einsteinium chemical element of atomic number 99 (symbol **Es**)
Éire Gaelic name for Ireland, and the Irish name of the Republic of Ireland □ **Éireann**
Eirene Gk Mythol. goddess of peace
eirenic (also **irenic**) aiming at peace
eirenicon var. of **irenicon**
Eisenhower, Dwight David (1890–1969), 34th president of the US 1953–61
Eisenstein, Sergei (Mikhailovich) (1898–1948), Soviet film director
eisteddfod pl. **eisteddfods** or **eisteddfodau** Welsh festival of music and poetry
ejection seat (also **ejector seat**)
ejusdem generis (also ***eiusdem generis***) of the same kind (L., ital.)
Ekaterinburg var. of **Yekaterinburg**
el- see **al-**
Elagabalus var. of **Heliogabalus**
El Al Israeli national airline
El Alamein site in Egypt of WWII battle (1942)
Elam ancient state in SW Iran □ **Elamite**
elan energy, style, and enthusiasm (not ital.) [Fr. *élan*]
élan vital life force in philosophy of Henri Bergson (Fr., ital.)
Elastoplast trademark sticking plaster (cap.)
E-layer (also **E-region**) layer of the ionosphere (hyphen, one cap.)
Elbrus peak in the Caucasus
Elburz Mountains mountain range in NW Iran
El Cid (*c.*1043–99), Spanish soldier; born *Rodrigo Díaz de Vivar*
eld 1 old age **2** the past
elder use **the Elder** when distinguishing between related people (*Bruegel the Elder*)
Elder Brethren the thirteen senior members of Trinity House
El Dorado 1 legendary country or city of gold **2** (also **eldorado**) pl. **El Dorados** or **eldorados** place of great abundance
eldritch weird and sinister or ghostly
elec. electricity or electrical
elector 1 voter **2** hist. German prince entitled to elect the Holy Roman Emperor (cap. in titles)
electress hist. wife of a German elector
electroencephalograph machine for measuring electrical activity in the brain
electrolyse (US **electrolyze**) treat by electrolysis
electromagnet, electromagnetic, electrometer (one word)
electromotive producing electric current
electron spin resonance (no hyphen)
electronvolt unit of energy (one word; abbrev. **eV**)
electroplate (one word; abbrev. **EP**)
electrostatic unit (abbrev. **e.s.u.**)
electrotype copy made by the deposition of copper on a mould
electuary arch. sweetened medicine
eleemosynary relating to or dependent on charity; charitable
elegiac like an elegy (not **-gaic**)
elegy 1 mournful poem, esp. a lament for the dead **2** poem in elegiac couplets
elenchus pl. **elenchi** Logic a logical refutation
elephantiasis condition in which a body part becomes grossly enlarged
Eleusinian mysteries ancient Greek rites

eleven (Roman numeral **xi** or **XI**) □ **elevenfold, eleventh**

Elgar, Sir Edward (William) (1857–1934), English composer

Elgin Marbles classical Greek sculptures brought to England by the 7th Earl of Elgin (Gk preferred term is **Parthenon Marbles**)

El Greco (1541–1614), Cretan-born Spanish painter; born *Domenikos Theotokopoulos*

Elia pseudonym of English writer Charles Lamb (1775–1834)

elicit evoke or draw out; cf. **illicit**

Elijah Hebrew prophet

Eliogabalus use **Heliogabalus**

Eliot 1 George (1819–80), English novelist; pseudonym of *Mary Ann Evans* **2** T(homas) S(tearns) (1888–1965), American-born British poet

elite (not ital.) [Fr. *élite*]

Eliz. Elizabeth (regnal year)

Ellice Islands former name for **Tuvalu**; cf. **Ellis Island**

Ellington, Duke (1899–1974), American jazz pianist and bandleader; born *Edward Kennedy Ellington*

ellipsis pl. **ellipses** omission of word or words (**...**)

Ellis Island island in the bay of New York, former entry point for immigrants to the US; cf. **Ellice Islands**

El Niño climatic changes affecting the equatorial Pacific every few years

elocution skill of clear and expressive speech; cf. **allocution**

Elohim a name for God in the Hebrew Bible

Eloise (lover of Abelard) use **Héloïse**

El Paso city in Texas

el-Qahira var. of **al-Qahira**

El Salvador country in Central America □ **Salvadorean**

Elsevier see **Elzevir**

Elsinore port in Denmark, setting for Shakespeare's *Hamlet*; Danish name **Helsingør**

ELT English language teaching

Elul (in the Jewish calendar) twelfth month of the civil and sixth of the religious year

el-Uqsur (also **al-Uqsur**) Arab. name for **Luxor**

elusive difficult to find, catch, or achieve; cf. **allusive, illusive**

elver young eel

Elysée Palace official residence in Paris of the French president; Fr. name **Palais de l'Elysée**

Elysium (also **Elysian Fields**) Gk Mythol. place where heroes went after death

elytron pl. **elytra** wing case of a beetle

Elzevir family of Dutch printers active 1581–1712 (modern publishing company is **Elsevier**)

em Printing **1** unit for measuring the width of printed matter, equal to the height of the type size being used **2** unit of measurement equal to twelve points; see also **em rule, en**

'em informal them (apostrophe)

email (also **e-mail**)

emalangeni pl. of **lilangeni**

embalmment (three *m*s; more usual noun is **embalming**)

embargo (**embargoes, embargoing, embargoed**)

embarras de richesses, embarras de choix embarrassment of riches (or choice) (Fr., ital.)

embarrass (two *r*s, two *s*s) □ **embarrassment**

embed (not **imbed**)

Ember day day for fasting and prayer in the Western Christian Church (one cap.)

embonpoint plumpness or fleshiness, esp. of a woman's bosom (not ital.)

embouchure way that a player applies the mouth to the mouthpiece of a musical instrument (not ital.)

embourgeoisement proliferation of middle-class values (Fr., ital.)

embrasure opening in a wall around a window or door, widening inwards

embrocation liquid rubbed on the body to relieve strains; cf. **imbrication**

embroglio use **imbroglio**

embryo pl. **embryos**

em dash another term for **em rule**

emend correct and revise a text; cf. **amend**

emerald green (two words, hyphen when attrib.)

emeritus having retired but allowed to

retain title as an honour
Emerson, Ralph Waldo (1803–82), American philosopher and poet.
EMF 1 electromagnetic field **2** European Monetary Fund.
emf (also **e.m.f.**) electromotive force
emigrant person who leaves their country to settle permanently in another; cf. **immigrant** □ **emigrate**
émigré person who has emigrated for political reasons (accents, not ital.)
Emilia-Romagna region of northern Italy (hyphen)
éminence grise person who exercises power without holding an official position (Fr., ital.)
eminent famous, respected; cf. **immanent, imminent**
emir (also **amir**) Muslim ruler (cap. in titles)
Emmanuel (also **Immanuel**) name given to Christ as the deliverer of Judah prophesied by Isaiah
Emmanuel College Cambridge
Emmental (also **Emmenthal**) hard Swiss cheese with holes in it
Emmet, Robert (1778–1803), Irish patriot
Emmy pl. **Emmys** US award for an outstanding television programme or performer
emollient softening or soothing the skin
emolument salary or fee from employment or office
emotional 1 relating to emotions **2** characterized by intense feeling
emotive arousing intense feeling
empanel (also **impanel**) (**empanelling, empanelled**; US one **-l-**) enrol (jury)
empassion, empassioned use **impassion, impassioned**
empathize (Brit. also **empathise**)
empathy ability to understand and share someone else's feelings; cf. **sympathy**
Empedocles (*c.*493–*c.*433 BC), Greek philosopher, born in Sicily
emperor (cap. in titles)
emphasis pl. **emphases**
emphasize (Brit. also **emphasise**)
Empire line style of women's clothing popular during the First Empire in France (1804–15) (one cap.)
Empire State Building skyscraper on Fifth Avenue, New York City (caps)
emporium pl. **emporia** or **emporiums**
empress (cap. in titles)
Empson, Sir William (1906–84), English poet and literary critic
emptor purchaser, buyer; cf. **caveat emptor** (L., ital.)
empty-handed (hyphen)
empyrean the highest part of heaven
em rule (also **em dash**) Brit. long dash (—) used in punctuation, roughly the width of the letter *M*; set with no space either side
EMS European Monetary System
EMU Economic and Monetary Union
emu[1] large flightless Australian bird
emu[2] **1** electric multiple unit (railway vehicle) **2** electromagnetic unit
en Printing unit of measurement equal to half an em, approximately the average width of typeset characters; see also **en rule, em**
enamel v. (**enamelling, enamelled**; US one **-l-**)
enamorato use **inamorato**
enamoured (US **enamored**)
en bloc all together or all at the same time (not ital.)
en brosse (of hair) short and bristly (Fr., ital.)
enc. enclosed or enclosure
Encaenia annual celebration at Oxford University in memory of founders and benefactors
encase (not **incase**)
enceinte pregnant (Fr., ital.)
encephalin var. of **enkephalin**
encephalitis inflammation of the brain (not **enkeph-**)
enchaînement Ballet sequence of steps or movements (Fr., ital.)
enchilada tortilla with a filling of meat or cheese
enchiridion pl. **enchiridions** or **enchiridia** book containing essential information on a subject
en clair in ordinary language rather than in code (Fr., ital.)
enclose, enclosure (not **in-**)

encomium pl. **encomiums** or **encomia** laudatory speech or piece of writing
en croute in a pastry crust (not ital.) [Fr. *en croûte*]
encrust, encumber (not **in-**)
Encyclopædia Britannica (abbrev. ***EB*** or ***Encycl. Brit.***)
encyclopedia (also **encyclopaedia**; not **encyclopædia** (arch.))
Encyclopédie French encyclopedia edited by Diderot 1751–76
encyclopédiste a writer of the *Encyclopédie*
en dash var. of **en rule**
en daube stewed, braised (Fr., ital.)
endeavour (US **endeavor**)
endemic regularly found in a certain area; cf. **epidemic**
Enderby Land part of Antarctica claimed by Australia
en déshabille in a state of undress (Fr., ital.)
endgame (one word)
end matter pages of a book, e.g. appendices and index, following the main text (two words)
endnote note at the end of a book or section (one word)
endorse (US & Law also **indorse**)
endoskeleton, endosperm (one word)
endpaper leaf at the beginning or end of a book (one word)
end point, end product, end result (two words)
endue (not **indue**)
end user (two words)
endways (also **endwise**) (one word)
Endymion 1 Gk Mythol. handsome young man, loved by the Moon (Selene) **2** (***Endymion***) poem by Keats (1818)
ENE east-north-east
en échelon arranged in an echelon (Fr., ital.)
enema pl. **enemas** or **enemata**
energize (Brit. also **energise**)
enervate drain of energy; cf. **innervate**
en face facing forwards (Fr., ital.)
en famille with one's family, or as a family (Fr., ital.)
enfant gâté person who is excessively flattered or indulged (Fr., ital.)
enfant terrible pl. ***enfants terribles*** person who behaves in an unconventional or controversial way (Fr., ital.)
enfeoff (under the feudal system) give property or land in exchange for service
en fête prepared for a party or celebration (Fr., ital.)
enforceable (not **-cable**)
enfranchise (not **-ize**)
ENG electronic news-gathering
engagé (of a writer or artist) committed to a cause (Fr., ital.)
Engels, Friedrich (1820–95), German socialist and political philosopher
engine room (two words)
English horn US term for **cor anglais**
English Pale, the hist. area in France or Ireland of English jurisdiction
engraft (not **ingraft**)
engrain var. of **ingrain**
engulf (not **ingulf**)
enjambement (also **enjambment**) (in verse) continuation of a sentence beyond the end of a line etc. (not ital.)
enkephalin (also **encephalin**) compound occurring in the brain
enkephalitis use **encephalitis**
Enlightenment, the European movement of the late 17th and 18th cents (cap.)
en masse in a group (not ital.)
Enniskillen town in Northern Ireland; the old spelling *Inniskilling* is used as a regimental name in the British army
ennui boredom (not ital.)
ennuyé (fem. ***ennuyée***) bored (Fr., ital.)
ENO English National Opera
enology US var. of **oenology**
enormity extreme seriousness of something bad; disp. large size, hugeness
enosis political union of Cyprus and Greece (lower case, not ital.)
en papillote cooked and served in a paper wrapper (Fr., ital.)
en passant incidentally (Fr., ital.)
en pension as a boarder or lodger (Fr., ital.)
en plein air in the open air (Fr., ital.)
en poste in an official diplomatic position (Fr., ital.)
en primeur (of wine) newly produced

and made available (Fr., ital.)
en prise Chess in a position to be taken (Fr., ital.)
enquire chiefly Brit. request information; cf. **inquire**
enquiry chiefly Brit. make a request for information; cf. **inquiry**
en rapport having a close and harmonious relationship (Fr., ital.)
enrol (US **enroll**) (**enrolling, enrolled**)
enrolment (US **enrollment**)
en route on the way (not ital.)
en rule (also **en dash**) Brit. a short dash, the width of an en, used esp. between figures (*the 1939–45 war*); set with no space either side
Enschede city in the Netherlands
ensheath (not **ensheathe**)
Ensor, James (Sydney), Baron (1860–1949), Belgian artist
ensue (**ensuing, ensued**)
en suite Brit. (of a bathroom) immediately adjoining a bedroom (not ital.)
ensure make certain that (something) will occur; cf. **assure, insure**
ENT ear, nose, and throat
entablature upper part of a classical building supported by columns
entablement platform supporting a statue, above the dado and base
Entebbe town in southern Uganda, the capital 1894–1962
entente (also ***entente cordiale***, Fr., ital.) informal alliance between states or factions
enterprise (not **-ize**)
enthral (US **enthrall**) (**enthralling, enthralled**)
entomology study of insects; cf. **etymology**
en tout cas parasol which also serves as an umbrella (Fr., ital.)
entozoon pl. **entozoa** internal parasite
entr'acte pl. **entr'actes** interval between acts of a play (not ital.)
en train under way (Fr., ital.)
entrammel (**entrammelling, entrammelled**; US one **-l-**) entangle or trap
entrap (**entrapping, entrapped**)
en travesti dressed as a member of the opposite sex (Fr., ital.)
entrechat Ballet vertical jump (Fr., ital.)
entrecôte steak cut off the sirloin (accent, not ital.)
entrée (accent, not ital.) **1** main course of a meal **2** dish served between the first and main courses at a formal dinner
entremets light dish served between two courses of a formal meal (Fr. sing., ital.)
entrench (not **intrench**)
entre nous between ourselves, privately (Fr., ital.)
entrepôt centre for import and export (accent, not ital.)
entrepreneur person taking on financial risks in the hope of profit □ **entrepreneurial**
entresol storey between the ground floor and the first floor (not ital.)
entrust (not **intrust**)
entryism infiltration of a political party
entryphone intercom at the entrance to a building (cap. as trademark)
E-number EU code number for food additives (hyphen)
enunciate say or pronounce clearly □ **enunciator**
enure 1 Law belong or be available to someone **2** var. of **inure**
enurn var. of **inurn**
envelop (**enveloping, enveloped**) cover or surround completely
envelope flat paper container for a letter
Enver Pasha (1881–1922), Turkish political and military leader
environment (three *ns*)
envoi (not ital.) **1** short stanza concluding a ballade **2** arch. author's concluding words
envoy messenger or representative on a diplomatic mission
enwrap (not **in-**)
enwreathe (not **enwreath** or **inwreathe**)
EOC Equal Opportunities Commission
Eocene second epoch of the Tertiary period
eo ipso by that very act or quality, thereby (L., ital.)
EOKA Greek-Cypriot liberation movement active in 1950s and 1970s
eolian US var. of **aeolian**
eon US or technical var. of **aeon**

Eos Gk Mythol. goddess of the dawn
EP 1 electroplate **2** European Parliament **3** extended-play (record or CD)
Ep. Epistle
EPA US Environmental Protection Agency
eparch chief bishop of an eparchy
eparchy province of the Orthodox Church
épater les bourgeois shock conventional people (Fr., ital.)
epaulette (US **epaulet**) ornamental shoulder piece
épée duelling and fencing sword (accents, not ital.)
epeirogeny (also **epeirogenesis**) Geol. regional uplift of an extensive area of the earth's crust
epenthesis pl. **epentheses** insertion of a sound or letter within a word, e.g. the *b* in *thimble*
epergne table ornament for holding fruit or flowers (not ital., no accent)
epexegesis pl. **epexegeses** addition of words to clarify meaning
Eph. Epistle to the Ephesians
ephah ancient Hebrew measure
ephedrine drug used to relieve asthma and hay fever
ephemera things existing or used for only a short time (not ital.)
ephemeris table or data file giving the calculated positions of a celestial object
ephemeron pl. **ephemerons** or **ephemera** insect living for only a day (not ital.)
Ephesians, Epistle to the book of the New Testament (abbrev. **Eph.**)
Ephesus ancient Greek city in Asia Minor □ **Ephesian**
ephod sleeveless garment worn by ancient Jewish priests
ephor senior magistrate in ancient Sparta
epicardium pl. **epicardia** Anat. membrane forming the innermost layer of the pericardium
epicedium pl. **epicedia** funeral ode
epicene of indeterminate sex
epicentre (US **epicenter**) point above the focus of an earthquake
epicure person devoted to fine food and drink (lower case)
Epicurean follower of Epicureanism (cap.)
epicurean person devoted to fine food and drink (lower case)
Epicureanism ancient school of Greek philosophy holding pleasure to be the highest good, founded by Epicurus (cap.)
epideictic designed to display rhetorical or oratorical skill
epidemic adj. (of an infectious disease) widespread in a community; cf. **endemic**
epidermis outer layer of skin
epiglottis flap of cartilage behind the root of the tongue
epigone pl. **epigones** or **epigoni** less distinguished follower or imitator
epigram 1 pithy saying or remark **2** witty short poem □ **epigrammatic**
epigraph inscription at the start of a book or chapter
epilogue (US also **epilog**) concluding part of a book or play
Epiphany occasion when Christ appeared to the Magi, celebrated on 6 January
epiphany moment of sudden great revelation (lower case)
epiphyte plant that grows on another plant
Epirot (also **Epirote**) inhabitant of Epirus
Epirus ancient country or modern region of NW Greece; mod. Gk name **Ipiros**
episcopal of or governed by bishops
Episcopal Church the Anglican Church in Scotland and the US
episcopalian 1 advocating government by bishops **2** of or belonging to an episcopal Church
Epistle to the Colossians, Epistle to the Ephesians, etc. see **Colossians, Epistle to the; Ephesians, Epistle to the**, etc.
epistolary (of a literary work) in the form of letters
epithalamium pl. **epithalamiums** or **epithalamia** song or poem celebrating a marriage

epithelium pl. **epithelia** Anat. thin tissue forming the outer layer of the body's surface
epitome 1 perfect example of a quality or type **2** summary of a written work
epitomize (Brit. also **epitomise**) **1** be a perfect example of **2** arch. summarize (a written work)
epizoic growing or living on the exterior of a living animal
epizoon pl. **epizoa** animal that lives on the body of another
epizootic (of disease) widespread in an animal population
E pluribus unum one out of many (the motto of the US) (L., ital.)
EPNS electroplated nickel silver
epode lyric poem written in couplets
eponym a person after whom a discovery, invention, etc. is named □ **eponymous**
EPOS electronic point of sale
epsilon the fifth letter of the Greek alphabet (**Ε, ε**), transliterated as 'e'
Epstein 1 Brian (1934–67), English manager of the Beatles **2** Sir Jacob (1880–1959), American-born British sculptor
Epstein–Barr virus herpesvirus causing glandular fever (en rule)
epyllion pl. **epyllia** poem resembling an epic poem in style, but shorter
epyornis use **aepyornis**
EQ adjustment of the levels of an audio signal; equalization
equable 1 calm and even-tempered **2** not fluctuating; cf. **equitable**
equal v. (**equalling, equalled**; US one **-l-**)
equalize (Brit. also **equalise**)
equals sign the symbol =; set with space before and after
equanimity calmness in a difficult situation □ **equanimous**
equator (lower case) □ **equatorial**
Equatorial Guinea small country of West Africa
equerry officer of the British royal household
eques sing. of **equites**
equestrian (fem. **equestrienne**) rider or performer on horseback
equilibrium pl. **equilibria** balance or calmness
equine relating to horses
equinox date at which day and night are of equal length □ **equinoctial**
equip (**equipping, equipped**)
equitable fair and impartial; cf. **equable**
equites (sing. **eques**) (in ancient Rome) wealthy class of citizens
equivocate use ambiguous language □ **equivocator**
equivoque expression with more than one meaning (not ital.)
ER 1 N. Amer. emergency room **2** King Edward [L. *Edwardus Rex*] **3** Queen Elizabeth [L. *Elizabetha Regina*]
Er the chemical element erbium (no point)
Erasmus, Desiderius (*c.*1469–1536), Dutch humanist and scholar; Dutch name *Gerhard Gerhards*
Erastianism doctrine that the state should have supremacy over the Church (wrongly attributed to Erastus)
Erastus (1524–83), Swiss theologian and physician; Swiss name *Thomas Lieber*
Erato the Muse of lyric poetry and hymns
Eratosthenes (*c.*275–194 BC), Greek scholar, geographer, and astronomer
erbium chemical element of atomic number 68 (symbol **Er**)
Erebus Gk Mythol. primeval god of darkness, son of Chaos
Erebus, Mount volcanic peak on Ross Island, Antarctica
Erechtheum temple on the Acropolis in Athens
E-region var. of **E-layer**
eremite Christian hermit or recluse □ **eremitic**
erethism excessive sensitivity of a part of the body
Erevan var. of **Yerevan**
Erewhon novel by Samuel Butler (1872)
erf pl. **erfs** or **erven** S. Afr. plot of land.
erg 1 Phys. unit of work or energy **2** pl. **ergs** or **areg** area of shifting sand dunes in the Sahara
ergo therefore (not ital.)
Ericsson, Leif (970–1020), Norse explorer, thought to have visited North America

Erie, Lake one of the five Great Lakes of North America
Eriksson, Sven-Göran (b.1948), Swedish coach of the England soccer team 2001–2006
Erin arch. or literary name for Ireland
Erinys pl. **Erinyes** Gk Mythol. a Fury
Eris Gk Mythol. the goddess of strife
eristic characterized by debate
Eritrea country in NE Africa, independent since 1993 □ **Eritrean**
Erl King (in Germanic mythology) a giant who lured children to the land of death
ERM Exchange Rate Mechanism
erne sea eagle
Ernie Brit. computer that selects prize-winning Premium Bond numbers
Eroica Symphony symphony by Beethoven (1804) [It. *Sinfonia Eroica*]
Eros Gk Mythol. god of love; Rom. equivalent **Cupid**
eroticize (Brit. also **eroticise**)
errant 1 straying from the accepted course or standard **2** travelling in search of adventure; cf. **arrant**
erratum pl. **errata 1** error in printing or writing **2** (**errata**) list of corrected errors in a book
Er Rif var. of **Rif Mountains**
erroneous (not **-ious**)
ersatz used as an inferior substitute for something else (not ital.)
Erse dated Scottish or Irish Gaelic
Erté (1892–1990), Russian-born French fashion designer; born *Romain de Tirtoff*
Ertebølle late Mesolithic culture in the western Baltic
eructation a belch
erupt explode; cf. **irrupt**
erven plural of **erf**
erysipelas disease characterized by raised red patches on the skin
erythrism abnormal redness in an animal's fur, plumage, or skin
Erzgebirge range of mountains between Germany and the Czech Republic
Erzurum city in NE Turkey
Es the chemical element einsteinium (no point)
ESA 1 Environmentally Sensitive Area **2** European Space Agency
escadrille French squadron of aircraft (not ital.)
escalade hist. scaling of fortified walls using ladders
escalate rapidly increase or intensify
escalator moving staircase (not **-er**)
escallop var. of **escalope** or **scallop**
escalope (also **escallop**) thin slice of boneless meat
escargot edible snail (not ital.)
escarpment long steep slope (not **escarpement**)
Escaut Fr. name for **Scheldt**
eschatology part of theology concerned with death and the destiny of the soul; cf. **scatology**
escheat reversion of property to the state or to a lord on the owner's dying without legal heirs
Escher, M(aurits) C(orneille) (1898–1972), Dutch graphic artist
eschew abstain from
eschscholzia (also **eschscholtzia**) kind of poppy
Escoffier, Georges-Auguste (1846–1935), French chef
Escorial monastery and palace in Spain
escritoire small writing desk (not ital.)
escudo pl. **escudos** basic monetary unit of the Cape Verde Islands and formerly of Portugal
escutcheon 1 shield or emblem bearing a coat of arms **2** metal plate around a keyhole etc.
Esdras 1 either of two books of the Apocrypha (**1, 2 Esdras**) **2** (in the Vulgate) the books of Ezra and Nehemiah (abbrev. **Esd.**)
ESE east-south-east
Esfahan var. of **Isfahan**
esker ridge of sediment deposited by glacier or ice sheet
Eskimo pl. same or **Eskimos**; use **Inuit** for peoples inhabiting northern Canada, Alaska, and Greenland; not **Esquimau** (arch.)
ESL English as a second language
ESN 1 dated educationally subnormal **2** electronic serial number

ESOL English for speakers of other languages
esophagus US var. of **oesophagus**
ESP extrasensory perception
esp. especially
espadrille light canvas shoe (not ital.)
espalier v. (**espaliering, espaliered**) train (tree or shrub) to grow against a wall
España Sp. name for **Spain**
especially (abbrev. **esp.**)
Esperanto language devised as an international medium of communication
espionage spying [Fr. *espionnage*]
espressivo Mus. with expression of feeling (not **expressivo**)
espresso pl. **espressos** small black coffee (not **expresso**)
esprit liveliness or wit (Fr., ital.)
esprit de corps pride and mutual loyalty in a group (Fr., ital.)
esprit de l'escalier phenomenon whereby a witty retort often comes to mind after the opportunity to make it has passed (Fr., ital.)
esprit fort pl. ***esprits forts*** strong-minded person (Fr., ital.)
Esquimau pl. **Esquimaux** arch. use **Eskimo**
esquire Brit. title appended to a man's name when no other title is used; N. Amer. appended to a lawyer's surname (abbrev. **Esq.**)
ESR electron spin resonance
Essene member of an ancient Jewish ascetic sect
EST Eastern Standard Time
est. 1 established **2** estimated
Established Church the Church of England or of Scotland
Establishment, the group in society exercising power and influence (cap.)
estaminet small cafe (Fr., ital.)
estancia cattle ranch in Latin America or the southern US (not ital.)
Estates General var. of **States General**
Estates of the Realm, the (also **the Three Estates**) **1** the Lords spiritual (the heads of the Church), the Lords temporal (the peerage), and the Commons **2** the Crown, the House of Lords, and the House of Commons
Esther book of the Old Testament (no abbrev.); part survives only in Greek and is included in the Apocrypha (abbrev. **Rest of Esth.**)
esthete etc. US spelling of **aesthete** etc.
estival etc. US spelling of **aestival** etc.
Estonia Baltic republic, independent since 1991 ◻ **Estonian**
estoppel Law principle by which a person cannot assert something contrary to their previous statements
Estragon character in *Waiting for Godot* by Samuel Beckett (1952)
estrogen etc. US var. of **oestrogen** etc.
estrus etc. US var. of **oestrus** etc.
e.s.u. electrostatic unit
esurient hungry
Eszett the character ß, representing a double *s* (Ger., ital.)
ET 1 (in North America) Eastern time **2** extraterrestrial
ETA 1 estimated time of arrival **2** Basque separatist movement in Spain [Basque *Euzkadi ta Azkatasuna* 'Basque homeland and liberty']
eta seventh letter of the Greek alphabet (**Η, η**), transliterated as 'e' or 'ē'
etagere (also **étagère**) piece of furniture for displaying ornaments (not ital.)
et al. and others (not ital. in general use; sometimes ital. in bibliographies) [L. *et alii*]
etalon Phys. device for producing interfering light beams (not ital.)
etc. et cetera (point; not **&c.**)
et cetera used at the end of a list to indicate that further, similar items are included (two words, not ital.)
etceteras extra items (one word)
Eternal City, the Rome
Etesian wind another term for **meltemi**
eth (also **edh**) Old English letter, Đ or ð; it was superseded by *th* but ð is now used to represent the dental fricatives ð and θ; cf. **thorn, wyn**
Ethelred II (*c.*969–1016), king of England 978–1016; known as **Ethelred the Unready** (= 'badly advised')
ether 1 liquid used as an anaesthetic etc. **2** (also **aether**) upper regions of sky
ethereal (not **etherial, aethereal**)
Etherege, Sir George (?1635–91),

English playwright

etherize (Brit. also **etherise**) hist. anaesthetize with ether

ethics 1 moral principles governing behaviour (treated as pl.) **2** study of moral principles (treated as sing.)

Ethiopia country in NE Africa; former name **Abyssinia** □ **Ethiopian**

ethnic relating to a group having a common national or cultural tradition; do not use to refer to non-white people as a whole

ethnology study of different peoples

ethology 1 study of human behaviour from a biological perspective **2** science of animal behaviour

etiolated 1 (of a plant) pale and weak due to a lack of light **2** feeble

etiology US var. of **aetiology**

Etna, Mount volcano in Sicily (not **Aetna**)

Eton College public school in Berkshire □ **Etonian**

etrier short rope ladder (not ital.) [Fr. *étrier*]

Etruria 1 ancient state of central Italy, the centre of the Etruscan civilization **2** pottery factory and village in Staffordshire

et seq. and what follows (ital.) [L. *et sequens*]

étude short musical composition (accent, not ital.)

etui dated case for needles, cosmetics, etc. (not ital.) [Fr. *étui*]

etymology study of the origin of words; cf. **entomology**

EU European Union

Eu the chemical element europium (no point)

Euboea Greek island in the Aegean; Gk name **Évvoia**

eucalyptus pl. **eucalyptuses** or **eucalypti** evergreen Australasian tree

Eucharist Christian service commemorating the Last Supper (cap.)

euchre North American card game

Euclid (*c.*300 BC), Greek mathematician □ **Euclidean**

eudaemonic (also **eudemonic**) conducive to happiness

eudaemonism (also **eudemonism**) system of ethics basing value on the likelihood of actions producing happiness

eugenics science of attempting to improve a population by controlled breeding (treated as sing.)

Eugénie (1826–1920), Spanish empress of France 1853–70 and wife of Napoleon III

euglena green single-celled freshwater organism

Euler 1 Leonhard (1707–83), Swiss mathematician **2** Ulf Svante von (1905–83), Swedish physiologist

Euler-Chelpin, Hans Karl August Simon von (1873–1964), German-born Swedish biochemist

eulogium pl. **eulogia** or **eulogiums** eulogy

eulogize (Brit. also **eulogise**) praise highly

Eumenides Gk Mythol. the Furies

eunuch man who has been castrated

euphemism mild expression substituted for blunt one □ **euphemistic, euphemistically**

euphonious pleasing to the ear

euphonium pl. **euphoniums** brass musical instrument

euphorbia plant

euphoria intense excitement and happiness

Euphrates river of SW Asia

euphuism highly elaborate way of writing or speaking [from *Euphues*, main character of two prose romances (1578–80) by John Lyly]

Eurasia land mass of Europe and Asia combined □ **Eurasian**

Euratom European Atomic Energy Community

eureka cry of joy on discovering something (not ital., not **heur-**)

eurhythmic in harmonious proportion

eurhythmics (also **eurhythmy**; US **eurythmics** or **eurythmy**) system of rhythmical movements to music; rock group is **the Eurythmics**

Euripides (480–*c.*406 BC), Greek dramatist

Euro- European (usu. capitalized and forming solid compounds)

euro[1] pl. **euros** or **euro** the unit of currency of several member states of the European Union and some other countries (lower case; symbol €)

euro[2] pl. **euros** kind of kangaroo (lower case)

European Commission group within EU which initiates Union action (abbrev. **EC**)

European Community association of European countries incorporated since 1993 in the EU (abbrev. **EC**)

European Economic Community association of western European countries set up by the Treaty of Rome (1957), now part of the EU (abbrev. **EEC**)

European Free Trade Association customs union of western European countries which are not members of the EU (abbrev. **EFTA**)

European Recovery Program official name for the **Marshall Plan**

European Union association of European countries which replaced the EC in 1993 (abbrev. **EU**)

Europe, Council of association of European states founded in 1949

europium chemical element of atomic number 63 (symbol **Eu**)

Europoort major European port in the Netherlands (one word)

Eurosceptic (cap., one word)

Eurostar trademark passenger rail service via the Channel Tunnel (cap., one word)

eurozone region formed by EU countries that have adopted the euro (one word, lower case)

Eurydice Gk Mythol. wife of Orpheus

eurythmics US var. of **eurhythmics**

Euskara the Basque language

Euterpe the Muse of flute playing

eV electronvolt(s)

evangelize (Brit. also **evangelise**)

evening star Venus (lower case)

Everest, Mount mountain in the Himalayas, the highest in the world (8,848 m, 29,028 ft)

Everglades area of marshland and coastal mangrove in Florida

evermore (one word)

every- see **any-**

everybody (one word)

everyday adj. happening or used every day (one word)

every day adv. each day (two words)

Everyman 1 typical human being (cap.) **2** character in 16th-cent. morality play

everyone every person (one word)

every one each one (two words)

everything all things (one word)

every thing each thing (two words)

everywhere (one word)

Evian 1 trademark still mineral water **2** spa town in eastern France

evildoer (one word)

Evita María Eva Duarte de Perón (see **Perón**)

Évvoia Gk name for **Euboea**

evzone kilted soldier of a Greek infantry regiment

ex 1 out of **2** excluding **3** pl. **exes, ex's** informal former husband, wife, etc.

ex. pl. **exx.** example

ex- former (generally forms hyphenated compounds): *ex-girlfriend*

exa- denoting a factor of 10^{18} (abbrev. **E**)

exaggerate (two gs)

exalt 1 think or speak very highly of **2** raise to a higher rank; cf. **exult** □ **exaltation**

exalté person who is elated or impassioned (Fr., ital.)

ex ante based on forecasts rather than actual results (L., ital.)

Excalibur King Arthur's magic sword (not ital.)

ex cathedra with the full authority of office (L., ital.)

excel (**excelling, excelled**)

excellency (**His, Your**, etc. **Excellency**) title or form of address for certain high officials of state or of the Roman Catholic Church

excentric see **eccentric**

exceptionable open to objection

exceptional 1 unusual, not typical **2** very good

excerpt short extract

exchangeable (not **-gable**)

exchequer a royal or national treasury; (**the Exchequer**) the account at the Bank of England into which public monies are paid
excise[1] n. tax on certain goods
excise[2] v. cut out (not **-ize**) □ **excision**
excitable (not **-eable**)
excl. excludes; excluding
exclamation mark (N. Amer. **exclamation point**)
excreta (not ital.; treated as sing. or pl.)
exculpate show or declare (someone) to be not guilty
excursus pl. same or **excursuses** detailed discussion of a point (not ital.)
ex-directory (hyphen)
ex dividend (of stocks or shares) not including the next dividend (two words; abbrev. **ex div.**)
exeat a permission from a college or school for temporary absence (not ital.)
executor (fem. **executrix**, pl. **executrices** or **executrixes**) **1** Law person or institution appointed to carry out terms of a will (abbrev. **exor**) **2** person who puts something into effect
exegesis pl. **exegeses** critical explanation or interpretation of a text
exegete person who interprets text
exemplar typical example or appropriate model
exempli gratia full form of **e.g.** (L., ital.)
exemplum pl. **exempla** example or mode (not ital.)
exenteration Med. removal of the eyeball
exequatur official recognition of a foreign state's representative (not ital.)
exequy 1 (**exequies**) funeral rites **2** funeral ode
exercise (not **-ize**)
exercise book, exercise yard (two words)
Exeter county town of Devon; Roman name **Isca**
exeunt (stage direction) they all leave (not ital.)
ex gratia from obligation rather than legal requirement (L., ital.)
ex hypothesi according to the hypothesis proposed (L., ital.)
exigent urgent □ **exigence, exigency**
exiguous very small
existence (not **-ance**)
exit (stage direction) he or she leaves (not ital.)
ex libris inscription on a bookplate (L., ital.)
ex nihilo out of nothing (L., ital.)
Exocet trademark anti-ship missile (cap.)
Exodus 1 (**the Exodus**) the departure of the Israelites from Egypt **2** second book of the Old Testament (abbrev. **Exod.**)
exodus mass departure of people (lower case)
ex officio by virtue of one's position or status (L., ital.)
exon Brit. officers of the Yeomen of the Guard
Exonian person from Exeter
exor executor (of a will) (no point)
exorbitant (not **exhor-**)
exorcise (also **exorcize**)
exordium pl. **exordiums** or **exordia** beginning of a discourse (not ital.)
exp 1 experience **2** (**Exp.**) experimental (in titles of periodicals) **3** expiry **4** Math. the exponential function raising *e* to the power of the given quantity **5** Photog. exposures
ex parte in the interests of one side only (L., ital.)
expatriate (one word; not **-iot**)
expeditious done quickly and efficiently
expertise expert skill or knowledge (not **-ize**)
expiate make amends or reparation for □ **expiable, expiation**
explicandum (also **explanandum**) pl. **explicanda** or **explananda** Philos. fact or expression which is to be explained
explicans (also **explanans**) pl. **explicanda** or **explanantia** Philos. explanation of a fact or expression
Expo pl. **Expos** large international exhibition (cap.)
exposé report revealing something discreditable (accent, not ital.)
ex post based on actual results rather than forecasts (L., ital.)
ex post facto with retrospective action or force (L., ital.)

expostulate express strong disapproval or disagreement □ **expostulator**
ex-president (hyphen; *ex-President* in titles)
expressible (not **-able**)
expressionism style of art (lower case)
expressivo, expresso use **espressivo, espresso**
ex-prime minister (one hyphen; but prefer **former prime minister**)
ex silentio based on lack of contrary evidence (L., ital.)
ext. 1 extension (in a telephone number) **2** exterior **3** external
extempore (also **extemporary** or **extemporaneous**) spoken or done without preparation
extemporize (Brit. also **extemporise**) compose or perform without preparation; improvise
extensible able to be extended; used in more technical contexts than **extendable**
extensor Anat. muscle (not **-er**)
extern 1 N. Amer. non-resident doctor in a hospital **2** nun in an enclosed order who is able to go on outside errands
externalize (Brit. also **externalise**)
extirpate destroy completely
extol (**extolling, extolled**)
extractable (not **-ible**)
extractor (not **-er**)
extracurricular, extramarital, extramural (one word)
extrados upper curve of an arch; cf. **intrados**
extraneous 1 irrelevant **2** of external origin
extraordinaire informal outstanding (after noun, not ital.)
extrasensory perception (abbrev. **ESP**)
extraterrestrial (one word)
extra virgin fine grade of olive oil (two words, hyphen when attrib.)
extremum pl. **extremums** or **extrema** Math. maximum or minimum value of a function
extrovert (Psychol. also **extravert**) □ **extroversion**
exult be triumphantly elated or jubilant; cf. **exalt** □ **exultant**
exuviae cast or sloughed skin of an animal (not ital.; treated as pl. or sing.)
ex-voto pl. **ex-votos** offering given to fulfil a vow (hyphen, not ital.)
exx. examples
Exxon Corporation oil company
eye v. (**eyeing** or **eying, eyed**)
eyeball, eyebrow, eyelash (one word)
eye level (two words)
eyelid, eyeliner, eyepatch, eyeshadow, eyesight (one word)
eye socket (two words)
eyesore, eyewitness (one word)
eyot var. of **ait**
eyrie (N. Amer. **aerie**) bird of prey's nest
eyrir pl. **aurar** monetary unit of Iceland
Eysenck, Hans (Jürgen) (1916–97), German-born British psychologist
Ezekiel 1 Hebrew prophet **2** book of the Old Testament (abbrev. **Ezek.**)
Ezra 1 Jewish priest and scribe **2** book of the Old Testament (no abbrev.)

F

F 1 pl. **Fs** or **F's** 6th letter of the alphabet **2** Fahrenheit: *60 °F* **3** farad(s) **4** female **5** the chemical element fluorine **6** Phys. force **7** franc(s)

f 1 Gram. feminine **2** femto- (10^{-15}) **3** Photog. focal length **4** Mus. forte **5** Electron. frequency **6** Math. function **7** furlong(s)

f. (point) pl. **ff. 1** folio(s) **2** following page

F faraday(s)

FA 1 informal Fanny Adams **2** Football Association

fa var. of **fah**

FAA 1 Federal Aviation Administration **2** Fleet Air Arm

Faber and Faber publishers

Fabergé, Peter Carl (1846–1920), Russian goldsmith and jeweller

Fabian member of the Fabian Society, a moderate socialist organization □ **Fabianism**

fabliau pl. **fabliaux** metrical tale in early French poetry (not ital.)

facade (not ital.) [Fr. *façade*]

faceache (one word)

Facebook trademark social networking website

facecloth (one word)

face cream, face flannel (two words)

facelift (one word)

face mask, face pack, face paint, face powder (two words)

faceted (not **facetted**)

facetiae dated **1** pornographic literature **2** witty sayings (not ital.)

face value (two words)

facia Brit. var. of **fascia** (exc. in anatomy)

facies Med. facial expression indicative of a disease

facile princeps by far the best (L., ital.)

façon de parler pl. ***façons de parler*** mere form of words (Fr., ital.)

facsimile (abbrev. **facs.**)

facta pl. of **factum**

factional relating to a faction

factious inclined to dissension

factitious artificially created

factorial Math. product of an integer and all the integers below it (symbol **!**)

factotum pl. **factotums** employee who does all kinds of work

factum pl. **factums** or **facta** Law **1** chiefly Canad. statement of the facts of a case **2** act or deed

facula pl. **faculae** Astron. bright region on the surface of the sun

FA Cup English soccer competition (cap.)

fado pl. **fados** type of Portuguese song

faeces (US **feces**) □ **faecal** (US **fecal**)

faerie (also **faery**) fairyland

Faerie Queene, The romance by Edmund Spenser (1590; 1596)

Faeroe Islands var. of **Faroe Islands**

fag end (two words)

faggot 1 Brit. ball of chopped liver **2** bundle of sticks (not **fagot**)

fah (also **fa**) Mus. note in tonic sol-fa

Fahrenheit (abbrev. **F**, **Fahr.**)

faience glazed ceramic ware (not ital.) [Fr. *faïence*]

fail-safe (hyphen)

fáilte welcome! (Ir., ital.)

fainéant arch. idle person (accent, not ital.)

Fairbanks 1 Douglas (Elton) (1883–1939, American actor; born *Julius Ullman* **2** Douglas (1909–2000), his son, also an actor; known as **Douglas Fairbanks Jr**

fair copy (two words)

Fairfax, Thomas, 3rd Baron Fairfax of Cameron (1612–71), English Parliamentary general

fair game (two words)

fairground (one word)

Fair Isle 1 one of the Shetland Islands **2** traditional design for knitwear

fair play, fair trade (two words)

fairway (one word)

fair-weather friend (hyphen)
fairyland (one word)
fairy story, fairy tale (two words, hyphen when attrib.)
fait accompli pl. **fait accomplis** something that has already happened or been decided (not ital.)
faith healer (two words)
fakir Muslim or Hindu religious ascetic (not **faquir**)
falafel (also **felafel**) dish of pulses formed into balls
Falange Spanish Fascist movement; cf. **Phalange** ◻ **Falangist**
Falasha Ethiopian Jew
falciparum the most severe form of malaria
faldstool folding chair used by a bishop
Falernian wine Italian wine prized in the ancient world
Falkland Islands group of British islands in the South Atlantic; Sp. name **Islas Malvinas** ◻ **Falkland Islander** (also **Falklander**)
Fall, the (also **the Fall of Man**) lapse of humans into state of sin
fall N. Amer. autumn (lower case)
Falla, Manuel de (1876–1946), Spanish composer and pianist
fal-lal piece of frippery
fall guy (two words)
fallible capable of making mistakes (not **-able**)
fallopian tubes tubes along which eggs travel to the uterus (lower case)
fallout n. (one word)
Falluja town in Iraq
falsetto pl. **falsettos**
Falstaffian resembling Sir John Falstaff, a fat jolly Shakespearean character
Falun Gong Chinese religious movement
familiarize (Brit. also **familiarise**)
famille Chinese enamelled porcelain with a specified predominant colour: ***famille jaune*** (yellow), ***famille noire*** (black), ***famille rose*** (red), ***famille verte*** (green) (ital.)
famulus pl. **famuli** assistant or servant of a magician or scholar
fan belt, fan club, (two words)
fandango pl. **fandangoes** or **fandangos** Spanish dance for two people
fane arch. temple or shrine
fanfaronade 1 arrogant talk **2** fanfare
fanlight (one word)
fanny 1 Brit. vulgar slang woman's genitals **2** N. Amer. informal person's buttocks
Fanny Adams (also **sweet Fanny Adams**) Brit. informal nothing at all
fantasia 1 musical composition with a free form **2** (***Fantasia***) Walt Disney film (1940)
fantasize (Brit. also **fantasise**)
fantasy not **phantasy** exc. in arch. or psychol. contexts
fanzine magazine for fans of a performer, group, etc. (one word)
FAO Food and Agriculture Organization
FAQ Comput. frequently asked questions
faquir use **fakir**
farad SI unit of electrical capacitance (abbrev. **F**) ◻ **faradaic** (or **faradic**)
Faraday, Michael (1791–1867), English physicist and chemist
faraday unit of electric charge (lower case; abbrev. ***F***)
farandole lively Provençal dance
farceur writer or performer of farces (not ital.)
Far East (caps) ◻ **Far Eastern**
farewell (one word)
far-fetched, far-flung (hyphen)
Far from the Madding Crowd novel by Thomas Hardy (1874)
farinaceous consisting of or containing starch
Faringdon town in Oxfordshire; cf. **Farringdon**
farman var. of **firman**
farmer's lung, farmers' market (note apostrophes)
farmhand, farmhouse, farmland, farmstead, farmyard (one word)
Farne Islands group of small islands off the coast of Northumberland
Faro seaport on the south coast of Portugal, capital of the Algarve
Fårö island in Sweden
faro gambling card game
Faroe Islands (also **Faeroe Islands**)

group of islands in the North Atlantic, belonging to Denmark but partly autonomous

far off, far out (two words, hyphenated when attrib.)

farouche sullen or shy (not ital.)

Farquhar, George (1678–1707), Irish dramatist

farrago pl. **farragos** or US **farragoes** confused mixture

far-reaching (hyphen)

Farringdon area of London; cf. **Faringdon**

Farsi the modern Persian language

far-sighted 1 prudently aware of future possibilities **2** N. Amer. long-sighted

farther, farthest Brit. further, furthest

fasces bundle of rods with a projecting axe blade, an emblem of authority in ancient Rome and Fascist Italy

fascia (Brit. also **facia** exc. in anatomy) pl. **fascias** or Anat. **fasciae**

fascicle 1 (also **fascicule**) separately published instalment of a book **2** (also **fasciculus**) Anat. & Biol. a bundle of nerves or muscle fibres

fasciitis Med. inflammation of the fascia of a muscle or organ

fascism, fascist usu. cap. in ref. to officially constituted parties, esp. in Italy 1922–43

Fassbinder, Rainer Werner (1946–82), German film director

fast forward (two words, hyphen as verb)

Fastnet rocky islet off SW Ireland

Fatah (also **al-Fatah**) Palestinian political and military organization

Fata Morgana mirage in the Strait of Messina

Fates, the Gk Mythol. three goddesses presiding over human destiny

father (cap. as name or form of address) **1** (**the Father**) the first person of the Trinity; God **2** (**Fathers** or **Fathers of the Church**) authoritative early Christian theologians

Father Christmas Brit. Santa Claus (caps)

father figure (two words)

father-in-law pl. **fathers-in-law** (hyphens)

Father of the Chapel Brit. shop steward of a printers' and journalists' trade union (caps; abbrev. **FoC**)

Father of the House longest-serving member of the House of Commons (caps)

Father's Day (caps, apostrophe)

Father Time (caps)

Fatiha (also **Fatihah**) first sura of the Koran

Fatima (*c.*606–32 AD), youngest daughter of the prophet Muhammad and wife of the fourth caliph, Ali

Fátima village in Portugal, scene of a reported sighting of the Virgin Mary

Fatimid member of a dynasty which ruled parts of northern Africa in the 10th–12th cents

fatso pl. **fatsos** fat person

fatwa ruling on a point of Islamic law (not ital.)

faubourg French suburb, esp. in Paris (not ital., cap. in names)

Faulkner, William (1897–1962), American novelist

fault-finding (hyphen)

faun Rom. Mythol. rural deity with a goat's horns, ears, legs, and tail; cf. **fawn**

fauna pl. **faunas** animals of a particular region or period; cf. **flora**

Fauntleroy boy hero of Frances Hodgson Burnett's novel *Little Lord Fauntleroy* (1886)

Fauré, Gabriel (Urbain) (1845–1924), French composer and organist

Faust (also **Faustus**) (died *c.*1540), German astronomer and necromancer, said to have sold his soul to the Devil □ **Faustian**

faute de mieux for want of a better alternative (Fr., ital.)

fauteuil armchair (not ital.)

Fauves painters following Fauvism (cap., not ital.)

Fauvism expressionistic style of painting in Paris from 1905 (cap.)

faux naïf affectedly simple or naive (Fr., ital.)

faux pas pl. **faux pas** embarrassing or tactless mistake (not ital.)

favela Brazilian shack or shanty town (ital.)

favour (US **favor**)

Fawkes, Guy (1570–1606), English Catholic conspirator

fawn n. **1** young deer **2** light brown

colour; cf. **faun.** v. show exaggerated flattery or affection

fax copy of a document transmitted by telecommunications links (lower case)

faze informal disturb or disconcert; cf. **phase**

fazenda estate in Portuguese-speaking country (ital.)

FBA Fellow of the British Academy

FBI Federal Bureau of Investigation

FC 1 Football Club **2** Forestry Commission

FCC US Federal Communications Commission

FCO Foreign and Commonwealth Office

FD Defender of the Faith [L. *Fidei Defensor*]

FDA US Food and Drug Administration

FDIC US Federal Deposit Insurance Corporation

FDR nickname of President Franklin Delano Roosevelt (see **Roosevelt**)

FE further education

Fe the chemical element iron (no point) [L. *ferrum*]

feasible (not **-able**)

feast day (two words)

feather bed (two words, hyphen as verb)

feather-light (hyphen)

featherweight boxing weight between bantamweight and lightweight (one word)

February (abbrev. **Feb.**)

fecal, feces US var. of **faecal, faeces**

fedayeen (also **fidayeen**) Arab guerrillas (cap. when used as proper name)

Federal Republic of Germany 1 official name of Germany **2** former name for West Germany

Federer, Roger (b.1981), Swiss tennis player

fed up (two words, hyphen when attrib.)

fee Law, hist. estate held on condition of feudal service; fief

feedback, feedstock (one word)

feel-good factor informal (hyphen)

fee simple Law permanent and absolute tenure in land

feet pl. of **foot**

fee tail Law tenure in land with restrictions about whom it may be willed to

feint n. & v. (make) deceptive or pretended attack. adj. (of paper) printed with faint lines

feisty spirited (not **-ie-**)

felafel var. of **falafel**

feldspar var. of **felspar**

Felixstowe port in Suffolk, England

fellah pl. **fellahin** Egyptian peasant

Fellini, Federico (1920–93), Italian film director

felloes outer rim of a wheel (not **fellies**)

fellow senior member of a college (lower case)

fellow citizen, fellow feeling, fellow man, fellow traveller (two words)

felo de se pl. ***felos de se*** suicide (Anglo-L., ital.)

felspar (also **feldspar**) rock-forming mineral

felucca sailing vessel used on the Nile

fem. female; feminine

female (abbrev. **f., fem.**)

feme covert Law, hist. married woman (not ital.)

feme sole Law, hist. woman without a husband, esp. one that is divorced (not ital.)

femme woman (Fr., ital.)

femme fatale pl. **femmes fatales** seductive woman (not ital.)

femto- denoting a factor of 10^{-15} (abbrev. **f**)

femur pl. **femurs** or **femora** bone of the thigh or upper hindlimb □ **femoral**

fencible hist. soldier who could be called up only for home service

fenestra pl. **fenestrae** small natural hole in a bone (not ital.)

fenestrated having a window or windows

feng shui Chinese system of laws governing spatial arrangement and orientation (lower case, not ital.)

Fenian 1 hist. member of the 19th-cent. revolutionary Irish Republican Brotherhood **2** offens. (in Ireland) Protestant name for a Catholic

fenugreek a spice

feoffee person given or entrusted with a freehold estate □ **feoffment**

ferae naturae Law (of animals) undomesticated or wild (L., ital.)

fer de lance pl. **fers de lance** or **fer de lances** large pit viper of Central and South America
Ferdinand (1452–1516), king of Castile 1474–1516 and of Aragon 1479–1516, husband of Isabella I
feringhee (in India and the Middle and Far East) foreigner or white person
Fermanagh county of Northern Ireland (abbrev. **Ferm.**)
Fermat, Pierre de (1601–65), French mathematician
fermata Mus. pause of unspecified length on a note or rest
Fermi, Enrico (1901–54), Italian-born American atomic physicist
fermi pl. same, unit of length equal to 10^{-15} metre (one femtometre)
Fermi–Dirac statistics Phys. type of quantum statistics used to describe systems of fermions (en rule)
fermion pl. **fermions** Phys. subatomic particle which has half-integral spin
fermium chemical element of atomic number 100 (symbol **Fm**)
Ferranti, Sebastian Ziani de (1864–1930), English electrical engineer
Ferrara city in northern Italy
Ferrari, Enzo (1898–1988), Italian car designer and manufacturer
ferrel use **ferrule**
ferret v. (**ferreting, ferreted**)
ferric Chem. of iron with a valency of three; of iron(III)
Ferris wheel fairground ride (one cap.)
ferrous 1 containing or consisting of iron **2** Chem. of iron with a valency of two; of iron(II)
ferrule ring or cap at the end of a handle, stick, etc. (not **ferrel**); cf. **ferule**
ferryman (one word)
fertilize (Brit. also **fertilise**)
ferule ruler formerly used for beating children; cf. **ferrule**
fervour (US **fervor**)
Fès var. of **Fez**
fess Heraldry an ordinary in the form of a broad horizontal stripe across the middle of the shield
fess point Heraldry a point at the centre of a shield
festa festival (It., ital.)
Festiniog use **Ffestiniog**
Festschrift pl. **Festschriften** or **Festschrifts** collection of writings published in honour of a scholar (cap., not ital.)
feta (also **fetta**) white Greek cheese
fetal (or chiefly in Brit. non-technical use **foetal**) relating to a fetus
fete n. Brit. fund-raising event. v. honour or entertain [Fr. *fête*]
fête champêtre pl. ***fêtes champêtres*** outdoor entertainment (Fr., ital.)
fête galante pl. ***fêtes galantes*** outdoor entertainment or festival as depicted in 18th-cent. painting (Fr., ital.)
fetid (also **foetid**) smelling extremely unpleasant
fetish (not **fetich**)
fetor (also **foetor**) strong unpleasant smell
fetta var. of **feta**
fettuccine pasta made in ribbons (not **-ini**)
fetus (or in Brit. non-technical use **foetus**) unborn offspring of a mammal
feu Sc. Law perpetual lease at a fixed rent (not ital.)
feu de joie pl. ***feux de joie*** ceremonial rifle salute (Fr., ital.)
Feuerbach, Ludwig (Andreas) (1804–72), German materialist philosopher
feuilleton part of a newspaper or magazine devoted to fiction or criticism (not ital.)
feverfew plant used in herbal medicine
Few, the RAF pilots who took part in the Battle of Britain (cap.)
Feydeau, Georges (1862–1921), French dramatist
Fez (also **Fès**) city in northern Morocco
fez pl. **fezzes** conical red hat worn by men in Muslim countries
ff (also **fff**) Mus. fortissimo (no point)
ff. (point) **1** folios **2** following pages
Ffestiniog see **Blaenau Ffestiniog**
Fg Off Flying Officer
f-hole f-shaped soundhole in violin, guitar, etc. (hyphen)
FHSA Family Health Services Authority
fiacre hist. carriage for public hire

fiancé man to whom a woman is engaged (accent, not ital.)
fiancée woman to whom a man is engaged (accent, not ital.)
fianchetto pl. **fianchettoes** Chess movement of a bishop to a long diagonal of the board (not ital.)
Fianna Fáil political party in the Republic of Ireland (accent, not ital.)
fiasco pl. **fiascos** complete failure
Fiat Italian car company
fiat formal decree or authorization (not ital.)
fiat lux let there be light (L., ital.)
Fibonacci, Leonardo (*c.*1170–*c.*1250), Italian mathematician
fibre (US **fiber**)
fibreboard, fibreglass (US **fiberboard, fiberglass**) (one word)
fibre optics (US **fiber optics**) (two words)
fibula pl. **fibulae** or **fibulas** Anat. outer of the two bones between the knee and the ankle
fiche microfiche (not ital.)
fichu woman's small shawl (not ital.)
fictile made of pottery
fictional relating to or occurring in fiction
fictitious imaginary or invented
fictive tech. relating to fiction
fidalgo pl. **fidalgos** Portuguese noble
fidayeen var. of **fedayeen**
fiddle-de-dee dated exclamation of impatience (two hyphens)
fiddle-faddle trivial matters; nonsense (hyphen)
Fidei Defensor (abbrev. ***Fid. Def., FD***) L. term for **Defender of the Faith** (ital.)
fideism doctrine that knowledge depends on faith or revelation
fidget v. (**fidgeting, fidgeted**)
Fido Fog Intensive Dispersal Operation, a WWII system for helping aircraft to land (one cap.)
fiducial tech. (of a point or line) assumed as a fixed basis of comparison
fiduciary Law involving trust
fidus Achates faithful friend or devoted follower (ital.) [L., lit. 'faithful Achates' (character from the *Aeneid* by Virgil)]
fief hist. estate held on condition of feudal service; fee □ **fiefdom**
field day, field glasses, field goal (two words)
field hockey US term for **hockey** (two words)
Fielding, Henry (1707–54), English novelist
field marshal, field mouse, field officer (two words)
Fields 1 Dame Gracie (1898–1979), English singer and comedienne; born *Grace Stansfield* **2** W. C. (1880–1946), American comedian; born *William Claude Dukenfield*
fieldwork (one word)
fieri facias Law a writ (L., ital; abbrev. ***fi. fa.***)
FIFA international governing body of soccer [Fr. *Fédération Internationale de Football Association*]
fifteen (Roman numeral **xv** or **XV**) □ **fifteenth**
fifth column group within a country who are working for its enemies (lower case)
Fifth-monarchy-man hist. member of a 17th-cent. sect expecting the Second Coming of Christ (two hyphens)
fifties (also **1950s**) decade (lower case, no apostrophe)
fifty hyphen in compound numbers, e.g. *fifty-one*; Roman numeral **l** or **L** □ **fiftieth**
fifty–fifty (also **50–50**) equal in share or probability (en rule)
fifty-year rule rule making public records available after fifty years, superseded in 1968 by the thirty-year rule
fig. 1 figure **2** figurative
fightback n. (one word)
fighter-bomber (hyphen)
fig leaf (two words)
figura pl. **figurae** person or thing representing a fact or ideal (not ital.)
figural figurative
figurant (fem. **figurante**) actor or ballet dancer in a minor role (not ital.)
figure (abbrev. **fig.**, pl. **figs.**)
figurehead (one word)
figure skating (two words)

Fiji country in the South Pacific consisting of some 840 islands ◻ **Fijian**
filabeg use **filibeg**
filagree use **filigree**
filename (one word)
filet boneless piece of meat (not ital.)
filet mignon tender piece of beef from the end of the undercut (not ital.)
filibeg kilt (not **fila-** or **phili-**)
filibuster prolonged speech which obstructs progress in a legislative assembly
filigree fine wire (not **fila-**)
filing cabinet (two words)
Filipina pl. **Filipinas** woman from the Philippines
Filipino pl. **Filipinos** **1** person from the Philippines **2** (also **Pilipino**) language of the Philippines
fille de chambre pl. ***filles de chambre*** chambermaid (Fr., ital.)
fille de joie pl. ***filles de joie*** prostitute (Fr., ital.)
fillet v. (**filleting, filleted**)
filling station (two words)
fillip stimulus or boost
fillister **1** rebate for holding a sash window **2** plane tool
Fillmore, Millard (1800–74), 13th president of the US 1850–3
film-maker, film-making (hyphen)
film noir genre of film marked by fatalism and menace (not ital.)
filmsetting Printing setting by projection on to photographic film (one word)
filo (US **phyllo**) pastry in very thin sheets
Filofax trademark (cap.)
filoselle silk used in embroidery (not ital.)
fils used after a surname to distinguish a son from his father (Fr., ital.); cf. ***père***
filter device for removing solid particles from a liquid; cf. **philtre**
filterable (not **filtrable**)
finale last part of a piece of music etc. (not ital.)
finalize (Brit. also **finalise**)
fin de siècle characteristic of the end of a century (Fr., ital., lower case)
fine champagne brandy from the Champagne district (Fr., ital., lower case)
Fine Gael political party in the Republic of Ireland (not ital.)
fines herbes mixed herbs (Fr., ital.)
finesse sublety and skill (not ital.)
fine-tooth comb var. of **fine-toothed comb, fine toothcomb**
fine-tune v. (hyphen)
Fingal's Cave cave on the island of Staffa in the Inner Hebrides
fingerboard (one word)
finger bowl (two words)
fingermark, fingernail (one word)
finger paint n. (two words, hyphen as verb)
fingerpick, fingerpost, fingerprint, fingertip (one word)
finicky (also **finicking** or **finical**) excessively fussy
finis the end (of a work etc.) (not ital.)
finishing line, finishing school, finishing touch (two words)
Finisterre **1** (**Finisterre, Cape**) promontory of NW Spain **2** former shipping forecast area; renamed **Fitzroy** in 2002
finito informal finished (not ital.)
Finland country on the Baltic Sea; Finnish name **Suomi**
Finn person from Finland ◻ **Finnish**
finnan haddock smoked haddock (lower case)
Finnegans Wake novel by James Joyce (1939) (no apostrophe)
Finn MacCool (also **Finn Mac Cumhaill**) legendary Irish hero
Finno-Ugric group of languages including Finnish and Hungarian
fino pl. **finos** dry sherry (not ital.)
fiord var. of **fjord**
fioritura Mus. embellishment of a melody
fiqh theory or philosophy of Islamic law (ital.)
fire alarm (two words)
firearm, fireball, firebomb, firebreak (one word)
fire brigade (two words)
firecracker (one word)
fire door, fire drill (two words)
fire-eater (hyphen)

fire engine, fire escape, fire extinguisher (two words)
firefighter prefer to **fireman**
firefly, fireguard, firelight (one word)
Firenze It. name for **Florence**
fireplace, firepower, fireproof (one word)
fire-raiser (hyphen)
fireside (one word)
fire station (two words)
firestorm (one word)
fire trap (two words)
firewall, firewater, firewood, firework (one word)
firing squad (two words)
firkin small cask used for liquids
firmament the heavens (lower case)
firman (also **farman**) hist. oriental sovereign's edict (lower case, not ital.)
firn crystalline or granular snow
First Adar see **Adar**
firstborn (one word)
first class (two words, hyphen when attrib.)
first-degree (hyphen)
first floor (two words, hyphen when attrib.) Brit. floor above the ground floor; N. Amer. ground floor
first-hand (hyphen; but **at first hand** two words)
First Lady wife of the president of the US (caps)
first minister leader of the Scottish parliament, Welsh assembly, and Northern Ireland assembly (cap. in titles)
first-rate (hyphen)
First Reich the Holy Roman Empire, 962–1806
First Republic the republican regime in France 1792–1804
First World War war of 1914–18 (caps; also called **World War I**)
Firth, J(ohn) R(upert) (1890–1960), English linguist
firth estuary (cap. in names)
fir tree (two words)
fiscal 1 relating to government revenue **2** chiefly N. Amer. relating to finance
fiscal year N. Amer. financial year
Fischer, Bobby (1943–2008), American chess player; full name *Robert James Fischer*
Fischer-Dieskau, Dietrich (1925–2012), German baritone
fishcake (one word)
fisherfolk, fisherman (one word)
fisheye (one word)
fish finger, fish hook (two words)
fishing line, fishing rod (two words)
fish kettle, fish knife (two words)
fishmeal, fishmonger, fishnet, fishtail, fishwife (one word)
fissile able to undergo nuclear fission
fission division or splitting into two or more parts; cf. **fusion**
fist fight (two words)
fisticuffs fighting with the fists
fistula pl. **fistulas** or **fistulae** passage within the body (not ital.)
fit v. **fitting, fitted** or US **fit.** n. arch. section of a poem (not **fytte**)
FitzGerald George Francis (1851–1901), Irish physicist (upper-case *G*)
Fitzgerald (lower-case *g*) **1** Edward (1809–83), English scholar and poet **2** Ella (1917–96), American jazz singer **3** F. Scott (1896–1940), American novelist; full name *Francis Scott Key Fitzgerald*
Fitzroy name since 2002 for shipping forecast area off NW Spain; formerly called **Finisterre**
Fitzwilliam College Cambridge
five (Roman numeral **v** or **V**) □ **fifth, fivefold**
five-a-side (two hyphens)
five-year plan (one hyphen, lower case)
fixed-doh system system of solmization in which C is called 'doh'
fizgig arch. silly or flirtatious girl
fjord (also **fiord**) narrow inlet of the sea
FL Florida (postal abbrev.)
fl. 1 floor **2** fluid
fl. abbrev. for *floruit* (ital., point, followed by a space)
Fla. Florida (official abbrev.)
flabbergast (not **-ghast**)
flack use **flak**
flag day (two words)
flagellum pl. **flagella** Biol. slender thread-like structure

flageolet 1 small flute-like instrument **2** French kidney bean
flagitious criminal, villainous
flag lieutenant, **flag officer** (two words)
flagpole, **flagship**, **flagstaff**, **flagstone** (one word)
flair 1 natural ability or talent **2** stylishness and originality; cf. **flare**
flak anti-aircraft fire (not **flack**)
flambé (of food) covered with spirits and set alight (accent, not ital.)
flambeau pl. **flambeaus** or **flambeaux** flaming torch (not ital.)
flamenco pl. **flamencos** style of Spanish music or dance
flameproof (one word)
flamethrower (one word)
flame tree (two words)
flamingo pl. **flamingos** or **flamingoes**
flammable easily set on fire (negative form is **non-flammable** not **inflammable**)
Flamsteed, John (1646–1719), English astronomer
Flanders region of Belgium, France, and the Netherlands; Fr. name **Flandre**, Flemish name **Vlaanderen**
flânerie aimless idle behaviour (Fr., ital.)
flâneur idler or lounger (Fr., ital.)
flannel v. (**flannelling**, **flannelled**) Brit. informal talk in empty or flattering way
flannelette fabric resembling flannel
flannelled (US also **flanneled**) wearing flannel
flapjack (one word)
flare n. bright light or signal. v. **1** burn or shine suddenly **2** gradually become wider; cf. **flair**
flare-up n. (hyphen, two words as verb)
flashbulb (one word)
flash card, **flash flood** (two words)
flashlight, **flashpoint** (one word)
flat Mus. (sign ♭)
flatfish, **flatmate**, **flatware**, **flatworm** (one word)
Flaubert, Gustave (1821–80), French novelist
flaunching cement or mortar around the base of a chimney pot
flaunt display ostentatiously; cf. **flout**
flautist (US **flutist**)
flavour (US **flavor**)
F-layer layer of the ionosphere (hyphen, one cap.)
flea market (two words)
fleapit (one word)
flèche slender spire (Fr., ital.)
fledgling (not **fledgeling**)
Fleming[1] **1** Sir Alexander (1881–1955), Scottish bacteriologist **2** Ian (Lancaster) (1908–64), English novelist
Fleming[2] **1** person from Flanders **2** Flemish-speaking person of northern and western Belgium; cf. **Walloon**
flense (also **flench**) cut up (a whale or seal)
fleshpots (one word)
flesh wound (two words)
fleur-de-lis (also **fleur-de-lys**) pl. **fleurs-de-lis** (in heraldry) stylized lily (not ital.)
fleuron pl. **fleurons** flower-shaped decoration
fleury var. of **flory**
flexible (not **-able**)
flexion (also **flection**) action of bending
flexitime (one word, lower case)
flexography method for printing on fabrics and plastics as well as on paper
flibbertigibbet frivolous person
flier var. of **flyer**
flintlock (one word)
Flintshire county of NE Wales
flip-flop sandal (hyphen)
FLN Front de Libération Nationale (Algerian group in war against France 1954–62)
floatation var. of **flotation**
floatplane (one word)
floccinaucinihilipilification action of estimating something as worthless
flocculent resembling tufts of wool
flocculus pl. **flocculi 1** Anat. small lobe on the cerebellum **2** (also **floccule**) small tuft
floe sheet of floating ice
Flood, the cap. in ref. to the Old Testament
floodgate, **floodlight**, **floodplain** (one word)
flood tide, **flood water** (two words)

floorboard (one word)
floor show (two words)
floozy (also **floozie**) informal promiscuous or flirtatious woman
flophouse US dosshouse
flor. abbrev. of ***floruit***; prefer ***fl.***
flora pl. **floras** plants of a particular region or period; cf. **fauna**
floreat let —— flourish (not ital.)
Florence city in west central Italy; It. name **Firenze** □ **Florentine**
flore pleno (of a plant variety) double-flowered (not ital.)
florescence process of flowering
floriated decorated with floral designs
Florida state in the south-eastern US (official abbrev. **Fla.**, postal **FL**)
florilegium pl. **florilegia** or **florilegiums** anthology (not ital.)
florin former British coin worth two shillings
Florio, John (*c.*1553–1625), English lexicographer
floruit (abbrev. ***fl.*** or ***flor.***) used with a period or set of dates to indicate when a historical figure lived or worked (ital., followed by space) [L., he or she flourished]
flory (also **fleury**) Heraldry decorated with fleurs-de-lis
flotation (also **floatation**)
flotsam wreckage of a ship or its cargo floating on or washed up by the sea; cf. **jetsam**
flourished see ***floruit***
flout openly disregard (a rule etc.); cf. **flaunt**
flow chart (two words)
flower bed (two words)
flowerpot (one word)
Flt Lt Flight Lieutenant
Flt Sgt Flight Sergeant
flu influenza (no apostrophe, no point)
flugelhorn brass musical instrument
fluid (abbrev. **fl.**)
fluky (also **flukey**) lucky
flummox informal bewilder
flunkey (also **flunky**) pl. **flunkeys, flunkies** liveried manservant or footman
fluorescent, **fluoride** (not **flour-**)
fluorine chemical element of atomic number 9 (symbol **F**)
fluorite mineral consisting of calcium fluoride
fluoroscope instrument for viewing X-ray images
fluorspar mineral consisting of calcium fluoride; fluorite
flutist US term for **flautist**
flyaway, flyblown, flycatcher (one word)
flyer (also **flier**)
fly fishing (two words, hyphen when attrib.)
fly half (two words)
flyleaf (one word)
Flynn, Errol (1909–59), Australian-born American actor; born *Leslie Thomas Flynn*
flyover, flypaper (one word)
fly-past, fly-post (hyphen)
flyweight boxing weight between light flyweight and bantamweight (one word)
flywheel (one word)
FM 1 Field Marshal **2** frequency modulation
Fm the chemical element fermium (no point)
fm fathom(s)
fn. footnote (but prefer **n**)
f-number Photog. ratio of the focal length of a camera lens to the diameter of the aperture being used for a particular shot (e.g. *f8*) (hyphen)
FO 1 Flying Officer **2** Foreign Office
fo. pl. **fos** or **fos.** folio (point)
f.o.b. free on board
focaccia flat Italian bread (not ital.)
Foch, Ferdinand (1851–1929), French general
fo'c'sle Naut. forecastle
focus n. pl. **focuses** or **foci**. v. **focusing, focused** or **focussing, focussed**
FoE Friends of the Earth
foehn var. of **föhn**
foetid var. of **fetid**
foetus see **fetus**
fogbound (one word)
fogey (also **fogy**) pl. **fogeys, fogies** old-fashioned or conservative person
Fogg, Phileas, hero of *Around the World*

in Eighty Days (1873) by Jules Verne
foghorn (one word)
föhn (also **foehn**) hot wind in the Alps (accent, not ital.)
foie gras short for **pâté de foie gras** (not ital.)
Fokine, Michel (1880–1942), Russian-born American dancer and choreographer; born *Mikhail Mikhailovich Fokine*
Fokker, Anthony Herman Gerard (1890–1939), Dutch-born American aircraft designer
fol. pl. **fols** or **fols.** folio (point)
-fold as a suffix forms one word (e.g. *threefold*) except after numerals (*10-fold*)
foliaceous resembling a leaf or leaves
folie à deux pl. ***folies à deux*** delusion shared by two people (Fr., ital.)
folie de grandeur delusions of grandeur (Fr., ital.)
Folies-Bergère variety theatre in Paris (hyphen, not ital.)
folio (abbrev. **f.**, **fo.**, or **fol.**) pl. **folios** **1** individual leaf of paper **2** page number **3** sheet of paper folded once to form two leaves (four pages) of a book
folium pl. **folia** thin leaf-like structure (not ital.)
folk dance (two words)
folklore (one word)
folk music, folk singer, folk song, folk tale (two words)
folkways traditional way of life of a community (one word)
follicle **1** sheath surrounding the root of a hair **2** Anat. small secretory cavity, sac, etc. ◻ **follicular**
following (abbrev. **f.**, pl. **ff.**)
follow-through, follow-up n. (hyphen, two words as verb)
fols (also **fols.**) folios
foment stir up (revolution or strife)
fondue dish in which pieces of food are dipped into a sauce (not **fondu**)
fons et origo source and origin of something (L., ital.)
font **1** receptacle in a church for the water used in baptism **2** (Brit. also **fount**) Printing set of type of one particular face or size
fontanelle (US **fontanel**) space between the bones of the skull in an infant
Fonteyn, Dame Margot (1919–91), English ballet dancer; born *Margaret Hookham*
foodstuff (one word)
foolhardy, foolproof (one word)
foolscap size of paper, about 330 × 200 (or 400) mm (one word)
fool's gold, fool's paradise (note apostrophe)
foot (abbrev. **ft**)
foot-and-mouth disease (hyphens)
football, footbridge, foothill, foothold, footlights (one word)
footnote additional piece of information at the bottom of a page (one word)
footpad, footpath, footplate, footprint, footrest (one word)
Footsie Brit. trademark informal term for **FTSE index** (cap.)
footsie amorous touching of feet
foot soldier (two words)
footsore, footstep, footstool, footway, footwear, footwork (one word)
f.o.r. free on rail
fora pl. of **forum**
foramen pl. **foramina** Anat. opening, hole, or passage (not ital.)
forasmuch as arch. because (two words)
forbear v. (past **forbore**; past part. **forborne**) refrain. n. use **forebear**
forbearance patient self-control (not **forebearance**)
forbid (**forbidding**; past **forbade** or **forbad**; past part. **forbidden**)
force-feed (hyphen)
force field (two words)
force majeure (Fr., ital.) **1** Law unforeseeable circumstances that prevent fulfilment of a contract **2** superior strength
forcemeat meat or vegetable stuffing (one word)
forceps pl. n. pincers or tweezers used in surgery etc.
Ford **1** Ford Madox (1873–1939), English novelist and editor; born *Ford Hermann Hueffer* **2** Gerald (Rudolph) (1913–2006), 38th president of the US 1974–7 **3** Henry (1863–1947), American

motor manufacturer **4** John (1586–*c.*1639), English dramatist
forearm (one word)
forebear ancestor (not **forbear**)
forebearance use **forbearance**
foreboding (not **forboding**)
forecast (not **forcast**)
forecastle (also **fo'c'sle**) forward part of a ship below the deck
foreclose (not **forclose**)
fore-edge outer vertical edge of the pages of a book (hyphen)
forefend use **forfend**
forefinger, forefoot, forefront (one word)
foregather gather together (not **forgather**)
forego (**foregoing, forewent**; past part. **foregone**) **1** arch. precede in place or time **2** var. of **forgo**
foreground, forehand, forehead (one word)
Foreign and Commonwealth Office full name of the Foreign Office (abbrev. **FCO**)
foreleg, forelock, foreman (one word)
forename preferable to **Christian name**, but **given name** is better in non-Western contexts
forenoon, forepaw, foreplay, forerunner (one word)
forensic 1 using scientific methods in investigating crime **2** of courts of law
foresee (not **forsee**) ◻ **foreseeable**
forestall (not **forstall**)
Forester, C. S. (1899–1966), English novelist; pseudonym of *Cecil Lewis Troughton Smith*
foretell (not **fortell**)
forever 1 (also **for ever**) for all future time **2** continually
forewarn (not **forwarn**)
foreword (not **forword**)
forfend arch. avert or prevent (not **forefend**)
forgather use **foregather**
forget (**forgetting, forgot**; past part. **forgotten** or chiefly US **forgot**)
forget-me-not (hyphens)
forgo (also **forego**) (**forgoing, forwent**; past part. **forgone**) go without
forint monetary unit of Hungary
forklift (one word)
formaldehyde gas used in solution as a preservative
formalin solution of formaldehyde used as a preservative
formalize (Brit. also **formalise**)
format v. (**formatting, formatted**)
forme (also US **form**) Printing body of type for printing
former the first of two; cf. **latter**
Formica trademark plastic laminate (cap.)
Formosa former name for Taiwan
formula pl. **formulae** (in scientific use) or **formulas** ◻ **formulaic**
Formula One international motor racing (caps)
forsake (past **forsook**; past part. **forsaken**) (not **foresake**)
forswear (not **foreswear**)
forte (not ital.) **1** person's strong point **2** Mus. loud or loudly (abbrev. **f**)
fortepiano early kind of piano (one word, not ital.)
forte piano Mus. loud and then soft (two words, not ital.; abbrev. **fp**)
forties (also **1940s**) decade (lower case, no apostrophe; as area of North Sea, cap.)
fortissimo Mus. very loud or loudly (abbrev. **ff**)
Fortran computer programming language
fortuitous happening by chance rather than intention
forty (not **fourty**) hyphen in compound numbers, e.g. *forty-one*; Roman numeral **xl** or **XL** ◻ **fortieth**
forum pl. **forums** or (in ref. to ancient Rome) **fora**
fos. folios (point)
fossa pl. **fossae** Anat. depression or hollow (not ital.)
Fosse Way Roman road (caps)
fossilize (Brit. also **fossilise**)
Foster 1 Sir Norman (Robert), Baron Foster of Thames Bank (b.1935), English architect **2** Stephen (Collins) (1826–64), American composer
Fotheringhay castle in Northamptonshire, England
Foucault, Michel (Paul) (1926–84), French philosopher ◻ **Foucauldian**

(also **Foucaultian**)
fouetté Ballet type of pirouette (Fr., ital.)
Foulah use **Fula**
foulard 1 thin soft material **2** tie or scarf made from foulard
foul-up n. (hyphen, two words as verb)
fount Brit. var. of **font**
four (Roman numeral **iv** or **IV**, archaic **iiii** or **IIII**) ◻ **fourfold, fourth**
Four Horsemen of the Apocalypse Conquest, Slaughter, Famine, and Death, riding white, red, black, and pale horses respectively (Rev. 6 1–8)
Fourier, Jean Baptiste Joseph (1768–1830), French mathematician
four-poster (hyphen)
fourscore, foursome (one word)
fourteen (Roman numeral **xiv** or **XIV**) ◻ **fourteenth**
Fourth Estate, the the press, journalism (caps)
Fourth of July (in the US) Independence Day
4to quarto
four-wheel drive (hyphen; abbrev. **4WD, f.w.d.**)
Fowler, Henry Watson (1858–1933) and Francis George (1870–1918), English lexicographers
Fox 1 Charles James (1749–1806), British statesman **2** George (1624–91), English preacher and founder of the Society of Friends (Quakers)
Foxe, John (1516–87), English religious writer
foxed (of a book or print) discoloured with brown spots
foxglove, foxhole, foxhound (one word)
fox hunting, fox terrier (two words)
foxtrot (one word)
FP former pupils
fp forte piano
f.p. freezing point (points)
FPA Family Planning Association
FPS Fellow of the Pharmaceutical Society of Great Britain
fps (also **f.p.s.**) **1** feet per second **2** foot-pound-second **3** frames per second
Fr (no point) **1** Father (as a title of priests) **2** the chemical element francium
Fr. (point) **1** France or French **2** Frau
fr. franc(s)
Fra title of an Italian monk or friar (no point)
fracas pl. same or US **fracases** noisy disturbance or quarrel
fractionalize (Brit. also **fractionalise**)
fractions hyphenate e.g. *two-thirds*, *three-quarters*, but write *one and a half* as separate words
fractious irritable or liable to squabble
fraenulum use **frenulum**
fraenum var. of **frenum**
Fragonard, Jean-Honoré (1732–1806), French painter
fraise strawberry (Fr., ital.)
Fraktur German style of black-letter type (cap., not ital.)
framboesia (US **frambesia**) Med. yaws
framboise raspberry (Fr., ital.)
frameable (also **framable**)
framework (one word)
franc basic monetary unit of France, Belgium, Switzerland, Luxembourg, and several other countries, replaced in France, Belgium, and Luxembourg by the euro in 2002 (abrev. **F** or **fr.**)
France[1] country in western Europe (abbrev. **Fr.**)
France[2], Anatole (1844–1924), French writer; pseudonym of *Jacques-Anatole-François Thibault*
Franche-Comté region of eastern France (hyphen)
franchise (not **-ize**)
Franciscan member of a Christian order founded by St Francis of Assisi
Francis of Assisi, St (*c.*1181–1226), Italian monk; born *Giovanni di Bernardone*
Francis of Sales, St (1567–1622), French bishop
Francis Xavier, St see **Xavier, St Francis**
francium chemical element of atomic number 87 (symbol **Fr**)
Franck, César (Auguste) (1822–90), Belgian-born French composer
Franco, Francisco (1892–1975), Spanish general, head of state 1939–75; title *el Caudillo*

Francophile person fond of France (cap.)
francophone French-speaking (lower case)
frangible fragile or brittle
frangipane almond-flavoured cream
frangipani American tree or shrub
franglais blend of French and English (not ital.)
Frankenstein scientist who creates monster in Mary Shelley's novel *Frankenstein, or, The Modern Prometheus* (1818)
Frankfort capital of Kentucky
Frankfurt (also **Frankfurt am Main**) city in western Germany
frankfurter smoked sausage (lower case)
frankincense resin burnt as incense
Franz Josef Land group of islands in the Arctic Ocean
frappé iced or semi-frozen drink (accent, not ital.)
Fraser river of British Columbia
frater dining room of a monastery
fraternize (Brit. also **fraternise**)
Frau pl. **Frauen** title for a married or widowed German-speaking woman (not ital.; abbrev. **Fr.**)
Fräulein title for an unmarried German-speaking woman (not ital.; abbrev. **Frl.**)
Fray Bentos port in Uruguay
Frazer, Sir James George (1854–1941), Scottish anthropologist
FRCS Fellow of the Royal College of Surgeons
Frederick I (*c.*1123–90), Holy Roman emperor 1152–90; known as **Frederick Barbarossa**
Fredericton capital of New Brunswick, Canada
free and easy (three words, hyphens when attrib.)
freebase, freebooter, freeborn (one word)
freedman hist. emancipated slave; cf. **freeman**
Freefone trademark Freephone
free-for-all (hyphens)
free-form (hyphen)
freehand, freehold, freelance, freeloader (one word)
freeman 1 person given the freedom of a city or borough **2** hist. person who is not a slave or serf; cf. **freedman**
Freemason (cap.) ◻ **Freemasonry**
Freephone (also trademark **Freefone**) (cap.)
free port (two words)
Freepost (cap.)
freer, freest compar. and superl. of **free**
free-range (hyphen)
free rein (not **free reign**)
freesia plant with colourful flowers
free-standing (hyphen)
freestyle, freethinker (one word)
Freetown capital of Sierra Leone
freeway, freewheel (one word)
freeze-dry, freeze-frame (hyphen)
freezing point (two words)
Frege, Gottlob (1848–1925), German philosopher and mathematician
Freiburg (also **Freiburg im Breisgau**) city in SW Germany
Freightliner Brit. trademark train carrying freight in containers
Frelimo nationalist liberation party of Mozambique
Fremantle port of Western Australia
French (abbrev. **Fr.**)
French bean, French dressing, French fries (one cap.)
French Guiana overseas department of France in South America
French kiss, French polish n. (two words, hyphen as verb)
French window (one cap.)
frenulum Anat. (not **fraenulum**)
frenum (also **fraenum**) Anat. frenulum
freon trademark hydrocarbon used in fridges etc. (lower case)
freq. frequent or frequently
fresco pl. **frescoes** or **frescos** painting done on wet plaster
freshman first-year student of either sex at university or (N. Amer.) at high school
fresh water (two words as noun, one word as adj.)
Fresnel, Augustin Jean (1788–1827), French physicist and civil engineer
fret (**fretting, fretted**)

fretboard, **fretsaw**, **fretwork** (one word)
Freud 1 Lucian (1922–2011), German-born British painter **2** Sigmund (1856–1939), Austrian psychotherapist □ **Freudian**
Freya Scand. Mythol. goddess of love and of the night
FRG Federal Republic of Germany
Fri. Friday
friable easily crumbled
fricandeau pl. **fricandeaux** slice of meat cut from the leg (not ital.)
fricassee (not ital., no accent) n. dish of meat in a thick white sauce. v. (**fricasseeing**, **fricasseed**) make fricassee of [Fr. *fricassée*]
fricative consonant made by the friction of breath in a narrow opening, e.g. *f*
Friday (abbrev. **Fri.**)
fridge (not **frig** or **'fridge**)
fridge-freezer (hyphen)
Friedman, Milton (1912–2006), American economist
frier use **fryer**
Friesian Brit. breed of black-and-white cattle
frieze 1 broad horizontal band decoration **2** Archit. part of an entablature between the architrave and the cornice
Frigga Scand. Mythol. wife of Odin
frigidarium pl. **frigidaria** cold room in an ancient Roman bath
Frink, Dame Elisabeth (1930–93), English sculptor
Frisbee trademark plastic disc skimmed through the air as a game
Frisia ancient region of NW Europe □ **Frisian**
frisson sudden strong feeling of excitement or fear (not ital.)
frites short for **pommes frites** (not ital.)
fritto misto dish of various foods deep-fried in batter (It., ital.)
Friuli-Venezia Giulia region of NE Italy (one hyphen)
frizzante (of wine) semi-sparkling (It., ital.)
Frl. Fräulein
fro as in 'to and fro' (not **froe**)
Frobisher, Sir Martin (*c.*1535–94), English explorer
frock coat (two words)
froe cleaving tool
Froebel, Friedrich (Wilhelm August) (1782–1852), German founder of the kindergarten system
frogman, **frogmarch**, **frogspawn** (one word)
froideur coolness or reserve (Fr., ital.)
frolic v. (**frolicking**, **frolicked**)
fromage cheese (Fr., ital.)
fromage blanc type of soft cheese with creamy sour taste (not ital.)
fromage frais type of smooth cheese resembling yogurt (not ital.)
Fronde (not ital.) **1** series of civil wars in 17th-cent. France **2** rebellious group in Fronde
frondeur member of the Fronde; political rebel (Fr., ital.)
frontbencher member of the cabinet or shadow cabinet, who sits on the front benches in the House of Commons (one word)
frontispiece illustration facing the title page of a book
front matter pages of a book, e.g. title page and preface, preceding the main text (two words)
front runner (two words) □ **front-running**
frostbite (one word)
frou-frou frills (hyphen, not ital.)
froward arch. difficult to deal with
frowsty Brit. stale, warm, and stuffy
frowzy (also **frowsy**) scruffy and neglected in appearance
FRS Fellow of the Royal Society
FRSE Fellow of the Royal Society of Edinburgh
fructose sugar found in honey and fruit
fructuous full of or producing fruit
frumenty (also **furmety**) dish of hulled wheat boiled in milk
frustum pl. **frusta** or **frustums** Geom. lower portion of a cone or pyramid
Fry 1 Christopher (Harris) (1907–2005), English dramatist **2** Elizabeth (1780–1845), English Quaker prison reformer **3** Roger (Eliot) (1866–1934), English art critic and painter
Frye, (Herman) Northrop (1912–91), Canadian literary critic
fryer container for frying food (not **frier**)
frying pan (two words)

fry-up n. (hyphen)
FS Flight Sergeant
FSA Fellow of the Society of Antiquaries
FSH follicle-stimulating hormone
f-stop camera setting (hyphen)
FT Financial Times
Ft Fort (in place names)
ft foot or feet
FTP Comput. n. file transfer protocol. v. (**FTP'ing, FTP'd**) transfer by FTP
FTSE index trademark (also **FT index**) list of share prices on the London Stock Exchange
Fuad I (1868–1936), sultan of Egypt 1917–22 and king 1922–36
fuchsia shrub with tubular flowers
fucus pl. **fuci** kind of seaweed
fuel v. (**fuelling, fuelled**; US one **-l-**)
fugacious tending to disappear; fleeting □ **fugacity**
fugleman hist. soldier standing in front of a regiment or company during drill
fugue Mus., Med. □ **fugal**
Führer (also **Fuehrer**) title assumed by Hitler as leader of Germany
Fujairah (also **al-Fujayrah**) member state of the United Arab Emirates
Fuji, Mount (also **Fujiyama**) dormant volcano in Japan
Fula language of Fulani people (not **Foulah**)
Fulani member of a West African people
Fulbright, (James) William (1905–95), American senator, founder of Fulbright scholarships
fulcrum pl. **fulcrums** or **fulcra**
fulfil (US **fulfill**) (**fulfilling, fulfilled**) □ **fulfilment** (US **fulfillment**)
fulgent shining brightly
fuliginous sooty; dusky
full back Sport (two words)
full-blooded, full-blown, full-bodied, full-frontal, full-grown, full-length (hyphen)
fullness (also **fulness**)
full-time adj. & adv. occupying or using all someone's working time (hyphen)
full time n. end of a game (two words)
fulmar gull-like seabird
fulsome excessively complimentary or flattering; disp. generous or abundant (not **fullsome**)
fumitory flowering plant
funambulist tightrope walker
function Math. (symbol **f**)
fundraiser, fundraising (one word)
funfair (one word)
fungus pl. **fungi** or **funguses**
funnel (**funnelling, funnelled**; US one **-l-**)
furbelow flounce on a skirt
Furies, the Gk Mythol. three goddesses (Alecto, Megaera, and Tisiphone) who cursed the guilty
furioso Mus. furiously and wildly
furlong an eighth of a mile, 220 yards (abbrev. **f, fur.**)
furmety var. of **frumenty**
Furnivall, Frederick (James) (1825–1910), English lexicographer
furore (US **furor**) outbreak of public anger or excitement
Furtwängler, Wilhelm (1886–1954), German conductor
fuselage main body of an aircraft
fusible (not **-able**)
fusil light musket
fusilier (N. Amer. also **fusileer**) soldier armed with a fusil
fusillade series of shots or missiles
fusion joining or blending to form a single entity; cf. **fission**
futhark (also **futhorc**) runic alphabet
futurism 1 concern with events and trends of the future **2** (**Futurism**) artistic movement of early 20th cent.
Fuzhou (also **Foochow**) port in SE China
fwd forward (no points)
f.w.d. (points) **1** four-wheel drive **2** front-wheel drive
fylfot swastika, esp. as an ancient symbol
fyrd English militia before 1066 (lower case)
FYROM Former Yugoslav Republic of Macedonia
fytte use **fit**

G

G 1 pl. **Gs** or **G's** 7th letter of the alphabet **2** gauss **3** giga- (10^9) **4** N. Amer. informal a grand ($1,000) **5** force exerted by the earth's gravitational field

g 1 Phys. acceleration due to gravity **2** Chem. gas **3** gelding **4** gram(s)

G8 Group of Eight (top industrial nations)

GA 1 general aviation **2** Georgia (postal abbrev.)

Ga the chemical element gallium (no point)

Ga. Georgia (official abbrev.; point)

GAA Gaelic Athletic Association

gabbro pl. **gabbros** kind of igneous rock

gaberdine (also N. Amer. **gabardine**) **1** smooth worsted or cotton cloth **2** hist. loose upper garment worn by Jews

Gabon country in West Africa □ **Gabonese**

Gaboon viper venomous African snake

Gaborone capital of Botswana

gadabout habitual pleasure-seeker (one word)

Gadarene involving a headlong or disastrous rush [Matt. 8:28–32]

Gaddafi (also **Qaddafi**), Colonel Mu'ammer Muhammad al- (1942–2011), Libyan head of state 1970–2011

gadfly (one word)

gadolinium chemical element of atomic number 64 (symbol **Gd**)

Gaea var. of **Gaia** (in sense 1)

Gael Gaelic-speaking person

Gaelic any of the Celtic languages of Scotland, Ireland, and the Isle of Man

Gaeltacht Irish-speaking region of Ireland

gaff 1 fishing spear **2** informal person's house

gaffe embarrassing blunder

gaga informal senile (one word)

Gagarin, Yuri (Alekseevich) (1934–68), Russian cosmonaut

gage¹ pledge

gage² US or technical var. of **gauge**

Gaia 1 (also **Gaea, Ge**) Gk Mythol. earth personified as a goddess **2** earth viewed as a vast self-regulating organism (in the **Gaia hypothesis**) □ **Gaian**

gaiety (US also **gayety**) cheerfulness, liveliness

gaillardia plant of the daisy family

gaily (not **gayly**)

Gainsborough, Thomas (1727–88), English painter

Gairloch area in NW Scotland; cf. **Gare Loch**

Gaitskell, Hugh (Todd Naylor) (1906–63), British Labour statesman

Gal. Epistle to the Galatians

gal. gallon(s)

galangal (also **galingale**) plant of the ginger family

galantine cold meat or fish in aspic

galanty show hist. performance of shadow theatre

Galapagos Islands archipelago off South America; Sp. name **Archipiélago de Colón**

Galatea Gk Mythol. **1** sea nymph **2** the statue brought to life by Pygmalion

Galaţi city in Romania

Galatia ancient region in Asia Minor

Galatians, Epistle to the book of the New Testament (abbrev. **Gal.**)

galaxy cap. in ref. to the galaxy of which the solar system is a part; lower case in ref. to other star systems

galena mineral

galère undesirable group (Fr., ital.)

Galicia 1 region of NW Spain **2** region of SE Poland and western Ukraine

Galilean¹ of Galileo Galilei

Galilean² of Galilee

Galilee northern part of ancient Palestine

Galilee, Sea of lake in northern Israel

Galileo Galilei (1564–1642), Italian

astronomer and physicist
galingale 1 kind of sedge **2** var. of **galangal**
galiot var. of **galliot**
galipot hardened pine resin; cf. **gallipot**
gall. gallon(s)
gall bladder (two words)
galley Printing, hist. oblong tray for holding set-up type
galley proof printer's proof in the form of long single-column strips
galliard hist. lively dance in triple time
Gallic 1 of France **2** of the Gauls
gallice in French (not ital.)
Gallicism French idiom
gallimaufry jumble or medley
galliot (also **galiot**) hist. Dutch cargo boat
Gallipoli peninsula in Turkey, site of a campaign of WWI; modern Turkish name **Gelibolu**
gallipot small pot formerly used for ointments etc.; cf. **galipot**
gallium chemical element of atomic number 31 (symbol **Ga**)
gallivant gad about
gallon (abbrev. **gal.**, **gall.**)
galloon ornamental strip of braid etc.
gallop v. (**galloping, galloped**) (of a horse) go at its fastest pace; cf. **galop** □ **galloper**
Galloway area of SW Scotland
galloway black hornless breed of beef cattle (lower case)
gallows (usu. treated as sing.)
gallstone (one word)
Gallup poll trademark assessment of public opinion by the questioning of a representative sample
galop ballroom dance; cf. **gallop**
galosh waterproof overshoe
galumph move noisily or clumsily
Galvani, Luigi (1737–98), Italian anatomist
galvanize (Brit. also **galvanise**)
Gama, Vasco da see **da Gama**
gambado (also **gambade**) pl. **gambadoes** or **gambados** horse's leap
Gambia (also **the Gambia**) country on the coast of West Africa
gambier extract of an Asian plant
gamboge gum resin used as a yellow pigment
gambol (**gambolling, gambolled**; US one **-l-**) frisk
game bird (two words)
gamekeeper (one word)
game plan, game point, game show, game theory (two words)
gamin dated street urchin
gamine n. attractively boyish girl. adj. (of a girl) attractively boyish
gamma 1 third letter of the Greek alphabet (**Γ**, **γ**), transliterated as 'g' **2** Phys. unit of magnetic field strength equal to 10^{-5} oersted
gamy (also **gamey**) having the strong flavour of game left till high
Ganapati another name for **Ganesh**
Gand Fr. name for **Ghent**
Gandhi (not **Ghandi**) **1** Mrs Indira (1917–84), Indian prime minister 1966–77 and 1980–4 **2** Mahatma (1869–1948), Indian nationalist leader; full name *Mohandas Karamchand Gandhi* **3** Rajiv (1944–91), Indian prime minister 1984–9
Ganesh (also **Ganesha**) elephant-headed Hindu deity; also called **Ganapati**
Ganges river of northern India and Bangladesh; Hindi name **Ganga**
ganglion pl. **ganglia** or **ganglions** Anat. swelling on a nerve fibre
gangue material in which ore is found
gangway (one word)
ganja marijuana
gantlet US var. of **gauntlet**²
Gantt chart chart showing the amount of work done (two *t*s)
Ganymede 1 Gk Mythol. handsome Trojan youth carried off to be Zeus' cup-bearer **2** moon of Jupiter
gaol, gaoler use **jail, jailer** exc. in historical contexts
Garamond a typeface
garbanzo pl. **garbanzos** N. Amer. chickpea
García Lorca see **Lorca**
García Márquez, Gabriel (1928–2014), Colombian novelist
garçon French waiter (ital.)
garçonnière bachelor's flat (Fr., ital.)
Garda 1 (in full **Garda Síochána**) police

force of the Irish Republic **2** pl. **Gardai** member of this

gardener person who works in a garden (not **gardner**)

gardenia tree or shrub (lower case)

Garden of Eden (caps)

Gardner, Ava (Lavinia) (1922–90), American actress

Gare Loch sea inlet in SW Scotland; cf. **Gairloch**

garfish long slender marine fish

garganey pl. same or **garganeys** duck

gargantuan enormous (lower case)

gargoyle grotesque carved face or figure

Garibaldi, Giuseppe (1807–82), Italian patriot

garibaldi pl. **garibaldis** currant biscuit

garlic pungent-tasting bulb □ **garlicky**

garrotte (also **garotte**; US **garrote**) strangle with a length of wire or cord

garryowen Rugby an up-and-under (lower case)

Garter King of Arms Heraldry principal King of Arms

gas n. pl. **gases** or chiefly US **gasses**. v. **gassing, gassed**

Gascogne Fr. name for **Gascony**

Gascon person from Gascony

gascon arch. boastful person (lower case)

gasconade extravagant boasting [Fr. *gasconnade*]

Gascony region of SW France; Fr. name **Gascogne**

gaseous (not **-ious**)

Gaskell, Mrs Elizabeth (Cleghorn) (1810–65), English novelist

gaslight, gaslit (one word)

gas mask (two words)

gasoline (also **gasolene**) N. Amer. petrol

Gastarbeiter pl. same or ***Gastarbeiters*** temporary worker, esp. in Germany (cap., ital.)

Gasthaus pl. ***Gasthäuser*** small German inn or hotel (cap., ital.)

Gasthof pl. ***Gasthöfe*** German hotel (cap., ital.)

gastroenteritis (one word)

gastropod kind of mollusc (not **gasteropod** (arch.))

gastropub pub specializing in good food (one word)

gasworks (one word)

gateau pl. **gateaus** or **gateaux** cake [Fr. *gâteau*]

gatecrash, gatefold, gatekeeper, gatepost, gateway (one word)

gather Bookbinding collect and put in order (the leaves or sheets of a book)

Gatling gun early type of machine gun

GATT General Agreement on Tariffs and Trade

gauche unsophisticated and awkward (not ital.)

gauche left (Fr., ital.)

gaucherie awkwardness (not ital.)

gaucho pl. **gauchos** South American cowboy

Gaudí, Antonio (1853–1926), Spanish architect; full name *Antonio Gaudí y Cornet*

Gaudier-Brzeska, Henri (1891–1915), French sculptor

gauge (US or technical also **gage**) measure

Gauguin, (Eugène Henri) Paul (1848–1903), French painter

Gaul 1 ancient region of Europe **2** inhabitant of this

gauleiter (lower case, not ital.) **1** hist. local official under Nazi rule **2** overbearing official

Gaulle, Charles de, see **de Gaulle**

Gauloise trademark French brand of cigarette

Gaunt former name for **Ghent**

gauntlet[1] long glove (not **gantlet**)

gauntlet[2] (US also **gantlet**) (in **run the gauntlet**) go through an intimidating crowd

gaur Indian wild ox

Gauss, Karl Friedrich (1777–1855), German mathematician and physicist

gauss pl. same or **gausses** unit of magnetic induction (abbrev. **G**)

Gautama, Siddhartha, see **Buddha**

Gautier, Théophile (1811–72), French writer

gavel auctioneer's or judge's hammer

gavial var. of **gharial**

gavotte French dance

Gawain knight of the Round Table

gay standard adj. for male homosexuals

in general contexts; do not use as a noun exc. in phrs such as **gays and lesbians**; other senses are now dated
gayety US var. of **gaiety**
Gay-Lussac, Joseph Louis (1778–1850), French chemist and physicist
Gaza Strip strip of coastal territory in Palestine, a self-governing enclave
gazebo pl. **gazebos** small building giving a good view
gazette, gazetteer (two *ts*)
gazpacho pl. **gazpachos** cold vegetable soup
gazump make a higher offer for a house than (someone whose offer has already been accepted)
GB 1 Great Britain **2** Comput. gigabyte(s)
Gb Comput. gigabit(s)
GBE Knight or Dame Grand Cross of the Order of the British Empire
GBH grievous bodily harm
Gbyte gigabyte(s)
GC George Cross
GCB Knight or Dame Grand Cross of the Order of the Bath
GCE General Certificate of Education
GCHQ Government Communications Headquarters
GCIE Knight Grand Commander of the Order of the Indian Empire
GCMG Knight or Dame Grand Cross of the Order of St Michael and St George
GCSE General Certificate of Secondary Education
GCVO Knight or Dame Grand Cross of the Royal Victorian Order
Gd the chemical element gadolinium (no point)
Gdańsk port in northern Poland; Ger. name **Danzig**
Gdns Gardens (no point)
GDP gross domestic product
GDR hist. German Democratic Republic (East Germany)
Ge[1] the chemical element germanium (no point)
Ge[2] Gk Mythol. another name for **Gaia**
gearbox (one word)
gear lever (two words)
gearwheel (one word)
gecko pl. **geckos** nocturnal lizard
gee-string use **G-string**
Ge'ez ancient language of Ethiopia
geezer informal old man; cf. **geyser**
Gehenna (in Judaism and the New Testament) hell
Geiger counter (also **Geiger-Müller counter**) device for measuring radioactivity
geisha pl. same or **geishas** Japanese hostess
Geissler tube tube producing a luminous electrical discharge
Geist spirit of an individual or group (Ger., cap., ital.)
gel n. jelly-like substance. v. (also **jell**) (**gelling, gelled**) set or become firmer
gelatin (also **gelatine**) **1** clear substance **2** high explosive
Gelderland province of the Netherlands (not **Guelder-**)
Gelibolu Turkish name for **Gallipoli**
gelsemium preparation made from jasmine, used in homeopathy
Gemara, the second part of the Talmud
Gemeinschaft social relations based on personal and family ties; cf. ***Gesellschaft*** (Ger., cap., ital.)
Gemini third sign of the zodiac □ **Geminian**
gemma pl. **gemmae** Biol. small cellular body or bud
gemütlich pleasant and cheerful (Ger., ital.)
Gemütlichkeit geniality, friendliness (Ger., cap., ital.)
Gen. 1 General **2** Genesis
gen. Gram. genitive
gendarme French paramilitary police officer (not ital.)
gendarmerie a force of gendarmes (not ital.)
genealogy line of descent (not **-ology**)
genera pl. of **genus**
general (cap. as military title; abbrev. **Gen.**)
General Assembly highest court of the Church of Scotland
general election (lower case)
generalia general principles (L., ital.)
generalissimo pl. **generalissimos** commander of a combined military

force

generalize (Brit. also **generalise**)

General Synod highest governing body of the Church of England

Generation X disaffected people born in the 1970s ◻ **Generation Xer**

generator (not **-er**)

Genesis first book of the Old Testament (abbrev. **Gen.**)

genesis origin or formation of something (lower case)

Genet, Jean (1910–86), French novelist and dramatist

genet catlike mammal; cf. **jennet**

Geneva city in Switzerland; Fr. name **Genève**

Geneva Convention international agreement concerning people captured in wartime (two caps)

Geneva, Lake lake on the French–Swiss border; Fr. name **Lac Léman**

genever (also **geneva**) Dutch gin (lower case)

Genghis Khan (1162–1227), founder of the Mongol empire; born *Temujin*

genie pl. **genii** or **genies** jinn or spirit in Arabian folklore

genitive Gram. case indicating possession or association (abbrev. **gen., genit.**)

genius 1 pl. **geniuses** exceptional natural ability; person with this **2** pl. **genii** spirit associated with a place

genius loci character or atmosphere of a place (L., ital.)

genizah storeroom at a synagogue

Genoa seaport in Italy; It. name **Genova** ◻ **Genoese**

genoa Sailing jib or foresail (lower case)

genre category of art or literature (not ital.)

gens pl. **gentes** related group of families, clan

Gent Flemish name for **Ghent**

genteel affectedly refined

Gentile person who is not Jewish or (hist.) Mormon

gentile indicating a nation or clan (lower case)

gentleman-at-arms bodyguards of the British monarch (hyphens)

Gentleman Usher of the Black Rod see **Black Rod**

gents, the men's public toilet (lower case)

genuflect bend one knee in respect ◻ **genuflection**

genus pl. **genera** class of things; Biol. principal taxonomic category (genus names are capitalized and italic)

Geo. George (regnal year)

Geoffrey of Monmouth (*c.*1100–*c.*1154), Welsh chronicler

Geordie person from Tyneside in NE England

Georgetown 1 capital of Guyana **2** part of Washington DC, site of **Georgetown University**

George Town 1 capital of the Cayman Islands **2** chief port of Malaysia

Georgia 1 country of SE Europe **2** state of the south-eastern US (official abbrev. **Ga.**, postal **GA**)

Georgian[1] of Georgia in SE Europe or the US

Georgian[2] of the reigns of the British kings George I–IV, esp. in ref. to architecture, or of the reigns of George V and VI, esp. in ref. to pastoral poetry of 1910–20

georgic poem concerned with agriculture or rural topics, esp. (the *Georgics*) a collection of four by Virgil

Ger. German; Germany

geranium pl. **geraniums** plant

Gerard, John (1545–1612), English herbalist

gerbil desert rodent (not **jerbil**)

gerfalcon use **gyrfalcon**

Géricault, (Jean Louis André) Théodore (1791–1824), French painter

German (abbrev. **Ger.**)

german having the same parents (*brother/sister-german*) (lower case)

German Democratic Republic official name for the former state of East Germany (abbrev. **GDR, DDR**)

germane relevant

germanium chemical element of atomic number 32 (symbol **Ge**)

Germanize (Brit. also **Germanise**) make German (cap.)

German measles one cap.; but prefer **rubella**

German shepherd Alsatian dog (one cap.)

Germany country in central Europe (abbrev. **Ger.**); Ger. name **Deutschland**
gerrymander unfairly manipulate the boundaries of (an electoral constituency) (not **jerry-**)
gerund Gram. verb form which functions as a noun, in English ending in *-ing*
gerundive Gram. Latin verb form that functions as an adjective meaning 'that should or must be done'
Gesellschaft social relations based on impersonal ties; cf. ***Gemeinschaft*** (Ger., cap., ital.)
gesso pl. **gessoes** gypsum used in painting and sculpture
gestalt Psychol. organized whole perceived as more than the sum of its parts (lower case)
Gestapo Nazi secret police
gesundheit good health! (lower case, not ital.)
get-at-able accessible (hyphens)
getaway n. (one word, two words as verb)
Gethsemane, Garden of garden where Jesus was betrayed
get-together n. (hyphen, two words as verb)
Getty, Jean Paul (1892–1976), American industrialist
Gettysburg town in Pennsylvania, scene of a battle and the **Gettysburg Address** by Lincoln in 1863
GeV gigaelectronvolt (10^9 electronvolts)
gewgaw showy thing of little value
geyser hot spring; cf. **geezer**
GG Governor General
Ghana country in Africa □ **Ghanaian**
gharial (also **gavial**) Indian crocodile
gharry pl. **gharries** Indian hired carriage
ghat 1 (in the Indian subcontinent) flight of steps leading down to a river **2** mountain pass
ghazi pl. ***ghazis*** Muslim fighter against non-Muslims (ital.)
ghee clarified butter used in Indian cooking (not **ghi**)
Gheg pl. same or **Ghegs** member of one of the two main ethnic groups of Albania; cf. **Tosk**
Ghent city in Belgium; Flemish name **Gent**, Fr. name **Gand**; former English name **Gaunt**
gherkin small pickled cucumber
ghetto pl. **ghettos**
ghettoize (Brit. also **ghettoise**)
ghi use **ghee**
Ghibelline member of the Italian medieval faction supporting the Holy Roman emperor; cf. **Guelph**
Ghiberti, Lorenzo (1378–1455), Italian sculptor and goldsmith
ghillie var. of **gillie**
Ghirlandaio (*c.*1448–94), Italian painter; born *Domenico di Tommaso Bigordi*
ghostwrite, ghostwriter (one word)
GHQ General Headquarters
ghyll var. of **gill**²
GHz gigahertz
GI pl. **GIs** US private soldier [*government* (or *general*) *issue*]
Giacometti, Alberto (1901–66), Swiss sculptor and painter
giant-killer, giant-killing (hyphen)
Giant's Causeway geological formation in Northern Ireland (note apostrophe)
giaour arch. Turkish name for a non-Muslim
Gib informal Gibraltar
gibbet v. (**gibbeting, gibbeted**)
Gibbon, Edward (1737–94), English historian
Gibbons 1 Grinling (1648–1721), Dutch-born English sculptor **2** Orlando (1583–1625), English composer
gibbous (of the moon) having the illuminated part greater than a semicircle
gibe see **jibe**
Gibraltar British overseas territory at the southern tip of Spain □ **Gibraltarian**
Gibran, Khalil (1883–1931), Lebanese-born American writer (not **Jubran**)
gibus collapsible top hat
Gide, André (Paul Guillaume) (1869–1951), French writer
Gideon 1 Israelite leader **2** member of **Gideons International**, an organization that distributes bibles
Gielgud, Sir (Arthur) John (1904–2000), English actor
GIF Comput. trademark in the UK format for image files
giga- denoting a factor of 10^9, or 2^{30} in

computing (abbrev. **G**)

gigabit Comput. one thousand million (10^9) or (strictly) 2^{30} bits (abbrev. **Gb**)

gigabyte Comput. one thousand million (10^9) or (strictly) 2^{30} bytes (abbrev. **GB**)

gigahertz one thousand million (10^9) cycles per second (abbrev. **GHz**)

gigawatt one thousand million (10^9) watts (abbrev. **GW**)

GIGO Comput. garbage in, garbage out

gigolo pl. **gigolos**

gigot leg of mutton or lamb (not ital.)

gigue lively dance

Gilbert, Sir W(illiam) S(chwenck) (1836–1911), English librettist □ **Gilbertian**

Gilbert and Ellice Islands former British colony consisting of the **Gilbert Islands** (now part of Kiribati) and the **Ellice Islands** (Tuvalu)

Gilead biblical area east of the River Jordan famous for its balm (Jer. 8:22)

Gilgamesh Babylonian epic

gill[1] quarter of a pint

gill[2] (also **ghyll**) deep ravine or narrow mountain stream

gill[3] (also **jill**) female ferret; cf. **hob**

gillie (also **ghillie**) **1** attendant on a hunting or fishing expedition **2** hist. Highland chief's attendant

gillyflower (also **gilliflower**) flower

gilt-edged (hyphen)

gimcrack showy but flimsy

gimp[1] (not **guimp** or **gymp**) **1** upholstery trimming **2** fishing line

gimp[2] offens. disabled person

ginger ale, **ginger beer** (two words)

gingerbread (one word)

ginger nut, **ginger snap**, **ginger wine** (two words)

ginglymus pl. **ginglymi** Anat. hinge-like joint, e.g. the elbow

ginkgo (also **gingko**) pl. **ginkgos** or **ginkgoes** Chinese tree

Giorgione (*c.*1478–1510), Italian painter; also called **Giorgio Barbarelli** or **Giorgio da Castelfranco**

Giotto (*c.*1267–1337), Italian painter; full name *Giotto di Bondone*

Giovanni de' Medici name of Pope Leo X

Gipsy var. of **Gypsy**

girandole branched support for candles (not ital.)

girasol (also **girasole**) reddish opal

gird (past and past part. **girded** or **girt**) encircle or secure

girl Friday junior female office worker (one cap.)

girlfriend (one word)

Girl Guide official term is now **Guide**

giro pl. **giros** system of electronic credit transfer, or a payment by this means

Gironde department of SW France

Girondist (also **Girondin**) moderate republican in the French Revolution

Giscard d'Estaing, Valéry (b.1926), president of France 1974–81

gismo use **gizmo**

gitano (fem. ***gitana***; pl. ***gitanos*** or ***gitanas***) Spanish Gypsy (ital.)

gîte holiday house in France (accent, not ital.)

Giuseppe Italian given name (not **Guiseppe**)

given name prefer to **Christian name** or **forename**

Giza city near Cairo, site of the Pyramids and the Sphinx; Arab. name **al-Jizah**

gizmo pl. **gizmos** device, gadget (not **gismo**)

Gk Greek

GLA Greater London Authority

glacé preserved in sugar (accent, not ital.)

gladiolus pl. **gladioli** plant

Gladstone, William Ewart (1809–98), British prime minister 1868–74, 1880–5, 1886, and 1892–4 □ **Gladstonian**

Gladstone bag (one cap.)

Glagolitic alphabet formerly used in writing some Slavic languages

glair preparation made from egg white

Glamorgan former county of South Wales (abbrev. **Glam.**); Welsh name **Morgannwg**

glamorize (Brit. also **glamorise**)

glamorous (not **glamour-**)

glamour (US also **glamor**)

glans pl. **glandes** Anat. rounded end of the penis or clitoris

glasnost (in the former USSR) wider dissemination of official information (not ital.)
glass-blowing (hyphen)
glassful pl. **glassfuls**
glasshouse, glassware (one word)
Glaswegian person from Glasgow
Glauber's salt form of sodium sulphate formerly used as a laxative (not **salts**)
glaucoma pl. **glaucomas** eye condition
glaucous 1 dull greyish-green or blue **2** covered with a powdery bloom
Glazunov, Aleksandr (Konstantinovich) (1865–1936), Russian composer
GLC hist. Greater London Council
glen write as separate word, e.g. *Glen Coe*, when referring to a glen (valley) itself rather than the settlement
Glencoe area in the Scottish Highlands where members of the MacDonald clan were massacred in 1692 by Campbells
Glendower, Owen (*c.*1354–*c.*1417), Welsh chief; Welsh name *Owain Glyndwr*
glengarry brimless Scottish hat
Glenlivet, Glenmorangie whiskies
Glenrothes town in eastern Scotland
glissade a slide down a steep slope
glissando pl. **glissandi** or **glissandos** Mus. slide between two notes
glissé (also ***pas glissé***) Ballet sliding movement (Fr. ital.)
glister sparkle, glitter (as in *All that glisters is not gold*)
globalization (Brit. also **globalisation**)
globetrotter (one word)
glockenspiel percussion instrument
glögg Scandinavian mulled wine (lower case, accent, not ital.)
Gloria 1 hymn beginning *Gloria in excelsis Deo* **2** doxology beginning *Gloria Patris*
Gloriana nickname of Queen Elizabeth I
Glorious Revolution, the replacement of James II by Mary II and her husband William of Orange in 1689
Glorious Twelfth, the 12 August, start of the grouse-shooting season in the UK
Gloucester city in SW England; old spelling **Gloster** was the name of an aircraft manufacturer
Gloucestershire county of SW England (abbrev. **Glos.**)
glovebox (one word)
glove compartment, glove puppet (two words)
glow-worm (hyphen)
gloxinia pl. **gloxinias** tropical plant
Gluck, Christoph Willibald von (1714–87), German composer
glue v. (**gluing** or **glueing, glued**) □ **gluey**
glue-sniffing (hyphen)
glühwein German mulled wine (lower case, not ital.)
gluten substance present in cereal grains
gluteus pl. **glutei** Anat. any of three muscles in each buttock, the largest being the **gluteus maximus**
glutinous having a sticky texture
glycaemia (US **glycemia**) presence of glucose in the blood
glycerine (US **glycerin**) liquid used in explosives, antifreeze, etc.
Glyndebourne estate in East Sussex, site of an annual opera festival
Glyndwr, Owain, see **Glendower**
Glynebwy Welsh name for **Ebbw Vale**
GM 1 General Motors **2** genetically modified **3** George Medal **4** grandmaster; Grand Master
gm gram(s) (but prefer **g**)
G-man informal **1** US FBI agent **2** Ir. political detective
GMO genetically modified organism
GMT Greenwich Mean Time
gn pl. **gns** guinea(s)
gnamma Austral. natural hole where rainwater collects
gneiss banded or laminated rock
gnocchi Italian dumplings (not ital.)
gnomic in the form of short maxims or aphorisms
gnosis knowledge of spiritual mysteries
gnostic (person) having esoteric mystical knowledge (cap. in ref. to Gnosticism)
Gnosticism ancient belief that knowledge of the supreme divine being enabled the redemption of the human spirit (cap.)
GNP gross national product

Gnr Mil. Gunner
gns guineas
gnu large African antelope, wildebeest
GNVQ General National Vocational Qualification
goalkeeper, **goalmouth**, **goalpost** (one word)
goatee small pointed beard
goatherd, **goatskin** (one word)
goat-like (hyphen)
gobbledygook (also **gobbledegook**) nonsense
Gobelin tapestry made at the Gobelins factory in Paris
gobemouche gullible listener (not ital.) [Fr. *gobe-mouches*]
go-between (hyphen)
Gobi Desert barren plateau of southern Mongolia and northern China
gobsmacked informal astonished (one word)
goby small fish
go-by in phr. **give someone the go-by** (hyphen)
GOC General Officer Commanding
go-cart var. of **go-kart**
god cap. in ref. to the monotheistic deity, but lower case for pronouns referring to him; lower case for the deities of polytheistic religions
Godard, Jean-Luc (b.1930), French film director
godawful (one word, lower case)
godchild (one word)
goddam (also **goddamn**, **goddamned**) (one word)
god-daughter (hyphen)
goddess (lower case)
godfather (one word)
God-fearing (hyphen, cap.)
godforsaken(one word, lower case)
God-given (hyphen, cap.)
godhead divine nature or essence; (**the Godhead**) God
godless, **godlike**, **godly** (one word)
godmother, **godparent** (one word)
God's acre a churchyard (one cap.)
godsend, **godson** (one word)
Godspeed (cap., one word)
Godthåb former name for **Nuuk**
Godunov, Boris (1550–1605), tsar of Russia 1598–1605
Goebbels, (Paul) Joseph (1897–1945), German Nazi leader (not **Göbbels**)
Goering, Hermann Wilhelm (also **Göring**) (1893–1946), German Nazi leader
Goethe, Johann Wolfgang von (1749–1832), German poet and dramatist □ **Goethean**
gofer informal dogsbody; cf. **gopher**
goffer crimp or emboss
Gog and Magog 1 (in the Bible) the names of enemies of God's people **2** pair of giants (or one giant, called **Gogmagog**) said to have inhabited Britain in ancient times
Gogh, Vincent Van, see **Van Gogh**
Goidelic group of Celtic languages including Irish, Scottish Gaelic, and Manx (cf. **Brythonic**); also called **Q-Celtic**
goings-on (hyphen)
go-kart (also **go-cart**) small lightweight racing car
Golan Heights range of hills on the border between Syria and Israel, annexed by Israel in 1981
Golconda source of wealth or advantage [ruined city near Hyderabad, famous for its diamonds]
gold chemical element of atomic number 79 (symbol **Au**)
gold-digger (hyphen)
golden age lower case in phrs such as *the golden age of rail travel*
Golders Green area of London (no apostrophe)
goldfield, **goldfish** (one word)
gold mine (two words) □ **gold miner**, **gold-mining**
gold rush (two words)
Goldsmiths College University of London (no apostrophe)
golf ball, **golf club**, **golf course** (two words)
Golgotha site of the crucifixion of Jesus; Calvary
Gollancz, Sir Victor (1893–1967), British publisher and philanthropist
golliwog black-faced doll (not **gollywog**)
GOM Grand Old Man (nickname of Gladstone)
Gomorrah town in Palestine destroyed by fire from heaven (Gen. 19:24)
Goncharov, Ivan (Aleksandrovich)

(1812–91), Russian novelist
Goncourt Edmond de (1822–96) and Jules de (1830–70), French novelists; Edmond founded the **Prix Goncourt**
Gond pl. same or **Gonds** member of a people of central India
Góngora, Luis de (1561–1627), Spanish poet; full name *Luis de Góngora y Argote*
gonorrhoea (US **gonorrhea**)
Gonville and Caius College Cambridge
goodbye (US also **goodby**) pl. **goodbyes** or **goodbys** (one word)
good-for-nothing (hyphens as noun and attrib. adj.; three words in e.g. *he was good for nothing except ...*)
Good Friday (two words, caps)
good humour, good nature (two words)
good-humoured, good-natured (hyphen)
goodness note apostrophe in **for goodness' sake**
goodnight (one word)
good-quality (hyphen as attrib. adj.)
Good Samaritan (caps)
goodwill (one word)
Google Internet search engine
google informal do an Internet search for (lower case)
googol ten raised to the power of a hundred (10^{100})
goose pl. **geese** or in sense 'tailor's smoothing iron' **gooses**
goosebumps, gooseflesh (one word)
goose-step (hyphen)
GOP Grand Old Party (nickname of the US Republican Party)
gopher 1 burrowing American rodent **2** kind of wood; cf. **gofer**
Gorbachev, Mikhail (Sergeevich) (b.1931), president of the USSR 1988–91
Gorbals district of Glasgow
Gordian knot tied by Gordius, cut through by Alexander the Great
Gordonstoun public school in Scotland
Gore-tex trademark breathable waterproof fabric
gorgio pl. **gorgios** Gypsy name for a non-Gypsy
gorgon Gk Mythol. female monster with snakes for hair (lower case)
Gorgonzola cheese (cap.)
Göring (also **Goering**), Hermann Wilhelm (1893–1946), German Nazi leader
Gorky[1] former name for **Nizhni Novgorod**
Gorky[2], Maxim (1868–1936), Russian writer; pseudonym of *Aleksei Maksimovich Peshkov*
gormandize (Brit. also **gormandise**) var. of **gourmandize**
Gorsedd council of Welsh bards and Druids
gory (not **-ey**)
go-slow n. (hyphen)
gospel cap. in ref. to the record of Christ's life in the first four books of the New Testament (*the Gospel of Luke*)
Gospel side north side of a church altar, at which the Gospel is read (one cap.)
Gosse, Sir Edmund (William) (1849–1928), English writer
gossip v. (**gossiping, gossiped**) □ **gossiper, gossipy**
Gotham 1 village in Nottinghamshire whose inhabitants were proverbial for their stupidity **2** (also **Gotham City**) nickname for New York City
Gothenburg seaport in SW Sweden; Swed. name **Göteborg**
Gothic style of architecture in the 12th–16th cents (cap.)
Gothick pseudo-arch. spelling of **Gothic** in sense 'portentously gloomy'
gotten past part. of **get**; in British English used only in *ill-gotten*, but common in N. Amer.
Götterdämmerung (Twilight of the Gods), last part of Wagner's *Der Ring des Nibelungen*
Göttingen town in Germany
gouache opaque watercolour
Gouda 1 town in the Netherlands **2** round Dutch cheese
goujons deep-fried strips of chicken or fish (not ital.)
gourami pl. same or **gouramis** tropical fish
gourd fleshy fruit with a hard skin
gourde monetary unit of Haiti

gourmand person fond of eating, sometimes to excess
gourmandize (also **gormandize**, Brit. also **-ise**) eat enthusiastically, esp. to excess
gourmet connoisseur of good food
goût taste (Fr., ital.)
gov. governor; government
government lower case even in ref. to the particular people in office (abbrev. **gov.**, **govt**)
governor general pl. **governors general** chief representative of the Crown in a Commonwealth country (lower case; abbrev. **GG**)
goy pl. **goyim** or **goys** derog. Jewish name for a non-Jew
Goya (1746–1828), Spanish painter and etcher; full name *Francisco José de Goya y Lucientes*
GP 1 general practitioner **2** Grand Prix
Gp Capt Group Captain
GPO 1 hist. (in the UK) General Post Office **2** (in the US) Government Printing Office
GPS Global Positioning System
GPU Soviet secret police agency 1922–3
GR King George [L. *Georgius Rex*]
Gr. Greece; Greek
gr. 1 grain(s) **2** gram(s) (but prefer **g**) **3** grey **4** gross
Graafian follicle Anat. structure in the ovary
graben pl. same or **grabens** Geol. depression of the earth's crust between faults
Gracchus, Tiberius Sempronius (*c.*163–133 BC) and his brother Gaius Sempronius (*c.*153–121 BC), Roman tribunes; known as **the Gracchi**
grace note Mus. (two words)
Graces, the Gk Mythol. three goddesses personifying charm, grace, and beauty
gradable (not **-eable**)
gradatim step by step (L., ital.)
gradus (also ***gradus ad Parnassum***) pl. ***graduses*** manual of classical prosody (L., ital.)
Graeae, the Gk Mythol. three sisters who guarded the gorgons
Graecism (also **Grecism**) Greek idiom
Graecize (also **Grecize**, Brit. **-ise**) make Greek
Graf German count (not ital. as part of name)
graffiti (sing. **graffito**) unauthorized writing on a wall etc.; cf. **sgraffito**
graham N. Amer. wholewheat (lower case)
Grahame, Kenneth (1859–1932), Scottish writer of children's stories
grail cap. in ref. to the Holy Grail
grain unit of weight equal to 1/5760 of a pound troy and 1/7000 of a pound avoirdupois (approx. 0.0648 grams) (abbrev. **gr.**)
Grainger, (George) Percy (Aldridge) (1882–1961), Australian-born American composer
gram (Brit. also **gramme**) metric unit of mass equal to one thousandth of a kilogram (abbrev. **g**)
graminivorous Zool. feeding on grass
Grammy pl. **Grammys** annual award given to recording artistes
grampus pl. **grampuses** killer whale or similar cetacean
Gram stain (also **Gram's stain**) Med. technique for distinguishing between two categories of bacteria (**Gram-positive** and **Gram-negative**)
Granada city in southern Spain; cf. **Grenada**
granadilla (also **grenadilla**) passion fruit
grandad (also **granddad**) grandfather
grandam (also **grandame**) arch. grandmother
grandchild (one word)
grand cru pl. ***grands crus*** wine of the best grade (Fr., ital.); cf. ***premier cru***
granddaughter (one word)
grand duchess, **grand duke** (two words, caps in titles)
grande dame influential or dignified woman
grande horizontale pl. ***grandes horizontales*** prostitute (Fr., ital.)
grandfather (one word)
Grand Guignol sensational or horrific drama (caps, not ital.)
grandiloquent pompous or extravagant in language or manner
grand jury (lower case)
grand mal serious form of epilepsy (not ital.); cf. **petit mal**

Grand Master head of an order of chivalry or of Freemasons (abbrev. **GM**)
grandmaster chess player of the highest class (abbrev. **GM**)
grandmother (one word)
grand-nephew, **grand-niece** (hyphen)
grandparent (one word)
Grand Prix pl. **Grands Prix** motor race (caps)
grand siècle reign of Louis XIV (Fr., ital.)
grandson (one word)
granivorous Zool. feeding on grain
Granny Smith eating apple (caps)
Grant, Ulysses S(impson) (1822–85), American general and 18th president of the US 1869–77
grant aid n. (two words, hyphen as verb)
grantee Law person to whom a grant or conveyance is made
granter person that grants something
Granth short for **Adi Granth**
grant-maintained (hyphen)
grantor Law person that makes a grant or conveyance
gran turismo pl. ***gran turismos*** high-performance car (It., ital.)
Granville-Barker, Harley (1877–1946), English dramatist, critic, and actor
grapefruit pl. same
grapeseed, **grapeshot**, **grapevine** (one word)
Grasmere village in Cumbria, home of William and Dorothy Wordsworth
Grass, Günter (Wilhelm) (1927–2015), German writer
Grasse town in SE France, centre of the French perfume industry
grasshopper, **grassland** (one word)
grass roots (two words, hyphen when attrib.)
gratia Dei by the grace of God (L., ital.)
gratin dish cooked au gratin (not ital.)
gratiné (also ***gratinée***) cooked au gratin (Fr., ital.)
gratis free of charge (not ital.)
grauwacke use **greywacke**
gravadlax var. of **gravlax**
gravamen pl. **gravamina** Law essence of a complaint or accusation
grave accent the mark ` placed over a letter
gravedigger (one word)
gravel v. (**gravelling**, **gravelled**; US one **-l-**) cover with gravel
Graves red or white wine from SW France
Graves' disease condition involving swelling of the neck and protrusion of the eyes (note apostrophe)
graveside, **gravestone**, **graveyard** (one word)
gravitas dignity or solemnity (L., ital.)
gravlax (also **gravadlax**) Scandinavian cured marinated salmon
gravure short for **photogravure**
Gray 1 Asa (1810–88), American botanist **2** Thomas (1716–71), English poet
gray[1] Phys. SI unit of the absorbed dose of ionizing radiation (abbrev. **Gy**)
gray[2] US var. of **grey**
grayling freshwater fish (not **grey-**)
Gray's Inn one of the four Inns of Court (caps)
graywacke US var. of **greywacke**
Graz city in southern Austria
grazier person who rears cattle or sheep
greasepaint, **greaseproof** (one word)
great-aunt (hyphen)
Great Britain England, Wales, and Scotland as a unit (abbrev. **GB**); see **Britain**
Great Dane large breed of dog (caps)
Greater Bairam Eid ul-Adha (see **Eid**)
greater jihad see **jihad**
Greater London, **Greater Manchester** (caps)
Great Lakes lakes Superior, Michigan, Huron, Erie, and Ontario, on the Canada–US border
Great Leap Forward attempted collectivization of industry and agriculture in China 1958–60
great-nephew, **great-niece** (hyphen)
Greats the Oxford BA final examination for honours in Literae Humaniores
Great Schism, the 1 breach between the Eastern and the Western Churches, 1054 **2** period (1378–1417) when the Western Church was divided by the creation of antipopes

great-uncle (hyphen)
Great War, the the First World War
Great Wen, the old nickname for London
Grecian use **Greek** with ref. to ancient architecture and artefacts
Grecism var. of **Graecism**
Greco, El see **El Greco**
Greece country in SE Europe (abbrev. **Gr.**); Gk name **Hellas**
Greek (abbrev. **Gr., Gk**)
Green concerned with the environment (cap.)
Green Cloth (in full **Board of Green Cloth**) Lord Steward's department of the royal household
Greene, (Henry) Graham (1904–91), English novelist
green fee (US **greens fee**) charge for playing golf
greenfield site previously undeveloped site; cf. **brownfield site**
greenfly pl. same or **greenflies**
greengage, **greengrocer**, **greenhorn**, **greenhouse** (one word)
greenhouse effect, **greenhouse gas** (lower case)
Greenland island NE of North America; Danish name **Grønland**, Inuit name **Kalaallit Nunaat**
Green Paper preliminary report of government proposals (caps)
Greenpeace environmental organization
greensand Geol. greenish kind of sandstone; (**the Greensand**) stratum deposited during the Cretaceous period
greens fee US var. of **green fee**
Greenwich Mean Time mean solar time at the Greenwich meridian (abbrev. **GMT**)
Greenwich Village district of New York City (caps)
greetings card (N. Amer. **greeting card**)
Gregorian calendar calendar introduced in 1582 by Pope Gregory XIII and still used today (one cap.); cf. **Julian calendar**
Gregorian chant (one cap.)
Grenada country in the Caribbean; cf. **Granada** □ **Grenadian**
grenadier hist. a soldier armed with grenades; (**Grenadiers** or **Grenadier Guards**) first regiment of the royal household infantry
grenadilla var. of **granadilla**
grenadine 1 sweet cordial made from pomegranates **2** silk fabric
Grenadine Islands chain of small islands in the Caribbean
Gresham, Sir Thomas (*c.*1519–79), English financier, proponent of **Gresham's law**, 'Bad money drives out good'
Greuze, Jean-Baptiste (1725–1805), French painter
Grey 1 Charles, 2nd Earl (1764–1845), British prime minister 1830–4 **2** Lady Jane (1537–54), queen of England 9–19 July 1553
grey (US **gray**)
Grey Friar friar of the Franciscan order
Greyfriars Hall Oxford
greyhen female black grouse (one word); cf. **blackcock**
greyhound (one word; US spelling is the same)
greywacke (US **graywacke**) Geol. dark sandstone (not **grauwacke**)
grief-stricken (hyphen)
Grieg, Edvard (1843–1907), Norwegian composer
grievous (not **-ious**)
griffin (also **gryphon**) mythical creature
griffon 1 terrier-like breed of dog **2** large vulture
gri-gri use **gris-gris**
grill device on a cooker
grille grating or screen of bars or wires
Grimm, Jacob (Ludwig Carl) (1785–1863) and Wilhelm (Carl) (1786–1859), German philologists and folklorists
grimoire book of magic spells
grimy dirty (not **-ey**)
grindstone (one word)
gringo pl. **gringos** derog. (in Latin America) white person
Griqua pl. same or **Griquas** member of a people of South Africa
grisaille method of painting in grey monochrome
grisette dated working-class French girl
gris-gris pl. same, African or Caribbean

charm or amulet (not **gri-gri**)
grisly causing horror; cf. **grizzly**
grissini Italian bread sticks (not ital.)
grizzly grey or grey-haired; cf. **grisly**
grizzly bear large brown bear (not **grisly**)
groat former English silver coin worth four pence
groats hulled or crushed grain, esp. oats
Gro-bag trademark for **growbag**
groin[1] **1** area between the abdomen and the thigh **2** Archit. edge formed by two intersecting vaults
groin[2] US var. of **groyne**
Gromyko, Andrei (Andreevich) (1909–89), Soviet statesman, foreign minister 1957–85, president 1985–8
Grønland Danish name for **Greenland**
Gropius, Walter (1883–1969), German-born American architect
grosbeak finch with a stout bill
groschen pl. same, former monetary unit of Austria
grosgrain heavy ribbed silk fabric
gros point type of embroidery
gross adj. without deduction of tax etc.; cf. **net**. n. **1** pl. same, twelve dozen; 144 **2** pl. **grosses** gross profit or income
Grosseteste, Robert (*c.*1175–1253), English churchman and scholar
Grosz, George (1893–1959), German painter and draughtsman
grosz pl. **groszy** or **grosze** monetary unit of Poland
Grote, George (1794–1871), English historian and politician
grotesque Printing family of 19th-cent. sans serif typefaces
grotesquerie grotesque quality or thing (not ital.)
Grotius, Hugo (1583–1645), Dutch jurist and diplomat; Latinized name of *Huig de Groot*
grotto pl. **grottoes** or **grottos** small picturesque cave
groundbreaking, groundsheet, groundsman, groundwater, groundwork (one word)
ground zero 1 point directly above or below an exploding nuclear bomb **2** (**Ground Zero**) site of the destroyed World Trade Center in New York
Group of Eight grouping of the eight leading industrial nations (abbrev. **G8**)
Grove, Sir George (1820–1900), English musicologist, founder of the *Dictionary of Music and Musicians* (current edition called the *New Grove Dictionary of Music and Musicians*)
grovel (**grovelling, grovelled**; US **-l-**)
groves of Academe the academic world (one cap.)
growbag (also trademark **Gro-bag**) bag containing potting compost
grown-up hyphen exc. as predic. adj.
groyne (US **groin**) barrier built out into the sea
Grozny city in SW Russia, capital of Chechnya
grt gross registered tonnage
Grub Street former street in London inhabited by impoverished journalists and writers
gruelling (US **grueling**)
Grundy, Mrs person with very conventional standards of propriety
Grünewald, Mathias (*c.*1460–1528), German painter; also called **Mathis Gothardt**
grungy (not **-ey**) **1** dirty **2** (of music) loud and distorted
Gruyère Swiss cheese (cap., accent)
gryphon var. of **griffin**
gs hist. guineas
gsm grams per square metre
Gstaad winter-sports resort in Switzerland
G-string skimpy undergarment (not **gee-string**)
GT high-performance car [abbrev. of **gran turismo**]
Gt Great: *Gt Britain*
guacamole dish of mashed avocado with chilli peppers etc.
Guadalajara 1 city in central Spain **2** city in west central Mexico
Guadalcanal island in the SW Pacific
Guadalupe 1 city in NE Mexico **2** town in SW Spain
Guadeloupe group of French islands in the Lesser Antilles □ **Guadeloupian**
guaiac resin from guaiacum tree

guaiacum tropical tree
Guam largest of the Mariana Islands ◻ **Guamanian**
Guangdong (also **Kwangtung**) province of southern China
Guangzhou (also **Kwangchow**) city in southern China; former name **Canton**
guano pl. **guanos** excrement of seabirds, used as fertilizer
Guantánamo Bay bay on the SE coast of Cuba, site of a US naval base (accent)
guarache use **huarache**
Guarani pl. same, member of an American Indian people of Paraguay
guarani pl. **guaranis** monetary unit of Paraguay
guarantor person that gives or acts as a guarantee
guaranty undertaking to answer for the payment or performance of another person's debt or obligation
guardhouse (one word)
Guardian, The UK newspaper (cap. and italic *The*)
guard rail (two words)
guardroom, **guardsman** (one word)
Guarneri family of Italian violin-makers based in Cremona
Guatemala country in Central America ◻ **Guatemalan**
Guatemala City capital of Guatemala
Guayaquil seaport in Ecuador
Guelderland use **Gelderland**
guelder rose flowering shrub
Guelph member of the Italian medieval faction supporting the Pope; cf. **Ghibelline** ◻ **Guelphic**
guerdon arch. reward or recompense
Guernica town in the Basque Country of Spain; full name **Guernica y Luno**
Guernsey second-largest of the Channel Islands
guernsey pl. **guernseys** thick sweater of oiled wool (lower case)
guerrilla (two *r*s, two *l*s)
guesstimate informal estimate based on a mixture of guesswork and calculation
guesswork (one word)
guest house, **guest worker** (two words)
Guevara, Che (1928–67), Argentinian revolutionary; full name *Ernesto Guevara de la Serna*
Guggenheim, Meyer (1828–1905), Swiss-born American industrialist
Guiana region in northern South America; cf. **Guyana**; see also **Dutch Guiana, French Guiana**
Guide member of the Guide Association
guidebook (one word)
guide dog (two words)
guideline (one word)
guidon pennant that narrows to a point or fork
guild association of craftsmen or merchants
guilder pl. same or **guilders** **1** former monetary unit of the Netherlands **2** hist. coin of the Netherlands, Germany, and Austria
guildhall meeting place of a guild or corporation; (**Guildhall**) the hall of the Corporation of the City of London
Guillain–Barré syndrome Med. disorder of the nerves (en rule)
Guillaume French given name
guillemets quotation marks « » of a type used in French etc. (not ital.)
guillemot kind of auk (seabird)
guilloche ornamentation resembling braided or interlaced ribbons
guillotine machine for beheading people
guimp use **gimp**[1]
guimpe hist. high-necked blouse or undergarment
Guinea country on the west coast of Africa ◻ **Guinean**
guinea sum of £1.05 (21 shillings), used esp. for professional fees (abbrev. **gn**)
Guinea–Bissau country on the west coast of Africa (en rule)
guinea fowl pl. same, African game bird (two words)
guinea pig (two words)
Guinevere wife of King Arthur
Guinness trademark dark Irish beer (two *n*s)
Guiseppe correct spelling is **Giuseppe**
Gujarat state of India ◻ **Gujarati**
Gujrat city in Pakistan

Gulag, the system of labour camps in the Soviet Union 1930–55 (cap.)
Gulbenkian, Calouste Sarkis (1869–1955), Turkish-born British oil magnate and philanthropist
gulden pl. same or **guldens** a guilder
gules Heraldry red (usu. after the noun)
gulf cap. in names (*the Gulf of Mexico, the Arabian Gulf*); (**the Gulf**) the Persian Gulf
Gulf Stream warm ocean current (caps)
Gulf War war in 1991 in which Iraqi forces were driven from Kuwait (caps)
Gulf War syndrome (two caps)
gulley pl. **gulleys** var. of **gully**
gullible easily deceived (not **-able**)
gully (also **gulley**) **1** ravine **2** Cricket fielding position
GUM 1 genito-urinary medicine **2** name of a Moscow department store
gum arabic, gum benzoin (two words)
Gumbo French-based patois spoken in Louisiana
gumbo pl. **gumbos** N. Amer. **1** okra **2** thick Cajun chicken or seafood soup
gumboot, gumshield (one word)
gum tree (two words)
gunboat (one word)
gun carriage, gun deck, gun dog (two words)
gunfight, gunfire (one word)
gung-ho eager for fighting or war (hyphen)
gunman, gunmetal (one word)
gunnel var. of **gunwale**
gunny N. Amer. coarse sacking
gunplay, gunpoint, gunpowder, gunrunner, gunship, gunshot (one word)
gun-shy (hyphen)
gunsight, gunslinger, gunsmith (one word)
Gunter's chain surveyor's measuring chain, 66 ft long
Gunther husband of Brunhild in the *Nibelungenlied*
gunwale (also **gunnel**) upper edge of the side of a boat
Guomindang var. of **Kuomintang**
Gurdjieff, George (Ivanovich) (1877–1949), Russian spiritual leader
gurdwara Sikh place of worship
Gurkha member of a Nepalese regiment in the British army
Gurmukhi script used by Sikhs for writing Punjabi
Gutenberg, Johannes (*c.*1400–68), German printer
gutta-percha hard latex from Malaysian tree (hyphen)
gutter blank space between facing pages of a book or adjacent columns of type
guttersnipe (one word)
guttural produced in the throat (not **gutter-**)
Guyana country in South America; cf. **Guiana** □ **Guyanese**
Guy Fawkes Night 5 November (no apostrophe)
GW gigawatt(s)
Gwent former county of SE Wales
GWR hist. Great Western Railway
Gwyn, Nell (1650–87), English actress; full name *Eleanor Gwyn*
Gwynedd county of NW Wales
Gy Phys. gray(s)
gybe (US **jibe**) Sailing change course
gymkhana children's riding competition
gymnasium pl. **gymnasiums** or **gymnasia** hall or building for gymnastics etc.
gymp use **gimp**[1]
gymslip (one word)
gynaecology (US **gynecology**) study of women's diseases
gynoecium pl. **gynoecia** Bot. female part of a flower
gypsum hydrated calcium sulphate
Gypsy (also **Gipsy**) cap. in ref. to the nomadic people; lower case in sense 'free spirit'
gyrfalcon arctic falcon (not **ger-**)
gyro pl. **gyros** gyroscope or gyrocompass
gyrus pl. **gyri** Anat. ridge or fold on the surface of the brain
GySgt Gunnery Sergeant
gyttja rich sediment at the bottom of a lake

H

H 1 pl. **Hs** or **H's** 8th letter of the alphabet **2** hard (grade of pencil lead) **3** height **4** henry(s) **5** Chem. enthalpy **6** the chemical element hydrogen **7** Phys. magnetic field strength **8** Mus. (in the German system) the note B natural

h 1 (of a horse's height) hand(s) **2** hecto- **3** hour(s)

h Phys. Planck's constant; (***ħ***) Planck's constant divided by 2π

Ha hahnium (no point)

ha hectare(s)

Haakon name of seven Norwegian kings; Norw. spelling **Håkon**

haar sea fog

Haarlem city in the Netherlands; cf. **Harlem**

Habakkuk 1 Hebrew minor prophet **2** book of the Old Testament (abbrev. **Hab.**)

Habana see **La Habana**

habdabs use **abdabs**

Habdalah (also **Havdalah**) Jewish ceremony marking the end of the Sabbath

habeas corpus Law writ requiring a person to be brought into court (not ital.)

habendum Law part of a deed stating the estate or quantity of interest to be granted (not ital.)

habile deft, skilful

habit-forming (hyphen)

habitué frequent visitor to a place (accent, not ital.)

Habsburg (also **Hapsburg**) major dynasty of central Europe

háček the mark ˇ placed over a letter

Hachette French publishers

hachis minced meat dish, hash (Fr., ital.)

hachures parallel lines for shading

hacienda large Spanish estate

hackberry purple berry

hackney pl. **hackneys 1** light horse **2** hired horse-drawn vehicle

hackney carriage Brit. official term for a taxi

hackneyed unoriginal and trite

hacksaw (one word)

Hades Gk Mythol. the underworld
□ **Hadean**

Hadith pl. same or **Hadiths** collection of sayings of the prophet Muhammad

Hadlee, Sir Richard (John) (b.1951), New Zealand cricketer

Hadrian's Wall (two caps)

haecceity Philos. quality of a thing that makes it unique

Haeckel, Ernst Heinrich (1834–1919), German biologist and philosopher

haem (US **heme**) Biochem. compound found in haemoglobin

haem-, haemato- (US **hem-, hemato-**) of blood

haematoma (US **hematoma**) pl. **haematomas** or **haematomata** Med. blood clot

haemo- (US **hemo-**) of blood

haemoglobin (US **hemoglobin**) red protein in the blood (abbrev. **Hb**)

haemorrhage (US **hemorrhage**) escape of blood from a ruptured blood vessel

haemorrhoids (US **hemorrhoids**) piles

haere mai Maori greeting (not ital.)

hafiz Muslim who knows the Koran by heart (not ital.)

hafnium chemical element of atomic number 72 (symbol **Hf**)

Haftorah pl. **Haftoroth** Judaism short reading from the Prophets following the reading from the Law (not **Haphtarah** or **Haphtorah**)

Haggadah (also **Aggadah**) pl. **Haggadoth** or **Haggadot** Judaism **1** text recited at the Seder during Passover **2** legend used to illustrate a point of the Law in the Talmud

Haggai 1 Hebrew minor prophet **2** book of the Old Testament (abbrev. **Hag.**)

haggis pl. same or **haggises** Scottish dish

Hagia Sophia Gk name for **St Sophia**

Hagiographa last of the three major divisions of the Hebrew scriptures (cap.)

hagiography 1 writing of the lives of saints **2** reverent biography

Hague, The seat of government of the Netherlands (*The* is always cap.); Du. name **Den Haag**; also called **'s-Gravenhage**

ha-ha ditch forming a boundary (hyphen)

ha ha sound of laughter (two words)

hahnium name formerly proposed for the chemical element **dubnium**, and also for **hassium**

Haig, Douglas, 1st Earl Haig of Bemersyde (1861–1928), British Field Marshal

haik outer wrap worn in North Africa (not **haick**)

haiku pl. same or **haikus** Japanese poem of seventeen syllables, in three lines (not **hokku**)

Haile Selassie (1892–1975), emperor of Ethiopia 1930–74; born *Tafari Makonnen*

Haileybury College English public school

hail-fellow-well-met showing excessive familiarity (hyphens)

Hail Mary pl. **Hail Marys** prayer

hailstone, hailstorm (one word)

Hainault area of Greater London

Hainaut province of southern Belgium

hairband, hairbrush, haircare (one word)

hairdo pl. **hairdos** informal hairstyle

hairdresser, hairdryer, hairgrip, hairline, hairnet, hairpiece, hairpin (one word)

hair-raising (hyphen)

hair's breadth (two words)

hair shirt (two words)

hair space very thin space (two words)

hairspray, hairstyle (one word)

hair trigger (two words)

Haiti country in the Caribbean, part of the island of Hispaniola □ **Haitian**

haji (also **hajji**) pl. **hajis** Muslim who has been to Mecca (cap. in titles)

hajj (also **haj**) Muslim pilgrimage to Mecca

Hakenkreuz swastika (Ger., cap., ital.)

hakim (in India and Muslim countries) traditional physician; judge or ruler

Hakluyt, Richard (*c.*1552–1616), English geographer and historian

Halacha (also **Halakha**) Jewish law

Halafian prehistoric culture of the Middle East

halal (of meat) prepared according to Muslim law

halberd (also **halbert**) combined spear and battleaxe

Hale–Bopp comet (en rule)

Haley, Bill (1925–81), American rock-and-roll singer; cf. **Halley**

half pl. **halves** usu. hyphenated in compounds (*half-cooked*; *half-dead*)

half a crown, half a dozen see **half-crown**

half-and-half (hyphens)

half an hour (three words; see also **half hour**)

half back (two words, one word in US)

half-baked (hyphen)

half binding bookbinding in which the spine and corners are bound in a different material to the rest of the cover (two words)

half board (two words; abbrev. **HB**)

half-bottle, half-brother, half-century, half-cocked (hyphen)

half-crown, half-dozen (hyphen), but **half a crown, half a dozen** (three words)

half-hearted (hyphen)

half hitch, half holiday, half hour (two words; see also **half an hour**)

half-inch, half-length, half-life, half-light (hyphen)

half mast, half measure (two words)

half-moon (hyphen)

half nelson (two words, lower case)

halfpenny (also **ha'penny**) pl. for separate coins **halfpennies**, for a sum of money **halfpence**

halfpennyworth (also **ha'p'orth**) as much as could be bought for a halfpenny

half price two words as noun (*at/for half price*); hyphen as adv. or attrib. adj.

half-sister, half-term, half-timbered, half-time (hyphen)

half-title short title of a book, printed on the right-hand page before the title page (hyphen)
halftone (one word) **1** image in which the tones of grey or colour are produced by dots **2** Mus., N. Amer. semitone
half-truth, half-volley (hyphen)
halfway (one word)
halfwit (one word) ◻ **half-witted**
half-yearly (hyphen)
Halicarnassus ancient Greek city in Asia Minor
halier pl. same or **haliers** monetary unit of Slovakia
haliotis pl. same, gastropod mollusc
halitosis bad breath
Halle city in east central Germany
Hallé, Sir Charles (1819–95), German-born conductor; born *Karl Halle*
hallelujah (also **alleluia**) God be praised!
Hallelujah Chorus part of the oratorio *Messiah* by Handel
Halley, Edmond (1656–1742), English astronomer, who identified **Halley's Comet**; cf. **Haley**
hallo var. of **hello**
halloo (**halloos, hallooing, hallooed**) (cry) inciting dogs to the chase
halloumi white cheese from Cyprus
Halloween (also **Hallowe'en**) 31 October
Hallstatt phase of the late Bronze Age and early Iron Age in Europe
hallux pl. **halluces** Anat. the big toe
hallway (one word)
halo pl. **haloes** or **halos** ◻ **haloed**
Hals, Frans (*c.*1580–1666), Dutch painter
halva (also **halvah**) Middle Eastern sweet
halve divide into two equal parts
halves pl. of **half**
halyard Naut. rope for raising and lowering a sail etc.
hamadryad 1 Gk & Rom. Mythol. wood nymph **2** king cobra
hamadryas pl. same, large Arabian and NE African baboon
hamartia fatal flaw of a tragic hero or heroine (not ital.)
Hamas militant Palestinian Islamic movement
Hameln modern name for a town in NW Germany, formerly called **Hamelin** (see **Pied Piper**)
ham-fisted (hyphen)
Hamite member of a group of North African peoples supposedly descended from Ham, son of Noah
Hamitic hypothetical language family formerly regarded as including Berber and ancient Egyptian
Hamlet tragedy by Shakespeare (abbrev. ***Haml.***)
hammam Turkish bath
Hammarskjöld, Dag (Hjalmar Agne Carl) (1905–61), Swedish diplomat and politician
hammer beam (two words)
hammerhead (one word)
Hammerstein, Oscar (1895–1960), American librettist; full name *Oscar Hammerstein II*
Hammett, (Samuel) Dashiell (1894–1961), American novelist
Hampshire county of southern England (abbrev. **Hants**)
Hampton Court palace on the Thames in London
hamster rodent (not **hampster**)
hamstring v. (past and past part. **hamstrung**)
hamza Arabic symbol (') representing a glottal stop, typographically largely equivalent to the Hebrew aleph or Greek lenis
hand measure of a horse's height (abbrev. **h**)
handbag, handball, handbasin, handbell, handbill, handbook, handbrake (one word)
h & c hot and cold (water)
handcart, handclap, handcraft (one word)
hand cream (two words)
Handel, George Frederick (1685–1759), German-born composer; born *Georg Friedrich Händel*
handful pl. **handfuls**
hand grenade (two words)
handgrip, handgun, handhold (one word)

handicapped in British English prefer **disabled** or, in ref. to mental disability, **having learning difficulties** or **learning-disabled**; still acceptable in American English
handicraft (one word)
handiwork (not **handy-**)
handkerchief pl. **handkerchiefs**
handlebar (one word)
Handley Page, Frederick, see **Page**
handlist, handmade, handmaiden (one word)
hand-me-down (hyphens)
handout, handover n. (one word, two words as verb)
hand-pick (hyphen)
handpump, handrail, handset (one word)
handsel var. of **hansel**
hands-free (hyphen)
handshake, handspan, handspring, handwriting (one word)
handyman (one word)
hang (past and past part. **hung** or in sense 'execute' **hanged**)
hangar building for aircraft
hanger 1 person who hangs something **2** coat hanger **3** wood on a hill
hanger-on pl. **hangers-on** (hyphen)
hang-glide, hang-glider (hyphen)
hangnail piece of torn skin at the root of a fingernail (not **agnail**)
hangover n. (one word, two words as verb)
Hang Seng index list of share prices on the Hong Kong Stock Exchange
hang-up n. (one word; two words as verb)
hanky-panky (hyphen)
Hanoi capital of Vietnam
Hanover city in NW Germany; Ger. name **Hannover** □ **Hanoverian**
Hansard (not ital.) verbatim record of debates in Parliament; formal name ***The Official Report of Parliamentary Debates***
Hanse medieval guild of merchants; (**the Hanse**) the Hanseatic League
Hanseatic League medieval association of north German cities
hansel (also **handsel**) arch. or US gift given at the beginning of the year
Hansen's disease leprosy
hansom hist. horse-drawn cab
Hants Hampshire (no point)
Hanukkah (also **Chanukah**) Jewish festival of lights in December
Hanuman Hinduism monkey-like semi-divine being
hanuman Indian langur monkey
hapax legomenon pl. **hapax legomena** term recorded only once (not ital.)
ha'penny var. of **halfpenny**
Haphtarah (also **Haphtorah**) use **Haftorah**
ha'p'orth var. of **halfpennyworth**
happi pl. **happis** loose Japanese coat
happy-go-lucky (hyphens)
happy hunting ground (three words)
Hapsburg var. of **Habsburg**
hara-kiri ritual suicide by disembowelment, as formerly practised in Japan; seppuku (not **hari-kari**)
haram forbidden by Islamic law
harangue (**harangued, haranguing**) lecture in a hectoring manner
Harare capital of Zimbabwe; former name (until 1982) **Salisbury**
harass (not **harr-**)
harbour (US **harbor**)
hardback (one word; abbrev. **HB, hb**)
hardball, hardbitten, hardboard (one word)
hard-boiled (hyphen)
hardcore (one word) **1** experimental popular music **2** explicit pornography
hard core (two words) **1** most committed members of a group **2** rubble used in building
hard-earned (hyphen)
Hardecanute (*c.*1019–42), Danish king of Denmark 1028–42 and England 1040–42
hard-hearted (hyphen)
hard hit (two words, hyphen when attrib.)
hard-hitting (hyphen)
Hardie, (James) Keir (1856–1915), Scottish Labour politician
hardihood (not **hardy-**)
hard line strict adherence to a policy (two words, hyphen when attrib.)

hardliner (one word)
hard-pressed (hyphen)
hard sign a double prime ″ used in transliterating Russian
hardware (one word)
hard-wearing, hard-wired (hyphen)
hardwood (one word)
hard-working (hyphen)
Hardy 1 Oliver (1892–1957), part of the American comedy duo Laurel and Hardy **2** Thomas (1840–1928), English novelist and poet
harebell (one word)
hare-brained (hyphen)
Harefoot, Harold, see **Harold I**
Hare Krishna member of the International Society for Krishna Consciousness
harelip avoid; use **cleft lip**
Hargreaves, James (1720–78), English inventor of the spinning jenny
haricot variety of French bean
Harijan member of the lowest Hindu caste (the **scheduled caste**, formerly known as **untouchables**)
hari-kari use **hara-kiri**
Haringey Greater London borough; cf. **Harringay**
hark 1 arch. listen **2** (**hark back to**) mention or remember
harken var. of **hearken**
Harlech village in Gwynedd, Wales
Harlem district of New York City; cf. **Haarlem**
Harlequin character in traditional pantomime and Italian *commedia dell'arte* (cap.)
harlequinade section of a traditional pantomime in which Harlequin played a leading role (lower case)
harlequin duck, harlequin fish (lower case)
harmattan dry West African wind
harmonize (Brit. also **harmonise**)
Harmsworth, Alfred Charles William, see **Northcliffe**
Harold I (d.1040), king of England 1037–40; known as **Harold Harefoot**
Harold II (*c.*1019–66), king of England 1066
Haroun-al-Raschid var. of **Harun ar-Rashid**
HarperCollins publishers (one word)
Harpers Ferry town in West Virginia (no apostrophe)
Harper's Magazine US magazine (apostrophe)
harquebus var. of **arquebus**
harridan bossy woman (two *r*s)
harrier 1 breed of hound used for hunting hares; (**Harriers**) team of cross-country runners **2** bird of prey
Harringay area of north London; cf. **Haringey**
Harrington man's short zipped jacket
Harris[1] southern part of the island of Lewis and Harris in the Outer Hebrides
Harris[2], Sir Arthur Travers (1892–1984), British Marshal of the RAF; known as **Bomber Harris**
Harris' hawk bird of prey (apostrophe)
Harrison 1 Benjamin (1833–1901), 23rd president of the US 1889–93 **2** William Henry (1773–1841), 9th president of the US 1841
Harris tweed trademark tweed from the island of Lewis and Harris
Harrods department store in London (no apostrophe)
Harrogate town in North Yorkshire
Harrow School public school in NW London ◻ **Harrovian**
Hart, Horace (1840–1916), printer to Oxford University 1883–1916
Harte, (Francis) Bret (1836–1902), American short-story writer
hartebeest large African antelope
Hartford state capital of Connecticut
Hartlepool port in NE England
hartshorn arch. ammonia solution used as smelling salts
harum-scarum (hyphen)
Harun ar-Rashid (also **Haroun-al-Raschid**) (763–809), caliph of Baghdad 786–809
haruspex pl. **haruspices** Roman official who interpreted omens by inspecting animals' entrails ◻ **haruspicy**
Harvard system another name for **author–date system**
Harvard University US university at Cambridge, Massachusetts

Harvey, William (1578–1657), English physician, discoverer of the circulation of the blood ◻ **Harveian**

Harz Mountains range of mountains in central Germany

has-been informal outmoded person (hyphen)

Hašek, Jaroslav (1883–1923), Czech novelist

hash the symbol #

Hashemite Kingdom of Jordan official name for **Jordan**

Hashemites Arab princely family claiming descent from Hashim, great-grandfather of Muhammad

hashish cannabis

hashtag 1 a topic on a social media website **2** the symbol #

Hasid (also **Chasid, Chassid**) pl. **Hasidim** adherent of Hasidism ◻ **Hasidic**

Hasidism (also **Chasidism, Chassidism**) mystical Jewish movement

hassium chemical element of atomic number 108 (symbol **Hs**)

hatband, hatbox (one word)

hatchback (one word)

hatchet-faced (hyphen)

hateable (not **hatable**)

hatha yoga exercises used in yoga

hatpin (one word)

Hatshepsut, Egyptian queen *c.*1503–1482 BC

hat-trick (hyphen)

hauberk full-length coat of mail

haulier 1 (N. Amer. **hauler**) person or company that transports goods by road **2** miner who moves coal within a mine

haulm Bot. stalk or stem

Hauptmann, Gerhart (1862–1946), German dramatist

Hausa pl. same or **Hausas** member of a people of Nigeria and Niger

hausfrau housewife (lower case, not ital.)

Haussmann, Georges-Eugène, Baron (1809–91), French architect of Paris

hautboy arch. form of **oboe**

Haut-Brion, Château claret (hyphen)

haute bourgeoisie the upper middle class (Fr., ital.)

haute couture high fashion (not ital.)

haute cuisine high-quality cooking (not ital.)

haute école advanced classical dressage (Fr., ital.)

Haute-Normandie region of northern France (hyphen)

hauteur haughtiness (not ital.)

haut monde fashionable society (Fr., ital.)

haut-relief Art high relief (Fr., ital.)

Havana 1 capital of Cuba; Sp. name **La Habana 2** cigar from Cuba

Havdalah var. of **Habdalah**

Havel, Václav (1936–2011), president of Czechoslovakia 1989–92 and of the Czech Republic 1993–2003

have-nots informal poor people (hyphen)

haver 1 Sc. talk foolishly **2** Brit. behave indecisively

Haverfordwest town in Pembrokeshire, Wales

havoc n. widespread destruction. v. (**havocking, havocked**) arch. lay waste to

Hawaii group of islands in the North Pacific, a state of the US (official abbrev. **Haw.**, postal **HI**) ◻ **Hawaiian**

Haw-Haw, Lord nickname of William Joyce, US-born German propagandist in WWII, executed 1946

hawk-eyed (hyphen)

hawklike (one word)

hawksbill tropical sea turtle

hawthorn thorny shrub or tree

Hawthorne, Nathaniel (1804–64), American novelist

hay country dance (not **hey**; but *Shepherd's Hey* by Percy Grainger)

Haydn, Franz Joseph (1732–1809), Austrian composer

hay fever (two words)

hayfield, hayloft, hayrick, hayseed, haystack, haywire (one word)

hazelnut (one word)

Hazlitt, William (1778–1830), English essayist

hazy (not **-ey**)

HB 1 half board **2** (also **hb**) hardback **3** hard black (grade of pencil lead)

Hb haemoglobin

HBM Her or His Britannic Majesty('s)
H-bomb hydrogen bomb (hyphen)
HC 1 Holy Communion **2** House of Commons **3** hydrocarbon
h.c. *honoris causa*
HCF Math. highest common factor
H.D. see **Doolittle**
HDTV high-definition television
HE 1 higher education **2** high explosive **3** His Eminence **4** His or Her Excellency
He the chemical element helium (no point)
headache (one word) □ **headachy**
headband, headboard, headcount, headdress, headgear, headhunt (one word)
headland, headlight, headlamp, headline, headlong (one word)
headman leader of a tribe (one word); cf. **headsman**
headmaster, headmistress (abbrev. **HM**) one word, although **Head Master** is the official title at certain schools; **head teacher** is now often preferred
head-on (hyphen)
headphone (one word)
headquarters (treated as sing. or pl.; abbrev. **HQ**)
headrest, headroom, headscarf (one word)
headsman executioner; cf. **headman**
headstone, headstrong (one word)
head teacher often preferred to **headmaster** or **headmistress**
headway, headwind (one word)
headword word beginning a separate entry in a dictionary etc.
healthcare (one word)
health centre, health farm, health food (two words)
health service, the Brit. the National Health Service (lower case)
hear! hear! used to express wholehearted agreement (not **here! here!**)
hearken (also **harken**) arch. listen
hearsay rumour (one word)
heartache (one word)
heart attack (two words)
heartbeat, heartbreak, heartbroken, heartburn (one word)
heart disease, heart failure (two words)
heartfelt, hearthrug, hearthstone, heartland (one word)
heart-lung machine, heart-rending (hyphen)
heartsease (also **heart's-ease**) wild pansy
heart-throb (hyphen)
heart-to-heart (hyphens)
heart-warming (hyphen)
heartwood (one word)
Heath, Sir Edward (Richard George) (1916–2005), British prime minister 1970–4
Heath Robinson ridiculously overcomplicated (no hyphen)
heatproof (one word)
heat-resistant, heat-seeking (hyphen)
heatstroke, heatwave (one word)
heave (past and past part. **heaved** or Naut. **hove**)
heave-ho (hyphen)
heaven cap. when equivalent to God or the gods; lower case as a place, in phrs, and in sense 'state of bliss'
heavenly, heavenly body, heavenly host (lower case)
heaven-sent (lower case, hyphen)
Heaviside, Oliver (1850–1925), English physicist and electrical engineer
Heaviside layer (also **Heaviside–Kennelly layer** (en rule)) the E-layer in the atmosphere
heavy-duty, heavy-footed, heavy-handed, heavy-hearted (hyphen)
heavyset (one word)
heavyweight heaviest category of boxing weight (one word)
Heb. 1 Epistle to the Hebrews **2** Hebrew
hebdomadal weekly
Hebrew (abbrev. **Heb.**)
Hebrew Bible sacred writings of Judaism, called by Christians the Old Testament, and comprising the Law (Torah), the Prophets, and the Hagiographa or Writings
Hebrews, Epistle to the book of the New Testament (abbrev. **Heb.**)
Hebrides group of islands off NW Scotland □ **Hebridean**

Hecate Gk Mythol. goddess associated with ghosts and sorcery
hecatomb great public sacrifice
heckelphone bass oboe
hectare metric unit equal to 10,000 square metres (2.471 acres) (abbrev. **ha**)
hecto- a hundred (abbrev. **h**)
hectogram (Brit. also **hectogramme**) 100 grams (abbrev. **hg**)
hectolitre (US **hectoliter**) 100 litres (abbrev. **hl**)
hectometre (US **hectometer**) 100 metres (abbrev. **hm**)
Hedda Gabler play by Ibsen (1890)
hedgehog, hedgerow (one word)
heebie-jeebies informal (hyphen)
Hegel, Georg Wilhelm Friedrich (1770–1831), German philosopher □ **Hegelian**
hegemony leadership or dominance
Hegira (also **Hejira**) Muhammad's departure from Mecca to Medina in AD 622, from which the Muslim era is reckoned [Arab. *hijra*]
Heidegger, Martin (1889–1976), German philosopher
Heidelberg city in SW Germany
Heidsieck a champagne
heigh-ho audible sigh (not **hey-ho**)
heil hail! (Ger., lower case, ital.); cf. ***Sieg Heil***
Heimlich manoeuvre procedure for dislodging an obstruction from a person's windpipe (one cap.)
Heimweh homesickness (Ger., cap., ital.)
Heine, (Christian Johann) Heinrich (1797–1856), German poet
Heinemann, William publishers
Heinz American food manufacturers
heir apparent pl. **heirs apparent** heir whose claim cannot be set aside by the birth of another heir; cf. **heir presumptive**
heir-at-law pl. **heirs-at-law** heir by right of blood (hyphens)
heir presumptive pl. **heirs presumptive** heir whose claim may be set aside by the birth of another heir; cf. **heir apparent**
Heisenberg, Werner Karl (1901–76), German physicist, discoverer of the **Heisenberg uncertainty principle**
Hejaz (also **Hijaz**) coastal region of western Saudi Arabia
Hejira var. of **Hegira**
Hekla active volcano in SW Iceland
Hel Norse world of the dead; goddess of the dead
HeLa cells strain of human cells maintained in tissue culture (two caps)
Heldentenor tenor with a powerful voice (Ger., cap., ital.)
Helensburgh town in SW Scotland (not **-borough**)
Helgoland Ger. name for **Heligoland**
heliacal Astron. denoting the first rising of a star or planet which occurs at the same time as the rising of the sun; cf. **helical**
helianthus pl. same or **helianthuses** sunflower or related plant
helical like a helix, spiral; cf. **heliacal**
helices pl. of **helix**
Helicon, Mount mountain in central Greece, traditional home of the Muses
Heligoland island off the coast of Germany; Ger. name **Helgoland**
Heliogabalus (also **Elagabalus**; not **Eliogabalus**) (AD 204–22), Roman emperor 218–22; born *Varius Avitus Bassianus*
helipad, heliport (one word)
helium chemical element of atomic number 2, a noble gas (symbol **He**)
helix pl. **helices**
hell (lower case)
Helladic of the Bronze Age cultures of mainland Greece (*c*.3000–1050 BC)
Hellas Gk name for **Greece**
hell-bent (hyphen)
Helle Gk Mythol. girl who flew on a golden ram but fell and drowned
Hellen Gk Mythol. ancestor of the Hellenes
Hellene a Greek □ **Hellenic**
Hellenize (Brit. also **Hellenise**)
Hellespont ancient name for the Dardanelles
hellfire, hellhole, hellhound (one word)
hello (also **hallo** or **hullo**) pl. **hellos**
Hell's Angel member of a motorcycle gang
helmeted (one *t*)

Helmholtz, Hermann Ludwig Ferdinand von (1821–94), German physiologist and physicist

helmsman (one word)

Héloïse (1098–1164), French abbess, lover of Abelard (not **Eloise**)

helpline (one word)

helpmate (also **helpmeet**) helpful companion (one word)

Helsingør Danish name for **Elsinore**

Helsinki capital of Finland; Swedish name **Helsingfors**

helter-skelter (hyphen)

Helvetia Latin name for **Switzerland**

hem-, hemato- US vars of **haem-, haemato-**

he-man (hyphen)

heme US var. of **haem**

Hemel Hempstead town in Hertfordshire, SE England

hemidemisemiquaver Mus., Brit. note having the value of half a demisemiquaver; N. Amer. **sixty-fourth note**

Hemingway, Ernest (Miller) (1899–1961), American novelist and journalist

hemistich half of a line of verse (not **-stitch**)

hemline (one word)

hemo- US var. of **haemo-**

hemstitch decorative stitch (one word)

Hen. Henry (regnal year)

henceforth, henceforward (one word)

hendiadys expression of a single idea by two words connected with 'and', e.g. *nice and warm*

Hendrix, Jimi (1942–70), American rock guitarist; full name *James Marshall Hendrix*

henge prehistoric monument

Hengist and Horsa (d.488 & d.455), semi-mythological Jutish leaders

henna reddish-brown dye □ **hennaed**

henpeck (one word)

Henry, O (1862–1910), American short-story writer; pseudonym of *William Sydney Porter*

henry pl. **henries** or **henrys** SI unit of inductance (lower case; abbrev. **H**)

Henry, King Shakespeare plays *The First Part of King Henry the Fourth, The Second Part of King Henry the Sixth*, etc. are abbreviated ***1 Hen. IV, 2 Hen. VI***, etc.

heortology study of Church festivals

Hephaestus Gk Mythol. god of fire and of craftsmen; Rom. equivalent **Vulcan**

Hepplewhite, George (d.1786), English cabinetmaker and furniture designer

heptahedron pl. **heptahedra** or **heptahedrons** solid figure with seven plane faces

Heptateuch first seven books of the Old Testament (Genesis to Judges)

Heracles Gk form of **Hercules**

Heraklion capital of Crete; mod. Gk name **Iráklion**

heraldic prefix with *a* not *an*

Heralds' College the College of Arms

herbaceous (not **-ious**)

herbarium pl. **herbaria** collection of dried plants (not ital.)

Hercegovina var. of **Herzegovina**

Herculaneum Roman town buried in the eruption of Vesuvius in AD 79

Herculean requiring or having great strength (cap.)

Hercules Gk & Rom. Mythol. hero of superhuman strength; Gk name **Heracles**

Hercynian Geol. mountain-forming period in the Upper Palaeozoic era

herdboy, herdsman (one word)

hereabout, hereabouts, hereafter, hereat, hereby (one word)

Herefordshire county of west central England

here! here! use **hear! hear!**

herein, hereinafter, hereinbefore, hereof (one word)

hereto, heretobefore, hereunder, hereunto, hereupon, herewith (one word)

Heriot-Watt University Edinburgh (hyphen)

heritor 1 Sc. Law proprietor of a heritable object **2** person who inherits

Her Majesty, Her Majesty's (caps; abbrev. **HM**)

hermeneutic concerning interpretation, esp. of the Bible or literary texts

hermeneutics study of hermeneutic interpretation (usu. treated as sing.)

Hermes Gk Mythol. messenger of the gods; Rom. equivalent **Mercury**
Hermitage, the art museum in St Petersburg
hero pl. **heroes** prefix with *a* not *an*
Herod name of rulers of ancient Palestine: **Herod the Great** (ruled 37–4 BC) ordered the massacre of the innocents; **Herod Antipas** (ruled 4 BC–AD 40) questioned Jesus □ **Herodian**
Herodotus (5th cent. BC), Greek historian
heroin narcotic drug
heroine chief female character
heroize (Brit. also **heroise**) make a hero of
hero worship (two words) □ **hero-worshipper**
herpes skin disease
herpesvirus viruses causing herpes etc. (one word)
herpes zoster shingles (two words)
Herr pl. **Herren** German equivalent of 'Mr' (not ital.; abbrev. **Hr.**)
Herrenvolk the German people, considered by the Nazis to be innately superior (Ger., cap., ital.)
herringbone stitch or pattern (one word)
Herriot, James (1916–95), English writer and veterinary surgeon; pseudonym of *James Alfred Wight*
Herrnhuter member of a Moravian Church (not ital.)
Her Royal Highness (caps; abbrev. **HRH**)
hers (no apostrophe)
Herschel 1 Sir (Frederick) William (1738–1822), German-born British astronomer **2** Sir John (Frederick William) (1792–1871), English astronomer and physicist
Herstmonceux town in East Sussex
Hertfordshire county of SE England (abbrev. **Herts.**)
Hertz, Heinrich Rudolf (1857–94), German physicist □ **Hertzian**
hertz pl. same, SI unit of frequency (abbrev. **Hz**)
Hertzsprung–Russell diagram Astron. graph plotting the absolute magnitudes of stars (en rule)
Herzegovina (also **Hercegovina**) southern part of Bosnia–Herzegovina □ **Herzegovinian**
Herzog, Werner (b.1942), German film director; born *Werner Stipetic*
Heshvan var. of **Hesvan**
Hesiod (*c.*700 BC), Greek poet
Hesperian 1 Gk Mythol. of the Hesperides **2** western
Hesperides Gk Mythol. nymphs who guarded a tree of golden apples
Hesperus the evening star; Venus
Hess, (Walther Richard) Rudolf (1894–1987), German Nazi leader
Hesse[1] state of western Germany
Hesse[2], Hermann (1877–1962), German-born Swiss novelist
Hessian of Hesse in Germany
hessian strong coarse fabric (lower case)
Hesvan (also **Chesvan, Heshvan**) (in the Jewish calendar) the second month of the civil and eighth of the religious year
hetaera (also **hetaira**) pl. **hetaeras** or **hetaerae**, or **hetairas** or **hetairai** ancient Greek courtesan
heterogeneous diverse or dissimilar (not **-genous**) □ **heterogeneity**
heteroousian person believing the first and second persons of the Trinity to be different; cf. **homoiousian, homoousian**
hetman pl. **hetmen** Polish or Cossack military commander
heureka use **eureka**
heuristic enabling a person to discover something for themselves
heuristics study and use of heuristic techniques (usu. treated as sing.)
HEW (US Department of) Health, Education, and Welfare
hew (past part. **hewn** or **hewed**)
hexahedron pl. **hexahedra** or **hexahedrons** solid figure with six plane faces
Hexateuch first six books of the Old Testament
hey see **hay**
Heyerdahl, Thor (1914–2002), Norwegian anthropologist
hey-ho use **heigh-ho**
hey presto (two words)
Hezbollah (also **Hizbullah**) extremist Shiite Muslim group

HF Phys. high frequency
Hf the chemical element hafnium (no point)
hf half
HFC pl. **HFCs** hydrofluorocarbon
HG 1 Her or His Grace **2** hist. Home Guard
Hg the chemical element mercury [mod. L. *hydrargyrum*]
hg hectogram(s)
HGV heavy goods vehicle
HH 1 extra hard (grade of pencil lead) **2** Her or His Highness **3** His Holiness **4** His or Her Honour
hh. (of a horse's height) hands
HI Hawaii (postal abbrev.)
hiatus pl. **hiatuses** pause or gap
Hiawatha legendary North American Indian, hero of Longfellow's poem *The Song of Hiawatha* (1855)
Hibernian Irish
hibiscus pl. same or **hibiscuses** plant of the mallow family
hiccup (also **hiccough**) (**hiccuping, hiccuped** or **hiccupping, hiccupped**)
hic jacet here lies (L., ital.)
Hickok, James Butler (1837–76), American frontiersman; known as **Wild Bill Hickok**
hidalgo pl. **hidalgos** Spanish gentleman
hide-and-seek game (hyphens)
hideaway n. hiding place (one word, two words as verb)
hidebound narrow-minded (one word)
hideout n. hiding place (one word, two words as verb)
hie (**hieing** or **hying, hied**) arch. go quickly
hieratic adj. of priests. n. ancient Egyptian writing of abridged hieroglyphics used by priests (lower case); cf. **demotic**
hieroglyph stylized picture used in ancient Egyptian writing systems □ **hieroglyphic**
hierogram (also **hierograph**) sacred inscription or symbol
hierolatry worship of saints or sacred things
hierology sacred literature or lore
hierophant person who interprets sacred or esoteric mysteries
hi-fi pl. **hi-fis** (equipment for) high-fidelity sound reproduction (hyphen)
higgledy-piggledy in disorder (hyphen)
Higgs boson (also **Higgs particle**) subatomic particle
highball drink (one word)
high-born (hyphen)
highbrow (one word)
High Church (caps; two words even when attrib.) □ **High Churchman**
high-class (hyphen)
high commission embassy of one Commonwealth country in another (cap. in proper names)
high court a supreme court of justice; (**the High Court** or **the High Court of Justice**) UK court of unlimited civil jurisdiction
Higher Scottish school exam (cap.)
highfalutin pompous (one word, no apostrophe)
high-flown, high-flyer, high-flying (hyphen)
high frequency (two words, hyphen when attrib.)
High German standard literary and spoken form of German
high-handed (hyphen)
high-hat Mus. var. of **hi-hat**
highjack use **hijack**
high jump, high jumper (two words)
Highland council area of Scotland
highland (also **highlands**) high or mountainous land; (**the Highlands**) northern part of Scotland □ **highlander**
high-level (hyphen)
highlight, highlighter (one word)
highly strung (two words)
high-minded (hyphen)
highness (cap. in **His/Your** etc. **Highness**)
high-octane, high-pitched (hyphen)
high-powered (hyphen)
high pressure (abbrev. **HP** or **h.p.**)
high profile n. (two words, hyphen as adj.)
high-rise, high-risk (hyphen)
high school 1 (in N. Amer. and Scotland) secondary school **2** (in the UK

exc. Scotland) grammar school or independent secondary school
high seas, the open ocean outside any country's jurisdiction (lower case)
high speed, high street, high tech, high technology, high water (two words, hyphen when attrib.)
highway, highwayman (one word)
HIH Her or His Imperial Highness
hi-hat (also **high-hat**) pair of foot-operated cymbals
hijab head covering worn in public by some Muslim women
hijack, hijacker (not **high-**)
Hijaz var. of **Hejaz**
hilarious (prefix with *a* not *an*)
Hilary term university term or session of the High Court beginning in January (one cap.)
hill (cap. in names, as *Box Hill*)
Hillary, Sir Edmund (Percival) (1919–2008), New Zealand mountaineer, who reached the summit of Mount Everest (1953)
hillbilly (one word)
hill-climber, hill-climbing (hyphen)
hill fort (two words)
hillside, hilltop, hillwalking, hillwalker (one word)
HIM Her or His Imperial Majesty
Himachal Pradesh state in northern India
Himalayas, the mountain system in southern Asia □ **Himalayan**
Himmler, Heinrich (1900–45), German Nazi leader
Hims see **Homs**
Hinayana name given by followers of Mahayana Buddhism to Theravada
Hindenburg Line German line of defence in WWI
Hindenburg, The German airship which crashed in 1937
hindlimb, hindmost, hindquarters, hindsight (one word)
Hindu pl. **Hindus** follower of Hinduism (not **Hindoo** (arch.))
Hindu Kush range of high mountains in Pakistan and Afghanistan
Hindustan hist. the Indian subcontinent
Hindustani Indian lingua franca
hinge v. (**hingeing** or **hinging, hinged**)
hinterland (one word)
hip bath, hip bone, hip flask, hip hop, hip joint (two words)
hippie chiefly N. Amer. var. of **hippy**
hippo pl. same or **hippos** hippopotamus
hippocampus pl. **hippocampi** Anat. part of the brain
hip pocket (two words)
Hippocrates (*c.*460–377 BC), Greek 'father of medicine'
Hippocratic oath (one cap.)
Hippocrene Gk Mythol. fountain on Mount Helicon sacred to the Muses
hippogriff mythical creature with the body of a horse and a griffin's wings and head (not **hippogryph**)
hippopotamus pl. **hippopotamuses** or **hippopotami**
hippy (also chiefly N. Amer. **hippie**) unconventional long-haired person
hiragana more cursive form of Japanese syllabic writing; cf. **katakana**
hircine goat-like
hireable (not **hirable**)
hire car (two words)
hire purchase (abbrev. **HP** or **h.p.**)
Hirohito (1901–89), emperor of Japan 1926–89; full name *Michinomiya Hirohito*
Hiroshima city in western Japan
Hirst, Damien (b.1965), English artist
His Eminence (caps; abbrev. **HE**)
His Majesty, His Majesty's (caps; abbrev. **HM**)
Hispanic 1 of Spain or Spanish-speaking countries **2** of Spanish-speaking people in the US
Hispanicize (Brit. also **Hispanicise**)
Hispaniola an island in the Caribbean now divided into the states of Haiti and the Dominican Republic
Hispanist expert in Hispanic language and culture (not **-icist**)
His Royal Highness (caps; abbrev. **HRH**)
hist. historic; historical
historic famous or important in history (prefix with *a* not *an*)
historical of or concerning history (prefix with *a* not *an*) □ **historically**

Hitchens, Ivon (1893–1979), English painter
hitch-hike, hitch-hiker (hyphen)
hi-tech using high technology (hyphen)
Hitler, Adolf (1889–1945), Austrian-born Nazi leader □ **Hitlerian**
hit list, hit man, hit parade, hit squad (two words)
HIV human immunodeficiency virus, a retrovirus which causes Aids (not **HIV virus**)
HIV-negative, HIV-positive (hyphen)
Hizbullah var. of **Hezbollah**
HK Hong Kong
HL House of Lords
hl hectolitre(s)
HM 1 headmaster or headmistress **2** heavy metal (music) **3** Her or His Majesty('s)
hm hectometre(s) (no point)
HMG Her or His Majesty's Government
HMI hist. Her or His Majesty's Inspector (of Schools)
HMO health maintenance organization
HMS Her or His Majesty's Ship
HMSO Her or His Majesty's Stationery Office
HNC Higher National Certificate
HND Higher National Diploma
Ho the chemical element holmium (no point)
ho. house
hoard store of money or possessions; cf. **horde**
hoar frost (two words)
hoarhound var. of **horehound**
hob male ferret; cf. **gill**[3]
Hobbema, Meindert (1638–1709), Dutch painter
Hobbes, Thomas (1588–1679), English philosopher □ **Hobbesian**
hobbit member of an imaginary race in stories by J. R. R. Tolkien (lower case)
hobbledehoy awkward youth (one word)
Hobbs, Sir Jack (1882–1963), English cricketer
hobby horse (two words)
hobgoblin, hobnail, hobnob (one word)
hobo pl. **hoboes** or **hobos** vagrant
Hoboken city in New Jersey
Hobson-Jobson assimilation of adopted foreign words to the sound pattern of the adopting language (hyphen)
Hobson's choice choice of taking what is offered or nothing at all (one cap.)
Ho Chi Minh, Vietnamese communist statesman (1890–1969), president of North Vietnam 1954–69
Ho Chi Minh City official name for **Saigon**
hockey the game played on grass is called **field hockey** in the US, where **hockey** refers to ice hockey
hocus (**hocussing, hocussed**) arch. **1** deceive **2** drug
hocus-pocus deception or trickery (hyphen)
Hodder & Stoughton publishers
hodgepodge US var. of **hotchpotch**
Hodgkin's disease disease of lymphatic tissues
hodiernal relating to the present day
Hoe[1] area of Plymouth in SW England
Hoe[2], Richard March (1812–86), American inventor
hoe v. (**hoeing, hoed**)
Hoek van Holland Du. name for **Hook of Holland**
Hoffman, Dustin (Lee) (b.1937), American actor
Hoffmann, Ernst Theodor Amadeus (1776–1822), German writer
Hofmann 1 August Wilhem von (1818–92), German chemist **2** Johan Christian Conrad von (1810–77), German theologian
Hofmannsthal, Hugo von (1874–1929), Austrian poet
hog 1 castrated pig **2** (also **hogg**) dial. young sheep
hogan traditional Navajo hut
Hogarth, William (1697–1764), English painter and engraver □ **Hogarthian**
hogg see **hog**
hoggin mixture of sand and gravel used in road-building
Hogmanay Sc. New Year's Eve
hogshead 1 large cask **2** measure of liquid volume equal to 52.5 imperial gallons for wine or 54 imperial gallons

for beer (abbrev. **hhd**)
Hohenzollern German dynasty, kings of Prussia 1701–1918 and German emperors 1871–1918
hoi polloi the common people (strictly, not **the hoi polloi**, as *hoi* = 'the'; not ital.)
hokey N. Amer. informal too sentimental or contrived
hokey-cokey communal song and dance (hyphen)
hokey-pokey (hyphen) **1** dated ice cream **2** US hokey-cokey
Hokkaido most northerly of the four main islands of Japan
hokku use **haiku**
hokum sentimental or trite material
Holarctic zoogeographical region comprising the Nearctic and Palaearctic regions
Holbein, Hans (1497–1543), German painter; known as **Holbein the Younger**
Hölderlin, (Johann Christian) Friedrich (1770–1843), German poet
hold-up n. a delay; a robbery (hyphen, two words as verb)
hole-in-one pl. **holes-in-one** Golf (hyphens)
holey having holes
Holi Hindu spring festival
Holiday, Billie (1915–59), American jazz singer; born *Eleanora Fagan*
holidaymaker (one word)
holier-than-thou (hyphens)
Holinshed, Raphael (died *c.*1580), English chronicler
Holland 1 use **the Netherlands** for the country (but **Holland** for the international soccer team); Holland is a former province now divided into **North Holland** and **South Holland** **2** former division of Lincolnshire
holland smooth linen (lower case)
hollandaise creamy sauce (lower case, not ital.)
Hollands arch. Dutch gin (cap.)
hollowware cookware or crockery (one word)
hollyhock plant (one word)
Hollywood district of Los Angeles
Holman Hunt, William, see **Hunt**
Holmes[1], Oliver Wendell (1809–94), American physician and writer
Holmes[2], Sherlock, private detective in stories by Sir Arthur Conan Doyle □ **Holmesian**
holmium chemical element of atomic number 67 (symbol **Ho**)
holocaust 1 wholesale slaughter; (**the Holocaust**) the mass murder of Jews by the Nazis **2** hist. Jewish offering burnt on an altar
Holocene Geol. the present epoch (from about 10,000 years ago); also called **Recent**
Holofernes (in the Apocrypha) Assyrian general killed by Judith
hologram three-dimensional image formed by a laser etc.
holograph manuscript handwritten by its author
Holstein breed of black-and-white cattle; Friesian
holus-bolus all at once (hyphen)
Holy Communion the Eucharist (caps; abbrev. **HC**)
Holy Cross Day the feast of the Exaltation of the Cross, 14 September
Holy Family, Holy Father, Holy Ghost (caps)
Holy Grail (cap.; lower case in sense 'something eagerly sought')
Holy Land (caps)
holy of holies inner chamber of the sanctuary in the Jewish Temple (lower case)
Holy Roman Empire empire under the medieval papacy (caps; abbrev. **HRE**)
Holy Rood Day 1 the feast of the Invention of the Cross, 3 May **2** Holy Cross Day
Holyroodhouse, Palace of Edinburgh
Holy Saturday the Saturday before Easter Sunday
Holy Scripture, Holy Spirit (caps)
Holy See the papacy or the papal court
holystone piece of soft sandstone for scouring a ship's deck (one word)
Holy Thursday 1 (in the Roman Catholic Church) Maundy Thursday **2** dated (in the Anglican Church) Ascension Day

Holy Trinity see **Trinity**
Holy Week week before Easter (caps)
Holywood town in County Down
homage public honour or respect [Fr. *hommage*]
hombre US informal a man (not ital.)
homburg man's felt hat (lower case)
homebody, homeboy, homegirl (one word)
home brew (two words) □ **home-brewed**
homebuyer, homecoming (one word)
Home Counties the English counties surrounding London
home-grown (hyphen)
Home Guard British citizen army organized in 1940 to defend the UK against invasion (abbrev. **HG**)
homeland (one word)
homely 1 Brit. simple but comfortable **2** N. Amer. unattractive
home-made (hyphen)
homemaker (one word)
Home Office British government department dealing with domestic affairs
home of lost causes Oxford University (lower case)
Home of the Hirsel of Coldstream, Baron, see **Douglas-Home**
homeopathy (also **homoeopathy**) system of complementary medicine □ **homeopath**
homeothermic (also **homoiothermic**) Zool. warm-blooded; cf. **poikilothermic**
homeowner (one word)
home page (two words)
Homer (8th cent. BC), Greek epic poet □ **Homeric**
home rule government of a place by its own citizens (caps in ref. to Ireland)
Home Secretary Secretary of State in charge of the Home Office (caps)
homesick, homespun, homestead (one word)
home town, home truth (two words)
homework, homeworker (one word)
homey comfortable and cosy (not **homy**)
homing (not **homeing**)
hominid Zool. primate of a family which includes humans
hominoid Zool. primate of a group which includes humans and the great apes
Homo Zool. genus of humans (not ital.)
homo pl. **homos** derog. homosexual man
homo pl. ***homines*** human being (L., ital.)
homoeopathy var. of **homeopathy**
homoerotic (one word)
homogeneous (also **homogenous**) all of the same kind □ **homogeneity**
homogenize (Brit. also **homogenise**) **1** make homogeneous **2** process (milk) so that the cream does not separate
homogenous 1 var. of **homogeneous 2** Biol., old-fashioned term for **homologous**
homogeny 1 var. of **homogeneity 2** Biol. dated similarity due to common descent
homograph each of two or more words spelled the same but having different meanings and origins
homoiothermic var. of **homeothermic**
homoiousian person believing God the Father and God the Son to be of like but not identical substance; cf. **heteroousian, homoousian**
homologous having a similar relative position or structure, corresponding
homologue (US also **homolog**) homologous thing
homonym each of two or more words having the same spelling but different meanings and origins
homoousian (also **homousian**) person believing God the Father and God the Son to be of the same substance; cf. **heteroousian, homoiousian**
homophone each of two or more words having the same pronunciation but different meanings, origins, or spelling
Homo sapiens species to which modern humans belong (L., ital.)
Homs (also **Hims**) city in Syria
homunculus (also **homuncule**) pl. **homunculi** or **homuncules** very small human or similar creature
homy use **homey**
Hon. (point) **1** Honorary **2** Honourable
honcho pl. **honchos** informal leader
Honduras country of Central America □ **Honduran**
Honecker, Erich (1912–94), East German head of state 1976–89

Honegger, Arthur (1892–1955), French composer, of Swiss descent
honey badger (two words)
honeybee, honeycomb, honeydew (one word)
honeyed (also **honied**) containing or coated with honey
honeymoon, honeypot, honeysuckle, honeytrap (one word)
Hong Kong former British dependency in SE China (abbrev. **HK**)
HongkongBank Hong Kong and Shanghai Banking Corporation (one word, two caps)
honied var. of **honeyed**
Honi soit qui mal y pense shame on him who thinks evil of it (the motto of the Order of the Garter; Fr., ital.)
honnête homme pl. ***honnêtes hommes*** gentleman (Fr., ital.)
honor, honorable US vars of **honour, honourable**
honorand person to be honoured
honorarium pl. **honorariums** or **honoraria** a nominal payment for professional services (not ital.)
honorary conferred as an honour (cap. in titles; abbrev. **Hon.**)
honorary secretary (abbrev. **Hon. Sec.**)
honoree N. Amer. person who is honoured at a ceremony etc.
honorific (title) given as a mark of respect
honoris causa as a mark of esteem (L., ital.)
honour (US **honor**)
honourable (US **honorable**) used (cap.) in the titles of an MP (with name of constituency), of a US judge or congressman, and of the son or daughter of a peer (abbrev. **Hon.**)
Hon. Sec. honorary secretary
Honshu largest of the four main islands of Japan
hoodoo (hoodoos, hoodooing, hoodooed)
hoodwink (one word)
hoof pl. **hoofs** or **hooves**
Hooghly river of India (not **Hugli**)
hookah oriental tobacco pipe
hook and eye (three words)
Hooke, Robert (1635–1703), English scientist, who formulated **Hooke's law**
Hooker, Sir Joseph Dalton (1817–1911), English botanist
Hook of Holland cape and port of the Netherlands; Du. name **Hoek van Holland**
hooky (also **hookey**) (in **play hooky**) play truant
hooping cough use **whooping cough**
hoopoe crested bird
hooray, hoorah vars of **hurrah**
Hooray Henry pl. **Hooray Henrys** or **Henries** lively young upper-class man
Hoover[1] Herbert (Clark) (1874–1964), 31st president of the US 1929–33
Hoover[2] trademark vacuum cleaner (cap.; lower case as verb)
hooves pl. of **hoof**
hopefully in a hopeful manner; disp. it is to be hoped that
Hopi pl. same or **Hopis** member of a Pueblo Indian people
Hopkins, Gerard Manley (1844–89), English poet
hop-o'-my-thumb a dwarf (hyphens)
hop-picker (hyphen)
Horace (65–8 BC), Roman poet; Latin name *Quintus Horatius Flaccus*
Horatius Cocles legendary Roman hero
horde large group of people; cf. **hoard**
horehound (also **hoarhound**) plant of the mint family
Hormuz (also **Ormuz**) Iranian island at the mouth of the Persian Gulf
hornblende mineral (not **-blend**)
Horn, Cape southernmost point of South America
hornpipe dance (one word)
horology 1 study and measurement of time **2** art of making timepieces
horror-stricken, horror-struck (hyphen)
horror vacui dislike of leaving empty spaces in a composition (L., ital.)
Horsa see **Hengist and Horsa**
hors concours engaged in a contest but not competing for a prize (Fr., ital.)
hors de combat out of action (Fr., ital.)
hors d'oeuvre pl. same or **hors**

d'oeuvres appetizer (not ital.)
horseback, horsebox (one word)
horse brass, horse chestnut (two words)
horse-drawn (hyphen)
horseflesh, horsefly (one word)
Horse Guards ceremonial mounted troops from the Household Cavalry (two words, caps)
Horse Guards Parade in Whitehall, London (three words)
horsehair, horseman, horseplay (one word)
horsepower pl. same (one word; abbrev. **h.p.**)
horse race, horse racing (two words)
horseradish, horseshoe (one word)
horse-trading (hyphen)
horsewhip, horsewoman (one word)
horsey (also **horsy**) resembling or fond of a horse or horses
horst Geol. raised elongated block between two faults
Horst Wessel Song official song of the German Nazi Party
hortus siccus pl. **horti sicci** collection of dried plants (not ital.)
hosanna (also **hosannah**) cry of praise
Hosanna Sunday arch. Palm Sunday
Hosea book of the Old Testament (abbrev. **Hos.**)
hosepipe (one word)
hospitalize (Brit. also **hospitalise**)
hospitaller (US **hospitaler**) member of a charitable religious order
hostelling (US **hosteling**) practice of staying in youth hostels □ **hosteller**
hostler var. of **ostler**
hotbed (one word)
hot-blooded (hyphen)
hotchpot Law reunion of properties so as to distribute them equally
hotchpotch (N. Amer. **hodgepodge**) confused mixture
hot cross bun (three words)
hot-desking (hyphen)
hotdog N. Amer. perform stunts (one word)
hot dog sausage in a roll (two words)
hotel cap. in names; prefix with *a* not *an*
hôtel de ville town hall (Fr., ital.)
hotelier hotel keeper (not ital.)
hotfoot, hothead, hothouse, hotline, hotlist (one word)
hot metal typesetting in which type is newly made each time from molten metal
hotplate, hotpot (one word)
hot rod, hot seat (two words)
hotshot (one word)
hot-tempered (hyphen)
Hottentot use **Khoikhoi** exc. in historical contexts or in the names of animals and plants
Houdini, Harry (1874–1926), Hungarian-born American escape artist; born *Erik Weisz*
houmous var. of **hummus**
houndstooth large dogtooth pattern
hour (abbrev. **h, hr**)
hourglass (one word)
houri pl. **houris** beautiful young woman in the Muslim Paradise
House, the informal **1** (in the UK) the House of Commons or Lords; (in the US) the House of Representatives **2** the Stock Exchange **3** Christ Church (Oxford college) **4** hist. the workhouse
house arrest (two words)
houseboat, housebound, houseboy, housebreaker (one word)
housecarl bodyguard of a Danish or early English king or noble
housecoat, housefly (one word)
houseful pl. **housefuls**
Household Cavalry two cavalry regiments responsible for guarding the monarch and royal palaces
householder, housekeeper, housemaid, houseman (one word)
house martin (two words)
housemaster, housemate, housemistress, housemother (one word)
House of Commons elected chamber of UK parliament (abbrev. **HC**)
House of Keys elected chamber of Tynwald (Isle of Man parliament)
House of Lords chamber of UK parliament composed of peers and bishops (abbrev. **HL**)
House of Representatives lower house of the US Congress (abbrev. **HR**)

house party, house plant (two words)
house-proud (hyphen)
houseroom (one word)
house-sit (hyphen)
house style company's preferred manner of presenting and laying out written material (two words)
housetop (one word)
house-train, house-warming (hyphen)
housewife, housework (one word)
Housman, A(lfred) E(dward) (1859–1936), English poet
hovercraft pl. same (one word)
Howard, Catherine (*c*.1521–42), fifth wife of Henry VIII (beheaded)
Howards End novel by E. M. Forster (1910) (no apostrophe)
howdah seat for riding on an elephant
how-do-you-do (also **how-de-do** or **how-d'ye-do**) informal awkward situation
howff Sc. favourite haunt, esp. a pub
howitzer gun for firing shells
howsoever (one word; in literary use also **howsoe'er**)
Hoxha, Enver (1908–85), Albanian Communist leader 1944–85
Hoxnian Geol. interglacial period of the Pleistocene in Britain
hoyden tomboy (not **hoiden**)
Hoyle, Edmond (1672–1769), English writer on card games; (**according to Hoyle**) according to the rules
h.p. (also **HP**) **1** high pressure **2** hire purchase **3** horsepower
HQ headquarters
HR 1 House of Representatives **2** Human Resources
Hr. Herr (point)
hr pl. **hrs** hour
Hradec Králové town in the Czech Republic; Ger. name **Königgrätz**
HRE Holy Roman Empire
HRH Her or His Royal Highness
HRT hormone replacement therapy
Hrvatska Croatian name for **Croatia**
hryvna (also **hryvnia**) monetary unit of Ukraine
Hs the chemical element hassium (no point)
HSBC Hong Kong and Shanghai Banking Corporation
HSE Health and Safety Executive
HSH Her or His Serene Highness
Hsian, Hsiang vars of **Xian, Xiang**
HST high-speed train
HT high tension
HTML Comput. Hypertext Markup Language
HTTP Comput. Hypertext Transport (or Transfer) Protocol
HUAC House Un-American Activities Committee
Huang Ho (also **Huang He**) Chin. name for the **Yellow River**
huarache Mexican leather sandal (not **guarache**)
Hubble, Edwin Powell (1889–1953), American astronomer, who proposed **Hubble's law** and **Hubble's constant**
hubble-bubble hookah (hyphen)
Hubble Space Telescope (caps)
hubcap (one word)
hubris (in Greek tragedy) excessive pride that leads to nemesis (not ital.)
huckaback strong linen or cotton fabric
Hudibras mock-heroic poem by Samuel Butler (1663–78) □ **hudibrastic**
Hudson Bay inland sea in NE Canada
Hudson's Bay Company British colonial trading company (apostrophe)
hugger-mugger confused, disorderly (hyphen)
Hugli use **Hooghly**
Hugo, Victor(-Marie) (1802–85), French novelist and dramatist
Huguenot French Protestant of the 16th–17th cents
hula hoop (also US trademark **Hula-Hoop**) hoop spun round the body
Hull port in NE England; official name **Kingston upon Hull**
hullabaloo commotion or fuss
hullo var. of **hello**
humanize (Brit. also **humanise**)
humankind (one word)
Humberside former county of NE England
humble-bee use **bumblebee**
Humboldt, Friedrich Heinrich

Alexander, Baron von (1769–1859), German explorer and scientist
humdrum dull (one word)
Hume, David (1711–76), Scottish philosopher and historian □ **Humean**
humerus pl. **humeri** bone of the upper arm or forelimb
hummingbird (one word)
hummus (also **houmous**) Middle Eastern chickpea dip; cf. **humus**
humorist, humorous (not **humour-**)
humour (US **humor**)
humpback, humpbacked (one word)
Humperdinck 1 Engelbert (1854–1921), German composer **2** Engelbert (b.1936), British pop singer; born *Arnold George Dorsey*
Humpty Dumpty egg-like nursery-rhyme character (caps, two words)
humus organic component of soil; cf. **hummus**
hunchback, hunchbacked (one word)
hundred pl. **hundreds** or with numeral or quantifying word **hundred** (hyphen in compound ordinal numbers, e.g. *hundred-and-first*; Roman numeral **c** or **C**) □ **hundredth**
hundredweight pl. same or **hundredweights** (abbrev. **cwt**) **1** (also **long hundredweight**) Brit. unit of weight equal to 112 lb **2** (also **short hundredweight**) US unit of weight equal to 100 lb **3** (also **metric hundredweight**) unit of weight equal to 50 kg
Hundred Years War war between France and England 1337–1453 (no apostrophe)
hung see **hang**
Hungary country in central Europe; Hungarian name **Magyarország** □ **Hungarian**
hunger march, hunger strike (two words)
hung-over (hyphen)
hunky-dory satisfactory, fine (hyphen; David Bowie album is *Hunky Dory*)
Hunt, (William) Holman (1827–1910), English Pre-Raphaelite painter
hunter-gatherer, hunter-killer (hyphen)
Huntingdon town in Cambridgeshire
Huntingdonshire former county of SE England
Huntington city in West Virginia
Huntington's disease hereditary brain disease
hurdy-gurdy musical instrument (hyphen)
hurling (also **hurley**) Irish game resembling hockey
hurly-burly boisterous activity (hyphen)
hurrah (also **hooray, hurray**) cry of joy
Hurricane WWII aircraft
hurricane tropical cyclone
Husain use **Hussein**
Husák, Gustáv (1913–91), president of Czechoslovakia 1975–89
Huss, John (*c.*1372–1415), Bohemian religious reformer; Czech name *Jan Hus*
hussar 1 soldier of a light cavalry regiment **2** 15th-cent. Hungarian light horseman
Hussein 1 ibn Talal (1935–99), king of Jordan 1953–99 **2** Saddam (1937–2006), Iraqi president and prime minister 1979–2003; full name *Saddam bin Hussein at-Takriti*
Husserl, Edmund (Gustav Albrecht) (1859–1938), German philosopher
Hutu pl. same or **Hutus** or **Bahutu** member of a people forming the majority population in Rwanda and Burundi
Huxley 1 Aldous (Leonard) (1894–1963), English novelist **2** Andrew Fielding (1917–2012), English physiologist **3** Sir Julian (Sorell) (1887–1975), English biologist **4** Thomas Henry (1825–95), English biologist
Huygens Christiaan (1629–95), Dutch mathematician and astronomer
HWM high-water mark
Hyades star cluster
hyaena var. of **hyena**
hybridize (Brit. also **hybridise**)
Hyde character in R. L. Stevenson's story *The Strange Case of Dr Jekyll and Mr Hyde* (1886)
Hyderabad 1 city in central India **2** city in SE Pakistan
hydrangea flowering shrub
hydrocarbon (one word; abbrev. **HC**)
hydrodynamics, hydroelectric,

hydrofoil (one word)
hydrogen chemical element of atomic number 1 (symbol **H**)
hydrolyse (US **hydrolyze**) Chem. break down by chemical reaction with water
hydrophobia extreme fear of water, esp. as a symptom of rabies
hydrotherapy (one word)
hyena (also **hyaena**; not **hyæna**) carnivorous African mammal
Hygieia Gk Mythol. goddess of health
hygiene, hygienic (not **-ei-**)
hying pres. part. of **hie**
Hyksos people who invaded Egypt *c.*1640 BC
Hymen Gk & Rom. Mythol. goddess of marriage □ **hymeneal**
hymen membrane which partially closes the opening of the vagina □ **hymenal**
hymn book (two words)
hypaesthesia (US **hypesthesia**) Med. diminished capacity for sensation
hypaethral (US **hypethral**) Archit. having no roof
hypallage transposition of the natural relations of elements in a proposition, e.g. *Melissa shook her doubtful curls*
hyperactive (one word)
hyperaemia (US **hyperemia**) Med. excess of blood
hyperaesthesia (US **hyperesthesia**) Med. excessive physical sensitivity
hyperbaton inversion of the normal order of words, e.g. *this I must see*
hyperbola pl. **hyperbolas** or **hyperbolae** Math. symmetrical open curve
hyperbole deliberate exaggeration
hypercorrect, hypercritical (one word)
hyperglycaemia (US **hyperglycemia**) Med. excess of glucose in the bloodstream
hyperlink, hypermarket (one word)
hypernym a superordinate; cf. **hyponym**
hyperreal, hypersensitive, hypertext, hyperventilate (one word)
hyphen sign (-) used to join words to indicate that they have a combined meaning or that they are grammatically linked, or to indicate word division at the end of a line
hypnotize (Brit. also **hypnotise**)
hypochondria chronic anxiety about one's health (not **-condria**)
hypocoristic denoting a pet name (not **-choristic**)
hypocrisy the claiming of higher standards than is the case
hypodermic syringe (not **hyper-**)
hypoglycaemia (US **hypoglycemia**) Med. deficiency of glucose in the bloodstream
hyponym word of more specific meaning than a general or superordinate term applicable to it; cf. **hypernym**
hypotaxis Gram. subordination of one clause to another; cf. **parataxis**
hypotenuse longest side of a right-angled triangle
hypothecate pledge (money) to a specific purpose
hypothermia abnormally low body temperature
hypothesis pl. **hypotheses** supposition or proposed explanation
hypothesize (Brit. also **hypothesise**)
hypoxaemia (US **hypoxemia**) Med. abnormally low concentration of oxygen in the blood
hysterectomy surgical removal of the womb
hysteresis Phys. phenomenon in which the value of a physical property lags behind changes in the effect causing it
hysteron proteron figure of speech in which the natural order of elements is reversed, e.g *'I die! I faint! I fail!'*
hysterotomy surgical incision into the womb
Hz hertz

I

I **1** pl. **Is** or **I's** 9th letter of the alphabet **2** electric current **3** the chemical element iodine **4** (**I.**) Island(s) or Isle(s) **5** (also **i**) Roman numeral for one **6** (**the I**) Philos. the ego

i Math. square root of minus one

IA Iowa (postal abbrev.)

Ia. Iowa (official abbrev.)

IAA indoleacetic acid

IAEA International Atomic Energy Agency

iambus (also **iamb**) pl. **iambuses** or **iambi** metrical foot of one short or unstressed syllable followed by one long or stressed □ **iambic**

Iaşi city in Romania; Ger. name **Jassy**

IATA International Air Transport Association

IB International Baccalaureate

ib. *ibidem* (not ital.)

IBA Independent Broadcasting Authority

Ibadan city in Nigeria; cf. **Abadan**

Ibárruri Gómez, Dolores (1895–1989), Republican leader in the Spanish Civil War; known as **La Pasionaria**

Iberia ancient name for the Iberian peninsula (Spain and Portugal)

ibex pl. **ibexes** wild mountain goat

IBF International Boxing Federation

ibidem in the same source (L., ital.; abbrev. **ibid.** or **ib.**)

I.Biol. Institute of Biology

ibis pl. **ibises** wading bird

Ibiza westernmost of the Balearic Islands □ **Ibizan**

Iblis (also **Eblis**) (in Islam) name for the Devil

IBM International Business Machines

Ibo var. of **Igbo**

IBRD International Bank for Reconstruction and Development

IBS irritable bowel syndrome

Ibsen, Henrik (1828–1906), Norwegian dramatist

ibuprofen drug (lower case)

IC **1** integrated circuit **2** internal-combustion

i/c **1** in charge of **2** in command

ICAO International Civil Aviation Organization

Icarus Gk Mythol. son of Daedalus, who flew too near the sun □ **Icarian**

ICBM intercontinental ballistic missile

ICC **1** International Chamber of Commerce **2** International Cricket Council **3** US Interstate Commerce Commission **4** International Criminal Court

ICE **1** Institution of Civil Engineers **2** internal-combustion engine

ice age cold period; (**the Ice Age**) series of glacial episodes during the Pleistocene period

ice axe, ice bag (two words)

iceberg, icebox (one word)

icebreaker (one word)

ice bucket, ice cap (two words)

ice-cold (hyphen)

ice cream, ice cube, ice field, ice floe, ice hockey, ice house (two words)

Iceland island country in the North Atlantic; Icelandic name **Island** □ **Icelander**

ice lolly (also **iced lolly**) (two words)

Iceni tribe of ancient Britons

ice pack, ice pick, ice rink, ice sheet, ice skate, ice skating (two words)

ICFTU International Confederation of Free Trade Unions

Ich dien I serve (motto of the Prince of Wales (Ger., ital.)

I.Chem.E. Institution of Chemical Engineers

I Ching ancient Chinese manual of divination

ichneumon parasitic wasp

ichor Gk Mythol. fluid in the veins of the gods
ichthyology study of fishes
ichthyornis fossil bird (lower case, not ital.)
ichthyosaur (also **ichthyosaurus**) fossil marine reptile (lower case, not ital.)
ICI Imperial Chemical Industries
Icknield Way pre-Roman track from Wiltshire to Norfolk
icon (sense 'devotional painting' also **ikon**)
iconize (Brit. also **iconise**)
iconostasis pl. **iconostases** screen with icons in an Eastern church
icosahedron pl. **icosahedra** or **icosahedrons** solid figure with twenty plane faces
ICRC International Committee of the Red Cross
ICT information and communications technology
ictus pl. same or **ictuses** rhythmical or metrical stress
ICU intensive-care unit
icy (not **-ey**)
ID 1 Idaho (postal abbrev.) **2** identification; identity
Id var. of **Eid**
id part of the mind (lower case)
id. *idem* (not ital.)
IDA International Development Association
Idaho state of the north-western US (official abbrev. **Ida.**, postal **ID**) ◻ **Idahoan**
idea'd (not **idead**)
idealize (Brit. also **idealise**)
idée fixe pl. ***idées fixes*** dominating idea (Fr., ital.)
idée reçue pl. ***idées reçues*** accepted idea (Fr., ital.)
idem the same person or source as mentioned before (L., ital.; abbrev. **id.**)
identikit (noun cap. as trademark)
ideogram (also **ideograph**) character representing an idea without indicating its pronunciation
ideographic of ideograms; cf. **idiographic**
ideological (not **idea-**)
ideologue dogmatic adherent of an ideology (not **idea-**)
ides (in the ancient Roman calendar) the 15th day of March, May, July, and October and the 13th of other months (pl., lower case)
idiographic of the discovery of particular scientific facts or processes; cf. **ideographic**
idiolect speech habits of a particular person
idiosyncrasy (not **-cy**) ◻ **idiosyncratic**
idiot savant pl. **idiot savants** or **idiots savants** person with learning difficulties but one particular gift (not ital.)
idolize (Brit. also **idolise**)
Id ul-Adha, Id ul-Fitr see **Eid**
idyll (not **idyl**) **1** blissful period **2** short description of a picturesque scene or incident ◻ **idyllic**
i.e. that is (points; preceded by a comma) [L. *id est*]
IEA International Energy Agency
iechyd da good health! cheers! (Welsh, ital.)
IEE Institution of Electrical Engineers
IEEE US Institute of Electrical and Electronics Engineers
Ieper Flemish name for **Ypres**
IF intermediate frequency
IFAD International Fund for Agricultural Development
IFC International Finance Corporation
iff Logic if and only if
Igbo (also **Ibo**) pl. same or **Igbos** member of a people of SE Nigeria
igloo pl. **igloos** snow house (not **iglu**)
Ignatius Loyola, St (1491–1556), Spanish founder of the Society of Jesus
igneous of or like fire
ignis fatuus pl. **ignes fatui** will-o'-the-wisp (not ital.)
ignitable (not **-ible**)
ignoramus pl. **ignoramuses**
ignoratio elenchi pl. ***ignorationes elenchi*** logical fallacy of refuting something not asserted (L., ital.)
ignotum per ignotius offering of an explanation that is harder to understand than the thing it is meant to explain (L., ital.)
iguana tropical American lizard

iguanodon dinosaur (not **-adon**)
i.h.p. indicated horsepower
IHS Jesus
IIII former Roman numeral for four (superseded by *IV*)
IJ, ij Dutch letter, alphabetized as *y*
IJssel, IJsselmeer river and lake in the Netherlands (one word, two caps)
ikebana art of Japanese flower arrangement
ikon see **icon**
IL Illinois (postal abbrev.)
ilang-ilang var. of **ylang-ylang**
Île-de-France region of France incorporating Paris
ileum pl. **ilea** third portion of the small intestine □ **ileac**
ileus painful intestinal obstruction
Iliad Greek epic poem ascribed to Homer
Ilium another name for **Troy**
ilium pl. **ilia** broad bone of the pelvis □ **iliac**
ilk (in **of that ilk, of his ilk,** etc.) of that type; (**of that ilk**) Sc. of the place or estate of the same name
Ill. Illinois (official abbrev.)
ill hyphen with participial adjectives: *ill-advised* | *ill-bred* | *ill-defined*
ill at ease (three words, hyphens when attrib.)
ill breeding, ill fame, ill feeling (two words)
illegal forbidden by law; cf. **illicit, unlawful**
ill-gotten (hyphen)
ill health (two words)
ill humour (two words) □ **ill-humoured**
illicit forbidden by law, rules, or custom; cf. **elicit, illegal, unlawful**
Illinoian Pleistocene glaciation in North America
Illinois state in the Middle West of the US (official abbrev. **Ill.**, postal **IL**) □ **Illinoisan**
ill-natured (hyphen) □ **ill nature**
ill-omened, ill-starred (hyphen)
ill-tempered (hyphen) □ **ill temper**
ill-treat, ill-treatment (hyphen)
illude trick; delude
Illuminati (not ital.) **1** 16th-cent. Spanish heretics **2** Bavarian secret society
illuminati people claiming special knowledge (lower case)
ill-use v. (hyphen, two words as noun)
illusive deceptive, illusory; cf. **allusive, elusive**
illustration (abbrev. **illus.**)
illustrator (not **-er**)
ill will (two words)
illywhacker Austral. small-time confidence trickster
ILO International Labour Organization
ILP Independent Labour Party
ILR Independent Local Radio
ILS instrument landing system
imaginable (not **-eable**)
imaginal of an image or imago
imagism school of poetry using precise images
imago pl. **imagos** or **imagines** adult stage of an insect
imam 1 leader of prayers in a mosque **2** (**Imam**) title of various Muslim leaders
Imam Bayildi Turkish aubergine dish (caps)
IMAP Internet Mail Access Protocol
IMAX trademark technique of widescreen cinematography
imbecile, imbecilic (not **-bi-**)
imbed use **embed**
imbrication overlapping arrangement like roof tiles; cf. **embrocation**
imbroglio pl. **imbroglios** confused or embarrassing situation (not ital., not **emb-**)
imbrue (**imbruing, imbrued**) stain
imbue (**imbuing, imbued**) inspire or permeate
I.Mech.E. Institution of Mechanical Engineers
IMF International Monetary Fund
I.Min.E. Institution of Mining Engineers
Immaculate Conception Roman Catholic doctrine of the Virgin Mary's conception (caps)

immanent inherent; cf. **eminent, imminent**
Immanuel var. of **Emmanuel**
immeasurable (not **-eable**)
Immelmann aerobatic manoeuvre (cap.)
immigrant person who comes from abroad to live permanently in another country; cf. **emigrant** □ **immigrate**
imminent about to happen; cf. **eminent, immanent**
immobilize (Brit. also **immobilise**)
immoral morally bad; cf. **amoral**
immortalize (Brit. also **immortalise**)
immortelle everlasting flower (not ital.)
Immortels, Les the members of the French Academy (ital.)
immovable (also **immoveable**)
immunize (Brit. also **immunise**)
immunocompromised, immunodeficiency, immunosuppression, immunotherapy (one word)
IMO International Maritime Organization
imp. 1 imperative **2** imperfect **3** imperial **4** impersonal **5** impression **6** imprimatur
impala pl. same, African antelope
impanel var. of **empanel**
impassable impossible to travel along or over
impasse deadlock (not ital.)
impassible incapable of suffering
impassion, impassioned (not **em-**)
impasto laying on paint thickly
impeccable (two *cs*; not **-ible**)
impedance resistance to alternating current (not **-ence**)
impedimenta bulky equipment (pl.)
impel (**impelling, impelled**) □ **impeller** (also **impellor**)
imperative mood of a verb expressing a command (abbrev. **imp.** or **imper.**)
imperator absolute ruler, emperor (not ital.)
imperfect tense denoting a past action not completed (abbrev. **imp.** or **imperf.**)
imperil (**imperilling, imperilled**; US one **-l-**)
imperium absolute power (not ital.)
impersonal pronoun pronoun without a definite referent or antecedent, in English *it*
impi pl. **impis** body of Zulu warriors
impinge (**impinging, impinged**) □ **impingement**
implausible (not **-able**)
imply (**implying, implied**) indicate by suggestion; cf. **infer**
impolder reclaim from the sea
impostor (also **imposter**) person who pretends to be someone else
imposture act of an impostor
impracticable impossible to carry out
impractical not sensible or realistic
impresario pl. **impresarios**
impression (abbrev. **imp.**) **1** printing of a number of copies of a book at one time **2** printed version of a book, esp. a reprint with few alterations
impressionism 1 19th-cent. movement in painting **2** impressionistic literary or artistic style
impressionist 1 exponent of impressionism **2** entertainer who impersonates others
impressionistic 1 based on subjective impressions **2** in the style of impressionism
imprimatur (not ital.) **1** official Roman Catholic licence to print a book (abbrev. **imp.**) **2** authoritative approval
imprint 1 printer's or publisher's name and details in a book **2** publisher's brand name
impro pl. **impros** improvisation
impromptu pl. **impromptus**
improvise (not **-ize**)
improviser (not **-or**)
I.Mun.E. Institution of Municipal Engineers
IN Indiana (postal abbrev.)
In the chemical element indium (no point)
in. inch(es)
in absentia in his, her, or their absence (L., ital.)
inadmissible (not **-able**)
inadvertent (not **-ant**)
inadvisable (not **-eable**)

inamorata female lover (not ital.)
inamorato pl. **inamoratos** male lover (not ital., not **enamor-**)
inapt unsuitable, inappropriate; cf. **inept**
inasmuch (one word)
inboard, inborn, inbound (one word)
inbox (one word)
inbred, inbreed, inbuilt (one word)
Inc. Incorporated
inc. including
Inca member of a South American Indian people ◻ **Incaic, Incan**
inca South American hummingbird (lower case)
in camera not in open court (not ital.)
Incarnation, the embodiment of God the Son as Jesus Christ
incase v. use **encase**
in case as a provision against (two words)
incense substance burned for its sweet smell (not **-ence**)
incentivize (Brit. also **incentivise**)
inch unit of measurement (not now in scientific use; abbrev. **in.**)
-in-chief (hyphens)
inchoate not fully formed or developed
incidentally (not **-tly**)
incipit opening of a manuscript, early printed book, or chanted liturgical text
incise mark with a cut (not **-ize**)
incl. including; inclusive
inclose, inclosure use **enclose, enclosure**
incognito pl. **incognitos** (having) an assumed or false identity
incognizant (also **incognisant**) lacking knowledge or awareness
incomer (one word)
income support, income tax (two words)
incoming (one word)
incommensurable not able to be judged by the same standards
incommensurate out of keeping or proportion
incommunicado unable or unwilling to communicate with others (not ital.)
incompatible (not **-able**)
inconnu pl. same, unknown person or thing (not ital.)
incontrovertible (not **-able**)
in-crowd (hyphen)
incrust use **encrust**
incubous having leaves which point forward and overlap
incubus pl. **incubi** male demon believed to have sex with sleeping women
incudes pl. of **incus**
inculturation (also **enculturation**)
incumber use **encumber**
incunabulum (also **incunable**) pl. **incunabula** book printed before 1501
incur (**incurring, incurred**)
incurve curve inwards (one word)
incus pl. **incudes** anvil-shaped bone in the middle ear
Ind. 1 Independent **2** India(n) **3** Indiana (official abbrev.)
ind. index
indefeasible not subject to being lost, annulled, or overturned
indefectible not liable to fail, end, or decay
indefensible not justifiable or able to be protected (not **-able, -c-**)
indefinite article non-specific determiner, in English *a* or *an*
indefinite pronoun pronoun without a particular referent, e.g. *anybody, something*
indent v. position (text) further from the margin than the main part of the text. n. space left by indenting text
indenture legal agreement, formerly esp. one binding an apprentice to a master
independence, independent (not **-ance, -ant**)
Independent, The UK newspaper (cap. and italic *The*)
in-depth (hyphen)
indestructible (not **-able**)
indeterminate vowel another name for **schwa**
index pl. **indexes** or esp. in technical use **indices** (abbrev. **ind.**)
Index Librorum Prohibitorum list of books formerly banned as contrary to Roman Catholic faith or morals
index-linked, index-linking (hyphen)

index locorum pl. **indices locorum** index of places (not ital.)
index nominum pl. **indices nominum** index of names (not ital.)
index rerum pl. **indices rerum** subject index (not ital.)
index verborum pl. **indices verborum** index of words (not ital.)
India country in southern Asia (abbrev. **Ind.**); Indian name **Bharat**
Indiaman pl. **Indiamen** hist. ship trading with India or the East or West Indies (cap.)
Indian for peoples of North America *American Indian* is still acceptable, although *Native American* is preferred in the US; use names of specific peoples where possible, and avoid *Indian* alone and *Red Indian*
Indiana state in the Midwest of the US (official abbrev. **Ind.**, postal **IN**) □ **Indianan**
Indianapolis state capital of Indiana
Indian ink (N. Amer. **India ink**) deep black ink
Indian rope trick (three words)
Indian subcontinent the part of Asia south of the Himalayas, divided between India, Pakistan, and Bangladesh (one cap.)
Indian summer (one cap.)
India paper 1 soft paper used for proofs of engravings **2** very thin paper used for Bibles
India rubber (also **indiarubber**)
Indic Sanskrit and the modern Indian languages descended from it
indicative mood of verbs expressing statement of fact (abbrev. **indic.**)
indicator (not **-er**)
indices see **index**
indicia signs or distinguishing marks (not ital.)
indict formally accuse of a crime; cf. **indite**
indie independent record label or film company (lower case; not **-y**)
indigenize (Brit. also **indigenise**)
indigestible (not **-able**)
indigo pl. **indigos** or **indigoes**
indiscreet revealing things that should be kept private or secret
indiscrete not divided into distinct parts
indispensable (not **-ible**)
indite arch. write, compose; cf. **indict**
indium chemical element of atomic number 49 (symbol **In**)
individualize (Brit. also **individualise**) give an individual character to
individuate distinguish from others, single out
Indo-Aryan 1 member of an Indo-European people who invaded NW India in the second millennium BC **2** another name for **Indic**
Indo-China Burma (Myanmar), Thailand, Malaya, Laos, Cambodia, and Vietnam □ **Indo-Chinese**
Indo-European 1 family of European and Asian languages or their ancestor **2** speaker of an Indo-European language
Indo-Iranian subfamily of Indo-European spoken in India and Iran
Indonesia SE Asian country consisting of many islands; former name **Dutch East Indies** □ **Indonesian**
indoor, indoors (one word)
indorse US & law var. of **endorse**
indraught, indrawn (one word)
indue use **endue**
industrialize (Brit. also **industrialise**)
Industrial Revolution (caps)
Indy motor racing round a banked oval circuit (cap.)
Indycar car used in Indy racing (cap., one word)
inédit unpublished work (Fr., ital.)
inedita unpublished writings (not ital.)
ineligible (not **-able**)
inept without skill, clumsy; cf. **inapt**
inequable not equal or evenly distributed
inequitable unfair, unjust
inescapable (not **-eable**)
in esse in actual existence (L., ital.)
inexhaustible (not **-able**)
in extenso in full, at length (L., ital.)
in extremis in an extremely difficult situation; at the point of death (L., ital.)
INF intermediate-range nuclear force(s)
inf. infinitive

infallible (not **-able**)
infanta eldest daughter of the monarch of Spain or, formerly, Portugal (not ital.)
infante a younger son of the monarch of Spain or, formerly, Portugal (not ital.)
infantilize (Brit. also **infantilise**)
infantryman (one word)
infer (**inferring, inferred**) deduce from evidence and reasoning; cf. **imply** ▫ **inferable** (also **inferrable**)
inference (not **-rr-**, **-ance**)
inferior another name for **subscript**
inferno pl. **infernos** large uncontrollable fire; (**the Inferno**) Hell, after Dante's *Inferno*
infield, infighting, infill (one word)
in fine in short, to sum up (L., ital.)
infinitive basic uninflected form of a verb (abbrev. **inf.** or **infin.**)
infinity (symbol ∞)
in flagrante delicto (also informal **in flagrante**) in the very act of wrong-doing (not ital.)
inflammable easily set on fire (prefer **flammable** for clarity)
inflater (also **inflator**)
inflection (Brit. also **inflexion**) grammatical termination or change in the form of a word
inflexible (not **-able**)
infra further on (in a book or article), below (L., ital.)
infra dig beneath one, demeaning (two words, not ital.)
infrared, infrasonic, infrasound, infrastructure (one word)
infringement (not **-ngment**)
infula pl. **infulae** ribbon on a bishop's mitre
infusible not able to be melted or fused
Ingenhousz, Jan (1730–99), Dutch scientist
ingenious clever and inventive
ingénue innocent or unsophisticated young woman (accent, not ital.)
ingenuity cleverness and inventiveness
ingenuous innocent and unsuspecting
inglenook space each side of a large fireplace (one word)
ingraft use **engraft**
ingrain (also **engrain**) firmly fix or establish
ingrain carpet reversible carpet
Ingres, Jean Auguste Dominique (1780–1867), French painter
in-group (hyphen)
ingrowing, ingrown, ingrowth (one word)
ingulf use **engulf**
inhabit (**inhabiting, inhabited**)
inherit (**inheriting, inherited**) ▫ **inheritor**
inhibit (**inhibiting, inhibited**)
in-house (hyphen)
initial v. (**initialling, initialled**; US one **-l-**)
initialism abbreviation consisting of initial letters pronounced separately (e.g. *BBC*); cf. **acronym**
initialize (Brit. also **initialise**)
initials spaced, with points (*D. H. Lawrence*)
initial teaching alphabet phonetic alphabet for learners (lower case; abbrev. **ITA**)
initiator (not **-er**)
in-joke (hyphen)
ink-blot test (one hyphen)
inkjet printer (not **ink-jet**)
inkling slight knowledge or suspicion
Inklings, the Oxford group including C. S. Lewis and J. R. R. Tolkien
inkstand, inkwell (one word)
INLA Irish National Liberation Army
inland revenue public revenue from income tax etc.; (**Inland Revenue**) UK government department
in-law relative by marriage (hyphen)
in-line adj. (hyphen)
in loco parentis in the place of a parent (L., ital.)
in medias res into the middle of a narrative (L., ital.)
in memoriam in memory of (L., ital.)
inner side of a sheet containing the second page
innervate supply with nerves; cf. **enervate**
inning division of a baseball game
innings pl. same or informal **inningses**

division of a cricket game; player's turn at batting
Inniskilling see **Enniskillen**
innkeeper (one word)
Innocents' Day 28 December (caps)
Inn of Court pl. **Inns of Court** each of four legal societies admitting people to the English bar (two caps)
Innsbruck city in western Austria
innuendo pl. **innuendoes** or **innuendos**
inoculate, inoculation (not **inn-**) □ **inoculator**
inpatient (one word)
in personam against or affecting a specific person only (L., ital.)
in potentia as a possibility, potentially (L., ital.)
in propria persona in his or her own person (L., ital.)
input v. (**inputting**; past and past part. **input** or **inputted**)
inquire Brit. make a formal investigation (cf. **enquire**); in US also means 'request information'
inquiry Brit. a formal investigation (cf. **enquiry**); in US also means 'a request for information'
inquisition prolonged questioning; (**the Inquisition**) the Spanish Inquisition
Inquisitor General head of the Spanish Inquisition (two words, caps)
inquorate without a quorum
in re Law in the legal case of; with regard to (L., ital.)
in rem Law imposing a general liability (L., ital.)
INRI *Iesus Nazarenus Rex Iudaeorum*, Jesus of Nazareth, King of the Jews
inroad, inrush (one word)
INS US Immigration and Naturalization Service
insectarium (also **insectary**) pl. **insectariums** or **insectaries** place where insects are kept and studied
inselberg pl. **inselbergs** isolated hill or mountain (lower case, not ital.)
insert 1 loose page or section in a magazine etc. **2** folded section of a book printed separately but bound in
INSET term-time training for teachers
inset n. **1** picture within the border of a larger one **2** insert in a magazine etc. v. (**insetting**; past and past part. **inset** or **insetted**) put in as an inset
inshallah if Allah wills it (not ital.) [Arab. *in šā' Allāh*]
inshore (one word)
insignia pl. same or **insignias**
insistence, insistent (not **-ance, -ant**)
in situ in the original place (L., ital.)
in so far (also **insofar**)
insole (one word)
insomuch (one word)
insouciance, insouciant (not ital.)
insourcing (one word)
inspector (cap. in titles; abbrev. **Insp.**)
inspector general pl. **inspectors general** or **inspector generals** (two words; caps in titles)
inspissate thicken or congeal □ **inspissator**
inst. 1 instant **2** institute; institution
install (Brit. also **instal**) (**installing, installed**)
installation (two *l*s)
instalment (US **installment**)
instant of the current month (abbrev. **inst.**)
instantaneous occurring or done instantly (not **-ious**) □ **instantaneity**
instanter at once (not ital.)
in statu pupillari under guardianship (L., ital.)
instauration restoration, renewal □ **instaurator**
instil (also **instill**) (**instilling, instilled**) □ **instillation, instilment**
institutionalize (Brit. also **institutionalise**)
in-store in a shop or store (hyphen)
in store about to happen (two words)
Inst.P. Institute of Physics
instructor (not **-er**)
instrumental Gram. case denoting a means or instrument (abbrev. **instr.**)
insula pl. **insulae** tenement in an ancient Roman city
insular 1 ignorant of or uninterested in the outside world **2** of a form of Latin handwriting used in Britain and Ireland in the early Middle Ages
insurable (not **-eable**)
insurance protection against a risk; see also **assurance**
insure arrange for compensation in the

event of damage to or loss of; cf. **assure, ensure** □ **insurable**
insurer (not **-or**)
inswinger (one word)
int. 1 interior **2** interjection **3** internal **4** international
intaglio n. pl. **intaglios 1** incised or engraved design **2** printing process in which the type or design is etched or engraved. v. (**intaglioes, intaglioing, intaglioed**) incise or engrave
integral sign Math. ∫
intel military intelligence
intellectualize (Brit. also **intellectualise**)
intelligentsia intellectuals or educated people (treated as sing. or pl.)
Intelsat trademark international organization which owns and operates the world-wide commercial communications satellite system
intensifier (also **intensive**) adverb used to give force or emphasis
intension internal content of a concept
intention aim or plan
inter (**interring, interred**) bury
inter. intermediate
inter- forming mainly solid compounds
inter-agency between agencies (hyphen)
inter alia among other things (not ital.)
inter alios among other people (not ital.)
interceptor (not **-er**)
interchangeable (not **-gable**)
intercity (one word) **1** between cities **2** (also trademark **InterCity**) denoting UK express passenger rail services
interest-free (hyphen)
interference (not **-ance**)
interjection exclamation (abbrev. **int.** or **interj.**)
interleaf extra leaf, usually a blank one, between the regular leaves of a book
interleave insert as an interleaf in
interline (also **interlineate**) insert words between the lines of
interlinear 1 written or printed between the lines **2** having the same text in different languages on alternate lines
interlingua 1 artificial language for machine translation **2** (**Interlingua**) particular artificial language with a Romance base
intermezzo pl. **intermezzi** or **intermezzos** Mus. short connecting instrumental movement
intermittent (not **-ant**)
intern n. (not **interne**) N. Amer. **1** recent medical graduate **2** trainee working for experience. v. imprison
internal-combustion engine (one hyphen)
internalize (Brit. also **internalise**)
International any of four associations for promoting socialist or communist action
International Bank for Reconstruction and Development official name for the **World Bank** (abbrev. **IBRD**)
international candle var. of **candle**
Internationale, the revolutionary song composed in France
internationalize (Brit. also **internationalise**)
International Phonetic Alphabet set of phonetic symbols (abbrev. **IPA**)
interne use **intern**
Internet (cap.)
internist N. Amer. specialist in internal diseases
interpellate interrupt parliamentary proceedings by demanding an explanation from
Interpol organization investigating international crimes
interpolate 1 interject **2** insert, esp. insert (something) in a book to give a false impression of its date □ **interpolator**
interpret (**interpreting, interpreted**)
interpretative (also **interpretive**)
interpreter (not **-or**)
interracial (one word)
interregnum pl. **interregnums** or **interregna** period between successive rulers or regimes; (**the Interregnum**) period between the execution of Charles I and the Restoration, 1649–60
interrelate, interrelationship (one word)

interrogation point (also **interrogation mark**) question mark
interrogative (abbrev. **interrog.**)
interrupter (also **interruptor**)
inter se between or among themselves (L., ital.)
inter vivos between living people (L., ital.)
interwar (one word)
intifada Palestinian uprising (lower case, not ital.)
intolerance, intolerant (not **-ence, -ent**)
in toto as a whole, overall (L., ital.)
intrados lower curve of an arch; cf. **extrados**
intranet local communications network (lower case)
intransitive Gram. not taking a direct object (abbrev. **intrans.**)
intrauterine (one word)
in tray tray for incoming documents (two words)
intrench use **entrench**
intrigant intriguer (not **-gu-**)
intro pl. **intros** introduction
introduction (abbrev. **introd.**)
intrust use **entrust**
Inuit indigenous people of northern Canada and parts of Greenland and Alaska (prefer to **Eskimo** unless people from Siberia are being included)
Inuk pl. **Inuit** member of the Inuit
Inuktitut (also **Inuktituk**) Inuit language
Inupiaq (also **Inupiat, Inupik**) pl. same, member or language of the Inuit of Alaska
inure 1 accustom **2** var. of **enure**
inurn (also **enurn**) place in an urn
in utero in the womb (L., ital.)
in vacuo in a vacuum (L., ital.)
inveigle persuade by deception or flattery □ **inveiglement**
inventor (not **-er**)
inverted comma another name for **quotation mark**
investor (not **-er**)
in vino veritas under the influence of alcohol a person tells the truth (L., ital.)
invisible (not **-able**)
in vitro in a test tube (L., ital.)
in vivo in a living organism (L., ital.)
-in-waiting (hyphens)
inward-looking (hyphen)
inwrap use **enwrap**
inwreathe use **enwreathe**
I/O input–output
IOC International Olympic Committee
iodine chemical element of atomic number 53 (symbol **I**)
iodize (Brit. also **iodise**)
IOM Isle of Man
Ionesco, Eugène (1912–94), Romanian-born French dramatist
Ionia classical name for the west coast of Asia Minor □ **Ionian**
Ionian Islands islands off the western coast of Greece
Ionic classical order of architecture
ionic of ions
ionize (Brit. also **ionise**)
iota ninth letter of the Greek alphabet (**Ι, ι**), transliterated as 'i'
iota subscript small iota written or printed beneath a long Greek vowel
IOU pl. **IOUs** signed document acknowledging a debt
IOW Isle of Wight
Iowa state in the Midwest of the US (official abbrev. **Ia.**, postal **IA**) □ **Iowan**
IPA 1 India Pale Ale **2** International Phonetic Alphabet **3** International Phonetic Association
IP address string identifying each computer attached to the Internet
ipecacuanha (also **ipecac**) drug from a dried rhizome
Iphigenia (also **Iphigeneia**) Gk Mythol. daughter sacrificed by Agamemnon
Ipiros mod. Gk name for **Epirus**
IPMS Institution of Professionals, Managers, and Specialists
IPO initial public offering
iPod trademark portable music player
IPR intellectual property rights
ipse dixit dogmatic and unproven statement (L., ital.)
ipsissima verba the precise words (L., ital.)
ipso facto by that very fact or act (L., ital.)

IQ intelligence quotient
Iqbal, Sir Muhammad (1877–1938), Indian poet, philosopher, and politician
IR infrared
Ir the chemical element iridium (no point)
IRA Irish Republican Army
Iráklion mod. Gk name for **Heraklion**
Iran country in the Middle East; former name **Persia** □ **Iranian**
Iran–Iraq War war of 1980–8 (en rule)
Iraq country in the Middle East
Iraqi pl. **Iraqis** person from Iraq
IRBM intermediate-range ballistic missile
IRC Internet Relay Chat
Ireland island west of Great Britain
Ireland, Republic of country comprising approx. four-fifths of Ireland; Irish name **Éire**
irenic var. of **eirenic**
irenicon (also **eirenicon**) proposal made to achieve peace
Irian Jaya province of Indonesia comprising half of New Guinea with adjacent islands
iridescent showing changing colours (one *r*)
iridium chemical element of atomic number 77 (symbol **Ir**)
Irish Free State name for the independent part of Ireland 1922–37
Irish Republic another name for the **Republic of Ireland**
Irkutsk chief city of Siberia
IRO 1 Inland Revenue Office **2** International Refugee Organization
iron chemical element of atomic number 26 (symbol **Fe**)
Iron Age (caps)
ironclad (one word)
Iron Curtain (caps)
ironing board (two words)
iron man 1 exceptionally strong man **2** (**Ironman**) trademark multi-event sporting contest
ironmaster, ironmonger (one word)
Ironsides 1 nickname for Oliver Cromwell **2** Cromwell's cavalry troopers
ironwork, ironworks (one word)
Iroquoian North American language family
Iroquois pl. same, member of a former North American Indian confederacy
Irrawaddy principal river of Burma (Myanmar)
irreconcilable (not **-eable**)
irredentist advocate of the restoration of a country's former territories (lower case)
irrefragable indisputable
irregardless use **regardless**
irregular (abbrev. **irreg.**)
irrelevant (not **-ent**)
irreparable (not **-pair-**)
irreplaceable (not **-cable**)
irresistible (not **-able**)
irrupt enter forcibly or suddenly; cf. **erupt**
IRS US Internal Revenue Service
Is. 1 (also **Isa.**) Isaiah **2** Island(s) **3** Isle(s)
ISA pl. **ISAs** individual savings account
isagogics introductory study (treated as sing.)
Isaiah book of the Old Testament (abbrev. **Is.** or **Isa.**)
ISBN pl. **ISBNs** international standard book number
Isca Latin name for **Exeter**
ISDN integrated services digital network
Iseult princess in medieval legend; also called **Isolde**
Isfahan (also **Esfahan**, **Ispahan**) city in central Iran
Isherwood, Christopher (William Bradshaw) (1904–86), British-born American novelist
Isidore of Seville, St (*c.*560–636), Spanish Doctor of the Church; also called *Isidorus Hispalensis*
Islam religion of Muslims □ **Islamize** (Brit. also **Islamise**)
Islamabad capital of Pakistan
Islamic □ **Islamicize** (Brit. also **Islamicise**)
Islamic Jihad (also **Jehad**) Muslim fundamentalist group
Islamist Islamic militant or fundamentalist
Islamophobia hatred or fear of Islam or Muslims (not **-ma-**)

Island Icelandic name for **Iceland**
island (cap. in names)
Islay southernmost of the Inner Hebrides
isle (cap. in names)
Isle of Man island in the Irish Sea, a British Crown possession having home rule (abbrev. **IOM**)
Isle of Wight island county off the south coast of England (abbrev. **IOW**)
Isles of Scilly another name for **Scilly Isles**
Ismaili pl. **Ismailis** member of a branch of Shiite Muslims
Isnik see **Iznik**
ISO[1] International Organization for Standardization [from Gk *isos* 'equal']
ISO[2] Imperial Service Order
isobar line on a map connecting points with the same atmospheric pressure
Isocrates (436–338 BC), Athenian orator
Isolde another name for **Iseult**
isosceles (of a triangle) having two of its three sides of an equal length
ISP Internet service provider
Ispahan var. of **Isfahan**
I spy children's game (two words)
Israel 1 country in the Middle East **2** northern kingdom of the Hebrews (*c.*930–721 BC) **3** the Hebrew nation or people
Israeli pl. **Israelis** person from Israel
Israelite member of the ancient Hebrew nation
ISSN pl. **ISSNs** international standard serial number
issue each of a regular series of publications
Istanbul port in Turkey; former names **Constantinople, Byzantium**
isthmian 1 of an isthmus **2** (**Isthmian**) of the Isthmus of Corinth
isthmus 1 pl. **isthmuses** strip of land with sea on either side (cap. in names) **2** pl. **isthmi** narrow organ or piece of tissue connecting two larger parts
IT information technology
ITA initial teaching alphabet
italic sloping typeface, like *this* (abbrev. **ital.**, pl. **itals** or **itals.**)
italicize (Brit. also **italicise**)
Italy country in southern Europe; It. name **Italia**
ITAR-Tass (also **ITAR-TASS**) official news agency of Russia; former name **Tass**
ITC Independent Television Commission
itemize (Brit. also **itemise**)
It girl young woman known for her socialite lifestyle (one cap.)
Ithaca 1 island off the western coast of Greece, the legendary home of Odysseus; mod. Gk name **Itháki 2** city in New York State
itinerary (not **-nery**)
ITN Independent Television News
its pron. of it (no apostrophe)
it's it is (apostrophe)
itsy-bitsy (also **itty-bitty**)
ITU International Telecommunication Union
ITV 1 Independent Television **2** (also **iTV**) interactive television
IU international unit
IUCN International Union for the Conservation of Nature
IUD 1 intrauterine death **2** intrauterine device
IUPAC International Union of Pure and Applied Chemistry
IV 1 (also **iv**) Roman numeral for four **2** intravenous(ly)
IVF *in vitro* fertilization
Ivory Coast former English name for **Côte d'Ivoire** □ **Ivorian**
Ivy League group of eastern US universities (caps) □ **Ivy Leaguer**
IWC International Whaling Commission
Iwo Jima small volcanic island in the western Pacific
IWW Industrial Workers of the World
Iyyar (in the Jewish calendar) eighth month of the civil and second of the religious year
Izmir seaport in western Turkey; former name **Smyrna**
Iznik 1 town in NW Turkey; former name **Nicaea. 2** (also **Isnik**) 16th- and 17th-cent. pottery and ceramic tiles produced at Iznik
Izvestia (also ***Izvestiya***) Russian daily newspaper

J

J 1 pl. **Js** or **J's** 10th letter of the alphabet **2** Cards jack **3** joule(s) **4** (**J.**) Journal **5** Law Mr Justice

j 1 arch. used instead of *i* as the Roman numeral for 'one' in final position (*iij*) **2** Med. (in prescriptions) one

j Electron. square root of minus one

JA Judge Advocate

Jabberwock monster in Lewis Carroll's nonsense poem *Jabberwocky*

jabot frill or ruffle on shirt or blouse

Jac. James (regnal year) [L. *Jacobus*]

jacana wading bird [Port. *jaçanã*]

jacaranda tropical American tree

jacinth reddish-orange gem

jack (lower case) **1** small version of a national flag **2** (**every man jack**) each and every person

jackanapes impertinent person (lower case)

Jack and Jill (not **Gill**)

jackaroo (also **jackeroo**) Austral. novice on sheep or cattle station

jackass (lower case) **1** stupid person **2** male donkey

jackboot, jackdaw (one word)

jackeroo var. of **jackaroo**

jacket v. (**jacketed, jacketing**)

Jack Frost personification of frost (caps)

jackfruit, jackhammer (one word)

Jackie O nickname of Jacqueline Kennedy Onassis

jack-in-the-box pl. **jack-in-the-boxes** (lower case)

Jack Ketch former nickname for the hangman

jackknife v. (**jackknifing, jackknifed**) (one word)

jack of all trades pl. **jacks of all trades** (lower case)

jack-o'-lantern pl. **jack-o'-lanterns** lantern made from a pumpkin (lower case)

jackpot, jackrabbit (one word)

Jack Russell small breed of terrier

Jackson 1 Andrew (1767–1845), 7th president of the US 1829–37; known as **Old Hickory 2** Thomas (1824–63), Confederate general; known as **Stonewall Jackson**

Jack Tar pl. **Jack Tars** a sailor (caps)

Jack the Lad, Jack the Ripper (caps)

Jacob Hebrew patriarch, brother of Esau

Jacobean 1 relating to reign of James I of England (1603–25) **2** relating to the Apostle St James

Jacobethan combining Elizabethan and Jacobean styles

Jacobi, Karl Gustav (1804–51), German mathematician □ **Jacobian**

Jacobin 1 extreme radical in French Revolution **2** Dominican friar □ **Jacobinical, Jacobinism**

jacobin pigeon with neck feathers resembling a cowl (lower case)

Jacobite supporter of deposed James II □ **Jacobitism**

Jacob sheep four-horned sheep of piebald breed

Jacob's ladder pl. **Jacob's ladders** plant with blue or white flowers

Jacob's staff pl. **Jacob's staffs** surveyor's rod

jaconet cotton cloth

jacquard 1 apparatus fitted to a loom **2** fabric with variegated pattern

jacquerie uprising or revolt (orig. in France 1357–8)

jactitation 1 restless tossing of the body **2** arch. false declaration that one is married

Jacuzzi pl. **Jacuzzis** trademark bath with under-water jets of water (cap.)

j'adoube Chess declaration by a player intending to adjust the placing of a chessman (Fr., ital.)

Jaeger trademark woollen fabric

jaeger kind of skua (seabird)

Jaffa 1 city in Israel; biblical name **Joppa**; Hebrew name **Yafo 2** kind of large orange

Jaffna city in Sri Lanka
JAG Judge Advocate General
Jagannatha form of Krishna whose image is dragged through streets on a chariot; formerly called **Juggernaut**
Jaguar UK car company, owned by Ford
jaguar large spotted cat of Central and South America
Jah Rastafarian name of God
Jahweh use **Yahweh**
jai alai Basque game played with wicker baskets
jail (Brit. also **gaol**, esp. in historical contexts)
jailbait, jailbird, jailbreak, jailhouse (one word)
Jain adherent of Jainism
Jainism non-theistic Indian religion
Jaipur city in India, capital of Rajasthan
Jakarta (also **Djakarta**) capital of Indonesia
jakes arch. a toilet
Jakobson, Roman Osipovich (1896–1982), Russian-born American linguist
Jalalabad city in Afghanistan
Jalal ad-Din ar-Rumi (1207–73), Persian founder of the order of whirling dervishes
Jalandhar var. of **Jullundur**
jalapeño pl. **jalapeños** hot green chilli pepper (accent)
jalfrezi pl. **jalfrezis** medium-hot Indian dish
jalousie slatted blind or shutter
jamb part of door frame
jambalaya Cajun rice dish
jamboree 1 large celebration or party **2** rally of Scouts or Guides
James epistle of the New Testament ascribed to St James the Just (no abbrev.)
James I (1566–1625), king of Scotland (as James VI) 1567–1625, and of England and Ireland 1603–25
Jamesian relating to the novelist Henry James
James II (1633–1701), king of England, Ireland, and (as James VII) Scotland 1685–8
Jameson Raid raid into Boer territory 1895–6, led by Dr L. S. Jameson
James, St 1 Apostle, brother of John; known as **St James the Great** **2** Apostle; known as **St James the Less** **3** leader of the early Christian Church; known as **St James the Just**
Jamestown British settlement established in Virginia in 1607
Jammu and Kashmir state of NW India
jam-packed (hyphen)
Jamshedpur city in NE India
Jan. January
Janáček, Leoš (1854–1928), Czech composer
Jane Doe pl. **Jane Does** N. Amer. anonymous female party in legal action
Jane Eyre novel by Charlotte Brontë (1847)
Janeite admirer of Jane Austen
Jane's yearbooks on aircraft, ships, etc.
janissary (also **janizary**) hist. member of Turkish Sultan's guard
jankers informal punishment for military offence
Jan Mayen Norwegian island in Arctic Ocean
Jansen, Cornelius Otto (1585–1638), Flemish founder of ascetic Roman Catholic movement □ **Jansenism**
Jansens (also **Janssen van Ceulen**) see **Johnson**
January (abbrev. **Jan.**)
Janus Roman god of doorways and gates, represented as having two faces
Jap offens. Japanese person
Japan country in east Asia; Japanese name **Nippon**
japan (**japanning, japanned**) lacquer with hard varnish
Japheth (in the Old Testament) son of Noah
japonica shrub of rose family (lower case)
jardinière (accent, not ital.) **1** ornamental pot or stand for plants **2** garnish of mixed vegetables
Jargonelle variety of pear (cap.)
jarl Norse or Danish chief
jarrah variety of eucalyptus tree
Jas. James
jaspé mottled or variegated (accent, not ital.)

Jassy Ger. name for **Iaşi**
JATO jet-assisted take-off
Java 1 island in Indonesia **2** trademark computer programming language □ **Javan, Javanese**
java N. Amer. informal coffee (not cap.)
jawbone (one word)
Jaycees American civic organization
jaywalk N. Amer. walk in road without regard for traffic (one word)
jazz age America in 1920s (lower case)
Jazzercise trademark type of fitness training (cap.)
JCB trademark mechanical excavator
JCL Comput. job control language
JCR Junior Common Room; (in Cambridge) Junior Combination Room
Jeanne d'Arc Fr. name of Joan of Arc
Jean Paul pseudonym of German novelist *Johann Paul Richter* (1763–1825)
jebel (also **djebel**) (in Middle East and North Africa) mountain or hill
Jedburgh town in southern Scotland
Jeddah (also **Jiddah**) port in Saudi Arabia
Jedi pl. **Jedis** member of knightly order in *Star Wars* films
jeep sturdy four-wheel-drive vehicle (cap. as trademark)
jeet kune do martial art (lower case, not ital.)
Jeeves, Reginald, butler in P. G. Wodehouse novels
Jeez (also **Jeeze** or **Geez**) exclamation
Jefferies, (John) Richard (1848–87), English writer and naturalist
Jefferson, Thomas (1743–1826), 3rd president of the US 1801–9
Jeffreys, George (*c.*1645–89), Welsh judge infamous for the Bloody Assizes
jehad var. of **jihad**
Jehoshaphat (also **Jehosaphat**) (in the Old Testament) king of Judah
Jehovah form of the Hebrew name of God
Jehovah's Witness member of fundamentalist Christian movement (two caps)
Jehu (in the Old Testament) king of Israel who drove his chariot furiously
jejune 1 simplistic and superficial **2** dry and uninteresting
jejunum part of small intestine
Jekyll 1 character in R. L. Stevenson's story *The Strange Case of Dr Jekyll and Mr Hyde* (1886) **2** Gertrude (1843–1932), English garden designer
jell v. var. of **gel**
jellaba var. of **djellaba**
jello (also trademark **Jell-O**) pl. **jellos** N. Amer. gelatin dessert
jelly baby, jelly bean (two words)
jellyfish pl. **jellyfish** or **jellyfishes**
jemmy burglar's crowbar
Jena town in central Germany
je ne sais quoi quality that cannot be described or named (Fr., ital.)
Jenkins's Ear, War of Anglo-Spanish war 1739
Jenner, Edward (1749–1823), English pioneer of vaccination
jennet small Spanish horse; cf. **genet**
jenny 1 spinning jenny **2** female donkey
jeopardize (Brit. also **jeopardise**)
Jephthah (in the Old Testament) judge of Israel
jequirity Indian vine
Jer. Jeremiah
jerbil use **gerbil**
jerboa desert rodent
jeremiad list of complaints (lower case)
Jeremiah 1 Hebrew major prophet **2** book of Old Testament (abbrev. **Jer.**) **3** pessimistic or complaining person
Jerez town in southern Spain
Jericho town on the West Bank, in the Old Testament a Canaanite city destroyed by the Israelites (not **Jerico**)
jeroboam wine bottle four times larger than ordinary bottle
Jerry derog. a German
jerry-builder, jerry-built (hyphen)
jerrycan (also **jerrican**) (one word)
jerrymander use **gerrymander**
Jersey Channel Island
jersey pl. **jerseys** knitted garment
Jerusalem city in Middle East sacred to Jews, Christians, and Muslims; declared its capital by Israel but not recognized as such by the UN
Jespersen, Otto Harry (1860–1943), Danish philologist

jessamine another term for **jasmine**
Jesse (in the Old Testament) father of David
jessie informal feeble man (lower case)
Jesuit member of the Society of Jesus, a Roman Catholic order ◻ **Jesuitical**
Jesus (also **Jesus Christ**; possessive **Jesus's** or arch. **Jesus'**; archaic vocative **Jesu**)
jet black (two words, hyphen when attrib.)
jeté Ballet jump with one leg extended outwards (Fr., ital.)
jetfoil (one word)
jet lag (two words) ◻ **jet-lagged**
jetliner (one word)
jet propulsion (two words) ◻ **jet-propelled**
jetsam goods that have been thrown overboard and washed ashore; cf. **flotsam**
jet set (two words, lower case) ◻ **jet-setter**
jet-ski v. (**jet-skiing, jet-skied**) (hyphen, two words as noun, cap. as trademark)
jet stream (two words, lower case)
jettison (**jettisoning, jettisoned**)
jeu d'esprit pl. ***jeux d'esprit*** light-hearted display of wit (Fr., ital.)
jeunesse dorée gilded youth (Fr., ital.)
jewel v. (**jewelling, jewelled**; US one **-l-**)
jeweller (US **jeweler**)
jewellery (US **jewelry**)
Jewess avoid: dated and offensive
Jew's harp small musical instrument held between teeth
Jezebel 1 (in the Old Testament) wife of Ahab, king of Israel **2** shameless woman
Jharkhand state of NE India
Jhelum river of Kashmir and Punjab
Jiang Jie Shi var. of **Chiang Kai-shek**
Jiangsu (also **Kiangsu**) province of eastern China
Jiangxi (also **Kiangsi**) province of SE China
jibba (also **djibbah, djibba**) Muslim man's long coat
jibe 1 (also **gibe**) taunt **2** Sailing US var. of **gybe 3** US agree
Jibuti use **Djibouti**
Jiddah var. of **Jeddah**
jiggery-pokery informal dishonest behaviour (hyphen)
jigsaw (one word)
jihad (also **jehad**) (among Muslims) war or struggle against unbelievers; (**greater jihad**) spiritual struggle within oneself against sin (lower case)
Jilin (also **Kirin**) province of NE China
jill var. of **gill**[3]
Jim Crow 1 former practice of segregating black people in the US **2** offens. black person
Jiménez de Cisneros (also **Ximenes de Cisneros**) (1436–1517), Spanish inquisitor
Jinan (also **Tsinan**) city in eastern China
jingo 1 pl. **jingoes** vociferous supporter of war **2** (**by jingo**) exclamation of surprise ◻ **jingoism, jingoistic**
jinn (also **djinn**) spirit in Arabian and Muslim mythology
Jinnah, Muhammad Ali (1876–1948), Indian statesman, founder of Pakistan
jinricksha (also **jinrikisha**) rickshaw
jinx source of bad luck
JIT (of manufacturing systems) just-in-time
jitterbug dance (one word)
jiu-jitsu var. of **ju-jitsu**
Jivaro pl. **Jivaros** member of indigenous people of Amazon jungle
Jnr junior (no point)
Joan of Arc, St French national heroine; known as **the Maid of Orleans**
Job 1 (in the Old Testament) man tried by undeserved misfortunes **2** book of the Old Testament (no abbrev.)
jobber (in UK Stock Exchange) person dealing with brokers (official term now **broker-dealer**)
jobcentre (one word)
job lot (two words)
job-share (hyphen)
jobsworth (one word)
jockstrap (one word)
Jodhpur city in western India
jodhpurs trousers worn for horse riding (lower case)
Jodrell Bank site in Cheshire of large

radio telescope
Joe Bloggs (N. Amer. **Joe Blow**) informal hypothetical average man
Joel **1** Hebrew minor prophet **2** book of the Old Testament (no abbrev.)
joey pl. **joeys** young kangaroo (lower case)
Jogjakarta var. of **Yogyakarta**
jogtrot slow trot (one word)
Johannesburg city in South Africa
Johannine relating to the Apostle St John the Evangelist
Johannisberg (also **Johannisberger**) variety of Riesling
John (1165–1216), king of England 1199–1216; known as **John Lackland**
John, St **1** Apostle; known as **St John the Evangelist** or **St John the Divine** **2** (also **John**) fourth Gospel **3** (also **John**) either of three New Testament epistles attributed to St John (**1 John, 2 John, 3 John**)
John Barleycorn personification of malt liquor
John Bull typical Englishman
John Chrysostom, St see **Chrysostom, St John**
John Doe pl. **John Does** N. Amer. anonymous male party in legal action
John Dory pl. **John Dories** edible fish of the Atlantic and Mediterranean
johnny pl. **johnnies** informal man, fellow (lower case)
johnny-come-lately pl. **johnny-come-latelys** informal newcomer or late starter (lower case)
John o'Groats village in extreme NE Scotland
Johns Hopkins US university and medical centre (no apostrophe)
Johnson **1** Andrew (1808–75), 17th president of the US 1865–9 **2** (also **Jansens** or **Janssen van Ceulen**) Cornelius (1593–*c.*1661), English-born Dutch painter **3** Lyndon Baines (1908–73), 36th president of the US 1963–9 **4** Samuel (1709–84), English writer and lexicographer; known as **Dr Johnson**
John the Baptist, St Jewish preacher and prophet
Johor (also **Johore**) state of Malaysia
joie de vivre exuberant enjoyment of life (Fr., ital.)
joinder Law the bringing together of parties
joined-up (hyphen)
joint-stock company Finance (hyphen)
jointure Law estate settled on wife for period during which she survives husband
jojoba oil from seeds of American shrub
jokey (not **joky**)
jolie laide pl. ***jolies laides*** fascinatingly ugly woman (Fr., ital.)
Jolly Roger pirate's flag (caps)
Jolson, Al (1886–1950), Russian-born American singer and actor; born *Asa Yoelson*
Jonah **1** Hebrew minor prophet, thrown overboard as bringer of bad luck and swallowed by great fish **2** book of the Old Testament (abbrev. **Jon.**)
Jonathan (in the Old Testament) son of Saul, noted for friendship with David
Joneses (in phr. **keep up with the Joneses**) informal try to emulate neighbours
jongleur itinerant minstrel (not ital.)
Jönköping city in southern Sweden
jonquil narcissus with yellow flowers
Jonson, Ben (1572–1637), English dramatist
Joplin **1** Janis (1943–70), US rock singer **2** Scott (1868–1917), US ragtime pianist
Joppa biblical name for **Jaffa**
Jordaens, Jacob (1593–1678), Flemish painter
Jordan country in the Middle East; official name **Hashemite Kingdom of Jordan** □ **Jordanian**
Jorvik Viking name for **York** (not **Yorvik**)
Josef K character in *The Trial* (1925) by Franz Kafka
Joseph **1** Hebrew patriarch, given coat of many colours **2** (**St Joseph**) husband of the Virgin Mary
Josephine (1763–1814), empress of France 1804–9
Joseph of Arimathea, St member of council at Jerusalem who buried Christ's body
Joshua **1** Israelite leader **2** book of Old

Testament (abbrev. **Josh.**)
Joshua tree yucca (spiky plant)
Josquin des Prez see **des Prez**
joss stick (two words)
jouissance pleasure or delight (not ital.)
Joule, James Prescott (1818–89), English physicist
joule SI unit of energy (lower case; abbrev. **J**)
journal (abbrev. in titles **J.**)
Journals, the record of daily proceedings in the Houses of Parliament
journeyman (one word)
Jove 1 Rom. Mythol. the god Jupiter **2** (**by Jove**) exclamation of surprise
Jovian 1 relating to the god Jupiter **2** relating to the planet Jupiter
Joyce, James (Augustine Aloysius) (1882–1941), Irish writer □ **Joycean**
joyride, joystick (one word)
JP Justice of the Peace
JPEG Comput. format for compressing images
Jr junior
Jubilate Psalm 100, beginning *Jubilate deo* 'rejoice in God' (not ital.)
Jubran use **Gibran**
Judaea (also **Judea**) southern part of ancient Palestine □ **Judaean** (also **Judean**)
Judaeo- (**Judeo-**) Jewish
Judah 1 Hebrew patriarch **2** southern part of ancient Palestine
Judaize (Brit. also **Judaise**) make or become Jewish
Judas 1 (also **Judas Iscariot**) Apostle who betrayed Christ **2** another name for **St Jude**
judas peephole in door (lower case)
Judas Maccabaeus Jewish leader of 2nd cent.
Jude, St Apostle, supposed brother of James; also known as **Judas**
judge (cap. in titles)
judge advocate pl. **judge advocates** barrister advising court martial and summing up case (abbrev. **JA**)
judge advocate general pl. **judge advocate generals** officer in control of courts martial (abbrev. **JAG**)
judgement (in legal contexts and N. Amer. **judgment**)
Judgement Day (caps; not **Judgment Day**)
Judges book of Old Testament (abbrev. **Judg.**)
judicial relating to law
judiciary judicial authorities
judicious well judged, careful
Judith 1 (in the Apocrypha) Israelite widow who seduced and killed the enemy general Holofernes **2** book of the Apocrypha (no abbrev.)
judo kind of unarmed combat (lower case)
Jugendstil art nouveau (Ger., cap., ital.)
Juggernaut old-fashioned name for **Jagannatha**
juggernaut large heavy truck (lower case)
Jugoslavia use **Yugoslavia**
jugular vein large vein in neck
ju-jitsu (also **jiu-jitsu**) Japanese system of unarmed combat (hyphen)
juju pl. **jujus** charm or fetish (one word)
jujube berry-like fruit (one word)
jukebox (one word)
julep 1 US drink of bourbon, sugar, and mint **2** drink made from sugar syrup, sometimes medicated
Julian 1 Roman emperor 360–3; known as **Julian the Apostate 2** of Julius Caesar
Julian calendar calendar introduced by Julius Caesar and superseded by the Gregorian calendar (one cap.)
Julian of Norwich (*c.*1342–*c.*1413), female English mystic
julienne food cut into short thin strips (not ital.)
Julius Caesar 1 Gaius (100–44 BC), Roman statesman **2** (***Julius Caesar***) Shakespeare play (abbrev. ***Jul. Caes.***)
Jullundur (also **Jalandhar**) city in NW India
July pl. **Julys** (no abbrev.)
jumble sale (two words)
jumbo pl. **jumbos**
jumbo jet Boeing 747 (two words, lower case)
jumped-up (hyphen)
jumping bean (two words)
jump jet (two words)
jump rope N. Amer. skipping rope (two words)

jump seat (two words)
jump-start v. (hyphen)
jumpsuit (one word)
Jun. Junior
June (no abbrev.)
Juneau capital of Alaska
Jung, Carl Gustav (1875–1961), Swiss psychologist □ **Jungian**
Jungfrau mountain in the Swiss Alps
junior (abbrev. **Jun.**, **Jnr**, or chiefly N. Amer. **Jr.**)
Junker German nobleman or aristocrat (Ger., cap., ital.)
junket v. (**junketing, junketed**)
junk food (two words)
junkie (or **junky**) informal drug addict
junk mail, junk shop (two words)
junkyard (one word)
Juno Rom. Mythol. wife of Jupiter
Junoesque (of a woman) tall and shapely
junta military or political group ruling country by force
junto pl. **juntos** political grouping or faction in 17th- and 18th-cent. Britain
Jupiter 1 Rom. Mythol. the supreme god (also called **Jove**; Gk equivalent **Zeus**) **2** fifth planet from the sun
Jura 1 mountain range on border of France and Switzerland **2** Scottish island, in Inner Hebrides
jural relating to law
Jurassic Geol. second period of Mesozoic era
jure divino by divine right (L., ital.)
jurisprudence theory or philosophy of law
juryman, jurywoman (one word)
jury-rigged having temporary makeshift rigging
jus[1] law (L., ital.)
jus[2] gravy or sauce from meat juices (Fr., ital.)
jus cogens norms of international law (L., ital.)
jus gentium international law (L., ital.)
just deserts (not **desserts**)
juste milieu pl. ***justes milieux*** judicious moderation (Fr., ital.)
Justice Clerk (also **Lord Justice Clerk**) (in Scotland) vice president of High Court of Justiciary
Justice of the Peace pl. **Justices of the Peace**
justiciar hist. a judge
justiciary chiefly Sc. a judge
justify Printing adjust line of type to form a straight edge at the margin
Justinian Byzantine emperor 527–65
jute rough fibre used for rope and sacking
Jutland peninsula of Denmark and northern Germany; Danish name **Jylland**
Juvenal (*c.*60–*c.*140), Roman satirist
juvenilia works produced by an author or artist while still young (not ital.)

K

K 1 pl. **Ks** or **K's** 11th letter of the alphabet **2** the chemical element potassium [mod. L. *kalium*] **3** kelvin(s) **4** kilobyte(s) **5** kilometre(s) **6** Chess king **7** Köchel (catalogue of Mozart's works) **8** informal thousand [f. *kilo-*]
k 1 a constant in a formula or equation, esp. (*k*) Boltzmann's constant **2** kilo-
K2 second-highest peak in the world, in the Karakoram range
ka (in ancient Egypt) supposed spiritual part of a person
Kaaba holy building in the centre of the Great Mosque at Mecca (not **Caaba**)
kabaddi Indian team game
Kabbalah (also **Kabbala, Cabbala,** or **Cabala**) ancient Jewish tradition of mystical interpretation of the Bible
Kabinett German wine of superior quality
kabob N. Amer. var. of **kebab**
kaboodle use **caboodle**
kabuki traditional Japanese drama
Kabul capital of Afghanistan
kachha var. of **kuccha**
kadai var. of **karahi**
Kádár, János (1912–89), Hungarian prime minister 1956–8 and 1961–5
Kaddish ancient Jewish prayer sequence
kadi var. of **cadi**
kaffeeklatsch social gathering with coffee (lower case, not ital.)
Kaffir S. Afr. offens. a black African; cf. **Kafir**
kaffiyeh var. of **keffiyeh**
Kafir member of a people of NE Afghanistan; cf. **Kaffir**
kafir Muslim's term for a non-Muslim (ital.)
Kafka, Franz (1883–1924), Czech novelist □ **Kafkaesque**
kaftan (also **caftan**) loose tunic or dress
kagoul var. of **cagoule**
Kahlo, Frida (1907–54), Mexican painter
Kahlúa trademark coffee-flavoured liqueur (accent)
kail var. of **kale**
Kailyard School var. of **Kaleyard School**
Kaiser, Georg (1878–1945), German dramatist
kaiser hist. the German emperor, the emperor of Austria, or the head of the Holy Roman Empire (cap. in titles)
Kaiserslautern city in Germany
kaizen Japanese business philosophy of continuous improvement (not ital.)
Kalaallit Nunaat Inuit name for **Greenland**
kala-azar tropical disease (hyphen)
Kalahari Desert arid plateau in southern Africa (caps)
Kalamazoo city in Michigan
Kalashnikov Russian sub-machine gun or rifle
kale (Sc. also **kail**) variety of cabbage
kaleidoscope (not **-ie-**)
kalends var. of **calends**
Kalevala collection of Finnish legends
Kaleyard School (also **Kailyard School**) 19th-cent. writers of fiction about local life in Scotland (caps)
Kalgoorlie gold-mining town in Western Australia
Kali Hindu goddess, wife of Shiva
Kalimantan southern part of the island of Borneo
Kaliningrad Russian port on the Baltic; former name **Königsberg**
kalmia evergreen shrub
Kalmyk (also **Kalmuck**) pl. same or **Kalmyks** member of a Buddhist people inhabiting Kalmykia in SW Russia
Kama the Hindu god of love
Kama Sutra ancient Sanskrit treatise on love and sex
Kamchatka mountainous peninsula of

the NE coast of Siberian Russia

kameez pl. same or **kameezes** long tunic worn in the Indian subcontinent

kamikaze Japanese suicide aircraft

Kampala capital of Uganda

Kampuchea former name for **Cambodia** 1976–89 □ **Kampuchean**

Kan. Kansas (official abbrev.)

kana Japanese syllabic writing system

Kanarese (also **Canarese**) pl. same, member of a people of Kanara, SW India

Kanchenjunga (also **Kangchenjunga**) third-highest mountain in the world, in the Himalayas

Kandahar city in southern Afghanistan

Kandinsky, Wassily (1866–1944), Russian painter

Kandy city in Sri Lanka □ **Kandyan**

Kangchenjunga var. of **Kanchenjunga**

KaNgwane former homeland in South Africa (one word, two caps)

kanji system of Japanese writing using Chinese characters

Kannada Dravidian language of Karnataka, SW India

Kanpur city in northern India; former name **Cawnpore**

Kansas state in the central US (official abbrev. **Kan.**, postal **KS**) □ **Kansan**

Kansas City two adjacent US cities, one in Kansas and the other in Missouri

Kant, Immanuel (1724–1804), German philosopher □ **Kantian**

KANU Kenya African National Union

kaolin fine white clay

kapellmeister director of an orchestra or choir (lower case, not ital.)

Kaposi's sarcoma Med. form of cancer (one cap.)

kappa fifth letter of the Greek alphabet (**Κ, κ**), transliterated as 'k'

kaput broken or ruined (not ital.) [Ger. *kaputt*]

karabiner (also **carabiner**) rock climber's coupling link

Karachi city in Pakistan

Karafuto Japanese name for the southern part of Sakhalin

karahi (also **kadai, karai**) pl. **karahis** two-handled Indian frying pan

Karaite member of a Jewish sect that interprets the scriptures literally

Karajan, Herbert von (1908–89), Austrian conductor

Karakoram mountain system from NE Afghanistan to Kashmir

Karakorum ancient city in central Mongolia

karakul (also **caracul**) **1** Asian sheep **2** cloth or fur from its fleece

karaoke entertainment of singing to a pre-recorded backing (not **kari-**)

karat see **carat**

karate form of unarmed combat

karate chop (two words, hyphen as verb)

Karbala city in southern Iraq

Karelia region on the border between Russia and Finland

Karen pl. same or **Karens** member of a people of SE Burma (Myanmar) and western Thailand

Kariba Dam dam on the Zambezi River between Zambia and Zimbabwe

Karl-Marx-Stadt former name for **Chemnitz**

Karlovy Vary spa town in the Czech Republic; German name **Karlsbad**

Karlsruhe town in western Germany

karma (in Buddhism and Hinduism) person's conduct seen as deciding their fate in future existences (not ital.)

karma yoga Hinduism selfless action (two words, not ital.)

Karnak site in Egypt of monuments of ancient Thebes; cf. **Carnac**

Karnataka state in SW India

Karnatic use **Carnatic**

Kärnten German name for **Carinthia**

Karoo (also **Karroo**) semi-desert plateau in South Africa

karoshi in Japan, death through overwork (not ital.)

Karoshthi (also **Karoshti**) one of the two oldest alphabets in the Indian subcontinent; cf. **Brahmi**

kart small motor-racing vehicle

kasbah (also **casbah**) citadel of a North African city

Kashmir region on the border of India and NE Pakistan □ **Kashmiri**

kashrut (also **kashruth**) Jewish law

concerning food and ritual objects
katabolism use **catabolism**
katakana angular form of Japanese syllabic writing; cf. **hiragana**
katana long samurai sword (not ital.)
Kathak northern Indian classical dancing with mime (cap.)
Kathakali southern Indian classical dancing with masks and mime (cap.)
katharevousa literary form of modern Greek (lower case); cf. **demotic**
Katharina character in Shakespeare's *The Taming of the Shrew*
Katharine characters in Shakespeare's *Love's Labour's Lost* and *Henry V*
Kathmandu capital of Nepal (not **Katmandu**)
kathode use **cathode**
Katowice city in SW Poland
Kattegat strait between Sweden and Denmark
katydid large North American cricket
Kauffmann, (Maria Anna Catherina) Angelica (1740–1807), Swiss painter
Kaunas city in southern Lithuania
Kaunda, Kenneth (David) (b.1924), president of Zambia 1964–91
kauri pl. **kauris** New Zealand tree
Kawasaki city on the SE coast of Honshu, Japan
kayak (**kayaks, kayaking, kayaked**) (use) a canoe of an Inuit type
Kazakhstan republic in central Asia □ **Kazakh**
KB 1 Comput. kilobyte(s) **2** King's Bench **3** Chess king's bishop
Kb Comput. kilobit
KBE Knight Commander of the Order of the British Empire
KBP Chess king's bishop's pawn
Kbps kilobits per second
Kbyte kilobyte(s)
KC King's Counsel
kc kilocycle(s)
kč (Czech) koruna
kcal kilocalorie(s)
KCB Knight Commander of the Order of the Bath
KCL King's College London
KCMG Knight Commander of the Order of St Michael and St George
kc/s kilocycles per second
KCVO Knight Commander of the Royal Victorian Order
kea New Zealand parrot
Kean, Edmund (1787–1833), English actor
Keane, Roy (b.1971), Irish footballer
Keats, John (1795–1821), English poet □ **Keatsian**
kebab (N. Amer. also **kabob**) food on a skewer or spit
Keble, John (1792–1866), English churchman, founder of **Keble College**, Oxford
Kedah state of NW Malaysia
kedgeree rice dish
Keele town in Staffordshire
keelhaul subject to old naval punishment (one word)
keelson (also **kelson**) structure fastening a ship's floor to its keel
keep-fit exercises to maintain physical fitness (hyphen)
keepnet, keepsake (one word)
keeshond Dutch breed of dog
Kefallinía mod. Gk name for **Cephalonia**
keffiyeh (also **kaffiyeh**) Arab headdress (not ital.)
Keflavik fishing port in Iceland
keftedes Greek meatballs (not ital.)
keiretsu pl. same, Japanese business conglomerate (not ital.)
Kelantan state of northern Malaysia
kelim var. of **kilim**
Kellogg Pact (also **Kellogg–Briand Pact**) 1928 treaty renouncing war
Kelmscott Press 1891–8, founded by William Morris
kelpie water spirit (not **-y**)
kelson var. of **keelson**
Kelt, Keltic use **Celt, Celtic**
Kelvin, William Thomson, 1st Baron (1824–1907), British physicist
kelvin SI unit of temperature (lower case; abbrev. **K**)
Kelvin scale temperature scale (one cap.)
Kempe, Margery (*c.*1373–*c.*1440), English mystic
Kempis see **Thomas à Kempis**

Kendal Green woollen cloth (caps)
kendo Japanese form of fencing with bamboo swords
Keneally, Thomas (Michael) (b.1935), Australian novelist
Kennedy 1 John F(itzgerald) (1917–63), 35th president of the US 1961–3 **2** Robert (Francis) (1925–68), US Attorney General 1961–4 **3** Edward (Moore) (1932–2009), US Senator
Kennedy, Cape name for **Cape Canaveral** 1963–73
kennel v. (**kennelling, kennelled**; US one **-l-**)
Kennelly layer (also **Kennelly–Heaviside layer**) another name for **E-layer**
Kent county in SE England □ **Kentish**
Kentucky state in the south-eastern US (official abbrev. **Ky.**, postal **KY**) □ **Kentuckian**
Kentucky Derby horse race (caps)
Kenya country in East Africa □ **Kenyan**
Kenyatta, Jomo (*c.*1891–1978), president of Kenya 1964–78
kepi pl. **kepis** French military peaked cap (no accent, not ital.) [Fr. *képi*]
Kepler, Johannes (1571–1630), German astronomer □ **Keplerian**
Kerala state on the coast of SW India □ **Keralite**
keratin constituent of hair, hoofs, etc.
kerb (US **curb**)
kerb-crawling (hyphen)
kerb drill (two words)
kerbside, kerbstone (one word)
kerfuffle commotion or fuss (not **cur-**)
Kerguelen Islands group of islands in the southern Indian Ocean
Kérkira mod. Gk name for **Corfu**
kermes red dye from scale insect
kern[1] Printing adjust spacing between characters to be printed
kern[2] (also **kerne**) hist. Irish foot soldier
kernel edible part of a nut (not **-al**)
Kernow Cornish name for **Cornwall**
kerosene (also **kerosine**) petroleum fuel
Kerouac, Jack (1922–69), American novelist and poet
kerseymere twilled woollen cloth
Kesey, Ken (Elton) (1935–2001), American novelist
Keswick town in Cumbria, NW England
ketchup (US also **catsup**; not **catchup** (arch.))
kettledrum (one word)
Keuper European rocks of Upper Triassic age
keV kilo-electronvolt(s)
key Caribbean island or reef
keyboard (one word)
key grip person in charge of a film crew's camera equipment (two words)
keyholder, keyhole (one word)
Key Largo resort island off the south coast of Florida
Keynes, John Maynard, 1st Baron (1883–1946), English economist □ **Keynesian**
keynote, keypad (one word)
key ring (two words)
Keys, House of see **House of Keys**
key signature (two words)
Key Stage fixed stage of UK national curriculum (caps)
Keystone US silent film company remembered for the Keystone Kops
keystone, keystroke (one word)
Key West city in southern Florida
keyword (one word)
KG Knight of the Order of the Garter
kg kilogram(s) (no point)
KGB state security police (1954–91) of the former USSR
Kgs Kings (in biblical references)
Khachaturian, Aram (Ilich) (1903–78), Soviet composer
Khakassia autonomous republic in south central Russia
khaki pl. **khakis** dull brownish-yellow colour or cloth (not ital.)
khalif use **caliph** exc. in specialist contexts
Khalsa the body of fully initiated Sikhs (cap., not ital.)
khamsin hot wind in Egypt
khan[1] title of rulers in central Asia, Afghanistan, etc. (cap. in titles)
khan[2] inn for travellers in the Middle East
Kharg Island small island at the head of the Persian Gulf
Khartoum capital of Sudan

khat leaves used as a stimulant
Khayyám see **Omar Khayyám**
Khedive viceroy of Egypt under Turkish rule 1867–1914 (cap.)
Khmer pl. same or **Khmers** ancient or modern inhabitant of Cambodia
Khmer Republic official name for **Cambodia** 1970–5
Khmer Rouge communist guerrilla organization ruling Cambodia 1975–9
Khoikhoi (also **Khoi**) pl. same, member of an indigenous people of southern Africa; use in preference to **Hottentot**
Khoisan southern African language family
Khomeini, Ruhollah (1900–89), Iranian Shiite Muslim leader; known as **Ayatollah Khomeini**
Khorramshahr oil port in western Iran
Khrushchev, Nikita (Sergeevich) (1894–1971), premier of the USSR 1958–64 □ **Khrushchevian**
khus-khus the extract vetiver; cf. **cous-cous**
Khyber Pass mountain pass between Pakistan and Afghanistan
kHz kilohertz (cap. *H*)
ki var. of **chi**
kiang Tibetan wild ass
Kiangsi var. of **Jiangxi**
Kiangsu var. of **Jiangsu**
kia ora New Zealand greeting
kibbutz pl. **kibbutzim** communal settlement in Israel
kibosh (in **put the kibosh on**) put an end to
kickback illicit payment for help (one word)
kick-boxing (hyphen)
kick-off n. (hyphen, two words as verb)
kickshaw fancy but insubstantial dish (one word)
kick-start (noun and verb; hyphen)
kidnap (**kidnapping, kidnapped**; US also one **-p-**) □ **kidnapper**
kidney bean (two words)
kidology deliberate teasing with untruths (one *d*)
Kiel naval port in northern Germany
kielbasa Polish garlic sausage
Kiel Canal waterway in NW Germany
Kieselguhr diatomaceous earth (two caps)
Kierkegaard, Søren (Aabye) (1813–55), Danish philosopher □ **Kierkegaardian**
Kiev capital of Ukraine; Ukrainian name **Kyiv**
Kigali capital of Rwanda
Kikuyu pl. same or **Kikuyus** member of a Kenyan people
Kilauea volcano on the island of Hawaii
kilderkin cask for liquids
kilim (also **kelim**) flat-woven carpet or rug (lower case)
Kilimanjaro, Mount extinct volcano in northern Tanzania
Kilkenny town and county in the Republic of Ireland
Killarney town in the Republic of Ireland
killick stone used as an anchor
killing field (two words)
killjoy (one word)
kilo pl. **kilos** kilogram
kilo- factor of 1,000, or 1,024 in computing (abbrev. **K**)
kilobit 1,024 bits of computer memory or data (abbrev. **Kb**)
kilobyte 1,024 bytes of computer memory or data (abbrev. **KB**)
kilocalorie 1,000 calories, one large calorie (abbrev. **kcal**)
kilocycle former unit, one kilohertz (abbrev. **kc**)
kilogram (also **kilogramme**) SI unit of mass equal to 1,000 grams (abbrev. **kg**)
kilohertz 1,000 cycles per second (abbrev. **kHz**)
kilojoule 1,000 joules (abbrev. **kJ**)
kilolitre (US **kiloliter**) 1,000 litres (abbrev. **kl**)
kilometre (US **kilometer**) 1,000 metres (abbrev. **km**)
kiloton (also **kilotonne**) 1,000 tons of TNT (abbrev. **kt**)
kilovolt 1,000 volts (abbrev. **kV**)
kilowatt 1,000 watts (abbrev. **kW**)
kilowatt-hour 1,000 watts per hour (hyphen; abbrev. **kWh**)
Kimberley 1 city in Northern Cape, South Africa **2** plateau region in Western Australia
Kim Il-sung (1912–94), first premier of

North Korea 1948–72 and president 1972–94

Kim Jong-il (1942–2011), president of North Korea 1994–2011

Kim Jong-un (b.1982/3), president of North Korea since 2011

kimono pl. **kimonos** Japanese robe with wide sleeves □ **kimonoed**

kinaesthesia (US **kinesthesia**) awareness of the parts of one's body □ **kinaesthetic**

Kincardineshire former county of eastern Scotland

kindergarten nursery school

kind-hearted (hyphen)

kinesis pl. **kineses** movement, motion

kinesthesia US var. of **kinaesthesia**

kinfolk var. of **kinsfolk**

king cap. in titles (*King Henry*) and often *the King*, but *king of the Visigoths*; style is *King Edward VI* or *King Edward the Sixth*, not *the VI* or *VIth*; chess abbrev. **K**

kingbird American flycatcher (one word)

King Charles spaniel (no apostrophe)

king cobra, king crab (two words)

kingfish large sporting fish (one word)

King James Bible (caps, no apostrophe)

King John Shakespeare play (abbrev. ***John***)

King Kong ape-like monster in film of 1933

King Lear Shakespeare play (abbrev. ***Lear***)

kingmaker (one word); see also **Warwick**

King of Arms a chief herald; the three Kings of Arms at the College of Arms are Garter, Clarenceux, and Norroy and Ulster

kingpin (one word)

king post upright post in a roof (two words)

King Richard the Second Shakespeare play (abbrev. ***Rich. II***)

King Richard the Third Shakespeare play (abbrev. ***Rich. III***)

Kings either of two books of the Old Testament (abbrev. **1 Kings, 2 Kings**)

king's bishop Chess (lower case, apostrophe)

King's College Cambridge (apostrophe)

King's College London (apostrophe, no comma)

King's Cross London and Sydney (apostrophe)

king-sized (also **king-size**) (hyphen)

king's knight Chess (lower case, apostrophe)

King's Langley, King's Lynn Hertfordshire and Norfolk (apostrophe)

kingsnake North American constrictor (one word)

king's pawn, king's rook Chess (lower case, apostrophe)

Kingsteignton town in Devon (one word)

Kingston 1 capital of Jamaica **2** port on Lake Ontario, Canada

Kingston upon Hull official name for **Hull** (no hyphens, two caps)

Kingston upon Thames town in Surrey (no hyphens, two caps)

Kingstown 1 capital of St Vincent **2** area of Dublin

Kingswinford town in the West Midlands (one word)

kinkajou nocturnal mammal of Central and South America

Kinross-shire former county of east central Scotland (hyphen)

kinsfolk (also **kinfolk**)

Kinshasa capital of the Democratic Republic of Congo (Zaire)

Kintyre peninsula on the west coast of Scotland

Kioto use **Kyoto**

kippa (also **kippah**) Orthodox Jew's skullcap (not ital.)

kirby grip (also trademark **Kirbigrip**) hairgrip

Kirchhoff, Gustav Robert (1824–87), German physicist

Kirghiz var. of **Kyrgyz**

Kirghizia (also **Kyrgyzia**) former name for **Kyrgyzstan**

Kiribati country in the SW Pacific including the Gilbert Islands

Kirin var. of **Jilin**

Kiritimati island in the Pacific Ocean

kirk Sc. church; (**the Kirk**) the Church of Scotland

Kirkcaldy town in Fife

Kirkcudbright town in Dumfries and Galloway
Kirkcudbrightshire former county of SW Scotland
Kirkuk city in northern Iraq
kirpan Sikh's short sword or knife
kirsch (also **kirschwasser**) cherry liqueur
Kisangani city in the Democratic Republic of Congo (Zaire)
Kishinyov Russ. name for **Chişinău**
Kislev (also **Kislew**) (in the Jewish calendar) third month of the civil and ninth of the religious year
kiss-curl (hyphen)
kissogram (also trademark **Kissagram**)
kist var. of **cist**
Kiswahili see **Swahili**
kitbag (one word)
kit car (two words)
kit-cat canvas used for life-size portraits showing the head, shoulders, and one or both hands (hyphen)
kitchen garden, **kitchen paper**, **kitchen roll** (two words)
kitchen-sink (of drama) depicting drab reality (hyphen)
Kitemark trademark kite-shaped mark on goods approved by the British Standards Institution (cap.)
kitsch objects in poor taste
Kitty Hawk town in North Carolina (two words)
Kitzbühel town in the Tyrol, Austria
kiwi pl. **kiwis** New Zealand bird
kiwi fruit pl. same, fruit with green flesh
kJ kilojoule(s) (one cap.)
KKK Ku Klux Klan
KKt Chess king's knight
KKtP Chess king's knight's pawn
KL Kuala Lumpur
kl kilolitre(s) (no point)
klaxon hooter (cap. as trademark)
Klee, Paul (1879–1940), Swiss painter
Kleenex pl. same or **Kleenexes** trademark (cap.)
Klein 1 Calvin (Richard) (b.1942), American fashion designer **2** Melanie (1882–1960), Austrian-born psychoanalyst
Klemperer, Otto (1885–1973), German-born conductor
klepht Greek independence fighter (lower case)
kleptomania recurrent urge to steal
Klerk, F. W. de, see **de Klerk**
klezmer traditional Jewish music
klieg light lamp used in filming
Klimt, Gustav (1862–1918), Austrian painter and designer
Klingon member of a humanoid alien species in *Star Trek*
Klondike tributary of the Yukon River in NW Canada (not **-dyke**)
Klosters winter-sports resort in Switzerland
klystron electron tube that generates microwaves
km kilometre(s) (no point)
K Mart US retail chain (caps, no hyphen)
km/h kilometres per hour
KN Chess king's knight
kn. knot(s) (point)
knackwurst (also **knockwurst**) German sausage (lower case)
knee breeches (two words)
kneecap (one word)
knee-deep, **knee-high** (hyphen)
kneehole (one word)
knee-jerk (hyphen)
kneel (past and past part. **knelt** or chiefly N. Amer. also **kneeled**)
knees-up (hyphen)
Knesset modern Israeli parliament
Knickerbocker New Yorker (cap.)
Knickerbocker Glory ice-cream dessert in a tall glass (caps)
knickerbockers breeches gathered at the knee or calf (lower case)
knickers 1 Brit. women's or girl's underpants **2** N. Amer. knickerbockers
knick-knack (also **nick-nack**) (hyphen)
knife-edge (hyphen)
knifepoint (one word)
knight (abbrev. **Kt**, **Knt**, in chess **N**)
knight bachelor pl. **knights bachelor** knight not belonging to any particular order
Knightbridge title of a Cambridge professorship (not **Knights-**)
knight errant pl. **knight errants** or

knights errant (two words)
Knightsbridge area of London
Knights Hospitaller military and religious order (not **Hospitallers**)
Knights Templar religious and military order (not **Templars**)
kniphofia red-hot poker (plant)
knit (past and past part. **knitted** or (esp. in the sense 'unite') **knit**)
knitting machine, knitting needle (two words)
knitwear (one word)
knobkerrie (also **knobkierie**) short stick with a knob at the top
knockabout (one word)
knock-back, knock-down n. (hyphen, two words as verb)
knock knees (two words) □ **knock-kneed**
knock-on adj. (hyphen, two words as verb)
knockout n. (one word, two words as verb)
knockwurst var. of **knackwurst**
Knole places in Kent and Somerset
Knole sofa (one cap.)
Knossos city of Minoan Crete (not **Cn-**)
knot pl. same or **knots** one nautical mile per hour (abbrev. **kn.**, **kt**)
knotgrass, knothole, knotweed, knotwork (one word)
know-all, know-how (hyphen)
knowledgeable (not **-gable**)
KNP Chess king's knight's pawn
knucklebone (one word)
knuckleduster (one word)
knurl small knob or ridge
Knut var. of **Canute**
Knutsford town in Cheshire
KO[1] kick-off
KO[2] (**KO's, KO'ing, KO'd**) (subject to) a knockout
koala (not **koala bear**)
Kobe port in central Japan, on Honshu
København Danish name for **Copenhagen**
kobo pl. same, monetary unit of Nigeria
Köchel number number in the complete catalogue of Mozart's works compiled by L. von Köchel (abbrev. **K**)
Kodály, Zoltán (1882–1967), Hungarian composer
Koestler, Arthur (1905–83), Hungarian-born British novelist
kofta pl. same or **koftas** Indian and Middle Eastern savoury ball
kohen (also **cohen**) pl. **kohanim** or **cohens** (in Judaism) member of a priestly caste
Koh-i-noor famous Indian diamond (hyphens, one cap.)
Kohl, Helmut (b.1930), Chancellor of the Federal Republic of Germany 1982–90 and of Germany 1990–8
kohl black powder used as eye make-up
kohlrabi pl. **kohlrabies** variety of cabbage
koi (also **koi carp**) pl. same, ornamental Japanese carp
koine Greek language between the classical and Byzantine eras (lower case, not ital.)
kola see **cola**
Kolkata official name for **Calcutta**
kolkhoz pl. same, **kolkhozes, kolkhozy** collective farm in the former USSR (not ital.)
Köln German name for **Cologne**
Kol Nidre Aramaic prayer sung on the eve of Yom Kippur
Komodo dragon large monitor lizard (one cap.)
Kondratiev, Nicolai D. (1892–*c.*1935), Russian economist
Königgrätz Ger. name for **Hradec Králové**
Königsberg former name for **Kaliningrad**
Kon-Tiki raft in which Thor Heyerdahl sailed from Peru to Polynesia (hyphen, caps)
kookaburra Australasian kingfisher
Kooning, Willem de, see **de Kooning**
Koori pl. **Kooris** an Australian Aboriginal (cap.)
kopek (also **copeck** or **kopeck**) monetary unit of Russia and some other countries of the former USSR
koppie (also **kopje**) S. Afr. small hill
Koran (also **Quran** or **Qur'an**) Islamic sacred book (not ital.) [Arab. *qur'ān*]
kore pl. **korai** Greek statue of a woman in long robes
Korea peninsular region of east Asia divided into North Korea (the **Demo-**

cratic People's Republic of Korea) and South Korea (the **Republic of Korea**) □ **Korean**

Korean War war 1950–3 between North and South Korea

korfball game similar to basketball

Kórinthos mod. Gk name for **Corinth**

Kortrijk city in western Belgium; French name **Courtrai**

koruna basic monetary unit of the Czech Republic and of Slovakia (abbrev. **kč** (Czech Republic), **ks** (Slovakia))

Kos (also **Cos**) Greek island in the SE Aegean

Kosciusko, Thaddeus (1746–1817), Polish soldier and patriot

kosher meeting the requirements of Jewish dietary law

Kosovo autonomous province of Serbia; Albanian name **Kosova** □ **Kosovan, Kosovar**

Kosygin, Aleksei (Nikolaevich) (1904–80), premier of the USSR 1964–80

Kotzebue, August von (1761–1819), German dramatist

koumiss fermented mare's milk

kourbash var. of **kurbash**

kouros pl. **kouroi** Greek statue of a young man

Kowloon peninsula on the SE coast of China, part of Hong Kong

kowtow act subserviently

Kozhikode seaport in SW India; former name **Calicut**

KP Chess king's pawn

kph (also **k.p.h.**) kilometres per hour (in scientific writing, use **km/h**)

KR Chess king's rook

Kr the chemical element krypton (no point)

kraal 1 traditional African enclosed village **2** enclosure for livestock

Krafft-Ebing, Richard von (1840–1902), German psychologist

kraft paper brown wrapping paper

Krakatoa volcanic island in Indonesia, scene of a great eruption in 1883; Indonesian name **Krakatau**

Kraków Pol. name for **Cracow**

kremlin Russian citadel; (**the Kremlin**) citadel in Moscow housing the Russian or USSR government

Kremlinology study of Russian or USSR policies (cap.)

Kreutzer, Rodolphe (1766–1831), German-French violinist; (the ***'Kreutzer' Sonata***) by Beethoven; (***The Kreutzer Sonata***) novella by Tolstoy

kriegspiel (lower case, not ital.) **1** war game **2** form of chess

Kriemhild Burgundian princess in the *Nibelungenlied*

krill pl. same, planktonic crustacean

Krishna Hindu god, the most important incarnation of Vishnu □ **Krishnaism**

Kristallnacht night of Nazi violence against Jews and their property, 9–10 November 1938 (cap., not ital.)

Kríti mod. Gk name for **Crete**

krona 1 pl. **kronor** monetary unit of Sweden **2** pl. **kronur** monetary unit of Iceland

krone pl. **kroner** monetary unit of Denmark and Norway

Kronos var. of **Cronus**

kroon pl. **kroons** or **krooni** monetary unit of Estonia until 2011

Kropotkin, Prince Peter (1842–1921), Russian anarchist

KRP Chess king's rook's pawn

Kru pl. same, member of a people of Liberia and Côte d'Ivoire (Ivory Coast)

Kruger, Stephanus Johannes Paulus (1825–1904), South African statesman

krugerrand South African gold coin (one word, lower case)

krummhorn (also **crumhorn**) medieval wind instrument

Krupp, Alfred (1812–87), German arms manufacturer

krypton chemical element of atomic number 36, a noble gas (symbol **Kr**)

KS 1 Kansas (postal abbrev.) **2** King's Scholar

ks (Slovakian) koruna

Kshatriya member of the Hindu military caste (cap., not ital.)

KStJ Knight of the Order of St John (no points, three caps)

KT 1 Knight of the Order of the Thistle **2** Knight Templar

Kt knight (no point)

kt (no point) **1** kiloton(s) **2** knot(s)

(unit of speed)
Kuala Lumpur capital of Malaysia
Kublai Khan (1216–94), Mongol emperor of China
Kubla Khan poem by Coleridge (1816)
kuccha (also **kachha**) short trousers worn by Sikhs
kudos honour for an achievement (sing., not ital.)
kudu pl. same or **kudus** African antelope
kudzu climbing plant
Kufic (also **Cufic**) early form of the Arabic alphabet
Kuiper belt solar system beyond Neptune (one cap.)
Ku Klux Klan (abbrev. **KKK**) US right-wing secret society (no hyphens, not **Klu**)
kukri pl. **kukris** curved Gurkha knife
kulak Russian peasant proprietor
Kultur German civilization and culture (cap., ital.)
Kulturkampf conflict 1872–87 between the German government and the papacy (cap., ital.)
Kumbh Mela Hindu festival held every twelve years
kümmel sweet liqueur (lower case, not ital., accent)
kumquat (also **cumquat**) citrus fruit like an orange
kuna pl. same or **kunas** monetary unit of Croatia
kundalini (in yoga) female energy at the base of the spine (not ital.)
Kundera, Milan (b.1929), Czech novelist
kung fu Chinese martial art (two words)
K'ung Fu-tzu see **Confucius**
Kuomintang (also **Guomindang**) Chinese nationalist party
kurbash (also **kourbash**) whip used for punishment in Turkey and Egypt
kurchatovium former name for **rutherfordium**
Kurd member of a people of Kurdistan, an area of the Middle East ◻ **Kurdish**
Kuril Islands (also **Kurile Islands** or **the Kurils**) chain of islands between the Sea of Okhotsk and the North Pacific
Kurosawa, Akira (1910–98), Japanese film director
kursaal hall for visitors at a spa (lower case, not ital.)
Kursk city in SW Russia
kurta (also **kurtha**) loose collarless shirt
Kuşadasi town in western Turkey
Kutch, Rann of salt marsh in the north-west of the Indian subcontinent
Kuwait country on the NW coast of the Persian Gulf ◻ **Kuwaiti**
Kuznets Basin (also **Kuznetsk**) industrial region of southern Russia
kV kilovolt(s) (one cap.)
kvass fermented Russian drink
kW kilowatt(s) (one cap.)
Kwa African language
kwacha monetary unit of Zambia and Malawi
KwaNdebele former homeland in South Africa for the Ndebele people (one word, two caps)
Kwangchow var. of **Guangzhou**
Kwangtung var. of **Guangdong**
kwanza pl. same or **kwanzas** monetary unit of Angola
Kwanzaa secular African American festival
kwashiorkor form of malnutrition
KwaZulu-Natal province of South Africa (hyphen, three caps)
kWh kilowatt-hour(s) (one cap.)
KY Kentucky (postal abbrev.)
Ky. Kentucky (official abbrev.)
kyat pl. same or **kyats** monetary unit of Burma (Myanmar)
Kyd, Thomas (1558–94), English dramatist
Kyiv Ukrainian name for **Kiev**
kylie Austral. a boomerang
kylin mythical composite animal
kylix pl. **kylikes** or **kylixes** Greek cup on a tall stem
Kyoto city in central Japan (not **Kioto**)
Kyrgyz (also **Kirghiz**) pl. same, member of a people of central Asia
Kyrgyzstan mountainous country in central Asia; former name **Kirghizia**, **Kyrgyzia**
Kyrie (also **Kyrie eleison**) 'Lord have mercy', an invocation used in Christian liturgies
kyu grade of proficiency in martial arts
Kyushu most southerly of the four main islands of Japan

L

L 1 pl. **Ls** or **L's** 12th letter of the alphabet **2** Chem. Avogadro's constant **3** Phys. inductance **4** (**L.**) Lake, Loch, or Lough **5** (**L.**) Latin **6** Brit. learner driver **7** (**L.**) Linnaeus **8** lire **9** (also **l**) Roman numeral for 50

l 1 left **2** length **3** Chem. liquid **4** litre(s)

l. 1 pl. **ll.** leaf **2** pl. **ll.** line **3** arch. pound(s) (money; placed after figures)

£ pound(s) (placed before figures, closed up) [initial letter of L. *libra* 'pound, balance']

LA 1 Library Association **2** Los Angeles **3** Louisiana (postal abbrev.)

La the chemical element lanthanum (no point)

La. Louisiana (official abbrev.)

la var. of **lah**

laager circle of wagons

label v. (**labelling, labelled**; US one **-l-**)

labial relating to the lips or a labium

labia majora, labia minora outer (or inner) folds of the vulva (not ital.)

labium pl. **labia** liplike structure

labor etc. US var. of **labour** etc.

Labor Day (in the US and Canada) the first Monday in September (caps)

Labor Party Australia (not **Labour**)

labour (US **labor**) cap. in a political context; abbrev. **Lab.**

laboured, labourer (US **labored, laborer**)

labour exchange, labour force (two words)

labour-intensive (hyphen)

Labour Party UK political party (caps)

Labrador[1] coastal region of eastern Canada

Labrador[2] breed of retriever (cap.)

labrum pl. **labra** structure corresponding to a lip

labyrinth (not **labi-**)

LAC Leading Aircraftman

lac resin

Lacedaemonian Spartan

lacemaking (one word)

lace-up adj. (hyphen, two words as verb)

Lachesis Gk Mythol. one of the three Fates

lachrymal (also **lacrimal**) connected with weeping or tears

lachrymose tearful or sad (not **lacri-**)

lackadaisical lacking enthusiasm

lackaday arch. expression of regret, grief, etc. (one word)

lackey pl. **lackeys** liveried servant

lacklustre (US **lackluster**)

Lac Léman Fr. name for **Lake Geneva**

Laconia (also **Lakonia**) region of Greece

La Coruña Sp. name for **Corunna**

lacquer (not **laquer**)

lacrimal var. of **lachrymal**

lacrimose use **lachrymose**

lacuna pl. **lacunae** or **lacunas** missing section

LACW Leading Aircraftwoman

lacy (not **-ey**)

ladder-back chair (hyphen)

laddie young boy (not **laddy**)

la-di-da (also **lah-di-dah**) pretentious or snobbish (hyphens)

ladies, the women's public toilet (lower case)

ladies' fingers okra (two words, apostrophe)

Ladin dialect of parts of Italy and Switzerland

Ladino language of some Sephardic Jews

ladino pl. **ladinos** clover grown as fodder (lower case)

lady cap. as title for peeresses etc.

Lady Chatterley's Lover novel by D. H. Lawrence (1928)

Lady Day 25 May, the feast of the Annunciation (caps)

lady-in-waiting pl. **ladies-in-waiting** (hyphens)

ladykiller, ladylike (one word)
Lady Margaret Hall Oxford college (abbrev. **LMH**)
ladyship (**Her/Your** etc. **Ladyship**) form of address for a titled woman (caps)
lady's maid pl. **ladies' maids** (apostrophe, no hyphen)
Ladysmith town in KwaZulu-Natal, South Africa
lady's slipper orchid (apostrophe)
Lafite, Château (in full **Lafite-Rothschild**) claret
La Fontaine, Jean de (1621–95), French poet
Lag b'Omer Jewish festival
La Gioconda another name for **Mona Lisa** (not ital.)
Lagos chief city of Nigeria
Lagrange, Joseph Louis, Comte de (1736–1813), French mathematician □ **Lagrangian**
LaGuardia airport, New York (one word, two caps)
lah (also **la**) Mus. note in tonic sol-fa
La Habana Sp. name for **Havana**
lah-di-dah var. of **la-di-da**
Lahore city in Pakistan
Laibach Ger. name for **Ljubljana**
laid-back (hyphen)
laid paper paper with a ribbed appearance; cf. **wove paper**
laissez-aller absence of restraint (hyphen, not ital.; not **laisser-**)
laissez-faire letting things take their own course (hyphen, not ital.; not **laisser-**)
laity lay people
lake (cap. in names)
Lake Baikal, Lake Erie, etc. see **Baikal, Lake**; **Erie, Lake**, etc.
Lake District, Lakeland region of Cumbria
Lake Poets Samuel Taylor Coleridge, Robert Southey, and William Wordsworth (two words, caps)
lakeside (one word)
Lake Wobegon fictional US town in the stories of Garrison Keillor (not **Woebegone**)
lakh pl. same or **lakhs** Ind. one hundred thousand; cf. **crore**
Lakonia var. of **Laconia**
Lallans Scottish literary form of English
Lalla Rookh novel by Thomas Moore (1817)
La Louvière city in SW Belgium
Lam. Lamentations
lama spiritual leader in Tibetan Buddhism; see also **Dalai Lama, Panchen Lama**; cf. **llama**
Lamaism Tibetan Buddhism (cap.)
Lamarck, Jean Baptiste de (1744–1829), French naturalist □ **Lamarckian**
lambada Brazilian dance
lambaste (also **lambast**) criticize harshly □ **lambasting**
lambda **1** eleventh letter of the Greek alphabet (Λ, λ), transliterated as 'l' **2** (λ) wavelength
lambskin (one word)
lamb's lettuce salad plant (two words, apostrophe)
lambswool (one word, no apostrophe)
LAMDA London Academy of Music and Dramatic Art
lamé fabric with metallic threads (accent, not ital.)
lamebrain, lamebrained (one word)
lamella pl. **lamellae** thin plate
Lamentations (in full **the Lamentations of Jeremiah**) book of the Old Testament (abbrev. **Lam.**)
lamia pl. **lamias** or **lamiae** **1** mythical monster with a woman's body **2** (**Lamia**) poem by Keats (1819)
lamina pl. **laminae** thin layer
Lammas (also **Lammas Day**) 1 August, formerly a harvest festival
lammergeier (also **lammergeyer**) large vulture
lamplight, lamplit (one word)
lamp post (two words)
lamprey pl. **lampreys** eel-like fish
lampshade (one word)
LAN Comput. local area network
Lanarkshire former county of SW central Scotland
Lancashire county of NW England (abbrev. **Lancs.**)
lance bombardier rank in a British

artillery regiment (cap. in titles; abbrev. **LBdr**)
lance corporal rank in the British army (cap. in titles; abbrev. **LCpl**)
Lancelot (also **Launcelot**) knight in Arthurian legend
lancet small surgical knife; (***The Lancet***) medical journal
Land pl. ***Länder*** province of Germany or Austria (cap., ital.)
landau type of horse-drawn carriage (lower case, not ital.)
landfall, landfill, landholder, landlady (one word)
landgrave hist. count with territorial jurisdiction (cap. in titles)
landing craft, landing gear, landing light, landing strip (two words)
Ländler Austrian folk dance (ital., cap., accent)
landline, landlocked, landlord, landlubber, landmark (one word)
land mass (two words)
landmine, landowner (one word)
Land Rover trademark rugged vehicle (two words)
landscape (of a format) wider than it is high; cf. **portrait**
Land's End tip of SW Cornwall
landslide, landslip (one word)
Landsmål another name for **Nynorsk**
langouste spiny lobster as food
langoustine Norway lobster as food
lang syne long ago (two words)
langue a language viewed as an abstract system (Fr., ital.); cf. ***parole***
langue de chat finger-shaped biscuit (no hyphens, not ital.)
Languedoc area of southern France
langue d'oc form of medieval French spoken south of the Loire (Fr., ital.)
Languedoc-Roussillon region of southern France (hyphen)
langue d'oïl form of medieval French spoken north of the Loire (Fr., ital.)
languor tiredness or inactivity □ **languorous**
langur long-tailed Asian monkey
laniard use **lanyard**
La Niña irregular changes in weather patterns of the equatorial Pacific, complementary to those of El Niño
lanolin fat in sheep's wool (not **-ine**)
lanthanum chemical element of atomic number 57 (symbol **La**)
lanthorn arch. lantern
lanyard short rope (not **laniard**)
Lanzarote one of the Canary Islands
Laodicean half-hearted
Laois (also **Laoighis, Leix**) county of the Republic of Ireland; former name **Queen's County**
Laos country in SE Asia □ **Laotian**
La Palma one of the Canary Islands
La Pasionaria see **Ibárruri Gómez**
La Paz 1 capital of Bolivia **2** city in Mexico
lap belt, lap dancing (two words)
lapdog (one word)
Laphroaig 1 village on Islay, Scotland **2** whisky
lapis lazuli (two words, not ital.)
Lapland region of northern Europe (one word)
Lapp prefer **Sami** in modern contexts
lapsang souchong tea
lapsus calami pl. same, slip of the pen (L., ital.)
lapsus linguae pl. same, slip of the tongue (L., ital.)
laptop (one word)
Laputa flying island in Swift's *Gulliver's Travels*
larboard Naut. arch. term for **port**
lardon (also **lardoon**) piece of bacon for larding
lares Roman household gods (lower case, not ital.); cf. **penates**
largesse (also **largess**) generosity in giving (not ital.)
larghetto pl. **larghettos** Mus. in a fairly slow tempo
largo pl. **largos** Mus. in a slow tempo
lari pl. same or **laris** monetary unit of Georgia
lariat rope used as a lasso
La Rioja autonomous region of northern Spain
La Rochefoucauld, François de Marsillac, Duc de (1613–80), French writer
La Rochelle town in western France
Larousse, Pierre (1817–75), French

lexicographer
larva pl. **larvae** immature form of an insect
larynx pl. **larynges** voice box □ **laryngeal, laryngitis**
Lascaux cave in SW France
lascivious lustful
laser device that generates an intense beam of light (lower case)
laserdisc (one word)
La Serenissima name for Venice
laser gun, laser printer (two words)
LaserVision trademark laserdisc reproduction system (one word, two caps)
Las Meninas paintings by Velázquez and Picasso (not ***-iñas***)
Las Palmas capital of the Canary Islands
Lassa fever acute viral disease (one cap.)
lassi Indian yogurt or buttermilk drink
lassie young girl (not **lassy**)
lasso n. pl. **lassos** or **lassoes**. v. **lassoes, lassoing, lassoed**
Lassus, Orlande de (*c.*1532–94), Flemish composer; Italian name *Orlando di Lasso*
last-ditch, last-gasp (hyphen)
Last Judgement (caps)
last post bugle call (lower case; it is 'sounded', not played)
Last Supper (caps)
Las Vegas city in Nevada (not **Los**)
lat pl. **lati** or **lats** monetary unit of Latvia
lat. latitude (no point in scientific work)
latecomer (one word)
lateish var. of **latish**
La Tène second phase of the European Iron Age
Lateran Council any of five general councils of the Western Church held between 1123 and 1512–17
latex pl. **latexes** or **latices** milky fluid in rubber tree
lath flat strip of wood
lathe machine for shaping wood etc.
lathi pl. **lathis** Ind. stick used by police
latices pl. of **latex**
latifundium pl. **latifundia** large landed estate or ranch
Latin America Spanish- or Portuguese-speaking parts of the American continent
Latin American (no hyphen even when attrib.)
Latin cross cross in which the lower vertical is the longest part (one cap.)
Latinize (Brit. also **Latinise**) (cap.)
Latino (fem. **Latina**) pl. **Latinos** or **Latinas** Latin American inhabitant of the US
latish (also **lateish**) fairly late
La Tour, Georges de (1593–1652), French painter
Latour, Château claret (two words)
latria RC Ch. supreme worship allowed to God alone; cf. **dulia**
La Trobe University, Melbourne
Latrobe 1 town in Pennsylvania **2** town in Tasmania
latte (also **caffè latte**) Italian white coffee (not ital.)
latter the second of two (not 'last in a series'); cf. **former**
latter-day (hyphen)
Latter-day Saints Mormons (two caps, one hyphen; abbrev. **LDS**)
latticework (one word)
Latvia country on the Baltic Sea; Latvian name **Latvija** □ **Latvian**
laughing gas, laughing stock (two words)
Launcelot var. of **Lancelot**
launch pad (two words)
launderette (also **laundrette**)
laundromat N. Amer. (trademark in the US) launderette
Laurel, (Arthur) Stan(ley Jefferson) (1890–1965), part of the American comedy duo Laurel and Hardy
laurelled (US **laureled**) honoured with a laurel or other award
Laurence 1 (Jean) Margaret (1926–87), Canadian novelist **2** Friar, character in Shakespeare's *Romeo and Juliet*
Laurentian Plateau the Canadian Shield (caps)
laurustinus Mediterranean evergreen (not **laure-**)
Lausanne town in SW Switzerland
lavabo pl. **lavabos** towel or basin used in ritual washing

Lavoisier, Antoine Laurent (1743–94), French scientist
law-abiding (hyphen)
lawbreaker, lawbreaking (one word)
law centre, law court (two words)
lawgiver, lawmaker (one word)
lawnmower (one word)
Lawrence 1 D(avid) H(erbert) (1885–1930), English writer **2** Sir Thomas (1769–1830), English painter **3** T(homas) E(dward) (1888–1935), British soldier and writer; known as **Lawrence of Arabia** □ **Lawrentian** (also **Lawrencian**)
Lawrence, St river in Canada
lawrencium chemical element of atomic number 103 (symbol **Lr**)
lawsuit (one word)
lay (**laying, laid**) place in horizontal position; cf. **lie**
layabout (one word)
lay brother (two words)
lay-by pl. **lay-bys** (hyphen)
lay figure artist's dummy (two words)
layman (one word)
La'youn (also **Laayoune**) capital of Western Sahara
layout, layover n. (one word, two words as verb)
layperson pl. **laypersons** or **laypeople** (one word)
lay reader, lay sister (two words)
lay-up n. (hyphen, two words as verb)
laywoman (one word)
lazaretto pl. **lazarettos** hist. isolation hospital (not ital.)
Lazio region of west central Italy
lazybones pl. same (one word)
lazy Susan revolving tray (one cap.)
lb 1 Cricket leg bye **2** pound(s) (in weight) [L. *libra*]
LBdr Lance Bombardier
LBO leveraged buyout
lbw Cricket leg before wicket
LC Lord Chancellor
l.c. 1 letter of credit **2** *loco citato* [L., 'in the place cited'] **3** lower case
LCD 1 liquid crystal display **2** lowest (or least) common denominator
LCJ Lord Chief Justice
LCM lowest (or least) common multiple
LCpl Lance Corporal
LD 1 N. Amer. learning disability; learning-disabled **2** lethal dose
Ld Lord
LDC less-developed country
Ldg Leading (in naval ranks)
L-driver learner driver (cap., hyphen)
LDS 1 Latter-Day Saints **2** Licentiate in Dental Surgery
LE language engineering
LEA Local Education Authority
lea open area of pasture; cf. **ley**
lead 1 chemical element of atomic number 82 (symbol **Pb**) **2** blank space between lines of type; (in hot-metal setting) metal strip creating this
leaded having lines separated by leads
leader another name for **leading article**
leaders dots or dashes across a page to guide the eye
lead-in n. introduction or preamble (hyphen, two words as verb)
leading amount of blank space between lines of print
leading aircraftman (or **leading aircraftwoman**) RAF rank (abbrev. **LAC, LACW**)
leading article (also **leader**) newspaper article giving the editorial opinion
lead-up n. period before an event (hyphen, two words as verb)
leaf pl. **leaves** single piece of paper; two pages back to back (abbrev. **l.**; pl. **ll.**)
leaflet v. (**leafleting, leafleted**)
Leakey family of Kenyan archaeologists and anthropologists
Leamington Spa town in Warwickshire; official name **Royal Leamington Spa**
lean v. (**leaning, leaned** or Brit. **leant**)
Leander 1 Gk Mythol. young man drowned swimming the Hellespont **2** rowing club in Henley-on-Thames
lean-to pl. **lean-tos** (hyphen)
leap v. (**leaping, leaped** or **leapt**)
leapfrog (one word)
leap year (two words)
Lear Shakespeare's *King Lear*
learn (**learned** or Brit. **learnt**)
learning curve, learning difficulties (two words)

learning disability (N. Amer. abbrev. **LD**) □ **learning-disabled**

leaseback, leasehold, leaseholder (one word)

least common denominator another name for **lowest common denominator** (abbrev. **LCD**)

least common multiple another name for **lowest common multiple** (abbrev. **LCM**)

leastways (also **leastwise**) at least

leatherjacket crane fly's larva (one word)

leatherneck US marine (one word)

Leavis, F(rank) R(aymond) (1895–1978), English literary critic □ **Leavisite**

Lebanon country in the Middle East (not **the Lebanon**) □ **Lebanese**

Lebensraum territory believed to be needed for expansion (Ger., cap., ital.)

Le Carré, John (b.1931), English novelist; pseudonym of *David John Moore Cornwell*

Leconte de Lisle, Charles Marie René (1818–94), French poet

Le Corbusier (1887–1965), French architect; born *Charles Édouard Jeanneret* □ **Corbusian**

lectern preacher's or lecturer's reading stand (not **-urn**)

lecythus pl. **lecythi** Greek narrow-necked vase

LED light-emitting diode

lederhosen leather shorts (lower case, not ital.)

Led Zeppelin English rock group

Lee–Enfield rifle (en rule)

Leeuwenhoek, Antoni van (1632–1723), Dutch naturalist

Leeward Islands group of islands in the Caribbean

leeway (one word)

Le Fanu, Joseph Sheridan (1814–73), Irish novelist

left 1 direction (abbrev. **l**) **2** (**the Left**) left-wing people (cap., treated as sing. or pl.)

Left Bank district of Paris (caps)

left hand (two words, hyphen when attrib.; abbrev. **l.h.**)

left-handed, left-hander (hyphen)

leftover (one word)

left wing (two words, hyphen when attrib.) □ **left-winger**

legalize (Brit. also **legalise**)

legato Mus. smooth

leg before wicket Cricket (no hyphens; abbrev. **lbw**)

leg bye Cricket (no hyphen; abbrev. **lb**)

Léger, Fernand (1881–1955), French painter

legerdemain sleight of hand (not ital.)

leger line (also **ledger line**) Mus. short line above or below the stave

Leghorn 1 old-fashioned name for **Livorno 2** breed of chicken

leghorn fine plaited straw (lower case)

legionnaire member of a legion (two *ns*, not ital.)

legionnaires' disease form of bacterial pneumonia (lower case, apostrophe)

Legion of Honour French order of distinction [Fr. *Légion d'honneur*]

legitimize (Brit. also **legitimise**)

Lego trademark toy of interlocking blocks

leg-of-mutton sleeve (two hyphens)

leg-pull, leg-pulling (hyphen)

legroom (one word)

leg side, leg slip Cricket (two words)

leg spin Cricket (two words) □ **leg-spinner**

leg stump Cricket (two words)

leg-up (hyphen)

leg warmer (two words)

legwork (one word)

Lehár, Franz (Ferencz) (1870–1948), Hungarian composer

Le Havre port in northern France (cap. *L* in English, lower case *l* in Fr.)

lei 1 Polynesian garland **2** pl. of **leu**

Leibniz, Gottfried Wilhelm (1646–1716), German philosopher (not **-itz**) □ **Leibnizian**

Leibovitz, Annie (b.1950), American photographer

Leicestershire county of central England (abbrev. **Leics.**)

Leiden (also **Leyden**) city in the west Netherlands

Leif Ericsson see **Ericsson**

Leighton, Frederic, 1st Baron Leighton of Stretton (1830–96), English artist

Leighton Buzzard town in Bedfordshire
Leinster province of the Republic of Ireland
Leipzig city in east central Germany
leishmaniasis tropical disease
leisurewear (one word)
leitmotif (also **leitmotiv**) recurrent theme (lower case, not ital.; not **-ive**)
Leix var. of **Laois**
Lely, Sir Peter (1618–80), Dutch painter
Le Mans town in NW France (cap. *L* in English, lower case *l* in Fr.)
Lemberg Ger. name for **Lviv**
lemma pl. **lemmas** or **lemmata** item treated in a dictionary
Lemmon, Jack (1925–2001), American actor; born *John Uhler*
lemongrass (one word)
lempira monetary unit of Honduras
lemur Madagascan primate
lending library (two words)
length (in horse racing abbrev. **l**)
lengthways (also **lengthwise**)
Lenin, Vladimir Ilich (1870–1924), first premier of the Soviet Union 1918–24; born *Vladimir Ilich Ulyanov*
Leningrad former name for **St Petersburg**
lenis pl. **lenes** smooth breathing mark in Greek, ʼ
Le Nôtre, André (1613–1700), French landscape gardener
Lent period preceding Easter (cap.) □ **Lenten**
lento pl. **lentos** Mus. to be performed slowly
Lent term university term or High Court session (one cap.)
Leo fifth sign of the zodiac □ **Leonian**
León city in northern Spain (accent)
Leonardo da Vinci (1452–1519), Italian painter
Leoncavallo, Ruggiero (1857–1919), Italian composer
leone monetary unit of Sierra Leone
Leonids annual meteor shower (cap.)
leopard skin (two words, hyphen when attrib.)
Léopoldville former name for **Kinshasa**
leper avoid in literal sense in modern-day contexts
Lepidoptera butterflies and moths □ **lepidopteran, lepidopterous**
leprechaun mischievous Irish sprite (not **lepra-**)
Lesbian person from Lesbos
lesbian homosexual woman (lower case)
Lesbos Greek island in Aegean; mod. Gk name **Lésvos**
lese-majesty treason or disrespect (not ital.) [Fr. *lèse-majesté*]
Lesotho country within South Africa
Lesser Bairam Eid ul-Fitr (see **Eid**)
lesser-known (hyphen)
Les Six (also **the Six**) Parisian composers of the early 20th cent.
Lésvos mod. Gk name for **Lesbos**
let-down n. disappointment (hyphen, two words as verb)
Lethe river in Hades □ **Lethean**
let-off, let-out n. (hyphen, two words as verb)
Lett (person from Latvia) use **Latvian** □ **Lettish**
letter bomb, letter box (two words)
letterform graphic form of a letter of the alphabet (one word)
letterhead printed heading on stationery (one word)
letterpress (one word) **1** printing by pressure on a raised image **2** Brit. text as opposed to illustrations
letterset printing to a cylinder and then to paper (one word)
letters patent open document conferring a right
let-up n. (hyphen)
Letzeburgesch (also **Letzebuergesch**) another name for **Luxemburgish**
leu pl. **lei** monetary unit of Romania
leucocyte (also **leukocyte**) colourless cell in blood and body fluids
leukaemia (US **leukemia**) malignant blood disease (not **-c-**)
Leuven town in Belgium; Fr. name **Louvain**
Lev. Leviticus
lev monetary unit of Bulgaria
Levant arch. eastern part of the Mediterranean □ **Levantine**
Levante four Mediterranean provinces

of Spain

levanter strong easterly wind in the Mediterranean (lower case)

levee (not ital., no accent) **1** formal reception **2** US river embankment

level v. (**levelling, levelled**; US one **-l-**)

level-headed (hyphen)

leveller (US **leveler**) **1** person or thing that levels **2** (**Leveller**) radical dissenter in the English Civil War

lever de rideau pl. ***levers de rideau*** curtain-raiser (Fr., ital.)

Leverhulme, 1st Viscount (1851–1925), English industrialist and philanthropist

Leverkusen city in western Germany

leviathan **1** sea monster **2** (***Leviathan***) book by Hobbes (1651)

Levi's trademark jeans manufactured by Levi Strauss & Co.

Lévi-Strauss, Claude (1908–2009), French social anthropologist

Leviticus third book of the Old Testament (abbrev. **Lev.**)

levy v. (**levying, levied**) ◻ **leviable**

Lewes[1] town in East Sussex

Lewes[2], George Henry (1817–78), English philosopher and critic

Lewis **1** C(live) S(taples) (1898–1963), British novelist and scholar **2** Jerry Lee (b.1935), American rock-and-roll singer **3** Meriwether (1774–1809), American explorer **4** (Harry) Sinclair (1885–1951), American novelist **5** (Percy) Wyndham (1882–1957), British writer and painter

Lewis and Harris (also **Lewis with Harris**) largest island of the Outer Hebrides

lexeme basic meaningful lexical unit

lexicography compilation of dictionaries

lexicology the study of words

lexicon **1** vocabulary of a person, language, or subject **2** dictionary, esp. of Greek, Hebrew, Syriac, or Arabic

lexis **1** total stock of words in a language **2** vocabulary, as opposed to grammar or syntax

lex loci the law of the relevant country (L., ital.)

lex talionis the law of retaliation in kind and degree (L., ital.)

ley **1** pasture used for a limited time; cf. **lea** **2** (also **ley line**) supposed straight line connecting prehistoric sites

Leyden var. of **Leiden**

Leyden jar early form of capacitor

Leyland cypress fast-growing conifer

leylandii pl. same, another name for **Leyland cypress** (lower case, not ital.)

LF low frequency

l.h. left hand

Lhasa capital of Tibet

Lhasa apso pl. **Lhasa apsos** breed of dog

LI **1** Light Infantry **2** Long Island

Li the chemical element lithium (no point)

liaise, liaison (two *i*s)

liana (also **liane**) tropical climbing plant

Lib. Liberal

Lib Dem Liberal Democrat

libeccio south-westerly wind west of Italy (not ital.)

libel n. written defamation. v. (**libelling, libelled**; US one **-l-**)

libellous (US **libelous**)

liberal (cap. in a political context; abbrev. **Lib.**)

liberalize (Brit. also **liberalise**)

Liberia country in West Africa ◻ **Liberian**

libertarian advocate of liberty

libertine dissolute person

Liberty Hall place where one may do as one likes (caps)

libido pl. **libidos** sex drive ◻ **libidinal**

Libra seventh sign of the zodiac ◻ **Libran**

library edition standard edition of an author's work

Library of Congress US national library, Washington DC

libretto pl. **libretti** or **librettos** text of an opera

Libreville capital of Gabon

Libya **1** country in North Africa **2** ancient North Africa west of Egypt ◻ **Libyan**

licence (US **license**) n. **1** official permit **2** freedom to behave without restraint

license v. grant a licence to ◻ **licensable, licenser** (also **licensor**)

licensed (also **licensed**)
licentiate holder of a certificate of competence
lichee use **lychee**
lichen simple plant
Lichfield town in Staffordshire
lichgate var. of **lychgate**
Lichtenstein, Roy (1923–97), American artist; cf. **Liechtenstein**
lickerish lecherous (not **liquorish** (arch.))
licorice US var. of **liquorice**
Lido island reef opposite Venice; full name **Lido di Malamocco**
lido pl. **lidos** public open-air swimming pool (lower case)
lie (**lying**; past **lay**, past part. **lain**) be in horizontal position; cf. **lay**
Liebfraumilch German white wine [Ger. *Liebfrauenmilch*]
Liebig, Justus, Baron von (1803–73), German chemist
Liechtenstein principality in the Alps; cf. **Lichtenstein** ▫ **Liechtensteiner**
lied pl. **lieder** German song (lower case, not ital.)
lie detector (two words)
Liège city and province of Belgium
Lietuva (also **Lietuvos Respublika**) Lithuanian name for **Lithuania**
lieu (in **in lieu of**) instead of (not ital.)
lieutenant army or navy rank (cap. in titles; abbrev. **Lieut.**, **Lt**) ▫ **lieutenancy**
lieutenant colonel, lieutenant commander, lieutenant general, lieutenant governor (two words, caps as title)
life assurance Brit. life insurance
lifebelt, lifeblood, lifeboat, lifebuoy (one word)
life cycle, life expectancy, life force, life form (two words)
life-giving (hyphen)
lifeguard (one word)
Life Guards regiment of the Household Cavalry
life history, life imprisonment, life insurance, life jacket (two words)
lifelike, lifeline, lifelong (one word)
life member, life peer, life raft (two words)
lifesaver (one word)
life sciences, life scientist, life sentence (two words)
life-size (also **life-sized**) (hyphen)
lifespan, lifestyle (one word)
life support (two words, hyphen when attrib.)
life-threatening (hyphen)
lifetime (one word)
lift-off n. (hyphen, two words as verb)
ligature 1 character consisting of joined letters, e.g. Æ, œ **2** stroke that joins adjacent letters **3** Mus. slur or tie
Ligeti, György Sándor (1923–2006), Hungarian composer
light[1] (past **lit**; past part. **lit** or **lighted**) provide with light
light[2] (**light on** or **upon**) (past and past part. **lit** or **lighted**) discover; settle
light bulb (two words)
light-emitting diode (abbrev. **LED**)
lightening making lighter; cf. **lightning**
lighthouse (one word)
light meter (two words)
lightning natural electrical discharge; cf. **lightening**
lightning conductor (two words)
lightproof, lightweight (one word)
light year (two words)
ligneous of wood, woody
-like established *-like* compounds are usually written as one word, except for those in which the first element ends in *-l*, which are hyphenated; newly formed words and words with first elements of several syllables have hyphens
likeable (also chiefly US **likable**)
likelihood (not **likelyhood**)
like-minded (hyphen)
Likud coalition of Israeli political parties
lilangeni pl. **emalangeni** monetary unit of Swaziland
Lille city in northern France
Lilliburlero old song
Lilliput country in *Gulliver's Travels* where everything is tiny ▫ **Lilliputian**
lilo (also trademark **Li-lo**) pl. **lilos** inflatable mattress
Lilongwe capital of Malawi
lily of the valley (no hyphens)
Lima capital of Peru

lima bean (lower case)
limbo[1] (lower case) **1** realm between heaven and hell **2** intermediate state
limbo[2] pl. **limbos** West Indian dance
Limburg former duchy, now provinces of Belgium and the Netherlands; Fr. name **Limbourg**
limelight (one word)
Limerick town and county of the Republic of Ireland
limerick humorous five-line poem (lower case)
limescale, limestone (one word)
Limey pl. **Limeys** informal British person (cap.); cf. **limy**
liminal relating to a boundary
Limited Brit. denoting a limited company (abbrev. **Ltd**)
limn depict or describe
limnology scientific study of lakes
Limoges city in west central France
Limousin 1 region of central France **2** French breed of beef cattle
limousine large luxurious car
Limpopo river of SE Africa
limy containing lime; cf. **Limey**
linage number of printed or written lines; cf. **lineage**
linchpin (also **lynchpin**) (one word)
Lincoln, Abraham (1809–65), 16th president of the US 1861–5
Lincolnshire county on the east coast of England (abbrev. **Lincs.**)
Lincoln's Inn one of the Inns of Court in London (caps)
Lindbergh, Charles (Augustus) (1902–74), American aviator
lineage ancestry or pedigree; cf. **linage**
lineament distinctive feature; cf. **liniment**
Linear A, Linear B two related forms of ancient writing discovered in Crete
line dancing, line drawing (two words)
linefeed advancing paper through a printer one line at a time (one word)
line manager (two words)
linenfold ornaments representing folds or scrolls (one word)
line-out n. (hyphen)
line printer (two words)
linesman (one word)
line-up n. (hyphen, two words as verb)
lingam (also **linga**) Hinduism phallus as a symbol of Shiva
lingerie women's underwear and nightclothes
lingua franca pl. **lingua francas** common language (not ital.)
linguine pasta in the form of ribbons (not **-ini**)
liniment embrocation; cf. **lineament**
lining numerals var. of **ranging numerals**
lining paper paper glued inside a book's cover
Linnaean relating to Linnaeus (but **Linnean Society**)
Linnaeus, Carolus (1707–78), Swedish founder of systematic botany and zoology; Latinized name of *Carl von Linné* (abbrev. **L., Linn.**)
Linnhe, Loch lake in the Scottish Highlands
lino pl. **linos** linoleum
linocut design carved in relief on a block of linoleum (one word)
Linotype trademark old type of composing machine
Linux trademark computer operating system
Linz city in northern Austria
lionheart (one word; cap. in names) □ **lionhearted**
lionize (Brit. also **lionise**)
Lions Club charitable society (no apostrophe)
lip gloss (two words)
Lipizzaner (also **Lippizaner**) breed of white horse
lipography scribal error of omitting letters
liposuction cosmetic surgery to remove fat
Lippi, Fra Filippo (*c.*1406–69) and his son Filippino (*c.*1457–1504), Italian painters
lip-read (hyphen)
lip salve (two words)
lipstick (one word)
liquefy (not **liquify**)
liqueur sweet alcoholic spirit (two *us*); cf. **liquor**

liquidambar tree yielding balsam (one word; not **-amber**)
liquidize (Brit. also **liquidise**)
liquify use **liquefy**
liquor alcoholic drink; cf. **liqueur**
liquorice (US **licorice**)
liquorish arch. var. of **lickerish**
lira pl. **lire** monetary unit of Turkey and formerly of Italy
Lisbon capital of Portugal; Port. name **Lisboa**
Lisburn city in Northern Ireland
lisente pl. of **sente**
lisle smooth cotton thread
lis pendens pending legal action (L., ital.)
lissom (also **lissome**) thin and supple
listening post (two words)
LISTSERV trademark in the US electronic mailing list
Liszt, Franz (1811–86), Hungarian composer □ **Lisztian**
lit. literally
litas pl. same, monetary unit of Lithuania
litchi chiefly US var. of **lychee**
lit. crit. literary criticism
liter US var. of **litre**
Literae Humaniores classics, philosophy, and ancient history at Oxford University (abbrev. **Lit. Hum.**)
literal misprint of a letter
literally (abbrev. **lit.**)
literati learned people (not ital.; not **litt-**)
literatim letter for letter (L., ital.)
lithium chemical element of atomic number 3 (symbol **Li**)
lithography printing from a treated flat surface that expels ink except where it is required
Lithuania country on the Baltic Sea; Lithuanian name **Lietuva, Lietuvos Respublika** □ **Lithuanian**
Lit. Hum. Literae Humaniores
litmus paper, litmus test (two words)
litotes ironical understatement using negation, e.g. 'no mean feat'
litre (US **liter**; abbrev. **l**)
LittD (also **Litt.D.**) Doctor of Letters; [L. *Litterarum Doctor*]
littérateur literary person (Fr., ital.)
Little Bighorn battle in which General Custer and his forces were defeated by Sioux warriors (1876)
Little, Brown publishers (comma)
Little Englander (two words, caps)
Little Lord Fauntleroy novel by Frances Hodgson Burnett (1886)
Little Rock state capital of Arkansas
Littré, Émile (1801–81), French lexicographer
liveable (US **livable**)
livelihood means of securing a living
livelong (of a period of time) entire
Liverpudlian person from Liverpool
livestock (one word)
live wire energetic person (two words)
living room (two words)
Livingston town in West Lothian, Scotland
Livingstone, David (1813–73), Scottish explorer
Livorno port in west central Italy; formerly also called **Leghorn**
livraison part of a work published in instalments (Fr., ital.)
Livy (59 BC–AD 17), Roman historian; Latin name *Titus Livius*
LJ pl. **LJJ** Lord Justice
Ljubljana capital of Slovenia; Ger. name **Laibach**
Lk. St Luke's Gospel
ll separate letter in Spanish and Welsh, alphabetized separately and not to be divided between lines; the Catalan letter group *-ll-* can be split
ll. (point) **1** leaves **2** lines
llama South American ruminant; cf. **lama**
Llandrindod Wells town in Powys, Wales
Llandudno town in Conwy, Wales
Llanelli town in Carmarthenshire, Wales
LLB Bachelor of Laws [L. *Legum Baccalaureus*]
LLD Doctor of Laws [L. *Legum Doctor*]
Llewelyn (d.1282), prince of Gwynedd; also known as **Llywelyn ap Gruffydd**
LLL the Shakespeare play *Love's Labour's Lost*
LLM Master of Laws [L. *Legum Magister*]

Lloyd George, David, 1st Earl Lloyd George of Dwyfor (1863–1945), British prime minister 1916–22
Lloyd's society of insurance underwriters in London
Lloyd's List daily London newsletter relating to shipping
Lloyd's Register (in full **Lloyd's Register of Shipping**) annual list of merchant ships
Lloyds TSB bank (no apostrophe)
Lloyd Webber, Sir Andrew, Baron Lloyd-Webber of Sydmonton (b.1948), English composer (hyphen in title)
Llywelyn ap Gruffydd see **Llewelyn**
LM 1 long metre **2** lunar module
lm lumen(s)
LMH Lady Margaret Hall (Oxford)
LMS hist. London Midland and Scottish (Railway)
LMT Local Mean Time
ln natural logarithm
LNER hist. London and North Eastern Railway
load line another name for **Plimsoll line**
loadstar, loadstone use **lodestar, lodestone**
loanword (one word)
loath (also **loth**) reluctant
loathe detest
loathsome repulsive (not **loathe-**)
lobotomize (Brit. also **lobotomise**)
lobster Newburg (one cap.)
lobster thermidor (lower case)
locale scene or locality
localize (Brit. also **localise**)
Locarno resort in southern Switzerland
loc. cit. in the passage or place already cited (not ital.) [L. *loco citato*]
loch Scottish lake (cap. in names)
Lochearnhead, Lochgilphead, Lochnagar places in Scotland
loci pl. of **locus**
Locke, John (1632–1704), English philosopher □ **Lockean**
Lockerbie town in Dumfries and Galloway, Scotland
lockjaw (one word)
lock-keeper (hyphen)
lockout, locksmith (one word)
lock-up n. (hyphen, two words as verb)
loco pl. **locos** locomotive
loco citato in the passage or place already cited (L., ital.)
locum tenens pl. **locum tenentes** doctor or cleric standing in for another (not ital.)
locus pl. **loci** place or position (not ital.)
locus classicus pl. ***loci classici*** most authoritative passage (L., ital.)
locus standi pl. ***loci standi*** legal right to bring an action (L., ital.)
lodestar star that one steers by (one word; not **load-**)
lodestone piece of magnetite (one word; not **load-**)
lodgement (US **lodgment**) location or lodging
lodging house (two words)
Łódź city in central Poland
loess deposit of wind-blown sediment
lo-fi (of recorded sound) low fidelity
log logarithm (no point)
$\log_e$ natural logarithm
logan rocking stone
logarithm (abbrev. **log**)
logbook (one word)
log cabin (two words)
loge theatre box (not ital.)
loggia open-sided gallery (not ital.)
login (also **logon**) n. act of logging in to a computer system (one word, two words as verb)
logjam (one word)
logo pl. **logos** identifying symbol
logoff var. of **logout**
logogram sign or character representing a word
logomachy dispute about words
logon var. of **login**
logorrhoea (US **logorrhea**) tendency to loquacity
Logos Chr. Theol. the Word of God
logout (also **logoff**) n. act of logging out of a computer system (one word, two words as verb)
logrolling N. Amer. exchanging political favours (one word)
Logroño town in northern Spain
Lohengrin (in medieval romances) the son of Perceval (Parsifal)

loiasis tropical African disease
loincloth (one word)
Loir river of NW France
Loire river of west central France
Lok Sabha lower house of the Indian Parliament; cf. **Rajya Sabha**
Lollard 14th-cent. follower of Wyclif
Lombard 1 member of a Germanic people who invaded Italy in the 6th cent. **2** person from Lombardy
Lombardy region of central northern Italy; It. name **Lombardia**
Lomé capital of Togo
Londonderry town and county of Northern Ireland; also called **Derry**
long. longitude (no point in scientific work)
longboat, longbow (one word)
longcase clock (two words)
long-distance adj. (hyphen)
longe var. of **lunge**²
longhand, longhorn (one word)
Longinus (*fl.* 1st cent. AD), Greek scholar
Long Island island of New York State (abbrev. **LI**)
longitude (abbrev. **l., long.** (no point in scientific work))
long jump, long jumper (two words)
long-life adj. (hyphen)
longlist (one word)
long mark another name for **macron**
long metre (abbrev. **LM**) **1** hymn metre **2** quatrain of iambic pentameters with alternate rhymes
Long Parliament English Parliament which sat Nov. 1640–Mar. 1653
long s obsolete form of lower-case *s*, written or printed as ſ, italic *ſ*; not used in final position
longship, longshore, longshoreman (one word)
long-sighted, long-standing (hyphen)
long term (two words as noun, hyphen as adj.)
long ton see **ton**
longueur tedious passage or time (not ital., two *us*)
longways (also **longwise**) lengthways (one word)
loofah fibrous matter used as a bath sponge (not **loofa, luffa**)
lookalike (one word)
looking glass (two words, but *Through the Looking-Glass* by Lewis Carroll)
lookout, lookup n. (one word, two words as verb)
loophole (one word)
Lope de Vega see **Vega**
lopsided (one word)
loquacious talkative
loquat small yellow fruit
loquitur he or she speaks (as a stage direction or to inform the reader) (L., ital.; abbrev. **loq.**)
Lorca, Federico García (1898–1936), Spanish writer
lord title given formally to barons, and may be substituted for Marquess, Earl, or Viscount; also prefixed to the given name of the younger son of a duke or marquess (cap. in titles; abbrev. **Ld**)
Lord Chamberlain official in charge of the royal household, formerly the licenser of plays
Lord Chancellor highest officer of the Crown (abbrev. **LC**)
Lord Chief Justice officer presiding over the Queen's Bench Division and the Court of Appeal (abbrev. **LCJ**)
Lord Fauntleroy see **Little Lord Fauntleroy**
Lord Justice pl. **Lords Justices** judge in the Court of Appeal (abbrev. **LJ**)
lord mayor (cap. in titles)
Lord Privy Seal senior cabinet minister without specified official duties
Lords, the the House of Lords
Lord's cricket ground in north London (apostrophe)
Lord's Day Sunday (caps)
lordship (**His/Your** etc. **Lordship**) form of address for a judge, bishop, or titled man
Lord's Prayer, Lord's Supper (caps)
Lords spiritual bishops in the House of Lords (one cap.)
Lords temporal House of Lords other than the bishops (one cap.)
Lorelei (siren said to live on) a rock on the bank of the Rhine
Lorentz, Hendrik Antoon (1853–1928), Dutch physicist

Lorenz, Konrad (Zacharias) (1903–89), Austrian zoologist
Lorenzo de' Medici (1449–92), Italian statesman and scholar
lorgnette (also **lorgnettes**) eyeglasses on a handle
loris pl. **lorises** small primate; cf. **lory**
Lorraine region of NE France; see also **Alsace-Lorraine**
Lorrain, Claude see **Claude Lorrain**
lory pl. **lories** small parrot; cf. **loris**
Los Angeles city in southern California (abbrev. **LA**)
loss adjuster (two words)
loss-leader (hyphen)
Lost Tribes ten tribes of Israel taken away to captivity in Assyria (caps)
loth var. of **loath**
Lothario pl. **Lotharios** womanizer
Lothian former local government region in Scotland, now divided into **East Lothian**, **Midlothian**, and **West Lothian**
loti pl. **maloti** monetary unit of Lesotho
lotus (not **lotos**) **1** water lily **2** mythical plant producing forgetfulness
lotus-eater person given to idleness and luxury (but 'The Lotos-Eaters' by Tennyson)
louche disreputable (not ital.)
loudhailer, **loudspeaker** (one word)
lough Irish lake (cap. in names)
Loughborough town in Leicestershire
Louis name of eighteen kings of France
louis (also **louis d'or**) pl. same, old French gold coin (lower case, not ital.)
Louisiana state in the southern US (official abbrev. **La.**, postal **LA**)
Louis Philippe (1773–1850), king of France 1830–48
Louisville city in northern Kentucky
lounge bar, **lounge suit** (two words)
lour (also **lower**) look angry or sullen
Lourdes town in SW France
Lourenço Marques former name for **Maputo**
Louth county of the Republic of Ireland
Louvain Fr. name for **Leuven**
Louvre museum and art gallery in Paris
louvre (US **louver**) slat in a shutter or door
lovable (also **loveable**)
lovebird (one word)
love–hate relationship (en rule)
love-in-a-mist, **love-in-idleness** plants (hyphens)
lovelock, **lovelorn**, **lovesick** (one word)
Love's Labour's Lost Shakespeare play (abbrev. ***LLL***)
low-born, **low-class** (hyphen)
lowbrow (one word)
Low Church (caps, two words even when attrib.) □ **Low Churchman**
Low Countries the Netherlands, Belgium, and Luxembourg
lower var. of **lour**
Lower Austria state of NE Austria
Lower California another name for **Baja California**
Lower Canada region of southern Quebec
lower case small letters as opposed to capital (upper-case) letters (abbrev. **l.c.**)
lower class (two words, hyphen when attrib.)
Lower Saxony state of NW Germany
lowest common denominator lowest common multiple of the denominators of vulgar fractions (abbrev. **LCD**)
lowest common multiple lowest quantity that is a multiple of given quantities (abbrev. **LCM**)
low frequency (two words, hyphen when attrib.)
Low German vernacular of northern Germany
low-key (hyphen)
lowland (also **lowlands**) low-lying country; (**the Lowlands**) Scotland south and east of the Highlands □ **lowlander**
Low Latin medieval and later forms of Latin (caps)
low-level, **low-loader**, **low-lying** (hyphen)
low profile n. (two words, hyphen as adj.)
Lowry 1 (Clarence) Malcolm (1909–57), English novelist **2** L(aurence) S(tephen) (1887–1976), English painter

Low Sunday first Sunday after Easter
lox 1 liquid oxygen **2** N. Amer. smoked salmon
Loyalist supporter of union between Great Britain and Northern Ireland (cap.)
LP 1 long-playing (record) **2** (also **l.p.**) low pressure
LPG liquefied petroleum gas
L-plate sign on a vehicle showing that the driver is a learner (cap., hyphen)
Lr the chemical element lawrencium (no point)
LS Linnean Society
l.s. left side
LSB Comput. least significant bit
LSD lysergic acid diethylamide, a hallucinogenic drug
l.s.d. (also **£.s.d.**) hist. pounds, shillings, and pence
LSE 1 London School of Economics **2** London Stock Exchange
L-shape, L-shaped (cap., hyphen)
LSO London Symphony Orchestra
Lt Lieutenant
LTA Lawn Tennis Association
Ltd (after a company name) Limited (no point)
Lu the chemical element lutetium (no point)
Luanda capital of Angola
luau pl. same or **luaus** Hawaiian party or feast
Lübeck port in northern Germany (not **Lue-**)
lubricious offensively sexual (not **-cous**)
Lubyanka (also **Lubianka**) building in Moscow
Lucan[1] (AD 39–65), Roman poet; Latin name *Marcus Annaeus Lucanus*
Lucan[2] of St Luke (not **-k-**)
Lucca city in west central Italy
Lucerne resort in Switzerland; Ger. name **Luzern**
lucerne (also **lucern**) alfalfa
Lucknow city in northern India
Lucr. Shakespeare's poem *The Rape of Lucrece*
lucre money
Lucretius (*c.*94–*c.*55 BC), Roman writer; Latin name *Titus Lucretius Carus*
Lucullan extremely luxurious
Luddite (cap.) □ **Luddism, Ludditism**
luffa use **loofah**
Luftwaffe the German air force (cap., not ital.)
luge (sport of riding) a light toboggan
Luger type of German automatic pistol (cap., trademark in the US)
Luggnagg island in Swift's *Gulliver's Travels*
lughole, lugsail, lugworm (one word)
Lukács, György (1885–1971), Hungarian philosopher
Luke, St 1 evangelist **2** (also **Luke**) third Gospel (no abbrev.)
lukewarm (one word)
luma pl. same or **lumas** monetary unit of Armenia
lumbar of the lower back
lumber v. move clumsily. n. **1** Brit. unused stored furniture etc. **2** N. Amer. sawn timber
lumberjack, lumberjacket (one word)
lumen SI unit of luminous flux (abbrev. **lm**)
Lumière, Auguste Marie Louis Nicholas (1862–1954) and Louis Jean (1864–1948), French pioneers of cinema
lumpenproletariat unpolitical lower orders of society (one word, lower case, not ital.)
lunch hour (two words)
lunchroom, lunchtime (one word)
lunette arched aperture or window
lunge[1] (**lunges, lungeing** or **lunging, lunged**) (make) a sudden forward movement
lunge[2] (also **longe**) (**lunges, lungeing, lunged**) (exercise a horse on) a long rein
lungi pl. **lungis** Indian and Burmese sarong-like garment
lunula pl. **lunulae 1** white area at the base of a fingernail **2** crescent-shaped Bronze Age necklace
lupin (N. Amer. **lupine**) plant with tall spikes of flowers
lupine of or like a wolf
lupus Med. ulcerous skin condition
Lusaka capital of Zambia
luscious rich and sweet (not **lush-**)

Lusitania 1 ancient Roman province in the Iberian peninsula **2** name for Portugal

Lusitania Cunard liner sunk in May 1915

lusophone Portuguese-speaking (lower case)

lustre (US **luster**)

lustrum pl. **lustra** or **lustrums** five-year period

lusus naturae pl. same or **lususes naturae** freak of nature (not ital.)

lutenist (also **lutanist**) lute player

lutetium (also **lutecium**) chemical element of atomic number 71 (symbol **Lu**)

Luther, Martin (1483–1546), German Protestant theologian

luthier maker of stringed musical instruments

Lutine Bell bell rung at Lloyd's in London for announcements (caps)

lutist another term for **lutenist** or **luthier**

Lutyens 1 (Agnes) Elisabeth (1906–83), English composer **2** Sir Edwin (Landseer) (1869–1944), English architect

lutz jump in skating

luvvie (also **luvvy**) informal effusive actor

lux pl. same, SI unit of illumination (abbrev. **lx**)

Luxembourg (Ger. name **Luxemburg**) **1** small country in western Europe **2** province of SE Belgium □ **Luxembourger, Luxembourgeois**

Luxemburg, Rosa (1871–1919), Polish-born German revolutionary leader

Luxemburgish language of Luxembourg; also called **Letzeburgesch**

Luxor city in eastern Egypt; Arab. name **el-Uqsur**

luxuriant thick and profuse

luxurious giving self-indulgent or sensual pleasure

Luzern Ger. name for **Lucerne**

Luzon largest island in the Philippines

LV luncheon voucher

Lviv city in western Ukraine; Russ. name **Lvov**; Pol. name **Lwów**; Ger. name **Lemberg**

lwei pl. same, monetary unit of Angola

LWM low-water mark

lx lux

LXX 1 Roman numeral for 70 **2** the Septuagint

lycée French secondary school (ital.)

Lyceum garden at Athens in which Aristotle taught

lychee (chiefly US also **litchi**) fruit with sweet-scented white flesh (not **lichee**)

lychgate (also **lichgate**) roofed gateway to a churchyard (one word)

Lycra trademark elastic polyurethane fabric

lyddite WWI explosive (two *ds*)

lying-in-state (two hyphens)

lyke wake night spent watching over a dead body; (**Lyke Wake Dirge**) medieval English song

Lyly, John (*c.*1554–1606), English writer; see also **euphuism**

Lyme disease form of arthritis contracted through ticks

lymph gland, lymph node (two words)

lymphoma pl. **lymphomas** or **lymphomata** cancer of the lymph nodes

lynch mob (two words)

lynchpin var. of **linchpin**

lynx wild cat with a short tail

Lyon (in full **Lord Lyon** or **Lyon King of Arms**) chief herald of Scotland

Lyons city in SE France; Fr. name **Lyon**

Lysenko, Trofim Denisovich (1898–1976), Soviet biologist

Lytton, 1st Baron (1803–73), British novelist and statesman; born *Edward George Earle Bulwer-Lytton*

M

M 1 pl. **Ms** or **M's** 13th letter of the alphabet **2** Cricket maiden over(s) **3** male **4** Master **5** mega- **6** Astron. Messier (catalogue of nebulae) **7** Chem. molar **8** Monsieur: *M Chirac* **9** motorway **10** (also **m**) Roman numeral for 1,000 [L. *mille*]

m 1 married **2** masculine **3** Phys. mass: $E = mc^2$ **4** metre(s) **5** mile(s) **6** milli-: *100 mA* **7** million(s) **8** minute(s)

m Chem. meta-

MA 1 Massachusetts (postal abbrev.) **2** Master of Arts [L. *Magister Artium*]

ma'am term of address for female royalty or more senior members of the police or armed forces

Maas Du. name for **Meuse**

Maasai var. of **Masai**

Maastricht city in the Netherlands, where an EU treaty on economic and monetary union was agreed in 1991

Mabinogion collection of Welsh tales of the 11th–13th cents

Mac trademark computer produced by the Apple company

Mac-, Mc- spelling is personal, and must be followed, as: MacDonald, Macdonald, McDonald, M[c]Donald, M'Donald; however spelled, traditionally alphabetized as *Mac-*

mac (also **mack**) mackintosh

macadam material for road-making

macadamia Australian tree or its nut

macadamized (Brit. also **macadamised**) covered with macadam

Macao former Portuguese dependency in China; Port. name **Macau**

macaque medium-sized monkey

macaroni 1 pasta in narrow tubes **2** 18th-cent. dandy

macaronic (of verse) mixing languages; (**macaronics**) macaronic verses

MacArthur, Dame Ellen (b.1976), English yachtswoman

Macassar 1 hist. men's hair oil **2** var. of **Makassar**

Macau Port. name for **Macao**

Macaulay 1 Dame (Emilie) Rose (1881–1958), English novelist **2** Thomas Babington, 1st Baron (1800–59), English historian

macaw long-tailed parrot

Macbeth 1 (*c.*1005–57), king of Scotland 1040–57 **2** (***Macbeth***) Shakespeare play (abbrev. ***Macb.***)

Maccabaeus see **Judas Maccabaeus**

Maccabees 1 hist. followers of Judas Maccabaeus **2** (in full **the Books of the Maccabees**) four books of Jewish history and theology; the first and second are in the Apocrypha (abbrev. **1 Macc., 2 Macc.**)

McCarthy Joseph (Raymond) (1909–57), American politician

McCarthyism campaign against alleged communists in the US in the 1950s

McCartney, Sir (James) Paul (b.1942), English pop musician

macchiato (also **caffè macchiato**) pl. **macchiatos** coffee with frothy milk

McCoy (in **the real McCoy**) the genuine article

McCullers, (Lula) Carson (1917–67), American writer

MacDiarmid, Hugh (1892–1978), Scottish poet; pseudonym of *Christopher Murray Grieve*

MacDonald 1 Flora (1722–90), Scottish Jacobite heroine **2** (James) Ramsay (1866–1937), British prime minister 1924, 1929–31, and 1931–5

McDonald's trademark fast-food chain (not **Mac-**, in spite of the 'Big Mac')

McDonnell Douglas US aircraft manufacturer (no hyphen)

MacDonnell Ranges mountains in Northern Territory, Australia

macédoine mixture of chopped fruit or vegetables (accent, not ital.)

Macedonia 1 (also **Macedon**) ancient

country **2** region in NE Greece **3** republic in the Balkans; also called **Former Yugoslav Republic of Macedonia**

McEwan, Ian (Russell) (b.1948), English novelist

McGill University Montreal, Canada

McGonagall, William (1830–1902), Scottish poet known for his bad verse

McGraw-Hill publishers (hyphen)

Mach 1 (or **Mach 2** etc.) used to indicate the speed of sound (or twice the speed of sound, etc.)

machete broad heavy knife

Machiavelli, Niccolò di Bernardo dei (1469–1527), Italian political philosopher □ **Machiavellian**

machicolation (in medieval fortifications) opening between corbels

machinable (not **-eable**)

machine gun n. (two words, hyphen as verb)

machine-readable (hyphen)

machine tool (two words) □ **machine-tooled**

machismo aggressive masculine pride

Machmeter instrument indicating airspeed (cap., one word)

Mach number ratio of the speed of a body to the speed of sound (*Mach 1, Mach 2*, etc.)

macho pl. **machos** aggressively masculine (person)

Machtpolitik power politics (Ger., cap., ital.)

Machu Picchu Inca town in Peru

Macintosh trademark computer produced by the Apple company; an Apple Mac

macintosh var. of **mackintosh**

McIntosh eating apple

mack var. of **mac**

Mackenzie, Sir (Edward Montague) Compton (1883–1972), English writer

mackerel (not **mackrel, mackeral**)

McKinley, William (1843–1901), 25th president of the US 1897–1901

Mackintosh, Charles Rennie (1868–1928), Scottish architect and designer

mackintosh (also **macintosh**) full-length raincoat

mackle blurred impression in printing

McLuhan, (Herbert) Marshall (1911–80), Canadian writer

Macmillan[1] (Maurice) Harold, 1st Earl of Stockton (1894–1986), British prime minister 1957–63

Macmillan[2] publishers

Macquarie River river in New South Wales, Australia

macramé knotting strings in patterns (accent, not ital.)

macro pl. **macros** single computer instruction that expands to a set

macroeconomics economics dealing with large-scale factors (one word)

macron mark ¯ indicating a long or stressed vowel

Madagascar island country off the east coast of Africa

madam polite term of address for a woman; (**Madam**) used at the start of a formal letter

Madame pl. **Mesdames** French equivalent of 'Mrs' (abbrev. **Mme**, pl. **Mmes**)

mad cow disease BSE (no hyphen)

Madeira 1 island in the Atlantic Ocean **2** fortified wine from Madeira

madeleine small sponge cake

Mademoiselle pl. **Mesdemoiselles** French equivalent of 'Miss' (abbrev. **Mlle**, pl. **Mlles**)

Madhya Pradesh state in central India

Madison, James (1751–1836), 4th president of the US 1809–17

Madonna[1] **1** (**the Madonna**) the Virgin Mary **2** (**madonna**) representation of the Virgin Mary

Madonna[2] (b.1958), American pop singer; born *Madonna Louise Ciccone*

Madras seaport on the east coast of India; official name **Chennai**

madras strong cotton fabric (lower case)

madrasa (also **madrasah**) Islamic college

Madrileño pl. **Madrileños** person from Madrid □ **Madrilenian**

Maeander ancient name for **Menderes**; cf. **meander**

Maecenas, Gaius (*c.*70–8 BC), Roman statesman

maelstrom powerful whirlpool (but *Descent into the Maelström* by Edgar Allan Poe, 1841)

maenad female follower of Bacchus
maestoso pl. **maestosos** Mus. performed in a majestic manner
maestro pl. **maestros** or **maestri** distinguished musician
Maeterlinck, Count Maurice (1862–1949), Belgian writer
Mafeking 1 former spelling of **Mafikeng 2** town in Manitoba, Canada
Mafia international criminal body
mafia group exerting sinister influence (lower case)
Mafikeng town in South Africa; former spelling **Mafeking**
mafioso pl. **mafiosi** member of the Mafia (not ital.)
magazines titles cited in italic
magdalen 1 arch. reformed prostitute **2** (**the Magdalen** or **the Magdalene**) St Mary Magdalene
Magdalen College Oxford
Magdalene College Cambridge
Magdalenian final Palaeolithic culture in Europe
Magellan, Ferdinand (*c.*1480–1521), Portuguese explorer
Maggiore, Lake lake in northern Italy and southern Switzerland
Maghreb (also **Maghrib**) region of North and NW Africa
Magi the 'wise men' from the East who brought gifts to the infant Jesus
magi pl. of **magus**
magic v. (**magicking, magicked**)
magick arch. spelling of **magic**
magilp var. of **megilp**
magistrates' court (note apostrophe)
Maglemosian northern European mesolithic culture
maglev system in which trains glide above a track (lower case)
magma pl. **magmas** or **magmata** hot semi-fluid below the earth's surface
Magna Carta (also **Magna Charta**) (not preceded by 'the')
magna cum laude with great distinction (L., ital.)
magnesium chemical element of atomic number 12 (symbol **Mg**)
magnetize (Brit. also **magnetise**)
magneto pl. **magnetos** small electric generator
Magnificat the hymn of the Virgin Mary used as a canticle
magnifying glass (two words)
magnum pl. **magnums** (lower case) **1** large wine bottle **2** gun firing powerful cartridges (cap. as US trademark)
magnum opus pl. **magnum opuses** or **magna opera** author's chief work (not ital.)
Magritte, René (François Ghislain) (1898–1967), Belgian painter
maguey agave plant
magus pl. **magi** member of a priestly caste of ancient Persia; see also **Magi**
Magyar member of a people settled in Hungary
Magyarország Hungarian name for **Hungary**
Mahabharata great Sanskrit epic
maharaja (also **maharajah**) hist. Indian prince (cap. in titles)
maharani (also **maharanee**) hist. maharaja's wife or widow (cap. in titles)
Maharashtra state in western India □ **Maharashtrian**
Maharishi Hindu sage
mahatma Ind. revered person (cap. in titles)
Mahayana major Buddhist tradition; cf. **Theravada**
Mahdi pl. **Mahdis** (person claiming to be) the final Islamic leader
Mahican (also **Mohican**) member of an American Indian people; cf. **Mohegan**
mah-jong (also **mah-jongg**) Chinese game (hyphen)
Mahler, Gustav (1860–1911), Austrian composer □ **Mahlerian**
mahlstick (also **maulstick**) painter's stick for steadying the hand
Mahomet use **Muhammad**
Mahometan arch. use **Muslim**
Mahon (also **Port Mahon**) capital of Minorca
mahout rider of elephants
Mahratti var. of **Marathi**
Maia 1 Gk Mythol. mother of Hermes **2** Rom. Mythol. goddess associated with Vulcan
maidan Ind. public open space

maidenhair, maidenhead (one word)
maiden name (two words)
mailbag, mailbox (one word)
mail merge, mail order (two words)
mailshot (one word)
Maimonides (1135–1204), Jewish scholar
Main river of SW Germany
Maine state of the north-eastern US (official abbrev. **Me.**, postal **ME**)
mainframe, mainland (one word)
main line n. (two words, hyphen when attrib., one word as verb)
mainmast, mainsail, mainspring, mainstay, mainstream (one word)
maiolica earthenware with decoration on a white tin glaze; cf. **majolica**
maisonette flat with a separate entrance [Fr. *maisonnette*]
maître d'hôtel (also **maître d'**) pl. **maîtres d'hôtel** or **maître d's** head waiter or hotel manager (not ital.)
Maj. Major
majesty impressiveness; royal power; (**His/Your** etc. **Majesty**) term of address to a sovereign
majlis parliament of Iran etc. (not ital.)
majolica 19th-cent. imitation of maiolica
major army and US air force rank (cap. in titles; abbrev. **Maj.**)
Majorca largest of the Balearic Islands; Sp. name **Mallorca**
major-domo pl. **major-domos** chief steward (hyphen)
major general army and US air force rank (cap. in titles; abbrev. **Maj. Gen.**)
majuscule large lettering, capital or uncial, with all letters the same height
Makarios III (1913–77), Greek Cypriot archbishop and first president of the republic of Cyprus 1960–77
Makassar (also **Macassar** or **Makasar**) former name for **Ujung Pandang**
makeable (also **makable**)
make-believe, make-do (hyphen)
makeover (one word)
makeready final preparation and adjustment for printing (one word)
makeshift (one word)
make-up n. (hyphen, two words as verb)
makeweight (one word)
Makkah Arab. name for **Mecca**
Mal. Malachi
Malabo capital of Equatorial Guinea
Malacca var. of **Melaka**
Malacca, Strait of channel between the Malay Peninsula and Sumatra
Malachi book of the Old Testament (abbrev. **Mal.**)
maladroit clumsy
mala fide (done) in bad faith (not ital.)
mala fides bad faith (not ital.)
Malaga seaport in southern Spain; Sp. name **Málaga**
Malagasy pl. same or **Malagasies** person from Madagascar
Malagasy Republic former name for **Madagascar**
malaise general unease
malapropism (also **malaprop**) mistaken use of a word
malapropos inopportune(ly) or inappropriate(ly) [Fr. *mal à propos*]
Malawi country of south central Africa □ **Malawian**
Malay member of a people of Malaysia and Indonesia
Malaya former country in SE Asia, now part of Malaysia
Malayalam language of Kerala, southern India
Malay Archipelago, Malay Peninsula (caps)
Malaysia country in SE Asia
Malcolm X (1925–65), American political activist; born *Malcolm Little*
mal de mer seasickness (Fr., ital.)
Maldives country consisting of islands in the Indian Ocean □ **Maldivian**
mal du siècle world-weariness (Fr., ital.)
Male capital of the Maldives
malefic causing harm □ **maleficence, maleficent**
malfeasance wrongdoing, in the US esp. by a public official; cf. **misfeasance**
Malherbe, François de (1555–1628), French poet
Mali country in West Africa □ **Malian**
Malibu resort in southern California

Malines Fr. name for **Mechelen**
Mallarmé, Stéphane (1842–98), French poet
malleus pl. **mallei** Anat. small bone in the inner ear
Mallorca Sp. name for **Majorca**
Malmesbury town in Wiltshire
Malmö city in SW Sweden
malmsey sweet Madeira wine
maloti pl. of **loti**
Malplaquet 1709 battle during the War of the Spanish Succession
malpractice (not **-ise**)
Malraux, André (1901–76), French writer
Malta island country in the Mediterranean
Maltese pl. same, (inhabitant) of Malta
Maltese cross cross with arms of even length broadening from the centre and with ends indented
Malthus, Thomas Robert (1766–1834), English economist □ **Malthusian**
Maluku Indonesian name for **Molucca Islands**
Malvinas, Islas Sp. name for **Falkland Islands**
mama (also **mamma**) one's mother
mamba venomous African snake
mambo pl. **mambos** Latin American dance
Mameluke member of the military regime that ruled Egypt 1250–1517
mamma[1] var. of **mama**
mamma[2] pl. **mammae** mammal's milk-secreting organ
Mammon wealth personified (cap.)
Man. Manitoba
man, mankind in sense 'human beings' prefer *the human race* or *humankind*; for compounds prefer gender-neutral terms, e.g. *firefighter* rather than *fireman*
Man, Isle of see **Isle of Man**
man about town (no hyphens)
manacle fetter
manageable (not **-gable**)
management (not **-gment**)
Managua capital of Nicaragua
manakin tropical American bird; cf. **manikin, mannequin, mannikin**
mañana tomorrow (Sp., ital.)
man-at-arms pl. **men-at-arms** (hyphens)
Manche, La English Channel (Fr., ital.)
Manchu member of a people from Manchuria
Manchukuo Manchuria as a Japanese puppet state 1932–45
Manchuria NE portion of China
Mancunian person from Manchester
Mandaean (also **Mandean**) member of a Gnostic sect
mandala circular symbol representing the universe
Mandalay port in Burma (Myanmar)
mandamus judicial writ to an inferior court (not ital.)
Mandarin modern standard Chinese
mandarin[1] official or bureaucrat (not **-ine**)
mandarin[2] (also **mandarine**) small citrus fruit
Mande pl. same or **Mandes** member of a group of West African peoples; also called **Manding, Mandingo**
Mandean var. of **Mandaean**
Mandela, Nelson (Rolihlahla) (1918–2013), South African statesman, president 1994–9
Mandelbrot, Benoît (1924–2010), French mathematician
mandible 1 jaw or jawbone **2** part of a bird's beak □ **mandibular**
Manding (also **Mandingo**) another name for **Mande**
Mandinka pl. same or **Mandinkas** member of a people of West Africa
mandola large mandolin
mandolin 1 musical instrument resembling a lute **2** (also **mandoline**) utensil for slicing vegetables
mandorla another name for **vesica piscis**
mandrel spindle in a lathe
mandrill large baboon
M&S Marks & Spencer (no spaces)
man-eater (hyphen)
manège enclosed area for training horses (accent, not ital.)
manent (sing. ***manet***) (stage direction) they remain (L., ital.)

manes Rom. Mythol. deified souls of dead ancestors (not ital.)
Manet, Édouard (1832–83), French painter
maneuver US var. of **manoeuvre**
man Friday male personal assistant (one cap.)
manganese chemical element of atomic number 25 (symbol **Mg**)
mangel (also **mangel-wurzel**) another name for **mangold**; cf. **mangle**
mangetout pl. same or **mangetouts** pea with an edible pod
mangle damage by tearing or cutting; cf. **mangel**
mango pl. **mangoes** or **mangos** fruit
mangold (also **mangel** or **mangel-wurzel**) beet with a large root
mangosteen tropical fruit
manhandle (one word)
Manhattan part of the city of New York
manhattan cocktail (lower case)
manhole (one word)
man-hour one person working for one hour (hyphen)
manhunt (one word)
manic depression (two words) ▫ **manic depressive**
Manichaeism (also **Manicheism**) dualistic religious system ▫ **Manichaean**
manifesto pl. **manifestos**
manifold many and various; cf. **manyfold**
manikin (also **mannikin**) jointed figure of the human body; cf. **manakin**, **mannequin**
Manila[1] capital of the Philippines
Manila[2] (also **Manilla**) **1** strong fibre **2** strong brown paper
manioc another name for **cassava**
Manipur state in the far east of India
Manitoba province of central Canada (abbrev. **Man.**, **Manit.**)
manitou (among some North American Indians) good or evil spirit
man-made hyphen; but alternatives such as 'artificial' or 'synthetic' may be preferable
manna food substance miraculously supplied to the Israelites
mannequin dummy for displaying clothes; cf. **manakin**, **manikin**
manner born, to the from *Hamlet*; British television series is *To the Manor Born*
Mannerism style of 16th-cent. Italian art (cap.)
mannerism habitual gesture
Mannheim port in SW Germany (not **Manheim**)
mannikin **1** small waxbill **2** var. of **manikin**; cf. **manakin**, **mannequin**
mano-a-mano pl. **mano-a-manos** head-to-head (hyphens, not ital, three words as adj. or adv.)
manoeuvrable (US **maneuverable**) (not **-œ-**)
manoeuvre (US **maneuver**) (not **-œ-**)
man-of-war (also **man-o'-war**) pl. **men-** armed sailing ship (hyphens)
ma non troppo Mus. but not too much
manpower (one word)
manqué (fem. also **manquée**) having failed to be the thing specified (not ital., placed after the noun)
Man Ray see **Ray** (sometimes alphabetized under *m-*)
Mans, Le see **Le Mans**
mansard roof with four sloping sides with two planes
mansion house house of a lord mayor or landed proprietor; (**the Mansion House**) official residence of the Lord Mayor of London
manslaughter (one word)
Mantegna, Andrea (1431–1506), Italian painter
mantelpiece (also **mantlepiece**) structure around a fireplace
mantelshelf (also **mantleshelf**) shelf above a fireplace
manteltree beam above a fireplace (not **mantle-**)
mantilla scarf worn by Spanish women
mantis pl. same or **mantises** insect
mantissa Math. part of a floating-point number which represents the significant digits
mantle woman's loose cloak
mantlepiece, mantleshelf vars of **mantelpiece, mantelshelf**
mantlet hist. woman's short loose cape (not **mantelet**)
mantling piece of heraldic drapery

mantrap (one word)
Mantua town in northern Italy; It. name **Mantova**
mantua hist. woman's gown (lower case)
manumit (manumitting, manumitted) release from slavery □ **manumission**
manus pl. same, Zool. hand (not ital.)
manuscript (abbrev. **MS**) **1** piece written by hand rather than typed or printed **2** author's text not yet published
manuscript paper paper printed with staves for music
manyfold by many times; cf. **manifold**
manzanilla pale dry sherry (lower case)
Maoism communist doctrines of Mao Zedong
Maori pl. same or **Maoris** member of the aboriginal people of New Zealand
Mao Zedong (also **Mao Tse-tung**) (1893–1976), chairman of the Communist Party of the Chinese People's Republic 1949–76
map-maker, map-making (hyphen)
Maputo capital of Mozambique; former name **Lourenço Marques**
maquillage cosmetics (not ital.)
Maquis, the French Resistance during WWII
maquis scrub vegetation of the Mediterranean coast
Mar. March
marabou large African stork
marabout Muslim holy man
Maranhão state of NE Brazil
maraschino pl. **maraschinos** sweet cherry liqueur
maraschino cherry cherry preserved in maraschino
Marat, Jean Paul (1743–93), French revolutionary
Marathi (also **Mahratti**) language of Maharashtra
Marathon town in Greece
marathon long-distance race (lower case)
Marbella resort town in southern Spain
marbling marking resembling marble, e.g. on the endpapers of a book
marc (spirit made from) the residue of crushed grapes
Marcan of St Mark or his Gospel (not **-k-**)
marcato Mus. played with emphasis
March (abbrev. **Mar.**)
Marche region of east central Italy
Marches area between England and Wales
marchesa pl. ***marchese*** Italian marchioness (ital. exc. as part of a name)
marchese pl. ***marchesi*** Italian marquess (ital. exc. as part of a name)
marchioness wife or widow of a marquess (cap. in titles)
Marconi, Guglielmo (1874–1937), Italian electrical engineer
Marco Polo (*c.*1254–*c.*1324), Italian traveller
Marcuse, Herbert (1898–1979), German-born American philosopher
Mardi Gras carnival held on Shrove Tuesday (not ital.)
mare pl. **maria** level plain on the moon
mare clausum pl. **maria clausa** sea under the jurisdiction of a particular country (not ital.)
mare liberum pl. **maria libera** part of the seas open to all nations (not ital.)
margarine (not **-gerine**)
margarita tequila cocktail (lower case)
Margaux, Château claret (two words)
margin (abbrev. **marg.**) the four margins of a page are called **back** or **gutter** (at the binding), **head** (at the top), **fore-edge** (opposite the binding), and **tail** (at the foot)
marginalia marginal notes (not ital.)
marginalize (Brit. also **marginalise**)
marguerite ox-eye daisy (lower case)
maria pl. of **mare**
Maria de' Medici see **Marie de Médicis**
mariage blanc pl. ***mariages blancs*** unconsummated marriage (Fr., ital.)
mariage de convenance pl. ***mariages de convenance*** marriage of convenience (Fr., ital.)
Marian of the Virgin Mary
Marie Antoinette (1755–93), French queen, wife of Louis XVI
Marie Celeste see ***Mary Celeste***

Marie de Médicis (1573–1642), queen of France; Italian name *Maria de' Medici*
marijuana (also **marihuana**) cannabis
marinade liquid mixture to flavour food before cooking
marinate soak in a marinade
Mariolatry idolatrous worship of the Virgin Mary (not **Mary-**)
Mariology theology dealing with the Virgin Mary (not **Mary-**)
marionette puppet on strings (not ital.) [Fr. *marionnette*]
Maritime Provinces New Brunswick, Nova Scotia, and Prince Edward Island (Canada)
marjoram culinary herb
mark[1] (before a numeral) particular model of car or aircraft; cf. **marque** (abbrev. **Mk**)
mark[2] former German monetary unit (abbrev. **Mk**)
Mark, St 1 Apostle **2** (also **Mark**) second Gospel (no abbrev.)
Mark Antony see **Antony**
markdown reduction in price (one word)
market garden, market gardener (two words)
market leader (two words)
marketplace (one word)
market research, market share, market town (two words)
markka former monetary unit of Finland
Marks & Spencer UK retail chain (abbrev. **M&S**)
marksman, marksmanship (one word)
marks of reference *, †, ‡, §, ¶, ||
markup (one word) **1** process or result of correcting text for printing **2** structural tags assigned to text
Marlborough, John Churchill, 1st Duke of (1650–1722), British general
marlin fish
marline rope for binding larger ropes
marlinspike (also **marlinespike**) tool for separating strands
Marlowe, Christopher (1564–93), English dramatist □ **Marlovian**
marmalade (not **marmel-**)
Marmara, Sea of small sea in NW Turkey
Marmite trademark dark savoury spread
marmite earthenware cooking pot
marmoset tropical American monkey
marmot burrowing rodent
Marne river of east central France
Maronite member of a Syrian Christian sect
marque make of car; cf. **mark**
marquee large tent
Marquesas Islands volcanic islands in the South Pacific □ **Marquesan**
marquess British nobleman ranking above an earl and below a duke (cap. in titles); cf. **marquis**
marquetry inlaid work
Márquez see **García Márquez**
marquis European nobleman ranking above a count and below a duke (cap. in titles); cf. **marquess**
Marquis de Sade see **Sade**
marquise wife or widow of a marquis (cap. in titles)
Marrakech (also **Marrakesh**) city in western Morocco
marriageable (not **-gable**)
marron glacé pl. **marrons glacés** sugared chestnut (not ital.)
marrowbone (one word)
Mars 1 Rom. Mythol. god of war; Gk equivalent **Ares 2** planet fourth from the sun
Marseillaise national anthem of France (not ital.) [Fr. *La Marseillaise*]
Marseilles city and port in southern France; Fr. name **Marseille**
marshal v. (**marshalling, marshalled**; US one **-l-**)
Marshall, George C(atlett) (1880–1959), American general
Marshall Islands two chains of islands in the NW Pacific
Marshall Plan US programme of aid to western Europe after WWII; official name **European Recovery Program**
Marsh Arab member of a people of southern Iraq (caps)
marshland (one word)
marshmallow confectionery (one word)

marsh mallow tall pink-flowered plant (two words)
Martello tower small circular fort
marten weasel; cf. **martin**
Martha's Vineyard island off the coast of Massachusetts
Martial (*c.*40–*c.*104 AD), Roman epigrammatist; Latin name *Marcus Valerius Martialis*
martin bird of swallow family; cf. **marten**
Martineau, Harriet (1802–76), English writer
martinet strict disciplinarian □ **martinettish**
martingale strap for keeping a horse's head down
Martini 1 trademark Italian vermouth **2** cocktail of gin and dry vermouth
Martinique French island in the Caribbean □ **Martiniquan**
Martinmas 11 November
martlet heraldic bird
martyrize (Brit. also **martyrise**)
marvel v. (**marvelling, marvelled**; US one **-l-**)
Marvell, Andrew (1621–78), English poet
marvellous (US **marvelous**)
Marx, Karl (Heinrich) (1818–83), German political philosopher
Marx Brothers American comedians, **Chico** (Leonard, 1886–1961), **Harpo** (Adolph Arthur, 1888–1964), **Groucho** (Julius Henry, 1890–1977), and **Zeppo** (Herbert, 1901–79) (caps)
Marxism–Leninism doctrine of Marx as developed by Lenin (en rule) □ **Marxist–Leninist**
Mary[1], mother of Jesus; known as **the (Blessed) Virgin Mary** or **St Mary**
Mary[2] **1** (1516–58), queen of England 1553–8; known as **Mary Tudor** or **Bloody Mary 2** (1662–94), queen of England 1689–94 (with her husband, William of Orange)
Mary, Queen of Scots queen of Scotland 1542–67; also known as **Mary Stuart**
Mary, St see **Mary**[1]
Mary Celeste abandoned ship found in the North Atlantic (name frequently reported as ***Marie Celeste***)
Maryland state of the eastern US (official abbrev. **Md.**, postal **MD**)
Marylebone area of London (but the church of St **Mary-le-Bone**)
Mary Magdalene, St follower of Jesus; see also **magdalen**
Masaccio, (1401–28), Italian painter
Masai (also **Maasai**) pl. same or **Masais** member of a people of Tanzania and Kenya
Mascagni, Pietro (1863–1945), Italian composer
mascaraed wearing mascara
Masefield, John (Edward) (1878–1967), English writer, Poet Laureate 1930–67
maser device to amplify radiation in the microwave range (lower case)
MASH US mobile army surgical hospital; (***M*A*S*H***) film and television series set in the Korean War
Mashonaland area of northern Zimbabwe
masjid mosque (ital.)
masker (also **masquer**) participant in a masquerade or masked ball
masking tape (two words)
masochism gratification from one's own pain
Mason–Dixon Line boundary between Maryland and Pennsylvania (en rule, caps)
Masonic relating to Freemasons (cap.)
Masonry Freemasonry
masonry mason's work; stonework
Masorah (also **Massorah**) text on the Hebrew Bible
Masorete (also **Massorete**) Jewish scholar contributing to the Masorah
masque form of dramatic entertainment of the 16th and 17th cents
masquer var. of **masker**
masquerade 1 wearing of disguise; false show **2** N. Amer. masked ball
Mass the Eucharist (cap.)
Mass. Massachusetts (point)
mass Phys. (symbol **m**)
Massachusetts state in the north-eastern US (double *s*, double *t*; official abbrev. **Mass.**, postal **MA**)
massacre slaughter of many people

masseur, **masseuse** (not ital.)
massif group of mountains (not ital.)
Massif Central mountainous plateau in south central France
Massorah, **Massorete** vars of **Masorah**, **Masorete**
mass-produced (hyphen) ◻ **mass production**
Master (cap. in degree titles; abbrev. **M**)
master-at-arms pl. **masters-at-arms** warrant officer on a ship (hyphens)
masterclass (one word)
master mariner seaman qualified as a captain (two words)
mastermind (one word)
master of ceremonies (no hyphens; abbrev. **MC**)
Master of the Rolls judge presiding over the Court of Appeal (Civil Division) (abbrev. **MR**)
masterpiece (one word)
Masters Tournament US golf competition (no apostrophe)
master stroke (two words)
master switch (two words)
masterwork (one word)
masthead (one word)
mastiff large strong dog
mat US var. of **matt**
Matabeleland former province of Rhodesia occupied by the Matabele (or Ndebele) people
matador bullfighter who kills the bull
matchbox, **matchlock**, **matchmaker** (one word)
match play, **match point** (two words)
matchstick, **matchwood** (one word)
maté (infusion of leaves from) a South American shrub (accent, not ital.)
matelot sailor (not ital.)
mater dolorosa the Virgin Mary sorrowing for the death of Christ (not ital.)
materfamilias pl. **matresfamilias** female head of a family (not ital.)
materialize (Brit. also **materialise**)
materia medica (study of) medicines (not ital.)
materiel military materials and equipment (no accent, not ital.) [Fr. *matériel*]
mathematics (also **maths**, N. Amer. **math**; abbrev. **math.**)
matinee afternoon performance (no accent) [Fr. *matinée*]
matins (also **mattins**) morning prayer service
Matisse, Henri (Emile Benoît) (1869–1954), French artist
Mato Grosso high plateau region of SW Brazil, divided into two states, **Mato Grosso** and **Mato Grosso do Sul**
matrix pl. **matrices** or **matrixes**
matronymic (also **metronymic**) name derived from that of a mother or female ancestor
Matt. St Matthew's Gospel
matt (also **matte** or US **mat**) without a shine
matte 1 impure product of smelting **2** mask to obscure part of an image **3** var. of **mat**
Matterhorn mountain in the Alps; Fr. name **Mont Cervin**, It. name **Monte Cervino**
matter-of-fact unemotional and practical (hyphens)
matter of fact fact rather than opinion or conjecture
Matthew, St 1 Apostle **2** (also **Matthew**) first Gospel (abbrev. **Matt.**)
Matthew Paris (*c.*1199–1259), English chronicler
Matthews, Sir Stanley (1915–2000), English footballer
Matthias, St Apostle, chosen to replace Judas
mattins var. of **matins**
mattress (two *ts*)
matzo (also **matzoh**) pl. **matzos** or **matzoth** crisp biscuit of unleavened bread
Maugham, (William) Somerset (1874–1965), British writer
Maui second-largest of the Hawaiian islands
maulana learned or pious Muslim
maulstick var. of **mahlstick**
Mau Mau Kenyan secret society of the 1950s
Maundy ceremony on the day before Good Friday (**Maundy Thursday**)
Maupassant, (Henri René Albert) Guy

de (1850–93), French writer
Mauretania ancient region of North Africa
Mauritania country in West Africa □ **Mauritanian**
Mauritius island country in the Indian Ocean □ **Mauritian**
mausoleum pl. **mausolea** or **mausoleums** impressive building for a tomb
maverick unorthodox person (lower case)
max. maximum (point)
maxi pl. **maxis** full-length skirt or dress
maxilla pl. **maxillae** jaw or jawbone
maximize (Brit. also **maximise**)
maximum pl. **maxima** or **maximums** greatest amount or extent (abbrev. **max.**)
Maxwell, James Clerk (1831–79), Scottish physicist (not **Clerk-Maxwell**)
maxwell unit of magnetic flux (lower case; abbrev. **Mx**)
Maxwell Davies see **Davies**
May fifth month (no abbrev.)
may hawthorn (lower case)
Maya pl. same or **Mayas** member of a Central American Indian people
maybe possibly (one word)
May bug cockchafer (cap., two words)
May Day 1 May (caps, two words)
Mayday international radio distress signal (cap., one word)
mayflower (one word) **1** trailing arbutus **2** (***Mayflower***) ship in which the Pilgrim Fathers sailed to America
mayfly (one word)
mayn't may not (one word, apostrophe)
mayonnaise salad dressing made with egg yolks (two *ns*)
mayor (cap. in titles)
maypole (one word, lower case)
May queen (two words, one cap.)
mayst (no apostrophe)
Mazarin, Jules (1602–61), French cardinal and statesman
Mazarin Bible first book printed from movable type (*c.*1450)
mazarine blue blue butterfly (lower case)
Mazatlán resort in Mexico
Mazdaism Zoroastrianism
mazel tov (among Jews) congratulations, good luck (ital.)
mazurka Polish dance in triple time
Mazzini, Giuseppe (1805–72), Italian nationalist leader
MB **1** Bachelor of Medicine [L. *Medicinae Baccalaureus*] **2** Manitoba (postal abbrev.) **3** Comput. megabyte(s)
Mb Comput. megabit(s)
MBA Master of Business Administration
Mbabane capital of Swaziland
mbar millibar(s)
MBE Member of the Order of the British Empire
Mbeki, Thabo (b.1942), South African president 1999–2008
MBO management buyout
Mbps megabits per second
Mbyte megabyte(s)
MC **1** pl. **MCs** Master of Ceremonies **2** Member of Congress **3** Military Cross **4** music cassette
Mc megacycle(s)
Mc- see **Mac-**
MCC Marylebone Cricket Club
mcg microgram(s)
MCh (also **MChir**, **M.Ch.**) Master of Surgery [L. *Magister Chirurgiae*]
mCi millicurie(s) (medial cap.)
MCom (also **M.Com.**) Master of Commerce
MCR Middle Common Room
Mc/s megacycles per second
MD **1** Doctor of Medicine [L. *Medicinae Doctor*] **2** Managing Director **3** Maryland (postal abbrev.) **4** musical director
Md the chemical element mendelevium (no point)
Md. Maryland (official abbrev.)
MDF medium density fibreboard
MDMA the drug Ecstasy, methylenedioxymethamphetamine
MDT Mountain Daylight Time
ME **1** Maine (postal abbrev.) **2** US Medical Examiner **3** Middle English **4** Brit. myalgic encephalomyelitis (chronic fatigue syndrome)
Me Maître (title of French advocate; no point)
Me. Maine (official abbrev.; point)
me (also **mi**) Mus. note in tonic sol-fa

mea culpa used to accept responsibility (not ital.) [L., 'by my fault']
meagre (US **meager**)
mealie (also **mielie**) S. Afr. maize
meal ticket (two words)
mealtime (one word)
mealy-mouthed afraid to speak honestly (hyphen)
means test n. (two words, hyphen as verb)
meantime (also **in the meantime**) meanwhile (one word)
mean time mean solar time, the time shown on a clock (two words)
meanwhile (also **in the meanwhile**) in the intervening period (one word)
measurable (not **-eable**)
measure 1 Printing width of a full line of print (abbrev. **meas.**) **2** N. Amer. bar of music
Measure for Measure Shakespeare play (abbrev. ***Meas. for M.***)
measuring tape (two words)
meatball (one word)
Meath county in the Republic of Ireland
Mecca city in Saudi Arabia, the holiest city of Islam; Arab. name **Makkah**
Meccano trademark toy for making mechanical models
mechanize (Brit. also **mechanise**)
Mechelen city in northern Belgium; Fr. name **Malines**
Mechlin lace lace made in Mechelen
MEcon (also **M.Econ.**) Master of Economics
MEd (also **M.Ed.**) Master of Education
med. 1 chiefly N. Amer. medical **2** medium
médaillon flat oval piece of meat or fish (Fr., ital.)
medal inscribed piece of metal; cf. **meddle**
medallion (two *l*s)
medallist (US **medalist**)
meddle interfere; cf. **medal**
Mede member of a people of Media
Medea Gk Mythol. wife of Jason, who killed her own children
Medellín city in Colombia (accent)
Media ancient region of Asia
media 1 means of mass communication (treated as sing. or pl.) **2** pl. of **medium**
mediaeval var. of **medieval**
Medicaid US federal system of health insurance for the poor
medical (abbrev. **med.**) □ **medically**
Medicare 1 US federal system of health insurance for the elderly **2** Canadian and Australian health-care scheme
Medici (also **de' Medici**) powerful Florentine family in the 15th–18th cents □ **Medicean**
medieval (also **mediaeval**)
Medina city in Saudi Arabia; Arab. name **al-Madinah**
medina walled part of a North African town
Mediterranean (one *t*, two *r*s)
medium (abbrev. **med.**) **1** pl. **media** or **mediums** channel of mass communication; see also **media 2** pl. **mediums** spiritualist
medley pl. **medleys**
Médoc 1 area of SW France **2** claret
meerkat southern African mongoose
meerschaum clay tobacco pipe
Meerut city in northern India
meeting place (two words)
mega- denoting a factor of one million (10^6), or 2^{20} in computing (abbrev. **M**)
megabit Comput. one million or (strictly) 1,048,576 bits (abbrev. **Mb**)
megabyte Comput. one million or (strictly) 1,048,576 bytes (abbrev. **MB**)
Megaera Gk Mythol. one of the Furies
megahertz pl. same, one million hertz (abbrev. **MHz**)
megapixel Comput. one million or (strictly) 1,048,576 pixels (abbrev. **MP**)
Megara city and port in ancient Greece
megaton (also **megatonne**) unit of explosive power
megavolt one million volts (abbrev. **MV**)
megawatt one million watts (abbrev. **MW**)
Megiddo ancient city in NW Palestine
Megillah book of the Hebrew scriptures
megilp (also **magilp**) vehicle for oil colours
Meiji Tenno (1852–1912), emperor of Japan 1868–1912; born *Mutsuhito*
meiosis pl. **meioses 1** litotes **2** Biol. cell division □ **meiotic**

Meissen 1 city in eastern Germany **2** Dresden china
Meistersinger pl. same or **Meistersingers** hist. member of a German poets' guild (cap., not ital.)
meitnerium chemical element of atomic number 109 (symbol **Mt**)
Mekong river of SE Asia
Melaka (also **Malacca**) state and city in Malaysia
Melanesia Solomon Islands, Vanuatu, New Caledonia, Fiji, and other islands
melange varied mixture (not ital., no accent) [Fr. *mélange*]
melee confused fight (not ital.) [Fr. *mêlée*]
Melos Greek island in the Aegean; mod. Gk name **Mílos**, Fr. and It. name **Milo**
Melpomene the Muse of tragedy
meltdown (one word)
meltemi summer wind in the eastern Mediterranean
melting point, melting pot (two words)
Melton Mowbray town in Leicestershire (two words)
meltwater (one word)
memento pl. **mementos** or **mementoes** souvenir (not **mom-**)
memento mori pl. same, object kept as a reminder of death (not ital.)
memo pl. **memos** memorandum
memoir personal historical account
memorabilia objects kept because of their associations
memorandum pl. **memoranda** or **memorandums** written message
memorialize (Brit. also **memorialise**)
memorize (Brit. also **memorise**)
Memphis 1 ancient city of Egypt **2** river port in Tennessee
memsahib Ind. married white woman
ménage household (accent, not ital.)
ménage à trois pl. ***ménages à trois*** household of a married couple and a lover (Fr., ital.)
menagerie collection of captive animals
menarche first menstruation
Mencken, H(enry) L(ouis) (1880–1956), American journalist and literary critic
mendacity untruthfulness; cf. **mendicity** □ **mendacious**
Mendel, Gregor Johann (1822–84), Moravian monk, the father of genetics □ **Mendelian**
Mendeleev, Dmitri (Ivanovich) (1834–1907), Russian chemist
mendelevium chemical element of atomic number 101 (symbol **Md**)
Mendelssohn, Felix (1809–47), German composer; full name *Jakob Ludwig Felix Mendelssohn-Bartholdy*
Menderes river of SW Turkey; ancient name **Maeander**
mendicity state of being a beggar; cf. **mendacity**
Menelaus Gk Mythol. king of Sparta, husband of Helen
menhaden North American fish
menhir upright prehistoric stone
meninges (sing. **meninx**) Anat. membranes enclosing the brain and spinal cord
meningitis inflammation of the meninges
meniscus pl. **menisci** Phys. curved upper surface of a liquid in a tube
Mennonite member of a Protestant sect in North America
menorah branched candelabrum used in Jewish worship; (**the Menorah**) candelabrum in the ancient temple of Jerusalem
Menorca Sp. name for **Minorca**
Mensa organization for people with high IQ scores (one cap.)
Menshevik hist. moderate opposed to the Bolsheviks
mens rea intention as part of a crime (L., ital.)
mens sana in corpore sano a sound mind in a sound body (L., ital.)
menswear (one word, no apostrophe)
mental defective, mental deficiency, mental handicap, mentally handicapped dated and offensive: express otherwise, e.g. in terms of 'learning difficulties'
menu pl. **menus**
Menuhin, Sir Yehudi (1916–99), American-born British violinist
meow var. of **miaow**
MEP Member of the European

Parliament

Mephistopheles evil spirit to whom Faust sold his soul in German legend □ **Mephistophelian** (also **Mephistophelean**)

Mercator projection map projection with all latitudes the same length as the equator

Mercedes-Benz German make of car (hyphen)

merchandise n. goods bought and sold. v. (also **merchandize**) promote the sale of

Merchant of Venice, The Shakespeare play (abbrev. ***Merch. V.***)

Merckx, Eddy (b.1945), Belgian racing cyclist

Mercurial of the planet Mercury

mercurial 1 subject to sudden changes of mood or mind **2** of the element mercury

Mercury 1 Rom. Mythol. messenger of the gods; Gk equivalent **Hermes 2** planet closest to the sun

mercury chemical element of atomic number 80 (symbol **Hg**)

merengue Caribbean dance music

meretricious superficially attractive but valueless

meringue sweet food

merino pl. **merinos** kind of sheep

Merionethshire former county of NW Wales

meritorious deserving reward or praise

Merlot French black wine grape (cap.)

Merovingian member of a Frankish dynasty *c.*500–750

Merriam-Webster publishers (hyphen)

merry-go-round (hyphens)

merrymaker, merrymaking (one word)

Merry Wives of Windsor, The Shakespeare play (abbrev. ***Merry W.***)

Merseyside former metropolitan county of NW England

Merthyr Tydfil town in South Wales

mésalliance misalliance (Fr., ital.)

mescal liquor distilled from agave

mescaline (also **mescalin**) intoxicating substance found in a cactus

Mesdames pl. of **Madame**

Mesdemoiselles pl. of **Mademoiselle**

mesmerize (Brit. also **mesmerise**)

Meso-America America from central Mexico to Nicaragua (hyphen, caps)

Mesolithic middle part of the Stone Age

Mesolóngion mod. Gk name for **Missolonghi**

Mesopotamia ancient region of SW Asia

Mesozoic Geol. era between the Palaeozoic and Cenozoic eras

Messeigneurs pl. of **Monseigneur**

Messerschmidt, Willy (1898–1978), German aircraft designer; full name *Wilhelm Emil Messerschmidt*

Messiaen, Olivier (Eugène Prosper Charles) (1908–92), French composer

Messiah promised deliverer of the Jewish nation; (the ***Messiah***) oratorio by Handel, 1742 (not ***The Messiah***)

messiah leader regarded as a saviour (lower case)

messianic of the Messiah or a messiah (lower case)

Messieurs pl. of **Monsieur**

Messrs pl. of **Mr** (no point)

mestizo (fem. **mestiza**; pl. **mestizos** or **mestizas**) Latin American of mixed race

metabolize (Brit. also **metabolise**)

metal v. (**metalling, metalled**; US one **-l-**)

metallize (Brit. also **metallise**, US also **metalize**)

metallurgy study of metals

metalware, metalwork, metalworking (one word)

metamorphosis pl. **metamorphoses** transformation □ **metamorphose**

metaphor figure of speech

metaphysical poets 17th-cent. poets using elaborate conceits (lower case)

metathesis pl. **metatheses** transposition of sounds or letters

metempsychosis pl. **metempsychoses** transmigration of the soul

meteorology study of weather

meter 1 measuring device **2** US var. of **metre**

methamphetamine illegal stimulant

méthode champenoise traditional way of making sparkling wine (Fr., ital.)

Methuselah (in the Old Testament) grandfather of Noah
methuselah large wine bottle (lower case)
métier occupation one is good at (accent, not ital.)
metonymy figure of speech substituting a part or attribute for the whole
metre (US **meter**) **1** SI unit of length (abbrev. **m**) **2** rhythm of a piece of poetry or music
metric royal see **royal**
metro pl. **metros** underground railway system; (***Le Métro***) Paris underground
metrology study of measurement
metronymic var. of **matronymic**
Metternich, Klemens Wenzel Nepomuk Lothar, Prince of Metternich-Winneburg-Beilstein (1773–1859), Austrian statesman
meunière cooked in butter with lemon and parsley (not ital.; after the noun)
Meuse river of France, Belgium, and the Netherlands; Du. name **Maas**
mews pl. same, row of stables converted into houses
Mexico country in North America □ **Mexican**
Meyerbeer, Giacomo (1791–1864), German composer; born *Jakob Liebmann Beer*
meze pl. same or **mezes** selection of Greek or Middle Eastern dishes (not ital.)
mezzanine storey between two others
mezza voce Mus. not using all one's vocal power
mezzo pl. **mezzos** Mus. singer with a voice between contralto and soprano
mezzo forte Mus. moderately loud(ly) (abbrev. **mf**)
Mezzogiorno southern Italy, including Sicily and Sardinia
mezzo piano Mus. moderately softly (abbrev. **mp**)
mezzo-relievo pl. **mezzo-relievos** Art half relief
mezzo-soprano pl. **mezzo-sopranos** another name for **mezzo** (hyphen)
mezzotint print made from an engraved plate giving areas of light and shade
MF **1** machine finish **2** medium frequency
mf mezzo forte
MFH Master of Foxhounds
MFN most favoured nation
MG **1** machine-glazed **2** machine gun **3** hist. Morris Garages (make of car)
Mg the chemical element magnesium (no point)
mg milligram(s)
MGM Metro-Goldwyn-Mayer, a film company
Mgr pl. **Mgrs** **1** Monseigneur **2** Monsignor
MHK Member of the House of Keys
MHR Member of the House of Representatives
MHz megahertz (two caps)
MI **1** Michigan (postal abbrev.) **2** Military Intelligence
mi Mus. var. of **me**
mi. mile(s) (point)
MI5 UK agency responsible for internal security; official name **Security Service**
MI6 UK agency responsible for counter-intelligence overseas; official name **Secret Intelligence Service**
miaow (also **meow**) cat's cry
miasma pl. **miasmas** unhealthy smell or vapour
Mic. Micah
mica shiny mineral
Micah **1** Hebrew minor prophet **2** book of the Old Testament (abbrev. **Mic.**)
Micawber, Wilkins, character in Dickens's novel *David Copperfield* (1850), an eternal optimist
Mich. Michigan (official abbrev.)
Michael, St archangel
Michaelmas 29 September
Michaelmas term university term or session of the High Court beginning in autumn (one cap.)
Michelangelo (1475–1564), Italian artist and poet; full name *Michelangelo Buonarroti*
Michelin, André (1853–1931) and Édouard (1859–1940), French industrialists
Michigan state in the northern US (official abbrev. **Mich.**, postal **MI**) □ **Michigander**

mickey (also **micky**) (in **take the mickey (out of)**) tease or ridicule
Mickey Finn drugged drink
Mickey Mouse Walt Disney cartoon character
Micmac (also **Mi'kmaq**) pl. same or **Micmacs** member of an American Indian people of Canada
micro pl. **micros** microcomputer or microprocessor
micro- (symbol **µ**) **1** small **2** factor of one millionth
microchip, microclimate, microcomputer (one word)
microeconomics economics concerned with single factors (one word)
microfiche, microfilm film containing minute photographs of a document
microgram one millionth of a gram (symbol **µg**)
microlitre (US also **microliter**) one millionth of a litre (symbol **µl**)
micrometer 1 gauge for measuring small distances or thicknesses **2** US var. of **micrometre**
micrometre (US **micrometer**) one millionth of a metre (symbol **µm**)
micron another name for **micrometre** (symbol **µ**)
Micronesia region of the western Pacific to the north of Melanesia and north and west of Polynesia
microorganism, microprocessor (one word)
microsecond one millionth of a second (symbol **µs**)
Microsoft trademark computer manufacturers (abbrev. **MS**)
mid generally forms open compounds (*the mid 17th century*), but hyphenated when attrib. (*mid-brown hair*)
mid-air (hyphen)
midbrain, midday (one word)
middle age (two words) □ **middle-aged**
Middle Ages period from the fall of the western Roman Empire (5th cent.) to the fall of Constantinople (1453), or more narrowly *c.*1000–1453
middlebrow (one word)
middle class (two words, hyphen when attrib.)
middle common room common room for graduate students (abbrev. **MCR**)
Middle East, Middle Eastern (no hyphen even when attrib.)
Middle England (caps)
Middle English English *c.*1150–*c.*1470 (abbrev. **ME**)
Middle European of central Europe (two caps, no hyphen even when attrib.)
middleman (one word)
middle of the road avoiding extremes (four words, hyphens when attrib.)
Middlesbrough port in NE England (not **-borough**)
Middlesex former county of SE England (abbrev. **Middx**)
middleweight boxing weight above welterweight (one word)
Middle West another name for **Midwest**
Mideast US name for **Middle East**
midfield central part of a soccer field (one word)
Midgard Norse Mythol. region in which human beings live
Mid Glamorgan former county of South Wales (two words, two caps)
MIDI musical instrument digital interface
Midi the south of France (not ital.)
midi pl. **midis** calf-length skirt or dress
Midland 1 central US **2** of the Midlands of England
Midlands, the inland counties of central England
midlife, midline (one word)
Midlothian council area of central Scotland (one word)
midnight (one word)
mid-off, mid-on Cricket (hyphen)
midriff region between the chest and the waist
midshipman pl. **midshipmen**
midships, midstream, midsummer (one word)
Midsummer Day (Brit. also **Midsummer's Day**) 24 June (caps)
Midsummer Night's Dream, A Shakespeare play (abbrev. ***Mids. N. D.***)
midterm, midway (one word)
Midway Islands two small islands and a coral atoll in the central Pacific

midweek (one word)
Midwest northern states of the US from Ohio to the Rocky Mountains
midwife pl. **midwives** nurse who assists women in childbirth □ **midwifery**
midwinter (one word)
mielie var. of **mealie**
mien appearance or manner (not ital.)
Mies van der Rohe, Ludwig (1886–1969), German-born architect and designer □ **Miesian**
MiG Russian aircraft designed by Mikoyan and Gurevich (two caps; individual models are cited with a hyphen, e.g. *MiG-15*)
mihrab niche in the wall of a mosque (ital.)
Mi'kmaq var. of **Micmac**
Míkonos mod. Gk name for **Mykonos**
mil one thousandth of an inch (no point)
Milan city in NW Italy; It. name **Milano**
milch cow source of easy profit (not **milk**)
mile (abbrev. **mi.**)
mileage (not **milage**)
mileometer var. of **milometer**
milepost, milestone (one word)
Milhaud, Darius (1892–1974), French composer
milieu pl. **milieux** or **milieus** social environment
militarize (Brit. also **militarise**)
Military Cross (abbrev. **MC**)
military-industrial complex (hyphen)
Military Medal (abbrev. **MM**)
militate have an effect; cf. **mitigate**
milkman, milkshake, milksop (one word)
Milky Way band of light crossing the night sky (caps)
Mill, John Stuart (1806–73), English philosopher and economist □ **Millian**
Millais, Sir John Everett (1829–96), English painter
Millay, Edna St Vincent (1892–1950), US poet
millefeuille layered puff-pastry cake (one word, not ital.)
millefiori ornamental glass (one word, not ital.)
millenarian of the Christian millennium (two *l*s, one *n*)
millenary of a thousand (two *l*s, one *n*)
millennium pl. **millennia** or **millenniums** one thousand years; (**the millennium**) prophesied thousand-year reign of Christ (lower case; two *l*s, two *n*s)
millepede use **millipede**
millesimal thousandth
Millet, Jean (François) (1814–75), French painter
Millett, Kate (b.1934), American feminist
milli- one-thousandth (forms unhyphenated words)
milliard billion
millibar cgs unit of atmospheric pressure (abbrev. **mbar**)
millieme Egyptian monetary unit
Milligan, Spike (1918–2002), British comedian and writer; born *Terence Alan Milligan*
milligram (also **milligramme**) (abbrev. **mg**)
millilitre (US **milliliter**) (abbrev. **ml**)
millimetre (US **millimeter**) (abbrev. **mm**)
million pl. **millions** or with numeral or quantifying word **million** a thousand thousands, 1,000,000 (abbrev. **m**; for millions of pounds write e.g. *£150m*)
millionaire (one *n*)
millipede (not **mille-**)
milliwatt one thousandth of a watt (abbrev. **mW**)
millpond, millstone, millstream (one word)
Mills & Boon trademark publishers of romantic novels
mill wheel (two words)
millworker, millwright (one word)
Milne, A(lan) A(lexander) (1882–1956), English writer for children
Milo Fr. and It name for **Melos**
milometer (also **mileometer**)
Mílos mod. Gk name for **Melos**
Milosevic, Slobodan (1941–2006), president of Serbia 1989–97 and of Yugoslavia 1997–2000

milreis pl. same, former monetary unit of Portugal and Brazil
Milton, John (1608–74), English poet □ **Miltonian, Miltonic**
Milton Keynes town in central England
Milwaukee city in SE Wisconsin
mimbar var. of ***minbar***
mimeograph obsolete duplicating machine
mimic v. (**mimicking, mimicked**) □ **mimicry**
min. **1** minim (fluid measure) **2** minimum **3** minute(s) (no point in scientific work)
minaret slender tower of a mosque □ **minareted**
minatory threatening
minbar (also ***mimbar***) steps in a mosque for preaching from (ital.)
mincemeat (one word)
mince pie (two words)
Mindanao second-largest island in the Philippines
Mindoro island in the Philippines
mindset (one word)
mine detector (two words)
minefield, minehunter, minelayer (one word)
Mineola town in Texas (one *n*); cf. **minneola**
mineralize (Brit. also **mineralise**)
mineralogy (not **-ology**)
mineral water (two words)
Minerva Rom. equivalent of **Athene**
mineshaft (one word)
minestrone soup with vegetables and pasta (not **-oni**)
minesweeper (one word)
Mini trademark model of car
mini pl. **minis** miniskirt (lower case)
miniature (not **-iture**)
miniaturize (Brit. also **miniaturise**)
minibus, minicab, minicomputer, minidisc (one word)
minikin small (person or thing)
minim **1** short vertical stroke in forming a letter **2** Mus., Brit. note with the value of two crotchets **3** one sixtieth of a fluid drachm (abbrev. **min.**)
minimize (Brit. also **minimise**)
minimum pl. **minima** or **minimums** smallest amount or extent (abbrev. **min.**)
miniseries, miniskirt (one word)
Minister of State, Minister of the Crown, Minister without Portfolio (two caps)
minivan (also trademark **Mini Van**)
miniver plain white fur
mink pl. same or **minks** stoat-like carnivore
minke small whale
Minn. Minnesota (official abbrev.)
Minneapolis city in SE Minnesota
minneola fruit (two *ns*); cf. **Mineola**
Minnesinger medieval German lyric poet (cap., not ital.)
Minnesota state in the north central US (official abbrev. **Minn.**, postal **MN**)
Minoan of a Bronze Age civilization of Crete
Minorca second-largest of the Balearic Islands; Sp. name **Menorca**
Minotaur Gk Mythol. creature who was half-man and half-bull
Minsk capital of Belarus
minuet (**minueting, minueted**) (perform) a stately dance in triple time
minuscule (not **mini-**) **1** tiny **2** in lower-case letters **3** of a small cursive script
minus sign the sign −
minute (abbrev. **m** or **min.**; no point in scientific work; symbol ′)
minutiae (also **minutia**) small details
Miocene fourth epoch of the Tertiary period
miosis (also **myosis**) constriction of the pupil of the eye
Mirabeau, Honoré Gabriel Riqueti, Comte de (1749–91), French revolutionary politician
mirabile dictu wonderful to relate (L., ital.)
mirepoix sautéed chopped vegetables (Fr., ital.)
mirk, mirky use **murk, murky**
Miró, Joan (1893–1983), Spanish painter
mirror image (two words)
MIRV intercontinental missile [*multiple*

independently targeted re-entry vehicle]
miry very muddy (not **-ey**)
misalliance unsuitable marriage; cf. ***mésalliance***
misandry hatred of the male sex
misanthropy dislike of humankind
miscegenation interbreeding
miscellanea miscellaneous items (pl.)
miscellaneous of various types or origins (abbrev. **misc.**)
miscellany pl. **miscellanies** book collecting items by different authors
mischievous (not **-ious**)
miscible forming a homogeneous mixture
misdemeanour (US **misdemeanor**)
mise en place preparation of cooking ingredients in advance (Fr., ital.)
mise en scène arrangement of scenery and properties (Fr., ital.)
miserere (lower case) **1** (musical setting of) Psalm 51 **2** another name for **misericord**
misericord ledge on the underside of a seat in a choir stall
misfeasance wrongful exercise of lawful authority; cf. **malfeasance**
mishit (one word)
mishmash (one word)
Mishnah first part of the Talmud ◻ **Mishnaic**
misogamy hatred of marriage
misogyny hatred of women by men
misprint error in printed text
Miss title of a girl or unmarried woman
Miss. Mississippi (official abbrev.)
mis-sell (hyphen)
missel thrush var. of **mistle thrush**
misshape, misshapen (one word)
Mississippi (two double *ss*, double *p*) **1** major river of North America **2** state of the southern US (official abbrev. **Miss.**, postal **MS**) ◻ **Mississippian**
Missolonghi city in western Greece (double *s*); mod. Gk name **Mesolóngion**
Missouri (double *s*) **1** one of the main tributaries of the Mississippi **2** state of the US (official abbrev. **Mo.**, postal **MO**) ◻ **Missourian**
misspeak, misspell, misspend, misstate (one word)
Mister Mr
mistle thrush (also **missel thrush**)
mistletoe plant with white berries (not **missel-**)
mistral strong cold wind in southern France (not ital.)
Mistress arch. Mrs
MIT Massachusetts Institute of Technology
miter US var. of **mitre**
Mithraism cult of the god **Mithras**, popular during the first three cents AD
Mithridates VI (also **Mithradates VI**) (*c.*132–63 BC), king of Pontus 120–63; known as **Mithridates the Great**
mithridatize (Brit. also **mithridatise**) make immune to poison by gradually increasing doses (lower case)
mitigate make less severe; cf. **militate**
Mitilíni mod. Gk name for **Mytilene**
mitre (US **miter**)
Mitsubishi Japanese car company
Mittelstand medium-sized companies (Ger., cap., ital.)
Mitterrand, François (Maurice Marie) (1916–96), French president 1981–95
Mixtec pl. same or **Mixtecs** member of a people of southern Mexico
mix-up n. (hyphen, two words as verb)
Mizoram state in NE India
mizzen (also **mizen, mizzenmast**, or **mizen**) mast aft of the mainmast
mizzensail (also **mizensail**) sail on a mizzen (one word)
Mk 1 hist. German mark **2** St Mark's Gospel **3** mark (of car, aircraft, etc.)
mks metre-kilogram-second
ml 1 mile(s) **2** millilitre(s)
MLA 1 Member of the Legislative Assembly **2** Modern Language Association (of America)
MLC Member of the Legislative Council
MLD minimum lethal dose
MLF multilateral nuclear force
MLitt Master of Letters [L. *Magister Litterarum*]
Mlle pl. **Mlles** Mademoiselle
MLR minimum lending rate
MM 1 Messieurs **2** Military Medal

mm millimetre(s)
Mme pl. **Mmes** Madame
m.m.f. magnetomotive force
MMR measles, mumps, and rubella
MMS Multimedia Messaging Service
MMus (also **M.Mus.**) Master of Music
MN 1 Merchant Navy **2** Minnesota (postal abbrev.)
Mn the chemical element manganese (no point)
Mn. Modern (with language names)
mnemonic pattern of letters which aids the memory
Mnemosyne mother of the Muses
MO 1 Comput. magneto-optical **2** Medical Officer **3** Missouri (postal abbrev.) **4** modus operandi **5** money order
Mo the chemical element molybdenum (no point)
Mo. Missouri (official abbrev.; point)
mo. N. Amer. month
-mo indicating book size according to the number of leaves per sheet
mobilize (Brit. also **mobilise**)
Möbius strip surface with one continuous side (one cap.)
Mobutu, Sese Seko (1930–97), president of Zaire (now the Democratic Republic of Congo) 1965–97
Moby-Dick novel by H. Melville, 1851 (hyphen)
moccasin soft leather shoe (two *c*s, one *s*)
Mocha port in Yemen
mocha type of coffee (lower case)
mock-heroic (hyphen)
mock turtle soup (three words)
mock-up n. (hyphen, two words as verb)
MoD Ministry of Defence
mod. modern
model v. (**modelling, modelled**; US one **-l-**)
modem Comput. device for modulation and demodulation
Modena city in northern Italy
Moderations first public examination in some faculties for the BA at Oxford (abbrev. **Mods**)
moderato pl. **moderatos** Mus. performed at a moderate pace
modern (abbrev. **mod.**, with language names **Mn.**)
moderne of a popularization of art deco (not ital.)
modern English English since about 1500
modernism, modernist (lower case)
modernize (Brit. also **modernise**)
modicum small quantity (no pl.)
Modigliani, Amedeo (1884–1920), Italian artist
modiste milliner or dressmaker (not ital.)
Mods Moderations
modus operandi pl. **modi operandi** way of doing something (not ital.; abbrev. **MO**)
modus vivendi pl. **modi vivendi** way of coexisting (not ital.)
Moët & Chandon trademark champagne
Mogadishu capital of Somalia
Mogul (also **Moghul** or **Mughal**) member of an Indian ruling dynasty, 16th–19th cents
mogul important or influential person (lower case)
MOH 1 Medical Officer of Health **2** Ministry of Health
Mohammed use **Muhammad**
Mohave Desert var. of **Mojave Desert**
Mohawk 1 pl. same or **Mohawks** member of an American Indian people **2** N. Amer. Mohican haircut
Mohegan (also **Mohican**) member of an American Indian people; cf. **Mahican**
Mohican 1 hairstyle with a single strip of hair down the middle of the head **2** var. of **Mahican** or **Mohegan**
Moholy-Nagy, László (1895–1946), Hungarian-born American artist
moidore old Portuguese gold coin
moiety each of two parts
moire (also **moiré**) silk with a rippled appearance (not ital.)
moisturize (Brit. also **moisturise**)
Moivre, Abraham de (1667–1754), French mathematician
Mojave Desert (also **Mohave**) desert in southern California
mol Chem. mole
molasses 1 uncrystallized juice from raw sugar **2** N. Amer. golden syrup

Mold town in NE Wales
mold US var. of **mould**
Moldau Ger. name for **Vltava**
Moldavia 1 former principality of SE Europe **2** another name for **Moldova**
Moldavian Romanian as spoken in Moldova
Moldova landlocked country in SE Europe; also called **Moldavia**
mole SI unit of amount of substance (abbrev. **mol**)
molehill, moleskin (one word)
Molière (1622–73), French dramatist; pseudonym of *Jean-Baptiste Poquelin*
moll Mus. minor (Ger., ital.)
mollusc (US **mollusk**)
Moloch Canaanite idol
Molotov, Vyacheslav (Mikhailovich) (1890–1986), Soviet statesman; born *Vyacheslav Mikhailovich Skryabin*
Molotov cocktail (one cap.)
molt US var. of **moult**
molto Mus. much, very
Molucca Islands island group in Indonesia; Indonesian name **Maluku** □ **Moluccan**
molybdenum chemical element of atomic number 42 (symbol **Mo**)
MoMA Museum of Modern Art, New York (three caps)
Mombasa city in SE Kenya (one *s*)
momentarily 1 for a very short time **2** N. Amer. very soon
momentum pl. **momenta** impetus
Mommsen, Theodor (1817–1903), German historian
Mon. Monday
Monaco coastal principality within France; see also **Monégasque**
Mona Lisa painting by Leonardo da Vinci; also called **La Gioconda**
monarch (always lower case)
monastery (not **-try**)
Mönchengladbach city in NW Germany
Monck, George, 1st Duke of Albemarle (1608–70), English general
mondaine fashionable or worldly (person) (Fr., ital.)
Monday (abbrev. **Mon.**)
Mondrian, Piet (1872–1944), Dutch painter; born *Pieter Cornelis Mondriaan*
Monégasque person from Monaco (not ital.)
Monet, Claude (1840–1926), French painter
monetize (Brit. also **monetise**) convert into currency
money pl. (in sense 'sums of money') **monies** or **moneys**
money box, money changer (two words)
moneyed (also **monied**)
moneylender, moneymaker (one word)
money order (two words; abbrev. **MO**)
Mongol person from Mongolia (do not use with reference to Down's syndrome)
Mongolia country of east Asia □ **Mongolian**
mongolism use **Down's syndrome**
Mongoloid of a division of humankind that includes Mongolians (do not use with reference to Down's syndrome)
mongoose pl. **mongooses**
monied var. of **moneyed**
monies pl. of **money**
moniker (also **monicker**) informal a name
Monk, Thelonious (Sphere) (1917–82), American jazz pianist
monkshood poisonous garden plant (one word, no apostrophe)
Monmouthshire county of SE Wales
monochrome in black and white or tones of one colour
monocoque vehicle structure with chassis integral to the body
monoecious Biol. having both the male and female reproductive organs in the same individual; cf. **dioecious**
monogamy marriage to one person at a time
monograph academic publication on a single subject
monogyny marriage to one woman at a time
monologue (not **-log**)
monopolize (Brit. also **monopolise**)
monotype 1 single print from a design in paint or ink **2** (**Monotype**) trademark

obsolete hot-metal typesetting machine

monounsaturated (no hyphen)

Monroe 1 James (1758–1831), 5th president of the US 1817–25 **2** Marilyn (1926–62), American actress; born *Norma Jean Mortenson*, later *Baker*

Monrovia capital of Liberia

Mons town in southern Belgium; Flemish name **Bergen**

Monseigneur pl. **Messeigneurs** title of a French prince or prelate (abbrev. **Mgr**, pl. **Mgrs**); cf. **Monsignor**

Monsieur pl. **Messieurs** French equivalent of 'Mr' (abbrev. **M**, pl. **MM**)

Monsignor pl. **Monsignori** title of various senior Roman Catholic posts (abbrev. **Mgr**, pl. **Mgrs**); cf. **Monseigneur**

mons pubis, mons Veneris fatty tissue over the joint of the pubic bones

Mont. Montana (official abbrev.)

Montagues Romeo's family in *Romeo and Juliet*; cf. **Capulets**

Montaigne, Michel (Eyquem) de (1533–92), French essayist

Montana state in the western US (official abbrev. **Mont.**, postal **MT**) ◻ **Montanan**

Mont Blanc peak in the Alps

Mont Cervin Fr. name for **Matterhorn**

Monte Carlo resort in Monaco

Monte Cervino It. name for **Matterhorn**

Montego Bay tourist resort in Jamaica

Montenegro republic in the Balkans; Serbian name **Crna Gora** ◻ **Montenegrin** (also **Montenegran**)

Monterey city in California

Monterrey city in NE Mexico

Montesquieu, Charles Louis de Secondat, Baron de La Brède et de (1689–1755), French philosopher

Montessori, Maria (1870–1952), Italian educationist

Monteverdi, Claudio (1567–1643), Italian composer

Montevideo capital of Uruguay

Montfort, Simon de, Earl of Leicester (*c.*1208–65), English soldier

Montgolfier, Joseph Michel (1740–1810) and Jacques Étienne (1745–99), French pioneers in hot-air ballooning

Montgomery 1 Bernard Law, 1st Viscount Montgomery of Alamein (1887–1976), British Field Marshal **2** L(ucy) M(aud) (1874–1942), Canadian novelist

Montgomeryshire former county of central Wales

month abbreviated Jan., Feb., Mar., Apr., Aug., Sept., Oct., Nov., Dec.; May, June, and July in full; style days of the month e.g. *25 January* (US *January 25*)

Montmartre, Montparnasse districts of Paris

Montpelier state capital of Vermont (one *l*)

Montpellier city in southern France (two *ls*)

Montreal port in Quebec; Fr. name **Montréal**

Montreux resort town in Switzerland

Montserrat one of the Leeward Islands ◻ **Montserratian**

moon cap. only in astronomical contexts; other planets' moons are lower case

moonbeam (one word)

Moonies derog. the Unification Church

moonlight n., v. (past and past part. **moonlighted**) (one word)

moonlit adj. (one word)

moonscape, moonshine, moonstone, moonstruck (one word)

Moor member of a NW African Muslim people ◻ **Moorish**

Moore 1 George (Augustus) (1852–1933), Irish novelist **2** G(eorge) E(dward) (1873–1958), English philosopher **3** Henry (Spencer) (1898–1986), English sculptor **4** Sir John (1761–1809), British general **5** Thomas (1779–1852), Irish poet

moorhen, moorland (one word)

moose pl. same

MOR middle-of-the-road

moraine rocks and sediment deposited by a glacier

moral concerned with right and wrong

morale confidence and discipline

moralize (Brit. also **moralise**)

Moral Rearmament Christian organization emphasizing integrity and respect (abbrev. **MRA**)

moratorium pl. **moratoriums** or **moratoria** temporary prohibition
Moravia region of the Czech Republic
Moray (also **Morayshire**) council area of northern Scotland
moray eel eel-like fish
morceau pl. **morceaux** short literary or musical composition (not ital.)
mordant sharply critical
mordent Mus. ornament of one rapid alternation of notes
More, Sir Thomas (1478–1535), English scholar and statesman; canonized as **St Thomas More**
Morecambe Bay inlet on the NW coast of England (not **-combe**)
morel edible fungus
morello pl. **morellos** sour cherry
mores customs and conventions (not ital.)
Morgannwg Welsh name for **Glamorgan**
morgue mortuary
MORI Market and Opinion Research International
moribund in terminal decline
Morisot, Berthe (Marie Pauline) (1841–95), French painter
Mormon member of the Church of Jesus Christ of Latter-day Saints
Moro pl. **Moros** Muslim inhabitant of the Philippines
Morocco country in NW Africa □ **Moroccan**
morocco pl. **moroccos** fine flexible leather (lower case)
morpheme Ling. meaningful unit that cannot be further divided (e.g. *in*, *come*, *-ing*, forming *incoming*)
Morpheus Rom. Mythol. god of sleep
morphology study of the forms of things
Morris 1 William (1834–96), English designer, craftsman, and writer **2** William Richard, see **Nuffield**
morris dance, morris dancer, morris dancing (two words, lower case)
Morrison, Toni (b.1931), American novelist; full name *Chloe Anthony Morrison*
Morse code system of light or sound signals (one cap.)
mortar board (two words)
mortgage (not **morg-**) □ **mortgageable**
mortgagee lender in a mortgage
mortgagor (also **mortgager**) borrower in a mortgage
mortise (also **mortice**) recess to receive a projection and lock parts together
mortmain Law status of lands held inalienably
Mosaic of Moses
mosaic (**mosaicks, mosaicking, mosaicked**) (decorate with) a design created using small pieces of stone, glass, etc.
Moscow capital of Russia; Russ. name **Moskva**
Mosel 1 river of NE France, Luxembourg, and Germany **2** Moselle wine
Moseley, Henry Gwyn Jeffreys (1887–1915), English physicist
Moselle 1 white wine from the valley of the Mosel **2** the Mosel
Moses (*fl. c.*14th–13th cents BC), Hebrew prophet and lawgiver
Moskva Russ. name for **Moscow**
Moslem use **Muslim**
Mosley, Sir Oswald (Ernald), 6th Baronet (1896–1980), English Fascist leader
mosque Muslim place of worship
mosquito pl. **mosquitoes**
Mossad secret intelligence service of Israel
mosso Mus. fast and with animation
Mostar city in Bosnia–Herzegovina
most favoured nation country granted favourable trading terms (abbrev. **MFN**)
Most Honourable title of marquesses, members of the Privy Council, and holders of the Order of the Bath
Most Reverend title of Anglican archbishops and Irish Roman Catholic bishops
MOT UK annual test for motor vehicles [*Ministry of Transport*]
mot witty remark (not ital.)
mothball (one word)
moth-eaten (hyphen)
mother (cap. as name or form of

address)
motherboard Comput. (one word)
Mother Earth (caps)
Mothering Sunday fourth Sunday in Lent (caps)
mother-in-law pl. **mothers-in-law** (hyphens)
motherland (one word)
Mother Nature (caps)
mother-of-pearl (hyphens)
Mother of the Chapel Brit. female shop steward of printers' and journalists' trade union (caps; abbrev. **MoC**)
Mother's Day in the UK, Mothering Sunday; in North America and South Africa, the second Sunday in May (caps, apostrophe)
Mother Superior head of a female religious community
Mother Teresa see **Teresa**
mother-to-be pl. **mothers-to-be** (hyphens)
motif dominant or recurring idea in a composition (not **-ive**)
mot juste pl. ***mots justes*** exactly appropriate word (Fr., ital.)
motley (**motlier, motliest**) incongruously varied
motocross cross-country motorcycle racing (not **motor-**)
moto perpetuo pl. **moto perpetui** Mus. fast instrumental piece
Motorail rail service transporting cars and their occupants
motorbike, motorboat, motorcade (one word)
motor car, motor coach (two words)
motorcycle, motorhome (one word)
motorize (Brit. also **motorise**)
motor neurone disease degenerative disease (three words)
motor racing, motor scooter, motor vehicle (two words)
motorway (one word)
Motown (also trademark **Tamla Motown**) pop/soul music, associated with Detroit
motte mound on the site of a castle
motto pl. **mottoes** or **mottos**
motu proprio pl. ***motu proprios*** edict issued by the Pope personally (L., ital.)
moue pouting expression (not ital.)
mouflon (also **moufflon**) wild sheep
moujik var. of **muzhik**
mould, moulder, moulding, mouldy (US **mold, molder**, etc.)
moules marinière mussels in a wine and onion sauce (not ital.)
Moulin Rouge cabaret in Montmartre, Paris
moult (US **molt**)
Mount (abbrev. **Mt**)
mountain ash, mountain bike, mountain goat (two words)
mountainside (one word)
Mount Ararat, Mount Helicon, etc. see **Ararat, Mount** etc.
Mountbatten, Louis (Francis Albert Victor Nicholas), 1st Earl Mountbatten of Burma (1900–79)
mountebank charlatan or trickster
Mountie member of the Royal Canadian Mounted Police (cap.)
Mount of Olives highest point in the range of hills to the east of Jerusalem
Mourne Mountains range of hills in SE Northern Ireland
mouse pl. **mice**; in the computing sense pl. **mice** or **mouses**
mousetrap (one word)
mousey var. of **mousy**
moussaka (also **mousaka**) Greek lamb dish
mousse frothy dish or preparation
mousseline fine fabric
mousseron edible mushroom
mousseux pl. same, sparkling (wine) (Fr., ital.)
Moussorgsky var. of **Mussorgsky**
moustache (US **mustache**)
Mousterian main culture of the Middle Palaeolithic period in Europe
mousy (also **mousey**)
mouthful pl. **mouthfuls**
mouthpart, mouthpiece, mouthwash (one word)
mouth-watering (hyphen)
mouton sheepskin made to resemble beaver fur or sealskin (not ital.)
Mouton-Rothschild, Château claret (hyphen)
movable (also **moveable**)

movable feast religious feast day that varies its date (Ernest Hemingway's memoir is *A Moveable Feast*)
moviegoer (one word)
mow (past part. **mowed** or **mown**)
Mozambique country on the east coast of southern Africa □ **Mozambican**
Mozart, (Johann Chrysostom) Wolfgang Amadeus (1756–91), Austrian composer □ **Mozartian**
mozzarella white Italian cheese
MP 1 megapixel **2** Member of Parliament **3** military police; military policeman
mp mezzo piano
m.p. melting point
MP3 pl. **MP3s** Comput. compressed sound file
MPC multimedia personal computer
MPEG Comput. international standard for video images
mpg (also **m.p.g.**) miles per gallon
mph (also **m.p.h.**) miles per hour
MPhil (also **M.Phil.**) Master of Philosophy
MPV multi-purpose vehicle
MR Master of the Rolls
Mr title used before a man's name (no point); see also **Messrs**
MRA Moral Rearmament
MRBM medium-range ballistic missile
MRC Medical Research Council
MRCP Member of the Royal College of Physicians
MRCVS Member of the Royal College of Veterinary Surgeons
MRI magnetic resonance imaging
MRIA Member of the Royal Irish Academy
MRM mechanically recovered meat
MRPhS Member of the Royal Pharmaceutical Society
Mrs title used before a married woman's name (no point)
MRSA methicillin-resistant *Staphylococcus aureus*, a strain of bacteria
Mrs Grundy see **Grundy, Mrs**
MS 1 pl. **MSS** manuscript **2** Master of Science **3** Master of Surgery **4** Master Seaman **5** Mississippi (postal abbrev.) **6** motor ship **7** multiple sclerosis
Ms title used before any woman's name
MSC Manpower Services Commission
MSc (also **M.Sc.**) Master of Science
MS-DOS trademark Microsoft disk operating system
MSG monosodium glutamate
Msgr pl. **Msgrs 1** Monseigneur **2** Monsignor
MSgt Master Sergeant
MSP Member of the Scottish Parliament
MSS manuscripts
MST Mountain Standard Time
MT 1 machine translation **2** Montana (postal abbrev.)
Mt (no point) **1** the chemical element meitnerium **2** pl. **Mts** Mount
MTech (also **M.Tech.**) Master of Technology
MTV trademark music television (channel)
mu 1 twelfth letter of the Greek alphabet (**Μ, μ**), transliterated as 'm' **2** (**μ**) micron **3** (**μ**) (in symbols for units) micro-
Mubarak, (Muhammad) Hosni (Said) (b.1928), Egyptian president 1981–2011
Much Ado about Nothing Shakespeare play (abbrev. ***Much Ado***)
mucous of or like mucus
mucus slimy secretion
mudbank, mudbath, mudflap, mudguard, mudlark, mudslide (one word)
Mudejar pl. **Mudejares** subject Muslim during the reconquest of the Iberian peninsula
muesli pl. **mueslis** mixture of cereals, fruit, and nuts
muezzin man who calls Muslims to prayer
muffin 1 (N. Amer. **English muffin**) flat circular roll eaten toasted **2** chiefly N. Amer. small domed spongy cake
mufti 1 pl. **muftis** Muslim legal expert **2** civilian dress
Mugabe, Robert (Gabriel) (b.1924), Zimbabwean prime minister 1980–7 and president since 1987
Mughal see **Mogul**
Muhammad (*c.*570–632), Arab prophet and founder of Islam (not **Mahomet** (arch.), **Mohammed**)
Muhammad Ali 1 (1769–1849),

Ottoman viceroy and pasha of Egypt 1805–49 **2** (b.1942), American boxer; born *Cassius Marcellus Clay*

Muhammadan (also **Mohammedan**) arch. Muslim (offensive to Muslims)

Muharram (celebration in) the first month of the Muslim calendar

Mühlhausen Ger. name for **Mulhouse**

mujahideen (also **mujahidin**) Islamic guerrilla fighters (not ital.) [Arab. *mujāhidīn*]

mujtahid Shiite authority on Islamic law (ital.)

mulatto pl. **mulattoes** or **mulattos** offens. person with one white and one black parent

mulct extract tax or a fine from

Mulhouse city in Alsace; Ger. name **Mühlhausen**

mull muslin used to join the back of a book to its cover

mullah Muslim man learned in theology and law (cap. in titles)

mullein plant with woolly leaves

mulligatawny spicy meat soup

Multan city in east central Pakistan

multangular having many angles (not **multi-**)

multiaxial having many axes (one word)

multichannel, multicoloured, multicultural, multidimensional, multidisciplinary (one word)

multi-ethnic (hyphen)

multifaceted, multimedia, multimillionaire, multinational (one word)

multi-occupancy, multi-occupation (hyphen)

multiple sclerosis chronic progressive disease (abbrev. **MS**)

multiplication sign the sign ×

multipurpose (one word)

multiracial (one word)

multistorey (one word)

multitasking, multitrack (one word)

multi-user (hyphen)

multum in parvo a great deal in a small space (L., ital.)

Mumbai official name for **Bombay**

mumbo jumbo (two words)

Munch, Edvard (1863–1944), Norwegian artist

Munchausen, Baron hero of a book of fantastic travellers' tales (1785) by Rudolph Erich Raspe

Munchausen's syndrome (also **Munchhausen syndrome**) **1** feigning severe illness to get hospital treatment **2** (**Munchausen's syndrome by proxy**) disorder marked by inducing illness in a child

Munich city in SE Germany; Ger. name **München**

muniments Law documents proving a title to land

Munro[1], Hector Hugh, see **Saki**

Munro[2] pl. **Munros** any of the 277 mountains in Scotland that are at least 3,000 feet high

Munster province of the Republic of Ireland

Münster city in NW Germany

muntjac small SE Asian deer

Muntz metal form of brass (not **Muntz's**)

Murcia autonomous region and city in SE Spain

Murillo, Bartolomé Esteban (*c*.1618–82), Spanish painter

murk, murky (not **mi-** (arch.))

Murmansk port in NW Russia

Murphy's Law anything that can go wrong will go wrong (caps)

Murrumbidgee river of SE Australia

MusB (also **Mus.B., Mus Bac**) Bachelor of Music [L. *Musicae Baccalaureus*]

muscadel var. of **muscatel**

Muscadelle white-wine grape (cap.)

Muscadet dry white French wine (cap.)

muscadine wine grape with a musky flavour (lower case)

Muscat capital of Oman

muscat (wine from) a variety of grape with a musky scent (lower case)

muscatel (also **muscadel**) (raisin from) a muscat grape (lower case)

muscle fibrous tissue; cf. **mussel**

muscly (not **-ey**)

muscovado pl. **muscovados** unrefined sugar

Muscovite person from Moscow

muscovite silver-grey form of mica (lower case)

Muscovy medieval principality in west central Russia

MusD (also **Mus.D., Mus Doc**) Doctor of Music [L. *Musicae Doctor*]
museology, museography science of organizing museums
Museveni, Yoweri (Kaguta) (b.1944), president of Uganda since 1986
Musharraf, Pervez (b.1943), president of Pakistan 2001–2008
musicale N. Amer. musical gathering or concert
Muslim follower of Islam (not **Moslem, Mussulman** (arch.))
mussel bivalve mollusc; cf. **muscle**
Mussolini, Benito (Amilcare Andrea) (1883–1945), Italian Fascist prime minister 1922–43; known as **Il Duce** ('the leader')
Mussorgsky (also **Moussorgsky**), Modest (Petrovich) (1839–81), Russian composer
Mussulman pl. **Mussulmans** or **Mussulmen** arch. use **Muslim**
must (also **musth**) frenzied state of rutting male elephants
mustache US var. of **moustache**
mustachios long or elaborate moustache (pl.) □ **mustachioed**
Mustique resort island in the northern Grenadines
mutatis mutandis making necessary alterations while not affecting the main point (L., ital.)
Mutsuhito see **Meiji Tenno**
mutualize (Brit. also **mutualise**)
mutuel US totalizator or pari-mutuel
muumuu Hawaiian woman's loose dress (one word)
muzak recorded background music (cap. as trademark)
muzhik (also **moujik**) hist. Russian peasant
MV 1 megavolt(s) **2** motor vessel **3** muzzle velocity
MVD secret police of the former USSR 1946–53
MVO Member of the Royal Victorian Order
MW 1 medium wave **2** megawatt(s)
mW milliwatt(s) (one cap.)
MWO Master Warrant Officer
Mx 1 maxwell(s) **2** Middlesex
MY motor yacht
myalgic encephalomyelitis chronic fatigue syndrome (abbrev. **ME**)
Myanmar see **Burma**
myasthenia muscle weakness
mycelium pl. **mycelia** part of a fungus
Mycenae ancient city in Greece
Mycenaean (also **Mycenean**) of a late Bronze Age civilization in Greece
Mykonos Greek island in the Aegean; mod. Gk name **Míkonos**
mynah (also **mynah bird** or **myna**) Asian and Australasian starling
myopia short-sightedness □ **myopic**
myrmecology study of ants
Myrmidon Gk Mythol. member of a people who followed Achilles to Troy
myrmidon powerful person's follower (lower case)
Myron (*fl.* *c.*480–440 BC), Greek sculptor
myrrh fragrant gum resin
Mysore city in the Indian state of Karnataka
mythicize (Brit. also **mythicise**)
mythologize (Brit. also **mythologise**)
mythopoeia making of myths □ **mythopoeic, mythopoetic**
mythos pl. **mythoi** myth or mythology (not ital.)
mythus pl. **mythi** myth (not ital.)
Mytilene chief town of Lesbos; mod. Gk name **Mitilíni**
myxoedema (US **myxedema**) swelling of skin and tissues associated with hypothyroidism
myxomatosis viral disease of rabbits

N

N 1 pl. **Ns** or **N's** 14th letter of the alphabet **2** Chess knight **3** New: *N Zealand* **4** newton(s) **5** the chemical element nitrogen **6** Chem. normal **7** North or Northern
n nano- (10^{-9})
n. pl. **nn. 1** Gram. neuter **2** note **3** noun
n unspecified or variable number
Na the chemical element sodium (no point) [mod. L. *natrium*]
n/a not applicable; not available
NAACP National Association for the Advancement of Colored People
NAAFI Navy, Army, and Air Force Institutes
naan var. of **nan**
Naas county town of Kildare
Nablus town in the West Bank
nabob official under the Mogul empire
Nabokov, Vladimir (Vladimirovich) (1899–1977), Russian-born American writer
nacelle aircraft engine casing
nacho pl. **nachos** tortilla chip
nacre mother-of-pearl □ **nacreous**
Nader, Ralph (b.1934), American lawyer and reformer
nadir lowest point; cf. **zenith**
naevus (US **nevus**) pl. **naevi** birthmark
NAFTA North American Free Trade Agreement
Nagaland state in NE India
Nagasaki city in SW Japan
Nagorno-Karabakh region of Azerbaijan
Nahuatl pl. same or **Nahuatls** member of a group of Central American peoples
Nahum 1 Hebrew minor prophet **2** book of the Old Testament (abbrev. **Nah.**)
naiad pl. **naiads** or **naiades** water nymph
naïf naive (person) (accent, not ital.)
nainsook soft cotton fabric
Naipaul, Sir V(idiadhar) S(urajprasad) (b.1932), Trinidadian writer
naira monetary unit of Nigeria
Nairnshire former county of NE Scotland
Nairobi capital of Kenya
naive (also **naïve**) innocent and unsophisticated
naivety (also **naïvety**) innocence or unsophistication [Fr. *naïveté*]
Najaf (also **an-Najaf**) city in Iraq
nakfa pl. same or **nakfas** monetary unit of Eritrea
Nama pl. same or **Namas** member of a people of South Africa and Namibia
Namaqualand region of SW Africa
namaskar traditional Indian gesture of greeting (not ital.)
namaste greeting said when making a namaskar (not ital.)
namby-pamby weak or ineffectual (hyphen)
nameable (not **namable**)
Namen Flemish name for **Namur**
nameplate (one word)
N. Amer. North America(n)
namesake (one word)
Namib Desert desert of SW Africa
Namibia country in southern Africa □ **Namibian**
Namur province and city in central Belgium; Flemish name **Namen**
nan (also **naan**) flat leavened bread
Nanak (1469–1539), founder of Sikhism; known as **Guru Nanak**
N & Q the journal *Notes and Queries*
nandrolone anabolic steroid
Nanjing (also **Nanking**) city in China
nankeen yellowish cotton cloth
nano- factor of 10^{-9} (abbrev. **n**)
nanometre (US **nanometer**) one thousand millionth of a metre (abbrev. **nm**)
nanosecond one thousand millionth of a second (abbrev. **ns**)

nanotechnology manipulation of individual atoms and molecules
Nansen, Fridtjof (1861–1930), Norwegian Arctic explorer
Nantes city in western France
Nantucket island off Massachusetts
naos pl. **naoi** inner sanctuary of a Greek temple (not ital.)
napa var. of **nappa**
napalm jelly used in incendiary bombs
naphtha flammable oil (not **naptha**)
Napier, John (1550–1617), Scottish mathematician □ **Napierian**
Naples city on the west coast of Italy; It. name **Napoli**
Napoleon (1769–1821), emperor of France 1804–14 and 1815; full name *Napoleon Bonaparte* □ **Napoleonic**
napoleon hist. gold twenty-franc coin (lower case)
Napoli It. name for **Naples**
nappa (also **napa**) soft leather
Narayan, R(asipuram) K(rishnaswamy) (1906–2001), Indian writer
Narayanan, K(ocheril) R(aman) (1920–2005), Indian president 1997–2002
Narbonne city in southern France
Narcissus Gk Mythol. youth who fell in love with his own reflection
narcissus pl. **narcissi** or **narcissuses** bulbous spring plant (lower case)
nares (sing. **naris**) Anat. & Zool. nostrils
narghile oriental tobacco pipe
Narragansett (also **Narraganset**) pl. same or **Narragansetts** member of an American Indian people
narrowband, narrowboat, narrowcast (one word)
narrow gauge (two words, hyphen when attrib.)
narrow-minded (hyphen)
narwhal small whale with a long tusk
NASA National Aeronautics and Space Administration
nasalize (Brit. also **nasalise**)
nascent just beginning to develop
NASDAQ US system for trading in securities [*National Association of Securities Dealers Automated Quotations*]
Nash 1 (Frederic) Ogden (1902–71), American poet **2** Richard (1674–1762), Welsh dandy; known as **Beau Nash**
Nashe, Thomas (1567–1601), English writer
Nashville state capital of Tennessee
Nasmyth, James (1808–90), Scottish engineer
Nassau 1 capital of the Bahamas **2** town and former duchy of western Germany
Nasser, Gamal Abdel (1918–70), Egyptian president 1956–70
nasturtium pl. **nasturtiums** plant with bright leaves
NASUWT National Association of Schoolmasters and Union of Women Teachers
Nat. 1 national **2** nationalist **3** natural
Natal former province of South Africa; see also **KwaZulu-Natal**
NATFHE National Association of Teachers in Further and Higher Education
National Enquirer US publication (not ***Inquirer***)
National Insurance (caps; abbrev. **NI**)
nationalist (abbrev. **Nat.**)
nationalize (Brit. also **nationalise**)
nation state (two words)
nationwide (one word)
native n. dated and offensive in ref. to non-white people; use only in contexts such as *a native of Boston*
Native American the preferred term in the US
NATO North Atlantic Treaty Organization
Nattier blue soft shade of blue
Natufian late Mesolithic culture of the Middle East
natural (abbrev. **Nat.**; musical symbol ♮)
naturalize (Brit. also **naturalise**)
natural logarithm (abbrev. **ln**)
naught 1 arch. nothing **2** N. Amer. var. of **nought**
Nauru island country in the SW Pacific □ **Nauruan**
nauseous affected with or causing nausea (not **-ious**)
Nausicaa girl in Homer's *Odyssey*
nautch traditional Indian dance
nautical mile (abbrev. **nm** or **n.m.**)

nautilus pl. **nautiluses** or **nautili** mollusc with a spiral shell
Nautilus first nuclear-powered submarine
Navajo (also **Navaho**) pl. same or **Navajos** member of a North American Indian people
Navan county town of Meath
Navaratri (also **Navaratra**) Hindu autumn festival
navarin lamb or mutton casserole (Fr., ital.)
Navarre autonomous region of northern Spain; Sp. name **Navarra** □ **Navarrese**
navy blue (two words, hyphen when attrib.)
nawab governor under the Mogul empire (cap. in titles)
Naxçivan Azerbaijani autonomous republic
Naxos Greek island in the Aegean
naysay (past and past part. **naysaid**) deny or oppose (one word)
Nazarene person from Nazareth; (**the Nazarene**) Jesus Christ
Nazca Lines huge abstract designs on a plain in Peru
Nazi pl. **Nazis** member of the National Socialist German Workers' Party □ **Naziism, Nazism**
Nazirite (also **Nazarite**) Hebrew who took vows of abstinence
NB 1 New Brunswick **2** *nota bene* (take note) [L.]
Nb the chemical element niobium (no point)
nb Cricket no-ball
NBA 1 National Basketball Association **2** US National Boxing Association **3** hist. net book agreement
NBC 1 US National Broadcasting Company **2** nuclear, biological, and chemical
NC 1 network computer **2** North Carolina
NC-17 for adults only (US film classification)
NCC National Curriculum Council
NCO non-commissioned officer
ND North Dakota (postal abbrev.)
Nd the chemical element neodymium (no point)
n.d. no date (in bibliographies)
N.Dak. North Dakota (official abbrev.; no space)
Ndebele pl. same or **Ndebeles** member of a people of Zimbabwe and South Africa
N'Djamena capital of Chad
NDL Norddeutscher Lloyd
NE 1 Nebraska (postal abbrev.) **2** (also **n/e**) new edition **3** New England **4** north-east(ern)
Ne the chemical element neon (no point)
né (of a man) born with the name that follows (accent, not ital.)
Neagh, Lough lake in Northern Ireland
Neanderthal extinct species of human (not **-tal**)
Neapolitan of Naples
neap tide tide with the least difference between high and low water (two words)
near (abbrev. **nr**)
nearby adj. situated close by. adv. (also **near by**) close by
Nearctic North America and Greenland as a zoogeographical region
Near East the countries between the Mediterranean and India
Near Eastern (no hyphen even when attrib.)
nearside (one word)
nearsighted N. Amer. short-sighted (one word)
Neath town in South Wales; Welsh name **Castell-Nedd**
neat's-foot oil oil used to dress leather (apostrophe, one hyphen)
NEB National Enterprise Board
NEB the *New English Bible*
Nebraska state in the central US (official abbrev. **Nebr.**, postal **NB**) □ **Nebraskan**
Nebuchadnezzar (*c.*630–562 BC), king of Babylon 605–562 BC
nebuchadnezzar very large wine bottle (lower case)
nebula pl. **nebulae** or **nebulas** cloud of gas or dust in outer space
nebulizer (Brit. also **nebuliser**) device for producing a fine spray
NEC 1 National Executive Committee **2** National Exhibition Centre

nécessaire case for small items (Fr., ital.)
necessary (one *c*, two *ss*)
necessitarian (also **necessarian**) believer in determinism
necessitate, necessitous, necessity (one *c*, two *ss*)
Neckar river of western Germany
Necker, Jacques (1732–1804), director general of French finances 1777–81, 1788–9
neckline, necktie (one word)
Nederland Du. name for **the Netherlands**
née (of a woman) born with the name that follows (accent, not ital.)
needlecord, needlecraft, needlepoint, needlework (one word)
ne'er never
ne'er-do-well (hyphens)
nefarious wicked or criminal
Nefertiti (also **Nofretete**) (14th cent. BC), Egyptian queen
negative (abbrev. **neg.**)
Negev arid region forming most of southern Israel
negligee woman's light dressing gown (not ital.) [Fr. *négligée*]
negligible (not **-able**)
negotiate, negotiation (not **-ci-**)
Negress avoid: dated and offensive
Negrillo pl. **Negrillos** member of an African people
Negrito pl. **Negritos** member of an Austronesian people
Negritude quality of being a black person (cap.); cf. **nigritude**
Negro pl. **Negroes** avoid: dated and offensive; see **black**
Negus hist. ruler of Ethiopia (cap.)
negus hist. hot drink of port, lemon, etc.
Nehemiah 1 (5th cent. BC), Hebrew leader **2** book of the Old Testament (abbrev. **Neh.**)
Nehru, Jawaharlal (1889–1964), Indian prime minister 1947–64; known as **Pandit Nehru**
neigh horse's whinnying sound
neighbour, neighbourhood, neighbourly (US **-bor-**)
Nejd arid plateau region in Saudi Arabia
nekton aquatic animals able to swim independently; cf. **plankton**
Nelson, Horatio, Viscount Nelson, Duke of Bronte (1758–1805), British admiral
nelson wrestling hold (lower case)
Nelspruit town in eastern South Africa
nematode unsegmented worm
nem. con. unanimously (ital.) [L. *nemine contradicente*]
nem. diss. with no one dissenting (ital.) [L. *nemine dissentiente*]
Nemean lion Gk Mythol. monstrous lion killed by Hercules
Nemesis agent of divine punishment
nemesis pl. **nemeses** inescapable agent of someone's downfall (lower case)
Nemo me impune lacessit no one attacks me with impunity (the motto of Scotland and the Order of the Thistle) (L., ital.)
Nennius (*fl.* *c.*800), Welsh chronicler
neo- new or revived form (hyphenated compounds retain caps of words that have them)
neoclassical, neocolonialism, neoconservative (one word)
neo-Darwinian (hyphen, one cap.)
neodymium chemical element of atomic number 60 (symbol **Nd**)
neo-fascist (hyphen, lower case)
neo-Georgian, neo-Gothic (hyphen, one cap.)
neo-impressionism (hyphen, lower case)
neo-Latin (hyphen, cap.)
neo-liberal (hyphen, lower case)
Neolithic later part of the Stone Age
neologism newly coined word
neo-Malthusianism, neo-Marxist (hyphen, one cap.)
neon chemical element of atomic number 10, a noble gas (symbol **Ne**)
neonatal (one word)
neo-Nazi (hyphen, one cap.)
neopaganism (one word, lower case)
neophyte person new to something
Neoplatonism ancient system combining Platonic thought with oriental mysticism (cap., one word)
neorealism (one word, lower case)
Neotropical Central and South America as a zoogeographical region (cap., one word) □ **neotropics**

Nepal country in the Himalayas
□ **Nepalese**
Nepali pl. same or **Nepalis** person from Nepal
nepenthes 1 (also **nepenthe**) drug in Homer's *Odyssey* **2** pitcher plant
neper unit for comparing power levels
ne plus ultra the perfect example of its kind (L., ital.)
Neptune 1 Rom. Mythol. god of the sea; Gk equivalent **Poseidon 2** eighth planet from the sun
neptunium chemical element of atomic number 93 (symbol **Np**)
NERC Natural Environment Research Council
Nereid Gk Mythol. sea nymph
nereid bristle worm (lower case)
Nernst, Walther Hermann (1864–1941), German physical chemist
Nero (AD 37–68), Roman emperor 54–68; Latin name *Nero Claudius Caesar Augustus Germanicus* □ **Neronian**
neroli essential oil from orange flowers
Neruda 1 Jan (1834–91), Czech writer **2** Pablo (1904–73), Chilean poet
nerve cell, nerve centre, nerve gas (two words)
nerve-racking (also **nerve-wracking**) (hyphen)
Nervi, Pier Luigi (1891–1979), Italian engineer and architect
Nesbit, E(dith) (1858–1924), English novelist
nescient ignorant □ **nescience**
nest box, nest egg (two words)
Nestlé Rowntree food manufacturer, part of *Société des Produits Nestlé SA* (accent)
net (Brit. also **nett**) remaining after deductions; cf. **gross**
Netanyahu, Benjamin (b.1949), Israeli prime minister 1996–9 and since 2009
netball (one word)
Netherlands, the 1 country in western Europe; **Holland** refers strictly to the western coastal provinces of the country; Du. name **Nederland 2** hist. the Low Countries
Netherlands Antilles two groups of Dutch islands in the Caribbean
netherworld the underworld, hell (one word)
netsuke pl. same or **netsukes** carved Japanese ornament
nett Brit. var. of **net**
network (one word)
Neuchâtel, Lake lake in Switzerland
Neufchâtel French cheese
Neumann, John von (1903–57), American computer pioneer
neume (also **neum**) (in plainsong) notes sung to a single syllable
neuralgia intense pain along a nerve
neurasthenia tiredness and irritability
neuritis inflammation of a peripheral nerve
neuron (also **neurone**) nerve cell
neuropathy disease of a peripheral nerve
neurosis pl. **neuroses** mental illness not caused by organic disease
neurotic affected by neurosis
neurotransmitter chemical substance that transfers nerve impulses
neuter (abbrev. **n.** or **neut.**)
neutralize (Brit. also **neutralise**)
neutrino pl. **neutrinos** neutral subatomic particle
neutron subatomic particle with no electric charge
Neva river in NW Russia
Nevada state of the western US (official abbrev. **Nev.**, postal **NV**) □ **Nevadan**
névé another name for **firn** (Fr., ital.)
never-ending (hyphen)
nevermore (one word)
Never-Never (hyphen) **1** desert country of the interior of Australia **2** (**the never-never**) hire purchase
Never-Never Land (one hyphen) **1** ideal country in *Peter Pan* **2** region of Northern Territory, Australia
Nevers city in central France
nevertheless (one word)
Neville, Richard see **Warwick**
Nevis one of the Leeward Islands, part of St Kitts and Nevis □ **Nevisian**
Nevsky, Alexander, see **Alexander Nevsky**
nevus US var. of **naevus**
New Age (caps, no hyphen even when attrib.)

Newark city in New Jersey
Newbery, John (1713–67), English printer
newborn (one word)
New Brunswick province on the SE coast of Canada
Newcastle-under-Lyme town in Staffordshire (hyphens)
Newcastle upon Tyne city in NE England (no hyphens)
New College Oxford (not simply **New**)
newcomer (one word)
New Deal measures in the US to counteract the Great Depression (caps)
New Delhi see **Delhi**
new edition (abbrev. **NE** or **n/e**)
New England US area of Maine, New Hampshire, Vermont, Massachusetts, Rhode Island, and Connecticut □ **New Englander**
New English Bible modern English translation of the Bible 1961–70 (abbrev. ***NEB***)
newfangled (one word)
New Forest area of heath and woodland in Hampshire
Newfoundland large island off the east coast of Canada (abbrev. **Nfdl**, postal **NF**) □ **Newfoundlander**
New Guinea island in the South Pacific, divided between Papua New Guinea and Irian Jaya □ **New Guinean**
New Hall Cambridge college
New Hampshire state in the north-eastern US (official and postal abbrev. **NH**) □ **New Hampshirite**
New Hebrides former name for **Vanuatu**
New International Version modern English translation of the Bible 1973–8 (abbrev. ***NIV***)
New Jersey state in the north-eastern US (official and postal abbrev. **NJ**) □ **New Jerseyan, New Jerseyite**
New Kingdom period of ancient Egyptian history (caps)
new-laid (hyphen)
New Latin Latin since the close of the Middle Ages (caps; abbrev. **NL**)
newly wed (two words, hyphen as noun)
New Mexico state in the south-western US (official abbrev. **N.Mex.**, postal **NM**) □ **New Mexican**
Newnham College Cambridge
New Orleans city and port in SE Louisiana (abbrev. **NO**)
Newport city in South Wales; Welsh name **Casnewyd**
Newport News city in SE Virginia
New Revised Standard Version modern English translation of the Bible 1990 (abbrev. ***NRSV***)
news agency (two words)
newsagent, newscaster, newsflash, newsgroup, newsletter (one word)
New South Wales state of SE Australia (abbrev. **NSW**)
newspaper, newspaperman (one word)
newspeak ambiguous euphemistic language (lower case)
newsprint, newsreader, newsreel, newsroom (one word)
news-sheet, news-stand (hyphen)
New Stone Age Neolithic period (caps)
New Style calculation of dates using the Gregorian calendar (caps; abbrev. **NS**); cf. **Old Style**
newsvendor, newsworthy (one word)
New Territories part of Hong Kong on mainland China
New Testament (not ital.; abbrev. **NT**)
Newton, Sir Isaac (1642–1727), English scientist □ **Newtonian**
newton SI unit of force (lower case; abbrev. **N**)
new wave new style of music, film, etc. (lower case)
New Year's Day 1 January (caps)
New Year's Eve 31 December (caps)
New York 1 (also **New York State**) state in the north-eastern US (official and postal abbrev. **NY**) **2** (also **New York City**) city in New York State (abbrev. **NY, NYC**)
New Yorker 1 person from New York (City) **2** (the ***New Yorker***) US magazine
New Zealand island country in the South Pacific (abbrev. **NZ**) □ **New Zealander**
next best, next door (two words, hyphen when attrib.)
next of kin (three words; treated as sing. or pl.)

nexus pl. same or **nexuses** connection or connected group
Nez Percé pl. same or **Nez Percés** member of an American Indian people
NF 1 National Front **2** Newfoundland
NFL US National Football League
Nfld Newfoundland
NFU National Farmers' Union
ngaio pl. **ngaios** New Zealand tree
Ngata, Sir Apirana Turupa (1874–1950), Maori leader and politician
NGO pl. **NGOs** non-governmental organization
ngoma (in East Africa) a dance (ital.)
Ngoni pl. same or **Ngonis** member of a people living in Malawi
ngoni pl. **ngonis** African drum
ngultrum pl. same, monetary unit of Bhutan
Nguni pl. same, member of a people of southern Africa
ngwee pl. same, monetary unit of Zambia
NH New Hampshire
NHS National Health Service
NI 1 National Insurance **2** Northern Ireland **3** the North Island (of New Zealand)
Ni the chemical element nickel (no point)
Niagara Falls 1 waterfalls on the Niagara River **2** city in upper New York State **3** city in southern Ontario
Niamey capital of Niger
Nibelungenlied 13th-cent. German poem; adaptations include Wagner's *Der Ring des Nibelungen*
NIC 1 National Insurance contribution **2** newly industrialized country
NiCad (also US trademark **Nicad**) type of battery or cell
Nicaea ancient city in Asia Minor, on the site of modern Iznik □ **Nicaean**
Nicam (also **NICAM**) digital system used in UK televisions
Nicaragua country in Central America □ **Nicaraguan**
Nicene Creed formal statement of Christian belief (caps)
niche recess (not **nich**)
nickel chemical element of atomic number 28 (symbol **Ni**)
Nicklaus, Jack (William) (b.1940), American golfer
nick-nack var. of **knick-knack**
nickname (one word)
Nicobar Islands see **Andaman and Nicobar Islands** □ **Nicobarese**
Niçois pl. same; fem. ***Niçoise***, pl. ***Niçoises*** n. person from Nice on the French Riviera. adj. of Nice; (of food) with tuna, olives, and tomatoes
Nicosia capital of Cyprus
niece (not **neice**)
niello black compound for filling in engraved designs □ **nielloed**
nielsbohrium former name for **bohrium**
Nielsen, Carl August (1865–1931), Danish composer
Nietzsche, Friedrich Wilhelm (1844–1900), German philosopher □ **Nietzschean**
Niflheim Norse underworld for those who died of old age or illness
Niger 1 river in NW Africa **2** country in West Africa
Niger–Congo large group of African languages (en rule)
Nigeria country on the coast of West Africa □ **Nigerian**
niggardly ungenerous, mean
nightcap, nightclothes, nightclub, nightdress, nightfall, nightgown (one word)
Nightingale, Florence (1820–1910), English nurse and medical reformer
nightingale small thrush with a melodious song
nightjar nocturnal bird with a distinctive call (one word)
nightlife (one word)
night light (two words)
nightmarish (not **-mareish**)
night owl, night safe, night school (two words)
nightshade plant with poisonous berries (one word)
night shift (two words)
nightshirt, nightspot, nightstick (one word)
night-time (hyphen)
night watch (two words)

nightwatchman, **nightwear** (one word)
nigritude blackness; cf. **Negritude**
nihil obstat Roman Catholic certificate that a book is not open to objection (L., ital.)
Nijinsky, Vaslav (Fomich) (1890–1950), Russian dancer and choreographer
Nijmegen town in the eastern Netherlands (not **Nymegen**)
Nike 1 Gk Mythol. goddess of victory **2** trademark make of sports goods
Nikkei index list of share prices on the Tokyo Stock Exchange
nil desperandum do not despair (not ital.)
nilgai large Indian antelope
Nilgiri Hills range of hills in Tamil Nadu, India
nimbostratus layer of low thick grey cloud (one word)
nimbus pl. **nimbi** or **nimbuses** large grey rain cloud
Nimby pl. **Nimbys** objector to developments in their own neighbourhood (cap.) ◻ **Nimbyism**
Nîmes city in southern France
niminy-piminy affectedly refined
Nin, Anaïs (1903–77), American writer
nincompoop foolish person (one word)
nine (Roman numeral **ix** or **IX**) ◻ **ninth**
9/11 US var. of **September 11**
ninepins skittles (one word)
nineteen (Roman numeral **xix** or **XIX**) ◻ **nineteenth**
nineties (also **1990s**) decade (lower case, no apostrophe)
ninety hyphen in compound numbers, e.g. *ninety-one*; Roman numeral **xc** or **XC** ◻ **ninetieth**
Nineveh ancient city on the Tigris
ninja exponent of **ninjutsu**, a Japanese espionage technique (not ital.)
niobium chemical element of atomic number 41 (symbol **Nb**)
nip and tuck (three words)
Nippon Japanese name for **Japan** ◻ **Nipponese**
NIREX Nuclear Industry Radioactive Waste Executive
nirvana transcendent state in Buddhism (lower case, not ital.)
Nisan (in the Jewish calendar) seventh month of the civil and first of the religious year
nisi taking effect only after conditions are met (not ital.)
Nissen hut corrugated iron hut (one cap.)
nitre (US **niter**) saltpetre
nitrogen chemical element of atomic number 7 (symbol **N**)
nitroglycerine (US also **nitroglycerin**) explosive yellow liquid (one word)
Niue island territory in the South Pacific
NIV the *New International Version* (of the Bible)
Nizam 1 title of the hereditary ruler of Hyderabad **2** (**the nizam**) the Turkish regular army
Nizhni Novgorod port in European Russia; former name **Gorky**
NJ New Jersey
Nkomo, Joshua (Mqabuko Nyongolo) (1917–99), Zimbabwean statesman
Nkrumah, Kwame (1909–72), Ghanaian president 1960–6
NKVD secret police agency in the former USSR 1934–46
NL New Latin
NM New Mexico
nm 1 nanometre(s) **2** (also **n.m.**) nautical mile
N.Mex. New Mexico (official abbrev.; no space)
nn. notes
NNE north-north-east
NNP net national product
NNW north-north-west
NO New Orleans
No¹ the chemical element nobelium (no point)
No² var. of **Noh**
No. US North
no pl. **noes** negative answer
no. pl. **nos** or **nos.** number [It. *numero*]
n.o. Cricket not out
Noachian of Noah
Noah's Ark (caps, not ital.)
no-ball Cricket (hyphen; abbrev. **nb**)
Nobel, Alfred Bernhard (1833–96), Swedish chemist and engineer

nobelium chemical element of atomic number 102 (symbol **No**)
Nobel Prize six annual international prizes, for work in physics, chemistry, physiology or medicine, literature, economics, and the promotion of peace (caps; awarded 'in' not 'for' a category)
nobiliary particle preposition forming part of a title of the nobility, e.g. French *de* or German *von*
noblesse oblige privilege entails responsibility (Fr., ital.)
nobody (one word); cf. **no one**
no-claims bonus (one hyphen)
nocturn part of Roman Catholic matins
nocturne (not ital. exc. in titles) **1** short romantic piano piece **2** picture of a night scene
Noel 1 Christmas **2** (often **Noël**) personal name
Nofretete var. of **Nefertiti**
no-go area (one hyphen)
Noh (also **No**) Japanese masked drama
noisette small piece of meat (not ital.)
noisome bad-smelling
nolens volens whether a person likes it or not (L., ital.)
noli me tangere warning about interference (L., ital.)
nolle prosequi formal notice of abandoning a lawsuit (L., ital.)
nom. 1 nominal **2** nominative
no man's land (three words, apostrophe)
nom de guerre pl. ***noms de guerre*** name assumed for fighting (Fr., ital.)
nom de plume pl. **noms de plume** pen name (not ital.)
nom de théâtre pl. ***noms de théâtre*** actor's stage name (Fr., ital.)
nomen second personal name of a citizen of ancient Rome, e.g. Marcus *Tullius* Cicero (not ital.)
nomenclature devising or choosing of names □ **nomenclator**
nomenklatura (beneficiaries of) the system of appointment to important posts in the former USSR (Russ., ital.)
nominative Gram. case expressing the subject of a verb (abbrev. **nom.**)
non- hyphenated in most compounds
nonagenarian person between 90 and 99 years old (not **nono-**)
nonce word word coined for one occasion only
nonchalant casually calm
non-commissioned officer officer of a rank not conferred by a commission (abbrev. **NCO**)
non compos mentis not sane (not ital.)
Nonconformist member of a Protestant church which dissents from the Church of England
nonconformist person whose behaviour differs from society's norms (lower case)
nondescript lacking distinctive characteristics
none treated as sing. or pl. depending on emphasis
nonentity unimportant person or thing
nones (in the ancient Roman calendar) the ninth day before the ides, counting inclusively (lower case)
nonesuch (also **nonsuch**) arch. incomparable person or thing
Nonesuch Press publishing company
nonet group of nine musicians
nonetheless (also **none the less**) nevertheless
non-Euclidean (one cap.)
nonfeasance failure to perform an act required by law (one word)
Nonjuror clergyman who refused to swear allegiance to William and Mary (cap., one word)
non licet unlawful (two words, not ital.)
non-lining numerals var. of **non-ranging numerals**
nonpareil having no equal
non placet negative vote (L., ital.)
nonplus (**nonplussing, nonplussed**) surprise and confuse
non possumus expression of an inability to act (L., ital.)
non-profit-making Brit. (two hyphens)
non-ranging numerals (also **non-lining numerals**) numerals with ascenders and descenders, as 123456789
non sequitur illogical conclusion (not ital.)
nonsuch var. of **nonesuch**
nonsuit Law stop (a lawsuit) because the

plaintiff has failed to make a case (one word)

non-U not characteristic of the upper classes (one cap., no point)

noonday (one word)

no one (two words); cf. **nobody**

Norddeutscher Lloyd shipping company (abbrev. **NDL**)

Nord-Pas-de-Calais region of northern France

Norfolk county of eastern England (abbrev. **Norf.**)

Norge Norw. name for **Norway**

normalize (Brit. also **normalise**)

Normandy former province of NW France, now divided into **Lower Normandy** (Basse-Normandie) and **Upper Normandy** (Haute-Normandie)

Norroy (in full **Norroy and Ulster**) Heraldry third King of Arms

north (abbrev. **N**)

North Africa (caps)

North African (no hyphen even when attrib.)

Northallerton town in North Yorkshire

North America continent comprising Canada, the US, Mexico, and the countries of Central America (abbrev. **N. Amer.**)

North American (no hyphen even when attrib.; abbrev. **N. Amer.**)

Northamptonshire county of central England (abbrev. **Northants**)

northbound (one word)

North Carolina state of the east central US (official and postal abbrev. **NC**) □ **North Carolinian**

Northcliffe, Alfred Charles William Harmsworth, 1st Viscount (1865–1922), British newspaper proprietor

north country England north of the Humber □ **north-countryman**

North Dakota state in the north central US (official abbrev. **N.Dak.**, postal **ND**) □ **North Dakotan**

north-east, north-eastern (hyphen; abbrev. **NE**)

northeaster wind (one word)

north-easterly, north-eastward (hyphen)

northern (abbrev. **N**)

northern hemisphere (lower case)

Northern Ireland province of the United Kingdom occupying the NE part of Ireland (abbrev. **NI**)

Northern Ireland Office UK government department (not **Northern Irish Office**)

Northern Irish (no hyphen even when attrib.)

Northern Lights another name for **aurora borealis** (caps)

Northern Territory state of north central Australia (abbrev. **NT**)

North Island, the more northerly of the two main islands of New Zealand

North Korea country occupying the northern part of Korea (see **Korea**)

north-north-east (two hyphens; abbrev. **NNE**)

north-north-west (two hyphens; abbrev. **NNW**)

North Pole (caps)

North Rhine-Westphalia state of western Germany (one hyphen)

North–South (en rule)

North Star (caps)

Northumberland county in NE England (abbrev. **Northumb.**)

Northumbria Northumberland, Durham, and Tyne and Wear

north-west, north-western (hyphen; abbrev. **NW**)

northwester wind (one word)

north-westerly (hyphen)

North-West Frontier Province province of NW Pakistan (one hyphen)

Northwest Territories territory of northern Canada (no hyphen)

north-westward (hyphen)

North Yorkshire county of NE England

Norway country in Scandinavia; Norw. name **Norge**

Norwegian (abbrev. **Norw.**)

nor'wester another term for **northwester** (one word, apostrophe)

nos (also **nos.**) pl. of **no.**

nosebag, nosebleed, nosedive, nosegay (one word)

nose job (two words)

nosey var. of **nosy**

nostalgie de la boue desire for

degradation (Fr., ital.)
Nostradamus (1503–66), French astrologer and physician; Latinized name of *Michel de Nostredame*
nostrum pl. **nostrums** quack remedy (not ital.)
nosy (also **nosey**) (**nosier, nosiest**) inquisitive
nosy parker overly inquisitive person (lower case)
nota bene mark well (abbrev. **NB**) (L., ital.)
notable (not **-eable**)
notarize (Brit. also **notarise**) have (a signature) attested by a notary
notary (in full **notary public**) pl. **notaries (public)** person authorized to perform certain legal formalities (abbrev. **NP**)
note footnote (abbrev. **n.**)
notebook, notecard, notecase, notepad, notepaper (one word)
noticeable (not **-cable**)
noticeboard (one word)
notorious well known for something bad □ **notoriety**
not proven Scottish verdict of insufficient evidence to establish guilt or innocence
Notre-Dame cathedral in Paris (hyphen)
Notre Dame university and town in Indiana (no hyphen)
Nottinghamshire county in central England (abbrev. **Notts.**)
Notting Hill district of NW central London (two words)
notwithstanding (one word)
Nouakchott capital of Mauritania
nougat sweet containing nuts
nought Brit. zero □ **noughth**
noughties informal decade 2000–9
noughts and crosses Brit. game of completing rows on a grid (three words)
noumenon pl. **noumena** (in Kantian philosophy) thing as it is in itself
noun (abbrev. **n.**)
nous (not ital.) **1** practical intelligence **2** Philos. mind or intellect
nouveau riche people who have recently acquired wealth (pl., not ital.)
nouveau roman style of French novel in the 1950s (ital.)
nouvelle cuisine light modern style of French cooking (not ital.)
nouvelle vague French film directors of the late 1950s and 1960s (ital.)
Nov. November
nova pl. **novae** or **novas** Astron. star suddenly very bright
Nova Scotia 1 peninsula on the SE coast of Canada **2** province of eastern Canada (abbrev. **NS**) □ **Nova Scotian**
novelist (one *l*)
novella short novel
November (abbrev. **Nov.**)
Novgorod city in NW Russia
novitiate (also **noviciate**) period of being a novice
novocaine (also trademark **Novocain**) another term for **procaine**
Novotný, Antonín (1904–75), Czechoslovak president 1957–68
nowadays (one word)
Nowel (also **Nowell**) arch. var. of **Noel**
nowhere (one word)
noxious harmful
NP notary public
Np the chemical element neptunium (no point)
n.p. 1 new paragraph **2** no place (of publication)
NPA Newspaper Publishers' Association
NPV net present value
nr near
NRA 1 US National Rifle Association **2** National Rivers Authority
NRSV the *New Revised Standard Version* (of the Bible)
NS New Style (dates or numbers)
NS new series (small caps)
ns nanosecond
n.s. not specified
n/s 1 not sufficient **2** non-smoker or -smoking
NSA US National Security Agency
NSB National Savings Bank
NSC US National Security Council
NSF US National Science Foundation
NSPCC National Association for the Prevention of Cruelty to Children
NSU non-specific urethritis

NSW New South Wales
NT 1 National Theatre **2** National Trust **3** New Testament **4** Northern Territory (Australia)
nth Math. unspecified member of a series (italic *n*)
NTP normal temperature and pressure
NU Nunavut (postal abbrev.)
nu thirteenth letter of the Greek alphabet (**N**, **ν**), transliterated as 'n'
nuance subtle difference
nubuck suede-like leather (lower case)
nucleus pl. **nuclei**
Nuffield, William Richard Morris, 1st Viscount (1877–1963), British motor manufacturer
nuit blanche pl. ***nuits blanches*** sleepless night (Fr., ital.)
Nuits-St-George red burgundy wine (hyphens)
NUJ National Union of Journalists
Nuku'alofa capital of Tonga
nulli secundus second to none (L., ital.)
NUM National Union of Mineworkers
number (abbrev. **no.**)
number cruncher, number plate (two words)
Numbers fourth book of the Old Testament (abbrev. **Num.**)
numbskull (also **numskull**)
numen pl. **numina** presiding spirit
numeraire measure of value or a standard for currency exchange (not ital., no accent) [Fr. *numéraire*]
numinous having a strong religious or spiritual quality
nunatak isolated rock projecting above snow
Nunavik northern part of Quebec in Canada
Nunavut Inuit territory of northern Canada (postal abbrev. **NU**)
Nunc Dimittis the Song of Simeon as a canticle
nuncio pl. **nuncios** papal ambassador
Nuremberg city in southern Germany; Ger. name **Nürnberg**
Nureyev, Rudolf (1939–93), Russian-born dancer and choreographer
Nurofen trademark ibuprofen
nursemaid (one word)
nursery rhyme, nursery school (two words)
nursing home (two words)
NUS National Union of Students
NUT National Union of Teachers
nut-brown (hyphen)
nutcase, nutcracker, nutshell (one word)
Nuuk capital of Greenland; former name **Godthåb**
nux vomica homeopathic preparation (two words, not ital.)
NV 1 Nevada (official abbrev.) **2** New Version
nvCJD new variant Creutzfeldt–Jakob disease (three caps)
NVI no value indicated
NVQ National Vocational Qualification
NW north-west(ern)
NY New York
Nyasaland former name for **Malawi**
NYC New York City
Nyerere, Julius Kambarage (1922–99), president of Tanganyika 1962–4 and of Tanzania 1964–85
nylon (lower case)
Nyman, Michael (b.1944), English composer
Nymegen use **Nijmegen**
nymphet (also **nymphette**) sexually mature young girl
Nynorsk literary form of Norwegian; cf. **Bokmål**
NYSE New York Stock Exchange
Nyx Gk Mythol. female personification of the night
NZ New Zealand

O

O 1 pl. **Os** or **O's** 15th letter of the alphabet **2** a human blood type **3** (**O.**) Ohio (official abbrev.) **4** order **5** Cricket over(s) **6** the chemical element oxygen

O' Irish patronymic prefix; means 'grandfather' (apostrophe)

o' short for 'of' (apostrophe; set closed up in common constructions, e.g. *o'clock*, but spaced in arch. and dial. uses such as *cock o' the walk*)

o- Chem. ortho-

Oahu third largest of the Hawaiian islands

Oaks, the annual horse race at Epsom Downs, England (treated as sing.)

OAM Medal of the Order of Australia

OAP old-age pensioner

OAPEC Organization of Arab Petroleum Exporting Countries

oarlock N. Amer. rowlock

oarsman, oarswoman (one word)

OAS Organization of American States

oasis pl. **oases** fertile spot in a desert

oast house conical brick building for drying hops (two words)

oatcake (one word)

Oates, Titus (1649–1705), English conspirator

oatmeal (one word)

OAU Organization of African Unity; now called **African Union**

Oaxaca state of southern Mexico or (in full **Oaxaca de Juárez**) its capital city

OB outside broadcast

ob. he or she died [L. *obiit*]

Obadiah 1 Hebrew minor prophet **2** book of the Old Testament (abbrev. **Obad.**)

Obama, Barack (Hussein) (b.1961), 44th president of the US since 2009

obbligato (US **obligato**) pl. **obbligatos** or **obbligati** Mus. instrumental part which must be played (abbrev. **obb.**)

OBE Officer of the Order of the British Empire

obeah (also **obi**) Caribbean sorcery

obeisance deferential respect

obelisk tapering tall pillar

obelus pl. **obeli** dagger-shaped reference mark, †

Oberammergau village in SW Germany

obi 1 sash worn with a kimono **2** var. of **obeah**

obiter dictum pl. ***obiter dicta*** judge's expression of opinion (L., ital.)

object lesson (two words)

objet d'art pl. ***objets d'art*** small artistic object (Fr., ital.)

objet trouvé pl. ***objets trouvés*** object found and displayed as a work of art (Fr., ital.)

obligato US var. of **obbligato**

obligee person to whom a legal obligation is owed

obliger person who does a favour

obligor person who owes a legal obligation

oblique Brit. slash or solidus /

obloquy strong public condemnation

oboe woodwind instrument □ **oboist**

Obote, (Apollo) Milton (1924–2005), Ugandan president 1966–71 and 1980–5

O'Brian, Patrick (1914–2000), British novelist; pseudonym of *Richard Patrick Russ*

O'Brien 1 Edna (b.1932), Irish writer **2** Flann (1911–66), Irish writer; pseudonym of *Brian O'Nolan*; wrote also as *Myles na Gopaleen*

obscurantism deliberate concealment of facts

obscurum per obscurius the obscure explained by the more obscure (L., ital.)

obsequies funeral rites

obsequious excessively attentive

observer (not **-or**)

obsessive–compulsive (en rule)

obsidian dark mineral

obsolescent becoming obsolete

obsolete no longer produced or used
obstreperous noisy and difficult to control
obstructor (not **-er**)
OC 1 Officer Commanding **2** Officer of the Order of Canada
OCAS Organization of Central American States
O'Casey, Sean (1880–1964), Irish dramatist
Occam, William of see **William of Occam**
Occam's razor (also **Ockham's razor**) principle of making no more assumptions than necessary
occasion, occasional (two *c*s)
Occident, the the countries of the West (cap.)
occidental 1 of the countries of the West **2** (**Occidental**) Westerner
occiput the back of the head □ **occipital**
Occitan language of Languedoc
occupancy, occupant, occupation, occupier, occupy (two *c*s)
occur (**occurring, occurred**) (two *c*s)
occurrence, occurrent (two *c*s, two *r*s)
oceanarium pl. **oceanariums** or **oceanaria**
Oceania islands of the Pacific Ocean
ocellus pl. **ocelli** insect's simple eye (not ital.)
ocelot South and Central American wild cat (one *l*)
ochlocracy mob rule
ochre (US **ocher**) earthy pigment
Ockham's razor var. of **Occam's razor**
o'clock (apostrophe, no spaces)
O'Connell, Daniel (1775–1847), Irish nationalist leader
O'Connor, (Mary) Flannery (1925–64), American writer
OCR optical character recognition
Oct. October
oct. octave; octavo
octagon shape with eight straight sides (not **octo-**)
octahedron pl. **octahedra** or **octahedrons** solid figure with eight plane faces
octameter line of eight metrical feet
octaroon var. of **octoroon**
octastyle Archit. having eight columns
octave (abbrev. **oct.**) **1** series of eight notes **2** stanza of eight lines **3** Fencing parrying position
Octavian see **Augustus**
octavo pl. **octavos** page size resulting from folding a sheet into eight leaves (abbrev. **8vo**, **8vo**, or **oct.**)
octennial recurring every eight years
octet first eight lines of a sonnet
October (abbrev. **Oct.**)
Octobrist hist. supporter of the tsar's reforms of 30 October 1905
octocentenary eight-hundredth anniversary □ **octocentennial**
octodecimo pl. **octodecimos** page size resulting from folding a sheet into eighteen leaves; eighteenmo (abbrev. **18mo**)
octogenarian person between 80 and 89 (not **octa-**)
octopus pl. **octopuses**
octoroon (also **octaroon**) person who is one-eighth black
octosyllable word or line with eight syllables
octroi pl. **octrois** municipal duty on goods (not ital.)
ocularist maker of artificial eyes
oculist ophthalmologist
oculus pl. **oculi** circular window or opening (not ital.)
OD (**OD's, OD'ing, OD'd**) (take) an overdose
odalisque concubine in a harem
Oddfellow member of a fraternity similar to the Freemasons
odd job (two words, hyphen when attrib.)
Odeon cinema chain
Odéon Paris theatre
odeon var. of **odeum**
Odessa coastal city in Ukraine
Odets, Clifford (1906–63), American dramatist
odeum (also **odeon**) pl. **odeums** or **odea** ancient building for musical performances (not ital.)
Odin (also **Woden** or **Wotan**) Scand. Mythol. supreme god
Odisha state in eastern India
odium widespread hatred

odometer (also **hodometer**) instrument for measuring distance travelled
odor US var. of **odour**
odorant substance that gives a particular smell (not **odour-**)
odoriferous smelly (not **odour-**)
odorize (Brit. also **odorise**) give an odour to (not **odour-**)
odorous having an odour (not **odour-**)
odour (US **odor**)
Odysseus king of Ithaca and central figure of the *Odyssey*
Odyssey Greek epic poem ascribed to Homer □ **Odyssean**
odyssey pl. **odysseys** long and eventful journey (lower case)
OE Old English
Oe oersted(s)
OECD Organization for Economic Cooperation and Development
OED the *Oxford English Dictionary*
oedema (US **edema**) excess of watery fluid in the tissues □ **oedematous**
Oedipus Gk Mythol. son of Jocasta and Laius, king of Thebes □ **Oedipal**
Oedipus complex child's supposed unconscious sexual desire for the parent of the opposite sex
oeil-de-boeuf pl. ***oeils-de-boeuf*** small round window (Fr., ital.)
oenology (US **enology**) study of wines
oenophile connoisseur of wines (not **eno-**)
Oersted, Hans Christian (1777–1851), Danish physicist
oersted unit of magnetic field strength (abbrev. **Oe**)
oesophagus (US **esophagus**) pl. **oesophagi** or **oesophaguses** the gullet □ **oesophageal**
oestrogen (US **estrogen**) hormone
oestrus (also **oestrum**) (US **estrus** or **estrum**) period of sexual fertility in female mammals □ **oestrous**
oeuvre artist's or composer's body of work (Fr., ital.)
OF old face
Ofcom Office of Communications, a regulatory body (one cap.)
Off. 1 Office **2** Officer
Offaly county in the Republic of Ireland
Offa's Dyke earthworks between England and Wales (caps; not **Dike**)
offbeat (one word)
off break Cricket (two words)
off-centre (hyphen)
off colour (two words, hyphen when attrib.)
offcut (one word)
off drive Cricket (two words)
Offenbach, Jacques (1819–80), German-born composer
offence (US **offense**)
offhand (one word)
Official Report of Parliamentary Debates, The official name for **Hansard**
officinal used in medicine
officious domineering in asserting authority
off-key, off-licence (hyphen)
offline, offload (one word)
off-peak, off-piste, off-price (hyphen)
offprint printed copy of an article from a collection (one word)
off-putting, off-road, off-screen (hyphen)
off season (two words, hyphen when attrib.)
offset n. printing in which ink is transferred from a plate or stone to a rubber surface and then to paper. v. (**offsetting, offset**) transfer an impression to the next leaf or sheet
offshoot, offshore, offside (one word)
off spin Cricket (two words) □ **off-spinner**
offspring pl. same (one word)
offstage (one word)
off stump Cricket (two words)
off-white (hyphen)
Ofgem Office of Gas and Electricity Markets, a regulatory body (one cap.)
Oflag German prison camp for officers (cap., not ital.)
OFr. Old French
Ofsted Office for Standards in Education (one cap.)
OFT Office of Fair Trading
oftentimes (one word)
oft-times (hyphen)

Ofwat Office of Water Services, a regulatory body (one cap.)
ogee S-shaped moulding □ **ogeed**
ogham (also **ogam**) ancient British and Irish alphabet
ogive Gothic arch
OGPU secret police agency in the former USSR 1923–34
ogre man-eating giant □ **ogreish** (also **ogrish**), **ogress**
OH Ohio (postal abbrev.)
OHG Old High German
O'Higgins, Bernardo (*c.*1778–1842), Chilean head of state 1817–23
Ohio state in the north-eastern US (official abbrev. **O.**, postal **OH**) □ **Ohioan**
Ohm, Georg Simon (1789–1854), German physicist
ohm SI unit of electrical resistance (symbol Ω)
ohmmeter instrument for measuring electrical resistance (one word, two *m*s)
OHMS on Her (or His) Majesty's Service
oidium pl. **oidia** fungal spore
OIEO offers in excess of
oilcake, oilcan, oilcloth (one word)
oil drum (two words)
oilfield (one word)
oil-fired (hyphen)
oil lamp, oil paint, oil painting, oil platform, oil rig (two words)
oilseed, oilskin (one word)
oil slick, oil tanker, oil well (two words)
Oireachtas legislature of the Irish Republic
OIRO offers in the region of
Ojibwa pl. same or **Ojibwas** member of an American Indian people (not **-way**)
OK[1] (also **okay**) adj. satisfactory. v. (**OK's, OK'ing, OK'd**) give approval to
OK[2] Oklahoma (postal abbrev.)
okapi pl. same or **okapis** member of the giraffe family
O'Keeffe, Georgia (1887–1986), American painter
Okhotsk, Sea of inlet of the Pacific on the east coast of Russia
Okinawa region in southern Japan
Oklahoma state in the south central US (official abbrev. **Okla.**, postal **OK**) □ **Oklahoman**
okra edible pods
OL Old Latin
old-age pension, old-age pensioner (hyphen)
Old Bailey the Central Criminal Court in London
old boy network (three words)
Old Church Slavonic oldest recorded Slavic language (caps)
Old English (caps) **1** English up to about 1150 (abbrev. **OE**) **2** English style of black letter
old face type design based on 15th-cent. roman type (lower case; abbrev. **OF**)
old-fashioned (hyphen)
Old French French up to about 1400 (caps; abbrev. **OFr.**)
Old High German High German up to about 1200 (caps; abbrev. **OHG**)
Old Kingdom period of ancient Egyptian history (caps)
Old Latin Latin before about 100 BC (caps; abbrev. **OL**)
Old Low German language of northern Germany and the Netherlands up to about 1200 (caps; abbrev. **OLG**)
Old Norse Scandinavian languages up to the 14th cent. (caps; abbrev. **ON**)
Old Pals Act (caps, no apostrophe)
Old Pretender, the James Stuart (1688–1766), son of James II
Old Saxon Old Low German of Saxony up to about 1200 (caps; abbrev. **OS**)
old school tie (three words)
Old Stone Age Palaeolithic period (caps)
Old Style calculation of dates using the Julian calendar (caps; abbrev. **OS**); cf. **New Style**
old-style numerals another term for **non-ranging numerals**
Old Testament (abbrev. **OT**)
old-time, old-timer (hyphen)
old wives' tale (three words)
Old World Europe, Asia, and Africa (caps)
old-world characteristic of former times (lower case, hyphen)
olé bravo! (Sp., ital.)

oleaceous of the olive family
oleaginous oily
oleiferous producing oil
oleograph print resembling an oil painting
O level hist. ordinary level (examination)
OLG Old Low German
oligarchy (rule by) a small controlling group
Oligocene the third epoch of the Tertiary period
oligopoly market with a small number of sellers
oligopsony market with a small number of buyers
olive branch, **olive drab**, **olive oil** (two words)
Olivier, Laurence (Kerr), Baron Olivier of Brighton (1907–89), English actor
Olmec pl. same or **Olmecs** member of a prehistoric Meso-American people
oloroso pl. **olorosos** medium-sweet sherry
Olympiad staging of the Olympic Games (cap.)
Olympic Games (caps)
OM Order of Merit
Omagh principal town of County Tyrone
Omaha city in eastern Nebraska
Oman country in the Arabian peninsula □ **Omani**
Omar Khayyám (d.1123), Persian poet, mathematician, and astronomer
ombudsman official investigating complaints; (**the Ombudsman**) the Parliamentary Commissioner for Administration
Omdurman city in central Sudan
omega last letter of the Greek alphabet (Ω, ω), transliterated as 'o' or 'ō'
omega-3 fatty acid unsaturated fatty acid in fish oils (one hyphen)
omelette (US **omelet**)
omertà Mafia code of silence (It., ital.)
omicron fifteenth letter of the Greek alphabet (**O**, **o**), transliterated as 'o'
omission (one *m*, two *ss*)
omnibus 1 volume containing works previously published separately **2** dated bus
omnidirectional, **omnipotent**, **omnipresent**, **omniscient** (one word)
omnium gatherum miscellaneous collection (not ital.)
omphalos pl. ***omphaloi*** centre or hub (Gk, ital.)
ON 1 Old Norse **2** Ontario (postal abbrev.)
Onassis 1 Aristotle (Socrates) (1906–75), Greek shipping magnate **2** Jacqueline Lee Bouvier Kennedy (1929–94), American First Lady; known as **Jackie O**
ONC Ordinary National Certificate
oncoming (one word)
oncost Brit. overhead expense (one word)
OND Ordinary National Diploma
Ondaatje, (Philip) Michael (b.1943), Sri Lankan-born Canadian writer
ondes martenot pl. same, electronic keyboard instrument (lower case)
on dit pl. ***on dits*** item of gossip (Fr., ital.)
on drive Cricket (two words)
one (Roman numeral **i** or **I**)
one-acter one-act play
one-dimensional (hyphen)
Oneida Community religious community in New York State
O'Neill, Eugene (Gladstone) (1888–1953), American dramatist
oneiric of dreams
oneiromancy interpretation of dreams to foretell the future
one-off, **one-piece** (hyphen)
oneself 1 reflexive or intensive pronoun **2** (**one's self**) one's personal entity
one-time former (hyphen)
one-to-one (also chiefly N. Amer. **one-on-one**) (hyphens)
one up having an advantage (two words)
one-upmanship (one hyphen)
ongoing (one word)
onion-skin paper fine translucent paper
online, **onlooker**, **onlooking** (one word)
o.n.o. or near(est) offer
on–off (en rule)
onomasiology study of terminology
onomastics study of proper names
onomatopoeia word formation from an

imitation of sound □ **onomatopoeic**
onrush (one word)
on-screen (hyphen)
onset beginning (one word)
on-set taking place on a film set (hyphen)
onshore, **onside**, **onstage** (one word)
on stream (two words)
on-street (hyphen)
Ontario province of eastern Canada (abbrev. **Ont.**, postal **ON**) □ **Ontarian**
on to (US & Math. **onto**)
ontology metaphysical study of the nature of being
oo- denoting an egg or ovum (forming solid compounds; not **oö-**)
oomiak use **umiak**
Oort, Jan Hendrik (1900–92), Dutch astronomer
Oostende Flemish name for **Ostend**
OP **1** observation post **2** opposite prompt **3** Order of Preachers (Dominican) [L. *Ordo Praedicatorum*] **4** organophosphate(s)
op. pl. **opp.** opus (before a number)
o.p. **1** out of print **2** overproof
op art art using patterns and colour to suggest movement
op. cit. in the work already cited (not ital.) [L. *opere citato*]
OPEC Organization of Petroleum Exporting Countries
op-ed newspaper page opposite the editorial page, containing features and opinion
open air (two words, hyphen when attrib.)
opencast mining from a level near the surface (one word)
open-heart surgery (one hyphen)
open-minded, **open-plan**, **open-topped** (hyphen)
open sesame magical formula (lower case, two words)
openwork ornamental work with patterns of holes (one word)
opera pl. of **opus**
opéra bouffe pl. ***opéras bouffes*** French comic opera (ital.)
opera buffa pl. ***opera buffas*** or ***opere buffe*** comic opera (It., ital.)
opéra comique opera with spoken dialogue (Fr., ital.)
opera glasses, **opera house** (two words)
opera seria pl. ***opera serias*** or ***opere serie*** opera on a classical or mythological theme (It., ital.)
operating system, **operating table**, **operating theatre** (two words)
operetta light opera
ophicleide old brass instrument
ophthalmic (not **opthal-**)
ophthalmic optician Brit. person qualified to examine eyesight, prescribe corrective lenses, and detect eye disease
ophthalmology study and treatment of diseases of the eye (not **opthal-**)
opinion poll (two words)
opopanax (also **opoponax**) essential oil or gum used in perfumery
Oporto principal city of northern Portugal; Port. name **Porto**
opossum American marsupial (one *p*, two *ss*)
opp. **1** opposite **2** opuses
Oppenheimer, Julius Robert (1904–67), American theoretical physicist
opponent, **opportune**, **opportunity** (two *ps*)
opposite font type set in a contrasting typeface, e.g. italic in roman or roman in italic
opposite prompt offstage area to the right of an actor facing the audience (abbrev. **OP**)
opposition, **oppress** (two *ps*)
oppress, **oppression**, **oppressive** (two *ps*, two *ss*)
optical centring positioning text on a page so that it appears to be centred though by measurement it is not
optimize (Brit. also **optimise**)
optimum pl. **optima** or **optimums**
optometrist N. Amer. ophthalmic optician
optometry occupation of an ophthalmic optician
opt-out n. (hyphen, two words as verb)
opus pl. **opuses** or **opera** musical composition (abbrev. **op.**)
Opus Dei trademark Roman Catholic organization (caps, not ital.)

opus Dei worship as a Christian duty to God (ital., one cap)
OR 1 operational research **2** Oregon (postal abbrev.) **3** other ranks
oral relating to the mouth or to speech; cf. **aural**
orangeade (one word)
Orange Free State province in central South Africa
Orangeman member of the **Orange Order**, a Protestant political society in Ireland
Orange, William of William III of Great Britain and Ireland
orangutan (also **orangutang**; not **orangoutang**) ape of Borneo and Sumatra
oratorio pl. **oratorios** narrative musical work for singers and orchestra (cap. and ital. in titles)
orca killer whale (lower case)
Orcadian of the Orkney Islands
orch. 1 orchestra **2** orchestrated by
orchid plant with showy flowers
orchidectomy surgical removal of a testicle
orchil red or violet dye from lichens
orchis orchid with a tuberous root
Orczy, Baroness Emmusca (1865–1947), Hungarian-born British novelist
ord. 1 order **2** ordinary
order 1 each of five classical styles of architecture, Doric, Ionic, Corinthian, Tuscan, and Composite (abbrev. **ord.**) **2** society of monks, knights, or honoured people (abbrev. **O**)
order book, **order form** (two words)
Order Paper Brit., Can. paper with the day's business of a legislative assembly (two words, caps)
ordinance authoritative order
ordinary seaman (abbrev. **OS**)
ordinate *y*-coordinate on a graph; cf. **abscissa**
ordnance artillery
ordnance datum mean sea level for Ordnance Survey
Ordnance Survey UK official survey organization (abbrev. **OS**)
ordonnance systematic arrangement of parts
Ordovician second period of the Palaeozoic era
øre pl. same, monetary unit of Denmark and Norway
öre pl. same, monetary unit of Sweden
oregano culinary herb
Oregon state in the north-western US (official abbrev. **Ore.** or **Oreg.**, postal **OR**) □ **Oregonian**
Oresteia trilogy by Aeschylus, 458 BC
Orestes Gk Mythol. son of Agamemnon and Clytemnestra
Øresund narrow channel between Sweden and Denmark
Orff, Carl (1895–1982), German composer
organdie (US **organdy**) fine cotton muslin
organize (Brit. also **organise**)
organon means of reasoning or system of thought
organophosphate synthetic compound (one word; abbrev. **OP**)
organum pl. **organa** (part in) an early kind of polyphonic music (not ital.)
organza thin stiff dress fabric
oriel upper-storey bay with a window
Oriel College Oxford
Orient, the the countries of the East
orient (Brit. also **orientate**) align or position in relation to the compass
oriental do not use of people; prefer **Asian** or specific terms such as **Chinese** or **Japanese**
orienteer participant in orienteering
orienteering cross-country sport using maps and a compass
oriflamme scarlet banner or knight's standard
orig. original; originally
origami Japanese art of folding paper
Origen (*c.*185–*c.*254), Christian scholar
Orinoco river in South America
oriole bird
Orissa former name for **Odisha**
Orkney (also **Orkney Islands**) group of islands off the NE tip of Scotland
Orleans city in central France; Fr. name **Orléans**
Ormazd another name for **Ahura Mazda**
ormolu gold-coloured alloy

Ormuz var. of **Hormuz**
orogeny formation of mountains
orography study of the formation of mountains
orotund (of a voice) resonant and imposing
orphan first line of a paragraph set as the last line of a page or column; cf. **widow**
Orpheus Gk Mythol. poet and lyrist who went to the underworld for Eurydice □ **Orphean**
Orphic of Orpheus or Orphism
Orphism mystic religion of ancient Greece
orphrey pl. **orphreys** ornamental stripe or border
orpiment yellow mineral
orpine (also **orpin**) purple-flowered plant
orrery clockwork model of the solar system
orris a preparation of the rootstock of an iris
ortanique cross between an orange and tangerine
Ortega y Gasset, José (1883–1955), Spanish philosopher
orthodox (cap. in ref. to the Orthodox Church or Orthodox Judaism)
Orthodox Church Christian Church originating in the Byzantine Empire
Orthodox Judaism strict traditional branch within Judaism
orthoepy (study of) correct or accepted pronunciation
orthogonal of or at right angles
orthography spelling system
orthopaedics (US **orthopedics**) correction of deformities of bones or muscles
Orvieto town in Umbria, central Italy
Orwell, George (1903–50), British writer; pseudonym of *Eric Arthur Blair* □ **Orwellian**
OS **1** Old Saxon **2** Old Style (dates or numbers) **3** operating system **4** Ordinary Seaman **5** Ordnance Survey **6** out of stock **7** outsize
Os the chemical element osmium (no point)
os old series (small caps)
os[1] pl. ***ossa*** Anat. a bone (L., ital.)
os[2] pl. ***ora*** Anat. opening or entrance (L., ital.)
Osaka city in central Japan
Osborne, John (James) (1929–94), English dramatist
Oscan extinct language of southern Italy
Oscar (trademark in the US) an Academy award
oscillate move back and forth regularly
osculate kiss
OSHA US Occupational Health and Safety Administration
osier small willow
Osiris god of ancient Egypt
Oslo capital of Norway; former name **Christiania**
Osman I (also **Othman**) (1259–1326), Turkish founder of the Ottoman (**Osmanli**) dynasty and empire
osmium chemical element of atomic number 76 (symbol **Os**)
osmosis gradual assimilation
Osnabrück city in NW Germany
osprey pl. **ospreys** fish-eating bird of prey
OSS US Office of Strategic Services
osseous consisting of or turned to bone
Ossetia region of the central Caucasus
Ossian legendary Irish warrior and bard
osso buco Italian stew of shin of veal (not **bucco**; not ital.)
OST original soundtrack
Ostend port in NW Belgium; Flemish name **Oostende**, Fr. **Ostende**
ostensible appearing to be true
ostensive indicating by demonstration
osteoarthritis, osteomyelitis, osteoporosis (one word)
Österreich Ger. name for **Austria**
ostinato pl. **ostinatos** or **ostinati** Mus. continually repeated musical phrase
ostler (also **hostler**) hist. man employed to look after horses at an inn
Ostmark former monetary unit of the German Democratic Republic
Ostpolitik hist. Western policy towards the communist bloc (cap., not ital.)
ostracize (Brit. also **ostracise**)
ostracon (also **ostrakon**) pl. **ostraca** or **ostraka** hist. potsherd used as a writing surface

Ostrogoth hist. member of the eastern branch of the Goths
Oświęcim Pol. name for **Auschwitz**
OT 1 occupational therapist; occupational therapy **2** Old Testament
Otago region of New Zealand, on the South Island
OTC 1 hist. Officers' Training Corps **2** over the counter
OTE on-target earnings
Othello Shakespeare play (abbrev. ***Oth.***)
other-worldly (hyphen)
Othman var. of **Osman I**
otiose serving no practical purpose
otorhinolaryngology study of diseases of the ear, nose, and throat (one word)
OTT over the top
ottava rima form of poetry consisting of stanzas of eight lines of ten or eleven syllables, rhyming *abababcc* (not ital.)
Ottawa federal capital of Canada
otto another name for **attar**
ottocento of the 19th century in Italy (not ital.)
Ottoman pl. **Ottomans** Turk of the Ottoman Empire
ottoman pl. **ottomans** low sofa with no back or arms (lower case)
Ottoman Empire Turkish empire from the 13th cent. to the end of WWI
Otway, Thomas (1652–85), English dramatist
OU Open University
Ouagadougou capital of Burkina
oubliette secret dungeon (not ital.)
oud Arab lute (not ital.)
Oudenarde 1708 battle in Flanders
Oudh (also **Audh** or **Awadh**) region of northern India
OUDS Oxford University Dramatic Society
ouguiya (also **ougiya**) (pl. same or **ouguiyas**) monetary unit of Mauritania
Ouida (1839–1908), English novelist; pseudonym of *Marie Louise de la Ramée*
Ouija board trademark in the US board used in seances
ounce unit of weight (not in scientific use; abbrev. **oz**)
OUP Oxford University Press
Our Father, Our Lady, Our Lord (caps)
ours (no apostrophe)
ourselves (not **ourself**)
Ouse name of several English rivers
ousel var. of **ouzel**
out and out absolute (three words, hyphens when attrib.)
outcast rejected person
outcaste person with no caste
Outer House (in full **the Outer House of the Court of Session**) (in Scotland) law court presided over by a single judge
Outer Mongolia former name for **Mongolia**
outerwear (one word)
out-group people not in an in-group (hyphen)
out island island away from the mainland (two words)
outmoded (one word)
out-of-body experience (two hyphens)
out of date (three words, hyphens when attrib.)
outpatient (one word)
output v. (**outputting**; past and past part. **output** or **outputted**)
outrageous (not **-gous**)
outré unusual and rather shocking (accent, not ital.)
out relief hist. assistance to poor people not in a workhouse (two words)
outsize (also **outsized**) very large
out-take section recorded but not included in the final version (hyphen)
out-talk, out-think, out-thrust (hyphen)
out tray tray for outgoing documents (two words)
Outward Bound trademark organization for adventure training
outward bound sailing away from home (two words)
outwith prep. Sc. outside
ouzel (also **ousel**) bird like a blackbird
ouzo pl. **ouzos** Greek aniseed-flavoured spirit
ova pl. of **ovum**
Oval Office US president's office in the White House (caps)

ovenproof (one word)
oven-ready (hyphen)
ovenware (one word)
overabundant (one word)
overage[1] (also **overaged**) over an age limit
overage[2] excess or surplus amount
overall 1 taking everything into account **2** (also **overalls**) one-piece protective garment
overcapitalize (Brit. also **overcapitalise**) (one word)
overdramatize (Brit. also **overdramatise**) (one word)
over easy N. Amer. (of an egg) fried on both sides (two words)
over-egg (in **over-egg the pudding**) go too far in embellishing something (hyphen)
over-elaborate, over-elaboration (hyphen)
overemphasize (Brit. also **overemphasise**) (one word)
over-exercise (hyphen)
overgeneralize (Brit. also **overgeneralise**) (one word)
Overijssel province of the east central Netherlands
overleaf on the other side of the page
over-optimism, over-optimistic, over-particular (hyphen)
overprint (one word)
over-refine, over-report, over-represent (hyphen)
overrun, overseer (one word)
overspecialize (Brit. also **overspecialise**) (one word)
overtype, overwrite (one word)
Ovid (43 BC–*c.*17 AD), Roman poet; Latin name *Publius Ovidius Naso* □ **Ovidian**
Oviedo city in NW Spain
ovolo pl. **ovoli** rounded architectural moulding (not ital.)
ovum pl. **ova** female reproductive cell
Owen 1 Robert (1771–1858), Welsh social reformer and industrialist **2** Wilfred (1893–1918), English poet
Owens, Jesse (1913–80), American athlete; born *James Cleveland Owens*
own brand (two words, hyphen when attrib.)
owner-occupier (hyphen)
own label (two words, hyphen when attrib.)
oxbow (one word)
Oxbridge Oxford and Cambridge universities regarded together
ox-eye daisy (one hyphen)
Oxfam British charity
Oxford city in central England (abbrev. **Oxf.**)
oxford thick cotton shirt fabric (lower case)
Oxford comma another name for **serial comma**
Oxford Group Christian movement advocating group discussion of personal problems (caps)
Oxford Movement Christian movement to restore Catholic ceremonial within the Church of England (caps)
Oxfordshire county of south central England (abbrev. **Oxon**)
Oxford University (two caps)
oxhide (one word)
oxidize (Brit. also **oxidise**)
Oxon (no point) **1** Oxfordshire **2** of Oxford University [L. *Oxonia* 'Oxford']
Oxonian person from Oxford
oxtail (one word)
ox tongue (two words)
oxyacetylene of a flame produced by mixing acetylene and oxygen
oxygen chemical element of atomic number 8 (symbol **O**)
oxygenize (Brit. also **oxygenise**)
oxymoron conjunction of apparently contradictory terms
oxytone having an acute accent on the last syllable; cf. **paroxytone**
oyez (also **oyes**) used to call for attention before an announcement
oy vey exclamation used by Yiddish-speakers (ital.)
oz ounce(s) (no point)
Ozalid trademark in the US photocopy made by a special process
Ozark Mountains highland plateau in the south central US
ozone-friendly (hyphen)
ozone hole, ozone layer (two words)
Ozymandias sonnet by Shelley, 1818
Ozzie use **Aussie**

P

P 1 pl. **Ps** or **P's** 16th letter of the alphabet **2** parking **3** Chess pawn **4** peta- (10^{15}) **5** the chemical element phosphorus **6** poise (unit of viscosity) **7** Law President **8** proprietary

p 1 penny or pence **2** Mus. piano (softly) **3** pico- (10^{-12}) **4** Phys. pressure **5** probability

p. pl. **pp.** page

p- Chem. para-

PA 1 Pennsylvania (postal abbrev.) **2** personal assistant **3** Press Association **4** public address **5** Publishers' Association

Pa (no point) **1** pascal(s) **2** the chemical element protactinium

Pa. Pennsylvania (official abbrev.: point)

p.a. per annum

paan (also **pan**) Ind. betel leaves

pa'anga pl. same, monetary unit of Tonga

Paarl town in SW South Africa

pabulum (also **pablum**) bland intellectual matter (not ital.)

PABX private automatic branch exchange

pace with due respect to (L., ital.)

pacemaker, pacesetter (one word)

pacey var. of **pacy**

pacha var. of **pasha**

Pachelbel, Johann (1653–1706), German composer

pachinko Japanese form of pinball (not ital.)

pachisi (also US trademark **parcheesi**) board game of Indian origin

pachyderm large mammal with thick skin

pacific peaceful (lower case)

Pacific Ocean largest of the world's oceans

Pacific Rim the small nations of east Asia bordering the Pacific Ocean (caps)

Pacino, Al (b.1940), American film actor; full name *Alfredo James Pacino*

package holiday (two words)

pack animal, pack drill (two words)

packet v. (**packeting, packeted**)

packhorse (one word)

pack ice (two words)

packing case (two words)

pack rat (two words)

Pac-Man trademark electronic computer game

pacy (also **pacey**) (**pacier, paciest**) fast

paddle boat, paddle steamer, paddle wheel (two words)

pademelon (also **paddymelon**) small wallaby

Paderewski, Ignacy Jan (1860–1941), Polish prime minister 1919

padlock (one word)

Padova It. name for **Padua**

padre chaplain or priest (not ital.)

padrone pl. **padrones** patron or master (not ital.)

padsaw small saw for cutting curves (one word)

pad thai Thai dish based on rice noodles (two words, not ital.)

Padua city in NE Italy; It. name **Padova**

paduasoy heavy corded or embossed silk fabric

paean song of praise or triumph; cf. **paeon**

paederast var. of **pederast**

paediatrics (US **pediatrics**) medicine dealing with children's diseases (treated as sing.) □ **paediatrician**

paedophile (US **pedophile**) person sexually attracted to children; cf. **pederast** □ **paedophilia**

paella Spanish rice dish (not ital.)

paeon metrical foot of one long and three short syllables; cf. **paean**

paeony var. of **peony**

Paganini, Niccolò (1782–1840), Italian violinist and composer

Page, Sir Frederick Handley

(1885–1962), English aircraft designer
page 1 one side of a leaf in a book etc.; (loosely) a leaf (abbrev. **p.**, pl. **pp.**) **2** section of data that can be displayed on a computer screen at one time
pageant procession for entertainment
pageboy (one word)
page proof printer's proof of a page to be published; cf. **galley proof**
paginate assign numbers to pages □ **pagination**
Pagliacci, I opera by Leoncavallo, 1892
Pagnol, Marcel (1895–1974), French dramatist, film director, and writer
Pahang state of Malaysia
Pahlavi (also **Pehlevi**) writing system used in ancient Persia
paid (abbrev. **pd**)
Paignton resort town in SW England
paillasse var. of **palliasse**
Paine, Thomas (1737–1809), English political writer
painkiller, painstaking (one word)
paintball game simulating military combat (one word)
paintbox (one word) **1** box holding dry paints **2** (**Paintbox**) trademark electronic system for video graphics
paintbrush, paintwork (one word)
pair-bond (hyphen)
paisa pl. **paise** monetary unit of India, Pakistan, and Nepal
Paisley town in central Scotland
paisley pattern of curved feather-shaped figures (lower case)
pajamas US var. of **pyjamas**
pak choi (N. Amer. **bok choy**) variety of Chinese cabbage
Pakeha NZ white New Zealander (cap.)
Pakhtun var. of **Pashtun**
Paki pl. **Pakis** offens. person from Pakistan
Pakistan country in the Indian subcontinent □ **Pakistani**
palace (cap. in proper names)
Palaearctic (also US **Palearctic**) northern Eurasia, North Africa, and parts of the Arabian peninsula as a zoogeographical region
palaeo- (US **paleo-**) older or ancient (forming solid compounds exc. with words beginning with a cap.)
Palaeocene (US **Paleocene**) earliest epoch of the Tertiary period
Palaeogene (US **Paleogene**) earlier part of the Tertiary period
palaeography (US **paleography**) study of ancient writing systems
Palaeolithic (US **Paleolithic**) early phase of the Stone Age
palaeontology (US **paleontology**) study of fossils
Palaeozoic (US **Paleozoic**) era between the Precambrian aeon and the Mezozoic era
palais de danse pl. same, dance hall (Fr., ital.)
Palais de l'Elysée Fr. name for **Elysée Palace**
palatable pleasant to taste (not **-eable**)
palatal of the palate
palate roof of the mouth; cf. **palette, pallet**
palatial spacious and splendid
palatinate hist. territory of a Count Palatine; (**the Palatinate**) territory of the Count Palatine of the Rhine
palatine[1] hist. having local authority similar to that of a sovereign (usu. after the noun; cap. in titles)
palatine[2] of the palate and surrounding area
Palau (also **Belau**) republic comprising a group of islands in the Pacific Ocean
palazzo pl. **palazzos** or **palazzi** Italian palace (not ital.)
Pale, the hist. the English Pale (cap.; lower case in **beyond the pale**)
Palearctic US var. of **Palaearctic**
paleo- etc. US var. of **palaeo-** etc.
Palermo capital of Sicily
Palestine territory in the Middle East □ **Palestinian**
Palestrina, Giovanni Pierluigi da (*c.*1525–94), Italian composer
palette board on which an artist mixes colours; cf. **palate, pallet**
palette knife (two words)
Palgrave, Francis Turner (1824–97), English anthologist
Pali language closely related to Sanskrit
palimony compensation to one of an unmarried couple after separation

palimpsest manuscript with writing superimposed on other writing
palindrome word or sequence reading the same backwards as forwards
palinode poem retracting something expressed in an earlier poem
Palladio, Andrea (1508–80), Italian architect □ **Palladian**
palladium chemical element of atomic number 46 (symbol **Pd**)
pall-bearer (hyphen)
pallet 1 straw mattress **2** platform for holding goods; cf. **palate, palette**
palletize (Brit. also **palletise**) place or transport on a pallet
palliasse (also **paillasse**) straw mattress
palliative relieving pain without removing its cause
pallium pl. **pallia** or **palliums** prelate's woollen vestment (not ital.)
Pall Mall London street (two words)
pall-mall old game of driving a ball down an alley (hyphen)
pallor paleness (not **-our**)
Palma (in full **Palma de Mallorca**) capital of the Balearic Islands
Palmerston, Henry John Temple, 3rd Viscount (1784–1865), British prime minister 1855–8 and 1859–65
palmette ornament like a palm leaf
palmetto pl. **palmettos** fan palm tree
palm oil (two words)
Palm Sunday Sunday before Easter (caps)
palmtop small hand-held computer (one word)
Palo Alto city in western California
Palomar, Mount mountain and astronomical observatory in California
palsgrave hist. a Count Palatine
Pamir Mountains mountain system of central Asia
pampas treeless South American plain (treated as sing. or pl.)
pampas grass (two words)
pamphlet v. (**pamphleting, pamphleted**)
Pamplona city in northern Spain
Pan Gk Mythol. god of flocks and herds
pan var. of **paan**
panacea remedy for all difficulties or diseases
panache flamboyant confidence
pan-African (hyphen)
Panama country in Central America □ **Panamanian**
panama hat of strawlike material (lower case)
pan-American, pan-Arabism (hyphen)
panatella long thin cigar (not **-tela**)
pancake (one word)
pancetta Italian cured belly of pork (not **-chetta**)
Panchen Lama Tibetan lama ranking after the Dalai Lama
pancreas pl. **pancreases** gland secreting digestive enzymes □ **pancreatic**
Pandaemonium abode of all the demons in Milton's *Paradise Lost*; cf. **pandemonium**
pandect complete body of laws; (**the Pandects**) 6th-cent. compendium of Roman civil law
pandemic prevalent everywhere
pandemonium wild disorder and confusion; cf. **Pandaemonium**
p. & h. N. Amer. postage and handling
pandit (also **pundit**) Hindu scholar (cap. in titles)
P & L profit and loss (account)
P. & M. Philip and Mary (regnal year)
P&O Peninsular and Oriental Steam Navigation Company (no spaces)
p. & p. Brit. postage and packing
paneer (also **panir**) milk curd cheese
panegyric speech or publication of praise
panel game (two words)
panelled, panelling, panellist (US one **-l-**)
panettone pl. **panettoni** Italian fruit bread (not ital., two *t*s)
pan-fry (hyphen)
pan-German (hyphen)
Pangloss optimistic person (cap.) □ **Panglossian**
panhandle N. Amer. narrow strip of territory
Panhellenic of all Greek people (cap., one word; not **pan-Hellenic**)

panic v. (**panicking, panicked**) □ **panicky**
panic attack, panic button (two words)
panic-monger, panic-stricken (hyphen)
panini (also **panino**) pl. same or **paninis** Italian-style sandwich (not ital.)
panir var. of **paneer**
Panjabi var. of **Punjabi**
panjandrum authoritative person (lower case)
Pankhurst, Mrs Emmeline (1858–1928), Christabel (1880–1958), and (Estelle) Sylvia (1882–1960), English suffragettes
pannikin small drinking cup (two *n*s)
pan pipes (two words; not **Pan's**)
pan-Slavism belief in the unification of all Slavic peoples (hyphen, one cap.)
Pantagruel giant in Rabelais's novel *Pantagruel* (1532) □ **Pantagruelian**
Pantaloon character in the *commedia dell'arte*
pantaloons baggy trousers (lower case)
pantheon temple to all the gods; (**the Pantheon**) circular temple in Rome; (**Panthéon**) circular building in Paris
pantihose var. of **pantyhose**
pantile curved roof tile (one word)
panto pl. **pantos** pantomime
pantograph instrument for copying on a different scale (not **panta-** or **penta-**)
pantyhose (also **pantihose**) N. Amer. women's tights
panzer German armoured unit (lower case, not ital.)
Paolozzi, Eduardo (Luigi) (1924–2005), Scottish artist
papabile fit to be pope (It., ital.)
papal of the pope (lower case)
Papal States the temporal dominions of the Pope
paparazzo pl. **paparazzi** photographer who pursues celebrities (not ital.)
papaw var. of **pawpaw**
papaya tropical fruit
paperback (one word; abbrev. **pb**)
paperchase (one word)
paper clip (two words)
paper-thin (hyphen)
paper tiger, paper trail (two words)
paperweight, paperwork (one word)
papier mâché mixture of paper and glue that dries hard (accents, not ital.)
papilla pl. **papillae** Anat. small rounded protuberance
papillon breed of toy dog (lower case)
pappardelle pasta in broad flat ribbons
Pap test test on a cervical smear to detect cancer
Papua SE part of New Guinea, now part of Papua New Guinea (the rest of the island is part of Irian Jaya)
Papua New Guinea country comprising half of New Guinea and some neighbouring islands (abbrev. **PNG**) □ **Papua New Guinean**
papyrology study of papyri
papyrus pl. **papyri** or **papyruses** ancient writing material
par standard number of golf strokes; cf. **parr**
par. pl. **pars** or **pars.** paragraph
Pará state in northern Brazil
para monetary unit of Bosnia-Herzegovina, Montenegro, and Serbia
para. pl. **paras** or **paras.** paragraph
parabola pl. **parabolas** or **parabolae**
Paracelsus (*c.*1493–1541), Swiss physician: born *Theophrastus Phillipus Aureolus Bombastus von Hohenheim*
paracetamol pl. same or **paracetamols** pain-relieving drug
Paraclete the Holy Spirit as advocate or counsellor
paradigm typical example or pattern
paradise heaven (cap. in ref. to the Garden of Eden)
paradisiacal (also **paradisaical, paradisal**, or **paradisical**) like paradise
paraffin (one *r*, two *f*s; not **-ine**)
paragraph distinct section of a text, indicated by a new line, indentation, or numbering (abbrev. **par.** or **para.**)
paragraph mark symbol, usually ¶, used as a reference mark or to mark a new paragraph or (in early manuscripts) section
Paraguay country in central South America □ **Paraguayan**

parakeet (also **parrakeet**) small green parrot
paralipomena (also **paraleipomena**) (sing. **paralipomenon**) **1** omissions added as a supplement **2** (**Paralipomena**) arch. Chronicles regarded as supplementary to Kings
paralipsis emphasis by professing to say little on a subject
parallel v. (**paralleling, paralleled**)
parallelepiped solid body with each face a parallelogram
parallel mark reference mark ||
paralogism piece of superficially logical reasoning
Paralympic Games international competition for disabled athletes
paralyse (US **paralyze**)
paralysis pl. **paralyses**
Paramaribo capital of Suriname
paramecium pl. **paramecia** Zool. single-celled freshwater animal (not **-moecium**)
paramedical, paramilitary (one word)
paranoia mental condition with delusions □ **paranoiac, paranoic**
paranormal (one word)
parapente gliding with an aerofoil parachute
parapet low protective wall on a high place □ **parapeted**
paraph flourish at the end of a signature
paraphernalia miscellaneous articles (treated as sing. or pl.)
paraphrase express in different words □ **paraphrastic**
paraprofessional, parapsychology (one word)
paraquat toxic fast-acting herbicide
pararhyme rhyme of consonants but not vowels
paras (also **paras.**) paragraphs
parasitize (Brit. also **parasitise**)
parataxis Gram. placing of clauses without indication of coordination or subordination; cf. **hypotaxis**
par avion by airmail (Fr., ital.)
Parcae Gk Mythol. the Fates
parcel v. (**parcelling, parcelled**; US one **-l-**)
parcel bomb, parcel post, parcel shelf (two words)
parcheesi see **pachisi**
parchment paper tough translucent paper (two words)
parens parentheses, round brackets
parenthesis 1 pl. **parentheses** insertion representing an explanation or afterthought (usu. marked off by brackets, dashes, or commas) **2** (**parentheses**) round brackets ( ) (abbrev. **parens**)
parenthesize (Brit. also **parenthesise**) insert as a parenthesis
parent–teacher association (en rule; abbrev. **PTA**)
parergon pl. **parerga** supplementary work
par excellence better or more than all others (usu. after a noun; not ital.)
parfait whipped cream dessert (not ital.)
parfumerie place making or selling perfume (Fr., ital.)
pargana subdivision of a district in India
parget (**pargeting, pargeted**) face with ornamental plaster
parhelion pl. **parhelia** bright spot either side of the sun
pariah 1 outcast **2** hist. member of a low or no caste in southern India
parietal of the wall of the body
pari-mutuel betting in which winners divide the losers' stakes (not ital.)
pari passu at the same rate (L., ital.)
Paris 1 capital of France **2** see **Matthew Paris**
Paris Commune communalistic government in Paris in 1871 (caps)
parishad Ind. council or assembly
Parisian (inhabitant) of Paris
Parisienne Parisian girl or woman (not ital.)
park-and-ride (hyphens)
Parker Bowles former surname of Camilla, Duchess of Cornwall, the wife of Prince Charles (no hyphen)
parking light, parking lot, parking meter, parking ticket (two words)
Parkinson's disease (also **parkinsonism**) progressive disease with tremor

Parkinson's law work expands to fill the time available
parkland (one word)
parkway (one word) **1** Brit. railway station with extensive parking **2** N. Amer. open landscaped highway
Parl. Parliament; Parliamentary
parlando Mus. in the manner of speech
parlay N. Amer. bet winnings to produce (a greater amount)
parley (**parleys, parleying, parleyed**) (hold) a conference between opposing sides
Parliament 1 highest legislature in the UK (abbrev. **Parl.**) **2** (**parliament**) a session of this; a similar legislature elsewhere
parliamentary private secretary (abbrev. **PPS**)
parlour (US **parlor**)
Parmesan hard Italian cheese (cap.)
Parnassus, Mount mountain in central Greece
Parnell, Charles Stewart (1846–91), Irish nationalist leader
parody v. (**parodying, parodied**)
parol Law expressed orally
parole conditional release before expiry of a jail sentence
parole linguistic behaviour of individuals on specific occasions (Fr., ital.); cf. ***langue***
paronomasia a play on words
paronym word cognate with another
Paros Greek island in the Aegean
paroxysm sudden attack of emotion or laughter
paroxytone having an acute accent on the penultimate syllable
parquet flooring of wooden blocks □ **parquetry**
Parr, Katherine (1512–48), last wife of Henry VIII (not **Catherine**)
parr pl. same, young salmon or trout; cf. **par**
parrakeet var. of **parakeet**
parramatta twill fabric
parricide killing or killer of a parent or close relative; cf. **patricide**
parrot v. (**parroting, parroted**)
pars paragraphs
parse resolve (a sentence) into its syntactic parts
parsec Astron. unit of distance equal to about 3.25 light years
Parsee adherent of Zoroastrianism, esp. in India
Parsifal 1 another name for **Perceval 2** (***Parsifal***) opera by Wagner (1879)
parsimonious mean with money
pars pro toto part taken as representative of the whole (L., ital.)
part (abbrev. **Pt**)
parterre level ornamental area in a garden
part exchange n. (two words, hyphen as verb)
Parthenon temple of Athene Parthenos on the Acropolis in Athens
Parthian shot another term for **parting shot**
partially sighted (two words)
partible Law divisible; to be divided equally (not **-able**)
participle verb form used as an adjective □ **participial**
particle word used with a verb to make a phrasal verb
particoloured (US **particolored**) of more than one colour (one word; not **party-**)
particularize (Brit. also **particularise**)
parting shot final remark on departure
parti pris pl. ***partis pris*** preconceived view (Fr., ital.)
partisan strong supporter (not **-zan**)
partita pl. **partitas** or **partite** musical suite
partitive construction indicating division into parts, as in *most of us*
part of speech (three words)
part-own, part-song, part-time (hyphen)
part way part of the way (two words)
party of political organizations, cap. only when integral to the name (*the Labour Party*; *party workers*)
partygoer (one word)
party line, party piece, party political, party wall (two words)
parvenu (fem. **parvenue**) upstart (not ital.)

Pasadena city in California
PASCAL computer programming language
Pascal, Blaise (1623–62), French scientist and philosopher
pascal SI unit of pressure (lower case, abbrev. **Pa**)
paschal of Easter or Passover
Paschal Lamb, the a name for Christ (caps)
pas de chat pl. same, Ballet jump raising each foot to the knee (Fr., ital.)
pas de deux pl. same, Ballet dance for two (Fr., ital.)
pas glissé var. of ***glissé***
pasha (also **pacha**) hist. high-ranking Turkish officer (cap. in titles)
pashmina shawl of fine goat's wool
Pashto (also **Pushtu**) language of the Pashtuns
Pashtun (also **Pakhtun**) member of a people of Pakistan and Afghanistan
paso doble pl. **paso dobles** ballroom dance based on marching
Pasolini, Pier Paolo (1922–75), Italian film director
pasque flower spring-flowering plant
pasquinade satire or lampoon
passable just good enough; cf. **passible**
passacaglia musical composition similar to a chaconne (not ital.)
passageway (one word)
passata thick sieved tomatoes (not ital.)
passbook (one word)
Passchendaele (also **Passendale**) scene in Belgium of trench warfare (1917)
passé out of date (accent, not ital.)
passementerie decorative textile trimming (Fr., ital.)
passepartout picture in a frame held together by tape (one word, not ital.)
passer-by pl. **passers-by** (hyphen)
pas seul Ballet solo dance (Fr., ital.)
passible capable of suffering; cf. **passable**
passim in various places throughout the text (L., ital.)
Passion, the the suffering and death of Christ (cap.)
Passion Sunday fifth Sunday in Lent, beginning **Passion Week**
passive with the grammatical subject the object of the action
pass key, pass mark (two words)
Passover major Jewish spring festival (cap., one word)
passport, password (one word)
pastel crayon made from powdered pigment; cf. **pastille** □ **pastellist**
Pasternak, Boris (Leonidovich) (1890–1960), Russian writer
paste-up copy consisting of different sections on a backing (hyphen)
Pasteur, Louis (1822–95), French scientist
pasteurize (Brit. also **pasteurise**)
pasticcio pl. **pasticcios** another term for **pastiche** (not ital.)
pastiche imitative work of art □ **pasticheur**
pastille small sweet or lozenge; cf. **pastel**
pastime (one *s*)
pastis pl. same, aniseed-flavoured aperitif (not ital.)
pastoral for grazing; of country life
pastorale pl. **pastorales** or **pastorali** instrumental composition in a pastoral style (not ital.)
past participle verb form in perfect and passive tenses
past perfect another term for **pluperfect**
pastrami smoked beef
pastureland (one word)
Pat. Patent
Patagonia region in southern Argentina and Chile □ **Patagonian**
patchouli aromatic oil from an Asian shrub
patchwork (one word)
pate person's head
pâté paste of seasoned meat, fish, etc. (two accents, not ital.)
pâte paste from which porcelain is made (Fr., ital., one accent)
pâté de campagne coarse pork and liver pâté
pâté de foie gras smooth pâté from fatted goose liver
patella pl. **patellae** kneecap
paten plate used during the Eucharist

patent government licence conferring a right (abbrev. **Pat.**)
Pater, Walter (Horatio) (1839–94), English writer
paterfamilias pl. **patresfamilias** father of a family (not ital.)
paternoster the Lord's Prayer (lower case)
Pathan former term for **Pashtun**
Pathé, Charles (1863–1957), French film pioneer
Pathétique piano sonata by Beethoven (in full *Grande sonate pathétique*); symphony by Tchaikovsky
pathfinder (one word)
pathos quality evoking pity or sadness; cf. **bathos**
pathway (one word)
patina film on the surface of metal
patio pl. **patios** paved outdoor area
patisserie (shop selling) cakes and pastries (not ital.) [Fr. *pâtisserie*]
Patmos Greek island in the Aegean Sea
Patna 1 city in NE India **2** long-grain rice
patois pl. same, regional dialect (not ital.)
patresfamilias pl. of **paterfamilias**
patricide killing or killer of one's own father; cf. **parricide**
patrol v. (**patrolling, patrolled**)
patrolman N. Amer. patrolling police officer (one word)
patronize (Brit. also **patronise**)
patronymic name derived from that of a father or male ancestor
Patten, Christopher (Francis), Baron Patten of Barnes (b.1944), English politician, Chancellor of Oxford University since 2003
patten hist. raised shoe or clog
paucity insufficient presence
Pauli, Wolfgang (1900–58), Austrian-born American physicist
Pauling, Linus Carl (1901–94), American chemist
pauperize (Brit. also **pauperise**)
paupiette rolled stuffed slice of meat or fish (not ital.)
Pausanias (2nd cent.), Greek geographer and historian
pavane (also **pavan**) slow stately dance
Pavarotti, Luciano (1935–2007), Italian operatic tenor
pavé jewellery setting with stones close together (accent, not ital.)
pavilion (one *l*)
paviour (also **pavior**) paving stone
Pavlov, Ivan (Petrovich) (1849–1936), Russian physiologist □ **Pavlovian**
Pavlova, Anna (Pavlovna) (1881–1931), Russian dancer
pavlova meringue dessert (lower case)
pawn Chess (abbrev. **P**)
pawnbroker, pawnshop (one word)
pawpaw (also **papaw**) another term for **papaya**
Pax Romana hist. the peace within the Roman Empire (caps)
pay as you earn deduction of income tax by the employer (abbrev. **PAYE**)
payback (one word)
pay bed, pay channel (two words)
pay cheque (US **paycheck**)
payday (one word)
PAYE pay as you earn
payload, paymaster (one word)
Paymaster General UK Treasury minister responsible for payments (caps; abbrev. **PMG**)
pay-off n. (hyphen, two words as verb)
payout n. (one word, two words as verb)
pay packet (two words)
PayPal trademark online payment business
pay-per-view (hyphens; abbrev. **PPV**)
payphone, payroll (one word)
paysage landscape in art (Fr., ital.)
Pays-Bas Fr. name for **the Netherlands**
Pays Basque Fr. name for **Basque Country**
Pays de la Loire region of western France
payslip (one word)
pay television, pay TV (two words)
pazazz var. of **pizzazz**
PB 1 Comput. petabyte(s) **2** *Pharmacopoeia Britannica* **3** Prayer Book
Pb the chemical element lead (no point) [L. *plumbum*]
pb paperback
PBX private branch exchange
PC 1 personal computer **2** police constable **3** politically correct; political

correctness **4** Privy Counsellor
p.c. per cent
PCB printed circuit board
P-Celtic another term for **Brythonic**
PCM pulse code modulation
PCN personal communications network
PCS 1 personal communications services **2** Sc. Principal Clerk of Session
pct. N. Amer. per cent
PCV passenger-carrying vehicle
PD 1 US Police Department **2** public domain
Pd the chemical element palladium (no point)
pd paid
PDA personal digital assistant
PDF Comput. format for capturing electronic documents
p.d.q. pretty damn quick
PDSA People's Dispensary for Sick Animals
PDT Pacific Daylight Time
PE 1 physical education **2** Prince Edward Island (postal abbrev.)
peaceable (not **-cable**)
peacekeeper, peacemaker (one word)
peace movement, peace offering, peace pipe (two words)
peacetime (one word)
peachick young pea fowl (one word)
peach Melba ice cream and peach dessert (one cap.; not **pêche**)
Peacock, Thomas Love (1785–1866), English writer
peacock (one word)
peafowl (one word)
pea green (two words, hyphen when attrib.)
peahen (one word)
pea jacket short double-breasted overcoat
Peak District hilly area in Derbyshire
Peake, Mervyn (Laurence) (1911–68), British writer and artist
peanut (one word)
pearl 1 lustrous round gem **2** Brit. another term for **picot**; cf. **purl**
pearl diver (two words)
Pearl Harbor harbour on Oahu, Hawaii (not **Harbour**)
Pearmain pear-shaped dessert apple with white flesh (cap.)
Pears, Sir Peter (1910–86), English operatic tenor
pear-shaped (hyphen)
pease pudding (two words)
pea-shooter (hyphen)
peatland (one word)
peat moss (two words)
peau de soie satin fabric (three words, not ital.)
peau d'orange pitted appearance of the skin (Fr., ital.)
pebble-dash Brit. mortar with pebbles in it (hyphen)
pecan nut similar to a walnut
peccadillo pl. **peccadilloes** or **peccadillos** minor fault (two *c*s, two *l*s)
peccary piglike mammal
peccavi pl. **peccavis** arch. acknowledgement of guilt (not ital.)
peck quarter of a bushel (abbrev. **pk**)
pecking order (two words)
Pecksniffian affecting virtue [after Mr *Pecksniff*, character in Dickens's *Martin Chuzzlewit*]
pecorino pl. **pecorinos** Italian ewes' milk cheese
Pécs city in SW Hungary
pectoral of the breast or chest
peculate embezzle
pecuniary of money
pedagogue teacher (not **-gog**)
pedal (**pedalling, pedalled**; US one **-l-**) (move by means of) a foot-operated lever; cf. **peddle**
pedal bin (two words)
pedalboard keyboard of pedals on an organ (one word)
pedal boat, pedal car, pedal cycle (two words)
pedaller (US **pedaler**) person pedalling a bike; cf. **peddler**
pedalo pl. **pedalos** or **pedaloes** Brit. small pedal-operated pleasure boat
peddle try to sell while going from place to place; cf. **pedal**
peddler var. of **pedlar**; cf. **pedaller**
pederast (also **paederast**) man who has sex with a boy; cf. **paedophile** □ **pederasty**
pedestal base for a statue, column, etc.

pedestrianize (Brit. also **pedestrianise**)
pediatrics US var. of **paediatrics**
pedlar (also **peddler**) itinerant trader; cf. **pedaller**
pedology soil science
pedometer instrument measuring distance travelled on foot
pedophile US var. of **paedophile**
Peeblesshire former county of southern Scotland
peekaboo (also **peek-a-boo**) hiding game played with a young child
peel (also **pele**) small square tower
peen (also **pein**) end of a hammer head opposite the face
peephole (one word)
peeping Tom voyeur (one cap.)
peep show (two words)
peer duke, marquess, earl, viscount, or baron
peer group (two words)
Peer Gynt play by Ibsen (1867); incidental music by Grieg
peer of the realm peer with the historical right to sit in the House of Lords
peer pressure, **peer review** (two words)
peewit lapwing (not **pewit**)
Pegasus Gk Mythol. winged horse
pegboard (US trademark **Peg-board**) board with holes for pegs
Peggotty family in Dickens's *David Copperfield*
Pehlevi var. of **Pahlavi**
PEI Prince Edward Island
Pei, I(eoh) M(ing) (b.1917), American architect
peignoir woman's light dressing gown
pein var. of **peen**
peine forte et dure medieval torture with heavy weights (Fr., ital.)
Peirce, Charles Sanders (1839–1914), American philosopher
Peisistratus var. of **Pisistratus**
pejorative expressing contempt or disapproval (not **perj-**)
peke Pekinese
Pekinese (also **Pekingese**) pl. same, small dog with long hair
Peking var. of **Beijing**
pekoe black tea
Pelagius (*c.*360–*c.*420), British or Irish monk □ **Pelagian**
pelargonium pl. **pelargonium** shrubby flowering plant
Pelé (b.1940), Brazilian footballer; born *Edson Arantes do Nascimento*
pele var. of **peel**
Pelée, Mount volcano on the island of Martinique
pelham type of bit for a horse (lower case)
pellagra deficiency disease
pell-mell in a disorderly manner (hyphen)
pellucid translucently clear
Peloponnese, the southern peninsula of Greece (one *p*, two *ns*); mod. Gk name **Pelopónnisos**
pelota Basque or Spanish racket game
peloton main group of cyclists in a race (not ital.)
pelvis pl. **pelvises** or **pelves** bony frame at the base of the spine
Pembrokeshire county of SW Wales (abbrev. **Pembs.**)
pemmican cake of pounded dried meat
PEN International Association of Poets, Playwrights, Editors, Essayists, and Novelists
Pen. Peninsula
penalize (Brit. also **penalise**)
penalty area, **penalty box**, **penalty kick** (two words)
Penang (also **Pinang**) island and state of Malaysia
penates Roman household gods (not ital.); see also **lares**
pence see **penny**
penchant strong liking (not ital.)
pencil v. (**pencilling**, **pencilled**; US one **-l-**)
pencil pusher (two words)
pencil sharpener (two words)
pendant piece of jewellery hanging on a chain
pendent hanging down
pendente lite during litigation (L., ital.)
Penderecki, Krzysztof (b.1933), Polish composer
penfriend (one word)
penguin flightless seabird

penicillin (one *n*, two *l*s)
peninsula n. projecting piece of land (abbrev. **Pen.**)
peninsular adj. of or constituting a peninsula
penis pl. **penises** or **penes**
penknife (one word)
Penn. (also **Penna.**) Pennsylvania
pen name (two words)
pennant tapering flag
penne pasta in short wide tubes
penni pl. **penniä** former monetary unit of Finland
penniless (not **penny-**)
Pennine Hills range of hills in northern England
pennon another term for **pennant**
penn'orth var. of **pennyworth**
Pennsylvania state of the north-eastern US (official abbrev. **Pa.**, postal **PA**) □ **Pennsylvanian**
Pennsylvania Dutch dialect of High German spoken in Pennsylvania
penny pl. for separate coins **pennies**, for a sum of money **pence** (abbrev. **p** (sing. and pl.), in pre-decimal currency **d**)
penny black first adhesive postage stamp (lower case)
penny-farthing early bicycle (hyphen)
pennyweight, pennyworth (one word)
pen pal (two words)
pensée a thought or aphorism (Fr., ital.)
pension small hotel in France (ital.)
pensione pl. ***pensioni*** small hotel in Italy (ital.)
pensionnat boarding school in France (ital.)
penstemon (also **pentstemon**) North American flowering plant
Pentagon headquarters of the US Department of Defense, near Washington DC
pentagon shape with five straight sides □ **pentagonal**
pentagram five-pointed star
pentahedron pl. **pentahedra** or **pentahedrons** solid figure with five plane faces
pentameter line of verse of five metrical feet
Pentateuch the first five books of the Old Testament (Genesis, Exodus, Leviticus, Numbers, and Deuteronomy)
Pentecost Christian festival on the seventeenth Sunday after Easter
Pentecostal of Christian groups emphasizing baptism in the Holy Spirit (cap.)
penthouse (one word)
pentimento pl. **pentimenti** visible trace of an earlier painting (not ital.)
pentstemon var. of **penstemon**
penultimate last but one
penumbra pl. **penumbrae** or **penumbras** partially shaded outer region of a shadow
peon pl. **peones** Spanish-American labourer (not ital.)
peony (also **paeony**) plant with showy flowers
people carrier (two words)
People's Republic of China official name of **China**
PEP 1 personal equity plan **2** Political and Economic Planning
peperoni var. of **pepperoni**
pepo pl. **pepos** watery fruit like a melon
pepperbox gun with revolving barrels (one word)
peppercorn, peppermint (one word)
pepperoni (also **peperoni**) sausage seasoned with pepper
pepper pot, pepper spray (two words)
Pepys, Samuel (1633–1703), English diarist
Per. Shakespeare's *Pericles*
per annum for each year (not ital.; abbrev. **p.a.**)
p/e ratio price–earnings ratio
per capita (also **per caput**) for each person (not ital.)
per cent (US **percent**) in or for every hundred (symbol **%**, but avoid in running text)
percentage number or amount in each hundred (one word)
percentile one hundredth of a statistical sample
perceptible (not **-able**)
Perceval 1 legendary figure associated with the Holy Grail; also called **Parsifal** **2** Spencer (1762–1812), British prime minister 1809–12

per contra on the other hand (not ital.)
per curiam by unanimous decision of a court (not ital.)
per diem for each day (not ital.)
père used after a surname to distinguish a father from a son of the same name (Fr., ital.); cf. ***fils***
Père David's deer large deer now found only in captivity
Père Lachaise Paris cemetery
Perelman, S(idney) J(oseph) (1904–79), American humorist
perennial (two *ns*)
Peres, Shimon (b.1923), Israeli prime minister 1984–6 and 1995–6; President since 2007
perestroika (in the former USSR) reform of the economic and political system (not ital.)
Pérez de Cuéllar, Javier (b.1920), Peruvian Secretary General of the United Nations 1982–91
perfect tense denoting a completed past action (abbrev. **perf.**)
perfecta N. Amer. bet on the correct prediction of the first two places in a race
perfect binding bookbinding in which the leaves are glued together after the back folds have been cut off
perfecter printing press that prints both sides of the paper at one pass (not **-or**)
perfectible (not **-able**) ◻ **perfectibility**
perfecting printing the second side of a sheet
perfecto pl. **perfectos** large cigar tapering at both ends
Pergamon Press publishing house, now a division of Elsevier Science Publishing
Pergamum ancient city in western Asia Minor ◻ **Pergamene**
peri pl. **peris** genie or fairy in Persian mythology
pericardium pl. **pericardia** Anat. membrane enclosing the heart
Pericles 1 (*c.*495–429 BC), Athenian statesman **2** (***Pericles***) Shakespeare play (abbrev. ***Per.***) ◻ **Periclean**
perigee point at which a moon or satellite is nearest the earth
Périgord area of SW France
perihelion pl. **perihelia** point at which a planet etc. is nearest the sun
perimeter continuous line forming a boundary
per incuriam Law through lack of regard to the law or the facts (L., ital.)
perineum pl. **perinea** area between the anus and the scrotum or vulva
period N. Amer. full stop
periodicals, titles of cited in ital.; preceding definite article to be roman lower case exc. in one-word titles (the *New York Review of Books*, *The Economist*)
peripatetic 1 travelling from place to place **2** (**Peripatetic**) Aristotelian
peripeteia sudden reversal of fortune
periphrasis pl. **periphrases** circumlocution ◻ **periphrastic**
peristyle row of columns round a space in a building
peritoneum pl. **peritoneums** or **peritonea** membrane lining the cavity of the abdomen ◻ **peritonitis**
periwig highly styled wig ◻ **periwigged**
periwinkle 1 plant with flat five-petalled flowers **2** winkle (mollusc)
permanent (not **-ant**)
Permian last period of the Palaeozoic era
per mille (also **per mil**) by a specified amount in every thousand (not ital.; symbol ‰)
permissible (not **-able**)
permit (**permitting, permitted**)
pernickety fussy
Perón 1 Eva (1919–52), Argentinian politician; full name *María Eva Duarte de Perón*; known as **Evita 2** Juan Domingo (1895–1974), Argentinian president 1946–55 and 1973–4
Perpendicular latest stage of English Gothic church architecture (cap.)
perpetrate carry out or commit; cf. **perpetuate** ◻ **perpetrator**
perpetuate cause to continue indefinitely; cf. **perpetrate** ◻ **perpetuator**
perpetuum mobile (L., ital.) **1** perpetual motion **2** Mus. another term for **moto perpetuo**
Perpignan city in southern France
per pro. (in full ***per procurationem***) through the agency of; see **pp**

perquisite right or privilege conferred by one's position; cf. **prerequisite**
Perrault, Charles (1628–1703), French writer
pers. Gram. person; personal
per se intrinsically (not ital.)
Perseids annual meteor shower
Persephone Gk Mythol. goddess carried off to the underworld; Rom. name **Proserpina**
perseverance (not **perserv-**, **-ence**)
Persia former name for **Iran**
persiflage light mockery or banter
persistence, **persistent** (not **-ance**, **-ant**)
persnickety N. Amer. term for **pernickety**
person pl. **people** or in official or formal contexts **persons** (Gram. abbrev. **pers.**)
persona pl. **personas** or **personae** perceived aspect of someone's character (not ital.)
persona grata pl. ***personae gratae*** person acceptable to certain others (L., ital.)
personality qualities forming a person's character; cf. **personalty**
personalize (Brit. also **personalise**)
personalty personal property; cf. **personality**
persona non grata pl. ***personae non gratae*** person unacceptable to certain others (L., ital.)
personnel staff employed (two *n*s)
Perspex trademark tough transparent plastic
perspicacious having ready insight and understanding
perspicuous clearly expressed and easily understood
PERT programme evaluation and review technique
Perth 1 town in eastern Scotland **2** capital of Western Australia
Perth and Kinross council area of central Scotland
Perthshire former county of central Scotland
pertinacious holding firmly to an opinion or course
pertinence, **pertinent** (not **-ance**, **-ant**)
Peru country in South America □ **Peruvian**
Perugia city in central Italy □ **Perugian**
peruke arch. wig or periwig (not **-que**)
pes pl. **pedes** Anat. the foot
peseta former monetary unit of Spain
pesewa monetary unit of Ghana
Peshawar capital of North-West Frontier Province, Pakistan
peso pl. **pesos** monetary unit of several Latin American countries and the Philippines
Pestalozzi, Johann Heinrich (1746–1827), Swiss educational reformer
Pet. Peter (in biblical references)
peta- denoting a factor of 10^{15} (abbrev. **P**)
petabyte Comput. one thousand million million (10^{15}) or strictly 2^{50} bytes (abbrev. **PB**)
Pétain, (Henri) Philippe (Omer) (1856–1951), French head of state 1940–2
pétanque French game similar to boule (accent, not ital.)
Peterhouse Cambridge college
Peterloo massacre attack on 16 August 1819 on a crowd in St Peter's Field, Manchester
Peter Pan **1** play by J. M. Barrie (1904) **2** (**Peter Pan**) person who remains youthful or childlike
Peter Principle members of a hierarchy are promoted until reaching a level at which they are incompetent
Peter's pence hist. tax on land paid to the papal see
Peter, St 1 Apostle; born *Simon* **2** (also **Peter**) either of two epistles in the New Testament (abbrev. **1 Pet.**, **2 Pet.**)
pétillant (of wine) slightly sparkling (Fr., ital.)
petit bourgeois pl. **petits bourgeois** (member) of the lower middle class (not ital.)
petite bourgeoisie the lower middle class (not ital.)
petit four pl. **petits fours** small fancy biscuit, cake, or sweet (not ital.)
petitio principii begging the question (L., ital.)
petit mal mild form of epilepsy (not ital.); cf. **grand mal**

petit pain pl. ***petits pains*** small bread roll (Fr., ital.)
petit point type of embroidery (not ital.)
petits pois small peas (not ital.)
pet name (two words)
Petrarch (1304–74), Italian poet; Italian name *Francesco Petrarca* □ **Petrarchan**
petrel seabird; cf. **petrol**
Petri dish dish for the culture of microorganisms
Petrie, Sir (William Matthew) Flinders (1853–1942), English archaeologist
petrochemical, petrochemistry, petrodollar (one word)
Petrograd former name (1914–24) for **St Petersburg**
petrol light fuel oil; cf. **petrel**
petroleum liquid mixture of hydrocarbons
Pétrus, Château claret
pettifogging placing undue emphasis on trivia
petty bourgeois Engl. form of **petit bourgeoise**
petty bourgeoisie Engl. form of **petite bourgeoisie**
petty officer naval non-commissioned rank (abbrev. **PO**)
Peugeot French make of car
Pevsner, Sir Nikolaus (1902–83), German-born British art historian
pewit use **peewit**
Pfc. Private First Class (one cap.)
PFD personal flotation device
pfennig pl. same or **pfennigs** former monetary unit of Germany
PFI private finance initiative
Pfizer pharmaceutical company
PG 1 parental guidance (UK film classification) **2** postgraduate
PGA Professional Golfers' Association
PGCE Postgraduate Certificate of Education
pH figure expressing acidity or alkalinity (one cap.)
Phaethon Gk Mythol. son of Helios the sun god
phaeton light horse-drawn carriage
Phalange right-wing party in Lebanon; cf. **Falange** □ **Phalangist**
phalanger lemur-like marsupial
phalanx 1 pl. **phalanxes** body of troops or police in close formation **2** pl. **phalanges** Anat. bone of the finger or toe
phallus pl. **phalli** or **phalluses** erect penis
Phanariot Greek official in Constantinople under the Ottoman Empire (cap.)
Phanerozoic the aeon covering the whole of time
phantasize arch. or Psychol. var. of **fantasize**
phantasmagoria sequence of images like that in a dream
phantast var. of **fantast**
phantasy arch. or Psychol. var. of **fantasy**
pharaoh (cap. in titles; not **-oah**) □ **pharaonic**
Pharisee member of a strict ancient Jewish sect □ **Pharisaic, Pharisaical, Pharisaism**
pharmaceutical of medicinal drugs
pharmacopoeia (US also **pharmacopeia**) official list of medicinal drugs
Pharos ancient lighthouse off the coast of Alexandria
pharyngeal (also **pharyngal**) of the pharynx
pharynx pl. **pharynges** cavity behind the nose and mouth
phase distinct period or stage; cf. **faze**
phatic of language used for social interaction rather than to convey information
PhD (also **Ph.D.**) Doctor of Philosophy [L. *Philosophiae Doctor*]
Phebe character in Shakespeare's *As You Like It* (not **Phoebe**)
Pheidippides (5th cent. BC), Athenian messenger sent to Sparta to ask for help after the Persian landing at Marathon
phenomenon pl. **phenomena**
phi 1 twenty-first letter of the Greek alphabet (**Φ**, **φ**), transliterated as 'ph' or, in modern Greek, 'f' **2** (φ) plane angle **3** (φ) polar coordinate
phial small glass bottle; cf. **vial**
Phi Beta Kappa US honorary academic society
Phidias (5th cent. BC), Athenian sculptor

Phil. **1** Epistle to the Philippians **2** Philadelphia **3** Philharmonic **4** Philosophy

Philadelphia chief city of Pennsylvania (abbrev. **Phil.**) □ **Philadelphian**

philately hobby of collecting postage stamps

Philemon, Epistle to book of the New Testament (abbrev. **Philem.**)

philharmonic devoted to music (cap. in the names of orchestras; abbrev. **Phil.**)

philhellene lover of Greece (one word)

philibeg use **filibeg**

Philip name of five kings of ancient Macedonia, six kings of France, five kings of Spain, and two saints (one *l*)

Philippi city in ancient Macedonia (one *l*, two *ps*)

Philippians, Epistle to the book of the New Testament (one *l*, two *ps*; abbrev. **Phil.**)

philippic bitter denunciation (one *l*, two *ps*; lower case)

Philippines country in SE Asia (one *l*, two *ps*)

Philips electronics manufacturer (one *l*)

Philistine member of a people of ancient Palestine

philistine person indifferent to culture (lower case) □ **philistinism**

Phillips trademark denoting a type of screw or screwdriver (two *l*s)

phillumenist collector of matchbox or matchbook labels (two *l*s)

philogynist admirer of women

philology study of the structure and development of languages

philosopher's stone mythical substance turning base metal into gold (lower case)

philosophize (Brit. also **philosophise**)

philosophy (abbrev. **Phil.**)

philtre (US **philter**) aphrodisiac drink; cf. **filter**

Phintias see **Damon**

Phiz (1815–82), English illustrator; pseudonym of *Hablot Knight Browne*

phlebitis inflammation of the walls of a vein

phlegm secretion of mucous membranes

phlegmatic stolidly calm

Phnom Penh capital of Cambodia

Phoebe female name; see also **Phebe**

Phoebus Gk Mythol. epithet of Apollo

Phoenicia ancient country on the shores of the eastern Mediterranean □ **Phoenician**

Phoenix state capital of Arizona

phoenix mythological bird that rose from its own ashes (lower case)

Phoenix and the Turtle, The Shakespeare poem (abbrev. ***Phoenix***)

phon unit of perceived loudness

phone telephone (not **'phone**)

phone book (two words)

phonecard (one word)

phone-in n. (hyphen, two words as verb)

phonemics study of the perceptually distinct sounds (**phonemes**) of languages (treated as sing.)

phonetics study and classification of speech sounds (treated as sing.)

phoney (N. Amer. **phony**) pl. **phoneys** or **phonies** fraudulent (person or thing)

phonics the teaching of reading through correlating sounds and alphabetic symbols (treated as sing.)

phonology study of the relationships between the sounds of a language

phosphorous of phosphorus

phosphorus chemical element of atomic number 15 (symbol **P**)

photo n. pl. **photos** a photograph. v. (**photoes, photoing, photoed**) take a photograph of

photocall, photochemical (one word)

photocomposition another term for **filmsetting** (one word)

photocopier, photocopy, photoelectric, photoessay (one word)

photo finish (two words)

photofit (one word)

photogravure (printing from) an image produced from a photographic negative transferred to a metal plate and etched in (one word)

photojournalism (one word)

photolithography (also **photolitho**) lithography using plates made photographically (one word)

photomontage montage from photographic images (one word)

photo-offset offset printing using plates made photographically (hyphen)

photo opportunity (two words)
photorealism artistic style (one word)
photosensitive (one word)
photo session (two words)
photosetter another term for **phototypesetter** (one word)
photosetting another term for **filmsetting** (one word)
photo shoot (two words)
photostat (**photostats, photostatting, photostatted**) type of machine for making photocopies on special paper (one word)
photostory strip cartoon with photographs instead of drawings (one word)
photosynthesize (Brit. also **photosynthesise**)
phototypesetter machine for filmsetting (one word)
phrase (abbrev. **phr.**, pl. **phrs** or **phrs.**)
phrase book (two words)
phraseology particular mode of expression
Phrygia ancient region of west central Asia Minor □ **Phrygian**
PHSE Physical, Health, and Social Education
phthisis arch. pulmonary tuberculosis
Phuket island and port of Thailand
phyla pl. of **phylum**
phylactery small box containing Hebrew texts
phyllo US var. of **filo**
phylloxera plant louse infesting vines
phylum pl. **phyla** taxonomic category in zoology and linguistics
physalis Cape gooseberry or Chinese lantern
physical education (abbrev. **PE**)
physical therapy US term for **physiotherapy**
physical training (abbrev. **PT**)
physician person qualified to practise medicine
physicist student of physics
physico-chemical (hyphen)
physics study of matter and energy (treated as sing.)
physio pl. **physios** physiotherapist
physiognomy person's facial features
physiotherapy (US **physical therapy**)
physique form and size of a person's body
pi **1** sixteenth letter of the Greek alphabet (Π, π), transliterated as 'p' **2** ratio of the circumference of a circle to its diameter, approx. 3.14159 **3** (π) the numerical value of pi **4** (Π) osmotic pressure **5** (Π) mathematical product
Piaget, Jean (1896–1980), Swiss psychologist
pianissimo pl. **pianissimos** or **pianissimi** Mus. (piece played) very softly
piano[1] pl. **pianos** large keyboard instrument
piano[2] pl. **pianos** or **piani** Mus. (piece played) softly (abbrev. **p**)
piano accordion (two words)
pianoforte formal a piano (one word)
piano-forte Mus. softly and then loudly (hyphen)
piano nobile first, main floor of a building (It., ital.)
piassava stout fibre from palm trees
piastre (US **piaster**) monetary unit of several Middle Eastern countries
piazza open square (not ital.)
pibroch type of music for bagpipes
pica **1** unit of type size and line length equal to 12 points (about ⅙ inch or 4.2 mm) **2** size of letter in typewriting with 10 characters to the inch (about 3.9 to the centimetre)
picador mounted bullfighter with a lance (not ital.)
Picardy region and former province of northern France □ **Picard**
picaresque of an episodic kind of fiction with a roguish hero (not ital.)
Picasso, Pablo (1881–1973), Spanish artist □ **Picassoesque**
Piccadilly street in central London
piccalilli pl. **piccalillies** or **piccalillis** spicy vegetable pickle
piccaninny (US **pickaninny**) offens. small black child
piccolo pl. **piccolos** small flute
pickaback use **piggyback**
pickaxe (US **pickax**) (one word)
pickelhaube hist. German soldier's spiked helmet (lower case, not ital.)
picket n. **1** person or group protesting

outside a workplace **2** (also **picquet**) soldier or squad performing a particular duty. v. (**picketing**, **picketed**) act as a picket outside

picket fence, **picket line** (two words)

picklock (one word)

pick-me-up tonic (hyphens)

pickpocket (one word)

pickup (one word, two words as verb) **1** truck with low sides **2** act of collecting

Pickwickian jovial, plump, or generous like Mr Pickwick in Dickens's *Pickwick Papers*; (of words) misunderstood or misused, esp. to avoid offence

picnic v. (**picnicking**, **picnicked**) □ **picnicker**

pico- factor of 10^{-12}

picot decorative loop in lace or embroidery

picquet see **picket**; cf. **piquet**

pictograph (also **pictogram**) pictorial symbol for a word or phrase

picture book, **picture postcard**, **picture rail**, **picture window** (two words)

pidgin 1 simplified and mixed form of language **2** (**Pidgin**) Tok Pisin; cf. **pigeon**

pi-dog var. of **pye-dog**

pie composed type that has been jumbled

piebald (horse) with patches of two colours, usu. black and white; cf. **skewbald**

pièce de résistance most remarkable feature or part (Fr., ital.)

piecemeal (one word)

piece rate (two words)

piecework (one word)

pie chart graph with a circle divided into sectors (two words)

piecrust (one word)

pied-à-terre pl. **pieds-à-terre** small residence for occasional use (not ital.)

Piedmont 1 region of NW Italy; It. name **Piemonte 2** hilly region of the eastern US □ **Piedmontese**

pie-dog var. of **pye-dog**

Pied Piper 1 person who entices people to follow them **2** 'The Pied Piper of Hamelin', poem by Robert Browning (1842)

Pierce, Franklin (1804–69), 14th president of the US 1853–7

pier glass large mirror (two words)

Piero della Francesca (1416–92), Italian painter

Pierrot stock male character in French pantomime (cap.)

pietà representation of the Virgin Mary holding the dead Christ (accent, not ital.)

pietas respect due to an ancestor, institution, etc. (L., ital.)

Pietermaritzburg capital of KwaZulu-Natal, South Africa

pietra dura mosaic work in semi-precious stones (It., ital.)

piezoelectricity (one word)

pigeon (not **pidg-**) **1** common bird **2** (**not my pigeon**) not my affair; cf. **pidgin**

pigeonhole (one word)

piggyback (one word; not **pickaback**)

pig-headed (hyphen)

pig iron (two words)

Pigmy, **pigmy** vars of **Pygmy**, **pygmy**

pigpen, **pigskin**, **pigsty**, **pigswill**, **pigtail** (one word)

pikestaff (one word)

pilaf (also **pilaff**) Middle Eastern dish based on rice or wheat (not ital.)

Pilate, Pontius (died *c.*36 AD), Roman procurator of Judaea *c.*26–*c.*36

Pilates system of exercises using special apparatus (cap.)

pilau rice Indian rice dish

pilcrow arch. term for **paragraph mark**

piledriver (one word)

pile-up crash involving several vehicles (hyphen, two words as verb)

pilgrim (cap. in ref. to the **Pilgrim Fathers**, the pioneers of British colonization of North America)

Pilipino var. of **Filipino**

pillar box (two words, hyphen when attrib.)

pillbox (two words)

pillowcase (one word)

pillow fight, **pillow lace** (two words)

pillowslip (one word)

pillule var. of **pilule**

pilot v. (**piloting**, **piloted**)

pilot light, **pilot officer**, **pilot whale** (two words)
Pilsen city in the western part of the Czech Republic; Czech name **Plzeň**
Pilsner (also **Pilsener**) lager beer (cap.)
pilule (also **pillule**) small pill
PIM personal information manager
pimento (also **pimiento**) pl. **pimentos** sweet red pepper
Pimm's trademark alcoholic drink (apostrophe)
PIN personal identification number (strictly, not **PIN number**)
pina colada cocktail [Sp. *piña colada*]
Pinang var. of **Penang**
pinball, **pinboard** (one word)
pince-nez eyeglasses with a nose clip (treated as sing. or pl.)
pincushion (one word)
Pindar (*c.*518–*c.*438 BC), Greek lyric poet □ **Pindaric**
pineapple (one word)
pine cone, **pine marten**, **pine nut** (two words)
Pinero, Sir Arthur Wing (1855–1934), English dramatist
pinewood (one word)
ping-pong (also US trademark **Ping-Pong**) table tennis (hyphen)
pinhead, **pinhole** (one word)
Pink Floyd English rock group
pinkie (also **pinky**) the little finger
pinking shears, **pinking scissors** (two words)
pin money (two words)
PIN number see **PIN**
pinochle North American card game
pinpoint, **pinprick**, **pinstripe** (one word)
pint one eighth of a gallon (in Britain 0.568 litre, in the US 0.473 litre for liquid measure and 0.551 litre for dry measure) (abbrev. **pt**)
pinto pl. **pintos** N. Amer. term for **piebald**
pin-up n. (hyphen, two words as verb)
Pinyin standard system of romanized spelling for Chinese; cf. **Wade–Giles**
pious devoutly religious; see also **Pius**
pipe band, **pipe bomb** (two words)
pipeclay (one word)
pipe cleaner, **pipe dream** (two words)
pipeline (one word)
pipe organ, **pipe rack** (two words)
pipe roll annual records of the British Exchequer in the 12th–19th cents
pipette laboratory tube with a bulb (not **-et**)
piping hot (two words, hyphen when attrib.)
pipit songbird (single *p*)
pippin dessert apple (double *p*, lower case)
piquant pleasantly sharp
pique irritation or resentment
piqué stiff ribbed fabric (accent, not ital.)
piqued irritated or resentful
piquet trick-taking card game; cf. **picquet**
Piraeus chief port of Athens
Pirandello, Luigi (1867–1936), Italian writer
Piranesi, Giovanni Battista (1720–78), Italian engraver
piranha voracious South American fish
pirouette spin on one foot
pis aller last resort (Fr., ital.)
Pisces twelfth sign of the zodiac □ **Piscean**
pisciculture breeding and rearing of fish
piscina pl. **piscinas** or **piscinae** stone basin for draining water used in the Mass (not ital.)
pisé building material of stiff earth (Fr., ital.)
Pisistratus (also **Peisistratus**) (*c.*600–*c.*527 BC), tyrant of Athens
pissaladière Provençal onion tart (accent, not ital.)
Pissarro, Camille (1830–1903), French artist
pistachio pl. **pistachios** edible pale green nut
piste ski run (not ital.)
pistil female organs of a flower
pistol (**pistolling, pistolled**; US one **-l-**) (shoot with) a small hand-held firearm
pistole old gold coin
pita N. Amer. var. of **pitta**
Pitcairn Islands British overseas territory in the South Pacific

pitch and putt form of miniature golf (three words)
pitch-and-toss gambling game of throwing coins at a mark (hyphens)
pitch-black, pitch-dark (hyphen)
pitchblende, pitchfork (one word)
piteous deserving or arousing pity
pitfall, pithead (one word)
pitiable, pitiful 1 deserving or arousing pity **2** contemptibly poor or small
Pitman, Sir Isaac (1813–97), English inventor of a shorthand system
Pitt 1 William, 1st Earl of Chatham (1708–78), British statesman; known as **Pitt the Elder 2** William (1759–1806), British prime minister 1783–1801 and 1804–6; known as **Pitt the Younger**
pitta (N. Amer. **pita**) flat hollow bread
Pitti art gallery and museum in Florence, housed in the Pitti Palace
Pitt-Rivers, Augustus Henry Lane Fox (1827–1900), English archaeologist and anthropologist
Pittsburgh city in SW Pennsylvania
più Mus. more; (**più forte**) a little more loudly; (**più mosso**) a little more softly (accent)
Pius 'pious', name taken by various popes
pivot v. (**pivoting, pivoted**)
pixel minute area of illumination on a display screen
pixelate (also **pixellate** or **pixilate**) divide into pixels
pixie (also **pixy**) small supernatural being □ **pixieish**
pixilated (also **pixillated**) bewildered, confused
pixilation (also **pixillation**) film technique of making real people look like animations
Pizarro, Francisco (*c.*1478–1541), Spanish conquistador
pizza dough base with a topping
pizzazz (also **pizazz**) vitality and glamour
pizzeria place selling pizzas
pizzicato pl. **pizzicatos** or **pizzicati** Mus. playing by plucking rather than bowing strings
PK psychokinesis
pk 1 pack **2** (also **Pk**) park **3** peak **4** peck(s)
pl. 1 (also **Pl.**) place **2** plate (in a book) **3** plural
PLA 1 People's Liberation Army **2** Port of London Authority
place (abbrev. **pl.** or **Pl.**)
place bet bet on a horse to come first, second, or third, or, in the US, first or second (two words) □ **place betting**
placebo pl. **placebos** medicine for psychological rather than physiological benefit
place mat, place name (two words)
placenta pl. **placentae** or **placentas**
place setting (two words)
placet affirmative vote (ital.) [L., 'it pleases']
plafond ornate ceiling (Fr., ital.)
plagiarism passing off another's ideas or work as one's own
plagiarize (Brit. also **plagiarise**)
plague v. (**plaguing, plagued**) □ **plaguy** (or **plaguey**)
plaice pl. same, flatfish
Plaid Cymru the Welsh Nationalist party
plainchant (one word)
plain clothes (two words, hyphen when attrib.)
plain sailing smooth and easy progress; cf. **plane sailing**
plainsong (one word)
plain text text not in code
plaintiff person bringing a lawsuit against another
plaintive sounding mournful
plait length of interlaced strands
planchet disc from which a coin is made
planchette small board on castors used in spiritualism
Planck's constant (also **Planck constant**) Phys. (symbol ***h***)
plane sailing calculation of a ship's position by assuming a plane surface; cf. **plain sailing**
planetarium pl. **planetariums** or **planetaria**
plankton microscopic organisms drifting in water; cf. **nekton**
planning permission (two words)
planographic of a printing process in

which the printing surface is flat
Plantagenet member of the English royal dynasty from Henry II to Richard III, 1154–1485
plantar of the sole of the foot
Plantin, Christophe (*c.*1520–89), French printer
plaque 1 ornamental tablet **2** deposit on teeth
plasterboard (one word)
plaster cast (two words)
plaster of Paris (three words, one cap.)
plasterwork (one word)
plasticine children's soft modelling material (cap. as trademark)
plasticize (Brit. also **plasticise**)
plasticky like plastic
plat du jour pl. ***plats du jour*** restaurant's dish of the day (Fr., ital.)
plate (abbrev. **pl.**) **1** sheet bearing an image from which multiple copies are printed **2** printed illustration, esp. on superior-quality paper
plateau n. pl. **plateaux** or **plateaus.** v. **plateaus, plateauing, plateaued**
plate glass (two words)
Plate, River estuary at the border between Argentina and Uruguay (*River* always cap.); Sp. name **Río de la Plata**
Plath, Sylvia (1932–63), American poet
platinize (Brit. also **platinise**) coat with platinum
platinum chemical element of atomic number 78 (symbol **Pt**)
platitudinize (Brit. also **platitudinise**)
Platonic of the Greek philosopher Plato (*c.*429–*c.*347 BC)
platonic intimate but not sexual (lower case)
Plattdeutsch Low German
platypus pl. **platypuses** Australian egg-laying mammal
platyrrhine denoting primates with a prehensile tail; cf. **catarrhine**
plausible (not **-able**)
Plautus, Titus Maccius (*c.*250–184 BC), Roman comic dramatist
play-act, play-actor (hyphen)
playback n. (one word, two words as verb)
playbill, playboy, playfellow, playgoer, playground, playgroup, playhouse (one word)
player-manager (hyphen)
playing card, playing field (two words)
playlist, playmaker, playmate (one word)
play-off n. (hyphen, two words as verb)
playpen, playroom, playschool, plaything, playtime, playwright (one word)
PlayStation trademark computer game (one word, two caps)
plaza public square (not ital.)
plc public limited company (lower case, no points)
plead (past and past part. **pleaded** or N. Amer. or dial. **pled**) in a law court one can *plead guilty* or *plead not guilty*; *plead innocent* is not a technical legal term
pleased as Punch (one cap.)
pleasurable (not **-eable**)
plebeian commoner in ancient Rome; member of the lower classes (not **-bian**)
plebiscite direct vote of an entire electorate
plectrum pl. **plectrums** or **plectra** item for plucking the strings of a guitar
pled see **plead**
Pleiades 1 Gk Mythol. the seven daughters of Atlas **2** cluster of stars
plein-air of a style of painting outdoors (Fr., ital.)
Pleistocene first epoch of the Quaternary period
plenipotentiary diplomat with full power to act
plenitude abundance (not **plenti-**)
pleonasm use of more words than are necessary □ **pleonastic**
pleura pl. **pleurae** membrane enveloping a lung
pleurisy inflammation of the pleurae
Plexiglas trademark, chiefly N. Amer. tough transparent plastic (one *s*)
plexus pl. same or **plexuses** network of nerves or vessels
plié Ballet an act of bending and straightening the knees (Fr., ital.)
pliers pincers (not **pliars**)
plimsoll (also **plimsole**) Brit. rubber-

soled canvas shoe (lower case)

Plimsoll line (also **Plimsoll mark**) mark on a ship's side showing the limit of legal submersion (cap.)

Pliny 1 (23–79), Roman statesman and scholar; Latin name *Gaius Plinius Secundus*; known as **Pliny the Elder 2** (*c.*61–*c.*112), Roman senator and writer; Latin name *Gaius Plinius Caecilius Secundus*; known as **Pliny the Younger**

Pliocene last epoch of the Tertiary period

plissé (fabric) treated to give a crinkled effect (accent, not ital.)

PLO Palestine Liberation Organization

plongeur menial kitchen assistant (Fr., ital.)

plosive consonant produced by stoppage then release of the airflow

Plotinus (*c.*205–70), Neoplatonic philosopher

plough (US **plow**) **1** farming implement **2** (**the Plough**) prominent formation of seven stars

ploughman (US **plowman**) but *Piers Plowman*, 14th-cent. poem by William Langland

ploughshare (US **plowshare**)

PLP Parliamentary Labour Party

PLR public lending right

plughole (one word)

plumb measure the depth of

plumbic Chem. of lead with a valency of four

plumb line (two words)

plumbous Chem. of lead with a valency of two

plummet (**plummeting**, **plummeted**)

pluperfect tense denoting completed past action (abbrev. **plup.**)

plural (abbrev. **pl.**)

pluralize (Brit. also **pluralise**)

plus pl. **pluses**

plus ça change (in full ***plus ça change, plus c'est la même chose***) used to express resigned acknowledgement of the immutability of things (ital.) [Fr., 'the more it changes, the more it stays the same']

plus fours (two words)

plus sign + (two words)

Plutarch (*c.*46–*c.*120), Greek biographer and philosopher; Latin name *Lucius Mestrius Plutarchus*

Pluto 1 Gk Mythol. god of the underworld **2** small planetary body orbiting the sun

□ **Plutonian**

plutocracy government by the wealthy

plutonium chemical element of atomic number 94 (symbol **Pu**)

plywood (one word)

Plzeň Czech name for **Pilsen**

PM 1 post mortem **2** prime minister **3** provost marshal

Pm the chemical element promethium (no point)

p.m. after noon (lower case, points) [L. *post meridiem*]

PMG 1 Paymaster General **2** Postmaster General

PMS premenstrual syndrome

PMT premenstrual tension

PNdB perceived noise decibel(s) (three caps)

pneumatic of air or gas under pressure

pneumatique Parisian system of conveying mail along tubes under pressure (not ital.)

pneumonic of the lungs

PNG Papua New Guinea

PO 1 Petty Officer **2** Pilot Officer **3** postal order **4** Post Office

Po the chemical element polonium (no point)

POA Prison Officers' Association

pocket v. (**pocketing**, **pocketed**)

pocketbook, **pocketknife** (one word)

pocketful pl. **pocketfuls**

pocket money, **pocket watch** (two words)

pockmark (one word)

poco Mus. a little

Pocomania Jamaican folk religion (cap.)

POD Pocket Oxford Dictionary (now called the *Pocket Oxford English Dictionary*)

Podgorica capital of Montenegro; former name **Titograd**

podiatry chiropody

podium pl. **podiums** or **podia** small platform to stand on

Podsnappery self-congratulatory philistinism, like that of Mr Podsnap in Dickens's *Our Mutual Friend*
podzol (also **podsol**) infertile acidic soil
Poe, Edgar Allan (1809–49), American writer
poems, titles of cited in roman in quotation marks unless long enough to be a separate publication, when ital.
poetaster writer of inferior poetry
poetess in general prefer **poet**
poeticize (Brit. also **poeticise**)
Poet Laureate pl. **Poets Laureate** or **Poet Laureates** (two words, caps)
Poets' Corner part of Westminster Abbey
po-faced (hyphen)
pogrom massacre of an ethnic group
poikilothermic Zool. cold-blooded; cf. **homeothermic**
poilu French soldier in WWI (not ital.)
Poincaré, Jules-Henri (1854–1912), French mathematician
poinsettia shrub with showy scarlet bracts (not **point-**, **-ta**)
point 1 full stop or decimal point; dot or small stroke in Semitic languages **2** unit for type sizes and spacing, in the UK and US traditionally 0.351 mm, in Europe 0.376 mm, standardized as ¹⁄₇₂ in. (0.356 mm) (abbrev. **pt**)
point-blank (hyphen)
point d'appui pl. ***points d'appui*** support or prop (Fr., ital.)
point duty (two words)
pointe Ballet tip of a toe (Fr., ital.)
pointillism painting technique using tiny dots of pure colours (lower case)
points of omission ellipsis ...
poise unit of dynamic viscosity (symbol **P**)
poisha pl. same, monetary unit of Bangladesh
poison pen letter (three words)
Poisson, Siméon-Denis (1781–1840), French mathematical physicist
Poitier, Sidney (b.1927), American actor
Poitiers city in west central France
Poitou former province of west central France
Poitou-Charentes region of western France (hyphen)
poker face impassive expression (two words) □ **poker-faced**
pokey 1 N. Amer. prison **2** var. of **poky**
pokie Austral. fruit machine
poky (also **pokey**) (**pokier, pokiest**) small and cramped □ **pokiness**
Pol. Polish
Poland country in central Europe; Pol. name **Polska**
Polaris 1 another name for **Pole Star 2** type of submarine-launched missile
polarize (Brit. also **polarise**)
Polaroid trademark plastic material that polarizes light
Pole 1 person from Poland **2** see **North Pole, South Pole**
pole location at the northern or southern ends of the earth's (or a celestial object's) axis of rotation (lower case exc. in *North Pole, South Pole* as geographical terms)
poleaxe (US also **poleax**) (one word)
polecat (one word)
polecat-ferret (hyphen)
Pole Star bright star located near the celestial north pole (caps)
pole vault (two words, hyphen as verb) □ **pole-vaulter**
police constable (two words; abbrev. **PC**)
police force (two words)
policeman (one word)
police officer (two words)
police sergeant (two words; abbrev. **PS**)
police state, police station (two words)
policewoman (one word)
policyholder (one word)
polio (also **poliomyelitis**) viral disease affecting the nervous system
Polish (abbrev. **Pol.**)
politburo pl. **politburos** communist policy-making committee; (**the Politbureau**) principal policy-making committee of the former USSR
politesse formal politeness (Fr., ital.)
politic v. (**politicking, politicked**)
political correctness, politically correct (abbrev. **PC**)

politicize (Brit. also **politicise**)
politico pl. **politicos** person with strong political views
polity form or process of civil government
polka (**polkas, polkaing, polkaed** or **polka'd**)
polka dot (two words, hyphen when attrib.) ◻ **polka-dotted**
pollack (also **pollock**) fish of the cod family
pollen count (two words)
polling booth, polling day, polling station (two words)
Pollock, (Paul) Jackson (1912–56), American painter
pollock var. of **pollack**
poll tax (two words)
Pollux Gk Mythol. twin brother of Castor; also called **Polydeuces**
Pollyanna excessively optimistic person (cap.) ◻ **Pollyannaish**
polonaise Polish dance (lower case)
polo neck (two words) ◻ **polo-necked**
polonium chemical element of atomic number 84 (symbol **Po**)
Pol Pot (*c.*1925–98), Cambodian leader of the Khmer Rouge, prime minister 1976–9
Polska Pol. name for **Poland**
poltergeist ghost responsible for physical disturbances
poly pl. **polys** hist. polytechnic (cap. in names)
poly- forms solid compounds
polyandry polygamy in which a woman has more than one husband
polyanthus pl. same, hybrid of the wild primrose and primulas
Polybius (*c.*200–*c.*118 BC), Greek historian
Polydeuces another name for **Pollux**
Polyfilla trademark plaster for small building repairs
polygamy practice of having more than one wife or husband at the same time
polygeny former theory that humans developed from more than one pair of ancestors
polyglot knowing or using several languages
polygyny polygamy in which a man has more than one wife
polyhedron pl. **polyhedra** or **polyhedrons** solid figure with many plane faces
Polyhymnia the Muse of mime
polymerize (Brit. also **polymerise**)
Polynesia region of the central Pacific including Hawaii, the Marquesas Islands, Samoa, the Cook Islands, and French Polynesia ◻ **Polynesian**
polynya open water surrounded by ice
polyp sedentary form of a coelenterate such as a sea anemone
polysemy coexistence of several meanings
polystyrene lightweight rigid foam
polysyllabic having more than one syllable ◻ **polysyllable**
polysynthetic of a language with complex words which may function as sentences
polytechnic hist. (cap. in names)
polythene light flexible synthetic resin
polyunsaturated (one word)
pomegranate spherical fruit (not **-granite**)
pomelo pl. **pomelos** large citrus fruit (not **pumm-**)
Pomeranian small dog (cap.)
pommel n. projecting part of a saddle. v. (**pommelling, pommelled**; US one **-l-**) another term for **pummel**
pommes frites very thin chips (not ital.)
Pommy Austral./NZ informal British person
Pompadour, Jeanne Antoinette Poisson, Marquise de (1721–64), French noblewoman; known as **Madame de Pompadour**
pompadour hairstyle with hair in a roll off the forehead (lower case)
Pompeii ancient city in western Italy, buried by an eruption of Mount Vesuvius in 79 AD (two *i*s) ◻ **Pompeiian**
Pompey (106–48 BC), Roman general and statesman; Latin name *Gnaeus Pompeius Magnus*; known as **Pompey the Great**
Pompidou, Georges (Jean Raymond) (1911–74), French prime minister 1962–8 and president 1969–74

Pompidou Centre cultural complex in Paris; also called **Beaubourg Centre**
pom-pom 1 (also **pompon**) woollen ball on a hat **2** WWII cannon (hyphen)
Ponce de León, Juan (*c.*1460–1521), Spanish explorer
poncho pl. **ponchos** cloak with a slit for the head
Pondicherry former name for Puducherry
pondweed (one word)
poniard small slim dagger
pons asinorum point at which many learners fail (ital.) [L., 'bridge of asses']
Pontefract cake flat round liquorice sweet (one cap., two words)
pontifex pl. **pontifices** member of the principal college of priests in ancient Rome
Pontifex Maximus (cap.) **1** head of the ancient Roman college of priests **2** the Pope
pontiff the Pope □ **pontifical**
Pont l'Évêque soft cheese from Normandy
Pontypridd town in South Wales
ponytail (one word)
pony-trekking (hyphen)
Pooh-Bah character in *The Mikado* by Gilbert and Sullivan (1885)
pooh-bah self-important holder of many offices (lower case)
pooh-pooh dismiss as foolish or impractical (not **poo-poo**)
pooja var. of **puja**
poolroom, poolside (one word)
Poona former name for **Pune**
poorhouse (one word)
Poor Law hist. law on the support of the poor (caps)
Pooterish self-important and narrow-minded (cap.)
POP 1 point of presence **2** Post Office Preferred
pop. population
popadom var. of **poppadom**
Pope, Alexander (1688–1744), English poet
pope cap. in titles and *the Pope*; lower case of the office and in ref. to more than one holder
Popocatépetl active volcano in Mexico
poppadom (also **poppadum** or **popadom**) piece of thin spiced bread made from lentils and fried
Popsicle N. Amer. trademark ice lolly
popsock (one word)
popularize (Brit. also **popularise**)
population (abbrev. **pop.**)
pop-up adj., n. (hyphen, two words as verb)
porcelain (not **-laine**) □ **porcellaneous, porcellanous**
pore (**pore over**) be absorbed in reading or studying; cf. **pour**
porphyria rare hereditary disease
Porphyry (*c.*232–303), Neoplatonist philosopher; born *Malchus*
porphyry hard rock with crystals
porridge but *Scott's Porage Oats*
Porsche, Ferdinand (1875–1951), Austrian car designer
Porson sloping Greek typeface
Port. Portuguese
port side of a ship on the left when one is facing forward; cf. **starboard, larboard**
Portakabin trademark portable building
Portaloo trademark portable building containing a toilet
portamento pl. **portamentos** or **portamenti** Mus. slide from one note to another
Port-au-Prince capital of Haiti (hyphens)
portcullis heavy grating lowered to block a gateway
Porte (in full **the Sublime Porte**) the Ottoman court at Constantinople
porte cochère gateway or entrance for vehicles (not ital.)
Port Elizabeth port in South Africa
portentous of or like a portent or omen (not **-ious**)
portfolio pl. **portfolios**
porthole (one word)
portico pl. **porticoes** or **porticos** structure of a roof supported by columns
portière curtain over a doorway (accent, not ital.)

Portlaoise (also **Portlaoighise**) county town of Laois in the Republic of Ireland
Port Louis capital of Mauritius
Port Mahon see **Mahon**
portmanteau pl. **portmanteaus** or **portmanteaux** large travelling bag
portmanteau word word combining the sound and meaning of two others
Port Moresby capital of Papua New Guinea
Porto Port. name for **Oporto**
Pôrto Alegre city in SE Brazil
portobello large flat mushroom (lower case)
Port-of-Spain capital of Trinidad and Tobago (hyphens)
Porto Novo capital of Benin
portrait (of a format) higher than it is wide; cf. **landscape**
Port Said port in Egypt, at the north end of the Suez Canal
Portsmouth port and naval base on the south coast of England
Portugal country occupying the western part of the Iberian peninsula
Portuguese pl. same (not **-gese**; abbrev. **Port.**)
Portuguese man-of-war floating coelenterate with a painful sting (one cap., two hyphens)
POS point of sale
Poseidon Gk Mythol. god of the sea; Rom. equivalent **Neptune**
Posen Ger. name for **Poznań**
poser 1 perplexing problem **2** another term for **poseur**
poseur affected person (not ital.)
posit (**positing, posited**)
posse hist. **1** body of men summoned to help a US sheriff **2** (also **posse comitatus**) body of men who could be summoned to help an English sheriff
possess, possession, possessive (two double *ss*)
post-bellum after a war, esp. the American Civil War (hyphen)
postbox, postcard (one word)
post-chaise hist. horse-drawn carriage for passengers and mail (hyphen)
post-classical (hyphen)
postcode (one word)
post-coital, post-date (hyphen)
postdoctoral (one word)
poste restante post office service of keeping mail until collected (two words, not ital.)
postface brief explanatory note at the end of a book (one word)
post-feminist (hyphen)
postgraduate (one word)
post-haste (hyphen)
post hoc after the event (not ital.)
post horn (two words)
posthumous occurring after death (not **postu-**)
Posthumus character in Shakespeare's *Cymbeline*
postilion (also **postillion**) rider of a horse drawing a coach
post-impressionism (hyphen, lower case)
post-industrial (hyphen)
Post-it trademark piece of paper with an adhesive strip (one cap., hyphen)
postlapsarian after the Fall of Man (one word)
postman, postmark (one word)
Postmaster General head of a postal service (title no longer used in the UK; abbrev. **PMG**)
postmodern, postmodernism (one word)
post-mortem (hyphen, not ital.)
postnatal (one word)
postnuptial (one word)
post office 1 public department or corporation responsible for postal services (caps as institution; abbrev. **PO**) **2** local office of the postal service
post office box (three words)
post-operative (hyphen)
post-paid, post-partum (hyphen)
postpositive (of a word) placed after the word that it relates to
postprandial after a meal (one word)
post-production (hyphen)
post room company department handling post (two words)
PostScript trademark computer language (one word, two caps)
postscript additional remark or piece of

information (one word; abbrev. **PS**)
post-structuralism, post-traumatic (hyphen)
post-viral (hyphen)
postvocalic (one word)
post-war (hyphen)
postwoman (one word)
posy small bunch of flowers (not **-ey**)
potage thick soup (Fr., ital.); cf. **pottage**
potassium chemical element of atomic number 19 (symbol **K**)
potato pl. **potatoes**
pot-au-feu pl. same, French soup of meat and vegetables (ital.)
pot belly (two words) □ **pot-bellied**
potboiler (one word)
pot-herb (hyphen)
pothole, pothunter (one word)
Potomac river of the eastern US
pot plant (two words)
potpourri pl. **potpourris** mixture of dried petals and spices
pot roast (two words, hyphen as verb)
Potsdam city in eastern Germany
potsherd broken piece of ceramic material (not **-shard**)
potshot (one word)
pottage arch. soup or stew; cf. **potage**
pottery 1 articles made of fired clay **2** (**the Potteries**) area around Stoke-on-Trent, Staffordshire
potto pl. **pottos** African nocturnal primate
pouffe (also **pouf**) cushioned footstool or low seat
Poulenc, Francis (Jean Marcel) (1899–1963), French composer
pound 1 unit of weight (not in scientific use; abbrev. **lb**) **2** (also **pound sterling**, pl. **pounds sterling**) monetary unit of the UK (symbol **£**) **3** monetary unit of several Middle Eastern countries, Cyprus, and Sudan
pound sign the symbol £ (placed before figures, closed up)
pour (cause to) flow in a steady stream; cf. **pore**
pourboire gratuity or tip (Fr., ital.)
pousse-café glass of layers of liqueurs, taken after coffee (Fr., ital.)
Poussin, Nicolas (1594–1665), French painter
poussin young chicken for eating (not ital.)
POW prisoner of war
powder blue (two words, hyphen when attrib.)
power base (two words)
powerboat (one word)
power broker (two words) □ **power-broking**
power cut (two words)
powerhouse, powerlifting (one word)
power line, power plant, power politics, power shower, power station, power steering (two words)
power walking (two words) □ **power-walk** v. & n., **power-walker** n.
powwow North American Indian ceremony (one word)
Powys county of east central Wales
Poznań city in NW Poland; Ger. name **Posen**
Pozsony Hungarian name for **Bratislava**
pp 1 (also **p.p.**) *per pro.*, through the agency of (when signing a letter on someone else's behalf; traditionally before the signer's name, but now often before the name of the person who has not signed) **2** Mus. pianissimo
pp. pages
PPE politics, philosophy, and economics (Oxford degree subject)
ppi pixels per inch
ppm 1 part(s) per million **2** page(s) per minute
PPP 1 politics, philosophy, and physiology (Oxford degree subject) **2** public-private partnership
PPS 1 additional postscript [L. *post-postscriptum*] **2** Parliamentary Private Secretary
PPV pay-per-view
PQ 1 Parti Québécois **2** Province of Quebec
PR 1 proportional representation **2** public relations **3** N. Amer. Puerto Rico
Pr the chemical element praseodymium (no point)
pr 1 pair **2** arch. per
practicable able to be done successfully
practical relating to practice rather than theory
practice n. process of practising.

v. US var. of **practise**

practician another name for **practitioner**

practise (US **practice**) v. regularly perform (an activity) to improve proficiency

practitioner person actively engaged in a pursuit or profession

Prado Spanish art gallery in Madrid

praenomen ancient Roman's personal name, e.g. *Marcus* Tullius Cicero (not ital.)

praepostor public school prefect (not **prepostor, -er**)

praesidium var. of **presidium**

praetor (US also **pretor**) ancient Roman magistrate □ **praetorian**

pragmatics study of language in context (usu. treated as sing.)

Prague capital of the Czech Republic; Czech name **Praha**

Praia capital of the Cape Verde Islands

Prakrit dialect of north and central India

Prandtl, Ludwig (1875–1953), German physicist

praseodymium chemical element of atomic number 59 (symbol **Pr**)

Pravda Russian daily newspaper

praxis practice as opposed to theory (not ital.)

prayer book (two words; caps in ref. to the Book of Common Prayer)

Prayer of Manasses book of the Apocrypha (abbrev. **Pr. of Man.**)

PRB Pre-Raphaelite Brotherhood

pre- generally forms solid compounds exc. where shown

preagricultural (one word)

preamble introductory part of a statute or deed

preamplifier, prearrange (one word)

prebendary (abbrev. **Preb.**)

pre-book (hyphen)

Precambrian earliest aeon of the earth's history

precancerous, precast (one word)

precede come or go before; cf. **proceed**

precentor leader of a congregation in singing or prayers

precession movement of the axis of a spinning body

pre-Christian (hyphen, one cap.)

preciosity excessive refinement

precipice steep rock face

precipitate done suddenly

precipitous dangerously steep

precis (no accent) n. pl. same, summary or abstract. v. (**precises, precising, precised**) summarize [Fr. *précis*]

precisian rigidly precise person

precision exactness

pre-classical (hyphen)

preclinical (one word)

precocious developed at an earlier age than usual

pre-Columbian (hyphen, one cap.)

preconceived, preconception, precondition, preconfigure (one word)

pre-Conquest, pre-cook, pre-cool (hyphen)

precursor forerunner (not **-er**)

pre-cut (hyphen)

predacious (also **predaceous**) predatory

predate[1] be a predator of (one word)

predate[2] occur earlier than (one word)

predawn, predecease (one word)

predecessor previous holder of a position

predefined, predestine, predetermine, predispose (one word)

predominant (not **-ent**)

predominantly (also **predominately**) for the most part

pre-echo, pre-eclampsia, pre-eminent, pre-empt, pre-emptive, pre-establish, pre-exist (hyphen)

pref. 1 preface **2** preference **3** preferred **4** prefix

prefab, prefabricate (one word)

preface introduction to a book, usu. stating its subject, scope, etc. (abbrev. **pref.**) □ **prefatory**

prefer (**preferring, preferred**)

preferable (one *r*)

preference (not **-ance**)

preferential (not **-cial**)

prefigure (one word)

prefix word, morpheme, or character

placed before another (abbrev. **pref.**)
preflight, preform, preheat, prehistoric, prehistory (one word)
pre-ignition, pre-industrial, pre-install (hyphen)
prejudge (one word)
preliminary matter (also **preliminaries** or **prelims**) pages preceding the main text of a book, including the title, contents, and preface
prelinguistic, preliterate, preload (one word)
premarital, prematch (one word)
pre-med N. Amer. premedical course (hyphen)
premedical, premedication, premenstrual (one word)
premier head of government; (in Australia and Canada) the chief minister of a state or province (cap. in titles)
premier cru pl. ***premiers crus*** wine of a superior grade (Fr., ital.); cf. ***grand cru***
premiere first performance (no accent, not ital.) [Fr. *première*]
premiership 1 position of a head of government **2** (**the Premiership** or **Premier League**) top division of professional soccer in England
premise (Brit. also **premiss**) previous statement from which another is inferred
premises house or building together with its land and outbuildings
premium pl. **premiums**
Premium Bond (also **Premium Savings Bond**) (caps)
premix, premodify, premolar, prenatal, prenuptial, preoccupation, preoccupy (one word)
pre-op preoperative (injection) (hyphen)
preoperative, preordain (one word)
pre-owned (hyphen)
prep. preposition
pre-pack, pre-package (hyphen)
prepaid, prepay (one word)
pre-plan (hyphen)
preposition (abbrev. **prep.**)
prepossessing (one word, two double *ss*)
prepostor use **praepostor**
preprandial (one word)
pre-prepare, pre-press (hyphen)
preprint, preprocess (one word)
pre-production (hyphen)
preprogram, prepubescent, prepublication (one word)
prequel story containing events preceding those in an earlier work
Pre-Raphaelite member of the **Pre-Raphaelite Brotherhood**, a group of 19th-cent. artists (hyphen, two caps)
pre-record (hyphen)
preregistration (one word)
pre-release (hyphen)
prerequisite thing required as a prior condition (one word); cf. **perquisite**
pre-Roman (hyphen, one cap.)
Pres. President
presbyopia age-related long-sightedness
presbyter elder of a Presbyterian Church
Presbyterian of a Christian Church locally administered by elders (cap.)
presbytery body of Christian elders and ministers (treated as sing. or pl.)
preschool (one word)
prescient showing knowledge in advance
pre-scientific (hyphen)
prescribable (not **-eable**)
prescribe advise and authorize the use of; cf. **proscribe**
preseason, preselect, preselector, presenile (one word)
present-day adj. (hyphen, two words as noun, e.g. *in the present day*)
presentiment intuitive feeling about the future
presentment formal presentation of information to a law court
preset (one word)
pre-shrunk (hyphen)
president cap. in titles (*President Bush*, but *the president of France*)
president-elect pl. **presidents-elect** (hyphen)
presidium (also **praesidium**) standing committee in a communist country; (**the Presidium**) committee in the former USSR

Presley, Elvis (Aaron) (1935–77), American singer
presoak (one word)
Presocratic (cap., one word)
press 1 printing press **2** business that prints or publishes books (cap. in names) **3** (**the press**) newspapers and journalists collectively
press agent (two words)
Pressburg German name for **Bratislava**
press conference (two words)
press cutting, **press gallery** (two words)
press gang n. (two words, hyphen as verb)
pressman (one word)
pressmark Brit. shelf mark in some older libraries (one word)
press proof final proof before a work goes to press
press release, **press stud** (two words)
press-up n. (hyphen)
pressure cooker (two words) □ **pressure-cook**
pressure group, **pressure point** (two words)
pressurize (Brit. also **pressurise**)
pressurized-water reactor (abbrev. **PWR**)
presswork 1 using of a printing press **2** printed matter
Prester John legendary medieval Christian king of Asia
prestidigitation conjuring
prestigious (not **-geous**, **-gous**)
prestissimo pl. **prestissimos** Mus. (piece played) very quickly
presto pl. **prestos** Mus. (piece played) quickly
Prestonpans town east of Edinburgh
prestressed (one word)
presumptive presumed in the absence of further information
presumptuous failing to observe appropriate limits in behaviour
presuppose, **presupposition** (one word)
Pret A Manger food chain (no accents, no hyphens, three caps)
prêt-à-porter ready-to-wear designer clothes (two accents, two hyphens, not ital.)
pre-tax, **pre-teen** (hyphen)
pretence (US **pretense**)
pretension claim to something (not **-tion**)
pre-tension apply tension to before manufacture or use
pretentious (not **-cious**, **-sious**)
preterite (US also **preterit**) simple past tense
preterition making mention of something by professing to omit it
preterm (one word)
preternatural (also **praeternatural**) beyond what is normal
pretest (one word)
pretor US var. of **praetor**
Pretoria administrative capital of South Africa
pretreat, **pretrial** (one word)
pretzel crisp salty biscuit in the form of a knot or stick
prevalent widespread (not **-velant**)
prevaricate speak or act evasively; cf. **procrastinate**
preventive (also **preventative**) designed to prevent something (not **-titive**)
prevocalic before a vowel (one word)
pre-vocational (hyphen)
Prévost d'Exiles, Antoine-François (1696–1763), French novelist; known as **Abbé Prévost**
pre-war (hyphen)
Prez, Josquin des, see **des Prez**
Pribilof Islands four islands in the Bering Sea
pricey (also **pricy**) (**pricier**, **priciest**) □ **priciness**
Pride's Purge exclusion or arrest of MPs opposed to a trial of Charles I, by Colonel Thomas Pride (1648) (two caps)
prie-dieu pl. **prie-dieux** piece of furniture for kneeling at prayer (hyphen, not ital.)
Priestley 1 J(ohn) B(oynton) (1894–1984), English writer **2** Joseph (1733–1804), English scientist and theologian
priestly of or befitting a priest
prima ballerina, **prima donna** (two words, not ital.)

primaeval var. of **primeval**
prima facie from a first impression (not ital., two words even when attrib.)
primate chief bishop of a province; (**Primate of All England**) the Archbishop of Canterbury; (**Primate of All Ireland**) each of the Archbishops (Catholic and Anglican) of Armagh; (**Primate of England**) the Archbishop of York
prime 1 symbol ′ written as a distinguishing mark or as a symbol for minutes **2** Fencing parrying position
prime minister cap. in titles (*Prime Minister Tony Blair*, but *the prime minister of Italy*); abbrev. **PM**
primeval (also **primaeval**; not **-æ-**) of the earliest time in history
primigravida pl. **primigravidae** Med. woman pregnant for the first time
primipara pl. **primiparae** Med. woman giving birth for the first time
primo pl. **primos** Mus. leading part in a duet
primogenitor earliest ancestor
primogeniture state of being the first-born child
primum mobile most important source of action (L., ital.)
Primus trademark portable cooking stove
primus inter pares first among equals (L., ital.)
prince (cap. in titles)
Prince Edward Island island province in the Gulf of St Lawrence, eastern Canada (abbrev. **PEI**)
Prince of Darkness, **Prince of Peace** (two caps)
Prince of Wales the heir apparent to the British throne (two caps)
Prince of Wales check large check pattern (no hyphens, no apostrophe)
Prince of Wales' feathers plume of three ostrich feathers as a crest (no hyphens, apostrophe)
Prince of Wales Island island in the Canadian Arctic (no hyphens, no apostrophe)
Prince Regent the future George IV, 1811–20 (caps)
Prince Rupert's Land another name for **Rupert's Land** (apostrophe)
princess (cap. in titles)
Princess Royal eldest daughter of a reigning monarch
Princeton University university at Princeton in New Jersey
principal first in order of importance (cap. in titles); cf. **principle**
principe (or ***principessa***) pl. ***principi*** or ***principesse*** Italian prince or princess (cap. in titles; not ital. as part of name)
principle fundamental truth or proposition; cf. **principal**
printer's mark logo serving as a printer's trademark
printery printing works
printhead Comput. component in a printer (one word)
printing (abbrev. **ptg**)
printing press (two words)
printing works business carrying on the printing of books, newspapers, etc. (two words, treated as sing. or pl.); cf. **printworks**
printmaker printer of pictures or designs (one word)
printout n. (one word, two words as verb)
print queue, **print run** (two words)
printworks factory for the printing of textiles (one word, treated as sing. or pl.); cf. **printing works**
prioritize (Brit. also **prioritise**)
prise (US **prize**) force apart or open
Priština capital of Kosovo, in Serbia
pristine in its original condition
Pritchett, Sir V(ictor) S(awdon) (1900–97), English writer
private (cap. in military titles; abbrev. **Pte**, US **Pvt.**)
private eye 1 private detective **2** (***Private Eye***) satirical UK magazine
privative Gram. indicating loss or absence
privatize (Brit. also **privatise**)
privilege special right or advantage (not **-elege**, **-ilige**)
Privy Council advisers appointed by a sovereign or Governor General (two words, caps)
privy counsellor (also **privy coun-**

cillor) member of a Privy Council (two words, lower case; abbrev. **PC**)
prix fixe meal of several courses at a fixed price (Fr., ital.)
prize 1 reward to a winner **2** US var. of **prise**
prizefight, prizefighter (one word)
prize-giving (hyphen)
prizewinner, prizewinning (one word)
PRO 1 Public Record Office **2** public relations officer
pro pl. **pros 1** an advantage **2** (a) professional
proactive controlling rather than just responding (one word)
pro-am involving professionals and amateurs (hyphen)
prob. probably
pro bono publico (not ital.) **1** for the public good **2** (usu. **pro bono**) N. Amer. (of legal work) undertaken without charge
proboscis pl. **probosces, proboscides,** or **proboscises**
procaine a local anaesthetic; novocaine
procedure (not **proceed-**)
proceed 1 begin a course of action **2** move forward; cf. **precede**
processor (not **-er**)
procès-verbal pl. ***procès-verbaux*** written report of proceedings (Fr., ital.)
pro-choice (hyphen)
Proconsul fossil hominoid primate
proconsul governor of an ancient Roman province
procrastinate delay or postpone action; cf. **prevaricate**
Procrustean enforcing uniformity or conformity (cap.)
Procter & Gamble company producing cosmetics, pharmaceuticals, etc.
proctor university official with disciplinary functions
procurator fiscal Scottish coroner and prosecutor (two words, lower case)
product Math. (symbol Π)
proem preface or preamble □ **proemial**
profession, professional (one *f*, two *s*s)
professionalize (Brit. also **professionalise**) make professional
professor (cap. in titles; abbrev. **Prof.**, but generally write in full)
profit v. (**profiting, profited**)
profiterole confection of cream-filled choux pastry with chocolate sauce
Pr. of Man. Prayer of Manasses
pro forma (not ital.; two words, no hyphen even when attrib.) **1** (done) as a matter of form **2** (invoice) sent in advance of or with goods
profoundly deaf prefer to **deaf mute**
progenitor ancestor or parent
progeniture (production of) offspring
prognosis pl. **prognoses** likely course, forecast
programmatic (two *m*s, in US also)
programme (US and Comput. **program**) v. (**programming, programmed**; US also one **-m-**)
programmer (not **programer**, even in N. Amer.)
pro hac vice for this occasion only (not ital.)
prohibit (**prohibiting, prohibited**) □ **prohibiter, prohibitor, prohibitory**
Prohibition cap. in ref. to the banning of alcohol, esp. in the US 1920–33 □ **Prohibitionist**
projector (not **-er**)
Prokofiev, Sergei (Sergeevich) (1891–1953), Russian composer
prolegomenon pl. **prolegomena** critical or discursive introduction to a book
prolepsis pl. **prolepses** anticipation and answering of objections
proletariat (also arch. **proletariate**)
prologue separate introductory section (not **-log**)
prom promenade concert; (**the Proms**) the Henry Wood Promenade Concerts
promethium chemical element of atomic number 61 (symbol **Pm**)
prominence, prominent (not **-ance, -ant**)
promisor person who makes a promise (one *s*)
promissory conveying a promise (two *s*s)
prompt side side of the stage where the prompter sits, usu. to the actor's left in the UK, right in the US (abbrev. **PS**)

pron. 1 pronoun **2** pronounced; pronunciation
pronoun (abbrev. **pron.**)
pronunciamento pl. **pronunciamentos** pronouncement or manifesto (not ital.)
pronunciation (not **pronounc-**; abbrev. **pron.**)
pro-nuncio pl. **pro-nuncios** papal ambassador without precedence over other ambassadors (hyphen)
proof trial impression for correction before final printing
proof positive (two words)
proofread, proofreader (one word)
proof sheet printer's proof (two words)
proof text biblical passage appealed to to support a theological argument (two words)
prop. 1 proposition **2** proprietor
propaedeutic introductory
propaganda 1 biased information promoting a cause **2** (**Propaganda**) committee of cardinals
propagandize (Brit. also **propagandise**)
propel (**propelling, propelled**)
propellant (substance) that propels something (not **-ent**)
propeller (also **propellor**)
propelling pencil (two words)
Propertius, Sextus (*c.*50–*c.*16 BC), Roman poet
prophecy n. a prediction
prophesy v. predict
Prophet 1 (**the Prophet**) Muhammad **2** (**the Prophets**) books of Isaiah, Jeremiah, Ezekiel, Daniel, and the twelve minor prophets
proprietary 1 of ownership; protected by a registered trademark **2** (**Proprietary**) Austral., S. Afr. used in the names of companies (after the individual name; abbrev. **Pty**)
pro rata proportional(ly) (not ital.)
prorate allocate pro rata (one word)
prorogue (**proroguing, prorogued**) discontinue a session of ▫ **prorogation**
proscenium pl. **prosceniums** or **proscenia** part of a stage in front of the curtain
prosciutto Italian cured ham (not ital.)
proscribe forbid; cf. **prescribe**
proselyte converted person ▫ **proselytism**
proselytize (Brit. also **proselytise**)
Proserpina (also **Proserpine**) Rom. name for **Persephone**
prosit (also ***prost***) good health! (ital.)
prosody patterns of rhythm and sound in poetry
prosopography collection or study of personal descriptions
prosopopoeia figure of speech in which a thing is personified or an imagined or absent person speaks
prospectus pl. **prospectuses** printed booklet advertising something
prost var. of ***prosit***
prostate gland releasing a component of semen; cf. **prostrate**
prosthesis pl. **prostheses** artificial body part
prostrate stretched on the ground face downwards; cf. **prostate**
protactinium chemical element of atomic number 91 (symbol **Pa**)
protagonist leading character in a play, novel, etc.; disp. supporter of a cause
pro tanto to that extent (not ital.)
protasis pl. **protases** Gram. clause expressing the condition in a conditional sentence; cf. **apodosis**
protean able to change frequently (lower case)
protector (not **-er**) **1** person or thing that protects **2** (**Protector** or **Lord Protector of the Commonwealth**) English head of state during the Commonwealth, 1653–9
protectorate 1 state protected and controlled by another **2** (usu. **Protectorate**) the position or period of a Protector, esp. in England 1653–9
protégé (fem. **protégée**) person guided and supported by another (accents, not ital.)
protein component of diet (not **-ie-**)
pro tem for the time being (not ital.) [L. *pro tempore*]
Proterozoic later part of the Precambrian aeon
Protestant, Protestantism (cap.)
Protestant Ascendancy hist. the

domination of Anglo-Irish Protestants in Ireland (caps)

Proteus Gk Mythol. sea god able to assume different shapes

prothalamium (also **prothalamion**) pl. **prothalamia** song or poem celebrating a forthcoming wedding; (**Prothalamion**) poem by Spenser (1596)

prothonotary var. of **protonotary**

protocol official procedure

Proto-Germanic ancient source of Germanic languages (hyphen)

Proto-Indo-European lost source of Indo-European languages (hyphens)

protolanguage hypothetical parent language (one word)

protonotary (also **prothonotary**) chief clerk in some law courts

protractor instrument for measuring angles (not **-er**)

protuberance, protuberant (not **protru-**)

Proudhon, Pierre Joseph (1809–65), French social philosopher

Proust, Marcel (1871–1922), French writer ◻ **Proustian**

Prov. 1 the Book of Proverbs **2** chiefly Canad. Province; Provincial

prove (past part. **proved** or **proven**) past part. forms are more or less interchangeable, with *proved* more common in British English; as adj. before a noun always *proven*

provenance place of origin

Provençal (language) of Provence (accent)

provençale cooked in tomatoes, garlic, and olive oil (after the noun; accent, not ital.)

Provence area of SE France

Provence-Alpes-Côte d'Azur region of SE France (two hyphens)

provenience US name for **provenance**

Proverbs (also **Book of Proverbs**) book of the Old Testament (abbrev. **Prov.**)

pro-vice-chancellor (two hyphens)

proving ground (two words)

proviso pl. **provisos** condition or qualification ◻ **provisory**

provost marshal head of military police (two words; abbrev. **PM**)

prox. proximo

proxime accessit second in an examination or for an award (L., ital.; abbrev. ***prox. acc.***)

proximo of next month (after the noun; not ital.; abbrev. **prox.**)

Prozac trademark drug used to treat depression

PRS 1 Performing Rights Society **2** President of the Royal Society

Prufrock, J. Alfred, narrator of T. S. Eliot's poem 'The Love Song of J. Alfred Prufrock' (1915)

Przewalski's horse Mongolian ancestor of the domestic horse

PS 1 police sergeant **2** pl. **PSS** postscript **3** private secretary **4** prompt side

Ps. 1 pl. **Pss.** Psalm **2** the Book of Psalms

psalm sacred song or hymn; (**Psalm**) one in the Book of Psalms ◻ **psalmist**

Psalms (also **Book of Psalms**) book of the Old Testament (abbrev. **Ps.**)

psalter (lower case) **1** (**the psalter**) the Book of Psalms **2** copy of this

psaltery old musical instrument like a dulcimer

p's and q's (also **Ps and Qs**)

PSBR public-sector borrowing requirement

psephology statistical study of voting

pseud. pseudonym

pseudepigrapha spurious or pseudonymous writings

pseudo pl. **pseudos** pretentious or insincere (person)

pseudonym fictitious name (abbrev. **pseud.**)

pseudoscience, pseudoscientific (one word)

pshaw exclamation of contempt or impatience

psi twenty-third letter of the Greek alphabet (Ψ, ψ), transliterated as 'ps'

p.s.i. pounds per square inch

psilocybin hallucinogenic alkaloid found in some toadstools

psittacine of parrots

psittacosis contagious disease of birds transmissible to humans

PSNI Police Service of Northern Ireland

psoriasis skin disease

PSS postscripts

Pss. pl. of **Ps.**
PST Pacific Standard Time
PSV public service vehicle
psych (also **psyche**) v.
psychedelic (not **psycho-**)
psycho pl. **psychos** psychopath
psychokinesis supposed moving of objects by mental effort (abbrev. **PK**)
psychologize (Brit. also **psychologise**)
psychosis pl. **psychoses**
psy-ops tactics intended to manipulate opponents (hyphen)
PT physical training
Pt the chemical element platinum (no point)
Pt. point (on maps)
pt pl. **pts 1** part **2** pint **3** point **4** port (side)
PTA 1 parent–teacher association **2** Passenger Transport Authority
ptarmigan northern grouse
Pte Private
pterodactyl late Jurassic pterosaur (not **ptera-**)
pterosaur prehistoric flying reptile
ptg printing
PTO please turn over
Ptolemy 1 member of a dynasty ruling Egypt 304–30 BC **2** 2nd-cent. Greek astronomer and geographer □ **Ptolemaic**
pts pl. of **pt**
PTSD post-traumatic stress disorder
Pty Proprietary (in company names)
Pu the chemical element plutonium (no point)
pub. 1 public **2** publication(s) **3** published; publisher
pubes 1 pl. same, lower abdomen in front of the pelvis **2** pl. of **pubis** **3** informal pubic hair
pubis pl. **pubes** each of two pelvic bones
public address system (three words)
publicize (Brit. also **publicise**)
public lending right right of authors to payment when their works are borrowed from UK public libraries (three words; abbrev. **PLR**)
publicly (not **-ally**)
publish, publisher (abbrev. **pub.**)
Publishers Association (no apostrophe; abbrev. **PA**)
publisher's binding standard binding in which an edition is supplied to booksellers (apostrophe)
Puccini, Giacomo (1858–1924), Italian composer
pudding-head (hyphen, but *The Tragedy of Pudd'nhead Wilson* by Mark Twain, 1894)
pudendum pl. **pudenda** woman's external genitals
Puducherry Union Territory and city of SE India; former name **Pondicherry**
Puebla state and city of Mexico
Pueblo pl. same or **Pueblos** member of an American Indian people
pueblo pl. **pueblos** village in Spain or Latin America
puerile childishly silly
Puerto Rico island of the Greater Antilles in the Caribbean □ **Puerto Rican**
puffball fungus (one word)
pufferfish (one word)
Puglia It. name for **Apulia**
Pugwash conferences international scientific conferences first held in Pugwash, a village in Nova Scotia
puisne Law presiding over a superior court but inferior to a chief justice
Puissance showjumping competition (cap.)
puissance power, strength (not ital.)
puja (also **pooja**) Hindu ceremonial offering
pukka (also **pukkah**) genuine
pul pl. **puls** or **puli** monetary unit of Afghanistan
pula pl. same, monetary unit of Botswana
Pulitzer, Joseph (1847–1911), Hungarian-born American newspaper proprietor, founder of the **Pulitzer Prize** for journalism
pull (print) a proof
pullback withdrawal of troops (one word, two words as verb)
pulley pl. **pulleys**
Pullman[1], Philip (b.1946), English writer
Pullman[2] pl. **Pullmans** comfortable railway carriage
pull-out adj., n. (hyphen, two words as verb)

pullover knitted garment (one word)
pull-up n. (hyphen, two words as verb)
pulp fiction popular or sensational fiction
pulverize (Brit. also **pulverise**)
pumice stone (two words)
pummel (**pummelling, pummelled**; US one **-l-**)
pummelo use **pomelo**
pumpkin large orange-yellow fruit (not **pumkin**)
punchbag, punchball, punchbowl (one word)
punch-drunk (hyphen)
punchline (one word)
punch-up (hyphen)
punctilio pl. **punctilios** fine point of conduct
punctus punctuation mark in a medieval manuscript; (***punctus elevatus***) mark like an inverted semicolon; (***punctus interrogatus***) mark of interrogation; (***punctus versus***) mark like a semicolon (L., ital.)
pundit 1 an expert **2** var. of **pandit**
Pune city in Maharashtra, western India; former name **Poona**
Punjab (also **the Punjab**) **1** region of NW India and Pakistan **2** province of Pakistan **3** state of India
Punjabi (also **Panjabi**) pl. **Punjabis** (inhabitant or language) of Punjab
punkah Ind. cloth or electric fan
pupa pl. **pupae** active immature form of insect
pupillage (also **pupilage**) state of being a pupil; Law apprenticeship to a member of the bar
pupil-master barrister in charge of a trainee (hyphen)
puppy dog, puppy fat, puppy love (two words)
Purana sacred Sanskrit text □ **Puranic**
purchasable (not **-eable**)
purdah seclusion of Muslim and Hindu women
puree (**pureeing, pureed**) (also **purée**) (make into) a smooth pulp of fruit or vegetables [Fr. *purée*]
Purgatory place of suffering before admission to heaven
purgatory mental anguish (lower case)
purify (not **purefy**)
Purim Jewish spring festival
Puritan strict Protestant of the 16th and 17th cents
puritan censorious person (lower case) □ **puritanical**
purl knitting stitch; cf. **pearl**
purlieus surrounding area
Purple Heart US military decoration (caps)
purposefully resolutely, with a strong purpose
purposely intentionally
purposively with a particular purpose
purslane edible fleshy-leaved plant (not **-lain, -laine**)
pursuivant officer of the College of Arms
purveyor (not **-er**)
pushbike (one word)
push-button (hyphen)
pushcart, pushchair (one word)
Pushkin, Aleksandr (Sergeevich) (1799–1837), Russian writer
pushover person easy to overcome; thing easy to do (one word, two words as verb)
push-start v., n. (hyphen)
Pushtu var. of **Pashto**
push-up n. (hyphen, two words as verb)
pusillanimous lacking courage
pussycat, pussyfoot (one word)
put place in a particular position; cf. **putt**
put-down n. (hyphen, two words as verb)
Putin, Vladimir (b.1952), Russian president 2000–8 and since 2012
putrefy (not **putrify**)
putsch violent coup (lower case, not ital.)
putt hit a golf ball gently into the hole; cf. **put**
puttee strip of cloth wound round the leg
putting green (two words)
putto pl. **putti** representation of a naked child (not ital.)
putty paste that hardens
PVC polyvinyl chloride
PVR personal video recorder
Pvt. 1 Private (in the US army) **2** private

(in company names)
PW policewoman
p.w. per week
Pwllheli town in Gwynedd, Wales
PWR pressurized-water reactor
PX post exchange
pya monetary unit of Burma (Myanmar)
pyaemia (US **pyemia**) form of blood poisoning
pye-dog (also **pie-dog** or **pi-dog**) stray mongrel, esp. in India
Pygmy (also **Pigmy**) member of a people of Africa or SE Asia
pygmy (also **pigmy**) small or insignificant person (lower case)
pyjamas (US **pajamas**)
pylon tall tower-like structure
Pynchon, Thomas (Ruggles) (b.1937), American novelist
Pyongyang capital of North Korea
pyorrhoea (US **pyorrhea**) gum inflammation
Pyramids cap. with ref. to major ancient Egyptian pyramids
Pyrenees mountains along the border between France and Spain □ **Pyrenean**
Pyrex trademark hard heat-resistant glass
pyrites (also **iron pyrites**, Mineralogy **pyrite**) shiny yellow mineral
pyromania obsessive desire to set fire to things □ **pyromaniac**
pyrotechnic of fireworks
pyrrhic metrical foot of two short or unaccented syllables (two *r*s)
pyrrhic victory victory won at too great a cost to the victor (lower case, two *r*s)
Pyrrho (*c.*365–*c.*270 BC), Greek philosopher □ **Pyrrhonism**
Pyrrhus (*c.*318–272 BC), king of Epirus, who had a **pyrrhic victory** against the Romans
Pythagoras (*c.*580–500 BC), Greek philosopher □ **Pythagorean**
Pythagoras' theorem (apostrophe, one *s*)
Pythia priestess of Apollo at Delphi □ **Pythian**
Pythias see **Damon**
Python Gk Mythol. serpent killed by Apollo
python large snake
Pythonesque resembling *Monty Python's Flying Circus*, a British comedy television series (cap.)
pythoness arch. witch able to foresee the future
pyx container for Eucharistic bread (not **pix**)

Q

Q[1] **1** pl. **Qs** or **Q's** 17th letter of the alphabet **2** quarter (of the financial year) **3** Chess queen **4** question

Q[2] pseudonym of Sir Arthur Quiller-Couch

q Phys. electric charge

QA quality assurance

Qaddafi var. of **Gaddafi**

Qantas Australian airline

Qatar sheikhdom on the Persian Gulf □ **Qatari**

Qattara Depression area of desert in NE Africa

qawwali style of Muslim devotional music

QB 1 Queen's Bench **2** Chess queen's bishop

QBP Chess queen's bishop's pawn

QC 1 quality control **2** Quebec (postal abbrev.) **3** Queen's Counsel (after the name, separated by a comma)

Q-Celtic another term for **Goidelic**

QED *quod erat demonstrandum* 'which was to be demonstrated'

qi var. of **chi**[2]

qiblah direction to which Muslims turn at prayer (ital.)

qigong Chinese system of exercise and breathing (not ital.)

Qin (also **Ch'in**) dynasty that ruled China 221–206 BC

Qing (also **Ch'ing**) dynasty that ruled China 1644–1912

qintar pl. **qintars** or **qindarka** monetary unit of Albania

QKt Chess queen's knight

QKtP Chess queen's knight's pawn

Qld Queensland

QM Quartermaster

QMG Quartermaster General

QMS Quartermaster Sergeant

QN Chess queen's knight

QNP Chess queen's knight's pawn

Qom (also **Qum**) city in central Iran

QP Chess queen's pawn

QPM Queen's Police Medal

QPR Queens Park Rangers (Football Club)

qq.v. *quae vide* 'which see' (refers to more than one place or source)

QR Chess queen's rook

qr 1 quarter(s) **2** quire(s)

QRP Chess queen's rook's pawn

QSO quasi-stellar object, quasar

qt quart(s)

q.t. (in **on the q.t.**) on the quiet

qua in the capacity of (not ital.)

Quaalude trademark sedative drug

quad bike off-road motorcycle (two words)

quadragenarian person between 40 and 49

Quadragesima first Sunday in Lent

Quadrantids annual meteor shower (cap.)

quadraphonic (also **quadrophonic**) (of sound) transmitted through four channels

quadrat small area selected as a sample

quadrate roughly square

quadrennial recurring every four years (two *n*s)

quadrennium pl. **quadrennia** or **quadrenniums** period of four years (two *n*s)

quadriceps pl. same, large thigh muscle

quadrille 1 dance performed by four couples **2** card game **3** ruled grid of small squares

quadrillion pl. **quadrillions** or (with numeral) same, 10^{15} or, formerly, 10^{24}

quadripartite consisting of four parts

quadriplegia paralysis of all four limbs

quadrivium medieval university course of arithmetic, geometry, astronomy, and music; cf. **trivium**

quadrophonic var. of **quadraphonic**

quaestor official in ancient Rome (not ital.)

quae vide full form of **qq.v.** (L., ital.)
quagga extinct zebra
quahog (also **quahaug**) N. Amer. large edible clam
Quai d'Orsay street in Paris, location of the ministry of foreign affairs
Quaker member of the Religious Society of Friends (cap.)
quale pl. **qualia** quality as perceived by a person (not ital.)
quango pl. **quangos** semi-public administrative body (lower case)
Quant, Mary (b.1934), English fashion designer
quantitative (also **quantitive**)
quantum pl. **quanta** discrete quantity of energy
quantum field theory (three words)
quantum mechanics (treated as sing.) □ **quantum-mechanical**
quantum meruit reasonable amount to be paid (L., ital.)
quark Phys. kind of subatomic particle
quarrel v. (**quarrelling, quarrelled**; US one **-l-**)
quart 1 one quarter of a gallon, two pints (abbrev. **qt**) **2** (also **quarte, carte**) Fencing parrying position
quarterback (one word)
quarter binding binding with the book's spine in a different material from the rest of the cover
quarter day (two words)
quarterdeck (one word)
quarter-final (hyphen)
Quarter Horse stocky agile breed of horse (caps)
quarter-hour, quarter-light (hyphen)
quarterly periodical published four times a year
quartermaster army officer responsible for supplies etc. (cap. in titles; abbrev. **QM**)
Quartermaster General head of an army department (caps; abbrev. **QMG**)
quartermaster sergeant (cap. in titles; abbrev. **QM**)
quarter note N. Amer. crotchet (two words)
quarter-pounder (hyphen)
quarter-tone Mus. half a semitone (hyphen)
quartet set of four people or things [Fr. *quartette*]
quartier district of a French city (ital.)
quarto pl. **quartos** page size from folding each printed sheet into four leaves (eight pages) (abbrev. **4to** or **4**^{to})
quasar Astron. quasi-stellar object
quasi-contract legal obligation independent of agreement (hyphen)
Quasimodo 1 hunchback in Victor Hugo's novel *Notre-Dame de Paris* (1831) **2** Salvatore (1901–68), Italian poet
quatercentenary four-hundredth anniversary (not **quarter-**)
quaternary 1 fourth **2** (**Quaternary**) most recent period in the Cenozoic era
quatrain stanza of four lines usually with alternate rhymes
quattrocento the 15th century in Italy (not ital., double *t*)
quay place for loading and unloading ships
quayside (one word)
Quebec province and city in eastern Canada (abbrev. **Que.**, postal **QC**); Fr. name **Québec** □ **Quebecker**
Quechua (also **Quecha, Quichua**) pl. same or **Quechuas** member of a South American Indian people
queen cap. in titles (*Queen Jane*) and often *the Queen*, but *queen of Castile*; style is *Queen Elizabeth II* or *Queen Elizabeth the Second*, not *the II* or *IIth*; chess abbrev. **Q**
queen post upright timber in a roof (two words)
Queens borough of New York City (no apostrophe)
Queensberry Rules standard rules of boxing
queen's bishop Chess (lower case, apostrophe)
Queens' College Cambridge college (named after two queens)
Queen's College, The Oxford college (named after one queen)
Queen's Counsel senior barrister (abbrev. **QC**)
Queen's County former name for **Laois**

queen-sized (also **queen-size**) (hyphen)
queen's knight Chess (lower case, apostrophe)
Queensland state in NE Australia (abbrev. **Qld**) □ **Queenslander**
queen's pawn, queen's rook Chess (lower case, apostrophe)
Queen's Speech (caps)
queensware cream-coloured Wedgwood pottery (one word, lower case)
quenelle ball of pounded fish or meat
question mark (two words)
questionnaire (two *ns*)
Quetta city in western Pakistan
quetzal monetary unit of Guatemala
Quetzalcóatl plumed serpent god of the Toltecs and Aztecs
queue v. (**queuing** or **queueing**, **queued**)
quiche baked savoury flan
Quichua var. of **Quechua**
quick-fire, quick-freeze (hyphen)
quicklime (one word)
quick march (two words)
quicksand, quickset, quicksilver, quickstep (one word)
quick-tempered, quick-witted (hyphen)
Quicunque vult the Athanasian Creed (ital.) [L., 'whosoever wishes (to be saved)', its opening words]
quid pl. same, informal one pound sterling
quiddity inherent nature or essence
quid pro quo pl. **quid pro quos** favour or advantage in return (not ital.)
quietus pl. **quietuses** death or cause of death (not ital.)
Quiller-Couch, Sir Arthur (Thomas) (1863–1944), English novelist; pseudonym **Q**
quin Brit. quintuplet; cf. **quint**
quincentenary (also **quincentennial**) five-hundredth anniversary
Quincey, Thomas De, see **De Quincey**
quincunx pl. **quincunxes** arrangement with four objects at the corners of a square or rectangle and one at its centre
Quine, Willard Van Orman (1908–2000), American philosopher
quinella bet on the prediction of the first two places in a race
quinine compound from cinchona bark
quinquagenarian person between 50 and 59
Quinquagesima Sunday before the beginning of Lent
quinquennial recurring every five years (two *ns*)
quinquennium pl. **quinquennia** or **quinquenniums** period of five years (two *ns*)
quinquereme ancient Roman and Greek galley
quinsy abscess in the tonsil region
quint **1** sequence of five cards of the same suit **2** N. Amer. quintuplet
quintal **1** one hundredweight or, formerly, 100 lb **2** 100 kg
quinte Fencing parrying position
quintet group of five persons or things [Fr. *quintette*]
Quintilian (*c.*35–*c.*96 AD), Roman rhetorician; Latin name *Marcus Fabius Quintilianus*
quintillion pl. **quintillions** or (with numeral) same, 10^{18} or, formerly, 10^{30}
quire (abbrev. **qr**) **1** four sheets of paper folded to form eight leaves (16 pages) **2** 25 (formerly 24) sheets of paper, one twentieth of a ream **3** collection of leaves one within another
quisling traitor, collaborator (lower case)
quit (**quitting**; past and past part. **quitted** or **quit**)
Quito capital of Ecuador
qui vive (in **on the qui vive**) on the lookout (not ital.)
Quixote see **Don Quixote**
quixotic idealistic and unrealistic (lower case)
quiz (**quizzes, quizzing, quizzed**)
quizmaster (one word)
Qum var. of **Qom**
Qumran region by the Dead Sea
quod erat demonstrandum which was to be demonstrated (L., ital.; abbrev. **QED**)
quodlibet medley of well-known tunes
quod vide full form of **q.v.** (L., ital.)
quoin wedge or device for locking a

letterpress forme into a chase

quoit 1 ring thrown at a peg in a game **2** (**quoits**) game with quoits (treated as sing.)

quokka small wallaby

quoll catlike marsupial

quondam former (not ital.)

Quorn trademark protein made from a fungus

quorum pl. **quorums** minimum number of members needed to make proceedings valid □ **quorate**

quota fixed number or amount

quotable (not **-eable**)

quotation mark each of a set of punctuation marks, single (‘ ’) or double (“ ”)

quotidian daily

Quran (also **Qur'an**) var. of **Koran** [Arab. *qur'ān*]

qursh pl. same, monetary unit of Saudi Arabia

q.v. *quod vide* 'which see' (refers to one place or source)

QWERTY standard layout of English-language keyboards

qy query

R

R 1 pl. **Rs** or **R's** 18th letter of the alphabet **2** rand **3** (in sport) Rangers or Rovers **4** Réaumur (obsolete temperature scale) **5** Regina or Rex **6** US Republican **7** Electron. resistance **8** roentgen(s) **9** Chess rook **10** Cricket run(s)

r 1 radius **2** recto **3** right **5** Law rule

r Statistics correlation coefficient

® registered as a trademark

RA 1 Astron. right ascension **2** Royal Academician; Royal Academy **3** Royal Artillery **4** Rugby Association

Ra[1] (also **Re**) Egyptian sun god

Ra[2] the chemical element radium (no point)

RAAF Royal Australian Air Force

Rabat capital of Morocco

rabbet N. Amer. rebate cut in wood

rabbi pl. **rabbis** Jewish scholar or teacher (cap. in titles)

rabbinic (also **rabinnical**) of rabbis or Jewish teachings

rabbit v. (**rabbiting, rabbited**)

rabbit punch (two words)

rabble-rouser (hyphen)

Rabelais, François (*c.*1494–1553), French satirist □ **Rabelaisian**

RAC 1 Royal Armoured Corps **2** Royal Automobile Club

raccoon (also **racoon**)

race major division of humankind (not used in technical contexts; prefer term such as **ethnic group**)

racecard, racecourse, racegoer, racehorse (one word)

race meeting (two words)

racetrack (one word)

rachis pl. **rachides** plant stem (not **rhachis**)

Rachmaninov, Sergei (Vasilevich) (1873–1943), Russian composer

Rachmanism exploitation and intimidation by a landlord

Racine, Jean (1639–99), French dramatist

racing car, racing driver (two words)

racism, racist (not **rasc-**)

rack noun 'framework for holding or storing things' or 'instrument of torture' is always **rack**, not **wrack**; verb 'torture by stretching on a rack' can be **rack** or **wrack**, as can phrs **rack and ruin, rack one's brains**; see also **wrack**

racket[1] (also **racquet**) rounded bat with strings

racket[2] (**racketing, racketed**) (make) a loud noise

rackets ball game (treated as sing.)

Rackham, Arthur (1867–1939), English illustrator

rack rent extortionate rent (two words)

raconteur (fem. **raconteuse**) (not ital.)

racoon var. of **raccoon**

racquet var. of **racket**[1]

racquetball North American ball game (one word)

racy (not **-ey**)

RAD Royal Academy of Dance (or Dancing)

rad 1 unit of absorbed dose of radiation **2** radian(s)

RADA Royal Academy of Dramatic Art

radar gun, radar trap (two words)

RADC Royal Army Dental Corps

Radcliffe, Mrs Ann (1764–1823), English novelist

Radhakrishnan, Sir Sarvepalli (1888–1975), Indian philosopher and statesman

radian SI unit of plane angles (abbrev. **rad**)

radiator (not **-er**)

radical fundamental; cf. **radicle**

radicalize (Brit. also **radicalise**)

radical sign Math. the symbol √

radicchio pl. **radicchios** variety of chicory

radices pl. of **radix**

radicle part of a plant embryo; cf. **radical**

radii pl. of **radius**
radio n. pl. **radios.** v. **radioes, radioing, radioed**
radioactive, radioactivity (one word)
radio astronomy, radio car (two words)
radiocarbon (one word)
radio-controlled (hyphen)
radiogram, radioimmunology, radioisotope (one word)
radiopaque (also **radio-opaque**) opaque to X-rays
radio-telephone, radio-telephony (hyphen)
radio telescope (two words)
radiotelex, radiotherapy (one word)
radium chemical element of atomic number 88 (symbol **Ra**)
radius pl. **radii** or **radiuses**
radix pl. **radices** base of a system
Radnorshire former county of eastern Wales
radon chemical element of atomic number 86, a noble gas (symbol **Rn**)
Raeburn, Sir Henry (1756–1823), Scottish portrait painter
RAF Royal Air Force
raffia fibre from a tropical tree (not **rafia, raphia**)
raga Indian musical mode
ragamuffin (also **raggamuffin**)
rag-and-bone man (two hyphens)
ragbag (one word)
rag doll (two words)
ragga dance music derived from reggae
raggamuffin var. of **ragamuffin**
ragged uneven because the lines are unjustified; (**ragged right** or **left**) aligned with the left (or right) margin
raggle-taggle (hyphen)
Ragnarök Scand. Mythol. final battle between the gods and the powers of evil
ragout meat stew (no accent, not ital.) [Fr. *ragoût*]
ragtag disorganized or incongruously varied; (**ragtag and bobtail**) disreputable or disorganized group (one word)
ragtime, ragtop (one word)
Ragusa former It. name for **Dubrovnik**
railbus, railcar, railcard, railhead, railroad (one word)
Railtrack former British railway company
railway, railwayman (one word)
rain check N. Amer. (two words)
raincoat, raindrop, rainfall, rainforest (one word)
rain gauge (two words)
rainproof, rainstorm, rainswept, rainwater, rainwear (one word)
raison d'état pl. ***raisons d'état*** purely political reason (Fr., ital.)
raison d'être pl. ***raisons d'être*** main reason for existence (Fr., ital.)
raita Indian side dish of yogurt
Raj, the British sovereignty in India
raja (also **rajah**) Indian prince (cap. in titles)
Rajasthan state in western India
□ **Rajasthani**
Rajput member of a Hindu military caste (cap.)
Rajya Sabha upper house of the Indian parliament; cf. **Lok Sabha**
rakhi pl. **rakhis** symbolic Indian bracelet
raki pl. **rakis** alcoholic spirit
Raksha Bandhan Indian festival
raku Japanese lead-glazed earthenware
Raleigh[1] state capital of North Carolina
Raleigh[2] (also **Ralegh**), Sir Walter (*c.*1552–1618), English explorer, courtier, and writer
rallentando pl. **rallentandos** or **rallentandi** Mus. with a gradual decrease in speed (abbrev. **rall.**)
rallycross (one word)
RAM 1 Comput. random-access memory **2** Royal Academy of Music
Ramadan (also **Ramadhan**) ninth month of the Muslim year, when fasting is observed from dawn to sunset
Raman, Sir Chandrasekhara Venkata (1888–1970), Indian physicist
Ramayana great Sanskrit epic
Rambo hero of the novel *First Blood* by David Morell (1972), popularized in films
Rambouillet town in northern France
RAMC Royal Army Medical Corps
Rameau, Jean-Philippe (1683–1764), French composer
ramekin small dish

Rameses (also **Ramses**) name of eleven Egyptian pharaohs
Ramillies 1706 battle near the Belgian village of Ramillies
ram raid n. (two words, hyphen as verb) □ **ram-raider**
ramrod (one word)
Ramsay, Allan (1713–84), Scottish portrait painter
Ramses var. of **Rameses**
Ramsey, Sir Alf (1920–99), English footballer and manager; full name *Alfred Ernest Ramsey*
RAN Royal Australian Navy
ranchero pl. **rancheros** N. Amer. worker on a ranch
rancour (US **rancor**) □ **rancorous**
rand monetary unit of South Africa
R & B rhythm and blues
R & D research and development
random access (two words, hyphen when attrib.)
randomize (Brit. also **randomise**)
R & R 1 rest and recreation **2** Med. rescue and resuscitation **3** (also **R 'n' R**) rock and roll
ranee use **rani**
rangatira Maori chief
range align at the end of successive lines
rangé having a settled lifestyle (Fr., ital.)
rangefinder (one word)
ranger 1 keeper of a park or forest **2** (**Ranger** or **Ranger Guide**) Brit. member of the senior branch of the Guides
ranging numerals (also **lining numerals**) numerals that align at the top and bottom, as 1234567890
Rangoon capital of Burma (Myanmar); Burmese name **Yangôn**
rani pl. **ranis** wife of a raja (cap. in titles; not **ranee**)
Ranjit Singh (1780–1839), founder of the Sikh state of Punjab; known as the **Lion of the Punjab**
Ranjitsinhji Vibhaji, Kumar Shri, Maharaja Jam Sahib of Navanagar (1872–1933), Indian cricketer and statesman
rank and file (three words, hyphen when attrib.; treated as pl.)
Rann of Kutch see **Kutch, Rann of**
Ransom, John Crowe (1888–1974), American writer
ransom sum demanded for the release of a captive
Ransome, Arthur (Michell) (1884–1967), English writer
ranunculus pl. **ranunculuses** or **ranunculi** plant of the buttercup family
RAOC Royal Army Ordnance Corps
RAPC Royal Army Pay Corps
Rape of Lucrece, The Shakespeare poem (abbrev. ***Lucr.***)
rape oil (two words)
rapeseed (one word)
Raphael (1483–1520), Italian artist; Italian name *Raffaello Sanzio*
raphia use **raffia**
rapid eye movement (three words; abbrev. **REM**)
rapid-fire (hyphen)
rappel (**rappelling, rappelled**) another term for **abseil**
rapport close and harmonious relationship (not ital.)
rapporteur person who reports on proceedings (not ital.)
rapprochement establishment of harmonious relations (not ital.)
rapt completely fascinated (not **wrapt**)
rara avis pl. ***rarae aves*** rare bird (L., ital.)
rarebit melted cheese on toast
rare earth element, rare earth metal (three words)
rarefied, rarefy (not **rari-**)
rarity (not **rare-**)
Rarotonga chief island of the Cook Islands □ **Rarotongan**
Ras al-Khaimah state and city of the United Arab Emirates
rase var. of **raze**
raspberry soft fruit (not **rasb-**)
Rasputin, Grigori (Efimovich) (1871–1916), Russian monk
Rasselas, Prince of Abyssinia, The History of novel by Dr Johnson (1759)
Rastafari Rastafarian movement
Rastafarian member of a religious movement of Jamaican origin
raster pattern of scanning lines
Rasumovsky Quartets three string

quartets by Beethoven
ratable var. of **rateable**
ratafia almond-flavoured liqueur or biscuit
ratatouille dish of vegetables (not ital.)
ratbag (one word)
ratchet v. (**ratcheting, ratcheted**)
rateable (also **ratable**)
ratepayer (one word)
Rathaus pl. ***Rathäuser*** town hall in a German-speaking country (cap., ital.)
rathskeller US beer hall or basement restaurant (lower case, not ital.)
ratio pl. **ratios**
ratio decidendi pl. ***rationes decidendi*** Law rule of law on which a decision is based (L., ital.)
rationale set of reasons or logical basis
rationalize (Brit. also **rationalise**)
ratlines small ropes for climbing rigging
rat pack, rat race, rat run (two words)
rat-tail (also **rat's tail**) narrow hairless tail (hyphen)
rattan thin jointed palm stems
rattlesnake (one word)
Rauschenberg, Robert (1925–2008), American artist
ravel (**ravelling, ravelled**; US one **-l-**)
Ravenna city in NE central Italy
ravioli filled pasta envelopes
Rawalpindi city in northern Pakistan
rawhide (one word)
Rawlplug trademark plastic sheath to hold a screw
Ray, Man (1890–1976), American photographer; born *Emmanuel Rudnitsky*
ray (also **re**) note in tonic sol-fa
Ray-Bans trademark brand of sunglasses
Rayleigh, John William Strutt, 3rd Baron (1842–1919), English physicist
raze (also **rase**) completely destroy
razor blade, razor wire (two words)
razor-sharp (hyphen)
razzmatazz (also **razzamatazz**)
Rb the chemical element rubidium (no point)
RBA Royal Society of British Artists
RBS Royal Society of British Sculptors
RC 1 racing club **2** Red Cross **3** reinforced concrete **4** resin-coated **5** resistance capacitance (or resistor/capacitor) **6** Roman Catholic
RCA 1 Radio Corporation of America **2** Royal College of Art
RCM Royal College of Music
RCMP Royal Canadian Mounted Police
RCN Royal College of Nursing
RCP Royal College of Physicians
RCS 1 Royal College of Scientists **2** Royal College of Surgeons **3** Royal Corps of Signals
RCVS Royal College of Veterinary Surgeons
RD 1 refer to drawer **2** Royal Naval Reserve Decoration
Rd Road
RDA 1 recommended daily (or dietary) allowance **2** Regional Development Agency
RDBMS relational database management system
RDC Rural District Council
RDF 1 radio direction-finder (or -finding) **2** US rapid deployment force
RDX type of high explosive
RE 1 Religious Education **2** Royal Engineers
Re 1 the chemical element rhenium (no point) **2** var. of **Ra**[1]
re[1] in the matter of (no point, not ital.)
re[2] var. of **ray**
re- usu. forming solid compounds exc. with words that begin with *e* or (sometimes) *r*
Read, Sir Herbert (Edward) (1893–1968), English critic
readapt, readdress (one word)
Reade, Charles (1814–84), English novelist
reader 1 person who reports on the merits of manuscripts or who provides critical comments on a text **2** proofreader **3** (**Reader**) university lecturer ranking next below professor
Reader's Digest Association publishing company; (***Reader's Digest***) periodical
reading age, reading desk, reading lamp, reading room (two words)
readjust, readmit (one word)
readopt (one word)

read-out n. (hyphen, two words as verb)
read-through n. (hyphen, two words as verb)
re-advertise (hyphen)
read–write adj. (en rule)
ready-made (hyphen)
ready-to-wear (of garment) not made to measure (hyphens; three words in general use)
reafforest reforest (one word)
Reagan, Ronald (Wilson) (1911–2004), 40th president of the US 1981–9
real monetary unit of Brazil
real estate agent N. Amer. (three words)
realign (one word)
realizable (Brit. also **realisable**; not **-eable**)
realize (Brit. also **realise**)
realpolitik politics based on practical considerations (lower case, not ital.)
realtor N. Amer. trademark estate agent
realty person's real property
ream 500 (formerly 480) sheets of paper (abbrev. **rm**)
rear admiral, rear commodore (two words; cap. in titles)
rearguard (one word)
rear-view mirror, rear-wheel drive (one hyphen)
Réaumur scale obsolete scale of temperature
Reb traditional Jewish courtesy title for a man (cap., used preceding the name)
rebarbative unattractive and objectionable
rebate 1 partial refund **2** step-shaped recess cut in a piece of wood
rebbe Hasidic rabbi (cap. in titles)
rebec (also **rebeck**) medieval stringed instrument
rebel v. (**rebelling, rebelled**)
rebellion, rebellious (two *l*s)
rebind replace the binding of
rebound (one word) **1** bounce back **2** past and past part. of **rebind**
rebus pl. **rebuses** puzzle with words represented by letters and pictures
REC Regional Electricity Company
rec recreation; recreation ground (no point)
recce (**recces, recceing, recced**) (make a) reconnaissance
recd received
receipt (not **-ceit**) **1** action of receiving; written or printed acknowledgement of this **2** arch. recipe
receivable (not **-eable**)
received pronunciation (lower case; abbrev. **RP**)
recension revised edition of a text
Recent Geol. the Holocene era (cap.)
receptor responsive organ or cell (not **-er**)
rechargeable (not **-gable**)
réchauffé dish of warmed-up leftovers (Fr., ital.)
recherché exotic or obscure (accent, not ital.)
recidivist convicted criminal who reoffends
recipe list of instructions for preparing a dish
recitativo pl. **recitativos** style of musical declamation
recognizable (Brit. also **recognisable**; not **-eable**)
recognizance (Brit. also **recognisance**)
recognize (Brit. also **recognise**)
recommend, recommendation (two *ms*)
reconcilable (not **-eable**)
reconnaissance (two *ns*, two *ss*)
reconnoitre (US **reconnoiter**) (two *ns*, no accent) [obs. Fr. *reconnoître*]
record-breaking, record-breaker (hyphen)
Recorder barrister serving as a part-time judge (cap.)
record player (two words)
recount[1] give an account of (one word)
recount[2] count again (one word)
recover return to normal (one word)
re-cover put another cover on (hyphen)
recreate create again, reproduce (one word)
recreation[1] activity for enjoyment (one word)
recreation[2] creating something again (one word)
recto pl. **rectos** right-hand page of an open book; front of a loose leaf (abbrev. **r**, ^{r}); cf. **verso**

rectrices (sing. **rectrix**) larger feathers of a bird's tail (not ital.)
rectum pl. **rectums** or **recta** final section of the large intestine
reculer pour mieux sauter withdraw to await a better opportunity (Fr., ital.)
recumbent lying down (not **-ant**)
recur (**recurring, recurred**)
recyclable (not **-eable**)
red cap. in ref. to communists or socialists
redaction editing a text for publication; version of a text
redbreast robin (one word)
red-brick (of a British university) founded in the late 19th or early 20th cent. (hyphen)
redcap (one word) **1** Brit. member of the military police **2** N. Amer. railway porter
red card n. Soccer (two words, hyphen as verb)
red carpet (two words, hyphen when attrib.)
redcoat hist. British soldier (one word)
redcurrant (one word)
Redding, Otis (1941–67), American soul singer
Redeemer, the Christ
red-eye effect in flash photography (hyphen)
red-figure type of ancient Greek pottery (hyphen)
redfish particular marine fish (one word)
red fish fish with dark flesh, as food (two words)
red flag symbol of socialist revolution or danger; (***the Red Flag***) Labour Party anthem
Redgauntlet novel by Sir Walter Scott (1824) (one word)
red–green (en rule with ref. to colour blindness)
red-handed (hyphen)
redhead ◻ **red-headed** (one word)
red-hot (hyphen)
redial (**redialling, redialled**; US one **-l-**)
rediffusion (two *f*s) **1** cable broadcasting **2** (**Rediffusion**) television company
Red Indian avoid: dated and offensive; see **American Indian**
redivivus reborn (not ital; after the noun)
red-letter day, red-light district (one hyphen)
redneck (one word)
redoubt fortification (not **-out**)
redoubtable formidable as an opponent
redpoll finch (one word)
red poll breed of cattle (two words)
redress remedy or set right (one word)
re-dress dress again (hyphen)
redshank sandpiper (one word)
redskin offens. (one word)
redstart songbird (one word)
reducible (not **-able, -eable**)
reductio ad absurdum disproof by an obviously absurd conclusion (L., ital.)
redundancy, redundant (not **-ency, -ent**)
redux brought back (not ital.; after the noun)
redwater cattle disease (one word)
redwing, redwood, redworm (one word)
Reebok sportswear company
reebok var. of **rhebok**
re-echo (hyphen)
Reed, Sir Carol (1906–76), English film director
reed bed (two words)
reedbuck (S. African also **rietbok**) kind of antelope (one word)
re-edit, re-educate (hyphen)
reef knot (two words)
re-elect (hyphen)
reel-to-reel (hyphens)
re-embark, re-emerge, re-equip, re-establish, re-evaluate (hyphen)
ref. 1 reference **2** refer to
refer (**referring, referred**)
referable (one *r*; not **-ible**)
referee v. (**refereeing, refereed**)
reference (abbrev. **ref.**)
reference book, reference library (two words)
reference marks see **marks of reference**
reference point (two words)
referendum pl. **referendums** or

referenda
referral (two *r*s)
refl. reflexive
reflection (not **reflexion** (arch.))
reflector (not **-er**)
reflet lustre or iridescence (Fr., ital.)
reflex word developed from a particular earlier form
reflexive Gram. referring back to the subject of the clause (abbrev. **refl.**)
reflexology system of massage
reform change to improve (one word)
re-form form again
reformation reforming an institution or practice; (**the Reformation**) the 16th-cent. movement to reform the Roman Catholic Church (one word)
re-formation forming again (hyphen)
Reform Judaism Judaism that has reformed much Orthodox ritual □ **Reform Jew**
refractor refracting lens (not **-er**)
refractory stubborn or unmanageable
refrangible able to be refracted
refrigerate, **refrigerator** (not **-dg-**)
refuel (**refuelling, refuelled**; US one **-l-**)
refurbish renovate and redecorate
refute disprove; disp. deny
reg. registered as a trademark (symbol ®)
regal of or fit for a monarch
regale entertain with talk or lavishly
regalia emblems of royalty (treated as sing. or pl.)
regalian of a monarch
regardless despite the prevailing circumstances (not **irregardless**)
regatta series of boat or yacht races
regd registered
regency period of government by a regent; (**the Regency**) in Britain 1811–20 or France 1715–23
Regent's Park park in London (apostrophe)
reggae popular music style originating in Jamaica
regime particular government
regimen prescribed course of treatment for health
regiment (cap. in names; abbrev. **Rgt**)
regimental sergeant major (cap. in titles; abbrev. **RSM**)
Regina reigning queen (cap.; after a name or in the titles of lawsuits)
regionalize (Brit. also **regionalise**)
regisseur ballet producer [Fr. *régisseur*]
register 1 correspondence of the position of printed matter on the two sides of a leaf or of colour components in a printed positive **2** variety of a language determined by context or purpose
registered nurse (abbrev. **RN**)
register office official term for **registry office**
registrable (not **-terable**)
registrar general government official responsible for a population census
registrary chief administrative officer of Cambridge University
registry office local government building for registering births, marriages, and deaths; official term **register office**
Regius professor holder of a university chair founded by a monarch or filled by Crown appointment (cap. *P* only in titles)
regret v. (**regretting, regretted**) □ **regretful**
regretfully in a regretful manner; disp. it is regrettable that ...
regrettable (two *t*s)
regrettably unfortunately; it is regrettable that ...
regs regulations
Regt Regiment
regularize (Brit. also **regularise**)
regulator (not **-er**)
Rehoboam king of ancient Israel *c.*930–*c.*915 BC
rehoboam wine bottle about six times the standard size (lower case)
Reich former German state (usu. refers to the Third Reich; cap., not ital.)
Reichstag former German legislature and current parliament building (cap., not ital.)
reify make more concrete or real
reign period of a monarch's rule; cf. **rein**
reignite ignite again (one word)
Reign of Terror, the period of the Terror during the French Revolution
reiki healing technique (not ital.)

reimburse, **reimport**, **reimpose** (one word)
Reims (also **Rheims**) city of northern France
rein strip attached to a horse's bit; cf. **reign**
reincarnate, **reincorporate** (one word)
reindeer pl. same or **reindeers**
reinfect, **reinflate**, **reinforce** (one word)
Reinhardt 1 Django (1910–53), Belgian jazz guitarist **2** Max (1873–1943), Austrian director and impresario; born *Max Goldmann*
reinsert etc. (one word)
Reith, John (Charles Walsham), 1st Baron (1889–1971), first director general (1927–38) of the BBC
reiver hist. Scottish Border raider
rejoin[1] join again (one word)
rejoin[2] say in reply (one word)
rejoinder a reply (one word)
rekey enter on a keyboard again (one word)
rel. relative
relater teller of a story; cf. **relator**
relative Gram. denoting a word that attaches a subordinate clause to an antecedent (abbrev. **rel.**)
relativity concept set out in Einstein's **special theory of relativity** (1905) and **general theory of relativity** (1915)
relativize (Brit. also **relativise**)
relator bringer of a public lawsuit about an abuse; cf. **relater**
releaser (Law **releasor**)
relevé Ballet an act of rising on the tips of the toes (Fr., accent, ital.)
reliable (not **-ly-**)
relic object surviving from an earlier time
relict thing surviving from an earlier period or in a primitive form
relief map map indicating hills and valleys by shading (two words)
relief printing printing from raised images, as in letterpress (two words)
relievo pl. **relievos** relief in moulding, carving, or stamping [It. *rilievo*]
religiose excessively religious
Religious Society of Friends official name for the Quakers
reliquary container for holy relics
reliquiae remains (not ital.)
REM rapid eye movement
R.E.M. US rock band (points)
rem pl. same, unit of effective absorbed radiation in tissue
remainder copy of a book left unsold
remanent remaining after the magnetizing field has been removed
remark comment
re-mark mark again (hyphen)
Remarque, Erich Maria (1898–1970), German-born American novelist
Rembrandt (1606–69), Dutch painter; full name *Rembrandt Harmensz van Rijn*
REME Royal Electrical and Mechanical Engineers
Remembrance Day (also **Remembrance Sunday**) Sunday nearest 11 November
remiges (sing. **remex**) bird's flight feathers (not ital.)
reminisce indulge in recollection of past events
remise Fencing make a second thrust after the first has failed (not **-ize**)
remissible forgivable (not **-able**)
remit (**remitting**, **remitted**) □ **remittance**
remodel (**remodelling**, **remodelled**; US one **-l-**)
remote control (two words)
remoulade salad dressing (not ital., no accent) [Fr. *rémoulade*]
remould (US **remold**)
removable (not **-eable**)
Renaissance 1 revival of European art and literature in the 14th–16th cents **2** (**renaissance**) revival or renewed interest; see also **renascence**
Renaissance man (one cap.)
renascence 1 revival of something dormant **2** (**Renascence**) another term for **Renaissance**
Renault French make of car
rencounter chance meeting
Rendell, Ruth (Barbara), Baroness Rendell of Babergh (1930–2015), English writer

rendezvous (**rendezvouses, rendezvousing, rendezvoused**)
renege go back on (not **renegue**)
Renfrewshire council area and former county of west central Scotland, divided into **Renfrewshire** and **East Renfrewshire**
renminbi system of currency in China
Renoir 1 Jean (1894–1979), French film director **2** (Pierre) Auguste (1841–1919), French painter
rent-a-car (hyphens)
rent-free (hyphen)
rentier person whose income derives from investments (not ital.)
renunciation formal rejection (not **renounc-**)
reoccupy, reoccur, reoffend, reopen (one word)
Rep. 1 Representative (in the US Congress) **2** Republic **3** US Republican
rep (no point) **1** representative **2** repertory **3** (also **repp**) ribbed fabric
repaginate renumber the pages of
repairable (esp. of something physical) possible to repair
reparable (esp. of an injury or loss) possible to rectify
repartee quick witty verbal exchange
repêchage contest between runners-up for a place in a final (accent, not ital.)
repel (**repelling, repelled**)
repellent (also **repellant**)
repentance, repentant (not **-tence, -tent**)
repertoire stock of items that a company or performer knows (not ital.)
repertory 1 performance of various items at short intervals **2** another term for **repertoire**
répétiteur person who teaches singers or ballet dancers their parts (Fr., ital.)
repetitive strain injury (three words; abbrev. **RSI**)
replaceable (not **-cable**)
replicator (not **-er**)
reply v. (**replying, replied**)
reportage reporting of news (not ital.)
repoussé (metalwork) hammered from the reverse side (accent, not ital.)
repp var. of **rep**
repr. 1 representing **2** reprint; reprinted
reprehensible (not **-able**)
represent act or speak on behalf of
re-present present again (hyphen)
representationalism 1 practice of representational art **2** another term for **representationism**
representationism doctrine that thought involves mental representations corresponding to external things
Representative US member of the House of Representatives (abbrev. **Rep.**)
represser person or thing that represses
repressor inhibitor of enzyme synthesis
reprint (abbrev. **repr.**) v. print again or in a different form, esp. with minor or no corrections. n. **1** act of reprinting a work; reprinted copy **2** another term for **offprint**
reprisal act of retaliation (not **-izal**)
reprise repeated musical passage (not **-ize**)
repro pl. **repros 1** reproduction of a document or image **2** imitative piece, copy
reproducible (not **-cable, -ceable**)
reprogram (also **reprogramme**) v. (**reprogramming, reprogrammed**; US also one **-m-**)
reprography (also **reprographics**) copying and reproducing of documents and graphic material
reproof[1] expression of blame (one word)
reproof[2] make a fresh proof of (one word)
reprove reprimand
Republican cap. in ref. to the US Republican Party (abbrev. **R**)
Republic Day in India, 26 January
republish publish again, esp. in a new edition
requiem Mass for the dead
requiescat prayer for the repose of a dead person (not ital.)
requiescat in pace may he or she rest in peace; (***requiescant in pace***) may they rest in peace (abbrev. **RIP**) (L., ital.)
reread (one word)
rerecord (one word)
reredos pl. same, ornamental screen behind an altar

rerelease, reroof, reroute (one word)
rerun (one word)
resaleable (not **-lable**)
resale price maintenance (three words; abbrev. **rpm**)
rescind revoke, cancel
réseau pl. **réseaux** network or grid (accent, not ital.)
resemblance (not **-ence**)
reserve keep back □ **reservable**
re-serve serve again (hyphen)
reservoir lake used as a source of water (not **resev-**)
res gestae matters relating to a particular law case (not ital.)
residence, resident (not **-ance, -ant**)
residuum pl. **residua** chemical residue (not ital.)
resign voluntarily leave a job or office
re-sign sign again (hyphen)
resilient (not **-ant**)
resin (**resining, resined**) (treat with) a sticky substance exuded by trees; cf. **rosin**
res ipsa loquitur principle that mere occurrence of an accident can imply negligence (not ital.)
resistance, resistant (not **-ence, -ant**)
resister person or thing that resists
resistor device having resistance to electric current
res judicata pl. **res judicatae** thing already decided (not ital.)
resoluble able to be resolved
re-soluble dissolvable again (hyphen)
resonator apparatus increasing resonance (not **-er**)
re-sort sort again (hyphen)
resource stock or supply
Respighi, Ottorino (1879–1936), Italian composer
respirator (not **-er**)
resplendent, respondent (not **-ant**)
responsible (not **-able**)
res publica the state, republic, or commonwealth (not ital.)
ressentiment suppressed envy and hatred (Fr., ital.)
restaurateur owner and manager of a restaurant (not **-rant-**)
rest cure, rest day, rest home, resting place (two words)
restharrow plant of the pea family (one word)
restorable (not **-eable**)
Restoration, the the re-establishment of Charles II as king of England, 1660
restraint of trade (three words)
restroom (one word)
resume begin again
résumé (accents, not ital.) **1** summary **2** N. Amer. curriculum vitae
Resurrection, the cap. in ref. to rising of Christ from the dead or the rising of the dead at the Last Judgement
resuscitate revive from unconsciousness □ **resuscitator**
ret. retired
retable (also **retablo**) pl. **retables** or **retablos** frame or shelf behind an altar
retail price index (three words; abbrev. **RPI**)
retardant (not **-ent**)
retd retired
reticulum pl. **reticula** fine network (not ital.)
retie, retighten (one word)
retime set a different time for (one word)
retina pl. **retinas** or **retinae**
retitle (one word)
retree damaged or defective paper
retriever dog for retrieving game
retroactive (one word)
retroflex (also **retroflexed**) pronounced with the tip of the tongue curled up
retroussé (of a nose) turned up (accent, not ital.)
retrovirus (one word)
retry (one word)
Reuben Hebrew patriarch, eldest son of Jacob
reunify (one word)
Réunion island in the Indian Ocean
reunion coming together after separation (one word)
reunite, reupholster, reuse (one word)
Reuters international news agency (no apostrophe)
Rev. 1 Revelation **2** (Brit. also **Revd**) Reverend **3** Review
rev. revised (by); reviser; revision

reveille signal to waken troops (not ital.)
revel v. (**revelling, revelled**; US one **-l-**) ◻ **reveller**
Revelation (in full the **Revelation of St John the Divine**) book of the New Testament (not **Revelations**; abbrev. **Rev.**)
reverence (not **-ance**)
Reverend the traditionally correct form is *the Reverend Joseph Bloggs, the Reverend J. Bloggs*, or *the Reverend Dr Bloggs*, not *Reverend Bloggs*; cap. *T* only in the official title of address, not in running text (abbrev. **Rev.** or Brit. **Revd**)
Reverend Mother Mother Superior of a convent
reverent showing deep respect
reverie (not **-ry**)
revers pl. same, turned-back edge of a garment (not ital.)
reversed block 1 design with illustration or lettering in white against a black background **2** block with contents transposed left-to-right for offset printing
reverse solidus a backslash \
reversible (not **-able**)
review 1 critical article in a newspaper or magazine **2** periodical (cap. in names; abbrev. **Rev.**); cf. **revue**
revise proof containing corrections made in an earlier proof (not **-ize**)
Revised Standard Version modern English version of the Bible 1946–57 (abbrev. **RSV**)
Revised Version version of the Bible based on the Authorized Version, 1881–95 (abbrev. **RV**)
revitalize (Brit. also **revitalise**)
reviver person or thing that revives
revivor hist. proceeding to revive a lawsuit
revoke cancel (a decree) ◻ **revocable, revocation, revocatory, revoker**
Revolution, the 1 cap. in ref. to a particular revolution depending on context **2** class struggle in Marxism
revolutionize (Brit. also **revolutionise**)
revue light theatrical entertainment; cf. **review**
rewritable (not **-eable**)
Rex (cap.) **1** reigning king (after a name or in the titles of lawsuits) **2** cat with curly fur
Reykjavik capital of Iceland
Reynard name for a fox (cap.; not **Ren-**)
Reynolds, Sir Joshua (1723–92), English painter
Rf the chemical element rutherfordium (no point)
RF radio frequency
RFA Royal Fleet Auxiliary
RFC 1 request for comment **2** hist. Royal Flying Corps **3** Rugby Football Club
RFP request for proposal
Rg the chemical element roentgenium (no point)
RGN Registered General Nurse
RGS Royal Geographical Society
Rh (no point) **1** rhesus (factor) **2** the chemical element rhodium
r.h. right hand
RHA Royal Horse Artillery
rhachis use **rachis**
Rhadamanthine showing inflexible justice, like **Rhadamanthus**, ruler in the underworld in Greek mythology
Rhaeto-Romance (also **Rhaeto-Romanic**) group of Romance dialects (caps, hyphen)
rhapsodize (Brit. also **rhapsodise**)
rhatany astringent root extract
rhebok (also **reebok**) small South African antelope (not **rhebuck**)
Rheims var. of **Reims**
Rhein Ger. name for **Rhine**
Rheingold, Das first part of Wagner's *Der Ring des Nibelungen* (1869)
Rheinland Ger. name for **Rhineland**
Rheinland-Pfalz Ger. name for **Rhineland-Palatinate**
Rhenish of the Rhine
rhenium chemical element of atomic number 75 (symbol **Re**)
rheostat electrical instrument for controlling a current
rhesus factor antigen on the red blood cells (abbrev. **Rh**)
rhesus monkey (also **rhesus macaque**)
rhesus-negative, rhesus-positive (hyphen)
Rhine river in western Europe; Ger.

name **Rhein**, Fr. name **Rhin**
Rhineland region of western Germany; Ger. name **Rheinland**
Rhineland-Palatinate state of western Germany; Ger. name **Rheinland-Pfalz**
rhinestone imitation diamond (lower case)
rhino pl. same or **rhinos**
rhinoceros pl. same or **rhinoceroses**
rhizome horizontal underground stem
rho seventeenth letter of the Greek alphabet (**Ρ**, **ρ**), transliterated as 'r'
Rhode Island state in the north-eastern US (official and postal abbrev. **RI**) □ **Rhode Islander**
Rhodes Greek island in the SE Aegean; mod. Gk name **Ródhos**
Rhodesia territory in southern Africa now divided into Zambia and Zimbabwe □ **Rhodesian**
Rhodes Scholarship scholarship at Oxford University (caps) □ **Rhodes scholar**
rhodium chemical element of atomic number 45 (symbol **Rh**)
rhododendron evergreen flowering shrub
rhombus pl. **rhombuses** or **rhombi** parallelogram with oblique angles and parallel sides
Rhondda district of South Wales
Rhône river in SW Europe
Rhône-Alpes region of SE France
rhotic pronouncing *r* before consonants and at the ends of words
RHS 1 Royal Historical Society **2** Royal Horticultural Society **3** Royal Humane Society
rhubarb plant with edible stalks
rhumb imaginary line on the earth's surface; point of the compass
rhumba var. of **rumba**
rhyme correspondence of sounds; cf. **rime**
rhythm pattern of movement or sound
rhythm and blues (abbrev. **R & B**)
RI 1 King and Emperor or Queen and Empress [L. *Rex et Imperator* or *Regina et Imperatrix*] **2** Rhode Island **3** Royal Institute (or Institution)
RIA Royal Irish Academy
rial (also **riyal**) **1** monetary unit of Iran and Oman **2** (usu. **riyal**) monetary unit of Saudi Arabia, Qatar, and Yemen
Rialto island in Venice
RIBA Royal Institute of British Architects
riband arch. ribbon (one *b*; see also **blue riband**)
ribbon (two *b*s)
ribcage (one word)
rib-eye cut of steak (hyphen)
riboflavin (also **riboflavine**) vitamin of the B complex
Ric. Richard (regnal year)
Ricardo, David (1772–1823), English political economist □ **Ricardian**
rice paper (two words)
ricercar (also **ricercare**) pl. **ricercars** or **ricercari** Mus. elaborate contrapuntal composition (not ital.)
Richard, Sir Cliff (b.1940), British pop singer; born *Harry Roger Webb*
Richard I (1157–99), king of England 1189–99; known as **Richard Coeur de Lion** or **Richard the Lionheart**
Richards 1 I(vor) A(rmstrong) (1893–1979), English literary critic **2** Keith (b.1943), English guitarist of the Rolling Stones **3** (Isaac) Vivian (b.1952), West Indian cricketer
Richelieu, Armand Jean du Plessis, duc de (1585–1642), French cardinal and statesman
Rich. II Shakespeare's *King Richard the Second*
Rich. III Shakespeare's *King Richard the Third*
Richter scale scale for the magnitude of an earthquake (one cap.)
Richthofen, Manfred, Freiherr von (1882–1918), German fighter pilot; known as **the Red Baron**
rickets disease caused by vitamin D deficiency (one *t*)
rickettsia pl. **rickettsiae** or **rickettsias** small bacterium causing typhus etc. (two *t*s)
rickety (one *t*)
rickshaw light vehicle drawn by a person (not **ricksha**)
ricochet v. (**ricocheting**, **ricocheted** or **ricochetting**, **ricochetted**)
ricotta soft white Italian cheese

RICS Royal Institution of Chartered Surveyors
riddance (two *ds*)
rideable (not **-able**)
ridge piece, ridge pole, ridge tent, ridge tile, ridge tree (two words)
ridgeway road along a ridge; (**the Ridgeway**) prehistoric trackway in southern England (one word)
Riefenstahl, Leni (1902–2003), German film-maker and photographer
riel monetary unit of Cambodia
Riemann, (Georg Friedrich) Bernhard (1826–66), German mathematician □ **Riemannian**
Riesling white-wine grape
rietbok S. Afr. var. of **reedbuck**
Rievaulx ruined abbey in North Yorkshire
riff-raff (hyphen)
rifle range, rifle shot (two words)
Rif Mountains (also **Er Rif**) mountain range of northern Morocco (one *f*)
Riga capital of Latvia
rigadoon lively dance for couples [Fr. *rigaudon*]
rigatoni pasta in the form of short fluted tubes (not **-one**)
right 1 direction (abbrev. **r** or **rt**) **2** (**the Right**) right-wing people (cap., treated as sing. or pl.)
right angle (two words) □ **right-angled**
Right Bank district of Paris (caps)
righteous morally right
right hand (two words, hyphen when attrib.; abbrev. **r.h.**)
right-handed, right-hander (hyphen)
right-hand man (one hyphen)
Right Honourable title given to Privy Counsellors and government ministers (caps)
Right Reverend title of bishops (abbrev. **Rt Revd** or **Rt Rev.**)
right wing (two words, hyphen when attrib.) □ **right-winger**
rigor 1 sudden shivering **2** US var. of **rigour**
rigor mortis stiffening of the body after death (not ital.)
rigorous (not **rigour-**)
rigour (US **rigor**) thoroughness
Rig Veda oldest of the Sanskrit Vedas
Rijksmuseum art gallery in Amsterdam
rijsttafel selection of rice dishes
Riksmål another name for **Bokmål**
rilievo see **relievo**
Rilke, Rainer Maria (1875–1926), Austrian poet; pseudonym of *René Karl Wilhelm Josef Maria Rilke*
rill small stream
rille (also **rill**) narrow fissure on the moon
Rimbaud, (Jean Nicholas) Arthur (1854–91), French poet
rime 1 frost **2** arch. var. of **rhyme**
Rime of the Ancient Mariner, The poem by Coleridge (1798)
Rimsky-Korsakov, Nikolai (Andreevich) (1844–1908), Russian composer
rinderpest infectious cattle disease
ring-a-ring o' roses children's singing game (two hyphens, apostrophe)
Ring des Nibelungen, Der see ***Nibelungenlied***
ringdove (one word)
ring fence (two words, hyphen as verb)
ringgit pl. same or **ringgits** monetary unit of Malaysia
ringleader (one word)
ringletted (double *t*)
ringmaster (one word)
ring pull, ring road (two words)
ringside, ringtone, ringworm (one word)
Rio de Janeiro state and city of eastern Brazil
Río de la Plata Sp. name for the **River Plate**
Rio Grande river of North America
Rio Grande do Norte, Rio Grande do Sul states of Brazil
Rioja wine from La Rioja, Spain
Riot Act, the (caps)
RIP 1 raster image processor **2** *requiescat in pace, requiescant in pace* (rest in peace)
ripcord (one word)
ripieno pl. **ripienos** or **ripieni** body of accompanying musicians in baroque music (not ital.)

rip-off n. (hyphen, two words as verb)
riposte quick clever reply
rip-roaring (hyphen)
rip tide (two words)
Rip Van Winkle hero of a story in Washington Irving's *Sketch Book* (1819–20)
rishi pl. **rishis** Hindu sage or saint
risible laughable
Risorgimento 19th-cent. movement for the unification of Italy (cap., not ital.)
risotto pl. **risottos** rice dish (one *s*, two *ts*)
risqué slightly indecent (accent, not ital.)
rissole fried savoury patty
ristorante pl. ***ristoranti*** Italian restaurant (ital.)
rit. Mus. ritardando; ritenuto
ritardando pl. **ritardandos** or **ritardandi** another term for **rallentando** (abbrev. **rit.**)
rite de passage pl. ***rites de passage*** rite of passage (Fr., ital.)
ritenuto pl. **ritenutos** or **ritenuti** Mus. (with) an immediate reduction of speed (abbrev. **rit.**)
rite of passage (three words)
ritornello pl. **ritornellos** or **ritornelli** Mus. short instrumental interlude in a vocal work
ritualize (Brit. also **ritualise**)
rival v. (**rivalling, rivalled**; US one **-l-**)
river 1 natural waterway (usu. cap. after the specific name, e.g. *Yellow River*; styles vary when it precedes the specific name) **2** track of white space down a printed page, the result of bad word-spacing
riverbank, riverboat, riverside (one word)
rivet v. (**riveting, riveted**)
riviera subtropical coastal region; (**the Riviera**) the Mediterranean coast near the border between France and Italy
rivière necklace of gems increasing in size (Fr., ital.)
Riyadh capital of Saudi Arabia
riyal var. of **rial**
RL rugby league
rly railway
RM 1 Royal Mail **2** Royal Marines
rm 1 ream **2** room
RMA Royal Military Academy
RMP Royal Military Police
r.m.s. root mean square
RMT National Union of Rail, Maritime, and Transport Workers
RN 1 Registered Nurse **2** Royal Navy
Rn the chemical element radon (no point)
RNA ribonucleic acid
RNAS Royal Naval Air Station
RNLI Royal National Lifeboat Institution
road (cap. in names; abbrev. **Rd**)
roadbed, roadblock (one word)
road fund licence (three words)
road hog (two words)
roadholding, roadhouse, roadkill (one word)
road manager, road map, road movie, road pricing, road rage (two words)
roadrunner, roadshow, roadside (one word)
road sign, road tax (two words)
road test n. (two words, hyphen as verb)
roadway, roadworks, roadworthy (one word)
roan soft sheepskin leather used in bookbinding
roaring forties the stormy ocean tracts between latitudes 40° and 50° south (lower case)
Robbe-Grillet, Alain (1922–2008), French novelist
Robben Island island off the coast of South Africa
Robbia see **della Robbia**
Robert the Bruce king of Scotland 1306–29
Robespierre, Maximilien François Marie Isidore de (1758–94), French revolutionary
Robin Goodfellow mischievous sprite or goblin
Robin Hood semi-legendary English medieval outlaw
robin redbreast (lower case)
Robinson, (William) Heath (1872–1944), English cartoonist and illustrator

Robinson Crusoe hero of Daniel Defoe's novel *Robinson Crusoe* (1719)
Rob Roy (1671–1734), Scottish outlaw, hero of Sir Walter Scott's novel *Rob Roy* (1817); born *Robert Macgregor*
ROC Royal Observer Corps
roc (also **rukh**) mythical bird in the *Arabian Nights*
roche moutonnée pl. ***roches moutonnées*** small outcrop of rock (Fr., ital.)
Rock, the Gibraltar
rock and roll (also **rock 'n' roll**) (three words even when attrib.) □ **rock and roller**
rock bottom n. (two words, hyphen when attrib.)
rock climbing (two words) □ **rock-climb, rock climber**
rock crystal (two words)
Rockefeller, John D(avison) (1839–1937), American industrialist and philanthropist
rocket v. (**rocketing, rocketed**)
rock face (two words)
rockfall, rockfish (one word)
rock garden (two words)
Rockies the Rocky Mountains
rocking chair, rocking horse, rocking stone (two words)
rock 'n' roll var. of **rock and roll**
rock plant, rock pool, rock salt (two words)
rockslide (one word)
rock solid (two words, hyphen when attrib.)
rococo elaborate baroque style of decoration (lower case; two single *c*s)
rodeo pl. **rodeos**
Rodgers, Richard (Charles) (1902–79), American composer
Ródhos mod. Gk name for **Rhodes**
Rodin, Auguste (1840–1917), French sculptor
rodomontade boastful talk (not **rhod-**)
roebuck (one word)
Roedean boarding school for girls, in southern England
roe deer (two words)
roentgen (also **röntgen**) former unit of radiation (abbrev. **R**)
roentgenium chemical element of atomic number 111 (symbol **Rg**)
Rogation Sunday Sunday preceding the **Rogation Days**, the three days before Ascension Day
Rogers 1 Ginger (1911–95), American actress and dancer; born *Virginia Katherine McMath* **2** Sir Richard (George) (b.1933), British architect
Roget, Peter Mark (1779–1869), English scholar, compiler of *Roget's Thesaurus of English Words and Phrases*, first published in 1852
rogues' gallery (apostrophe after the *s*)
Rohmer, Eric (1920–2010), French film director and critic; born *Jean-Marie Maurice Scherer*
role actor's part [Fr. *rôle*]
role model, role play, role playing, role reversal (two words)
Rolfing massage technique (cap.)
Rolland, Romain (1866–1944), French writer
rollback n. (one word, two words as verb)
roll call (two words)
rollerball trademark in the UK type of ballpoint pen (one word)
Rollerblade trademark in-line skate □ **rollerblader**
roller coaster (two words)
roller skate n. (two words, hyphen as verb) □ **roller skater, roller skating**
rolling pin, rolling stock, rolling stone (two words)
rollmop (one word)
roll-on adj., n. (hyphen, two words as verb)
roll-on roll-off denoting a ferry that vehicles drive directly on and off (two hyphens; abbrev. **ro-ro**)
roll-out n. (hyphen, two words as verb)
rollover n. (one word, two words as verb)
Rolls-Royce luxury car (two caps, hyphen)
roll-top desk (one hyphen)
roly-poly (hyphen)
ROM read-only memory
Rom pl. **Roma** Gypsy
Rom. Epistle to the Romans
rom. roman (type)
Roma 1 It. name for **Rome 2** pl. of **Rom**

Romaic vernacular of modern Greece
romaji romanized spelling system for Japanese
Roman denoting the alphabet used for English and most other European languages (cap.)
roman type of a plain upright kind used in ordinary print (lower case; abbrev. **rom.**)
roman-à-clef pl. ***romans-à-clef*** novel about real people using invented names (Fr., ital.)
Roman Catholic (no hyphen even when attrib.; abbrev. **RC**)
Roman Catholic Church (all caps for the organization or its hierarchy)
Romance (of) the languages descended from Latin (cap.)
romance tale of chivalry or events remote from everyday life; love story (lower case)
Roman de la rose French allegorical poem of the 13th cent.
Rom. & Jul. Shakespeare's *Romeo and Juliet*
Roman Empire (caps)
Romanesque style of architecture before 1200 (cap.)
roman-fleuve pl. ***romans-fleuves*** novel describing the lives of many connected characters; sequence of related novels (Fr., ital.)
Romania (also **Rumania**) country in SE Europe (not **Roumania** (arch.)) □ **Romanian**
Romanic another name for **Romance**
Romanize (also **Romanise**) make Roman Catholic (cap.)
romanize (Brit. also **romanise**) put into roman type or the Roman alphabet (lower case)
Roman numeral letter representing a number, I = 1, V = 5, X = 10, L = 50, C = 100, D = 500, M = 1,000
Romano strong hard cheese
Romanov dynasty that ruled in Russia 1613–1917 (not **-of, -off**)
Romans, Epistle to the book of the New Testament (abbrev. **Rom.**)
Romansh (also **Rumansh**) language spoken in part of Switzerland
Romantic of romanticism (cap.)
romanticism artistic movement emphasizing subjectivity and the individual (lower case)
romanticize (Brit. also **romanticise**)
Romany language of the Gypsies
Rome capital of Italy; It. name **Roma**
Romeo pl. **Romeos** passionate male lover (cap.)
Romeo and Juliet Shakespeare play (abbrev. ***Rom. & Jul.***)
Rome, Treaty of treaty setting up the European Economic Community
Romney, George (1734–1802), English portrait painter
Romney Marsh area in Kent
Ronaldsway airport on the Isle of Man
Roncesvalles 778 battle in northern Spain
rondavel circular African dwelling
ronde circular dance (not ital.)
rondeau pl. **rondeaux** poem with two rhymes throughout and the opening words used twice as a refrain (not ital.)
rondel form of rondeau
rondo pl. **rondos** musical form with a recurring leading theme
rone Sc. roof gutter
Röntgen, Wilhelm Conrad (1845–1923), German physicist
röntgen var. of **roentgen**
roo pl. **roos** kangaroo
roof pl. **roofs** (not **rooves**)
roof garden (two words)
roofscape, rooftop (one word)
rook Chess (abbrev. **R**)
roomful pl. **roomfuls**
rooming house (two words)
room-mate (hyphen)
room service, room temperature (two words)
Roosevelt 1 (Anna) Eleanor (1884–1962), American humanitarian and diplomat **2** Franklin D(elano) (1882–1945), 32nd president of the US 1933–45 **3** Theodore (1858–1919), 26th president of the US 1901–9
root canal, root crop, root directory (two words)
root mean square (three words, hyphen when attrib.; abbrev. **rms**)
root sign Math. the symbol √

rootstock (one word)
root vegetable (two words)
rooves use **roofs**
ropeable (also **ropable**)
rope ladder (two words)
ropeway (one word)
ropy (also **ropey**) (**ropier, ropiest**)
Roquefort trademark in the US blue ewes' milk cheese
ro-ro roll-on roll-off
rorqual baleen whale
Rorschach test psychological test using ink blots
rosaceous of the rose family
Rosalind character in Shakespeare's *As You Like It*
Rosaline character in Shakespeare's *Love's Labour's Lost* and *Romeo and Juliet*
rosarian cultivator of roses
rosarium pl. **rosariums** or **rosaria** rose garden (not ital.)
rosary (beads for counting) a series of Roman Catholic devotions
rosé light pink wine (accent, not ital.)
Roseau capital of Dominica in the Caribbean
rosebay (also **rosebay willowherb**)
Rosebery, Archibald Philip Primrose, 5th Earl of (1847–1929), British prime minister 1894–5
rose bowl (two words)
rosebud (one word)
rose garden, rose hip (two words)
Rosencrantz and Guildenstern characters in Shakespeare's *Hamlet*; ***Rosencrantz and Guildenstern are Dead*** is a play by Tom Stoppard (1966)
Rosencranz, Johann Karl Friedrich (1805–79), German philosopher
Rosencreuz, Christian, see **Rosicrucian**
rose of Jericho (one cap.)
Rosetta Stone inscribed stone found near Rosetta on the Nile (two caps)
rose water, rose window (two words)
rosewood (one word)
Rosh Hashana (also **Rosh Hashanah**) Jewish New Year festival
Roshi pl. **Roshis** leader of a community of Zen Buddhist monks
Rosicrucian member of a 17th- and 18th-cent. occult society, said to have been started by a mythical 15th-cent. knight Christian Rosenkreuz
rosin (**rosining, rosined**) (treat with) a kind of resin
Roskilde port in Denmark
RoSPA Royal Society for the Prevention of Accidents
Rossellini, Roberto (1906–77), Italian film director
Rossetti 1 Christina (Georgina) (1830–94), English poet **2** Dante Gabriel (1828–82), English painter and poet
Rossini, Gioacchino Antonio (1792–1868), Italian composer
Rostand, Edmond (1868–1918), French dramatist
rösti pl. same, grated potato cake (accent, not ital.; not **roesti**)
rostrum pl. **rostra** or **rostrums** raised platform for a speaker
rosy (not **-ey**)
rota 1 Brit. roster **2** (**the Rota**) supreme court of the Roman Catholic Church
Rotary trademark (in full **Rotary International**) society of business and professional people □ **Rotarian**
Rotary club local branch of Rotary (one cap.)
rotary press printing press that prints on paper between rotating cylinders
rotator (not **-er**)
rotavator (also **rotovator**) tilling machine with rotating blades (cap. as trademark)
rote mechanical repetition of something to be learned
Rothko, Mark (1903–70), American painter; born *Marcus Rothkovich*
Rothschild, Meyer Amschel (1743–1812), German financier
rotisserie restaurant specializing in roasts (not ital., no accent) [Fr. *rôtisserie*]
rotogravure printing system using a rotary press with intaglio cylinders
rotor rotary part
rotovator var. of **rotavator**
Rottweiler powerful black-and-tan dog
rotunda round building or room; (**the Rotunda**) the Pantheon in Rome

Rouault, Georges (Henri) (1871–1958), French artist
rouble (also US **ruble**) monetary unit of Russia and some other republics of the former USSR
roué debauched man (accent, not ital.)
Rouen port in NW France
rouge et noir gambling card game (Fr., ital.)
rough and ready, rough and tumble (three words, hyphens when attrib.)
rough breathing see **breathing**
roughcast (one word)
rough-hewn (hyphen)
roughneck (one word)
rough pull proof pulled by hand on inferior paper for correction purposes
rough-rider (hyphen)
roughshod (one word)
roulade dish cooked or served in a rolled shape (not ital.)
rouleau pl. **rouleaux** or **rouleaus** cylindrical packet of coins (not ital.)
Roumania use **Romania**
Roumelia var. of **Rumelia**
roundabout n., adj. (one word, two words as prep. or adv.)
round brackets Brit. brackets of the form ( )
roundel small disc
roundelay simple song with a refrain
Roundhead (cap., one word)
roundhouse (one word)
round robin (two words)
Round Table table around which King Arthur and his knights met
round table assembly for discussion (lower case, hyphen when attrib.)
round-up n. (hyphen, two words as verb)
roundwood, roundworm (one word)
rouseabout Austral./NZ farm labourer (one word); cf. **roustabout**
Rousseau 1 Henri (Julien) (1844–1910), French painter; known as **le Douanier** ('customs officer') **2** Jean-Jacques (1712–78), French philosopher and writer **3** (Pierre Étienne) Théodore (1812–67), French painter
Roussillon former province of southern France, now part of Languedoc-Roussillon
roustabout unskilled or casual labourer; cf. **rouseabout**
rout 1 cause to retreat in disorder **2** find and force from a place
route n. course from one point to another (abbrev. **rte**). v. (**routeing** or **routing, routed**) direct along a route
routier French long-distance lorry driver (Fr., ital.)
Routiers, Les network of independent restaurants, hotels, etc.
routinize (Brit. also **routinise**)
Routledge publishers
roux pl. same, mixture of melted fat and flour (not ital.)
ROV remotely operated vehicle
rowboat N. Amer. rowing boat (one word)
Rowe, Nicholas (1674–1718), English dramatist
rowel (**rowelling, rowelled**; US one **-l-**) (urge on with) a spiked disc at the end of a spur
rowing boat, rowing machine (two words)
Rowling, J(oanne) K(athleen) (b.1965), English novelist
rowlock (one word)
Roxburghe Club exclusive club for bibliophiles
Roxburghshire former county of the Scottish Borders
Royal (cap. in titles; abbrev. **R**)
royal 1 (in full **metric royal**) paper size, 636 × 480 mm **2** royal octavo or quarto
Royal Commission (caps)
royalist supporter of monarchy; (**Royalist**) supporter of the King in the English Civil War
Royal Leamington Spa official name for **Leamington Spa**
royal octavo book size, 234 × 156 mm
royal quarto book size, 312 × 237 mm
Royal Tunbridge Wells official name for **Tunbridge Wells**
Royal Welch Fusiliers, Royal Welch Regiment (not **Welsh**)
RP 1 read for press **2** received pronunciation **3** reprint
RPI retail price index
rpm (also **r.p.m.**) **1** resale price mainten-

ance **2** revolutions per minute
RPO Royal Philharmonic Orchestra
rpt 1 repeat **2** report
RPV remotely piloted vehicle
RRP recommended retail price
RS 1 US received standard **2** Royal Scots
Rs. rupee(s)
r.s. right side
RSA 1 Republic of South Africa **2** Royal Scottish Academy; Royal Scottish Academician **3** Royal Society of Arts
RSC 1 Royal Shakespeare Company **2** Royal Society of Chemistry
RSE Royal Society of Edinburgh
RSFSR Russian Soviet Federative Socialist Republic
RSI repetitive strain injury
RSJ rolled steel joist
RSM Regimental Sergeant Major
RSNC Royal Society for Nature Conservation
RSPB Royal Society for the Protection of Birds
RSPCA Royal Society for the Prevention of Cruelty to Children
RSV Revised Standard Version (of the Bible)
RSVP *répondez s'il vous plaît*, 'please reply' (Fr.)
RT 1 radio-telegraphy **2** radio-telephony **3** received text
rt right
RTA road traffic accident
RTÉ Radio Telefís Éireann
rte route
RTF rich text format
Rt Hon. Right Honourable
Rt Revd (also **Rt Rev.**) Right Reverend
RU rugby union
Ru the chemical element ruthenium (no point)
Rubáiyát of Omar Khayyám, The collection of Persian poetry translated by Edward Fitzgerald (1859)
Rub' al-Khali vast desert in the Arabian peninsula
rubato pl. **rubatos** or **rubati** Mus. deviation from strict tempo
rubberize (Brit. also **rubberise**)
rubberneck (one word)
rubber stamp n. (two words, hyphen as verb)
Rubbra, (Charles) Edmund (1901–86), English composer
rub-down n. (hyphen, two words as verb)
rubella German measles; cf. **rubeola**
Rubenesque (of a woman's figure) full and rounded (not **Rubens-**)
Rubens, Sir Peter Paul (1577–1640), Flemish painter
rubeola measles; cf. **rubella**
Rubicon 1 stream in NE Italy, the boundary between Italy and Cisalpine Gaul **2** point of no return
rubicon decisive win in piquet (lower case)
rubicund ruddy
rubidium chemical element of atomic number 37 (symbol **Rb**)
Rubik's cube trademark plastic cube puzzle
Rubinstein 1 Anton (Grigorevich) (1829–94), Russian composer and pianist **2** Artur (1888–1982), Polish-born pianist **3** Helena (1882–1965), Polish-born beautician
ruble var. of **rouble**
rubric heading on a document
RUC hist. Royal Ulster Constabulary
ruche frill or decorative pleat
rucksack (one word)
rue (**rueing** or **ruing**, **rued**) bitterly regret
ruffe (also **ruff**) freshwater fish
rufiyaa pl. same, monetary unit of the Maldives
rufous reddish brown
Rugbeian member of Rugby School
rugby (also **rugby football**) (lower case)
rugby league (lower case; abbrev. **RL**)
rugby union (lower case; abbrev. **RU**)
Ruhr region in western Germany
Ruisdael (also **Ruysdael**), Jacob van (*c.*1628–82), Dutch landscape painter
rukh another term for **roc**
Rule, Britannia (comma)
Rumania var. of **Romania**
Rumansh var. of **Romansh**
rumba (also **rhumba**) (**rumbas**, **rumbaing**, **rumbaed** or **rumba'd**)
Rumelia (also **Roumelia**) territories in

Europe which formerly belonged to the Ottoman Empire
rumen pl. **rumens** or **rumina** ruminant's first stomach
rumour (US **rumor**)
rumour-monger (US **rumormonger**)
Rumpelstiltskin dwarf in German folklore
Rump Parliament the part of the Long Parliament which continued to sit after Pride's Purge in 1648
rumpus pl. **rumpuses**
runabout light vehicle for short journeys (one word)
runaround, the evasive treatment (one word)
runaway n., adj. (one word, two words as verb)
runcible spoon curved fork with outer prong for cutting (lower case)
rundown 1 analysis or summary **2** (usu. **run-down**) neglected; in poor condition; rather unwell
rune letter of an ancient Germanic alphabet □ **runic**
run-in n. (hyphen)
runner-up pl. **runners-up** (hyphen)
running foot (also **running footline**) text at the bottom of each page of a book or chapter
running head (also **running headline**) text at the top of each page of a book or chapter
running mate (two words)
Runnymede meadow on the south bank of the Thames where King John signed Magna Carta in 1215
run-off n. (hyphen, two words as verb)
run-of-the-mill adj. (hyphens, four words as noun)
run-on adj. without a break or new paragraph (hyphen, two words as verb)
run-out n. (hyphen, two words as verb)
run-through n. brief outline or summary (hyphen, two words as verb)
runtime (one word)
run-up n. (hyphen, two words as verb)
runway (one word)
Runyon, (Alfred) Damon (1884–1946), American writer
rupee monetary unit of India, Pakistan, Sri Lanka, Nepal, Mauritius, and the Seychelles
Rupert's Land (also **Prince Rupert's Land**) historical region of Canada (apostrophe)
rupiah monetary unit of Indonesia
ruralize (Brit. also **ruralise**)
Ruritania imaginary kingdom in central Europe in the novels of Anthony Hope (1863–1933) □ **Ruritanian**
Rushdie, (Ahmed) Salman (b.1947), Indian-born British novelist
rus in urbe illusion of countryside in a city (L., ital.)
Ruskin, John (1819–1900), English art and social critic
Russell 1 Bertrand (Arthur William), 3rd Earl Russell (1872–1970), British philosopher **2** John, 1st Earl Russell (1792–1878), British prime minister 1846–52 and 1865–6
Russell Group association of some UK universities (caps)
Russia country in northern Asia and eastern Europe; official name **Russian Federation**
Russia leather durable calfskin leather used in bookbinding
Russian Orthodox Church, **Russian Revolution** (caps)
Russian roulette (one cap.)
rustproof (one word)
rutabaga N. Amer. swede
Ruth book of the Old Testament (no abbrev.)
ruthenium chemical element of atomic number 44 (symbol **Ru**)
rutherfordium chemical element of atomic number 104 (symbol **Rf**)
Rwenzori (also **Ruwenzori**) mountain range in central Africa
Ruysdael var. of **Ruisdael**
RV Revised Version (of the Bible)
Rwanda country in central Africa; official name **Rwandese Republic** □ **Rwandan**
Ry Railway
Ryder Cup golf tournament
ryegrass (one word)
ryokan traditional Japanese inn
Ryukyu Islands chain of Japanese islands in the western Pacific

S

S 1 pl. **Ss** or **S's** 19th letter of the alphabet **2** pl. **SS** (esp. in Catholic use) Saint **3** siemens **4** South or Southern **5** the chemical element sulphur **6** Svedberg(s)

s 1 Math. (in formulae) distance **2** second(s) **3** Law section (of an act) **4** Gram. singular **5** Chem. solid **6** (in genealogies) son(s) **7** succeeded

s. shilling(s)

's 1 abbrev. of Du. *des* 'of the', as in *'s-Gravenhage* (The Hague) **2** arch. (in oaths) God's: *'sblood*

$ dollar(s) (placed before figures, closed up)

SA 1 Salvation Army **2** (Sp.) *sociedad anónima*, (Port.) *sociedade anónima*, (Fr.) *société anonyme*, public limited company **3** South Africa **4** South America **5** South Australia **6** *Sturmabteilung* (the Brownshirts)

s.a. *sine anno* (without date)

Saar river of Germany and France; Fr. name **Sarre**

Saarbrücken city in western Germany

Saarland state of western Germany

Sabaean member of an ancient Semitic people

Sabah state of Malaysia

sabbatarian (lower case)

Sabbath day of religious observance and rest (cap.)

saber US var. of **sabre**

Sabine member of an ancient people in Italy

Sabin vaccine vaccine against poliomyelitis

sabot wooden shoe (not ital.)

sabra Jew born in Israel

sabre (US **saber**)

sabretooth (also **sabre-toothed tiger**; US **sabertooth** or **saber-toothed tiger**)

sabreur cavalryman or fencer using a sabre (not ital.)

SAC Senior Aircraftman

sac hollow structure

saccharin artificial sweetener

saccharine 1 excessively sweet or sentimental **2** another term for **saccharin**

saccharometer hydrometer for measuring sugar content (not **-imeter**)

sachem American Indian chief

Sachertorte pl. ***Sachertorten*** Viennese chocolate gateau (Ger., ital.)

Sachsen Ger. name for **Saxony**

sackbut early form of trombone

sackcloth (one word)

sack race (two words)

Sackville-West, Vita (1892–1962), English writer; full name *Victoria Mary Sackville-West*

Sacramento state capital of California

sacré bleu expression of surprise, dismay, etc. (Fr., ital.)

Sacred College the College of Cardinals

sacrilege (not **sacre-**, **-lige**)

sacrilegious (not **-religious**, **-riligious**)

SACW Senior Aircraftwoman

SAD seasonal affective disorder

Sadat, (Muhammad) Anwar al- (1918–81), Egyptian president 1970–81

Saddam Hussein see **Hussein**

saddleback, saddlebag, saddlecloth (one word)

saddle horse, saddle shoe, saddle soap (two words)

saddle-sore adj. (hyphen, two words as noun)

saddle stitch, saddle tree (two words)

Sadducee member of a Jewish sect at the time of Christ □ **Sadducean**

Sade, Donatien Alphonse François, Comte de (1740–1814), French writer; known as the **Marquis de Sade**

sadhu Hindu sage or ascetic

Sadler's Wells Theatre London theatre (one *d*)

sadomasochism (one word; abbrev. **SM**)

sae stamped addressed envelope
safari pl. **safaris**
safe conduct (two words)
safe deposit (two words, hyphen when attrib.)
safeguard (one word)
safekeeping (one word)
safety deposit (two words, hyphen when attrib.)
S. Afr. South Africa(n)
saga long story of heroic achievement; medieval prose narrative in Old Norse or Old Icelandic
saggar (also **sagger**) protective box used in making ceramics
Sagittarius ninth sign of the zodiac (two *ts*) □ **Sagittarian**
sago pl. **sagos** edible starch
saguaro pl. **saguaros** giant cactus (not **sahuaro**)
Sahara Desert (also **the Sahara**) desert in North Africa
Sahel semi-arid region of North Africa □ **Sahelian**
sahib Ind. polite term of address for a man (cap. in titles)
Saigon city in Vietnam; official name **Ho Chi Minh City**
sailboard, sailboat, sailcloth (one word)
sailer vessel of a specified power or manner of sailing; cf. **sailor**
sailing boat, sailing ship (two words)
sailmaker (one word)
sailor person who sails; cf. **sailer**
sailplane glider designed for sustained flight (one word)
sainfoin fodder plant
Sainsbury's UK supermarket chain, **J Sainsbury plc** (apostrophe)
saint (cap. in titles; abbrev. **S** or **St**)
St Albans, St Andrews UK towns (no apostrophe)
St Andrew's cross X-shaped cross (apostrophe)
St Anne's College Oxford (apostrophe)
St Anselm etc. see **Anselm, St**
St Anthony's cross T-shaped cross (apostrophe)
St Anthony's fire the skin disease erysipelas (apostrophe)
St Antony's College Oxford (apostrophe)
St Bartholomew's Day Massacre (caps, apostrophe)
St Benet's Hall college affiliated to Oxford University (apostrophe)
St Bernard large breed of dog
St Bernard Pass either of two passes across the Alps, the **Great St Bernard Pass**, on the Swiss–Italian border, and the **Little St Bernard Pass**, on the French–Italian border
St Catharine's College Cambridge (apostrophe)
St Catherine's College Oxford (apostrophe)
St Christopher and Nevis, Federation of official name for **St Kitts and Nevis**
St Clements non-alcoholic cocktail (no apostrophe)
St Cross College Oxford
St David's small city in SW Wales (apostrophe); Welsh name **Tyddewi**
Saint-Denis (hyphen) **1** suburb of Paris **2** capital of Réunion
Sainte-Beuve, Charles Augustin (1804–69), French writer (hyphen)
St Edmund Hall Oxford college
St Edmund's College Cambridge (apostrophe)
St Elmo's fire electrical phenomenon during storms (apostrophe)
St-Émilion claret (hyphen)
St-Estèphe claret (hyphen)
St-Étienne city in SE central France (hyphen)
St Eustatius island in the Caribbean
Saint-Exupéry, Antoine (Marie Roger de) (1900–44), French writer and aviator
St George's capital of Grenada (apostrophe)
St George's Channel channel between Wales and Ireland (apostrophe)
St George's cross +-shaped cross (apostrophe)
St Gotthard Pass pass in the Alps in Switzerland
St Helena island in the South Atlantic □ **St Helenian**
St Helens town in NW England (no apostrophe)

St Helens, Mount active volcano in the state of Washington
St Helier capital of Jersey
St James's Palace royal palace in London (apostrophe)
St John 1 island in the Caribbean **2** city in New Brunswick, eastern Canada
St John Ambulance voluntary organization (not **St John's**)
St John's (apostrophe) **1** capital of Antigua and Barbuda **2** capital of Newfoundland
St John's College Oxford, Cambridge
St John's wort plant or shrub with yellow flowers (two caps)
St-Julien claret (hyphen)
St Kilda island group of the Outer Hebrides
St Kitts and Nevis country in the Caribbean consisting of two islands (no apostrophe; official name **Federation of St Christopher and Nevis**)
Saint Laurent, Yves (Mathieu) (1936–2008), French couturier
St Lawrence River river of North America
St Leger annual flat horse race
St Louis city in eastern Missouri
St Lucia country in the Caribbean □ **St Lucian**
St Luke's summer period of fine weather in October (apostrophe)
St Malo coastal town in Brittany
St Mark's Cathedral cathedral church of Venice
St Martin small island in the Caribbean
St Martin-in-the-Fields London church (hyphens)
St Martin's summer period of fine weather in November (apostrophe)
St Moritz resort in SE Switzerland
St-Nazaire town in NW France (hyphen)
St Paul state capital of Minnesota
saintpaulia African violet
St Paul's Cathedral cathedral on Ludgate Hill, London
St Peter Port town in Guernsey (not **St Peter's**)
St Petersburg seaport in NW Russia; former names **Petrograd, Leningrad**
St Peter's fish (apostrophe)
St Pierre and Miquelon group of French islands in the North Atlantic
St Pölten city in NE Austria
Saint-Saëns, (Charles) Camille (1835–1921), French composer
Saint-Simon 1 Claude-Henri de Rouvroy, Comte de (1760–1825), French social reformer and philosopher **2** Louis de Rouvroy, Duc de (1675–1755), French writer
St Sophia monument of Byzantine architecture in Istanbul; also called **Hagia Sophia, Santa Sophia**
St Stephens name for the House of Commons (no apostrophe)
St Swithin's Day 15 July (apostrophe)
St Thomas island in the Caribbean
St Trinian's fictional girls' school (apostrophe)
St-Tropez resort on the coast of southern France (hyphen)
St Vincent, Cape headland in SW Portugal
St Vincent and the Grenadines island state in the Caribbean
St Vitus's dance (apostrophe)
saith arch. (he or she) says
saithe fish of the cod family
Saiva member of one of the main branches of Hinduism □ **Saivite**
sake Japanese fermented drink
Sakharov, Andrei (Dmitrievich) (1921–89), Russian nuclear physicist and civil rights campaigner
Saki (1870–1916), British writer; pseudonym of *Hector Hugh Munro*
saki pl. **sakis** tropical American monkey
Sakti var. of **Shakti**
salaam (gesture of) greeting (not ital.)
salable US var. of **saleable**
salad cream, salad days, salad dressing (two words)
salade another name for **sallet**
salade niçoise pl. ***salades niçoises*** salad with tuna, hard-boiled eggs, and olives (Fr., ital.)
Saladin (1137–93), sultan of Egypt and Syria 1174–93; Arab. name *Salah-ad-Din Yusuf ibn Ayyub*
salami pl. same or **salamis**

Salamis island to the west of Athens
Salammbô novel by Flaubert (1862)
salariat salaried white-collar workers
salaryman (one word)
saleable (US **salable**)
Salem 1 state capital of Oregon **2** city in NE Massachusetts **3** city in Tamil Nadu
saleroom (one word)
salesman, salesperson, salesroom, saleswoman (one word)
Salic law law excluding females from dynastic succession
salient most noticeable or important
Salieri, Antonio (1750–1825), Italian composer
Salinger, J(erome) D(avid) (1919–2010), American writer
Salisbury 1 city in Wiltshire, southern England **2** former name for **Harare**
sallet hist. light helmet
Sallust (86–35 BC), Roman historian and politician; Latin name *Gaius Sallustius Crispus*
Sally Lunn teacake (caps)
salmagundi pl. **salmagundis** dish of seasoned chopped meat
salmanazar large wine bottle (lower case)
salmi pl. **salmis** rich game casserole
salmon trout (two words)
Salomon Brothers US investment bank (not **Sol-**)
salon 1 reception room **2** (**Salon**) annual art exhibition in Paris
Salon des Refusés 1863 Paris exhibition displaying pictures rejected by the Salon (Fr., ital.)
Salonica former name for **Thessaloníki**
Salop former name for **Shropshire** □ **Salopian**
salopettes padded trousers worn for skiing
salpicon chopped mixture bound in a thick sauce (not ital.)
salsa 1 Latin American dance music **2** spicy sauce
salsa verde sauce made with parsley etc. (not ital.)
salsify edible plant
SALT Strategic Arms Limitation Talks
saltarello pl. **saltarellos** or **saltarelli** Italian or Spanish dance (not ital.)
salt cellar, salt fish (two words)
saltimbocca dish of rolled veal or poultry (not ital.)
Salt Lake City capital of Utah (three caps)
salt lick, salt marsh, salt pan (two words)
saltpetre (US **saltpeter**) (one word)
salt water (two words, one word when attrib.)
saluki pl. **salukis** tall swift dog
salutary beneficial (not **-ory**)
salutatory of the nature of a salutation
Salvador 1 port in eastern Brazil **2** see **El Salvador**
Salvadorean (also **Salvadorian**) of El Salvador
salvageable (not **-gable**)
Salvation Army (abbrev. **SA**)
Salvationist member of the Salvation Army
salver tray; cf. **salvor**
salvo pl. **salvos** or **salvoes** simultaneous discharge of guns
sal volatile smelling salts
salvor person engaged in salvage; cf. **salver**
salwar (also **shalwar**) trousers worn by women from the Indian subcontinent
Salzburg city in Austria
Salzkammergut resort area in Austria
SAM surface-to-air missile
Sam. Samuel (in biblical references)
Samara city in SW central Russia
Samaritan 1 (usu. **good Samaritan**) charitable person **2** (**the Samaritans**) organization assisting suicidal people
samarium chemical element of atomic number 62 (symbol **Sm**)
Samarkand (also **Samarqand**) city in eastern Uzbekistan
Samarra city in Iraq
samba v. (**sambaing, sambaed** or **samba'd**)
Sam Browne belt with a shoulder strap
sambuca aniseed-flavoured liqueur
S. Amer. South America(n)
samey (**samier, samiest**) □ **sameyness**
Samhain 1 November, a Celtic festival
Sami (pl.) a people of northern Scandinavia; the term by which the Lapps prefer to be known

Samian of Samos
samisen (also **shamisen**) Japanese lute
samite hist. rich silk fabric
samizdat clandestine publication of banned material (not ital.)
Samnite member of an ancient people of southern Italy
Samoa group of Polynesian islands divided between American Samoa and the state of Samoa □ **Samoan**
Samos Greek island in the Aegean
Samoyed member of a people of northern Siberia
sampan small boat used in the Far East
samphire edible plant
samsara (in Hunduism and Buddhism) the material world; the cycle of life and rebirth
samskara Hindu purificatory ceremony
Samson exceptionally strong Israelite
Samuel 1 Hebrew prophet **2** either of two books of the Old Testament (abbrev. **1 Sam.**, **2 Sam.**)
samurai pl. same or **samurais**, member of a military caste in feudal Japan
SAN storage area network
San (also **Santo**) Spanish and Italian title for a male saint
Sana'a (also **Sanaa**) capital of Yemen
San Andreas fault fault line through California (two caps)
sanatorium pl. **sanatoriums** or **sanatoria**
sanatory conducive to health; cf. **sanitary**
Sancerre French white wine (cap.)
Sancho Panza squire of Don Quixote
sanctum pl. **sanctums** sacred or private place
sanctum sanctorum pl. **sancta sanctorum** or **sanctum sanctorums** holy of holies in the Jewish temple (not ital.)
Sand, George (1804–76), French novelist; pseudonym of *Amandine-Aurore Lucille Dupin*
sandal light shoe □ **sandalled** (US **sandaled**)
sandalwood (one word)
sandarac gum resin
sandbag, sandbank, sandbar, sandblast, sandboy, sandcastle (one word)
sand eel, sand flea (two words)
sandhi Gram. process whereby the form of a word changes as a result of its position
sandhill, sandhopper (one word)
Sandhurst training college for officers for the British army
Sandinista member of a left-wing organization in Nicaragua
sandpaper, sandpiper, sandpit, sandstone, sandstorm (one word)
sandwich (not **-witch**)
sandwich board, sandwich course (two words)
San Francisco city on the coast of California (not **-sisco**) □ **San Franciscan**
sangar (also **sanga**) small protected military structure
sang-de-boeuf deep red colour on Chinese porcelain (Fr., ital.)
sangfroid composure or coolness under pressure (one word, not ital.)
sangha the Buddhist monastic order
Sangiovese Italian red wine (cap.)
sanguinary bloody, involving bloodshed
sanguine cheerfully optimistic
sanguineous arch. of or containing blood
Sanhedrin (also **Sanhedrim**) highest court of justice in ancient Jerusalem
sanitarium pl. **sanitariums** or **sanitaria** US var. of **sanatorium**
sanitary of conditions affecting hygiene and health; cf. **sanatory**
sanitaryware (one word)
sanitize (Brit. also **sanitise**)
San Jose city in western California
San José capital of Costa Rica
San Juan capital of Puerto Rico
San Marino tiny republic within Italy
sannyasi (also **sanyasi** or **sannyasin**) pl. same, Hindu mendicant
sans without (Fr., ital.)
San Salvador capital of El Salvador
sans-culotte lower-class republican during the French Revolution (not ital.)
sansevieria (also **sanseveria**) plant in the agave family
Sanskrit (abbrev. **Skt**)
sans serif style of type without serifs

(two words; not **san serif**)
Santa Italian, Spanish, and Portuguese title for a female saint (abbrev. **Sta**)
Santa Ana 1 city and volcano in El Salvador **2** city in southern California
Santa Claus (not **Klaus**)
Santa Fe (also **Santa Fé**) **1** state capital of New Mexico **2** city in northern Argentina
Santa Fé de Bogotá official name for **Bogotá**
Santander port in northern Spain
Santa Sophia another name for **St Sophia**
Santayana, George (1863–1952), Spanish philosopher and writer; born *Jorge Augustin Nicolás Ruiz de Santayana*
santeria Afro-Cuban religious cult
Santiago capital of Chile
Santiago de Compostela city in NW Spain
Santiago de Cuba port in SE Cuba
santim monetary unit of Latvia
Santo var. of **San** or **São**
Santo Domingo capital of the Dominican Republic
sanyasi var. of **sannyasi**
São (also **Santo**) Portuguese title for a male saint
Saône river of eastern France
São Paulo state and city of southern Brazil
São Tomé and Príncipe country consisting of two main islands and several smaller ones in the Gulf of Guinea
sapper military engineer; soldier in the corps of Royal Engineers (cap. in titles; abbrev. **Spr**)
Sapphic of Sappho (cap.)
sapphic of lesbians or lesbianism (lower case)
sapphism lesbianism (lower case)
Sappho (early 7th cent. BC), female Greek lyric poet
Sapporo city in northern Japan (two *p*s)
SAR search and rescue
saraband (also **sarabande**) stately Spanish dance
Saragossa city in northern Spain; Sp. name **Zaragoza**
Sarajevo capital of Bosnia-Herzegovina
sarape var. of **serape**
Sarawak state of Malaysia
sarcenet var. of **sarsenet**
sarcoma pl. **sarcomas** or **sarcomata** malignant tumour
sarcophagus pl. **sarcophagi** stone coffin
Sardinia Italian island; It. name **Sardegna**
Sargasso Sea region of the western Atlantic Ocean
sargassum (also **sargasso**) brown seaweed
Sargent 1 John Singer (1856–1925), American painter **2** Sir (Henry) Malcolm (Watts) (1895–1967), English conductor
sari (also **saree**) pl. **saris** or **sarees**
sarin nerve gas
sarong piece of cloth wrapped round the body and tucked in
saros Astron. period of about eighteen years between repetitions of eclipses
Sarre Fr. name for **Saar**
sarrusophone wind instrument similar to a saxophone
SARS severe acute respiratory syndrome
sarsaparilla flavouring for drinks (not **sarspa-**)
sarsen boulder used for prehistoric monuments
sarsenet (also **sarcenet**) silk fabric
Sartre, Jean-Paul (1905–80), French philosopher and writer
Sarum old name for Salisbury, still used for its diocese
SAS Special Air Service
SASE self-addressed stamped envelope
Saskatchewan 1 province of central Canada (abbrev. **Sask.**) **2** river of Canada
Saskatoon city in south central Saskatchewan
sassafras North American tree
Sassanian (also **Sasanian** or **Sassanid**) member of a Persian dynasty ruling 3rd cent. AD–651
Sassenach Sc., Ir. English person
Sassoon, Siegfried (Lorraine) (1886–1967), English writer

SAT pl. **SATs** **1** standard assessment task **2** US trademark Scholastic Aptitude Test
Sat. Saturday
Satan the Devil (cap.)
satanic, satanism (lower case)
satay (also **saté**) Indonesian and Malaysian dish of meat on a skewer
SATB Mus. soprano, alto, tenor, bass
satcom satellite communications
sateen glossy cotton fabric
satellite (two *l*s)
Sati Hinduism wife of Shiva
sati (also **suttee**) pl. **satis** or **suttees** Indian widow's act of throwing herself on her husband's funeral pyre
Satie, Erik (Alfred Leslie) (1866–1925), French composer
satinette (also **satinet**) fabric similar to satin
satire use of humour, exaggeration, or ridicule to expose stupidity or vice ◻ **satiric, satirical**
satirize (Brit. also **satirise**)
satisfice do the minimum required
satnav navigation using satellite information
satrap provincial governor in the ancient Persian empire
satrapy province governed by a satrap
Satsuma **1** former province of SW Japan **2** pottery from Satsuma
satsuma kind of tangerine (lower case)
Saturday (abbrev. **Sat.**)
Saturn **1** Rom. Mythol. ancient god; Gk equivalent **Cronus** **2** sixth planet from the sun ◻ **Saturnian**
Saturnalia (treated as sing. or pl.) **1** ancient Roman festival of Saturn **2** (**saturnalia**) occasion of wild revelry ◻ **saturnalian**
saturnine gloomy in character (lower case)
Saturn V launch vehicle for the Apollo space missions of 1968–72
satyagraha passive resistance as advocated by Gandhi (not ital.)
satyr lustful drunken Greek woodland god ◻ **satyric**
saucepan (one word)
saucier chef who prepares sauces (Fr., ital.)
saucisson French sausage (ital.)
Saudi pl. **Saudis** person from Saudi Arabia; member of its ruling dynasty
Saudi Arabia country in SW Asia ◻ **Saudi Arabian**
sauerkraut pickled cabbage (not ital.)
Saumur French sparkling wine (cap.)
sausage dog, sausage meat, sausage roll (two words)
Saussure, Ferdinand de (1857–1913), Swiss linguistics scholar
sauté (**sautéing, sautéed** or **sautéd**) (accent)
Sauternes sweet white French wine from Sauternes (cap.)
sauve qui peut general stampede (ital.) [Fr., 'let him save himself who can']
Sauveterrian early Mesolithic culture of Europe
Sauvignon (also **Sauvignon Blanc**) white wine (cap.)
savable var. of **saveable**
Savai'i (also **Savaii**) largest of the Samoan islands
Savannah port in Georgia (US)
savannah (also **savanna**) grassy plain
savant learned person (not ital.)
savante learned woman (not ital.)
saveable (also **savable**)
Savile Row London street known for its tailors
savin type of juniper
savings account, savings bank, savings certificate (one word)
saviour (US **savior**)
savoir faire ability to act or speak appropriately (Fr., ital.)
Savonarola, Girolamo (1452–98), Italian religious reformer
savory **1** culinary herb **2** US var. of **savoury**
savour (US **savor**)
savoury (US **savory**)
Savoy area of SE France ◻ **Savoyard**
savoy cabbage with densely wrinkled leaves (lower case)
saw (past part. **sawn** or chiefly N. Amer. **sawed**) cut with a saw
sawbones pl. same, informal doctor or surgeon (one word)

sawdust, sawhorse, sawmill (one word)
sawn-off (N. Amer. **sawed-off**)
sawtooth (also **sawtoothed**) adj. (one word)
sax 1 saxophone **2** (also **zax**) small saw for roof tiles
saxe light blue colour
Saxe-Coburg-Gotha name of the British royal house 1901–17
Saxony state and former kingdom of Germany; Ger. name **Sachsen**
saxony fine kind of wool (lower case)
saxophone wind instrument (not **saxa-**)
SAYE save as you earn
say-so n. (hyphen)
Sb the chemical element antimony (no point) [L. *stibium*]
SBS Special Boat Service (or Section)
SC 1 South Carolina **2** special constable **3** supercalendered
Sc the chemical element scandium (no point)
s.c. small capital(s)
***sc.* 1** *scilicet* **2** *sculpsit*
scabies contagious skin disease
scabious plant of the teasel family
scabrous scabby; indecent
Scafell Pike mountain in the Lake District
scagliola plasterwork imitating stone (not ital.)
scalable (also **scaleable**)
scalar having only magnitude, not direction
scalawag N. Amer. var. of **scallywag**
scald v. injure with hot liquid or steam. n. var. of **skald**
scaler person or thing that scales
Scaliger 1 Joseph Justus (1540–1609), French scholar **2** Julius Caesar (1484–1558), Italian-born French scholar and physician
scallion N. Amer. long-necked onion
scallop mollusc (not **scollop**)
scalloped having a decorative edging
scallywag (N. Amer. also **scalawag**)
scaly (not **-ey**)
scampi (treated as sing. or pl.)
scandalize (Brit. also **scandalise**)
Scandinavia peninsula in NW Europe (not **Scanda-**)
scandium chemical element of atomic number 21 (symbol **Sc**)
scansion rhythm of a line of verse
Scapa Flow strait in the Orkney Islands
scapegoat, scapegrace (one word)
scaramouch arch. boastful but cowardly person
Scarborough port in North Yorkshire (not **-brough**)
scarecrow, scaremonger (one word)
scare quotes quotation marks around an unusual or arguably inaccurate use
scarf pl. **scarves** or **scarfs** covering for the neck or head ▫ **scarfed** (also **scarved**)
scarlatina (also **scarletina**) scarlet fever
Scarlatti 1 (Pietro) Alessandro (Gaspare) (1660–1725), Italian composer **2** (Giuseppe) Domenico (1685–1757), Italian composer, his son
Scarlet Pimpernel assumed name of the hero of novels by Baroness Orczy
scarlet pimpernel small plant with scarlet flowers (lower case)
Scart socket for connecting video equipment (one cap.)
scarves pl. of **scarf**
scary (not **-ey**)
scatology preoccupation with excretion; cf. **eschatology**
scatterbrain, scattergun, scattershot (one word)
scazon another term for **choliamb**
ScD (also **Sc.D.**) Doctor of Science [L. *Scientiae Doctor*]
SCE Scottish Certificate of Education
scena scene in an Italian opera (not ital.)
scenario pl. **scenarios**
sceptic, sceptical (N. Amer. **skeptic, skeptical**) lower case even with ref. to ancient philosophers
sceptre (US **scepter**)
sch. 1 scholar **2** school **3** schooner
Schadenfreude malicious glee in others' misfortunes (Ger., cap., ital.)
schappe fabric from waste silk
schedule list of events and their times
scheduled caste official name in India for the lowest caste
Scheele, Carl Wilhelm (1742–86), Swedish chemist

Scheherazade 1 narrator of the *Arabian Nights* **2** (***Scheherazade***) symphonic suite by Rimsky-Korsakov (1888) **3** (***Schéhérazade***) song cycle with music by Ravel (1903)

Scheldt (also **Schelde**) river of northern Europe; Fr. name **Escaut**

schema pl. **schemata** or **schemas** outline or model of a plan or theory

schematize (Brit. also **schematise**)

schemozzle var. of **shemozzle**

Schengen agreement European agreement on border controls

scherzando pl. **scherzandos** or **scherzandi** Mus. (passage played) in a playful manner

scherzo pl. **scherzos** or **scherzi** Mus. vigorous, light, or playful composition

Schiaparelli 1 Elsa (1896–1973), Italian-born French fashion designer **2** Giovanni Virginio (1835–1910), Italian astronomer

Schiele, Egon (1890–1918), Austrian artist

Schiller, (Johann Christoph) Friedrich von (1759–1805), German writer

schilling former monetary unit of Austria

Schindler, Oskar (1908–74), German industrialist

schipperke small black tailless dog

schism split or division

schist coarse-grained rock

schizophrenia mental disorder

Schlegel, August Wilhelm von (1767–1845), German poet and critic

schlemiel N. Amer. informal stupid or hapless person

schlep (also **schlepp**) (**schlepping**, **schlepped**) N. Amer. informal walk or carry with difficulty

Schleswig-Holstein state of NW Germany (hyphen)

Schlick, Moritz (1882–1936), German philosopher and physicist

Schliemann, Heinrich (1822–90), German archaeologist

schlock N. Amer. informal inferior material, rubbish

schloss castle in Germany or Austria (not ital.; cap. in names)

schmaltz excessive sentimentality (not **-lz**)

schmuck N. Amer. informal contemptible person

schnapps strong alcoholic spirit

schnauzer German breed of dog

schnitzel thin slice of veal; see also **Wiener schnitzel**

Schoenberg, Arnold (1874–1951), Austrian-born American composer

scholar (abbrev. **sch.**)

Scholar-Gipsy, The poem by Matthew Arnold (1853)

scholasticism (lower case)

scholiast hist. commentator on ancient or classical literature

scholium pl. **scholia** hist. scholiast's marginal note or explanatory comment

school (abbrev. **sch.**; cap. in names)

school age (two words, hyphen when attrib.)

schoolboy, schoolchild, schooldays, schoolfellow, schoolgirl, schoolhouse (one word)

school inspector (also **schools inspector**) (two words)

school-leaver (hyphen)

school-leaving age (one hyphen)

schoolman, schoolmaster, schoolmate, schoolmistress, schoolroom, schoolteacher (one word)

school year (two words)

Schopenhauer, Arthur (1788–1860), German philosopher

schottische slow polka (not ital.)

Schröder, Gerhard (b.1944), Chancellor of Germany 1998–2005

Schrödinger, Erwin (1887–1961), Austrian theoretical physicist

schtum var. of **shtum**

Schubert, Franz (Peter) (1797–1828), Austrian composer

Schulz, Charles (1922–2000), American cartoonist

Schumacher 1 E(rnst) F(riedrich) (1911–77), German economist and conservationist **2** Michael (b.1969), German racing driver

Schumann, Robert (Alexander) (1810–56), German composer

schuss Skiing (make) a straight downhill run

Schütz, Heinrich (1585–1672), German composer
Schutzstaffel Nazi SS (Ger., cap., ital.)
schwa unstressed vowel, as in *a*go (IPA symbol ə; not **sheva, shwa**)
Schwaben Ger. name for **Swabia**
Schwäbisch Gmünd city in SW Germany
Schwann, Theodor Ambrose Hubert (1810–82), German physiologist
Schwarzenegger, Arnold (b.1947), Austrian-born American actor and politician
Schwarzkopf, Dame (Olga Maria) Elisabeth (Friederike) (1915–2006), German operatic soprano
Schwarzwald Ger. name for the **Black Forest**
Schweinfurt city in western Germany
Schweitzer, Albert (1875–1965), German theologian and medical missionary
Schweiz Ger. name for **Switzerland**
Schwerin city in NE Germany
Schwyz canton and city in Switzerland
sciagraphy (also **skiagraphy**) use of shading to show perspective
sciatica pain affecting the back and hip
Scientology trademark (cap.)
sci-fi science fiction (hyphen)
scilicet that is to say, namely (L., ital.; abbrev. ***sc.***)
Scilly Isles (also **Isles of Scilly** or **the Scillies**) group of islands off the south-western tip of England □ **Scillonian**
scimitar sword with a curved blade
scintilla tiny trace or spark
scintillate (two *l*s)
scion (not **cion**) **1** young shoot or twig **2** descendant of a notable family
scirocco var. of **sirocco**
SCM 1 State Certified Midwife **2** Student Christian Movement
Scolar Press publishers (not **Scholar**)
SCONUL Society of College, National, & University Libraries
scordatura altering the normal tuning of a stringed instrument (It., ital.)
score Bookbinding break the surface of a board to help folding
scoreboard, **scorecard**, **scoreline**, **scoresheet** (one word)
scoria pl. **scoriae** fragment of basaltic lava (not ital.) □ **scoriaceous**
Scorpio eighth sign of the zodiac □ **Scorpian**
Scot person from Scotland
Scot. Scotland; Scottish
scot and lot hist. tax levied by a municipal corporation
Scotch Scottish; use only in fixed compounds such as *Scotch broth* and *Scotch mist*, and as noun meaning *Scotch whisky*; do not use of people
Scotchgard trademark preparation for giving a waterproof finish
Scotch tape trademark transparent adhesive tape
scot-free (lower case, hyphen)
Scoticism var. of **Scotticism**
Scotland Office UK government department (not **Scottish Office**)
Scots (of) the form of English used in Scotland; Scottish
Scotsman, **Scotswoman** (not **Scotch-**)
Scots pine, **Scots fir** (not **Scotch**)
Scott 1 Sir George Gilbert (1811–78), English architect **2** Sir Giles Gilbert (1880–1960), English architect, his grandson
Scotticism (also **Scoticism**) Scottish word or expression
Scottie Scottish terrier
Scottish of Scotland (the usual word; abbrev. **Sc.**); cf. **Scotch, Scots**
Scottish Borders council area of southern Scotland
Scouse dialect or accent of Liverpool
Scouser person from Liverpool
Scout member of the Scout Association
scout person sent ahead to gather information
Scout Association worldwide youth organization fostering self-sufficiency
Scouter adult in the Scout Association
scoutmaster male leader of a group of Scouts (official term **Scout leader**)
SCPO Senior Chief Petty Officer
SCPS Society of Civil and Public Servants
SCR Senior Common (or Combination) Room

Scrabble trademark board game involving building up words
scrapbook (one word)
scrap dealer (two words)
scrapheap (one word)
scrapie disease of sheep
scrap merchant, scrap metal, scrap paper (two words)
scrapyard (one word)
scratch card, scratch pad (two words)
screenplay (one word)
screen print n. design produced by forcing ink through a prepared screen (two words, hyphen as verb)
screen saver (two words)
screen test (two words, hyphen as verb)
screenwash, screenwriter (one word)
screwball, screwdriver (one word)
screw top (two words, hyphen when attrib.) □ **screw-topped**
screw-up n. (hyphen, two words as verb)
Scriabin (also **Skryabin**), Aleksandr (Nikolaevich) (1872–1915), Russian composer and pianist
script 1 handwriting as distinct from print **2** printed type imitating handwriting **3** written text of a play or film
scriptorium pl. **scriptoria** or **scriptoriums** room set apart for writing
scriptural (lower case)
scripture cap. in ref. to the body of Judaeo-Christian sacred writings
scriptwriter (one word)
scroll bar (two words)
scrollwork (one word)
Scrooge 1 Ebenezer, miserly curmudgeon in Charles Dickens's *A Christmas Carol* (1843) **2** mean person
scrotum pl. **scrota** or **scrotums**
scruple hist. weight equal to 20 grains
scrutinize (Brit. also **scrutinise**)
SCSI small computer system interface
scuba-dive (hyphen) □ **scuba diver** n., **scuba diving** n. (two words)
Scud missile (one cap.)
scullcap (one word)
sculpsit he or she sculpted (it) (L., ital.; abbrev. ***sc.***)
sculpt create as sculpture (not **sculp**)
sculptor person who sculpts (not **-er**)
Scylla Gk Mythol. sea monster across a channel from the whirlpool Charybdis
Scythia ancient region of SE Europe and Asia
SD South Dakota (postal abbrev.)
sd sewed (of books)
s.d. *sine die*
S.Dak. South Dakota (official abbrev.; no space)
SDI US Strategic Defense Initiative
SDLP Social Democratic and Labour Party
SDP Social Democratic Party
SE south-east(ern)
Se the chemical element selenium (no point)
SEA Single European Act
sea (cap. in names)
sea bass (two words)
seabed, seabird, seaboard (one word)
seaborgium chemical element of atomic number 106 (symbol **Sg**)
seaborne (one word)
sea bream, sea breeze, sea captain (two words)
SeaCat trademark large catamaran used as a ferry (one word, two caps)
sea change, sea chest, sea cow, sea cucumber, sea eagle (two words)
seafarer, seafaring, seafood, seafront, seagoing (one word)
sea green (two words, hyphen when attrib.)
seagull (one word)
sea holly, sea horse (two words)
Sea Island cotton (three words, two caps)
seakale (one word)
SEAL (also **Seal**) member of an elite force within the US Navy
sea lane, sea legs, sea level (two words)
sealing wax (two words)
sea lion, sea loch (two words)
Sea Lord either of two senior officers in the Royal Navy (caps)
sealpoint markings on a Siamese cat (one word)
sealskin (one word)
Sealyham wire-haired terrier
seaman (one word)
sea mile (two words)
seamstress woman who sews (not **sempstress**)

Seanad (also **Seanad Éireann**) upper House of Parliament in Ireland
seance an attempt to contact the dead [Fr. *séance*]
Sea of Azov, Sea of Galilee, etc. see **Azov, Sea of; Galilee, Sea of,** etc.
seaplane, seaport (one word)
sea power (two words)
SEAQ Stock Exchange Automated Quotations
sear (also **sere**) withered
search engine (two words)
searchlight (one word)
search party, search warrant (two words)
sea room, sea salt (two words)
seascape (one word)
Sea Scout member of the maritime branch of the Scout Association (caps)
sea serpent, sea shanty (two words)
seashell, seashore, seasick, seaside (one word)
sea slug, sea snail, sea snake (two words)
seasonable usual for or appropriate to a particular season
seasonal relating to a particular season; fluctuating or restricted according to the season
seasonal affective disorder (abbrev. **SAD**)
seasons, names of lower case except when personified or addressed
season ticket (two words)
SEAT Spanish make of car
seat belt (two words)
SEATO South East Asia Treaty Organization
sea trout (two words)
Seattle city in the state of Washington
sea urchin, sea wall (two words)
seawater, seaway, seaweed, seaworthy (one word)
Sebastopol naval base in Ukraine; Ukrainian and Russ. name **Sevastopol**
Sebat (also **Shebat, Shevat**) (in the Jewish calendar) the fifth month of the civil and eleventh of the religious year
SEC US Securities and Exchange Commission
Sec. Secretary
sec¹ secant
sec² (of wine) dry (not ital.)
sec. second(s) (no point in scientific work)
SECAM television system in France and eastern Europe [Fr. *séquentiel couleur à mémoire*]
secateurs pruning clippers
secco painting on dry plaster (not ital.)
Sechuana var. of **Setswana**
second SI unit of time (abbrev. **s, sec.**; no point in scientific work; symbol ″)
Second Adar see **Adar**
second best, second class (two words, hyphen when attrib.)
Second Coming Chr. Theol. the prophesied return of Christ (caps)
second-degree (hyphen)
seconde Fencing parrying position
second-guess (hyphen)
second-hand 1 previously owned **2** (in **at second hand**) by hearsay
second hand hand of a clock (two words)
second in command (three words)
Second Isaiah name for **Deutero-Isaiah**
second lieutenant (cap. in titles)
secondo pl. **secondi** Mus. lower part in a duet
second-rate (hyphen)
Second Reich the German Empire, 1871–1918
Second World War 1939–45 war (caps; also called **World War II**)
secretaire small writing desk (not ital.)
secretariat permanent administrative department
secretary general pl. **secretary generals** (two words)
Secretary of State (caps) **1** head of a major UK government department **2** head of the US State Department **3** Canadian minister responsible for a specific area within a department
secrete 1 discharge **2** hide
section (abbrev. **s, sect.**)
section mark mark § (plural §§) used e.g. as a mark for footnotes or to indicate a section of a book
secularize (Brit. also **secularise**)

secund Bot. arranged on one side only
Securitate internal security force of Romania 1948–89
securitize (Brit. also **securitise**)
Seder Jewish ceremony at the beginning of Passover
sederunt Sc. sitting of an assembly (not ital.)
Sedgemoor 1685 battle on the plain of Sedgemoor in Somerset
sedilia (sing. **sedile**) stone seats in a church for the clergy
see often ital. in indexes and reference books to distinguish it from the words being treated
seedbed (one word)
seed cake, seed capital, seed corn (two words)
seedeater (one word)
seed head, seed money, seed pearl, seed potato (two words)
seedsman (one word)
Seeing Eye dog N. Amer. trademark guide dog (three words, two caps)
See of Rome the Holy See
see-saw (hyphen)
seethe boil, bubble (not **seeth**)
see-through transparent (hyphen)
segue (**segueing, segued**) (make) an uninterrupted transition
seguidilla Spanish dance in triple time
Sehnsucht wistful longing (Ger., cap., ital.)
seicento the 17th century in Italy (not ital.)
seiche disturbance in water level
seif long narrow sand dune
seigneur (also **seignior**) feudal lord
seigniorage (also **seignorage**) government profit made by issuing currency
seigniory (also **seigneury**) feudal lordship
Seine river of northern France
seine vertical fishing net
seisin (also **seizin**) freehold possession
seismic of earthquakes
sei whale small rorqual
seize (not **-ie-**) **1** grab **2** (**be seized of** or **be seised of**) be in legal possession of
Sekt German sparkling white wine (cap., ital.)
Selangor state of Malaysia
Selborne, The Natural History of book by Gilbert White (1789)
selector (not **-er**)
Selene Gk Mythol. goddess of the moon
selenium chemical element of atomic number 34 (symbol **Se**)
self- forms hyphenated compounds exc. in *selfmate, selfsame*
self-conscious (hyphen, but *unselfconscious*)
selfmate chess problem (one word)
Selfridges UK department stores (no apostrophe)
selfsame (one word)
Seljuk Turkish ruler of Asia Minor 11th–13th cents □ **Seljukian**
Selkirkshire former county of SE Scotland
Sellafield site of a nuclear power station in Cumbria
sell-by date (one hyphen)
sell-off n. (hyphen, two words as verb)
Sellotape trademark transparent adhesive tape
sell-out, sell-through n. (hyphen, two words as verb)
selvedge (chiefly N. Amer. also **selvage**) edge preventing woven fabric from unravelling
SEM scanning electron microscope
semantics branch of linguistics and logic concerned with meaning (usu. treated as sing.)
semasiology branch of knowledge concerned with meanings and the terms that represent them
semblance (not **-ence**)
semeiology, semeiotics use **semiology, semiotics**
Semele Gk Mythol. mother, by Zeus, of Dionysus
semi pl. **semis 1** Brit. semi-detached house **2** semi-final **3** N. Amer. semi-trailer
semi-acoustic, semi-annual (hyphen)
semiaquatic (one word)
semi-automatic, semi-autonomous, semi-basement (hyphen)
semibold typeface with strokes less thick than bold (one word)
semibreve, semicircle, semicircular (one word)

semi-classical (hyphen)
semicolon punctuation mark (;) indicating a pause more pronounced than that of a comma (one word)
semiconducting, semiconductor (one word)
semi-conscious, semi-cylinder, semi-darkness (hyphen)
semidemisemiquaver another term for **hemidemisemiquaver** (one word)
semi-deponent, semi-detached, semi-final, semi-fluid, semi-literate (hyphen)
Sémillon white wine (cap.)
semimetal, semimetallic (one word)
semi-modal, semi-monthly, semi-official (hyphen)
semiology another term for **semiotics** (not **semeiology**)
semi-opaque (hyphen)
semiotics study of signs and symbols (treated as sing.; not **semeiotics**)
semi-permanent (hyphen)
semipermeable (one word)
semi-precious, semi-pro, semi-professional (hyphen)
semiquaver (one word)
semi-retired, semi-skilled, semi-skimmed, semi-solid (hyphen)
semitone (one word)
semi-trailer, semi-transparent (hyphen)
semivowel (one word)
semper fidelis always faithful (L., ital.)
semplice Mus. in a simple style
sempre Mus. always, throughout
sempstress use **seamstress**
Semtex plastic explosive (cap.)
SEN State Enrolled Nurse
Sen. 1 Senate **2** Senator **3** Senior
sen pl. same, monetary unit of Brunei, Cambodia, Malaysia, and Indonesia, and formerly of Japan
senate (cap. in names; abbrev. **Sen.**)
senator (cap. in titles; abbrev. **Sen.**)
senatus consultum pl. ***senatus consulta*** decree of the ancient Roman senate (L., ital.)
send-off, send-up n. (hyphen, two words as verb)
sene pl. same or **senes** monetary unit of Samoa
Seneca 1 Lucius Annaeus (*c.*4 BC–AD 65), Roman statesman, philosopher, and dramatist; known as **Seneca the Younger 2** Marcus (or Lucius) Annaeus (*c.*55 BC–*c.*39 AD), Roman rhetorician; known as **Seneca the Elder**
Senegal country in West Africa
□ **Senegalese**
seneschal steward of a medieval great house
senhor (pl. **senhores**) Portuguese man, Mr (cap. in titles; abbrev. **Sr**)
senhora Portuguese married or mature woman, Mrs (cap. in titles; abbrev. **Sra**)
senhorita Portuguese unmarried or young woman or girl, Miss (cap. in titles; abbrev. **Srta**)
senior (abbrev. **Snr, Sr, Sen.**, or **Senr**)
senior master sergeant (cap. in titles; abbrev. **SMSgt**)
Senior Service the Royal Navy (caps)
seniti pl. same, monetary unit of Tonga
sennet trumpet call (in Elizabethan stage directions)
sennight arch. week
sennit 1 plaited straw etc. for hats **2** var. of **sinnet**
Señor pl. **Señores** Spanish man, Mr (cap.; abbrev. **Sr**)
Señora Spanish married or mature woman, Mrs (cap.; abbrev. **Sra**)
Señorita Spanish unmarried or young woman or girl, Miss (cap.; abbrev. **Srta**)
Senr Senior
sensa pl. of **sensum**
sensationalize (Brit. also **sensationalise**)
sensei pl. same, (in Japan) teacher (not ital.)
sensitize (Brit. also **sensitise**)
sensor detecting or measuring device (not **-er**)
sensual gratifying the physical senses; cf. **sensuous**
sensu lato in the broad sense (L., ital.)
sensum pl. **sensa** sense datum (not ital.)
sensuous relating to the senses rather than the intellect; cf. **sensual**

sensu stricto strictly speaking, in the narrow sense (L., ital.)
sente pl. **lisente** monetary unit of Lesotho
sentence adverb adverb expressing an attitude to the content of the sentence
sentimentalize (Brit. also **sentimentalise**)
Seoul capital of South Korea
separate (not **-erate**) □ **separable, separator**
Sephardi pl. **Sephardim** Jew of Iberian descent □ **Sephardic**
sepoy hist. Indian soldier under European command
seppuku (in Japan) hara-kiri (not ital.)
Sept. 1 September **2** Septuagint
sept subdivision of a clan
septa pl. of **septum**
September (abbrev. **Sept.**)
September 11 date in 2001 on which airliners were flown into the World Trade Center and the Pentagon; also called **9/11**
septennial recurring every seven years (two *ns*)
septennium pl. **septennia** or **septenniums** period of seven years (two *ns*)
septet group of seven musicians
septicaemia (US **septicemia**) blood poisoning
septillion pl. **septillions** or (with numeral) same, 10^{24} or, formerly, 10^{42}
septime Fencing parrying position
septuagenarian person between 70 and 79
Septuagesima third Sunday before Lent
Septuagint Greek version of the Old Testament including the Apocrypha (abbrev. **LXX, Sept.**)
septum pl. **septa** partition between two bodily chambers
sepulchre (US **sepulcher**)
seq. pl. **seqq.** (in) what follows (not ital.) [L. *sequens*, (pl.) *sequentes*]
sequel work that continues the story
sequela pl. **sequelae** condition arising from a previous disease or injury
sequoia California redwood
ser. series
sera pl. of **serum**
seraglio pl. **seraglios 1** harem **2** (**the Seraglio**) the Sultan's court at Constantinople
serai another term for **caravanserai**
serape (also **sarape**) shawl or blanket worn as a cloak by Latin Americans
seraph pl. **seraphim** or **seraphs**
Serb person from Serbia
Serbia republic in the Balkans, formerly part of Yugoslavia; Serbian name **Srbija**
Serbian Slavic language of Serbia, written in the Cyrillic alphabet
Serbo-Croat (also **Serbo-Croatian**) Serbian and Croatian treated as a single language (use the more specific terms in present-day contexts)
Sercial Madeira made from the Sercial grape
sere var. of **sear**
sergeant (cap. in titles; abbrev. **Sgt**; see also **serjeant**)
sergeant-at-arms var. of **serjeant-at-arms**
sergeant major (two words, caps in titles; abbrev. **SM**)
serial 1 story or play in regular instalments **2** (**serials**) periodicals (in a library)
serial comma comma when used before 'and' at the end of lists, e.g. the second comma in *red, white, and blue*
serialize (Brit. also **serialise**)
seriatim one after another, point by point (not ital.)
series pl. same (abbrev. **ser.**)
serif slight projection finishing off a stroke of a letter □ **serifed**
serio-comic (hyphen)
serjeant sergeant in the Foot Guards (cap. in titles)
serjeant-at-arms (also **sergeant-at-arms**) pl. **serjeants-at-arms** official of a legislative assembly (hyphens)
serjeant-at-law pl. **serjeants-at-law** hist. barrister of the highest rank (hyphens)
sermonize (Brit. also **sermonise**)
serpent large snake; (**the Serpent**) biblical name for Satan

serpentine like a snake; (**the Serpentine**) lake in Hyde Park, London
SERPS state earnings-related pension scheme
serum pl. **sera** or **serums**
serviceable (not **-cable**)
serviceman, servicewoman (one word)
service provider (two words)
servingman, servingwoman (two words)
servo pl. **servos** servomechanism or servomotor
servomechanism powered mechanism with higher energy output than energy input (one word)
servomotor motive element in a servomechanism (one word)
sesame plant with edible seeds; see also **open sesame**
Sesotho Bantu language
sesquicentenary (also **sesquicentennial**) one-hundred-and-fiftieth anniversary
sesquipedalian polysyllabic
sesterce pl. **sesterces** or **sestertii** ancient Roman coin
sestet last six lines of a sonnet
set Printing **1** amount of spacing in type controlling the distance between letters **2** width of a piece of type; cf. **sett**
set-aside n. (hyphen, two words as verb)
setback n. (one word, two words as verb)
set-off unwanted transference of ink from one printed sheet or page to another (hyphen)
Setswana (also **Sechuana**) Bantu language
sett 1 badger's burrow **2** granite paving block
settler person who settles in a place
settlor person who makes a legal settlement
set-to n. pl. **set-tos** (hyphen, two words as verb)
set-up n. (hyphen, two words as verb)
Seurat, Georges Pierre (1859–91), French painter
Sevastopol Ukrainian and Russ. name for **Sebastopol**
seven (Roman numeral **vii** or **VII**) □ **sevenfold, seventh**
seven deadly sins pride, covetousness, lust, anger, gluttony, envy, and sloth (lower case)
seven seas all the oceans of the world (conventionally the Arctic, Antarctic, North Pacific, South Pacific, North Atlantic, South Atlantic, and Indian Oceans) (lower case)
seventeen (Roman numeral **xvii** or **XVII**) □ **seventeenth**
Seventh-Day Adventist member of a strict Protestant sect (three caps, one hyphen)
seventies (also **1970s**) decade (lower case, no apostrophe)
seventy hyphen in compound numbers, e.g. *seventy-one*; Roman numeral **lii** or **LII** □ **seventieth**
Seven Wonders of the World the pyramids of Egypt, the Hanging Gardens of Babylon, the Mausoleum of Halicarnassus, the temple of Artemis at Ephesus, the Colossus of Rhodes, the statue of Zeus at Olympia, and the Pharos of Alexandria (or, in some versions, the walls of Babylon) (caps)
Seven Years War 1756–63 European war (caps, no apostrophe)
severance (not **-ence**)
Seville city in southern Spain; Sp. name **Sevilla**
Sèvres fine French porcelain
sewage waste in sewers
sewerage 1 drainage by sewers **2** US sewage
sewing the sewing of each book section to its neighbours; cf. **stitching**
sewing machine (two words)
sex use **gender** in ref. to social or cultural differences
sexagenarian person between 60 and 69
Sexagesima second Sunday before Lent
sexcentenary six-hundredth anniversary
sexennial recurring every six years (two *ns*)
sexennium pl. **sexennia** or **sexenniums** period of six years (two *ns*)
sextet group of six musicians
sextillion pl. **sextillions** or (with numeral) same, 10^{21} or, formerly, 10^{36}

sexto pl. **sextos** page size resulting from folding a sheet into six leaves (abbrev. **6mo**)
sextodecimo pl. **sextodecimos** page size resulting from folding a sheet into sixteen leaves; sixteenmo (abbrev. **16mo**)
sexualize (Brit. also **sexualise**)
Seychelles (also **the Seychelles**) country consisting of islands in the Indian Ocean ◻ **Seychellois** (pl. same)
Seymour, Jane (*c.*1509–37), third wife of Henry VIII (died)
Sezession (also **Secession**) 19th-cent. German and Austrian art movement
SF 1 San Francisco **2** science fiction **3** Sinn Fein
s.f. *sub finem*
SFA 1 Scottish Football Association **2** Securities and Futures Authority
SFO Serious Fraud Office
sforzando (also **sforzato**) pl. **sforzandos** or **sforzandi** Mus. with sudden emphasis (abbrev. **sf** or **sfz**)
sfumato painting with softened outlines or hazy forms (It., ital.)
SFX special effects
SG 1 Solicitor General **2** specific gravity
Sg the chemical element seaborgium (no point)
sgd signed
SGML Standard Generalized Markup Language
sgraffito pl. **sgraffiti** decoration made by scratching a surface to expose another colour below (not ital.)
's-Gravenhage Du. name for **The Hague**
Sgt Sergeant
sh. shilling(s)
Shaanxi (also **Shensi**) province of central China
shadow-box spar with an imaginary opponent (hyphen)
shadowland (one word)
shagpile (one word)
shagreen sharkskin
shah former monarch of Iran (cap. in titles)
shahada (also ***shahadah***) Muslim profession of faith (ital.)
shaikh var. of **sheikh**
shakeable (also **shakable**)
shakedown n. (one word, two words as verb)
shake-out n. (hyphen, two words as verb)
Shakespeare, William (1564–1616), English dramatist ◻ **Shakespearean** (also **Shakespearian**)
shake-up n. (hyphen, two words as verb)
shako pl. **shakos** military hat
Shakti (also **Sakti**) Hinduism female principle of divine energy ◻ **Saktism**
shaky, shaly (not **-ey**)
shallot small bulb like an onion
shalom Jewish salutation (not ital.)
Shalott, The Lady of poem by Tennyson (1833)
shalwar var. of **salwar**
shaman pl. **shamans**
shamefaced (one word)
shammy (leather) informal term for **chamois**
Shandong (also **Shantung**) province of eastern China
Shanghai city on the east coast of China
shanghai (**shanghaiing, shanghaied**) force to join a ship's crew
Shangri-La Tibetan utopia in James Hilton's novel *Lost Horizon* (1933) (two caps, hyphen)
Shantung var. of **Shandong**
shantung silk dress fabric (lower case)
shanty (arch. or US **chantey** or **chanty**) sailors' work song
shanty town (two words)
Shanxi (also **Shansi**) province of north central China
SHAPE Supreme Headquarters Allied Powers Europe
shapeable (also **shapable**)
shareable (also **sharable**)
sharecropper, shareholder, shareware (one word)
sharia (also **shariah** or **shariat**) Islamic canonical law (not ital.)
sharif descendant of Muhammad through his daughter Fatima (not **shereef** or **sherif**) ◻ **sharifian**
Sharjah member state of the United Arab Emirates; Arab. name **Ash Shariqah**
sharkskin (one word)

sharon fruit persimmon (lower case)
sharp Mus. (sign ♯)
Sharp 1 Becky, character in Thackeray's *Vanity Fair* **2** Cecil (James) (1859–1924), English collector of folk songs
Sharpe 1 Richard, hero of a series of books by Bernard Cornwell **2** Tom (1928–2013), English novelist
Shar Pei pl. **Shar Peis** Chinese breed of dog (two words, caps)
Sharpeville South African township
sharpshooter (one word)
Shatt al-Arab river of SW Asia
Shavian of George Bernard Shaw
Shavuot (also **Shavuoth**) major Jewish festival
Shaw, George Bernard (1856–1950), Irish writer
shaykh var. of **sheikh**
shchi Russian cabbage soup
s/he she or he (closed up)
sheaf pl. **sheaves**
shealing var. of **shieling**
shear (past part. **shorn** or **sheared**) cut off; remove hair etc. from; cf. **sheer**
shearwater seabird (one word)
sheath n. close-fitting cover
sheathe v. put into a sheath
Shebat var. of **Sebat**
shebeen unlicensed place selling alcohol
she-devil (hyphen)
Sheela-na-gig medieval female stone figure
sheep dip (two words)
sheepdog, **sheepfold** (one word)
sheepshank knot for shortening a rope (one word)
sheepskin (one word)
sheer n. **1** unmitigated **2** perpendicular **3** diaphanous. v. swerve or change course; cf. **shear**
sheerlegs hoisting apparatus (one word, treated as sing.)
sheikh (also **shaikh**, **shaykh**, or **sheik**) Arab leader (cap. in titles)
shekel monetary unit of Israel
shelduck pl. same or **shelducks** large duck, the male of which is sometimes called a **sheldrake**
shelf pl. **shelves** □ **shelf-like**
shelf-ful pl. **shelf-fuls**
shelf life, shelf mark, shelf room (two words)
shellac (**shellacks, shellacking, shellacked**) (varnish with) a lac resin
Shelley 1 Mary (Wollstonecraft) (1797–1851), English writer **2** Percy Bysshe (1792–1822), English poet
shellfire, shellfish (one word)
shell-like (hyphen)
shell shock (two words) □ **shell-shocked**
shell suit (two words)
Shelta secret language based on Irish
sheltie (also **shelty**) Shetland pony or sheepdog (lower case)
shelves pl. of **shelf**
shemozzle (also **schemozzle**) chaos or confusion
Shenandoah river of Virginia
shenanigans dishonest activity or manoeuvring
Shensi var. of **Shaanxi**
Shepheardes Calendar, The poem by Spenser (1589) (several subsequent editions have different spellings)
shepherd's pie, shepherd's purse (apostrophe before the *s*)
sherbet (not **-bert**)
shereef, sherif use **sharif**
sheriff (one *r*, two *f*s)
Sherman, William Tecumseh (1820–91), American general
Sherpa pl. same or **Sherpas** member of a Himalayan people
's-Hertogenbosch city in the southern Netherlands
Shetland (also **Shetland Islands**) group of islands off the north coast of Scotland; (**Shetland**) council area of Scotland
sheva use **schwa**
Shevardnadze, Eduard (Amvrosievich) (1928–2014), head of state of Georgia 1992–2003
Shevat var. of **Sebat**
shew old-fashioned and Scots law var. of **show**
shewbread loaves placed in the Jewish Temple
Shia (also **Shi'a, Shiah**) pl. same or **Shias** (adherent of) one of the two main branches of Islam; cf. **Sunni**

shiatsu therapy in which pressure is applied with the hands to certain points on the body
shibboleth custom etc. distinguishing a particular group of people (two *b*s)
shieling (also **shealing**) Highland hut
shift work (two words)
shih-tzu dog with long silky hair (hyphen)
shiitake (also **shitake**) mushroom
Shiite (also **Shi'ite**) adherent of the Shia branch of Islam □ **Shiism**
Shikoku smallest of the four main islands of Japan
shiksa non-Jewish girl or woman
shillelagh thick blackthorn stick
shilling (abbrev. **s.** or **sh.**; symbol /-)
shilly-shally (hyphen)
Shin Bet (also **Shin Beth**) principal security service of Israel
shin bone (two words)
shindy noisy disturbance; lively party
Shinkansen pl. same, Japanese high-speed railway system (cap., not ital.)
shinny N. Amer. informal form of ice hockey
shin pad, shin splints (two words)
Shinto Japanese religion □ **Shintoism**
shinty Scottish game resembling hockey
shiny (not **-ey**)
shipboard (one word)
ship-breaker (hyphen)
shipbroker, shipbuilder, shipload, shipmate, shipowner (one word)
shipping agent, shipping office (two words)
ship's biscuit (apostrophe before the *s*)
shipshape (one word)
ships, names of to be ital.
shipwreck, shipwright, shipyard (one word)
Shiraz 1 city in central Iran **2** grape and red wine
shire county, shire horse (two words)
Shires, the rural parts of England
shirt dress, shirt front (two words)
shirtsleeve (one word)
shirt tail (two words)
shirtwaister (one word)
shish kebab (two words)
shitake var. of **shiitake**
Shiva (also **Siva**) Hindu god
shiva (also **shivah**) Jewish period of mourning (lower case, not ital.)
shivaree US var. of **charivari**
SHM simple harmonic motion
Shoah, the Jewish name for the Holocaust
shock absorber (two words)
shock tactics, shock therapy, shock troops, shock wave (two words)
shoeblack, shoebox, shoehorn, shoelace, shoemaker, shoeshine, shoestring (one word)
shoe tree (two words)
shogun hereditary commander in feudal Japan (cap. in titles)
shooting brake (also **shooting break**) estate car (two words)
shoot-out n. (hyphen, two words as verb)
shopfitter, shopfront, shopkeeper, shoplifting (one word)
shop-soiled (hyphen)
shopworker, shopworn (one word)
shorebird, shoreline (one word)
shorn see **shear**
shortbread, shortcake (one word)
short change, short circuit n. (two words, hyphen as verb)
shortcoming, shortcrust (one word)
shortcut (one word)
short-distance adj. (hyphen)
shortfall, shorthair, shorthand (one word)
short-handed (hyphen)
shorthold, shorthorn, shortlist (one word)
short-lived (hyphen)
short mark breve indicating a short vowel (two words)
short metre metrical pattern for hymns (two words; abbrev. **SM**)
short-sighted, short-sleeved, short-staffed (hyphen)
short term (two words as noun, hyphen as adj.)
short title abbreviated form of the title of a book or document
short ton see **ton**
Shostakovich, Dmitri (Dmitrievich) (1906–75), Russian composer

shotgun (one word)
shot-put, shot-putter, shot-putting (hyphen)
shoulder charge n. (two words, hyphen as verb)
shoulder head (also **shoulder headline**) supplementary running head, usually of section, paragraph, or line numbers, or listing the first and last entry on a page
shoulder note marginal note at the top outer corner of the page
shove-halfpenny (hyphen)
shovel v. (**shovelling, shovelled**; US one **-l-**)
shovelboard (one word)
shoveler (also **shoveller**) **1** kind of duck **2** (Brit. usu. **shoveller**) person or thing that shovels
show (past part. **shown** or **showed**) see also **shew**
showband, showbiz, showboat (one word)
show business (two words)
showcase, showdown (one word)
showerproof (one word)
showgirl, showground (one word)
show home, show house (two words)
showjumping, showman (one word)
show-off n. (hyphen, two words as verb)
showpiece, showplace, showroom (one word)
showstopper (one word)
show time, show trial (two words)
s.h.p. shaft horsepower
shrieval of a sheriff
shrilly in a shrill manner
shrink-fit, shrink-resistant, shrink-wrap (hyphen)
shrivel (**shrivelling, shrivelled**; US one **-l-**)
Shropshire county of England, on the border with Wales
Shrove Tuesday the day before Ash Wednesday, the last of the three days of **Shrovetide**
shtum (also **schtum**) informal silent
shufti pl. **shuftis** quick look or reconnoitre
shutdown n. (one word, two words as verb)
Shute, Nevil (1899–1960), English novelist; pseudonym of *Nevil Shute Norway*
shut-eye (hyphen)
shut-off n. (hyphen, two words as verb)
shutout phase of play in which the opposition is prevented from scoring (one word, two words as verb)
shut-out bid pre-emptive bid in bridge (one hyphen)
shuttlecock (one word)
s.h.v. *sub hac voce* or *sub hoc verbo* 'under this word' [L.]
shwa use **schwa**
shy (**shyer, shyest**) ◻ **shyly, shyness**
Shylock 1 Jewish moneylender in Shakespeare's *Merchant of Venice* **2** extortionate moneylender
shyster unscrupulous lawyer or business person
SI 1 the international system of measurement [Fr. *Système International*] **2** statutory instrument
Si the chemical element silicon (no point)
si Mus. another term for **te**
sialagogue (also **sialogogue**) drug that promotes salivation
Siam former name for **Thailand**
Siamese pl. same, use **Thai** exc. in compounds such as *Siamese cat*
Siamese twins use **conjoined twins**
Sian var. of **Xian**
SIB Securities and Investment Board
Sibelius, Jean (1865–1957), Finnish composer; born *Johan Julius Christian Sibelius*
sibilant hissing speech sound, e.g. *s*
sibyl prophetess in ancient times; cf. **Sybil**
sibylline like a sibyl
Sibylline books collection of oracles in ancient Rome (one cap.)
sic used or spelled as given (ital.; in brackets after a copied or quoted word) [L., 'thus, so']
sice 1 six on dice **2** var. of **syce**
Sichuan (also **Szechuan** or **Szechwan**) province of west central China
Sicilian Vespers massacre of French inhabitants of Sicily in 1282

Sicily Italian island in the Mediterranean; It. name **Sicilia** ◻ **Sicilian**
sick bag (two words)
sickbay, sickbed (one word)
sick building syndrome (three words)
Sickert, Walter Richard (1860–1942), British painter
sick headache, sick leave (two words)
sickle-cell anaemia (one hyphen)
sick-making (hyphen)
sick note, sick pay (two words)
sickroom (one word)
sic transit gloria mundi thus passes the glory of the world (L., ital.)
Siddhartha Gautama see **Buddha**
sidearm (one word) **1** performed with a motion of the arm from the side of the body **2** weapon worn at a person's side
sidebar N. Amer. short newspaper or magazine article alongside and supplementing a longer one (one word)
side bet (two words)
sideboard, sideburn, sidecar (one word)
side chapel, side door, side drum, side effect (two words)
side head heading or subheading set full left to the margin
side issue (two words)
sidekick, sidelamp, sidelight, sideline, sidelong (one word)
side note marginal note
side-on (hyphen)
side road (two words)
side-saddle (hyphen)
side salad (two words)
sideshow, sidestep (one word)
side-splitting (hyphen)
side stream tributary stream (two words)
sidestream smoke cigarette smoke that passes into the air (two words)
side street (two words)
sidestroke, sideswipe (one word)
side table (two words)
sidetrack (one word)
side view (two words)
sidewalk, sidewall, sideways (one word)
side whiskers (two words)
sidewind move in a series of S-shaped curves (one word)
side wind wind blowing from one side (two words)
sidewinder rattlesnake that sidewinds (one word)
Sidgwick & Jackson publishers
Sidney, Sir Philip (1554–86), English poet, courtier, and soldier
SIDS sudden infant death syndrome
siege (not **-ei-**)
Siegfried 1 hero of the first part of the *Nibelungenlied* **2** (***Siegfried***) third part of Wagner's *Der Ring des Nibelungen* (1876)
Siegfried Line German WWII line of defence (caps)
Sieg Heil Nazi victory salute (Ger., caps, ital.)
Siemens German electronics and engineering company
siemens SI unit of conductance (lower case, abbrev. **S**)
Siena city in west central Italy (one *n*) ◻ **Sienese**
sienna earth pigment used in painting (two *ns*)
sierra mountain chain (cap. in names)
Sierra Leone country in West Africa ◻ **Sierra Leonean**
sieve (not **-ei-**)
sievert SI unit of dose equivalent (abbrev. **Sv**)
SIG special interest group
Sig. Signor
sig. pl. **sigs** or **sigs.** signature
sight-read (hyphen)
sightseeing, sightworthy (one word)
sigil symbol with supposed magical power
SIGINT signals intelligence
siglum pl. **sigla** letter or symbol denoting a particular manuscript or text
sigma eighteenth letter of the Greek alphabet (**Σ, σ**), transliterated as 's'
Sig.na Signorina
signal v. (**signalling, signalled**; US one **-l-**) ◻ **signaller**
signal box (two words)

signary syllabic or alphabetic symbols of a language
signatory party to an agreement
signature (abbrev. **sig.**) **1** printed sheet folded into leaves **2** letter or figure on each sheet of a book as a guide to binding **3** Mus. group of sharps and flats after the clef indicating the key
signed (abbrev. **sgd**)
sign language (two words)
sign-off n. (hyphen, two words as verb)
Signor (also **Signore**) pl. **Signori** Italian equivalent of 'Mr' (cap.; abbrev. **Sig.**)
Signora pl. **Signore** Italian married or mature woman, Mrs (cap.; abbrev. **Sig.ra**)
Signorina pl. **Signorine** Italian unmarried or young woman or girl, Miss (cap.; abbrev. **Sig.na**)
signory another term for **seigniory**
signpost, **signwriter** (one word)
Sig.ra Signora
sigs (also **sigs.**) signatures
Sikh member of a monotheistic religion founded in Punjab (cap.) ◻ **Sikhism**
Sikkim state of NE India ◻ **Sikkimese**
Sikorski, Władysław (1881–1943), Polish general and statesman
Sikorsky, Igor (Ivanovich) (1889–1972), Russian-born aircraft designer
silhouette dark shape against a brighter background
silicon chemical element of atomic number 14 (symbol **Si**)
silicone synthetic material used e.g. in breast implants
Silicon Valley area between San Jose and Palo Alto in California
silkworm (one word)
sill (also chiefly Building **cill**)
silo pl. **silos**
Silurian third period of the Palaeozoic era
silvan var. of **sylvan**
silver chemical element of atomic number 47 (symbol **Ag**)
silverback, **silverfish** (one word)
silver Latin literary Latin AD 14–mid second cent. (one cap.)
silverpoint, **silverside**, **silversmith**, **silverware** (one word)
silviculture (also **sylviculture**) the cultivation of trees
SIM smart card inside a mobile phone
simile figure of speech involving a comparison
Simla city in NE India
simon-pure completely genuine (lower case, hyphen)
simoom (also **simoon**) hot dry desert wind
simpatico likeable; compatible (not ital.)
simpliciter simply, unconditionally (L., ital.)
simulacrum pl. **simulacra** or **simulacrums** image, representation
simulator (not **-er**)
simultaneous (not **-ious**)
sin sine (no point)
Sinai 1 peninsula in NE Egypt **2** (**Mount Sinai**) mountain in the south of Sinai ◻ **Sinaitic**
Sinbad the Sailor (also **Sindbad**) hero of a tale in the *Arabian Nights*
Sind province of SE Pakistan
Sindhi pl. **Sindhis** person from Sind
sine Math. (abbrev. **sin**)
sine anno without a date (L., ital.; abbrev. ***s.a.***)
sine die with no appointed date for resumption (L., ital.; abbrev. ***s.d.***)
sine loco, anno, vel nomine without the place, year, or name (L., ital.; abbrev. ***s.l.a.n.***)
sine loco et anno without the place and date, without an imprint (L., ital.; abbrev. ***s.l.e.a.***)
sine nomine without a (printer's) name (L., ital.; abbrev. ***s.n.***)
sine qua non essential condition (L., ital.)
sinfonia symphony; baroque overture
sinfonia concertante 18th-cent. concerto
sinfonietta short symphony
sing. singular
singalong (one word)
Singapore country in SE Asia ◻ **Singaporean**
singe v. (**singeing**, **singed**)

singer-songwriter (hyphen)
Singh Sikh title or surname
Singhalese var. of **Sinhalese**
sing-song (hyphen)
singular (abbrev. **s** or **sing.**)
sinh hyperbolic sign (no point)
Sinhalese (also **Singhalese, Sinhala**; not **Cingalese**) pl. same, member of the majority people of Sri Lanka
sinister Heraldry on the bearer's left-hand side, i.e. the right as it is depicted; cf. **dexter**
sink (past **sank**; past part. **sunk**) use **sunken** only as an adj.
sinnet (also **sennit**) Naut. braided cordage
Sinn Fein political party seeking a united republican Ireland (abbrev. **SF**) □ **Sinn Feiner** [Ir. *Sinn Féin*]
Sino- Chinese (and): *Sino-Japanese*
sinology study of China and Chinese
Sintra (also **Cintra**) town near Lisbon
sinus pl. **sinuses** Anat.
Sion var. of **Zion**
Siouan family of North American Indian languages
Sioux pl. same, member of a North American Indian people
siphon (also **syphon**)
sir (cap. in titles)
Sirach another name for **Ecclesiasticus** (abbrev. **Sir.**)
Siracusa see **Syracuse**
siren Gk Mythol. (lower case)
sirocco (also **scirocco**) pl. **siroccos** hot wind blowing from North Africa
sirup US var. of **syrup**
SIS Secret Intelligence Service
sissy (Brit. also **cissy**)
sister (cap. in the title of a nun or nurse)
sister-german pl. **sisters-german** arch. sister sharing both parents (hyphen)
sister-in-law pl. **sisters-in-law** (hyphens)
Sistine Chapel chapel in the Vatican
Sisyphean impossible to complete, like the eternal task of Sisyphus in Greek mythology (cap.)
sitcom (one word)
sit-in n. (hyphen, two words as verb)
sitrep report on the current military situation (one word)
sits vac situations vacant (no points)
sitting room (two words)
sit-up exercise involving sitting up (hyphen)
Sitwell 1 Dame Edith (Louisa) (1887–1964), English poet and critic **2** Osbert (1892–1969), English poet **3** Sacheverell (1897–1988), English poet
Siva var. of **Shiva**
Sivan (in the Jewish calendar) the ninth month of the civil and third of the religious year
six (Roman numeral **vi** or **VI**) □ **sixfold, sixth**
sixain six-line stanza
Six Counties the counties of Northern Ireland
Six Day War 5–10 June 1967 (no hyphen)
six-gun, six-pack (hyphen)
sixpence, sixpenny (one word)
six-shooter (hyphen)
sixte Fencing parrying position
sixteen (Roman numeral **xvi** or **XVI**) □ **sixteenth**
sixteenmo pl. **sixteenmos** another term for **sextodecimo**
sixteenth note N. Amer. semiquaver
sixth constituting number six
sixth form (two words, hyphen when attrib.) □ **sixth-former**
sixties (also **1960s**) decade (lower case, no apostrophe)
sixty hyphen in compound numbers, e.g. *sixty-one*; Roman numeral **lx** or **LX** □ **sixtieth**
sixty-fourmo pl. **sixty-fourmos** page size resulting from folding a sheet into sixty-four leaves (abbrev. **64mo**)
sixty-fourth note Mus., N. Amer. hemidemisemiquaver
sixty-four thousand dollar question (one hyphen)
sizeable (also **sizable**)
sizeism (not **sizism**)
SJ Society of Jesus
Sjælland Danish name for **Zealand**
sjambok long stiff South African whip
SK Saskatchewan (postal abbrev.)

Skagerrak strait separating Norway and Denmark
skald (also **scald**) ancient Scandinavian poet and reciter
skateboard, skatepark (one word)
skating rink (two words)
skean dhu dagger worn as part of Highland dress (two words, not ital.)
skein 1 length of thread or yarn **2** V-shaped formation of geese or swans
skeptic, skeptical US vars of **sceptic, sceptical**
sketchbook (one word)
sketch map, sketch pad (two words)
skeuomorph imitation of a work in another medium
skewbald horse with patches of two colours, usu. white and a colour other than black; cf. **piebald**
ski (**skis, skiing, skied**)
skiagraphy var. of **sciagraphy**
skidpan (one word)
skid row (two words, lower case)
skier 1 person who skis **2** var. of **skyer**
skiing sport of travelling on skis (no hyphen)
skijoring sport of being pulled along on skis (one word)
ski jump, ski jumper, ski jumping (two words)
skilful (US **skillful**)
ski lift (two words)
skill-less (hyphen)
skincare (one word)
skin-deep (hyphen)
skin diving swimming under water without a diving suit (two words) □ **skin-dive, skin-diver**
skinflint, skinfold (one word)
skin graft (two words)
skinhead (one word)
Skinner, Burrhus Frederic (1904–90), American psychologist
skintight (one word)
ski-plane aeroplane with skis for landing on snow or ice (hyphen)
ski pole (two words)
skipping rope (two words)
skirting board (two words)
skol (also ***skoal***) said before drinking (ital.)
Skopje capital of the republic of Macedonia
Skryabin var. of **Scriabin**
Skt Sanskrit
skulduggery (also **skullduggery**)
skullcap (one word)
sky blue (two words, hyphen when attrib.)
skydiving (one word)
Skye island of the Inner Hebrides
skyer (also **skier**) Cricket hit that goes very high
skyjack, skylark, skylight, skyline, skyrocket, skyscraper, skywriting (one word)
slainte said before drinking (ital.) [Gaelic *slàinte*]
slalom ski race down a winding course with poles
s.l.a.n. *sine loco, anno, vel nomine*
slander spoken defamation □ **slanderous**
slapdash (one word)
slap-happy (hyphen)
slapstick (one word)
slap-up (hyphen)
slash oblique stroke (/) in printing or writing, solidus; see also **backslash**
slaughterhouse (one word)
Slavic (also **Slavonic**) branch of the Indo-European language family
SLBM submarine-launched ballistic missile
s.l.e.a. *sine loco et anno*
sledgehammer (one word)
sleeping bag, sleeping car, sleeping draught, sleeping pill, sleeping sickness (two words)
sleep-out n. (hyphen, two words as verb)
sleepover n. (one word, two words as verb)
sleepwalk (one word)
sleigh sledge drawn by horses or reindeer
sleight of hand (not **slight**)
sleuth-hound (hyphen)
slew (also **slue**) turn or slide uncontrollably
slily var. of **slyly**
slimline (one word)
slingback, slingshot (one word)
slipcase close-fitting case for a book,

open at one side (one word)
slip knot (two words)
slip-on adj., n. (hyphen, two words as verb)
slip road (two words)
slipshod, slipstream, slipware, slipway (one word)
Sloane[1], Sir Hans (1660–1753), Irish physician and naturalist
Sloane[2] (also **Sloane Ranger**) upper-class young woman □ **Sloaney**
sloe-eyed (hyphen)
slo-mo slow motion (hyphen)
sloping fractions vulgar fractions with an oblique stroke, e.g. ¾
Slough town to the west of London
slough n. **1** a swamp **2** a situation without progress. v. cast off, shed
Slough of Despond 1 deep boggy place in John Bunyan's *The Pilgrim's Progress* **2** hopeless depression
Slovak 1 Slovakian **2** Slavic language of Slovakia
Slovakia country in central Europe, formerly part of Czechoslovakia □ **Slovakian**
Slovene (also **Slovenian**) **1** person from Slovenia **2** Slavic language of Slovenia
Slovenia country in SE Europe, formerly a republic of Yugoslavia
slowcoach (one word)
slowdown n. (one word, two words as verb)
slow motion (two words, hyphen when attrib.)
slow-worm (hyphen)
SLR 1 self-loading rifle **2** Photog. single-lens reflex
slue var. of **slew**
sluice gate (two words)
slur Mus. curved line linking notes to be sung to one syllable or played legato
slyly (also **slily**)
SM 1 sadomasochism **2** Sergeant Major **3** short metre
Sm the chemical element samarium (no point)
small-bore (hyphen)
small capital capital letter the same height as a lower-case x, like THIS (abbrev. **s.c.**)
small caps small capitals
small claims court (three words)
smallholding (one word)
small letter lower-case letter
small-minded (hyphen)
smallpox (one word)
small print printed matter in a small typeface
smart alec (chiefly N. Amer. also **smart aleck**) □ **smart-alecky**
smartphone (one word)
SME small to medium-sized enterprise
Smelfungus Sterne's name for Smollett (one *l*)
smell (past and past part. **smelled** or **smelt**)
Smetana, Bedřich (1824–84), Czech composer
smetana sour cream
smidgen (also **smidgeon** or **smidgin**)
smiley (not **-ly**) (**smilier, smiliest**)
Smith 1 Adam (1723–90), Scottish economist and philosopher **2** Stevie (1902–71), English writer; pseudonym of *Florence Margaret Smith* **3** Sydney (1771–1845), English churchman and essayist
Smithsonian Institution foundation in Washington DC
smokable (also **smokeable**)
smokehouse, smokescreen, smokestack (one word)
smoky (not **-ey**)
smolder US var. of **smoulder**
Smollett, Tobias (George) (1721–71), Scottish novelist
smooth adj., v. (as verb also **smoothe**)
smooth breathing see **breathing**
smoothie (not **-y**) **1** man with a smooth manner **2** puréed fruit drink
smooth talk n. (two words, hyphen as verb) □ **smooth-talker**
smorgasbord range of open sandwiches and delicacies
smorzando Mus. dying away
smoulder (US **smolder**)
smriti pl. ***smritis*** Hindu text containing traditional teachings (ital.)
SMS Short Message (or Messaging) Service
SMSgt Senior Master Sergeant

SMTP Simple Mail Transfer (or Transport) Protocol
Smuts, Jan (Christiaan) (1870–1950), South African prime minister 1919–24 and 1939–48
Smyrna ancient city on the site of modern Izmir in Turkey
Sn the chemical element tin (no point) [L. *stannum*]
s.n. *sine nomine*
snake charmer (two words)
snakehead, snakepit, snakeskin (one word)
snaky (not **-ey**)
snapdragon, snapshot (one word)
sneak (past and past part. **sneaked** or US informal **snuck**)
snivel (**snivelling, snivelled**; US one **-l-**)
snorkel v. (**snorkelling, snorkelled**; US one **-l-**) (not **schnorkel**)
Snorri Sturluson (1178–1241), Icelandic historian and poet
snowball (one word)
snow-blind (hyphen)
snowblower, snowboard, snowbound (one word)
snow-capped (hyphen)
Snowdon mountain in NW Wales; Welsh name **Yr Wyddfa**
snowdrift, snowdrop, snowfall, snowfield, snowflake (one word)
snow goose, snow hole, snow leopard, snow line (two words)
snowman, snowmobile, snowplough, snowscape, snowshoe, snowstorm (one word)
snow-white (hyphen)
SNP Scottish National Party
Snr Senior
snuck informal US past and past part. of **sneak**
snuffbox (one word)
So. South
so var. of **soh**
so-and-so pl. **so-and-sos** (hyphens; one cap. in names, as *Mr So-and-so*)
Soane, Sir John (1753–1837), English architect
soapbox (one word)
soap bubble, soap flakes, soap opera, soap powder (two words)
soapstone, soapsuds (one word)
SOAS School of Oriental and African Studies
Soave Italian white wine (cap.)
sobriquet (also **soubriquet**) nickname
Soc. 1 Socialist **2** Society
socage (also **soccage**) form of feudal tenure
so-called hyphen before a noun, but two words in phrs such as *the crown wheel is so called because of its shape*
soccer the unambiguous term around the world, but prefer **football** in British contexts
socialism, socialist lower case; cap. in party names
socialize (Brit. also **socialise**)
sociedad anónima public limited company (abbrev. **SA**) (Sp., ital.)
sociedade anónima public limited company (abbrev. **SA**) (Port., ital.)
società per azioni public limited company (abbrev. **SpA**) (It., ital.)
société anonyme public limited company (abbrev. **SA**) (Fr., ital.)
society (cap. in names; abbrev. **Soc.**)
Society of Jesus official name for the Jesuits (abbrev. **SJ**)
sociobiology, sociocultural (one word)
socio-economic (hyphen)
sociolinguistics, sociopolitical (one word)
Socrates (469–399 BC), Greek philosopher
sodium chemical element of atomic number 11 (symbol **Na**)
Sodom town in Palestine destroyed by fire from heaven (Gen. 19:24)
sodomize (Brit. also **sodomise**)
Sodor medieval diocese comprising the Hebrides and the Isle of Man
Sodor and Man Anglican diocese of the Isle of Man
SOE Special Operations Executive
SOED the *Shorter Oxford English Dictionary*
Sofia capital of Bulgaria
S. of S. Song of Songs
softback another term for **paperback** (one word)

softball (one word)
soft-boiled, soft-centred (hyphen)
soft-core adj. (hyphen)
softcover another term for **paperback** (one word)
soft-hearted (hyphen)
S. of III Ch. Song of the Three Children (Apocrypha)
soft hyphen hyphen to be displayed or typeset only at the end of a line
softie (also **softy**)
soft pedal, soft sell n. (two words, hyphen as verb)
soft sign single prime ′ used in transliterating Russian
soft-spoken (hyphen)
software, softwood (one word)
softy var. of **softie**
sogo shosha pl. same, large diverse Japanese company (two words, ital.)
soh (also **so** or **sol**) Mus. note in tonic sol-fa
SoHo area of New York
Soho area of London
soi-disant self-styled (Fr., ital.)
soigné (fem. **soignée**) well groomed (Fr., ital.)
soirée evening party (accent, not ital.)
sol¹ var. of **soh**
sol² pl. **soles** monetary unit of Peru
sola fem. of **solus**
solarium pl. **solariums** or **solaria**
solatium pl. **solatia** compensatory or consolatory gift (not ital.)
sola topi sun hat made of pith
solecism grammatical mistake
solemnize (Brit. also **solemnise**)
sol-fa (**sol-fas, sol-faing, sol-faed**) (hyphen)
solfège another term for **solfeggio** (not ital.)
solfeggio pl. **solfeggi** exercise in singing sol-fa syllables (not ital.)
soli see **solo**
solicit (**soliciting, solicited**)
Solicitor General pl. **Solicitors General** (two words, caps; abbrev. **SG**)
solid (of text) set without extra space between the lines or characters
Solidarity trade union movement in Poland; Pol. name **Solidarność**
solid state (two words, hyphen when attrib.)
solidus pl. **solidi** a slash /
soliloquy speech made when alone or not addressed to others ◻ **soliloquist, soliloquize** (Brit. also **soliloquise**)
Soliman var. of **Suleiman I**
solipsism 1 view that the self is all that can be known to exist **2** selfishness
solmization (Brit. also **solmisation**)
solo n. **1** pl. **solos** thing done alone **2** pl. **solos** or **soli** music or dance for one performer. v. (**soloes, soloing, soloed**) perform a solo
Solomon king of ancient Israel *c.*970–*c.*930 BC ◻ **Solomonic**
Solomon Islands country consisting of a group of islands in the SW Pacific ◻ **Solomon Islander**
Solon (*c.*630–*c.*560 BC), Athenian statesman and lawgiver
Solti, Sir Georg (1912–97), Hungarian-born British conductor
solubilize (Brit. also **solubilise**)
soluble able to be dissolved or solved
solus (fem. **sola**) alone or unaccompanied (not ital.)
Solutrean period between the Aurignacian and Magdalenian
solvable able to be solved (not **-eable**)
solvent (not **-ant**)
Solyman var. of **Suleiman I**
Solzhenitsyn, Alexander (1918–2008), Russian novelist; Russian name *Aleksandr Isaevich Solzhenitsyn*
Som. Somerset
som pl. same, monetary unit of Kyrgyzstan and Uzbekistan
Somali pl. same or **Somalis** member of a people of Somalia
Somalia country in the Horn of Africa ◻ **Somalian**
sombre (US **somber**)
sombrero pl. **sombreros**
some- see **any-**
somebody (one word)
some day (also **someday**) (one word)
somehow, someone (one word)
someplace chiefly N. Amer. somewhere (one word)
somersault (not **summer-** (arch.))

Somerset county of SW England (abbrev. **Som.**)
Somerville College Oxford
something (one word)
sometime adv., adj. (one word)
sometimes adv. (one word)
someway adv. chiefly N. Amer. (one word)
somewhat, somewhere (one word)
Somme river of northern France
sommelier wine waiter (not ital.)
somoni pl. same or **somonis** monetary unit of Tajikistan
Somoza 1 Anastasio (1896–1956), president of Nicaragua 1937–47 and 1951–6; full name *Anastasio Somoza García* **2** Anastasio (1925–80), president of Nicaragua 1967–79; full name *Anastasio Somoza Debayle* **3** Luis (1922–67), president of Nicaragua 1957–63; full name *Luis Somoza Debayle*
Son, the Christ
Sondheim, Stephen (Joshua) (b.1930), American composer and lyricist
son et lumière night-time entertainment using lighting effects and recorded sound (accent, not ital.)
Song (also **Sung**) dynasty that ruled in China 960–1279
songbird, songbook (one word)
song cycle (two words)
Song of Songs (also **Song of Solomon**) book of the Old Testament (abbrev. **S. of S.**)
Song of the Three Children book of the Apocrypha (abbrev. **S. of III Ch.**)
songs, titles of cited in roman in quotation marks
song thrush (two words)
songwriter (one word)
son-in-law pl. **sons-in-law** (hyphens)
Sonn. Shakespeare's *Sonnets*
sonnet fourteen-line poem with a formal rhyme scheme
Son of Man Jesus Christ (caps)
sooth truth
soothe gently calm
soothsayer (one word)
Sophocles (*c.*496–406 BC), Greek dramatist
sophomore N. Amer. second-year student
sopranino pl. **sopraninos** instrument higher than a soprano
soprano pl. **sopranos** highest singing voice; instrument with a high pitch
Sorb member of a Slavic people
sorb fruit of the service tree (lower case)
Sorbian Slavic language of the Sorbs
Sorbonne seat of the faculties of science and literature of the University of Paris
sordino pl. **sordini** mute for a musical instrument (not ital.)
sorel male fallow deer in its third year; cf. **sorrel**
sorghum cereal (not **-gum**)
sorrel 1 plant used in salads **2** horse with a light reddish-brown coat; cf. **sorel**
Sorrento town facing the Bay of Naples
sortes divination or the seeking of guidance by chance selection; (***sortes Biblicae***) from random passages of the Bible (L., ital.)
sortie v. (**sortieing, sortied**)
sortilege foretelling the future by lots
sorts characters from a font of type
SOS pl. **SOSs** code signal of extreme distress
so-so neither good nor bad (hyphen)
sostenuto pl. **sostenutos** Mus. (passage) in a sustained or prolonged manner
Sotheby's international auctioneers (apostrophe; formerly **Sotheby Parke Bernet**)
sotto voce in a quiet voice (not ital.)
sou former French coin of low value
soubrette maidservant's role in comedy (not ital.)
soubriquet var. of **sobriquet**
souchong fine black China tea
souffle blowing sound heard through a stethoscope
soufflé light spongy baked dish (accent, not ital.)
souk (also **suq**) Arab bazaar (not **suk, sukh**)
soulless, soulmate (one word)
soul music (two words)
soul-searching (hyphen)
sound barrier, sound bite (two words)
soundboard, soundbox (one word)

sound card (two words)
soundcheck (one word)
sound effect, sound engineer (two words)
sounding board, sounding line (two words)
soundproof (one word)
sound shift, sound system (two words)
soundtrack (one word)
sound wave (two words)
soupçon small quantity (not ital.)
sourcebook (one word)
sourdough, sourpuss (one word)
Sousa, John Philip (1854–1932), American composer and conductor
south (abbrev. **S** or **So.**)
South Africa country occupying the southernmost part of Africa (abbrev. **SA** or **S. Afr.**)
South African (no hyphen even when attrib.; abbrev. **S. Afr.**)
South America (abbrev. **S. Amer.**)
South American (no hyphen even when attrib.; abbrev. **S. Amer.**)
South Australia state of central southern Australia (abbrev. **SA**)
southbound (one word)
South Carolin
Atlantic coast (official and postal abbrev. **SC**) □ **South Carolinian**
South Dakota state in the north central US (official abbrev. **S.Dak.**, postal **SD**) □ **South Dakotan**
south-east, south-eastern (hyphen; abbrev. **SE**)
South East Asia (US **Southeast Asia**)
southeaster wind (one word)
south-easterly, south-eastward (hyphen)
southern (abbrev. **S**)
Southern Comfort trademark whisky-based US drink
southern hemisphere (lower case)
Southern Lights another term for **aurora australis** (caps)
Southey, Robert (1774–1843), English poet
South Island, the more southerly of the two main islands of New Zealand
South Korea country occupying the southern part of Korea (see **Korea**)
southpaw left-handed boxer (one word)
South Pole (caps)
south-south-east (two hyphens; abbrev. **SSE**)
south-south-west (two hyphens; abbrev. **SSW**)
South Sudan country in NE Africa, independent since 2011
south-west, south-western (hyphen; abbrev. **SW**)
southwester wind (one word)
south-westerly, south-westward (hyphen)
souvlaki pl. **souvlakia** or **souvlakis** Greek skewered meat
sou'wester waterproof hat (apostrophe)
sovereign 1 supreme ruler, esp. a monarch **2** former British gold coin worth one pound
Soviet (citizen) of the former USSR
soviet elected council in the former USSR (lower case)
Soviet Union former federation of Communist republics; full name **Union of Soviet Socialist Republics**
sow (past **sowed**; past part. **sown** or **sowed**) plant (seed)
Soweto large urban area south-west of Johannesburg □ **Sowetan**
soybean (also **soya bean**)
Soyinka, Wole (b.1934), Nigerian writer
Soyuz series of manned Soviet spacecraft
Sp. Spanish
sp. pl. **spp.** species (sing.)
SpA (It.) *società per azioni*, public limited company
Spa town in eastern Belgium
spa mineral spring (lower case)
space age, space bar (two words)
spacecraft (one word)
space flight (two words)
spaceman (one word)
space probe, space race, space rocket (two words)
spaceship (one word)
space shuttle, space station (two words)
space–time (en rule)
space travel (two words)
spacewalk (one word)
spacewoman (one word)
spacey (also **spacy**) (**spacier, spaciest**)

spacial var. of **spatial**
SPAD signal passed at danger
spadework (one word)
spaghetti (treated as sing. or pl.; not **-getti**)
spaghetti bolognese (lower case; not **-naise**)
Spain country in SW Europe; Sp. name **España**
Spam trademark tinned meat product (cap.)
spam inappropriate Internet messages sent to a large number of users (lower case)
spandex stretchy fabric (lower case)
Spanish (abbrev. **Sp.**)
Spanish America parts of America once colonized by Spaniards
Spanish Armada (caps)
Spanish Inquisition ecclesiastical court (caps)
Spanish Town town in Jamaica
sparagmos ritual dismemberment in Greek tragedy (ital.)
Sparta city in southern Greece; mod. Gk name **Spartí**
Spartan of Sparta
spartan austere or lacking in comfort (lower case)
spastic avoid; use **person with cerebral palsy**
spatial (also **spacial**)
spatio-temporal (hyphen)
Spätlese pl. **Spätleses** or **Spätlesen** good-quality German white wine (cap., accent, not ital.)
SPCK Society for Promoting Christian Knowledge
speakeasy (one word)
Speaker, the presiding officer in the House of Commons (cap.)
spear carrier actor with a walk-on part (two words)
speargun, spearhead, spearmint (one word)
spec[1] (in **on spec**) without any specific plan or instructions
spec[2] (**speccing, specced**) (construct to) a specification
spec. specifically
speciality (US & Med. **specialty**)
specialize (Brit. also **specialise**)
special sort character not normally included in a font, e.g. a symbol or a letter with an accent
specie money in the form of coins
species pl. same (abbrev. **sp.**, pl. **spp.**; species names are lower case)
specific epithet second element in the Latin binomial name of a species
specific name Latin binomial name of a species, the generic name followed by the specific epithet
spectre (US **specter**)
spectrum pl. **spectra**
speculum pl. **specula** instrument for dilating part of the body
speech act, speech day, speech sound, speech therapy (two words)
speech-impaired prefer to **dumb**
speech-writer (hyphen)
speed v. (past and past part. **sped** or in sense 'exceed the speed limit' **speeded**)
speedboat (one word)
speed limit (two words)
speed-read (hyphen)
speedway, speedwell, speedwriting (one word)
spell (past and past part. **spelled** or Brit. **spelt**)
spellbind, spellbound, spellcheck, spellchecker (one word)
spelling bee, spelling checker (two words)
Spencer 1 Herbert (1820–1903), English philosopher and sociologist **2** Sir Stanley (1891–1959), English painter
Spencerian of a style of sloping handwriting
Spengler, Oswald (1880–1936), German philosopher
Spenser, Edmund (*c.*1552–99), English poet □ **Spenserian**
Spenserian stanza eight iambic pentameters followed by an alexandrine, rhyming *ababbcbcc*
spermatozoon pl. **spermatozoa**
spew expel large quantities of (not **spue** (arch.))
SPF sun protection factor

Sphinx 1 Gk Mythol. winged monster **2** huge stone figure near the Pyramids in Egypt; cf. **Sphynx**
sphygmomanometer instrument for measuring blood pressure
Sphynx breed of hairless cat; cf. **sphinx**
spick and span (also **spic and span**)
spicy (not **-ey**)
spiderman builder who works at great heights (one word)
Spider-Man superhuman cartoon character (hyphen)
spiderweb (one word)
Spielberg, Steven (b.1947), American film director and producer
spifflicate (also **spiflicate**) treat roughly, destroy
spiky (not **-ey**)
spill (past and past part. **spilled** or **spilt**)
spillover n. (one word, two words as verb)
spina bifida (two words, not ital.)
spin dryer (two words) □ **spin-dry**
spine-chiller, spine-chilling (hyphen)
spin-off by-product or incidental result (hyphen)
Spinoza, Baruch (or Benedict) de (1632–77), Dutch philosopher □ **Spinozism**
spinster avoid exc. in historical contexts
spiny (not **-ey**)
spiraea (chiefly US also **spirea**) shrub of the rose family
spiral v. (**spiralling, spiralled**; US one **-l-**)
spiritual of the human spirit
spiritualism (lower case)
spiritualize (Brit. also **spiritualise**)
spirituous arch. containing much alcohol
spirochaete (US **spirochete**) spirally twisted bacterium
spirt use **spurt**
Spitfire WWII aircraft
spitfire person with a fiery temperament (lower case)
Spithead channel between the Isle of Wight and mainland England
Spitsbergen Norwegian island in the Arctic Ocean (not **Spitz-**)
spitz breed of small dog
splashback, splashboard, splashdown n. (one word, two words as verb)
splendour (US **splendor**)
split infinitive construction with an adverb between the *to* of an infinitive and the verb
Spode trademark pottery or porcelain made at the factories of Josiah Spode (1755–1827) or his successors
spoil (past and past part. **spoiled** or Brit. **spoilt**)
spoilsport (one word)
spokesman, spokesperson, spokeswoman (one word)
spondee metrical foot of two long (or stressed) syllables □ **spondaic**
sponge v. (**sponging** or **spongeing, sponged**) □ **spongeable**
spongy (not **-ey**)
sponsor (not **-er**)
spontaneous (not **-ious**) □ **spontaneity**
spoonerism accidental transposition of the initial sounds of words (lower case)
spoon-feed (hyphen)
spoonful pl. **spoonfuls**
sportif interested in or suitable for sports (Fr., ital.)
sportive playful
sports car (two words)
sports jacket (US **sport jacket**) (two words)
sportsman, sportsperson, sportswear, sportswoman (one word)
sport utility vehicle (no hyphen; abbrev. **SUV**)
spot check n. (two words, hyphen as verb)
spotlight (one word)
spp. species (pl.)
SPQR (L.) *Senatus Populusque Romanus*, the Senate and people of Rome
Spr Sapper
Sprachgefühl intuitive feeling for the idiom of a language (Ger., cap., ital.)
spreadeagle stretch with arms and legs extended (one word)
spread eagle emblem of an eagle with legs and wings extended (two words)
spreadsheet (one word)
Sprechgesang (also ***Sprechstimme***) dramatic vocalization between speech and song (Ger., cap., ital.)

sprezzatura studied carelessness (It., ital.)
sprightly (not **spritely**)
spring[1] season (lower case)
spring[2] (past **sprang** or chiefly N. Amer. **sprung**; past part. **sprung**) move suddenly upwards or forwards
springboard (one word)
springbok 1 southern African gazelle **2** (**the Springboks**) the South African rugby union team
spring clean n. (two words, hyphen as verb)
Springsteen, Bruce (b.1949), American rock artist
springtail wingless insect (one word)
springtide springtime (one word)
spring tide tide with the greatest difference between low and high water (two words)
springtime (one word)
sprinkled edges cut edges of books sprinkled with coloured ink
spritely use **sprightly**
sprung rhythm poetic metre with each foot having one stressed syllable followed by a varying number of unstressed ones
spry (**spryer, spryest**) □ **spryly, spryness**
spue use **spew**
spumante Italian sparkling wine (lower case, not ital.)
spumoni (also **spumone**) N. Amer. layered ice cream dessert (not ital.)
spurrey (also **spurry**) pl. **spurreys** plant of the pink family
spurt (not **spirt** (arch.))
sputnik early Soviet artificial satellite (lower case)
spyglass, spyhole, spymaster (one word)
sq. square
SQL Structured Query Language
squacco heron small crested heron
squaddie (also **squaddy**) Brit. private soldier
squadron leader (cap. in titles; abbrev. **Sqn Ldr**)
square n. **1** open area surrounded by buildings (cap. in names; abbrev. **Sq.**) **2** the part of the cover of a bound book which projects beyond the pages. adj. denoting a unit of measurement (abbrev. **sq.**)
square brackets Brit. the marks [ ]
square root (two words)
squat (assume) a crouching position
squatt larva used as anglers' bait
squaw offens. American Indian woman or wife
squeegee (**squeegeeing, squeegeed**) (clean with) a rubber-edged scraping implement
squirearchy landowners as a class (not **-rarchy**)
squirrel v. (**squirrelling, squirrelled**; US one **-l-**)
Sr 1 Senhor **2** Senior **3** Señor **4** the chemical element strontium (no point)
sr steradian(s)
SRA Strategic Rail Authority
Sra 1 Senhora **2** Señora
Srbija Serbian name for **Serbia**
Srebrenica town in Bosnia–Herzegovina
Sri Lanka island country off the SE coast of India; former name **Ceylon** □ **Sri Lankan**
Srinagar city in NW India
SRN State Registered Nurse
SRO 1 self-regulatory organization **2** standing room only
Srta 1 Senhorita **2** Señorita
SS[1] **1** Saints **2** social security **3** steamship
SS[2] Nazi special police force [Ger. *Schutzstaffel*]
SSAFA Soldiers', Sailors', and Airmen's Families Association
SSC US Solicitor in the Supreme Court
SSE south-south-east
SSL Secure Sockets Layer
SSP statutory sick pay
ssp. subspecies (sing.)
sspp. subspecies (pl.)
SSR Soviet Socialist Republic
SSRC Social Science Research Council
SSRI selective serotonin reuptake inhibitor
SSSI Site of Special Scientific Interest
SSW south-south-west
St 1 Saint (alphabetize as *Saint*) **2** (also

ST) stokes
St. Street (point)
st 1 (usu. **st.**) stanza **2** stone (in weight) **3** stumped by
Sta Santa (female saint) (no point)
Sta. Station
Stabat Mater Latin hymn on the suffering of the Virgin Mary at the Crucifixion [L., 'the Mother was standing']
stabbing 1 wire stitching near the back edge of a closed section or pamphlet **2** the piercing of a book section prior to sewing or stitching
stabilize (Brit. also **stabilise**)
stablemate (one word)
staccato pl. **staccatos** Mus. (passage played) with each note separate
stadium 1 pl. **stadiums** sports ground **2** pl. **stadia** ancient Greek or Roman measure of length; ancient racing track
stadtholder (also **stadholder**) hist. chief magistrate of the United Provinces of the Netherlands (not ital., cap. in titles)
Staël, de Madame, see **de Staël**
staff Mus. Brit. var. of **stave**
Staffordshire county of central England (abbrev. **Staffs.**)
staffroom (one word)
stagecoach, stagecraft (one word)
stage direction, stage door, stage fright (two words)
stagehand (one word)
stage-manage (hyphen) □ **stage management, stage manager**
stage name, stage play (two words)
stage-struck (hyphen)
staghorn, staghound (one word)
stagy (also **stagey**) excessively theatrical
staid sedate; cf. **stayed**
staircase, stairlift (one word)
stair rod (two words)
stairway, stairwell (one word)
stakeholder (one word)
Stakhanovite exceptionally productive worker in the former USSR (cap.)
stalactite mineral structure hanging from the roof of a cave
Stalag WWII German prison camp (cap., not ital.)
stalagmite mineral structure rising from the floor of a cave
stalemate (one word)
Stalin, Joseph (1879–1953), General Secretary of the Communist Party of the USSR 1922–53; born *Iosif Vissarionovich Dzhugashvili* □ **Stalinism**
Stalingrad former name for **Volgograd**
stalking horse (two words)
stallholder (one word)
Stamboul arch. name for **Istanbul**
stamp collecting, stamp duty (two words)
stamped addressed envelope (no comma; abbrev. **SAE**)
stanch US var. of **staunch**²
standard-bearer (hyphen)
standardize (Brit. also **standardise**)
standby pl. **standbys** (one word)
stand-down, stand-in n. (hyphen, two words as verb)
stand-off deadlock (hyphen)
stand-off half rugby halfback
stand-offish (hyphen)
standout outstanding person or thing (one word)
standpipe, standpoint, standstill (one word)
stand-up (of comedy) involving standing in front of an audience (hyphen)
Stanislavsky, Konstantin (Sergeevich) (1863–1938), Russian theatre director and actor; born *Konstantin Sergeevich Alekseev*
Stanley knife trademark knife with a short retractable blade (one cap.)
Stansted international airport NE of London (not **-stead**)
stanza group of lines forming a metrical unit (abbrev. **st.**) □ **stanzaed**
stapes pl. same, bone in the ear
starboard side of a ship on the right when one is facing forward; cf. **port**
starburst, stardust, starfish, stargazer, starlight (one word)
stare decisis Law principle of determining points according to precedent (L., ital.)
Star of David six-pointed figure used as a Jewish symbol (two caps)

Stars and Stripes the US flag (treated as sing.)
starship (one word)
star sign (two words)
Star-Spangled Banner the US national anthem (one hyphen, caps)
star-struck, **star-studded** (hyphen)
START Strategic Arms Reduction Talks
starting block, **starting gate**, **starting point**, **starting post**, **starting price** (two words)
start-up n. (hyphen, two words as verb)
Star Wars informal the US Strategic Defense Initiative
Stasi internal security force of the former German Democratic Republic
stasis inactivity or equilibrium
stat. statute
state nation or territory under one government (often cap. as an abstract concept, as in 'Church and State')
State Department the US government department dealing with foreign affairs
Staten Island borough of New York City
state of the art (four words, hyphens when attrib.)
stater ancient Greek coin
stateroom (one word)
States, the 1 the US **2** the legislative body in Jersey, Guernsey, and Alderney
States General (also **Estates General**) hist. legislative body in the Netherlands and in France to 1789
stateside N. Amer. of, in, or to the US (one word, lower case)
statesman, **stateswoman** (one word)
station (cap. in names; abbrev. **Sta.**)
stationary not moving
stationer seller of paper, pens, and other writing materials
stationery writing materials
stationmaster (one word)
Stations of the Cross (two caps)
station wagon (two words)
statistics 1 science of collecting and analysing large quantities of data (treated as sing.) **2** pieces of data for statistical study (treated as pl.)
stator stationary portion of an electric generator or motor
statuary statues collectively
status quo the existing state of affairs (not ital.)
status quo ante the state of affairs previously existing (not ital.)
statute written law passed by a legislative body (abbrev. **stat.**)
statutory (not **-ary**)
staunch[1] loyal and committed
staunch[2] (chiefly US also **stanch**) stop the flow of
stave 1 verse or stanza of a poem **2** (also **staff**) Brit. set of parallel lines for writing music on
stave rhyme alliteration in old Germanic poetry
stay-at-home (hyphens)
stayed remained; stopped; cf. **staid**
STD 1 Doctor of Sacred Theology [L. *Sanctae Theologiae Doctor*] **2** sexually transmitted disease **3** subscriber trunk dialling
Ste (Fr.) *Sainte*, female saint
steak au poivre peppered steak (not ital.)
steak Diane thin slices of steak fried with seasoning (one cap.)
steakhouse (one word)
steak knife (two words)
steak tartare raw minced steak and eggs
steam age, **steam bath** (two words)
steamboat (one word)
steam engine, **steam hammer**, **steam iron** (two words)
steamroll, **steamroller** (one word)
steamship (one word; abbrev. **SS**)
steatopygia accumulation of fat on the buttocks □ **steatopygous**
Steele, Sir Richard (1672–1729), Irish writer
steelwork, **steelworker**, **steelworks**, **steelyard** (one word)
steenbok (also **steinbok**) small African antelope
steeplechase, **steeplejack** (one word)
steering wheel (two words)
stegosaur (also **stegosaurus**) dinosaur with bony plates along the back (lower case)
Stein, Gertrude (1874–1946), American writer

Steinbeck, John (Ernst) (1902–68), American novelist
steinbock pl. same or **steinbocks** Alpine ibex
steinbok var. of **steenbok**
stela pl. **stelae** upright stone slab
Stella Maris female protector at sea (caps)
Stellenbosch university town in South Africa
stemma pl. **stemmata** family tree
stencil v. (**stencilling, stencilled**; US one **-l-**)
Stendhal (1783–1842), French novelist; pseudonym of *Marie Henri Beyle*
Sten gun sub-machine gun (one cap.)
stentorian having a powerful voice (lower case)
stepbrother, stepchild, stepdaughter, stepfather (one word)
Steph. Stephen (regnal year)
Stephen 1 (*c.*1097–1154), king of England 1135–54 **2** Sir Leslie (1832–1904), English biographer and critic
Stephenson 1 George (1781–1848), English engineer **2** Robert (1803–59), English engineer
stepladder, stepmother (one word)
step-parent (hyphen)
steppe extensive flat grassland
stepping stone (two words)
stepsister, stepson (one word)
steradian SI unit of solid angles (abbrev. **sr**)
stere unit of volume
stereo pl. **stereos 1** stereotype (printing plate) **2** music player producing stereophonic sound
stereophonic (of sound recording) using two or more channels
stereotype relief printing plate cast in a mould made from composed type
sterilize (Brit. also **sterilise**)
sterling British money (abbrev. **stg**)
Sterne, Laurence (1713–68), Irish novelist
sternum pl. **sternums** or **sterna** the breastbone
stet (not ital.) **1** let it stand (instruction to ignore a proof correction) **2** (**stetting, stetted**) write 'stet' against
Stetson US trademark hat (cap.)
Stettin Ger. name for **Szczecin**
Stevens, Wallace (1879–1955), American poet
Stevenson, Robert Louis (Balfour) (1850–94), Scottish writer
Stewart 1 Sir Jackie (b.1939), British motor-racing driver; born *John Young Stewart* **2** James (Maitland) (1908–97), American actor
Stewartry, the the Kirkcudbright district of Galloway
stg sterling
stichomythia dialogue in alternate lines of verse
stick-in-the-mud n. (hyphens)
Stieglitz, Alfred (1864–1946), American photographer
stigma pl. **stigmas** or in Christian use **stigmata 1** mark of disgrace **2** marks corresponding to those left on Christ's body by the Crucifixion **3** the ancient Greek character ς
stigmatize (Brit. also **stigmatise**)
stilb unit of luminance
stilboestrol (US **stilbestrol**) powerful synthetic oestrogen
stile 1 steps over a gate etc. **2** vertical piece in a door or window frame; cf. **style**
stiletto pl. **stilettos**
stillbirth, stillborn (one word)
still life pl. **still lifes** (two words, hyphen when attrib.)
Stilton trademark kind of cheese
stimulator (not **-er**)
stimulus pl. **stimuli**
stink (past **stank** or **stunk**; past part. **stunk**)
stir-crazy, stir-fry (hyphen)
Stirling[1] city in central Scotland
Stirling[2] **1** James (1692–1770), Scottish mathematician **2** Sir James Fraser (1926–92), Scottish architect
stitching sewing together of all the sections of a book in a single operation; cf. **sewing**
stoa classical portico or roofed colonnade; (**the Stoa**) hall in Athens where Zeno founded Stoicism

stockbreeder, stockbroker (one word)
stock car, stock company, stock control, stock cube (two words)
stock exchange (two words, cap. as proper name)
Stockhausen, Karlheinz (1928–2007), German composer
stockholder (one word)
Stockholm capital of Sweden
stockinet (also **stockinette**) loosely knitted stretch fabric
stock-in-trade (hyphens)
stockjobber, stocklist, stockman (one word)
stock market (two words)
stockpile, stockpot, stockroom, stocktaking, stockyard (one word)
stoep S. Afr. veranda; cf. **stoop, stoup**
Stoic follower of Stoicism
stoic stoical (person) (lower case)
stoical enduring pain without complaint
Stoicism ancient philosophical school founded at Athens by Zeno
stoicism endurance of pain without complaint (lower case)
Stoke-on-Trent city in central England (hyphens)
stokes pl. same, cgs unit of kinematic viscosity (abbrev. **St** or **ST**)
Stokowski, Leopold (1882–1977), British-born American conductor
STOL short take-off and landing
stone 1 pl. same, Brit. unit of weight equal to 14 lb (6.25 kg) (abbrev. **st**) **2** Printing sheet on which pages of type are made up
Stone Age (caps)
stone dead (two words)
stoneground, stonemason (one word)
stonewall obstruct by evasion or uncooperativeness (one word)
stoneware, stonewashed, stonework (one word)
stony (not **-ey**)
stoop 1 posture with the head or body forwards and downwards **2** N. Amer. porch with steps in front of a house **3** var. of **stoup**; cf. **stoep**
stopcock, stopgap (one word)
stop–go (en rule)
stop-off n. (hyphen, two words as verb)
stopover n. (one word, two words as verb)
Stoppard, Sir Tom (b.1937), British dramatist; born *Thomas Straussler*
stop press late news inserted in a newspaper at the time of printing (two words, hyphen when attrib.)
stop–start adj. (en rule; hyphens in adj. **stop-and-start**)
stop valve (two words)
stopwatch (one word)
store card (two words)
storefront, storehouse, storekeeper, storeroom (one word)
storey (N. Amer. also **story**) pl. **storeys** or **stories** level of a building
storeyed (N. Amer. also **storied**) having a specified number of storeys
storied celebrated in story
storm cloud, storm drain, storm troops (two words)
Storting the Norwegian parliament
story 1 account of something imaginary **2** N. Amer. var. of **storey**
storyboard, storybook, storyline, storyteller (one word)
stotinka pl. **stotinki** monetary unit of Bulgaria
stoup (also **stoop**) basin for holy water; cf. **stoep**
stowaway n. (one word, two words as verb)
Stowe[1] public school in Buckinghamshire
Stowe[2] Harriet (Elizabeth) Beecher (1811–96), American novelist
Stow-on-the-Wold town in Gloucestershire (hyphens)
STP 1 Professor of Sacred Theology [L. *Sacrae Theologiae Professor*] **2** standard temperature and pressure
Str. Strait(s)
str. stroke (oar)
Strachey, (Giles) Lytton (1880–1932), English biographer
Stradivari, Antonio (*c.*1644–1737), Italian violin-maker
Stradivarius violin made by Stradivari
straight extending uniformly in one direction; cf. **strait**

straight away 1 (also **straightaway**) immediately **2** (**straightaway**) N. Amer. moving in a straight line
straightforward (one word)
straightjacket, straight-laced vars of **straitjacket, strait-laced**
strait 1 (also **straits**) narrow passage of water (cap. in names; abbrev. **Str.**) **2** (**straits**) trouble or difficulty; cf. **straight**
straitened characterized by poverty
straitjacket (also **straightjacket**)
strait-laced (also **straight-laced**)
Straits Settlements British Crown Colony in SE Asia 1867–1946
stranglehold (one word)
Stranraer port in SW Scotland
strappado pl. **strappados** hist. form of torture
Strasberg, Lee (1901–82), American actor, director, and teacher
Strasbourg city in Alsace; Ger. name **Strassburg**
strata pl. of **stratum**
Strategic Defense Initiative (abbrev. **SDI**) projected US system of defence using satellites; now the **Ballistic Missile Defense Organization**
Stratford-upon-Avon town in Warwickshire (hyphens) □ **Stratfordian**
Strathclyde former local government region in SW Scotland
strathspey Scottish dance (lower case)
stratocumulus kind of cloud (one word)
stratosphere earth's upper atmosphere (lower case)
stratum pl. **strata** layer of rock
stratus cloud forming a horizontal grey sheet
Strauss 1 Johann (1804–49), Austrian composer; known as **Strauss the Elder** **2** Johann (1825–99), Austrian composer; known as **Strauss the Younger** **3** Richard (1864–1949), German composer
Stravinsky, Igor (Fyodorovich) (1882–1971), Russian-born composer
streamline (one word)
stream of consciousness (three words, hyphen when attrib.)
Streatfeild, Noel (1895–1986), English writer (not **-field**)
street (cap. in names; abbrev. **St.**)
streetcar (one word)
street light (two words)
streetwalker, streetwise (one word)
streptococcus pl. **streptococci** kind of bacterium
stretto pl. **stretti** Mus. (passage performed) in a quicker time
strew (past part. **strewn** or **strewed**)
strewth (also **struth**) expressing surprise or dismay (not **'s-**)
stria pl. **striae** linear mark
stride (past **strode**; past part. **strode** or **stridden**)
stridor harshness of sound
strike-breaker (hyphen)
strike force (two words)
Strindberg, (Johan) August (1849–1912), Swedish writer □ **Strindbergian**
stringendo pl. **stringendos** or **stringendi** Mus. (passage performed) with increasing speed
strip-search (hyphen)
striptease (one word)
stripy (not **-ey**)
strive (past **strove** or **strived**; past part. **striven** or **strived**)
stroganoff dish in which the main ingredient is cooked in sour cream (lower case, often after a noun)
strong-arm adj., v. (hyphen)
strongbox, stronghold, strongman (one word)
strongpoint specially fortified position
strong point something at which one excels
strongroom (one word)
strontium chemical element of atomic number 38 (symbol **Sr**)
strophe first section in an ancient Greek choral ode; section of a lyric poem □ **strophic**
strove past of **strive**
strudel dessert of pastry round a fruit filling (lower case, not ital.)
struth var. of **strewth**
strychnine poisonous alkaloid (not **-nin**)
Sts Saints

Stuart[1] name of the family ruling Scotland 1371–1714 and Britain 1603–39 and 1660–1714
Stuart[2] Charles Edward (1720–88), pretender to the British throne; known as **Bonnie Prince Charlie**
stucco (**stuccoes, stuccoing, stuccoed**) (coat or decorate with) fine plaster
stuck-up informal snobbishly aloof (hyphen)
studio pl. **studios**
stumbling block (two words)
stuntman, stuntwoman (one word)
stupa dome-shaped Buddhist shrine (not ital.)
stupefy (not **-ify**)
Sturmabteilung Nazi Brownshirts (Ger., ital.; abbrev. **SA**)
Sturm und Drang German literary and artistic movement in the late 18th cent. (two caps, ital.)
Stuttgart city in western Germany
sty[1] enclosure for pigs
sty[2] (also **stye**) pl. **sties** or **styes** inflamed swelling on the eyelid
Stygian (cap.) **1** of the River Styx **2** very dark
style manner or way of doing something; see also **house style**; cf. **stile**
style sheet editor's list of forms preferred in a text; Comput. file for standardizing documents (two words)
stylize (Brit. also **stylise**)
stylus pl. **styli** or **styluses**
stymie (**stymieing, stymied**) hinder the progress of (not **stimy**)
styptic capable of stopping bleeding
Styx Gk Mythol. river in the underworld
subacid, subalpine (one word)
subaltern army officer below the rank of captain
sub-aqua, sub-aquatic (hyphen)
subaqueous (one word)
subarctic (also **sub-Arctic**)
subatomic (one word)
sub-basement, sub-breed (hyphen)
subcategory, subclass, subclause, subcommittee, subconscious, subcontinent (one word)
subcontract, subculture, subdirectory, subdivide, subdominant (one word)
subedit check, correct, and improve before printing (one word)
subfamily (one word)
sub finem towards the end (L., ital.)
subfusc dark clothing worn for examinations at some universities
subgenus, subgroup (one word)
subheading (also **subhead**) heading of a subsection
subhuman (one word)
sub judice under judicial consideration (L., ital.)
subjunctive mood of verbs expressing what is imagined, wished, or possible (abbrev. **subj.**)
subkingdom, sublanguage, sublease (one word)
sub-lessee, sub-lessor (hyphen)
sublet (one word)
sub lieutenant (two words, cap. as title; abbrev. **Sub-Lt**)
Sublime Porte see **Porte**
sublunar within the moon's orbit
sublunary belonging to this world
sub-machine gun (one hyphen)
submarine, submenu, submicroscopic, subnormal (one word)
subplot subordinate plot (one word)
subpoena (**subpoenas, subpoenaing, subpoenaed** or **subpoena'd**) (summon with) a writ ordering a person to attend a court
sub-postmaster, sub-postmistress, sub-post office (hyphen)
subregion (one word)
sub rosa in secret (L., ital.)
subroutine (one word)
sub-Saharan (hyphen, one cap.)
subscript (of a letter, figure, or symbol) printed or written below the line
subsection division of a section (abbrev. **subsec.**)
subsense subsidiary sense of a word in a dictionary
subset (one word)
subsidize (Brit. also **subsidise**)
subsoil, subsonic (one word)

sub specie aeternitatis viewed in relation to the eternal (L., ital.)
subspecies (abbrev. **subsp.** or **ssp.**)
substandard, **substation**, **subtenant**, **subterranean**, **subtext**, **subtitle** (one word)
subtly (not **-ey**)
subtotal, **subtropical**, **subtropics**, **subtype** (one word)
sub voce see **s.v.**
subway (one word)
sub-zero (hyphen)
succès de scandale success due to notoriety (Fr., ital.)
succès d'estime critical success (Fr., ital.)
Succoth (also **Sukkot**, **Sukkoth**) Jewish festival, the Feast of Tabernacles
succour (US **succor**) help, aid
succubus pl. **succubi** female demon
suchlike (one word)
sucre monetary unit of Ecuador until 2000
Sudan 1 country in NE Africa (not **the Sudan**) **2** vast region of North Africa □ **Sudanese**
Sudetenland area in the Czech Republic, on the border with Germany
sudoku number puzzle (one word, not ital.)
Sudra member of the lowest Hindu caste
sue (suing, sued) □ **suable**
suede leather with a velvety nap (no accent)
Suetonius (*c*.69–*c*.150 AD), Roman biographer and historian; Latin name *Gaius Suetonius Tranquillus*
suffix morpheme at the end of a word forming a derivative (abbrev. **suff.**)
Suffolk county of eastern England (abbrev. **Suff.**)
Sufi pl. **Sufis** Muslim ascetic and mystic
sugar beet, **sugar cane**, **sugar cube**, **sugar daddy** (two words)
sugarloaf conical mass of sugar (one word, but *Sugar Loaf Mountain*, Brazil)
sugar lump (two words)
sugarplum (one word)
sugar snap, **sugar soap** (two words)
suggestible (not **-able**)
sui generis unique (L., ital.)
sui juris of age, independent (L., ital.)
Suisse Fr. name for **Switzerland**
suitcase (one word)
suite set of rooms, furniture, or pieces of music
suk (also **sukh**) use **souk**
Sukarno, Achmad (1901–70), Indonesian president 1945–67
sukiyaki Japanese dish of flash-fried meat (one word)
Sukkot (also **Sukkoth**) var. of **Succoth**
Sulawesi island in Indonesia; former name **Celebes**
Sulaymaniyah (also **Sulaimaniya**) town in NE Iraq
Suleiman I (also **Soliman** or **Solyman**) (*c*.1494–1566), sultan of the Ottoman Empire 1520–66
Sullivan, Sir Arthur (Seymour) (1842–1900), English composer
sulphate, **sulphide**, **sulphite** (US & Chem. **sulf-**)
sulphur (US & Chem. **sulfur**) chemical element of atomic number 16 (symbol **S**)
sulphuric, **sulphurous** (US & Chem. **sulfuric**, **sulfurous**)
sultan (cap. in titles) Muslim sovereign; (**the Sultan**) the former sultan of Turkey
sultana 1 small seedless raisin **2** sultan's wife (cap. in titles)
sumac (also **sumach**) ornamental shrub
Sumer ancient region in present-day Iraq □ **Sumerian**
summa pl. **summae** summary of a subject (not ital.)
summarize (Brit. also **summarise**)
summer season (lower case)
summer house (two words)
summersault use **somersault**
summertime season of summer (one word)
summer time UK time adjusted to an hour ahead of standard time (two words; lower case, but *British Summer Time*)
summons pl. **summonses**
summum bonum the supreme good (L., ital.)
sumo pl. **sumos** (participant in) a

Japanese form of wrestling
Sun. Sunday
sun cap. only in astronomical contexts; the suns of other solar systems are lower case
sunbathe, sunbeam, sunbed, sunblock (one word)
sun bonnet (two words)
sunburn, sunburst (one word)
sun cream (two words)
sundae ice cream dessert
Sunday (abbrev. **Sun.**)
sun deck (two words)
sundial, sundown, sundress, sunflower (one word)
sun-dried (hyphen)
Sung var. of **Song**
sunglasses (one word)
sun hat (two words)
sunk past part. of **sink**
sunken adj. having sunk; at a lower level
Sun King Louis XIV of France
sun-kissed (hyphen)
sunlamp, sunlight, sunlit (one word)
sun lounge (two words)
sunlounger (one word)
Sunna traditional portion of Muslim law based on Muhammad's words or acts
Sunni pl. same or **Sunnis** (adherent of) one of the two main branches of Islam; cf. **Shia**
sunrise, sunroof, sunscreen, sunset, sunshade, sunshine, sunspot, sunstroke, suntan, suntrap, sunup (one word)
Sun, The UK newspaper (cap. and italic *The*)
sun visor (two words)
Sun Yat-sen (also **Sun Yixian**) (1866–1925), Chinese Kuomintang statesman
Suomi Finnish name for **Finland**
sup. *supra*
super- forms solid compounds exc. for *super-duper*
Super Bowl trademark American football championship game (two words, caps)
supercalendered (of paper) given a highly glazed finish (abbrev. **SC**)
supercargo pl. **supercargoes** or **supercargos** owner's representative on a merchant ship
supercede use **supersede**
super-duper (hyphen)
superego pl. **superegos** part of the mind responsible for the conscience
superficies pl. same, surface or appearance
superintendent (cap. in titles; abbrev. **Supt**; not **-ant**)
superior another term for **superscript**
superlative (abbrev. **superl.**)
superlunary celestial
superman ideal or exceptional man (lower case; cap. as cartoon character)
superordinate word whose meaning includes the meaning of one or more other words
superscript (of a letter, figure, or symbol) printed or written above the line
supersede (not **-cede**)
supervise (not **-ize**)
supervisor (not **-er, -izor**)
supplely (also **supply**)
supplement extra section added to a published work (abbrev. **suppl.**)
suppositious based on assumption
supposititious substituted, not genuine
suppress (two *ps*)
supra earlier in a book or article, above (L., ital.; abbrev. **sup.**)
supremacism advocacy of supremacy
suprematism Russian abstract art movement
supreme dish served in a rich cream sauce [Fr. *suprême*]
Supreme Court (in full **Supreme Court of Judicature**) final court of appeal in the UK for civil cases
supremo pl. **supremos**
Supt Superintendent
suq var. of **souk**
sura (also **surah**) section of the Koran (cap. in references)
surah 1 twilled silk fabric **2** var. of **sura**
Surat city in Gujarat in western India
Sûreté (also **Sûreté nationale**) French police department of criminal investigation
surety person taking responsibility for another's action
surfboard (one word)
surf-riding (hyphen)

surgeon general pl. **surgeons general** head of US public health service (lower case)
Suriname (also **Surinam**) country on the NE coast of South America □ **Surinamer, Surinamese**
surmise conjecture (not **-ize**)
surplice white linen vestment
surplus excess of production or supply
surprise (not **sup-**, **-ize**)
surrealism (lower case)
Surrey county of SE England (abbrev. **Surr.**)
surrey pl. **surreys** light four-wheeled carriage (lower case)
surtitle trademark in the US caption projected above an opera stage
surtout hist. man's greatcoat
surveillance (two *l*s)
surveyor, survivor (not **-er**)
Susa ancient city of SW Asia
Susanna book of the Apocrypha (abbrev. **Sus.**)
susceptible (not **-able**)
Susquehanna river of the north-eastern US
Sussex former county of southern England, now divided into **East Sussex** and **West Sussex** (abbrev. **Suss.**)
sustenance food and drink
Sutherland former county of northern Scotland
Sutlej river of India and Pakistan
sutra aphorism in Sanskrit literature
suttee var. of **sati**
SUV sport utility vehicle
Suva capital of Fiji
Suwannee (also **Swanee**) river of the south-eastern US
Suzman, Helen (1917–2009), South African politician
Suzuki 1 method of teaching the violin **2** Japanese vehicle manufacturer
Sv sievert(s)
s.v. under the specified word [L. *sub verbo* or *sub voce*]
Svedberg (also **Svedberg unit**) unit of time used in expressing sedimentation coefficients (abbrev. **S**)
svelte slender and elegant
Sven var. of **Sweyn I**
Svengali person exercising a sinister influence over another (cap.)
Sverige Swed. name for **Sweden**
S-VHS super video home system
Svizzera It. name for **Switzerland**
SW south-west(ern)
Swabia former duchy of medieval Germany; Ger. name **Schwaben** □ **Swabian**
Swahili pl. same **1** Bantu language; also called **Kiswahili 2** member of a people of Zanzibar and nearby
swami pl. **swamis** Hindu religious teacher
Swammerdam, Jan (1637–80), Dutch naturalist
Swanee var. of **Suwannee** (the correct form in *Swanee whistle* and in the song 'Swanee River')
swansdown, swansong (one word)
swan-upping annual marking of swans on the Thames (hyphen)
swap (also **swop**) exchange
swapfile (one word)
SWAPO South West Africa People's Organization
swaraj hist. Indian independence (ital.)
swash (of a capital or other character) ornamental
swat hit sharply with a flat object; cf. **swot**
swathe[1] (chiefly N. Amer. also **swath**) row of mown grass etc.
swathe[2] (wrap in) a strip of fabric
Swazi pl. same or **Swazis** member of a people of Swaziland and South Africa
Swaziland kingdom in southern Africa
swear word (two words)
sweat (past and past part. **sweated** or N. Amer. **sweat**)
sweatband (one word)
sweat gland (two words)
sweatpants, sweatshirt, sweatshop, sweatsuit (one word)
Swed. Swedish
Swede person from Sweden
swede root vegetable (lower case)
Sweden Scandinavian country; Swed. name **Sverige**
Swedenborg, Emanuel (1688–1772),

Swedish scientist and philosopher □ **Swedenborgian**
Swedish (abbrev. **Swed.**)
Sweeney, the Brit. informal the flying squad
sweepstake (one word)
sweet-and-sour (hyphens)
sweetbread, sweetcorn, sweetheart, sweetmeal, sweetmeat (one word)
sweet briar (two words)
sweet pea (two words)
sweet talk n. (two words, hyphen as verb)
sweet tooth pl. **sweet tooths** (two words) □ **sweet-toothed**
sweet william garden plant (two words, lower case)
swell (past part. **swollen** or **swelled**)
swept-back, swept-up adj. (hyphen)
Sweyn I (also **Sven**) (d.1014), king of Denmark *c.*985–1014; known as **Sweyn Forkbeard**
SWG standard wire gauge
Swift, Jonathan (1667–1745), Irish satirist and Anglican cleric
swim (past **swam**; past part. **swum**)
swimming bath, swimming costume, swimming pool, swimming trunks (two words)
swimsuit, swimwear (one word)
Swinburne, Algernon Charles (1837–1909), English poet
swine 1 pl. same, pig **2** pl. same or **swines** contemptible person
swine fever (two words)
swineherd (one word)
swing bridge, swing door (two words)
swingeing hard or severe
swinging lively and fashionable
swing state US state where voters are liable to swing from one political party to another (two words)
swing-wing (of an aircraft) having a wing that can move from a right-angled to a swept-back position (hyphen)
swipe card (two words)
switchback, switchblade, switchboard (one word)
Swithin, St (also **Swithun**) (d.862), English ecclesiastic
Switzerland country in central Europe; Fr. name **Suisse**, Ger. **Schweiz**, It. **Svizzera**, L. **Helvetia**
swivel v. (**swivelling, swivelled**; US one **-l-**)
swizz (also **swiz**) pl. **swizzes** disappointing thing, swindle
swop var. of **swap**
sword dance (two words)
swordfish, swordplay, swordsman (one word)
swot study assiduously; cf. **swat**
swung dash the symbol ~
SY steam yacht
sybaritic fond of sensual pleasure
Sybil female name; cf. **sibyl**
sycamore 1 maple with winged fruits **2** (also **sycomore**) fig tree (in the Bible)
syce (also **sice**) Ind. a groom
Sydenham, Thomas (*c.*1624–89), English physician, known as 'the English Hippocrates'
Sydney capital of New South Wales
syllabary set of characters representing syllables
syllabi pl. of **syllabus**
syllabification (also **syllabication**)
syllabize (Brit. also **syllabise**)
syllable unit of pronunciation
syllabub whipped cream dessert
syllabus pl. **syllabuses** or **syllabi** subjects in a course
syllepsis pl. **syllepses** connection of a word to two others of which it grammatically suits only one (e.g. *neither they nor it is working*) □ **sylleptic**
syllogism example of reasoning with two premises and a conclusion
sylphlike (one word)
sylvan (also **silvan**) wooded or rural
Sylvaner German white wine (cap.)
sylviculture var. of **silviculture**
symbiosis pl. **symbioses**
symbolize (Brit. also **symbolise**)
symmetrical, symmetry (two *ms*)
Symons, Julian (Gustave) (1912–94), English writer
sympathique in tune with another person (Fr., ital.)
sympathize (Brit. also **sympathise**)
sympathy pity and sorrow for someone else's misfortune; cf. **empathy**
symposium pl. **symposia** or **sympo-**

siums conference or drinking party
synaesthesia (US **synesthesia**) production of one kind of sense impression by stimulating a different sense
synagogue building for Jewish worship
sync (also **synch**) synchronization
synchronic concerned with something as it exists at one time; cf. **diachronic**
synchronize (Brit. also **synchronise**)
syncline Geol. fold of rock with upward-sloping strata; cf. **anticline**
syncope omission of sounds or letters within a word
syncretize (Brit. also **syncretise**)
synecdoche figure of speech representing a part by a whole or vice versa (e.g. *England lost by six wickets*)
syneresis (Brit. also **synaeresis**) pl. **synereses** contraction of separate vowels into a diphthong or single vowel
synergy (also **synergism**) interaction to produce a whole greater than the sum of the parts
synesthesia US var. of **synaesthesia**
Synge, J. M. (1871–1909), Irish dramatist; full name *Edmund John Millington Synge*
synonym word meaning the same as another □ **synonymous**
synopsis pl. **synopses** summary or general survey
Synoptic Gospels Matthew, Mark, and Luke, which relate events from a similar point of view
syntax arrangement of words and phrases to form sentences □ **syntactic**
synthesis pl. **syntheses**
synthesize (also **synthetize**, Brit. also **synthesise** or **synthetise**)
syphon var. of **siphon**
Syracuse 1 port in Sicily; It. name **Siracusa 2** city in New York State □ **Syracusan**
Syrah red wine from the Shiraz grape
Syria country in the Middle East □ **Syrian**
Syriac dialect of Aramaic
syringe v. (**syringing**, **syringed**)
syrinx pl. **syrinxes** set of pan pipes
syrup (US also **sirup**)
systematic methodical
systematize (Brit. also **systematise**)
Système International see **SI**
systemic of a whole system
systemize (Brit. also **systemise**)
systems analyst (two words)
systole phase of the heartbeat when the muscle contracts □ **systolic**
syzygy astronomical conjunction
Szczecin city in NW Poland; Ger. name **Stettin**
Szechuan (also **Szechwan**) var. of **Sichuan**
Szent-Györgyi, Albert von (1893–1986), Hungarian-born American biochemist
Szilard, Leo (1898–1964), Hungarian-born American physicist and molecular biologist

T

T 1 pl. **Ts** or **T's** 20th letter of the alphabet **2** tera- (10^{12}) **3** tesla **4** (in sport) Town **5** Chem. tritium

t ton(s)

T temperature

TA Territorial Army

Ta the chemical element tantalum (no point)

t/a trading as

TAB 1 Austral. & NZ Totalizator Agency Board **2** typhoid–paratyphoid A and B vaccine

tabac French tobacconist's shop (ital.)

Tabasco[1] state of SE Mexico

Tabasco[2] trademark pungent sauce

tabbouleh Arab salad with cracked wheat

tabernacle tent used as a sanctuary for the Ark of the Covenant

Tabernacles, Feast of Jewish festival of Succoth

tabla pair of small hand drums

tablature musical notation indicating fingering rather than pitch

tableau pl. **tableaux** group of figures representing a scene (not ital.)

tableau vivant pl. ***tableaux vivants*** tableau with real people (Fr., ital.)

tablecloth (one word)

table d'hôte set meal (accent, not ital.)

tableland (one word)

tablespoon large spoon for serving food; measurement in cookery (one word; abbrev. **tbsp** or **tbs**)

table tennis (two words)

tabletop, tableware (one word)

taboo pl. **taboos** (not **tabu** exc. in anthropology)

tabor hist. small drum (not **-our**)

tabouret (US **taboret**) low stool or small table

tabula rasa pl. ***tabulae rasae*** absence of preconceived or innate ideas (L., ital.)

tabulator facility for advancing to a set position in tabular work

tac-au-tac Fencing parry combined with a riposte (not ital.)

tacet Mus. indicating that a voice or instrument is silent (not ital.)

tachism (also **tachisme**) French style of painting using dabs of colour (not ital.)

tachograph tachometer providing a record over time

tachometer instrument for measuring the speed of an engine

tachygraphy ancient or medieval shorthand

tachymeter theodolite for rapid measuring of distances

Tacitus (*c.*56–*c.*120 AD), Roman historian; full name *Publius*, or *Gaius*, *Cornelius Tacitus*

taco pl. **tacos** tortilla with a filling

Tadjik, Tadzhik vars of **Tajik**

Tadzhikistan var. of **Tajikistan**

tae-bo trademark exercise system combining aerobics and kick-boxing

taedium vitae weariness of life (L., ital.)

tae kwon do Korean martial art (three words)

taenia (US **tenia**) pl. **taeniae** or **taenias** fillet between a Doric architrave and frieze

taffeta crisp lustrous fabric

taffrail rail around a ship's stern

Tagalog member of a people of the Philippines; their language

tagine (also **tajine**) North African stew

tagliatelle pasta in narrow ribbons (not **-lli**)

Tagore, Rabindranath (1861–1941), Indian writer and philosopher

tag question question formed by a statement with an interrogative formula such as *isn't it?*

Tagus river in the Iberian peninsula; Sp.

name **Tajo**, Port. name **Tejo**
tahini (also **tahina**) paste made from ground sesame seeds
Tahiti island in the South Pacific □ **Tahitian**
tahr (also **thar**) goat-like mammal
Tai family of SE Asian languages
t'ai chi ch'uan (also **t'ai chi**) Chinese martial art
tail blank space at the bottom of a page
tailback, tailboard (one word)
tail end (two words, hyphen when attrib.) □ **tail-ender** (Cricket)
tail feather, tail fin (two words)
tailgate (one word)
Tailleferre, Germaine (1892–1983), French composer and pianist
tailless (one word)
tail light (two words)
tailor person who makes clothes (not **taylor**)
tailor-made (hyphen)
tailpiece small decorative design at the foot of a page or the end of a chapter or book (one word)
tailpipe, tailplane, tailspin, tailwind (one word)
Taino extinct Caribbean language
taipan 1 foreign head of a business in China **2** venomous Australian snake
Taipei capital of Taiwan
Taiping Rebellion uprising against the Qing dynasty in China 1850–64
Taiwan island country off the SE coast of China □ **Taiwanese**
Tajik (also **Tadjik** or **Tadzhik**) member of a people of Tajikistan
Tajikistan (also **Tadzhikistan**) republic in central Asia
tajine var. of **tagine**
Taj Mahal mausoleum at Agra in northern India
Tajo Sp. name for **Tagus**
takable (also **takeable**)
take amount of copy set up at one time or by one compositor
takeaway n. (one word, two words as verb)
take back transfer (text) to the previous line (abbrev. **t.b.**)
take-home pay (one hyphen)
take-off n. (hyphen, two words as verb)
takeout N. Amer. takeaway (one word, two words as verb)
takeover n. (one word, two words as verb)
take over transfer (text) to the next line (abbrev. **t.o.**)
take-up n. (hyphen, two words as verb)
Taleban var. of **Taliban**
talebearer (one word)
taleggio soft Italian cheese
tales writ for summoning substitute jurors (not ital.)
talesman juror summoned by a tales (one word); cf. **talisman**
tale teller (two words) □ **tale-telling**
tali pl. of **talus**
Taliban (also **Taleban**) fundamentalist Muslim movement of Afghanistan
Taliesin (*fl.* 550), Welsh bard
talipes Med. club foot
talisman pl. **talismans** good-luck charm; cf. **talesman**
talk radio, talk show (two words)
Tallahassee state capital of Florida
tallboy tall chest of drawers (one word)
Talleyrand, Charles Maurice de (1754–1838), French statesman; full surname *Talleyrand-Périgord*
Tallinn capital of Estonia
Tallis, Thomas (*c.*1505–85), English composer
tallith fringed shawl worn by Jewish men at prayer
tally-ho (**tally-hoes, tally-hoing, tally-hoed**) (hyphen)
Talmud body of Jewish law and legend
talus pl. **tali** large bone in the ankle
tamable var. of **tameable**
tamarillo pl. **tamarillos** egg-shaped red fruit
tamarin South American monkey
tamarind tree with pods used in Asian cookery
tamarisk shrub with a feathery appearance
tambour 1 hist. small drum **2** circular frame for embroidery
tamboura (also **tambura**) Balkan lute or mandoline
tambourin Provençal drum

tambourine percussion instrument with metal discs
tameable (also **tamable**)
Tamerlane (also **Tamburlaine**) (1336–1405), Mongol ruler of Samarkand 1369–1405
Tamil member of a people of South India and Sri Lanka □ **Tamilian**
Tamil Nadu state in SE India
Taming of the Shrew, The Shakespeare play (abbrev. ***Tam. Shr.***)
Tamla Motown see **Motown**
Tammany (also **Tammany Hall**) US organization within the Democratic Party
Tammuz[1] Mesopotamian god
Tammuz[2] var. of **Thammuz**
Tam o' Shanter poem by Robert Burns (1791) (three words, apostrophe)
tam-o'-shanter cap with a bobble (lower case, hyphens, apostrophe)
Tampa resort in Florida
Tampax pl. same, trademark sanitary tampon
Tampere city in SW Finland
tampion (also **tompion**) stopper for a gun muzzle
tampon absorbent plug
Tam. Shr. Shakespeare's *The Taming of the Shrew*
tan tangent (no point)
Tánaiste deputy prime minister of Ireland
tandoori cooked using a **tandoor** (clay oven)
Tanganyika former country in East Africa, the mainland part of Tanzania
tangelo pl. **tangelos** tangerine and grapefruit hybrid
tangent Math. (abbrev. **tan**)
tangerine small citrus fruit
tangible perceptible by touch
Tangier seaport in northern Morocco (not **-iers**)
tango n. pl. **tangos**. v. **tangoes, tangoing, tangoed**
tanh hyperbolic tangent (no point)
tanka pl. same or **tankas** Japanese poem in five lines and thirty-one syllables (not ital.)
Tannhäuser 1 (*c.*1200–*c.*1270), German poet **2** (***Tannhäuser***) opera by Wagner (1845)
tannoy public address system (cap. as trademark)
tantalize (Brit. also **tantalise**)
tantalum chemical element of atomic number 73 (symbol **Ta**)
Tantalus Lydian king punished with unreachable fruit and water
tantalus lockable stand for decanters (lower case)
tant mieux so much the better (Fr., ital.)
tant pis so much the worse (Fr., ital.)
tantra Hindu or Buddhist mystical text
Tanzania country in East Africa □ **Tanzanian**
Taoiseach prime minister of Ireland
Taoism (also **Daoism**) Chinese philosophy based on the writings of Lao-tzu
Taormina town in Sicily
Tao-te-Ching (also **Daodejing**) central Taoist text
tap dance n. (two words, hyphen as verb) □ **tap dancer, tap-dancing**
tape machine, tape measure (two words)
tapenade olive paste [Fr. *tapénade*]
tape recorder (two words) □ **tape-record, tape recording**
tapeworm (one word)
taproom, taproot (one word)
Tarabulus al-Gharb, Tarabulus Ash-Sham see **Tripoli**
taradiddle (also **tarradiddle**) petty lie
taramasalata fish-roe paste
tarantella (also **tarantelle**) whirling dance
tarantula large hairy spider
Tardenoisian late Mesolithic culture of west and central Europe
Tardis time machine in the TV series *Doctor Who*
target v. (**targeting, targeted**)
tariff duty on imports or exports (one *r*, two *f*s)
tarmac (noun cap. as trademark; verb **tarmacking, tarmacked**)
tarmacadam (lower case)
taro pl. **taros** plant with edible starchy corms
tarot game played with **the Tarot**, a set

of playing cards for fortune-telling
tarpaulin waterproof cloth
Tarpeian Rock cliff in ancient Rome
tarradiddle var. of **taradiddle**
tarragon culinary herb
Tarragona city in north-eastern Spain
tarsus pl. **tarsi** Anat. group of small bones forming the ankle and upper foot
Tartar hist. member of conquering central Asian forces in the 13th and 14th cents; cf. **Tatar** □ **Tartarian**
tartar[1] fierce or intractable person
tartar[2] hard deposit on the teeth
tartare served raw (after the noun)
tartare sauce (also **tartar sauce**) mayonnaise mixed with onions, gherkins, and capers
Tartarus part of the Greek underworld where the wicked suffered punishment □ **Tartarean**
Tartary historical region of Asia and eastern Europe
Tartuffe religious hypocrite; (***Le Tartuffe***) play by Molière (1669)
Tas. Tasmania
taser weapon firing electrified barbs
Tashkent capital of Uzbekistan
task force (two words)
taskmaster, taskmistress (one word)
Tasmania state and island of Australia (abbrev. **Tas.**) □ **Tasmanian**
Tass former name for **ITAR-Tass**
tassel (not **tassle**)
tasselled (US **tasseled**)
taste bud (two words)
tastevin shallow cup for tasting wine (Fr., ital.)
Tatar member of a Turkic people of **Tatarstan**, an autonomous republic in European Russia; cf. **Tartar**
Tate Gallery national museum of art in London, renamed **Tate Britain** in 2000
Tate Modern museum of modern art in London
tatterdemalion tattered, dilapidated
tattersall checked woollen fabric (lower case)
Tattersalls English firm of horse auctioneers (no apostrophe)
tattoo (**tattoos, tattooing, tattooed**)
tau nineteenth letter of the Greek alphabet (**Τ**, **τ**), transliterated as 't'
tau cross T-shaped cross
taught past and past part. of **teach**
Taurus second sign of the zodiac □ **Taurean**
taut tight, not slack
tautology the saying of the same thing in different words
Tavener, Sir John (Kenneth) (1944–2013), English composer
taverna small Greek restaurant (not ital.)
Taverner, John (*c.*1490–1545), English composer
tawny (not **-ey**)
tax-free (hyphen)
taxi n. pl. **taxis**. v. **taxies, taxiing** or **taxying, taxied**
taxicab, taxiway (one word)
taxon pl. **taxa** taxonomic group
taxpayer (one word)
Taylor 1 Dame Elizabeth (1932–2011), American actress **2** Zachary (1784–1850), 12th president of the US 1849–50
taylor use **tailor**
Taylor Institute (also **the Taylorian**) library in Oxford
tazza shallow wine cup (not ital.)
TB 1 terabyte(s) **2** tubercle bacillus; tuberculosis
Tb the chemical element terbium (no point)
t.b. take back
TBA to be announced (or arranged)
TBC to be confirmed
Tbilisi capital of Georgia; former name **Tiflis**
T-bone (hyphen)
tbsp (also **tbs**) pl. same or **tbsps** tablespoon
Tc the chemical element technetium (no point)
TCD Trinity College, Dublin
Tchaikovsky, Pyotr (Ilich) (1840–93), Russian composer
TD 1 Teachta Dála, Member of the Dáil **2** technical drawing **3** Territorial (Officer's) Decoration **4** Amer. Football touchdown

Te the chemical element tellurium (no point)
te (N. Amer. **ti**) Mus. note in tonic sol-fa
teabag (one word)
tea break (two words)
teacake (one word)
tea ceremony, tea chest (two words)
Teachta Dála pl. **Teachtai Dála** member of the Irish Dáil (abbrev. **TD**)
tea cosy (two words)
teacup (one word)
tea dance, tea garden, tea leaf (two words)
teammate (one word)
teamster N. Amer. truck driver; (**Teamsters Union**) a union including truck drivers and warehouse workers
teamwork (one word)
tea party, tea planter (two words)
teapot (one word)
teapoy small three-legged table
tearaway wild person (one word)
teardrop (one word)
tear duct, tear gas (two words)
tear-jerker (hyphen)
tear sheet page that can be removed from a newspaper, magazine, or book for separate use
tease (not **-ze**)
teasel (also **teazle**) tall plant with spiny flower heads
Teasmade trademark automatic tea-maker
teaspoon small spoon for stirring hot drinks; measurement in cookery (one word; abbrev. **tsp**)
teatime (one word)
tea towel, tea tray (two words)
teazle var. of **teasle**
Tebet (also **Tevet**) (in the Jewish calendar) fourth month of the civil and tenth of the religious year
tech (also **tec**) **1** Brit. technical college **2** technology
technetium chemical element of atomic number 43 (symbol **Tc**)
Technicolor trademark process of colour cinematography
technicolored (Brit. also **technicoloured**) vividly coloured
teddy bear (two words, lower case)
Teddy boy (two words, one cap.)
Te Deum ancient hymn (L., ital.)
tee-hee (**tee-heeing, tee-heed**) titter (hyphen)
teenage, teenaged, teenager (one word)
teepee var. of **tepee**
tee shirt var. of **T-shirt**
Teesside industrial region in NE England
teetotal avoiding alcohol (abbrev. **TT**)
teetotaller (US **teetotaler**)
TEFL teaching of English as a foreign language
Teflon trademark synthetic resin used as a non-stick coating
Tegucigalpa capital of Honduras
Tehran (also **Teheran**) capital of Iran
Teilhard de Chardin, Pierre (1881–1955), French Jesuit philosopher and palaeontologist
Tejo Port. name for **Tagus**
Te Kanawa, Dame Kiri (Janette) (b.1944), New Zealand operatic soprano
tel. telephone
telamon pl. **telamones** male figure as an architectural support (not ital.)
Tel Aviv (also **Tel Aviv-Jaffa**) city on the coast of Israel
telco pl. **telcos** telecommunications company
telebanking (one word)
telecoms (also **telecomms**) telecommunications (treated as sing.)
teleconference, teleconferencing (one word)
Telegu var. of **Telugu**
Telemann, Georg Philipp (1681–1767), German composer
telemarketing (one word)
Telemessage trademark message sent by telephone or telex and delivered in written form
téléphérique cableway; cable car (Fr., ital.)
telephone (abbrev. **tel.**)
telephoto pl. **telephotos** lens with long focal length
teletex enhanced version of telex
teletext news and information service (lower case)

telethon long television programme to raise money
televise (not **-ize**) ▫ **televisable**
telex international system of telegraphy
Telford, Thomas (1757–1834), Scottish civil engineer
Tell el-Amarna site of the ruins of the ancient Egyptian capital Akhetaten
telling-off pl. **tellings-off** (hyphen)
telltale (one word)
tellurian (inhabitant) of the earth
tellurium chemical element of atomic number 52 (symbol **Te**)
telnet computer network protocol
Telstar first active communications satellite
Telugu (also **Telegu**) pl. same or **Telugus** member of a people of Andhra Pradesh, India
Téméraire, The Fighting painting by Turner (1839)
temp. in or from the time of (not ital.) [L. *tempore*]
Temp. Shakespeare's *The Tempest*
tempera method of painting with an emulsion
temperance (not **-ence**)
temperature (symbol ***T***)
tempest 1 violent storm **2** (***The Tempest***) Shakespeare play (abbrev. ***Temp.***)
Templar member of the Knights Templar
template rigid piece used as a pattern (not **templet**)
tempo pl. **tempos** or **tempi** speed of a passage of music
temporary not permanent (not **-pory**)
temporize (Brit. also **temporise**)
tempo rubato Mus. another name for **rubato**
Tempranillo Spanish red-wine grape
tempura Japanese dish of fish or vegetables fried in batter
ten (Roman numeral **x** or **X**) ▫ **tenfold, tenth**
ten. tenuto
Ten Commandments the rules of conduct given by God to Moses (caps)
tendency (not **-ancy**)
tendentious intended to promote a particular point of view
tenderfoot pl. **tenderfoots** or **tenderfeet** newcomer or novice (one word)
tenderize (Brit. also **tenderise**)
tenderloin (one word)
tendinitis (also **tendonitis**) inflammation of a tendon
Tendulkar, Sachin (b.1973), Indian cricketer
Tenerife largest of the Canary Islands
tenesi pl. same, monetary unit of Turkmenistan
tenet principle or belief (not **-ent**)
tenge pl. same or **tenges** monetary unit of Kazakhstan
Teniers 1 David (1610–90), Flemish painter; known as **David Teniers the Younger 2** David (1582–1649), Flemish painter, his father
Tennessee 1 river in the south-eastern US **2** state in the central south-eastern US (official abbrev. **Tenn.**, postal **TN**) ▫ **Tennessean** (also **Tennesseean**)
Tenniel, Sir John (1820–1914), English illustrator and cartoonist
Tenno pl. **Tennos** the Emperor of Japan (cap.; see also **Meiji Tenno**)
Tennyson, Alfred, 1st Baron Tennyson of Aldworth and Freshwater (1809–92), English poet ▫ **Tennysonian**
Tenochtitlán ancient Aztec capital
tenor (not **-our**)
tenpin bowling (two words)
tense set of verb forms indicating the time of the action
tenterhooks (one word)
tenuto pl. **tenutos** or **tenuti** (note or chord) held for its full time value (abbrev. **ten.**)
Tenzing Norgay (1914–86), Sherpa mountaineer
Teotihuacán city of pre-Columbian America
tepee (also **teepee** or **tipi**) conical American Indian tent
tequila alcoholic spirit made from agave
Ter. Terrace
terabyte Comput. 10^{12} or (strictly) 2^{40} bytes (abbrev. **TB**)
teraphim ancient Semitic cult objects (not ital; treated as pl. or sing.)

terawatt 10^{12} watts or a trillion megawatts
terbium chemical element of atomic number 65 (symbol **Tb**)
terce Christian office said at the third daytime hour
tercel (also **tiercel**) male hawk (female is called a **falcon**)
tercentenary (also **tercentennial**) three-hundredth anniversary
tercet group of three lines of verse
Terence (*c.*190–159 BC), Roman comic dramatist; Latin name *Publius Terentius Afer*
Teresa 1 (**Mother Teresa**) (1910–97), Roman Catholic nun and missionary; born *Agnes Gonxha Bojaxhiu* **2** (**St Teresa of Ávila**) (1515–82), Spanish Carmelite nun and mystic **3** (**St Teresa of Lisieux**) (1873–97), French Carmelite nun; born *Marie-Françoise Thérèse Martin*
tergiversate equivocate □ **tergiversator**
termagant bad-tempered or overbearing woman
terminator (not **-er**)
terminus pl. **termini** or **terminuses**
terminus ad quem finishing point (L., ital.)
terminus ante quem latest possible date (L., ital.)
terminus a quo starting point (L., ital.)
terminus post quem earliest possible date (L., ital.)
Terpsichore the Muse of lyric poetry and dance
terpsichorean of dancing (lower case)
Terr. Territory
terra alba pulverized gypsum (not ital.)
terrace (cap. in names; abbrev. **Ter.**)
terracotta (one word; two *r*s, two *t*s)
terra firma dry land (not ital.)
terrain stretch of land; cf. **terrane**
terra incognita unknown territory (not ital.)
terrane Geol. distinctive fault-bounded area; cf. **terrain**
terrapin freshwater turtle (two *r*s)
terrarium pl. **terrariums** or **terraria** vivarium for smaller land animals (not ital.)
terra rossa reddish Mediterranean soil (not ital.)
terra sigillata astringent clay (not ital.)
terrazzo flooring material with marble or granite chips (not ital.)
terret (also **territ**) loop for driving reins
terre verte greyish-green pigment (two words, not ital.)
territory (cap. in names; abbrev. **Terr.**)
Terror, the period of the French Revolution 1793–4 (cap.)
terrorize (Brit. also **terrorise**)
tertium quid third thing ill-defined but known to exist (not ital.)
Terylene trademark textile fibre
terza rima triplets rhyming *aba*, *bcb*, etc. (not ital.)
terzetto pl. **terzettos** or **terzetti** vocal or instrumental trio (not ital.)
Tesco UK food retailer (not **Tesco's**)
TESL teaching of English as a second language
tesla SI unit of magnetic flux density (lower case; abbrev. **T**)
TESOL teaching of English to speakers of other languages
TESSA tax-exempt special savings account replaced in 1999 by the ISA
tessellate (US also **tesselate**) decorate with mosaics (two *ss*, two *ls*) □ **tessellation**
tessera pl. **tesserae** piece used in mosaics
tessitura Mus. range of a vocal part
Tess of the D'Urbervilles novel by Hardy (1891)
Testament division of the Bible (cap.)
testator Law person who has made a will (not **-er**)
test drive n. (two words, hyphen as verb)
testis pl. **testes**
Test match (one cap.)
test tube (two words, hyphen when attrib.)
tête-à-tête pl. same or **tête-à-têtes** (accents, hyphens, not ital.)
tête-bêche (of a postage stamp) printed upside down or sideways (accents, hyphen, ital.)
Tetragrammaton Hebrew name of

God written in four letters, YHVH or YHWH (cap.)

tetrahedron pl. **tetrahedra** or **tetrahedrons**

tetralogy four related literary or operatic works

tetrameter verse of four measures

tetraplegia another term for **quadriplegia**

tetrastich four lines of verse

tetrasyllable word of four syllables

tetri pl. same or **tetris** monetary unit of Georgia

Tevere It. name for **Tiber**

Texas state in the southern US (official abbrev. **Tex.**, postal **TX**) ◻ **Texan**

textbook (one word)

text message, **text messaging** (two words)

textured vegetable protein (abbrev. **TVP**)

texturize (Brit. also **texturise**)

textus receptus the received text (L., ital.)

TGV French high-speed train [*train à grande vitesse*]

TGWU Transport and General Workers' Union

Th the chemical element thorium (no point)

Th. Thursday

Thackeray, William Makepeace (1811–63), British novelist

Thai pl. same or **Thais** native of Thailand

Thailand kingdom in SE Asia; former name **Siam**

thaler old German silver coin

Thalia the Muse of comedy

thallium chemical element of atomic number 81 (symbol **Ti**)

Thames river of southern England

Thammuz (also **Tammuz**) (in the Jewish calendar) the tenth month of the civil and fourth of the religious year

thankfully in a thankful manner; disp. fortunately

thanksgiving (one word) **1** expression of gratitude to God **2** (**Thanksgiving** or **Thanksgiving Day**) North American national holiday, the fourth Thursday in November in the US

thank you (two words, hyphen when attrib.)

thar var. of **tahr**

the cap. and ital. if part of a work's title; lower case in names of events, groups, etc.; see also **periodicals, titles of**

theatre (US **theater**)

theatregoer (one word)

theatre-in-the-round (hyphens)

thebe pl. same, monetary unit of Botswana

Thebes 1 city in Greece; mod. Gk name **Thívai 2** Greek name for an ancient city of Upper Egypt ◻ **Theban**

thé dansant pl. ***thés dansants*** tea dance (Fr., ital.)

thee arch. you (sing. obj.)

thegn English thane

their of them; cf. **there, they're**

theirs (no apostrophe; cf. **there's**)

theism belief in the existence of a god or gods, spec. of a creator who intervenes in the universe; cf. **deism**

themself avoid; use **themselves, himself, herself**

Theocritus (*c.*310–*c.*250 BC), Greek poet

theodolite surveying instrument

theologize (Brit. also **theologise**)

Theophrastus (*c.*370–*c.*287 BC), Greek philosopher and scientist

theorbo pl. **theorbos** large lute

theorem proposition proved by reasoning (not **-um**)

theorize (Brit. also **theorise**)

theory supposition or system of ideas

therapeutic (not **-put-**)

Theravada more conservative tradition of Buddhism; cf. **Mahayana**

there to or at that place; cf. **their, they're**

thereat, thereafter (one word)

therefor arch. for that purpose

therefore for that reason (math. symbol ∴)

therein, thereinafter, thereinbefore, thereof (one word)

there's there is (apostrophe); cf. **theirs**

Theresa, Mother, Thérèse of Lisieux, St, see **Teresa**

Thermopylae pass between the mountains and the sea in Greece

Thermos trademark vacuum flask
thesaurus pl. **thesauri** or **thesauruses** book that lists words in groups of synonyms
thesis pl. **theses** titles in roman, in quotation marks
Thessalonians, Epistle to the either of two books of the New Testament (abbrev. **1 Thess., 2 Thess.**)
Thessaloníki seaport in NE Greece; Latin name **Thessalonica**
Thessaly region of NE Greece; mod. Gk name **Thessalí** ◻ **Thessalian**
theta eighth letter of the Greek alphabet (**Θ, θ**), transliterated as 'th'
they're they are; cf. **their, there**
thiamine (also **thiamin**) B vitamin
thickhead, thickset (one word)
thick-skinned, thick-skulled (hyphen)
thick space one third of an em space
thief pl. **thieves**
thimbleful pl. **thimblefuls**
Thimphu (also **Thimbu**) capital of Bhutan
thine arch. yours or (before a vowel) your (sing.)
thingamabob (also **thingamajig**) unnamed person or thing; thingummy
thingummy unnamed person or thing
think tank (two words)
thin space one fifth of an em space
third best, third class (two words, hyphen when attrib.)
third-degree, third-generation, third-hand (hyphen)
third party (two words, hyphen when attrib.)
third-rate (hyphen)
Third Reich the Nazi regime, 1933–45
Third World (caps, no hyphen even when attrib.; **developing countries** is often preferred)
thirteen (Roman numeral **xiii** or **XIII**) ◻ **thirteenth**
thirties (also **1930s**) decade (lower case, no apostrophe)
thirty hyphen in compound numbers, e.g. *thirty-one*; Roman numeral **xxx** or **XXX** ◻ **thirtieth**
Thirty-Nine Articles doctrines accepted by the Church of England (three caps, one hyphen)
thirty-second note Mus., chiefly N. Amer. demisemiquaver
thirty-twomo pl. **thirty-twomos** page size resulting from folding each sheet into thirty-two leaves (abbrev. **32mo**)
Thirty Years War European war of 1618–48 (caps, no apostrophe)
Thívai see **Thebes**
tho' though (apostrophe)
Thomas, St Apostle; known as **Doubting Thomas**
Thomas à Kempis (*c.*1380–1471), German theologian
Thomism doctrine of St Thomas Aquinas
Thompson 1 Daley (b.1958), English athlete **2** Emma (b.1959), English actress **3** Flora (Jane) (1876–1947), English writer **4** Francis (1859–1907), English poet
Thomson 1 Sir George Paget (1892–1975), English physicist **2** James (1700–48), Scottish poet, probable author of 'Rule, Britannia' **3** James (1834–82), Scottish poet, author of 'The City of Dreadful Night' **4** Sir Joseph John (1856–1940), English atomic physicist **5** Roy Herbert, 1st Baron Thomson of Fleet (1894–1976), Canadian-born British newspaper proprietor **6** Sir Willliam, see **Kelvin**
Thomson's gazelle (not **Thompson's**)
thorax pl. **thoraces** or **thoraxes** body between the neck and abdomen or tail ◻ **thoracic**
Thoreau, Henry David (1817–62), American writer
thorium chemical element of atomic number 90 (symbol **Th**)
thorn Old English and Icelandic runic letter, Þ, þ or ƀ, ƀ, representing the dental fricatives /ð/ and /θ/; superseded by *th*; cf. **eth, wyn**
thorough bass basso continuo (two words)
thoroughbred, thoroughfare, thoroughgoing (one word)
Thorshavn var. of **Tórshavn**
Thos Thomas (no point)
thou[1] arch. you (sing. subj.)

thou² pl. same or **thous** informal thousand (no point)
thought-provoking (hyphen)
thousand pl. **thousands** or (with numeral or quantifying word) same (hyphen in compound ordinal numbers, e.g. *thousand-and-first*; Roman numeral **m** or **M**) □ **thousandth**
Thousand and One Nights another name for ***Arabian Nights***
thrall □ **thraldom**
threadbare (one word)
Threadneedle Street street in the City of London, location of the Bank of England
threadworm (one word)
three (Roman numeral **iii** or **III**) □ **threefold, threesome**
three-card trick, three-colour process (one hyphen)
three-dimensional (hyphen)
Three Estates, the see **Estates of the Realm, the**
3G third-generation
Three Graces Gk Mythol. the Graces
threepence, threepenny (one word)
three-point turn (one hyphen)
three-quarter adj., n. (hyphen)
three quarters n., adv. (two words)
three Rs reading, writing, and arithmetic (no apostrophe)
threescore sixty; (**threescore and ten**) seventy (one word)
Three Wise Men the Magi (caps)
threnody (also **threnode**) lament
threshold (one *h*)
thrips (also **thrip**) pl. **thrips** plant pest
thrive (**thriving**, past **throve** or **thrived**; past part. **thriven** or **thrived**)
thrombosis pl. **thromboses**
throughput (one word)
Through the Looking-Glass book by Lewis Carroll (1871)
throughway (also **thruway**) N. Amer. major road or motorway
throwaway adj. (one word, two words as verb)
throwback n. (one word, two words as verb)
throw-in n. (hyphen, two words as verb)
thruway var. of **throughway**
Thucydides (*c.*455–*c.*400 BC), Greek historian
Thug hist. assassin in India (cap.)
thug violent person
thuggee hist. practice of the Thugs (lower case)
Thule 1 country north of Britain described by the ancient explorer Pytheas **2** settlement in NW Greenland
thulium chemical element of atomic number 69 (symbol **Tm**)
thumb index (two words) □ **thumb-indexed**
thumbnail, thumbprint, thumbscrew, thumbtack (one word)
Thummim see **Urim and Thummim**
thunderbolt, thunderclap, thundercloud, thunderstorm (one word)
Thuringia state of central Germany; Ger. name **Thüringen**
Thursday (abbrev. **Th., Thurs.**)
thy (also **thine** before a vowel) arch. your (sing.)
thyme culinary herb
thymus pl. **thymi** Anat. organ in the neck
Ti the chemical element titanium (no point)
ti var. of **te**
Tia Maria trademark coffee-flavoured rum liqueur
Tiananmen Square square in Beijing, China
tiara □ **tiaraed** (also **tiara'd**)
Tiber river of central Italy; It. name **Tevere**
Tiberius (42 BC–AD 37), Roman emperor AD 14–37; Latin name *Tiberius Julius Caesar Augustus* □ **Tiberian**
Tibet country in Asia; Chinese name **Xizang** □ **Tibetan**
tibia pl. **tibiae** or **tibias** inner bone between the knee and the ankle
Tibullus, Albius (*c.*50–19 BC), Roman poet
tic muscle contraction
tic douloureux facial neuralgia (two words, not ital.)
tick Brit. mark (✓) to indicate that an item in a text is correct

ticket v. (**ticketing, ticketed**)
ticket office (two words)
tic-tac (also **tick-tack**) manual semaphore used at racecourses (hyphen)
tic-tac-toe (also **tick-tack-toe**) N. Amer. noughts and crosses (hyphens)
tidbit US var. of **titbit**
tiddlywink (US **tiddledywink**)
tideland, tideline, tidemark (one word)
tide rip, tide table (two words)
tidewater, tideway (one word)
tie (**tying, tied**)
tie-back cord to hold something back (hyphen, two words as verb)
tie beam (two words)
tiebreaker (also **tiebreak**) (one word)
tie-dye (hyphen)
tie-in n. (hyphen, two words as verb)
tiepin (one word)
Tiepolo, Giovanni Battista (1696–1770), Italian painter
tier row or level
tierce 1 another name for **terce 2** organ stop **3** Fencing parrying position
tiercel var. of **tercel**
Tierra del Fuego island at the southern extremity of South America
tie-up n. (hyphen, two words as verb)
TIFF Comput. tagged image file format
Tiffany, Louis Comfort (1848–1933), American glass-maker and interior decorator
tiffany thin gauze muslin (lower case)
tiffin Ind. snack or light lunch
Tiflis former name for **Tbilisi**
Tiger balm trademark mentholated ointment (cap.)
tigerish (not **tigr-**)
tigerwood (one word)
tight-fisted, tight-lipped (hyphen)
tightrope (one word)
Tigray (also **Tigre**) province of Ethiopia
Tigre 1 language of Eritrea and parts of Sudan; cf. **Tigrinya 2** another name for **Tigray**
Tigrinya language of Tigray; cf. **Tigre**
Tigris river in SW Asia
Tijuana town in NW Mexico
tika another term for **tilak**; cf. **tikka**
tike var. of **tyke**
tiki pl. **tikis** NZ large wooden or small greenstone image of a human figure
tikka Indian dish of pieces of marinated meat or vegetables; cf. **tika**
tilak mark worn on a Hindu's forehead
tilde accent ˜ placed over a Spanish *n* or Portuguese *a* or *o*, or used in phonetic transcriptions to indicate nasalization
Tim. Timothy (in biblical references)
timbal arch. kettledrum
timbale 1 moulded minced meat or fish **2** (**timbales**) paired Latin American cylindrical drums
timbre character of a musical sound or voice
Timbuktu (also **Timbuctoo**) town in northern Mali; Fr. name **Tombouctou**
time cap. when personified; time of day in numerals with full point (colon in US) where time contains minutes or hours, as 9.35, 09.35, but spelled out in phrs such as 'half past ten'
time and motion study (four words)
time bomb, time capsule (two words)
time-consuming, time-honoured (hyphen)
time frame (two words)
timekeeper, timekeeping (one word)
time lag, time limit (two words)
timeline (one word)
time lock, time machine, time off (two words)
timeout a brief break in play or activity (one word)
time out time for rest or recreation (two words)
timepiece, timescale, timeshare (one word)
time-sharing (hyphen)
time sheet, time signal, time signature, time span (two words)
times table (two words)
Times, The UK newspaper (cap. and italic *The*)
timetable (one word)
time travel, time trial, time warp, time zone (two words)
Timon of Athens Shakespeare play (abbrev. ***Timon***)
Timor island in the southern Malay

Archipelago ◻ **Timorese**
Timor Leste official name for **East Timor**
Timothy, Epistle to either of two books of the New Testament (abbrev. **1 Tim., 2 Tim.**)
timpani (also **tympani**) orchestral kettledrums (pl.) ◻ **timpanist**
tin chemical element of atomic number 50 (symbol **Sn**)
tinfoil (one word)
tinge v. (**tinging** or **tingeing, tinged**)
tin Lizzie early Ford car (one cap.)
tinnitus Med. ringing in the ears
tin opener (two words)
Tin Pan Alley the world of composers and publishers of popular music (three caps)
tinplate, tinpot (one word)
tinselled (US **tinseled**)
tinsmith (one word)
Tintagel village in northern Cornwall
tintinnabulation ringing or tinkling sound (double *n*)
Tintoretto (1518–94), Italian painter; born *Jacopo Robusti*
tip-in basketball score
tip in stick (a page) into a book with a line of paste down its inner margin
tip-off n. (hyphen, two words as verb)
Tipperary county in the Republic of Ireland
tippet long cape or scarf
Tippett, Sir Michael (Kemp) (1905–98), English composer
Tipp-Ex n. trademark correction fluid. v. (**tippex**) delete with Tipp-Ex
tiptoe (**tiptoeing, tiptoed**) (one word)
tip-top (hyphen)
tiramisu Italian dessert
Tirana (also **Tiranë**) capital of Albania
tire US var. of **tyre**
Tir-na-nog Irish equivalent of Elysium (one cap., two hyphens)
tiro var. of **tyro**
Tirol Ger. name for **Tyrol**
'tis it is (apostrophe)
Tishri (also **Tisri**) (in the Jewish calendar) the first month of the civil and seventh of the religious year
Tisiphone Gk Mythol. one of the Furies
Tit. Epistle to Titus
Tit. A. Shakespeare's *Titus Andronicus*
Titan Gk Mythol. any of the older gods who preceded the Olympians
titan person or thing of very great strength or importance (lower case)
Titanic British liner that sank on her maiden voyage in 1912
titanic exceptionally strong or great
titanium chemical element of atomic number 22 (symbol **Ti**)
titbit (US **tidbit**)
tit for tat (three words)
Titian (*c.*1488–1576), Italian painter; Italian name *Tiziano Vecellio* ◻ **Titianesque**
titillate excite pleasurably (two *l*s)
titivate make minor enhancements to (not **titt-**)
title page page at the beginning of a book giving the title, author, and publisher
titles articles, chapters, shorter poems, songs to be cited in roman, in quotation marks; books, periodicals, epic poems, plays, operas, symphonies, ballets, in italic; works of art, pieces of music in ital. if named by the creator, roman in quotation marks if popularly identified as such by others
title verso reverse of a title page
titmouse pl. **titmice**
Tito (1892–1980), Yugoslav prime minister 1945–53 and president 1953–80; born *Josip Broz*
Titograd former name for **Podgorica**
tittle-tattle (hyphen)
tittup (**tittuping, tittuped** or **tittupping, tittupped**) move jerkily
Titus Andronicus Shakespeare play (abbrev. ***Tit. A.***)
Titus, Epistle to book of the New Testament (abbrev. **Tit.**)
T-junction (cap., hyphen)
Tl the chemical element thallium (no point)
Tlemcen city in NW Algeria
TLS the *Times Literary Supplement*
T-lymphocyte Physiol. lymphocyte participating in the immune response
TM transcendental meditation (trademark in the US)

Tm the chemical element thulium (no point)
™ trademark (indicates that rights are claimed but that the mark is not registered)
tmesis pl. **tmeses** separation of parts of a word by an intervening word (e.g. *out-bloody-rageous*)
TMT technology, media, and telecom (or telecommunications) company
TN Tennessee (postal abbrev.)
tn 1 US ton(s) **2** town
TNT trinitrotoluene, a high explosive
t.o. take over
toad-in-the-hole (hyphens)
toadstool (one word)
to and fro (three words)
toastmaster (one word)
tobacco pl. **tobaccos**
Tobago smaller island of Trinidad and Tobago □ **Tobagonian**
Tobit book of the Apocrypha (abbrev. **Tob.**)
toboggan (two *g*s)
toccata musical composition to display keyboard technique (two *c*s, one *t*)
Toc H society promoting Christian fellowship and social service (no point)
Tocharian 1 member of a central Asian people of the 1st millennium AD **2** (**Tocharian A, Tocharian B**) two extinct languages of the Tocharians
tocsin arch. alarm bell or signal
today (one word)
to-do n. (hyphen)
toe v. (**toeing, toed**)
toea pl. same, monetary unit of Papua New Guinea
toecap, toehold, toenail, toerag (one word)
toffee (not **toffy** (arch.))
toga □ **toga'd**
Togo country in West Africa □ **Togolese**
toilet lavatory
toilette washing and dressing (not ital.)
toing and froing (three words)
Tokay sweet Hungarian wine; Hungarian name **Tokaji**
Tokyo capital of Japan; former name **Edo**
Tolkien, J(ohn) R(onald) R(euel) (1892–1973), British writer
tollbooth (also **tolbooth**) (one word)
toll bridge, toll gate, toll house, toll road (two words)
Tolstoy, Count Leo (1828–1910), Russian writer; Russian name *Lev Nikolaevich Tolstoi*
Toltec member of a people in Mexico before the Aztecs
tomahawk light American Indian axe
tomatillo pl. **tomatillos** edible purple or yellow fruit
tomato pl. **tomatoes** □ **tomatoey**
tombola lottery using a revolving drum
tombolo pl. **tombolos** bar of sand or shingle joining an island to the mainland
Tombouctou Fr. name for **Timbuktu**
tomboy (one word)
tombstone (one word)
tomcat, tomcod (one word)
tomfool, tomfoolery (one word)
Tommy pl. **Tommies** British private soldier (cap.)
tommy gun (two words, lower case)
tommyrot (one word, lower case)
tompion var. of **tampion**
tomtit small bird (one word)
tom-tom drum (hyphen)
ton (abbrev. **t**, US also **tn**) unit of weight: (also **long ton**) 2,240 lb (1016.05 kg); (also **short ton**) N. Amer. 2,000 lb (907.19 kg); (also **metric ton**) 1,000 kilograms (2,205 lb); cf. **tonne**
ton fashionable style (Fr., ital.)
tondo pl. **tondi** circular painting or relief (not ital.)
tone-deaf (hyphen)
tonepad (one word)
Tonga country in the South Pacific □ **Tongan**
tonga light horse-drawn vehicle in India (lower case)
tongue v. (**tonguing, tongued**)
tongue-in-cheek (hyphens)
tonic sol-fa (one hyphen)
tonne metric ton, 1,000 kg (abbrev. **t**; use **ton** in informal phrs such as *weigh a ton*)
tonneau part of a car occupied by the back seats (not ital.)
tonsillectomy, tonsillitis (two *l*s)
Tony pl. **Tonys** US theatre award (cap.)

tony N. Amer. classy (not **-ey**)
toolbar, toolbox (one word)
tooling ornamentation of a leather book cover with impressed designs
toolkit, toolmaker, toolset (one word)
toothache, toothbrush (one word)
toothcomb (in phr. **fine toothcomb**; also **fine-tooth comb, fine-toothed comb**)
toothpaste, toothpick (one word)
tooth powder (two words)
topcoat (one word)
topgallant ship's mast above the topmast (one word)
top-heavy (hyphen)
topi pl. **topis** sola topi
topknot, topmast (one word)
top-notch (hyphen)
toponym place name □ **toponymy**
topos pl. **topoi** traditional theme or formula in literature (not ital.)
topsail, topside, topsoil, topspin (one word)
topsy-turvy (hyphen)
top-up n. (hyphen, two words as verb)
Torah the first five books of the Hebrew scriptures
torc (also **torque**) ornament worn by ancient Gauls and Britons
torchère tall stand for a candlestick (accent, not ital.)
torchlight, torchlit (one word)
toreador bullfighter, esp. one on horseback (not ital.)
torero pl. **toreros** bullfighter, esp. one on foot (not ital.)
toreutics making designs in relief or intaglio (treated as sing.)
tori pl. of **torus**
Torino It. name for **Turin**
tormentor (not **-er**)
tornado pl. **tornadoes**; pl. of the military aircraft is **Tornados**
torpedo (**torpedoes, torpedoing, torpedoed**)
torque 1 force causing rotation **2** var. of **torc**
Torquemada, Tomás de (*c.*1420–98), Spanish Grand Inquisitor
Torricelli, Evangelista (1608–47), Italian mathematician and physicist □ **Torricellian**
Tórshavn (also **Thorshavn**) capital of the Faroe Islands
torso pl. **torsos** or US also **torsi**
tort wrongful act leading to legal liability
torte pl. **torten** or **tortes** sweet cake or tart (not ital.)
tortfeasor person who commits a tort
tortilla 1 Mexican flat maize pancake **2** Spanish omelette
tortious constituting a tort; cf. **tortuous, torturous**
tortoiseshell (one word)
tortuous full of twists and turns; cf. **tortious, torturous**
torturous involving pain or suffering; cf. **tortious, tortuous**
torus pl. **tori** or **toruses** geometric surface shaped like a doughnut
Tory member of the British Conservative Party (cap.)
Toscana It. name for **Tuscany**
Toscanini, Arturo (1867–1957), Italian conductor
Tosk pl. same or **Tosks** member of one of the two main ethnic groups of Albania; cf. **Gheg**
toss-up n. (hyphen, two words as verb)
total v. (**totalling, totalled**; US one **-l-**)
totalizator (Brit. also **totalisator**) device recording bets and apportioning winnings (**-s-** in *Horserace Totalisator Board*)
Tote, the Brit. trademark system of betting
touch-and-go (hyphens)
touchdown (one word; abbrev. **TD**)
touché used to acknowledge a hit (accent, not ital.)
touchline, touchpaper, touchstone (one word)
touch-tone, touch-type (hyphen)
touch-up n. (hyphen, two words as verb)
Toulon port in southern France
Toulouse city in SW France
Toulouse-Lautrec, Henri (Marie Raymond) de (1864–1901), French painter and lithographer
toupee small hairpiece (not **toupet**)
touraco var. of **turaco**
tour de force pl. **tours de force** highly skilled performance (not ital.)

tour d'horizon pl. ***tours d'horizon*** extensive survey (Fr., ital.)
Tourette's syndrome neurological disorder with tics and vocalizations
Tournai town in Belgium; Flemish name **Doornik**
tournedos pl. same, small round cut of beef fillet
tourney pl. **tourneys** medieval joust
tourniquet device for stopping the flow of blood
Toussaint L'Ouverture François Dominique (*c.*1743–1803), Haitian revolutionary leader
tout court with no addition or qualification (Fr., ital.)
tout de suite immediately (Fr., ital.)
tovarish (also **tovarich**) (in the former USSR) comrade
towel v. (**towelling, towelled**; US one **-l-**)
Tower of Babel see **Babel, Tower of**
towline (one word)
town (abbrev. **tn**)
town councillor, town hall, town house (two words)
townie informal person who lives in a town
town planning (two words)
townscape, townsfolk, townsman, townspeople, townswoman (one word)
towpath, towplane (one word)
tow rope (two words)
toxaemia (US **toxemia**) blood poisoning
toxin a poison (not **-ine**)
toxophilite student or lover of archery
toy boy (two words)
toymaker, toyshop (one word)
toytown adj. (one word)
Tpr Trooper
tr. translated (by); translation; translator
Trâblous see **Tripoli**
Trabzon port on the Black Sea in Turkey; also called **Trebizond**
traceable (not **-cable**)
trachea pl. **tracheae** or **tracheas** windpipe ▫ **tracheitis**
tracheotomy (also **tracheostomy**) incision in the windpipe to aid breathing
trackball (also **tracker ball**) ball in a holder rotated to move a cursor
track record, track shoe (two words)
trackside, tracksuit, trackway (one word)
Tractarianism another name for **Oxford Movement** (cap.)
tractor (not **-er**)
tradable (not **-eable**)
trade book commercial book for general sale
trade edition edition for general sale rather than for book clubs or specialist suppliers
trade-in n. (hyphen, two words as verb)
trademark (one word in general use; two words in British legal contexts)
trade name (two words)
trade-off n. (hyphen, two words as verb)
tradesman, tradespeople (one word)
Trades Union Congress (abbrev. **TUC**)
trade union (Brit. also **trades union**)
traffic v. (**trafficking, trafficked**) ▫ **trafficker**
tragedian actor in or author of tragedies
tragedienne female tragedian (not ital., no accent) [Fr. *tragédienne*]
tragicomedy work containing elements of tragedy and comedy
trahison des clercs betrayal of standards by writers, academics, or artists (Fr., ital.)
trailblazer (one word)
train oil, train set (two words)
trainspotter, trainspotting (one word)
train station use **station** or **railway station**
traipse walk wearily or reluctantly (not **trapse**)
trait distinguishing characteristic
traiteur French delicatessen (ital.)
Trajan (*c.*53–117 AD), Roman emperor 98–117; Latin name *Marcus Ulpius Traianus*
tramcar, tramline (one word)
tramontana (also **tramontane**) cold north wind in Italy and the Adriatic
trampoline sprung sheet for acrobatics (not **-ene**)
tramway (one word)
tranche portion, esp. of money (not ital.)

Tr. & Cr. Shakespeare's *Troilus and Cressida*
tranquillity (US **tranquility**)
tranquillize (Brit. also **tranquillise**; US **tranquilize**)
trans. 1 translated (by); translation; translator **2** transitive
transalpine on the northern side of the Alps (lower case exc. in **Transalpine Gaul**)
transatlantic beyond or crossing the Atlantic (one word, no cap.)
transceiver device able to transmit and receive communications
transcontinental (one word)
transcript written or printed version of words originally in another medium
transexual var. of **transsexual**
trans-fatty acid (one hyphen)
transfer (**transferring, transferred**) □ **transferable, transferee, transference, transferor** (chiefly Law), **transferral, transferrer**
transfiguration complete change into something more spiritual; (**the Transfiguration**) Christ's appearance in radiant glory to three of his disciples
tranship var. of **trans-ship**
transistor (not **-er**)
transit v. (**transiting, transited**)
transitive Gram. taking a direct object (abbrev. **trans.**)
Transjordan former name of the region now forming the main part of Jordan
Transkei former homeland in South Africa for the Xhosa
translatable (not **-eable**)
translator (not **-er**)
transliterate represent in a different alphabet or writing system
transonic (also **trans-sonic**) of speeds close to that of sound
trans-Pacific (hyphen, one cap.)
transparence, transparency, transparent (not **-an-**)
transpontine on the south side of the Thames or the US side of the Atlantic; cf. **cispontine**
transsexual (also **transexual**) person who feels that they belong to the opposite sex
trans-ship (also **tranship**) transfer from one ship etc. to another □ **trans-shipment**
trans-sonic var. of **transonic**
Transvaal (also **the Transvaal**) former province in South Africa
Transylvania region of NW Romania □ **Transylvanian**
trapdoor (one word)
trapezium pl. **trapezia** or **trapeziums** **1** Brit. quadrilateral with one pair of sides parallel **2** N. Amer. quadrilateral with no sides parallel
trapezoid 1 Brit. quadrilateral with no sides parallel **2** N. Amer. quadrilateral with one pair of sides parallel
trattoria Italian restaurant (not ital.)
trauma pl. **traumas** or **traumata**
traumatize (Brit. also **traumatise**)
travail (engage in) laborious effort
travel v. (**travelling, travelled**; US one **-l-**)
travelator (also **travolator**, trademark **Trav-o-lator**) moving walkway
traveller (US **traveler**) cap. in ref. to Gypsies or other travelling people
traveller's cheque, traveller's tale (apostrophe before the *s*)
travelogue work recounting travels (not **-log**)
travel-sick (hyphen)
travel sickness (two words)
travesty v. (**travestying, travestied**)
travolator var. of **travelator**
trayf var. of ***trefa***
tread (past **trod**; past part. **trodden** or **trod**)
treadmill (one word)
treasury 1 funds or revenue **2** (**Treasury**) government department responsible for public expenditure
treatise written work dealing with a subject systematically (not **-ize**)
Trebizond another name for **Trabzon**
trecento the 14th century in Italy (not ital.)
treeline (one word)
treenail (also **trenail** or US **trunnel**) wooden nail for fastening timbers
treetop (one word)
trefa (also ***trayf***) not kosher (ital.)
trek (**trekking, trekked**) (not **treck**)
trelliswork (one word)

tremolo (also **tremolando**) pl. **tremolos** or **tremolandi** Mus. wavering effect in a tone
tremor (not **-our**)
trenail var. of **treenail**
trench coat (two words)
trendsetter, trendsetting (one word)
trente et quarante another term for ***rouge et noir*** (Fr., ital.)
Trentino-Alto Adige region of NE Italy (hyphen)
Trento city in northern Italy; former English name **Trent**
Trenton state capital of New Jersey
trepan (**trepanning, trepanned**) (perforate with) a surgical saw formerly used on the skull
trepang sea cucumber
Trèves Fr. name for **Trier**
TRH Their Royal Highnesses
Triad secret Chinese criminal society
triad group or set of three
triage assessment of degree of medical urgency (not ital.)
trial v. (**trialling, trialled**; US one **-l-**)
trialist (Brit. also **triallist**) participant in a sports or motorcycle trial
trialogue conversation between three people (not **-log**)
Triassic earliest period of the Mesozoic era
tribe in contemporary contexts prefer terms such as **community** or **people**
tribesman, tribespeople, tribeswoman (one word)
tribrach metrical foot of three short or unstressed syllables
tribunal (not **-eral**)
tricentenary, tricentennial another name for **tercentenary**
triceps pl. same, large muscle at the back of the upper arm
triceratops large dinosaur with three horns (lower case)
tricolour (US **tricolor**)
tricorn (also **tricorne**) hat with a brim turned up on three sides
Trident long-range ballistic missile
trident three-pronged spear
Tridentine of the Council of Trent (Trento), 1545–63, which redefined Roman Catholic doctrine
triennial recurring every three years (two *ns*)
triennium pl. **triennia** or **trienniums** period of three years (two *ns*)
Trier city in western Germany; French name **Trèves**
trier person who tries
Trieste city in NE Italy
triffid giant predatory plant in ***The Day of the Triffids*** by John Wyndham (1951)
trifid split into three
trigger-happy (hyphen)
trigraph group of three letters representing one sound
trihedron pl. **trihedra** or **trihedrons** solid figure with three sides or faces
trilby soft felt hat (lower case) □ **trilbied**
trillion pl. **trillions** or with numeral or quantifying word **trillion** a million million (1,000,000,000,000); Brit. dated a million million million (1,000,000,000,000,000,000)
trilogy group of three related literary works
trimeter line of verse consisting of three metrical feet
Trinidad larger island of **Trinidad and Tobago**, a country in the Caribbean □ **Trinidadian**
Trinitarian believer in the doctrine of the Trinity (cap.)
Trinity (also **Holy Trinity**) the three persons of the Christian Godhead
trinity group of three (lower case)
Trinity Brethren the members of Trinity House
Trinity College Oxford, Cambridge, Dublin
Trinity Hall Cambridge college
Trinity House association responsible for buoys and lighthouses around England and Wales
Trinity Sunday next Sunday after Pentecost
Trinity term university term or session of the High Court beginning after Easter (one cap.)
trio pl. **trios**
triphthong three vowels pronounced in one syllable (not **tripthong**)

Tripitaka the sacred canon of Theravada Buddhism
Triplex trademark safety glass
triplex N. Amer. building divided into three residences
Tripoli 1 capital of Libya; Arab. name **Tarabulus al-Gharb 2** port in NW Lebanon; Arab. name **Tarabulus Ash-Sham, Trâblous**
tripoli rottenstone (powder or paste for polishing metal)
tripos final honours BA examination at Cambridge (lower case)
triptych picture or carving on three panels
trireme ancient war galley with three banks of oars
triskaidekaphobia extreme superstition about the number thirteen
Tristan 1 another name for **Tristram 2** (***Tristan und Isolde***) opera by Wagner (1865)
Tristan da Cunha island in the South Atlantic
tristesse melancholy sadness (not ital.)
Tristram (in medieval legend) a knight who was the lover of Iseult
trisyllable word or metrical foot of three syllables
tritium radioactive isotope of hydrogen (symbol **T**)
triumvir pl. **triumvirs** or **triumviri** each of three equal public officers in ancient Rome ◻ **triumvirate**
trivialize (Brit. also **trivialise**)
trivium medieval university course of grammar, rhetoric, and logic; cf. **quadrivium**
tRNA transfer RNA
trochee metrical foot of one long or stressed syllable followed by one short or unstressed syllable ◻ **trochaic**
Trockenbeerenauslese sweet German white wine (cap., not ital.)
Troilus 1 Gk Mythol. Trojan prince killed by Achilles **2** (***Troilus and Cressida***) Shakespeare play (abbrev. ***Tr. & Cr.***) **3** (***Troilus and Criseyde***) Chaucer poem
Trojan Horse (caps)
trolley (not **-ly**)
trolleybus (one word)
trolley car (two words)
trollop promiscuous woman
Trollope, Anthony (1815–82), English novelist
trompe l'œil pl. ***trompe l'œils*** visual illusion in art (Fr., ital.)
Tromsø city of Arctic Norway
Trondheim town in central Norway
troop 1 unit of cavalry or artillery; group of a particular kind; cf. **troupe 2** (**troops**) soldiers or armed forces
trooper private soldier in a cavalry or armoured unit (abbrev. **Tpr**)
trope word or expression used figuratively
tropic of Cancer, tropic of Capricorn (one cap.)
tropology the figurative use of language
troppo Mus. too much
Trossachs valley in central Scotland
Trotsky, Leon (1879–1940), Russian revolutionary; born *Lev Davidovich Bronshtein* ◻ **Trotskyism, Trotskyist, Trotskyite** (derog.)
troublemaker, troubleshooter (one word)
Troubles, the periods of civil war or unrest in Ireland
troupe group of touring entertainers; cf. **troop**
trousseau pl. **trousseaux** or **trousseaus** clothes and other items collected by a bride (not ital.)
trouvaille lucky find (Fr., ital.)
trouvère medieval French poet (accent, not ital.)
trowel v. (**trowelling, trowelled**; US one **-l-**)
Troy (in Homeric legend) city besieged by the Greeks
troy (in full **troy weight**) system of weights with a pound of 12 oz or 5,760 grains (lower case)
Troyes 1 town in northern France **2** see **Chrétien de Troyes**
Trucial States former name for **United Arab Emirates**
Trudeau, Pierre (Elliott) (1919–2000), prime minister of Canada 1968–79 and 1980–4
Trueman, Fred (1931–2006), English cricketer

Truffaut, François (1932–84), French film director
Truman, Harry S. (1884–1972), 33rd president of the US 1945–53
trumpet v. (**trumpeting**, **trumpeted**)
trunnel US var. of **treenail**
try-out n. (hyphen, two words as verb)
tryst private romantic rendezvous
TS pl. **TSS** typescript
tsar (also **czar** or **tzar**) emperor of Russia before 1917 (cap. in titles)
tsarevich (also **czarevich** or **tzarevich**) tsar's eldest son (cap. in titles)
tsarina (also **czarina** or **tzarina**) empress of Russia before 1917 (cap. in titles)
Tsaritsyn former name for **Volgograd**
tsetse Africa bloodsucking fly
TSgt Technical Sergeant
TSH thyroid-stimulating hormone
T-shirt (also **tee shirt**)
tsp pl. same or **tsps** teaspoon
T-square instrument for drawing or testing right angles (hyphen)
TSS typescripts
tsunami pl. same or **tsunamis** large sea wave caused by an earthquake etc.
Tswana pl. same, **Tswanas**, or **Batswana** member of a southern African people
TT **1** teetotal; teetotaller **2** Tourist Trophy (motorcycle-racing competition in the Isle of Man) **3** tuberculin-tested
TTS text-to-speech
TU Trade Union
Tuareg pl. same or **Tuaregs** member of a Berber people
Tube, the trademark the London underground
tuberculin-tested (hyphen; abbrev. **TT**)
tuberculosis (abbrev. **TB**)
tuberose Mexican plant with white waxy flowers
tuberous like or having a tuber
TUC Trades Union Congress
Tucson city in SE Arizona
Tudor member of the English royal dynasty 1485–1603
Tuesday (abbrev. **Tues.**)
tug of war (three words)
tugrik pl. same or **tugriks** monetary unit of Mongolia
tuile thin curved biscuit (not ital.)
Tuileries formal gardens next to the Louvre in Paris
tularaemia (US **tularemia**) infectious bacterial disease
tulle soft fine fabric
tumbledown (one word)
tumble dryer (also **tumble drier**) (two words) □ **tumble-dry**
tumbleweed (one word)
tumbril (also **tumbrel**) hist. open cart
tumour (US **tumor**) □ **tumorous**
tumulus pl. **tumuli** ancient burial mound (not ital.)
tun large beer or wine cask
tunable (not **-eable**)
Tunbridge Wells spa town in Kent; official name **Royal Tunbridge Wells**
tungsten chemical element of atomic number 74 (symbol **W**)
tuning fork, tuning peg (two words)
Tunisia country in North Africa; capital, Tunis □ **Tunisian**
tunnel v. (**tunnelling**, **tunnelled**; US one **-l-**) □ **tunneller**
Tupamaro pl. **Tupamaros** Uruguyan Marxist guerrilla
Tupelo city in NE Mississippi
tupelo pl. **tupelos** timber tree
Tupi pl. same or **Tupis** member of a group of peoples of the Amazon valley □ **Tupian**
Tupi-Guarani South American Indian language family (hyphen)
Tupolev, Andrei (1888–1972), Russian aeronautical engineer
tuppence, tuppenny vars of **twopence, twopenny**
Tupperware trademark range of plastic storage containers
turaco (also **touraco**) pl. **turacos** African bird
turbid (of a liquid) cloudy; (of language or style) confused or obscure; cf. **turgid**
turbo pl. **turbos** turbocharger
turboboost, turbocharge, turbocharger (one word)
turbofan, turbojet, turboprop (one word)
turbot pl. same or **turbots** flatfish

turbulence, turbulent (not **-ance, -ant**)
Turco- (also **Turko-**) Turkish (and); of Turkey
Turcoman var. of **Turkoman**
turf pl. **turfs** or **turves**
Turgenev, Ivan (Sergeevich) (1818–83), Russian writer
turgid swollen and distended; (of language or style) tediously pompous or bombastic; cf. **turbid**
Turin city in NW Italy; It. name **Torino**
Turing, Alan Mathison (1912–54), English mathematician
Turkestan (also **Turkistan**) region of central Asia
Turkey country in western Asia with a small enclave in SE Europe; Turk. name **Türkiye**
turkey pl. **turkeys**
turkey cock (two words)
Turki group of languages of central Asia
Turkic group of languages of west and central Asia
Turkish Turkic language of Turkey
Turkish bath, Turkish delight (one cap.)
Turkistan var. of **Turkestan**
Turkmen pl. same or **Turkmens** member of a group of peoples in Turkmenistan
Turkmenistan republic in central Asia
Turko- var. of **Turco-**
Turkoman (also **Turcoman**) pl. **Turkomans 1** another name for **Turkmen 2** richly coloured rug
Turks and Caicos Islands British overseas territory in the Caribbean
Turku port in SW Finland; Swed. name **Åbo**
turmeric yellow spice (not **tum-**)
turnabout, turnaround, turnback n. (one word, two words as verb)
turncoat (one word)
turned comma opening quotation mark ‘ resembling an upside-down comma
turned sort Printing sort printed upside down or on its side
Turner, J(oseph) M(allord) W(illiam) (1775–1851), English painter
turning circle, turning point (two words)
turnkey (one word)
turn-line final part of a paragraph or other section of text, which is carried over to a separate line (hyphen)
turn-off, turn-on n. (hyphen, two words as verb)
turnout, turnover n. (one word, two words as verb)
turnpike, turnstile, turntable (one word)
turn-up n. (hyphen, two words as verb)
turtle dove (two words)
turtleneck (one word)
turves pl. of **turf**
Tuscany region of west central Italy; It. name **Toscana** □ **Tuscan**
Tussaud, Madame (1761–1850), French founder of Madame Tussaud's waxworks
tussore coarse silk (not **tussah**)
Tutankhamen (also **Tutankhamun**) (died *c.*1352 BC), Egyptian pharaoh, reigned *c.*1361–*c.*1352 BC
tutee pupil of a tutor
Tutsi pl. same or **Tutsis** member of a people forming a minority of the population of Rwanda and Burundi
tutti pl. **tuttis** Mus. (passage performed) with all voices or instruments together
tutti-frutti pl. **tutti-fruttis** ice cream with mixed fruit (hyphen)
Tutu, Desmond (Mpilo) (b.1931), South African clergyman
tutu ballerina's costume of bodice and skirt
Tuvalu country in the SW Pacific; former name **Ellice Islands** □ **Tuvaluan**
tu-whit tu-whoo tawny owl's cry (two hyphens, no comma)
tuxedo pl. **tuxedos** or **tuxedoes** N. Amer. man's dinner jacket □ **tuxedoed**
tuyère nozzle for forcing air into a furnace (accent, not ital.)
TV 1 television **2** transvestite
TVP textured vegetable protein
Twain, Mark (1835–1910), American novelist and humorist; pseudonym of *Samuel Langhorne Clemens*
'twas arch. it was (apostrophe)
twee (**tweer, tweest**)

Tweedledum and Tweedledee virtually indistinguishable pair (two caps)
tweet n. & v. (make) a posting on the social media website Twitter
twelfth constituting number twelve
Twelfth Night 1 6 January **2** (***Twelfth Night***) Shakespeare play (abbrev. ***Twel. N.***)
twelve (Roman numeral **xii** or **XII**) ◻ **twelvefold**
twelve-bore (hyphen)
twelvemo pl. **twelvemos** another name for **duodecimo**
twelvemonth (one word)
twenties (also **1920s**) decade (lower case, no apostrophe)
twenty (hyphen in compound numbers, e.g. *twenty-one, twenty-third*; Roman numeral **xx** or **XX**) ◻ **twentieth, twentyfold**
twenty-fourmo pl. **twenty-fourmos** page size resulting from folding a sheet into twenty-four leaves (abbrev. **24mo**)
24/7 (also **24–7**) twenty-four hours a day, seven days a week (en rule)
twentymo pl. **twentymos** page size resulting from folding a sheet into twenty leaves (abbrev. **20mo**)
Twenty-Six Counties the counties of the Republic of Ireland (caps)
twerp silly person (not **twirp**)
twilight, twilit (one word)
twinge v. (**twingeing** or **twinging, twinged**)
twinset (one word)
twirp use **twerp**
Twitter n. trademark social media website (lower case as verb)
'twixt arch. betwixt, between (apostrophe)
two (Roman numeral **ii** or **II**) ◻ **twofold, twosome**
two-dimensional (hyphen)
Two Gentlemen of Verona, The Shakespeare play (abbrev. ***Two Gent.***)
twopence (also **tuppence**) Brit. two pence, before decimalization
twopenny (also **tuppenny**) Brit. costing two pence, before decimalization
TX Texas (postal abbrev.)
Tyddewi Welsh name for **St David's**
tying present participle of **tie**
tyke (also **tike**) mischievous child
Tyler 1 John (1790–1862), 10th president of the US 1841–5 **2** Wat (d.1381), English leader of the Peasants' Revolt of 1381
tympan (in letterpress printing) layer of packing between the platen and paper to be printed
tympani var. of **timpani**
tympanum pl. **tympanums** or **tympana** **1** eardrum **2** Archit. centre of a pediment ◻ **tympanic**
Tyndale, William (*c.*1494–1536), English translator of the Bible
Tyndall, John (1820–93), Irish physicist
Tyne and Wear former metropolitan county of NE England
Tyneside conurbation on the banks of the River Tyne, in NE England
Tynwald parliament of the Isle of Man
type printed characters or letters; character for printing
typecast, typeface (one word)
type founder, type foundry, type metal (two words)
typescript copy of a text produced on a computer or typewriter (abbrev. **TS**)
typeset (**typesetting, typeset**) (one word) ◻ **typesetter**
typewriter, typewriting, typewritten (one word)
typo pl. **typos** typographical error
typography 1 style and appearance of printed matter **2** setting and arranging of type or data and printing from them
tyrannize (Brit. also **tyrannise**) (two *n*s)
tyrannosaur (also **tyrannosaurus**) carnivorous dinosaur (lower case, not ital.; one cap. in **Tyrannosaurus rex**)
Tyre port in southern Lebanon ◻ **Tyrian**
tyre (US **tire**) rubber covering round a wheel
tyro (also **tiro**) pl. **tyros** beginner
Tyrol Alpine state of western Austria; Ger. name **Tirol** ◻ **Tyrolean, Tyrolese**
Tyrone county of Northern Ireland
Tyrrhenian Sea Mediterranean between mainland Italy and Sicily and Sardinia
tzar etc. vars of **tsar** etc.
tzatziki Greek yogurt dish
tzigane pl. same or **tziganes** Hungarian Gypsy (lower case)
Tzotzil pl. same or **Tzotzils** member of a people of southern Mexico

U

U 1 pl. **Us** or **U's** 21st letter of the alphabet **2** (in sport) United **3** universal (UK film classification) **4** upper class: *U and non-U* **5** the chemical element uranium **6** Burmese equivalent of 'Mr': *U Thant*
u micro- (10^{-6})
U2 Irish rock group
U-2 US reconnaissance aircraft
UAE United Arab Emirates
UB40 card formerly issued to unemployed people in the UK
U-bend (cap., hyphen)
Übermensch Nietzschean superman (Ger., cap., ital.)
ubiety condition of being in a definite place
ubi supra in the place above (L., ital.; abbrev. ***u.s.***)
U-boat (cap., hyphen)
UC University College
u.c. upper case
UCAS Universities and Colleges Admissions Service
UCC Universal Copyright Convention
Uccello, Paolo (*c.*1397–1475), Italian painter; born *Paolo di Dono*
UCD University College Dublin
UCL University College London
UCLA University of California at Los Angeles
UDA Ulster Defence Association
UDC 1 Urban Development Corporation **2** hist. Urban District Council
UDI unilateral declaration of independence
Udmurtia (also **Udmurt Republic**) autonomous republic in central Russia
udon Japanese pasta in strips (not ital.)
UDR hist. Ulster Defence Regiment
UEA University of East Anglia
UEFA Union of European Football Associations
Uffizi art gallery in Florence
UFO pl. **UFOs** unidentified flying object
ufology study of UFOs (lower case)
Uganda country in East Africa □ **Ugandan**
Ugli fruit pl. same, trademark hybrid of a grapefruit and a tangerine (one cap.)
Ugric (also **Ugrian**) of the language family including Hungarian
UHF ultra-high frequency
UHT ultra heat treated
u.i. *ut infra*
Uighur member of a Turkic people of NW China
uillean pipes Irish bagpipes (lower case)
uitlander S. Afr. foreigner or outsider
ujamaa Tanzanian system of village cooperatives
Ujung Pandang seaport in Indonesia; former name **Makassar**
UK United Kingdom
UKAEA United Kingdom Atomic Energy Authority
ukase tsarist decree; peremptory command
ukiyo-e style of Japanese art (ital., hyphen)
Ukraine country in eastern Europe (not **the Ukraine**) □ **Ukrainian**
ukulele (also **ukelele**) small four-stringed guitar
Ulan Bator (also **Ulaanbaatar**) capital of Mongolia
ulema (also ***ulama***) body of Muslim scholars (ital.; treated as sing. or pl.)
Ulfilas (also **Wulfila**) (*c.*311–*c.*381), bishop and translator
Ullswater lake in Cumbria (not **Ulles-**)
ulna pl. **ulnae** or **ulnas** longer of the bones in the forearm
Ulster former province of Ireland; (in general use) Northern Ireland □ **Ulsterman, Ulsterwoman**
ulster man's overcoat (lower case)
ult. 1 ultimate **2** ultimo

ultima Thule distant unknown region (L., ital.)
ultimatum pl. **ultimatums** or **ultimata**
ultimo of last month (after the noun; abbrev. **ult.** or **ulto**)
ultra heat treated (no hyphens; abbrev. **UHT**)
ultra-high frequency (one hyphen; abbrev. **UHF**)
ultraist holder of extreme opinions
ultralight, ultramicroscope, ultramicroscopic (one word)
ultramontane (one word) **1** advocating supreme papal authority **2** on the other side of the Alps
ultramundane existing outside the known universe (one word)
ultrashort, ultrasonic, ultrasound, ultraviolet (one word)
ultra vires beyond one's legal authority (not ital.)
Uluru official name for **Ayers Rock**
Ulysses Roman name for **Odysseus**
Umayyad member of an early Muslim dynasty
umbel Bot. flower cluster
umbilicus pl. **umbilici** or **umbilicuses**
umbo pl. **umbones** or **umbos** boss on a shield
umbra pl. **umbras** or **umbrae** inner region of a shadow
Umbria region of central Italy
□ **Umbrian**
umiak Eskimo open boat (not **oomiak**)
umlaut mark ¨ used over a vowel, e.g. in German, to indicate a different vowel quality
umma (also ***ummah***) whole Muslim community (ital.)
Umm al-Qaiwain state and city of the United Arab Emirates
UMTS Universal Mobile Telephone System
UN United Nations
un- forms solid compounds exc. with words beginning with a cap.
'un one, an individual (apostrophe)
UNA United Nations Association
una corda Mus. using the piano's soft pedal
un-American (hyphen, cap.)
unbeknown (also **unbeknownst**)
unbiased (one *s*)
unbound (of printed sheets) not bound together; (of a bound book) not provided with a proper cover
unbridgeable (not **-gable**)
uncalled for, uncared for (two words, hyphen when attrib.)
unchristian (one word, no cap.)
uncial in a majuscule script with rounded unjoined letters
Uncle Sam personification of the US (caps)
UNCSTD United Nations Conference on Science and Technology for Development
UNCTAD United Nations Conference on Trade and Development
unctuous ingratiatingly oily (not **-ious**)
under- usu. forms solid compounds exc. with most words beginning with *r* and in age categories, as *the under-thirties*
underage too young to do something legally (one word)
undercover adj., adv. (one word)
under-fives children less than five years old (hyphen)
underground adv. & adj. beneath the ground (one word)
Underground, the Brit. underground railway, esp. the one in London
Under Milk Wood radio drama by Dylan Thomas (1954) (three words)
underrate (one word)
under-record, under-rehearsed, under-report, under-represent, under-resourced (hyphen)
undersecretary (one word; cap. in titles)
underwater adj., adv. (one word)
under way (Naut. also **underway**) in or into motion (not **weigh**)
underweight (one word)
UNDP United Nations Development Programme
undreamed of (Brit. also **undreamt of**) (two words, hyphen when attrib.)
UNDRO United Nations Disaster Relief Office
un-English (hyphen, cap.)
UNEP United Nations Environment Programme

unequalled (US **unequaled**)
UNESCO United Nations Educational, Scientific, and Cultural Organization
unexceptionable not open to objection
unexceptional not out of the ordinary
unfavourable (US **unfavorable**)
unfocused (also **unfocussed**)
unforeseeable, unforeseen (not **-fors-**)
UNFPA United Nations Fund for Population Activities
unget-at-able (two hyphens)
ungulate Zool. hoofed mammal
UNHCR United Nation High Commissioner for Refugees
unheard of (two words, hyphen when attrib.)
unheimlich uncanny, weird (Ger., ital.)
unhoped for (two words, hyphen when attrib.)
uni pl. **unis** university
Uniate (also **Uniat**) of a Catholic community in eastern Europe and the Near East that retains its own liturgy
UNICEF United Nations Children's (Emergency) Fund
unidea'd (apostrophe)
UNIDO United Nations Industrial Development Organization
Unification Church evangelistic religious and political organization; members are sometimes referred to as **Moonies** (derog.)
uninterested not interested; cf. **disinterested**
union catalogue list of the combined holdings of several libraries
Unionist cap. in ref. to person favouring the union of Northern Ireland with Great Britain
unionize (Brit. also **unionise**)
Union Jack (also **Union flag**) national flag of the UK (orig. a small Union flag flown as the jack of a ship)
Union of Myanmar official name for **Burma**
Union of Serbia and Montenegro federation of the republics of Serbia and Montenegro
Union of Soviet Socialist Republics (abbrev. **USSR**)
Union Territory territory of India administered by the central government (caps)
UNISON UK trade union
UNITA Angolan nationalist movement
UNITAR United Nations Institute for Training and Research
Unitarian person who rejects the Christian doctrine of the Trinity
United Arab Emirates independent state on the Persian Gulf (abbrev. **UAE**)
United Arab Republic former political union established by Egypt and Syria, latterly Egypt alone (abbrev. **UAR**)
United Artists US film production company
United Kingdom England, Wales, Scotland, and Northern Ireland as a political unit (abbrev. **UK**)
United Reformed Church (not **United Reform Church**; abbrev. **URC**)
United States, United States of America (abbrev. **US** or **USA**)
unitholder person with an investment in a unit trust (one word)
unitize (Brit. also **unitise**)
unit trust (two words)
Univ. University
Universal US film production company
Universal Copyright Convention international copyright agreement (abbrev. **UCC**)
universalize (Brit. also **universalise**)
Universal Time (also **Universal Time Coordinated**) another name for **Greenwich Mean Time** (abbrev. **UT**)
university (cap. in names; abbrev. **Univ.**)
University College London (no comma; abbrev. **UCL**)
Unix trademark computer operating system
Unknown Soldier (also **Unknown Warrior**) unidentified representative of the armed services given a memorial (caps)
unlabelled (US **unlabeled**)
unlawful forbidden by law or rules; cf. **illegal, illicit**
unlicensed (also **unlicenced**)
unlikeable (also **unlikable**)
unlived in, unlooked for (two words, hyphen when attrib.)

unlovable (also **unloveable**)
unmistakable (also **unmistakeable**)
UNO United Nations Organization (use **UN**)
unpaged not having the pages numbered
unperson pl. **unpersons** person whose existence is denied or ignored
unpractised (US **unpracticed**)
unputdownable (one word)
unravel (**unravelling, unravelled**; US one **-l-**)
unrecognizable (Brit. also **unrecognisable**; not **-eable**)
unrivalled (US **unrivaled**)
UNRWA United Nations Relief and Works Agency
unsaleable (US **unsalable**)
unsewn binding another name for **perfect binding**
unshakeable (also **unshakable**)
unskilful (US **unskillful**)
unsociable not enjoying the company of others; cf. **antisocial, unsocial**
unsocial (of working hours) socially inconvenient; cf. **antisocial, unsociable**
Untermensch pl. ***Untermenschen*** person considered inferior (Ger., ital.)
unthaw best avoided; in N. Amer. means 'melt or thaw', in Brit. **unthawed** means 'still frozen'
untouchable avoid in senses relating to the traditional Hindu caste system; the official term is **scheduled caste**
untrammelled (US **untrammeled**)
up-and-coming, up-and-over adj. (hyphens)
up-and-under n. (hyphens)
Upanishad Hindu sacred treatise (cap.)
upbeat n., adj. (one word)
upbringing, upcoming, upcountry, update (one word)
Updike, John (Hoyer) (1932–2009), American writer
updraught, upend, upfield (one word)
upfront adj. bold and frank (one word)
up front adv. at the front (two words)
upgrade, uphill, upkeep, upland, upmarket (one word)
upper case capital letters (abbrev. **u.c.**)
upper class (two words, hyphen when attrib.)
uppercut (one word)
upper house higher house in a bicameral parliament; (**the Upper House**) the House of Lords
upper middle class (three words, hyphens when attrib.)
Upper Volta former name for **Burkina**
Uppsala city in eastern Sweden
upright, upriver (one word)
UPS uninterruptible power supply
ups-a-daisy var. of **upsy-daisy**
upside down (two words, hyphen when attrib.)
upsilon twentieth letter of the Greek alphabet (**Υ, υ**), transliterated as 'u' or 'y'
upslope, upstage, upstairs, upstate, upstream (one word)
upsy-daisy (also **ups-a-daisy**) said to a child who has fallen
uptempo, uptight, uptime (one word)
up to date, up to the minute (hyphens when attrib.)
uptown, upturn (one word)
UPU Universal Postal Union
uPVC unplasticized polyvinyl chloride
upwardly mobile (two words, even when attrib.)
upwind (one word)
Ural Mountains (also **the Urals**) mountain range in northern Russia
Urania the Muse of astronomy
uranium chemical element of atomic number 92 (symbol **U**)
Uranus 1 Gk Mythol. god of heaven or the sky **2** seventh planet from the sun
urban of a town or city
urbane courteous and refined
urbanize (Brit. also **urbanise**)
URC United Reformed Church
Urdu language related to Hindi, with many Persian and Arabic words
urethra pl. **urethrae** or **urethras**
Urim and Thummim hist. two objects on the breastplate of a Jewish high priest (caps, both words pl.)
URL pl. **URLs** Comput. uniform (or universal) resource locator

urtext pl. **urtexte** or **urtexts** original version of a text (lower case, not ital.)

Uruguay country in South America □ **Uruguayan**

urus another name for **aurochs**

US 1 undersecretary **2** United States

***u.s.* 1** *ubi supra* **2** *ut supra*

USA United States of America (prefer **US**)

usable (also **useable**)

USAF United States Air Force

USD United States dollars

use-by date (one hyphen)

Usenet Internet service consisting of newsgroups (cap.)

user-friendly (hyphen)

user interface (two words)

username (one word)

USM Unlisted Securities Market

USN United States Navy

USP unique selling point

usquebaugh whisky (not ital.)

USS United States Ship

USSR Union of Soviet Socialist Republics

usu. usually

usucaption (also **usucapion**) Roman Law acquisition of a right to property by possession of it

usufruct Roman Law right to use another's property

UT 1 Universal Time **2** Utah (postal abbrev.)

Utah state in the western US (official abbrev. **Ut.**, postal **UT**) □ **Utahan**

utahraptor dinosaur (lower case)

UTC Universal Time Coordinated

Utd United

uterus pl. **uteri** or **uteruses**

utilitarianism (lower case)

utilize (Brit. also **utilise**)

ut infra as below (L., ital.; abbrev. ***u.i.***)

utopia imagined place of perfection, (lower case; in ref. to Sir Thomas More's *Utopia* (1516), cap.)

utopian (lower case)

Utrecht city and province in the central Netherlands

Utrillo, Maurice (1883–1955), French painter

ut supra as above (L., ital.; abbrev. ***u.s.***)

Uttarakhand state in northern India; former name Uttaranchal

Uttar Pradesh state in northern India

U-turn (cap., hyphen)

UUC Ulster Unionist Council

UV ultraviolet

UVA ultraviolet radiation of relatively long wavelengths

UVB ultraviolet radiation of relatively short wavelengths

UVC ultraviolet radiation of very short wavelengths

uvula pl. **uvulae** or **uvulas** Anat. fleshy part at the back of the soft palate

uxorial of a wife

uxorious very fond of one's wife

Uzbek member of a people of Uzbekistan

Uzbekistan republic in central Asia

Uzi Israeli sub-machine gun (cap.)

V

V **1** pl. **Vs** or **V's** 22nd letter of the alphabet **2** the chemical element vanadium **3** voltage or potential difference **4** volt(s) **5** Math. (in formulae) volume **6** (also v) Roman numeral for five

v verso

v. **1** verb **2** pl. **vv.** verse **3** very **4** vide **5** pl. **vv.** volume (prefer **vol.**)

v velocity

V-1, V-2 WWII German flying bombs (hyphen)

V-8 (also **V-6**) configuration of internal-combustion engine (cap., hyphen)

VA **1** Order of Victoria and Albert **2** US Veterans' Administration **3** Vicar Apostolic **4** Virginia (postal abbrev.)

Va. Virginia (official abbrev.)

vaccinate, vaccine (two *c*s)

vacillate (one *c*, two *l*s)

vacuum **1** pl. **vacuums** or **vacua** space devoid of matter **2** pl. **vacuums** vacuum cleaner

vacuum cleaner (two words) □ **vacuum-clean**

vacuum flask (two words)

vacuum-pack (hyphen)

VAD Voluntary Aid Detachment

vade mecum pl. **vade mecums** handbook or guide (two words, not ital.)

Vaduz capital of Liechtenstein

vagina pl. **vaginas** or **vaginae**

vainglory, vainglorious (one word)

Vaishnava member of one of the main branches of Hinduism

Vaisya (also **Vaishya**) member of the Hindu caste comprising merchants and farmers

valance (also **valence**) length of drapery round a bed

vale valley (cap. in names)

vale farewell (L., ital.)

valence[1] US var. of **valency**

valence[2] var. of **valance**

Valencia **1** city and region in eastern Spain **2** city in northern Venezuela

Valenciennes type of bobbin lace

valency (US **valence**) chiefly Brit. combining power of a chemical element

valentine card or message sent on St Valentine's Day (lower case)

Valera, Eamon de, see **de Valera**

Valerian (d.260), Roman emperor 253–60; Latin name *Publius Licinius Valerianius*

valerian (drug from) a Eurasian plant

Valéry, (Ambroise) Paul (Toussaint Jules) (1871–1945), French writer

valet (**valeting, valeted**) (attend to a man as) a personal servant responsible for clothing

valeta var. of **veleta**

valetudinarian person unduly anxious about their health

Valhalla Scand. Mythol. palace in which heroes killed in battle feast with Odin

Valium trademark the drug diazepam

Valkyrie Scand. Mythol. each of twelve handmaidens of Odin

Valladolid city in northern Spain

Valle d'Aosta Alpine region in NW Italy

Valletta capital of Malta

valley pl. **valleys** (cap. in names)

Valois **1** medieval duchy of northern France **2** French royal house 1328–1589

valorize (Brit. also **valorise**) give value or validity to

valour (US **valor**) □ **valorous**

Valparaíso principal port of Chile

Valpolicella Italian red wine from the Val Policella district

valse waltz (not ital., cap. in titles)

value added tax (three words; abbrev. **VAT**)

value judgement (two words)

valuta value of one currency in relation to another

van, van de, van den, van der capitalization as prefix to proper names is personal, and must be followed; Dutch names are usually lower case, Flemish and South African names may be capitalized; alphabetize under *V* in English texts

vanadium chemical element of atomic number 23 (symbol **V**)

Van Allen belt, Van Allen layer (two caps)

Vanbrugh, Sir John (1664–1726), English architect and dramatist

Van Buren, Martin (1782–1862), 8th president of the US 1837–41 (two caps)

Vancouver system reference system in which each bibliographical source is assigned a number, which is then used to cite that source in text

V&A Victoria and Albert Museum (no spaces)

Vandal member of a Germanic people

vandal person who deliberately damages property

vandalize (Brit. also **vandalise**)

van de, van den, van der see **van**

van de Graaff generator machine for generating electrostatic charge (one cap.)

Vanderbilt, Cornelius (1794–1877), American businessman and philanthropist

Van der Hum South African liqueur (two caps)

Van der Post, Sir Laurens (Jan) (1906–96), South African explorer and writer (two caps)

van der Waals forces weak electrostatic forces between uncharged particles (one cap.)

van de Velde (one cap.) **1** name of a family of Dutch painters **2** Henry (Clemens) (1863–1957), Belgian architect and designer

Van Diemen's Land former name for **Tasmania** (apostrophe; not **-man's**)

Van Dyck (also **Vandyke**), Sir Anthony (1599–1641), Flemish painter

Vandyke 1 broad lace or linen collar **2** neat pointed beard

Vandyke brown deep rich brown

Van Eyck, Jan (*c.*1370–1441), Flemish painter (two caps)

Van Gogh, Vincent (Willem) (1853–90), Dutch painter (two caps)

vanishing point (two words)

vanitas still-life painting with symbols of death (L., ital.)

Vanity Fair 1 the world regarded as a place of frivolity (orig. with ref. to Bunyan's *Pilgrim's Progress*) **2** (***Vanity Fair***) novel by Thackeray (1847–8); magazine

Vanuatu country consisting of a group of islands in the SW Pacific; former name **New Hebrides** □ **Vanuatuan**

vaporetto pl. **vaporetti** or **vaporettos** motor boat providing public transport in Venice (not ital.)

vaporize (Brit. also **vaporise**) (not **-our-**)

vapour (US **vapor**) □ **vaporous**

vaquero pl. **vaqueros** cowboy (not ital.)

var. pl. **vars** or **vars. 1** variant **2** variety

Varanasi city on the Ganges, in Uttar Pradesh; former name **Benares**

Varangian guard bodyguard of the later Byzantine emperors

Varese town in Lombardy

Varèse, Edgard (1883–1965), French-born American composer

Vargas, Getúlio Dornelles (1883–1954), Brazilian president 1930–45 and 1951–4

Vargas Llosa, (Jorge) Mario (Pedro) (b.1936), Peruvian writer

variables Math. usu. set in ital.

varia lectio pl. ***variae lectiones*** variant reading (L., ital.; abbrev. ***v.l.***)

varifocal (one word)

variorum pl. **variorums** (edition) having notes from various editors or commentators, or including variant readings

Varna port in eastern Bulgaria

varna each of the four Hindu castes (not ital.)

vars (also **vars.**) pl. of **var.**

vas pl. **vasa** vessel or duct

Vasco da Gama see **da Gama**

vas deferens pl. **vasa deferentia** duct conveying sperm to the urethra

Vaseline trademark petroleum jelly

VAT value added tax

Vatican, the palace and official residence of the Pope in Rome

Vatican City independent papal state in Rome
vatu pl. same, monetary unit of Vanuatu
Vaud canton in western Switzerland; Ger. name **Waadt**
Vaughan 1 Henry (1621–95), Welsh poet **2** Sarah (Lois) (1924–90), American jazz singer and pianist
Vaughan Williams, Ralph (1872–1958), English composer
vb verb
vbl verbal
VC pl. **VCs 1** vice chairman **2** vice chancellor **3** vice consul **4** Victoria Cross
VCH Victoria County History
V-chip programmable chip in a television (cap., hyphen)
vCJD variant CJD
VCR pl. **VCRs** video cassette recorder
VD venereal disease
v.d. various dates
VDT pl. **VDTs** visual display terminal
VDU pl. **VDUs** visual display unit
vectors Math. set in bold
VED vehicle excise duty
Veda collection of early Indian scripture □ **Vedic**
Vedanta Hindu philosophy
VE Day 8 May, marking the WWII Allied victory in Europe (no hyphen)
Vedda pl. same or **Veddas** member of an aboriginal people of Sri Lanka
Vega, Lope de (1562–1635), Spanish writer; full name *Lope Felix de Vega Carpio*
veggie burger (also trademark **Vegeburger**) vegetarian patty resembling a hamburger
veinous having prominent veins; cf. **venous**
vela pl. of **velum**
velar speech sound pronounced with the tongue near the soft palate
Velázquez, Diego Rodríguez de Silva y (1599–1660), Spanish painter
Velázquez de Cuéllar, Diego (*c.*1465–1524), Spanish conquistador
Velcro trademark fastener made of strips that adhere when pressed together
veld (also **veldt**) open grassland in southern Africa
Velde, van de see **van de Velde**
veleta (also **valeta**) ballroom dance in triple time
velleity wish not strong enough to be acted on
vellum fine parchment
vellum paper high-quality paper resembling vellum
velocity (symbol ***v***)
velodrome cycle-racing track
velour (also **velours**) plush woven fabric
velouté white sauce (accent, not ital.)
velum pl. **vela** Anat. soft palate
Ven. Venerable
vena cava pl. **venae cavae** vein carrying blood into the heart (not ital.)
venal bribable, corrupt; cf. **venial**
Ven. & Ad. Shakespeare's *Venus and Adonis*
vendetta blood feud
vendeuse saleswoman (Fr., ital.)
vending machine (two words)
vendor (US also **vender**)
venepuncture (US also **venipuncture**) puncture of a vein as a medical procedure
Venerable (abbrev. **Ven.**) **1** title given to an Anglican archdeacon **2** title given to a person of a degree of sanctity in the Roman Catholic Church
Venetia region of NE Italy; It. name **Veneto**
Venetian person from Venice
venetian blind (lower case)
Venetian glass, Venetian red, Venetian window (one cap.)
Venezuela republic in South America □ **Venezuelan**
vengeance (not **-gance**)
venial pardonable; cf. **venal**
Venice city in NE Italy; It. name **Venezia**
venipuncture US var. of **venepuncture**
Venn diagram (one cap.)
venous of the veins; cf. **veinous** □ **venosity**
ventilator (not **-er**)
ventre à terre at full speed (Fr., ital.)
ventriloquize (Brit. also **ventriloquise**)
Venturi, Robert (Charles) (b.1925), American architect

venturi pl. **venturis** short piece of tube between wider sections (lower case)

Venus 1 Rom. Mythol. goddess of love; Gk equivalent **Aphrodite 2** second planet from the sun □ **Venusian**

Venus and Adonis Shakespeare poem (abbrev. ***Ven. & Ad.***)

Venus de Milo classical sculpture of Aphrodite (not ital.)

Venus flytrap (also **Venus's flytrap**) carnivorous bog plant

Venus's comb, Venus's flower basket, Venus's girdle, Venus's looking glass (apostrophe *s*)

Veracruz state and city of Mexico

veranda (also **verandah**) □ **verandaed**

verb (abbrev. **v.** or **vb**)

verbal functioning as a verb (abbrev. **vbl**)

verbalize (Brit. also **verbalise**)

verbal noun noun formed from and sharing some of the constructions of a verb (abbrev. **vbl n.**)

verbatim word for word (not ital.)

verboten forbidden (Ger., ital.)

verbum satis sapienti a word to the wise suffices (L., ital.; abbrev. **verb. sap.**)

verd-antique green ornamental marble (hyphen)

Verdelho pl. **Verdelhos** white wine or Madeira made from the Verdelho grape

verderer judicial officer of a royal forest

Verdicchio pl. **Verdicchios** Italian white wine made from the Verdicchio grape

verdigris green patina on copper (not **verde-**)

verger (arch. also **virger**) church caretaker

Vergil var. of **Virgil**

verglas thin coating of ice (not **-glass**)

verisimilitude appearance of being true or real (one *s*)

verism extreme naturalism in art or literature

verismo realism in late 19th-cent. opera and other arts (not ital.)

vérité realistic genre of film, television, or radio (Fr., ital.)

verity true principle or belief

Verlaine, Paul (1844–96), French poet

Vermeer, Jan (1632–75), Dutch painter

vermeil gilded silver or bronze

vermicelli (not **-lle**) **1** pasta in the form of threads **2** shreds of chocolate for decorating cakes

vermilion brilliant red (not **-ll-**)

Vermont state in the north-eastern US (official abbrev. **Vt.**, postal **VT**) □ **Vermonter**

vermouth wine flavoured with herbs (lower case)

Verne, Jules (1828–1905), French novelist

vernier small movable scale on a fixed main scale

vernissage private view of paintings before public exhibition (Fr., ital.)

Veronese, Paolo (*c.*1528–88), Italian painter; born *Paolo Caliari*

veronica (lower case) **1** herbaceous plant **2** cloth supposedly impressed with an image of Christ's face

veronique prepared or garnished with grapes (after the noun, not ital., no account)

Verrazano-Narrows Bridge suspension bridge across New York harbour (hyphen)

verruca pl. **verrucae** or **verrucas** wart on the foot (two *r*s, one *c*)

Versace, Gianni (1946–97), Italian fashion designer

Versailles palace near the town of Versailles, south-west of Paris

vers de société verse about polite society (Fr., ital.)

verse 1 writing with a metrical rhythm **2** group of lines forming a metrical unit (abbrev. **v.**)

versicle short verse said or sung by the minister in a church service

vers libre free verse (Fr., ital.)

verso pl. **versos** left-hand page of an open book; back of a loose leaf (abbrev. **v** or ^{v}); cf. **recto**

verst Russian measure of length (not ital.)

versus (not ital.; abbrev. **v.** or **vs**)

vertebra pl. **vertebrae**

vertex pl. **vertices** or **vertexes** highest point

vertu var. of **virtu**

Verulamium Roman name for **St Albans**
Verwoerd, Hendrik (Frensch) (1901–66), South African prime minister 1958–66
very (abbrev. **v.**)
Very light flare fired from a pistol (one cap.)
Very Reverend title given to an Anglican dean (abbrev. **Very Revd**)
Vesak most important Buddhist festival
vesica piscis pl. **vesicae piscis** pointed oval architectural feature (not ital.)
Vespa trademark Italian motor scooter
Vespasian (AD 9–79), Roman emperor 69–79; Latin name *Titus Flavius Vespasianus*
Vespucci, Amerigo (1451–1512), Italian merchant and explorer
Vesta Roman goddess of the hearth and household
vesta wooden or wax match (lower case)
Vestal Virgin (caps)
Veterans Day US public holiday (no apostrophe)
veterinarian N. Amer. veterinary surgeon
veterinary of the diseases and injuries of animals
vetiver (also **vetivert**) fragrant root extract
veto (**vetoes, vetoing, vetoed**)
Veuve Clicquot champagne
vexillology study of flags (three *l*s)
VFR visual flight rules
VG **1** very good **2** Vicar General
VGA videographics array
VHF very high frequency
VHS video home system
VHS-C VHS compact (hyphen)
VI Virgin Islands
via through, by way of (not ital.)
via dolorosa painful journey or process; (**the Via Dolorosa**) route between Jerusalem and Calvary (not ital.)
Viagra trademark male potency drug
vial small container for medicines etc.; cf. **phial**
via media middle way or compromise (L., ital.)
vibrato Mus. rapid slight variation in pitch
vibrator (not **-er**)
viburnum pl. **viburnums** flowering shrub
Vic. (also **Vict.**) Victoria (regnal year)
vicar apostolic (cap. in titles; abbrev. **VA**) **1** Roman Catholic missionary **2** titular bishop
vicar general pl. **vicars general** assistant to an Anglican bishop or archbishop; Roman Catholic bishop's representative (cap. in titles; abbrev. **VG**)
vice[1] (US **vise**) metal gripping tool □ **vice-like**
vice[2] as a substitute for (not ital.)
vice admiral (two words, caps in titles; abbrev. **VA**)
vice chairman, vice chancellor, vice consul (two words, caps in titles; abbrev. **VC**)
vicegerent person exercising delegated power (one word, cap. in titles)
Vicenza city in NE Italy
vice president (two words, caps in titles; abbrev. **VP**)
vice-presidential (hyphen)
vicereine viceroy's wife; female viceroy (one word, cap. in titles)
viceroy (one word, cap. in titles) □ **viceregal, viceroyal**
viceroyalty position or territory of a viceroy (one word)
vice versa (two words, not ital.)
Vichy town in south central France
vichyssoise creamy potato and leek soup
vicomte French viscount (cap. in titles; not ital. as part of name)
vicomtesse French viscountess (cap. in titles; not ital. as part of name)
Vict. var. of **Vic.**
victimize (Brit. also **victimise**)
Victoria[1] **1** state of SE Australia **2** capital of British Columbia, the Seychelles, and Hong Kong
Victoria[2] (1819–1901), queen of Great Britain and Ireland 1837–1901 and empress of India 1876–1901
victoria horse-drawn carriage (lower case)
Victoria, Lake (also **Victoria Nyanza**) largest lake in Africa
Victoria Cross (caps; abbrev. **VC**)
Victoria plum, Victoria sandwich,

Victoria sponge (one cap.)
victor ludorum overall male sports champion (not ital.)
victrix ludorum overall female sports champion (not ital.)
victual v. (**victualling, victualled**; US one **-l-**) ◻ **victualler** (US **victualer**)
vicuña wild relative of the llama (accent)
vide see, consult (not ital.; abbrev. **v.**)
videlicet namely, that is to say (not ital.; abbrev. **viz.**)
video n. pl. **videos**. v. **videos, videoing, videoed**
video camera (two words)
videocassette recorder (two words; abbrev. **VCR**)
videoconference, videodisc, videofit (one word)
video game, video nasty (two words)
videophone (one word)
video piracy (two words)
VideoPlus trademark system for recording from a television (one word, two caps)
video recorder (two words)
videotape (one word)
vie (**vying, vied**) compete
Vienna capital of Austria; Ger. name **Wien** ◻ **Viennese**
Vientiane capital of Laos
Vietcong pl. same, member of the Communist guerrilla movement in Vietnam 1954–75
Vietminh pl. same, member of the Vietnamese independence movement that fought against the French
Vietnam country in SE Asia ◻ **Vietnamese**
vieux jeu old-fashioned, hackneyed (Fr., ital.)
viewdata TV news and information service
viewfinder, viewgraph, viewpoint, viewport (one word)
VIFF technique of vertical take-off
Vigée-Lebrun, (Marie Louise) Élisabeth (1755–1842), French painter
vigesimal of or based on the number twenty
vigilante self-appointed law enforcer ◻ **vigilantism**
vignette 1 small illustration or portrait photograph without a definite border **2** small ornamental design filling a space on a page **3** brief account
vigorish excessive interest on a loan
vigorous (not **-our-**)
vigour (US **vigor**)
vihara Buddhist temple or monastery (ital.)
Viking (cap.)
Vila (also **Port Vila**) capital of Vanuatu
vilayet Turkish province (ital.)
vilify (not **-ll-, vile-**)
Villa, Pancho (1878–1923), Mexican revolutionary; born *Doroteo Arango*
villain wicked person; cf. **villein**
Villa-Lobos, Heitor (1887–1959), Brazilian composer
villanella pl. **villanelle** or **villanellas** rustic Italian part-song (not ital.)
villanelle pastoral or lyrical poem of nineteen lines with only two rhymes and some repeated lines
villein feudal serf; cf. **villain**
Vilnius capital of Lithuania
VIN vehicle identification number
vinaigrette salad dressing
Vinci, Leonardo da, see **Leonardo da Vinci**
vindaloo pl. **vindaloos** hot Indian dish
vin de pays (also ***vin du pays***) pl. ***vins de pays*** French wine of a particular locality and quality (ital.)
vin de table pl. ***vins de table*** French table wine (ital.)
vineyard (not **vinyard**)
vingt-et-un the card game pontoon (Fr., ital., hyphens)
vin ordinaire pl. ***vins ordinaires*** cheap French table wine (ital.)
Viognier white wine from the Viognier grape
viola da gamba (also **viol da gamba**) bass viol (not ital.)
violator (not **-er**)
violoncello (not **violin-**)
VIP pl. **VIPs** very important person
virago pl. **viragos** or **viragoes** domineering or bad-tempered woman
Virchow, Rudolf Karl (1821–1902), German pathologist

virelay short lyric poem in stanzas with two rhymes, the end rhyme of one being the main rhyme of the next
virger arch. var. of **verger**
Virgil (also **Vergil**) (70–19 BC), Roman poet; Latin name *Publius Vergilius Maro* □ **Virgilian**
Virginia state of the eastern US (official abbrev. **Va.**, postal **VA**) □ **Virginian**
Virginia creeper, Virginia reel (one cap.)
Virgin Islands group of Caribbean islands (abbrev. **VI**)
Virgin Queen, the Elizabeth I (caps)
Virgo sixth sign of the zodiac □ **Virgoan**
virgo intacta girl or woman who has never had sexual intercourse (L., ital.)
virgule another term for **slash**
virtu (also **vertu**) knowledge of the fine arts (not ital.)
virtualize (Brit. also **virtualise**)
virtuoso pl. **virtuosi** or **virtuosos**
virus pl. **viruses**
Vis. Viscount
visa (**visas, visaing, visaed** or **visa'd**)
vis-à-vis in relation to (hyphens, accent, not ital.)
Visc. Viscount
viscera (sing. **viscus**) internal organs
viscose synthetic fabric
viscount British nobleman ranking between an earl and a baron (cap. in titles; abbrev. **Vis.** or **Visc.**)
viscountess wife or widow of a viscount, or woman holding the rank of viscount (cap. in titles)
viscous sticky
viscus sing. of **viscera**
vise US var. of **vice**[1]
Vishnu Hindu god
Visigoth member of the branch of the Goths that ruled in Spain before the Moors □ **Visigothic**
visitor (but *The Young Visiters* by Daisy Ashford, 1919)
visitors' book (apostrophe after *s*)
visor (also **vizor**)
vista view □ **vistaed**
visualize (Brit. also **visualise**)
vitalize (Brit. also **vitalise**)
vitiate spoil or impair □ **vitiator**
Vitoria city in NE Spain
Vitória port in eastern Brazil
vitreous of glass, glassy
vitriol bitter criticism
vituperation bitter abuse
viva (**vivas, vivaing, vivaed** or **viva'd**) (subject to) a viva voce examination
vivace Mus. in a lively or brisk manner
vivarium pl. **vivaria** enclosure for animals (not ital.)
viva voce oral (examination) (two words even when attrib., not ital.)
vive la difference long live the difference (between the sexes) [Fr. *vive la différence*]
viverrid mammal of the civet family (two *r*s)
viz. namely, videlicet (point, not ital., preceded by a comma)
vizier hist. high official in Ottoman Turkey
vizor var. of **visor**
vizsla Hungarian breed of dog (lower case)
VJ pl. **VJs** video jockey
VJ Day Victory over Japan Day, 15 Aug. 1945 (no hyphen)
v.l. *varia lectio* (variant reading)
Vlaanderen Flemish name for **Flanders**
Vlaminck, Maurice de (1876–1958), French painter
VLF very low frequency
Vltava river of the Czech Republic; Ger. name **Moldau**
V-neck (cap., hyphen)
VO Royal Victorian Order
voc. vocative
vocabulary (abbrev. **vocab.**)
vocal cords (not **chords**)
vocalese style of singing to jazz tunes
vocalise singing exercise using individual syllables
vocalize (Brit. also **vocalise**) utter, express in words
vocative grammatical case used in addressing or invoking (abbrev. **voc.**)
Vodafone mobile telecommunications company
vogue n. prevailing fashion. v. (**vogueing** or **voguing, vogued**) dance imitating a model on a catwalk □ **voguish**
voice box (two words)

voicemail (one word)
voice-over text of a film etc. spoken off-screen (hyphen)
voila there you are! (not ital.) [Fr. *voilà*]
voile semi-transparent fabric
voir dire (also **voire dire**) Law preliminary examination of a witness or potential juror (two words, not ital.)
vol. pl. **vols** or **vols.** volume
Volapük artificial language
vol-au-vent small filled case of puff pastry (hyphens, not ital.)
volcanism (also **vulcanism**) volcanic activity
volcano pl. **volcanoes** or **volcanos**
volcanology (also **vulcanology**) study of volcanoes
Volga river of Russia
Volgograd city in SW Russia; former names **Tsaritsyn, Stalingrad**
Völkerwanderung migration of Germanic and Slavic peoples into Europe (Ger., cap., ital.)
völkisch (also ***volkisch***) populist or nationalist (Ger., ital.)
Volkswagen German make of car (abbrev. **VW**)
volley (**volleys, volleying, volleyed**)
volleyball (one word)
Volpone play by Ben Jonson (1606)
vols (also **vols.**) volumes
volt 1 SI unit of electromotive force (abbrev. **V**) **2** var. of **volte**
Voltaire (1694–1778), French writer; pseudonym of *François-Marie Arouet* □ **Voltairean**
volte (also **volt**) Fencing sudden movement to escape a thrust
volte-face act of turning around to face the other way; complete reversal (hyphen, not ital.)
voltmeter (one word)
volume (abbrev. **vol.**) **1** book forming part of a work or series **2** single book **3** consecutive series of issues of a periodical
voluntarism (also **voluntaryism**) principle of relying on voluntary action
vomit v. (**vomiting, vomited**)
von as prefix to proper names usu. lower case for German names, sometimes capitalized for Swiss (ignored for alphabetization); **vom, von dem, von den, von der** are also usu. lower case but are retained for alphabetization
Vonnegut, Kurt (1922–2007), American writer
von Neumann, John, see **Neumann, John von**
von Sternberg, Josef (1894–1969), Austrian-born American film director (usu. alphabetized thus)
voodoo (**voodoos, voodooing, voodooed**)
Voortrekker hist. Afrikaner pioneer (cap.)
vortal Internet directory of links for a particular industry
vortex pl. **vortexes** or **vortices** whirling mass
Vorticism British art movement of the early 20th cent. (cap.)
Vosges mountain system of eastern France
voting booth (two words)
voussoir wedge-shaped stone in an arch (not ital.)
Vouvray French white wine
vowel speech sound with vibration of the vocal cords but without audible friction
vox angelica tremolo organ stop (not ital.)
vox humana voice-like organ stop (not ital.)
vox pop Brit. popular opinion expressed in informal interviews
vox populi majority opinion or belief (not ital.)
voyager person making a voyage
voyageur hist. Canadian boatman transporting goods and passengers to trading posts (not ital.)
voyeur person who watches others' sexual activity
VP pl. **VPs** vice president
VPN pl. **VPNs** virtual private network
VR 1 Queen Victoria [L. *Victoria Regina*] **2** pl. **VRs** variant reading **3** virtual reality
VRML Comput. virtual reality modelling language
VS Veterinary Surgeon
vs versus

V-sign (cap., hyphen)
VSO Voluntary Service Overseas
VSOP very special old pale (brandy)
VT Vermont (postal abbrev.)
Vt. Vermont (official abbrev.)
VTO vertical take-off
VTOL vertical take-off and landing
VTR pl. **VTRs** video tape recorder
Vuillard, (Jean) Édouard (1868–1940), French artist
Vulcan Rom. Mythol. god of fire; Gk equivalent **Hephaestus**
vulcanism var. of **volcanism**
vulcanize (Brit. also **vulcanise**) harden by treatment with sulphur at a high temperature
vulcanology var. of **volcanology**
vulgar fraction fraction expressed by a numerator and denominator
vulgarize (Brit. also **vulgarise**)
vulgar Latin informal Latin of classical times (one cap.)
Vulgate the principal Latin version of the Bible (abbrev. **Vulg.**)
vulgate common or colloquial speech; accepted text of an author (lower case)
vulpine of or like a fox
vv. **1** verses **2** volumes
vv.ll. *variae lectiones* (variant readings)
VW Volkswagen
v.y. various years
vying present participle of **vie**

W

W 1 pl. **Ws** or **W's** 23rd letter of the alphabet **2** watt(s) **3** West or Western **4** Cricket wicket(s) **5** the chemical element tungsten [mod. L. *wolframium*]

w 1 weight **2** Cricket wide(s) **3** (also **w/**) with

WA 1 Washington (postal abbrev.) **2** Western Australia

Waadt Ger. name for **Vaud**

Waaf member of the Women's Auxiliary Air Force, 1939–48

wabble use **wobble**

WAC US Women's Army Corps

wacky (also **whacky**) funny in an odd way

wadeable (also **wadable**)

Wade–Giles system of romanized spelling for transliterating Chinese, largely superseded by Pinyin (en rule)

wadi pl. **wadis** channel that is dry exc. in the rainy season

WAF Women in the (US) Air Force

Waffen SS combat units of the Nazi SS in WWII

wage earner, wage slave (two words)

Wagga Wagga town in New South Wales

Wagner, (Wilhelm) Richard (1813–83), German composer □ **Wagnerian**

wagon (Brit. also **waggon**)

wagon-lit pl. **wagons-lits** sleeping car on a continental railway (not ital.)

wagonload (one word)

wagon train (two words)

wagtail bird (one word)

Wahhabi (also **Wahabi**) pl. **Wahhabis** member of a strict Sunni Muslim sect □ **Wahhabism**

wah-wah fluctuating musical effect (hyphen)

Waikato longest river of New Zealand

Waikiki Hawaiian beach resort

Wain, John (Barrington) (1925–94), English writer

wainscot (also **wainscoting** or **wainscotting**) wooden panelling used to line the walls of a room □ **wainscoted** (also **wainscotted**)

wainwright hist. wagon-builder

WAIS Comput. wide area information service

waistband, waistcoat, waistline (one word)

waist-deep, waist-high (hyphen)

waiting list, waiting room (two words)

waive refrain from insisting on; cf. **wave**

waiver instance of waiving a right or claim; document recording this

wake (past **woke** or US, dial., or arch. **waked**; past part. **woken** or US, dial., or arch. **waked**)

wakeboarding (one word)

Walachia var. of **Wallachia**

Waldenses puritan religious sect (pl.) □ **Waldensian**

Waldorf salad (one cap.)

Waldsterben death of forest trees because of atmospheric pollution (Ger., cap., ital.)

wale ridge on cloth such as corduroy

wale knot (also **wall knot**) knot at the end of a rope

Waler breed of horse from New South Wales

Wales principality of the UK; Welsh name **Cymru**

Wałęsa, Lech (b.1943), Polish president 1990–5

Wales Office UK government department (not **Welsh Office**)

walkabout n. (one word, two words as verb)

walkathon (one word)

walkie-talkie (hyphen; not **walky-talky**)

walk-in adj. (hyphen, two words as verb)

walking frame, walking shoe,

walking stick, walking tour (two words)
Walkman pl. **Walkmans** or **Walkmen** trademark personal stereo
walk-on adj. (hyphen, two words as verb)
walkout, walkover n. (one word, two words as verb)
walk-through adj. (hyphen, two words as verb)
Walküre, Die second part of Wagner's *Der Ring des Nibelungen* (1870)
walkway (one word)
Wallace 1 Alfred Russel (1823–1913), English naturalist **2** (Richard Horatio) Edgar (1875–1932), English writer **3** Sir William (*c*.1270–1305), Scottish national hero
Wallachia (also **Walachia**) former principality of SE Europe □ **Wallachian**
wallah informal person doing a specified thing (not **-a**)
wall bar (two words)
wallchart, wallcovering (one word)
wall eye (two words) □ **wall-eyed**
wallflower (one word)
wall game form of football played at Eton (two words, lower case)
Wallis, Sir Barnes Neville (1887–1979), English inventor
wall knot var. of **wale knot**
Wall of Death fairground sideshow (two caps)
Walloon member of a French-speaking people of Belgium and northern France; cf. **Fleming**[2]
wall painting (two words)
wallpaper (one word)
Wall Street street where the New York Stock Exchange is located
Wal-Mart US retail chain (hyphen)
Walpole 1 Horace, 4th Earl of Orford (1717–97), English writer and politician **2** Sir Robert, 1st Earl of Orford (1676–1745), British statesman
Walpurgis night night of 30 April, when witches meet with the Devil in German folklore (one cap.); Ger. name **Walpurgisnacht**
Walton 1 Izaak (1593–1683), English writer **2** Sir William (Turner) (1902–83), English composer
Walvis Bay port in Namibia
WAN pl. **WANs** Comput. wide area network
wanderlust (one word, lower case)
Wanganui port in New Zealand
Wankel engine rotary internal-combustion engine (one cap.)
wannabe aspiring person (not **-bee**)
WAP Wireless Application Protocol
wapiti pl. **wapitis** North American red deer
war artist, war baby, war bride (two words)
Warburg 1 Aby (Moritz) (1866–1929), German art historian **2** Otto Heinrich (1883–1970), German biochemist
war chest, war crime, war cry, war dance (two words)
Wardour Street London street associated with the British film industry
wardroom commissioned officers' mess on a warship (one word)
war game, war grave (two words)
warhead (one word)
Warhol, Andy (*c*.1928–87), American artist; born *Andrew Warhola* □ **Warholian**
warhorse, warlike, warlock, warlord, warmonger (one word)
warm-hearted (hyphen)
warm-up n. (hyphen, two words as verb)
Warne 1 Frederick, publishers **2** Shane (Keith) (b.1969), Australian cricketer
warpaint, warpath, warplane (one word)
war poet (two words)
warranter person who warrants something
warrant officer (cap. in titles; abbrev. **WO**)
warrantor person or company providing a warranty
warrigal (also **warragal**) Austral. **1** dingo dog **2** wild horse
Warsaw capital of Poland; Pol. name **Warszawa**
warship (one word)
warthog (one word)
wartime (one word)
war-torn (hyphen)
Warwick, Richard Neville, Earl of

(1428–71), English statesman; known as **Warwick the Kingmaker**
Warwickshire county of central England (abbrev. **War.**)
Wash. Washington (official abbrev.)
washbasin, washboard, washday (one word)
washed out, washed up (two words, hyphen when attrib.)
washer-up pl. **washers-up** (hyphen)
washerwoman (one word)
wash-hand basin (one hyphen)
wash house (two words)
washing line, washing machine, washing powder (two words)
Washington[1] **1** (also **Washington State**) state of the north-western US (official abbrev. **Wash.**, postal **WA**) **2** (also **Washington DC**) capital of the US (no comma) **3** town in NE England □ **Washingtonian**
Washington[2] **1** Booker T(aliaferro) (1856–1915), American educationist **2** George (1732–99), 1st president of the US 1789–97
washing-up (hyphen)
washout, washroom, washstand, washtub (one word)
Wasp (also **WASP**) N. Amer. white Anglo-Saxon Protestant
wastebasket (one word)
waste bin (two words)
wasteland (one word, but *The Waste Land* by T. S. Eliot, 1922)
wastepaper basket (two words)
waste pipe (two words)
watchdog, watchfire, watchmaker, watchman, watchtower, watchword (one word)
waterbed, waterbird (one word)
water biscuit, water boatman (two words)
waterborne (one word)
water cannon, water chestnut, water clock (two words)
water closet (two words; abbrev. **WC**)
watercolour (US **watercolor**) (one word, but *The Royal Society of Painters in Water Colours*)
water cooler (two words)
watercourse, watercress, waterfall, waterfowl, waterfront (one word)
Watergate 1970s US political scandal (one word)
waterhen, waterhole (one word)
water ice (two words)
watering can, watering hole, watering place (two words)
water jump, water level, water lily (two words)
waterline, waterlogged (one word)
water main (two words)
watermark faint design in some kinds of paper (one word)
water meadow (two words)
watermelon, watermill (one word)
water nymph, water pipe, water pistol, water polo (two words)
waterproof (one word)
water rat, water rate (two words)
water-resistant (hyphen)
watershed, waterside (one word)
waterski (**waterskis, waterskiing, waterskied**) □ **waterskier**
water slide, water snake, water softener, water sports (two words)
waterspout (one word)
water table (two words)
watertight (one word)
water torture, water tower, water vole (two words)
waterway, waterweed, waterwheel, waterworks (one word)
watt SI unit of power (lower case; abbrev. **W**)
Watteau, Jean Antoine (1684–1721), French painter
Waugh, Evelyn (Arthur St John) (1903–66), English novelist
wave move to and fro; cf. **waive**
waveband, waveform, wavefront, wavelength (one word)
wavy (not **-ey**)
waxcloth, waxwork (one word)
waybill, wayfarer, waylay (one word)
Wayne, John (1907–79), American actor; born *Marion Michael Morrison*
waypoint, wayside (one word)
way station (two words)
wayzgoose pl. **wayzgooses** hist. printing house's annual summer outing
Wb weber(s)

WBA 1 West Bromwich Albion **2** World Boxing Association
WBC World Boxing Council
WC 1 pl. **WCs** water closet **2** West Central (London postal district)
WCC World Council of Churches
WEA Workers' Educational Association
weal (also chiefly Med. **wheal**) red swollen mark
Weald district including parts of Kent, Surrey, and East Sussex □ **Wealden**
weaponize (Brit. also **weaponise**)
Wear river of northern England
wear (low dam) use **weir**
weasel v. (**weaselling, weaselled**; US one **-l-**)
weather-beaten (hyphen)
weatherboard, weatherbound, weathercock (one word)
weather forecast, weather forecaster (two words)
weathergirl, weatherman, weatherproof, weathervane (one word)
weave (past **wove**; past part. **woven** or **wove**) form (fabric); *weave* meaning 'move from side to side' inflects regularly
Web, the the World Wide Web
Webb 1 (Gladys) Mary (1881–1927), English novelist **2** (Martha) Beatrice (1858–1943) and Sidney (James), Baron Passfield (1859–1947), English socialists and economists
webcam (one word, lower case, cap. as US trademark)
Weber 1 Carl Maria (Friedrich Ernst) von (1786–1826), German composer **2** Max (1864–1920), German economist and sociologist **3** Wilhelm Eduard (1804–91), German physicist
weber SI unit of magnetic flux (lower case; abbrev. **Wb**)
Webern, Anton (Friedrich Ernst) von (1883–1945), Austrian composer
weblog, webmaster (one word, lower case)
web offset offset printing from continuous paper on a reel (two words)
web page (two words, lower case)
website (one word, lower case)
Webster 1 John (*c.*1580–*c.*1625), English dramatist **2** Noah (1758–1843), American lexicographer
Wed. Wednesday
Wedgwood trademark ceramic ware made orig. by the English potter Josiah Wedgwood (not **-dge-**)
Wednesday (abbrev. **Wed.** or **Weds.**)
week (abbrev. **wk**)
weekday, weekend (one word)
weekly newspaper or periodical issued every week
weepie sentimental film, song, etc.
weepy tearful, inclined to weep
weevil small beetle □ **weevily**
w.e.f. with effect from
Wehrmacht the German armed forces 1921–45 (cap., ital.)
Weidenfeld & Nicolson publishers
weighbridge (one word)
weigh-in n. (hyphen, two words as verb)
weight (abbrev. **wt**)
weightlifting (one word)
weight training (two words)
weight-watcher (hyphen, lower case, but *Weight Watchers*, trademark of an organization for slimmers)
Weil, Simone (1909–43), French essayist and philosopher
Weill, Kurt (1900–50), German composer
Weimaraner breed of dog (cap.)
Weimar Republic the German republic of 1919–33
weir low dam across a river (not **wear**)
weird (not **wie-**)
Weismann, August Friedrich Leopold (1834–1914), German biologist
Weizmann, Chaim (Azriel) (1874–1952), first Israeli president 1949–52
welch var. of **welsh**
Welch Fusiliers, Welch Regiment (not **Welsh**)
welcome (one *l*; cf. **Wellcome Trust**)
welfare state (lower case)
Welkom town in central South Africa
well usu. two words with participial adjectives after the verb, hyphen when attrib.: *people who are well adjusted* | *well-adjusted people*
well-being (hyphen)
Wellcome Trust health charity (two *l*s)
Welles, (George) Orson (1915–85),

American film director and actor
well head (two words)
well heeled (two words, hyphen when attrib.)
wellie var. of **welly**
Wellington[1] capital of New Zealand
Wellington[2] Arthur Wellesley, 1st Duke of (1769–1852), British soldier and prime minister 1828–30 and 1834; known as **the Iron Duke**
wellington knee-length waterproof boot (lower case)
well known (two words, hyphen when attrib.)
well-nigh (hyphen)
well off wealthy (two words, hyphen when attrib.)
Wells, H(erbert) G(eorge) (1866–1946), English novelist
wellspring (one word)
well-to-do wealthy (hyphens)
well-wisher (hyphen)
well woman denoting a clinic for women's health (attrib., two words)
welly (also **wellie**) **1** wellington **2** informal power or vigour
Welsh of Wales
welsh (also **welch**) fail to honour an obligation
Welsh rarebit (also **Welsh rabbit**) melted cheese on toast
Weltanschauung pl. ***Weltanschauungen*** particular philosophy or view of life (Ger., cap., ital.)
welterweight boxing weight between lightweight and middleweight (one word)
Weltschmerz melancholy and world-weariness (Ger., cap., ital.)
Wenceslas (also **Wenceslaus**) **1** (1361–1419), king of Bohemia 1378–1419 **2** (**St Wenceslas** or **Good King Wenceslas**) (*c.*907–29), patron saint of the Czech Republic
Wendy house toy house for children to play in (one cap.)
Wensleydale crumbly white cheese
werewolf pl. **werewolves** (not **werwolf**)
Wesley, John (1703–91) and Charles (1707–88), English preachers □ **Wesleyan**
west (abbrev. **W**; cap. in ref. to Europe and North America, or in contrast with the former communist states of eastern Europe)
West Africa (caps)
West Bank region west of the River Jordan, occupied by Israel after the Six Day War of 1967 (caps)
westbound (one word)
West Country the south-western counties of England (caps)
West End area of London (caps)
western (abbrev. **W**; cap. in ref. to Europe and North America, or in contrast with the former communist states of eastern Europe)
Western Australia state of Australia (abbrev. **WA**)
Western Church the Christian Church originating in the Latin Church
Western Empire western part of the Roman Empire after its division in AD 395
western hemisphere (lower case)
Western Isles council area of Scotland, consisting of the Outer Hebrides
westernize (Brit. also **westernise**)
West Germany the Federal Republic of Germany, reunited with East Germany in 1990
West Highland terrier (two caps)
West Indies islands between the Caribbean and the Atlantic (abbrev. **WI**) □ **West Indian**
West Lothian council area of east central Scotland
Westmorland former county of NW England (not **-more-**)
Weston-super-Mare resort in SW England (hyphens, two caps)
West Sussex county of SE England (caps)
West Virginia state of the eastern US (official abbrev. **W.Va.**, postal **WV**) □ **West Virginian**
wet v. (past and past part. **wet** or **wetted**)
wetland, wetsuit (one word)
w.f. wrong font
WFTU World Federation of Trade Unions
Wg Cdr Wing Commander
whaleboat, whalebone (one word)
wharf pl. **wharves** or **wharfs**

whatever (one word; in emphatic use also two words)
Whatman paper English handmade drawing paper
whatnot, whatsit, whatsoever (one word)
wheal chiefly Med. var. of **weal**
wheatear, wheatgerm, wheatmeal (one word)
Wheatstone bridge simple circuit for measuring electrical resistance
wheelbarrow, wheelbase, wheelchair, wheelhouse (one word)
wheeler-dealer (hyphen)
wheel lock (two words)
wheelspin, wheelwright (one word)
whence from where (strictly, avoid **from whence**)
whenever (one word; in emphatic use also two words)
whensoever (one word)
whereabouts, whereas, whereby, whereof, wheresoever, whereupon (one word)
wherever (one word; in emphatic use also two words)
wherewithal means or resources (one word; not **-all**)
whichever, whichsoever (one word)
Whig member of a British political party succeeded by the Liberal Party (cap.)
whilst Brit. prefer **while**
whimsy (also **whimsey**) pl. **whimsies** or **whimseys**
whinge v. (**whingeing, whinged**)
whinny (not **-ey**)
whipcord, whiplash (one word)
whipper-in pl. **whippers-in**
whippersnapper (one word)
whippoorwill American nightjar (one word)
whipsaw, whipstitch, whipstock (one word)
whir (also **whirr**) v. (**whirring, whirred**)
whirligig spinning toy (not **-ly-**)
whirlpool, whirlwind (one word)
whirlybird helicopter
whirr var. of **whir**
whisky 1 (Ir. & US **whiskey**) spirit distilled from grain **2** (**whiskey**) code word for the letter W
whistle-blower, whistle-stop (hyphen)
Whitaker's Almanack annual handbook originally published by J. Whitaker & Sons (not ***-tt-***, ***-nac***)
Whitby town on the coast of North Yorkshire
white accepted term (lower case) as an adj. for light-skinned people; do not use as a noun; some prefer to use words, e.g. **European**, which relate to geographical origin rather than skin colour; **Caucasian** is chiefly US
whitebait, whiteboard (one word)
white book 1 official government report bound in white **2** (**White Book**) book of rules for the Supreme Court in England and Wales
whitecap (one word)
whitefish pl. same or **whitefishes** a fish of the salmon family (one word)
white fish fish with pale flesh (two words)
Whitehall London street with many government offices
Whitehorse capital of Yukon Territory
White Horse, Vale of valley and district in Oxfordshire (not **of the**)
white-hot (hyphen)
White House 1 the official residence of the US president **2** the Russian parliament building
white-out dense blizzard (hyphen)
White Paper UK government report giving information or proposals (caps)
White Russia former name for **Belarus**
White Russian 1 opponent of the Bolsheviks during the Russian Civil War **2** dated Belarusian
whitethorn, whitethroat, whitewash (one word)
whitish (not **-eish**)
Whitsun (also **Whitsuntide**) period including Whit Sunday
Whit Sunday (US **Whitsunday**) seventh Sunday after Easter
whizz (also chiefly N. Amer. **whiz**)
whizz-kid (also **whiz-kid**) (hyphen)
WHO World Health Organization
Who, the English rock group
whoa command to stop

whodunnit (US **whodunit**) story about a murder investigation
whoever (one word; in emphatic use also two words)
wholefood, wholegrain, wholehearted, wholemeal (one word)
whole note N. Amer. semibreve
wholesale, wholescale, wholesome, wholewheat (one word)
whomever, whomsoever (one word)
whoopee cushion (not **-ie**)
whooping cough (not **hoop-**)
whorehouse, whoremonger (one word)
whosesoever, whosoever (one word)
who's who directory of facts about notable people; (***Who's Who***) annual biographical reference publication
why pl. **whys**
whydah African weaver bird (not **whi-**)
why ever (two words)
Whymper Edward (1840–1911), English mountaineer
WI 1 West Indies **2** Wisconsin (postal abbrev.) **3** Women's Institute
Wicca modern witchcraft ▫ **Wiccan**
wicketkeeper (one word)
widdershins Sc. anticlockwise; cf. **deasil**
wideawake soft felt hat (one word)
wide awake fully awake (two words, hyphen when attrib.)
wide-body (also **wide-bodied**) (hyphen)
widescreen, widespread (one word)
wide-eyed, wide-ranging (hyphen)
widgeon var. of **wigeon**
widow last word or short line of a paragraph set as the first line of a page or column; cf. **orphan**
Wien Ger. name for **Vienna**
wiener N. Amer. frankfurter
Wiener schnitzel (one cap.)
Wiesbaden city in western Germany
Wi-Fi trademark facility allowing computers, smartphones, etc. to connect to the Internet wirelessly
wigeon (also **widgeon**) kind of duck
Wight, Isle of see **Isle of Wight**
Wigtownshire former county of SW Scotland
wildcat (one word)
Wilde, Oscar (Fingal O'Flahertie Wills) (1854–1900), Irish writer and wit
wildebeest pl. same or **wildebeests** another name for **gnu**
wildfire (one word)
wild flower (two words)
wildfowl (one word)
wild goose chase (three words)
wildlife, wildwood (one word)
wilful (US **willful**)
Wilhelmshaven port in NW Germany
Will. William (regnal year)
Willemstad former capital of the Netherlands Antilles
William I (*c.*1027–87), king of England 1066–87; known as **William the Conqueror**
William II (*c.*1060–1100), king of England 1087–1100; known as **William Rufus**
William III (1650–1702), king of Great Britain and Ireland 1689–1702; known as **William of Orange**
William of Occam (also **Ockham**) (*c.*1285–1349), English philosopher
will-o'-the-wisp (hyphens, apostrophe)
willow pattern (two words, hyphen when attrib.)
willpower (one word)
willy-nilly (hyphen)
willy-willy Austral. whirlwind or dust storm (hyphen)
Wilson 1 (James) Harold, Baron Wilson of Rievaulx (1916–95), British prime minister 1964–70 and 1974–6 **2** (Thomas) Woodrow (1856–1924), 28th president of the US 1913–21
Wiltshire county of southern England (abbrev. **Wilts.**)
Wimpey trademark construction company
Wimpy trademark fast-food chain
Wimsey, Lord Peter, character in novels by Dorothy L. Sayers
wincey pl. **winceys** light twilled fabric
Winchester 1 city in southern England **2** trademark repeating rifle **3** (in full **Winchester disk** or **drive**) disk drive in a sealed unit
winchester large cylindrical bottle (lower case)
Winckelmann, Johann (Joachim) (1717–68), German archaeologist and art historian

windbag, windbound, windbreak, windburn, windcheater (one word)
wind chill (two words even when attrib.)
Windermere lake in Cumbria (not **Lake W-**)
windfall (one word)
wind farm (two words)
Windhoek capital of Namibia
windjammer, windmill (one word)
window box, window dressing, window frame, window ledge (two words)
windowpane (one word)
Windows trademark operating system for personal computers (treated as sing.)
window-shop (hyphen)
windowsill (one word)
windpipe, windproof (one word)
windscreen (N. Amer. **windshield**) (one word)
windsock, windstorm, windsurfer, windsurfing, windswept (one word)
wind tunnel, wind turbine (two words)
Windward Islands islands in the eastern Caribbean
wine bar, wine bottle, wine box, wine cellar, wine glass (two words)
wineglassful pl. **wineglassfuls**
winegrower (one word)
wine list (two words)
winemaker, winemaking, wineskin (one word)
wine tasting, wine vinegar, wine waiter (two words)
winey (also **winy**) resembling wine
wingbeat (one word)
wing commander (cap. in titles; abbrev. **Wg Cdr**)
Winged Victory winged statue of the goddess Nike (caps)
wingspan, wingspread, wingstroke (one word)
Winnie-the-Pooh toy bear in stories by A. A. Milne (hyphens, two caps)
wino pl. **winos** alcoholic
winter season (lower case)
wintergreen (pungent oil from) a North American plant (one word)
winterize (Brit. also **winterise**) adapt for cold weather
Winter's Tale, The Shakespeare play (abbrev. ***Wint. T.***)
wintertide, wintertime (one word)
wintry (also **wintery**)
win–win situation (en rule)
WIP work in progress
wipeout n. (one word, two words as verb)
WIPO World Intellectual Property Organization
wireline, wiretapping (one word)
wiry (not **-ey**)
Wisconsin state in the northern US (official abbrev. **Wis.**, postal **WI**) □ **Wisconsinite**
Wisden Cricketers' Almanack annual cricketing handbook (not **-er's, -ac**)
Wisdom of Solomon book of the Apocrypha (abbrev. **Wisd.**)
wiseacre, wisecrack (one word)
wisent European bison
wishbone (one word)
wish fulfilment (two words)
wishy-washy (hyphen)
Wissenschaft pursuit of knowledge and scholarship (Ger., cap., ital.)
wisteria (also **wistaria**) climbing shrub
witch elm var. of **wych elm**
witches' sabbath (lower case, apostrophe)
witchetty grub edible larva (not **-ety**)
witch hazel (also **wych hazel**) (astringent lotion from) a shrub
witch-hunt (hyphen)
withal in addition (not **-all**)
withhold (two *hs*)
without (abbrev. **w/o**)
withy (also **withe**) pl. **withies** or **withes** flexible willow branch
witness box (N. Amer. **witness stand**) (two words)
Wittenberg town in eastern Germany
Wittgenstein, Ludwig (Josef Johann) (1889–1951), Austrian-born British philosopher □ **Wittgensteinian**
Witwatersrand region of South Africa
wivern use **wyvern**
wizened shrivelled (not **weaz-**)
wk pl. **wks** week

Wm William
Wm. & Mar. William and Mary (regnal year)
WMD weapon of mass destruction
WML Comput. Wireless Markup Language
WMO World Meteorological Organization
WNW west-north-west
WO Warrant Officer
w/o without
wobbegong (also **wobbegon**) Australian shark
wobble (not **wabble** (arch.)) □ **wobbly**
Wodehouse, Sir P(elham) G(renville) (1881–1975), English writer
Woden another name for **Odin**
woebegone miserable-looking (but 'Lake Wobegon' in the stories of Garrison Keillor)
wok bowl-shaped frying pan
Wolf, Hugo (Philipp Jakob) (1860–1903), Austrian composer
Wolfe **1** James (1727–59), British general **2** Thomas (Clayton) (1900–38), American novelist **3** Tom (b.1931), American writer
wolfhound (one word)
wolfram tungsten or its ore
Wolfson College Oxford, Cambridge
wolf whistle n. (two words, hyphen as verb)
Wollaston, William Hyde (1766–1828), English scientist
Wollstonecraft, Mary (1759–97), English writer
Wolsey, Thomas (*c.*1474–1530), English churchman and statesman; known as **Cardinal Wolsey**
womanize (Brit. also **womanise**)
womankind (also **womenkind**)
women's lib, women's liberation, women's movement (lower case)
womenswear (one word)
wonderland (one word)
wonderstruck (also **wonder-stricken**)
wondrous (not **wonder-**)
woodbine (not **-bind**) **1** Brit. honeysuckle **2** N. Amer. Virginia creeper
woodblock, woodcarving, woodchip (one word)
woodchuck North American marmot (one word)
woodcock pl. same, woodland bird (one word)
woodcut print made from a design cut in a block of wood, formerly much used for book illustrations (one word)
Woodhouse surname of Emma in Jane Austen's *Emma*
woodland, woodlark, woodlouse, woodman (one word)
wood nymph (two words)
woodpecker (one word)
wood pigeon (two words)
woodpile (one word)
wood pulp reduced wood fibre used to make paper (two words)
woodshed, woodsman, woodsmoke, woodturning, woodwind, woodwork, woodworm (one word)
Woolf, Virginia (1882–1941), English writer; born *Adeline Virginia Stephen*
woollen (US **woolen**)
Woolley, Sir (Charles) Leonard (1880–1960), English archaeologist
woolly (two *ls*)
Woolmark quality symbol for wool (cap.)
Woolsack Lord Chancellor's seat in the House of Lords (cap.)
wool-sorters' disease pulmonary anthrax (one hyphen, note apostrophe)
Woolworths retail chain (no apostrophe)
woonerf pl. **woonerven** or **woonerfs** road with traffic calming (not ital.)
Wooster, Bertie, character in the stories of P. G. Wodehouse
Worcester **1** cathedral city in western England **2** trademark in the US porcelain made at Worcester
Worcester sauce (also **Worcestershire sauce**)
Worcestershire county of west central England (abbrev. **Worcs.**)
wordbook study book containing words and meanings (one word)
word break (also **word division**) point at which a word is hyphenated at the end of a line
wordplay (one word)

word processor ◻ **word-process, word processing**
word search (two words)
wordsmith (one word)
Wordsworth, William (1770–1850), English poet, Poet Laureate 1843–50 ◻ **Wordsworthian**
workaday, workaholic (one word)
workbench, workbook, workday (one word)
work ethic, work experience (two words)
workfare, workflow, workforce, workhorse, workhouse (one word)
working class (two words, hyphen when attrib.)
workingman N. Amer. manual worker (one word)
Working Time Directive (three words, caps)
workload, workman, workmate (one word)
workout n. (one word, two words as verb)
workpeople (one word)
work permit (two words)
workpiece, workplace (one word)
work rate (two words)
workroom, worksheet, workshop, workspace, workstation (one word)
work surface (two words)
worktop (one word)
work-to-rule n. (hyphens, three words as verb)
World Bank international banking organization controlling aid and loans; official name **International Bank for Reconstruction and Development**
world-class, world-famous, world-shaking, world-weary (hyphen)
World War I (abbrev. **WWI**)
World War II (abbrev. **WWII**)
worldwide (one word)
World Wide Fund for Nature (abbrev. **WWF**; not **Worldwide**)
World Wide Web (three words, caps; abbrev. **WWW**)
WORM Comput. write once read many
worm-eaten (hyphen)
wormhole (one word)
worm's-eye view (one hyphen, apostrophe before the *s*)
wormwood (one word) **1** woody shrub **2** bitterness or grief
worn out (two words, hyphen when attrib.)
worry beads (two words)
worship (**worshipping, worshipped**; US also one **-p-**; cap. in *His/Her/Your Worship*) ◻ **worshipper** (US also **worshiper**)
Wörterbuch dictionary (Ger., cap., ital.)
worthwhile one word when used before a noun; either one or two words after a noun
Wotan another name for **Odin**
would-be adj. (hyphen)
Woulfe bottle glass bottle for passing gases through liquids
wove paper paper with a uniform unlined surface; cf. **laid paper**
Wozzeck opera by Berg (1925) based on *Woyzeck*, fragmentary play by Georg Büchner (1837)
WP word processing; word processor
w.p. weather permitting
WPC woman police constable
wpm (also **w.p.m.**) words per minute
WRAC hist. Women's Royal Army Corps
wrack 1 (also **rack**) mass of fast-moving cloud **2** brown seaweed **3** see **rack**
WRAF hist. Women's Royal Air Force
Wrangel Island island off NE Russia
wrangle long complicated dispute
wrap-around extending round at the edges or sides (hyphen)
wrapping paper (two words)
wrasse pl. same or **wrasses** marine fish
wrath anger; cf. **wroth**
wreak (past **wreaked**); **wrought**, as in *wrought havoc*, is an arch. past tense of **work**
wreath n. arrangement of flowers etc.
wreathe v. cover or surround
Wren hist. member of the Women's Royal Naval Service (cap.)
wrinkly (not **-ey**)
wristband, wristwatch (one word)
writable (not **-eable**)
write-off n. (hyphen, two words as verb)
write-protect (hyphen)
writer-in-residence pl. **writers-in-residence** (hyphens)
write-up n. (hyphen, two words as verb)

writing case, writing desk, writing pad, writing paper (two words)

WRNS hist. Women's Royal Naval Service

Wrocław city in western Poland; Ger. name **Breslau**

wrongdoer, wrongdoing (one word)

wrong font the wrong size or style of font (abbrev. **w.f.**)

wrong-foot v. (hyphen)

wrong-headed (hyphen)

wroth angry; cf. **wrath**

wrought iron (two words, hyphen when attrib.)

WRVS Women's Royal Voluntary Service

wry (**wryer, wryest** or **wrier, wriest**) □ **wryly, wryness**

wrybill, wryneck birds (one word)

WSW west-south-west

wt weight

WTO World Trade Organization

Wulfila var. of **Ulfilas**

Wunderkammer pl. ***Wunderkammern*** place exhibiting curiosities (Ger., cap., ital.)

wunderkind pl. **wunderkinds** or **wunderkinder** person achieving great success when young (lower case, not ital.; not **won-**)

wurst German sausage (lower case, not ital.)

Wuthering Heights novel by Emily Brontë (1846)

WV West Virginia (postal abbrev.)

W.Va. West Virginia (official abbrev.; no space)

WWI World War I

WWII World War II

WWF 1 World Wide Fund for Nature **2** World Wrestling Federation

WWW World Wide Web (lower case in Internet addresses)

WY Wyoming (postal abbrev.)

wych elm (also **witch elm**)

Wycherley, William (*c.*1640–1716), English dramatist

wych hazel var. of **witch hazel**

Wyclif (also **Wycliffe**), John (*c.*1330–84), English religious reformer

Wycliffe Hall theological college, part of Oxford University

Wykehamist member of Winchester College

wynn (also **wyn**) Old and Middle English runic letter Ƿ, ƿ, replaced by *w* (not **wen**); cf. **eth, thorn**

Wyndham, John (1903–69), English writer

Wyndham Lewis, Percy (1882–1957), English writer and painter

Wynkyn de Worde (1471–1534), early printer in London

Wyoming state in the west central US (official abbrev. **Wyo.**, postal **WY**) □ **Wyomingite**

WYSIWYG (of on-screen text) in a form exactly corresponding to its appearance in printout [*what you see is what you get*]

wyvern heraldic dragon (not **wivern** (arch.))

X

X **1** pl. **Xs** or **X's** 24th letter of the alphabet **2** for adults only (former film classification, in the UK now *18* and in the US *NC-17*) **3** (also **x**) Roman numeral for ten

x Math. **1** first unknown quantity in an algebraic expression **2** principal or horizontal axis in a system of coordinates

Xanadu pl. **Xanadus** idealized magnificent place

Xanthian Marbles ancient sculptures found in Turkey (caps)

Xanthippe **1** wife of Socrates **2** bad-tempered woman

Xavier, St Francis (1506–52), Spanish Catholic missionary; known as **the Apostle of the Indies**

X chromosome (cap., two words)

Xe the chemical element xenon (no point)

xebec (also **zebec**) hist. Mediterranean sailing ship

Xenakis, Iannis (1922–2001), French composer

xenograft tissue graft or organ transplant from a different species

xenon chemical element of atomic number 54, a noble gas (symbol **Xe**)

Xenophanes (*c.*570–*c.*480 BC), Greek philosopher

xenophobia fear or dislike of foreigners

Xenophon (*c.*435–*c.*354 BC), Greek historian and military leader

xenotransplantation tissue grafting or organ transplantation from a different species

xeric having very dry conditions

xerography dry copying process using electrically charged powder

Xerox n. trademark copying process. v. (**xerox**) copy using the Xerox process

Xerxes I (*c.*519–465 BC), king of Persia 486–465 BC

x-height height of a lower-case x, considered characteristic of a typeface or script

Xhosa pl. same or **Xhosas** member of a South African people

XHTML Comput. Extensible Hypertext Markup Language

xi fourteenth letter of the Greek alphabet (Ξ, ξ), transliterated as 'x'

Xian (also **Hsian** or **Sian**) city in central China

Xiang (also **Hsiang**) dialect of Chinese

Ximenes de Cisneros var. of **Jiménez de Cisneros**

xiphoid sword-shaped

Xizang Chin. name for **Tibet**

XL **1** Roman numeral for 40 **2** extra large

Xmas Christmas

XML Comput. Extensible Markup Language

xoanon pl. **xoana** ancient Greek primitive wooden image of a deity

X-rated, X-ray (cap., hyphen)

xref. pl. **xrefs** or **xrefs.** cross reference

xu pl. same, monetary unit of Vietnam

XXXX former Roman numeral for 40 (superseded by **XL**)

xylography engraving on wood or printing from woodblocks

xylophone percussion instrument with graduated wooden bars

xystus pl. **xysti** long portico used in ancient Greece for exercise

Y

Y **1** pl. **Ys** or **Y's** 25th letter of the alphabet **2** yen **3** the chemical element yttrium
y year(s)
y Math. **1** second unknown quantity in an algebraic expression **2** secondary or vertical axis in a system of coordinates
¥ yen(s) (placed before figures, closed up)
yachtsman, yachtswoman (one word)
Yafo Hebrew name for **Jaffa**
Yahoo brutish creature in Swift's *Gulliver's Travels*
Yahoo! Internet company (exclamation mark)
yahoo rude or violent person (lower case)
Yahweh form of the Hebrew name for God (not **Jahweh**)
Yajur Veda Veda based on a collection of sacrificial formulae
yak¹ (**yakking, yakked**) talk at length about trivia
yak² pl. same or **yaks** large shaggy ox
Yakutsk city in eastern Russia
yakuza pl. same, Japanese gangster (not ital.)
Yale trademark type of lock
Yale University university at New Haven, Connecticut
Yamamoto, Isoroku (1884–1943), Japanese admiral
Yamato-e style of early Japanese painting (cap., ital., hyphen)
Yamoussoukro capital of Côte d'Ivoire (Ivory Coast)
Yangon Burmese name for **Rangoon**
Yangtze (also **Chang Jiang**) principal river of China
Yankee an American, esp. inhabitant of one of the northern states (cap.)
Yanomami (also **Yanomamö**) pl. same, member of an American Indian people of Venezuela and Brazil
Yanqui (in Latin America) person from the US
Yaoundé capital of Cameroon
yapp form of bookbinding with a projecting limp leather cover
yarborough bridge or whist hand with no card above nine (lower case)
yard (abbrev. **yd**)
yardarm (one word)
Yardie member of a Jamaican criminal gang (cap.)
yardstick (one word)
yarmulke (also **yarmulka**) Jewish man's skullcap
Yaroslavl port in European Russia
yashmak veil worn by some Muslim women
YB Year Book
Yb the chemical element ytterbium (no point)
Y chromosome (cap., two words)
yclept arch. called (one word)
yd pl. **yds** yard
ye **1** arch. you (pl.) **2** (also **y^e**) the (in approximating 15th- to 17th-cent. works)
year (abbrev. **y** or **yr**)
yearbook (one word; but **Year Book**, law reports, abbrev. **YB**)
year end (two words, hyphen when attrib.)
year-on-year (hyphens)
year-round (hyphen)
Yeats, W(illiam) B(utler) (1865–1939), Irish poet
Yekaterinburg (also **Ekaterinburg**) city in central Russia
yellowfin, yellowhammer (one word)
Yellowknife capital of the Northwest Territories, Canada
Yellow Pages trademark business telephone directory
Yellow River second-largest river in China; Chin. name **Huang Ho**
Yellowstone National Park national park in NW Wyoming and Montana

Yeltsin, Boris (Nikolaevich) (1931–2007), Russian president 1991–9
Yemen country in the Arabian peninsula □ **Yemeni**
yen pl. same, monetary unit of Japan (abbrev. **Y**, symbol **¥**)
Yeoman Usher pl. **Yeoman Ushers** deputy of Black Rod
Yeoman Warder pl. **Yeoman Warders** warder at the Tower of London
yerba (also **yerba maté**) another name for **maté**
Yerevan (also **Erevan**) capital of Armenia
yes pl. **yeses** or **yesses**
yes-man (hyphen)
yesterday, yesteryear (one word)
yeti pl. **yetis**
Yevtushenko, Yevgeni (Aleksandrovich) (b.1933), Russian poet
Y-fronts trademark (cap., hyphen)
Yggdrasil Scand. Mythol. huge ash tree at the centre of the earth
YHA Youth Hostels Association
ylang-ylang (also **ilang-ilang**) essential oil from flowers
YMCA Young Men's Christian Association
Ynys Môn Welsh name for **Anglesey**
yobbo pl. **yobboes** or **yobbos**
yodel v. (**yodelling, yodelled**; US one **-l-**)
yogh Middle English letter Ȝ, ȝ or Ʒ, ʒ, used mainly where modern English has *gh* or *y*
yogi pl. **yogis** practitioner of yoga
yogurt (also **yoghurt** or **yoghourt**)
Yogyakarta (also **Jogjakarta**) city in Java, Indonesia
Yoknapatawpha County fictional Mississippian county in the stories of William Faulkner
Yokohama seaport on Honshu, Japan
Yom Kippur Jewish religious fast, the Day of Atonement
Yonge, Charlotte Mary (1823–1901), English novelist
York city in northern England; Roman name **Eboracum**, Viking name **Jorvik**
Yorkshire former county of northern England, divided into the county of North Yorkshire and a number of unitary authorities (abbrev. **Yorks.**)
Yoruba pl. same or **Yorubas** member of a people of SW Nigeria and Benin
Yorvik use **Jorvik**
Yosemite National Park national park in central California
Young, Brigham (1801–77), American Mormon leader
Young Pretender, the Charles Edward Stuart (1720–88)
Young Turk 1 member of a revolutionary party in the Ottoman Empire **2** young radical
Yourcenar, Marguerite (1903–87), French writer
yours (no apostrophe; abbrev. **yrs**)
yourself pl. **yourselves**
youth hostel (two words, hyphen as verb)
yo-yo n. (trademark in the UK) pl. **yo-yos**. v. **yo-yoes, yo-yoing, yo-yoed**
Ypres town in NW Belgium; Flemish name **Ieper**
Yquem, Château d' Sauternes
yr 1 year(s) **2** younger **3** your
yrs 1 years **2** yours
Yr Wyddfa Welsh name for **Snowdon**
YT Yukon Territory (postal abbrev.)
y^t that (superscript *t*, in approximating 15th- to 17th-cent. works)
ytterbium chemical element of atomic number 70 (symbol **Yb**)
yttrium chemical element of atomic number 39 (symbol **Y**)
Yuan dynasty ruling China 1279–1368
yuan pl. same, monetary unit of China
Yucatán state of SE Mexico (accent)
yucca plant of the agave family (two *c*s)
Yugoslavia former federal republic in SE Europe (not **Jugoslavia** (arch.))
Yukon Territory territory of NW Canada (postal abbrev. **YK**)
Yule, Yuletide Christmas (cap.)
Yupik pl. same or **Yupiks** member of an Eskimo people of Siberia and Alaska
yuppie (also **yuppy**) young urban professional
YWCA Young Women's Christian Association

Z

Z **1** pl. **Zs** or **Z's** 26th letter of the alphabet **2** Chem. atomic number

z Math. **1** third unknown quantity in an algebraic expression **2** third axis in a three-dimensional system of coordinates

zabaglione Italian dessert made with egg yolks and Marsala

Zagreb capital of Croatia

zaibatsu pl. same, large Japanese business conglomerate (ital.)

Zaire (also **Zaïre**) former name for the **Democratic Republic of Congo** □ **Zairean** (also **Zairian**)

Zaïre tragedy by Voltaire (1732)

zaire pl. same, former monetary unit of Zaire (lower case)

Zaire River the Congo River

Zakynthos Greek island; mod. Gk name **Zákinthos**; also called **Zante**

Zambezi river of East Africa

Zambia country in central Africa □ **Zambian**

zamindar (also **zemindar**) hist. Indian landowner leasing to tenants (not ital.)

Zante another name for **Zakynthos**

ZANU Zimbabwe African National Union

ZANU–PF Zimbabwe African National Union–Patriotic Front (en rule)

Zanzibar island part of Tanzania □ **Zanzibari**

Zapata, Emiliano (1879–1919), Mexican revolutionary

zapateado pl. ***zapateados*** flamenco dance (Sp., ital.)

Zappa, Frank (1940–93), American rock musician

ZAPU Zimbabwe African People's Union

Zaragoza Sp. name for **Saragossa**

Zarathustra Avestan name for Zoroaster □ **Zarathustrian**

zarzuela **1** Spanish musical comedy **2** Spanish fish stew

Zealand principal island of Denmark; Danish name **Sjælland**; cf. **Zeeland**

Zealot member of an ancient Jewish sect

zealot fanatical person (lower case)

zebec var. of **xebec**

Zechariah book of the Old Testament (not **Zach-**; abbrev. **Zech.**)

Zeebrugge seaport in Belgium

Zeeland province of the Netherlands; cf. **Zealand**

Zeffirelli, Franco (b.1923), Italian director; born *Gianfranco Corsi*

Zeiss German optical instrument company

zeitgeist defining spirit or mood of a period (lower case, not ital.)

zemindar var. of **zamindar**

Zen Japanese school of Buddhism

zenana women's part of an Indian or Iranian house

Zend an interpretation of the Avesta

Zend-Avesta Zoroastrian sacred writings

Zener cards cards used in ESP research (one cap.)

zenith highest point; cf. **nadir**

Zeno **1** (*fl.* 5th cent. BC), Greek philosopher, member of the Eleatic school **2** (*c.*335–*c.*263 BC), Greek philosopher, founder of Stoicism; known as **Zeno of Citium**

Zephaniah book of the Old Testament (abbrev. **Zeph.**)

zephyr gentle breeze

Zeppelin **1** Ferdinand (Adolf August Heinrich), Count von (1838–1917), German aviation pioneer **2** hist. German dirigible airship

Zermatt Alpine resort in Switzerland

zero n. pl. **zeros** nought. v. (**zeroes, zeroing, zeroed**) adjust to zero

zeroth immediately preceding the first

zeta sixth letter of the Greek alphabet (**Z**, ζ), transliterated as 'z'

zeugma application of a word to two others in different senses (e.g. *he took his hat and his leave*) □ **zeugmatic**

Zeus Gk Mythol. the supreme god; Rom. equivalent **Jupiter**
ZEV pl. **ZEVs** zero-emission vehicle
zho use **dzo**
Zhou (also **Chou**) dynasty which ruled in China 11th cent. BC–256 BC
Zhou Enlai (also **Chou En-lai**) (1898–1976), Chinese prime minister 1949–76
Zia ul-Haq, Muhammad (1924–88), Pakistani president 1978–88
Ziegfeld, Florenz (1869–1932), American theatre manager
ZIF socket socket for electronic devices
ziggurat Mesopotamian stepped tower
zigzag (one word)
zilla administrative district in India
Zimbabwe country in SE Africa □ **Zimbabwean**
Zimmer trademark walking frame
zinc chemical element of atomic number 30 (symbol **Zn**)
zinco pl. **zincos** etched letterpress printing plate made of zinc
Zinfandel red or blush wine made from the Zinfandel grape
Zinnemann, Fred (1907–97), Austrian-born American film director
Zion (also **Sion**) hill of Jerusalem
Zionism (not **S-**)
zip code (also **ZIP code**) US postal code
ziplock (also trademark **Ziploc**) denoting a sealable plastic bag
zip-up adj. (hyphen, two words as verb)
zircaloy (also **zircalloy**) alloy used as cladding for nuclear-reactor fuel
zirconium chemical element of atomic number 40 (symbol **Zr**)
zloty pl. same or **zlotys** monetary unit of Poland
Zn the chemical element zinc (no point)
zodiac, the (lower case)
Zoffany, Johann (*c.*1733–1810), German-born painter
Zog I (1895–1961), king of Albania 1928–39; full name *Ahmed Bey Zogu*
Zollverein 19th-cent. German customs union (cap., ital.)
zombie corpse supposedly revived by witchcraft □ **zombielike**
zookeeper (one word)
zoological names genera, species, and subspecies to be ital., all other divisions roman; specific epithets to be lower case, even when derived from names
zoonosis pl. **zoonoses** disease transmissible to humans from animals
zori pl. **zoris** Japanese shoe (not ital.)
Zoroaster (*c.*628–*c.*551 BC), Persian founder of Zoroastrianism; Avestan name **Zarathustra**
Zouave member of a French light-infantry corps
zouaves women's tapering trousers (lower case)
Zoug Fr. name for **Zug**
zouk style of popular music
ZPG zero population growth
Zr the chemical element zirconium (no point)
Zsigmondy, Richard Adolph (1865–1929), Austrian-born German chemist
zucchetto pl. **zucchettos** Roman Catholic cleric's skullcap (not ital.)
zucchini pl. same or **zucchinis** N. Amer. courgette
Zug canton and city in Switzerland; Fr. name **Zoug**
zugzwang chess position in which any move is disadvantageous (lower case, not ital.)
Zuider Zee former large shallow inlet of the North Sea, in the Netherlands
Zulu pl. **Zulus**
Zululand hist. area of South Africa
Zuni (also **Zuñi**) pl. same or **Zunis** member of a people of New Mexico
Zurbarán, Francisco de (1598–1664), Spanish painter
Zurich city in north central Switzerland; Ger. name **Zürich**
zwieback rusk or biscuit of bread
Zwingli, Ulrich (1484–1531), Swiss Protestant reformer □ **Zwinglian**
zydeco dance music from Louisiana
Zyklon B hydrogen cyanide released from small tablets
zymurgy study or practice of fermentation in brewing etc.

Appendices

Proofreading marks

Below is a list of the most commonly used proofreading marks. See also the British Standard Institution's BS 5261-2: *Copy Preparation and Proof Correction—Part 2* (2005), which may be obtained from the BSI.

Instruction	Mark in text	Mark in margin
Correction is concluded	None	/ or ⋏
Insert matter indicated in the margin	⋏	New matter followed by ⋏
Insert additional matter identified by a letter in a diamond	⋏	◇A ⋏; write matter to be inserted at any convenient position on the page, preceded by the corresponding letter ◇A
Delete	/ through a single character or ⊢⊣ through multiple characters to be deleted	δ
Close up and delete space between characters or words	⁀‿ connecting characters	⁀‿/
Substitute character(s)	/ through a single character or ⊢⊣ through multiple characters	New character(s) followed by /
Substitute or insert full point or decimal point	/ through character or ⋏ between characters	⊙/ or ⊙⋏
Substitute or insert colon	/ through character or ⋏ between characters	(:)/ or (:)⋏
Substitute or insert semicolon	/ through character or ⋏ between characters	;/ or ;⋏
Substitute or insert comma	/ through character or ⋏ between characters	,/ or ,⋏
Substitute or insert solidus (oblique)	/ through character or ⋏ between characters	(/)/ or (/)⋏

Instruction	Mark in text	Mark in margin
Substitute or insert character in superior (superscript) position	/ through character or ⋏ between characters	⋎/ or ⋎ under character, e.g. $\overset{2}{⋎}$/ or $\overset{2}{⋎}$
Substitute or insert character in inferior (subscript) position	/ through character or ⋏ between characters	⋏ or ⋏ over character, e.g. $\underset{2}{⋏}$ or $^{2}⋏$
Substitute or insert opening or closing parenthesis, square bracket, or brace	/ through character or ⋏ between characters	(/)/ or (/)/ or [/]/ or { / }/
Substitute or insert hyphen	/ through character or ⋏ between characters	|–| / or |–| ⋏
Substitute or insert rule	/ through character or ⋏ between characters	Give the size of rule |1 em|/ or |4 mm|⋏
Set in or change to bold type	~~~ under character(s) to be set or changed	~~~ /
Set in or change to bold italic type	≈≈≈ under character(s) to be set or changed	⊔̰ /
Set in or change to italic	— under character(s) to be set or changed	⊔ /
Change bold to roman type	Encircle character(s) to be changed	~~+~~ /
Change bold italic to roman type	Encircle character(s) to be changed	⊔̰+ /
Change italic to roman type	Encircle character(s) to be changed	⊔+ /
Set in or change to capital letters	≡ under character(s) to be set or changed	≡/
Change capital letters to lower-case letters	Encircle character(s) to be changed	≢/
Set in or change to small capital letters	= under character(s) to be set or changed	=/
Set in or change to capital letters for initial letter and small capital letters for the rest of the word	≡ under initial letter and = under rest of the word	≡ =/
Change small capital letters to lower-case letters	Encircle character(s) to be changed	≠/
Start new paragraph	__⌐	__⌐ /

Instruction	Mark in text	Mark in margin
Run on	⌒	⊂/
Transpose characters or words	⊔⊓ around and between characters or words	⊔⊓/
Transpose lines	⊏ around and between lines	⊏/
Transpose a number of lines	③ ② ① around and between lines	To be used when the sequence cannot be clearly indicated otherwise. Each line to be transposed should be numbered
Invert type	Encircle character to be inverted	↻/
Centre	[/] enclosing matter to be centred	[/]/
Insert or substitute space between characters or words	⋏ between characters or / through characters	Y⋏ or Y/
Reduce space between characters or words	| between characters or words affected	⊤/
Equalize space between characters or words	| between characters or words affected	X/
Close up to normal interlinear spacing	(each side of column, linking lines)	Linking symbols are placed in the margins
Insert space between lines or paragraphs	≻— or —≺ each side of column between lines	Marginal marks extend between lines of text
Reduce space between lines or paragraphs	←— or —→ each side of column between lines	Marginal marks extend between the lines of text
Take over character(s), word(s), or line to next line, column, or page	⊏	Textual mark surrounds matter to be taken over and extends into the margin
Take back character(s), word(s), or line to previous line, column, or page	⊐	Textual mark surrounds matter to be taken back and extends into the margin
Insert or substitute em space, en space, thin space, or fixed space	□ (em), ⊠ (en), ♀ or ‡ (thin), Y (fixed)	□ /, ⊠ /, ♀⋏, ‡⋏, Y⋏
Indent	⊏	⊏/ (verticals indicate alignment)

Instruction	Mark in text	Mark in margin
Cancel indent	⅃	⅃ / (verticals indicate alignment)
Move matter specified distance to the right	[enclosing matter to be moved to the right] →|	⌐⅃ /
Move matter specified distance to the left	|← [enclosing matter to be moved to the left]	⅃ /
Correct vertical alignment	||	|| /
Correct horizontal alignment	Single line above and below misaligned matter, e.g. misaligned	= /
Correction made in error. Leave unchanged	under characters to remain - - - - - - - - -	(✓) /
Remove extraneous mark(s) or replace damaged character(s)	Encircle mark(s) to be removed or character(s) to be changed	× /
Wrong font. Replace by character(s) of correct font	Encircle character(s) to be changed	(×) /
Query something in the text	Encircle word(s) affected	(?) /

Glossary of printing and publishing terms

accent a mark on a letter that indicates pitch, stress, or vowel quality.

acknowledgements (US **acknowledgments**) a statement at the beginning of a book expressing the author's or publisher's gratitude to others for ideas or assistance or for permission to use copyright material.

afterword a short concluding section in a book, typically written by someone other than the author.

appendix (also **annex**) a section of subsidiary matter at the end of a book or document.

Arabic numeral any of the numerals 0, 1, 2, 3, 4, 5, 6, 7, 8, 9; cf. **Roman numeral**.

artwork illustrations, figures, photographs, or other non-textual material.

ascender a part of a letter that extends above the level of the top of an *x* (as in *b* and *d*).

ASCII American Standard Code for Information Interchange, used as a standard format in the transfer of text between computers.

back matter another term for **end matter**.

bibliography a list of books or other texts that are referred to in a work or that contain material of related interest, typically printed as an appendix.

bitmap image graphics file made up of **pixels**.

blad a promotional booklet of pages from a forthcoming book.

bleed (of an illustration or design) be printed so that it runs off the page.

block capitals plain capital letters.

block quotation another term for **displayed quotation**.

bold (also **boldface**) a style of type with thick strokes, as **here**.

caption a title or brief explanation accompanying an illustration, in particular one shown beneath or beside the image.

cancel a new page or section inserted in a book to replace the original text.

caret a mark ^, ʌ used to indicate a proposed insertion in a text.

case-bound (also **cased**) (of a book) hardback.

cast-off an estimate of the number of pages a given amount of copy will make given the specified design.

catchline an eye-catching line of type, such as a slogan or headline.

CMYK (cyan, magenta, yellow, and key (black)) the four process (primary) colours used in colour printing.

code 1 in editing, any means of identifying the elements of text such as headings, lists, and displayed matter. **2** in **markup languages**, see **tag**.

collate 1 assemble folded sections of a book in the correct sequence ready for binding. **2** verify the number and order of the sheets of a book. **3** bring together editorial changes from different sources and combine the amendments on a single master copy.

colophon a publisher's emblem, usually appearing on the title page of a book.

computer-to-plate process whereby the image of the **PDF** file is transferred direct to the printing plate for offset printing.

content management system a software repository for digital assets (text, images, numerical data, audio, video, and animation) coded in a neutral format with XML tags to facilitate output in multiple media.

copy matter to be published, in particular the text before or after it is copy-edited.

copy-edit prepare the text for publication by checking its consistency and accuracy and identifying elements requiring special attention during the production process.

copy-fitting adjusting text to fit the available space on a page proof.

copyright the exclusive legal right to print, publish, perform, film, or record literary, artistic, or musical material.

copyright page another term for **title page verso**.

corrigenda (singular **corrigendum**) a list of errors in a printed book that is fixed to or printed in the book.

credits acknowledgements expressing gratitude for permission to use images.

cue a number, letter, or symbol placed in the text to direct the reader to a footnote or endnote.

dele mark (a part of a text) for deletion.

descender a part of a letter that extends below the level of the base of an *x* (as in *g* and *p*).

desktop publishing the process of laying out pages on-screen.

diacritic an accent or similar sign which is written above, below, or through a letter to indicate pitch, stress, or vowel quality.

digital artwork images created with graphics/image-editing software, or a digital camera, or by scanning an **original** to produce electronic files.

digraph 1 a combination of two letters representing one sound, as in *ph* and *ey*. **2** another term for **ligature**.

displayed quotation a quotation that is broken off from the text to begin on a new line, often set in smaller type.

drop capital (also **drop initial**) a large capital letter at the beginning of a section of text, occupying more than the depth of one line.

DTP short for **desktop publishing**.

dummy a mock-up of a book or the layout of a page.

duotone a half-tone illustration made from a single original with two different colours.

dust jacket another term for **jacket**.

edition a version of a book at its first publication and at every following publication for which more than minor changes are made.

em a unit for measuring the width of printed matter, originally reckoned as the width of a capital roman M in the typeface in use, but in digital fonts equal to the current typesize.

embedded another term for **run on**; matter that is integrated in the text such as a graphics file.

em rule (also **em dash**) a long dash (—).

en a unit of horizontal space equal to half an **em**.

en rule (also **en dash**) a short dash (–), used in particular to elide ranges of figures.

end matter (also **back matter**) material that supplements the text and is placed after it.

endnote a note printed at the end of a book or section of a book.

endpaper a leaf of paper fixed to the inside of the cover at the beginning or end of a hardback book.

epigraph a quotation placed at the beginning of a volume, part, or chapter.

epilogue an author's short concluding comment on the text.

EPUB open-source standard and file format for ebooks.

errata slip (singular **erratum slip**) a list of errors and their corrections inserted loose in a book.

even working a situation whereby the text of a book fits neatly into the allotted number of pages so that there are no blank pages at the end.

face short for **typeface**.

fascicle (also **fascicule**) a separately published section of a very long book.

figure an illustration (often a diagram or other line drawing) that is integrated into the text.

flatten compress the digital layers that make up an image into a single plane.

flush aligned with the left- or right-hand edge of the text.

flyleaf a blank page at the beginning or end of a book.

folio **1** a sheet of typescript. **2** the page number in a printed book.

font (also **fount**) a set of type of one particular face and size.

footer text that is repeated at the foot of the page, such as the page number.

footnote a note printed at the bottom of a page within the text area and above the **footer**.

foreword a recommendation of the work written by someone other than the author, printed before the main text.

frontispiece an illustration that faces the title page.

front matter another term for **preliminary matter**.

full out aligned (or 'flush') with the left- or right-hand edge of the text.

gathering a group of signatures or leaves bound together in the production of a book.

gutter the blank space between facing pages of a book or between adjacent columns of type.

hair space a very thin space between characters, as, for example, between multiplied units of measure or consecutive punctuation marks; Unicode code point U+200A HAIR SPACE.

half-title the first page of the preliminary matter of a book, bearing only the work's title.

half-tone a reproduction of an image in which the various tones of grey or colour are produced by variously sized dots of ink.

hard hyphen a nonbreaking hyphen that is keyed and appears whether the word containing it is split across the end of a line or not; cf. **soft hyphen**.

header text that is repeated at the top of a page, such as a chapter title or main heading.

heading a title at the head of a page, a section of a book, or a table.

headword a word that begins a separate entry in a reference work.

HTML Hypertext Markup Language, a standardized coding system for tagging text files to achieve formatting, graphic, and hyperlink effects on websites.

imposition the layout on the quad sheet of the pages of a publication so that when the sheet is printed and folded they will fall in the correct order.

impression a particular printed version of a book, especially one reprinted with no or only minor alteration.

imprint the name and other details of a book's publisher.

inferior another term for **subscript**.

infographic clear visual representation of otherwise complex data.

ISBN International Standard Book Number.

ISSN International Standard Serial Number.

italic a sloping style of type like *this*.

jacket (also **dust jacket**) a removable paper cover, generally with a decorative design, used to protect a book.

JPEG a **bitmap** file format that compresses the image data to produce a smaller file.

justified (of text) adjusted so as to fill the width of the text area and align at the left and right margins.

kern a part of a printed character that overlaps its neighbours.

kerning adjustment of the spacing between characters in a piece of text.

label explanatory description of a feature in an illustration.

landscape a format of printed matter which is wider than it is high; cf. **portrait**.

leader line a labelled line added to an illustration to point out a salient feature.

leaders a series of dots or dashes across the page to guide the eye.

leading the amount of blank space between lines of print.

leaf a single sheet of paper, forming two pages in a book.

legend another term for **caption**.

lettering 1 decorative letters inscribed on e.g. a book cover. **2** see **label**.

ligature a character consisting of two or more joined letters (e.g. æ, œ, fi, ffl).

line artwork graphic material, such as a map, diagram, or graph, consisting of solid lines or other shapes on a white background, as opposed to a **half-tone**.

linefeed the distance from the bottom of one line of type to the bottom of the next.

lithography printing from a flat surface treated to repel the ink except where it is required for printing.

lower case small letters as opposed to capital letters (**upper case**).

margin the white space around the text area on a page.

markup 1 the process or result of correcting text in preparation for printing. **2** the tags or codes used in **markup languages** such as **HTML**.

markup language a system for coding text so that content can be described for output in print or digital media; an example is **HTML**.

minuscule of or in lower-case letters.

moral rights the right of an author or artist to protect the integrity and paternity of their work.

note a piece of explanatory or additional information printed at the end of a section or in the end matter of the publication (**endnote**) or at the foot of the page (**footnote**).

octavo (abbrev. **8vo**) a size of book page that results from folding each printed sheet into eight leaves (sixteen pages).

offprint a printed copy of an individual article or essay that originally appeared as part of a larger publication.

offset a method of printing in which ink is transferred from a plate or stone to a uniform rubber surface and from that to the paper.

opening a double-page spread (see **spread**).

original artwork in physical form that can be captured for reproduction digitally by photography or scanning.

orphan the first line of a paragraph set as the last line of a page or column, considered undesirable.

overmatter material that cannot be accommodated in a work.

Oxford comma another term for **serial comma**.

page proof pages composed in **DTP** software with all the elements, e.g. text, running heads, and images, laid out in the final form.

Pantone® a system for matching colours, used in specifying printing inks.

parentheses (also **parens**) round brackets ().

PDF Portable Document Format, a file format for capturing and sending electronic documents in exactly the intended format.

pica a unit of type size and line length equal to 12 points (about ⅙ inch or 4.2 mm).

picture library agency that represents the creators or the assigned copyright holders of images and sells licences for the images it holds.

pitch the density of typed or printed characters on a line.

pixel picture element; single physical point in a **bitmap** image.

plate 1 a sheet of metal, plastic, etc. bearing an image of type or illustrations from which multiple copies are printed. **2** a photograph or other illustration that is separated from the text, especially one on superior-quality paper.

point a unit of measurement for type sizes and spacing, in the UK and US traditionally 0.351 mm, in Europe 0.376 mm, now standardized as 1/72 in. (0.356 mm).

portrait a format of printed matter which is higher than it is wide; cf. **landscape**.

preliminary matter (also **prelims**) the pages preceding the main text of a book, including the title page, title page verso, contents page, and preface.

preface a section in the preliminary matter where the author sets out the purpose, scope, and content of the book.

proof a trial impression of typeset text, which is checked for errors before final printing.

proof-edit process whereby unedited material that is laid out in pages is corrected.

proofread read proofs, mark any errors, and make a final check of the material.

quad sheet the large sheet of paper that is printed with text and then folded and cut to produce separate leaves.

quarto (abbrev. **4to**) a size of book page resulting from folding each printed sheet into four leaves (eight pages).

ragged right (of text) justified only at the left margin, with the result that the width of lines is variable.

range (with reference to type) align or be aligned, especially at the ends of successive lines.

raster image see **bitmap image**.

ream 500 (formerly 480) sheets of paper.

recto the right-hand page of a spread, having an odd page number; cf. **verso**.

register 1 the exact correspondence of the position of colour components in a printed positive. **2** the exact correspondence of the position of printed matter on the two sides of a leaf.

reprint a republication of a book for which no corrections or only minor corrections are made.

resolution number of dots or pixels in a given area, measured in dots per inch (dpi) or pixels per inch (ppi).

RGB (red, green, blue) colour model used by computer monitors to display colours, which therefore render differently to **CYMK** colour printing processes.

roman an upright style of type used for text that requires no special emphasis or distinction.

Roman numeral any of the letters representing numbers in the Roman numerical system (I or i = 1, V or v = 5, X or x = 10, etc.); cf. **Arabic numeral**.

round brackets parentheses ().

running head (or **running foot**) a book title, chapter title, or other heading which appears at the top (or bottom) of every page or spread.

running sheets a set of unbound pages that are checked to ensure that the correct order has been achieved.

run on (also **run in**) continued on the same line as the preceding matter, rather than broken off or displayed.

sans serif a style of type without **serifs**.

serial comma (also **Oxford comma**) a comma used after the penultimate item in a list of three or more items, before 'and' or 'or'.

serif a slight projection finishing off a stroke of a letter, as in T contrasted with T.

signature 1 a group of pages formed by folding a single sheet. **2** a letter or figure printed at the foot of one or more pages of each sheet of a book as a guide in binding.

small capitals capital letters which are of the same height as a lower-case x in the same typeface, as in THIS STYLE OF TYPE.

soft hyphen a hyphen inserted automatically into a word when it is divided at the end of a line of text, sometimes shown as the symbol.

special sort a generic term for a symbol or accented character.

spread (also **double-page spread**) a pair of pages (left-hand and right-hand) exposed when a book is opened at random, in particular a pair of pages designed as an entity, as in an illustrated book; cf. **opening**.

style sheet 1 house style guidance for authors and editors on the client's preferred forms of text, such as variations in spelling, hyphenation, and capitalization, and treatment of references, lists, quotations, and numbers. **2** a list of the word-processor or **DTP** styles used in a particular project.

subscript (of a letter, figure, or symbol) written or printed below the line.

superscript (also **superior**) (of a letter, figure, or symbol) written or printed above the line.

table an arrangement of data in columns and rows.

tag 1 a set of plain text characters used in **markup languages** to describe content, e.g. <H1> to signify a main heading. **2** another term for an artwork **cue**.

text area the part of the page in which the text and images of the book are accommodated; the area inside the margins.

title page a page at the beginning of a book containing the complete title and subtitle of the work, the name of the author or editor, and the publisher's name.

title page verso the verso of the title page, on which is printed the statements and clauses that establish the copyright of the material, the identity of the work, and its publication history.

turn-line (also **turnover**) **1** the part of a line of verse or quoted material, a bibliographical citation, etc. that has to be carried over on to a new line. **2** the last line of a paragraph.

type characters or letters that are printed or shown on a screen.

typeface a particular design of type.

typescript the text of a publication in paper form.

typeset arrange or generate the type or data for a piece of text to be published.

typography 1 the style and appearance of printed text. **2** the process of setting and arranging text in type for printing.

Unicode an international encoding system by which each letter, digit, and symbol is assigned a unique numeric value that applies across different platforms and programs.

upper case capital letters as opposed to small letters (**lower case**).

vector image a graphics file with mathematical descriptions of the objects within, e.g. a line or the boundary of a shape.

verso the left-hand page of a spread, having an even page number; cf. **recto**.

widow a last word or short last line of a paragraph falling at the top of a page or column, considered undesirable.

x-height the height of a lower-case x, considered characteristic of a given typeface or script.

XML Extensible Markup Language, a system that allows users to define their own customized markup languages, especially in order to display documents on websites.

Appendix 3: Prime Ministers of Great Britain and of the United Kingdom

[1721]–1742	Sir Robert Walpole
1742–1743	Earl of Wilmington
1743–1754	Henry Pelham
1754–1756	Duke of Newcastle
1756–1757	Duke of Devonshire
1757–1762	Duke of Newcastle
1762–1763	Earl of Bute
1763–1765	George Grenville
1765–1766	Marquess of Rockingham
1766–1768	William Pitt the Elder
1768–1770	Duke of Grafton
1770–1782	Lord North
1782	Marquess of Rockingham
1782–1783	Earl of Shelburne
1783	Duke of Portland
1783–1801	William Pitt the Younger
1801–1804	Henry Addington
1804–1806	William Pitt the Younger
1806–1807	Lord William Grenville
1807–1809	Duke of Portland
1809–1812	Spencer Perceval
1812–1827	Earl of Liverpool
1827	George Canning
1827–1828	Viscount Goderich
1828–1830	Duke of Wellington
1830–1834	Earl Grey
1834	Viscount Melbourne
1834	Duke of Wellington
1834–1835	Sir Robert Peel
1835–1841	Viscount Melbourne
1841–1846	Sir Robert Peel
1846–1852	Lord John Russell
1852	Earl of Derby
1852–1855	Earl of Aberdeen
1855–1858	Viscount Palmerston
1858–1859	Earl of Derby
1859–1865	Viscount Palmerston
1865–1866	Earl Russell
1866–1868	Earl of Derby
1868	Benjamin Disraeli
1868–1874	William Ewart Gladstone
1874–1880	Benjamin Disraeli
1880–1885	William Ewart Gladstone
1885–1886	Marquess of Salisbury
1886	William Ewart Gladstone
1886–1892	Marquess of Salisbury
1892–1894	William Ewart Gladstone
1894–1895	Earl of Rosebery
1895–1902	Marquess of Salisbury
1902–1905	Arthur James Balfour
1905–1908	Sir Henry Campbell-Bannerman
1908–1916	Herbert Henry Asquith
1916–1922	David Lloyd George
1922–1923	Andrew Bonar Law
1923–1924	Stanley Baldwin
1924	James Ramsay MacDonald
1924–1929	Stanley Baldwin
1929–1935	James Ramsay MacDonald
1935–1937	Stanley Baldwin
1937–1940	Neville Chamberlain
1940–1945	Winston Churchill
1945–1951	Clement Attlee
1951–1955	Sir Winston Churchill
1955–1957	Sir Anthony Eden
1957–1963	Harold Macmillan
1963–1964	Sir Alec Douglas-Home
1964–1970	Harold Wilson
1970–1974	Edward Heath

1974–1976	Harold Wilson	1990–1997	John Major
1976–1979	James Callaghan	1997–2007	Tony Blair
1979–1990	Margaret Thatcher	2007–2010	Gordon Brown
		2010–	David Cameron

Appendix 4: **Presidents of the United States of America**

1789–1797	1. George Washington
1797–1801	2. John Adams
1801–1809	3. Thomas Jefferson
1809–1817	4. James Madison
1817–1825	5. James Monroe
1825–1829	6. John Quincy Adams
1829–1837	7. Andrew Jackson
1837–1841	8. Martin Van Buren
1841	9. William H. Harrison
1841–1845	10. John Tyler
1845–1849	11. James K. Polk
1849–1850	12. Zachary Taylor
1850–1853	13. Millard Fillmore
1853–1857	14. Franklin Pierce
1857–1861	15. James Buchanan
1861–1865	16. Abraham Lincoln
1865–1869	17. Andrew Johnson
1869–1877	18. Ulysses S. Grant
1877–1881	19. Rutherford B. Hayes
1881	20. James A. Garfield
1881–1885	21. Chester A. Arthur
1885–1889	22. Grover Cleveland
1889–1893	23. Benjamin Harrison
1893–1897	24. Grover Cleveland
1897–1901	25. William McKinley
1901–1909	26. Theodore Roosevelt
1909–1913	27. William H. Taft
1913–1921	28. Woodrow Wilson
1921–1923	29. Warren G. Harding
1923–1929	30. Calvin Coolidge
1929–1933	31. Herbert Hoover
1933–1945	32. Franklin D. Roosevelt
1945–1953	33. Harry S. Truman
1953–1961	34. Dwight D. Eisenhower
1961–1963	35. John F. Kennedy
1963–1969	36. Lyndon B. Johnson
1969–1974	37. Richard Nixon
1974–1977	38. Gerald Ford
1977–1981	39. Jimmy Carter
1981–1989	40. Ronald Reagan
1989–1993	41. George Bush
1993–2001	42. Bill Clinton
2001–2009	43. George W. Bush
2009–	44. Barack Obama

Appendix 5: **Members of the European Union**

The European Union (EU) originated as the European Economic Community (EEC), an economic association of western European countries set up by the Treaty of Rome (1957). The European Community (EC) was formed in 1967 from the European Economic Community, the European Coal and Steel Community, and the European Atomic Energy Community (Euratom). It was encompassed by the European Union on 1 November 1993, when the Maastricht Treaty on European economic and monetary union came into force.

Founder members (1957)
Belgium†
France†
Italy†
Luxembourg†
Netherlands†
Federal Republic of Germany†

Joined 1973
Denmark
Republic of Ireland†
UK

Joined 1981
Greece†

Joined 1986
Spain†
Portugal†

Joined 1995
Austria†
Finland†
Sweden

Joined 2004
Cyprus*†
Czech Republic
Estonia†
Hungary
Latvia†
Lithuania
Malta†
Poland
Slovakia†
Slovenia†

Joined 2007
Bulgaria
Romania

Joined 2013
Croatia

†national currency is the euro

*excluding the Turkish Republic of Northern Cyprus

Appendix 6: **Greek alphabet**

Α	α	alpha	a
Β	β	beta	b
Γ	γ	gamma	g
Δ	δ	delta	d
Ε	ϵ	epsilon	e
Ζ	ζ	zeta	z
Η	η	eta	ē
Θ	θ	theta	th
Ι	ι	iota	i
Κ	κ	kappa	k
Λ	λ	lambda	l
Μ	μ	mu	m
Ν	ν	nu	n
Ξ	ξ	xi	x
Ο	ο	omicron	o
Π	π	pi	p
Ρ	ρ	rho	r, rh
Σ	σ	(ς final) sigma	s
Τ	τ	tau	t
Υ	υ	upsilon	u, y
Φ	ϕ	phi	ph
Χ	χ	chi	kh
Ψ	ψ	psi	ps
Ω	ω	omega	ō

Appendix 7: **Diacritics, accents, and special sorts**

á, é	acute
æ	ae ligature
&	ampersand
Æ, æ, ᚫ	Old English ash
Å, å	Scandinavian circled a
*	asterisk
⁂	asterism
@	at sign
ʿ	Arabic ayn, Hebrew ayin
\	backslash
( )	round brackets, parentheses
[ ]	square brackets
{ }	curly brackets, braces
< >	angle brackets
⟨ ⟩	narrow angle brackets
⟦ ⟧	double brackets
ă, ĕ	breve
^	caret
¢	cent sign
ç	cedilla
☧	chi-rho
â, î	circumflex
©	copyright
†	dagger/obelus
‡	double dagger
°	degree
₰	delete
ä, ü	diaeresis/umlaut
„	ditto mark
$	dollar sign
...	ellipsis/omission dots
—	em dash
–	en dash
ß	German *Eszett*
Ð, ð, ð	Old English eth
€	euro sign
¡	Spanish inverted exclamation mark
♭	flat sign
/	forward slash/solidus
à, è	grave
᾿	Greek smooth breathing/lenis
῾	Greek rough breathing/asper
«	opening guillemets
»	closing guillemets
ǎ, č	háček
ʾ	Arabic hamza, Hebrew aleph
#	hash
ę, ǫ	hook, ogonek
ᾳ, ῃ	Greek iota subscript
ſ	archaic long s
ā, ē	macron
Ø, ø	Scandinavian crossed o
œ	oe ligature
¶	paragraph mark
𝄐	pause mark
%	per cent
‰	per mille
£	pound sign
′	prime/minute
″	double prime/second

¿	Spanish inverted question mark	ã, ñ	tilde
ə	schwa	®	trademark
§	section mark	‖	tramlines
♯	sharp sign	ü, ï	umlaut/diaeresis
‐	sloping/soft hyphen	Ƿ, ƿ	Old English wyn
~	swung dash	¥	yen sign
Þ, þ, Þ, Þ	Old English thorn	Ȝ, ȝ	Old English yogh

Appendix 8: **Mathematical symbols**

∞	infinity	$\gg$	much greater than
$\int$	integral	$\ll$	much less than
$\sum$	summation	$\geq$	greater than or equal to
π	pi	$\leq$	less than or equal to
$\prod$	product	$\wedge$	vector product
$=$	equal to	$\varnothing$	the empty set
$\neq$	not equal to	$+$	plus
$\equiv$	identically equal to	$-$	minus
$\not\equiv$	not identically equal to	$\pm$	plus or minus
$\approx$	approximately equal to	$\mp$	minus or plus
$\not\approx$	not approximately equal to	$p!$	factorial p
$\sim$	equivalent to, of the order of	$'$	prime
$\nsim$	not equivalent to, not of the order of	$''$	double prime
$\propto$	proportional to	$^\circ$	degree
$\rightarrow$	approaches	$\angle$	angle
$>$	greater than	$:$	ratio
$\not>$	not greater than	$::$	proportion
$<$	less than	$\therefore$	therefore, hence
$\not<$	not less than	$\because$	because

Appendix 9: **SI units**

1. Base units

Physical quantity	Name	Abbreviation or symbol
length	metre	m
mass	kilogram	kg
time	second	s
electric current	ampere	A
temperature	kelvin	K
amount of substance	mole	mol
luminous intensity	candela	cd

2. Supplementary units

Physical quantity	Name	Abbreviation or symbol
plane angle	radian	rad
solid angle	steradian	sr

3. Derived units with special names

Physical quantity	Name	Abbreviation or symbol
frequency	hertz	Hz
energy	joule	J
force	newton	N
power	watt	W
pressure	pascal	Pa
electric charge	coulomb	C
electromotive force	volt	V
electric resistance	ohm	Ω
electric conductance	siemens	S
electric capacitance	farad	F
magnetic flux	weber	Wb
inductance	henry	H
magnetic flux density	tesla	T
luminous flux	lumen	lm
illumination	lux	lx

Appendix 10: **Metric prefixes**

	Abbreviation	Factors
deca-	da	10
hecto-	h	10^2
kilo-	k	10^3
mega-	M	10^6
giga-	G	10^9
tera-	T	10^{12}
peta-	P	10^{15}
exa-	E	10^{18}

	Abbreviation	Factors
deci-	d	10^{-1}
centi-	c	10^{-2}
milli-	m	10^{-3}
micro-	μ	10^{-6}
nano-	n	10^{-9}
pico-	p	10^{-12}
femto-	f	10^{-15}
atto-	a	10^{-18}

Appendix 11: **Chemical elements**

Element	Symbol	Atomic no.	Element	Symbol	Atomic no.	Element	Symbol	Atomic no.
actinium	Ac	89	germanium	Ge	32	potassium	K	19
aluminium	Al	13	gold	Au	79	praseodymium	Pr	59
americium	Am	95	hafnium	Hf	72	promethium	Pm	61
antimony	Sb	51	hassium	Hs	108	protactinium	Pa	91
argon	Ar	18	helium	He	2	radium	Ra	88
arsenic	As	33	holmium	Ho	67	radon	Rn	86
astatine	At	85	hydrogen	H	1	rhenium	Re	75
barium	Ba	56	indium	In	49	rhodium	Rh	45
berkelium	Bk	97	iodine	I	53	roentgenium	Rg	111
beryllium	Be	4	iridium	Ir	77	rubidium	Rb	37
bismuth	Bi	83	iron	Fe	26	ruthenium	Ru	44
bohrium	Bh	107	krypton	Kr	36	rutherfordium	Rf	104
boron	B	5	lanthanum	La	57	samarium	Sm	62
bromine	Br	35	lawrencium	Lr	103	scandium	Sc	21
cadmium	Cd	48	lead	Pb	82	seaborgium	Sg	106
caesium	Cs	55	lithium	Li	3	selenium	Se	34
calcium	Ca	20	livermorium	Lv	116	silicon	Si	14
californium	Cf	98	lutetium	Lu	71	silver	Ag	47
carbon	C	6	magnesium	Mg	12	sodium	Na	11
cerium	Ce	58	manganese	Mn	25	strontium	Sr	38
chlorine	Cl	17	meitnerium	Mt	109	sulphur	S	16
chromium	Cr	24	mendelevium	Md	101	tantalum	Ta	73
cobalt	Co	27	mercury	Hg	80	technetium	Tc	43
copernicium	Cn	112	molybdenum	Mo	42	tellurium	Te	52
copper	Cu	29	neodymium	Nd	60	terbium	Tb	65
curium	Cm	96	neon	Ne	10	thallium	Tl	81
darmstadtium	Ds	110	neptunium	Np	93	thorium	Th	90
dubnium	Db	105	nickel	Ni	28	thulium	Tm	69
dysprosium	Dy	66	niobium	Nb	41	tin	Sn	50
einsteinium	Es	99	nitrogen	N	7	titanium	Ti	22
erbium	Er	68	nobelium	No	102	tungsten	W	74
europium	Eu	63	osmium	Os	76	uranium	U	92
fermium	Fm	100	oxygen	O	8	vanadium	V	23
flerovium	Fl	114	palladium	Pd	46	xenon	Xe	54
fluorine	F	9	phosphorus	P	15	ytterbium	Yb	70
francium	Fr	87	platinum	Pt	78	yttrium	Y	39
gadolinium	Gd	64	plutonium	Pu	94	zinc	Zn	30
gallium	Ga	31	polonium	Po	84	zirconium	Zr	40

Appendix 1 Chemical elements

Index

The index entries appear in word-by-word alphabetical order.
Page references in italics indicate illustrations.